This volume of 456 entries marks the completion of the *Dictionary of North Carolina Biography*, the most comprehensive state project of its kind. Taken together, the six volumes provide information on more than three thousand notable North Carolinians—native and adopted—whose accomplishments and occasional misdeeds span four centuries. A planned supplementary volume will bring the *Dictionary* up to date and will include an index to all the volumes.

The *Dictionary* contains the first comprehensive biographical information for many of these individuals. Included are native North Carolinians, no matter in what area they made their contributions, and non-natives whose contributions were made in North Carolina. All persons included are deceased.

Explorers, inventors, engineers, writers, chemists, business leaders, architects, artists, musicians, colonial leaders, military figures, national and state officials, and outstanding teachers and clergymen are among those recognized. And there are the infamous and eccentric—pirates, criminals, a hermit, and the man who weighed more than one thousand pounds. Averaging about eight hundred words, each sketch includes the full name of the subject, dates and places of birth and death (when known), family connections, a career description, and a bibliography. Most of the sketches are based on manuscript and contemporary printed sources that are rare or difficult to find. Some research was conducted in Europe.

William S. Powell has been working on the *Dictionary* since 1971 with the help of approximately 1,500 volunteer contributors.

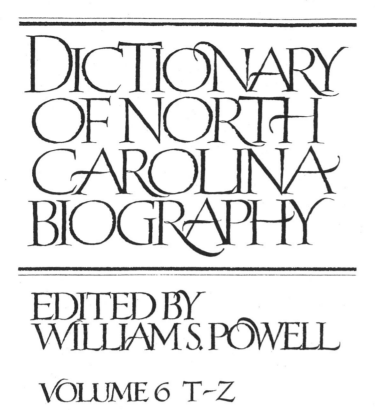

DICTIONARY OF NORTH CAROLINA BIOGRAPHY

EDITED BY WILLIAM S. POWELL

VOLUME 6 T-Z

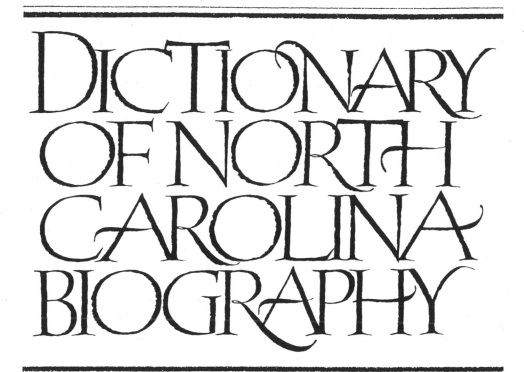

DICTIONARY OF NORTH CAROLINA BIOGRAPHY

EDITED BY WILLIAM S. POWELL

VOLUME 6 T-Z

The University of North Carolina Press

Chapel Hill and London

The paper in this book meets the guidelines for
permanence and durability of the Committee on
Production Guidelines for Book Longevity of the
Council on Library Resources.

Library of Congress Cataloging-in-Publication Data
Dictionary of North Carolina Biography
    Includes bibliographical references.
    1. North Carolina—Biography—Dictionaries. I. Powell,
William Stevens, 1919– .
CT252.D5   920′.0756   79-10106
ISBN 0-8078-1329-X (vol. 1)
ISBN 0-8078-1656-6 (vol. 2)
ISBN 0-8078-1806-2 (vol. 3)
ISBN 0-8078-1918-2 (vol. 4)
ISBN 0-8078-2100-4 (vol. 5)
ISBN 0-8078-2225-6 (vol. 6)

00 99 98 97 96   5 4 3 2 1

In Memory of

James Isaac Copeland
5 May 1910–12 November 1995

Chalmers Gaston Davidson
6 June 1907–25 June 1994

George Elliot London
19 August 1912–30 March 1993

John Davenport Neville
15 August 1942–13 February 1993

Mattie Erma Edwards Parker
3 November 1905–4 July 1995

Joseph Carlyle Sitterson
17 January 1911–19 May 1995

whose scholarly assistance contributed
to the usefulness of the *Dictionary of
North Carolina Biography*

Acknowledgments

With this sixth and concluding volume I once more heartily thank the North Carolina Society of the Cincinnati for its generous grant to The University of North Carolina Press in support of publication costs. Armistead Maupin presented the cause most convincingly to the members.

At the University of North Carolina Press, editors C. David Perry and Pamela Upton and director Kate D. Torrey were constantly alert on behalf of the *DNCB*. Copyeditor Stevie Champion continued with this volume, as with the previous ones, to delight me with her penetrating questions when something needed to be explained. Her keen eye for inconsistencies and words that needed to be clarified helped to improve the text immeasurably.

The staffs of the North Carolina Collection, the Southern Historical Collection, and the General Reference desk at the university libraries in Chapel Hill and the staff at the State Archives in Raleigh were all generous in their responses to my inquiries.

And most basic of all, the diligent research and writing by contributors across the state and around the country made this volume possible.

My wife, Virginia Waldrop Powell, has stuck faithfully to the role she long ago volunteered to play in this undertaking: she sometimes looks up answers to some of the questions that I raise; she tells me when something is not expressed clearly; and she is a first-rate proofreader. Alas, however, I have not been able to persuade her to write a single biography herself.

Dictionary of North Carolina Biography

Taliaferro, Hardin Edwards (1811–2 Nov. 1875), humorist and preacher, was born in Surry County, the youngest of nine children of Charles and Sallie Burroughs Taliaferro. The Taliaferros, their surname an anglicization of the Norman-French Taillefer, established themselves in England about 1200. The American branch came from Robert Taliaferro, an immigrant to Virginia before 1645. Brothers and sisters of Hardin, known in his youth as Mark Hardin, were John, Elizabeth, Charles, Mary, Richard, Dickerson, Benjamin, and Sallie. In the mountains of Surry County, the well-to-do Taliaferros, linked by ties of friendship and marriage to the family of Governor Jesse Franklin, were leaders in cultural and political affairs. Young Taliaferro worked at the local tub mills, read books from the large library of his neighbor Meshack Franklin, observed the unrestrained antics of the natives, and listened to their tall tales. In 1829 he followed his older brothers Charles and Richard, both Baptist ministers, to Roane (now Loudon) County in eastern Tennessee, where he became a tanner and farmer. Two years later he was baptized and attended an academy in nearby Madisonville, where in 1834 he married Elizabeth Henderson and was ordained to preach.

He moved to Talladega, Ala., in the fall of 1835 and for the next twenty years served a number of churches in the Coosa River Association. Beginning in 1849, Taliaferro passed through a "great spiritual conflict," the nature of which he disclosed in his first book, *The Grace of God Magnified* (1857). "Salvation by grace and grace alone was ever thereafter his perpetual theme," reported his brother-in-law Samuel Henderson, also a Baptist preacher. By January 1856 Taliaferro had located in Tuskegee to assist Henderson in editing the weekly *South Western Baptist*.

In the summer of 1857 he returned for the last time to Surry County, a visit that sparked memories of his boyhood days along Fisher River. Back in Alabama, he began "to write down some of the scenes and stories of that age and section" in a series of comic sketches published as *Fisher's River (North Carolina) Scenes and Characters, by "Skitt," "Who Was Raised Thar"* (1859). The book is one of the most joyous expressions of antebellum Southern humor. In using the actual names of his friends and acquaintances, however, Taliaferro did not endear himself to the Surry County folk, whom he called "a healthy, hardy, honest, uneducated set of pioneers." Even his proud boast that he was one "raised among them who knows their worth every way" was insufficient apology for hilarious yarns in which uncultivated yokels told staggering (if delightful) lies, fought, got drunk, and indulged themselves in outrageous shenanigans. In Tuskegee, the pseudonym "Skitt" protected the laughter-loving author of *Fisher's River* from being identified as the prominent Baptist editor and churchman.

In 1862 Taliaferro gave up his editorial post at the *South Western Baptist* and stayed on in the Tuskegee area for a decade as minister to several churches. He then moved back to Loudon, where he died. He was survived by his wife and two married daughters, Nancy J. Ham and Adelaide Weaver.

SEE: Richard Walser, "Biblio-Biography of Skitt Taliaferro," *North Carolina Historical Review* 55 (1978).

RICHARD WALSER

Tannahill, Mary Harvey (11 Jan. 1863–21 June 1951), artist, was born at the family home Kinderhook, in Warren County, the daughter of Robert and Sallie Jones Sims Tannahill. Her father had business connections in Petersburg, Va., was a major in the Confederate army, and in 1865 took his family to New York City, where he was a cotton factor and served as president of the New York Cotton Exchange (1880–82). The family lived at 44 East 65th Street but also had a residence in Englewood, N.J., and a summer home at Lake Mahopac near Peekskill, N.Y. They frequently visited in Warrenton, N.C., and Petersburg, Va. The Tannahill children were educated in private schools. Mary's interest in art was encouraged, and she studied with J. Alden Weir, John Twachtman, Henry Siddons Mowbray, Kenyon Cox, and Arthur Wesley Dow. Initially she used watercolors on ivory and came to be recognized as a skilled miniaturist; as such, she joined the Pennsylvania Society of Miniature Painters. She soon began to work with tempera, oils, woodcuts (or color blocks, as she called them), batik, and embroidery.

Prior to World War I she studied in Europe; in Germany, where the attractive blond, almost six feet tall, was assumed to be English, she was mistreated in public. Returning home, she passed the winters in New York and summers in Provincetown on Cape Cod beginning in 1916. The availability of inexpensive studios, the opportunity to enjoy the company of other artists, and exhibitions by the Provincetown Art Association led her to spend more than thirty summers there.

Over a forty-year period Mary Tannahill's work appeared in numerous exhibitions—the American and New York Water Color Clubs, the Brooklyn Museum of Art, Knoedler Galleries, the American Society of Miniature Painters, the Provincetown Art Association, the Art Students League, the Society of Independent Artists, the Peachtree Gallery in Atlanta, the North Carolina Professional Artists' Club, and others. In 1938 the Greenville County, S.C., Museum of Art included works by her in an exhibition entitled "Eight Southern Women," which was also shown by the Gibbes Art Gallery in Charleston. Her works are now held by numerous museums and by members of her family.

She never married and spent her final years in Warrenton, where she was at the time of her death. She was buried in the Old Blandford Church Cemetery, Petersburg.

SEE: *Atlanta Journal and Constitution*, 7 June 1985; James Payne Beckwith, Jr., to William S. Powell, 8 May 1986; Mantle Fieldings, *Dictionary of American Painters, Sculp-*

tors, and Engravers (1986); John William Leonard, ed., *Woman's Who's Who of America* (1914); Gladys G. Lippincott, News Release, "Peachtree Gallery Opens Mary H. Tannahill Retrospective," 22 Apr. 1985; Peachtree Gallery, Atlanta, *Gallery Glimpses* 2 (Spring 1985); Chris Petteys, *Dictionary of Women Artists: An International Dictionary of Women Artists Born before 1900* (1985); Raleigh *News and Observer*, 4 Dec. 1931, 19 Dec. 1937.

WILLIAM S. POWELL

Tarrant, Edward H[enry?] (1796 or 1799–2 Aug. 1858), soldier, Indian fighter, and Texas official, was born in North Carolina, probably in Caswell County, as one Henry Tarrant was active there between 1799 and 1801. Manlove Tarrant served as ensign to captain with the Second North Carolina Battalion from 1776 until his retirement on 1 June 1778. When Edward Tarrant was young his family moved to Tennessee. During the War of 1812 he joined a militia unit in Kentucky for a six-month enlistment and attained the rank of corporal. Discharged on 20 May 1815, he returned to Tennessee and studied law. By the early 1820s he was living in Henry County near the Kentucky state line, where he served as colonel of the local militia, organized the first Masonic lodge in the county seat, and by 1827 was sheriff. In 1829 he was a resident of Henderson County, where he held minor public office.

Tarrant was among the Tennessee volunteers who went to Texas in 1835, ostensibly to support the fight for independence, but no record has been found to substantiate any service by him. Nevertheless, he received 4,605½ acres of land in Red River County in the northeastern part of the state, on 2 Mar. 1836, simply by virtue of the fact that he was residing in Texas at the time of independence, and he soon established his family, slaves, and hired hands there.

Tarrant was elected a member of the Second Congress of the Republic of Texas, serving between 17 Oct. and 11 Nov. 1837; he resigned to command troops on the frontier in quelling Indian troubles. As a brigadier general he led his men to victory in the Battle of Village Creek in 1841, thereby opening new territory to settlement. Tarrant County, of which Fort Worth is now the county seat, was named in his honor. He also was a member of the statehood convention in 1845. Following service in the War with Mexico, Tarrant again was elected to the state legislature, serving in the third and fourth sessions, and to the position of chief justice of Red River County.

Retiring to his plantation near Italy in Ellis County, Tarrant spent his final years. At the time of his death he happened to be at Fort Belknap, where he also owned property, but was buried at his plantation. In 1928 the Daughters of the Republic of Texas had his remains removed to Pioneer Rest Cemetery in Fort Worth.

SEE: *Biographical Directory of Texas Conventions and Congresses* (1941); Robert L. and Pauline H. Jones, "Edward H. Tarrant," *Southwestern Historical Quarterly* 69 (January 1966); Katharine Kerr Kendall, comp., *Caswell County, North Carolina, Deed Books, 1777–1817* (1989); Texas Young Lawyers Association, *Young Lawyers at Texas Independence* (1986); Walter P. Webb, ed., *The Handbook of Texas*, vol. 2 (1953).

JOSEPH L. PRICE

Tate, Frederick Nelson (5 Sept. 1867–12 June 1945), High Point civic leader and pioneer furniture manufacturer, was born at Owen Sound, Ontario, Canada, the son of Mary Ann and Edward Tate. About 1871 the elder Tate settled his family in Jamestown, N.C., and engaged in farming. His oldest son, John Hall Tate (*see below*), was also a furniture manufacturer. Fred Tate was educated in the Jamestown area but sought his fortune in nearby High Point. After a brief period as store clerk, Tate became associated with the Southern Railway Company. In 1887 he was appointed clerk in the freight department, and in 1891 he became general agent, a position he held for fifteen years—even after entering into a private business venture. Convinced of the potential of the burgeoning furniture industry in High Point, Tate organized the Continental Furniture Company in 1901. He became president, treasurer, and general manager; he remained president until his death.

Continental specialized in the manufacture of solid wood bedroom and dining room furniture of superior quality. The woods used were predominantly mahogany, maple, and cherry. Tate was personally involved in all phases of the manufacturing process. He sought perfection in the selection of wood, in joinery, in cabinet fitting, in finishing, and in styling. The Continental line was widely sold in the eastern United States and shipped throughout the country, especially into the metropolitan areas of New York, Chicago, San Francisco, and Boston. Known and advertised as "Continental Superior Quality," Tate's solid hardwood furniture was beautiful, but relatively expensive in an industry where many manufacturers catered to the popular market. Nevertheless, the Continental Furniture Company, at its height, employed some 150 skilled workers in buildings totaling 150,000 square feet and had an annual production of $2 million. Upon Tate's death his associates carried on the Continental tradition of excellence until the mid-1950s, when the company was sold to Burlington Industries, which phased it out.

Tate's cabinet craft brought immeasurable prestige to the furniture industry centered around High Point and earned him a national reputation. But his contributions to the industry and to his city did not end with the success of his own company. In his long career he was president of the High Point Chamber of Commerce, the Manufacturers Club, the Southern Furniture Manufacturers Association, and the National Furniture Manufacturers Council. His efforts to improve the quality of life of his fellow citizens were no less impressive. Tate served six years as mayor of High Point, ten years as a public school commissioner, sixteen years as chairman of the Wesley Memorial Methodist Church Stewards, and several years as an influential YMCA board president. He was also a Mason, Odd Fellow, Elk, and Rotarian. Describing Fred Tate as "pioneering in spirit, steadfast in faith, generous almost to a fault, and courageous in leadership," the High Point Chamber of Commerce honored him in 1944 by a plaque that said in part: "He came to High Point when it was a village and by his immense vitality, keen vision, arresting leadership, and greatness of heart, he has been a dynamic force in helping to build its industries, its public and semi-public institutions and its citizenship." This seems an apt characterization of a busy man's busy life.

Despite his numerous business and civic responsibilities, Tate found ample time for his family, to which he was devoted. In 1891 he married Estelle Field, of High Point, an alumna of Greensboro College. They had four daughters—Mabel Alice (1892–1964), Kathryn (1894–1968), Frances (1896–1900), and Marjorie (1906–67). Tate was interred in the family plot, Oakwood Memorial Cemetery, High Point.

SEE: Fred Flagler, Jr., "History of High Point," in *High Point, North Carolina: "Then and Now"* (1951); High Point

Chamber of Commerce, plaque, 19 Dec. 1944; Mrs. Richard D. Hartley, granddaughter of Tate, completed questionnaire.

MAX R. WILLIAMS

Tate, James (*d. 1795*), schoolmaster and clergyman, went to Wilmington, N.C., from Ireland in 1760 and opened the first classical school in North Carolina under Presbyterian influence. He initially resided in a tenement on Front Street but later bought a house on the south side of Princess between Front and Second. Tate also owned a tract known as the Four Mile House located near the Race Ground.

The Reverend Mr. Tate never affiliated himself with one congregation. Instead, he preached anywhere people were desirous of the gospel. He was especially active in the area around Black and South Rivers. In the struggle between Great Britain and the colonies Tate served as a member of the Wilmington Committee of Safety in 1775. In October of the same year he became chaplain to the First North Carolina Regiment and later to the Fourth regiment. It was in this capacity that he served with the American troops at Germantown in 1777. Being a staunch Whig, he found it necessary to move from Wilmington to the Hawfields section of Orange County, where he continued his preaching and teaching.

After the war Tate returned to Wilmington, where he opposed the confiscation of Tory property and ratification of the new Federal Constitution. He was particularly distressed that there was to be no mint in each state of the new nation. Tate died a bachelor. It is probable that he had relatives in the Wilmington area as well as in Orange County. However, he only mentioned one, George Lawson, in his will.

SEE: Walter Clark, ed., *State Records of North Carolina*, vols. 13, 15–19, 22 (1896–1905); William Henry Foote, *Sketches of North Carolina: Historical and Biographical* (1846); Edgar W. Knight, *Public Education in the South* (1922); Donald Lennon and Ida Brooks Kellam, *Wilmington Town Book, 1743–1778* (1973); Elizabeth McKoy, *Early New Hanover County Records* (1973); Griffith J. McRee, *Life and Correspondence of James Iredell*, 2 vols. (1857–58); New Hanover County Wills, vol. 5 (North Carolina State Archives, Raleigh); William L. Saunders, ed., *Colonial Records of North Carolina*, vol. 10 (1890).

H. KENNETH STEPHENS II

Tate, John Hall (*7 Apr. 1861–8 Apr. 1930*), pioneer furniture manufacturer, was born in Kilsyth, Ontario, Canada, the son of Edward (1822–83) and Mary A. Tate (1831–1920). His father was a native of England and his mother of Ireland. Both were Presbyterians who were married in Canada and in 1871 moved to a farm near Jamestown, N.C., where Tate became a farmer and cabinetmaker. No record has been found of young John Tate's education, but perhaps like his younger brothers he attended school in Jamestown.

John Tate and two of his three brothers were among the earliest furniture manufacturers in High Point. There Ernest A. Snow, a lumberman, who sold lumber to a furniture manufacturer in Baltimore, returned home and realized to the full extent the great increase in the value of lumber when it was made into furniture. To establish a factory to provide furniture, Tate in the spring of 1889 invested $3,000 and so did Thomas F. Wrenn; Snow agreed to provide lumber and he also became a partner. Tate was president and his brother, Albert E., was secretary and treasurer. Around the first of July the High Point Furniture Company began shipping bedroom suites consisting of a bed, dresser, and washstand which sold for $7.50. Demand grew and in the first year sales amounted to $75,000. Labor was available from the surrounding area, lumber was plentiful in the forests of Piedmont North Carolina, and there were excellent rail connections. These advantages led a number of men to open new factories, all of which flourished. Tate sold his interest in the first factory and in 1893 organized the Tate Furniture Company, of which his brother Albert was secretary-treasurer. He also assisted others in establishing factories and frequently invested in them himself. He was generous with his resources, led in founding the YMCA, and was highly regarded in the community.

Tate's first wife was Narcissa Spencer, who died in 1900; they were the parents of a daughter, Genevieve (m. Dorsey Brockett). In 1906 he married Hattie Gavin of Newton; their only child died in infancy. Tate was buried in Oakwood Cemetery, High Point.

SEE: *The Building and the Builders of a City: High Point, North Carolina* (1947); *Charlotte Observer*, 9 Apr. 1930; J. J. Farris, *High Point, North Carolina: A Brief Summary of Its Manufacturing Enterprises, Together with Sketches of Those Who Have Built Them* (1900 [portrait]) and *High Point, North Carolina* (1911?); *Greensboro Daily News*, 9 Apr. 1930; Robert F. Hicks, Jr., " 'The Spirit of Enterprise': The History of High Point's Formative Period, 1851–1926" (master's thesis, University of North Carolina at Greensboro, 1989); *High Point Enterprise*, 9 Apr. 1930; *North Carolina Biography*, vol. 3 (1928).

WILLIAM S. POWELL

Tate, Samuel McDowell (*6 Sept. 1830–25 June 1897*), merchant, soldier, railroad official, and legislator, was born in Morganton. Of French-Huguenot and Scots-Irish heritage, he was the eldest son of David, who for many years represented Burke County in both houses of the North Carolina General Assembly, and Susan Maria Tate. After his father's death in 1836, Samuel attended private schools in North Carolina and Pennsylvania, his mother's native state. Completing his schooling, he established himself in Philadelphia as a merchant. In 1850 he went back to Burke County and set up a thriving business selling general merchandise.

Soon after his return to the state, Tate became involved with the Western North Carolina Railroad. Colonel Charles Fisher of Salisbury contracted in 1854 to build the first section of the road from Salisbury to Morganton, and Tate worked for him as an agent and as manager of the railroad's various financial interests. During this time Tate also served as a federal census taker for Burke County, and from 1856 to 1860 he was the postmaster of Morganton. In addition, he was a justice of the peace for twenty-five years.

In 1861, after the outbreak of war, Tate volunteered for service in the Confederate army and was appointed captain of Company D, Sixth North Carolina Regiment. Commissioned and promoted to the rank of major on 20 May 1862, he was advanced to lieutenant colonel on 2 July 1863 at Gettysburg. There he assumed command of the Sixth North Carolina Regiment after the death of Colonel Isaac E. Avery and led his troops up Cemetery Hill and in the battle on Cemetery Ridge. This continued to command the Sixth regiment until the close of the war.

When the Civil War ended, Tate made his way back to Morganton, where the stockholders of the Western North Carolina Railroad elected him to the presidency of the disorganized and bankrupt organization. As president, Tate repaired and rebuilt the railroad, revamped the old rolling stock, and straightened out its financial affairs. Governor William W. Holden removed him from the presidency in 1865, but Governor Jonathan Worth restored him to that position in 1866. He was again ousted by the Holden-appointed board of directors in 1868 but continued to act as the financial agent of the stockholders and as the trustee for payment of debts.

In 1874 Tate sold his stock in the Western North Carolina Railroad, resigned all his connections with the railroad, and was elected to the North Carolina House of Commons from Burke County. During this term in the General Assembly he sponsored a bill that would allow the state to assume control of the Western North Carolina Railroad. The bill passed, and Tate was elected as commissioner to reorganize the railroad. He also was the author of a bill providing for convict labor on works of internal improvement, and in 1875 the stockholders of the Western North Carolina Railroad appointed him as the overseer of its convict workforce. Another notable accomplishment in his first term was the founding of the Western Insane Asylum in Morganton. Tate also served on the committee for internal improvement, the Railroad Commission, the rules committee, and the finance committee, of which he was chairman. He was again elected chairman of the finance commmittee in 1880, 1882, and 1884.

His public service was not confined to the legislature. In 1886 Comptroller of the Currency William Lee Trenholm appointed Tate examiner of national banks in the district extending from West Virginia to Florida. In 1891 he worked hard to bring the North Carolina School for the Deaf to Morganton. The next year Governor Thomas Holt named him state treasurer of North Carolina following the death of Donald W. Bain; he served until December 1894, when he sought election to the post but was defeated.

Tate was tainted by scandal during his campaign for state treasurer. The *Progressive Farmer* Advance Sheet claimed to have evidence that he had been in partnership with Littlefield, Swepson and Company to bring pressure to bear upon the legislature in order to secure the sale of bonds for railroads. Tate was berated in the press, he was investigated twice by a legislative commission, his bank books were examined, and he lost the election, but he was not found guilty of any wrongdoing. After his defeat, he retired from public life.

A Presbyterian and staunch Democrat, Tate gained a reputation as a person of solid judgment. The *Legislative Biographical Sketchbook* of 1883 describes him as a "quiet, old-fashioned Jeffersonian Democrat; sound, logical, practical, and worthy to be carefully considered."

In 1866 he married Jennie Pearson, the daughter of Robert Pearson, a bank president and merchant in Morganton and the first president of the Western North Carolina Railroad. The Tates had ten children: Franklin Pierce, Sue Virginia, Wilhelmina, Samuel McDowell, Jr., Alexander, Claude, Maude, Irene, Howard Wilson, and Charles Gordon. Tate died in Morganton; he and his wife were buried in Forest Hill Cemetery.

SEE: Walter Clark, ed., *Histories of the Several Regiments and Battalions from North Carolina in the Great War*, vols. 1, 3–5 (1901 [portrait]); Jerome Dowd, *Sketches of Prominent Living North Carolinians* (1888); Weymouth T. Jordan, comp., *North Carolina Troops, 1861–1865: A Roster*, vol. 4 (1973); Elizabeth Kincaid and Fred Crawford, *Spotlight on Burke* (1971); *Legislative Biographical Sketchbook* (1883); Morganton *News-Herald*, 25 June 1897, 27 Oct. 1969; Notes of Mrs. Charles Gordon Tate (Burke County Library, Morganton); Samuel McDowell Tate Papers (Southern Historical Collection, University of North Carolina, Chapel Hill); W. F. Tomlinson, *Biography of State Officials, Members of the General Assembly of North Carolina* (1893); Ina and John J. Van Noppen, *Western North Carolina since the Civil War* (1973).

ELAINE DOERSCHUK PRUITT

Tatham, William *(13 Apr. 1752–22 Feb. 1819),* clerk, merchant, soldier, lawyer, legislator, surveyor, engineer, civil servant, author, book and map collector, and cartographer, was born in the County of Cumberland, England. The eldest of five children of Sandford and Elizabeth Tatham, he spent much of his early life with relatives and received little formal education. When he was sixteen his father, rector of Hutton-in-the-Forest and vicar of Appleby, sent him to Virginia to learn the tobacco trade. Young Tatham was apprenticed to the mercantile firm of Carter and Trent, located on the James River in Amherst County. After five years as a clerk with the firm he launched an unsuccessful mercantile venture of his own. Following some military service on the frontier and in Virginia during the Revolution, he went to North Carolina and studied law with William R. Davie; he was admitted to the bar in that state in 1784. Later he was licensed to practice law in Virginia and the Southwest Territory. In 1786 Tatham, along with John Willis and others, founded the town of Lumberton, N.C. Tatham laid out the town and served as one of the original trustees. The next year the voters in Robeson County sent him to the state legislature, and in 1788 he was commissioned lieutenant colonel of the Fayetteville militia district.

By this time he had developed a keen interest in surveying, canal construction, cartography, and the collection of historical, political, and geographic information. After practicing law briefly in Knoxville in 1793, he journeyed to Philadelphia, where he met Josef de Jaudenes, the Spanish chargé, who had been involved in intrigue to separate the backcountry. Tatham convinced Jaudenes that he possessed much knowledge, influence, and material that would be of interest to the Spanish government. The Spanish chargé provided Tatham with expense money and letters of introduction and sent him to Spain in the latter part of 1795. However, with the ratification of Pinckney's Treaty, which represented a change in Spain's policy regarding its possessions in North America, the Spanish government considered Tatham's materials and information of little value and asked him to leave the country in the summer of 1796. That August, instead of returning to the United States, he sailed to England, where he spent the next eight years. During this period he wrote numerous books and essays on agriculture, commerce, canal construction and irrigation projects, and architecture. His most noted, and still a classical work, was *An Historical and Practical Essay on the Culture and Commerce of Tobacco* (London, 1800). In 1802 he was elected to membership in the Royal Society of Arts.

He returned to Virginia at the beginning of Jefferson's second term as president and spent most of the remainder of his life surveying and drawing up proposals for inland canals, fortifications, lighthouses, and communication systems designed to promote the defense and commerce of the Chesapeake Bay area, including Albemarle Sound. In February 1806 the Treasury Department appointed Tatham, Thomas Coles, and Jonathan Price (both North Carolinians) commissioners to survey the coast of North Carolina from Cape Hatteras to Cape Fear. After completing this task, and immediately following the *Chesapeake* affair off the coast of Norfolk in June 1807, Tatham was employed by Jefferson to observe and report daily on the movements and activities of British ships in the Chesapeake Bay. This episode encouraged Tatham to seek additional public employment and exert greater efforts to provide Presidents Jefferson and Madison with acceptable proposals for coastwise inland navigation, fortifications, and gunboats designed to protect the Chesapeake area. His pleas and proposals fell on deaf ears until war was declared in 1812. Although sixty years old, he hurried to Washington and was employed as topographical engineer in the War Department until 1815.

After the war his health began to fail and he became intemperate in his drinking habits. His frequent requests for public employment were ignored until June 1817, when the secretary of war appointed him military storekeeper at the U.S. Arsenal near Richmond. Unable to serve adequately even in this capacity, he resigned in December. He spent his last few destitute years trying to revive a proposal he had made periodically since 1806—that the federal government purchase his vast collection of maps, documents, and instruments. It has been said that Tatham was the first to define the functions of a national library. In an effort to survive, he apparently sold and lost much of his collection. When the Virginia legislature finally agreed to purchase his collection after his death, little was left. Tatham committed suicide on Richmond's Capitol Square by stepping in front of the muzzle of one of the cannons firing the sundown salute in honor of Washington. He never married and left no children. A portrait painted in 1779 is at the North Carolina Division of Archives and History in Raleigh.

SEE: Elizabeth G. McPherson, ed., "Letters of William Tatham," *William and Mary Quarterly* 16, 2d ser. (April, July 1936); G. Melvin Herndon, *William Tatham, 1752–1819: American Versatile* (1973); Norman Lois Peterson, ed., *Defense of Norfolk in 1807 as Told by William Tatham, Wataugan* (1947).

G. MELVIN HERNDON

Tatom, Absalom (1742–20 Dec. 1802), military leader, delegate to the Constitutional Convention of 1788, and a member of Congress, was born in Granville County. He first appears in North Carolina records as a sergeant in the local militia in 1763. On 1 Sept. 1775, in anticipation of the Revolutionary War, he was commissioned first lieutenant in the First North Carolina Continental Regiment; he was promoted to captain on 19 June 1776. The reason for his resignation in the fall, on 19 September, is unknown, but on 15 Aug. 1778 he enlisted in state service as assistant quartermaster and keeper of the arsenal at Hillsborough. Before the end of the year he also became contractor for the town. He resigned both positions when commissioned major of the detachment of North Carolina Light Horse on 12 Feb. 1779, but in July he was named clerk of the Randolph County Court and later in the year was elected to represent that county in the House of Commons. The latter position was invalidated, however, as he was already county clerk. In 1781 he appears as district auditor for Hillsborough.

Why Tatom was there is not clear, but at the Battle of Elizabethtown in August 1781 he was captured by Tories but escaped under cover of darkness. In 1782 the Continental Congress named him one of three commissioners to survey lands to be granted to Continental soldiers in the western territory that later became Tennessee. For a time he was actually in the West, where one of his servants was captured by Indians, yet it was also in 1782 that Tatom served as private secretary to Governor Thomas

Burke and as the state tobacco agent. Clearly a busy man and one of many talents, in May 1785 he was elected surveyor of North Carolina by the Continental Congress and soon afterwards was named by the state as a commissioner to sign paper money. In 1788 he was a delegate to the Constitutional Convention as well as the Hillsborough borough representative in the legislature. He served in the next six sessions as well but died shortly before the end of the last one.

Tatom's name does not appear in the 1790 census for North Carolina, but at the time of the 1800 tally of Orange County he was recorded as being over forty-five years of age and owning eight slaves but having no family. Following a brief illness he died in Raleigh during the 1802 legislative session and was buried in the Old City Cemetery.

Available records make no mention of Tatom's family, marital status, or religious affiliation, although it is known that he was a member of the Grand Order of Masons, Eagle Lodge No. 19 (now No. 71) at Hillsborough. He served as senior grand warden pro tem of the Grand Lodge on 25 Jan. 1795.

SEE: John L. Cheney, Jr., ed., *North Carolina Government, 1585–1979* (1981); Walter Clark, ed., *Colonial Records of North Carolina*, vol. 10 (1890); Don Higginbotham, ed., *The Papers of James Iredell*, vol. 2 (1976); William L. Saunders, *State Records of North Carolina*, vols. 12–13 (1895–96), 15–22 (1898–1907), 24–25 (1905–6); Frederick G. Speidel, *North Carolina Masons in the American Revolution* (1975); *Who Was Who in America*, historical vol. (1967).

NEIL C. PENNYWITT

Tatum, Howell (1753–9 Sept. 1822), officer in the Revolution and War of 1812, merchant, engineer, and lawyer, attorney general, and superior court judge in Tennessee, was the son of Joshua and Amey Tatum of Halifax County. There was a younger son James, who rose to a lieutenancy in the North Carolina Continental Line.

Howell Tatum's combat career was entirely with the First Regiment, North Carolina Continental Line, elements of which saw service in both the Northern and Southern Departments under Colonel Thomas Clarke. His ratings were as follows: ensign, 1 Sept. 1775; second lieutenant and lieutenant, 4 Jan. and 28 Mar. 1776; and second captain, 3 Apr. 1777. Captured at Charles Town with other North Carolina officers and men on 12 May 1780, Tatum was exchanged on parole on 14 June 1781. He accepted command of a troop of horse in the First Regiment about January 1782 but on 20 May resigned from the army. Ironically he had attempted to do so on 3 Apr. 1780—five weeks prior to his capture: in a letter to Brigadier General Jethro Sumner he pointed out that his originally adequate patrimony at the war's beginning had become so dissipated through lack of pay that he was reduced "to little better than Poverty." Nevertheless, Tatum emerged from the conflict with a major's brevet, and in due course Military Land Warrant number 340 allotted him 3,565 acres for seventy-eight months' service. A charter member of the North Carolina Society of the Cincinnati, founded at Hillsborough in October 1783, Tatum early in 1787 succeeded the Reverend Adam Boyd as the society's secretary, a post that he probably retained until he left the state.

During this period Tatum may have taken up surveying, and he must have studied law, for on 17 Dec. 1787 his name was among several put forward by the House of Commons for the position of judge in Davidson County [Tenn.]. He was not appointed and at about this time migrated to the new Territory South of the Ohio (Tennessee).

On 28 May and 5 June 1790 Congressman Hugh Williamson and Timothy Bloodworth of North Carolina endorsed Tatum's name to President Washington as a proper man for secretary of the territory, and on the latter date a one-time superior officer in the First North Carolina Regiment, Congressman John B. Ashe, recommended him warmly for a territorial judgeship, with the suggestion that Washington might himself recollect this ex-Continental. Nothing resulted from these overtures. But at Nashville on 5 Dec. 1790, Tatum's former Revolutionary compatriot, Governor William Blount, made him one of the initial appointees licensed to practice law in the new territory. On 27 Oct. 1792 the governor also named Tatum lieutenant colonel of Davidson County (Tenn.).

From at least 1793 to perhaps the outbreak of the War of 1812 Tatum engaged in general merchandising at Nashville, with transactions extending as far afield as eastern North Carolina. Some of his more than 150 accounts included those of such regionally prominent personalities as Andrew Jackson, John McNairy, and James Robertson. From January 1802 he operated in partnership with George M. Deaderick.

At the first General Assembly of the territory, staged at Knoxville in August 1794, a treasury department was established, and Tatum was made treasurer for the Mero (western) District of Middle Tennessee, a post he filled until sometime in 1796. In that year the legislature appointed him attorney general for Mero District, to succeed Andrew Jackson, a position that Tatum held until 12 May 1797. On that date he was named to a judgeship in the superior court of law and equity at Nashville, succeeding John McNairy—a post for which Jackson had recommended him to President Washington the preceding 8 February in these words: "Mr. Tatum is an old officer who has faced all the stormy showers of war, and faithfully served and fought for his Country, his Abilities equal to any other Charactor [sic] in the state Except [John] Overton and I may add [John] Rea, he is a man of great firmness and much Esteemed by all who know him." Tatum occupied this bench until his resignation on 20 Sept. 1798 (to be succeeded by Jackson).

In November 1803 Tatum at Jackson's request was witness to an altercation between the judge and William Maclin, the Tennessee secretary of state. The encounter, which degenerated into a caning and brick heaving, constituted one of the episodes resurrected in the anti-Jackson campaign leaflet by Dr. James L. Armstrong, *Reminiscences; or, An Extract from the Catalogue of General Jackson's Juvenile Indiscretions . . .* (ca. 1827). From about 1807 Tatum held from the legislature an appointment as commissioner of land claims in disputes arising between North Carolina and Tennessee.

In December 1812 Jackson as major general of Tennessee militia appointed Tatum his chief engineer for the march towards Natchez. He does not seem to have been with Jackson during the Creek campaign but was with him at Camp Jackson in the Creek Nation during the summer of 1814, when the commander was fashioning the treaty with those Indians. Upon Jackson's appointment as major general, U.S. Army, he picked Tatum as his topographical engineer for the New Orleans campaign, subordinate to the chief engineer Major Arsène L. Latour. Tatum's own journal, embodied in his report to the secretary of war pro tem, James Monroe, covered the period from 6 July 1814 to 20 Jan. 1815. Tatum called the artillery bombardment of 1 Jan. 1815 before New Orleans the worst he had experienced, surpassing that of the British forces against Charles Town in 1780.

On 21 Jan. 1815 Jackson wrote the secretary of war that Tatum, nearing age sixty-two, had "exhibited all the ardor of youth in the hour of peril." Tatum dated his field report at New Orleans, 20 Feb. 1815, and on 15 June resigned from military service. In a dispute over certain events of the New Orleans campaign Jackson in 1817 referred his interrogators to Tatum's journal as the work of a man "whose impartiality is proverbial."

Returning to the Nashville area, Tatum settled on his lands in Rutherford County. At this juncture he was appointed military storekeeper for the national government, in Nashville, and held the post for a year or so. His brother-in-law Stephen Cantrell later declared: "I heard him refuse to apply for a pension when requested by his friends, on the ground that he was then Military Storekeeper and receiving pay from the Government for his services in that Capacity and that he did not want to receive pay from the Government in two Capacities at the same time."

On 24 Dec. 1795 Tatum married Rosannah Wendel (ca. 1777–post–1854) in Davidson County, Tenn., and took up residence in Nashville. The couple had several children, of whom the name only of Edwin M. Tatum is known. On 28 Sept. 1812 the parents were divorced by act of the General Assembly. In 1828 Mrs. Tatum married Anderson Claxton and with her son moved to Fort Smith, Ark. Tatum died in Nashville of rheumatism and palsy. His estate, administered by Stephen Cantrell, was appraised at $11,839.28. He was interred with military honors by the Nashville Guards, but the gravestone in City Cemetery is marked simply "H. T." There is no known likeness of Tatum, nor are his religious and political affiliations known.

SEE: John S. Bassett, ed., *Correspondence of Andrew Jackson*, vols. 1–2, 6 (1926–35); Bassett, ed., "Major Howell Tatum's Journal While Acting Topographical Engineer (1814) to General Jackson," *Smith College Studies in History* 7 (1921–22); Mary S. Blakemore, *Narrative Genealogy of the Stewarts of Sequatchie Valley, Tennessee* (1960); C. E. Carter, ed., *Territorial Papers of the United States*, vol. 4 (1936); Walter Clark, ed., *State Records of North Carolina*, vols. 14–20 (1899–1902); R. D. W. Connor, comp., *Documentary History of the University of North Carolina*, vol. 2 (1953); Curtis C. Davis, *Revolution's Godchild* (1976); P. J. Hamilton, *Colonial Mobile* (1897); A. C. Holt, "Economic and Social Beginnings of Tennessee," *Tennessee Historical Quarterly* 8 (April 1924); Sarah Lemmon, ed., *Pettigrew Papers*, vol. 1 (1971); *Nashville Whig*, 11 Sept. 1822; Samuel C. Williams, *Phases of the History of the Supreme Court of Tennessee* (1944).

CURTIS CARROLL DAVIS

Tatum, James Moore (22 Aug. 1913–23 July 1959), star athlete, football coach, and university athletic director, was born at McColl, S.C., the youngest of five sons of Walter Robert and Jessie Carmichael Tatum. His father was a general merchant-banker-farmer. His mother was descended from Highland Scots who settled in Dillon, S.C. When Jim was twelve, his father died leaving nine children to be educated.

Young Jim enrolled at The University of North Carolina under the persuasion and with the financial aid of an uncle, William Donald Carmichael, Jr., of New York City, who was a vice-president of the Liggett and Meyers Tobacco Company. A sandlot player whose personal temperament earned him the sobriquet "Sunny Jim," Tatum starred as a catcher, outfielder, and hitter; won two All-American mentions, and became an All-Southern tackle (1934) as a deceptively quick six-foot, four-inch 220-pounder under the coaching of "Chuck" Collins and Carl Snavely. After his graduation from the university in 1935, he immediately followed Snavely to Cornell University as his assistant football coach and Cornell's head baseball coach. One of his baseball teams went to the eastern regional finals.

Tatum returned to The University of North Carolina as director of freshman athletics in 1939, became head coach for one year (1942), and then joined the navy and learned the Split-T formation as an assistant to Don Faurot, the system's founder, at Iowa Pre-Flight. He was head coach at Jacksonville Naval Station for one season (1945) with a 9–2 record before being tapped as head football coach for the University of Oklahoma, where one of his assistants was Charles (Bud) Wilkinson. Jim Tatum was credited with laying the groundwork for that school's phenomenal reign in football. His 1946 Oklahoma team won eight games and lost three; it beat North Carolina State University, 34–14, in the 'Gator Bowl.

From Oklahoma, he went to the University of Maryland in 1947 as head coach and athletic director. During nine years, he built the Terps from a shambles into a football power that won the National Championship in 1953, when Tatum was named Coach of the Year. Five of his Maryland teams played in postseason bowls, winning two (against Missouri and Tennessee), losing two (both to his old Oklahoma coached by his former assistant, Bud Wilkinson), and tying one (with Georgia).

On his second return to his alma mater, in 1956 (at a substantial cut in salary), he faced problems, one being a defeatist attitude among Tar Heels after a cycle of lean seasons. In striving for the goodwill of students, faculty, and administration, he reorganized and expanded the university's Educational Foundation—the source of athletic grants-in-aid—until it enjoyed enthusiastic and spirited alumni support, which long outlived him. Except for an occasional golf game as a recreational release, he devoted himself single-mindedly to his football teams. Nights and weekends were spent in tireless recruiting. Summers went to clinics and public appearances calculated to knit more solidly the relationship between football and other university programs. He experienced the only losing season of his career (2–7–1) in 1956 but came back in 1957 with a 6–4 record, which included upset victories over otherwise undefeated Navy, traditional rival Duke, Miami, and Clemson. The 6–4 record was repeated in 1958.

For all the acclaim his victories brought, Tatum also felt thorns among the roses. Maryland was criticized for overemphasizing football; in one year the school awarded 93 scholarships, averaging $944 each, to Tatum's players. The University of North Carolina student newspaper greeted him as "this parasitic monster of open professionalism." When his student supporters demanded an election to recall the editors, Sunny Jim came to the defense of the free press and dismissed the incident as a "tempest in an ink pot."

When his singular devotion to football prompted the same student paper to take him to task for "playing to win and win alone," the supremely self-confident coach commented: "Winning isn't the most important thing—it's the only thing."

Win he did. During fourteen years of coaching and as athletic director of three top universities, he built from the bottom on each assignment and compiled a record of 100 wins, 34 losses, and 7 ties. Dick Herbert, former sports editor of the Raleigh News and Observer and a discerning commentator on athletics, noted these special Tatum strengths: "brilliance in devising defensive tactics ... ability to organize ... work with alumni ... [and] one of the top recruiters in football." Herbert said that there had been "few like him" and noted "a degree of genius about

him." Tatum was enshrined on 12 June 1975 in the South Carolina Athletic Hall of Fame.

Jim Hickey, who succeeded him at The University of North Carolina, said: "He was very flambouyant, a great salesman. He believed in himself completely ... completely in command." Tatum assistants who went on to top coaching jobs included Bud Wilkinson at Oklahoma, Warren Giese at the University of South Carolina, Eddie Teague at The Citadel, Tommy Mont at Maryland, Bill Meek at Kansas, and George Barclay at Washington and Lee and at The University of North Carolina.

On 7 May 1938 Tatum married Edna Sumrell, of Ayden, the daughter of Barnes and Minnie Dixon Sumrell. Her father was an automobile dealer in Greenville and Ayden and a Pitt County farmer. Jim and Edna Tatum had a son, James Moore Jr., and two daughters, Mrs. Paul (Rebecca T.) Hilstad of Minneapolis, Minn., and Mrs. Ronald W. (Reid T.) Merritt of Chapel Hill. All were graduated from The University of North Carolina. The son and one son-in-law earned law degrees at Chapel Hill, and the other son-in-law took a law degree at Duke University.

While visiting in Canada with fellow coaches Clyde (Peahead) Walker of Montreal and Frank Howard of Clemson, S.C., Tatum apparently contracted an overwhelming viral infection, which also hospitalized his wife. One week after entering Memorial Hospital in Chapel Hill, the big, rugged veteran of so many physical campaigns succumbed. His wife threw off the virus.

Tatum was Methodist. He was buried in the shade of a tree beside a walkway in the Old Chapel Hill Cemetery.

SEE: George Lynn Cross, *Presidents Can't Punt: The OU Football Tradition* (1977); *Durham Sun*, 11 Aug. 1959; *New York Times*, 19 Jan. 1947; Bob Quincy, *The Jim Tatum Story* (1960); Raleigh *News and Observer*, 21 Jan., 25 July 1959; *Raleigh Times*, 30 Mar. 1960; *Shelby Daily Star*, 5 Nov. 1957; *Time* magazine, 3 Aug. 1959; Jake Wade, *Jim Moore Tatum* (1960); *Winston-Salem Journal*, 18 Oct. 1957.

JACK RILEY

Taylor, Charles Elisha (28 Oct. 1842–5 Nov. 1915), Baptist minister and college president, was born in Richmond, Va., the son of James Barnett and Mary Williams Taylor. His father, who was born in England, was the first corresponding secretary of the Foreign Mission Board of the Southern Baptist Convention. His mother was the daughter of the Reverend Elisha Williams, who had served in the American Revolution, and his wife's great-grandfather was Rector Elisha Williams, president of Yale College.

At age fifteen Taylor entered Richmond College but left to join the Confederate army the day Virginia passed the Ordinance of Secession. He served with the Tenth Virginia and with the Signal and Secret Service Bureau in Richmond. After the Civil War, he opened a school for a short time and then entered the University of Virginia at Charlottesville. He was graduated with a B.Litt. in 1870. After spending a few months in Europe, he accepted the position of professor of Latin and German at Wake Forest College. He served in this capacity from 1870 to 1883. In 1883–84 he was professor of Latin and moral philosophy. He received honorary doctorates from Richmond College, The University of North Carolina, and Mercer University.

He was ordained on 23 Apr. 1871 by Washington Manly Wingate, president of Wake Forest College. Assisting him was James B. Taylor, the father of Charles Elisha. On occasion he filled the pulpit of the Wake Forest Baptist Church and served surrounding Baptist churches at Franklinton, Louisburg, and Perry's Chapel. Thirteen years later, on

11 Nov. 1884, the Wake Forest board of trustees met in Raleigh and elected Taylor president to fill the vacancy created by the resignation of Thomas Henderson Pritchard.

Taylor's primary contribution to the college was a movement (begun in 1875 while he was still a professor) to increase its endowment. As president he kept a steady appeal before the Baptist people to help Wake Forest. In 1883 he made an extensive trip among the Baptists in the North and was successful in interesting J. A. Bostwick to contribute Standard Oil Company stock as an endowment to the college. The initial donation was followed by others: $12,000 in 1885, $50,000 in 1886, and $13,000 in 1891. These large donations and thousands of smaller ones formed the basis on which the college grew. The endowment increased from about $100,000 to more than $300,000 during Taylor's administration.

The curriculum of the school grew as Taylor introduced the elective system in 1887 The School of Law was organized in 1894 and the School of Medicine in 1902. A number of departments were added: Modern Language in 1888, Religion in 1896, History and Political Science in 1898, Physics in 1899, and both Education and Physical Culture in 1900. Faculty increased from seven professors to seventeen and the student enrollment from 150 to 328. Three new buildings were erected with adequate lighting, running water, and comfortable seats in the classrooms. Special attention was paid to the campus with the planting of magnolias and other trees and shrubs and the building of a rock wall around the property.

Taylor was an outspoken proponent of public school education. His articles in the *Biblical Recorder*, later appearing in a volume entitled *How Far Should a State Undertake to Educate?* (1894), were very influential in this area. He also suggested the formation of an orphanage association, contributed to its success, and "put hope, courage, and inspiration into the heart of [John Haymes] Mills."

In addition to his articles and weekly reports to the *Biblical Recorder* and essays, biographical sketches, and sermons in the *Wake Forest Student* and the *North Carolina Baptist Historical Papers*, Taylor published a poem—"Gilbert Stone, the Millionaire"—in 1891. His most notable work was *The Story of Yates the Missionary . . .* (1898). He also wrote an article that appeared in *Baptist, Why and Why Not . . .* (1900) and two undated pamphlets, *A Familiar Talk with Young Men and a Symposium* and *What Were the Best Things Wake Forest Did for Me*. He compiled the college's first alumni directory, *General Catalogue of Wake Forest College North Carolina, 1834–5–1891–2* (1892), which contains much information of a biographical nature.

Highly esteemed by southern educators, Taylor was awarded a doctor of divinity by Richmond College (now University of Richmond) in 1884, a doctor of laws by The University of North Carolina in 1889, and a doctor of laws by Mercer University in 1898.

Taylor married Mary Hinton Pritchard, the daughter of John Lamb Pritchard, on 11 Sept. 1873. The couple had one son, Charles Elisha, Jr., and six daughters: Mary Pritchard, Ethel (Mrs. Charles Christopher Crittenden), Fanny (Mrs. J. Hendren Gorrell), Janie (Mrs. William D. Duke), Agnes (Mrs. Aubrey Hawkins), and Edith (Mrs. Elliott B. Earnshaw).

After his retirement as president of Wake Forest College in 1905, Taylor continued to teach as professor of moral philosophy until his death a few hours after suffering a severe heart attack. His funeral was conducted by Willis Richard Cullom and W. N. Johnson, pastor of the Wake Forest Baptist Church. He was buried in the cemetery at Wake Forest.

SEE: Samuel A. Ashe, ed., *Biographical History of North Carolina*, vol. 1 (1917); *Nat. Cyc. Am. Biog.*, vol. 25 (1935); Raleigh, *Biblical Recorder*, 10 Nov. 1915; Charles E. Taylor Papers (Baptist Historical Collection, Wake Forest University, Winston-Salem [portrait]); *Wake Forest Student*, Taylor Memorial Issue, 35 (March 1916 [portrait]); Davis E. Woolley, ed., *Southern Baptist Encyclopedia*, vol. 2 (1958).

JOHN WOODARD

Taylor, Eben-Ezer (*ca. 1660–February 1720*), clergyman, was born in England and moved to South Carolina at an undetermined date as a minister to the dissenters in that colony. There he gained the attention of the governor, Sir Nathaniel Johnson, who persuaded him to obtain Anglican orders. Taylor returned to England in 1711 and was ordained. Later in the year he received the King's Bounty for his passage back to America and was appointed missionary for the Society for the Propagation of the Gospel in Foreign Parts to serve in South Carolina. After he was named rector of St. Andrew's Parish, Ashley River, his career promptly became marred by controversy. He was accused of continuing to talk like a Presbyterian, "railing" in his sermons, neglecting his attire, and quarreling with the vestry over financial matters.

In the fall of 1717 he moved to North Carolina, where he remained until his death three years later. His fellow missionary, the Reverend John Urmston, not always reliable in his comments, reported to officials of the Society for the Propagation of the Gospel in London on 12 October that Taylor, who had recently arrived, was aged and infirm and "not able to ride five miles were it to gain the world." Taylor himself reported to the Society's secretary on 23 April 1719 that he was living at Esquire Duckenfield's on the southwestern shore of Chowan Precinct. Duckenfield was "the gentleman with whom I lived most of the year and whose house was our church all the year." Urmston referred to these accommodations as a "fourth of a chamber for an apartment and the liberty of a large room to preach." William Duckenfield, who died about February 1722, was a prominent early citizen in what is now Bertie County.

While Taylor was living at Duckenfield's, a question arose as to the status of slaves who became Christians. After two slaves belonging to Duckenfield were baptized, a rumor spread in the neighborhood that baptized slaves were thereby freed. Duckenfield refused to allow any more baptisms until a law could be passed in England that no slave would become free because he was baptized. Possibly as a result of this difficulty, Taylor seems to have moved.

At the end of 1719 Urmston said that "brother Taylor" had changed his habitation a dozen times since arriving in North Carolina and such were his trials that he wished himself back in South Carolina. Nevertheless, the hardworking missionary soon came to an unfortunate end. On 25 Apr. 1720 Urmston reported to his superiors in London that in February "his fellow laborer" had died of exposure from being in an open boat for ten days going from Bath Town to Core Sound. The boatmen buried the deceased on Harbor Island at the mouth of the Neuse River and then rifled his chests. There was suspicion of foul play, and two of the men were tried and convicted of taking a large sum of money from a chest belonging to Taylor.

Rev. Eben-Ezer Taylor married a woman named Agnes. They may have been the parents of a daughter, as he mentioned his son-in-law, Gowen London, in his will. His wife did not return to South Carolina with him after his ordination but remained in the west of England, perhaps at or near Exeter. His will was dated 21 Apr. 1711, shortly before he left Charles Town for England. He bequeathed his library to whichever son of his three brothers entered the ministry. One of the brothers, Benjamin, had been a missionary in South Carolina for a brief time. On 16 Sept. 1720, John Walker, a merchant in Barbadoes (and probably the husband of Taylor's sister) but "at present sojourning in North Carolina," was administrator of the Reverend Mr. Taylor and gave power of attorney to Colonel Maurice Moore and John Porter to receive money due the estate.

Taylor's lengthy will cited significant sums of money plus interest due him from various individuals, some of whom bore prominent names in South Carolina. This suggests that he lent money. He also willed his plantation on Forster Creek, merchandise, a slave, an Indian woman and her son, and generous sums of money to members of his family, including cousins Samuel and Elenor Cross.

SEE: S. Charles Bolton, *Southern Anglicanism: The Church of England in Colonial South Carolina* (1982); J. Bryan Grimes, ed., *Abstract of North Carolina Wills* (1910); Margaret Hofmann, *Chowan Precinct, North Carolina, 1696–1723: Abstract of Deed Books* (1972); William W. Manross, *S.P.G. Papers in the Lambeth Palace Library* (1965); William L. Saunders, ed., *Colonial Records of North Carolina*, vol. 2 (1890); Eben-Ezer Taylor will (North Carolina State Archives, Raleigh).

CLAIBORNE T. SMITH, JR.

Taylor, Hannis *(12 Sept. 1851–26 Dec. 1922)*, lawyer, scholar, and diplomat, was born in New Bern, the son of Susan Stevenson and Richard Nixon Taylor, a merchant. He was the grandson of Mary Hannis and William Taylor, Scottish immigrants, and of Elizabeth Sears and James C. Stevenson of New Bern.

Young Taylor had just completed a classical elementary education at New Bern Academy when civil war came to the North Carolina sound region. In March 1862 he and his family fled inland to Chapel Hill, where they were safe from Union troops. There Taylor continued his studies during the years 1862–65 with Cornelia Phillips Spencer and in 1865 with Dr. Alexander Wilson. After the family moved to Raleigh in 1866, Hannis completed his preparatory studies at Lovejoy's School (1866–67) and then entered The University of North Carolina in July 1867, but family financial straits forced him to withdraw after nine months of study. He returned with the family to New Bern and there, with his ambition fixed on a legal career, served as a law clerk under John N. Washington. When Washington died in 1869 and tuberculosis began to claim many lives in the New Bern area, Taylor's parents decided to move to Point Clear, Ala., where the father hoped to obtain work in the production of naval stores. Shortly after arriving, Taylor's mother died, and as a result his father seemed unable to function. In December 1870 Hannis moved the family—the father, four brothers, and two sisters—across the bay to Mobile and thus became head of a household at age twenty.

In Mobile, Taylor worked as a law clerk on a modest salary before gaining admittance to the Alabama bar in 1872. With credentials to practice, he first served as solicitor of neighboring Baldwin County but within a year had turned to private practice. As a man of legal and public activities in Alabama, he gained a regional reputation for his avid if fruitless attacks on the federal antilottery law (*Ex parte Rapier*, 143 U.S. 93–103) and for his advocacy of industrialism and other New South programs. He rewrote the Mobile city charter in a way that kept the city from being liable for its Reconstruction debts. Soon he had a name in international scholarship circles as the Ala-

bamian who wrote *Origin and Growth of the English Constitution* (2 vols., 1889, 1898), for which the University of Edinburgh honored him with the L.L.D. degree. Because of this work and his association with the conservative branch of the Democratic party, Taylor was chosen president of the Alabama state bar (1891) and, during Grover Cleveland's second administration, was appointed minister to Spain (1893–97). During and after his Madrid tenure, Taylor's strong advocacy of American intervention in Cuba offended the administrations of Grover Cleveland and William McKinley. Even so, Taylor received considerable attention for his expansionist views; when the Spanish-American War was concluded, he attempted to use this reputation to win election to the U.S. House of Representatives from Alabama's First District. He lost in the Democratic primary in 1898 and again in 1900, owing chiefly to his having married Leonora LeBaron, who belonged to a prominent Roman Catholic family in Mobile.

Frustrated over chances for personal advancement in the South, Taylor moved to Washington, D.C., in 1902. He taught part-time in the law school of George Washington University and practiced before the U.S. Supreme Court. More important, he became a Republican publicist, supporting Theodore Roosevelt and his progressivist policies and publishing many articles in the *North American Review* and other prestigious journals. Taylor also served as special adviser to the Spanish Treaty Claims Commission (1903–10) and as American counsel to the Alaskan Boundary Tribunal (1903). He gave similar support to William Howard Taft but levied constant criticism at Woodrow Wilson, especially regarding Wilson's use of the militia in World War I (*Cox v. Wood*, 247 U.S. 3–7). Soon after failing to win an appointment in Warren G. Harding's administration, Taylor died of Bright's disease. He had become a Roman Catholic nine years earlier. He was buried at Fort Lincoln Cemetery in Maryland but very near Washington. Surviving him were his wife, three sons—Alfred R., Hannis Joseph, and Charles LeBaron—and two daughters, Mary L. T. Hunt and Hannah T. Bayly.

Aside from some one hundred articles and *The English Constitution*, Taylor's major writings include *A Treatise on International Public Law* (1901); *Jurisdiction and Procedure of the Supreme Court* (1905); *The Science of Jurisprudence* (1908), which Oliver Wendell Holmes castigated for its plagiarism; *The Origin and Growth of the American Constitution* (1911), advancing the strange thesis that Pelatiah Webster was the architect of the U.S. Constitution; and *Due Process of Law* (1917).

SEE: Mary L. T. Hunt, "Memoirs of a Diplomat's Daughter" (possession of Tennant S. McWilliams, Birmingham, Ala.); Tennant S. McWilliams, *Hannis Taylor: New Southerner as American* (1977); Richard V. Taylor, "A Voice for Alabama: An Autobiography" (possession of Mrs. Luther Bewley, Birmingham, Ala.).

TENNANT S. MCWILLIAMS

Taylor, Haywood Maurice *(11 May 1898–21 Oct. 1960)*, toxicologist and biochemist, was born near Tarboro, Edgecombe County, the son of David Dawson and Margaret Elizabeth Brown Taylor. His studies at The University of North Carolina were interrupted by service in the army during World War I, when he was a first lieutenant. He was graduated in 1920 with a B.S. degree, then received the M.S. in 1921 and the Ph.D. in 1924. At the university he was an instructor in chemistry and pharmacy in 1920–25; he also taught science at the Chapel Hill High School in 1921–22.

Taylor was a research chemist with E. R. Squibb and Sons in New York and then head of the department of chemistry at the Wilmer Ophthalmological Institute at the Johns Hopkins Hospital and Medical School before joining the original staff of the Duke University Medical Center when it opened in 1930. Widely known as a toxicologist, he was professor of biochemistry at Duke and in 1950 became professor of toxicology. He served as a consultant to the North Carolina Bureau of Investigation and to the North Carolina Medical Examiners System. During World War II he was appointed gas consultant to the state Office of Civilian Defense.

He married Alice Lee Brown of Chadbourn on 29 Oct. 1922, and they had two daughters, Alice Lee and Martha Anne. An Episcopalian, he was buried in Maplewood Cemetery, Durham.

SEE: Alumni Files (University of North Carolina, Chapel Hill); Maurice M. Bursey, *Carolina Chemists* (1982 [portrait]); *Durham Morning Herald*, 2 Oct. 1960; Daniel L. Grant, *Alumni History of the University of North Carolina* (1924); Raleigh *News and Observer*, 3 Sept. 1942; *Who's Who in the South and Southwest* (1959).

WILLIAM S. POWELL

Taylor, Hoyt Patrick, Sr. *(11 June 1890–11 Apr. 1964)*, lieutenant governor, state senator, and attorney, was born in Winton, the Hertford County seat, the son of Simeon Pipkin and Kate Ward Taylor, of Scots-Irish ancestry. His mother was the sister of Hallet (Hot Stuff) Ward, a former congressman from Washington, N.C. Young Taylor attended Winton High School and Academy and Horner Military School. After graduating in 1906 he had intended to enter The University of North Carolina, but "economic circumstances" thwarted that ambition. Instead, he went to work for his father, who was in the timber and lumber business and was an expert timber cruiser, for two years, mainly in the Pender County area.

At age seventeen Taylor took a job as a hotel clerk at the Colonial Inn in Wilmington. About a year later he became a clerk at the old Lafayette Hotel in Fayetteville, where a representative of the Fred Harvey hotel chain persuaded him to accept a clerk position in Needles, Calif. Taylor remained there for two years before homesickness and an urge to study law lured him back to North Carolina in 1912. That summer he worked as a vacation relief hotel clerk in Raleigh, Rocky Mount, and Morehead City. In the fall, the twenty-two-year-old, armed with only a high school diploma, enrolled at Wake Forest College Law School. There he established a close friendship with a fellow student, Roland S. Pruette. Six months before Taylor was graduated, Pruette received his law degree and went to Wadesboro to establish a practice. During his final months at Wake Forest, Taylor became familiar with the Anson County town and county seat largely because of Pruette's anecdotes and descriptions of the place. After receiving his law degree and admission to the state bar in February 1914, he also moved to Wadesboro and began working in the law office of Fred J. Cox.

Two weeks after joining Cox, Taylor won a civil case. About sixteen months later he formed his own practice, which eventually became known as a breeding ground for young lawyers who later branched out on their own. His office became the firm of Taylor, Kitchin and Taylor, which included former Eighth Congressional District Representative A. Paul Kitchin and Taylor's son, H. Patrick Taylor, Jr., who followed in his father's footsteps by working his way up the General Assembly ladder and

reaching the lieutenant governorship in 1969. The elder Taylor continued to practice law in Wadesboro until the advent of World War I.

Taylor entered the U.S. Army in May 1917, completed officers' training at a camp in Fort Ogelthorpe, Ga., and became a second lieutenant. In January 1918 he began a ninety-day program to prepare him for overseas service. In April he was assigned to the 371st Infantry Regiment, a black unit led by white officers, and sailed for France. Under French command, Taylor and his regiment were first positioned in the Argonne Forest region on 2 June. On 12 September they were sent to the Champagne sector. About two weeks later First Lieutenant Taylor was wounded after being gassed and struck on his right side by shrapnel. Concerned about his injuries, the battalion commander instructed him to withdraw from combat, but Taylor chose to stay with his company for two more days. On 29 Mar. 1919 he was promoted to captain and awarded the Purple Heart and Silver Star for gallantry in combat by General John J. Pershing. His regiment received the French Fourragère.

On returning to Wadesboro in 1919, Taylor discovered that he had been elected mayor of the town; he served until 1921. On 28 June 1923 he married Inez Wooten of Chadbourn, Columbus County. In addition to Hoyt Patrick, Jr., the couple were the parents of Caroline Corbett and Frank Wooten. Caroline studied at the Julliard School of Music in New York City; having performed solo on a number of occasions with the North Carolina Symphony orchestra, first at age ten, she eventually became a world renowned pianist. Her brother Frank was ill most of his life and died young, whereas Pat became a key player in North Carolina politics for about two decades.

Until 1936 Taylor remained a political fixture in Anson County, serving as county attorney and chairman of the Anson County Democratic executive committee. In 1936 he was elected to represent the Nineteenth Senatorial District in the General Assembly and began his tenure by serving in the special session of that year. During the 1937 regular session Lieutenant Governor Wilkins P. Horton appointed him chairman of the committee on institutions for the blind and later chairman of the calendar committee. Taylor returned to the senate for the 1938 special session and was reelected and installed as chairman of the finance committee for the 1939 regular session. Due to Anson County's rotation with a neighboring county for the district's senate seat, he did not reappear in Raleigh until the 1943 session. He was named chairman of the appropriations committee before that session convened. Taylor remained on the advisory budget commission and division of purchase and contract in 1943–44; he had previously served on the commission and division in 1939–40. His work received much praise; at the end of the 1939 and 1943 sessions, members of the state press voted him the most valuable member of the senate.

In 1945 Taylor became a legislative assistant to Governor R. Gregg Cherry. On 4 Nov. 1948 he was elected lieutenant governor and W. Kerr Scott was elected governor. It is noteworthy that twenty years later, Taylor's son Patrick was elected lieutenant governor and Scott's son Robert became governor. While lieutenant governor Taylor was also chairman of the state board of education and of Meredith College's board of trustees. He had been a member of The University of North Carolina board of trustees since 1939.

After completing his term Taylor returned to Wadesboro and continued practicing law. He maintained his involvement as a member of the Wadesboro Rotary and Executive Clubs, and of Anson County Post No. 31,

American Legion, of which he was a charter member. Additionally, he belonged to Woodmen of the World, Phi Delta Phi legal fraternity, the Ancient Free and Accepted Masons, the Carolina Consistory, and the Oasis Temple of the Shrine. For about twenty-five years he taught the Baracca Class at the First Baptist Church, Wadesboro, where he served on the board of deacons. At age seventy-three Taylor died at his home; he was buried in Eastview Cemetery.

SEE: Mary L. Medley, *History of Anson County, 1750–1976* (1976); *North Carolina Manual* (1951); William S. Powell, ed., *North Carolina Lives* (1962); Raleigh *News and Observer*, 30 June 1947, 10 Jan. 1949, 11 Mar. 1951, 13 Apr. 1964; Hoyt Patrick Taylor, Jr., personal contact.

BENJAMIN A. JOLLY

Taylor, James Fauntleroy *(21 Sept. 1821–31 Aug. 1903)*, state librarian, the son of North Carolina attorney general James Fauntleroy and Eliza Leonora Taylor, was born in Raleigh. He attended The University of North Carolina, where he joined the Dialectic Society, and was graduated with the A.B. degree in 1841. The university, as was frequently done, granted him an unearned A.M. degree in 1844. Taylor read law and obtained a license but never practiced. In February 1843 the trustees of the state library appointed him state librarian, a position he held until February 1854. He was the first person to manage the library on a full-time basis. On 30 Oct. 1850 Governor Charles Manly selected him to prepare North Carolina's exhibit at the Exposition of the Industry of All Nations, held in 1851 at the Crystal Palace in London.

A member of the Historical Society of North Carolina, Taylor in 1870 was appointed to a committee to obtain from Mrs. David Lowry Swain books and manuscripts claimed by the society. During the Civil War he was a petty officer on the blockade-runner *Ad-Vance*. An active Republican, Taylor served as a trustee of The University of North Carolina in 1868 and from 1870 to 1874. He considered himself a Roman Catholic but was not active in a specific church. He enjoyed writing poetry, for which he gained some recognition, and referred to himself as the "bard of Rhamkatte." Taylor died in Raleigh, never having married, and was buried in Oakwood Cemetery.

SEE: Dialectic Society, *Catalogue of the Members of the Dialectic Society, Instituted in the University of North Carolina June 3, 1795, Together with Historical Sketches* (1890); H. G. Jones, *For History's Sake: The Preservation and Publication of North Carolina History, 1663–1903* (1966); Letter Book of Governor Charles Manly (North Carolina State Archives, Raleigh); Raleigh *News and Observer*, 2 Sept. 1903; Raleigh *North Carolinian*, 3 Sept. 1903; Glen Tucker, *Zeb Vance: Champion of Personal Freedom* (1965); Wake County Estates Records, 1772–1941 (North Carolina State Archives, Raleigh).

MAURY YORK

Taylor, James Peyton *(20 Oct. 1839–9 Dec. 1928)*, Confederate soldier and teacher, was born near Pittsboro, the son of the Reverend William Peter, a Methodist minister, and Mary High Taylor. He was graduated from The University of North Carolina in 1859 and taught school in Pittsboro during the years 1859–61 and 1865–66. On 11 June 1860 he married Virginia Morris Hanks, who was also a schoolteacher.

From 15 Apr. 1861 until serious health problems arose,

he served with North Carolina troops in Virginia, first as a private and then as a corporal. Although present, his unit took virtually no part in the fighting at Seven Pines, but it was heavily engaged at Malvern Hill. Sometime prior to 10 July 1862 he was discharged after providing a substitute. In 1863 Governor Zebulon B. Vance detailed Taylor for service as assistant adjutant and inspector general of the Twelfth Brigade, North Carolina militia, with the rank of major.

Taylor and his wife and young daughter, Helen Euphemia, called Effie, moved to Texas in 1866. Soon other members of the family from North Carolina joined them: Mrs. Taylor's brother, John Wesley Hanks; her sister Louise Hanks, who married Joseph P. Underwood; and an uncle, Dr. Anthony Morris. James P. Taylor farmed briefly on the San Bernard River at a place they named Bernadine. Moving to Brazoria County, both Taylor and his wife resumed teaching—in Brazoria in 1867 and Columbia in 1868. In time they built a spacious, two-story house on what was called "the Avenue" between East and West Columbia. There they erected a separate building and opened a private school. Taylor also taught there between 1867 and 1872, when he became principal of the first public school in Texas, a post he retained until 1910, when he was elected county superintendent of schools. After serving for four years he retired. Three hundred former students attended a celebration of the Taylors' fiftieth wedding anniversary in June 1910.

SEE: James A. Creighton, *A Narrative History of Brazoria County* (1975); Daniel L. Grant, *Alumni History of the University of North Carolina* (1924); Weymouth T. Jordan, comp., *North Carolina Troops, 1861–1865: A Roster*, vols. 5 (1975), 9 (1983).

WILLIAM S. POWELL

Taylor, John Louis *(1 Mar. 1769–29 Jan. 1829)*, chief justice and legislator, was born in London of Irish parentage. Orphaned, he came to America at age twelve with an older brother, James, who helped finance his studies at William and Mary College, Williamsburg, Va. For lack of funds, he left school before graduation and settled in North Carolina, where he studied law by himself without a tutor. Admitted to the bar in 1788, he began practicing in Fayetteville. In 1790 he was an unsuccessful candidate for the post of state solicitor general, to be appointed by the General Assembly. Five years later he also failed in his application to be North Carolina's attorney general. Meanwhile, in 1792 he was a presidential elector and was sent to the 1792 House of Commons by the borough town of Fayetteville. He was reelected in 1794 and 1795. The next year he moved to New Bern.

In 1798 the Assembly named him a judge of the superior courts. Under an 1810 act the other judges in July 1811 chose him as their presiding officer or so-called "chief justice." This necessitated his moving to Raleigh. He sold his fine home at New Bern and in Raleigh built a residence, Elmwood, about 1813. In 1822 he opened "the first place for legal education in North Carolina which might be called a law school." When the Supreme Court of North Carolina was established, Taylor became on 1 Jan. 1819 its first chief justice, a position he retained until his death at his Raleigh home. He was buried nearby.

Taylor was the first reporter of the state supreme court and published several volumes of its decisions. The author of textbooks and other works, he was a member of a commission to revise the state's statutes. From 1793 to 1818 he was a trustee of The University of North Carolina.

Georgetown University conferred on him the honorary doctor of laws degree. A Federalist in politics, he was an orator of note. He opposed the importation of slaves and supported measures to encourage trade and improve the administration of justice.

While residing at Fayetteville Taylor joined Phoenix Lodge, Ancient Free and Accepted Masons, and was one of its two delegates to the Grand Lodge Communication there in December 1793. He was elected junior grand warden and the next year was advanced to senior grand warden.

At New Bern he affiliated with St. John's Lodge. In 1799 he was made deputy grand master, an office he held for two years. In 1802, at age thirty-three, he became grand master and was twice reelected. He was the 1807 worshipful master of St. John's Lodge and from 1814 to 1817 served again as grand master. Taylor worked diligently and spoke frequently in behalf of Masonic principles. When he retired from the grand mastership, two lodges were named for him. Portraits of him were hung in the headquarters of the Grand Lodge of North Carolina at Raleigh and the Masonic Temple at New Bern.

Taylor's first wife was Julia Rowan, by whom he had one daughter, Julia Rowan. After her death he married, on 16 Aug. 1797, Jane Gaston, by whom he had a son, John L., and a daughter, Margaret Ann. He bequeathed his Raleigh home to his brother-in-law, William Gaston, who lived there until his own death.

SEE: Gertrude S. Carraway, *Years of Light* (1944); John L. Cheney, Jr., ed., *North Carolina Government, 1585–1979* (1981); *DAB*, vol. 9 (1936); Marshal De Lancey Haywood, *Builders of the Old North State* (1968); *Nocalore* 8 (1938 [portrait]); *North Carolina Reports, 1826–1830* (1900); *North Carolina University Magazine* 9 (March 1860).

GERTRUDE S. CARRAWAY

Taylor, Marble Nash *(183?–1894),* preacher and Civil War figure, is believed to have been born in Bedford County, Va. Said to have been orphaned as a child and reared by the Reverend Morgan Closs of Hillsborough, N.C., Taylor applied and was rejected for both Baptist and Methodist ministries in the late 1840s. Accepted by the North Carolina Methodist Conference in 1850, he received annual assignments in various eastern North Carolina localities prior to his appointment in late 1860 to the small church on Hatteras Island. He married Catherine Munroe of Cumberland County in 1857, and they had a daughter.

Taylor was the only clergyman on Hatteras at the time of the Union assault there in August 1861 and was reported in the state press to have given aid to the Federal landing parties that seized the island. He was the first islander to take the pledge of allegiance to the Union and was instrumental in fostering a cooperative attitude among fellow Hatteras residents towards the Federal forces.

In the early fall of 1861 Taylor entered into an alliance with Charles Henry Foster, a Maine native but lately of Murfreesboro, N.C., for the purpose of forming a Unionist government for that portion of North Carolina under Federal occupation. It was arranged that Taylor should exercise the powers of governor and that Foster would seek election as Second District congressman. The scheme was launched with a "convention" at Hatteras church on 12 October and the creation of a "provisional state government," which was evidently neither endorsed nor discouraged by Federal military officials. Following a brief "relief mission" to New York in November seeking aid for distressed islanders, Foster and Taylor returned to Hatteras and held a "constitutional convention" at which Taylor was formally named governor. As his first official act, Taylor drafted ordinances calling for a late November congressional election for Hatteras and adjacent Union-occupied portions of the Outer Banks. In the balloting on 28 November, candidate Foster, running unopposed, garnered a few score votes and hurried away to Washington to claim his seat in the Thirty-seventh Congress.

Despite a sympathetic Northern press, the Hatteras scheme made no headway in Washington. Foster's credentials were hooted off the floor of the Elections Committee. Further elections on the Outer Banks in January and February 1862 failed to add credence to the enterprise, and Taylor seems to have taken no further part in Foster's political machinations. In March a Boston journalist found Taylor living unpretentiously on Hatteras Island, "a well-meaning" man who would be "one of the last to lay claim to that which he did not believe himself entitled to." A few weeks later the Lincoln administration named Edward Stanly military governor of North Carolina. Taylor appears to have remained at Hatteras in the role of minister until the war's end.

The Reconstruction regime appointed Taylor "keeper of the poor house" at Fayetteville. Evidently he stayed in that town for about fifteen years, "respected as a man of earnest and strong convictions, honest and well-meaning, though misguided as to politics in the opinion of most." Around 1880 he is said to have turned up in western Moore County peddling fruit trees and living in a shack made of scraps from a sawmill. Long after his death there he was remembered locally as "a dour, taciturn" man who read much, talked little, and was addressed as "governor" to the end.

SEE: Norman D. Brown, "A Union Election in North Carolina," *North Carolina Historical Review* 43 (October 1966); Ben D. McNeill, *The Hatterasman* (1958); *New York Times*, 27 Oct. 1861; "North Carolina Review," Raleigh *News and Observer*, 4 Sept. 1910; Washington, D.C., *National Republican*, 2 Jan. 1862.

THOMAS C. PARRAMORE

Taylor, Robert Robinson *(8 June 1868–7 Dec. 1942),* architect, was born in Wilmington, the son of Henry, a wealthy mulatto house carpenter, and Emilie Taylor, also mulatto. His father later was described as an able black contractor and builder who constructed public commercial and residential buildings; he also built large cargo ships for the Caribbean island trade. Taylor was educated at the Williston School and Gregory Institute, the latter operated by the American Missionary Association, both in Wilmington. He was graduated at the head of his class. After entering the Massachusetts Institute of Technology in 1888, he was graduated in 1892 with the B.S. degree in architecture, the first black to do so.

While at MIT Taylor came to the attention of Booker T. Washington, of the Tuskegee Normal and Industrial Institute in Alabama, who persuaded him to join the staff at Tuskegee in the winter of 1892–93 to transform the Industrial Program into a Department of Mechanical Industries. His first appointment was as instructor in architecture. He became the institute's architect and designed and directed the construction of forty-five buildings on the campus between 1900 and 1913; the structures that he designed between 1913 and 1932, however, were contracted to a firm in Birmingham, Ala. Taylor's favorite building was the chapel, constructed between 1895 and 1898 entirely with student labor and student-made bricks. He also designed other buildings in Alabama and in Arkansas, Mississippi, Ohio, North Carolina, South Carolina, Tennessee, and Virginia.

Taylor left Tuskegee in 1899 to join a large architectural firm in Cleveland, Ohio, where he may also have been briefly in 1892, but after a few years Washington persuaded him to return. In 1911 he was invited to deliver an address at the fiftieth anniversary of the Massachusetts Institute of Technology; it was published in *Technology and Industrial Efficiency* as "The Scientific Development of the Negro." At Tuskegee he served as director of the department of mechanical industries and as general superintendent of industries before becoming vice-principal of the institute in 1925. From time to time he also was acting principal. By invitation in 1929, he went to Africa to prepare plans for and establish the program of industrial training for the Booker T. Washington Agricultural Institute in Kakata, Monrovia, Liberia, and to determine the type of buildings to be erected. In the same year Lincoln University in Pennsylvania awarded him the honorary doctor of science degree.

In addition to his work at Tuskegee and in Liberia, Taylor designed buildings for other institutions including the Carnegie Library at Livingstone College, Salisbury. He also designed churches, office buildings, and homes. In 1928 he worked with the Hoover Commission in the reconstruction of flooded areas in the Mississippi Valley.

Following his retirement, about 1935, Taylor returned to his birthplace and spent the remainder of his life in Wilmington. Continuing his interest in civic affairs, he was appointed by Governors J. C. B. Ehringhaus in 1936 and J. Melville Broughton in 1942 to successive terms on the board of trustees of the Fayetteville State Teachers College, the first black to hold such a position. The science building on the campus was named in his honor. He had been a member of the Society of Arts of Boston, American Economic Society, Masonic order, and other groups. In Tuskegee he belonged to the local Business League and was active in the Educational Association of Teachers and other educational, business, and professional organizations.

During his retirement Taylor frequently returned to Tuskegee, and it was there, while attending a service in the chapel, that he died. Taylor and his wife, Nellie C., were the parents of three sons and two daughters. He was buried in Pine Forest Cemetery, Wilmington.

SEE: *Charlotte Observer*, 8 Jan. 1983; Massachusetts Institute of Technology, Institute Archives and Special Collections, registrar's record; New Hanover County census returns, 1870; Clement Richardson, ed., *National Cyclopedia of the Colored Race* (1919 [portrait]); *Technology and Industrial Efficiency* (1911); Tuskegee Institute Archives, "Robert Robinson Taylor (1868–1942)," January 1942; Ellen Weiss, "Robert R. Taylor of Tuskegee: An Early Black American Architect," *Arris* 2 (1991 [portrait]).

WILLIAM S. POWELL

Taylor, Simon Bruton (*16 Mar. 1834–27 Jan. 1929*), Confederate officer, merchant, public official, and farmer, was born on a farm in southern Lenoir County, the son of Stanton and Nancy Bruton Taylor. His father died when Simon was seven years old, and he and an older brother contributed to the family's support. The brother opened a store in Kinston and Simon became his helper. The younger Taylor also became a member of the local militia and afterwards was identified with "the Onslow Dough and Roadies" in Onslow County not far from his birthplace.

On the eve of the Civil War these men constituted Company A, Thirty-fifth North Carolina Regiment, and re-

ceived training at Camp Mangum near Raleigh. He was commissioned first lieutenant on 6 Sept. 1861. The regiment first came under fire in March 1862, when New Bern fell to the enemy. The regiment was reorganized, and Taylor became captain of Company A on 21 Apr. 1862. Following the victory at Chancellorsville, 2–3 May 1863, he was promoted to major on 15 June and served with the regiment in battles in Virginia. His old company participated in the many exchanges of Harpers Ferry, as it changed hands repeatedly. In these exchanges, the men of Company A were among those who waded the James River three times in nine days. Following the battles at Antietam and Fredericksburg members of the regiment expressed their sympathy for the people of the area by raising a large collection for the relief of those who had lost property and supplies during the battles.

The regiment returned to North Carolina to participate in the liberation of Plymouth on 20 Apr. 1864 and expected to be involved in the freeing of New Bern soon afterwards. Instead, it was called to help defend Richmond, while Plymouth shortly was retaken by Union forces. During this time, however, Taylor was advanced to lieutenant colonel on 18 June 1864. At Five Forks in Virginia about 1 Apr. 1865, he received a serious bullet wound in the arm and leg, was captured, and held prisoner. Nevertheless, he was given excellent medical attention and later expressed gratitude for his treatment.

Three of Taylor's brothers were killed in action, including Guilford, with whom he had expected to return to the mercantile business. Taylor moved to Onslow County to be among those with whom he had served in the war and opened a store on the shore of Catherine Lake. It flourished and for more than sixty years was a major enterprise of the area. He engaged in the naval stores trade, providing employment and a market for countless small producers. He also lent support to an academy that was established in the community, and he served as a county commissioner, county treasurer, and a justice of the peace. Although farming was merely a sideline with him, he practiced advanced methods for the time and supported the Farmers Alliance.

In 1866 Taylor married Sallie Murrill, the daughter of a leading plantation owner near Catherine Lake. They had three daughters: Annie, Mattie (died in infancy), and Lucy Bruton. Taylor was a member of the Disciples of Christ. After the death of his wife as a result of an uncontrollable runaway horse, Taylor married the widow Nancy Murrill Hoyt.

SEE: J. Parsons Brown, *The Commonwealth of Onslow: A History* (1960); Walter Clark, ed., *Histories of the Several Regiments from North Carolina in the Great War, 1861–1865*, vol. 2 (1901); Weymouth T. Jordan, comp., *North Carolina Troops, 1861–1865: A Roster*, vol. 9 (1983); Raleigh *News and Observer*, 22 Jan. 1928, 28 Jan. 1929, 3 Feb. 1929 (Ben Dixon MacNeill, "Cellar and Garret").

A. M. FOUNTAIN

Taylor, Walter Frank (*4 Apr. 1889–28 Sept. 1977*), lawyer, legislator, and civic leader, the son of Luther and Ettie Crow Taylor, was born on a cotton farm four miles from Faison. When he was fifteen the family moved into town, where the father bought a mercantile business. Young Frank attended Faison Academy and in the fall of 1907 entered the University of North Carolina, where he did well; during his final two years he was a licentiate in Latin. Called upon by his classmates, he took part in intercollegiate debating and was voted best debater in his class. He was associate editor of the *Yackety Yack*, manager of the baseball team, and a member of Phi Beta Kappa and the Golden Fleece.

After graduation he worked in his father's store for a year before returning to Chapel Hill to enter law school. He passed the state bar examination in February 1914, received the LL.B. degree in June, was awarded the Callaghan Law Prize, won the Senior Law Class Thesis Prize, and accepted a position as law clerk to John D. Langston and Matt H. Allen of Goldsboro. By the fall of 1914 he was a member of the firm of Langston, Allen and Taylor. He became a member of the American Bar Association and the North Carolina Bar Association, serving the latter as president in 1943–44.

In 1915 Taylor accepted a seat on the The University of North Carolina Board of Trustees, where, except for the years 1931–41, he remained until 1971, when the governing body of the university was changed to a board of governors. At that time he became a member of the board of trustees for the Chapel Hill campus. For twenty-five years he sat on the powerful executive committee. He also served as president of the Alumni Association and on the John Motley Morehead Scholarship Committee.

Taylor's third great area of service was in the General Assembly, first in the senate (1921) and then in the house (1939–52), where he was elected speaker for the 1951 session. He was chairman of the Motor Transportation Commission and a member of the Recodification Commission, Commission to Rewrite Insurance Laws, Committee for Improving the Administration of Justice, State Advisory Budget Commission, and Board of Contracts and Awards. In 1953 Governor William B. Umstead selected him as the governor's legislative counsel in the General Assembly. At various times he was offered a seat on the North Carolina Supreme Court, an appointment to fill an unexpired U.S. Senate term, and the position of treasurer of North Carolina. These he declined, preferring to return home to practice law. He was labeled "conservative" or "liberal" according to the whims of certain politicians. In 1950, when labor unions tried to defeat him because of his stand against the closed shop, he still won election. Described as "a liberal with no wild ideas," he himself said, "I believe in . . . [government] that gives as many services as possible within its means. I do not believe in deficit spending . . . the government should live within a balanced budget."

As a civic leader his activities were varied and numerous. He served on and was sometimes chairman of the boards of the Goldsboro Public Library, Goldsboro Board of Aldermen, Board of St. Paul's Methodist Church, local Kiwanis Club, Wayne County Fair Association, and Community Chest. He also was a director of the Bank of Wayne and a trustee of North Carolina Central College, Durham.

On 16 Dec. 1933 he married Elizabeth Gibson of Faison, formerly of Gibson. They had one daughter, Katharine (Mrs. William F. Baldridge). When he was over eighty, Taylor developed cancer of the liver and died at Wayne Memorial Hospital. Funeral services were held at St. Paul's Church with burial in Willow Dale Cemetery, Goldsboro. A portrait of him was hung in the North Carolina Bar Association headquarters, Raleigh.

SEE: John L. Cheney, Jr., ed., *North Carolina Government, 1585–1974* (1975); *Goldsboro News Argus*, 25 Apr. 1965, 28 Sept. 1977; Daniel L. Grant, *Alumni History of the University of North Carolina* (1924); *North Carolina Bar Association Reports*, vol. 46 (1944); *North Carolina Manual* (1951); Raleigh *News and Observer*, 17 Dec. 1950, 29 Sept. 1977.

ERMA WILLIAMS GLOVER

Taylor, William *(March 1743–16 June 1819)*, early state official, was born in Southampton County, Va., the son of William and Lucy Vaughan Taylor. On the death of his father in 1772, young Taylor inherited two plantations and eight slaves. Apparently soon afterwards he moved to Dobbs (now Wayne) County, N.C. Three years later he was a delegate to the Fifth Provincial Congress (November–December 1775). In June 1776, on the eve of the Revolution, the Council of Safety heard that Taylor and another man were "disaffected to the Common Cause and are endeavouring to dissuade the people from associating in defence of their Liberties." The sheriff of Dobbs County was instructed to bring them before the Council, and a little later it was ordered that their personal property be inventoried. The records do not report further on this case, but Taylor family tradition says that the two men were tried and convicted, whereupon the judge joined people in the county in a successful petition that Taylor be pardoned.

This escapade appears to have produced a thorough change of sentiment in Taylor. He served as a member of the Council of State in 1777 and in a dozen sessions of the General Assembly between 1785 and 1802, representing at different times Wayne, Glasgow, or Greene County as names and boundaries were altered while he continued to occupy the same house. He was elected to still another term in the Assembly but died before the session convened. He had been a delegate to the Constitutional Convention of 1788.

Taylor was married three times. By his first wife, Celeya Edwards, he had twelve children; there were two by his second wife and three by his third. Taylor and his wives are said to have been buried in the Lemuel Hill family cemetery about half a mile north of the site of his home.

SEE: John L. Cheney, Jr., ed., *North Carolina Government, 1584–1979* (1981); Mary Daniels Johnston, ed., *Heritage of Wayne County, North Carolina* (1982); William L. Saunders, ed., *Colonial Records of North Carolina*, vol. 10 (1890).

WILLIAM S. POWELL

Teach, Edward. *See* **Blackbeard.**

Teer, Nello Leguy *(24 Aug. 1888–28 Aug. 1963)*, construction contractor, was born in rural Orange County, the son of George Washington and Nannie Elizabeth Thompson Teer. His family moved to Durham in 1889, and there the elder Teer, in partnership with A. A. Holder, owned and operated a brickyard. In 1907 the partners became road construction contractors and built the highway between Chapel Hill and Durham.

Nello Teer's formal education was limited to the third grade in the Durham public schools. At an early age he began working in his father's brickyard, where, about 1905, he was involved in an accident that resulted in the loss of his right hand. Having helped on road construction jobs, Teer took over the equipment and goodwill of his father's partnership in 1909 and began to dream, work, and plan for his own business in the construction industry. Among his early projects he graded the sites for several Durham showplace residences—those of Benjamin N. Duke, J. Ed Stagg, and Clinton W. Toms. He also hauled limestone for construction at The University of North Carolina, built culverts, set out shrubbery, and did small grading jobs.

Teer organized his own grading construction company, the Nello L. Teer Company, in 1901 with headquarters in Durham; it was still operating continuously under that name well into the 1990s. Working at first with equipment, mainly mules, temporarily rented and later purchased from his father, Teer developed his business into a worldwide operation involving many millions in capital and annual expenses.

The company's first big contract was the grading of the Hanes Athletic Field at Trinity College in Durham about 1910. Teer then contracted with the Duke family to "revise and improve the road bed alignment and trestle structure" of the Durham and Southern Railway, owned by the Dukes. Subsequently he built approaches to bridges in Durham County and was awarded contracts for highway construction in adjacent Orange, Granville, and Person counties and later in Rockingham County. With the expansion of North Carolina's highway system under Governor Cameron Morrison and his commissioner, Frank Page, in 1921, the Teer firm was one of the leading contractors, at one time having 147 highway miles under construction simultaneously. The company built roads all over the state and eventually constructed more than 12,000 miles of roads in the United States and abroad.

Alert to promote highway interests, Teer was host in 1924 to the historic Pan American Highway Commission at a barbecue in Yanceyville at which more than 7,000 were present, many of them from foreign countries. With the creation of Duke University in the same year, the Teer Company was chosen for much of the grading of the new campus, including Duke stadium. In the same period it did the excavating and grading for Kenan Stadium at The University of North Carolina and the million-dollar Washington Duke Hotel, Durham's tallest building at the time.

In 1926 Teer realized that working with mules (he once owned 400) was unsatisfactory, and he became one of the first Southern contractors completely to mechanize his operations. This process continued; before Teer retired from active duty in 1952, most travel by officials and employees was in their own airplanes.

During and following World War II the Teer Company held contracts for many mammoth jobs including reservoirs, power plants, and missile sites in Kentucky, Virginia, Tennessee, and Florida; tunnels were built for railroads, rivers were diverted through mountains of earth and rock, quarry operations on the eastern seaboard were begun and expanded, and asphalt plants were put into operation. The company received early contracts for work in many foreign countries, notably the Moroccan Air Base in Africa; uncounted air bases and cantonments were constructed in record time. It built 180 miles of the highly acclaimed Blue Ridge Parkway, a job beset with many problems caused by weather and terrain. Turnpikes became one of Teer's major interests, a natural extension of the road-building experiences in North Carolina. He did large sections of the West Virginia, the Pennsylvania, Maine, and Massachusetts turnpikes. He built the U.S. Marine base at Cherry Point and six outlying auxiliary fields, Camp Butner, the Beaufort Marine Air Base, and the air station at Edenton.

Projects in Iceland, Guatemala, Nicaragua, and Panama and the ultimate establishment of a subsidiary in Central America suggest the extent of the company's operations. Teer was always noted for the use of innovative equipment and was hailed by road builders everywhere for his leadership in his field. This resulted in his being elected to a term as president of the American Road Builders Association, of which he was a member for more than forty years.

By 1952, when Nello Teer retired as president, he had built the company into a million-dollar-a-year business. Remaining chairman of the board, he was succeeded by

his sons: Nello L. Teer, Jr., became president and Dillard Teer vice-president and secretary-treasurer.

In the early years of his business Teer built a headquarters complex on ninety-two acres four miles north of Durham. There he had maintenance shops, stables for the prize show horses he owned, and pastures for his large herd of Guernsey cows. In 1950 he acquired controlling interest in the Durham and Southern Railway, operating from Durham to Dunn, and he served as director and executive vice-president until his death. He consistently demonstrated humanitarian concern for those who worked for him, used the best obtainable auditors to keep his records, insisted on the very best treatment for all of his equipment, whether mules or machinery, and spent all of his time working at his jobs with a dedication and tenacity that were contagious. He was an active member of the Duke Memorial United Methodist Church and of the Democratic party but never ran for public office.

Teer was married on 16 Sept. 1909 in Durham to Gertrude Adcock, and they had six children: Nello L., Jr., Robert Dillard, Mary Elizabeth (Mrs. Isaac Emerson Harris, Jr.), Margaret Gaynelle (Mrs. William P. Farthing, Jr.), Nellene (died in infancy), and Marion Page (died in early childhood). He died in Watts Hospital, Durham, from injuries in an automobile accident and was interred in the family mausoleum in the New Maplewood Cemetery.

SEE: *America's Builders* (1954); *Durham Morning Herald*, 29 Aug. 1963, *Durham Sun*, 28 Aug. 1963; *The Earth Mover* 8 (September 1921); *Nat. Cyc. Am. Biog.*, vol. 50 (1968 [portrait]); Raleigh *News and Observer*, 7 Mar. 1976.

C. SYLVESTER GREEN

Telfair, Alexander (*ca. 1738–21 July 1786*), Loyalist, was born at Town Head in Kirkcudbright on the Firth of Solway, southwestern Scotland. He came to America in 1759 with his brothers Edward, Hugh, and William. The Telfairs were first associated with John and Thomas Gilchrist, Scottish merchants in Suffolk, Va., who had extensive business dealings in the new North Carolina towns of Halifax and Tarboro. Edward Telfair, who seems to have been the oldest of the brothers, appeared in the North Carolina records in 1761, when he witnessed the conveyances for many lots when Tarboro was laid out. The act of the Assembly establishing the town has been lost, but it is possible that he was one of the original commissioners. In 1763 Telfair was referred to as a merchant in Halifax. In 1766 he moved to Savannah, where he later enjoyed a distinguished career as a member of the Continental Congress and governor of Georgia. William Telfair also settled in Georgia; his strong Loyalist stand was a source of embarrassment to his brother, who had cast his lot with the colonies. When the British occupied Savannah in 1779, an attempt was made to reestablish the royal government in Georgia. William was appointed a member of the Council, a commissioner of claims, and a commissioner to obtain the property of active Whigs.

Alexander Telfair relocated in Halifax in 1765 and, together with his brother Hugh, built up a successful mercantile business. A contemporary described him as a man of character and probity. In 1775 he had prospered enough to invest a thousand pounds in Richard Henderson's Transylvania Company. While in Halifax, the Telfair brothers dealt with John Hamilton and Company, Longroup merchants located in Gould Square.

Married to an American, Alexander was uncertain as to his course of action when the Revolution broke out. He was a member of the local Committee of Safety in the summer of 1776 and was a member of a committee to state the amount the province of North Carolina had spent on the United Colonies in order to transmit the same to the Continental Congress. In the summer of 1777 the state of North Carolina required oaths of allegiance to the new government. This Telfair could not bring himself to do, and he, along with other Loyalists, was given sixty days to dispose of his property and leave the state. Because few ships were available for the numerous persons who wanted to go, Telfair bought a brigantine at Beaufort and, outfitting the vessel at his own expense, named it *The Brothers*. The delays in preparation threatened to prevent their leaving within the prescribed time so Telfair obtained a twenty-day extension from Governor Richard Caswell, a fellow Mason and a friend in happier days. The ship set sail on 6 Aug. 1777, carrying Hugh Telfair, Alexander and his wife and children, several other Tory families, and some Negro slaves. The most prominent passenger was Martin Howard, chief justice of North Carolina. The party sailed for New York, then in British hands, and was stopped twice by American privateers on the way. Hugh remained in New York while the rest of the party went on to England in a British convoy. In London, the ship was claimed by an earlier owner and was sold at a fraction of its purchase price. Alexander returned to America in 1779 and for three years was in business in New York and then Charles Town, S.C. On his return to England in 1782, he attempted to establish himself in Liverpool but lost what property remained to him. Here he committed suicide in 1786. Anthony Warwick, a fellow Tory who had been a merchant in Tarboro some years before, was of the opinion that Telfair had become despondent over his failure to obtain adequate compensation from the British government for his financial losses in North Carolina.

While in North Carolina Telfair had married Paulina, the daughter of Thomas Hall of Edgecombe County. Her sister Elizabeth was the wife of John Thompson, a Tory innkeeper in Halifax town who went into exile. Another sister, Dolly, married Ralph MacNair, a Scottish merchant settled in Hillsborough who also became a Loyalist. Thomas H. Hall, of Tarboro, nephew to Mrs. Telfair, was a member of Congress for many years.

On her husband's death, Paulina Telfair was left with five small children. She went to live with her mother-in-law, Mrs. Margaret Blair Telfair, in Scotland and eventually obtained a small pension from the British government. In 1798 she and her family returned to North Carolina and bought a small property near Tarboro. She was still living in 1816, when she sold her land in Edgecombe and moved to Pitt County. According to census records and the deeds of Pitt and Edgecombe counties, Alexander and Paulina Telfair had three sons, Thomas, Hugh, and David Alexander. The last named was a physician and died in Bath, Beaufort County, in 1831. Dr. Alexander F. Telfair of Johnston County was a grandson of Alexander Telfair, as was David A. Telfair, an officer in the Confederate States Navy. While in England both Alexander Telfair and his wife were painted by Sir Joshua Reynolds; the portraits are in the possession of their North Carolina descendants.

SEE: Edgecombe County Wills and Deeds (courthouse, Tarboro); Halifax County Deeds (courthouse, Halifax); Laura MacMillan, comp., *North Carolina Portrait Index* (1963); Thomas Parramore, *Launching the Craft: The First Half Century of Freemasonry in North Carolina* (1975); Alexander Telfair and Pauline Telfair, Memorials (Loyalist Claims; xerox copies, North Carolina State Archives, Raleigh).

CLAIBORNE T. SMITH, JR.

Tenney, Samuel Mills *(25 Oct. 1871–23 Dec. 1939)*, minister and curator, was born at Crockett, Tex., the son of Samuel Fisher and Sarah Mills Tenney. On 18 Feb. 1897 he married Mary Frances McWhorter, and the couple had three sons: Samuel McWhorter, Robert Paul Warfield, and Warren William.

He was graduated from Southwestern Presbyterian University, Clarksville, Tenn., in 1891 with the degree of M.A. After a year at the Southwestern Divinity School, he transferred to Princeton Theological Seminary, completing his course there in 1894. Ordained by the Eastern Texas Presbytery on 15 Sept. 1893, he later became stated supply and afterwards pastor of the Presbyterian Church at Longview, Tex. Subsequent to his departure from Longview in 1899, he served other Texas churches until 1923, his longest pastorate being at Rusk, 1910–23. While at Rusk he acted as chaplain for the state prison in addition to his work with the local church.

In 1923 Tenney became pastor-at-large for the Eastern Texas Presbytery. Following his entire loss of hearing in 1924, he engaged in activities related to the work of the Presbyterian Historical Society of the Synod of Texas which he had been instrumental in organizing in 1902. In 1926 the General Assembly of the Presbyterian Church in the United States took over the collections of that society, together with similar personal holdings of Dr. Tenney and in the next year established the Historical Foundation of the Presbyterian and Reformed Churches, which it located at Montreat, N.C. The General Assembly elected Tenney administrative head of the new institution with the title of curator. For the next thirteen years he devoted himself to the development of this work, with Mrs. Tenney (Litt.D., Austin College, 1938) acting as assistant curator. By the time of his death the Historical Foundation had gained international recognition.

He received the Litt.D. degree from Davidson College (1937) and D.D. (1918) and Litt.D. (1938) degrees from Austin College and was the author of *Souvenir of the General Assembly of the Presbyterian Church, U.S.* (1924) and *Presbyterians: Who They Are* (1927). Tenney died at Asheville and was buried in Crockett, Tex. His portrait and papers are in the Historical Foundation at Montreat.

SEE: Louisville, Ky., *Christian Observer*, 3 Jan. 1940; Thomas H. Spence, Jr., *The Historical Foundation and Its Treasures* (rev. ed., 1960 [portrait]); S. M. Tenney, "A Brief Autobiography of Rev. S. M. Tenney, D.D." (manuscript in the Historical Foundation, Montreat, N.C.).

THOMAS H. SPENCE, JR.

Terrell, Saunders (Sonny Terry) *(24 Oct. 1911–11 Mar. 1986)*, blind black singer and harmonica player, was born in Greensboro, Ga., but in 1915 moved to Rockingham, N.C., where he was reared. He was partially blinded in an accident in 1922, came to be known as Sonny Terry, and met similarly blind guitarist Fulton Allen (Blind Boy Fuller) in 1934. Moving to Durham, Terry frequently played on the streets around East Pettigrew with both Fuller and blind Gary Davis, occasionally as a trio. By the time he was nineteen he was traveling with medicine shows and soon afterwards played in tobacco warehouses in Durham.

From December 1937 to June 1940 Terry accompanied the popular Blind Boy Fuller on songs from every recording session, held in Columbia, S.C., Memphis, and Chicago, as well as in the more usual New York. Terry made his first commercial recordings under his own name in March 1940, on one track from which Fuller accompanied him on guitar; this was the only time Fuller deigned to accompany another artist on record.

In 1938, by chance, Terry was heard by John Hammond, an executive with Columbia Records, who persuaded him to attend the Spirituals to Swing concert being staged at Carnegie Hall. Terry's manager was J. B. Long from Elon College, who also managed Blind Boy Fuller, who died in 1941. Long chose a guitarist from nearby Burlington, Walter Brown McGhee, to fill Fuller's role, even billing him as Blind Boy Fuller No. 2 on record. Terry came to replace McGhee's regular harmonica player, and when Terry was invited to perform at a concert in Washington, D.C., in 1942, he chose "Brownie" McGhee to accompany him. At this point, both men accepted offers to play in New York and did not return to North Carolina for over thirty years.

As Brownie McGhee and Sonny Terry they became the best-known duo in the blues-folk scene, and, playing together, they became part of a very small group of black folk artists who made their living from their music in the white market. Once in New York, Terry was frequently in demand for recording sessions. He also appeared on Broadway in *Finian's Rainbow* and with McGhee in *Cat on a Hot Tin Roof* and Steve Martin's film, *The Jerk*. Terry provided some of the sound-track music for *The Color Purple*. He rode the folk boom in the late 1950s and 1960s, touring extensively with McGhee throughout the world.

Terry made his home in Queens, Long Island, N.Y., with his wife, Emma. They had no children.

SEE: Bruce Bastin, *Crying for the Carolinas* (1971); Kent Cooper, *The Harp Style of Sonny Terry* (1975); *Durham Morning Herald* (24 Jan. 1980); Raleigh *News and Observer*, 13 Mar. 1986; Happy Traum, ed., *Guitar Styles of Brownie McGhee* (1971).

BRUCE BASTIN

Terry, John Skally (*19 Nov. 1894–30 June 1953*), professor and friend of Thomas Wolfe, was born in Rockingham, the son of Jennie Skally and Edgar Burton Terry, both natives of Richmond County. His father was a merchant. Besides his older sister Bessie, he had three younger brothers: Edgar Burton, Jr., Harvey Stansill, and Charles Gibbons. He completed high school in Laurens, S.C., then for more than two years worked in railroad offices to earn college expenses, and in 1914 entered The University of North Carolina, where he participated in a wide range of extracurricular activities, including all the campus publications. His 270-pound physique prevented his engaging in athletics. In September 1916 he met freshman Thomas Wolfe at a meeting of the Dialectic Literary Society, took a special interest in him, and the following year solicited several youthful poems from Wolfe for the *University Magazine*. They were Wolfe's first published writing. Terry was graduated in 1918, returned to Chapel Hill for two years of medical school, and spent a seventh year at the university as a graduate student in English.

After receiving an M.A. in English from Columbia University in 1922, he was for twelve years associated with *School*, a weekly newspaper serving the New York City public school system, eventually becoming its editor. In 1925 he joined the Department of English at the Washington Square College of New York University and from then until his death taught English composition, biography, and creative writing, mostly in the evening college. Off and on, between 1924 and 1930, Wolfe also taught there. During 1929–30 Terry was one of the editors of the Children's Book Club. Meanwhile, he wrote and edited early film monographs and contributed to professional journals.

In 1936 the artist Letterio Calapai suggested that he try his hand at watercolors, and his success and pleasure were such that he began studying art at New York University under Constant van de Wall. His work was exhibited in New York and Chapel Hill in 1939 and again in New York in 1943. On early sketching trips he often was accompanied by Wolfe, who lived near him in Brooklyn.

After Wolfe's death in 1938, Terry continued his friendship with the family and in 1943 wrote an introduction to and edited *Thomas Wolfe's Letters to His Mother Julia Elizabeth Wolfe*. Shortly before Mrs. Wolfe's death in 1945, she spoke to Terry's students in New York—an event that prompted him to organize the Thomas Wolfe Biography Club at the university. From reminiscences by Wolfe's friends at club meetings, Terry began to collect materials for a biography, but so inundated did he become in the data gathering that it is doubtful he would ever have completed the work, though he announced a month before he died that soon he would issue the first of four projected volumes. In Wolfe's *The Web and the Rock* (1939) Terry is satirically portrayed as Jerry Alsop. He was buried at Eastside Cemetery, Rockingham. He was a Methodist and a Democrat. His family donated his paintings to New York University and his books, papers, and the oil portrait by Constant van de Wall to The University of North Carolina.

SEE: Alumni Files (University of North Carolina, Chapel Hill); Don Bishop, in *Winston-Salem Journal and Sentinel*, 25 May 1947; LeGette Blythe, in *Charlotte Observer*, 20 June 1947; *International Who's Who Supplement* (June 1949); Isaac S. London, in *Rockingham Post-Dispatch*, 9 July 1953; Ed Wallace, in *New York World-Telegram*, 16 May 1947; Hilton G. West, in *Greensboro Daily News*, 4 June 1939;

RICHARD WALSER

Terry, Sonny. *See* **Terrell, Saunders.**

Terry, William Leake (*27 Sept. 1850–4 Nov. 1917*), Arkansas lawyer and U.S. congressman, was born near Wadesboro, Anson County, the son of William Leake and Mary Parsons Terry. He was related to Colonel W. A. Terry of the Stonewall Brigade, David D. Terry of the California Supreme Court, Colonel Frank P. Leake of Mississippi, and Congressman Walter Leake Steele of North Carolina. His family moved to Tippah County, Miss., in 1857. In 1861, after the death of his wife, the elder Leake went to Arkansas, taking young William with him. In 1864 the father died, leaving William in the hands of an uncle, Colonel Francis A. Terry. Colonel Terry sent William back to North Carolina to Bingham Military Academy and then to Trinity College, where he was graduated in 1872, delivering the valedictorian address.

After a brief study of the law, William returned to Arkansas and was admitted to the Arkansas bar in 1873. He served on the Little Rock city council (1878–79), as city attorney (1879–85), and in the state senate (1879 and 1881). Leake was elected to the U.S. Congress in 1891 and held his seat for the next ten years. A ranking Democrat on the House Judiciary Committee, he was a constant thorn in the side of House Speaker Thomas B. (Czar) Reed. He was defeated for reelection in 1900.

Terry was well known for his legal abilities; "the strongest trial lawyer in the state," one colleague called him. In appearance he was "tall, slender, and handsome. He was blond with an unusually fair complexion." He was married twice: first to Mollie C. Dixon (1875–95), with whom he had three sons, and to Florence Forshe, with whom he had a daughter. His son David D. also served in the House of Representatives. A Roman Catholic, William Leake Terry was buried at Calvary Cemetery, Little Rock.

SEE: *Biog. Dir. Am. Cong.* (1950); Fay Hempstead, *Historical Review of Arkansas* (1911); Little Rock *Arkansas Gazette*, 5 Nov. 1917; Memorial and Tribute, *Arkansas Supreme Court Reports*, 136 Ark. 618 (quotations).

MICHAEL B. DOUGAN

Tew, Charles Courtenay *(17 Oct. 1827–17 Sept. 1862)*, teacher and Confederate officer, was born of French Huguenot descent in Charleston, S.C., the son of Henry Slade and Caroline Jane Courtenay Tew. After attending the common schools of South Carolina, he entered the South Carolina Military Academy (now The Citadel) in 1842 and was graduated in 1846 first in his class. The next year he joined the faculty of the Columbia branch of the academy to teach history, belles lettres, and ethics, a post he held until 1852. Also an accomplished teacher of French and competent in the use of several other languages, he spent the following year in Europe and then returned to The Citadel. In 1854 he was appointed superintendent of the South Carolina Arsenal Academy, Columbia, where he remained until 1859, when he resigned and moved to Hillsborough, N.C.

Anticipating a need in the South for men with military training, Tew signed a contract to establish the Hillsborough Military Academy. There he was joined by J. S. Gillard, also a Citadel graduate, in the operation of this four-year school for boys. Its barracks had a capacity of 125 cadets. Tew was granted the rank of colonel in the North Carolina militia, and each of the teachers was commissioned captain. Fifteen months later, at the beginning of the Civil War, Tew and all of the teachers were called to active duty. Early in 1861 Governor John W. Ellis asked Tew and Daniel H. Hill of the Charlotte Military Academy to draw up a list of military supplies that the state might soon need. With this list in hand, Colonel Charles C. Tew was sent to the North to purchase them. For a short time before North Carolina seceded from the Union, Tew was commander of Fort Macon. His initial rank was major, but he was soon made a colonel and commanded the Second North Carolina Regiment.

Tew saw action at Harpers Ferry and in the Antietam campaign. He was killed at the Battle of Sharpsburg. At the request of Governor Henry T. Clark, Senator William T. Dortch, and others, Tew had recently set in motion the steps to resign from the army and return to train young men at the Hillsborough academy. His death occurred, of course, before final action could be taken in this case.

Several accounts of his death were circulated. General John B. Gordon saw him fall in advance of the Confederate line while the two were on reconnaissance and believed he had died instantly. Another report said that he was mortally wounded and died the next day. For several years after the war a former Union soldier, apparently in an attempt to get money, wrote tantalizing letters to the family saying that Tew was alive. Tew's aged father went to Washington to obtain permission and visited the Dry Tortugas government prison in the Gulf of Mexico off the southwestern coast of Florida in a vain search for his son. Finally in October 1874 a silver cup that Colonel Tew had in his possession at his death was returned to the family by a Union captain. Tew also had had with him a sword that had been presented to him by the arsenal cadets as well as a fine watch, but they were never returned. Neither Tew's wife nor his father, it was reported, "long survived the harrowing anxieties to which mercenary sensationalism had basely subjected them." In 1885 a former Union soldier wrote to one of Tew's daughters relating the details of his death on the battlefield at which time he was still holding his sword. In 1891 a former member of Tew's regiment called at the office of the *News and Observer* in Raleigh and reported that he and two other men, both of whom were later killed in battle, had buried Tew's body, together with his sword, on the field of Sharpsburg.

In 1854 Courtenay Tew, as he was known by his family, married Elizabeth Faust Tradewell of Columbia, S.C. They had five children: Elizabeth Caroline, Emma Louise, James Tradewell, Charles Matthew, and Ella Glass.

SEE: O. J. Bond, *The Story of the Citadel* (1936); Louis H. Manarin, comp., *North Carolina Troops, 1861–1865: A Roster*, vol. 3 (1971); Charles Courtenay Tew Papers (North Carolina State Archives, Raleigh [portrait]); John P. Thomas, *The History of the South Carolina Military Academy* (1893); Noble J. Tolbert, ed., *The Papers of John Willis Ellis* (1964); Stephen B. Weeks Scrapbook, vol. 8 (North Carolina Collection, University of North Carolina, Chapel Hill).

WILLIAM S. POWELL

Thackston, James *(d. 1792)*, was a rather suspect figure of secondary importance in North Carolina mercantile, political, and military affairs throughout the Revolutionary period. Thackston (occasionally spelled Thaxton) first appears in 1768 as a captain of the Orange County militia. That he is first noted in a fairly significant position indicates that he may have belonged to the class of non-native officeholders who went to the colony. Indeed, Thackston soon began to associate himself with the so-called Courthouse Ring composed of people of that description. By 1769 he was engaged in tobacco and hemp production in Orange County. That year he opened a store on Churton Street in Hillsborough in partnership with William Johnston.

During the riot at the September court of 1770 Edmund Fanning sought refuge in their establishment, which the Regulators "instantly beset, demolishing the windows and threw dirt and stones or brickbats into the house." The merchants became active in their opposition to the mob, signing a petition to Governor William Tryon on 30 Sept. 1770. The memorialists requested forceful measures against the Regulators, "a set of men . . . whom we have long considered as dangerous to society and as pursuing every measure destructive of Peace and good Government." Thackston journeyed to New Bern in March 1771 to testify against the "backwoods Revolutionaries" at the Special Court of Oyer and Terminer. On 1 May 1771 he raised a company of sixty-two Orange County militiamen, which served in the Alamance campaign.

This slight military experience was sufficient to secure an appointment as colonel of minutemen for the Hillsborough District in September 1775 for Thackston, who had established a residence between Lindley's Mill and Rocky River in southern Orange County. With this command, theoretically five hundred men, he participated in the Moore's Creek campaign, occupying Cross Creek in order to prevent an orderly Loyalist retreat. Afterwards the New England papers celebrated him as a hero of the battle. Unfortunately, it was the apogee of his Revolutionary career.

After that success Thackston received an appointment as lieutenant colonel of the Fourth North Carolina Continental Regiment under Thomas Polk on 15 Apr. 1776. Before the unit could be raised Thackston took Robert Howe's Second Regiment to Charles Town, where it helped repulse the British siege during June 1776. Returning to the state, he commenced recruiting activities, and on 22 Apr. 1777 the Fourth regiment marched north to serve under George Washington.

From all appearances an inept field leader, Thackston by the summer of 1776 found himself in charge of the camp at Peytonsburg, Va., where new recruits from North Carolina were assembled. Even this assignment proved difficult, for the lieutenant colonel failed in most of his efforts to acquire provisions for the outpost. In November he removed himself from active duty due to poor health, but by February 1779 he had recovered so that he could serve under Benjamin Lincoln in South Carolina. Soon he was back in his home state, however, supervising the discharge of soldiers at Cross Creek during the summer.

After Horatio Gates's debacle at Camden in August 1780, the Board of War authorized Thackston to assemble new recruits and repatriated deserters at Hillsborough. By mid-November he had amassed but sixteen men, not counting himself. Not surprisingly, he was one of the Continental officers ordered by Congress to retire on half pay effective 1 Jan. 1781 due to the lack of a proper command.

Lord Cornwallis's invasion of North Carolina restored Thackston to duty. Once General Nathanael Greene had safely retreated across the Dan River, he placed Thackston in charge of the thirty Continentals from the state still with the Southern Department. The lieutenant colonel served throughout the Guilford Court House campaign, but in July 1781 he left the army when Greene charged him with misrepresenting the position and arrangement of his troops. Thereafter he served in various roles, was captured and exchanged, and retired for a second time on 26 Apr. 1782. Two years later he proudly joined the Order of the Cincinnati, and on 14 Mar. 1786 the veteran of such an undistinguished career received 4,352 acres in Tennessee as a reward.

Thackston reestablished his mercantile operations on New Street in Fayetteville, near the scene of his greatest military exploit. He won election to the House of Commons for the session of 1787, during which term he accomplished little other than to win the legislative stationery contract for his firm. In December he unsuccessfully sought appointment as brigadier general from the Fayetteville District. By 1790 the veteran resided there, owning nine slaves but having no family. Although his exact date of death is unknown, an inventory of Thackston's estate was commissioned on 11 Apr. 1792. In sum, his career was active but his record uninspiring.

SEE: Walter Clark, ed., *State Records of North Carolina*, vol. 11 (1895), vols. 14–22 (1896–1907); Hugh T. Lefler and Paul Wager, eds., *Orange County, 1752–1952* (1953); Hugh F. Rankin, *The North Carolina Continentals* (1971); William L. Saunders, ed., *Colonial Records of North Carolina*, vols. 7–8, 10 (1890).

ARTHUR C. MENIUS

Thaden, Louise Marcellus McPhetridge *(12 Nov. 1905–9 Nov. 1979),* businesswoman and aviatrix, was born in Bentonville, Ark., the daughter of Roy Fry and Edna Hobbs McPhetridge. She attended the University of Arkansas (1921–25), where she switched her major from journalism to physical education and premedicine, making it impossible to graduate without extensive extra work. Beginning a career in aviation, she was manager of the D. C. Warren Company, airplane distributors, in 1928–29 and worked in public relations at Pittsburgh Aviation Industries, Inc. during the period 1930–31. Afterwards she assisted in developing the National Air Marking Program for the Bureau of Air Commerce covering much of the western United States, flying her own plane and persuading cities to paint their names atop large buildings for easier identification from the air. For a time she was

factory representative of the Beech Aircraft Corporation and of the Porterfield Aircraft Company. She next was purchasing agent for the Thaden Engineering Company, involved in plastics research and development, and vice-president and director of Thaden Molding Corporation. Active in the Motor Corps of the American Red Cross from 1946 to 1952, she became a lieutenant colonel in the Civil Air Patrol in 1949. In 1959 she was made chairman of the National Commanders Training Commission and served as a command pilot.

When she flew her 180-horsepower plane to an altitude of 20,260 feet in 1928, she was higher than any woman had been before. She also held the record for solo endurance (1929), speed (1929), refueling endurance (1932), light plane speed (1934), East-West speed (1936), and 100 km. speed (1938). She won the first woman's derby in 1929 and the Bendix Transcontinental Trophy Race in 1936, the first year women were allowed to enter the contest, when she flew a Beech Staggerwing from New York to Los Angeles in fifteen hours, setting a new coast-to-coast record. Also in 1936 she received the Harmon Trophy from the Federation Aeronautique Internationale as outstanding aviatrix. Louise Thaden was elected to the Aviation Hall of Fame. Her book, *High, Wide and Frightened*, a first-person account of her early days with airplanes, was published in 1938.

A charter member of the Ninety-Nines, an international organization of women pilots, she also held membership in the Veteran Air Pilots, OX5 Club, Silver Wings, and Defense Advisory Committee on Women in the Services. She was secretary of the National Aeronautic Association in 1937–38.

She married Herbert von Thaden in 1928, and they had two children, William and Patricia, both of whom became pilots. She and her husband played a significant role in the development of all-metal airplanes. In 1956 the Thadens moved to High Point, N.C., and became the owners of Thaden Engineering, a company engaged in development engineering in plastics. After a time they also began to make reinforced plastic furniture. After her husband's death in 1969, Mrs. Thaden continued the business. She died in High Point, where a memorial service for her was held in St. Mary's Episcopal Church.

SEE: Jean Adams and Margaret Kimball, *Heroines of the Sky* (1942); *Charlotte Observer*, 7 July 1974; *Durham Morning Herald*, 13 Aug. 1973; Don Dwiggins, *They Flew the Bendix Race* (1965); *Greensboro Daily News*, 11 Nov. 1979; William S. Powell, ed., *North Carolina Lives* (1962); *Raleigh News and Observer*, 12 Nov. 1979; *Tar Heel* 6 (July / August 1978); *Who's Who of American Women*, vol. 1 (1958).

WILLIAM S. POWELL

Thomas, Charles Randolph *(7 Feb. 1827–18 Feb. 1891),* lawyer and congressman, was born in Beaufort, the son of Marcus and Elizabeth Duncan Thomas. His father was a wealthy shipowner and merchant, and Charles received the best education available in antebellum North Carolina, graduating from The University of North Carolina in 1849. He read law with Judge Richmond M. Pearson, tutor of many of the state's illustrious attorneys, and was admitted to the bar in 1850.

Thomas once declared that he was born a Whig, "and after some study and reflection about politics, he supported that had he lived in the time of Hamilton, he would have been a Federalist." When the Whig party disintegrated, he supported the Democrats "until that party went for secession and disunion." He won his first political office in 1861 as a Unionist delegate to the secession convention but lost his bid for a seat in the Confederate Congress in 1861. From 1862 to 1864 he was chief clerk of the state senate. Named secretary of state by the assembly in January 1865, he served until the end of the war, when provisional governor W. W. Holden appointed him to the same position; he left the post at the end of 1865. From 1868 to 1870 he was a judge of the superior court, and in 1868 he was a trustee of The University of North Carolina. He had no military record during the Civil War.

After the war, he became active in the affairs of the Atlantic and North Carolina Railroad, of which the state was a part owner. In 1867 he was appointed president of the railroad. The next year Thomas was elected a superior court judge on the Republican slate.

Before he had completed his term on the bench, the Republicans of the Second Congressional District nominated Thomas for the House of Representatives. Based in New Bern and running in a heavily black, Republican district, he was elected in 1870 and reelected in 1872. Opposition within the Republican party denied him a third nomination in 1874. As a director of the Atlantic and North Carolina Railroad (an office he continued to hold while in Congress), Thomas had defied the railroad policy of the Republican governor, Tod R. Caldwell, who in the spring of 1874 removed Thomas and five other directors, appointing a new board led by political rivals of Thomas. Thomas was further weakened by the strong feeling among many black voters that a Negro nominee ought to be chosen for the Second District seat. In the end the nomination went to black legislator John A. Hyman.

Thomas formally broke with the Republican party in the campaign of 1876. He announced that he would support the Democratic candidates for president and governor, even as he affirmed his Whiggish principles and defended his vote in Congress for the Civil Rights Act of 1875. In a speech in New Bern he said that he considered both "Bourbon" Democracy and "Radical" Republicanism to be dangerous extremes. He returned to the private practice of law, never again holding a partisan political office.

Thomas's wife was Emily Pitkin, described as a Northern woman, and they had five sons, one of whom, Charles Randolph, Jr., also served in Congress. Thomas died in New Bern shortly after his sixty-fourth birthday and was buried in Cedar Grove Cemetery. He was a member of the Presbyterian church.

SEE: Eric Anderson, "Race and Politics in North Carolina, 1872–1901: The 'Black Second' Congressional District" (Ph.D. diss., University of Chicago, 1978); *Biog. Dir. Am. Cong.* (1961); Daniel L. Grant, *Alumni History of the University of North Carolina* (1924); J. G. de Roulhac Hamilton, *Reconstruction in North Carolina* (1914); John G. McCormick, "Personnel of the Convention of 1861," *James Sprunt Historical Monographs*, No. 1 (1900); *North Carolina Biography*, vol. 6 (1919); *Newbernian*, 2 Sept. 1876.

ERIC D. ANDERSON

Thomas, Charles Randolph, Jr. *(21 Aug. 1861–8 Mar. 1931),* congressman, was born in Beaufort, Carteret County, the son of Emily Pitkin and Charles Randolph Thomas. He attended New Bern Academy and Emerson Institute, Washington, D.C., prior to his graduation from The University of North Carolina in 1881. He then studied law with his father and at the law school of Judges R. P. Dick and John H. Dillard in Greensboro. In 1882 he was admitted to the bar and commenced practice in New Bern. He was a member of the state House of Representatives in 1887 and the attorney for Craven County from 1890 to 1896.

In 1893 Thomas was named a trustee of The University of North Carolina, and in 1896 he was a member of the Democratic state executive committee and a presidential elector on the ticket of Bryan and Sewall. As a Democrat, he was elected to Congress in 1888 and served five terms between 4 Mar. 1889 and 3 Mar. 1911. In 1924 his party named him a delegate to its national convention in New York City. The following year, because of his wife's health, they moved to Waynesville but spent most of their winters in Norfolk, Va. Thomas gave many valuable books to the city library in Waynesville. In Norfolk he was a vestryman at Christ Episcopal Church.

Thomas's first wife, whom he married in 1887, was Laura Pasteur Davis, of Beaufort, the daughter of Major James C. Davis. Following her death on 30 May 1889 he married Mary Ruffin, the daughter of Judge Thomas Ruffin of Hillsborough. Thomas died in Norfolk and was buried in Cedar Grove Cemetery, New Bern. He was survived by two sons, Charles Randolph III, an engineer in Chicago, and Frank T., of Norfolk, and by three brothers, the Reverend Frederick D., the Reverend James A., and the Reverend John S. Thomas.

SEE: *Biog. Dir. Am. Cong.* (1961); *Greensboro Daily News*, 10 Mar. 1931; *Legislative Biographical Sketch Book* (1887); *National Magazine*, August 1906; *New Bern Journal*, 19 Feb. 1891; *New York Times*, 10 Mar. 1931; Raleigh *News and Observer*, 10 Mar. 1931.

MARY BODMAN KENNER

Thomas, James Augustus *(6 Mar. 1862–10 Sept. 1940),* tobacco merchant, benefactor, and Asian specialist, was born in Lawsonville, Rockingham County. His grandfather and his father, Henry Evans Thomas, were both tobacco men; his mother was Cornelia Carolina Jones Thomas. The younger Thomas literally grew up in the tobacco business, having gone to work in a Reidsville tobacco warehouse at age ten; his first wage was twenty-five cents a day. In 1881 he was graduated from Eastman National Business College, Poughkeepsie, N.Y.

Thomas traveled all over the United States as a tobacco salesman, but his most important position came with the British-American Tobacco Company, Ltd., which he joined at its inception in 1902 and represented as managing director in China from 1914 until his retirement in 1922. There Thomas supervised the building of factories that employed thousands of Chinese workers. He was largely responsible for the introduction of American cigarettes into China, as well as Australia, New Zealand, India, Japan, Tasmania, and India. He also introduced Western ways into many countries in the Orient.

In all, Thomas spent twenty-six years in China. Very active in that country's commercial and educational life, he founded the Chinese-American Bank of Commerce and two schools for Chinese children. He witnessed a turbulent period in China's history, having been there during the Boxer Rebellion, the Russo-Japanese War, and the beginning of the Chinese Revolution in 1911. Long afterwards he described his experiences in two books: *A Pioneer Tobacco Merchant in the Orient* (1928) and *Trailing Trade a Million Miles* (1931).

For his varied activities in China, Thomas received numerous awards and recognition. A life member of the Chinese Red Cross, he was decorated in 1905 by the Dalai Lama and the Empress Dowager of China, who made him a Crystal Button Mandarin. He also was decorated 6th and 3rd classes, Order of the Golden Harvest and Order of the Jade, Red Cravat with White and Blue Borders (China), in 1937. Thomas was treasurer of China Famine

Relief, U.S.A., Inc., chairman of China Child Welfare, Inc., and a trustee of the Shanghai American School and the American Hospital of Istanbul. He was a director of the China Society of America and a member of the Church Committee for China Relief and of the Council on Foreign Relations in New York. In addition, he belonged to the American Academy of Political Science, American Institute of Pacific Relations, American Museum of Natural History, English Speaking Union, Japan Society of New York, and Omicron Delta Kappa. A Presbyterian Mason (32), he was a member of the following clubs: India House, Manursing Island, American Yacht Club, Apawamic, China Club of Seattle, American Club of Shanghai, and Thatched House of London.

On his retirement Thomas moved to White Plains, N.Y., where he lived for the balance of his life. His association with the Duke family had given him a keen interest in Duke University, to which he donated in 1928 his Far East library, one of the choicest collections of its kind in the world, a result of thirty years of careful selection. He became a member of the Duke University Board of Trustees in 1936 and served as chairman of the Duke Memorial Fund to erect a memorial to Washington Duke and his sons Benjamin N. and James B. Duke. He made repeated purchases of rare books on Oriental life for the university, many of which he bought from Arthur Probsthain, an Oriental bookseller and publisher in London.

Thomas's first wife, Anna Branson of Durham, died in November 1918, only seven months after their marriage. He then married Dorothy Quincy Hancock Read on 21 Nov. 1922, and they had two children, James Augustus, Jr., and Eleanor Lansing.

SEE: *New York Times*, 11 Apr. 1940; James A. Thomas, *A Pioneer Tobacco Merchant in the Orient* (1928) and *Trailing Trade a Million Miles* (1931); Introduction to James Augustus Thomas Papers and Thomas Papers (Manuscript Department, Duke University Library, Durham).

AUGUSTUS MERRIMON BURNS III

Thomas, James Houston (*22 Sept. 1808–4 Aug. 1876*), congressman and lawyer, was born in Iredell County, the son of Isaac J., a physician, and Asenath Houston Thomas. Called Houston, he was seven years old when he moved with his parents to Tennessee, where he attended rural schools. In 1830 he was graduated from Jackson College in Columbia, Maury County, Tenn. He then studied law, was admitted to the bar in 1831, and began practicing in Columbia. On 17 Aug. 1843 he became a law partner of James K. Polk, whose family had migrated to Maury County from North Carolina a few years prior to the arrival of the Thomas family. Elected district attorney general in 1836, he served until 1842. While Polk was president of the United States (1845–49), Thomas wrote to him on many occasions concerning cases in which his firm was involved. As a Democrat Thomas served in the U.S. House of Representatives during the Thirtieth and Thirty-first Congresses (4 Mar. 1847–3 Mar. 1851). Although unsuccessful in his 1850 bid for a third term, he was again elected in 1858 and held his seat from 4 Mar. 1859 to 3 Mar. 1861.

On 17 Jan. 1861, when the possibility of secession was being widely considered, Thomas spoke in Congress in favor of remaining in the Union "with dignity" if possible, but he was critical of the North for its attitude towards the South. The Southern states, he insisted his colleagues, had a common interest and a common destiny that Southerners would protect "peaceably if we can but forcibly if we must." His words were printed and distributed in Tennessee as well as in other Southern states.

Having supported the governor of Tennessee in bringing about secession, Thomas was elected to the Provisional Confederate Congress. He was an outspoken Southern nationalist and urged the invasion of Kentucky, where it was anticipated backing would be found for the Confederacy. He served only one term, however, after which, in February 1862, he returned to his law practice in Columbia. After Nashville, together with much of central Tennessee, was occupied by Federal troops, Thomas moved to Alabama. Returning home in 1864, he was arrested for treason and imprisoned until the end of the war by Unionist officials who held power in the state. Afterwards he moved to Fayetteville, Tenn., forty miles southeast of Columbia, to practice law and was living there at the time of his death. His body was returned to Maury County for burial in the cemetery of St. John's Episcopal Church at Ashwood, of which he was a member.

Thomas was married on 20 Dec. 1832 to Margaret Meeds Stephens (1810–49), the daughter of the Reverend Daniel Stephens, D.D., rector of St. Peter's Episcopal Church in Columbia. Their children were James David (1833–34); James Daniel (1835–99), a Confederate captain of engineers; Margaret Stephens (August–September 1839); and Mary Catherine (1844–1920).

SEE. *Biog. Dir. Am. Cong.* (1951); William Bruce, *History of Maury County, Tennessee* (1955); Richard N. Current, ed., *Encyclopedia of the Confederacy*, vol. 4 (1993); Fred Lee Hawkins, Jr., comp., *Maury County, Tennessee, Cemeteries* (1989); Marise Lightfoot and Evelyn Shackelford, comps., *They Passed This Way*, vol. 2, "Maury County, Tennessee Death Records" (1989); Robert M. McBride and Dan M. Robinson, *Biographical Directory of the Tennessee General Assembly*, vol. 1 (1975); Leonidas L. Polk, *Handbook of North Carolina* (1879); Jon L. Wakelyn, *Biographical Dictionary of the Confederacy* (1977); Herbert Weaver and others, eds., *Correspondence of James K. Polk*, vols. 1–8 (1969–93).

WILLIAM S. POWELL

Thomas, John (*11 Oct. 1705–3 Dec. 1788*), religious leader, justice, and militia officer, was born in Nansemond County, Va., the son of John and Mary Lawrence Thomas. Educated locally, he was "bred a Churchman," but after settling in North Carolina about 1740 he was converted to the Baptist faith by Dr. Josiah Hart in 1748. In 1756 Thomas founded and was first pastor of the Tosneot Baptist Church, the first of any denomination in lower Edgecombe County. On 24 Sept. 1759 the county court licensed the meetinghouse recently completed on his upper plantation near Tosneot Swamp.

In 1760–62 he allied his church briefly with the distant Charleston Baptist Association, but on 6 Nov. 1769 he became a founder and signer of the covenant of Kehukee Baptist Association at its first formal meeting in Halifax County. On 17 Sept. 1772 he was named to the committee selected to present a complimentary address of the association to Governor Josiah Martin at New Bern. His last appearance noted in the surviving minutes was 20 Oct. 1777, when he was elected moderator and directed the special committee that drew up the Articles of Marriage still reflected in the ceremonies of the Southern Baptists.

In the course of his evangelical career he assisted, on 2 May 1772, Elders Morgan Edwards (Baptist historian from Rhode Island), John Moore, and John Meglamre in ordaining William Burgess as pastor of Kehukee Baptist Church. On 24 Sept. 1773, "through the goodness of God, and the instrumentality of Elder John Thomas," a reformation was accomplished at the Red Banks Baptist Church in Pitt County, and in 1776 he and the Reverend

John Thomas, Jr., constituted the Flat Swamp Baptist Church in Martin County, also ordaining John Page to the pastorate. Early in 1777 he helped to reorganize the Lower Fishing Creek Baptist Church in Halifax County. With the assistance of Elder John Page, he constituted the Lower Town Creek Baptist Church and installed Elder Joshua Barnes as its first pastor on 17 Sept. 1780. He and Elder Barnes constituted Little Contentnea Baptist Church in Greene County on 10 Aug. 1785, it having been for some years a branch of the Tosneot church. Although Elder Thomas's home church remained in "a languid situation" for a time after his death, it was destined to fill many years of renewed prominence into the late twentieth century as the Wilson Primitive Baptist Church.

On 11 Oct. 1749 Governor Gabriel Johnston and the colonial Council at New Bern appointed John Thomas a justice of the peace, and the surviving minutes of the Edgecombe County Court reveal that he was in regular attendance at Council meetings from 17 June 1758 to 18 Oct. 1775. Although reappointed by the General Assembly on 23 Dec. 1776, he withdrew from the bench and devoted himself to ministerial duties and public service. His name appears on a road or bridge commission almost yearly between 1767 and 1786, and he served as captain of militia in his district from 1761 until after 1774.

A successful planter, Thomas accumulated around 1,800 acres and at least nine slaves. His considerable household goods, livestock, and home-distilled or fermented beverages enabled him to provide hospitable entertainment for the frequent visitors in his community on church or public business. The inventory of his estate listed twenty-four books by title, principally of a religious nature, and suggest his intellectual preparation for his long and useful career.

The Reverend Morgan Edwards, who visited Thomas in 1772, recorded that his host was married about 1732 to Christenater Roberts (1712–96), the daughter of Thomas and Mary Roberts of Nansemond County. They had six children: the Reverend John, Jr., (1733–1807), who married (1) Patience Williams and (2) Elizabeth Jones; the Reverend Jonathan (1735–75), who married Mary Hilliard; Obedience (1737–88); Major Theophilus (1740–1803), who married Mary Rogers; Millicent (1742–before 1788); and Theresa (1744–ca. 1826), who married (1) the merchant Theophilus Hill and (2) Don Manuel Marchal of St. Augustine.

SEE: Lemuel Burkitt and Jesse Read, *A Concise History of the Kehukee Baptist Association* (1803); M. A. Huggins, *A History of North Carolina Baptists* (1967); George W. Paschal, *History of North Carolina Baptists*, 2 vols. (1930, 1955), and "Morgan Edwards' Materials towards a History of the Baptists in the Province of North Carolina," *North Carolina Historical Review* 7 (July 1930); William L. Saunders, ed., *Colonial Records of North Carolina*, vol. 5 (1887); J. Kelly Turner and John L. Bridgers, Jr., *History of Edgecombe County, North Carolina* (1920).

HUGH BUCKNER JOHNSTON

Thomas, John Warwick *(27 June 1800–17 May 1871),* founder of Thomasville, politician, and educator, was born in Caswell County, the son of Robert and Margaret Warwick Thomas. Because many in Margaret's family spelled their name Warrick, following the popular English pronunciation, numerous descendants continue to use the phonetic spelling. Robert Thomas died in 1810 leaving his widow with six children. John matured young and in late 1817 pursued his interest in mining to Davidson County, where gold, silver, and other valuable min-

erals were found. He engaged in mining, both personally and in business partnerships, for many years. At the home of Moses Lambeth, who lived on large landholdings in the place much later called Cedar Ledge, he fell in love with the daughter Mary (Polly) with whom he eloped on 25 Jan. 1818. Earlier the same month his mother became the second wife of Daniel Merrill, a Revolutionary War veteran who lived a few miles southeast in Randolph County. In 1823 Moses Lambeth ceded to Thomas a large tract of his home place for the consideration of love and affection. Soon Thomas erected a substantial frame house there for his growing family; the house with remodelings was occupied until 1976.

Active in public affairs, Thomas was named one of nine trustees of Fair Grove Methodist Church, which was less than a mile from his home. In 1830 he entered politics and was elected a county representative in the 1831 General Assembly. He was returned as a senator in 1842, 1848, 1854, and 1860. An outspoken Whig, he strongly supported his party's promotion of internal improvements. In 1849 he voted for the bill obligating the state to build a railroad from Goldsboro to Charlotte via Raleigh, Greensboro, and Salisbury. He was chairman of a committee that sold more stock in Davidson than was sold in any other county. Because the survey passed two miles north of his home, he purchased a large piece of land centered by the proposed route and with his sons contracted to construct three railroad sections towards Lexington. He soon had started a town with a large frame store in the center and a mill near the east edge where both grist and lumber were produced. On 23 Oct. 1852 the *Greensborough Patriot* announced the gathering at Thomas Depot on Saturday, 30 October, to be addressed by six named leading North Carolina Whigs promoting the candidacy of General Winfield Scott for president and William A. Graham, a recent state governor, for vice-president. From this first printed naming, the town counts 1852 as its founding date.

Workers came from all around to clear the heavily wooded area, prepare the roadbed, build houses for their families, and provide necessary services. The Thomasville post office was established in 1853 with mail distribution from a desk in the Thomas store. In 1857 the town was incorporated by the General Assembly. Other events that year included the erection of a large house for the Thomas family west of the store on Main Street, the arrival of two shoe manufacturing firms from Bush Hill (Archdale) so as to be better served by the newly completed railroad, and the relocation of the Glen Anna Female Seminary from its place two miles south to the large brick building on East Main Street north of the railroad.

Families moved to the town to provide schooling for their children. Thomas's continuing interest in education dated to his youth, when schooling for those without means was hard to get. But from his many speeches published in the *Greensborough Patriot* during his political years, one finds him well read and using excellent English. When Davidson County first established public schools in 1843, Thomas was one of ten men named to the school board and elected their chairman the first two years. As president of Glen Anna in its new town location, he secured a faculty of highly trained Northern teachers. Both the culture and the prosperity of the area benefited from the seminary's activities and programs.

As a Methodist from Fair Grove, he gave his church a lot north of the railroad for a building and was equally generous to the few Baptists, who received a lot on Randolph Street south of the railroad. Thomas became a member of Richland Lodge No. 214, Ancient Free and Accepted Masons, when it was organized in 1860. He and his sons were active in this strong lodge. He soon gave it a lot on Randolph Street on which they erected a large meeting place also used for many other community purposes. Following Thomas's death a tribute of respect from this Thomasville lodge was published in the *Raleigh Sentinel*. The white-clad students of the seminary followed his bier from the nearby Methodist church to the Thomasville Cemetery. He had given this large cemetery tract to the town in 1860, when the need arose. A portrait was hung in the city council room in the Thomasville municipal building. Six sons and three daughters grew up in the Main Street house.

SEE: Caswell County Records, Yanceyville; Davidson County Board of Education Minutes, 1843 and following years; Davidson County Records, Lexington; Glen Anna Female Seminary Catalogue, 1858; *Greensborough Patriot* (1857 and other years); *Raleigh Sentinel*, 31 May 1871; John H. Wheeler, *Historical Sketches of North Carolina* (1851).

MARY G. MATTHEWS

Thomas, Micajah, Jr. *(3 Jan. 1757–26 Sept. 1788)*, planter, taverner, clerk of court, justice, and legislator, was the son of Captain Micajah (13 Feb. 1726–14 Nov. 1769) and Mourning Dixon Thomas. His father was a native of Nansemond County, Va., a prominent planter, merchant, justice, and militia officer in what was then Edgecombe County, N.C. The first court in Nash County, formed in 1777 from Edgecombe, was held on 29 Jan. 1778 at the home of Micajah, Jr., who was unanimously chosen clerk in April but resigned on 5 October. In April 1780 he sold the commissioners three acres south of Peachtree Creek on which the first permanent courthouse for the new county was erected in 1784. Thomas represented Nash County in the legislature in 1780, 1782–85, and 1787. He also became a justice of the county court on 8 Apr. 1783.

His will, dated 17 May 1788, was unusual not only for the disposal of 88 slaves, 25,000 acres of land, and a great deal of personal wealth, but also for the excessive litigation that it engendered for many years as an indirect result of his unusual domestic life. He provided abundantly for all four of his illegitimate daughters, and the three by Ann Jackson were to "have a good education and be brought up in a genteel manner" until aged eighteen or married, meanwhile living with their mother "in the new house." Several other family connections were also treated generously, and his blacksmith, Lewis, and "trusty servant old Peter" were given their freedom, their wives, and a lifetime means of support.

The handsome two-story Thomas residence, erected east of the courthouse on Washington Street in the summer of 1788, was sold out of the family in 1830 and thereafter served variously as a private residence, a hotel, and finally a storehouse before being demolished in 1976. A detailed inventory of the Thomas estate indicates that this house was attractively furnished with walnut and mahogany furniture, a library, considerable sterling silver and pewterware, and other evidence of wealth.

The almost novelistic details of Thomas's private life began with the tentative bond he made on 5 June 1776 to marry Elizabeth Crafford of Surry County, Va. They never married, however, and their child, Mary Thomas Crafford, was born out of wedlock; she became the wife of Archibald Cocke of Surry County on 5 Sept. 1793. On 7 Jan. 1778 Micajah Thomas married as his only wife Anne Hawkins (5 June 1759–12 Mar. 1781), the daughter of Colonel Philemon and Delia Martin Hawkins of Bute County, N.C. Their two children, Barsheba and Philemon Thomas, inherited their mother's tuberculosis and died in infancy.

In 1784 the widower Micajah Thomas introduced upon the Nash County scene a charming mistress, Ann Jackson, who, in due time, presented him with three daughters whose maturing physical and cultural endowments were enhanced by their outstanding inheritances of both slaves and land. In the course of events their illegitimate births offered no impediment to the matrimonial attentions of the most eligible young bachelors of Nash and adjacent counties.

Thomas's will was recorded on 10 Nov. 1788 and placed in the care of executor William Boddie the property intended for his three daughters, resident in Nash County. Executors Benjamin Hawkins and Shadrach Rutland were to supervise the Northampton County estate of daughter Mary Thomas Crafford.

After the marriage of Ann Jackson in 1791 to general and state senator William Arrington (2 Mar. 1766–24 Sept. 1812), Arrington secured from the Nash County Court on 13 Nov. 1792 the guardianship of Thomas's "three reputed Daughters," now Arrington's stepdaughters. In the spring of 1793 he instituted against the executors the first of the lawsuits over the Thomas estate that would involve the family intermittently for the next twenty-five years.

The situation became more complicated in 1799, when the General Assembly passed an act that entitled illegitimate brothers and sisters to inherit from each other as if they were legitimate. Ann Jackson Arrington died in 1804; her married but childless daughter, Mourning Thomas Branch, died in 1805 and this daughter's husband, James Branch, died in 1807. William Arrington died in 1812. The legal problems were basically (1) how much of one-third of the Micajah Thomas estate might be recovered from James Branch or his executor, John Branch, by the heirs-at-law of his late wife, Mourning Branch, and (2) how much of the total estate or the income therefrom might have remained improperly in the hands of guardian William Arrington or in those of his administrator, Joseph Arrington.

The subsequent developments and their solutions can be understood better after a proper identification of the three children of Ann Jackson and Micajah Thomas: (1) Mourning Thomas Jackson (4 May 1785–1805), married first Thomas M. Alston on 12 Oct. 1802 and second James Branch (brother of Governor John Branch) on 14 Dec. 1803; as a widower, Branch married second Martha Hilliard on 26 Sept. 1806 and died about 1 Nov. 1807. (2) Margaret Thomas Jackson (4 May 1785–9 June 1866) married General Joseph John (Jack) Alston on 7 Oct. 1802. (3) Temperance Thomas Jackson (14 Sept. 1787–after 1840) married James Wright Alston.

Of the four later children that Ann Jackson had by William Arrington: (1) Mary Arrington Jackson (b. 29 Aug. 1790) married first Captain James M. Nicholson (d. May 1809) on 11 Dec. 1806 and second General Joseph Arrington. (2) John D. Arrington (b. 4 May 1792), married Joanna Williams Drake on 28 Jan. 1812. (3) William Arrington, Jr., married Ann Brinkley. (4) Martha Arrington (7 Nov. 1795–20 June 1870) married in 1812 her stepbrother Lawrence Battle (20 Mar. 1788–30 Aug. 1841).

Then in December 1804 General Arrington married as his second wife Mrs. Mary Williams Battle (1768–3 Sept. 1816), the widow of Captain William Battle, by whom he had two additional children: (1) Ann Arrington (1805–1825), married Peyton Randolph Tunstall in 1822. (2) Colonel Nicholas Williams Arrington (25 Dec. 1807–14 Feb. 1865), married Temperance Arrington Drake on 18 Apr. 1827 and is reputed to have become the most famous Arrington in Nash and its environs.

At its July 1810 term the North Carolina Supreme Court reviewed an appeal of *Alston and Wife v. Branch and Arrington* from the Halifax County Court and decided that

James Branch and his heirs had been correct in maintaining their title to the land, slaves, and moneys heired by his first wife, Mourning Thomas Jackson. In the case of *Arrington* v. *Battle* as appealed from the Nash County Court to the January 1813 term of the Supreme Court, it was determined that both parties were liable for the charges of the county clerk. Joseph Arrington would return the slave woman and her increase and pay all other costs of the suit, and Lawrence Battle would restore to Arrington the purchase price of £250.

The lawsuit of *Branch* v. *Arrington* concerning income and interest from the Macajah Thomas estate was introduced into the Halifax County Court of Equity at the April 1815 term and was heard in July 1815 by the state supreme court. The state court ruled that guardian William Arrington and his successor were bound to report annually all interest and other income from the estate of their wards "after the deduction of just charges." The case of *Arrington* v. *Arrington Heirs* from the Nash County Court was heard by the same session of the supreme court, which decided that only the lands acquired by William Arrington after signing the marriage contract with Mrs. Mary Battle on 10 Dec. 1804 were subject by law to her claim of dower.

On 18 June 1816 the litigation of *Arrington and Others* v. *John Alston* was instituted in the Nash County Court on the issue that the slaves and other personal property bequeathed by Micajah Thomas to Mourning Jackson Branch in 1788 had been in a different clause from the real property and by all applicable law and equity should have reverted in equal shares to her legitimate and illegitimate heirs by blood (i.e., all the living children of the late Ann Jackson Arrington, including the never-identified first four who were "born out of wedlock" and bore the surname Monroe). The July 1818 term of the North Carolina Supreme Court rendered judgment that this personal estate belonged to the aforesaid "heirs at law."

What appears to have been the last litigation over the Micajah Thomas estate was begun in the Nash County Court of September 1820, and concluded without further involvement of the state supreme court, for the recovery and division of Mourning Branch's real property consisting of 3,025 acres worth $5,166 on Peachtree and Pig Basket creeks and of 540 acres worth $5,215 north of Tar River at Rocky Branch. On 14 Dec. and 19 Mar. 1821 twelve tracts in six shares of 594 acres each were finally divided among her two half brothers and the husbands representing her two whole and two half sisters.

SEE: John B. Boddie, *Virginia Historical Genealogies* (1954); John L. Cheney, Jr., ed., *North Carolina Government, 1585–1974* (1975); Walter Clark, ed., *State Records of North Carolina*, vols. 6, 8–9 (1888–90); William L. Saunders, ed., *State Records of North Carolina*, vols. 12, 15–17, 19–20, 24 (1895–1905); *Tarboro Free Press*, 11 July 1828; Wills and deeds of Edgecombe County, Tarboro, and of Nash County, Nashville; *Wilson Daily Times*, 1–15 Dec. 1953, 24, 27 Apr., 11 Oct. 1954, 14–20 July 1955, 27 Sept. 1956, 21–30 Dec. 1957.

HUGH BUCKNER JOHNSTON

Thomas, Perley Albert (*17 Sept. 1874–28 Apr. 1959*), High Point industrialist, was born in the London area of Ontario, Canada, the son of Margaret Cunningham and John Andrew Thomas. His father was a carpenter and farmer. Young Thomas received an elementary school education, which he supplemented with correspondence courses. Always an imaginative, practical draftsman-engineer, he learned the manufacture of streetcars in Detroit and later became chief engineer of the Kuhlman Car Company of Cleveland, Ohio. In 1909 he moved to High Point as chief engineer of the Southern Car Company.

After the company closed in 1914, P. A. Thomas began to produce replacement parts for streetcars. Initially this effort involved the manufacture of wooden parts and was linked to the furniture industry, which was gaining importance in High Point. In 1917 he founded his own company, the Thomas Car Works, to construct streetcars; it employed thirty workmen, and its first order was for four cars by the neighboring city of Winston-Salem. Fire destroyed Thomas's facilities in 1921, but he rebuilt, realizing great success in the 1920s. Two of his biggest orders in these years were for 150 cars for New Orleans and 100 for Detroit. The market for streetcars declined after 1930 with the depression and ensuing downturn in the popularity of streetcars as a means of transportation. In the 1930s the company began to produce bus transport equipment. In 1936, when Thomas bid on school buses for the first time, he convinced buyers to adopt all-steel construction instead of a composite (wood reinforced with steel). He also innovated a new safety door that swung outward, thus incorporating a feature of the streetcar design that he had previously used. These changes were a breakthrough in school bus manufacture and secured the future of Thomas Car Works.

During World War II Thomas Car Works, now largely converted from a wood to a metal industry, handled large orders from the U.S. Army. Among the items manufactured were metal pontoons for barges and bridges, metal bodies for radar equipment, and buses. The company also performed body repairs on army vehicles and for these services received a citation from the Ordinance Section, U.S. Army. By 1950 Thomas Car Works, which had always been a family corporation, operated a modern assembly line manned by 350 skilled laborers. At full production the output reached 1,700 buses per year. Aside from the chassis and engine, the materials were processed and installed at the plant.

Perley A. Thomas retired from active management of the company in the 1950s but retained the title of president until his death. But the Thomas story continued to unfold. In 1978, under the third generation of family management, Thomas of High Point occupied 125 acres, had 400,000 square feet of plant facilities, and produced approximately 6,000 units for world distribution. In addition, plants in Canada and Ecuador manufactured buses for those markets.

Shy and taciturn except when animated by an exciting idea, Thomas was an excellent supervisor and a diligent worker. His hobby was designing and making bedroom and dining room furniture of cherry, mahogany, and oak. He was also active in civic affairs as a member of the First Baptist Church, an Elk, a Mason, and a Shriner.

In February 1897 Thomas married Margaret Milne. At one time or another all of their children—Melva T., Mary, J. Willard, and J. Norman—were involved in the management of the business. The Thomas family provided significant economic diversification in High Point, a city where some would contend that textiles and furniture have been too dominant. Thomas died in Jacksonville, Fla., where he was interred in Greenlawn Cemetery. In addition to his offspring, he was survived by his second wife, Joan Madden Thomas.

SEE: *High Point Enterprise*, 28 Apr. 1959; *Pioneer Days and Progress of High Point, N.C., 1859–1948* (1948); Mrs. Melva T. Price to Max R. Williams, 19 Dec. 1978; J. Norman Thomas, personal contact, 25 Nov. 1978.

MAX R. WILLIAMS

Thomas, William Holland (5 Feb. 1805–10 May 1893), white chief of the Eastern Band of the Cherokee Indians, legislator, and Confederate officer, was born in rural Haywood County shortly after the death of his father, Richard Thomas. Raised by his mother, Temperance Calvert Thomas, he was forced to start working at age thirteen in a store owned by Congressman Felix Walker in Cherokee territory. By 1823 Thomas was able to open his own store in Qualla Town. His knowledge of the Cherokee language enabled him to prosper, and by the late 1820s he owned three stores and large tracts of land in the western part of the state.

During this time Thomas became a good friend of Yonaguska, the principal chief of the Cherokee who chose to remain under white rule following the land cession and treaty of 1819. As a result of this friendship, the young white man was adopted into the Cherokee tribe and given the name Wil-Usdi (Little Will) because of his small size. He not only continued his businesses, but he also began to read law and act as the attorney for the North Carolina Cherokee. Thomas's first major action on their behalf was to draw up a simple plan of government that allowed them to coordinate their responses to government policies.

The relationship between the federal government and the Cherokee reached a critical stage after the signing of the Treaty of New Echota, which provided that all members of the Cherokee nation must move to the West. The North Carolina Cherokee maintained that they were exempted from the removal order and contracted with Thomas to represent them in Washington. The assignment lasted from 1836 to 1848, and Thomas often spent months at a time in Washington. Despite his commitment to the Cherokee cause, he openly speculated in lands made available for sale by the Cherokee removal. He also aided the U.S. Army in its efforts to locate Cherokee from other states who hid in North Carolina to escape removal. These contradictory actions, ironically, served to strengthen his position with the Cherokee, local whites, and the federal government.

The significance of Thomas's activities during this period cannot be underestimated. Immediately after removal he spent some of his own money to feed and clothe many Cherokee. He defended his support of the Indians' cause, asserting that "when entrusted with defending the rights of white or red man I hope I shall always be found faithful to my trust and act worthy of the confidence reposed in me without regard to consequences. The Indians are as much entitled to their rights as I am to mine." Recognizing Thomas's devotion to the tribe, the dying chief Yonaguska named Thomas the new leader of the North Carolina Cherokee in April 1839. This job encouraged Thomas to continue his efforts to secure for his people a proportionate share of the moneys promised the Cherokee by the New Echota agreement. He finally succeeded in July 1848, when the U.S. government recognized the Eastern Band of the Cherokee and allowed most of their claims to treaty awards. By 1840 Thomas had also purchased in his name—the state of North Carolina did not allow the Cherokee to sign contracts—50,000 acres that would form the major portion of the future Qualla Boundary home of the Eastern Cherokee.

His assistance to the Cherokee and his large landholdings made Thomas an influential figure in western North Carolina. He entered politics and served continuously in the North Carolina state senate from 1849 to 1861. A Democrat, Thomas was an active member of the Committee on Internal Improvements and served as chairman for four terms. He consistently sponsored or supported legislation to improve the transportation system of the western portion of the state including such projects as plank roads and the Western North Carolina Railroad. These same years were a time of change in his personal life. He increasingly neglected his business interests and became "land poor" and deeply in debt; in 1857, at age fifty-two, he married Sarah Jane Burney Love, the daughter of a wealthy Haywood County man. Their three children—William H., Jr. (b. 1858), James R. (b. 1860), and Sarah L. (b. 1862)—soon gave him even greater personal responsibilities.

The Civil War added new challenges to Thomas's life. He was an ardent Southern patriot and voted for secession at the state convention in May 1861. After returning home, he persuaded the Cherokee to support the Confederacy and organized a home guard group. In April 1862 he joined the Confederate army and was named captain of a company that included many Cherokee. That September the company took part in a skirmish at Baptist Gap in eastern Tennessee, which ended with some Cherokee scalping wounded Union soldiers. Thomas was soon promoted to colonel and placed in command of the Sixty-ninth North Carolina Regiment with several companies of Cherokee in the unit. This force, known as Thomas's Legion, served as the major line of defense between the Federal presence in eastern Tennessee and Confederate North Carolina. Thomas was one of the last Confederates to surrender, along with General James G. Martin, in Waynesville on 10 May 1865.

His career after the war was one of increasing personal and financial difficulties. The demands of the conflict led to a physical and emotional collapse. In March 1867 Thomas was declared insane and confined to the state asylum in Raleigh. His businesses failed and creditors began to dismantle his empire; for example, the sheriff of Cherokee County sold off more than 115,000 acres of Thomas's land in 1869 alone. Even the Cherokee had to go to court to secure control of their land from his creditors. Thomas still experienced periods of mental stability and related many of the Cherokee myths to researcher James Mooney. He died in the state mental hospital in Morganton and was buried in the public cemetery in Waynesville. Thomas was the one individual most responsible for the creation of the Eastern Band of the Cherokee and a consistent champion of the economic development of the mountain region of North Carolina.

SEE: Walter Clark, ed., *Histories of the Several Regiments and Battalions from North Carolina*, vols. 1, 3–4 (1901); Richard W. Iobst, "William Holland Thomas and the Cherokee Claims," in Duane H. King, ed., *The Cherokee Nation: A Troubled History* (1979); James Mooney, *Myths of the Cherokees* (1902 [portrait]); Mattie Russell, "Devil in the Smokies: The White Man's Nature and the Indian's Fate," *South Atlantic Quarterly* 73 (Winter 1974), and "William Holland Thomas: White Chief of the North Carolina Cherokees" (Ph.D. diss., Duke University, 1956); William H. Thomas manuscripts (Manuscript Department, Duke University Library, Durham, and Western Carolina University Library, Cullowhee).

GORDON B. MCKINNEY

Thomlinson, Thomas (November 1732–23 or 24 Sept. 1805), schoolmaster, the son of John Thomlinson, was born at Evening-Hill in the parish of Thursby, Cumberland County, England, and was master of Uldale School nearby from 1752 to 1762. At the invitation of a brother who owned a plantation near New Bern, he decided to migrate and establish a school in North Carolina. Arriving in New Bern in December 1763, he began classes on

1 January 1764. He "immediately got as many scholars as he could instruct" and received so many additional requests that he needed an assistant. The Reverend James Reed, rector of Christ Church Parish, excited about the presence of a schoolmaster and the prospects of a schoolhouse, wrote that "during 11 years Residence in this province I have not found any man so well qualified for the Care of a school as Mr. Tomlinson." He was "not only a good scholar but a man of good conduct." A year later, in 1765, Governor William Tryon informed the Society for the Propagation of the Gospel in Foreign Parts that Thomlinson was "the only person of repute of that profession in the country."

Thomlinson not only became the first "regular settled Schoolmaster" in the province, but also the first instructor of the colony's newly incorporated free school. In 1764, shortly after his arrival, the Assembly passed an act for the construction of a schoolhouse. Two years later it placed the school on a sound foundation by naming trustees and providing a source of revenue. Reed reported that the schoolmaster was ready to make New Bern his permanent home. At that time Thomlinson was living in an ordinary (inn or tavern), which he found distasteful, but it kept his expenses down as the owners sent two children to his school. Reed believed that the young schoolmaster needed "a house of his own in the honorable state of matrimony." Thomlinson's salary came to approximately £60 sterling. In addition, the parish hired him as a lay reader for £12, and the Society for the Propagation of the Gospel granted him a stipend of £15. Because £100 per annum was considered an adequate income, Thomlinson could almost live in comfort, except that his fees were not always paid promptly.

For the first seven years of its existence, the school prospered and Thomlinson was praised for his teaching. He even hired an assistant, James Macartney, in 1767, when his enrollment reached eighty scholars. He generally averaged sixty students, who came from all over the province. By 1770 Thomlinson noted a decline in enrollment; the school was becoming too much of a local institution. He gave as the principal reasons "the advanced price of Boarding in this place, and the extreme scarcity of our currency." At about the same time a dissenting minister in Wilmington had opened an academy and Thomlinson lost six boys who lived in the Lower Cape Fear area. But what apparently hurt the school most was Thomlinson's discipline and expulsion of two unruly children, the offspring of two trustees. The Reverend Mr. Reed reported that when the schoolmaster began classes, he had been "apprized of the excessive Indulgence of American Parents, and the great difficulty of keeping up a proper discipline; more especially as his school consisted of numbers of both sexes." Thomlinson had thus proceeded with caution, but to maintain order in the school he had finally found it necessary to discipline the two youngsters and had thus committed a "sin against the Holy Ghost, never to be forgiven."

He managed to maintain the school for about a year, but during that time a majority of the trustees were pressuring him to resign first by removing the poor children from the school's foundation, which lowered his income, and then by encouraging Thomlinson's former assistant to set up school. Both schemes failed and, finally, in September 1771 the trustees dismissed him on the basis of neglect—an unfounded charge. The new governor, Josiah Martin, protested but could do nothing about the case. Thomlinson apparently kept the school until April 1772. He managed to recover over £235 owed to him by threatening a suit. Remaining in New Bern, he became a merchant and by the time of his death had accumulated con-

siderable wealth. He endowed four schools in his native Cumberland County, including the celebrated Wigton Grammar School where the endowment still exists. Presumably he is the one of this name listed in the 1790 census of Craven County in a household consisting of himself, a free white female (his wife?), and four slaves. His wife, Elizabeth, died in 1801, naming Boneta Macartney her sole executrix.

SEE: Alonzo T. Dill, *Governor Tryon and His Palace* (1955); Elizabeth Kaye, "The Case of Thomas Thomlinson," *Historical Magazine of the Protestant Episcopal Church* 5 (March 1936); Memorial tablets in Uldale and Thursby parish churches, Cumberland, England; William S. Powell, ed., *The Correspondence of William Tryon*, 2 vols. (1980); *Raleigh Register*, 12 Oct. 1802; William L. Saunders, ed., *Colonial Records of North Carolina*, vols. 7, 9–10 (1890); *William and Mary Quarterly* 2, 2d. ser. (October 1922).

ALICE E. MATHEWS

Thompson, Cyrus (*8 Feb. 1855–20 Nov. 1930*), secretary of state, legislator, physician, teacher, agriculturist, and orator, was born at Gregory Forks near Richlands, the son of Franklin, Sr., and Leah Brown Thompson. Franklin Thompson, Jr., and R. D. Thompson were brothers of Cyrus.

Young Thompson's parents sent him to a preparatory school in Raleigh, and from there he went to Randolph-Macon College, Ashland, Va., and was graduated in 1876. He studied medicine at the University of Virginia Medical School and at the University of Louisiana (now the School of Medicine of Tulane University), where he received a medical degree in 1878. He established a medical practice first in Richlands but after 1881 in Jacksonville, the county seat. Recognizing in 1893 that his income was insufficient to support his family, he taught school for several years and for a time afterwards he farmed extensively. Throughout his life he retained an interest in farming, and as a prominent agriculturist he took a leadership role in the Farmers Alliance, serving as its state lecturer.

Interested in politics, Thompson represented Onslow County as a Democrat in the North Carolina House of Representatives in 1883 and in the North Carolina Senate in 1885. From 1895 to 1897 he was a trustee of The University of North Carolina. In 1896 he was elected secretary of state on the Republican ticket and served under Governor Daniel L. Russell from 1897 to 1901. Although not elected, he received the Populist vote for U.S. senator in 1897 and the Republican and Progressive vote in 1913. He was a presidential elector in the balloting of President Herbert Hoover in 1928.

Resuming his medical practice in Jacksonville in 1904, Thompson was a Fellow of the Medical Society of North Carolina from that time until his death. He was the Onslow County superintendent of health during the years 1905–8 and 1911–12 and the county medical examiner during World War I. Thompson was named to the North Carolina Medical Corps by the surgeon general of the United States, and from 1913 to 1930 he was a member of the State Board of Health (president, 1918). He served several terms as president of the Medical Society of North Carolina and held the same position in the Tri-State Medical Association and the Seaboard Medical Society.

Thompson enjoyed a reputation as an orator, often displaying both eloquence and humor. One of his best known speech-making feats occurred during the term of Governor Thomas W. Bickett (1917–21), who was much interested in requiring patent medicines to display labels declaring their ingredients. The measure was opposed by the manufacturers of patent medicines, who sent their New York attorney to debate the issue before the senate. Representing the governor at a crowded senate hearing, Dr. Thompson defeated the opposition lawyer.

In 1882 he married Florence Garland Kent, of Richmond, Va., the daughter of Charles E. Kent. They had ten children: Florence Kent, Cyrus, Virginia Garland, Charles Edward, Gertrude, Lorimer Wilder, Marguerite, Franklin, Horace Kent, and Minnetta Gordon. Dr. and Mrs. Thompson were buried in the family cemetery near his birthplace at Gregory Forks.

SEE: J. Parsons Brown, *The Commonwealth of Onslow: A History* (1960); John L. Cheney, Jr., ed., *North Carolina Government, 1585–1979* (1981); P. L. Pittman, *Gregory Forks: History* (1978); *Southern Medicine and Surgery* 92 (December 1930); *Transactions of the Medical Society of the State of North Carolina* (1931 [portrait]); *Who Was Who in America*, vol. 1 (1981). There is a photograph in the Tucker Littleton Collection (North Carolina State Archives, Raleigh).

TUCKER REED LITTLETON

Thompson, David Matthew *(5 June 1844–26 June 1926)*, educator, better known as D. Matt Thompson, was born near Long's Mill in Randolph County, the son of Samuel and Elizabeth Moser Thompson. He attended the county's public schools and then a private school until the Civil War intervened. During the war he served first in the Third North Carolina Regiment, an infantry unit, and later in the Nineteenth North Carolina Regiment, a cavalry detachment. He was wounded on the third day at Gettysburg and later in a cavalry engagement at Deep Bottom. Attaining the rank of sergeant, he was slated for a commission but did not receive it because of the unsettled state of affairs just before Appomattox.

As soon as possible after the war Thompson continued his education with the aim of becoming a teacher. He went to Sylvan Academy, near Snow Hill in Alamance County, and then to Cook County Normal, in Chicago, under the direction of Colonel Francis Parker.

He taught at Sylvan before founding Aurora Academy, in Alamance, where he taught until elected principal of Sylvan, which by then was Sylvan High School. In 1872 he became principal of Rock Spring Seminary at Denver, Lincoln County, and in the next twelve years built it into one of the more successful schools of the era. In 1884 he assumed the principalship of Piedmont Academy, Lincolnton, a position he held until 1890, when he went to Gainesville, Fla., to become superintendent of the graded schools there. He had been chairman of the new board of education in Lincoln County until he left for Florida.

In 1891 the citizens of Statesville voted to establish a graded school system, and D. Matt Thompson, already thinking of leaving Florida because of his wife's health, was recalled to his native state to head the newly created system. For nearly thirty years his name was synonymous with educational development in the Iredell County seat. On 20 Nov. 1920 he was hit by an automobile while crossing a Statesville street, and soon afterwards his sons, acting as his attorneys, made arrangements for him to resign his post; he died six years later in the state hospital at Morganton.

His long service in the same position was at the time something of a record in school work. When he went to Statesville in 1891 there were only 407 white pupils and 172 "colored" pupils, with a brick building in the process of construction on Mulberry Street and another small house for the blacks on Green Street. By 1920 a second elementary school for whites had been built on Davie Avenue and a new one for blacks on Garfield Street, to be known as Morningside. After 1907 the white schools were expanded to include high school work and before 1920 there were eleven grades. When he was struck down, a new high school was being built on West Front Street; it later became D. Matt Thompson Junior High School.

Those who knew D. Matt Thompson recalled him best as a strict disciplinarian, one of the large number of such schoolmen engendered by the Civil War expedience. They were impressed by the drums he used as the pupils lined up to march in and out of the building in military fashion.

Thompson lived before the days of civic clubs in Statesville, but he was very active in such organizations as the North Carolina Teachers Association, at one time heading the superintendent's division. A Methodist, he was for thirty years a steward in Broad Street Methodist Church and for fifteen years secretary of the Western North Carolina Conference Board of Missions. On 2 Aug. 1872, before moving to Lincoln County, he married Lizzie [Mary Elizabeth] Rice of Randolph County. They had three sons: Holland, professor of history in the City College of New York; Walter Holland, superintendent of the Children's Home in Winston-Salem; and Dorman, Statesville attorney and representative in the General Assembly for Iredell County. D. Matt Thompson was buried in Oakwood Cemetery, Statesville.

SEE: Statesville *Landmark*, 1891–1920, especially his obituary, 2 July 1926.

HOMER M. KEEVER

Thompson, Holland McTyeire *(30 July 1873–21 Oct. 1940)*, historian of the New South, was born in Randolph County to D. Matt and Mary Elizabeth Rice Thompson. Reared in Denver, Lincolnton, and Statesville, where his father was for many years principal and superintendent of public schools, he received the Ph.B. degree at The University of North Carolina in 1895 and for the next four years was a high school principal at Concord. There he was in a position to observe the rapid transfer of population from farms to the textile industry and the attendant social changes. On the basis of an essay on that subject Thompson was awarded a fellowship to Columbia University and, like so many other young southern teachers of the time, went north for advanced studies, receiving his doctorate in 1906. He then was appointed assistant professor of history at the College of the City of New York, with which he had been associated since 1901 as tutor and instructor. Thompson later stated that he accepted the position in New York on the advice of Charles D. McIver, who suggested that he, like Walter Hines Page, could do the state of North Carolina more good out of it than in it.

Thompson remained at the College of the City of New York until his sudden death at his home nearly forty years later. He became a full professor in 1920 and was active in the administrative affairs of his department, the college, and a number of academic organizations including the American Association of University Professors, of which he was a charter member. Although his writings and interests were eclectic, Thompson made the New South the subject of many articles and reviews as well as of two of his best-known books. *From Cotton Field to Cotton Mill: A Study of the Industrial Transition in North Carolina* (1906), his doctoral dissertation, based largely on firsthand investigation, achieved something of the status of a classic. The *New South: A Chronicle of Social and Industrial Revolution* (Yale Chronicles of America Series, 1919) was praised by William K. Boyd at the time of its publication for its "catholicity of spirit" and "descriptive value." According to Boyd, "as a brief and suggestive survey of the rise of a civilization the book is unsurpassed."

Although not profound, Thompson's *The Age of Invention: A Chronicle of Mechanical Conquest* (Yale Chronicles of America Series, 1921) was a popular work. Thompson also delivered numerous speeches and scholarly papers and contributed many articles and reviews on diverse subjects to journals, both popular and scholarly, and to encyclopedias and reference works. Simultaneously with his academic life, he enjoyed a productive and lucrative career as an editor. He served as editor-in-chief of *The Book of Knowledge*, a children's encyclopedia, published in twenty volumes in 1910–11 and several times revised. He worked in an editorial capacity with commercial publishers and popular magazines, most notably the *Review of Reviews*. In the course of such editorial work he collaborated on, contributed to, or edited a number of textbooks, pictorial histories, symposia on current subjects, and the like. In this category are works such as *History of Our Land* (1911), *Prisons of the Civil War* (1911), *The People and the Trusts* (1912), *The United States* (1915), *The World War* (3 vols., 1920), and *Lands and People* (1929–30).

One of the first historians to make the New South a field of study, Thompson maintained a lifelong interest in North Carolina and in the work of the social sciences pertinent to the social, industrial, and racial problems of the state. He visited regularly and was said to be contemplating retirement in Chapel Hill for the writing of a comprehensive history of the New South at the time of his death. He received a gold medal for distinguished service to education at the Philadelphia Sesquicentennial Exposition of 1926 and an honorary doctorate from The University of North Carolina in 1935. Thompson married Isobel Graham Aitken of New York in 1905 and they had one son, Lawrence. Vigorous and square-built, he was described as a man of "genial spirit" with a "penchant for conversing upon the South and her problems." Named for the Methodist bishop Holland McTyeire, Thompson early in life dropped both the family faith and the middle name that it had inspired. At death, his remains were cremated and the ashes scattered at the base of the Davie poplar in Chapel Hill.

Though his contributions to historical scholarship were by no means insignificant, Thompson is perhaps best characterized as a social commentator or higher type of journalist, skilled as a graceful essayist and interpreter of broad trends. Unlike the next generation of southern scholars, his dedication to progress did not override his genteel detachment or lead him to complete repudiation of inherited traditions. The civilization of the New South, which had clearly emerged by 1920, was, he believed, a natural evolution of the Old South and not a sharp new departure. A cautious optimist, his life was representative of the success wrung from the northern, urban, professional world by some southerners of his generation, and in temper his writings represent something of a link between the values of the Old South and the hustling progressive spirit of the early twentieth century.

SEE: *American Historical Review*, vol. 46 (January 1941); *Greensboro Daily News*, 15 Feb. 1925; *Journal of Southern History*, vol. 7 (February 1941); *New York Herald Tribune*, 22 Oct. 1940; *New York Times*, 22 Oct. 1940; *Who Was Who in America*, vol. 1 (1981).

CLYDE WILSON

Thompson, Jacob (*15 May 1810–24 Mar. 1885*), Mississippi congressman, secretary of the interior, and Confederate agent in Canada, was born in Leasburg, Caswell County, one of nine children of Nicholas and Lucretia Van Hook Thompson. His father's tanning business and his mother's estate had placed the family in comfortable circumstances, and it was the hope of Jacob's parents that he would enter the ministry, a vocation for which he had no ambition. Graduating in 1831 from The University of North Carolina, he remained at Chapel Hill as a postgraduate tutor. Eighteen months later he resigned in order to read law in the Greensboro office of Judge John M. Dick. On his admission to the bar in 1835, Thompson, concluding that the best opportunity for a young attorney lay on the frontier, decided to relocate in Mississippi; all but one of his eight siblings eventually moved to that state.

A chance encounter with his older brother, Young, at Columbus, Miss., persuaded Jacob to establish himself at Pontotoc in the area newly ceded by the Chickasaws in the Jackson Indian removal program. He quickly prospered, although at first his legal practice was devoted mostly to conveyances. In addition to his main career, Thompson acquired within a few years three substantial plantations. Making his home in Oxford after his initial period in Mississippi, he became a pillar of the local Episcopal church and a benefactor of the state university. In 1840 he married Catharine Jones, the daughter of a wealthy planter. Because of her very tender age she was sent to France to complete her education, but on her return she blossomed into an outstanding social figure; the couple had one son, Caswell Macon.

Thompson launched his political career shortly after reaching Mississippi. He established a public reputation by vigorously opposing state endorsement of $5 million in Union Bank bonds, a position that proved to be sound when the institution subsequently defaulted; he later urged the state to repudiate the obligation. Narrowly defeated for attorney general in 1837, just two years after his arrival, he was elected as a Democrat to Congress in 1839, a victory that began for Thompson six consecutive House terms concluded in 1851, when he was turned out by a strong Whig tide in Mississippi. From 1845 on he was influential in the House by virtue of his successive chairmanships of the Public Lands and Indian Affairs committees, assignments that furnished valuable experience for a future secretary of the interior.

Thompson's first significant impact on national politics came in 1844, when he backed the efforts of Robert J. Walker and others to deny the Democratic nomination to the antiexpansionist former president, Martin Van Buren. On the election of James K. Polk, Thompson was instrumental in persuading the new president to name Walker to head the Treasury Department. But Thompson's friendship for Walker foundered when he discovered that his fellow Mississippian had withheld from him an interim gubernatorial appointment to Walker's old Senate seat. The rupture between the two men was never healed, and Thompson became increasingly identified with the Democrats' proslavery wing; he opposed the Henry Clay compromise proposals of 1850 despite substantial Mississippi support for them. Ironically, late in life Thompson came to regret that he had helped thwart Clay's 1844 bid for the presidency.

After leaving the House of Representatives, he declined President Franklin Pierce's offer of the Havana consulate, which was then considered to be a political prize. In 1856 he stood aside from a Senate race so that Jefferson Davis might win the seat. The following year he was given the Interior Department by President James Buchanan. From the first Thompson was a strong figure in a decidedly prosouthern cabinet; he vigorously asserted his authority over the hitherto largely autonomous bureaus of his own department. Unfortunately, however, his stewardship was clouded in 1860–61 by the discovery that a subordinate clerk, Goddard Bailey, had exchanged $557,000 in Indian Trust Fund bonds for worthless drafts of the Russell, Majors, and Waddell Company on the War Department. Secretary of War John B. Floyd was disgraced by the scandal—Bailey was a relative who had tried to help Floyd escape the consequences of his misplaced faith in Russell, Majors, and Waddell—but a five-member special House committee absolved Thompson of any responsibility. It was for other reasons that Thompson left the administration at the beginning of 1861.

As a states' rights man he had indicated at the outset of the secession crisis that he would stand by Mississippi, but he tried to exert influence within the national government for as long as possible. It was President Buchanan's decision to dispatch the *Star of the West* to Charleston, S.C., without Thompson's foreknowledge, which persuaded the latter to withdraw.

Back in Mississippi Thompson made a desultory, and unsuccessful, race for governor before undertaking military service in several different capacities. His army career ended when, as inspector under Lieutenant General John C. Pemberton, he was captured at Vicksburg and paroled. Elected to the Mississippi legislature in the fall of 1863, Thompson was summoned to Richmond by Confederate president Jefferson Davis early the next year. Sent to Canada, Thompson spent the last year of the war vainly attempting—with or without copperhead support—to arrange mass Confederate escapes from prisoner-of-war camps in the Great Lakes area. He steadfastly disavowed any complicity in plots to burn Northern cities and maintained that the 1864 raid on St. Albans, Vt., was carried out against his orders. At the close of the war he and other Confederate leaders were charged with coconspiracy in the Lincoln assassination, and a $25,000 reward was posted for his capture. Consequently Thompson and his wife passed several years in England before it was safe for them to return first to Oxford, where their home had been destroyed in the war, and shortly thereafter to Memphis, Tenn.

In the 1870s Thompson came again to public notice when the scandal-beset Grant administration sued him for $2 million to recover the Floyd-Bailey losses. Clearly a partisan effort to divert attention from the War Department's Belknap scandals, the suit was quietly dropped after the 1876 election. However, the sources of the Thompsons' affluent postwar lifestyle have yet to be explained fully. Had he indeed invested his wife's dowry—"a trunk full of gold" according to family tradition—in English securities, or had he embezzled vast Confederate funds entrusted to him in Canada as charged by William C. Davis?

An ambitious, calculating man of ability, Jacob Thompson remains strikingly obscure considering his antebellum political prominence in both Mississippi and Washington. On his death in Memphis he left behind remarkably little material on which to base a definitive study of his career.

SEE: J. F. H. Claiborne, *Mississippi as a Province, Territory, and State* (1880); William C. Davis, "The Conduct of 'Mr. Thompson,'" *Civil War Times Illustrated* 9 (May 1970); Seymour J. Frank, "The Conspiracy to Implicate the Confederate Leaders in Lincoln's Assassination," *Mississippi Valley Historical Review* 40 (1953–54); Historical Society of Trinity College, *An Annual Publication of Historical Papers*, ser. 7 (1898); Trinity, Springs, Mississippi Kalindrum, 11 May 1851; Guy McLean, "The *Georgian* Affair: An Incident of the American Civil War," *Canadian Historical Review* 42 (1961); Dorothy Zollicoffer Oldham, "Life of Jacob Thompson" (master's thesis, University of Mississippi, 1930); P. L. Rainwater, ed., "Letters to and from Jacob Thompson," *Journal of Southern History* 6 (February 1940); James E. Winston, "The Lost Commission: A Study in Mississippi History," *Mississippi Valley Historical Review* 5 (1917–18).

RICHARD G. STONE, JR.

Thomson, John *(1690–1753)*, Presbyterian clergyman, teacher, and writer, was born in Northern Ireland and baptized in 1691. On 1 Mar. 1706 he entered the University of Glasgow, Scotland, from which he was graduated with the M.A. degree in 1710–11. Licensed to preach by the Presbytery of Armagh in Northern Ireland on 23 June 1713, he moved with his family to Virginia in 1715, disembarking at Yorktown just nine years after the Presbyterian church had been formally organized in the American colonies. He settled among relatives and on 24 Sept. 1717 became a member of the New Castle Presbytery, one of four that constituted the newly formed Synod of Philadelphia. Thomson frequently served as moderator of the courts of the church of which he was a member and in 1719 and 1722 of the Synod of Philadelphia. He was the first to recommend to the synod the adoption of the Westminster Assembly (1641–48) Standards (*Confession of Faith, Larger and Shorter Catechisms*, and the *Book of Church Order*) as the constitution of the Presbyterian church. This was formerly done in 1729. He is also credited with authorship of *The Directory of Worship*, which was later incorporated into the constitution.

Following his ordination in April 1717, Thomson began his ministry at Lewes, Del. For thirty-five years he served churches in Delaware, Pennsylvania, and Virginia—possibly even after he settled in North Carolina in midcentury. A controversial figure, he often engaged in polemics, written and spoken, with peers and sometimes with parishioners. He was outspoken and adequately endowed with Scottish sagacity equal to every situation.

The minutes of the General Synod of Philadelphia record that in May 1744 many people in North Carolina reported their "desolate condition" and requested that a minister be stationed among them. It was ordered that the Reverend Mr. Thomson respond, and it is assumed that he did. He moved to North Carolina in 1751, intending to remain; he built a cabin in present Iredell County near Mount Mourne not far from the home of his son-in-law, Samuel Baker. Not only did he prove to be a vigorous and persuasive preacher, but also he had an eye for desirable land, some of which was held for eventual church uses. Land in the area was rapidly being taken up, and he acquired three grants of 640 acres each on various creeks. Early deeds indicate that he actually surveyed some of the tracts himself. As new settlers arrived this land was made available to them.

With the location of his home as a central point, Thomson established a number of stands or outpost preaching stations—one was under a great poplar tree near the present Davidson College, and another, near Fourth Creek, became the prominent First Presbyterian Church in Statesville. Deeds dated 1753 suggest that he served Cathey's Meeting House, a landmark for the region. Another stand became Third Creek Presbyterian Church, and the town of Concord developed around another. He visited the settlements in which Centre, Hopewell, Sugaw Creek, Poplar Tent, and Thyatira churches developed. The significance of this is that all of these stands became influential Presbyterian churches, and from them or the communities in which they were located have come some of the most powerful and distinguished citizens of North Carolina.

Thomson's marriage took place in Ireland in or about 1715. His wife's name is unknown, but she may have been a Miss Osborne. They had one child, a daughter, before arriving in America, and they were the parents of eleven more before her death in 1733 or 1734. His second wife was Mary McKean Reid, widow of Thomas Reid of Octorara, Pa. To them was born one child, Hannah, in 1735.

Thomson died on the eve of the French and Indian War when Indian raids on frontier settlements were common. This may account for his burial beneath the floor of his cabin, where his son-in-law, Samuel Baker, was also buried. The site eventually became known as Baker's Grave Yard, and it was surrounded by a rough rock wall. In 1963 it disappeared under the waters of Lake Norman, after the construction of Cowan's Ford Dam on the Catawba River and the removal of the graves and stone markers to the cemetery of old Centre Church near Mount Mourne.

Thomson was the author of several publications, one of which was printed in Philadelphia by Benjamin Franklin and one in Williamsburg, Va., by William Parks. Among them were *An Overture Presented to the Reverend Synod of Dissenting Ministers* (1729), *An Essay Upon the Faith of Assurance* (1740), *The Doctrine of Convictions Set in a Clear Light* (1741), *Poor Orphan's Legacy* (1743), written on the occasion of the death of his first wife, *An Appendix, Containing the Articles of the Church of England* (1749), and *An Explication of the Shorter Catechism* (1749). The latter, printed in Williamsburg, Va., has been acclaimed as the first Presbyterian book published in the South.

SEE: C. A. Hanna, *The Scotch-Irish*, vol. 2 (1902); John G. Herndon, *John Thomson: Presbyterian Constitutionalist* (1943); James A. Livernier and Douglas R. Wilmes, eds., *American Writers before 1800*, vol. 3 (1983); *National Union Catalog, Pre-1956 Inprints*, vol. 592 (1978); Worth S. Ray, *The Mecklenburg Signers' Neighbors* (1962); E. F. Rockwell, "Gospel Pioneers in Western North Carolina," *Historical Magazine* (1869); Clifton K. Shipton and James E. Mooney, eds., *National Index of American Imprints through 1800: The Short Title Evans* (1969); Charles W. Sommerville, *History of Hopewell Presbyterian Church* (1939).

HAROLD J. DUDLEY

Thomson, John W. (*1811–6 Mar. 1836*), Texas pioneer, was born in North Carolina, probably in Orange or Johnston County. He migrated to Tennessee and in 1835 joined a group that was traveling to Texas. Arriving there in January 1836, Thomson went initially to the town of Washington. From there he moved to San Antonio de Bexar, enlisted as a private in the Texas army medical corps, and was assigned to David Crockett's company. He died with Crockett at the Alamo. In 1883 a special act of the Texas legislature enabled Thomson's heirs to receive a grant of 3,036 acres of public land.

SEE: Houston *Telegraph and Texas Register*, 24 Mar. 1836; Records of the Alamo Chapel, San Antonio, Tex.; State of Texas, *Special Laws, Eighteenth Legislature*, no. 10 (1883); Amelia W. Williams, "A Critical Study of the Siege of the Alamo and the Personnel of Its Defenders," *Southwestern Historical Quarterly* 37 (1933–34). Records in the Alamo Chapel indicate that a portrait of Thomson was owned by Mr. and Mrs. George Cook, Sunnymeade Drive, Bellemeade, Nashville, Tenn., but efforts to verify this have not been successful.

R. H. DETRICK

Thorington, James (*7 May 1816–13 June 1887*), lawyer, congressman, and diplomat, was born in Wilmington, the son of John A. Thorington, a Protestant Irishman. In 1827 he moved with his parents to Montgomery, Ala., where he attended the common schools. He was enrolled at a Fayetteville, N.C., military school from 1830 until it was destroyed by fire in 1832. Afterwards he entered the University of Alabama at Tuscaloosa and in 1835 began to study law in his father's Montgomery office. He soon moved to St. Louis, Mo., where he was followed by the entire family. He then set out trading and trapping on the Missouri and Columbia rivers and for two years traveled the frontier, spending six months in the company of the legendary Christopher (Kit) Carson.

In 1839 Thorington returned to Missouri and the family again relocated—this time to Davenport, Iowa, where the young frontiersman set up a law practice. Elected mayor of Davenport in 1842, he served four terms (1843–47). He also was probate judge of Scott County (1843–51) and clerk of the district court (1846–54). In 1854 Thorington ran for Congress as an antislavery Whig, handily defeating Iowa's former Democratic governor, Stephen Hempstead. Shortly after his election in 1855, the new legislator, along with other prominent antislavery Whigs, joined the Republican party. This made Thorington the first Republican congressman from Iowa.

Thorington's greatest achievement in the House of Representatives was passage of the Iowa Land Grant Bill of 1856, which provided that four million acres of federal land be given to the state as an incentive for railroad development. Iowa acted quickly, making huge land grants to railroads for the purpose of developing east-to-west trunk lines. Yet this singular accomplishment was the ultimate cause of Thorington's downfall. Many resented the generous grants, especially persons in towns that were not beneficiaries of the new lines. Denied renomination, the former congressman made an unsuccessful run for the U.S. Senate in 1858. Though his national political aspirations were ended, he remained involved in Scott County, serving as sheriff (1859–63) and recorder (1864–68).

Thorington was rewarded for his strong Republicanism when President Ulysses S. Grant appointed him consul to Aspinwall, Colombia, on 21 Jan. 1873. On 27 May he was named commercial agent to the city. That June the new consul achieved notoriety for his refusal to withdraw American protection from the *Virginius*, a ship of U.S. registry charged by the Spanish with shipping arms to Cuban revolutionaries. Thorington arranged for the vessel to leave Colombian waters accompanied by the U.S. warship *The Kansas* under the watchful eyes of the crew of the Spanish gunboat *Bazan*. He was praised for "protect[ing] the Stars and Stripes in Columbian waters." Unfortunately, five months later the *Virginius* was captured in international waters near Jamaica and fifty-three crew and passengers, some Americans, were executed by the Spanish as pirates. The resulting dispute required international arbitration, with the Spanish government paying $80,000 to the families of the American victims. Thorington continued as consul until 21 Oct. 1882, when he returned to Davenport.

Thorington was active in a number of organizations, including the Odd Fellows, the Masons, and the Scott County Pioneer Settlers Society. He married Vermont-born Mary Parker and they had seven children: James, Jr. (a surgeon), Monroe P. (a soldier), Mary, Sarah, Naomi, Ella, and Jessie. Thorington died while visiting a daughter in Santa Fe, N.Mex., and was returned to Davenport for burial in Oakdale Cemetery.

SEE: *Biog. Dir. Am. Cong.* (1989); *Biographical History and Portrait Gallery of Scott County, Iowa* (1895, repr. 1989);

Census of Scott County, Iowa (1850, 1860, 1870); George W. Cullum, *Biographical Register of the Officers and Graduates of the U.S. Military Academy*, vol. 3 (1891); Benjamin F. Gue, *History of Iowa from the Earliest Times to the Beginning of the Twentieth Century*, vol. 4 (1903); Louis B. Ketz, ed., *Dictionary of American History*, rev. ed., vol. 7 (1976); Charles Lanman, *Biographical Annals of the Civil Government of the United States during Its First Century* (1876, repr. 1976); *Tenth Annual Reunion of the Graduates of the U.S. Military Academy* (1879); Joseph F. Wall, *Iowa: A Bicentennial History* (1978); *Who Was Who in America*, vol. 2 (1950).

RONNIE W. FAULKNER

Thornton, Francis Alexander (*1 Apr. 1797–29 June 1869*), planter and legislator, was born in Warren County, the son of Francis and Drucilla Jones Ransom Thornton. His mother, a maternal aunt of Nathaniel Macon, married Plummer Willis after the death of her first husband and moved to Tennessee. Francis Thornton attended Warren Academy and in 1813 entered The University of North Carolina. Early in 1814 he was involved in a student uprising opposing university president Robert H. Chapman's peace views during the War of 1812. Among other things, the students cut off the hair of Chapman's horse's tail and took his gate off its hinges. For these and other misdeeds Thornton appears to have been among a group of students who were dismissed.

Entering politics, he represented his county in the House of Commons for the sessions of 1821, 1822, 1848–49, and 1850–51. He was a delegate in 1850 to the Democratic National Convention, which nominated Franklin Pierce for the presidency. He also represented Warren County in the secession convention of 1861–62 and in the Constitutional Convention of the same time. As his last public service he represented Warren County in the state senate in 1866–67. Kemp P. Battle, who met Thornton at the secession convention, described him as "a neighbor of Nat. Macon, a mild-mannered, gentlemanly, venerable man . . . tho' he was a fire-eating Secessionist."

Thornton in 1822 married Ann Swepson Boyd, the daughter of Richard and Panthea Burwell Boyd of Mecklenburg County, Va. After her death he married her first cousin, Lucy Nelson Boyd, the daughter of Robert Boyd. By his first wife, he was the father of two sons, George and Plummer, who both died in young manhood. Only one child of the second marriage, Robert Boyd, grew to maturity. Thornton was buried in a family cemetery on his Roanoke River plantation in the Oakville section of Warren County.

SEE: Kemp P. Battle, *History of the University of North Carolina*, vol. 1 (1907); John L. Cheney, Jr., ed., *North Carolina Government, 1585–1974* (1975); Daniel L. Grant, *Alumni History of the University of North Carolina* (1924); John G. McCormick, "Personnel of the Convention of 1861," *James Sprunt Historical Monographs*, No. 1 (1900); Wills, Deeds, and Estate Records, Warren County (courthouse, Warrenton).

CLAIBORNE T. SMITH, JR.

Thornton, Mary Lindsay (*12 June 1891–27 Sept. 1973*), first librarian of the North Carolina Collection at The University of North Carolina, was born in Cuckoo House, built by her maternal great-great grandfather in Louisa County, Va. The first of the children of William Borcy and Elizabeth Pendleton Thornton, she moved with the family to Salisbury when she was nine and to Atlanta, Ga., four years later. As a child she did not like the name she

was given at birth, Mary Louise, and chose Mary Lindsay, her paternal grandmother's name. Without going through any formality she simply proclaimed that to be her name. She was graduated from the Atlanta Girls High School and the Carnegie Library School of Atlanta (afterwards the Emory University Library and still later the Division of Library and Information Management).

In 1917, fresh out of library school, she became the librarian of the North Carolina Collection. The university librarian, L. R. Wilson, had pulled together the North Carolina material in his custody and placed it in a small upstairs corner room in the library, the building that later became Hill Music Hall. The collection contained about 1,000 books and 500 pamphlets. Miss Thornton began cataloguing the material in a thorough, analytical fashion, seeking to bring out all that was in the books, as there was so little material at hand. The result was a card catalogue that became virtually an index of every issue of the periodicals and of many of the books as well. Thorough cataloguing became the permanent policy of the collection. In 1918 the university trustees purchased from Stephen B. Weeks his collection of 10,000 volumes of North Caroliniana, and soon a bequest of about 1,200 volumes from Kemp P. Battle further enlarged it.

In processing the new material, Miss Thornton became familiar with the broad acquisition policy developed by Weeks, and from that time until her retirement forty years later she diligently sought to acquire North Caroliniana in all its forms—books, pamphlets, broadsides, serials, government documents, maps, and pictures—just as Weeks had done. To this list she added assorted university "keepsakes" as they were found in campus buildings or contributed by alumni and friends. The collection for a time also contained the university archives. The success of her efforts was demonstrated by the recognized completeness of the collection. By 1958, when she retired, it contained more than 150,000 items and had attained nationwide recognition as a model state collection.

Although she had library training when she went to Chapel Hill, Miss Thornton did not have a formal degree, and in her thirties she began freshman courses at the university. In 1939 she was graduated with a B.A. degree and membership in Phi Beta Kappa, and in 1943 she received the M.A. degree with a major in history, writing a thesis on "Public Printing in North Carolina from 1749 to 1815."

Mary Thornton was friendly, energetic, and enthusiastic. Because she was open-minded and objective in her acquisition policy, the North Carolina Collection came to include scores of books, pamphlets, broadsides, and ephemeral material on such topics as labor unrest, the activity of blacks, minor political parties, and various other issues that a less diligent collector of her day might have ignored as unimportant. Her development of the carefully mounted and organized clipping files and the indexed literary scrapbooks produced sources for which countless people have expressed gratitude. She was, in brief, a scholar-librarian.

Another valuable characteristic was her ability to win the friendship of potential donors. Of course, the university setting and the subject of the collection undoubtedly helped, but it was her enthusiasm and her obvious care for the material that contributed to the decision of John Sprunt Hill, Bruce Cotten, the family of Thomas Wolfe, and others to make significant additions of North Caroliniana as well as donate money to the North Carolina Collection.

Miss Thornton wrote a number of articles published in the North Carolina Historical Review and other journals. From the time of her arrival until shortly before her retirement she compiled for publication the annual bibliography of North Carolina books. She was the author of two very useful bibliographies published by The University of North Carolina Press in 1954 and 1958. The first, *Official Publications of the Colony and State of North Carolina, 1749–1939*, describes and locates thousands of government documents in eighteen depositories. A particularly useful aspect of this bibliography was its concise statements on the origin and development, particularly name changes, of assorted colonial and state agencies. At the time there was no other convenient source for that information. Her second book, *A Bibliography of North Carolina, 1589–1956*, lists over 15,000 items. It was virtually a main-entry catalogue of the North Carolina Collection as it then existed. The inclusion of serial publications made it especially useful.

Her thorough professional competence gave her assurance and confidence in her work that masked a deep-seated shyness and reserve. Because of this, and because of her responsibility in caring for an invalid mother through many years of illness, she stayed close to home, seldom going away to meetings and refusing to speak publicly about her work and her research. Nevertheless, almost every summer she visited Pawley's Island, S.C., for a change of scenery.

Miss Thornton's quiet but effective contribution through her work with the collection and her writing about it and North Carolina continued into retirement as long as her health permitted. For many years she managed the collection in her care with little or no assistance; she was responsible for book selection and ordering, cataloguing, reference, and circulation. Later she had the help of some student assistants and finally one or two other staff members. The collection, nevertheless, served generation after generation of university students, as well as countless readers and researchers of every category.

She died in Chapel Hill at age eighty-two and was buried in the town cemetery.

SEE: *Asheville Citizen-Times*, 4 Nov. 1951; *Chapel Hill Weekly*, 18 Dec. 1953, 4 Feb. 1955, 5 May, 7 July 1958; Citation by Friends of the Library, 2 May 1958 (clipping files, North Carolina Collection, University of North Carolina, Chapel Hill); Memorial address read at a meeting of the faculty (files, Secretary of the Faculty, University of North Carolina, Chapel Hill); Raleigh *News and Observer*, 2 Nov. 1951, 13 Dec. 1953.

WILLIAM S. POWELL

Thorp, Robert Taylor *(12 Mar. 1850–26 Nov. 1938)*, lawyer and congressman, was born in the Goshen District of Granville County near Oxford, the son of Benjamin Person, a moderately wealthy farmer, and Ann Eliza Norman Thorp. He attended Horner Military Academy in Oxford and was graduated in 1870 from the law department of the University of Virginia, where he won the medal of the Jefferson Debating Society. Admitted to the bar, he established a practice in Boydton, Mecklenburg County, Va., in 1871 and also was commonwealth attorney for the county from 1877 to 1895.

Elected twice to Congress as a Democrat, Thorp served from 2 May 1896 to 3 Mar. 1897 and from 23 Mar. 1898 to 4 Mar. 1899. An unsuccessful candidate for reelection, he moved to Norfolk and practiced law until 1934, when he made a home in Virginia Beach. In 1911 he became referee in bankruptcy in the federal district in which Norfolk lay. He was said to have been "regarded as one of the most brilliant members of the bar this section ever has known." An Episcopalian, he married Lucy Brent, and they had a son, Roland. He died at his home in Virginia Beach and was buried in Forest Lawn Cemetery, Norfolk.

SEE: *Biog. Dir. Am. Cong.* (1971); Granville County census returns, 1850; *History of Virginia*, vol. 6, Virginia Biography by a special staff of writers (1924); *Richmond Times-Dispatch*, 27 Nov. 1938.

WILLIAM S. POWELL

Thorpe, Earlie Endris *(9 Nov. 1924–30 Jan. 1989)*, historian and college professor, was born in Durham, the son of Eural Endris and Vina Dean Thorpe. He served in the U.S. Army in the European theater (1944–46) and in 1948 was graduated from North Carolina College, in Durham, from which he received a master's degree the next year. In 1953 he was awarded the Ph.D. degree by Ohio State University; his dissertation was entitled "Negro Historiography in the United States."

Thorpe taught at Stowe Teachers College, St. Louis, Mo. (1951–52), Alabama A. and M. College, Normal (1952–55), and Southern University, Baton Rouge, La. (1955–62). In 1962 he returned to his alma mater, by then North Carolina Central University, where he spent the remainder of his career as chairman of the Department of History and Social Science. He was visiting professor of history at Duke University in 1969–70 and of Afro-American Studies at Harvard University in 1971. Thorpe was the author of *Negro Historians in the United States* (1958), *The Desertion of Man: A Critique of Philosophy of History* (1958), *The Mind of the Negro: An Intellectual History of Afro-Americans* (1961), *Eros and Freedom in Southern Life and Thought* (1967), *The Central Theme of Black History* (1969), *The Old South: A Psychohistory* (1972), *African Americans and the Sacred: Spirituals, Slave Religion, and Symbolism* (1982), *Slave Religion, Spirituals, and C. J. Jung* (1983), and *A Concise History of North Carolina Central University* (1984). He also was editor of the ten-booklet series "The Black Experience in America." Thorpe married Martha Vivian Branch, and they had two daughters, Rita Harrington and Gloria Earl.

SEE: *Directory of American Scholars-History* (1978); "Historical News and Notices," *Journal of Southern History* 55 (May 1989); James A. Page and Jae M. Roh, *Selected Black American, African, and Caribbean Authors* (1985); *Who's Who among Black Americans* (1985).

WILLIAM S. POWELL

Thorpe, James Francis *(28 May 1888–28 Mar. 1953)*, perhaps the greatest performer in the history of sport, spent the summers of 1909 and 1910 in North Carolina as a baseball player in the Eastern Carolina League. As a result of his participation, first with the Rocky Mount Railroaders and later with the Fayetteville Highlanders, he was forced, in January 1913, to forfeit the many awards he had won during the summer of 1912 in the Olympic competition held in Sweden. Despite the petitions of hundreds of thousands of people throughout the world, as well as the commonly held belief that Thorpe played Carolina baseball not for financial gain but for love of competition, the awards are today not in the possession of his heirs and his name does not appear in official Olympic records.

A descendant of Black Hawk, the Sac and Fox warrior from whom the Black Hawk War of 1831–32 derived its name, Thorpe was born in a cabin in Indian territory near the present city of Prague, Okla. He was educated at four institutions: two schools near his birthplace, Haskell Institute, and the U.S. Indian Industrial School (commonly known as the Carlisle Indian School). At the Pennsylvania school, which he entered in 1904, he gained fame in a variety of sports; in football he earned All-American honors in 1908, 1911, and 1912. The 198 points that he scored in 1912 remain the highest total ever amassed by a college player in a single season.

In July 1912, representing the United States, he easily won the pentathlon and the decathlon track and field events in Olympic competition—the lone athlete ever to triumph in both. After the loss of his awards six months later, he left Carlisle to sign a baseball contract with the National League's New York Giants, for which he performed during most of his ten-season professional baseball career (1913–22). As a major league outfielder and first baseman, he compiled a batting average of .252 during six seasons of play. In 1915 he embarked on a fifteen-year career in professional football, starring for a number of teams including the Canton Bulldogs, New York Giants, and Oorang Indians. In 1920 he was president of the American Professional Football Association, forerunner of the National Football League.

After his retirement from professional athletics in 1929, Thorpe enjoyed little prosperity. He worked in a variety of jobs—among them as movie actor, master of ceremonies, and day laborer—but none brought him financial success or security. In 1945 he entered the Merchant Marines and spent the duration of World War II serving his country. In 1950 the Associated Press voted him both the outstanding football player and the outstanding male athlete of the half century, and in 1951 Warner Brothers starred Burt Lancaster in the role of *Jim Thorpe—All-American*, a much-publicized motion picture.

Following difficulties with alcohol, heart ailments, and cancer, he succumbed to a heart attack in Lomita, Calif. His third wife, present at his death, subsequently arranged for his body to be transported to the city of Jim Thorpe, Pa., where an impressive tomb marks his resting place. In death, as in life, he remains a charismatic legend without peer in the annals of sport.

SEE: Wilbur J. Gobrecht, *Jim Thorpe: Carlisle Indian* (1972); R. W. Reising, *Jim Thorpe: The Story of an American Indian* (1974) and *Jim Thorpe: Tar Heel* (1974); Gene Schoor, *The Jim Thorpe Story* (1951); John Steckbeck, *Fabulous Redmen* (1951).

R. W. REISING

Throop, George Higby (Gregory Seaworthy)

(1818–2 Mar. 1896), schoolmaster and novelist, was born in Willsboro, N.Y., the youngest of six children of George Throop, Sr., a manufacturer and storekeeper. His mother, the elder Throop's second wife, died soon after his birth. He was named Higby but eventually appropriated his father's given name and relegated his own to a middle initial. A student of the classics and an avid reader of literature, he attended the University of Vermont at Burlington in 1835–36 and afterwards possibly another college. After an unhappy marriage that was soon broken up, he spent a number of years during the 1840s working as a schoolmaster and mariner, occupations reflected in his later fiction.

In 1849, and perhaps earlier, Throop's career as an itinerant schoolmaster brought him to the Coastal Plains of North Carolina, an area that stirred his greatest creative achievements. He may have taught first at a plantation near Hertford, but it is certain that at least from March until October 1849 he taught at Scotch Hall, the plantation of Cullen Capehart near Merry Hill in Bertie County. During the last months he accompanied his pupils, their family, and their servants to the Capehart summer home at Nags Head. His sojourn in North Carolina may have been the happiest of his sad life.

After his brief but stimulating residence with the Capeharts, Throop ostensibly spent a few years in Philadelphia overseeing the publication of his three novels. Under the nom de plume "Gregory Seaworthy," he first brought out a book that he wrote while still living in North Carolina: *Nag's Head; or, Two Months Among "The Bankers": A Story of Sea-Shore Life and Manners* (1850). Published by A. Hart of Philadelphia but with the dedication page signed from "Merry Hill, Bertie County, N.C.," this book may be loosely termed a novel but is more accurately a memoir, in the guise of fiction, of the author's summer on the Outer Banks. Although devoid of plot and sustained characterization, it captures the spirit of a mid-nineteenth century seashore holiday and offers revealing glimpses of the coastal area, its lore, and its inhabitants. *Nag's Head* also represents the first novel concerned with contemporary times in North Carolina.

Although his first literary effort did not receive much attention, Throop was so encouraged by a letter from Washington Irving expressing interest in the book and by a few other favorable notices that he soon completed another work. With a dedication letter dated 15 Dec. 1850 in Philadelphia and using the same pseudonym and publisher as before, he brought out this second work the following year: *Bertie; or, Life in the Old Field: A Humorous Novel* (1851). Set chiefly at "Cypress Shore" in North Carolina, in reality the Capehart plantation on the banks of Albemarle Sound, this remarkably good-humored novel deftly intertwines several romances against a background of antebellum plantation life. Far more sophisticated than *Nag's Head* in plot and characterization, *Bertie* ranks as a masterpiece of nineteenth-century North Carolina fiction and was called by a *Godey's Lady's Book* reviewer "one of the best American novels of its day." Like its predecessor, however, it was largely ignored by literary critics and the general public.

In Philadelphia the next year Throop signed the preface for his third book, *Lynde Weiss* (1852), a strongly autobiographical novel published by Lippincott, Grambo and Company under his own name. But this work contains no references to North Carolina.

Throop's efforts as an author brought him little fame and no fortune, however, so the luckless wanderer rambled on to wherever he could find employment as a schoolmaster. In 1853 he spent some time in Georgia, but prior to the Civil War he settled in Hampshire County in what became eastern West Virginia.

In West Virginia, though a well-liked teacher and an accomplished singer and composer of lyrics and tunes, Throop lived out his days in obscurity and poverty, debilitated by alcoholism. Around 1888, when he could no longer teach, he learned of a previously unknown son, Edward H. Palmer, of Boston, who had taken the name of his stepfather. Palmer provided an allowance of twenty dollars monthly, which supported Throop as a boarder in the homes of various citizens of Bloomery, the site of his last teaching assignment, until his death. He was buried in the Presbyterian Church cemetery on Bloomery Run, where his grave was finally marked in August 1955 by the Pioneer Teachers Association of Hampshire County, W.Va.

SEE: David Stick, *The Outer Banks of North Carolina, 1584–1958* (1958); Richard Walser, Introduction to a facsimile reissue of *Nag's Head* and *Bertie* (1958) and "The Mysterious Case of George Higby Throop (1818–1896); or, The Search for the Author of the Novels *Nag's Head*, *Bertie*, and *Lynde Weiss*," *North Carolina Historical Review* 33 (1956).

W. KEATS SPARROW

Tiernan, Frances Christine Fisher *(5 July 1846–24 Mar. 1920)*, writer whose pen name was Christian Reid, was born in Salisbury, the oldest of three children of Colonel Charles Fredric and Elizabeth Ruth Caldwell Fisher. Her younger brother and sister were Fredric and Annie. Both paternal and maternal forebears were among the first settlers and leading citizens of Rowan County. Her father, killed at the first Battle of Manassas in 1861, had studied at Yale and was a railroad promoter, member of the General Assembly, and publisher of the *Western Carolinian*. Fort Fisher at the mouth of the Cape Fear River was named in his honor. Her mother died early, and the three children were brought up by their aunt Christine Fisher, a recluse and an occasional writer who in the 1850s converted to Roman Catholicism from the Episcopal faith. Except for a semester at St. Mary's College in Raleigh, Frances Fisher was educated by her aunt and, with her, vacationed in the North Carolina mountains. In 1868 she and her sister followed her aunt and brother into the Catholic church.

Her first writings were for pleasure, but during the difficult times of Reconstruction she turned to her pen for a livelihood, assuming a pseudonym of indeterminate gender and unpretentiousness. Aristocratic and aloof in manner, she shrank from personal publicity. *Valerie Aylmer*, her first published book though not the first written, quickly sold over 8,000 copies and brought her to the attention of southern writers like Paul Hamilton Hayne. Eminently representative of the marketable "polite literature" of the day, *Valerie Aylmer* and its successors inculcated grace and good manners in an "exalted tone" of "virginal delicacy." Her disposition was to look back to genteel antebellum times, devoid of gaucheries and degraded conditions of life, her humorless, stereotyped characters endlessly engaged in the complications and misunderstandings of courtship, the women either haughty and proud or pure and mistreated, the men either profligate and devious or worthy and underestimated. Frequently both men and women were energetically engaged in fortune hunting. *Morton House*, her second published work, she often said was her favorite. But it is her tenth book, *"The Land of the Sky"; or, Adventures in Mountain By-Ways*, a story of summer North Carolina travelers amusing themselves with scenery and mild flirtations, that is best remembered. During this period, her short stories and serialized novelettes were constantly appearing in such widely read magazines as *Appleton's Journal* and *Lippincott's Monthly*. Then in 1879, feeling the need to gather fresh material for fiction, she went to Europe on money she had earned. A partisan Catholic tendency, contributing neither to her rarefied talents nor to her popularity with readers, began to permeate her books in the 1880s.

In the summer of 1887, at age forty-one, she caught the fancy of James Marquis Tiernan, a Baltimore widower who was in Salisbury on business in his capacity as a mineralogist. They were married in New Orleans on 29 December and set out for Mexico, where he had mining interests. For most of the next ten years they lived there but, when Tiernan became ill, returned to Salisbury, where he died in January 1898. In 1909 Mrs. Tiernan received the Laetare medal for her contributions, as a Catholic, to American life. Several years later, with her husband's mines no longer operating, she resumed writing, though weary and motivated only by the income to be received, to support her brother's children, her afflicted sister, and her aging aunt. She died of pneumonia and was buried in Chestnut Hill Cemetery, Salisbury.

The settings of Mrs. Tiernan's forty-six published works, most of them novels, are quite varied. *"The Land of the Sky"* (1876), *A Summer Idyl* (1878), *A Child of Mary* (1885), *Roslyn's Fortune* (1885), *His Victory* (1887), *Fairy Gold* (1897), *The Secret Bequest* (1915), and *The Wargrave Trust* (1921) are set in North Carolina. Unspecified plantation backgrounds are provided for *Morton House* (1871), *A Daughter of Bohemia* (1873), *Bonny Kate* (1878), and *Mabel Lee* (1895). Other stories of the South are *Hearts and Hands* (1875), White Sulpher Springs, West Va.; *Philip's Restitution* (1888), New Orleans; *A Little Maid of Arcady* (1893), Virginia and New Orleans; and *A Far-Away Princess* (1914), Maryland. The selections in *Ebb-Tide and Other Stories* (1872) and *Nina's Atonement and Other Stories* (1873) are set mainly in the South. Having locales in American small towns are *A Question of Honor* (1875), *After Many Days* (1877), and *A Gentle Belle* (1879). *Véra's Charge* (1907) and *Noël: A Christmas Story* (1910) take place in New York City. Those with a change in settings are *Valerie Aylmer* (1870), Baltimore, Louisiana, Cuba, and France; *Miss Churchill* (1887), North Carolina, Florence, and Venice; *A Comedy of Elopement* (1893), Florida and Italy; and *Weighed in the Balance* (1900), France and America. European novels are *Carmen's Inheritance* (1873), Paris; *Heart of Steel* (1883), Rome; *Armine* (1884), Paris; *A Woman of Fortune* (1896), Paris and Rome; *Princess Nadine* (1908), France; *The Light of the Vision* (1911), France; and *The Daughter of a Star* (1913), London. Novels of Mexico are *A Cast of Fortune* (1890); *Carmela* (1891); *Lost Lode* (1892), a "travel romance"; *The Land of the Sun* (1894); *Lady of Las Cruces* (1895); *The Picture of Las Cruces* (1896); and *A Daughter of the Sierra* (1903). Haiti is the scene of *A Man of the Family* (1897) and Santo Domingo that of *The Chase of an Heiress* (1898). Her only play, *Under the Southern Cross* (1900), is a drama of the Civil War; *A Coin of Sacrifice* (1909) is a religious short story. No copy of *Out of Deep Depths* (1916) has been cited.

SEE: Kate Harbes Becker, *Biography of Christian Reid* (1941); *Catholic Encyclopedia*, vol. 17, supp. I (1922); Anne Heagney, *The Magic Pen*, a juvenile biography (1949); Archibald Henderson, *North Carolina: The Old North State and the New*, vol. 2 (1941); *Library of Southern Literature*, vol. 12 (1910); *North Carolina Authors: A Selective Handbook* (1952); *North Carolina Fiction* (1958); *Notable American Women*, vol. 3 (1971); *Who's Who in America* (1920–21).

RICHARD WALSER

Tillett, Charles Walter, Jr. *(6 Feb. 1888–23 Dec. 1952)*, attorney and civic leader, was born in Mangum, Richmond County, the son of Carrie Patterson and Charles W. Tillett. He attended the Charlotte public schools and Webb School at Bell Buckle, Tenn., from which he was graduated in 1905. At The University of North Carolina, where he received the A.B. degree in 1909, he was elected to membership in Phi Beta Kappa and the Order of the Golden Fleece; he was an intercollegiate debater and president of the Dialectic Society. He also studied law at the university, was admitted to the bar in 1911, and established a practice in Charlotte. In 1918 he entered the Officers' Training Corps; commissioned in the Fiftieth Infantry, he was discharged as a captain in 1919.

As a member of the school board in Charlotte, Tillett was noted for his championship of a fair distribution of public school funds for the benefit of black children. He was a leader in the Citizens Library Movement, which obtained state support for countywide library service, and in Charlotte he served on the board of directors of the Symphony Society and helped to establish the Mint Museum of Art. Perhaps the one act that brought him most forcefully to public attention occurred in Charlotte in May

1926, when a Committee of One Hundred, a Fundamentalist group, met to plan steps to secure legislation that would prohibit the schools of North Carolina from teaching the theory of evolution. During a brief pause in the proceedings, while the Resolutions Committee was temporarily off the floor, Tillett and a group of his friends, all university alumni, received permission to speak. Tillett taunted the Fundamentalists by asking whether they intended to destroy free speech and free thought. Reportedly his remark "brought on a tumult" and in large measure contributed to the failure of this committee to achieve its objective. Tillett also spoke effectively before legislative committees on behalf of freedom of research and teaching. North Carolina was spared the infamy that befell several other states on this question.

After World War II Tillett became a champion of "peace by world law." As an observer, he attended the 1945 conference in San Francisco at which the United Nations Charter was adopted and reported on the proceedings for the *Charlotte News*. He later spoke and wrote extensively in support of the United Nations, and his writings were reprinted and widely distributed. On his own initiative as well as through membership in the American Bar Association, Tillett succeeded in defeating a proposed amendment to the Constitution offered in 1952 by Senator John W. Bricker of Ohio and more than sixty others that would have imposed far-reaching restrictions on the treaty-making powers of the U.S. president and the Senate. (The amendment proposed that the House of Representatives and each of the state legislatures have the right to reject a treaty.) His testimony before the Senate Committee on Foreign Relations undoubtedly contributed to the failure of this proposal.

He was a Presbyterian and an active Democrat, attending the Democratic National Convention of 1944. In 1917 he married Gladys Love Avery, and they had three children: Charles W. III, M.D., Gladys (Mrs. William I. Coddington), and Sara Avery (Mrs. William Wayt Thomas, Jr.).

SEE: *Charlotte Observer*, 24 Dec. 1952; William B. Gatewood, "Politics and Piety in North Carolina: The Fundamentalist Crusade at High Tide, 1925–1927," *North Carolina Historical Review* 42 (July 1965); Daniel L. Grant, *Alumni History of the University of North Carolina* (1924); *Proceedings of the . . . North Carolina Bar Association*, vol. 37 (1935 [portrait]); Raleigh *News and Observer*, 24 Dec. 1952; *Who Was Who in America* (1960); *Who's Who in the South and Southwest* (1950).

JAMES B. CRAIGHILL

Tillett, Gladys Love Avery (*19 Mar. 1892–21 Sept. 1984*), political leader and proponent of equal rights for women, was born in Morganton. Her parents were Judge A. C. Avery of the North Carolina Supreme Court and his wife, Sarah Love Thomas. Her paternal great-grandfather, Waightstill Avery, was the first attorney general of the state. On her mother's side her great-grandfather was William Holland Thomas, white chief of the Cherokee Indians. She was graduated from the North Carolina College for Women in 1915, where she was influenced by Professor Harriet Elliott, and received a second bachelor's degree from The University of North Carolina in 1917 with a major in political science. She became interested in the issue of women's rights, and while her husband was serving in the army during World War I she continued her studies at Columbia University; in New York she also engaged in social work.

Her interest in politics never wavered throughout her

life. From 1920 until her death, she cast her ballot for every Democratic presidential nominee. While her husband, an important Charlotte lawyer and onetime president of the state bar, pursued his professional career with an occasional foray into support of some public cause, Gladys Tillett pursued a career in politics.

In Charlotte she was active with the YWCA and the Business and Professional Women's Club and also performed with the Charlotte Little Theater. Beginning in the 1930s Mrs. Tillett held numerous positions in the Democratic party and in 1936 was director of the Speakers Bureau of the Women's Division of the Democratic National Committee—a post she held again in 1940. This required her to find thousands of speakers for different women's groups nationwide.

In 1943 she became the first woman to be named assistant to the chairman of the Democratic National Convention. The next year she became the first woman to address the convention, and she returned to address it again in 1948. Her work as an observer at the 1945 founding conference of the United Nations in San Francisco helped her when she worked with UNESCO in 1949.

These national activities kept her in the spotlight and busy, but she did make time for other activities. She served on the State Board of Elections and organized the first county League of Women Voters in North Carolina. From 1961 to 1966 she was a delegate to the United Nations Commission on the Status of Women, and in the 1970s she was active in support of the Equal Rights Amendment. She once remarked to a reporter: "It's my highest ambition to be free and equal. I may have missed it by a few years, but I want it to end that way." She found sincere satisfaction in politics. "Women in the South are very interested in politics and very active," she once observed. "This is all nonsense about the Southern woman devoting herself exclusively to home activities."

Mrs. Tillett was awarded LL.D. degrees from the Woman's College in Greensboro and The University of North Carolina and the L.H.D. degree from Queens College. In 1917 she married Charles Walter Tillett, Jr., of Charlotte, and they had three children: Charles W. III, Gladys, and Sara. A Presbyterian, she was buried in Elmwood Cemetery, Charlotte.

SEE: *Charlotte News*, 20 July 1944; *Charlotte Observer*, 8 Oct. 1933, 27 Sept. 1936, 12 Sept. 1945, 4 July 1974, 24 Sept. 1984; Helen D. Harrison, "Famous Women of North Carolina" (typescript, North Carolina Collection, Chapel Hill); *New York Times*, 3 Oct. 1984; Raleigh *News and Observer*, 2 Feb. 1975; *University Report* (University of North Carolina at Chapel Hill), vol. 32 (January 1985).

CAROLYN ROFF

Tilley, Nannie May (*29 May 1899–4 Oct. 1988*), professor and historian, was born on a tobacco farm at Bahama, Durham County, the daughter of Roscoe and Lucy Roberts Tilley. She was graduated from the North Carolina College for Women (now the University of North Carolina at Greensboro) in 1920. From 1921 to 1930 she was principal of an elementary school in Durham County and in the summer during a part of that time did graduate work at Duke University, from which she received the master's degree in 1931. From 1930 to 1935 she taught history at Western Carolina Teachers College after which she won admitted to the doctoral program at Duke University, where she became head of the manuscript collection until 1947. She was also the compiler of the *Guide to the Manuscript Collections in the Duke University Library* (1947). Awarded a doctorate by Duke in 1947, she promptly became professor of history at East Texas State Teachers College; she was the head of its history department during the period 1950–58. In 1958–59 she taught at Del Mar College, Corpus Christi, Tex., and from 1959 to 1964 she was historian of the R. J. Reynolds Tobacco Company in Winston-Salem.

Her lifelong interest in tobacco was reflected in her two major works: *The Bright-Tobacco Industry, 1860–1929* (1948) and *The R. J. Reynolds Tobacco Company* (1985), both published by The University of North Carolina Press. She also wrote other books including a history of the Trinity College Historical Society and articles for scholarly journals. A pioneer member of the Southern Historical Association, she sat on the editorial boards of the *Journal of Southern History* and *Agricultural History*. After a long illness she died in Commerce, Tex., where she had lived since 1947.

SEE: *Directory of American Scholars*, vol. 1 (1969), *Duke Alumni Register*, vol. 39 (May 1943); *Journal of Southern History* 55 (May 1989).

WILLIAM S. POWELL

Tillinghast, John Huske (*19 Sept. 1835–10 Jan. 1933*), clergyman and Confederate chaplain, was born in Hillsborough, the son of Samuel Willard and Jane Burgin Norwood Tillinghast. His father was a native of Uxbridge, Mass., and his mother was born in Hillsborough. Young Tillinghast attended the Bingham School at The Oaks before studying at The University of North Carolina from 1853 to 1854. Between 1855 and 1857 he was at Hampden-Sydney College, in Virginia, from which he received a bachelor's degree. For brief periods he taught in Professor Ralph H. Graves's school at Belmont in Granville County and as a private tutor in Spartanburg, S.C. He studied for two years at the Episcopal Theological Seminary, Alexandria, Va., but with the invasion of that state by the Federal army during the Civil War he left and was ordained deacon in Wilmington by Bishop Thomas Atkinson of North Carolina in July 1861, a few days after the first Battle of Manassas. From August 1861 to May 1862 he was in charge of St. Thomas Church, Rutherfordton. His commission as chaplain with the Forty-fourth Regiment, North Carolina Troops, was dated 28 Mar. 1862, the day the regiment was activated; he resigned on 27 Oct. 1863.

Tillinghast received military training at Camp Mangum near Raleigh after which the regiment went to Tarboro and then to Greenville. It saw its first action at Tranter's Creek and was sent to Petersburg, Va., on 5 July 1862. From there it served in southeastern Virginia and eastern North Carolina. In March 1863 Tillinghast participated in the unsuccessful campaign to recapture New Bern and Washington. In the spring the regiment returned to Virginia for service in the vicinity of Richmond and suffered significant losses at Bristoe Station in October.

After leaving the army Tillinghast became assistant rector at Trinity Church, Mobile, Ala., but he returned to North Carolina in 1865 and served churches in Clinton and Salisbury. In 1872–82 he was at two churches in Richland County, S.C., before becoming rector of St. John's Church, Charleston. Later he returned to several churches in Richland County before retiring to Eastover in the diocese of Upper South Carolina where he died.

Tillinghast married Sarah Wilkins; their children were Mildred Lewis, John Wilkins, William Norwood, Jane Norwood, Mary Anderson, and Robina Bingham. At the time of his death at age ninety-seven, the Reverend Mr. Tillinghast was the oldest alumnus of The University of North Carolina, the oldest ex-chaplain of the Confederate army, and the oldest priest in the Episcopal church.

SEE: Chapel Hill, *Daily Tar Heel*, 4 May 1932; *General Catalogue of the Officers and Students of Hampden-Sidney College, Virginia, 1770–1906* [1908]; Daniel L. Grant, *Alumni History of the University of North Carolina* (1924); Weymouth T. Jordan, comp., *North Carolina Troops, 1861–1865: A Roster*, vol. 10 (1985); *Living Church*, 6 Feb. 1932 [portrait]; Raleigh *News and Observer*, 13 Jan. 1933.

WILLIAM S. POWELL

Timberlake, Edwin Walter (*4 July 1854–2 Jan. 1933*), lawyer and judge, was born in Franklin County, the son of R. H. and Mary A. Harris Timberlake. His father was a country doctor, and young Edwin traveled around with him and observed firsthand the poverty and hardships of his area. When his family moved to the town of Wake Forest, Timberlake entered college. He was graduated from Wake Forest College in 1873 and from the law school of the University of Virginia, Charlottesville, in 1876.

He began to practice law in Louisburg in 1877 as a Republican. The Democratic party's dominance in the state from 1872 to 1894 closed the avenue of judicial advancement to Republican lawyers, but in 1894 the Populists fused with the Republicans and became the majority party. On this occasion Timberlake was nominated by his friends as superior court judge of his district. During his eight years of service (1 Jan. 1895 to 1 Jan. 1903), he made numerous acquaintances over the state. In 1904 he moved his family back to Wake Forest, where he remained for the rest of his life.

Timberlake was a Baptist and a member of the Odd Fellows and Masonic order. He served as chairman of the Wake County Draft Board in 1917 and 1918 and was a member of the Wake Forest College Board of Trustees from 1896 until his death. On 27 May 1879 he married Ada Lee Simmons, the daughter of Professor William Gaston and Mary Foote Simmons. They had three children: Mary Lee, Mrs. Phil M. Utley, and Edward Walter.

Judge Timberlake died at his home in Wake Forest. His funeral services were conducted by Drs. Willis Richard Cullom and J. W. Lynch at the Wake Forest Baptist Church. He was buried in the cemetery at Wake Forest.

SEE: H. M. London, ed., *Proceedings of the Thirty-fifth Annual Session of the North Carolina Bar Association* (1933); Raleigh, *Biblical Recorder*, 12 Oct. 1881, 11 Jan. 1833; *Wake Forest Alumni Directory* (1961).

JOHN R. WOODARD

Tippett, James Sterling (*7 Sept. 1885–20 Feb. 1958*), author and educator of English and Scottish ancestry, was born in Memphis, Mo., in the three-room house of his parents, Everett and Mary Montgomery Tippett. Both families were of pre-Revolutionary pioneer stock and pushed westward, settling in Missouri soon after it became a state. Young Tippett's grandfather Montgomery had bought 160 acres of farmland, and he remembered stories his grandmother told of first living in a sod house. When he was five, his father, a blacksmith, moved the family to a sixty-acre farm in Scotland County, where young Tippett's formal education began in a country school. He had already learned to read from pages of the *Memphis Reveille* pasted on the wood box in the kitchen. For the rest of his life there was usually a book in his hand or in his pocket.

Tippett loved the country and school and early decided that he wanted to be a teacher. This ambition was realized, when at seventeen, having graduated from the Memphis High School, he was hired to teach all the grades in a country school. From that beginning he progressed to high school teacher, principal, and / or superintendent in Lancaster, Huntsville, Fayette, and Kansas City. In summers he attended The University of Missouri, earning a B.S. degree in 1915.

From Kansas City he moved in 1918 to Nashville, Tenn., as principal of the Peabody Demonstration School. Four years later he went to the Lincoln School of Teachers College in New York as teacher and special investigator. Of this experience he wrote: "That was a wonderful school. Teachers and children were painting, modeling, building, acting in plays, doing all sorts of interesting things in connection with their learning, so I did things, too; I began to write for children." Two of his early books, *The Singing Farmer* (1927) and *I Live in a City* (1927), appeared while he was in New York. He also edited *Curriculum Making in an Elementary School*, compiled by the Lincoln School staff and published by Ginn and Company. In 1928 he became assistant professor of education at the University of Pittsburgh, and from 1930 to 1932 he was dean of the faculty at the Avon School for Boys in Connecticut.

After a year of free-lance writing and lecturing he went as curriculum adviser to the Parker School District in Greenville, S.C. Here he edited *Schools for a Growing Democracy*, also published by Ginn. In 1939 he moved to Chapel Hill, where he had taught in the summer of 1932 and 1933. He bought four wooded acres from his neighbor and friend, Paul Green, and built the home he lived in the rest of his life.

Tippett had intended to give all his time to writing but was soon pressed into service teaching Saturday classes for teachers, extension and correspondence courses, and summer school classes. When North Carolina schools added the twelfth grade, he headed the committee that worked out the new program. His contribution to education was recognized by the Horace Mann League in 1972, when it added his name to the North Carolina Educational Hall of Fame. From 1939 until his death he was listed in The University of North Carolina catalogue as visiting professor of education, a position that kept him in touch with the profession he loved and left time for the writing he wished to do.

A flexible schedule allowed him to indulge his love of gardening, where he wielded a wicked hoe. In one of his poems he asks: "Who should make a garden? He who loves the soil And outdoor toil. Who does not fear a calloused hand; Who cannot bear To let weeds stand Where plants should be. One like me Should make a garden." There was also time for writing both textbooks and stories and verses for children. His simple poems were widely used in readers, language books, music books, anthologies, and teachers' guides, and in 1973 Harper and Row brought out a selection of over fifty of "The Best Loved Poems of James S. Tippett" under the title *Crickety Cricket.*

He found Chapel Hill particularly congenial to his interests and once said he liked it because every year it renewed its youth. He died at his home and his ashes, as he had requested, were scattered in his woods.

In 1929 he married Martha Louise Kelly, who had taught with him at Peabody and in Lincoln School and who survived him. A registered Democrat with liberal leanings, he was a member of the Presbyterian church. His other publications included *I Go A-Traveling* (1929), *Busy Carpenters* (1929), *I Spend the Summer* (1930), *Toys and Toymakers* (1931), *A World to Know* (1933), *Henry and the Garden* (1936), *Stories About Henry* (1936), *Shadow and the Stocking* (1937), *I Live (1937), The Picnic* (1938), *Paths to Conservation* (1939), *Henry and His Friends* (1939), *Counting the Days* (1940), *I Know Some Little Animals* (1941), *Christmas Magic* (1942), *Here and There with Henry* (1944), *Tools for*

Andy (1951), *Abraham Lincoln* (1951), *Jesus Lights the Sabbath Lamp* (1953), and *Search for Sammie* (1954).

SEE: Chapel Hill *News Leader*, 20 Feb. 1958; *Durham Morning Herald*, 21 Feb. 1958; *North Carolina Authors: A Selective Handbook* (1942); *Who's Who in the South and Southwest* (1969).

MARTHA K. TIPPETT

Tipton, John (13 Aug. 1730–April 1813), North Carolina, Virginia, and Tennessee statesman, was born in Baltimore, Md., the son of Jonathan II and Elizabeth Tipton. He was the brother of Joseph Tipton, who was a delegate to the North Carolina Constitutional Convention in 1788 and served in the North Carolina Continental Line during the Revolutionary War; the father of Samuel Tipton, who served in the Tennessee house from 1801 to 1805 and founded Duffield Academy in Elizabethton, Tenn.; the grandfather of Jonathan Caswell Tipton, who served in the Tennessee house, and Abraham Tipton, who served in the Tennessee senate; and the great-grandfather of Albert Jackson Tipton, who served in the Tennessee house as a member of the Know-Nothing party.

Early in his life Tipton moved to Virginia, where he was a founder of Woodstock in Dunmore (later Shenandoah) County, a justice of the peace for Beckford Parish, and county sheriff. He was an organizer and signer of the Independence Resolution of Woodstock and served in Lord Dunmore's War under Andrew Lewis in 1774. Active in Virginia politics, Tipton served in the House of Burgesses in 1774 and the House of Delegates in 1776–77 and 1778–81. Although over forty, Tipton was a recruiting officer for the Continental army and fought throughout the Revolutionary War with seven of his sons.

Tipton followed his brother Joseph, who had emigrated from Virginia around 1775, to North Carolina sometime in the early 1780s and immediately became involved in politics. A leader in the establishment of the state of Franklin, he represented Washington County in the Franklin conventions of 1784 and 1785. Tipton, however, was among the first Franklinites to resume allegiance to North Carolina and became a political opponent to the state of Franklin leader, John Sevier. Elected to the North Carolina General Assembly over Sevier, he served as a senator in 1786 and 1788. Tipton's and Sevier's western North Carolina factions were involved in a civil war for three years, with each holding court and establishing militias. Court records and official papers were carried off by raiding parties from both sides. Tipton's forces were finally victorious at a battle near his Jonesboro, Tenn., home in 1788.

A delegate to the 1788 North Carolina Constitutional Convention in Hillsborough, Tipton voted against ratifying the federal constitution. Granted 750 acres before the convention and 1,000 after it, he owned 2,750 acres of land, according to convention records.

When North Carolina ceded the Tennessee lands to the United States in 1789, Tipton, no longer a North Carolinian, continued to be active politically, serving as a member of the House of the Territory of the United States South of the Ohio River. Likewise, he quickly became involved in Tennessee government, representing Washington County in the first and second Tennessee General Assemblies. He also helped draft the Tennessee constitution at the 1796 convention.

Tipton married Mary Butler, the daughter of Thomas Butler, about 1760. They had nine sons: Samuel, Benjamin, Abraham, William, Isaac, Jacob, John, Thomas, and Jonathan III. He married Mrs. Martha Denton Moore, the daughter of Abraham Denton and the widow of James Moore, on 22 July 1779. They had a son, Abraham.

An Episcopalian, Tipton was a trustee of Washington College in 1795. He died at his home near Johnson City, Tenn., and was buried at the Tipton homeplace on Sinclair Creek near the Washington-Carter County line.

SEE: Robert M. McBride and Dan M. Robison, *Biographical Dictionary of the Tennessee General Assembly*, vol. 1 (1975); Seldon Nelson, "The Tipton Family of Tennessee," East Tennessee Historical Society, *Publications*, vol. 1 (1929); William C. Pool, "An Economic Interpretation of the Ratification of the Federal Constitution in North Carolina," *North Carolina Historical Review* 27 (1950); *Who Was Who in America*, historical vol. (1963).

PATRICIA J. MILLER

Tisdale, William (*29 May 1734–ca. 1796*), silversmith, judge of the admiralty court for the Port of Beaufort, and engraver of the Great Seal of the State of North Carolina, was born the second son of Ebenezer and Hope Basset Tisdale of Lebanon, Conn. Following his brother Nathan (A.B. 1749) to Harvard, he entered with the class of 1755 on a Hollis Scholarship. Tisdale was, according to classmate John Adams, one of the best students in that exceptional class, but he left college before the end of his first year. His connection with North Carolina was fostered by the relationship he had with the Trumbull family of Lebanon with whom he corresponded for some twenty years. In 1762 he wrote to Colonel Jonathan Trumbull in Boston inquiring about the debts of one Antipas Trumbull, of New Bern, who died in that North Carolina town in 1770. From that later date William Tisdale begins to appear frequently in the North Carolina records, as he seems to have moved quickly into the political sphere of the area. In 1771 he was a juror and grand juror for Craven County, and late in the same year he was a member of the Assembly. On 9 Sept. 1775 he was appointed by the Provincial Congress to the Committee of Safety for New Bern, and a month later he was elected to Congress, which, on 20 Oct. 1775, employed him to engrave plates for bills of credit and designated him "silversmith" in the Act. In 1779 Tisdale was paid £150 for engraving the Great Seal of the new state, and the next year he was one of the commissioners to supervise the issuing of the new paper money.

During the late 1770s Tisdale was occupied not only with the practice of his artistic trade but also with affairs of a public nature, which took up much of his time. On 11 Mar. 1777 he was appointed a justice of the peace, and the following 30 April Governor Richard Caswell signed his commission as judge of the admiralty court for the Port of Beaufort. However, in 1781 a petition was presented to the Assembly to suspend him as judge of the court of admiralty, and in July 1781 Tisdale was so suspended until the charges of bribery and corruption were refuted. The committee of propositions and grievances recommended that the resolution of July 1781 be rescinded, but the house rejected this recommendation. On 17 Apr. 1782 he sent an address to the legislature asking it to reconsider its earlier vote, but once again he was refused. Finally, on 5 Nov. 1784, his resignation as justice of the peace was accepted by the legislature. Yet the next year Tisdale was elected a member of the General Assembly representing New Bern and was subsequently appointed to several committees.

The census of 1790 showed the household of William Tisdale to consist of one white male over sixteen, one male under sixteen, three white females, and three slaves. Unfortunately it gives no clues as to the names of his (pre-

sumed) wife and children. Several deeds in which he was involved from 1794 to 1796 appear in Craven County documents, but his name does not show up in North Carolina records after the later date, and his will was not recorded in Craven County.

SEE: Walter Clark, ed., *State Records of North Carolina*, vols. 11, 16–17, 19, 26 (1895–1906); George Barton Cutten, *Silversmiths of North Carolina* (1973); William L. Saunders, ed., *Colonial Records of North Carolina*, vol. 10 (1890); Clifford K. Shipton, *Sibley's Harvard Graduates*, vol. 13, 1751–55 (1965).

NEIL C. PENNYWITT

Todd, Furney Albert (*3 Oct. 1921–3 Mar. 1991*), plant pathologist and broadcaster, was born in Wake County, the son of Willie D. and Mayne B. Todd. In 1943 he was graduated from North Carolina State College, where as a student he worked in the Plant Pathology Department laboratory. He entered graduate school but decided that he preferred to work with tobacco rather than continue to study. In 1945 he accepted a position with the U.S. Department of Agriculture as a tobacco pathologist at the McCullers Research Station south of Raleigh involved in plant bed disease control, breeding, rotation studies, and chemical soil treatment. In 1955 he took a newly created post as extension tobacco disease specialist at North Carolina State College and began an on-farm applied research program that became known as "Extension-Research on Wheels." In that position he developed a successful pest management program called R-6-P (Reduce Six Pests).

For a number of years Todd recorded a daily farm broadcast for the Tobacco Radio Network that was heard in South Carolina, Virginia, Georgia, Kentucky, and Florida, as well as North Carolina. He also appeared on a monthly farm show broadcast over WRAL-TV in Raleigh. In 1960 he visited Germany, Switzerland, and France to help tobacco growers combat widespread field outbreaks of blue mold and spent three weeks there assisting in planning control measures. In 1970 he was named "Man of the Year in Service to North Carolina Agriculture" by the *Progressive Farmer* magazine. *Tobacco International* magazine picked him as one of eight Men of the Year in 1977, and in 1978 he became one of the first two "Philip Morris Extension Specialists." In the latter year he also was named a Fellow in the American Phytopathological Society. Todd was the author or coauthor of more than six hundred scientific articles, extension bulletins, circulars, and leaflets.

He married Anne Liles of Zebulon, and they became the parents of Furney A., Jr., Richard, Anita, Elizabeth, and Judy. A member of Wendell Baptist Church, Todd was buried at Greenmount Cemetery, Wendell.

SEE: Raleigh *News and Observer*, 3 Apr. 1977, 4 Mar. 1991; Furney A. Todd file (Archives, North Carolina State University Library, Raleigh); *Wall Street Journal*, 26 Mar. 1980.

MAURICE TOLER

Tolson, John Jarvis III (Jack) (*22 Oct. 1915–2 Dec. 1991*), army officer and pioneer in the use of helicopters in combat, was born in New Bern, the son of John Jarvis and Lillian Bartling Tolson. He attended The University of North Carolina in 1932–33 before entering the U.S. Military Academy, from which he was graduated in 1937. In the same year he also was graduated from the Chemical Warfare School and later from the Army Parachute School (1941), Air and Command Staff School (1947), British Staff College (1951), Army War College (1953), and Army Aviation School (1956). He rose in grade from second lieutenant (1937) to lieutenant general (1968).

Serving in Hawaii and the southwestern Pacific between 1937 and 1946, he assisted in activating the 503d Parachute Infantry Regiment in 1943 and jumped with it at the retaking of Corregidor—the first airborne assault operation of U.S. forces in the Pacific. Following a tour of duty in Japan after World War II he served on the staff and faculty of the Air University in Alabama (1946–49) and with the 325th Airborne Infantry Regiment (1949–50). He then was with the 82d Airborne Division for a time and in 1952 served as the U.S. airborne-infantry representative to the United Kingdom.

Between 1953 and 1955 he was assigned to the office of the Assistant Chief of Staff, G-3, Department of the Army. He directed the airborne-army aviation department, Infantry School (1955–56), and was assistant commandant, U.S. Army Aviation School (1957–59); deputy director, army aviation, office of the Deputy Chief of Staff Operations, Department of the Army (1959–61); chief, Military Assistance Advisory Group (Ethiopia) (1961–63); director, army aviation, office of the assistant chief of staff of force development, Department of the Army (1963–65); commanding general, U.S. Army Aviation Center, and commandant, Army Aviation School, Fort Rucker, Ala. (1965–67); commanding general, First Cavalry Division (air mobile), Vietnam, which he led during the Tet offensive and the relief of Khe Sanh (1967–68); commanding general of the Eighteenth Airborne Corps (promoted to lieutenant general, 1 Aug. 1968) and of Fort Bragg (1968–71); and deputy commanding general, Continental Army Command (1971–73).

In Vietnam General Tolson and his staff formed and led what has been called "the most deadly unit ever sent to war . . . helicopter-borne sky troops, fast-moving, hard-hitting, true descendants of the horse-riding cavalry." He was awarded the Distinguished Service Cross, Distinguished Service Medal with two oak leaf clusters, Silver Star, Legion of Merit with two oak leaf clusters, Distinguished Flying Cross, Bronze Star, Air Medal with forty-four oak leaf clusters, Army Commendation Medal, Purple Heart, Combat Infantry badge, and numerous unit and area ribbons. In 1975 he was named to the Army Aviation Hall of Fame. Tolson retired in 1973 and made his home in Raleigh.

While commanding general of the Eighteenth Airborne Corps at Fort Bragg, Tolson began the army's first drug rehabilitation program. After retirement he became secretary of the North Carolina Department of Military and Veterans Affairs (1973–77), which created the Emergency Operations Center in 1974. The General Assembly in 1973 established an Energy Crisis Study Commission, a cabinet-level panel that Tolson served as chairman.

Tolson married Margaret Jordan Young in 1947, and they became the parents of David Chillingsworth, John Jarvis IV, and Harriet Boykin. He died of a heart attack in Raleigh and was buried in Arlington National Cemetery. He had been a lay reader in the Episcopal church.

SEE: John L. Cheney, Jr., ed., *North Carolina Government, 1585–1979* (1981); Memory F. Mitchell, ed., *Addresses and Public Papers of James Elbert Holshouser, Jr., Governor of North Carolina, 1973–1977* (1978 [portrait]); *North Carolina Manual* (1975); Raleigh *News and Observer*, 2, 25 Aug. 1968, 3, 10 Dec. 1991 [portrait]; *Who's Who in America* (1980).

WILLIAM S. POWELL

Tomes (Tems, Thomes, Tums), Francis (ca. 1633–June 1712), Council member, justice, customs collector, and prominent Quaker, moved from Virginia to the North Carolina colony, then called Albemarle, about 1664. He had migrated to Virginia in 1649 and lived for nine years in Martin's Brandon, Charles City County, where he was an indentured servant to one Francis Grey. About 1658 he moved to Ware Neck, Surry County, Va., where he lived until his removal to Albemarle. In Surry County he served in a militia force that brought the Weyanoke Indians to the English settlements for protection against the Nansemond Indians, who had killed the Weyanoke king. He also served with the detachment that returned the Weyanokes to their town when danger had passed.

Tomes soon became prominent in Albemarle. In 1672 he was identified as a justice of the peace by William Edmundson, the Quaker missionary who visited Albemarle that year. A deposition made by Tomes in the 1690s indicates that he held some office of importance as early as 1669. In February 1683/84 he was a justice of the county court, then the highest court of law in the colony. By November 1684, and probably as early as the preceding February, he was a member of the Council. He appears to have served on the Council continuously from that time until 1705, although there may have been short gaps in his service that are not indicated in the sparse surviving records of the period. As Council member Tomes was ex officio justice of various courts held by the Council, which included the Palatine's Court, the General Court, and the Court of Chancery. From February 1683/84 through February 1684/85 he was a justice of the county court, on which several Council members as well as others ordinarily sat.

In 1695 Tomes was commissioned customs collector for the colony. He also was a collector of quit rents in the late 1690s. Earlier in that decade he was clerk of the Perquimans Precinct Court. The length of his service in those capacities is unknown.

Tomes was one of the earliest and most influential Quakers in Albemarle. He and his wife, Priscilla, were converted in 1672 by William Edmundson, who made his first visit to the colony that year. Tomes and his wife were so moved by Edmundson's first sermon in Albemarle that they invited him to hold his next service in their home, which he did. For many years the Perquimans Monthly Meeting was held regularly in Tomes's home, which frequently was also the site of quarterly and yearly meetings. When Edmundson again visited Albemarle in 1676, he was entertained in Tomes's home, where he again preached. Other missionaries, including George Fox and Thomas Story, also were entertained and preached there. In 1706 Tomes donated to the Perquimans meeting an acre of land on which by that time a meetinghouse had been built. In 1707 Tomes, like many other Quakers, suffered distraint of property, apparently for refusing to pay the recently imposed tithe to support the Anglican church. No doubt his religion was the primary factor in ending Tomes's public career, which came to a close when discriminatory restrictions on Quakers and other dissenters replaced the religious toleration earlier characterizing the colony.

Tomes lived in Perquimans Precinct, where he owned more than a thousand acres of land. He was married three times. His first wife, Priscilla, bore him seven children: Penelope, Mary, Francis, Priscilla, Joseph, and twins Joshua and Caleb. The eldest child, Penelope, was born in December 1668 and the twins, who were the youngest, were born in 1679. Tomes's second wife was Abigail Lacy, the widow of John Lacy and previously the widow of William Charles. That marriage took place in May 1683. Abigail, who bore Tomes a daughter also named Priscilla, died in March 1687/88. Tomes subsequently married Mary Nicholson, who had no children.

Of Tomes's eight children, only four—Mary, Francis, Joshua, and the second Priscilla—appear to have lived to maturity. Those four married and had children of their own. Mary married Gabriel Newby, the son of William Newby of Nansemond County, Va. Francis, first married Margaret Bogue Lawrence, the widow of William Lawrence. His second wife was named Rebecca. He died in 1729. Joshua married, first, Sarah Gosby, the daughter of John and Hannah Gosby, and second, Rebecca Jones Sutton, the daughter of Peter Jones and the widow of Joseph Sutton. Joshua died in 1732. Priscilla's first husband was John Nicholson, the son of Christopher and Hannah Nicholson. She later married John Kinse, the son of John and Catherine Kinse of Nansemond County, Va.

On his death at age seventy-nine Francis Tomes was survived by his widow, Mary (d. ca. December 1717), by sons Francis and Joshua, and by daughters Mary and Priscilla.

SEE: J. Bryan Grimes, ed., *Abstract of North Carolina Wills* (1910); J. R. B. Hathaway, ed., *North Carolina Historical and Genealogical Register* (1900–1903); William W. Hinshaw, comp., *Encyclopedia of American Quaker Genealogy*, vol. 1 (1936–50); Minutes and Records of the Perquimans Monthly Meeting and the Symons Creek Monthly Meeting of the Society of Friends in North Carolina, 1680–1762 (Guilford College Library, Greensboro); North Carolina State Archives (Raleigh), esp. Albemarle Book of Warrants and Surveys (1681–1706), Colonial Court Records (boxes 139, 148, 189, 192), Council Minutes, Wills, Inventories (1677–1701), Perquimans Births, Marriages, Deaths, and Flesh Marks (1659–1739, 1701–1820), Perquimans Deeds (Book A, microfilm), Perquimans Precinct Court Minutes (1688–93, 1698–1706), and Wills of Gabriel Newby (1735), Francis Tomes (1712), Francis Tomes, Jr. (1729), Joshua Tomes (1732), Mary Tomes (1717/18); Mattie Erma E. Parker, ed., *North Carolina Higher-Court Records, 1670–1696* and *1697–1701* (1968 and 1971); William S. Price, Jr., ed., *North Carolina Higher-Court Records, 1702–1708* (1974); William L. Saunders, ed., *Colonial Records of North Carolina*, vol. 1 (1886); Thomas Story, *Journal* (1747); *Virginia Magazine of History and Biography*, vol. 8 (July 1900); Ellen Goode Winslow, *History of Perquimans County* (1931).

MATTIE ERMA E. PARKER

Tomlinson, Ambrose Jessup (*22 Sept. 1865–2 Oct. 1943*), charismatic clergyman and sectarian leader, was born near Westfield, Ind., about twenty miles north of Indianapolis. One of six children, he was the only son of Milton and Delilah Tomlinson. The elder Tomlinson had migrated to Indiana from the vicinity of High Point, N.C., and it was in his father's native state that A. J. Tomlinson was later to begin his work as a holiness evangelist and sectarian organizer.

On 24 Apr. 1889 he married Mary Jane Taylor, one of thirteen children of a prosperous Quaker farm family living near Rushville, Ind. The Tomlinsons had four children: Halcy (1891), Homer (1892), Iris (1895), and Milton (1906).

A profoundly religious Quaker, Tomlinson was a restless wanderer and a constant seeker after higher spiritual truths. During the 1890s he roamed from Maine to Georgia as a colporteur for the American Bible Society. His travels on several occasions took him to the mountains of North Carolina, and in May 1899 he moved his family to the southwestern corner of that state, settling briefly at Murphey and then for a protracted period at Culbertson. There he operated a small orphanage on his farm and be-

gan publication of a religious monthly entitled *Samson's Foxes*.

Tomlinson's literacy and piety won him the respect of the mountain folk of the region. In 1903 he was persuaded to join the Holiness Church at Camp Creek in Cherokee County. He was soon ordained and appointed pastor of the little holiness congregation, freeing its earlier leadership to engage in evangelistic work. In December 1904 he moved his family to Cleveland in Bradley County, Tenn., approximately fifty miles from Camp Creek; he continued, however, to serve as pastor of the Camp Creek church. Within a year Tomlinson and other evangelists, among them R. G. Spurling, Jr., and W. F. Bryant, had established five small holiness congregations in the rural mountainous region where Tennessee, Georgia, and North Carolina converge; Tomlinson served as the pastor for three of these.

On 26 and 27 Jan. 1906 representatives from these scattered congregations met at Camp Creek and united them into a loose confederation known as the Holiness church. Gradually the center of this burgeoning sect's work shifted from southwestern North Carolina to the area around Cleveland, Tenn. On 9 Jan. 1907 the Second General Assembly of the Holiness church convened at Union Grove near Cleveland. Delegates to this convocation voted to change the name of the organization to the Church of God. By this time Tomlinson had emerged as the informal leader of the sect.

A major theological change occurred within the Church of God in late 1907 and early 1908, when many of its members were converted to pentecostalism and came to regard the baptism in the Holy Spirit, signified by speaking in tongues, as the ultimate religious experience. Tomlinson's own "baptism in the Spirit" on 12 Jan. 1908 effectively sealed the theological destiny of the rapidly growing sect.

Delegates to the 1909 annual assembly of the Church of God voted to create the position of general overseer and named A. J. Tomlinson to the post. His appointment was little more than a formal recognition of what had already become a reality. Tomlinson was at this time probably the most able and energetic man in the organization, and his gifts had naturally resulted in his emergence as leader of the group long before 1909. Under his leadership, the church had grown rapidly, by 1910 having some 1,005 members in 31 churches scattered throughout the Southeast.

As general overseer Tomlinson broadened the scope of his activities. In addition to fulfilling his ministerial responsibilities, he made frequent evangelist tours and in 1910 became editor of the sect's first newspaper, the *Evening Light and Church of God Evangel*, known later as the *Church of God Evangel*. His successful work as evangelist, administrator, and editor resulted in 1914 in his election as general overseer for life. By 1920 he exercised almost absolute authority in the church. At the zenith of his power, however, Tomlinson's authority was challenged by disgruntled elements within the Church of God. Perhaps his almost unlimited power made him too autocratic, overwork may have clouded his judgment, or the changing character of the sect may have required a different type of leader. In any case, by the early 1920s he was under fire from several quarters for abusing his authority and mismanaging church funds. In 1921 and 1922 new administrative offices, curtailing the general overseer's authority, were created over Tomlinson's objections. In 1923 the Church's Committee on Better Government charged him with misappropriation of $14,000, and that July the Council of Elders removed him from office.

Indignant at his removal, Tomlinson immediately organized another group, proclaiming it the legitimate standard bearer of the Church of God; its members regarded his opponents within the original organization as schismatics. Litigation then ensued in the Tennessee courts over who had legitimate claim to the name Church of God and the legal right to funds that came to Cleveland, Tenn., addressed to that body. On 15 July 1927 the Tennessee Supreme Court decided in favor of Tomlinson's opponents. As a result, on 8 Apr. 1929, the defeated faction adopted the name the Tomlinson Church of God. This sect flourished under Tomlinson's leadership, but following his death it too was racked with dissension because of a power struggle between Milton and Homer Tomlinson for control of their father's church. Milton ultimately emerged the victor in this contest, becoming general overseer, while Homer, expelled from the organization, went to New York and organized the Church of God World Headquarters.

On 6 Mar. 1953 the Tomlinson Church of God changed its name to the Church of God of Prophecy. Later this organization developed the Fields of the Woods shrine in Cherokee County, where by the early 1970s more than $2 million had been spent to mark the spot at which A. J. Tomlinson had, after much prayer, come to regard the holiness congregation at Camp Creek as the Church of God of biblical prophecy.

A. J. Tomlinson was buried in Fort Hill Cemetery at Cleveland, the eastern Tennessee town that had become the headquarters of the two pentecostal sects over which he had presided and the home of the pentecostal college that was named in his honor. Although his reputation was somewhat marred by the struggle that occurred within the Church of God—Cleveland, Tenn., in the early 1920s, he was one of the most important figures in the classical pentecostal revival of the early twentieth century.

SEE: Charles W. Conn, *Like a Might Army, Moves the Church of God* (1955); *New York Times*, 3 Oct. 1943; Vinson Synan, *The Holiness-Pentecostal Movement in the United States* (1971); Homer A. Tomlinson, *Mountain of the Lord's House* (1941) and *There Shall Be Wings*, part 1 of 7 (1941); Homer A. Tomlinson, ed., *Diary of A. J. Tomlinson*, 3 vols. (1949–55)

ROBERT F. MARTIN

Tomlinson, Sidney Halstead, Sr. *(4 May 1876–15 Mar. 1949)*, High Point furniture manufacturer, was born at Bush Hill (now Archdale) in Randolph County. He was descended from a pioneer Quaker family that emigrated from England to America in 1752 in search of religious liberty. The progenitors of the Tomlinson family in America were Josiah and Olive Unthank Tomlinson (the great-great-grandparents of S. H. Tomlinson, Sr.), who landed at Charleston, S.C. In 1786 their eldest son William Allen, who had married Martha Coppock, relocated in Piedmont North Carolina. William Allen Tomlinson became the first landowner in the Quaker settlement of Bush Hill, having received a grant of three hundred acres from Governor Samuel Johnston. He and his progeny engaged in farming and light industry, operating a tannery throughout most of the nineteenth century and for many years a shoe factory in conjunction with the tannery. The Tomlinson family was characterized by industry, thrift, and prosperity; its members were devoted to the Quaker faith and to the cause of education.

Allen Josiah Tomlinson, the father of S. H. Tomlinson, took a prominent part in the work of Maryland Quakers who sought to promote elementary and normal school education among their North Carolina brethren. He

founded the successful Sylvan Academy at Cane Creek in Alamance County. In 1869, during his junior year at Haverford College, he became principal of the Friends' Academy in Damascus, Ohio. There he met and married Anna Fawcett, a daughter of Simeon and Deborah Fawcett. In time, Tomlinson and his bride returned to North Carolina, where he taught school and operated the family tannery. After his death it was reported that "Allen Josiah Tomlinson was teacher and friend in general to the young people of the state. He was a genial spirit wherever he went. His good judgment and consideration for others brought him many duties in church and neighborhood. His influence and impression on the lives of his students were an ever-widening circle going on and on."

It was to this rich birthright that Sidney Halstead Tomlinson was born. Inspired by the lore of family legend, he early demonstrated ability and the desire to excel. He was educated at Old Trinity (a school that was later moved to Durham and became the nucleus of Duke University) and at Guilford College, where, in 1898, he received the B.S. degree in business administration and accounting. At Guilford he was a student leader in a variety of campus activities. After graduation he became a salesman for the Globe Home Furniture Company of High Point, then the largest company of its kind in the South.

Two years later, while in his mid-twenties, he launched an independent career that proved to be both innovative and highly successful. His efforts led in two directions—the more imaginative marketing of furniture products and furniture manufacturing. First, in light of his experience as a Globe salesman, Tomlinson responded to the need for better methods; he trained men in the marketing of furniture by organizing a sales agency. This agency, located in High Point, employed several traveling professionals who sold High Point furniture throughout the South. The step from selling furniture to manufacturing was a logical one. In 1900, with capital resulting from the sale of the family tannery and shoe factory following his father's death, S. H. Tomlinson organized the Tomlinson Chair Manufacturing Company. With capital estimated at between $8,000 and $10,000, the company began production in a two-story, sheet-iron covered building with 18,000 square feet of space. The total volume of business in the first year's operation was $48,000. In this venture Finley Tomlinson, an uncle, was initially president, and S. H. Tomlinson was secretary and treasurer. Soon "Mr. S. H.," as he was known to his employees and associates, became president of the Tomlinson Chair Manufacturing Company (later Tomlinson of High Point and then Tomlinson Furniture), a position he held until his death nearly half a century later. In 1904 he persuaded his brother, Charles F. Tomlinson, to join the company as secretary and treasurer. This vital partnership was disrupted when Charles died in 1943.

The growth of the Tomlinson company was remarkable. In 1911 the Tomlinsons bought the Globe Home Furniture plant, which occupied an entire city block. Over a four-year period the plant was remodeled, and the Tomlinsons had the facilities to enter the highly competitive national market. In 1916 the company innovated the manufacture of dining and living room suites of matching design. Tomlinson furniture, already characterized by excellent craftsmanship, achieved more distinctive styling year after year until the line was fully developed. Period furniture became a company hallmark as fine adaptations of eighteenth-century English, French, and American styles were produced. To display this furniture to advantage the Tomlinsons had, in a prophetic move in 1909, opened High Point's first furniture exhibition. Subsequently the company pioneered the later industrywide practice of displaying its line in gallery form. With excellence in design and craftsmanship, imaginative marketing, and good management, the Tomlinson name gained national and even international prominence. At the time of his death S. H. Tomlinson had approximately eight hundred employees and a modern physical plant with a floor space covering eleven acres. The company maintained two permanent displays—one at the Chicago Merchandise Mart and the other at the Tomlinson Exhibition Building in High Point. A local anecdote—whether true or apocryphal—suggests the fame of Tomlinson furniture. It seems that a wealthy High Pointer was determined to furnish her home with the world's finest furniture. After extensive shopping abroad, she selected an elegant suite offered by a fashionable Paris gallery. The furniture was purchased and imported at great expense. Only after the arrival of this elegant living and dining room suite was it discovered that the manufacturer was Tomlinson of High Point.

Active in civic and church affairs, S. H. Tomlinson was a founder of the High Point YMCA. He was an original stockholder-director of the High Point Hotel Company and a charter member of the Emerywood Country Club. True to his Quaker heritage, he was a member of High Point's Friends Meeting, but he maintained his interest in his ancestral meeting at Springfield, where he was a birthright member. For many years he was vice-president of the Springfield Memorial Association and instrumental in establishing an endowment for that venerable Quaker institution. In politics he was a Democrat who believed in economic self-determination.

In December 1904 Tomlinson married Ethel May Diffee of High Point. Their children were James Diffee, Gertrude Diffee, William Allen, and Sidney Halstead, Jr. The latter sons became president and vice-president, respectively, of Tomlinson Furniture. The elder Tomlinson was interred in the Springfield Friends Burial Ground.

SEE: *North Carolina Biography*, vol. 3 (1929); *Pioneer Days and Progress of High Point, N.C., 1859–1948* (1949?); William Allen Tomlinson, personal contact, May 15, 1975; *Tomlinson News*, September 1949.

MAX R. WILLIAMS

Tompkins, Daniel Augustus (*12 Oct. 1851–18 Oct. 1914*), engineer, industrialist, and newspaper publisher, was born in Edgefield County, S.C., to DeWitt Clinton and Hannah Virginia Smyly Tompkins. After attending the local schools and Edgefield Academy, he entered the University of South Carolina in 1867. Two years later he transferred to Renssalear Polytechnic Institute in Troy, N.Y., and was graduated with a civil engineering degree in 1873.

Alexander Lyman Holley, who introduced the Bessemer process of making steel to the United States, hired Tompkins during school vacations to work as a draftsman in the Troy steel works of John A. Griswold and Company. Upon graduation Tompkins worked for Holley for a year in New York City as a designer and private secretary. Holley then sent Tompkins to Bethlehem, Pa., where he was a machinist for John Fritz at the Bethlehem Iron Works. At the end of five years Tompkins had become a master machinist. Fritz arranged for him to go to Westphalia, Germany, to supervise the installation of a hoop mill at the Schwerte Iron Works. Returning from Germany in late 1879, Tompkins worked as a draftsman in the Bethlehem Iron Works until September 1881, when he moved to Crystal City, Mo., and was employed for almost two years as a master machinist for the Crystal Plate Glass Company.

In March 1883 Tompkins went to Charlotte, which became his permanent home, as agent for the Westinghouse Machine Company. In that capacity he installed steam engines in the Carolinas and received a commission on each engine sold. The arrangement led to the formation of the D. A. Tompkins Company in partnership with R. M. Miller, Sr. One of the first engines Tompkins installed was in a cottonseed oil mill belonging to Fred Oliver. Tompkins and Oliver combined to organize the Southern Cotton Oil Company, which took over its competitor, the American Cotton Oil Company. They built eight mills in 1887 before dissolving the partnership and selling their interest in the company. In the same year the D. A. Tompkins Company incorporated and Tompkins, the major shareholder, served as its engineer. By 1889 the company was involved in the construction of mills and electric plants. It had, by 1910, helped build at least 250 cotton oil mills, 150 electric plants, and 100 cotton mills.

During the early years of his interest in cotton mills Tompkins acted only as contractor, but soon he promoted the building of mills by encouraging local communities to raise money for that purpose on a subscription basis. In the decade before 1900 he acquired three cotton mills: Atherton Mill in Dilworth, High Shoals Mills in Gaston County, and Edgefield Manufacturing Company in Edgefield, S.C.

Tompkins's considerable textile holdings led to his appointment by President William McKinley to the U.S. Industrial Commission in 1899. The next year he joined the National Association of Manufacturers, in which he played a policy-making role. Numerous articles appeared under his name in the *Manufacturers Record*. Instrumental in the founding of the textile school at North Carolina State University and a member of the board of trustees for over twenty years, Tompkins encouraged the development of similar programs at Clemson University and in Mississippi and Texas. He was president of the Manufacturers' Club in Charlotte, belonged to the Engineers' Club in New York City, and was a director of the Equitable Life Insurance Company. Tompkins was a lifelong Democrat.

He owned a controlling interest in three newspapers: the *Charlotte Daily Observer* (formerly the Charlotte *Chronicle*), Charlotte *Evening News*, and Greenville (S.C.) *News*. The Observer Printing House, also owned by Tompkins, published many pamphlets and speeches under his name, as well as several books: *Cotton Mill Processes and Calculations* (1899), *Cotton Mill Commercial Features* (1899), *American Commerce: Its Expansion* (1900), *Cotton Values in Textile Fabrics* (1900), *Cotton and Cotton Oil* (1901), and *History of Mecklenburg County and the City of Charlotte from 1740 to 1903* (1903). Tompkins apparently did not write the books and articles on which his name appeared as author but employed ghostwriters. The *History* was written by Charles Lee Coon, Alexander J. McKelway, and Bruce Craven. E. W. Thompson, an engineer in Tompkins's employ, wrote the technical books.

Tompkins's newspapers and publishing firm served him as mouthpieces in his role as a major spokesman for the industrial New South. His biographer, George T. Winston, said, "Anything, everything, and everybody—all the world—was grist in the voracious Tompkins mill of industrialism." Tompkins's outspoken opposition to compulsory public education, child labor legislation, wage/hour regulation, and restricted immigration was calculated to maximize profits and to ensure a continuous supply of cheap labor for southern mills. He saw the unionization movement as an effort of New England mill owners to put their southern counterparts out of business. In 1911 Clark Howell of the *Atlanta Constitution* said of Tompkins, "He perhaps has done more to stimulate the cotton mill development of the South than any living man."

Tompkins's fiancée died in 1884 and he never married. Due to declining health he retired from active involvement in his business in 1910 and moved to his summer home in Montreat in 1912. He died of a paralytic condition two years later and was buried in Elmwood Cemetery, Charlotte. The public library in Edgefield, S.C., and the former textile building at North Carolina State University were named for him.

SEE: Samuel A. Ashe, ed., *Biographical History of North Carolina*, vol. 1 (1905); *Charlotte Daily Observer*, 19 Oct. 1914; Howard B. Clay, "Daniel Augustus Tompkins: An American Bourbon" (Ph.D. diss., University of North Carolina, 1950); William P. Jacobs, *The Pioneer* (1935); *Who Was Who in America*, vol. 1 (1967); George T. Winston, *Daniel Augustus Tompkins: A Builder of the New South* (1920).

BRENDA MARKS EAGLES

Tompkins, John Franklin, Jr. *(b. 1823)*, agriculturist and physician, was born in Edgecombe County, the son of John F. and Rosanna Spruill Tompkins. His mother's brother, George Evans Spruill, was a graduate of Yale University and for several sessions represented Halifax County in the House of Commons. Richard Hines, an uncle by marriage, was a member of Congress. The father of young Tompkins died when he was an infant, and he was reared by his mother and her relations. He attended The University of North Carolina for the session of 1840–41 from Nash County, where his mother was then living. After leaving the university he studied medicine, though where is unknown.

By 1847 Dr. John Tompkins had located in Washington, Beaufort County, and there became a close friend of William L. Kennedy. He acted as second for Kennedy in his duel with Fenner S. Satterthwaite, also a resident of Washington. The duel, arising out of a political argument, was fought at Spring Church, Greenesville County, Va., twenty miles north of Halifax, N.C., on 24 Feb. 1847. Bishop Joseph B. Cheshire, in his book *Nonnulla*, published the documents relating to this duel, including letters written by Tompkins in his capacity as second, as an example of the duelling code of the antebellum period. Tompkins had great admiration for Kennedy, and when his only son was born in 1850, he named him William Lee Kennedy Tompkins. The boy died in childhood.

In 1846 Tompkins married Caroline Crawford Bonner, the daughter of Joseph and Sallie Ann Crawford Bonner of Bath. By the time of the census of 1850 he had left Washington and was residing in the former rectory of St. Thomas Church in his wife's native town. He appears to have given up the practice of medicine and to have turned his attention to agriculture. It is likely that in the course of his medical studies, Tompkins had some exposure to chemistry, then a new science. In April 1852 he brought out in Bath the first issue of the *Farmer's Journal*, published monthly and devoted to "improvements in agriculture, horticulture and the household arts." Principally because of the initiative taken by Tompkins, a meeting was held in Raleigh in October 1852 at which the North Carolina Agricultural Society was organized. Plans were made to hold a state fair the following year.

Though Tompkins was the most able of the editors of farm journals appearing in the state at the time, the publication was not a financial success. In an attempt to improve this situation, he moved to Raleigh in August 1853. There he rented a house near the city called Sharon, which was owned by Thomas Ruffin, a major supporter

of his efforts. In addition to editing the *Farmer's Journal*, Tompkins taught elementary, agricultural, and experimental chemistry at the well-known J. M. Lovejoy Academy in Raleigh and made himself available to farmers who wished to bring soil for analysis. His financial plight did not improve, and by the third volume, William D. Cooke, proprietor of the *Southern Weekly Post*, had bought the *Farmer's Journal*. By the last issue, in December 1854, Tompkins had turned the editorship over to Cooke, who continued publication the following year under the name, *Carolina Cultivator*. Cooke incurred heavy losses in taking over the *Farmer's Journal*.

Late in 1854 Tompkins sold all of his household furniture and surrendered his Raleigh lease. He disappeared from the North Carolina records at this time, and his later career and the date of his death are unknown. According to the records of the Bonner family, however, he was survived by two daughters: Sallie and Rose Spruill who later married, respectively, Bennett Flanner Mayhew and Marion Grubbs.

SEE: Kemp P. Battle, *History of the University of North Carolina*, vol., 1 (1907); Cornelius O. Cathey, *Agricultural Developments in North Carolina, 1783–1860* (1956); Edgecombe County Deeds and Wills (Courthouse, Tarboro); Guion G. Johnson, *Ante-Bellum North Carolina* (1937); Wesley H. Wallace, "North Carolina's Agricultural Journals, 1838–1861," *North Carolina Historical Review* 36 (July 1959).

CLAIBORNE T. SMITH, JR.

Toms, Clinton White *(2 Oct. 1868–29 Aug. 1936)*, teacher, school superintendent, businessman, and philanthropist, was born in Hertford, Perquimans County, the son of Zachariah and Susan Baker Toms. In 1889 he was graduated from The University of North Carolina and in the fall began teaching at the Plymouth High School at Plymouth, Washington County. He left in 1892 for Durham to teach in the newly opened Morehead School (also called the Durham Graded School until the opening of the new Durham Graded School building in 1894). Toms was soon made principal of the school and a trustee of the Durham public schools, which at that time retained a distinctly private character, relying heavily on private contributions and tuition. In June 1894 he was elected superintendent of the Durham public schools.

In the late 1890s Toms gained considerable notice around the state as a progressive educator. He introduced the first course of manual training in a white school in North Carolina and brought in a teacher from the Pratt Institute in New York to teach it. In 1896 he spoke to the State Teachers Assembly at Asheville on manual training. He also introduced such "novel features" as current events and North Carolina history to the curriculum of the graded school and succeeded in acquiring Peabody funds to support the new programs.

Less well known were his efforts to improve educational opportunities for blacks in Durham. In 1896 Toms opened a new graded school building for blacks and installed the same manual training program he had begun in the white school, as well as the standard academic curriculum. The year before he had obtained Peabody funds for that purpose, and in September 1896 he convinced Washington Duke to contribute money for the purchase of new desks for the school.

It was in the final years in Durham that Toms became associated with the Duke family. Washington Duke had been involved for some time in local educational affairs, and so Toms naturally had many occasions to deal with him. Toms solicited contributions from Washington Duke to serve a variety of needs: new desks and materials and a night school for working people in Durham. The night school was taught by regular graded school faculty, but, unlike the day school, no tuition was charged. Toms also consulted Duke on political matters that might affect the schools.

Toms became associated with Benjamin Newton Duke, the son of Washington Duke and the brother of James Buchanan Duke, through his work as a trustee of the Oxford Orphans Asylum at Oxford, Granville County. He and Benjamin Duke both served as state-appointed trustees for the Masonic order throughout the 1890s, and the two made several trips together to Oxford in 1896 and 1897. During this time Benjamin Duke became better acquainted with Toms's abilities.

In February 1897 Toms was elected to the chair of pedagogy at The University of North Carolina. But he did not have much chance to make an impression there, for on 1 Sept. 1897 he received a note from Ben Duke requesting a meeting "to talk important business matters." The next day Duke offered to make Toms the manager of the Durham plant of the American Tobacco Company. Toms readily accepted the position and began work in October. He had clearly mastered the technical aspects of tobacco manufacturing within a year and a half, though little is known of his business activities in Durham or later in New York. With the formal dissolution of the American Tobacco Company in 1911, Toms moved to New York City as executive vice-president of the Liggett and Meyers Company (also operated by the Duke family). He became president of the company in 1928 and held that position until his death.

Despite his residency in New York, Toms remained active in North Carolina affairs. Appointed a trustee of Trinity College (later Duke University) in 1901, he continued to serve until business pressures and poor health forced him to resign in 1932. Actually, Toms acted more as an agent for the Duke family than simply as a trustee of the college. When presidents John C. Kilgo or William P. Few wished to approach the Dukes for a donation, most often they contacted Toms first for his opinion and then arranged an appointment through him with Benjamin Duke. Toms also interceded with the Dukes for others regarding a variety of requests.

A philanthropist in his own right, Toms began by helping individuals who needed financial aid for their schooling. Later he established scholarship funds at The University of North Carolina and Duke University. He also contributed to a variety of causes in Durham and in his hometown, Hertford.

Toms married Mary Newby of Hertford in 1891. Though living in New York for many years, he was a lifelong member of the Duke Memorial Methodist Episcopal Church in Durham. He also helped found the Durham Public Library in 1896. He died in New York and was buried in Durham.

SEE: *Biennial Report of the Superintendent of Public Instruction* (1898); Duke University *Alumni Register*, vols. 11 (December 1926), 13 (June 1927), 23 (September 1936); Robert F. Durden, *The Dukes of Durham* (1975); *Durham Daily Sun*, 1 May 1896; *Durham Globe*, 9 (portrait), 11 July 1895; *Durham Morning Herald*, 30–31 Aug., 1, 9 Sept. 1936; Daniel L. Grant, *Alumni History of the University of North Carolina* (1924); *New York Times*, 30 Aug. 1936 (portrait); *North Carolina Biography*, vol. 5 (1941); Raleigh *News and Observer*, 9 July 1895; Raleigh *North Carolinian*, 21 May 1896 (portrait); *Washington Post*, 30 Aug. 1936; Superintendent of Public Instruction Letter Book HH (North Carolina State Archives, Raleigh). Also William Kenneth Boyd, Benjamin Newton Duke, Washington Duke, William Preston Few, John Carlisle Kilgo, and James Augustus Thomas manuscripts (Manuscript Department, Duke University Library, Durham); Frank Porter Graham manuscripts (Southern Historical Collection, University of North Carolina, Chapel Hill).

WAYNE K. DURRILL

Toomer, Henry *(7 Aug. 1738–[between 22 Dec. 1798 and 19 Mar.] 1799)*, Wilmington Safety Committee member, army commissary, financier and bail bondsman, and merchant, was born in Charleston, S.C., the second son of Joshua and Mary Bonneau Toomer. Following his wife's death Joshua moved in 1747 with his son Henry to Wilmington. There Henry Toomer achieved considerable financial success; in 1790 he owned fifty-one slaves.

In 1752 Toomer was a member of George Merrick's militia company. His first appearance in court was as a juror in 1761. He posted his first security bonds in the court in December 1765 and posted at least another thirty-three by the time of his last recorded action in August 1793. His activities in the real estate market were first documented in 1765; by 1798 the records show at least thirty-five such transactions, many of which were for land that he held for only a few years. In 1766 Toomer was among those who signed letters relating to the Stamp Act rejection by the citizens of Wilmington, and he was a signer of the letter to Governor William Tryon in July 1766.

Named inspector for Wilmington in 1767, Toomer was reappointed in 1768, 1769, 1772, 1773, and 1785. He ran unsuccessfully for sheriff in 1774. On 3 July 1775 he was elected to the Wilmington Safety Committee, of which he remained a member through its last recorded meeting on 9 Feb. 1776. He also served on the committee to take a census of all white male and free mulatto inhabitants of the town of Wilmington between the ages of sixteen and sixty.

His first recorded action as a commissary during the Revolutionary War was in August 1775, when he furnished beef. By January 1776 Toomer was responsible for providing a barracks for regulars to use as a hospital as well as the nurses for the hospital. In March 1776 the Provincial Council officially designated him a commissioner for the district of Wilmington, and in June the Council of Safety appointed him commissary to the detachment of militia from the Halifax Brigade. During this time he was also a captain in command of militia companies. In April 1777 the senate named him a marshal for the Port of Brunswick. That July he was selected one of the commissioners to take possession of estates of those opposing the Revolution, but in May 1780 he joined other Wilmington merchants in protesting to the Assembly that the canceling of debts owed to the English would lead to the loss of future credit to North Carolina merchants. In August 1777 Toomer was named a commissioner for the ship *Washington*, and later that year he was appointed with William Hooper to sell the ship. The next year he was assigned to the commission to regulate the pilot fees at Cape Fear bar. In May 1779 he was designated deputy quartermaster by the senate. His final recorded commissary action was in April 1780.

In 1784 Toomer was named both to a committee to purchase land for a jail in Wilmington and to a commission to lay out a town adjoining Fort Johnston on the Cape Fear River. From 1786 until his death he apparently served as coroner in Wilmington, a post his father had filled soon after his arrival. He also provided funds for other traders when money was scarce or unavailable from other sources.

Toomer married three times. His first wife was Mary Vanderhorst, of Charleston, S.C., by whom he had a son, Anthony B. He next wed Mary Grainger, of Wilmington, and they had a daughter, Mary J. He and his third wife,

Magdalene Mary De Rossett (b. 2 Feb. 1762) of Wilmington, were the parents of Eliza, Anthony, John De Rossett, Lewis D., and Mary Fullerton.

SEE: Walter Clark, ed., *State Records of North Carolina*, vols. 11–15 (1895–98), 20 (1904), 24 (1905); Mae B. Graves, comp., *New Hanover County Abstracts of Wills* (1981); Elizabeth F. McKoy, *Early Wilmington Block by Block from 1733 On* (1967); Catherine De Rosset Meares, comp., *Annals of the De Rosset Family: Huguenot Immigrants to the Province of North Carolina Early in the Eighteenth Century* (1906?); William L. Saunders, ed., *Colonial Records of North Carolina*, vol. 7, 10 (1890); Alexander M. Walker, comp., *New Hanover County Court Minutes: [Part 1], 1738–1769* (1958), *Part 2, 1771–1785* (1959), *Part 3, 1786–1793* (1960), and *Part 4, 1794–1800* (1962).

WILLIAM S. SMITH, JR.

Toomer, John De Rossett (*13 Mar. 1784–27 Sept. 1856*), attorney, legislator, and superior court judge, was born in Wilmington, the son of Henry and Magdalene Mary De Rossett Toomer. Henry Toomer, who moved from South Carolina to Wilmington with his father, Joshua Toomer, in 1747, was a member of the Wilmington Safety Committee in 1775 and 1776. Magdalene, his third wife, was the daughter of Dr. Moses John and Mary Ivy De Rossett. After attending The University of North Carolina, John D. Toomer began to practice law in Wilmington. In 1815 he was county attorney. He moved to Cumberland County and was living in Fayetteville in 1824.

The General Assembly elected Toomer a superior court judge on 18 Dec. 1818 to fill a vacancy created when several superior court judges were sent to the state supreme court, but he resigned in 1819. Eight years later, in 1827, he was elected to the General Assembly to replace Robert Strange, who had resigned. Appointed an associate justice of the supreme court by the governor on 8 May 1829, Toomer resigned on 1 December of the same year. In June 1835 he was a delegate to the constitutional convention. He was elected a judge of the superior court on 7 Jan. 1837 and served until 1840, when he resigned because of ill health. Sometime after this he moved from Fayetteville to Pittsboro, where he died.

In Wilmington on 9 Dec. 1805 Toomer married Maria J. Rhett Swann, who was born on 13 May 1787 in New Hanover County to John and Sarah Moore Swann. Sarah was the daughter of Brigadier General James Moore. The children named in Toomer's will were John, Henry, Duncan, Frederick, Lucy, Eliza (m. Thomas Hill), Sarah Ann (m. Albert Torrence), and Mary (m. Warren Winslow).

Both Toomer and his wife were buried in Pittsboro.

SEE: Carrie L. Broughton, comp., *Marriage and Death Notices from the Raleigh Register and North Carolina State Gazette*, 16 Dec. 1805, 18 Oct. 1856; Chatham County Will Book C; John L. Cheney, Jr., ed., *North Carolina Government, 1585–1974* (1975); Crockette W. Hewlett, comp., "Attorneys of New Hanover Co.," 1976 (photocopy, Wilmington Public Library); Ida B. Kellam records (Wilmington); Leora H. McEachern and Isabel M. Williams, eds., *Wilmington–New Hanover Safety Committee Minutes, 1774–1776* (1974); Wilmington *Daily Herald*, 30 Sept. 1856; New Hanover County Court Minutes, 19 June 1799 (microfilm, Cape Fear Technical Institute Library); New Hanover County Deed Book P; New Hanover County Will Book AD; St. James Church Register, Wilmington.

IDA B. KELLAM
LEORA HIATT MCEACHERN

Toon, Thomas Fentress (*10 June 1840–19 Feb. 1902*), farmer, teacher, soldier, and superintendent of public instruction, was born in Columbus County, the son of Anthony and Mary McMillan Fentress Toon. He attended county schools and Wake Forest College. When the Civil War began during his senior year, he enlisted immediately but completed the term and was graduated with high honors.

On receiving his diploma, Toon joined the Columbus Guards No. 2, which later became a part of the Twentieth North Carolina. He was elected first lieutenant in his company, and a month later his men chose him captain. Toon's command served in various campaigns of Robert D. Jackson, Jubal Early, and John B. Gordon, during which his distinguished performance led to his elevation to colonel in 1863. At Spottsylvania General R. D. Johnston was injured, and Toon was temporarily promoted to brigadier general; he returned to the rank of colonel when Johnston was well enough to resume command. Wounded several times during the war, Toon was permanently removed from the fighting ranks during the attack on Fort Stedman in March 1865.

After the war he returned to Columbus County, where he had a many-sided career in teaching, farming, and working for the Atlantic Coast Line Railway system. He also served as county school examiner, mayor of Fair Bluff, and member of the state legislature (lower house, 1881–82; senate, 1883–84).

In January 1866 Toon married Carrie E. Smith, the daughter of Alva Smith of Fair Bluff. They had two sons and three daughters. After his wife's death Toon married, in 1891, Rebecca Cobb Ward and moved to Lumberton in Robeson County. Well known in her own right, the new Mrs. Toon was chosen first superintendent of Robeson Baptist Women's Missionary Union at the time of its creation in 1896 and served for five years. Her husband taught at the Robeson Institute.

In 1900 North Carolina elected as its governor Charles B. Aycock, who planned to revamp and drastically improve the state's education system. Aycock called T. F. Toon to Raleigh to become state superintendent of public instruction. These two men and Charles D. McIver made plans to canvass the state in order to gain support for the "Declaration against Illiteracy." During the strenuous campaign Toon contracted an illness that ended his career in 1902. He was a Democrat and a Baptist. Of him his church people said: he was "a humble and faithful servant of His Master and Lord, an exemplary father and companion and a statesman of rare merit."

SEE: Edgar W. Knight, *Public School Education in North Carolina* (1916); Robert C. Lawrence, *The State of Robeson* (1939); Lumberton *Robesonian*, 26 Feb. 1951; *Minutes of the Baptist State Convention* (1902); C. Beauregard Poland, *Twentieth-Century Statesmen: North Carolina Political Leaders, 1900–1901* (n.d. [portrait]); Raleigh *News and Observer*, 20 Feb. 1902; Ezra J. Warner, *Generals in Gray: Lives of the Confederate Commanders* (1959); *Who Was Who in America, 1897–1942* (1981); Marcus J. Wright, *General Officers of the Confederate Army* (1911).

MAUD THOMAS SMITH

Torrey, Reuben Archer (*28 Jan. 1856–26 Oct. 1928*), evangelist, author, and Fundamentalist, was born in Hoboken, N.J., the son of Reuben Slay ton and Elizabeth Ann Swift Torrey. He was graduated in 1875 from Yale University, where he also received a divinity degree. As a liberal theologian he was a pastor in Garrettsville, Ohio, but left to study theology at Leipzig and Erlangen, Germany. Unlike others who became even more liberal in German universities, Torrey returned home more conservative. In the 1880s he took up pastorates in Minneapolis and contributed to the Fundamentalist foundations soon to be built upon by W. B. Riley and later by Riley successor Billy Graham.

In Minneapolis Torrey came to the attention of Dwight Moody, who invited him to Chicago in 1889 to be the first superintendent of Moody's Chicago Training Institute—later called the Moody Bible Institute—which had been cofounded by Asheville's W. J. Erdman. In 1894 he also became pastor of the Chicago Avenue Church, later Moody Memorial Church. When Moody became too ill to continue his Kansas City revival, he asked Torrey to complete it. In 1902 Torrey took the Fundamentalist movement worldwide when he succeeded the late Moody on a preaching tour to Australia, New Zealand, Tasmania, India, China, Japan, England, Scotland, Ireland, Germany, and France.

Even earlier Torrey had begun to influence Tar Heel thought when in June 1896 he addressed the Southern Students' Conference, attended by a number of North Carolinians. By 1900 he was a familiar figure in North Carolina, in part through attendance at the annual Montreat Bible Conferences in Black Mountain. Begun in 1897, these meetings were modeled in part on Tar Heel James H. Brookes's Fundamentalist Niagara Bible Conferences in which Torrey played a supporting role. Torrey's addresses at Montreat were circulated in North Carolina and the Southeast through Weston R. Gales's *The Revival*, a premillenial prohibitionist promotional periodical published at Montreat. Torrey established a conference center in Pennsylvania but in 1926 settled in Asheville and continued his work from there.

His published addresses accented the fundamentals of his faith, especially creationism, the second coming of Christ, and an inerrant Bible. One North Carolinian whom Torrey influenced was Salisbury's young First Baptist prohibitionist pastor, Ralph E. Neighbor, who later was one of the founders of the Fundamentalist Baptist Bible Union and of the northern separatist General Association of Regular Baptist Churches. When Torrey's ministry became worldwide in scope, he took with him as his song leader and associate a Moody Bible Institute musician, Charles Alexander, who had introduced Moody's millenarian message to Marshall, Bryson City, Waynesville, and the Cherokee Indian reservation at least a decade earlier than Torrey advanced it at Montreat.

Torrey's influence in North Carolina was not restricted to Montreat, subscribers to *The Revival*, or North Carolinians attending Princeton Seminary who heard him speak when university president Woodrow Wilson reluctantly permitted him to preach to the student body. Torrey succeeded Amzi Dixon, a Shelby native and world renowned evangelist, as editor of a series of booklets subsidized by a wealthy Californian to accent Fundamentalism. Between 1910 and 1915 thousands of booklets entitled *The Fundamentals* were sent to pastors, Sunday school superintendents, and others throughout North Carolina. The state's 1920s conflict over the teaching of evolution was one of the fruits of this activity.

From 1912 to 1924 Torrey became involved with the Bible Institute of Los Angeles, patterned after his own Moody Bible Institute. Torrey was dean of the Los Angeles institute, where he and Amzi Dixon delivered annual lectures. The new medium of radio was adopted and in time produced "The Old Fashioned Revival Hour," to which young Billy Graham listened in Charlotte and through which Jerry Falwell was converted in Virginia.

It was when he left California in 1926 that Torrey chose Asheville as his retirement home. He then conducted revivals at the First Presbyterian Church and around North Carolina and the Southeast. Torrey married Clara B. Swift of Ohio, and they had five children: Edith Clare, Blanche, Reuben Archer, Elizabeth, and Margaret.

Torrey's published works include *How I Bring Men to Christ* (1893), *Baptism with the Holy Spirit* (1895), *What the Bible Teaches* (1898), *Divine Origin of the Bible* (1899), *How to Promote and Conduct a Successful Revival* (1901), *How to Work for Christ* (1901), *Revival Addresses* (1903), *Talks to Men* (1904), *Studies in the Life and Teachings of Our Lord* (1909), *The Fundamental Doctrines of the Christian Faith* (1919), *Is the Bible the Inerrant World of God?* (1922), and *How to Get the Gold out of the Word of God* (1925).

SEE: *American Literary Yearbook*, vol. 1 (1919); *Charlotte Observer*, 27 Oct. 1928; G. T. B. Davis, *Torrey and Alexander* (1905); *Greensboro Daily News*, 27 Oct. 1928; R. Harkness, *Reuben Archer Torrey: The Man, His Message* (1929); Erwin L. Lueker, ed., *Lutheran Cyclopedia* (1954); *Nat. Cyc. Am. Biog.*, vol. 21 (1931); Ernest R. Sandeen, *The Roots of Fundamentalism* (1970); *Who Was Who among American Authors*, vol. 2 (1976).

JAMES LUTZWEILER

Tossy, Janos. *See* **Schonwald, Johann Tossy.**

Totten, Henry Roland (*6 Nov. 1892–9 Feb. 1974*), botanist and professor, was born in Matthews, the son of William Theophilus and Jeannette Frances Barham Totten. He attended the Yadkin Collegiate Institute and in 1913 was graduated from The University of North Carolina, from which he also received the M.A. (1914) and Ph.D. (1923) degrees. His graduate work was under the direction of Professor W. C. Coker. Totten was an instructor in botany in Chapel Hill between 1914 and 1917. Following enlistment in the Reserve Officer Training Corps in World War I, he was commissioned second lieutenant (1917), was stationed at Camp Jackson, S.C., with the field artillery (1917–18), and served in France (1918–19). He was a graduate student at the University of Paris in 1919. Totten retained his army reserve commission; he entered World War II as a captain and rose to lieutenant colonel. Returning to his post as instructor in botany in 1919, he became assistant professor (1923–25), associate professor (1925–29), and professor (1929–63). He retired in 1963.

A dedicated teacher of general botany, pharmacognosy, dendrology, and taxonomy, Professor Totten helped train two generations of pharmacists. His research interests were in the fungi, ferns, and vascular flora, while his primary interest was in the taxonomy of the woody plants of the southeastern United States. His outstanding publications include *Trees of the Southeastern States* (1916, 1937) with W. C. Coker and "Fagaceae" for the *Manual of the Vascular Flora of the Carolinas* (1968). A member of many professional organizations, he was particularly active in the Elisha Mitchell Scientific Society, North Carolina Academy of Science, Association of Southeastern Biologists, and Southern Appalachian Botanical Club. A leader in wildflower preservation, he also was influential in the establishment of garden clubs in North Carolina.

After the retirement of W. C. Coker, Totten became director of the arboretum on the university campus, and it was his interest and efforts that helped procure the site of the North Carolina Botanical Garden in Chapel Hill. He won numerous awards for teaching and for distinguished contributions to the training of pharmacists and received an honorary doctorate of laws from Atlantic Christian College. His greatest pleasure, however, resulted from the naming of an oak in his honor, *Quercus totteni*, by Lionel Melvin. He also was noted for his fondness in roaming the fields and woods with his students, friends, and his dogs.

A Methodist, he was married in 1923 to Addie Williams, who joined him in his work, particularly with garden clubs.

SEE: Daniel L. Grant, *Alumni History of the University of North Carolina* (1924); Mary F. Henderson, ed., *Social Register of North Carolina* (1936); William S. Powell, ed., *North Carolina Lives* (1962); University of North Carolina, Faculty Council, Minutes, "Henry Roland Totten," 19 Apr. 1974; *Who's Who in the South and Southwest* (1967).

WILLIAM S. POWELL

Totten, William Theophilus (*13 Feb. 1862–26 Nov. 1936*), minister, educator, and president of Yadkin Collegiate Institute (later Yadkin College) for twenty-six years, was born in Rockingham County, the eldest son of the Reverend John Henry and Margaret Frances Smith Totten. Both his father and an uncle, the Reverend Felix M. Totten, were members of the North Carolina Annual Conference of the Methodist Protestant Church, and a brother, the Reverend J. Felix Totten, joined the North Carolina Conference of the Methodist Episcopal Church, South.

William T. Totten attended local schools and Oak Ridge Institute, from which he was graduated in 1881. Afterwards he was graduated from Yadkin College and taught at Pilot Mountain, Yadkin College, and other places in North Carolina. He was the last Methodist Protestant minister to obtain a degree from Yadkin College. He was admitted to the conference of his denomination in 1885 and was ordained in 1888. He served charges in Albemarle, Halifax, LaGrange, Mecklenburg County, Greenville, Shiloh, Catawba, Mocksville, Union Grove, and Draper. In 1898 he personally assumed responsibility for the indebtedness of Yadkin College and for the next twenty-six years conducted the school as Yadkin Collegiate Institute. After the institute closed in 1924, when it was consolidated with High Point College, Totten was again given ministerial assignments in the Methodist Protestant Conference.

He married Mrs. Jeannette Barham Daniel of Pleasant Hill in 1891, and they had three children: Henry Roland, John T., and Lucy Battle. After his wife's death in July 1923, he married Callie Tarkington of Chowan County in 1925. She died in 1929, and in 1931 he married Mrs. Ella Norman Cobb, of Halifax, Va., who died in 1936. Totten died at Yadkin College and was buried there.

SEE: Virginia G. Fick, *Country College on the Yadkin* (1984); Greensboro, *Methodist Protestant Herald*, 4 Feb. 1937; Nolan B. Harmon, ed., *Encyclopedia of World Methodism* (1974); *Journal of the North Carolina Annual Conference of the Methodist Protestant Church*; Olin B. Michael, *Yadkin College, 1846–1924: A Historic Sketch* (1939).

RALPH HARDEE RIVES

Tourgée, Albion Winegar (*2 May 1838–21 May 1905*), carpetbagger, judge, writer, and equalitarian crusader, was born in Williamsfield, Ohio, the son of a Methodist farm family that migrated to the Western Reserve from Massachusetts. His father, Valentine, was a descendant of seventeenth-century French Huguenot immigrants, and his mother, Louise Emma Winegar, was of colonial Swiss ancestry. Albion attended high school in Lee, Mass., and alternately taught school and attended Kingsville Acad-

emy in Ohio. He was enrolled at Rochester University from the fall of 1859 until his enlistment in the Union army in May 1861. Paralyzed by a severe back injury received in the Battle of Manassas, he was medically discharged, but in July 1862 he reenlisted as an infantry lieutenant. He participated in the Battle of Perryville, was captured, and spent four months in Confederate prisons. He was exchanged and took part in the Battle of Chickamauga. In December 1863, still troubled by his back injury, he left the service. For the remainder of the war he served as a journalist, studied law, earned his M.A. at Rochester University, and taught school. In 1863 he married Emma Lodoilska Kilbourne; their only child, a daughter, Lodoilska (Aimee), was born in 1870.

Impressed by the needs and opportunities of the postwar South, the Tourgées migrated to North Carolina in 1865 and leased a nursery near Greensboro. Tourgée's hostility toward Confederates and his equalitarian ideals soon impelled him into Reconstruction politics and an alliance with the state's small faction of consistent Unionists. In 1866 he organized Loyal Reconstruction Leagues, championed Negro rights and a radical Reconstruction, published and edited two radical newspapers, and attended the Philadelphia Southern Loyalist Convention. The enfranchisement of the blacks in 1867 opened a new opportunity, and Tourgée was elected to the constitutional convention of 1868 and became one of its most influential delegates and a vigorous promoter of political, legal, and economic reform. He is considered especially responsible for the judicial reforms of the Reconstruction constitution. From 1868 to 1870 he served as one of three code commissioners rewriting the state's law, and in 1868 he was elected a state superior court judge.

During his six years as a judge, Tourgée provoked intense opposition with his outspoken, effective, and equalitarian Republicanism. Like all Republicans of Yankee origin, he was stigmatized as a carpetbagger and was considered "for many years the most thoroughly hated man in North Carolina." His judicial circuit was a center of racial conflict and Ku Klux Klan atrocities, including the brutal assassinations of Wyatt Outlaw and John Walter Stephens in Alamance and Caswell counties respectively. Nonetheless, Tourgée also won recognition for his ability, candor, and courage. He was an excellent judge, and his role in reforming the law brought praise. Becoming one of Greensboro's leading citizens, he was active in a variety of community affairs and was a founder of the Negro school that became Bennett College. He promoted industrial and railroad development and conducted one of the region's early wood-turning industries. Despite ostracism, persecution, and frequent danger, Tourgée proved himself an able and involved citizen of his adopted state, and much in his conduct and achievement demanded respect. There were some remarkable exchanges of mutual admiration between Tourgée and his Southern foes, but Reconstruction politics and the issue of race drove an implacable wedge between them.

Following his judgeship Tourgée was often denied electoral opportunity within his own party because of his Yankee origins. He was, however, elected to the constitutional convention of 1875, where he played a central role. In 1876 he moved to Raleigh as a federal pension agent, and in 1878 his anonymous "C" letters, which humorously exploited Democratic party factionalism, won statewide attention. In the same year, having finally obtained a Republican nomination, he was beaten as a congressional candidate. Convinced that he would never be anything but an alien in the "redeemed" South and probably anticipating an adverse reaction to his forthcoming novel, Tourgée decided to leave.

In 1879 he moved to Colorado and an editorial post with the Denver *Evening Times*. His largely autobiographical novel on Reconstruction, *A Fool's Errand by One of the Fools*, appeared that year and, becoming a sensational success, brought a small fortune and a new career. Five years earlier Tourgée had published a first novel, *Toinette: A Tale of the South*, which dealt with race relations in the slave South, and in 1880 he completed a second Reconstruction novel, *Bricks Without Straw*. Three additional novels on the Civil War period followed, but Tourgée's two Reconstruction novels were the high point of his literary career. His intense concern and immense knowledge of the subject had combined with sufficient literary skill to produce powerful portrayals of conditions, issues, and character types in the Reconstruction South. Recent historical writing has largely confirmed Tourgée's analysis, and *A Fool's Errand* and *Bricks Without Straw* remain historical classics.

In 1881 Tourgée purchased a new home in Mayville, N.Y., on the shores of Lake Chautauqua. From 1881 to 1884 he published and edited a weekly literary magazine, *Our Continent*, which exhausted his fortune. He wrote a variety of additional novels, most of which dealt with the Lake Erie region, and he continued his journalistic work and lectured on the lyceum circuit. Remaining an ardent Republican, he was also a critic of modern industrial society, and his novel, *Murvale Eastman: Christian Socialist* (1890), has been considered "the most carefully considered novel of Christian socialism" ever written. His articles on a variety of social issues appeared in most of the leading journals, and from 1888 to 1898 he wrote a weekly editorial column entitled "A Bystander's Notes" for the Chicago *Inter Ocean*. This column typified Tourgée's incessant crusade for social reform and justice. It delved into practically every issue of the times, but his primary concern remained the race question, and he was without a doubt the nation's leading white advocate of racial equality and justice. In his editorials, essays, and books as well as his public and private affairs, he was forever exposing and denouncing white racism. He lobbied for federal aid to education and a federal election law to that end, he presented the only equalitarian position at the Lake Mohonk Conference on the Negro in 1890, and he worked with black leaders in such endeavors as the founding of the Afro American League and the passage of the Ohio antilynching law of 1896. He founded his own civil rights association in 1891 and was appointed chief counsel by Louisiana black leaders in a legal struggle that culminated in another defeat, the *Plessy v. Ferguson* segregation decision of 1896.

After writing a Republican campaign pamphlet for the election of 1896, *The War of the Standards*, Tourgée was appointed consul to Bordeaux, France, where he served until his death. His body was returned to Mayville, N.Y., and among those in attendance at his funeral were a number of the nation's black leaders. In November 1905 the black Niagara Movement sponsored nationwide memorial services in behalf of "Three Friends of Freedom"—William Lloyd Garrison, Frederick Douglass, and Albion W. Tourgée.

SEE: Daniel Aaron, *The Unwritten War: American Writers and the Civil War* (1973); Samuel A. Ashe, ed., *Biographical History of North Carolina*, vol. 4 (1906); William A. Devin, "Footprints of a Carpetbagger," *Torch* 17 (1944); Dean H. Keller, "A Checklist of the Writings of Albion W. Tourgée (1838–1905)," *Studies in Bibliography: Papers of the Bibliographical Society of the University of Virginia*, vol. 18 (1965); Russel B. Nye, "Judge Tourgée and Reconstruction," *Ohio State Archaeological and Historical Quarterly* 50 (1941);

Otto H. Olsen, *Carpetbagger's Crusade: The Life of Albion Winegar Tourgée* (1965) and "Albion W. Tourgée: Carpetbagger," *North Carolina Historical Review* 40 (1963); Albion W. Tourgée Papers, Chautauqua County Historical Society, Westfield, N.Y. (available on microfilm), and Tourgée's Reconstruction novels; Edmund Wilson, *Patriotic Gore: Studies in the Literature of the Civil War* (1962).

OTTO H. OLSEN

Towe, Kenneth Crawford *(19 Jan. 1893–6 Jan. 1978)*, chemical company executive, was born in Elizabeth City to the Reverend William (1865–1946), a Methodist circuit rider, and Katherine Crawford Towe (1868–1942). Educated at public schools in Elizabeth City, Towe worked in a post office, grocery store, and lumber, textile, and paper mills before attending Trinity College (now Duke University) during 1914–17. In 1917 he enlisted in the army. He attended the officers' training camp at Fort Oglethorpe, Ga., and was commissioned a second lieutenant in the Quartermaster Corps. He served at Camp Jackson, S.C., and at the General Intermediate Storage Depot, Gievres, France. Discharged a captain in July 1919, he began working as secretary to the chief executive of Roanoke Mills in Roanoke Rapids.

In 1923 Towe became head buyer for the Childs Restaurant chain in New York City. Three years later he joined the American Cyanamid Company in New York and began a thirty-two-year career in the accounting department. He was named assistant treasurer in 1928, treasurer and a director in 1939, vice-president of finance in 1945, and president in January 1952. In 1957 he was elected chairman of the board, a position he held until his retirement in April 1958.

Towe served as a director of the Campbell Soup Company, Duke Power Company, Morgan Guaranty Trust Company, Putnam Trust Company, Boys' Club of America, and Michigan Gas Utilities Company and as a trustee of the Columbia-Presbyterian Medical Center, the National Safety Council, Duke University, and the Duke Endowment. He was a member of the National Association of Manufacturers, the Newcomen Society of America, the Masonic order (Shriner), Omicron Delta Kappa, and Kappa Alpha. Towe was a Methodist.

On 28 Apr. 1934, in Bethesda, Md., he married Elizabeth McCarn. They had three sons: Kenneth McCarn, Rolf Harvey, and Teri Noel. Towe died in Greenwich, Conn., his home for forty years, and was buried in Rocky Mount.

SEE: Duke Endowment, *Annual Report of the Duke Endowment* (1977); *Fortune* magazine, June 1952; *Nat. Cyc. Am. Biog.*, current vol. 1, 1953–59 (1960); *New York Times*, 8 Jan. 1978; Raleigh *News and Observer*, 13 Nov. 1957.

SUZANNE S. LEVY

Town, Ithiel *(3 Oct. 1784–13 June 1844)*, architect, was born in Thompson, Conn., to Archelaus and Martha Johnson Town. An ancestor was William Towne, who was in Salem, Mass., as early as 1640. Archelaus, a farmer, died when Ithiel was only eight and the lad, as soon as possible, went to work as a house carpenter and schoolteacher. Going to Boston, he attended a school conducted by Asher Benjamin, an architect and writer of books on the subject, thus receiving as good training as was available in the country at that time.

His career began with the construction of Center Church on the New Haven, Conn., green, a project in which he showed ability as a designer and engineer and familiarity with classical architectural designs. In 1814 he was commissioned to design and build Trinity Church on the same green, and this work established his reputation. On 28 Jan. 1820 he received a patent for a new system of constructing wooden bridges, known as the Town Lattice Truss, and during this period he was busy not only in working on public buildings and residences but also in supervising the construction of bridges. Among others, he built a bridge across the James River near Richmond, Va., and one in North Carolina. From this time on he apparently had ample means. In 1827–28 he was a partner of Martin E. Thompson in New York.

Town was one of the great leaders of Greek Revival architecture in the United States. According to the diary of Alexander Jackson Davis, he designed the Greek Revival asylum building on the grounds on which the Cathedral of St. John the Divine in New York was later built. He assisted William P. Elliot in designing the first wing, facing F Street, of the Patent Office in Washington, D.C., now the home of the National Portrait Gallery and the National Collection of Fine Arts of the Smithsonian Institution. It has been called "one of the noblest examples of the Greek mode in the Classical Revival style of architecture to appear in this country."

In 1829 Town formed a partnership with Alexander Jackson Davis, with offices in New York. The firm of Town and Davis became one of the best as well as the best known in the country. Some of its important works were the City Hall in Hartford, Conn., and the state capitols of Connecticut, Indiana, and North Carolina. In August 1833 Town and Davis were engaged to work on the capitol at Raleigh. "They modified and greatly improved the earlier design, giving the Capitol essentially its present appearance and plan." They established the form of rooms in the building and clarified "the discipline of architectural style." During the building of the capitol there were thirteen commissioners and five directly responsible architects, so many must be credited with its completion. In the state archives at Raleigh are receipts for "architectural services rendered the Board of Commissioners for rebuilding the Capitol of North Carolina." These were signed by Ithiel Town in 1834. The legislature that convened at the end of 1834 criticized the expenditures of the board, and the new board severed connections with the firm of Town and Davis to effect economies, leaving work on the capitol to David Paton, an architect who had recently arrived from Scotland, and whom Town and Davis had chosen as their representative in work on the capitol.

Town traveled in Europe in 1829–30 with Samuel F. B. Morse, who selected him as one of the two representatives of architecture in the founding of the National Academy of Design in New York City. A portrait of him, painted by Nathaniel Jocelyn (1796–1881) between 1830 and 1840, is in the academy's possession. The dimensions are thirty-six inches by twenty-nine inches, and the subject is seated, head to the left, with both hands showing. It was a gift to the academy in 1941 of George Dudley Seymour of New Haven, Conn.

Town published *The Outlines of a Plan for Establishing in New York an Academy of the Fine Arts* (1835) and *A Detail of Some Particular Services Performed in America . . . 1776–1779: From a Journal Kept on Board H.M.S. Rainbow, by Commodore Sir George Collier* (1835). The latter was based on material he bought in England. He had an immense library of 11,000 volumes plus thousands of loose engravings, medieval manuscripts, incunabula, objects of art, and old prints. For many years this was the finest collection relating to architecture and the fine arts in the United States. Five catalogues were issued for the sale after his death. Part of the collection went to Yale University.

Town never married but had a daughter, Etha (1809–71), who bore his name and lived with him. Her mother was also named Etha. The daughter married Dr. William T. Peters in 1826, and they had eight children. Town died in New Haven, where he always maintained his home, although he was associated with New York both professionally and socially. He was buried in Grove Street Cemetery, the grave being marked by a simple marble headstone.

SEE: *Appleton's Cyclopedia of American Biography*, vol. 6 (1887); Marshall W. Butt, *Portsmouth under Four Flags, 1752–1970* (1971); *DAB*, vol. 9 (1964); William Dunlap, *History of the Rise and Progress of the Arts of Design in the United States*, vol. 3 (1965); Cecil D. Elliott, "The North Carolina State Capitol," *Southern Architect* (June and July 1958); Roger Hale Newton, *Town and Davis, Architects: Pioneers in American Revivalist Architecture, 1812–1870* (1942); William B. O'Neal, *Architectural Drawing in Virginia, 1819–1969* (1969); George Dudley Seymour, *New Haven* (1942); Leaflets—*The Capitol of North Carolina* (n.d.) and *National Collection of Fine Arts (&) National Portrait Gallery* (1968); Town letters and scrapbook (Yale University Library, New Haven, Conn.). Other sources include material gathered in research at the American Institute of Architects Library, The Octagon, Washington, D.C.; Archives of the State of North Carolina, Raleigh, N.C.; and Catalog of American Portraits, National Portrait Gallery, Washington, D.C.

CAROLINE HOLMES BIVINS

Townsend, Newman Alexander *(1 May 1882–11 Apr. 1951)*, lawyer, legislator, judge, and federal official, was born in the community of Raynham, Robeson County, the son of the Reverend Jackson and Sarah Melissa Oliver Townsend. The Townsend family had emigrated from the parish of Raynham in Norfolk, England. He attended Oak Ridge Military Institute and was graduated from The University of North Carolina in 1905, studied law there in 1905–6, and was admitted to the bar in February 1906. He was president of his senior class and, selected a member of the all-southern football team of 1904, was considered one of the greatest ends ever to attend the university. He began to practice law in Dunn, where he was mayor in 1911–12, town attorney during the period 1917–21, and represented Harnett County in the General Assembly sessions of 1921, 1923, 1925, and 1927. From 1927 to 1930 he was a superior court judge and in 1930–31 served as executive counsel to Governor O. Max Gardner.

In 1934 Townsend went to Washington, D.C., as a special assistant attorney general of the United States to work with the assistant solicitor general in the Department of Justice and to organize a new office in that department to perform special tasks for the president. His principal duties pertained to executive orders, a position that brought him into association with President Franklin D. Roosevelt. The *New York Times*, for example, reported on 7 May 1939 that Townsend had conferred with Roosevelt on government reorganization. Although he intended to remain in this position for only six months, he stayed nine years. Among his most significant acts were negotiating acceptance of Paul Mellon's National Gallery of Art gift and preparing the legal argument that rationalized lend-lease in 1940. Apparently he also played a key role in the preparation of Roosevelt's deed of gift establishing the presidential library. Townsend was exceedingly modest about his role in Washington, and there was little if no contemporary recognition of his contributions, nor did his name appear in the standard biographical volumes of the time.

In 1944 Townsend joined the Washington law firm of Gardner, Morrison, and Rogers, of which he later became a partner. He married Myrtle Agnes Wade of Dunn in 1909, and they had three children: Newman A., Jr., Benjamin O., and Sarah Margaret. He died in Washington and was buried in Greenwood Cemetery, Dunn.

SEE: *Asheville Citizen*, 12 Apr. 1951; Chapel Hill, *Daily Tar Heel*, 24 Mar. 1932; Daniel L. Grant, *Alumni History of the University of North Carolina* (1924); Philip Kopper, Chevy Chase, Md., to William S. Powell, 15 July 1990; *New York Times*, 12 Apr. 1951; *North Carolina Manual* (1927); Raleigh *News and Observer*, 7 Oct. 1934, 14 Jan. 1944, 12 Apr. 1951; *The State* magazine, 20 Aug. 1938; *Washington Post*, 12 Apr. 1951.

WILLIAM S. POWELL

Trent, Josiah Charles *(7 Aug. 1914–10 Dec. 1948)*, surgeon and historian of medicine, was born in Okmulgee, Okla., the youngest of four children, to parents of English ancestry. His father, Josiah Charles Trent, was a native of Arkansas and a merchant who traded with both settlers and Indians and who used his store as a bank. His mother, Mary Simpson Trent, was a native of Mississippi and a music teacher. Although his father died when Trent was a boy, he attended public schools in Okmulgee and matriculated at Duke University, graduating in 1934 at age nineteen. He began his study of medicine at the University of Pennsylvania, where, beyond the general run of medical courses, he developed particular interests in surgical pathology and the history of medicine. Awarded the M.D. with honors from Pennsylvania in 1938, he took a medical internship at Ford Hospital in Detroit. During this year he and his wife began the collections of rare books in the fields of medicine and literature that were one expression of Dr. Trent's conviction that current medicine is most successfully practiced and understood by persons who are knowledgeable of its history.

In 1939 Trent began a six-year residency at the Duke University School of Medicine. He developed a special interest in the services that supported surgery, organizing a blood bank for the hospital and advocating establishment of a Division of Anesthesiology in the School of Medicine. In 1941 he underwent surgery for an abdominal mass that was identified as an abdominal lymphosarcoma. During the next seven years, while the disease was held in check, he published fifty papers, forty-three on the history of medicine. The specifically surgical papers reported on the value, or disvalue, of specific operative procedures. The majority of the history papers were titled *Thumbnail Sketches of Eminent Physicians*, reflecting his belief that young physicians should know the ideals and accomplishments of the profession as expressed in the lives of its most successful practitioners. The articles frequently were grouped in series such as "The Evolution of the Aseptic Principle in Surgery," "The Story of Yellow Fever," "Obstetrics and Gynecology in America," and "Chapters in the History of Thoracic Surgery." By this device his historical teaching moved beyond the biographical to become a means of describing the parameters of entire fields. He used this device in an elective career for medical students as well as in his publications.

On completion of his residency, Trent was offered a choice of positions at Duke: to become a junior member of the Department of Surgery in general surgery or to develop as head a Division of Thoracic Surgery. He opted for the second alternative, asking for two years in which to gain additional training, and was appointed instructor in thoracic surgery at the University of Michigan under Dr. John Alexander. At Michigan he accumulated both operative and administrative experience in the management of thoracic surgical cases. In 1946, however, he underwent an operation to relieve intracranial pressure resulting from his lymphosarcoma. He soon was released from his position at Michigan, at his request, to return to Duke and organize the Division of Thoracic Surgery. The essence of his administrative technique was cooperation. He correlated the work of his division with the parallel group in the Department of Medicine and broadened his program by instituting joint conferences in tuberculosis sanatoria. Trent stepped up his involvement with the history of medicine, presenting papers at the American Association of the History of Medicine and the Grolier Club in 1948. He arranged the session on the history of medicine at the annual meeting of the American Medical Association according to his personal philosophy. At the session, participants who had made important contributions to medicine described their work, and subsequent discussion focused on the concept of progress in medicine. Beginning in January 1948 he served as a trustee of Lincoln Hospital, which originally had been a gift of his wife's family for the care of blacks in Durham. In November, however, his disease became widely disseminated, and he died in Durham the following month.

Trent's professional affiliations reflected his dual interests in surgery and the history of medicine. He was a member of the Durham-Orange County Medical Society (secretary-treasurer, 1947–48), Founders Group of the American Board of Thoracic Surgery, American Board of Surgery, Society of University of Surgeons, American College of Surgeons, National Tuberculosis Association, and National Trudeau Society. He dropped his membership in the Southern Medical Association because he felt that it discriminated against black physicians. Trent also served on the editorial boards of the *North Carolina Medical Journal* and the *Journal of the History of Medicine and Allied Sciences* and was honorary consultant of the Army Medical Library. Memberships in the American Association of the History of Medicine, Charaka Club, and Grolier Club reflected his interest in the history of medicine and in collecting books and manuscripts.

Trent was a Democrat in politics and a member of the Methodist church. In 1938 he married Mary Duke Biddle of Durham, and they had four daughters: Mary Duke Trent Jones, Sarah Elizabeth Trent Harris, Rebecca Gray Trent Kirkland, and Barbara Biddle Trent Kimbrell. In 1945 they gave their collection of Walt Whitman materials to Duke University in order to promote student interest in and use of original sources. Following his death Mrs. Trent donated their larger collection—4,000 volumes and 2,000 manuscripts on the history of medicine—to the Duke University School of Medicine for the same purposes. In an era of medical specialization, Dr. Trent insisted, the education of the whole person must not be neglected. The collection was housed in the Trent Room of the library of the Duke University Medical Center, where his bust and portrait were displayed and his collected works made available.

SEE: *Bulletin of the History of Medicine*, no. 23 (1949); *Journal of the History of Medicine and Allied Sciences* 3 (1948 [portrait]); *Nat. Cyc. Am. Biog.*, vol. 36 (1950 [portrait]); *North Carolina Medical Journal* 10 (1949).

JAMES F. GIFFORD

Tribble, Harold Wayland *(18 Nov. 1899–17 June 1986)*, theologian and educator, was born in Charlottesville, Va., the third son and sixth child of Henry Wise and Estelle

Carlton Rawlings Tribble. At the time of his birth, his fa- ther, a Baptist minister, was president of Rawlings Insti- tute, a college at Charlottesville for women. In 1909 the family moved to Lake City, Fla., where Henry Wise Trib- ble became president of Columbia College (later absorbed by Stetson University). Young Harold received his early education in the primary and secondary schools operated by Rawlings Institute and Columbia College. After two years at Columbia College (1915–17) at the collegiate level, he entered Richmond College (later the University of Richmond), where he was awarded the A.B. degree in 1919. At Richmond he played varsity basketball and dur- ing his senior year was editor-in-chief of the weekly stu- dent newspaper, the *Collegian*. He also served in the Stu- dent Army Training Corps at Richmond and at Platts- burg, N.Y.

In 1919, at age twenty, he was ordained into the Baptist ministry and entered Southern Baptist Theological Semi- nary, Louisville, Ky., where he received the Th.M. degree in 1922 and the Th.D., summa cum laude, in 1925. Con- tinuing formal study, he earned the M.A. degree in phi- losophy at the University of Louisville in 1927. Three years later he began the first of several periods of study abroad, enrolling at the University of Edinburgh, in Scot- land, which awarded him the Ph.D. degree in 1937. He at- tended the University of Bonn, Germany, in 1931 and the University of Basel, Switzerland, in 1936.

Meanwhile, Tribble had been appointed assistant pro- fessor of theology (1925) and then a full professor (1929) at Southern Baptist Theological Seminary. During the twenties and thirties he served as pastor of Baptist churches in Cropper, Christiansburg, New Castle, and Simpsonville, Ky. Throughout his career he was widely in demand on college campuses as a preacher for special oc- casions such as religious emphasis weeks and commence- ments. While teaching at the seminary he wrote three books—*Our Doctrines* (1929), *From Adam to Moses* (1934), and *Salvation* (1940)—and revised E. Y. Mullins's *The Bap- tist Faith* (1935). He was also the author of many articles published in theological journals.

Moving from teaching to educational administration, Tribble became president of Andover Newton Theologi- cal School, Newton Center, Mass., in 1947. A year before he accepted this position, an event had occurred in North Carolina that would later take him there for the culmina- tion of his career as an educational administrator. In 1946 the Z. Smith Reynolds Foundation of Winston-Salem of- fered to give Wake Forest College $350,000 a year in per- petuity on condition that the college be moved from its lo- cation in Wake County to Winston-Salem and that an adequate plant be built to care for at least two thousand students. Wake Forest and the Baptist State Convention of North Carolina, its sponsoring body, accepted the offer, and a campaign to raise the needed funds was launched.

On 29 Apr. 1949, after several heart attacks, Thurman Delna Kitchin, president of Wake Forest College, resigned so a younger, more active leader could be sought. Already well known to the trustees, Tribble on 4 May 1950 was elected to succeed Kitchin with the clear understanding that he would vigorously pursue the campaign to move the institution to Winston-Salem. The *Winston-Salem Jour- nal* welcomed the "eminent minister-educator-adminis- trator" to North Carolina, declaring that "His presence and personality stimulated new confidence in the re- moval project." The Raleigh *News and Observer* noted after the opening of the fall semester the "cordial admiration atmosphere" between the students and faculty and their new president.

In his inaugural address Tribble declared that the de- velopment of the college into a university was "inescapa-

bly implicit in the removal and enlargement program." He foresaw Wake Forest as "including all the areas of learning that are essential in culture at its best, and some schools or departments devoted to scholarly specializa- tion, and a graduate school of first rank." The *Biblical Re- corder* quoted President Gordon Gray of The University of North Carolina as saying: "This is a case of a fortunate meeting of the college and the man. . . . Harold Tribble has, in abundance, integrity, vision, passion, and a sound concept of the role of education in this changing world."

The task of fund-raising went so well that ground- breaking exercises, with President Harry S Truman as the principal speaker, were held on 15 Oct. 1951. But Tribble's administration was not destined always to be peaceful and harmonious. Some alumni still opposed the move, and as the prospect grew nearer they refused to accept it. Many believed, albeit without foundation, that Tribble opposed the athletic program and intended to deempha- size it. Moreover, certain segments of the Baptist State Convention felt that the college was not following Baptist traditions. Tribble's aggressiveness and sometimes abra- sive personality offended some of those with whom he worked, including several members of the board of trustees. On 16 Nov. 1955 the president of the board ap- pointed a nine-man committee to study the "serious mat- ters involving the College and its administration." After seven more months of bitter controversy both within and outside the board, the trustees defeated—20–13—a resolu- tion to discharge Tribble as president.

Despite the turmoil, fund-raising and building con- tinued, enabling the school to open on the new $19.5 mil- lion campus on 18 June 1956. But this did not end the president's troubles. The trustees, responding to student pressure and Tribble's recommendation, voted to allow dancing on the new campus, only to have the Baptist State Convention force them to rescind the action. Trib- ble's later proposal to modify the requirements for mem- bership on the board of trustees, all of whom had to be North Carolina Baptists, by allowing up to sixteen of the thirty-six to be non-Baptists and non–North Carolinians failed by a narrow margin to gain the convention's ap- proval. Although defeated at the meeting, Tribble re- ceived, as reported in *Old Gold and Black*, a "tumultuous reception from the student body . . . on his return from the Baptist State Convention in Wilmington." He thanked the assembled students, expressing confidence that the pro- posal to liberalize relations with the convention "would win in the future" because "what we are doing is for a better Wake Forest College and that is our destiny."

During Tribble's administration the total assets of the institution grew from $10,454,000 to $91,267,900 and the annual budget from $1,573,444 to $13,587,000. The library budget rose from $40,700 to $532,000. The student body, despite higher requirements for admission, grew from 1,750 to more than 3,000, and the proportionate increase in the faculty was larger. In 1950 only 43 percent of the faculty held a doctoral degree, whereas in 1967 the figure was 72 percent. Under his leadership, the student body had been racially integrated and the curriculum ex- panded to include, among many new features, graduate study in the arts and sciences. In January 1967 the trustees recognized the development that had occurred by chang- ing the name of the institution to Wake Forest University. That June Tribble retired after the stormiest yet most pro- ductive period in the school's history.

He received the honorary degrees of D.D., Stetson Uni- versity (1930), and LL.D., Union University (1939), Wake Forest College (1948), University of Richmond (1949), Duke University (1952), and The University of North Car- olina (1952). On 10 June 1925 he married Nelle Louise

Futch (1898–1984), of Lake City, Fla., a 1925 graduate of the Women's Missionary Union Training School, Louisville, Ky. They had three children: Harold Wayland, Jr., of Long Island, N.Y., a clergyman; Betty May (Mrs. Richard C. Barnett), of Winston-Salem, an educator; and Barbara Ann (Mrs. Harvey R. Holding), of Atlanta, Ga., an artist. A Rotarian and a Mason, Tribble was also a member of Phi Beta Kappa, Omicron Delta Kappa, Kappa Sigma, Tau Kappa Alpha, Wake Forest Baptist Church, and the Old Town Club. Golf was his hobby. His official Wake Forest portrait, which was hung in the classroom building named for him, was painted by Belgian artist Alfred Jonniaux. After retiring he lived in Blowing Rock, Port St. Lucie, Fla., and the Moravian Home in Winston-Salem. A memorial service was held at Wake Forest University on 15 June 1986.

SEE: Betty May Tribble Barnett, personal contact, 15 Feb. 1987; Raleigh, *Biblical Recorder*, 9 Dec. 1950; Raleigh *News and Observer*, 24 Sept. 1950, 6 Nov. 1960; Bynum Shaw, "A History of the Presidency of Wake Forest University" (typescript) and Harold Wayland Tribble Papers (Wake Forest University Archives, Winston-Salem); Harold W. Tribble, *A Seventeen Year Report of the Administration of Wake Forest University* (1967); "Wake Forest University: A Proposal: An Interview with Dr. Tribble," *Wake Forest Magazine*, June 1963; *Who's Who in America* (1966–67); *Winston-Salem Journal*, 10 Aug. 1950, 18 June 1986; Winston-Salem *Journal and Sentinel*, 3 Sept. 1950; Winston-Salem, *Old Gold and Black*, 18 Nov. 1963.

HENRY S. STROUPE

Trigg, Harold Leonard *(15 Dec. 1893–29 Aug. 1978),* educator and college president, was born in Lynchburg, Va., the son of Frank and Ellen Preston Taylor Trigg. After attending Princess Anne High School, Md., he earned a B.A. degree from Morgan State College, Baltimore (1913), an M.A. degree at Syracuse University (1918), and several years later a doctorate in education at Columbia University. Following his graduation from Morgan State, Trigg taught mathematics at Bennett College, Greensboro, for three years. He served a year in the U.S. Army (1918–19), achieving the rank of sergeant major. After his discharge from the army, he took the position of professor of education at New Orleans College.

In 1921 Trigg moved to North Carolina, where he made his home for the next fifty years. After teaching at Winston-Salem Teachers' College for two years, he was principal of Berry O'Kelly School, Method (1923–26). He returned to Winston-Salem in 1926 to become principal of Columbian Heights Schools. His work in education was recognized in 1928, when he was appointed to the State Department of Public Instruction as supervisor of Negro high schools. Trigg held this position for eleven years except for a leave of absence to serve as associate director of the National Survey of Vocational Education and Guidance for Negroes in the U.S. Office of Education (1936–37).

On 13 Oct. 1939 Trigg was elected president of Elizabeth City State Teachers' College. When he assumed the presidency, the college was in the process of changing from a two-year to a four-year school, which he successfully completed. Despite wartime conditions during most of his administration, enrollment increased by 33 percent. On 25 Sept. 1945 President Trigg left his position to become associate executive director of the Southern Regional Council, Inc., with headquarters in Atlanta, whose primary objective was to improve racial and economic conditions in the thirteen southern states. After two years he resigned to accept the presidency of St. Augustine's

College, Raleigh. Trigg was the first black and the first layman to hold this office since the founding of the college in 1867. During his administration (1947–55), academic standards were raised, the physical plant was enlarged and improved, and the Penick Hall of Science was built. Following his resignation as president on 6 Jan. 1955, Trigg became a lecturer at Livingstone College, Salisbury, continuing in the post until 1975. During this period he made his home in Greensboro, where he became an active member of the Church of the Redeemer.

In 1949 Governor Kerr Scott appointed Trigg to the State Board of Education, making him the first black to serve on that board. Regarding the appointment, the Asheville *Citizen-Times* commented: "Because of his wide experience as a teacher in the State, and his consequent knowledge of educational problems, in general and as they apply to his race, it seems to be the unanimous agreement that Dr. Trigg is admirably qualified." He remained on the board until 1973.

Trigg married Geraldine L. Nelson of Savannah, Ga., on 16 Sept. 1920, and they had three children: Leota Nelson, Mrs. Melva Camille Currier, and Dr. Harold L., Jr. In 1940 his alma mater, Morgan College, awarded him the honorary degree of doctor of education. An Episcopalian, he served on the board of directors of the National Conference of Christians and Jews. He was a member of the National Council of Family Relations, a thirty-third degree Mason, and a Democrat. In 1978 the Greensboro *Daily News* observed that Trigg's death was "a profound loss to Greensboro and to North Carolina. His career as one of the state's outstanding black educators touched both the public schools and higher education, distinguishing both by his leadership." He was buried in Forest Lawn Cemetery, Greensboro.

SEE: Asheville *Citizen-Times*, 24 Apr. 1949; Greensboro *Daily News*, 26 Apr. 1949, 1 and 4 Sept. 1978; *Journals of the Diocese of North Carolina* (1947–55); William S. Powell, ed., *North Carolina Lives* (1962); Raleigh *News and Observer*, 14 Oct. 1939, 24 Nov. 1945, 14 Jan. 1955, 30 Aug. 1978; *Who's Who in the South and Southwest* (1947).

LAWRENCE F. LONDON

Trollinger, Benjamin Newton *(27 Oct. 1810–26 Sept. 1862),* textile manufacturer and business adventurer, was born in the community of Haw River in Orange (now Alamance) County, the son of Joseph John and Elizabeth Rony Trollinger. The Trollingers of Haw River were descended from Adam Trollinger, who was born near the Rhine in Germany and settled on the west bank of Haw River about 1745.

Benjamin N. Trollinger was a member of the North Carolina General Assembly in the 1836 session. Eight years later, in 1844, he built one of the first cotton mills in present-day Alamance County. A promoter of internal improvements, he was a great supporter of the North Carolina Railroad. He and his partner and brother-in-law, Dr. D. A. Montgomery, were large contractors for the railroad in Alamance, Orange, Wake, and Johnston counties. They made brick and built bridges over Haw River, Back Creek, and both crossings of the Eno River at Hillsborough. They also ran a steam sawmill at Asbury and Cary, Wake County, for the purpose of cutting ties for the railroad.

The North Carolina Railroad wanted to locate its repair and maintenance shops on land slightly west of what is now Burlington and were shocked when they found that people in western Alamance could not be persuaded to sell their land. Had not Ben Trollinger come to the rescue at this point, the county might have lost the shops altogether. The railroad, he said, could build shops on his property two miles west of Graham. The railroad accepted this offer after acquiring several other tracts. This land, totaling 632 acres, cost the railroad $6,748.

After the railroad was completed, Trollinger built a hotel at Haw River with the hope that it would become a stopping place for the trains. However, another hotel went up at Company Shops, and the Trollinger hotel failed. Being a man of great energy, Ben Trollinger did not stop but went to Clayton, Johnston County, and began producing spirits of turpentine. This enterprise proved profitable, and, needing a larger area in which to work, he moved to Richmond County, where he and his father bought 5,000 acres of pine land in order to produce turpentine there. The operation was successful, but when the Civil War began in 1861, foreseeing that the Confederacy would need salt, he started two separate salt works south of Wilmington.

There, in the summer of 1862, he became ill with yellow fever. He died and was buried at Haw River.

Trollinger married Nancy Elizabeth Montgomery, and they had a son and two daughters: John, Sallie, and Mary Frances.

SEE: Ruth Blackwelder, *The Age of Orange* (1961); Julian Hughes, *Development of the Textile Industry in Alamance County* (1965); S. W. Stockard, *The History of Alamance* (1900); Walter Whitaker, *Centennial History of Alamance County* (1949).

LARRY W. FUQUA

Trotter, John Scott (*14 June 1908–30 Oct. 1975*), musician, was born in Charlotte, the son of John Scott and Lelia Bias Trotter. He attended local schools, studied piano under Ida Moore Alexander, and in 1925 he entered The University of North Carolina. In Chapel Hill he joined a dance band formed by his childhood friend, Hal Kemp. Kemp had entered the university in 1922 and was graduated in 1926, but Trotter withdrew near the end of his first year to join Kemp's band as pianist and arranger, a position he held until 1936. In Charlotte Kemp and Trotter provided music for Epworth League meetings and attracted considerable attention because of their musical ability.

In 1936 Trotter was in California orchestrating songs for Paramount Picture's *Pennies from Heaven* when he met Bing Crosby and began a seventeen-year association. Trotter became music director for the Crosby radio show and later for the Crosby television show. He did the arrangement for Crosby's popular recording, "White Christmas." For ten years (1954–64) Trotter was music director for George Gobel's television show. He was also music director of "The Kraft Music Hall," "Philco Radio Time," and "The Chesterfield Show." Trotter was twice nominated for awards: once for an Emmy for his music in a "Peanuts" special on television and once in 1970 for an Academy Award for music in the film, *A Boy Named Charlie Brown*.

He died of cancer in Mount Sinai Hospital, Hollywood, and was buried in Sharon Memorial Park, Charlotte. Surviving him were a sister, Mrs. Margaret Kinghorn, of California, and two brothers, William of Charlotte and Robert of Eugene, Oreg.

SEE: *Charlotte Observer*, 21 Jan. 1940, 31 Oct. 1975, 7 Feb. 1976; Calvin Jarrett, "Tar Heel Musical Stars," *Music Journal* 29 (January 1971); *New York Times*, 31 Oct. 1975.

ROSAMOND PUTZEL

Trousdale, William (*23 Sept. 1790–27 Mar. 1872*), soldier, statesman, and ambassador, was born in Orange County, the son of James and Elizabeth Dobbins Trousdale. James Trousdale had commanded a company of North Carolina Patriots in the American Revolution. In return for his services, the state of North Carolina granted him 640 acres of land in the Tennessee Territory, where he moved his family, including young William, in 1796.

Trousdale grew up accustomed to the deprivations and wilds of frontier life. The educational advantages available to him were very limited, but with the influx of civilization there came improved facilities. Over the years he received instruction from the Reverend Gideon Blackburn and later John Hall, both fine scholars of that area and time. In 1813, while Trousdale was a pupil under Dr. Blackburn, the Creek Indians began hostilities in Tennessee. Trousdale entered Captain William Edward's company of mounted riflemen and was soon elected a third lieutenant. He fought under General John Coffee in the Battle of Tallashatchee and a short time later served under General Andrew Jackson at the Battle of Talledega, where he gained notice for his daring and bravery.

When the Creek War was over, Trousdale returned home briefly, only to reenter service in 1814 following the burning of Washington, D.C., by the British. He enrolled in George Elliott's company of Tennessee volunteers and served as a private throughout his enlistment despite numerous offers of a staff position. His company was part of General Jackson's army that surrounded the Spanish fort at Pensacola, Fla., on 6 Nov. 1814. Trousdale was directly responsible for the recruiting of volunteers requested by Jackson to storm the fort. Fortunately this action was unnecessary, as the fort surrendered prior to the hour of battle. The army was then moved to New Orleans to prevent the city's capture by the British. On 23 Dec. 1814 Coffee's brigade came into contact with the British force, and the company in which Trousdale served was credited with the capture of a number of British officers and troops. Trousdale also participated in the battles of 27 Dec. 1814 and 1 and 8 Jan. 1815. At the end of the conflict he returned to Tennessee to finish his studies under John Hall. He later read law and in 1820 was admitted to the bar.

In 1836 Trousdale volunteered his services in the quelling of the Indian uprising in Florida. At the command of a Tennessee regiment with the rank of colonel, he proceeded to Florida and participated in two set battles and several skirmishes. In these actions he distinguished himself by his fearlessness. Jackson offered him an appointment as brigadier general in the U.S. Army following the end of hostilities, but Trousdale declined, stating that he desired no connection with the army except in times of war.

In 1847, with the Mexican War pending, President James K. Polk commissioned Trousdale a colonel of infantry and assigned him to General Winfield Scott's army. Landing in Mexico on 13 June 1847 after the outbreak of the war, Trousdale engaged the enemy at the Battle of Contreras on 19 July 1847. However, he became most noted for his actions in the Battle of Molino del Rey on 8–13 September. On the twelfth of September his regiment bore the brunt of the Mexican attack and repulsed the enemy. Although Colonel Trousdale was badly wounded with his right arm shattered by two rifle balls, he maintained his position with great firmness, repulsed an enemy assault, stormed an enemy battery, and turned the guns on its retreating defenders. This decisive action virtually ended the Mexican War. Trousdale returned to private life, but on 20 Aug. 1848, "for gallant and meritorious conduct," he was made a brigadier general by brevet in the U.S. Army on the appointment of President Polk.

In 1849 General Trousdale, after losing in congressional elections in earlier years, was nominated by the Democrats for the governorship of Tennessee. He won this post but was defeated for reelection by a small margin in 1851. On 24 May 1853 President Franklin Pierce appointed him to the prestigious post of ambassador to Brazil. During the four years he served, he induced the Brazilian government to open up the Amazon River to commerce and extended the friendly relations between that country and the United States. At the termination of this service, Trousdale retired and began to nurse a rheumatic affliction that had long caused him pain. During the Civil War he cast his sympathies with those of his state but was unable to serve the Confederate cause due to physical decrepitude.

In March 1872 Trousdale contracted pneumonia, which impaired his health and his physical powers. His death at age eighty-three was mourned by the entire state. In 1827 he had married Mary Ann Bugg, who bore him seven children: Maria Louisa, Caroline Valeria, Belvederia Adelaid, Ophelia Alice, Charles William, Julius Augustus, and Frances Elizabeth.

SEE: Robert M. McBride and others, eds., *Biographical Directory of the Tennessee General Assembly*, vol. 1 (1975); J. A. Trousdale, "History of the Life of General William Trousdale," *Tennessee Historical Magazine* 2 (June 1916); Karl Truesdell, *The Trousdale Genealogy* (1952); Robert H. White, ed., *Messages of the Governors of Tennessee*, vol. 4 (1957).

CLAUDE H. SNOW, JR.

Truett, George Washington *(6 May 1867–7 July 1944)*, clergyman, was born on a farm near Hayesville, Clay County, the seventh child of Charles Levi and Mary Rebecca Kimsey Truett. His father, a native of Buncombe County, was of English and Scots-Irish ancestry; his mother, of Scots-Irish descent, was the daughter of James Kimsey and the niece of Elijah Kimsey, both well-known Baptist preachers in the North Carolina mountains. Charles Levi Truett's family lived in Cherokee County at the time the older children were born but later moved to Clay to take advantage of the better educational opportunities available there. Although his circumstances ranged between poverty and simple comfort, he always supplied his family with books and periodicals suitable for a religiously oriented household.

From 1875 to 1885 George Washington Truett attended Hicksville Academy (later called Hayesville Academy), operated by John O. Hicks, a highly regarded schoolmaster. By the time Truett was eighteen, he had completed all of the courses offered by the academy and wanted to go to college to study law. Needing money, he began teaching in a one-room public school on Crooked Creek in Towns County, Ga., just over the state line from his North Carolina home. In 1887 he founded and became principal of Hiawassee Academy in Towns County. The next year an impromptu speech before the Georgia Baptist Convention about his school brought him to public attention. He so stirred his hearers that they determined to support the school, and one even offered to pay his expenses if he would attend Mercer University. Many have believed that the clear diction and sharp pronunciation that characterized Truett's speaking then and afterwards may be attributed in part to the fact that at home he practiced pronouncing every word distinctly, forcing his lips to do their part, for the benefit of his deaf brother, who depended on lip reading.

In the summer of 1889 Truett followed his parents to Whitewright, Grayson County, Tex., where they had migrated early that year. That fall he entered Grayson Junior College in Whitewright, and the next year he was ordained to the ministry by the Whitewright Baptist Church. From 1890 to 1893 he was financial secretary of Baylor University, traveling for twenty-three months and raising $92,000 to free the university of debt. For the next four years he was a student at Baylor, receiving the A.B. degree in 1897. Baylor awarded him the D.D. degree only two years later and a few years after that elected him to the presidency, which he declined. The LL.D. degree was conferred by Alabama, Baylor, and Southern Methodist.

While a student at Baylor, Truett was pastor of East Waco Baptist Church. In 1897 he became pastor of First Baptist Church, Dallas, Tex., a position he held until his death forty-seven years later. During his pastorate membership increased from 715 to 7,804; a total of 19,531 new members were received, and total contributions exceeded $6 million

It was in the period of World War I that Truett reached his peak as preacher, pastor, and world-renowned leader. From the first an outspoken supporter of the war effort as a struggle of democracy against autocracy, he held noonday religious services in the Palace Theater in downtown Dallas for the convenience of people at work. By appointment of President Woodrow Wilson he spent six months in Europe in 1918 preaching a message of "patriotism and religion" to the Allied armies and navies. On 16 May 1920 he delivered from the steps of the capitol in Washington a memorable address on religious liberty. In 1921 he began broadcasting services by radio, one of the first in the nation to do so.

From 1927 to 1930 Truett was president of the Southern Baptist Convention. During the Great Depression it was he who led the convention to determine to repay one hundred cents on the dollar on the debts of its agencies. In the summer of 1930 he went on a preaching tour in South America, and in 1934 he was the sole American speaker on the program of the Spurgeon Centenary in England. The successes achieved on these two occasions assured his election as president of the Baptist World Alliance at Berlin in 1934. From then until the end of his term in 1939, he preached and conferred all over the world.

Truett was a trustee of Baylor University; of Southwestern Baptist Theological Seminary, Fort Worth; and of Baylor Hospital, Dallas. For one week each summer for thirty-seven years he preached at the Cowboy Camp Meetings held in the Davis Mountain country of western Texas. He returned frequently to North Carolina, especially to Ridgecrest, and once told a Raleigh audience: "Every thought of North Carolina, my native land, warms my heart to the depths. The spirit of the people is the great thing about them." The *Charlotte Observer* called him "America's greatest preacher," and Josephus Daniels said in 1936 that Truett was "the greatest living North Carolinian." In 1937 the Baptist State Convention of North Carolina acquired the Truett home near Hayesville by deed in order to preserve it as a memorial. Dozens of religious, educational, and healing institutional buildings over the South and abroad bear his name.

Although Truett wrote little intended for publication, others have compiled and edited ten volumes of his sermons, two volumes of his addresses, and two volumes of his annual Christmas messages, which were originally personal letters to friends. His authorized biography (Powhatan W. James, *George W. Truett—A Biography*) has appeared in six issues, five by the Macmillan Company, New York (1939–45), and the sixth by the Broadman Press, Nashville (1953).

However sophisticated his audience, Truett's basic orientation and figures of speech remained rural. The effect of his haunting voice, clear as a bell and under complete control, was enhanced by his striking appearance. Soon after moving to Dallas he went quail hunting with two friends, one of whom was fatally wounded by the accidental discharge of Truett's gun. Because he never used humor in the pulpit and maintained an air of quiet dignity that bordered on detachment, the legend arose that he never smiled after the accident. The truth is that by age twenty-three, years before the tragedy, "he already had the serious and solemn dignity that always marked his platform presence." In informal circles he had a "most infectious and frequent smile" and a keen sense of humor. Surprisingly, he never learned to drive an automobile, and his only hobby was collecting books.

On 28 June 1894 Truett married Josephine Jenkins, the daughter of Judge W. H. Jenkins, a resident of Waco and chairman of the Baylor trustees. The Truetts had three daughters: Jessie (Mrs. Powhatan W. James), Mary (Mrs. Thomas W. Gilliam), and Annie Sallee (Mrs. Robert L. Milliken). Truett was buried in the Grove Hill Cemetery, but some months later his body was moved to the more spacious Hillcrest Memorial Cemetery, both in Dallas.

SEE: *Dallas Morning News*, 8–11 July 1944 (portrait); *Encyclopedia of Southern Baptists*, vol. 2 (1958); Margaret Walker Freel, *Our Heritage: The People of Cherokee County, North Carolina, 1540–1955* (1956); Powhatan W. James, *George W. Truett: A Biography* (1939 [portrait]); Leon McBeth, *The First Baptist Church of Dallas* (1968 [portrait]); Loulie Latimer Owens, "Dr. George W. Truett Probably Best-known Baptist in History," *Charity and Children*, 16 May 1957; Raleigh, *Biblical Recorder*, 12 Feb. 1966 (portrait); Raleigh *News and Observer*, 8 Apr. 1958; George Washington Truett, Baptist voices of yesterday, Recordings (Historical Commission, Southern Baptist Convention, Nashville); George Washington Truett Papers (Baptist Historical Collection, Wake Forest University, Winston-Salem); *Who's Who in America, 1942–1943*.

HENRY S. STROUPE

Tryon, William (*1729–27 Jan. 1788*), professional soldier and governor of the province of North Carolina and New York on the eve of the Revolution, was born at Norbury Park in Surrey, England. His father was Charles Tryon, of Bulwick, Northamptonshire, who descended from a family that had fled Spanish persecution in the Lowlands and established itself in England in trade and shipping. His mother was Lady Mary Shirley, the daughter of Robert Shirley, first Earl Ferrers. Through her relatives the Tryons appear to have enjoyed some connections at court.

Young Tryon began his career in the army. In 1751 he was commissioned a lieutenant in the First Regiment of Foot Guards. Marriage with Margaret Wake of London's fashionable West End in 1757 brought him her fortune of £30,000 and additional connections with the ruling caste of Great Britain. His wife was related to Wills Hill, second Viscount Hillsborough, who became First Lord of Trade and Plantations in 1763 and Secretary of State for the Colonies when that office was created in 1768. By 1758 Tryon had risen to lieutenant colonel in his regiment, but soon a new opportunity appeared that Hillsborough may well have opened for him. Aged Governor Arthur Dobbs of North Carolina asked for retirement in 1764, and Tryon was promptly named lieutenant governor, with instructions to proceed to North Carolina and relieve the old man if he could return for his health in the British Isles. Tryon sold Norbury Park, resigned his commission, and sailed in the snow *Friendship* with his wife and small

daughter Margaret, arriving at Cape Fear on 10 Oct. 1764. Tryon now cooled his heels while Dobbs delayed his departure.

On the death of Dobbs at Cape Fear on 28 Mar. 1765, Tryon took over his duties and was commissioned governor a few months later. His first problem was to deal with the turmoil that followed passage of the Stamp Act. Demonstrations were held during the summer and fall in the principal ports. A crowd at Wilmington, only a few miles from Tryon's residence at Brunswick, caught the Crown-appointed stamp tax collector at his lodgings and forced him to resign the office. When the packets of stamped paper arrived in November, the captain of H.M. sloop *Diligence* refused to land them because of threatened violence ashore.

Tryon did not favor the tax because he believed it would drain the province of specie. He went so far as to offer to pay the tax for taverns in the larger communities and for the legal documents on which he was entitled to collect fees. He demanded compliance with the law, but there was little he could do, lacking vessels to patrol the sound ports. Early in 1766, after he had seized three vessels that arrived at Cape Fear without stamped papers, his home was surrounded by four to five hundred armed men. Despite Tryon's determination, Cornelius Harnett and other leaders were able to free the vessels and keep the deeper water ports of Brunswick and Wilmington also open.

In June 1766 Tryon formally announced repeal of the Stamp Act and an end to the conflict. From the struggle he and the eastern North Carolinians emerged with mutual respect. What he hoped to do now was move along with matters he considered of first priority for the province—one being the location of the capital, not at the southeastern tip of North Carolina, but in the most central coastal town, New Bern. There he proposed to build a governor's house at which he would reside and the Council would meet. For this purpose he had brought with him on the *Friendship* "a very worthy . . . master builder," John Hawks.

Since the early part of the century, the capital had been moved about from one town to another. Tryon felt that "the late great indulgences granted to the colonies"—meaning repeal of the Stamp Act—would help induce the North Carolinians to pay for an expensive building. On 7 Dec. 1766 the Assembly passed by a large majority an appropriation of £5,000 with which to purchase lots in New Bern and begin construction. A month later Tryon and "John Hawks of Newbern Architect" signed a contract, and at the time Hawks estimated the total cost of the edifice and dependencies at £15,000. On 15 Jan. 1768 the additional money was voted. By mid-1770 the building was sufficiently completed for the Tryons to move in. The first Assembly session to use the structure convened in New Bern on 5 Dec. 1770.

"Tryon's Palace," as it became known, was to be paid for almost entirely by a poll tax, which bore far harder on the small farmer, particularly in the western counties, than on the merchants and plantation owners of the eastern counties. Western North Carolina had long seethed with grievances—dishonest officials, uncertain land titles, nonconformist resentment, and lack of equal representation in the lower house, to name a few. The heavy poll tax for a "palace" inflamed all these grievances, and the backcountry dissidents, who called themselves Regulators, began to grow in numbers and boldness. In 1768 Tryon led a small militia force to put down a riot at Hillsborough, but the violence persisted.

In the spring of 1771 Tryon and the eastern leaders determined to muster a large force, equipped with cannon, for a full-scale expedition against the Regulators. The result was that Tryon's column, numbering about 1,100 militia, put to flight some 2,000 Regulators on 16 May 1771. The clash took place on the Alamance River near the present city of Burlington. Of the Regulators, 20 were killed and possibly 100 were wounded. The militia lost 9 killed and 61 wounded. Tryon hanged one Regulator leader, James Few, but most of the others escaped to northern provinces. The governor offered pardons to the rank and file, and 6,000 came forward to take the oath.

Tryon's tour of duty in North Carolina should not be judged solely in the light of Alamance. He proved an able administrator, and his dispatches reflect vividly what he saw as the need for the province's economic development. He sought establishment of a postal system to the north. He supported measures to link the backcountry with the Cape Fear River's head of navigation. He achieved the unprecedented running of boundaries with western South Carolina and the Cherokee nation. He urged the establishment of Queen's College in Charlotte, and he signed a law (later disallowed) to permit performance of the marriage rite by Presbyterian ministers.

While on the Alamance expedition, Tryon learned that his wish to become governor of New York had been approved, as John Murray, Earl of Dunmore, was leaving the position to become governor of Virginia. Tryon sailed from New Bern in the sloop *Sukey* and arrived in New York port on 8 July 1771.

Here, too, he won respect as an administrator. In his first message to the Assembly, he urged strengthening of the militia and support for New York Hospital. He gave a large tract of land to establish King's College, which became Columbia University. He attempted to pacify the violent dispute that had broken out between New York and New Hampshire over conflicting grants in the territory known as Vermont. Unhappily, on 29 Dec. 1773, in a disastrous fire at Fort George, his residence, he lost all his personal effects, including an extensive library. For the loss, the Crown granted him £5,000 compensation.

For consultation on the New York–New Hampshire dispute and other problems, his superiors summoned him to London, and he sailed in April 1774 in the packet *Mercury* for a stay of nearly a year in England. When he returned to New York on 25 June 1775, he found all the colonies in arms and General George Washington appointed commander-in-chief of a growing Continental army. Washington and Tryon arrived in New York on the same day (though not at the same hour), each receiving a warm welcome from his supporters in that city of divided loyalties.

Washington immediately warned Major General Philip Schuyler that Tryon should be carefully watched because of his many adherents among New York Loyalists. He would not hesitate to order Tryon's seizure, said Washington, if he felt it necessary, but the arrest of a Crown official being "quite a new Thing and of exceeding great Importance," he preferred to have guidance from the Continental Congress. John Adams's diary reports a desultory debate on the matter beginning on 5 October, but Congress ended up taking no action.

Possibly having learned of the debate, Tryon went aboard the sloop *Halifax* in New York harbor on 19 October. Later he moved to the ship *Dutchess of Gordon*, where he remained until the Howe brothers captured the city in September 1776. No question now remained of continuing the civil administration, and in April of the following year he assumed command of a corps of Loyalists. His health was not good, and he had already asked permission to return to England if he could not have a military command of army regulars.

On 5 June 1778 Tryon was named colonel of the Seventieth (or Surrey) Regiment with the additional rank of major general "in America." His military exploits consisted chiefly in launching raids against Washington's supply bases in Connecticut. His troops savagely burned the town of Fairfield, and he wrote an indiscreet letter avowing his wish to put the torch to every safety committeeman's house in the area. The Reverend John Vardill, a British agent, wrote William Eden, chief of British espionage, that the statement "has made him very odious & ridiculous."

Tryon's governorship, no more than nominal since the outbreak of war, officially came to an end in 1780 with the appointment of James Robertson as the last of New York's colonial governors. Early that year a "very severe gout" impelled Tryon to return to England. He had made a dubious purchase of several thousand acres from the Mohawk Indians, all of which were expropriated by the state of New York. He had hoped for royal rewards, but for his services was merely made colonel of the Twenty-ninth Foot and promoted to lieutenant general on the retired list.

Tryon was a study in flawed ability and capacity for leadership. Vardill called him "a Gentleman of Integrity & Fortitude . . . made by his *Vanity* a Dupe to every flattering Impostor . . . too much guided by personal Resentment to be trusted." He died at his home on Upper Grosvenor Street and was buried in the churchyard at Twickenham, Surrey. No authenticated portrait of him has been found. A facsimile of his coat of arms is printed in Haywood's *Governor William Tryon and His Administration of the Province of North Carolina*. His only son died in infancy in North Carolina, and his daughter never married, so there are no descendants.

SEE: D. B. Barger, "Governor Tryon's House in Fort George," *New York History* 35 (1954); A. T. Dill, *Governor Tryon and His Palace* (1955); *Gentleman's Magazine*, December 1757, February 1788; Marshall De Lancey Haywood, *Governor William Tryon and His Administration in the Province of North Carolina* (1903); Solomon Henner, *The Career of William Tryon as Governor of the Province of New York, 1771–1780* (1968); Paul D. Nelson, *William Tryon and the Course of Empire* (1990); E. B. O'Callaghan, ed., *Documents Relative to the Colonial History of the State of New-York*, vol. 8 (1857); William S. Powell, ed., *The Correspondence of William Tryon and Other Selected Papers*, 2 vols. (1980–81); William S. Powell and others, eds., *The Regulators in North Carolina: A Documentary History, 1759–1776* (1971); William L. Saunders, ed., *Colonial Records of North Carolina*, vols. 7–8 (1890).

ALONZO THOMAS DILL

Tsali (Charley) (*d. 25 Nov. 1838*), a full-blooded Cherokee farmer, resided with his family near the mouth of the Nantahala River in western North Carolina at the time of the 1835 Cherokee census. Apparently of middle age, he was illiterate in both Cherokee and English and would no doubt have remained obscure except for a dramatic episode occurring when the U.S. Army attempted to remove him and his family from their homeland.

On 29 Dec. 1835 a small faction of the Cherokee Nation signed a treaty at New Echota, Ga., giving up its land in the eastern United States and agreeing to move to the West within two years of the treaty's ratification. (It was ratified on 23 May 1836.) The North Carolina Cherokee had not signed the treaty and, like tribal members everywhere, were reluctant to accept its terms. Nonetheless, by the fall of 1838 the army had supervised the removal of thousands of Cherokee, and only a few hundred remained in North Carolina—some legally and a handful of others, including Tsali and his family, as fugitives hiding in the Great Smoky Mountains near present-day Bryson City. On 1 November Second Lieutenant Andrew Jackson Smith and three enlisted men found the site where Tsali's group was camped. The soldiers were accompanied by William Holland Thomas, a local merchant who served as agent for the Oconaluftee Cherokee, a band that claimed legal right to stay in the state. Smith and his men apprehended Tsali's band without resistance. The captives, numbering five men and seven women and children, apparently consisted of Tsali, his wife, brother, sons, and their families.

On the morning of 2 Nov. 1838 the soldiers left William Thomas and began escorting the Indians to an army camp. Various published and oral accounts dating from a much later period claim that the soldiers mistreated their captives; one says that they prodded Tsali's wife with a bayonet to make her move more quickly, another that they inadvertently caused the death of Tsali's youngest child. The whites who were closest to the events, however, said nothing about mistreatment. Whatever the truth, about sunset several male Indians suddenly turned on their escort, killed one soldier outright, wounded two others (one mortally), and attacked Lieutenant Smith, who escaped only because of "the spirit & activity of my horse." The Indians then slipped away into the surrounding mountain forests. It is not certain what part, if any, Tsali played in the attack.

Major General Winfield Scott, the officer in charge of the Cherokee removal, ordered Colonel William Stanhope Foster of the Fourth U.S. Infantry Regiment to apprehend Tsali's band and execute those responsible for the killings. Foster was assisted by William Thomas, the Oconaluftee Indians, and a group of fugitive Cherokees led by Euchella (Oo cha lah or Utsala), a former neighbor of Tsali. Apparently Foster, through Thomas, indicated that Euchella and his people might remain in North Carolina with the Oconaluftee Cherokee if they assisted in capturing the killers. By 23 November the army's Cherokee allies had seized all of the fugitives except Tsali and had executed three adult males by a firing squad. They quickly apprehended Tsali as well and executed him in a similar manner at noon on the twenty-fifth.

Since the late nineteenth century, a legendary Tsali has grown to far more significant proportions than the real figure ever attained. He has usually been portrayed as a hero, nobly resisting enforced removal and the soldiers' brutality. According to some accounts, Colonel Foster and Thomas promised Tsali that if he gave himself up to face execution, the remaining Cherokee in North Carolina, including Euchella's band, could stay indefinitely. Thus, the story goes, he surrendered voluntarily and suffered martyrdom so that his people could stay in their homeland. Many years later they and their descendants formed the Eastern Band of Cherokee and acquired the Qualla Boundary Reservation in western North Carolina. Today Tsali is eulogized in many published and oral accounts and, most spectacularly, in the outdoor drama *Unto These Hills*, staged each summer on the reservation in Cherokee, N.C.

SEE: John Preston Arthur, *Western North Carolina* (1914); John R. Finger, "The Saga of Tsali: Legend Versus Reality," *North Carolina Historical Review* 56 (January 1979); Col. William S. Foster to Major Gen. Winfield Scott, 15, 19, 24 Nov. 1838, 3 Dec. 1838 (all in Major Gen. Winfield Scott to Adjutant General, 28 Dec. 1838, National Archives, RG 94); Kermit Hunter, *Unto These Hills: A Drama of the Cherokees* (1950); Paul Kutsche, "The Tsali Legend: Culture Heroes and Historiography," *Ethnohistory* 10 (1963); Lt. C. H.

Larned to Major Gen. Winfield Scott, 5 Nov. 1838 (National Archives, RG 75 [Cherokee Emig.]); James Mooney, "Myths of the Cherokee," *19th Annual Report of the Bureau of American Ethnology* (1900); Mattie Russell, "William Holland Thomas: White Chief of the North Carolina Cherokees" (Ph.D. diss., Duke University, 1956); Major Gen. Winfield Scott to War Department, 6 Nov. 1838, Scott to Col. William S. Foster, 7 Nov. 1838, and Lt. Andrew Jackson Smith to Lt. C. H. Larned, 5 Nov. 1838 (National Archives, RG 75 [Cherokee Emig.]); William Holland Thomas, *Argument in Support of the Claims of the Cherokee Indians . . .* (1839).

JOHN R. FINGER

Tucker, Glenn Irving *(30 Nov. 1892–26 Oct. 1976)*, author and historian, was born in Tampico, Ind., to William W. and Bertha Clark Tucker. Reared in Greencastle, Ind., where his father practiced medicine, he was graduated from DePauw University in 1914 and the Columbia University School of Journalism in 1915. He was a reporter for newspapers in Illinois, Wisconsin, Indiana, New Jersey, and New York and a White House correspondent for the *New York World* during the Wilson, Harding, and Coolidge administrations. Tucker left journalism to work in advertising for N. W. Ayer and Son in Philadelphia; later he was vice-president of Thornley and Jones in New York and then director of public relations for the Radio Corporation of America.

In 1948 Tucker retired and moved to Flat Rock, N.C., where he grew apples and began to research the popular histories he had always wanted to write. In the ensuing twenty-eight years he was the author of fourteen books, beginning with *Poltroons and Patriots: A Popular Account of the War of 1812* (1954).

Tucker was an unprecedented three-time winner of the Mayflower Cup Award for *Tecumseh: Vision of Glory* (1956), *Dawn Like Thunder: The Barbary Wars and the Birth of the U.S. Navy* (1963), and *Zeb Vance: Champion of Personal Freedom* (1966). He received the Fletcher Pratt Award for *Chicamauga: Bloody Battle in the West* (1961), the Thomas Wolfe Memorial Award for Distinguished Writing in 1956, the Historians Cup Award of the Western North Carolina Historical Association in 1958, and the Harry S Truman Award for meritorious achievement in the field of Civil War history in 1968. President of both the North Carolina Literary and Historical Association and the Western North Carolina Historical Association in 1965, he was the recipient of an honorary doctor of literature degree from his alma mater, DePauw University (1960), and an honorary doctor of letters degree from The University of North Carolina (1966), where he was cited for his "careful research, spritely style, and his sense of the dramatic in history and biography."

His other publications include *High Tide at Gettysburg* (1958), *Hancock the Superb* (1960), *Front Rank* (1962), *Lee and Longstreet at Gettysburg* (1968), *The War of 1812: A Compact History* (1969), *Mad Anthony Wayne and the New Nation* (1973), and numerous articles in *Civil War Times Illustrated* and the *North Carolina Historical Review*. His writings consistently received critical acclaim.

Tucker married Dorothy Gail Thomas on 10 Nov. 1917, and they had two sons: William T. and Richard C. The Tuckers moved from Flat Rock to Fairview, a suburb of Asheville, in 1966. Tucker died in an Asheville hospital at age eighty-three. He had been a member of the Republican party and the Methodist church.

SEE: *Asheville Citizen*, 28 Oct. 1976; William S. Powell, ed., *North Carolina Lives* (1962); Raleigh *News and Observer*, 28,

30 Oct. 1976; Glenn Irving Tucker Papers (Southern Historical Collection, University of North Carolina, Chapel Hill).

BRENDA MARKS EAGLE

Tucker, Joel W. *(1820–post–1868),* Methodist clergyman and controversialist, a native of Virginia, was one of those individuals who appear from virtually unknown origins, reveal a flash of brilliance, and then disappear in obscurity. In 1845 he was received on trial as a minister in the North Carolina Conference of the Methodist Episcopal Church, South. In his first year in the active ministry, he was assigned to the Guilford Circuit. Between 1845 and 1850 he served churches in Greensboro, Beaufort, Plymouth, and Whiteville. Afterwards he succeeded to the largest churches in North Carolina Methodism at Washington, New Bern, Wilmington, Wilson, Raleigh, and Fayetteville. He was examined before a committee of clergymen at the December 1860 meeting of the church's North Carolina Conference and approved to be made an elder.

In 1868 Tucker was serving as the presiding elder of the New Bern District when his ministerial career came to an abrupt end. The official record for the year merely notes, "Joel W. Tucker . . . was expelled for immorality." His whereabouts thereafter are unknown. But by the time of his dismissal, he had become one of the more prominent Methodist clergymen in North Carolina. In 1866, for example, when he was assigned to the Methodist church in Wilson, he was named to the Board of Missions and was also chosen to preach the funeral sermon of an elderly, highly respected clergyman.

His flash of brilliance came during the course of the Civil War, when he was located at the Methodist church in Fayetteville. In quick succession he gave three sermons that were published and distributed throughout the South as comforting, if stern, theological interpretations of the place of the Confederacy in divine history. In one of the sermons, *God's Providence in War,* delivered to his congregation in Fayetteville on Friday, 16 May 1862, a general Confederate fast day, Tucker saw the ongoing war as "a conflict of truth with error—of the Bible with Northern infidelity—of pure christianity with Northern fanaticism—of liberty with despotism—of right with might." In the next, *God Sovereign and Man Free* (1862), he prayed "for the success of our cause; for the triumph of our armies," arguing that God could "answer our petitions, because he has sovereign control of the bodies and souls of men." These two sermons expressed succinctly and clearly the epitome of Southern wartime religious ideology, making Tucker momentarily one of the most popular and lauded prophets of the wartime South. The third published sermon, *Guilt and Punishment of Extortion,* preached on 7 Sept. 1862, was directed at extortioners who caused serious price inflation and contributed to the scarcity of certain goods. Tucker suggested means of controlling them. All of these were printed in Fayetteville at the office of the *Presbyterian,* a journal of that denomination.

At the time of the 1850 census, when he was living in Plymouth, N.C., his wife was twenty-year-old Penelope, a native of North Carolina. No children were recorded.

SEE: Methodist Episcopal Church, South, *Minutes of the Annual Conferences* (1845–68); Joel W. Tucker, *God Sovereign and Men Free: A Discourse* (1862), *God's Providence in War: A Sermon Delivered . . . in Fayetteville, N.C., on Friday, May 16, 1862* (1862), and *Guilt and Punishment of Extortion: A Sermon* (1862).

LARRY E. TISE

Tucker, Rufus Sylvester *(5 Apr. 1829–4 Aug. 1894),* merchant and planter, was born in Raleigh, the third son of three children of Ruffin, a prominent merchant of his native Wake County, and Lucinda M. Sledge Tucker of Franklin County. Having received his preliminary education at the academy in Raleigh under the distinguished guidance of J. M. Lovejoy, he entered The University of North Carolina in 1844, receiving the A.B. degree in 1848 and the A.M. degree in 1868. On leaving the university in 1848, he entered his father's mercantile business, serving as a clerk until his father's death in 1851, at which time Tucker with his two brothers inherited the business.

On 23 Apr. 1861 he entered the Confederate army as a captain with an appointment by Governor John W. Ellis to be quartermaster and commissary for the Raleigh post. Resigning this position in the fall, he raised, captained, and mustered into service on 12 Feb. 1862 a company of North Carolina volunteers known as the Wake Rangers, Company I, Forty-first Regiment (or Third Cavalry). He served primarily in the eastern part of the state, where he received distinguished mention for distinguished gallantry in the Battle of Washington in September 1862. Shortly after this engagement he was promoted major but resigned on 20 December. The next year he accepted an appointment as assistant adjutant general, serving both General Daniel G. Fowle and his successor, Brigadier General R. C. Gatlin, until Tucker resigned in October 1863. November 1864 saw Major Tucker's election as principal clerk in the House of Commons for the 1864–65 session. Although he was suggested as a gubernatorial possibility in 1888, he never sought political office.

After the war he devoted himself to his mercantile business, expanding its operations until it became the leading dry goods house in the state. When in February 1883 Tucker retired from the business, its successful tradition was continued by his son-in-law, James Boylan, and his associates.

Having achieved success in business, Tucker turned largely to agriculture, profitably operating a valuable plantation in Pitt County while developing 540 acres in the Raleigh vicinity, known as Camp Mangum, into one of the finest farms in the state. His civic concern was evident in the gift of Tucker Hall, Raleigh's first public amusement building, dedicated by former Governor David L. Swain in 1867. Active in forming the Raleigh Chamber of Commerce, Tucker was chosen its first president in 1887.

His experience in managing the affairs of railroads, banks, and other institutions of a quasi-public nature was considerable. For more than thirty years he was a director of the Institution for the Deaf, Dumb and Blind at Raleigh, serving part of that time as its board president. He was a director of the North Carolina, Raleigh and Gaston, Raleigh and Augusta, and Carolina Central Railroads, in addition to being the largest private stockholder in the Atlantic and North Carolina Railroad. With his very considerable agricultural and real estate holdings, Tucker was reputed to be Raleigh's wealthiest citizen. He demonstrated a genuine enthusiasm for agricultural interests, munificent private hospitality, and humanitarian concerns.

Tucker died at his home in Raleigh, with funeral services in Christ Church, where he had been an active vestryman for more than twenty years. He was buried beside his parents in Oakwood Cemetery, Raleigh. Survivors were his widow, formerly Florence E. Perkins of Pitt County, whom he had married in 1856; five daughters, Bessie, Sarah, Minnie, Florence, and Margaret; and a son, William Ruffin.

SEE: Samuel A. Ashe, ed., *Biographical History of North Carolina*, vol. 7 (1908 [portrait]), and *Cyclopedia of Eminent and Representative Men of the Carolinas*, vol. 2 (1892); Jerome Dowd, *Sketches of Prominent Living North Carolinians* (1888); Raleigh *News and Observer*, 27 Mar. 1888, 5 Aug. 1894, R. S. Tucker Papers (North Carolina State Archives, Raleigh); Stephen B. Weeks Scrapbook, vol. 3 (North Carolina Collection, University of North Carolina, Chapel Hill).

SUSAN TUCKER HATCHER

Tucker, Starling *(ca. 1766–3 Jan. 1834)*, South Carolina congressman and general, was born in Halifax County, N.C. His father, William Willis (Billy) Tucker, whose will of 8 Nov. 1770 was probated at the February 1771 term of Halifax court, left all to Starling's mother, Priscilla Doyle Tucker. If she remarried, the estate was to be divided equally among her and the children: Martha, Mary, Starling, and Fanny. A witness, Henry Haws Tucker, may have been related. For a second husband Priscilla in time chose the Virginian Thomas Clark. Before the household moved to South Carolina at the end of the American Revolution, Starling's half-brother William was born.

Endowed with native intelligence but perhaps little formal education, Starling Tucker began farming the Mountain Creek (now Enoree) section of Laurens District (now County) near Tucker's Mill on Enoree River. The ambitious Tucker married Levinia Higgins on 8 Oct. 1789 and eventually owned land on both sides of the stream. The couple as many as eleven neighboring Higgins households are recorded in the census of 1790. By 1800 Major Starling Tucker, at least on paper, commanded the upper battalion, Enoree Regiment, South Carolina militia. Without ever any enumerated children of their own, the Tuckers at this time had two slaves to help, and by 1820 five individuals of their establishment were engaged in agricultural work and one person performed manufacturing, perhaps milling. *The Biographical Directory of the Senate of the State of South Carolina, 1776–1964* credits Tucker with having become a justice of the peace, a justice of the quorum, and a commissioner of free schools. He represented Laurens in the state house of representatives (1801–6) and state senate (1806–17) until he resigned to go to Congress; he was succeeded as senator by his half brother William Clark, who in 1810 had received a four-year appointment as the state's surveyor general.

The War of 1812 did not scathe South Carolina, but it did bring about the chance for Tucker as a lieutenant colonel to train from 1 Mar. to 1 Apr. 1814 at Camp Alston in coastal Beaufort County, 210 miles by baggage wagon from his home. Commanding a readiness detachment of the Second Brigade, First Division, South Carolina militia, the backcountry colonel got along well with his men but poorly with Governor Joseph Alston. When Alston had him court-martialed and suspended from authority for ten months, "the whole affair made Starling Tucker subsequently Brigadier of the Tenth Brigade, Major General Fifth Division, and a Member of Congress."

One of the candidates he defeated to get to Washington was Anderson Crenshaw, the first graduate of South Carolina College. Through seven terms, from the Fifteenth Congress through the Twenty-first (1817–31), no representative from South Carolina exceeded Starling Tucker in being consistently returned to Washington. Living there modestly and persuaded "that he rendered his constituents more justice than he should do by talking or trying to talk, he attended punctually and voted regularly yet in silence until 4 Feb. 1822, when he took the floor of the House of Representatives to denounce an apportion-

ment bill that threatened to short-change South Carolina. Thereafter he was less and less reticent to set forth his thinking, dominated by strict construction of the U.S. Constitution. Internal improvements were his pet anathema. Except in the Fifteenth Congress when assigned to a committee on expenditures in the War Department and in the second session of the Twentieth when assigned to a select committee on the militia, Tucker was uniformly placed on the committee on elections.

Less than three years after retiring from Congress, he died at about age sixty. His wife died on 16 July 1855 in her eighty-sixth year. Their well-preserved twin graves occupied a walled plot on private ground in later wooded surroundings a mile west of Enoree, S.C. Proud of his personal worth and usefulness in life, his Laurens friends had their sentiments inscribed atop the marble over his grave, to the memory of General Sterling Tucker. There is little question, however, that he habitually signed his given name as Starling.

SEE: *Biog. Dir. Am. Cong.* (1961); Benj. Elliott and Martin Strobel, *The Militia System of South Carolina* (1835); Perry M. Goldman and James S. Young, *The United States Congressional Directories, 1789–1840* (1973); *Heads of Families at the First Census of the U.S. Taken in the Year 1790: South Carolina* (1966); John Bolton O'Neall, *Biographical Sketches of the Bench and Bar of S.C.*, vol. 2 (1859; reprint, 1975); Emily Bellinger Reynolds and Joan Reynolds Faunt, *Biographical Directory of the Senate of the State of South Carolina, 1776–1964* (1964); Billy Willis Tucker, record of will of 8 Nov. 1770 (Superior Court, Halifax, N.C.); Starling Tucker file, Tucker's regiment, S.C. militia, War of 1812 (National Archives); Starling Tucker and Levinia Tucker tombstone inscriptions (transcriptions furnished by Mildred Brownlee, Laurens, S.C.); U.S. Census records, Laurens District, S.C., 1800, 1810, 1820, and Laurens County, S.C., 1830 (National Archives, microcopies M32, roll 50; M252, roll 61; M33, roll 121; and M19, roll 69); U.S. Congress proceedings: *Annals of the Congress of the United States*, 15th Cong. through 1st sess., 18th Cong., vols. 31–41 (1854–56); *Journals of the House of Representatives of the United States*, 15th through 21st Cong., 14 vols. (1817–31); *Register of the Debates in Congress*, 18th Cong., 2d sess., through 21st Cong., vols. 4–7 (1825–31).

H. B. FANT

Tucker, Tilghman Mayfield *(5 Feb. 1802–30 Apr. 1859)*, congressman and governor of Mississippi, was born near Lime Stone Springs, the son of John, a farmer, and Margaret Mayfield Tucker. The family moved to Mississippi when he was young, and for a time he worked as a blacksmith before studying law under Daniel W. Wright in Hamilton, Monroe County. After receiving a license he moved to Columbus in the newly created adjoining Lowndes County and established a thriving practice. Elected to the lower house of the legislature in 1831, he served until 1836, when he was elected to the state senate. He remained there until 1842.

On 1 Nov. 1841 Tucker was elected governor as a Democrat by a mere eight votes over his Whig opponent and was inaugurated on 10 Jan. 1842. In May he attended a dinner in honor of Dr. James Hagan, editor of the *Vicksburg Sentinel*, where he was one of the speakers. Because of his remarks, the governor received a challenge to a duel from former senator Sargeant S. Prentiss, who inquired whether Tucker approved of Hagan's editorials attacking Prentiss. General John A. Quitman represented Prentiss in delivering a series of thirteen very formal but interesting notes exchanged between the two men. Dueling as a means of settling a question of honor had virtually ended, and rhetoric in this case, with each participant in the dispute employing language to save face and as well, perhaps, his life, seems to have ended the matter. There was no duel of bullets, only words. Prentiss, a native of Maine, soon moved to New Orleans.

As governor, Tucker was concerned with legislative repudiation of Union Bank bonds, completion of the new Executive Mansion, and reapportionment of his state's congressional representation. At the end of his two-year term in 1843, he was elected to Congress, where he served during the period 1843–45. He soon retired to his plantation, Cottonwood, in Louisiana.

Tucker was married in 1829 to Sarah F. McBee and after her death to Martha A. Conger in 1854. He died while visiting his father in Marion County, Ala., and was buried there.

SEE: *Biog. Dir. Am. Cong.* (1961); Virginia Quitman McNealus, *Code Duello: Letters Concerning the Prentiss-Tucker Duel of 1842* (1931); *Nat. Cyc. Am. Biog.*, vol. 13 (1906); Dunbar Rowland, *Encyclopedia of Mississippi History*, vol. 2 (1907); *Who Was Who in America*, vol. 1 (1967).

WILLIAM S. POWELL

Tucker, William Feimster (*9 May 1827–15 Sept. 1881*), Confederate brigade commander, teacher, lawyer, and legislator, was born in Iredell County. After study at Emory and Henry College he began teaching in Houston, Miss. In 1851, soon after his arrival, he met and married Martha Josephine Shackleford, the daughter of Henry Shackleford, a wealthy landowner of Okolona, Miss.

Shortly after his marriage Tucker abandoned teaching and opened a law practice in Houston. Politically active, he campaigned hard for John C. Breckinridge in 1860. When Breckinridge lost, Tucker, believing that war was inevitable, began organizing and training a militia unit in Houston known as the Chickasaw Guards. This unit, commanded by Tucker, answered Governor John J. Pettus's call in January 1861 and moved against the Federal garrison in Pensacola.

In March 1861 Captain Tucker and the Chickasaw Guards were mustered into the Confederate army as Company K, Eleventh Mississippi Regiment. Immediately they were ordered to Virginia and fought under General Barnard E. Bee at First Manassas. After this battle, Tucker returned to Mississippi and, using his Company K as a nucleus, recruited the Forty-first Mississippi Regiment. On 8 May 1862 he was mustered its colonel. The regiment distinguished itself in its first battle at Perryville in October 1862, although suffering severe casualties. Tucker was among those wounded. The Forty-first Mississippi continued to see action as a part of James R. Chalmers's brigade in the Army of Tennessee, fighting at Murfreesboro, Chickamauga, and Missionary Ridge. At Chickamauga Tucker and his regiment were again cited for distinguished service.

On 1 Mar. 1864 Tucker was promoted to brigadier general, commanding Chalmers's old brigade (Seventh, Ninth, Tenth, Forty-first, Forty-fourth Mississippi Infantry Regiments and the Ninth Mississippi Sharpshooter Battalion). In the ensuing Atlanta campaign, he led the brigade until his arm was shattered during the Battle of Resaca on 14 May 1864. This wound forced his retirement from field service, but the end of the war found him commanding the District of Southern Mississippi and East Louisiana.

Tucker resumed his law practice after the war and moved to Okolona. There he prospered as a lawyer and

soon returned to politics. A participant in the violent upheavals and controversies that marked Mississippi politics in the 1870s, he served in the state legislature in 1876 and again in 1878. He was one of the members of the committee that initiated impeachment proceedings against Governor Adelbert Ames.

On 14 Sept. 1881 Tucker was assassinated at his residence. Two men were arrested for his murder but were not convicted. He was buried in Okolona Cemetery.

SEE: Clement A. Evans, ed., *Confederate Military History*, vol. 7 (1899); R. Henderson, "W. F. Tucker" (Mississippi Division of Archives and History, Jackson); Dunbar Rowland, *History of Mississippi* (1925); William F. Tucker Papers (Manuscript Department, Duke University Library, Durham, and Southern Historical Collection, University of North Carolina, Chapel Hill).

N. C. HUGHES, JR.

Tufts, Edgar (*4 Dec. 1869–6 Jan. 1923*), Presbyterian minister and educator, was born at Kirkwood, Ga., the son of Joseph F. A. and Anna Robinson Tufts. In 1898 he married Mary Elizabeth Hall, of Hampden-Sydney, Va., who survived him. They were the parents of Edgar Hall, Margaret, and Mary.

Tufts was graduated from Washington and Lee University in 1894 with the A.B. degree and from Union Theological Seminary in Virginia in 1897. Concord Presbytery ordained him to the ministry on 26 Sept. 1897, after which he served as evangelist for Watauga County while residing at Banner Elk (1897–1901). During 1901–2 he was pastor of the Presbyterian church at Hazelhurst, Ga., returning in 1902 to Banner Elk, where he remained until his death. For a portion of this time he also supplied the Blowing Rock, Newland, Linville, and Pineola churches.

In 1898 Tufts began a school at Banner Elk that eventually became Lees-McRae Institute and then Lees-McRae Junior College (1929). He established Grace Hospital at Banner Elk in 1907 and what was later known as Grandfather Home for Children in 1914. From 1916 to 1922 he supervised publication of the *Pinnacles*, a periodical promoting these institutions. After his death, the Edgar Tufts Memorial Association was set up for the oversight of the school, hospital, and home. His son, Edgar Hall Tufts (1899–1942), was the first president of the association and served as administrative head of the school and, later, college. The Reverend Edgar Tufts died at Banner Elk and was buried in Banner Elk Cemetery. His portrait was hung at Lees-McRae College, but few of his papers were preserved.

SEE: *Ministerial Directory of the Presbyterian Church, U.S., 1861–1941* (1942); *Pinnacles*, April 1927; *Presbyterian Standard*, 24 Jan. 1923; Edgar Tufts, *Souvenir, Lees-McRae Institute* (1919); Margaret Tufts, *To the Lees-McRae College Alumni* (1975).

THOMAS H. SPENCE, JR.

Tufts, James Walker (*11 Feb. 1835–2 Feb. 1902*), businessman, resort developer, and philanthropist, was born in Charlestown, Mass., of English ancestry. One of his forebears, William Brewster, went to Plymouth on the *Mayflower* in 1620. The son of Leonard and Hepzibah Fosdick Tufts, he attended the primary school of Miss Putnam and the Training Field School of Masters Baker and Swan. At age fifteen he became an apprentice to Samuel Kidder and Company, druggists in Charlestown. Enterprising and ambitious, he opened his own pharmacy in

Somerville, Mass., in 1856 and later expanded to Medford, where he eventually resided, and to Boston, Winchester, and Woburn, Mass.

Within six years of launching his business career, Tufts had patented and begun to manufacture in Boston his Arctic Soda Apparatus, the perfection of which had involved much experimentation. He disposed of his drugstores in order to concentrate on this new venture. Phenomenally successful, he ultimately sold more soda fountains than all of his competitors combined. The firm of James W. Tufts also produced a complete line of soda fountain supplies, including extracts. Italian marble and silver-plated fixtures were used in the elaborately constructed fountains, one of which Tufts displayed at the Philadelphia Centennial Exposition. As a by-product of the silver-plating process, he designed and sold silver-plated pitchers, dolls, dishes, and the like. In 1891 his firm merged with the three largest manufacturers in the United States to form the American Soda Fountain Company, of which Tufts remained president for the rest of his life. A genuine interest in the lot of his workers prompted him to build, in Charlestown in 1890, the model tenements known as the Bunker Hill Terraces and to establish the next year the James W. Tufts Mutual Benefit Association in his Boston factory. He was an early supporter of the nine-hour working day.

About 1880 Tufts's health, which had never been robust, began to be impaired by the demands of his business, and he started traveling in the winter to places like Bermuda and Florida. He was troubled by the thought that most working-class New Englanders could not afford such long trips. On returning from one of his journeys he joined with Edward Everett Hale, the author and Unitarian minister, in forming the Invalid Aid Society for the purpose of founding a community where semi-invalids could go for recuperation and rest. Tufts declined the presidency of this organization, however, deciding instead to undertake the project alone. At that juncture Benjamin Asbury Goodridge, a Bostonian who frequently wintered in Southern Pines, N.C., spoke persuasively to Tufts about the potential of the Sandhills area. In June 1895 Tufts visited Southern Pines, founded several years earlier by John T. Patrick as a health resort. Patrick took him on a tour of the Sandhills, giving him an opportunity to survey a tract of land in Moore County owned by the Page brothers of Aberdeen. In an interview with Henry A. Page on 21 June, he learned that he could buy 5,000 acres of this land for a dollar an acre. Tufts was agreeable to the transaction, and the first transfer was made the next month. Work on clearing the land started at once. In Boston Tufts consulted landscape architect Frederick Law Olmsted, who drew up plans for a village. As public buildings, cottages, and the Holly Inn were built, Olmsted's associate Warren H. Manning supervised the planting of the first of some 222,000 trees and shrubs. By January 1896 streets had been graded, electricity and a telephone system had been installed, the Holly Inn had been opened, and an electric railroad to Southern Pines had been largely completed in order to link the village with the Seaboard Airline Railway. Pamphlets describing the mild climate of the region, the attractive features of the new community, and the advantages for invalids on small incomes were circulated in New England. The location was ideal, for it could be easily reached by people who had neither the time nor the money to go as far as Florida. In November 1895 Tufts succinctly summed up his objective: "My work is of semi-philanthropic character, yet I desire it to appear in the light of a business venture enterprise."

Local people originally called the new community Tuftown, and there were several changes—Pinalia, Sundalia,

Pine-alia—before the name Pinehurst was adopted. The idea of a health resort soon gave way to one of a recreation center as Tufts came to appreciate the growing popularity of golf in the United States. In 1897 a nine-hole golf course was built under the direction of D. LeRoy Culver. A small clubhouse was added, and for two seasons John Dunn Tucker served as the golf professional. In December 1900 the well-known Scottish golfer Donald J. Ross arrived in Pinehurst to take charge of all matters pertaining to the sport. The Carolina Hotel, which remained for many years the largest hotel in North Carolina, opened in January 1901. Since the turn of the century Pinehurst and golf have been synonymous, and the village founded by Tufts came to rank as one of the major winter resorts in the United States.

Tufts belonged to the Republican party and to the Unitarian church. He was a director of the North End Union, a vice-president of the Training Field School Association, and a member of the Twentieth-Century Club and the Lend-a-Hand Society of New England; he also held many other positions of trust. On 30 Oct. 1862 he married Mary Emma Clough, the daughter of Samuel and Martha Ayer Clough of Medford, Mass., by whom he had three sons and one daughter. He died of heart failure in his apartment at the Carolina Hotel and was buried in the family plot in Oak Grove Cemetery, Medford.

A portrait of Tufts owned by a grandson, Richard S. Tufts of Pinehurst, reveals a man of short stature and medium build with brown eyes and hair; typical of the times, he wore a full beard. For many years he faithfully kept a diary that provides insights into his social consciousness and philanthropic bent. Tufts's extensive papers are located in the archives wing of Given Memorial Library, Pinehurst.

SEE: Boston *Daily Advertiser*, 8 Feb. 1902; B. H. Butler, "James Walter Tufts" (unpublished sketch, Duke University Library, Durham); Charlestown, Mass., *Enterprise*, 8 Feb. 1902; Moore County Deed Books 13–14 (Moore County Courthouse, Carthage); *Pinehurst Outlook*, 18 Feb. 1898, 7 Feb. 1902 [portrait], 10 Mar. 1944, 6 Nov. 1945; Raleigh *News and Observer*, 13 Dec. 1970, 1 Oct. 1972; Southern Pines *Pilot*, 29 Nov. 1935, 6 Dec. 1940; R. W. Tufts, *The Scottish Invasion* (1962); Manly W. Wellman, *The County of Moore, 1847–1947* (1962).

CHARLES H. BOWMAN, JR.

Tufts, Leonard (30 June 1870–19 Feb. 1945), resort developer and geneticist, was born in Medford, Mass., the son of James Walker and Mary Emma Clough Tufts. He attended the Medford public schools until the age of fifteen, when he entered Stone's Private School in Boston. He later enrolled at the Albert Hale School prior to matriculating at the Massachusetts Institute of Technology to study mechanical engineering. A member of the class of 1894, Tufts left MIT before completing his last year in order to join the staff of the American Soda Fountain Company, in Boston, of which his father was president. He soon became a vice-president and director of the company. When his father, the founder and owner of Pinehurst, N.C., died in 1902, Leonard Tufts inherited a resort village growing renowned because of its golf.

In 1904 he relinquished his executive position in Boston and moved with his family to Pinehurst, where he took up permanent residence as full-time director of the resort. One of the first steps that Tufts took to put the operation on a sound financial footing was to abandon his father's policy of retaining ownership of all Pinehurst real estate. He began selling lots in the village and in 1907 turned the first profit in the resort's twelve-year history. Tufts applied the money towards construction of a sand- and clay-surfaced road to Southern Pines, six miles away. Thereafter he demonstrated an ardent interest in road building not only in his area but also in North Carolina generally.

Tufts also raised Ayrshire cattle and Berkshire hogs on a large scale; his dairy farm, established to supply milk and butter to Pinehurst hotels, was considered one of the finest in the state. His superior livestock was displayed at the annual fair that he operated in Pinehurst. With the number of people visiting his resort always increasing, Tufts opted to buy 6,000 acres of nearby land where he could develop a satellite community. A real estate venture at Knollwood accordingly was launched under his guidance, as was the golf club at Mid Pines. He organized the holdings inherited from his father as Pinehurst, Incorporated, chartered under state law. This private enterprise he controlled as president, but a village council was chosen each year from among residents to act in an advisory capacity to Tufts and his business associates.

In 1919 Governor Thomas W. Bickett offered Tufts a seat on the State Highway Commission but he declined the position. The gubernatorial gesture derived from a recognition of Tufts's role as a pioneer in the construction of modern highways in North Carolina. He was, indeed, chairman of the county Good Roads Committee. As the head of a thriving resort as well, he identified five priorities for the enterprise: transportation, buildings, food, fun, and beauty. New golf courses, riding trails, a trotting track, a livery stable, and many other facilities were built before he retired in 1929 because of illness and turned over the management of Pinehurst, Incorporated, to his eldest son, Richard S. Tufts.

Leonard Tufts devoted the rest of his life to developing better cattle-breeding methods. After years of experimentation he found a technique that was 70 percent successful in producing good calves. His complicated formula, known as the Regression Index, was adopted in January 1945 by the Ayrshires Breeders Association. Several pamphlets on livestock resulted from his genetic studies, for which he was nationally respected.

Tufts held a variety of offices over the years. At one time or other he was president and director of the Ayrshires Breeders Association, Carolina-Virginia Ayrshire Association, and North Carolina State Fair Association; president of the Southern Berkshire Congress, Capital Highway Association, Continental Field Trial Club, and Pinehurst Jockey Club; director of the U.S. Seniors Golf Association, National Dairy Association, and U.S. Good Roads Association; and member of the Society of Mayflower Descendants, Massachusetts Historical and Genealogical Society, Tin Whistles, and Kiwanis Club. In addition, he was a director of numerous North Carolina agricultural, educational, and charitable organizations. He belonged to the Democratic party and to the Unitarian church.

On 14 June 1895 Tufts married Gertrude Ware Sise, the daughter of Albert Fleetford and Edith Ware Sise of Medford, by whom he had three sons and one daughter. He died of virus pneumonia at Moore County Hospital, Pinehurst, and was buried in the family plot in Mount Hope Cemetery, Southern Pines. At the time of his death author Struthers Burt commented on his personal attributes: "Always one remembers some especial characteristic of a man or woman. There was Leonard Tufts' quiet manner and then, his sudden, illumined smile, in his eyes and on his lips. He was invariably interested in the other person. A real interest [it was], rare and noticeable and valuable beyond measure."

In a portrait owned by Richard S. Tufts of Pinehurst, the elder Tufts appears as a distinguished man with brown hair and blue eyes; he was of medium height and somewhat stocky in build. His papers are located in the archive wing of the Given Memorial Library, Pinehurst.

SEE: B. H. Butler, "James Walter Tufts" (unpublished sketch, Duke University Library, Durham); Charlestown, Mass., *Enterprise*, 8 Feb. 1902; Moore County Deed Books, 35, 37 (Moore County Courthouse, Carthage); *Pinehurst Outlook*, 23 Feb. 1945; Raleigh *News and Observer*, 13 Dec. 1970, 1 Oct. 1972; Southern Pines *Pilot*, 5 Aug. 1921, 3 May 1929, 29 Nov. 1935, 6 Dec. 1940, 23 Feb. 1945; R. S. Tufts, personal contact, 11 Oct. 1975; Manly W. Wellman, *The County of Moore, 1847–1947* (1962).

CHARLES H. BOWMAN, JR.

Tull, John Graham (20 Nov. 1816–28 Apr. 1870), physician and surgeon, the son of Isaac and Eliza Graham Tull, was born in Lenoir County, near Kinston. He was graduated from The University of North Carolina in 1836 and from the University of Pennsylvania School of Medicine in 1839. Dr. Tull then spent several years studying in Paris hospitals before establishing a practice in New Bern. He participated in the reorganization of the Medical Society of North Carolina in 1849 and later served on the first State Board of Medical Examiners, which was appointed in 1859. Tull continued his successful practice in New Bern until the town was captured by Federal troops in 1862. Subsequently he moved to Philadelphia, where, in 1864, he became an acting assistant surgeon in the U.S. Army, serving until the military hospital closed in 1865. For the rest of his life he practiced in Philadelphia, where he was buried.

On 9 Mar. 1845 Tull married Julia West Hollister, and they had sixteen children, twelve boys and four girls. Among his surviving children were John Tull, who became a pharmacist in Waynesville, and Dr. Montrose Graham Tull, who practiced in Philadelphia.

SEE: Archives (University of Pennsylvania, Philadelphia); Medical Society of the State of North Carolina, *Transactions* 10 (1859); U.S. Census, 1850, Craven County.

DOROTHY LONG

Turlington, Edgar Willis (24 Oct. 1891–27 Sept. 1959), lawyer, was born in Smithfield, the son of Ira Thomas and Hortense Mary Rose Turlington. After graduation from The University of North Carolina in 1911, he became a Rhodes Scholar at Oxford (1911–14), receiving M.A. and B.C.L. degrees in 1914 after having attained first class honors in the School of Jurisprudence in 1913. Returning to Chapel Hill, he was a graduate student in 1915–16 and an instructor in Latin and English in 1915–17. Turlington then joined the Department of State, where he was a special assistant (1917–20); assistant solicitor (1920–25); legal adviser to the American delegation at the Conference on Near Eastern Affairs at Lausanne and to the American high commissioner in Constantinople (1923); assistant chief, Division of Near Eastern Affairs (1925); legal adviser to the American ambassador in Havana (1930–32); chief counsel, Mexican Claims Commission (1935–38); member of the advisory commission, Harvard Research in International Law (1935–42); and chairman, District of Columbia branch, Commission to Study the Organization of Peace (1944–45).

In 1947 he became a partner in the law firm of Peaslee and Turlington, in Washington, D.C., where he was a member of the Alabama and District of Columbia bar and was licensed to practice before the Supreme Court. He was active in numerous professional organizations, societies, and councils and was the author of two books: *Mexico and Her Foreign Creditors* (1930) and *Neutrality: The World War Period* (1936).

Turlington married Catherine Isabel Hackett in 1926, and they had three daughters: Sylvia, Ellen Rigby, and Barbara. Early in life he was a Presbyterian but became a Unitarian.

SEE: Alumni Files (University of North Carolina, Chapel Hill; Daniel L. Grant, *Alumni History of The University of North Carolina* (1924); Raleigh *News and Observer*, 28 Sept. 1959; Catherine I. Turlington, *Three to Make Ready* (1948); *Who's Who in the South and Southwest* (1950).

WILLIAM S. POWELL

Turlington, Zebulon Vance *(8 Jan. 1877–16 Nov. 1969)*, lawyer, was born in Johnston County, the son of Eli and Sarah Woodall Turlington. After attending Turlington Institute, a noted school operated by his brother in Smithfield, he taught for two years at nearby Benson and for one five-month term in Ashe County. He studied law at The University of North Carolina (1898–99) and opened an office to practice law in Mooresville, Iredell County, on 21 Aug. 1900. Turlington served as clerk and treasurer of the town in 1900–1901, and from 1900 for sixty years he also was the town attorney. For ten years he was the county attorney. His political initiation occurred when he began many years of service on the county Democratic committee. He represented Iredell County in the General Assembly terms of 1905, 1905–8, 1909, 1911, 1923, 1925, 1927, and 1939.

In the legislature Turlington was chairman of the house committee on appropriations in 1911. In 1923 he was the author of a prohibition bill widely referred to as the Turlington Act, the bill that made North Carolina legally dry; it remained in effect until 1967. At the next session he was chairman of the committee on roads at a time when the state was engaged in a significant road-building program.

An active Presbyterian, he was a Sunday School superintendent for nineteen years, an elder in his church, and president of the Board of Regents of Barium Springs Presbyterian Orphanage. In 1902 he married Mary Howard Rankin, and they had two daughters, Mary Howard and Sarah Woodall. An infant daughter died in 1903 and a son in 1911. Turlington's funeral was held in the First Presbyterian Church, Mooresville, where he was buried in Willow Valley Cemetery.

SEE: John L. Cheney, Jr., ed., *North Carolina Government, 1584–1979* (1981); *Durham Morning Herald*, 8 Jan. 1967; Daniel L. Grant, *Alumni History of the University of North Carolina* (1924); W. J. Haselden, *Mooresville: The Early Years* (1961); *North Carolina Biography*, vol. 4 (1928 [portrait]); Raleigh *News and Observer*, 19 Nov. 1969.

WILLIAM S. POWELL

Turner, Benjamin Sterling *(17 Mar. 1825–21 Mar. 1894)*, Alabama congressman during Reconstruction, was born near Weldon, Halifax County, of unknown parents. A slave, he moved to Selma, Ala., with his master in 1830. Although he had no formal schooling, he managed to obtain a fair education surreptitiously. As a slave of Dr. J. T. Coo, a Selma hotel owner, Turner was regarded as "a remarkably efficient and intelligent servant."

After obtaining his freedom, probably as a result of the Emancipation Proclamation, he developed a prosperous livery stable business and was elected Dallas County tax collector in 1867. On 22 Dec. 1868 he won a seat on the Selma City Council but resigned on 6 Sept. 1869. In September 1870 he was chosen foreman of Central Fire Company, No. 2, in Selma, a unit consisting of forty members. Nominated unanimously by the Republican party in 1870 for the First District seat from Alabama in the Forty-second Congress, Turner sold his horse to finance his campaign and won the election handily.

In Congress Turner introduced legislation aimed at stimulating the South's economy, and he stressed this need in his appeal for a public building program to aid war-devastated Selma. Other bills that he introduced were designed to restore political and legal rights to ex-Confederates generally and to some of his Dallas County constituents in particular, but they were not approved by Congress. His speech, *Public Buildings in Selma, Alabama—The Refunding of the Cotton Tax*, was printed as a pamphlet in 1872. This and other speeches reveal an unbiased concern for all of his constituents. During his tenure in the House Turner was described by the Washington correspondent for the New York *Globe* as "a big broad-shouldered man with a large nose and curly hair." He also observed that Turner was "very quiet, always present (when the House was in session) . . . and among Republican colleagues has a considerable reputation for good sense and political sagacity."

Although he received the Republican nomination in 1872, Turner was the victim of a split in party ranks that resulted in his defeat as a candidate for reelection to Congress, a loss that marked the end of his political career above the local level. Unwilling to engage in political infighting, he returned to Dallas County in March 1873 and confined himself largely to farming and civic affairs; however, he did not abandon local politics.

He served as an election official for Selma municipal elections in 1875, 1877, and 1891 and won a seat on the Selma City Council in 1885. When his two-year term ended, he chose not to seek reelection. In 1880 he was an Alabama delegate to the Republican National Convention in Chicago. Turner died in Selma, where he was buried in Live Oak Cemetery.

SEE: *Biog. Dir. Am. Cong.* (1961); Maurice Christopher, *America's Black Congressmen* (1971); John W. DuBose, *Alabama's Tragic Decade: Ten Years of Alabama, 1865–1874* (1940); John Hardy, *Selma: Her Institutions and Her Men* (1957); *International Library of Negro Life and History: Historical Negro Biographies* (1967); Walter M. Jackson, *The Story of Selma* (1954); Rayford W. Logan and Michael R. Winston, eds., *Dictionary of American Negro Biography* (1982); Annjennette Sophie McFarlin, *Black Congressional Reconstruction Orators and Their Orations, 1869–1879* (1976 [portrait]).

ALVA W. STEWART

Turner, Daniel *(21 Sept. 1796–21 July 1860)*, soldier, lawyer, congressman, teacher, and engineer, was born near Warrenton, Warren County, one of four children of James and Mary Anderson Turner. His mother died when he was five. His father was active in North Carolina politics, serving as governor (1802–5) and a U.S. senator (1805–16). After preparatory studies at the Warrenton Male Academy, Daniel Turner became a cadet at West Point on 19 July 1813; he was graduated in the class of 1814 at age eighteen. Commissioned a second lieutenant of artillery, he served during the last months of the War of 1812 as an assistant engineer on the defenses of New York. Resigning his commission in May 1815, soon after the war ended, he attended the College of William and Mary for two years before returning home to practice law.

Turner represented Warren in the General Assembly for five terms (1819–23) and was a captain in the North Carolina militia (1819–27). In the Assembly he followed an independent course, voting to support internal improvements and to create Davidson as a county in the western section of the state, neither popular votes in Warren.

When Weldon Edwards retired from Congress in 1827, Turner was elected to replace him as representative of the Granville District. In Washington he lived at Mr. Dowson's, No. 2, on Capitol Hill with Nathaniel Macon, Thomas H. Hall, and John Randolph. Turner, who served on the Committee on Expenditures in the War Department, made little mark in the House and did not stand for reelection. In both 1834 and 1835 the Assembly elected him a councillor of state, and in 1835 he was a delegate at the Baltimore Democratic convention. In 1836 he was a member of the State Central Committee supporting the ticket of Martin Van Buren and Richard M. Johnson.

The principal of the Warrenton Female Seminary, Nelson Graves, was dismissed in 1847, apparently because of his abolitionist sentiments, and Turner was given the position, which he held until 1854. During this period the former congressman was in financial trouble, and his friends tried to find a political appointment for him. One of the last presidential acts of James K. Polk was to nominate Turner for the job of collector of revenue at San Francisco, but the Senate blocked confirmation. In 1854 President Franklin Pierce appointed him superintendent of public works at the Mare Island Navy Yard, Calif., a post Turner held from 16 Sept. 1854 until his death.

Turner married Anna Key, the daughter of Francis Scott Key, and they had a large family of daughters. He died in California and was buried at the Mare Island Naval Cemetery.

SEE: *Biog. Dir. Am. Cong.* (1971); John L. Cheney, Jr., ed., *North Carolina Government, 1585–1979* (1981); G. W. Cullum, *Biographical Register of Officers and Graduates of the United States Military Academy*, vol. 1 (1868); Key-Cutts-Turner Papers (Library of Congress, Washington, D.C.); *Library of Congress Information Bulletin*, no. 49 (2 July 1990); G. W. McIver, "North Carolinians at West Point before the Civil War," *North Carolina Historical Review* 8 (1930); Lizzie W. Montgomery, *Sketches of Old Warrenton, North Carolina* (1924); Manly W. Wellman, *The County of Warren, North Carolina, 1586–1917* (1959).

DANIEL M. MCFARLAND

Turner, Henry Gray (*20 Mar. 1839–9 June 1904*), congressman, legislator, and Confederate officer, was born near the young community of Henderson in the part of Franklin County that became Vance County in 1881. He was the son of Archibald Adams and Mary Anne Howze Turner who moved to North Carolina from Frederick County, Va. Young Henry is said to have enrolled at The University of North Carolina but withdrew shortly afterwards because of illness. He then entered the University of Virginia, but after the death of his father in 1857, he left and became principal of an academy in Brooks County, Ga.

On 6 May 1862 Turner enlisted as a private in the Georgia infantry but soon transferred as a second lieutenant to the Twenty-third Regiment, North Carolina Volunteers, in which his brother was also an officer. In August he was elected captain of Company H. At the Battle of Gettysburg in July 1863 he was struck in the left shoulder by a rifle ball and taken prisoner. Following preliminary

treatment in an army hospital, he was held first at Johnson's Island, Ohio, then at Point Lookout, Md., and finally at Fort Delaware, Del., from where he was cleared for exchange. Arriving in Richmond, Va., he was examined by Confederate surgeons in October 1864 and sent to the Confederate hospital at Kittrell Springs, N.C. Still unable to return to duty, he spent some time at his old home in Henderson and was continued on leave until the end of the war.

Returning to Georgia, he was admitted to the bar and on 18 June 1865 married Lavinia Calhoun Morton, the daughter of Judge James Oliver Morton. Turner entered politics as a delegate to the state Democratic convention in 1872, and between 1874 and 1879 he was a member of the Georgia House of Representatives. As a legislator in 1879, in a case that attracted considerable attention, he managed the impeachment trial of several state officials charged with improper use of public funds. In 1880 he was elected to Congress, where he served seven consecutive terms between 1881 and 1897. In 1890 he contributed a chapter entitled "Reconstruction in Georgia" to *Why the Solid South? or Reconstruction and Its Result*, edited by Alabama congressman Hilary A. Herbert; published in Baltimore, this work contained chapters by other southern congressmen.

Appointed to the Georgia Supreme Court, Turner served from 1903 until declining health obliged him to resign. Returning home from Baltimore, where he had gone to consult physicians about his health, he died in Raleigh at the home of his brother, Dr. Vines E. Turner. His body was returned to his home in Quitman, where he was buried in West End Cemetery. Turner County, created in 1905, was named in his honor. He was survived by a daughter and two sons.

SEE: Samuel A. Ashe, ed., *Biographical History of North Carolina*, vol. 6 (1907); *Atlanta Constitution*, 16 June 1871–30 Dec. 1880; I. W. Avery, *History of Georgia from 1850 to 1881* (1881); Walter Clark, ed., *Histories of the Several Regiments and Battalions from North Carolina in the Great War*, vol. 2 (1901 [portrait]); H. W. J. Ham, ed., *Representative Georgians: Biographical Sketches of Men in Public Life* (1887); Folks Huxford, ed., *History of Brooks County, Georgia* (1948 [portrait]); Weymouth T. Jordan, comp., *North Carolina Troops, 1861–1865: A Roster*, vol. 7 (1979); "Memorial of Hon. Henry G. Turner," in *Reports of Cases Decided in the Supreme Court of the State of Georgia at the March Term, 1904: Georgia Supreme Court Reports*, vol. 120 (1904); *Nat. Cyc. Am. Biog.*, vol. 3 (1893 [portrait]); William J. Northen, *Men of Mark in Georgia*, vol. 4 (1908 [portrait]); U.S. census returns, Franklin (1840) and Granville (1850) Counties (microfilm, North Carolina Collection, University of North Carolina, Chapel Hill).

H. B. FANT

Turner, Jacob (*ca. 1745–4 Oct. 1777*), Revolutionary hero, was probably born in Southampton County, Va., before his father Thomas moved to Warren County (then Bute), N.C. Turner first appears in the records in January 1775, when he was appointed captain in Alston's company. On 23 June of the same year he was elected to the Bute County Committee of Safety. When the Third North Carolina Battalion was created by the Provincial Congress at Halifax on 11 Apr. 1776, Turner was appointed fifth captain in the regiment. The following year, in response to urgent pressure from the Continental army in the North, the North Carolina Continentals were ordered to rendezvous at Halifax. The Third Regiment was the first to arrive. The officers met at Martin's Tavern, where several disputes over rank took place. One argument was settled by recognizing Turner as first captain of the regiment.

On 1 Sept. 1777 General Jethro Sumner, in camp at Wilmington, Del., wrote to General George Washington for the commission of major for Jacob Turner, in the room of Major Samuel Lockhart. Before this request could be acted on, the Third North Carolina Regiment, on 11 September, went into action at Brandywine, where the Continental army unsuccessfully attempted to thwart Sir William Howe's march on Philadelphia. Turner distinguished himself by his gallantry in the early stage of this battle. When the British occupied Philadelphia, the greater part of their army encamped at Germantown, then a small village northwest of the city. Washington decided to attack the camp on 4 Oct. 1777. During this engagement Captain Turner was felled by musket fire. He was buried in the Upper Burying Ground in Germantown in a common grave with Colonel Henry Irwin, Adjutant Lucas, and six privates, all killed on the same day. Many years later, a monument was erected over the graves through the efforts of John Fanning Watson, author of the *Annals of Philadelphia*, himself then a resident of Germantown.

Turner died unmarried. In the fall of 1777 the Assembly of North Carolina granted Thomas Turner £170 for the losses incurred by his son, Captain Jacob Turner, deceased. At a commission to settle army accounts for the North Carolina Continental Line held in Warrenton in 1786, further payment was made to Thomas Turner on behalf of the captain. His younger brother, James Turner, later governor of the state, was granted Captain Jacob Turner's bounty land warrant for 3,840 acres of Tennessee land. Judge Walter Clark published the diary of one Captain Turner from 19 Aug. 1777 to 27 Aug. 1778 in the *State Records of North Carolina*, printing it "because of the light it throws upon the condition and management of our troops." Clark was in error in attributing this to Captain Jacob Turner; indeed, nothing in the diary indicates that this Turner was a native of North Carolina. John H. Wheeler in his *History of North Carolina* incorrectly placed Captain Jacob Turner in Bertie County.

SEE: *Bute County Committee of Safety Minutes, 1775–1776* (1977); Walter Clark, ed., *State Records of North Carolina*, vols. 10–13, 16–17 (1890–99); National Archives, carded service record; Hugh F. Rankin, *The North Carolina Continentals* (1971); Phillips Russell, *North Carolina in the Revolutionary War* (1965).

CLAIBORNE T. SMITH, JR.

Turner, James (20 Dec. 1766–15 Jan. 1824), farmer, legislator, U.S. senator, and governor, was born in the part of Bute County that became Warren County in 1779. His father, Thomas, a farmer, had lived in Granville County since at least 1754; Bute was formed from Granville in 1764. By 1790 James Turner had twenty slaves; two plantations, Bloomsbury near Warrenton and Oakland near Williamsboro, were associated with the family.

Turner received scant education in local academies. As a teenager he served as a private in a local volunteer company that marched with General Nathanael Greene's army in 1781 during the last campaign of the Revolutionary War. An older neighbor, Nathaniel Macon, was in the same company, and a circle of young men soon forged ties of political interest that lasted a lifetime. By the time that Turner was elected without opposition as a Warren County member of the House of Commons in 1797, he was already identified with the "Warren junto," the name applied to Macon's adherents.

Turner served three terms in the house and then went to the state senate in 1801. He was reelected in 1802, and when governor-elect John B. Ashe died before taking office, Turner was the legislature's choice for governor. He was reelected for one-year terms in 1803, 1804, and 1805. His terms coincided with a period when the Jeffersonian Republican party took a firm grip on state affairs. His three gubernatorial messages to the Assembly were noteworthy mainly for their short passages expressing the Jeffersonian belief that education was a necessity for a free society. But they were devoid of concrete suggestions for public support of education and were not acted upon by the legislature.

When Montford Stokes declined to serve after having been elected, the state legislature sent Turner to the U.S. Senate on 21 Nov. 1805. Turner resigned as governor to join a Washington delegation from North Carolina dominated by Macon, then Speaker of the U.S. House of Representatives.

Although he stayed in a Capitol Hill boardinghouse that was also quarters for Macon, Turner showed some independence from his friend when Macon became a leader of a "Quid" Republican opposition to Jeffersonian policies. He embraced the Louisiana Purchase and staunchly supported the conduct of the War of 1812, unlike his North Carolina colleague, David Stone. Turner did not play an active role in Senate affairs, only being listed once as a committee member and that on the Committee on Enrolled Bills.

His service was increasingly mortgaged to bad health, and when he was unable to leave for the session of 1816, he sent a letter of resignation, dated 21 Nov. 1816, to Governor William Miller, another Warren County neighbor. Turner took no further active part in politics and died at Bloomsbury, where he was buried.

Turner was married three times and survived by his third wife. In 1783 he married Mary Anderson of Warrenton, and they had four children: Thomas, Daniel, Rebecca, and Mary. She died in 1802, leaving, according to her obituary, "a smiling race of pratlers." Anna Cochran became Turner's second wife in 1803; she died in 1806. He married Elizabeth Johnston, widow of Dr. William Johnston, in 1810, and they had two daughters. Their daughter Rebecca married George E. Badger, of Hillsborough, later a congressmen and secretary of the navy in the administration of President Benjamin Harrison. Turner's son Daniel was a graduate of the U.S. Military Academy, an officer in the War of 1812, and a congressman in 1827–29.

SEE: Samuel A. Ashe, ed., *Biographical History of North Carolina*, vol. 3 (1906); *Biog. Dir. Am. Cong.* (1971); John L. Cheney, Jr., ed., *North Carolina Government, 1585–1979* (1981); William E. Dodd, *Life of Nathaniel Macon* (1903); D. H. Gilpatrick, *Jeffersonian Democracy in North Carolina* (1931); Perry Goldman and James S. Young, *United States Congressional Directories, 1789–1840* (1973); Lois S. Neal, *Abstracts of Vital Records of Raleigh, North Carolina: Newspapers, 1799–1819* (1979).

ROY PARKER, JR.

Turner, Jesse (3 Oct. 1805–22 Nov. 1894), pioneer Arkansas lawyer, politician, and industrialist, was born in Orange County. His family, of Scots-Irish descent, emigrated from County Downs, Ireland, in 1750 to Lancaster, Pa., moving south to North Carolina in subsequent years. Young Jesse attended The University of North Carolina in 1824, studying law under William McCauley. He moved to Alabama in 1830, staying but a short time before continuing on to Arkansas and settling at Van Buren in 1831.

A Whig in politics, Turner played a major role in a political party that never elected a governor or congressman in Arkansas. Nevertheless, he was a state legislator in 1838, a delegate to the Whig convention in 1840, a visitor to West Point in 1841, and district attorney for western Arkansas during the period 1851–54. He retired from active politics in the late 1850s, when the state Whig party disintegrated. Turning his attention to economic development, Turner was instrumental in the organization of the Little Rock and Fort Smith Railroad, serving as its president from 1857 until after the Civil War. A promoter of educational betterment, he sat on the Van Buren School Board and the Crawford Institute board.

Turner led the opposition to secession in western Arkansas. Elected to the secession convention, he forcefully opposed withdrawal from the Union from both a practical and theoretical standpoint, denying completely the legitimacy of the doctrine of peaceful secession. The firing on Fort Sumter caused him to alter his position. He voted for the ordinance while continuing to assert that he had actually supported an "act of revolution" rather than of secession. Turner played only a minor role during the Confederate period. When Federal control was extended over the state, he came to terms with the Unionists, announcing in a public letter that the war was lost and slavery must be abandoned.

His primary interest in the Reconstruction years was the revival of his cherished Little Rock and Fort Smith Railroad. However, financial problems overwhelmed the company, and Turner was forced to take a seat as vice-president in a reorganization that gave northern capitalists control of the road. He returned to politics briefly in 1866 and again in 1874 as a state senator. As a Democrat he attended his party's national convention in 1876. In 1878 he was appointed to fill an unexpired term as associate justice of the state supreme court. A much respected figure in Arkansas politics, he had "a fine commanding appearance" and possessed a library of over 1,500 books.

In 1842 Turner married Violet P. Drennen, who died the same year. In 1855 he married Rebecca J. Allen, who gave him one son, Jesse, Jr. He was buried in Van Buren.

SEE: Alfred Holt Carrigan, "Reminiscences of the Secession Convention," *Publications of the Arkansas Historical Association*, vol. 1 (1906); Clara B. Eno, *History of Crawford County* (n.d.); George H. Thompson, *Arkansas and Reconstruction* (1976); "Tribute by U. M. Rose and Ben T. DuVal," 60 Ark. 621 (1895); Jesse Turner Papers (Duke University Archives, Durham); J. S. Utley, "Graves of Eminent Men," *Publications of the Arkansas Historical Association*, vol. 2 (1908).

MICHAEL B. DOUGAN

Turner, John (ca. 1802–1844), Texas pioneer, politician, soldier, and jurist, was born in North Carolina but, like others of the time, was taken by his parents to Tennessee as a youth. From there he emigrated to Texas in 1834. On 20 June 1835 he received title to one league and one labor (a Spanish land unit measuring 177 acres) of land in what became Live Oak County, seventy miles south of San Antonio.

On 1 Feb. 1836 Turner was elected to represent the San Patricio community in the constitutional convention. After the convention adjourned, he joined the Army of Texas. His land was overrun by the army of the Mexican dictator, Santa Anna. Turner served under General Thomas Jefferson Green, a native of Warren County, N.C., and was apparently engaged in procuring horses and supplies for the army.

Following the success of the Texas Revolution, Turner was elected to the house of representatives of the new Republic of Texas. After his service in the government, he returned to the San Patricio municipality and was appointed county judge by Sam Houston. Turner left San Patricio in 1839 and settled near Houston, where he resided until his death.

SEE: Louis Waltz Kemp, *Signers of the Texas Declaration of Independence* (1944); Walter P. Webb, ed., *Handbook of Texas*, vol. 2 (1952).

JOSEPH L. PRICE

Turner, John Clyde (31 Mar. 1879–1 Feb. 1974), Baptist minister, scholar, and author, was born in Iredell County, the son of John and Nancy Tuck Turner who were of English descent. He first attended the three-month annual sessions of Ebenezer Academy, where the students ranged in ages from six to twenty-one years. The school's emphasis on writing the beautiful Spencerian style, strict discipline, a thorough mastery of Webster's Blue-Backed Speller, and arithmetic fundamentals laid a sound foundation for his later advances in education. When Clyde Turner was nine, his father was elected treasurer of Iredell County and the family moved to Statesville, where the boy attended the city school.

In 1899 he received the A.B. degree from Wake Forest College. At the end of his senior year he was awarded the valedictory by his class and was the featured anniversary orator for the Euzelian Literary Society, two of the most coveted honors bestowed upon any graduating senior. Also a popular athlete, he was catcher for the college baseball team in his final year. His avid interest in Wake Forest College sports continued until his death.

Turner taught in the Durham High School for three years (1899–1901) and was an instructor at the Oxford Masonic Orphanage for one year (1901–2). In 1902 he enrolled at Southern Baptist Theological Seminary, in Louisville, Ky., where he received the Th.M. degree in 1905. While at the seminary he was a student pastor of the Baptist church at Fisherville, Ky. (1902–5). Thereafter he was pastor of the First Baptist church at Newport, Ky. (1905–7) and minister of Tattnall Square Baptist Church in Macon, Ga. (1907–10).

Turner's most illustrious pastorate was his thirty-eight years of service in the First Baptist Church in Greensboro, N.C. (4 Dec. 1910–48). There he demonstrated a brilliant ability in church finance, offering sound business judgment and assisting the congregation in clearing its overwhelming monetary obligation in seven years. He gave generously himself and insisted that the church should appropriate as much to benevolence and missions as it did to local expenses. The Greensboro church was the state's largest contributor to the mission program of Southern Baptists. Even during the depression years of the thirties, it could be counted on for its unmatched stewardship. Turner was a dynamic preacher and developed a strong religious educational program at the church, which experienced a phenomenal growth both in membership and in spiritual depth while he was pastor. Under Turner's leadership the First Baptist Church was instrumental in founding many other churches in the North Carolina Piedmont and was fondly known as the "Mother of Churches."

A participant in important local civic affairs, Turner remained sensitive to the activities of the Baptist denomination in spite of his ninety-five years. He was respected as the "Grand Old Man" of the ministry, leaving a significant list of accomplishments. He served with distinction as president of the North Carolina Baptist State Convention for four terms (1929–32); as a trustee of the Southern Baptist Theological Seminary for twenty-five years, two of which as chairman of the board; and as a trustee of Wake Forest College for twenty-five years. Turner wrote six books. *These Things We Believe*, the basic doctrinal text of more than 12 million Southern Baptists, was perhaps the most noteworthy. He also was the author of *Soul-Winning Doctrines, The Gospel of the Grace of God, Our Baptist Heritage, The New Testament Doctrines of the Church*, and *Century of Service: A History of the First Baptist Church, Greensboro, N.C.*

He married Bertha May Hicks of Raleigh (30 May 1873–5 Nov. 1962). An able Bible scholar and Sunday school teacher, she also made significant contributions as president of the Woman's Missionary Union of North Carolina for seven years. The Turners had no children of their own, but they maintained an interest in the adolescent age and lived vicariously in the youth programs of their church.

He died in Raleigh and was buried in Oakwood Cemetery. A dual portrait of Dr. and Mrs. Turner is in the First Baptist Church, Greensboro.

SEE: *Charlotte Observer*, 2 Feb. 1974; *Greensboro Daily News*, 3 Mar. 1956, 26 Mar. 1965, 10 Jan., 20 Mar. 1971, 2 Feb. 1974; *Greensboro Record*, 1 Feb. 1974; Raleigh, *Biblical Recorder*, 9 Feb. 1974; *Raleigh Times*, 2 Feb. 1974; *Statesville Record and Landmark*, 12 Sept. 1967; J. Clyde Turner, *The New Testament Doctrine of the Church* (1951); *Woman's Missionary Union Annual* (1963).

IRMA RAGAN HOLLAND

Turner, Josiah, Jr. (*27 Dec. 1821–26 Oct. 1901*), Confederate congressman, editor, and militant foe of Reconstruction, was born in Hillsborough, the eldest son of Josiah and Eliza Evans Turner. The father, a longtime sheriff and large landowner in Orange County, sent his son to the Caldwell Institute at Greensboro and then for a year to The University of North Carolina. After two years of legal study in Hillsborough, Josiah, Jr., was admitted to the bar in about 1845. He soon built up a large practice, based partly on his father's influence and partly on his own sharp wit and tongue. In 1856 he married Sophie Devereux, of Raleigh, who bore him four sons and a daughter.

Turner's political career opened with his election to the state House of Commons as a Whig in 1852. He was reelected in 1854, defeated for the state senate in 1856, then elected senator in 1858 and 1860. Turner was ardent to the point of excess in every cause he took up. This included his opposition to secession; but once the decision was made, he raised a company of cavalry for the Confederate service and became its captain. Severely wounded in April 1862, he was disabled from further service and subsequently resigned his commission. In 1863 he was elected to the Confederate Congress as a peace candidate and opponent of the Davis administration. He delivered as promised, opposing conscription, impressment, taxation, and the suspension of habeas corpus so outspokenly as to be assigned to the "lunatic fringe" of that congress. In November 1865, as an old opponent of secession, he was elected to the Federal Congress but, in company with the others chosen at that time, was denied his seat. In 1866 and 1867 he was appointed a director of the state-owned North Carolina Railroad, and in 1867 he was elected its president.

At the end of the war Turner set himself resolutely against all but the most minimal divergence from the old order. Never one to do things by halves, he became the most caustic and uncompromising enemy of congressional Reconstruction when it made its appearance in 1867.

Late the next year, with funds borrowed from industrialist George W. Swepson, Turner bought the Raleigh *Sentinel* and made it the leading Conservative newspaper in the state. Here lay his major lifework, flaying the Republican administration of Governor William W. Holden with loosely substantiated charges of fraud and dictatorship, ridiculing its supporters for their real or imaginary foibles, often with outrageously clever nicknames, and lending encouragement to every Conservative opposition device including the Ku Klux Klan. (Holden's rival Raleigh *Standard* referred to Turner as King of the Ku Klux, but there is no evidence that he was ever more than an apologist for the order.) Turner was a master of polemical journalism at a time when that style was in high fashion. Other papers took their lead from the *Sentinel* when they did not quote it directly, and he thereby contributed as much as anyone in the state to the overthrow of Governor Holden in 1870. This was all the more pleasant for Turner, as he had been briefly imprisoned by the governor's militia earlier that year owing to the blunder of one of its commanding officers.

But Turner's victory proved his undoing. Erratic and even destructive by temperament, he belonged congenitally to the opposition. Fellow Conservatives mistrusted him and he turned against them. He declined a congressional nomination in 1872, apparently expecting a U.S. senatorship that did not materialize, and the congressional nomination was denied him two years later. As a delegate to the Conservative-oriented constitutional convention of 1875, he outdid his fellows in denouncing past Republican measures. A year later he sold his newspaper, still encumbered with debt despite its previous popularity and large circulation. He was defeated in a bid for the state senate in 1876, endorsed by the Republicans, then ran unsuccessfully for Congress as an independent in 1878. He was elected to the lower house of the legislature in 1878, however, only to be expelled for disorderly ad hominem attacks upon his colleagues. After another failed congressional race in 1884, Turner flirted with populism in the 1890s and ended his life a Republican. An Episcopalian, he died at his home in Hillsborough, where he was buried in the churchyard of St. Matthew's Church. The North Carolina Collection in Chapel Hill has a portrait of him.

SEE: Thomas Alexander and Richard E. Beringer, *The Anatomy of the Confederate Congress* (1972); Samuel A. Ashe, ed., *Biographical History of North Carolina*, vol. 3 (1906); *DAB*, vol. 19 (1936); Jonathan Daniels, *Prince of Carpetbaggers* (1958); Raleigh *News and Observer*, 27 Oct. 1901; Josiah Turner Papers (Manuscript Department, Duke University Library, Durham, and Southern Historical Collection, University of North Carolina, Chapel Hill).

ALLEN W. TRELEASE

Turner, Vines Edmunds (*19 Jan. 1837–11 May 1914*), dentist, businessman, Confederate soldier, and civic leader, was born in Franklin County, the son of Archibald Adams, a farmer and businessman, and Mary Anne Howze Turner. His most distinguished brother was Henry Gray Turner, a congressman from Georgia and associate justice of the Georgia Supreme Court. As a young man, Vines Turner attended the Henderson Male Academy until he went into the hardware business with his father in Henderson. At age nineteen, he enrolled in the Baltimore College of Dental Surgery, from which he was graduated with a D.D.S. degree in March 1858.

Returning to Henderson, Turner practiced dentistry until the Civil War broke out in 1861. He immediately enlisted in the Granville Rifles and served until commissioned a second lieutenant in Company G, Twenty-third North Carolina Infantry Regiment, on 11 June 1861. Due to his superior performance, he was selected as adjutant of the regiment on 10 May 1862. He fought in the battles at Williamsburg, Mechanicsville, South Mountain, Sharpsburg, Fredericksburg, and Cold Harbor. He was wounded at Cold Harbor on 27 June 1862 and received a minor injury at Mechanicsville when his horse was killed and fell on him. Beginning in the spring of 1863, Turner served successively as a captain on the staffs of General Stephen D. Ramseur, General John Pegram, and General James A. Walker. His military career ended when General Walker surrendered at Appomattox.

After the war Turner resumed his dental practice in Henderson. On 24 Sept. 1868 he married Zene H. Lassiter, who died on 26 May 1869. Around 1870 he moved to Raleigh and in September 1874 married Love Gales Root, the daughter of Charles B. and Anna Freeman Gales Root. Dr. and Mrs. Turner had three children: Charles Root, who became a physician and dentist; Mary Archer, who married Henry Merryman Wilson; and Henry Gray, who became a physician and surgeon.

Active in many professional organizations, Turner was a charter member and served for two terms as president of the North Carolina Dental Society. From 1894 until his death, he was president of the Board of Dental Examiners of North Carolina; he was also president of the Southern Dental Association. In 1887 and 1904 he was vice-president of the Third and Fourth International Medical Congresses at Washington, D.C., and St. Louis, and in 1893 he sat on many committees at the Columbian Dental Congress in Chicago. He was elected president of the National Association of Dental Examiners in 1901. In the National Dental Association, he served as treasurer (1904–6) and president (1908). President Woodrow Wilson appointed him an assistant dental surgeon (1913) and a member of the Examining Board of Dental Surgeons, Dental Reserve Corps, U.S. Army.

In addition, Vines Turner was involved in the business and social life of Raleigh. He was a director of the North Carolina Railroad Company (1894–96 and 1901–6) and a founder of the Raleigh Street Railway, serving as its president for three years. Later he was a director of the Raleigh Electric Company, which bought the Raleigh Street Railway. For almost twenty-five years, he was a director of the Raleigh Savings Bank. Turner was one of the founders of the Capital Club and a member of the William G. Hill Masonic Lodge, No. 218. An Episcopalian, he belonged to Christ Church. He was an active Democrat.

Turner died of edema of the lungs and heart failure due to diabetes mellitus. He was buried in Raleigh.

SEE: Samuel A. Ashe, ed., *Biographical History of North Carolina*, vol. 6 (1907); Walter Clark, ed., *Histories of the Several Regiments and Battalions from North Carolina in the Great War*, vol. 2 (1901 [portrait]); Compiled Service Records (U.S. National Archives Microfilm, North Carolina State Archives, Raleigh); *Dental Cosmos*, obituary (July 1914); Clement A. Evans, ed., *Confederate Military History*, vol. 4 (1899); Weymouth T. Jordan, comp., *North Carolina Troops, 1861–1865: A Roster*, vol. 7 (1979); *Nat. Cyc. Am. Biog.*, vol. 14 (1892); *North Carolina Yearbook* (1912); Raleigh *Daily Sentinel*, 16 Sept. 1874; Raleigh Savings Banks Records, Wake County Estate Records, William G. Hill Lodge Roster of Members (North Carolina Archives, Raleigh).

CAROL DALTON DEATON

Turner, Wilfred Dent (*30 Jan. 1855–8 Nov. 1933*), lawyer, legislator, lieutenant governor, and businessman, was born at Turnersburg, Iredell County, the son of Wilfred and Dorcas Tomlinson Turner. His grandfather, Samuel Turner, moved to North Carolina from Port Tobacco, Md., in 1818. His father was a member of the House of Commons in the 1852 General Assembly and was a pioneer in the establishment of a cotton manufacturing business on Rocky Creek in the present community of Turnersburg. The Turners and Tomlinsons were prominent families in the northern section of the county where both the community and the township were named for the Turners.

His early education was in the old-field schools of the county, Olin Academy, and Mount Airy High School. From Trinity College in Durham he received the B.A. degree in 1876 and the M.A. degree in 1879. After completing his undergraduate work he returned to the county and began to read law under Judge Robert F. Armfield in Statesville; later, without a teacher, he studied further and received a license to practice. In July 1877 he began a fifty-six-year legal career in Statesville.

Turner's successful political career opened in 1887, when he served in the state senate; he was returned for the sessions of 1889, 1891, and 1917. In 1900, as a candidate for lieutenant governor, he teamed up with gubernatorial candidate Charles B. Aycock. The Aycock-Turner victory swept the last power of Fusion rule from office for the Democrats. As lieutenant governor from 1901 to 1905, one of Turner's significant duties as president of the senate was presiding at the impeachment proceedings in 1901 against Chief Justice David M. Furches, a fellow Iredell County citizen, but of the Republican party. Turner's fairness in the trial was viewed as a demonstration of the soundness of his leadership at a time of rampant partisan politics. Although few historians link Turner with Aycock's administration, his prior service in the state senate was helpful in securing passage of the governor's legislative proposals.

In addition to successful legal and political careers, Turner had an active role in industry and finance in his home area. He was president of the Commercial National Bank and of the Imperial Furniture Company, chief organizer of the Monbo Manufacturing Company on the Catawba River, and secretary-treasurer of the Armfield Veneer Company. A prominent churchman, he was chairman of the Board of Stewards of Broad Street Methodist Church, teacher of the Men's Bible Class, and for forty years chairman of the church's board of trustees. He served on the board of trustees of Trinity College and later of Duke University for twenty-three years and was a member of the board of trustees of the North Carolina College for Women. At the time of his death he was president of the Iredell County Bar Association and a member of the North Carolina Bar Association. He was a former county attorney. From 1931 to 1933 he practiced law as the senior member of the firm of Turner, Moss and Winberry.

Turner was viewed as conservative, solid, and sound, and one who proved his heritage. He was not considered a brilliant advocate, but he commanded wide respect and received broad political support for his integrity and ability. He was married three times—first, in 1878, to Ida Lanier, who died in 1894. They had four children: Mrs. W. A. Colvert, Laura L., Mrs. James F. Robertson, and Jack. In 1897 he married Julie H. McCall, who died in 1925; their children were Mrs. W. A. Tucker and Dent. In 1927 he married Mrs. Sarah F. Goff.

Following an illness of ten days Turner died of acute nephritis at age seventy-eight and was buried in Oakwood Cemetery, Statesville. There is a portrait of him at Broad Street Methodist Church.

SEE: Samuel A. Ashe, ed., *Biographical History of North Carolina*, vol. 6 (1907); John L. Cheney, Jr., ed., *North Carolina Government, 1585–1974* (1974); *Proceedings of the Thirty-sixth Annual Session of the North Carolina Bar Association*, vol. 36 (1934); *Statesville Landmark*, 10 Nov. 1933; *Who Was Who in America*, vol. 1 (1943).

T. HARRY GATTON

Turrentine, John William (5 July 1880–11 July 1966), chemist, was born in Company Shops (later renamed Burlington), the son of William Holt and Ella Anvil Rea Turrentine and a descendant of Alexander Turrentine, a migrant from Ireland who settled in North Carolina in 1761. He attended The University of North Carolina, receiving the Ph.B. degree in 1901 and the M.S. degree in 1902. He was awarded the Ph.D. degree in inorganic chemistry from Cornell University in 1908 and the honorary degree of doctor of agriculture from North Carolina State College (now North Carolina State University) at Raleigh in 1954.

Turrentine was an instructor in chemistry at Lafayette College (1902–5), an assistant at Cornell University (1905–8), and an instructor at Wesleyan College in Connecticut (1908–11). In 1911 he went to work for the Bureau of Soils in the U.S. Department of Agriculture. In that post Turrentine solved the problem of extracting potash from kelp; and when potash importation from Germany ceased in 1914, he was assigned the task of designing, constructing, and operating a plant for this purpose. During the project Turrentine invented a process for the crystallization of potash salts, which revolutionized the potash industry, and developed a procedure for obtaining iodine and decoloring carbon as by-products. He also developed a new method for recovering iodine from dilute solution that proved to be commercially practical. After the plant ceased operations in 1922, he returned to Washington to direct the government's potash studies.

In 1935 Turrentine became president and chairman of the board of directors of the American Potash Institute, founded by American potash producers and importers for scientific research and publicity. He officiated in this capacity until 1950, when he became president emeritus and a consultant of the institute. During his presidency, the work of the organization was greatly expanded, and approximately $500,000 was expended for basic research through fellowships and grants-in-aid to universities and agricultural colleges. In addition, his membership in the American Chemical Society dated from 1902; he also belonged to the American Institute of Chemical Engineers, American Society of Agronomy, Soil Science Society of America, and American Planning and Civic Association. He was a U.S. delegate to the International Congress on Pure and Applied Chemistry when it met in Madrid in 1934 and in Rome in 1938. In 1937 he received the gold medal of the Académie d'Agriculture de France for his work with potash. Turrentine was the author of numerous books and articles on potash and allied subjects including "Potash in North America," published in *American Chemical Society Monograph No. 91.* An excellent photograph of the chemist appeared on the cover of the 13 Dec. 1948 issue of *Chemical Engineering News.*

Turrentine donated twenty acres of his father's former plantation to the Burlington City School System and was present on 7 Nov. 1960 when the institution built on the site was opened and named the Turrentine Junior High School in honor of his parents. He married a Burlington woman in 1926 and she died in 1948. They had no children. Turrentine resided in Washington, D.C., until his death. He and his wife were buried in Pine Hill Cemetery, Burlington.

SEE: Alumni Files (University of North Carolina, Chapel Hill); Burlington *Daily Times-News*, 11 July 1966; *Chemical Abstracts: Decennial Index: Authors*, vols. 1–10 (1907–16), 21–30 (1927–36), 31–40 (1937@2-46); *Chemical Abstracts: Fifth Decennial Index: Authors*, vols. 41–50 (1947–56); *Chemical Engineering News*, vol. 26 (13 Dec. 1948); *Who Was Who in America*, vol. 7 (1981).

DURWARD T. STOKES

Turrentine, Morgan Clower (17 Sept. 1800–15 July 1881), pioneer missionary of the Methodist Episcopal church to the Indian territory in the southwestern United States, was born in Orange County. His parents were James and Catherine Clower Turrentine, and his paternal grandparents were Samuel and Mary Bryant Turrentine. Morgan's brothers and sisters were William, Samuel, George, Allen Augustus, Daniel Clower, James Samuel, Thomas C., Joseph Tarpley, Sarah, Frances L., Elizabeth, and Nancy L. When Morgan was only a few years old, the James Turrentine and Clower families moved to Georgia, settling near Milledgeville, where the youth grew to manhood.

The religious background of the Turrentines was Presbyterian, but Morgan chose the Methodist Episcopal church and was ordained into its ministry. Being physically strong and a fearless crusader of religion, he was dispatched by his church to carry Christianity to the western Indians. On numerous hazardous journeys through the wilderness, he arrived at the villages of the red men, slept in their huts or tents, ate their food, learned to communicate with them, and cultivated their friendship with considerable success. Only on one occasion did he face failure. Several Indians became intoxicated during the absence of their chief and decided to burn the minister at the stake. Just before the fire was lighted, the chief returned and stopped the execution.

Turrentine made many other journeys during his ministry. He frequently visited his numerous relatives, especially his brother, General Daniel Clower Turrentine, who had settled in Gadsden, Ala., after being instrumental in founding that town. The minister also returned to his native state occasionally, but his lifework was primarily with the Indians and with congregations in Georgia and Alabama.

In 1835 he married Lydia Mary Rothwell of Woodford Plantation in Brunswick (now Columbus) County. Their children were Mary C., Sarah, and John Rothwell. His wife died in 1837, and two years later he married Julia Elizabeth Flowers; their children were Frances Virginia, Eugenia, and Frederick. The missionary died in Wilmington while visiting his son John; he was buried there in Oakdale Cemetery.

SEE: Census returns, Brunswick County, 1850 (microfilm, North Carolina State Archives, Raleigh); Deeds, Births, Marriages, and Wills (Brunswick County Courthouse, Bolivia, and Orange County Courthouse, Hillsborough); *New Orleans Christian Advocate*, 4 Oct. 1877; *Southern Christian Advocate*, 24 Dec. 1847; George Ruford Turrentine, *The Turrentine Family* (1952).

DURWARD T. STOKES

Turrentine, Samuel Bryant (15 Nov. 1861–11 Apr. 1940), clergyman and educator, was born in Chatham County, the son of William Holt and Annie Amy Stroud Turrentine and a great-grandson of Alexander Turrentine, who immigrated to North Carolina from Ireland about 1761. After spending his boyhood on a farm, Turrentine attended The University of North Carolina, receiving the A.B. degree in 1884 and the master's degree in 1887. On 4 Jan. 1888 he married Sallie Leonora Atwater; he then undertook theological studies at Vanderbilt University, Yale University, and the University of Chicago. Trinity College (now Duke University) awarded him the doctor of divinity degree in 1900. While pursuing graduate studies, Turrentine was associated with the Union Academy in Chatham County, assisted as superintendent of public instruction in adjoining Orange County, and served as associate professor at the Cartersville Institute in Georgia.

After his ordination into the ministry of the Methodist Episcopal Church, South, in 1890, Turrentine served North Carolina Methodist pastorates at the Centenary Church, Winston (1891–95); Trinity Church, Charlotte (1895–97); West Market Street Church, Greensboro (1900–1904); and First Church, Salisbury (1908–10). He also was presiding elder of the Charlotte District (1897–1900), of the Greensboro District (1904–8), and of the Shelby District (1910–13). In addition, he was a delegate to the General Conference of the Methodist Episcopal Church, South, in 1902 and to the General Conference of the Methodist Episcopal Church in 1906. For many years he served as a trustee of Trinity College and was the senior member of the board of trustees when Trinity became Duke University.

Intensely interested in Greensboro College, Turrentine was instrumental in the rebuilding of the school after a disastrous fire on 18 Feb. 1904. He also worked with the college alumnae in a lengthy fund-raising drive with the ultimate result that Greensboro College was purchased and presented to the North Carolina and the Western North Carolina Conferences of the Methodist Episcopal church. In 1913 Turrentine was elected president of the college and devoted the remainder of his life to its affairs. During his administration facilities were greatly expanded, with a consequent increase in enrollment and accreditation. In 1921 he pursued further graduate work at Columbia University during the summer and was a coorganizer of the North Carolina College Conference. After becoming president emeritus of Greensboro College in 1935, he served as professor of Bible (1935–39) and special lecturer in Bible (1940). Also in 1940 he was one of the founders of the Turrentine Family Association in America.

Turrentine was a Mason and a Democrat. His children were Samuel Bryant, Jr., Annie Leonore, Carney Gray, Wilburn Clinton, Julian Atwater, and Walter William. He was the author of *A Romance of Education: A Narrative, Including Recollections and Other Facts, Connected with Greensboro College* (1946). He was buried in Green Hill Cemetery, Greensboro.

SEE: Ethel Stephens Arnett, *Greensboro, North Carolina* (1955); Daniel L. Grant, *Alumni History of the University of North Carolina* (1924); *Minutes of the North Carolina Conference* and *Minutes of the Western North Carolina Conference*, both of the Methodist Episcopal Church, South, for the years of his ministry (1890–1949); George Ruford Turrentine, *The Turrentine Family* (1954); *Who Was Who in America*, vol. 3 (1966).

DURWARD T. STOKES

Twitty, Panthea Massenburg *(7 Sept. 1912–21 Oct. 1977)*, photographer, ceramist, and historical writer, was born in Warrenton, the daughter of Nancy B. White and John B. Massenburg. She was educated in local schools, studied art in White Plains, N.Y., and attended Columbia University, Cooper Union, and Georgiana Studio of De-

sign. She was active in the United Daughters of the Confederacy as chairman of the monuments and markers committee, compiler of historical records, and historical writer for Children of the Confederacy programs. In 1957 she wrote *Confederate History of Warren County*, and at other times she supplied information and photographs for books published by others. Certified by the National Ceramics Association, she taught ceramics at Halifax Technical Institute and Vance-Granville Community College and operated a ceramics shop at "Reedy Rill," her home in Warren County.

She married Henry Fitts Twitty II in 1941, and they had two children: Panthea Anne (Crawford) and William Henry. A member of the Episcopal church, she was buried in Warrenton.

SEE: Lewis Joel Gregory, *Twitty Family in America* (1976); *Warren Record*, 27 Oct. 1977.

WILLIAM S. POWELL

Twitty, Sallie Duke Drake *(28 July 1835–26 July 1923)*, teacher and school administrator, was born at the Fitts Place, her mother's family home, near Oakville, Warren County, the daughter of Matthew Mann and Winnifred Fitts Drake. She attended private schools in Oakville and Warrenton and was graduated from the Warrenton Female College. Afterwards she studied at Patapsco Institute in Ellicott City, Md.

On the last day of 1862 Sallie Duke Drake married John Eldridge Twitty, a young Confederate corporal. By now promoted to sergeant, he was mortally wounded at the Battle of Spotsylvania Court House, on 12 May 1864, and on the twenty-first he died in enemy hands in Carver Hospital, Washington, D.C. He was buried in the recently established Arlington Cemetery on the grounds of General Robert E. Lee's former home. In November 1865, however, his remains were transferred to the Fitts family cemetery in Warren County. Mrs. Twitty became the model Confederate widow—she wore black, in mourning for her husband, for the remainder of her life and worked to support herself by teaching and in caring for surviving Confederate veterans. She also was a leader in organizing the United Daughters of the Confederacy.

Mrs. Robert Jones, a teacher in Warrenton for many years, was also widowed, and she and Sallie Twitty were employed after the war as teachers in the Warrenton Female College for the year 1868–69. The college closed at the end of the term, and the two women, acting as coprincipals, opened a school for girls in May 1869. Formally termed Warren High School, it was known locally simply as "Mrs. Jones's and Mrs. Twitty's School." When Mrs. Jones remarried in 1873, the school was closed, and Mrs. Twitty became governess in the family of Elias Carr, who was chief executive of the state for the term 1893–97. The Carr family's home was Bracebridge Hall in Edgecombe County, but they had a summer house in Warrenton, and there, in the summers between 1873 and 1880, Mrs. Twitty operated a school for small boys. She then taught English in the Wilson Collegiate Institute in Wilson for the term 1880–81. She was an English teacher and lady principal in charge of the preparatory department in Wilson Collegiate Institute (1881–85), Oxford Female Seminary (1885–89 and 1893–1915), and Luray Female Institute, Luray, Va. (1889–93).

As lady principal she was second in authority to the president, ready to assume charge of the college in his absence. At all times she rang the rising bell, inspected the rooms and the person of each student, presided over the meals in the dining hall, conducted religious worship in the chapel, gave the instructions for the day, taught her own classes, led the students on a daily walk, saw to it that they were all safely in their rooms for study and quiet, and rang the bell for retiring. She was in charge of student discipline and conduct on the college grounds and in the town.

It was her responsibility in these finishing schools to train girls from childhood to adulthood in all the accomplishments of womanly life, which in those days meant presiding over a home and family or teaching school. She was expected to form her pupils by her own example. She taught simple subjects to students ranging from six-year-old beginners to mature young women, but she taught them thoroughly. She was a stern disciplinarian. For instance, she gave four lessons a week in spelling to each student, and no student was graduated until she could pass with a perfect mark Mrs. Twitty's examination of ninety-nine words.

When she retired on 25 May 1915, the senior class at Oxford College presented a portrait of her to the school. A member of the graduating class, who spoke on the occasion, characterized the gift as a symbol of the love and devotion "her girls" had felt for their teacher over a period of forty-seven years. In retirement she lived at the home of Mr. and Mrs. George R. Scoggin in Warrenton, and at her death at age eighty-eight she was buried beside her soldier husband in the Fitts family cemetery in Warren County. A devout member of the Methodist church all of her life, she favored the Democratic party and was a leader in the United Daughters of the Confederacy, whose Warrenton chapter was named in her honor.

SEE: *Ellicott City Bicentennial Journal*, Summer–Fall 1972; James Harris Fitts, *Genealogy of the Fitts or Fitz Family* (1897); Emma Hales, "Address at Presentation of Portrait of Mrs. S. D. Twitty to Oxford College, May 25, 1915" (Oxford College records, State Archives, Raleigh); Robert B. House, *Miss Sue and the Sheriff* (1941); Weymouth T. Jordan, comp., *North Carolina Troops, 1861–1865: A Roster*, vol. 5 (1975); *Oxford Ledger*, 3 Aug. 1923; Harry W. Strickler, *A Short History of Page County, Virginia* (1957); *Wilson Advance*, 9 June 1882–6 June 1884.

ROBERT B. HOUSE

Tyler, Margaret Ridley Long (*26 Mar. 1917–30 Mar. 1991*), teacher and preservationist, was born in Roanoke Rapids, the daughter of Thomas W. M., a physician, and Maria Greenough Burgwyn Long. She attended St. Mary's College and was graduated from The University of North Carolina in 1938. The following year she also received a degree in library science. She taught English and mathematics and was librarian in the public schools of Bertie County for thirty years. In 1941 she married John Edward Tyler of Roxobel, and they had three children: Margaret Ridley (m. James E. Smith), John Cotten Pierce, and Ethel Leonard Gregory Tyler Hand.

Mrs. Tyler achieved wide recognition for her leadership in the preservation and restoration of Hope Plantation, the 1803 home of Governor David Stone in Bertie County. She was instrumental in raising funds for this community undertaking, as well as in decorating the house and acquiring furnishings. Especially noteworthy was the replication of the large library of late-eighteenth and early-nineteenth-century books held by Stone. Her work and the completed project came to be regarded as a model for similar programs.

An Episcopalian, Mrs. Tyler was buried in the family cemetery at Oaklana, the family home near St. Mark's Church, Roxobel, where the funeral was held.

SEE: Alumni Files (University of North Carolina, Chapel Hill [portrait]); Greenville *Daily Reflector*, 4 Apr. 1991; Raleigh *News and Observer*, 31 Mar. 1991; *Roanoke Rapids Herald*, 31 Mar. 1991.

CLAIBORNE T. SMITH, JR.

Tyson, Bryan (*1830–1909*), controversialist and Unionist, was born in the Brower's Mill community of southeastern Randolph County, the son of Aaron Tyson, a relatively prominent farmer, slaveholder, and Quaker expatriot. Tyson claimed that his controversial actions during the Civil War resulted from a divine revelation that occurred in 1848 on his eighteenth birthday and a series of visions and visitations he experienced thereafter. In 1860 he owned a farm implement manufacturing firm located on his farm in the "Gold Region" of Moore County and four slaves.

Animated by a series of visions and his inherited favoritism for what he called the "yeoman class," Tyson decided in March 1862 to wage a one-man war against the twin threats of abolitionism and secessionism. He saw both as the major moral and political menaces to the existence of the United States. By summer he had written a lengthy book that he entitled *A Ray of Light; or, A Treatise on the Sectional Troubles Religiously and Morally Considered*, which came off the press in August as deriving from Brower's Mills and as being published by the author; actually, the book was clandestinely printed in Raleigh by F. K. Strother. The volume was a vicious attack on Abolitionists in the North and on the secessionist leadership of the Confederacy. It also contained the argument that the problem of union greatly overshadowed in importance the problem of slavery; therefore, all agitation on the latter issue should cease, with the institution of slavery left intact until the Union could be permanently and safely reestablished. Southerners were urged to end their war and return immediately to the Union to avoid inevitable defeat.

A Ray of Light was proscribed by Confederate and state authorities before it could be widely distributed; yet among the North Carolinians who received copies, it became an instant object of debate between those favorable to the Union and those inclined to support the Confederacy. It articulated the views of a vast number of North Carolinians from the Piedmont region who opposed the war and resisted the efforts of Governor Zebulon B. Vance to prosecute it. In mid-September Tyson was arrested at Carthage (the county seat of Moore County) for expressing incendiary views and was marched off to Raleigh as a Confederate conscript. Due to the timely intervention of powerful friends, he was granted an exemption from the army on the grounds that he would be more valuable to the Confederacy as a manufacturer of farm implements. While in Raleigh he had a circular printed defending his views. The circular and copies of his book were mailed to Jefferson Davis and other Confederate leaders. He then boarded a train for Richmond and began distributing his book by hand to the passengers and was soon arrested. After a brief confinement in Raleigh he was brought before Governor Vance, who agreed to his release on the condition that he not further circulate or promote his inflammatory views.

Tyson did not long desist. Back in his own county, he joined the militant Unionist underground and wrote letters to Confederate soldiers urging them to desert and return home. When the General Assembly convened in the winter of 1863, he sent a copy of his book and circular to each member urging them to take steps to end the war. Following this act he fled to Snow Camp, in Chatham County, where he received assistance in making his way through the Confederate lines in eastern North Carolina to New Bern and thence to New York. By 14 April he was in Washington, D.C., where, as a reward for his efforts on behalf of the Union cause in the South, he was given a job in the Treasury Department.

Soon after his arrival in Washington, Tyson advertised widely through the news media the existence of a strong Unionist element in the South, especially in North Carolina. He wrote Abraham Lincoln urging the president to assist him in fortifying and spreading the Union cause in the South and among captured Confederate soldiers. He later suggested to Lincoln that it would be wise for the administration to reject its radical abolitionist wing in favor of cooperating with Northern Democrats and Southern Unionists.

Snubbed by Lincoln, Tyson gradually made contacts with the Democratic party leadership, and by the end of 1863 he was corresponding with such copperhead notables as Charles Mason and Samuel F. B. Morse, both leaders of the Democratic propaganda organization called the Society for the Diffusion of Political Knowledge.

In the summer of 1863 William Woods Holden, editor of the Raleigh *North Carolina Standard*, launched the peace movement, an unsuccessful effort on the part of militant and covert Unionists to lead the state out of the Confederacy and back into the Union. Tyson played a role in this movement by issuing a broadside to be clandestinely distributed calling for North Carolina to be the first in a succession of Southern states to secede from the Confederacy and return to the Union. He also issued in the North a sixty-page pamphlet, entitled *The Institution of Slavery in the Southern States, Religiously and Morally Considered in Connection with Our Sectional Troubles*, which urged Northern readers to reject the abolitionist element in the current administration—thereby encouraging and strengthening Southern Unionists in their struggle against the Confederacy—and Southern readers to stop all support of the Confederacy and let the secessionist ship of state sink.

Upon the publication in August 1864 of his pamphlet, *Object of the Administration in Prosecuting the War*—which was marked "Approved by the National Democratic Resident Executive Committee"—Tyson resigned his position as clerk at the Treasury Department to campaign full-time for George B. McClellan's election. In this pamphlet, he charged that Lincoln and the radicals had perverted the true purpose of the war from a crusade to save the Union into an unconstitutional social revolution to free the slaves. To accomplish this end, he argued, they had pursued a deliberate policy of sabotaging all efforts made by Southern Unionists to overthrow the Confederacy and reestablish the Union because of the fear that this action would receive support from Northern Democrats and moderate Republicans, thereby jeopardizing the radicals' plan for emancipation. As examples of this negative policy, Tyson cited the Emancipation Proclamation, the dismissal of General McClellan, a Democrat, and the selection of General Benjamin F. Butler, who was hated in the South for his harsh administration of occupied Louisiana, to take charge of the Union Army Department of North Carolina and Virginia at the time of the peace movement of 1863, thus alienating the masses in North Carolina from the Union cause and dampening their enthusiasm for the peace movement. Tyson claimed that had the war been prosecuted strictly on constitutional principles, it would have ended long before in favor of the Union with the saving of thousands of lives. He declared that the "deluded, fanatical, and suicidal" Lincoln administration—which had made war on Southern Unionists—was "nothing but a John Brown raid upon a large scale" and should be "hurled from power."

On the reelection of Lincoln in November 1864, Tyson's career as a political agitator largely came to an end. He had failed in his single-minded mission to unseat the Secessionists in the South and the Radical Republicans (or Abolitionists, as he generally called them) in the North. His chief significance lay in his ability to articulate the views of thousands of North Carolinians and other Southerners who opposed secession and who, through resistance to Confederate authorities and desertion from the Confederate army, effectively hampered the Southern cause. Until his flight from North Carolina, he was the best-known proponent of their perspective. Following his flight, from his governmental post in Washington and as a result of his acceptance by Unionists in the North, he was able to assist many like-minded North Carolinians in finding their way from the South or occasionally from Federal detention camps into the Union army or to relatives in Indiana and other northwestern states. He is also important for the light his writings and letters shed on the activities and goals of the peace movement in North Carolina and on the interplay between Southern Unionists, Northern Democrats, the Radical Republicans, and the Lincoln administration.

After the war, Tyson gradually built up a profitable mail contract business. By the mid-1870s he had numerous mail routes in most of the southern and southwestern states including Texas, Nevada, and California. At the same time, he operated a "pension agency" in Washington that serviced war pension and mail claims against the government. While in the West, he became interested in inventing a device that would profitably extract silver and gold from the discarded ore piled about the mines. In all, Tyson received fourteen patents on his inventions, but, due to a disastrous law suit related to his mail contract business, he had to declare bankruptcy in 1883 and largely give up his dreams of being a successful inventor. Until 1894, when he returned permanently to North Carolina, he made a bare subsistence servicing soldiers' pension claims against the government.

During the postwar years, Tyson retained a lively interest in politics. He supported Andrew Johnson against the radicals, wrote a political tract for the Democrats in the 1872 campaign, and worked for the election of Grover Cleveland in 1884. Reflecting a progressive temperament, he championed woman suffrage, adoption of the Fourteenth Amendment, Negro suffrage, higher wages for labor, and equal rights before the law for blacks.

On Cleveland's election in 1884, Tyson hoped to overcome his poverty through appointment to a government post as a reward for his long and extraordinary service to the Democratic party. To his dismay and anger, a reward was never forthcoming because Cleveland feared offending his southern Democratic allies, almost all of whom were ex-Confederates, by allowing a "traitor" like Tyson to benefit from Democratic munificence.

Tyson's spent his last fifteen years in Carthage and nearby communities where he busied himself writing articles and essays in support of the new People's party, about his experiments in agriculture, and about economic issues. To the end, he never received aid or recompense from the federal government for his sacrifice on behalf of the Union cause during the Civil War.

SEE: William T. Auman, "North Carolina's Inner Civil War: Randolph County" (master's thesis, University of

North Carolina at Greensboro, 1978); "Interesting From North Carolina," *New York Times*, 1 May 1863; Letter to the editor, Washington *Chronicle*, 2 July 1869; Tyson to Lincoln, 30 Apr., 1 May 1863, 8 Feb. 1864 (Abraham Lincoln Papers, Library of Congress, Washington, D.C.); Tyson to Greeley, 21 Mar. 1865 (Horace Greeley Papers, Library of Congress, Washington, D.C.); Tyson to Morse, 23 Nov. 1863 (Samuel F. B. Morse Papers, Library of Congress, Washington, D.C.); Tyson to Cleveland, 8 Jan., 16 Dec. 1884, 9 Feb. 1885, 25, 29 Oct. 1886 (Grover Cleveland Papers, Library of Congress, Washington, D.C.); Tyson to Mason (Charles Mason Papers, Iowa State Archives, Des Moines); Bryan Tyson Papers (Manuscript Department, Duke University Library, Durham, and Library of Congress, Washington, D.C.); Robert and Newton D. Woody Papers (Manuscript Department, Duke University Library, Durham).

LARRY E. TISE
WILLIAM T. AUMAN

Tyson, Lawrence Davis (*4 July 1861–24 Aug. 1929*), soldier, lawyer, financier, and U.S. senator from Tennessee, was born on his father's plantation near Greenville, N.C. His ancestors had been in Pitt County since the 1720s, and he was the first son of Richard L. (d. 1879) and Margaret L. Turnage Tyson. His father, a cotton planter, owned twenty-one slaves and a substantial plantation in 1860 at age twenty-five and served briefly in the Confederate army. Shortly after the war, young L. D. Tyson received his initial education at a country school on the family farm with his two younger sisters, Julia and Ellen. War and emancipation greatly diminished his father's net worth, but the family's economic circumstances by 1870 remained well above average. Tyson entered Greenville Academy in 1873. At age seventeen he secured employment in Salisbury but soon won an appointment to West Point by competitive examination. Enrolling at the military academy in 1879, he was graduated in 1883 ranking fifty-first of fifty-two students, a standing that did not foreshadow his distinguished career.

Posted to the western frontier as a second lieutenant with the Ninth Infantry, he took part in various campaigns against the Apache Indians, including the capture of Geronimo. On 10 Feb. 1886 Tyson married Betty Humes McGhee, the daughter of Charles McGhee, a leading southern railroad financier of Knoxville. From 1891 to 1895 Tyson, by then a first lieutenant, was professor of military science at the University of Tennessee in Knoxville. Simultaneously studying law at the university, he received an LL.B. degree in 1894. Two years later he resigned his regular army commission to begin a law practice in Knoxville and become president of the Nashville Street Railway Company, the first of many business ventures he would found or head.

The trumpet sounded again for Tyson in the brief Spanish-American War of 1898. He received a presidential appointment as colonel of volunteer infantry, recruited and trained a regiment, took it to Puerto Rico, and served as military governor of a portion of that island for several months before being mustered out of the active service in mid-1899.

Returning to Knoxville, Tyson resumed his law practice for a few years but became increasingly involved in businesses of various sorts as well as politics and, to lesser extent, military matters. In textiles, he established and was president of the Knoxville Cotton Mills, Tennessee Mills, and Knoxville Spinning Company. He became a key officer in several coal- and iron-mining companies, a manufacturing concern, and a real estate company. He was a

director of a number of other corporations and two banks. From 1902 to 1908 he was a brigadier general and inspector general of the Tennessee National Guard. He served in the Tennessee House of Representatives as a Democrat from 1903 to 1905 and was the first person to be chosen speaker in his initial term. There he obtained the first state funding for the University of Tennessee. A delegate to the Democratic National Convention in 1908, he was an unsuccessful candidate for the U.S. Senate in 1913, being defeated in the Tennessee legislature by a handful of votes.

When the United States entered World War I, he was quartermaster general of the Tennessee National Guard. He volunteered again, and the governor placed him in command of all state guardsmen. Soon he received a commission as brigadier general in the national army and command of the Fifty-ninth Brigade of the Thirtieth Division, the "Old Hickory" division. After training in South Carolina, the brigade embarked for France in May 1918 and fought alongside British forces in Belgium in July and August. The brigade of 8,000 men persevered in nearly continuous combat through 20 Oct. 1918, suffering losses of 3,000 killed or wounded. In the Somme offensive General Tyson's brigade, during three days of terrific fighting in late September, broke through the Germans' Hindenburg defensive line, at perhaps its strongest point, defeating two enemy divisions. Members of the Thirtieth Division earned twelve Congressional Medals of Honor in World War I, more than any other division, and troops in Tyson's brigade received nine of the dozen decorations. The general himself was awarded the Distinguished Service Medal.

Back home in Knoxville after the war, Tyson resumed his many business activities, became president and publisher of the *Knoxville Sentinel* after buying the newspaper, and plunged again into politics. His state's Democrats boosted him as nominee for vice-president in 1920, but he withdrew his name and seconded that of Franklin D. Roosevelt. In 1924 he won election as a U.S. senator in the term 1925–31. On Capitol Hill he led a fight to carry the Tyson-Fitzgerald Act over a presidential veto and give retirement benefits to disabled emergency officers from World War I. In addition to veterans' welfare, his other chief concerns in the Senate were national defense, world peace and the world court, and economic development of the South.

Among Tyson's other interests were his family, the Episcopal church, the Masonic order, and the American Association of Cotton Manufacturers, of which he became president in 1923. He and his wife gave municipal parks to two Tennessee cities. Tyson died at a sanatorium in Stafford, Pa., before his senatorial term was completed. Fellow senators and other colleagues eulogized him as courageous, frank and open, refined and gentlemanly, highly capable yet modest, and a man of integrity.

SEE: *Biog. Dir. Am. Cong.* (1989); Census returns, 1860, 1870, Pitt County (microfilm, North Carolina State Archives, Raleigh); *DAB*, vol. 19 (1936); *Nat. Cyc. Am. Biog.*, vol. 21 (1931 [portrait]); *Lawrence D. Tyson: Memorial Addresses Delivered in the Senate and House . . .* (U.S., 71st Congress, Sen. Doc. 27, 1929); Lawrence Davis Tyson Papers (Southern Historical Collection, University of North Carolina, Chapel Hill); University of Tennessee *Record*, vol. 13 (Memorial number, 1930); *Who Was Who in America*, vol. 1 (1943).

RICHARD F. KNAPP

Umstead, John Wesley, Jr. (*7 Apr. 1884–21 Aug. 1968*), legislator and advocate of education and mental health, was born in Durham County, the son of John Wesley, a

Confederate veteran, farmer, and politician, and Lulie Elizabeth Lunsford Umstead. His brother, William B., was a congressman, U.S. senator, and governor of North Carolina. John W., Jr., was educated in the Durham city schools and at age fifteen entered The University of North Carolina, where he excelled in history and French. Awarded the Bingham medal for debating in 1908, he was permanent secretary of his class of 1909 and president of the Debating Union. He was a classmate and roommate of Frank Porter Graham, subsequently president of the university. The 1909 *Yackety Yack*, the yearbook, characterized Umstead as "a speaker, a money-maker, a student, and above all else a worker. He is ultra-emotional, abnormally enthusiastic and a loud laugher; but he is grounded right, and will do something some day, if work counts."

Following graduation he joined the Southern Life and Trust Company in Greensboro and ultimately the Jefferson Standard Life Insurance Company, where he earned admission to the Million Dollar Club in 1953. He became one of Jefferson Standard's most successful insurance executives before retiring in 1955 after forty-three years with the firm.

In 1931 voters sent Umstead to the North Carolina Senate for one term. He then lobbied for North Carolina insurance companies during the 1933, 1935, and 1937 sessions before being again elected to the senate for the 1939 term. Although defeated in a bid for a seat in the North Carolina House of Representatives in 1940, Umstead—representing Orange County—was elected to the house the next year; he served continuously until ill health forced his resignation in March 1963. In the legislature he introduced more than 230 bills and resolutions, of which almost 60 percent were enacted. At one time or another Umstead sat on all major committees in the General Assembly and was directly responsible for some of the most beneficial legislation enacted during his twenty-two-year tenure.

When his son, Captain John W. Umstead III, was killed in action in the Pacific Theater in World War II, Umstead was deeply affected, and the incident changed the course of his life. "When my boy was killed, I figured it was punishment for having frittered away my talents. I decided to devote the rest of my life to public service."

Umstead's major interests as a legislator were education, mental institutions, and the rehabilitation of young criminals (first offenders). In 1945 he was picked to head a small subcommittee to investigate conditions at Dorothea Dix Mental Hospital in Raleigh. He was so appalled by the terrible conditions at all state mental institutions that he made it his lifework to improve services at these hospitals. Umstead was particularly disturbed by the "almost criminal neglect" of the mentally ill, as emphasis was on providing space for the confinement of the emotionally ill rather than on rehabilitating or curing the patient. He succeeded in bringing about many reforms in mental hospitals and in 1962 helped establish at Camp Butner a mental hospital serving twenty-one counties in North Carolina. The state purchased the abandoned World War II camp of 1,700 acres and a hospital building for one dollar and then spent $1.5 million to develop the facility. Umstead also sponsored an Alcoholics Center at Butner and set up the Butner Youth Center—an experiment in the rehabilitation of youthful first offenders. Chairman of the State Hospital Board of Control, he worked tirelessly to raise the standards of medical education and to stimulate the growth of the medical center at The University of North Carolina.

John Umstead had a lifelong desire to achieve equality of opportunity in education for all North Carolinians. He gave unbounded energy and time to the support of a nine-month school term and was the author of legislation establishing twelve nine-month school years for every child in the state. He advocated compulsory attendance in public schools and fashioned the bill that required all children between six and sixteen to attend school, with absences under the supervision of a truant officer. Umstead lightened the load of pupils per teacher by limiting the student-teacher ratio to 30:1. He was a leader in raising teachers' pay and in modernizing the prison system. All of these reforms were permanent and significant forward steps in the cause of public education. For many years Umstead was a trustee of The University of North Carolina and constantly fought for improvements there. From 1933 onward, he furnished free room and board to approximately 125 needy young men who attended the university. He also provided, in memory of his son John, the funds to send two young men annually from a North Carolina orphanage. For his services to the state Umstead was awarded an honorary doctor of laws degree from the university in 1957.

A member of the North Carolina Grange and the Farm Bureau, Umstead voted for increased appropriations for agricultural research, vocational education, and agricultural extension courses. He was a member of the board of the American Fund for Psychiatry, North Carolina Association for Mental Health, American Heart Association, and North Carolina Association for Retarded Children; Kiwanis International, the North Carolina Symphony Society, and Sons of the American Revolution; and the Shriners, Elks Club, and Methodist church. Umstead combined his legislative skills with an idealistic dedication to improve life for his fellow citizens. He reserved his major services for those people who did not vote—"the boys and girls in public schools across North Carolina, the young and old at the mental hospitals which he built, and the students at the University of North Carolina."

Umstead married Sally Hunter Reade of Person County on 20 Jan. 1914, and they had four children: Frank Graham, John W. III, Sarah Elizabeth, and Ann Reade. He was buried in the Old Chapel Hill Cemetery.

SEE: *Chapel Hill Weekly*, 30 June 1944, 22 Jan. 1954, 17 Feb. 1956, 7 June 1957, 23 Apr. 1959, 11 Dec. 1968; *Charlotte Observer*, 30 Nov. 1958; *Durham Morning Herald*, 5 July 1958, 15 Mar. 1963; Frank Porter Graham Papers (Southern Historical Collection, University of North Carolina, Chapel Hill); *Greensboro Daily News*, 19 Dec. 1943, 19 Apr. 1962; Raleigh *News and Observer*, 27 Feb. 1943, 21 Dec. 1944, 13 Jan. 1952, 14, 17 Mar. 1963, 22 Aug. 1968; John Wesley Umstead Papers (Southern Historical Collection, University of North Carolina, Chapel Hill).

JULIAN M. PLEASANTS

Umstead, William Bradley (*13 May 1895–7 Nov. 1954*), attorney, congressman, and North Carolina governor, was born on a farm in Mangum Township, Durham County. His mother, Lulie Lunsford Umstead, the daughter of a prosperous farmer, was active in civic and religious affairs in her community. His father, John W., was a farmer, legislator, and longtime member of the Durham County Board of Education. William B. Umstead spent his early childhood on a farm, where he performed all the duties expected of the average country boy. His prized possession was a black mare named Robbie, whom he raised and kept until her death at age thirty-three.

After completing nine years at Mangum School, he attended Durham High School. In 1916 he was graduated from The University of North Carolina, where his fellow students recognized his debating prowess, skill in campus politics, and fondness for quoting poetry. From his undergraduate days until his death, Umstead loved the university and was never happier than when in its service. In recognition of this interest, he was chosen president of The University of North Carolina Alumni Association and a trustee of the Consolidated University.

Umstead taught school in Kinston for one year before beginning active duty in the army. As a second lieutenant in the 317th Machine Gun Battalion, a part of the "Wild Cat" Division, he served overseas for almost a year during World War I. A few months after his discharge in March 1919, he entered law school at Trinity College (now Duke University). Receiving a license to practice law in August 1920, he launched his legal career in Durham in July 1921.

He entered politics in 1922, when he was elected prosecuting attorney of the Durham County Recorder's Court. After serving for four years, Umstead won the office of solicitor for the Tenth Judicial District. His popularity with voters in the Sixth Congressional District earned him a seat in the U.S. House of Representatives in November 1932. In Washington he took a special interest in rural electrification, soil conservation, and the Farm Home Administration. He was instrumental in securing passage of a bill appropriating funds for enlarging facilities at the Tobacco Experiment Station in Oxford, N.C., for the study of tobacco will and other diseases. As chairman of the subcommittee on appropriations for the Navy Department, he introduced several appropriations measures and led the fight for their passage on the House floor.

At the end of his third term Umstead resigned his seat and resumed his law practice in Durham. In 1944 he returned to the political arena as manager of the gubernatorial campaign of R. Gregg Cherry of Gastonia. Following Cherry's election, Umstead accepted the chairmanship of the state Democratic executive committee, a position he held until November 1946. Early the next year Governor Cherry appointed him to serve the unexpired term of the late senator Josiah W. Bailey. Seeking a full Senate term in 1948, Umstead faced a formidable opponent in former governor J. Melville Broughton. Umstead's loss by a small margin was the first and only defeat of his political career.

Returning to Durham in November 1948, he practiced law until the spring of 1952, when he received the Democratic nomination for governor. Elected by an overwhelming majority, he took the oath of office on 8 Jan. 1953. In his inaugural address he submitted several recommendations to the General Assembly: a 10 percent salary increase for public school teachers and administrators retroactive to 1 July 1952, passage of a bill requiring mechanical inspection of all motor vehicles in the state and establishment of a drivers' training program in every public high school, submission of bond issues to construct facilities for the treatment and education of the mentally ill and to build additional school facilities, and a statewide referendum on whether to legalize the sale of intoxicating liquor.

One of Umstead's chief interests was reorganization of the State Board of Paroles, a recommendation approved by the 1953 General Assembly. He lost no time in appointing the three-member board and conferred with it frequently on the adoption of new policies that stressed uniform and fair parole consideration for prisoners in the state's penal institutions.

When the U.S. Supreme Court ruled in the landmark Brown v. Board of Education decision of 17 May 1954 that "the doctrine of separate but equal has no place in the field of public education," Umstead's calm reaction was in the state's tradition of reasoned moderation. He reluctantly accepted the decision and appointed a nineteen-member commission, chaired by Thomas J. Pearsall of Rocky Mount, to study the school situation and submit its recommendations to the 1955 General Assembly. Largely because of Umstead's leadership on this issue, irresponsible and intemperate actions were averted.

Probably his most significant appointment as governor was that of Sam J. Ervin, Jr., of Morganton, a University of North Carolina classmate who was then an associate justice of the North Carolina Supreme Court, to fill the unexpired term of Senator Clyde R. Hoey when he died in May 1954. Ervin held his Senate seat for twenty years, gaining national prominence as chairman of the Senate Select Committee on Presidential Campaign Activities, which investigated the widely publicized Watergate affair in 1973 and 1974. Earlier in his term Umstead had appointed Alton A. Lennon of Wilmington to complete the unexpired term of U.S. senator Willis Smith of Raleigh following his death on 26 June 1953.

Physically frail, Umstead spent several months of his abbreviated term as governor in a hospital bed. Two days after his inauguration he suffered a heart attack and had deep chest congestion verging on pneumonia. Admitted to Watts Hospital in Durham on 10 January, he was unable to return to his office until 21 May. Against the advice of physicians and friends, he doggedly discharged his responsibilities as chief executive, often discussing issues of state with legislative leaders and executive department heads from his bed in the Executive Mansion. After three weeks' hospitalization in October 1954, Umstead returned to Raleigh on the twenty-fifth. When a severe cold failed to respond to treatment, he was again hospitalized. His cold quickly turned to pneumonia, and he died of congestive heart failure. Funeral rites were held on 9 November at Trinity Methodist Church, Durham, where Umstead had been an active lay leader; burial was in the Mount Tabor Methodist Church cemetery near his home community of Bahama in Mangum Township.

Although Umstead lacked the charisma and boldness of a colorful leader, his courageous devotion to duty and his intense concern for the state's welfare served as a commendable example for his successors.

He married Merle Davis of Rutherford County on 5 Sept. 1929, and they had a daughter, Merle Bradley. A portrait of Umstead hangs in the Executive Mansion.

SEE: David L. Corbitt, ed., *Public Addresses, Letters, and Papers of William Bradley Umstead, Governor of North Carolina, 1953–54* (1957); *Durham Morning Herald*, 8 Nov. 1954; *New York Times*, 8 Nov. 1954; North Carolina General Assembly, *Joint Session of the General Assembly of North Carolina Honoring the Memory of the Late Governor William B. Umstead, March 15, 1955* (1955).

A. W. STEWART

Underwood, Norman (2 Sept. 1862–17 June 1930), building contractor, was born in Youngstown, Ohio, of English and Irish ancestry. His parents were Mary Jones and Wright A. Underwood. After attending the public schools of Wood County, Ohio, he moved to Knoxville, Tenn., where he worked in construction for approximately fourteen years. He then became the general superintendent for the contracting firm of D. Getoz in Durham, N.C., between 1897 and 1899. Moving to the Golden Belt Manufacturing Company, he was superintendent of construction until 1901, when he began his own firm in Durham. Hill C. Linthicum, a noted architect, stated that Underwood was "the principal builder in this area at one time" and described Underwood's work for him as "excellent."

Underwood constructed buildings on three college campuses. At Trinity College they included Craven Memorial Hall (1898), the library (1902), Alspaugh Hall (1902), and West Duke Building—also called the Academic Building—(1911), and at The University of North Carolina, Howell Hall (1906), the president's home (1907), Davie Hall (1908), and Peabody Hall (1912). The president's home on East Franklin Street in Chapel Hill was a copy of the North Carolina Building at the Jamestown Exposition of 1907. When the decision was reached to dismantle some buildings at Trinity College and reconstruct them on the campus of Kittrell College, the materials were moved by rail to Kittrell, where students were hired and assistance was given by a black licensed architect.

Construction in Durham by Underwood's firm included the U.S. Post Office—also called the Federal building—(1906) (site of the Hill building), the Trust building (1905), Durham Public Library (1921), the Southern Conservatory of Music, the Academy of Music (reportedly the largest stage south of Baltimore), the Underwood building, the Temple building (1904), Duke Memorial Methodist Church (1907–14), Watts Hospital (the two buildings with stucco exterior on the east side), and the Public Service Company building (formerly the Durham Sun building). His firm constructed near Van Straaten's the five-storied B. N. Duke building, which burned soon after completion. The Trust building, erected for the Durham Bank and Trust Company, was the first in that area of the state to use reinforced concrete and at the time of its construction was reported to be the tallest building in North Carolina. Underwood built several fine homes in Durham including that of J. E. Stagg (1911), J. M. Morehead, H. A. Foushee, B. N. Duke (Four Acres, 1910), and Victor S. Bryant (1924).

Active in civic affairs, Underwood was a member of the Durham Board of Aldermen and served as the police and fire commissioner. At the time of his death he sat on the city board of adjustments, whose five members worked with the city building inspector. In addition, he was a trustee of the Southern Conservatory of Music and a member of the board of directors of Durham Iron Works. When Underwood was elected the first president of the Carolinas Branch of the Associated General Contractors of America in 1922, the thirty-five charter members included such prominent contractors as George W. Kane and Nello L. Teer. Previously he had served as president of the Builders Exchange of North Carolina. He was a charter member of the Durham Rotary Club (1915) and belonged to the Knights of Pythias and the Independent Order of Odd Fellows. When the Hope Valley Country Club was organized in 1927, Underwood was among the charter members. At the huge Duke Memorial Methodist Church, which his firm built, Underwood was a trustee and a member of the Board of Stewards.

He married Elsie E. Ward in Bowling Green, Ohio, on 6 Mar. 1882. His home was located at the present site of University Apartments on Duke University Road, then known as Rigsbee Road. Underwood Avenue in this area was named for him.

Underwood died at Watts Hospital at age sixty-seven. He was survived by his widow, his daughter May Almina Underwood Rigsbee, and sons Norman Bruce, Harrison Aubrey, and Robert Ward. Another son, Daniel Maurice, had died in 1921 after an elevator shaft accident. Norman Underwood's funeral was held at his home by the pastor and former pastor of Duke Memorial Methodist Church. He was buried in Maplewood Cemetery, Durham, at the end of the main entrance road. There was a portrait of him but its location is unknown.

SEE: *The City of Durham Illustrated* (1910); Alice R. Cotten to B. W. C. Roberts, 10 Dec. 1976; Wyatt T. Dixon, *Ninety Years of Duke Memorial Church* (1977); *Durham Daily Sun*, 27 Feb., 19 Mar., 28 May 1904, 29 June 1904; *Durham Morning Herald*, 18–19, 21 June 1930; *Durham Sun*, 17 Jan., 6 Mar. 1964, 20 Sept. 1968, and 22 Aug. 1970; John Baxton Flowers III and Marguerite Schumann, *Bull Durham and Beyond* (1976); William King, personal contact, 5 Dec. 1976; Marguerite E. Schumann, *The First State University— A Walking Guide* (1972) and *Stones, Bricks, and Faces: A Walking Guide to Duke University* (1976); *Who's Who in the South* (1927).

B. W. C. ROBERTS

Upchurch, John Jordan *(26 Mar. 1820–18 Jan. 1887),* founder of the Ancient Order of United Workmen, was born on a farm in Franklin County, one of four children of Ambrose and Elizabeth Hill Upchurch. After 1824, when his father was shot and killed by his wife's brother-in-law, Upchurch and his mother first lived with his grandfather Upchurch and then on a small farm purchased by his grandfather Hill. He received a limited education "as the opportunity offered." In 1837 he left the farm to learn the trade of millwright but gave it up because he was too frail. Subsequently, he was apprenticed as a carpenter but again discovered that he was not strong enough for the occupation and took employment at Henderson as a clerk until 1841.

On 1 June 1841 Upchurch married Angelina Zeigenfuss Green, a Pennsylvanian, the niece of John Zeigenfuss. About the same time, Zeigenfuss and Upchurch opened a hotel in Raleigh. Under the influence of the temperance movement, they converted it into what Upchurch called "the first temperance house" south of the Mason-Dixon Line. When business fell off, they had to close the hotel, and Zeigenfuss went back to Pennsylvania in 1844. In the meantime, Upchurch had learned to be an engraver and a silversmith and briefly operated an engraving shop. Leaving Raleigh in late 1845, he was unsuccessful in finding suitable permanent employment. For a brief period, he acted as a horse tamer and horse trader in Georgia, South Carolina, and North Carolina and accumulated resources with which to support a move to Pennsylvania in October 1846.

There Upchurch took a job first with the Philadelphia and Reading Railroad and later with the Catasauqua Iron Works. Still later he went to work for the Mine Hill and Schuylkill Haven Railroad, where he remained for thirteen years as foreman and master mechanic. In June 1864, when train workers struck after management refused to meet their demands, Upchurch ran the railroad with men provided by the War Department. Two weeks later the strike was broken. Concluding that the strike was not in the best interest of workers, Upchurch determined to develop a system that would harmonize the interests of capital and labor. In January 1865 he became involved in an unsuccessful venture with an oil company. He went to Alabama in 1866 to work with a railroad company but soon moved back to Pennsylvania because of his health. After holding two short-term jobs in Pennsylvania, he took a position with the Atlantic and Great Western Railroad in Meadville, Pa., in April 1868.

At Meadville Upchurch joined the League of Friendship, Supreme Mechanical Order of the Sun. The Meadville lodge soon split, and Upchurch took the lead in organizing Jefferson Lodge No. 1 of the Ancient Order of the United Workmen on 27 Oct. 1868. Objectives of the order were to "create and foster a more friendly and cooperative feeling" among those who had a common interest and to use all possible "legitimate means" to adjust differences that might arise between employers and employees. Strikes were to be countenanced only when "absolutely necessary." In addition, the order was authorized to provide life insurance for members. A year later, when a per capita assessment of one dollar was levied to pay death benefits to members, the order was transformed into a fraternal benefit society that became a model for other similar societies. After early dissension in the AOUW unity was attained in 1873, and Upchurch was named past supreme master workman. Growth of the AOUW and other fraternal societies was stimulated by the need of workers for aid in the payment of expenses related to sickness, old age, and death. Because of his association with the AOUW, Upchurch is generally regarded as the founder of the mutual benefit system, which by 1919 included two hundred fraternal societies in the United States and Canada with some 9 million members. Throughout the country he was greeted as "Father" Upchurch and hailed as a benefactor.

In 1873 Upchurch moved to Missouri and worked for a number of employers until 1881; from 1881 to 1887 he apparently had no regular employment. While making an extensive tour of the West in 1885, he was introduced as the founder of "poor man's insurance, the widow's support, and the orphan's help." In 1886 he made a similar tour in the East including visits to Boston and Philadelphia. In Philadelphia he said that the AOUW had done more to cure poverty and degradation than any other group. His autobiography, *Life, Labor, and Travels of Father J. J. Upchurch*, was edited and published after his death.

Upchurch was the father of fifteen children, eleven boys and four girls. Throughout his life he had difficulties because of his large family, ill health, and irregular employment. He died at Steelville, Mo., and was buried at Bellefontaine Cemetery, St. Louis.

SEE: Walter Basye, *History and Operation of Fraternal Insurance* (1919); *Life, Labor, and Travels of Father J. J. Upchurch, Founder of the Ancient Order of United Workmen, Written by Himself* (1887); Arthur Preuss, comp., *A Dictionary of Secret and Other Societies* (1924); Raleigh *News and Observer*, 6 Feb. 1938; M. W. Sackett, *Early History of Fraternal Beneficiary Societies in America* (1914); *Saint Louis Globe-Democrat*, 19 Jan. 1887.

JOHN M. MARTIN

Urmston, John (1662?–November 1731), Anglican clergyman and schoolmaster, was born in Lancashire, England, the home of his family for centuries. The names of his parents and the college where he received his liberal education are unknown. After having lived "many years in divers foreign countries," he returned to England and entered the priesthood. He was ordained in the chapel of Fulham Palace by Henry Compton, bishop of London, on 17 Feb. 1694/95. From about this time until the end of the century Urmston was master of a school at Kensington, where he taught Latin, probably Greek, French, possibly Italian, writing, arithmetic, and drawing. From his experience in the school, he prepared and published *The London Spellingbook: Being a Most Easie and Regular Method of Teaching to Spell, Read and Write True English*, which ran through four editions between 1700 and 1710. Also in 1710 he published his octavo grammar, *A New Help to the Accidence, With a Preface, Shewing the Right Method of School Teaching*.

Presumably Urmston performed the office of chaplain to his school. If so, his first clerical appointment independent of the school occurred in 1702. When the navy was activated preparatory to the War of the Spanish Succession, the bishop of London recommended Urmston to the lord high admiral. He entered as chaplain aboard HMS *Woolwich* on 23 Feb. 1701/2 but was discharged from the appointment half a year later at his own request and that of the merchants in the Russia Company with whom he then accepted a chaplaincy. Urmston took up this appointment in the hope that he might be "an instrument of great good" among the English mercantile communities in Moscow and Archangel. By March 1702/3 he was at Moscow, and by September at Archangel. Finding that he was not permitted to extend his services to the native Russians, he sent back to London a number of Greek testaments and liturgies with which he had been furnished by the Society for the Propagation of the Gospel in Foreign Parts for distribution among them. Armed, instead, with practical books, Bibles, prayer books, and catechisms, Urmston focused his attention on the English merchant fleet and servants of the Russia Company at Archangel and artificers, sailors, and soldiers in the employ of Peter the Great at Voronezh, Azov, and on the Baltic. In 1704 he was made a corresponding member of the Society for Promoting Christian Knowledge, but in the same year English trade at Archangel fell off by a third, and his chaplaincy in the Russian Company shortly afterwards came to an end.

Returning to London, Urmston became curate of East Ham in Essex in 1706. During this curacy he gave serious consideration to becoming a missionary in America, for which work he was recommended to the SPG by the bishop of London in August 1709. The vicars of East Ham and Barking testified to Urmston's pious, sober, and exemplary life, his conformity to the rubric of the Book of Common Prayer, and to the faithful discharge of his duties while curate. One of the society's missionaries, William Gordon, had just returned from North Carolina, and when the society offered Gordon's vacant place to Urmston, he accepted it. After several months of hesitation caused by the fears of his wife, Urmston departed for North Carolina with her, their three small children, and two indentured transportees in the spring of 1710, having first subscribed the Act of Uniformity and having secured from the bishop of London a letter recommending him to the Lords Proprietors as a person of worth, fully qualified as a minister.

Once in the colony Urmston discovered that its vestry acts had but weakly established the Church of England in North Carolina. Local vestries had begun building a few church edifices but had left them unfinished and abandoned to decay. Parishes were unable to raise the small stipend of £30 per annum to pay their ministers, and no glebes had been set aside for their maintenance. In Urmston's field of labor, Chowan and Perquimans Precincts, the boundaries of the parishes were contiguous with those of the precincts, and in the case of Chowan extended southward across Albemarle Sound to take in the settlements on the southern shore and westward across Roanoke River to include the long-established plantations on Salmon Creek and Cashie River. Public roads in the province were little more than the Indian routes they had been prior to European settlement, and public ferries were practically nonexistent.

As though these circumstances were not sufficiently daunting, Urmston found the inhabitants divided into two armed factions struggling for control of the government. Of the two, one faction was strongly supported by dissenters. Then, in his second year, a massacre in the southern settlements of Bath County provoked an Indian war that lasted four years. In this turbulent frontier Urmston was expected to acquire and farm a plantation so as to raise a crop to support himself and family and at the same time to travel through the two precincts preaching and administering the sacraments among a population whose general attitudes seem to have ranged from indifference to resentment. Urmston's predecessors, John Blair, William Gordon, and James Adams, like his later contemporary, Giles Rainsford, were all defeated by conditions in North Carolina and abandoned their missions after brief stays lasting from six to twenty-four months (Adams dying as he was awaiting passage to England).

A minister of a saintly disposition could have borne the situation in the province with greater grace than Urmston, who was not of a saintly disposition. Indeed, his temperament more nearly matched that of his parishioners, and that, in the final analysis, may account for his having successfully persevered in his mission for eleven years. It might account, as well, for the judgment that his mission enjoyed but a marred success. Probably it is not literally true, as Colonel John Barnwell reported in 1712, that after drinking a considerable quantity of punch those in attendance at the General Assembly stripped stark naked and boxed two and two—the governor with a militia colonel, Urmston with the speaker of the house, the provost marshal with a burgess, and so forth. Nevertheless, even the floating of such a rumor is suggestive of Urmston's determination to hold his own among the rough and ready gentry who controlled the provincial government.

Although one doubts the boxing scene that Barnwell said was described to him, it is true that Urmston waited on the Assembly when it was in session. He served as its chaplain, and he lobbied for the interests of the Church of England. His influence on the vestry act of 1711 appears to have been weak, for though that act ended the power of vestries to dismiss their ministers at will, a provision for which Urmston was a stickler, it failed to stipulate that ministers be of the vestry, which was among his desiderata. It also failed to clarify the role of readers in the services of the church or to address the common problem of uncanonical marriages, all of concern to Urmston. He had better success with the 1715 vestry act, which, while it did nothing to curb the presumptuousness of readers, stipulated that ministers were to be constituent members of the vestry, ordered the vestries to post the church's table of marriages, imposed a fine for uncanonical marriages, and established fees for marriages solemnized by the clergy. His personal influence on the supplemental vestry act of 1720 is evident in the section requiring his parishioners to pay him that portion of his stipend that had lain in arrears for a decade.

Urmston had less success with the Lords Proprietors. Before departing for North Carolina, he had tried to persuade the Duke of Beaufort to appoint him his chaplain in the colony, and he unsuccessfully renewed his efforts in 1712 after Beaufort succeeded as palatine at the Proprietary board. Whatever chance of victory he might have had in his application to be appointed provincial deputy to Sir John Colleton was ruined by a "very tart" letter he wrote to Colleton in 1711, and Urmston was not surprised in 1715 that John Danson was "mightily offended" by one of the missionary's letters to him. In fact, the Proprietors desired Urmston to write them no longer until he should write more like a missionary and less like a spy to the country he lived in.

Although settled in Chowan Precinct on an Albemarle Sound plantation southeast of Edenton, Urmston saw more of North Carolina than the Proprietors apparently realized. He was forbidden by the vestry act to absent himself from his duties in his parish more than one-sixth of the Sundays in the year without permission of his church wardens and vestrymen to officiate in vacant neighboring parishes. Nonetheless, he appears to have journeyed annually to Pasquotank and Currituck Precincts, whose parishes had been left vacant by the death of the Reverend James Adams shortly after Urmston's arrival in the colony. Similarly, once the Tuscarora Indian war was over, he traveled through Bath County in 1716 and 1717 preaching, baptizing, and catechizing. Unfortunately, reports of Urmston's missionary activities, his *notitia parochialis*, survive for periods approximating only about four of his eleven years of residence in North Carolina. But even this incomplete record shows that Urmston carried his mission into all precincts of both Albemarle and Bath counties. Because the baptism of 660 souls into the Church of England represents results of only slightly more than one-third of his whole mission, that total should probably be at least doubled when speaking of the success or failure of his ministry.

The exaggeration native to Urmston's satirical epistolary style leads one to suppose that he, with his family, was not nearly so often in danger of starving (i.e., perishing) as he claimed. The entire colony, however, suffered actual want during the Tuscarora war and had to accept relief from Virginia. Following the war, grain crops failed throughout the colony in 1716, and a widespread murrain decimated the livestock in 1717. Consequently Urmston's complaints should not be dismissed out of hand. Similarly, the vestry minutes for Chowan Precinct (subsequently St. Paul's Parish) reveal that the vestry was, indeed, dilatory from the beginning in paying Urmston the agreed-upon stipend. By the opening of 1715 his stipend was in arrears by £110, which, by the simple expedient of not meeting again until May 1717, the vestry avoided paying him. At the same time, Urmston's man of business in London appears to have failed or to have defalcated, thereby losing such of Urmston's money as he held. Edward Moseley, Urmston's chief creditor as well as his neighbor and one of his church wardens, was too astute to accept an assignment of the arrears in payment of Urmston's debt to him. Although as church warden Moseley could have obliged the Chowan vestry to meet, he probably knew too well what chance of success he would have with them, short of an action at law—a process Urmston declined to take for fear of injuring the infant establishment.

Urmston's junior missionary and fellow Lancastrian, Giles Rainsford, whose discretion seems to have been younger than his years, began his mission in North Carolina by fishing in these troubled waters and making invidious contrasts of the two. Having reinforced popular sentiment in Chowan Precinct by publicly stating that missionaries ought to live off the salaries paid them by the SPG and not expect pay from the parish, Rainsford wrote to tell the society how beloved he was in the precinct. However, when shortly thereafter his vestry failed to meet and provide a stipend for him, after he overdrew his accounts and had his bills of exchange protested in London, after he received a rebuke from the SPG, and after he became familiar with the pinch of hunger, Rainsford abandoned his parish. He left North Carolina denouncing the population as liars, slanderers, traducers, ingrates, and hinderers of Divine service. His disgruntled departure fulfilled Urmston's prophecy to that effect but did nothing to relieve the situation that had been exacerbated by the younger missionary. After Rainsford's campaign against Urmston, Urmston was able to gather the canonical number of communicants required to celebrate the Lord's Supper in Chowan Precinct only twice between 1715 and 1719.

In response to Urmston's frequent appeals to the SPG for relief, the society in 1715 induced Governor Charles Eden to intervene with the vestries to settle their accounts with Urmston. This the Pasquotank Precinct parish did in 1716. The Chowan vestry voted in 1717 that £50 be raised and paid towards its arrears but failed to enforce its order. In the interim, at Urmston's urging, the SPG voted on 16 Nov. 1716 to allow him to return to England and formally notified him of the permission in a letter dated 17 December sent to him via Boston. The history of this letter remains mysterious. The years 1717, 1718, and 1719 passed without Urmston having any news of the society. On 18 Oct. 1719 Mrs. Urmston died, her heart broken, he declared, "through our ill usage and our comfortless way of living." Urmston wrote the society threatening to return in the spring of 1720 to plead his case before them *viva voce* since his letters remained unanswered. Then, surprisingly, on 7 Feb. 1720, the 1716 letter was put into his hands three years after permission to return to England had been granted and three months after the death of the wife, who had begged in vain to be allowed to take her children and return home with or without him. Urmston, who originally assumed the letter to be erroneously dated, was staggered. The following month, during court week, he went out and got drunk along with Major John Plowman, William Charleton, Esq., and others in the presence of Chief Justice Frederick Jones, who laid an information against them; all were fined. Worse yet, Urmston's son Thomas, now on the eve of his majority, broke out of control, got the serving maid with child, and, having been turned out by his father for his undutiful behavior, went to the northern edge of the precinct to take up the independent life of a bachelor. Despairingly, Urmston wrote in February 1721 begging to be allowed a word from the secretary of the SPG. "I cannot hear from England," he cried; "I am buried alive in this hell of a hole."

Finally, in March 1721, Urmston gave Edward Moseley a power of attorney to collect the £138 owing him from the Chowan vestry. He left North Carolina for London in early April in order to appeal in person to the missionary society that had replied to none of his letters during the past five years. Governor Eden, alarmed at and highly displeased with Urmston's apparent association with Moseley, his political foe, wrote the society to say that Urmston had needlessly deserted his parish without informing a single provincial authority, on which account Eden was withholding the usual letter testimonial. A poisonous, anonymous letter denouncing Urmston as a notorious drunkard given to lewdness and swearing also followed him to London. One feels the letter to be a malicious invention, but it is possible, of course, that the writer had heard gossip of Thomas Urmston's behavior and mistakenly attributed to the father the son's scandalous conduct. The society took no notice of the anonymous letter, but it filed Governor Eden's letter for future reference.

In July 1721 Urmston informed the society of his arrival and expressed his intention of remaining in England if he could not return to North Carolina under terms better than his original ones. He seems to have used his leave to look about in London for a new place among the five hundred livings the city boasted. Urmston apparently discussed some of his prospects with the society's secretary, who helped him in his unsuccessful bid to go to Jamaica in 1721 in the entourage of the newly appointed governor, the Duke of Portland. When similar efforts also failed, Urmston applied to the society at the end of his year's

leave, in June 1722, to be sent back to North Carolina. The society had concluded already that Urmston had left the colony with no intention of returning. It now refreshed its memory of Eden's remark that Urmston had needlessly deserted his parish and informed Urmston that, having already filled his vacancy, the society had no occasion for his service. He immediately made successful application to the bishop of London to license him for Virginia. Then, drawing on the King's Bounty on 29 June 1722 for £20 to defray his passage, Urmston set sail via New England. In Boston he hoped for appointment to the city's new Episcopal church but found that it was reserved for one of the church's own converts from Congregationalism who had gone to England for ordination. Pushing on to New York, he narrowly missed becoming chaplain to the fort and assistant to the Reverend William Vezey, commissary in that colony to the bishop of London. Then, learning that the incumbent of Christ Church, Philadelphia, had returned to England for his health, Urmston hastened there and was gladly received. Little apprehending that he was about to fall afoul of the Jacobites, Urmston wrote friends in England to intercede on his behalf for a permanent appointment from the bishop of London.

The Jacobites, or nonjuring clergy, had refused to withdraw their allegiance from James II and his descendants in the male line. They regarded as apostates all bishops who had sworn allegiance to William and Mary, as well as all successor bishops who had transferred their allegiance to the Hanoverian line. Playing at a dangerous game on behalf of a discredited doctrine, the nonjurors erected a shadow church and consecrated secret titular bishops for every see in England who were to replace their regularly consecrated counterparts should the Stuart pretenders ever seize the crown of England. Just as Urmston sailed for Boston in 1722, two nonjuring shadow bishops for America were consecrated. The first of these was Richard Welton, who had become vicar of East Ham three years after Urmston left it as curate in 1710. Welton had gained notoriety for having put up an altarpiece portraying a Last Supper in which Jesus was given the face of that idol of the Tory party, Henry Sacheverell; Saint John the Beloved was pictured as a mere boy with the countenance of Prince James Edward Stuart, and Judas bore the likeness of White Kennett, Whiggish bishop of Peterborough (the painter scrupling to put in the face of Bishop Gilbert Burnet). The second "American bishop" consecrated was John Talbot, who appears to have known Urmston ever since the two had served as navy chaplains in 1702. In 1715, while temporarily filling the vacancy of Christ Church, Philadelphia, Talbot had written to Urmston in North Carolina expressing surprise that he was still alive in "that dismal swamp" and inviting him to come north where there were several churches he might serve.

Talbot's regular station was at Burlington, N.J., from which he labored mightily, at least through the reign of Queen Anne, to secure a regularly consecrated bishop for America. It was owing to him that the SPG purchased property at Burlington in 1712 to serve as a residence for the anticipated bishop. Talbot dropped his campaign for an American bishop when the house of Hanover succeeded to the throne. Then, when the opportunity arose for his own consecration by the nonjurors, he was unable to resist it. One supposes the septuagenarian Talbot to have been drawn into this folly by Welton. The aged Ralph Taylor, "greatly weakened both in body and mind" (who had himself received nonjuring consecration little more than a year earlier), consecrated Welton *solus*, and he and Welton then consecrated Talbot in the summer of 1722.

Having returned to America in November 1722, Talbot convened the clergy of Pennsylvania at Chichester in October 1723, at which time an unnamed clergyman criticized the missionaries who had recommended Urmston to Christ Church. Talbot and four others sent a message on 23 October to the Christ Church vestry stating that they would concur in Urmston's removal from the parish providing the vestry filed a complaint with the convention and applied for its assistance. The vestry accepted the invitation. Urmston was forced out of Christ Church by December 1723 ("starved out," according to Talbot), and Talbot supplied the vacancy while Welton was sent for from England. Welton arrived in Philadelphia in June 1724, bringing with him engravings of his notorious altarpiece, and in July was given charge of Christ Church, where "he entered at once upon his duties and secretly ordained clergymen, exercising the functions and wearing the robes of a bishop." Civil and ecclesiastical authorities in the northern colonies, alarmed at Jacobite developments in their jurisdictions, wrote to warn their superiors in England. Urmston, of undoubted "duty and affection to His Majesty King George," was among the several who wrote warning of the danger. In the end, Welton was ordered back to England under a writ of privy seal in 1725; he fled, instead, to Lisbon, where he died in August 1726. Talbot was removed from his missionary status for disaffection to the government in October 1724 and died at Burlington in 1727.

Urmston, against whom Talbot's biographers have railed for a century and a half as the chief instrument of Talbot's downfall (no one seems to have regretted Dr. Welton), went from Philadelphia to North Carolina by way of Maryland and Virginia. After selling his plantation on Albemarle Sound and settling his affairs, he returned to Maryland. Here he was inducted into St. Stephen's Parish, Cecil County, on the eastern shore in 1724. Urmston appears to have lived quietly at St. Stephen's during the lifetime of Christopher Wilkinson, "a truly good man" and the bishop of London's commissary on the eastern shore. On Wilkinson's death in 1729, Jacob Henderson, the bishop's commissary on the western shore, assumed jurisdiction over all Church of England clergy in the colony. In June 1730 Henderson held a visitation of the eastern shore clergy. When examining Urmston's credentials, Henderson noted his lack of the letter testimonial that the irritated Eden had withheld in 1721. Further, it was Henderson's opinion that Urmston was drunk, and on the following day he gave Urmston an admonition. Despite this, in July Urmston joined other eastern shore clergymen in an address to the bishop of London accepting Henderson as commissary over them.

Meanwhile, Henderson earmarked Urmston for removal from his parish. By October 1730 the vestry of St. Stephen's began drawing up complaints against Urmston, alleging (according to Henderson) frequent drunkenness. By August 1731 Henderson had removed Urmston from his priestly function in the parish. The vestry then asked the governor to induct a new minister, speaking in the petition of Urmston's conduct in a general charge as "too shameful to mention." Its only specific charge against Urmston was the disingenuous one that he had not exercised his clerical function for two months (suppressing the fact that Henderson had silenced him). Urmston is said to have officiated at Appoquinimy and Lewes in Delaware after he was silenced in Maryland. Despite Urmston's apparent acceptance of his sentence, Henderson, who had knowingly acted without proper authority, justifiably feared that Urmston might bring an action at law that would raise in Maryland a nerve-wracking inquiry into the question of the doubtful legal basis for the bishop of London's claim to American jurisdiction similar to the one that had been raised in Barbados only a few years earlier. Urmston's consultation with lawyers and continued occupation of the vicarage and glebe belonging to St. Stephen's Parish were ominous signs. He soon vacated the premises by death.

In November 1731 Urmston's manservant, in going out to visit a neighbor, left the sixty-nine-year-old clergyman sitting by the fire. When the servant returned, he found his master's body on the hearth, his pipe by his side, his head burned off in the fireplace. Henderson's relief over his narrow escape, greater than his love of strict truth, allowed him to *suppose* to the bishop of London that Urmston had met his death by falling into the fire in a drunken fit. The names of Mrs. Urmston and the two younger children are unknown. Urmston was survived by his son and administrator, Thomas, who had remained in America on the family's return to England in 1721.

Urmston's reputation in North Carolina has suffered greatly at the hands of Victorian church historians and biographers of John Talbot. Probably it is true that his mordant wit was grounded in a morose spirit. Certainly it is true that he was publicly drunk in the spring of 1720 and probably true that he routinely enjoyed wines and punches in an age when ale was a lady's usual breakfast drink. It is likely that he was treated contemptuously by many of those who were technically his parishioners and whom he is said to have scolded. One must remember that whereas it is generally believed that there was little organized dissent and opposition to the Church of England in early eighteenth-century North Carolina outside the Quaker community, there was probably a much larger body of unorganized dissent and opposition than is usually recognized. In England, where there was an active press to publish the polemical writings and controversies between the establishment and dissent, the parson's hatred of dissent and the dissenters' contempt for the parson are clearly visible. Although no press was available to record those same passions in early eighteenth-century North Carolina, such evidences as are available in official dispatches and missionaries' letters show that they were in place and were active.

Within the contemporary establishment in the colony, both civil and ecclesiastical, Urmston's faults were recognized, but so were his virtues. Governor Edward Hyde, in a confidential aside written in 1712, believed that Urmston's reception in the colony was "purely owing to himself and his unfortunate temper which noways suits with the humors of the natural born people of America." This is the harshest failing assigned to him by his superiors in the colony. His vestry, in 1714, informed the SPG that "His great Pains and universal Dilligence to keep together those of our Church hath had good success," and Governor Eden told the society in the same year that Urmston "is really an honest painstaking Gentleman and worthy your care." While Eden believed Urmston's economic difficulties stemmed from the fact that "he has been but a moderate conductor of his affairs," he reported in 1717 that he "does all he is able in the discharge of his function and spares for no pains."

There is never a hint, never a suggestion, that Urmston's North Carolina mission was marred by a lewd life or habits of dissipation. True, if one chooses to give credence to an anonymous letter (the hallmark of the blackguard), one can slander his North Carolina mission into the ground. The preponderance of evidence, however, leads one to feel Dr. Francis L. Hawks judged falsely when he ruled that Urmston "did more to retard the spread of Christianity and the growth of the Church of England in Carolina, than any and all other names combined." Had Urmston done nothing more than help secure the vestry act of 1715, which provided the foundation for firm establishment of the Church of England in North Carolina, he is owed a better opinion than that by his successors in the American Episcopal church.

With reference to Urmston's post–1722 reputation in the northern colonies, it is clear that he was considered to have a good moral character during the year he spent in London in 1721 and 1722. The secretary of the Society for the Propagation of the Gospel, who knew him both personally and through his correspondence, did not hesitate to recommend him for ecclesiastical appointment, and the bishop of London did not hesitate to license Urmston for further ministry in America. Was there a real change in his character in 1723? Did the absence of a wife and family weaken Urmston's sense of social restraint when he entered the climacteric of his seventh decade? One wishes that the testimonials against his character had been expressed in specific terms rather than as general condemnations, for they require careful investigation and not mere acceptance or dismissal. When they are investigated, it should be borne in mind that the testimonials against his character in 1723 and 1730 appear to have been solicited by Talbot in Philadelphia and possibly invited by Henderson in Maryland. Full and impartial inquiry ought to be made before judging his experiences in those places.

SEE: *Manuscript sources*: Admiralty Records, Accounting Departments, Ships' Musters, Ser. I, 1688–1783—*HMS Woolwich* (ADM.36/4617B), and Court of Chancery, Town Depositions (C.24/1292, Pt. 2, Harper v. Hart, and C.24/1299, Pt. 2, Honnor v. Honnor) (Public Record Office, Kew and London); Bishop of London Ordination Register (MS.9535/3) (Guildhall Library, London); Chowan County Deed Books, vols. B and C (North Carolina State Archives, Raleigh); Inventory of Rev. John Urmston, Cecil County, 2 Feb. 1731/32 and Additional Inventory, 27 May 1734 (Maryland Hall of Records, Annapolis); Rawlinson Manuscripts B, no. 376, f. 286 (Bodleian Library, Oxford); St. Paul's Parish Vestry Minutes, Edenton (microfilm, North Carolina State Archives, Raleigh); SPG Journals, vols. 1–4, 1701–24, and Letterbooks, Ser. A, vols. 1, 5–16 (Rhodes House Library, Oxford). *Printed sources*: *An Account of the Propagation of the Gospel in Foreign Parts* (1704, 1893); E. Ingress Bell, "Richard Welton (1671?–1726)," in *Dictionary of National Biography*, vol. 20 (1968); *British Museum Catalog of Printed Books* (entries for Urmston), vol. 335 (1986); Cecil Headlam, ed., *Calendar of State Papers: America and the West Indies*, vol. 28, item 674 (1928); Gerald Fothergill, *List of Emigrant Ministers to America, 1690–1811* (1904); Francis Lister Hawks, *History of North Carolina*, vol. 2 (1858); David Humphreys, *An Historical Account of the Incorporated Society for the Propagation of the Gospel in Foreign Parts* (1730); Edgar Legare Pennington, *Apostle of New Jersey: John Talbot, 1645–1727* (1938); *Pennsylvania Gazette*, 18 Nov. 1731, abstracted in *Pennsylvania Magazine of History and Biography* 11 (1887); William S. Perry, ed., *Historical Collections Relating to the American Colonial Church*, vol. 4, *Maryland, 1694–1775* (1878); Nelson W. Rightmyer, "The Character of the Anglican Clergy of Colonial Maryland," in *Maryland Historical Magazine* 44 (1949); *Russkoe Istoricheskoe Obschestvo*, vol. 29 (1884); William L. Saunders, ed., *Colonial Records of North Carolina*, vols. 1–2 (1986); *The Term Catalogs, 1688–1700*, vol. 3 (1906), "The Tw... ... ... P... ... ... Letters of Colonel John Barnwell," in *South Carolina Historical and Genealogical Magazine* 9 (1908)

GEORGE STEVENSON

Usteneka (*fl. 1758–69*), Cherokee leader, is referred to in some sources as Ostenaco, Autositty, Ustonekka, Outacite, Outacity, and Judd's Friend. There seems to be no substantial agreement among sources as to whether these names all refer to the same man or to several different men. The confusion is complicated by the caption under a contemporary print of Sir Joshua Reynolds's portrait of three Cherokee Indians that lists two of the men as "Outacite or Man-Killer; who sets up the War Whoop" and "Austenace, or King, a great warrior." Outacite is Cherokee for "Mankiller," a title of respect.

Usteneka was a prominent leader of the Overhill Cherokee who lived in far western North Carolina (now eastern Tennessee) during the eighteenth century and figured in several treaties and conferences with the North Carolina, South Carolina, and Virginia governments as well as in the Cherokee War of 1760–61. He may have been the chief of the Cherokee town of Tomotley and was probably second in command of the Overhill tribes, which were under Ouconnostotah after 1760. He was also a contemporary of the better-known North Carolina Cherokee, Attakullakulla.

Usteneka's name first appears in the white settlers' history as a member of various delegations to show the Cherokee's desire to continue trade relations with the British and pledge allegiance to King George II during the French and Indian Wars. Two such trips were recorded to Charles Town before 1758. There is also evidence that Usteneka led a band of eighty Indians into Virginia at the request of that colony's representative, Edward Guest, in an expedition against warring Shawnees. Despite the efforts of some Cherokee, particularly Attakullakulla, and some British officials, relations between the two groups were severely strained by the fall of 1759. In one incident, a delegation of Cherokee was forced to go all the way to Charles Town to demand ammunition that had been promised them. The British, fearful of supplying gunpowder to potential enemies, had assumed that they would not make the long trip. Usteneka is listed as one of this expedition of Indians. At one point during the journey Usteneka left, and it was suggested that he was arranging for an ambush of the British Indian agent, but this is doubtful as the ambush never occurred. Relations with the Cherokee continued to break down until the British found themselves engaged in serious warfare in 1760 and 1761, referred to as the Cherokee War. On 26 Sept. 1759 Usteneka and Ouconnostotah raised the British flag at Nucassee Town, a Cherokee village, and sent a peace delegation to William Bull, South Carolina's Indian representative. The Indians' demand for complete destruction of Fort Prince George was not acceptable to the South Carolina government, and a final peace was not arranged until a year later.

In early 1760 Usteneka was influential in getting Kanagataucko chosen "emporor" or head of all the Cherokee, despite Attakullakulla's known desire for the position. At this time Usteneka was made second in command of the Overhill Indians. In 1761 he and seventy other Cherokee went to Williamsburg, Va. While there, Usteneka pled with the British authorities to be taken to England, a sign of high prestige among the Cherokee; he finally went with two other warriors. Unfortunately for the Indians, their interpreter died during the voyage. But the language barrier did not prevent Usteneka from dining with Henry Ellis, meeting Oliver Goldsmith, having his portrait painted by Sir Joshua Reynolds, being received at court, or returning home in November 1762 thoroughly pro-British.

Usteneka is mentioned as a Cherokee warrior again in 1764, when he agreed to help the English in their conflict against Pontiac and the Creeks. He led an unsuccessful expedition to capture a large French convoy of supplies to Pontiac but was rewarded £900 for the capture of two French planters. Usteneka is noted as a peacemaker and spokesman for the British in the various conflicts between the "cracker" settlers and the Indians that occurred in the years following the French and Indian War. In 1768 he was a signer of the important Hard Labor Boundary agreement, instigated by the Cherokee and surveyed and arranged by Governor William Tryon. This treaty set a line from the Reedy River in South Carolina to Chiswell's Lead Mine (near present-day Wytheville, Va.) as the furthest point white settlement could be allowed, in accordance with the Proclamation of 1763. The last mention of Usteneka is as a Cherokee representative to another meeting, held with the white settlers in January 1769 at Charles Town.

SEE: John R. Alden, *John Stuart and the Southern Colonial Frontier, 1754–75* (1944); Stanley J. Folmsbee and others, *History of Tennessee*, vol. 1 (1960); Wilbur R. Jacobs, ed., *The Appalachian Indian Frontier: The Edmond Atkins Report and Plan of 1755* (1967); William S. Powell, ed., *The Correspondence of William Tryon and Other Selected Papers*, 2 vols. (1980–81).

MARY NELLE TROTMAN

Vail, Edward (*6 Aug. 1717–5 June 1777*), colonial official and member of a large and active family, joined his brother John in 1749 in petitioning the Chowan County Court for permission to operate a mill near Sandy Point. Edward was one of six men who raised troops in North Carolina in 1754 to help defend Virginia during the French and Indian War; they were part of the first troops recruited in British America to fight outside their own territory in defense of a common cause. Vail also represented Chowan County in the Assembly in 1754–62, 1770–71, and 1773–74. Locally he was a member of the county court in 1756 as well as one of five trustees named in 1767 to erect the brick courthouse in Edenton that still stands.

As a colonel, Vail accompanied Governor William Tryon in the 1771 expedition against the Regulators. With the approach of the American Revolution he was one of eight members of the North Carolina Committee of Correspondence in 1768, 1773, and 1774. Remaining active in the militia, Vail was appointed brigadier general of the Edenton District in April 1776 and reelected within a month of his death.

Vail and his wife Susannah, whose maiden name is unknown, had four sons: Thomas, Frederick, Jeremiah, and Edward. Susannah was among the fifty-one "patriotic ladies" who participated in the Edenton Tea Party on 24 Oct. 1774.

SEE: John L. Cheney, Jr., ed., *North Carolina Government, 1585–1974* (1974); J. R. B. Hathaway, ed., *North Carolina Historical and Genealogical Register*, vols. 1–2 (1900–1901); William S. Powell, ed., *The Correspondence of William Tryon and Other Selected Papers*, vol. 2 (1981); William L. Saunders, ed., *Colonial Records of North Carolina*, vols. 5–7, 9–10 (1887–90); Vail family Bible (possession of Lillian Smith Hough, Eden, N.C.); *Virginia Gazette*, 19 July 1754, 4 July 1767, 24 May 1770, 3 Nov. 1774.

WILLIAM S. SMITH, JR.

Vail, Jeremiah (*d. pre–10 Sept. 1741*), local and provincial official, one of several of this name, began to be involved in a number of land transactions and other legal causes in Chowan County beginning in 1697, when he bought 560 acres of land on Albemarle Sound; in 1709 he acquired 560 additional acres adjoining the property of Edward Moseley, his brother-in-law. In 1719 Vail engaged in land transactions with another brother-in-law, John Lillington, and was then identified as a mariner. He was a frequent witness to deeds, wills, and other documents in the 1730s.

Vail married Mary Lillington Swann, the widow of Samuel Swann, after 10 July 1707. They had seven children: Moseley, Mary, Jeremiah, Jr., Edward, Martha, John, and Sarah Elizabeth—neither the order nor the dates of their births are known. Because sons Jeremiah and Edward also had sons named Jeremiah, much of the data now available cannot be attributed with certainty to any one of them. The several contemporary persons of this name exemplify the difficulty frequently encountered by those who try to reconstruct the life of colonial North Carolinians. One Jeremiah Vail was a member of the Assembly in 1727, and another one served in 1755–60. The complications began in 1728, when one Jeremiah Vail was granted 320 acres of land on New Topsail Sound in New Hanover County. In 1737 a Jeremiah Vail, Hanah Nuggent, Frances Tool, and William Bailey were charged with "stripping themselves naked and going into the water together in the face of the town." For this offense, the males were bound over to the next court, whereas the two females were sentenced "to be carried to the publick whipping post and there to receive ten lashes on her back well laid." Insofar as the subject of this sketch is concerned, however, the swimming caper seems more the action of a younger man than of one probably near sixty.

In March 1743, at a time when many of the residents of the northern part of the colony were moving to the newly opened Cape Fear section, Jeremiah Vail, Jr., successfully petitioned the Council for 400 acres in New Hanover County to which he had moved by 2 June 1740. Two years later he acquired another 400 acres by petition. Following the passage of a bill in the General Assembly in 1745 to regulate conditions in the county, Vail was hired to make the official survey of the recently chartered town of Wilmington. His survey was designated by a law of 1754 as the official one of Wilmington. In 1749 Jeremiah Vail was named one of three commissioners to erect public buildings in New Bern as a seat of provincial government.

Vail was appointed in 1752 to be inspector of exported goods from the Neuse River and was designated as well to serve as receiver of the impost or duty in Carteret County for all goods, wares, merchandise, wine, and distilled liquors imported or brought into Carteret. Although he served with distinction in the Assembly in 1753 as deputy clerk of the Council and as chairman of the Assembly committee of public accounts, by 1757 a bill was introduced into the lower house to replace him as receiver of duties on wine, rum, and other spirituous liquors and to more effactually oblige receivers of duties to account for and pay them. Despite his promise in December 1757 to pay in full the balance due on his duty accounts, the assets of his estate were sold in 1764 to satisfy public debts.

SEE: John L. Cheney, Jr., ed., *North Carolina Government, 1585–1979* (1981); Walter Clark, ed., *State Records of North Carolina*, vols. 23, 25 (1904, 1906); J. R. B. Hathaway, ed., *North Carolina Historical and Genealogical Register*, 3 vols. (1900–1903); Weynette Parks Haun, ed., *Chowan County, North Carolina: County Court Minutes, Pleas and Quarter Sessions, 1735–1738, 1746–1748* (1983); William L. Saunders, ed., *Colonial Records of North Carolina*, vols. 2, 4–6 (1886–88).

WILLIAM S. SMITH, JR.

Valentiner, William Reinhold *(2 May 1880–6 Sept. 1958)*, art historian and museum director, was born in Karlsruhe, Germany, the youngest of four children of Wilhelm and Anna Isis Lepsius Valentiner. His father was the director of the observatory and professor of astronomical sciences at the University of Heidelberg. The boy's mother became ill while he was young, and the children were sent off to board with other people. Valentiner studied at the University of Leipzig and at the University of Heidelberg, from which he received a doctorate in 1905. He was an assistant to several of the most famous European art museum directors before moving to the United States in 1908 to become curator of decorative arts at the Metropolitan Museum of Art, a post he held until 1914.

During World War I Valentiner served in the German army. Remaining in Germany after the war, he worked at the Kaiser Friedrich Museum from 1918 to 1921. He and Marie Cecilia Odefey were married in Berlin on 10 Dec. 1919 and had one daughter, Brigetta (Mrs. Harry Bertoia). In 1921 Valentiner returned to the United States to serve as adviser (later director) of the Detroit Institute of Arts, where he stayed until 1944. He became a U.S. citizen in 1935. After two years of partial retirement, he resumed his work, first at the Los Angeles County Museum and then at the Getty Museum.

In 1955 Valentiner became the first director of the North Carolina Museum of Art in Raleigh. His prestige and knowledge helped the new state art museum get under way on a sound footing. In 1957 he received the Order of Merit, the highest award for cultural achievement given by the Federal Republic of Germany. In the summer of 1958 Valentiner became ill in Munich while on a research trip. He was hospitalized for about two months, then returned to New York. He resigned as director of the North Carolina Museum of Art on 28 August and a short time later died in New York of arteriosclerosis complicated by pneumonia. His body was cremated.

The entire art world mourned the death of Valentiner. He had been a prolific writer and lecturer on art, specializing in Rembrandt and Leonardo da Vinci. His services as adviser and director of numerous art museums had greatly contributed to the preservation and increased knowledge of art and artists.

SEE: *Nat. Cyc. Am. Biog.*, vol. 48 (1965); North Carolina Museum of Art, *Masterpieces of Art, in Memory of William R. Valentiner . . .* (1959); *Who Was Who in America*, vol. 3 (1960).

ALICE R. COTTEN

Vance, Robert Brank *(1793–6 Nov. 1827)*, physician and congressman, was born on Reems Creek, near Asheville in Buncombe County, one of eight children of David (1745–1813) and Priscilla Brank (1756–1836) Vance. His father was a surveyor, teacher, and farmer who, as an officer in the Revolution, saw service at Brandywine, Germantown, Monmouth, Valley Forge, and King's Mountain; he also served in the Assembly several terms, was first clerk of court for Buncombe, and held the rank of colonel in the local militia. Two nephews of Robert Brank Vance became congressmen. One of them was a general in the Confederate army and the other, Zebulon Baird Vance, was North Carolina's Civil War governor and a U.S. senator.

Robert Brank Vance was educated at Newton Academy in Asheville and studied medicine at the school of Dr. Charles Harris in Cabarrus County. He began to practice in Asheville in 1818 but soon realized that he was physically unsuited to conduct his profession. One of his legs was six inches shorter than the other, and his lameness made it difficult for him to attend his patients. Fortunately, winnings from a lottery allowed him to retire and devote himself to literature, history, and politics.

In the election of 1821 Vance challenged incumbent Felix Walker of the Twelfth (Burke County) Congressional District. Old and long-winded, Walker was called "Talking to Buncombe" in Washington, where his dull speeches were notorious. Nevertheless, the congressman, who had been a friend of Daniel Boone and was a veteran of the Revolution and Indian wars, defeated the young doctor. In a rematch two years later the count was apparently even. When required to break the tie, the sheriffs of the district gave the victory to the younger man.

Congressman Vance was active in the campaign to reform the state constitution. In April 1824 he was the only member of the North Carolina delegation to support the act authorizing a survey of possible federally financed roads and canals. In February 1825, when the disputed presidential race was decided by the House, he was one of the two congressmen from his state to support Andrew Jackson. During his one term on Capitol Hill he served on the Revolutionary Pensions Committee.

Four men announced as candidates to represent the Burke district in 1825, when Walker and Vance were joined on the ticket by Samuel P. Carson of Burke and James Graham of Rutherford. Before election day Walker withdrew in favor of Carson, and Carson won the race. This prematurely forced Vance into an unwelcomed retirement. Two years later he tried to unseat Carson. It was a vituperative contest seldom equaled in the mountain district. In Asheville Vance called his opponent a coward. A few days later in Morganton, Carson's hometown, where the crowd obviously contained many of Carson's kin, Vance insulted Carson's father. Carson held his temper until after the election, which he won by a wide margin. Then Carson challenged Vance to a duel. Vance realized his danger and wrote his will: "anticipating in a few days a probable exit from this earthly theatre," he divided his property. His library of some five hundred volumes he inventoried and left to three friends who were to help "in the affair of honour now pending."

The duel took place at Saluda Gap in November 1827. Dr. Vance was fatally wounded. His gun was not fired, and some said he had deliberately courted death. He was buried in the family burial ground at Reems Creek. The former congressman had never married.

SEE: John P. Arthur, *Western North Carolina: A History* (1914); *Biog. Dir. Am. Cong.* (1971); Frontis W. Johnston, ed., *The Papers of Zebulon Baird Vance*, vol. 1 (1963); Daniel M. McFarland, "Politics in the Good Old Days Was a Serious Proposition," *The State* magazine, 31 Mar. 1951; Daniel M. McFarland, "Rip Van Winkle: Political Evolution in North Carolina, 1815–1835" (Ph.D. diss., University of Pennsylvania, 1954); James Meehan, "Duelist's Legacy Started a Library," *The State* magazine, March 1973; Zebulon Baird Vance Papers (North Carolina State Archives, Raleigh).

DANIEL M. McFARLAND

Vance, Robert Brank *(24 Apr. 1828–28 Nov. 1899)*, Confederate general and politician, was born at the family home at Reems Creek, near Asheville in Buncombe County. He was the son of Captain David (1792–1844) and Mira Margaret Baird Vance, the nephew of Congressman Robert Brank Vance, and the brother of Governor Zebulon Baird Vance. His formal education was limited, but he did attend the local country schools and was taught by his mother at home, where he had access to the extensive library left by his uncle.

At age twenty Vance was elected clerk of the Buncombe County Court of Common Pleas and Quarter Sessions, a post held by his father until his death. He maintained the office until 1858, when he declined reelection in order to become a merchant in Asheville.

Like his brother, Vance was an ardent follower of the political philosophy of Henry Clay and the Whigs. As the Civil War approached, he maintained strong Unionist sympathies and was an avid supporter of John Bell, the Constitutional Union party candidate for president in 1860. But when the conflict did come, he offered his services to the Confederacy, forming the Buncombe County Life Guard, which later became Company H of the Twenty-ninth North Carolina Infantry. After the training period at Camp Patton in Asheville, Vance was unanimously chosen as the division's colonel, and he and his men were dispatched to East Tennessee to guard the bridges on the Bristol-Chattanooga road from raiders. In February 1862 they were moved to Cumberland Gap, where they saw their first real action at the battle on 24 March. On 30 Dec. 1862 Vance's division was the first into action at the Battle of Murfreesboro and suffered heavy casualties; the colonel's own horse was killed beneath him by a shell. Vance was commended for his meritorious service by his superior, General John P. McCown, leading to his commission by Jefferson Davis as brigadier general.

On his recovery from a lengthy case of typhoid fever, Vance was put under the command of General Braxton Bragg, who placed him in charge of the North Carolina–Tennessee mountains, a difficult assignment as the terrain was very rough and anti-Confederate sentiment was high. Here they were to harass the Union flanks and disrupt the flow of enemy supplies. On one such mission in January 1864 they managed to capture a major supply train going to General Ambrose Burnside's troops near Knoxville, but on trying to remove the wagons to North Carolina, Vance and virtually all his troops were taken prisoner at Crosby's Creek. Confined in Union prisons in Nashville, Louisville, Fort Chase (Ohio), and Fort Delaware, Crosby was given a special parole by President Abraham Lincoln to buy clothing for other Confederate prisoners. This was achieved largely at the instigation of the Reverend Nathaniel G. Taylor, who had been a prisoner under Vance in Tennessee but was well treated and later released. On 14 Mar. 1865 Vance was given a full pardon and allowed to return to North Carolina on condition that he not fight again.

In 1872 he was elected as a Democrat to the congressional seat earlier held by his uncle and his brother. During his six terms in office he obtained appropriations to get mail delivery daily in every county in his district and to have the French Broad River dredged from Brevard to Asheville for transportation purposes. He served on the Committee on Pensions for Veterans of the War of 1812, the Committee on Coinage, and the Committee on Patents, which he chaired for four terms. Declining reelection in 1884, he was appointed assistant commissioner of patents by President Grover Cleveland and held the post through Cleveland's first administration. Vance ended his political career as a member of the North Carolina General Assembly (1893–96).

He was married twice, first to Harriet V. McElroy on 13 May 1851 (d. 20 Mar. 1885) and then to Lizzie R. Cook on 15 Dec. 1892. He had six children, all by his first marriage, of whom three sons and a daughter survived to adulthood.

Vance was a member of the Knights Templar and the Freemasons, serving for two terms as grand master of the North Carolina Masons (1868–69). He helped found the Asheville chapter of the Sons of Temperance and was grand worthy patriarch of the state organization. A devout member of the Methodist Episcopal Church, South, he was elected many times to its General Conferences; he served as secretary-treasurer of the Holston Conference College and was chosen as a representative to the Ecumenical Methodist Conference, London, in 1881 though he was unable to attend. He was also an accomplished poet and published collections under the titles *Heart Throbs from the Mountains, Oneka; or, The White Plume of the Cherokee,* and *Shadows of Mountain Life,* among others.

He died at his farm at Alexander, near Asheville, and was buried at Riverside Cemetery, Asheville.

SEE: John P. Arthur, *Western North Carolina: A History* (1914); Samuel A. Ashe, ed., *Biographical History of North Carolina,* vol. 6 (1907); *Asheville Citizen,* 7 Oct. 1960, 31 July 1961; John G. Barrett, *The Civil War in North Carolina* (1963); *Biog. Dir. Am. Cong.* (1961); Jerome Dowd, *Sketches of Prominant Living North Carolinians* (1888); R. N. Price, *Holston Methodism* (1913); W. F. Tomlinson, *State Officers and the General Assembly of North Carolina, 1893* (1893).

MARTIN REIDINGER

Vance, Rupert Bayless *(15 Mar. 1899–25 Aug. 1975),* university professor and sociologist, was born in Plumerville, a community in central Arkansas located only a short distance from Conway. He was the oldest of four children of Walter Johnson and Lula Mary Bayless Vance. His father owned a general store in the village and a beef and dairy farm where the family lived.

At age three Vance was stricken with poliomyelitis, which left both legs paralyzed and forced him to use crutches. His mother, who had been a schoolteacher, helped him adjust to his handicap and supervised his early education. After entering public school in the fourth grade at age ten, he was always at the head of his class. A love of reading acquired while very young became his main diversion. The family bought the works of Scott, Dickens, Eliot, and Irving by the set in an effort to satiate his literary appetite. As an adult he was an avid reader of fiction, poetry, treatises on art, philosophy, science, and history.

On completing high school Vance entered Henderson-Brown College (now Hendrix); he was graduated as valedictorian in 1920 with an A.B. degree and majors in English and the social sciences. He then won a fellowship for a year's study at Vanderbilt University, which awarded him a master's degree in economics. At Vanderbilt he became acquainted with the colorful and well-known Conservative, Professor Gus Dyer—an experience, Vance reportedly said, humorously, that almost turned him to radicalism.

Accepting a teaching position in Talihina, Okla., Vance taught English in the high school and served as principal for two years. From 1923 to 1926 he also taught English in South Georgia College, a junior college located in McRae, but during this time he decided to study sociology. Vance was familiar with the work being done at The University of North Carolina under the leadership of Professor Howard W. Odum, especially at the Institute for Research in Social Science, which Odum had established. In 1926 Vance entered The University of North Carolina and the next year was granted a teaching fellowship. In 1928 he was awarded the doctorate and received appointments to the staff of Odum's institute and to the faculty of the Department of Sociology. Though subsequently offered attractive appointments elsewhere, Vance remained with the university.

His doctoral dissertation, published in 1929 under the title *Human Factors in Cotton Culture*, was the first of three major classics that he wrote. For *Human Geography of the South*, which was recognized as a masterpiece in American social science on its publication in 1932, the North Carolina Literary and Historical Association awarded Vance the Mayflower Cup in 1933. *All These People: The Nation's Human Resources in the South*, appearing in 1945, was promptly acclaimed by population experts as a model of its kind. This book was destined to be read not only by scholars, but by governors, legislators, and editors as well. It won for Vance the Lord and Taylor Design for Living Award.

Professor George Tindall, in a memorial presented to the university's Faculty Council (17 Oct. 1975), noted that in addition to his major writings Vance had been a collaborator in the writing and editing of four other books, the author of a dozen monographs and nearly one hundred articles, and the compiler of an annotated bibliography of travel accounts. The bibliography of "The Twentieth-Century South as Viewed by English-speaking Travelers, 1900–1955," with its excellent introductory essay, was published as one section of Thomas D. Clark's two-volume *Travels in the New South*. Vance's contribution is a bibliographical tour de force. Tindall also noted the diversity of Vance's scholarship. The Raleigh *News and Observer* called attention to Vance's ability to appeal to different age levels, citing his *Exploring the South*, written with Marjorie Bond and John Ivey, as a text for eighth-grade students.

For a number of years Vance was a member of the board of governors of The University of North Carolina Press. He served on the administrative board of the Graduate School and was appointed to a number of other university committees. Of particular delight to him was his editorial association with *Social Forces*.

On the national scene he served at various times as a consultant to the National Resources Planning Board, Rosenwald Fund, Social Science Research Council, National Institutes of Health, Bureau of the Census, and United Nations. "His studies directly influenced the farm tenancy programs of the New Deal and the *Report on Economic Conditions of the South,* prepared in 1934 by the National Emergency Council at the request of President Roosevelt." Professionally, Vance was president of the Southern Sociological Society (1938), American Sociological Society (1944), and Population Association of America (1952).

Vance "won national and international distinction as a scholar who broke new ground in many fields." Though he identified himself strongly with the South and was in a sense a "professional Southerner," he was neither a parochial sentimentalist nor an agrarian romantic. Instead, he was a "realist who believed the South's destiny was, and should be, to enter the mainstream of an urbanized national society." His hope was that the South could retain some of its rural and small-town quality of life while avoiding the worst of the big-city problems.

He held summer teaching appointments at several universities, was a visiting professor at Louisiana State University for a year, and accepted a number of invitations from universities to deliver lectures. At The University of North Carolina he was named a Kenan professor in 1945, and he received honorary doctorates from the university, Hendrix College, and the University of Arkansas. In 1963 The University of North Carolina bestowed on him the Thomas Jefferson Award for exemplifying in his life and work "the best tradition and spirit of Thomas Jefferson."

As a teacher Vance was held in highly regard by his students. He was master of the subject matter and a lecturer whose comments often sparkled with touches of humor.

As a colleague he was understanding and cheerfully gave of himself to all who sought his counsel. He directed numerous doctoral dissertations and retained a keen interest in the careers of his former students.

In 1930 Vance married Rheba Cecile Usher, a native of Bennettsville, S.C., and in so doing took one of the most fortunate steps of his life. The two had met as fellow students, both having arrived at Chapel Hill in the same year, and for forty-five years they remained a devoted and remarkable couple. The Vances had three sons: David Rupert, Donald Ernest, and Victor Stuart. In the last years of his life Vance's physical condition deteriorated noticeably, confining him to a wheelchair. On 21 August he suffered a slight stroke; respiratory complications developed, and he died four days later, survived by his wife and sons.

SEE: Almonte C. Howell, *The Kenan Professorships* (1956); *International Encyclopedia of the Social Sciences: Biographical Supplement* (1979); "A Memorial Presented to the Faculty Council of the University of North Carolina, October 17, 1975" (University Archives, Chapel Hill); Raleigh *News and Observer*, 9 July 1950; *Who's Who in America*, 1968–69.

J. ISAAC COPELAND

Vance, Zebulon Baird *(13 May 1830–14 Apr. 1894)*, Confederate soldier, governor of North Carolina, congressman, and U.S. senator, was the third child and second son of David and Mira Baird Vance. He was born in the old homestead in Buncombe County, on Reems Creek, about twelve miles north of Asheville. After attending the neighborhood schools, he enrolled in 1843 (at age thirteen) in Washington College, near Jonesboro in eastern Tennessee, but withdrew the next year on the death of his father, who left a widow and seven children. In search of better educational opportunities Mrs. Vance moved to Asheville and put her children in school there. In 1850 Vance read law briefly under John W. Woodfin and in July 1851 arrived at The University of North Carolina to continue his legal studies. The next year, after being licensed to practice in the state's county courts, he returned to Asheville and was immediately elected solicitor for Buncombe County. In 1853 he was admitted to practice in the superior courts. Yet law never brought forth his best endeavors. For Vance law was primarily preparation for politics, which was his passion. Success in the courtroom was usually the result of wit, humor, boisterous eloquence, and clever retorts, not knowledge of the law. He understood people better than he did judicial matters.

Vance entered North Carolina politics as a Henry Clay Whig but on the dissolution of his party aligned himself with the American or Know-Nothing party. In 1858, after serving one term (1854) in the lower house of the North Carolina legislature, he was elected to the Thirty-fifth Congress to fill the vacancy caused by the resignation of Thomas L. Clingman. He also won a seat in the Thirty-sixth Congress (1859–61), the last before the disruption of the Union.

Vance never questioned the legality of secession, only its wisdom under certain circumstances. In fact, his was a powerful voice in behalf of union up to the firing on Fort Sumter and President Abraham Lincoln's call for troops. These were the circumstances that changed his plea from that of union to that of secession.

Refusing all overtures to be a candidate for the Confederate Congress Vance raised a company of "Rough and Ready Guards" and on 1 May 1861 marched off to war with a captain's commission. By June the "Guards" had become Company F, Fourteenth North Carolina Regiment, and were on duty in Virginia. In August Vance was elected colonel of the Twenty-sixth North Carolina, which he ably led in battle at New Bern in March 1862 and shortly afterwards in the Seven Days fighting before Richmond.

Although Vance was a good combat officer, he could not remove himself completely from politics. Thus he gladly accepted the Conservative party nomination for governor in 1862. The Conservatives, composed primarily of old-line Union Whigs, were led by W. W. Holden, editor of the *North Carolina Standard* and a bitter critic of President Jefferson Davis. The Confederate party, as the Democrats called themselves, selected "original secessionist" and railroad executive William Johnston of Mecklenburg County. The result was an overwhelming victory for Vance but not a verdict for reunion. It was more an expression of dissatisfaction with state and Confederate leadership and trying war conditions.

As war governor Vance worked hard to provide North Carolina troops and civilians with necessary arms, clothing, and food. At the same time he strongly defended the wartime rights of the state and its citizens. These efforts endeared him to his own people but oftentimes brought him into sharp dispute with the Davis administration. Vance objected strenuously to the Confederate conscription and impressment of property laws, the suspension of the writ of habeas corpus, discrimination against North Carolinians in the appointment and promotion of commissioned officers, and the use of Virginia officers in the state. Other controversies between the governor and Richmond centered around North Carolina's efforts to clothe its troops in the Confederate army and its ownership of blockade-runners. But there were no quarrels with Confederate officials when the governor turned his attention to the difficult task of returning army deserters to the ranks. Instead, Vance found himself in conflict with Chief Justice Richmond M. Pearson of the state supreme court who discharged many defendants on the grounds that the governor had no authority to arrest either deserters or recusant conscripts.

Disaffection in North Carolina manifested itself not only in desertion and draft evasion but also in the peace movement of 1863–64 led by Holden. Fearful of this development, Vance denounced it strongly and then broke with his erstwhile political ally. Thereupon Holden announced his candidacy for the governorship in 1864. The gubernatorial race of that year was a bitter one, but Vance won by a very convincing majority. From the moment of his reelection until the end of the war the next spring the governor worked untiringly for the Confederate cause. In early 1865 he refused to cooperate with a group in the Confederate Congress calling for peace on the basis of separate state action. However, on 10 April, having been informed that Confederate troops of General Joseph E. Johnston would soon have to evacuate Raleigh, Vance began the transfer of state records and military stores to Graham, Greensboro, and Salisbury. Two days later, with the capital unprotected and William T. Sherman's army rapidly advancing on the city from the east, he sent ex-governors David L. Swain and William A. Graham to open negotiations with the Union general. When the commissioners failed to return at the appointed time, late afternoon, the governor decided to leave Raleigh, which he did around midnight. After spending the remainder of the evening at General Robert F. Hoke's camp about eight miles from the city, he proceeded to Hillsborough and from there to Greensboro and thence to Charlotte by rail to talk with President Davis. Vance then returned to Greensboro. He was there when it was announced that General Johnston on 26 April had surrendered his forces to Sherman at the James Bennett farmhouse near Dur-

ham. On receipt of this news the governor issued his final proclamation to the people of North Carolina and then surrendered himself to Union general John M. Schofield. The general, having no orders for Vance's arrest, told him to go to Statesville, where Mrs. Vance and their children had sought safety. But early on the morning of 13 May the governor was arrested at his Statesville home. It was his thirty-fifth birthday. He was sent to Washington, D.C., and on the twentieth placed in the Old Capitol Prison where he remained until paroled on 6 July. No reason was ever given for his forty-seven-day imprisonment, and no charge was ever brought against him.

On 3 June 1865, in compliance with President Andrew Johnson's amnesty proclamation of 29 May and while still in prison, Vance filed an application for pardon. It was granted on 11 Mar. 1867. In the meantime he had returned to North Carolina and formed a law partnership in Charlotte. He was elected to the U.S. Senate in 1870, but due to the disabilities placed on ex-Confederates under the Fourteenth Amendment he was unable to take his seat in Congress. Later freed of political encumbrances, Vance accepted the Democratic (formerly Conservative) nomination for governor in 1876. His Republican opponent, Judge Thomas Settle of Rockingham County, was a very able man. The candidates agreed on a joint stumping tour of the state beginning at Rutherfordton in late July and lasting for three months. The debates, combined with the partisan bitterness of the times, made the campaign one of the most dramatic political contests in North Carolina history. Huge crowds gathered at campaign stops. Vance won, but his margin of victory was narrow. His third term as governor was noteworthy not only because it marked the end of Reconstruction in the state but also because of gains made in public education and railroad building.

Vance served only two years of his four-year term, as he was elected to the U.S. Senate by the General Assembly in 1878 on the expiration of A. S. Merrimon's term. Reelected in 1885 and 1891, he held his seat until his death. During his senatorial career Vance stoutly defended the interests of the South but at the same time harbored little bitterness towards the North. It was his misfortune, however, to be known as an opposition senator. He resisted much of the important legislation of the period, and no constructive enactment of the Senate is associated with his name.

Vance's health began to fail in 1889 with the removal of one of his eyes. He died five years later of a stroke at his home in Washington. He was buried in Asheville. Vance was married twice. His first wife, Harriette Espy of Quaker Meadows, Burke County, whom he married on 3 Aug. 1853, bore him four sons: Robert Espy (b. 1854, died young), Charles Noel (b. 1856), David Mitchell (b. 1857), and Zebulon Baird, Jr. (b. 1860). She died in 1878. In 1880 he married a widow, Florence Steele Martin of Louisville, Ky., who survived him. They had no children.

Vance's engaging personality and lengthy public career gained for him an admiration from North Carolinians that no other state official has ever enjoyed. To the multitude especially he was a beloved leader. Ex-Confederate soldiers and their families were not quick to forget his efforts to care for them in time of war and how he defended their liberties and preserved their honor. As his funeral train moved westward through the state, thousands of humble people lined the tracks to pay their last respects to one whom they loved and admired very much.

SEE: *DAB*, vol. 19 (1936); Clement Dowd, *Life of Zebulon B. Vance* (1897); Frontis W. Johnston, ed., *The Papers of Zebulon Baird Vance*, vol. 1 (1963); Joe A. Mobley, ed., *The Papers of Zebulon Baird Vance*, vol. 2 (1995); Glen Tucker, *Zeb Vance: Champion of Personal Freedom* (1965 [portrait]); Richard E. Yates, *The Confederacy and Zeb Vance* (1958).

JOHN G. BARRETT

Vanderbilt, George Washington (*14 Nov. 1862–6 Mar. 1914*), heir of a portion of the family fortune acquired in railroad development, turned his interests to agriculture and forestry and became outstanding in both. Born in New Dorp (now Richmond Borough), Staten Island, N.Y., the youngest son of William Henry and Maria Louisa Kissam Vanderbilt, he was educated by tutors and through world travel. Shy and serious, he cared little for finance but nevertheless increased his inherited fortune during his lifetime.

Fascinated by the mountains of western Carolina, Vanderbilt began buying land south and southeast of Asheville in 1889. Eventually his holdings amounted to 130,000 acres, including Mount Pisgah (5,721 ft.), from the top of which may be seen points in South Carolina, Georgia, Tennessee, and Virginia, as well as in North Carolina. Within this area he sought the ideal spot for what he anticipated would be the most beautiful country home in the nation. Having studied architecture, forestry, and landscape gardening, he devoted himself wholeheartedly to the exciting task ahead. Working closely with architect Richard Morris Hunt, he developed plans that anticipated expansive views from every possible window. Temporary structures were raised to examine the view where windows would be, and in other ways as well Vanderbilt superintended the construction, the final cost of which was reported to have been $3 million. He invested millions more in improving the estate, which he named "Biltmore." Frederick Law Olmsted, designer of Central Park in New York City and of the capitol grounds in Washington, D.C., was engaged to develop plans for the estate grounds. Until the death of his widowed mother in 1896, Vanderbilt lived with her in New York. Although he inherited her Fifth Avenue mansion, the thirty-four-year-old Vanderbilt then went to live in his North Carolina château. On 2 June 1898 he married Edith Stuyvesant Dresser, of Newport, R.I., who proved to be a valued aide in the unique work he anticipated.

Vanderbilt became a scientific farmer and stockbreeder, as well as one of the pioneers in scientific forestry in America. His pedigreed hogs, raised for sale in local markets, were a significant improvement over the unimproved stock found in most of the mountain region. The milk production of one of his Jersey cows broke all records, and the milk and ice cream from his dairies were sold across a wide area. The significance of the example he set for improving livestock would be difficult to overestimate.

The Biltmore Nursery, featuring trees and plants of the Appalachian region, became an important part of the output of the Vanderbilt estate. A portion of his woodland was developed for pleasure—with bridle paths following the interesting terrain and picnic shelters conveniently located. Roads were also built to ensure the movement of fire-fighting equipment in case of forest fires.

Gifford Pinchot was the first superintendent of the wooded estate, and in 1898 he went on to become head of the U.S. Division of Forestry. Vanderbilt founded the Biltmore School of Forestry on his estate, where large numbers of young men received training. He planned and built the model village of Biltmore as a center for the employees on his property, as well as All Souls Church. He bought another home in Washington, D.C. but spent most of his time in the North Carolina mountains, overseeing the work of the estate, studying trees, bird, and animals, or doing research in his large library, which held many books on nature. He spoke eight languages and had a reading acquaintance with Hebrew and Sanscrit.

In the early 1900s Vanderbilt sold the timber rights in Pisgah Forest to the Carr Lumber Company for $12 an acre, the contract extending over a twenty-year period. During those years the estate netted about $870,000. Vanderbilt directed that weak and undesirable trees be removed first and that after an area had been selectively cut over, new trees be planted. Forests were to be "managed" and kept in constant production. He maintained that "private ownership of any resource necessary to the general welfare carries with it the moral obligation of faithful stewardship to the public." He stressed that he had "stuck to forestry from the beginning and I shall not forsake it now. For me to impair the future usefulness of Pisgah Forest in order to somewhat increase present revenues, would be bad business policy. But apart from that, it would be bad citizenship, as I see it, no man is a good citizen who destroys for selfish ends a good forest."

Vanderbilt might have received a much higher price for the timber if he had waived restrictions under this sale as to methods of cutting, but he required that the techniques of practical forestry be followed. An observer commented: "Pisgah Forest, its mountainous slopes clothed in an unbroken mantle of protective tree growth is his monument. He transformed it by nearly a quarter of a century's efficient fire protection from a forest characterized by scanty young growth, thin humus covering, and impoverished soil, as the result of injury it had received in former years from excessive grazing and recurrent fires, to one whose silvicultural condition is probably unequaled in the Southern Appalachians."

Among his benefactions, Vanderbilt in 1888 erected and presented to the New York Free Circulating Library (later New York Public Library) its Jackson Square Branch and gave to Columbia University the site on which the Teachers College was built. He also built a private museum in New York City, gave it art objects that he had collected all over the world, and presented it to the American Fine Arts Society. He offered to sell the major portion of his forest land to the United States for a forest preserve, but the offer was not accepted until 1916, after his death, when the government bought an 80,600-tract from Mrs. Vanderbilt to form the nucleus of Pisgah National Forest.

Following an operation for appendicitis about a week previously, Vanderbilt died at his Washington home of "a weak heart." In addition to his wife, he was survived by a daughter, Cornelia Stuyvesant. His body was placed in the family vault at New Dorp, Staten Island.

SEE: *American Forestry*, June 1914; *American Homes and Gardens*, July 1909; *Asheville Citizen-Times*, 27 Feb. 1949; *Greensboro Daily News*, 8 Feb. 1959; *Harper's Weekly*, 28 July 1900; *New York Sun*, 7 Mar. 1914; *New York Times*, 7–8 Mar. 1914; *New York Tribune*, 7 Mar. 1914; Gifford Pinchot, *Biltmore Forest . . . An Account of Its Treatment and the Results of the First Year's Work* (1893); *Travel*, April 1911; Arthur T. Vanderbilt II, *Fortune's Children* (1989); *Who's Who in America* (1912–13).

JOE L. MORGAN

Van Landingham, Mary Oates Spratt (*14 Sept. 1852–24 Dec. 1937*), cultural leader, speaker, and author, was born in Charlotte, the daughter of Charles E. and Margaret Lowery Oates Spratt. On 18 Dec. 1873 she married John Van Landingham, a young hardware merchant, and they established their home at 500 East Avenue, where she resided until her death sixty-four years later. They had four children, three of whom survived: Ralph, Norma (Mrs. Jacob Binder), and John Henry.

A descendant of colonial and Revolutionary Mecklenburg County ancestors, Mary Oates Van Landingham became active in a number of patriotic organizations. A member of the National Society of the Daughters of the American Revolution, she was elected vice-president general in 1913. On three occasions she declined to be a candidate for president general. She frequently held office in the local chapter, however, and was state regent three times. She was also a member of the North Carolina Society of Colonial Dames, of which she was vice-president. On 6 Mar. 1900 she became the first woman invited to address the Mecklenburg Historical Society. Speaking on "The Native Literature of North Carolina," she compared the literary production of the state with that of its neighbors, Virginia and South Carolina. North Carolina's record was not impressive, Mrs. Van Landingham concluded. "Could it be," she asked, "that being located between Virginia and South Carolina, our people for so long have been furnished such conspicuous illustrations of self-appreciation that they have, by contrast, learned modesty and silence? Where there are mountains of conceit, there are apt to be valleys of humility." Widely reported in the press, her words became a popular characterization of the state's cultural status.

She also was the first woman to address the State Literary and Historical Association when, in 1900, she presented a paper entitled "The Encouragement of Art as an Aid to History and Literature." She took an interest in the North Carolina Folklore Society and attended meetings in Raleigh on its behalf. As an active member of these and other organizations, Mrs. Van Landingham took the lead in the erection of markers and otherwise publicizing a number of historic places and people in the state. Reared in the Episcopal church, she held offices at the parish and diocesan levels and was especially effective in raising funds for St. Peters Hospital.

Writing on topics of both current and historical interest, her contributions to state and regional newspapers were well received, with mention made of her "unusual literary accomplishment, of smooth style and wise judgment." At a time when it was considered complimentary, she was described as having "the mind of a man" and a "mind that can grasp the political and economic conditions of the country." As a memorial to her husband, who died in 1915, she published a selection of her writings under the title *Glowing Embers* (1922). Included were pieces she had written for newspaper publication, reviews read to book clubs, addresses to literary societies and church organizations, and comments at the unveiling of historical markers. She dealt with an impressive variety of subjects—among them the responsibilities of women, architecture, treaties with Japan, the ethics of politics, and government ownership of railroads.

Mrs. Van Landingham died two weeks after suffering a stroke of paralysis. Funeral services were held at St. Peter's Episcopal Church, Charlotte, and she was buried in Elmwood Cemetery.

SEE: *Charlotte Observer*, 25 June 1933 (portrait), 26 Dec. 1937 (portrait); Margaret Wootten Collier, ed., *Biographies of Representative Women of the South, 1861–1925*, vol. 3 (1925).

WILLIAM S. POWELL

Van Loon, Elizabeth (*5 Feb. 1843?–6 Feb. 1893?*), author, apparently was born in Yancey County. That she grew up there is attested by an explicit statement in one of her works, *Hampton Mead* (p. 140), and from the fact that members of the Bailey family in Yancey remember that she was described by their ancestors as a relative. Whether her family name was Bailey, or Hampton, or some other, cannot be established. Of her education, nothing is known.

She wrote four novels, each published by T. B. Peterson and Brothers of Philadelphia: *The Shadow of Hampton Mead* (1878), *A Heart Twice Won; or, Second Love* (1878), *Under the Willows; or, The Three Countesses* (1879), and *The Mystery of Allanwold* (1880). The first of these is set in the mountains of North Carolina, apparently in Yancey County, whose geographic features and minor place-names are recognizable to those familiar with the county. *The Shadow of Hampton Mead* was also published in paperback (from the same type) by Royal Publishing Company of Philadelphia, undated, as *The White Slave*.

By 1870 she had married Benjamin Franklin Van Loon, and they were residents of Memphis, Tenn. By 1885 they were living in Knoxville, Tenn., where they remained until her death. Van Loon disappears from the records, but Elizabeth was buried in the Van Loon cemetery at the site of Campbellite Church on Middlebrook Pike (Ball Camp), Knoxville. The cemetery is located on land that Van Loon deeded to the church. Their only child, a daughter named Frankie, married Henry Goosie and has numerous descendants in the Knoxville area.

SEE: Knoxville city directories, 1871–74; Tennessee census records; Elizabeth Van Loon, *The Shadow of Hampton Mead* (1878).

LLOYD R. BAILEY, SR.

Vann, Preston Stewart (*1870–27 Apr. 1954*), educational administrator, was born in Sampson County, the youngest of twelve children of Kedar and Louisa Robinson Vann. He received his early education at Coharie Academy—an institution of which his father had been one of the principal founders—and Scotland Neck Military Academy. In 1893 he enrolled in Wake Forest College, which awarded him both the A.B. and L.L.B. degrees in 1897.

After spending a short term at Harvard University, where he earned certificates in education, Vann devoted the next quarter century of his career to education and educational administration. He taught Latin, mathematics, and science at Chowan Female Institute, Murfreesboro, from 1897 to 1902 before service with the following institutions: principal, Robeson Institute (1903–7) and Liberty-Piedmont Institute (1907–9); superintendent, Davidson County Schools (1909–15), Gates County Schools (1917–18), and Pasquotank County Schools (1918–20); and president, Chowan College (1920–23). Thereafter, he spent several years as southern regional representative for the J. B. Lippincott Publishing Company, Philadelphia.

Vann's major contribution as a secondary school administrator—in both the public and private sectors—was to garner support for the expansion and improvement of the physical facilities of these institutions. He delighted in being a "builder." Thus, no less than forty-eight new schools were erected during his six-year tenure with the Davidson County system, including the first three high schools to be established in the county. Earlier, he had rallied support—especially among area Baptists—for the fledgling Robeson Institute (Lumberton) and the Liberty-Piedmont Institute (Wallburg).

The primary objective of his tenure as president of Chowan College was to raise educational standards so the institution could attain the highest possible accreditation rating by the State Board of Education. Accordingly, he enlisted the assistance of the school's trustees and patrons for the necessary renovations and construction projects and for upgrading curriculum requirements. Although his goal was not realized until two years after his resignation, Vann initiated the project and secured the approval of Chowan's governing board and patrons to carry it out.

Vann married Katherine Lee Alley of Petersburg, Va., on 12 Oct. 1897. They had no children. A devoted Baptist and active in numerous civic, professional, and fraternal organizations, Vann spent his later years in Charlotte. There his remains were interred in Forest Lawn Cemetery.

SEE: Biographical file on Preston Stewart Vann (records, Wake Forest College Alumni Association, Winston-Salem); "Minutes of Board of Trustees, Chowan College," 1920–23; Mrs. J. A. Yarbrough, "Interesting Carolina People," *Charlotte Observer*, 22 Feb. 1942.

R. HARGUS TAYLOR

Vann, Richard Tilman *(24 Nov. 1851–25 July 1941)*, teacher, clergyman, and college president, was born on a farm near Winton, Hertford County, the seventh of nine children of Albert Gallatin and Harriet Gatling Vann. When he was not quite twelve years old, he lost both arms in a cane mill, the left just below the elbow and the right just below the shoulder. His mother had died when he was five, and though his father lived until 1877, Vann was informally adopted in 1868, at the time he entered Buckhorn Academy, by a cousin, Rowena Vann Savage, and her husband, the Reverend R. R. Savage. Largely through their efforts, he was able to enter Wake Forest College, where he was graduated in 1873 at the head of his class. In 1873–74 and again in 1875–76 he attended the Southern Baptist Theological Seminary, then located in Greenville, S.C. Later, Furman University conferred on him the degree of doctor of divinity.

Between the two sessions at the seminary, Vann was ordained at the Mount Tabor church, Murfreesboro. For two years (1877–79) he taught in the Academy for Girls, Scotland Neck, then spent the next two years as a state missionary pastor. Afterwards he taught for two more years in the Chowan Baptist Female Institute, also serving the Murfreesboro church as interim pastor from January to October 1883. His pastorates thereafter were Wake Forest (1883–89), Edenton (1889–91), and Scotland Neck (1891–1900).

In Scotland Neck his sermons were sometimes published in the local weekly newspaper, but occasionally, moved by righteous indignation, he appealed to a wider audience. In response to an uncritical 1894 eulogy of Confederate general Jubal A. Early in the *Wilmington Messenger*, Vann launched a stinging rebuke to the editor. Granting Early's valor during the Civil War, he criticized the editor's failure to note Early's "long connection with that grizzly horror," the Louisiana lottery. "Is it quite the thing," he wondered, "to set him forth before our youth as one of 'the breed of noble bloods?'" The editor, though claiming "no stomach for this fight," placed alongside Vann's response two columns of rebuttal. Although again assailing Early in his final sally, Vann directed his most ringing retort at the editor's implication that Vann was among the "younger portion of our people" who, owing to "envy of [their] good fortune, . . . turn up their noses at their betters." Indignant, Vann responded that the shaft, if personal, "flew wild. . . . All my brothers (four) volunteered in the Southern army and stayed there till the end came; no, two of them did; the other two fill soldiers' graves."

In 1900 Vann began his life's great work, the presidency of the Baptist Female University (renamed, after much debate, Meredith College in 1909). It would have been a staggering undertaking even for a veteran administrator. The young school had no endowment and a debt of $43,000. The effects of the financial panic of the nineties were still being felt and increased the difficulties of the new school. There were more courses leading to the A.B. degree in the 1899–1900 catalogue than the small faculty could possibly manage, and even the degree of M.A. was offered. Vann's extraordinary ability as a preacher was already recognized: "brilliant," "scholarly," "devout" were among the terms applied to him. However, he had had no experience in administration. Yet the same indomitable spirit, the same courageous faith that refused to be handicapped by the loss of his arms kept him from discouragement when faced with seemingly insuperable obstacles.

Beginning immediately to work toward erasing the $43,000 debt, Vann devised a letter-writing campaign to seek larger donations and undertook personally, from 1900 to 1904, an intensive travel schedule in the belief that small gifts from the many were essential to bond Baptists to the young institution. After celebrating victory in February 1904, Vann's administration made amazing progress. The value of the property increased from $75,000 to $289,050, and an endowment of $127,000 was accumulated. The enrollment rose from 220 to 383 despite the discontinuance of the departments of business and education, the first nine years of the preparatory department, and the M.A. degree. From a "female university" with rather vague requirements for entrance and graduation it became a women's college that commanded respect in academic circles.

During his presidency Vann spoke with increasing authority on a broader range of issues. Before his Meredith career, he was once quoted as stating, "I am opposed to educating woman *as* woman. I am in favor of *education*. The idea that woman acts by intuition and man by reason degrades the woman." By 1911, however, Vann could amplify that statement: they should be educated not to "refine and fit [them] for the drawing room," but because of women's "pervasive and dominating influence on the individual," an influence that must be made to "count for most in creating the highest types of public institutions and civic witness." Still unsure whether or when women should be granted the vote, Vann insisted that they had earned their education as a right: monuments to Civil War dead were proper, he granted; yet "what of their wives and sisters and mothers, who stayed at home and served and starved and smiled through a dumb and endless agony?" If they were dead, their daughters were "here and begging us only to give [them] a chance." He urged Southern Baptists, therefore, not only to establish colleges for women, but also to endow them.

With other prominent Baptists, he questioned the state's support for institutions of higher education, arguing that the money should go to the common schools. And he strongly advocated prohibition, once calculating that the "billions of dollars spent for drinks and an equal sum in crime from whiskey" would "build twenty schoolhouses in each [North Carolina] county and pay their teachers [for] ten years."

Vann's service in Christian education did not end when he resigned as president of Meredith. Just as fifteen years earlier he had been called to head a new enterprise, so now the denomination called him to a new work. The executive secretaryship of the newly established Educational Board of the Baptist State Convention, a position he held until 1924, when he became associate secretary. With this new responsibility, his public role shifted. Often in the past an advocate for educational causes or a critic of societal practices, Vann now was looked to as a conciliator. His most prominent challenge in reconciling opposing factions came in the early 1920s, when Wake Forest College president W. L. Poteat's teaching of evolution in his science classes threatened to divide irrevocably not only North Carolina's Baptists, but also their counterparts throughout the South. As attacks on Poteat intensified in 1922, Vann arranged for Poteat to lecture at a series of Baptist Association meetings, hoping to reassure skeptics of the scientist's Christian piety. Later, with the issue still dominant, Poteat was invited to speak to the December 1922 North Carolina Baptist State Convention. In an eloquent address on "Christianity and Enlightenment," he insisted that "[m]anifestly science cannot discredit faith."

Vann introduced President Poteat to the convention, and as Poteat left the rostrum, Vann stepped forward to lead the applauding hosts in a healing chorus of "All Hail the Power of Jesus' Name." But the issue was not so quickly laid to rest. Early in 1925, as secretary of the North Carolina Baptist State Convention's Board of Education, Vann was asked to address the Southern Baptist Educational Conference in Memphis. His assignment was to discuss what attitude the college, on whose grounds the battle between Fundamentalists and Modernists seemed destined to be fought, should take "towards the contestants and the issues involved." In "a brilliant address," as it was hailed, Vann urged a clearer definition of terms, in particular of the word "evolution"; a rejection of extremism ("fundamentalism and modernism are not necessarily exclusive of one another and should not be made so"); recognition of the role of men in interpreting God's revelations and the progressive nature of revelation itself; and the necessity of Baptists' granting to scientists the same freedom of investigating God's universe that Protestant individuals prized in investigating, for themselves, God's written word.

In an author's note appended to the published address, Vann made clear both his neutral position in the controversy and his purpose as a mediator: rather than attempting a scholarly discussion of issues, he offered "only a popular appeal to the moderates of both sides in the pending controversy, in the hope of bringing about larger tolerance and a working harmony." Vann wrote, he stated, "as one who has accepted no theory of evolution, nor lined up with the extremists of either side; who holds firmly every fundamental doctrine of the evangelical faith, but is open to every new truth that may be discovered."

On 21 Oct. 1885, while pastor at Wake Forest, Vann married Ella Rogers McVeigh, who had been a fellow instructor at the Chowan Institute. She was an honor graduate of Hollins College and had also taught at a private academy before her marriage. The couple had five children: William Harvey, Albert Gallatin, Dorothy McDowell, Elizabeth Rogers, and Richard Thaddeus.

In 1926 the Baptist State Convention elected Vann secretary of benevolence, a position he held until 1940. Despite stating in 1927 that the loss of his arms, as well as "partial failure of eyes since 1894," largely curtailed his ability to read and write, "and therefore anything like authorship of books or written sermons," Vann, at the urging of friends and family, did assemble a collection of sermons, *The Things Not Seen*, which was published in 1931. This "affliction of the head and eyes" had, however, forced him in 1907 to decline, with great regret, the chair of homiletics at the Southern Baptist Theological Seminary. Nevertheless, he was able to serve extended terms as trustee of that institution (1909–24) and Wake Forest College

(1894–1928), as well as twice accept the vice-presidency of the Baptist State Convention.

Vann was seldom sidelined by his handicap when the challenge of game or sport was presented to him. Not only was he a champion high and long jumper in college and later an enthusiastic mountain climber; he also excelled at croquet (he used a long handled mallet, strapped to his left forearm).

After funeral services at the First Baptist Church of Raleigh, he was buried in the family plot in Scotland Neck, where he had served his longest pastorate. His portrait hangs in the Meredith College building named for his longtime friend and Baptist colleague: the Livingston Johnson Administration Building.

SEE: *Annuals of the North Carolina Baptist State Convention* (1900–1915); *Catalogues* of the Baptist Female University, the Baptist University for Women, and Meredith College (1900–1915); Helen C. A. Dixon, *A. C. Dixon: A Romance of Preaching* (1931); *Encyclopedia of Southern Baptists* (1958); M. L. Johnson, *A History of Meredith College*, 2d ed. (1972); Memphis *Commercial Appeal* (3–6 Feb. 1925); Thomas Parramore, "Red-Tie Bill and the Wingless Bird: Tar Heel Baptists and the Evolution Controversy," *Faculty Distinguished Lectures, 1964–81*, Meredith College (1982); W. L. Poteat Papers (Baptist Historical Collection, Wake Forest University, Winston-Salem); Raleigh *Biblical Recorder* (1870–1942); Raleigh *News and Observer*, 27 Dec. 1905, 10 Dec. 1922; *Scotland Neck Democrat* (14 Feb. 1895); Richard Tilman Vann Papers (Meredith College Library, Raleigh, and Baptist Historical Collection, Wake Forest University, Winston-Salem); Vann family correspondence and papers (private collection); R. T. Vann and family (personal contact); *Who Was Who in America*, 1897–1942.

MARY LYNCH JOHNSON
HARRIET V. HOLMES

Vann, Robert Lee (27 Aug. 1879–24 Oct. 1940), newspaper editor, was born in Ahoskie to Lucy Peoples, who named him for his great-grandfather, Robert Lee, and for her first employer, Albert Vann. His father is unknown. At age six Vann moved to Harrellsville, where his mother cooked for a prominent white family. After graduation from the Springfield Colored School in 1892, he spent several years working for his mother's new husband, who farmed in the Red Hill section. During the summer of 1895 Vann was a janitor and part-time clerk for Harrellsville's black postmaster. He attended the Baptist-affiliated Waters Training School in Winton from the fall of 1895 until his graduation as valedictorian in 1901. Vann first went north in the summer of 1898 to be a waiter in Boston's Copley Square Hotel.

In the fall of 1901 he enrolled in Wayland Academy, the preparatory school of Virginia Union University, and the next year he entered the university. He won a scholarship to Western University of Pennsylvania in 1903 and was graduated in 1906. At Western, where he had been the first black editor of the student journal, *The Courant*, Vann completed law school in 1909. As a student he worked as a waiter, dining car porter, and clerk in city government and became involved in Republican politics. He passed the Pennsylvania bar in 1909 and opened a law practice early in 1910 as one of only five Negro attorneys in Pittsburgh.

As counsel to the incorporation of the Pittsburgh *Courier* in May 1910, Vann received stock in the new black newspaper. The first treasurer of the *Courier* and a contributor, he became its editor in the fall of 1910; he remained the paper's editor, treasurer, and legal counsel until his death. He also continued to practice law.

Vann editorially advocated improvements in all phases of Negro life, but he generally agreed with the economic views of Booker T. Washington. His biographer called him basically "pragmatic and conservative in his outlook." He had checkered relations with major black organizations, however. From 1926 to 1929 he waged a campaign against James Weldon Johnson and W. E. B. DuBois for their handling of funds for the National Association for the Advancement of Colored People. After initially supporting A. Philip Randolph, Vann criticized him in 1929 as the main obstacle to organizing the Brotherhood of Sleeping Car Porters. On many other occasions he supported the NAACP and the National Urban League.

Throughout his adult life Vann was active in politics. As a reward for supporting the winning mayoral candidate in Pittsburgh, he served as fourth assistant city solicitor from 1917 to 1921. In 1921 and again in 1927 he ran unsuccessfully for the Allegheny County Court of Common Pleas. A loyal Republican, he was an alternate delegate to the national convention in 1920 and an alternate delegate-at-large in 1924. Disappointed at his treatment by the Republican administration in the 1920s, disheartened by the disarray of the state party, and troubled by the economy under President Herbert Hoover, Vann in 1932 advocated blacks' "turning the picture of Lincoln to the wall" and switched his allegiance to the Democratic party and Franklin Roosevelt's New Deal. For his work on the Colored Advisory Committee of the Democratic National Committee in 1932, he was appointed a special assistant to Attorney General Homer L. Cummings. He was not a member of the "black cabinet," and in 1936 he resigned because of his lack of influence. Later in the year he was a delegate to the Democratic National Convention. In 1940 Vann supported Republican Wendell Wilkie because he opposed a third term and believed that Roosevelt had done little to aid blacks economically or to assist them in the military.

Vann also engaged in many unsuccessful business ventures such as *The Competitor* magazine in 1920, a Negro bank in 1925, and a stint with a brokerage firm in 1928. The *Courier*, however, prospered under his direction and became the nation's largest Negro weekly newspaper with a circulation of 250,000. In 1939 Vann started the Interstate United Newspaper Company to sell advertisements for the Negro press.

A Baptist, Vann belonged to the Masons, Alpha Phi Alpha, Sigma Pi Phi, the National Bar Association of which he was president, and after 1939 the Pittsburgh Chamber of Commerce. On 17 Feb. 1919 he married Jessie Ellen Matthews. He died of abdominal cancer and was buried in a mausoleum at Homewood Cemetery, Pittsburgh. After his death schools were named for him in Ahoskie and Pittsburgh, scholarships were established with his bequests to Virginia Union University and the University of Pittsburgh, the Robert L. Vann Memorial Tower was built at Virginia Union University, and the Liberty ship *Robert L. Vann* was launched on 10 Oct. 1943.

SEE: James H. Brewer, "Robert Lee Vann and the *Pittsburgh Courier*" (M.A. thesis, University of Pittsburgh, 1941); Andrew Buni, *Robert L. Vann of the Pittsburgh Courier* (1974); *Who's Who in Colored America* (1941–44).

                                                                        CHARLES W. EAGLES

Van Noppen, Charles Leonard *(7 Jan 1869–15 June 1938)*, businessman, publisher, and political reformer, was born at Wemelding, Zeeland, Holland, the son of Cornelius Martin and Johanna Maria Cappon Van Noppen. His parents immigrated to the United States in 1874, set-

tling first in Michigan and in 1877 near Greensboro, where they became members of the Society of Friends and sent their boys to the New Garden Boarding School (now Guilford College). While a teenager, Charles Leonard Van Noppen attended The University of North Carolina, graduating about the same time that his parents died in 1887. Early in life he gained national distinction as a book salesman, enabling him to assume responsibility for educating his two brothers, John J. and Leonard Charles. He was associated with such prestigious firms as Charles Scribner's Sons and the Yale University Press.

Often taking time from his extensive business interests to support education and public works, Van Noppen was contemptuous of businessmen who lacked a sense of civic responsibility. In 1899 he gave his services to establish a fund to construct an Alumni building for The University of North Carolina, and in 1903 he spearheaded a campaign to save the Greensboro Female College from foreclosure. He claimed to have also played a major role in obtaining a new post office building for Greensboro in 1933. The business achievement that he took the greatest pride in was his work in organizing and promoting the Security Life and Annuity Company, which merged with the Jefferson Standard Life Insurance Company. He was president of the Southern Light Improvement Company, which was associated with the Tungstolier Company of Ohio and had the sole contract to sell the company's tungsten lamps in the Southeast. He was an agent for the Camden Land and Cattle Company, and he had a number of real estate interests in Georgia and North Carolina. By 1913 his estate was worth well over a quarter of a million dollars.

Van Noppen was the publisher and principal supporter of Samuel A'Court Ashe's *Biographical History of North Carolina*, issued in eight volumes between 1905 and 1917. In 1907 Van Noppen recognized the talent of the young Stephen Beauregard Weeks, who has been hailed as the state's first professional historian, and brought Weeks into the enterprise as associate editor. At the same time he was active in a campaign against the so-called Mecklenberg Declaration of Independence. He wrote and published a number of pamphlets between 1908 and 1912 opposing the declaration, which he proclaimed an 1892 forgery. He also supported Leonard Charles Van Noppen's literary endeavors; by 1913 he had invested $10,000 in his brother and in 1917 he published Leonard Charles's translation of Joost van den Vondel's *Lucifer*.

Despite his many business interests Van Noppen considered himself a Jeffersonian Democrat; he adopted for his own political creed the motto "equal rights to all, special privileges to none." In 1914 at the Progressive Democratic convention he proposed the adoption of a woman's suffrage plank, and from 1930 until his death he campaigned against special banking rates for corporations. In 1932 he was a candidate for the newly created Sixth Congressional District comprised of Guilford, Alamance, Orange, and Durham Counties. His campaign pledge of "Human Rights above Dollar Rights" opposed corporations, particularly the tobacco companies and their lawyer friends. He also urged support for public education and came out in favor of the League of Nations. In his 1936 bid for Congress he continued his attacks against corporations. Singling out John and William Umstead, he repeated his vitriolic comments of 1932 referring to the Umsteads as "John the Ox and Bill the Ass."

Throughout much of his adult life Van Noppen resorted to the printing press to publicize the causes in which he believed. Among the earliest was *The Manhood and Intelligence of North Carolina Should Stand for Truth and Justice, Truth and Justice for the History of North Carolina, The*

Mecklenburg Resolves of May 31, 1775 v. The Mecklenburg Declaration of May 20, 1775 (1908). Near the end of his life he wrote *Are the People Being Enslaved by the Banks? If So, What Are We Going to Do about It?* (1930), *The Industrial Banks Must Be Destroyed! Exposed as Racketeers! Bills for the Legislature to Consider* (1930), *The People Be Damned: The Shame of Greensboro* (1930), *The Impending Crisis* (1933), *Killing the Goose, Then What?* (1936), and *Death in Cellophane* (1937).

In appearance Charles L. Van Noppen was less Byronic and a good deal stouter than his brother, Leonard C. In all respects he looked like what he was: a successful businessman and a native of Holland. He maintained his home in Greensboro, where he married Addie Donnell in 1896. He was pleased that his four children were college graduates. As he was getting off a bus, Van Noppen was struck and killed by an automobile. He was survived by his wife and children: Mrs. George Howard, Mrs. Robert P. Wilson, Charlotte, and Donnell.

SEE: *Charlotte Daily Observer*, 5, 8 June 1914; Daniel L. Grant, *Alumni History of the University of North Carolina* (1924); *National Union Catalog*, vol. 629 (1979); Raleigh *News and Observer*, 5 June 1914, 22 Sept. 1931, 8 May 1935, 16 June 1938; Charles Leonard Van Noppen Papers (Manuscript Department, Duke University Library, Durham).

D. A. YANCHISIN

Van Noppen, Leonard Charles *(9 Jan. 1868–21 July 1935)*, poet, literary expert, and translator, was born at Wemeldinge, Zeeland, Holland. His parents, Cornelius Martin and Johanna Maria Cappon Van Noppen, immigrated to the United States settling first in Michigan in 1874 and then near Greensboro in 1877, where they became members of the Society of Friends and their three boys, Charles Leonard, John J., and Leonard Charles, attended the New Garden Boarding School. Both parents of Leonard Charles Van Noppen died within a few months of each other in 1887. His brother, Charles Leonard, sent him to the renamed Friends School, Guilford College. He received an A.B. degree from Guilford in 1890, a B.Litt. from The University of North Carolina in 1892, and an M.A. from Haverford College in 1893. He returned to The University of North Carolina in 1893 to study law. Although he was licensed, he never practiced, having found literary endeavors more suited to his temperament.

For two years he attended lectures at the University of Utrecht and the University of Leiden, where he immersed himself in the study of Dutch literature. On his return to the United States he published his translation of Joost van den Vondel's *Lucifer* in 1898. It was heralded as a major literary event. The parallels between this first English translation of *Lucifer* and *Paradise Lost* led some critics to pronounce Milton a plagiarist. The translation was of such a fine quality that Henry Hadley set it to music, and the New York Philharmonic Orchestra presented two performances of it in Carnegie Hall. Van Noppen translated two other Vondel works, *Sampson* and *Adam in Banishment*, which reinforced the claims of Vondel's influence on Milton.

Because of his translations, Van Noppen became well known as an authority on Dutch literature. He presented lectures at Princeton University, Johns Hopkins University, the Lowell Institute of Boston, and a number of other institutions, and from 1913 to 1917 he was the first Queen Wilhelmina Lecturer at Columbia University. He was made an honorary member of the Society of Netherlands Literature, and at various times before 1918 he continued his studies at the Dutch universities.

Although preoccupied by his literary endeavors, Van Noppen had brief stints as a journalist in Cincinnati, Pittsburgh, and New York City, and at various times he was a private secretary to Justice John Woodward of Jamestown, N.Y., Major William J. Gaynor of New York City, and Nathan L. Miller, who later became governor of New York. In 1913 he read his own poem, "The Vision—The Palace of Peace," at the dedication of the Carnegie Peace Palace at The Hague and in 1916 presented his "Abraham Lincoln: An Elegy" at the dedication of Lincoln Memorial University. On his first visit to Holland Van Noppen became a Boer sympathizer. He returned to the United States with Boer propaganda and translated the Independence Proclamation of Martinus Theunis Steyn, president of the Orange Free State. During his second trip to Europe he met African statesman Paul Kruger in Paris, and he assisted the Boer Press Bureau at Dordecht.

After the United States became involved in World War I, he enlisted as a lieutenant in the U.S. Naval Reserve. Appointed assistant naval attaché at The Hague, he was reputed to have carried on some secret work. He held the same post for eight months at the U.S. embassy in London. In 1919 his collection of war poems, *The Challenge*, was published first in Great Britain and then in the United States. In London it was praised by Laurence Binyon, Sydney Brooks, and Thomas Hardy. Van Noppen spent the remainder of his life working on an epic poem, "Cosmorama: A Symphonic Poem of Evolution," sometimes referred to under the title "An Epic of the Cell from Protoplasm to Deity."

Van Noppen had the well-proportioned physique and physical capability of an athlete. Although he favored a Byronic appearance in dress and demeanor, his face also presented the qualities of strength and stolidity that are usually associated with the Dutch character. He possessed a dynamic and outgoing personality that generally made him a focus at social gatherings. His poetry was popular during his lifetime, especially before and during World War I in the midst of a neo-romantic revival. His poetry appeared in the *Christian Quarterly*, *Current Opinion*, and *Independent*, and his work was reviewed in the major magazines and newspapers including *The Times* of London.

On 28 Sept. 1902 he married Adah Maude Stanton Becker, of Jamestown, N.Y., a former journalist who turned to editing his work after their marriage. They had no children. Van Noppen died at age sixty-seven in Glen Cove, Long Island. After her husband's death, Adah Van Noppen spent the remainder of her life preparing Van Noppen's manuscript of his epic "Cosmorama" for publication until her own death in Cambridge, N.Y., on 25 Feb. 1944.

SEE: Samuel A. Ashe, ed., *Biographical History of North Carolina*, vol. 5 (1906); *Bookman* 50 (1919); Daniel L. Grant, *Alumni History of the University of North Carolina* (1924); *Nat. Cyc. Am. Biog.*, vol. 26 (1937 [portrait]); *New York Times*, 25 Feb. 1944; *Publisher's Weekly*, 3 Aug. 1935; Raleigh *News and Observer*, 4 Aug. 1935; Charles Leonard Van Noppen, *Killing the Goose, Then What?* (1936); Leonard Charles Van Noppen Papers (Southern Historical Collection, University of North Carolina, Chapel Hill); *Who Was Who in America*, vol. 1 (1943).

D. A. YANCHISIN

VanPoole, Gideon McDonald *(2 Sept. 1872–12 Apr. 1950)*, physician and eye, ear, nose, and throat specialist, was born in Salisbury, the son of Otho and Lucretia Lentz VanPoole. In 1894 he entered The University of North

Carolina, where he studied medicine in 1895–96; he received a medical degree from the University of Maryland in 1899. An acting U.S. Army assistant surgeon in 1900, he served in the Boxer uprising in China and afterwards was promoted to first lieutenant.

VanPoole was back in the United States from 1902 to 1905, when he married Margaret van Schenck van Dyke. Between 1905 and 1907 he was in the Philippines, where he was promoted to captain in 1906. Returning to the United States in 1907, he became a major in the medical corps in 1910. He next served in Hawaii (1913–16) and on the Mexican border. When the United States began preparations for World War I, he became an instructor at Fort Benjamin Harrison, Ind., and Camp Greenleaf, Ga. Promoted to lieutenant colonel in 1917, he took Evacuation Hospital No. 6 to France; there he was engaged in two battles on the front line and was decorated by the French government. He was advanced to colonel in the medical corps in 1918 and returned from France the next year. Because of physical disability, he retired from the army in 1920.

Moving to Honolulu, he served on the staff of Queen's, St. Francis, Kapiolani Maternity and Children's, and Kuakini hospitals and the Leahi Home for chronic invalids. In 1933 and 1936 he was a member of the House of Delegates of the American Medical Association, and in 1934–35 he was president of the Hawaii Territorial Medical Association. In 1942 he represented The University of North Carolina at the inauguration of the new president of the University of Hawaii.

Dr. VanPoole was a member of the American Academy of Ophthalmology and Otolaryngology, American Bronchoscopic Society, American Ophthalmological Society, Association for Research in Ophthalmology, International College of Surgeons, and American Broncho-Esophagological Association. He also was a specialist certified by the American Board of Ophthalmology and the American Board of Otolaryngology.

SEE: Alumni Files (University of North Carolina, Chapel Hill); Daniel L. Grant, *Alumni History of the University of North Carolina* (1924); *Honolulu Advertiser*, 13 Apr. 1950, 5 Aug. 1951; *Honolulu Star-Bulletin*, 25 May 1959; *Journal of the American Medical Association* 143 (24 June 1950); *Men of Hawaii*, vol. 5 (1935).

WILLIAM S. POWELL

Van Vleck, Jacob (13 Mar. 1751–3 July 1831), Moravian bishop, was born in New York City, the third oldest of seven children. His father, Henricus (Henry) Van Vleck, was a merchant and realtor in New York City; his mother, Jannetje Cargyle Van Vleck, was from Isle, Scotland. Van Vleck obtained his early education at Nazareth, Pa, and attended the theological seminary at Barby, Saxony, between 1771 and 1779. At this time he sought experience at the Single Brothers House in Christiansbrunn, Pa. His abilities were recognized, and by 1781 he was appointed chaplain and superintendent of the Brothers House at Bethlehem, Pa. Here he became secretary of the General Board.

Perhaps in appreciation for the Moravians allowing the Brothers House to be used as a hospital on two occasions during the American Revolution, George Washington in 1782 visited Bethlehem, where he was entertained by sacred music, vocal and instrumental. Jacob Van Vleck played the organ in the chapel while cake and wine were served. Van Vleck had a fondness for music and was a pianist, organist, and violinist, as well as a composer. The music he wrote was in the classical tradition. His father's

admiration for him was evidenced in his will in 1784; it stated, "And unto my dear Son, Jacob, I give my Silver pocket watch which I leave him in Remembrance of His Father who ever had singular joy in his said son's Spiritual prosperity."

In 1789, while a delegate to the synod in Herrnhut, Van Vleck married Ann Elizabeth Staehle (Lisetta Stackly), from Bern, Switzerland, and of Moravian parentage, who was teaching in Herrnhut. They had two children, William Henry (15 Nov. 1790–19 Jan. 1853) and Charles Anthony (4 Nov. 1794–21 Dec. 1845). Both sons entered the ministry, and Charles Anthony served as bishop in Salem. In 1881 Jacob's grandson, Henry Jacob Van Vleck, was also consecrated a bishop.

On returning to America Van Vleck became principal of the Young Ladies' Seminary, in Bethlehem, which had approximately 80 students enrolled. By 1797 the boarding school had 365 students, including the niece of George Washington and the children of other prominent families. New applications were not even considered. Van Vleck remained in his post until 1800. Two years later he was appointed principal of the boys' school, Nazareth Hall. He had become the head pastor at Bethlehem in 1799.

In 1811 he was transferred to Lititz, Pa., and in 1812 he was sent to Salem, N.C. Arriving in Salem on 14 November, he and his wife resided at the Gemein Haus. One of three administrators for the Southern Province in the Provincial Helpers Conference (later known as the Provincial Elders Conference), Van Vleck became chairman of this group by 16 November. Also beginning in 1812 he served as pastor of the Salem congregation, preaching in German and English and leading song services (*singstunden*).

Van Vleck traveled to Bethlehem, Pa., where on 2 May 1815 he was consecrated bishop, thus becoming the first American-born Moravian bishop. In 1816 he was listed as a member of the North Carolina Bible Society, a statewide religious organization. In 1822 his wife was elected by the fifty-six charter members as president of the Female Missionary Society. Later that year Van Vleck asked to be relieved of his duties at Salem, and after ten years' residence there he and his wife returned to Bethlehem. She died on 24 Nov. 1829. Jacob Van Vleck died at age eighty and was buried in the married men's section of the Moravian cemetery in Bethlehem. A photograph of his portrait is in the Old Salem research files, Winston-Salem.

SEE: François J. de Chastellux, *Travels in North-America, in the Years 1780, 1781, and 1782*, vol. 2 (1787); Adelaide L. Fries, ed., *Records of the Moravians in North Carolina*, vol. 7 (1947); J. Taylor Hamilton, *A History of the Church Known as the Moravian Church* (1900); Levin T. Reichel, *The Moravians in North Carolina* (1857); William C. Reichel, *History of the Rise, Programs, and Present Conditions of the Bethlehem Female Seminary with a Catalogue of Its Pupils, 1785–1858* (1858); Jane Van Vleck, *Ancestry and Descendants of Tielman Van Vleeck in Niew Amsterdam* (1955).

B. W. C. ROBERTS

Vardell, Charles Gildersleeve (19 Aug. 1893–19 Oct. 1962), music educator and composer, was born in Salisbury, the only son of Charles Graves, a Presbyterian minister, and Linda Lee Rumple Vardell. He grew up in Red Springs, where his father founded and was the first president of Flora Macdonald College. From his mother, who was an accomplished pianist, a graduate of the New England Conservatory of Music, and dean of music at Flora Macdonald, he inherited his musical aptitude, and from her he received his first piano instruction. Awarded an A.B. degree from Princeton University in 1914, he spent the next two years at the Institute of Musical Art (now the Julliard School), in New York City, where he studied harmony and composition under the renowned Percy Goetschius and piano under Herbert Fryer. He received a piano diploma in 1915 and the artists and teachers diploma in 1916 with highest honors. Vardell was master of music at the Hotchkiss School (Lakeville, Conn.) in 1916–17 and, during World War I, YMCA secretary at Fort Oglethorpe, Ga., in 1918. In 1919 he returned to Red Springs, N.C., as dean of music at Flora Macdonald College.

In 1923 Vardell moved to Winston-Salem to head the piano department at Salem College. He taught at The University of North Carolina during the summers of 1926 and 1927 and at Cornell University during the summer of 1930. From 1928 to 1951 he was dean of Salem's School of Music, which he developed from a small department into an outstanding school whose graduates, all of whom had at least one course under the dean, performed so well in their profession that they brought national recognition to the college. Vardell's fine, innate musicianship and scholarship combined with enthusiasm and a genial personality caused him to excel as a teacher of piano and organ and to inspire his many students, who eagerly looked forward to their individual lessons. He himself continued to perform as piano recitalist, as accompanist, and as organist-choir director first at Reynolds Presbyterian, then at the First Presbyterian, Home Moravian, and Centenary Methodist Churches in the city. Active in community musical movements, he sat on the board of directors of the Winston-Salem Symphony, the local Civic Music Association, and the Arts Council. While living in Winston-Salem he was president of the North Carolina Music Teachers Association; he served a term as regional vice-president of the National Association of Schools of Music and for many years was a member of its Commission on Curricula. A member of the American Guild of Organists, he earned the associate degree (AAGO) during his first years in Salem.

Vardell spent the academic year 1937–38 in residence at the Eastman School of Music (Rochester, N.Y.), from which he received an M.A. (1938) and a Ph.D. in composition (1940). He wrote his "Carolinian" symphony while at Eastman, where it was introduced on 28 Apr. 1938 at the Festival of American Music; the work was performed by the Philadelphia Symphony in 1940. Vardell's thesis was a composition for orchestra, "Nocturne Picaresque."

In 1951 Vardell returned to Flora Macdonald as dean of the Music Conservatory. He became president of the college in 1959, the year before it merged with Presbyterian Junior College to form St. Andrews in Laurinburg. He was a key figure in smoothing the transition, and it was his special task to plan the School of Music, of which he served as dean from 1960 until his death.

Vacations at Blowing Rock each summer from early childhood fostered Vardell's lifelong interest in North Carolina versions of the early English ballads and folk tunes that had been preserved for over two centuries in the isolation of the mountain region. These songs and their modal harmonies formed the basis for many of his compositions. Vardell was a pioneer in the movement among American composers to use their native tunes, yet he was also a product of his time. His compositions use harmonic progressions and orchestral color that were modern when he was writing. His remarkable gifts of improvisation at the keyboard were thoroughly enjoyed by his audience during college convocations or club programs.

Vardell won the Shirley cup for music composed by North Carolinians in 1921, 1923, and 1926, which gave him permanent possession of the cup. Among his published works are a Concert Gavotte (piano), 1924; "Dark Days or Fair" (song), 1926; "The Inimitable Lovers" (cantata), 1928; Christmas Evocation (anthem), 1932; "Joe Clark Steps Out" (a short symphonic sketch that has proved a favorite with many orchestras and has been recorded by the Eastman-Rochester Symphony, Howard Hanson conducting), 1937; "Song in the Wilderness" (a cantata about the early Moravians in North Carolina with the poem by Paul Green), 1947; and "Lullaby in the Manger" (anthem), 1950. Many of his works, including his "Carolinian" symphony, remain unpublished; all have been placed in the Charles G. Vardell Collection at the Moravian Music Foundation (Winston-Salem), and scores and parts are available from the foundation.

On 16 June 1920 Vardell married Eleanor Matilda Ferrill, a singer and musician in her own right. Their children were Margaret Ferrill (Mrs. Clemens Sandresky) and Julia Eleanor, who died in infancy. An outstanding composer, Margaret V. Sandresky continued her family's musical heritage.

Vardell was an elder in the First Presbyterian Church, Winston-Salem. He was a member of the Winston-Salem Torch Club and of the Rotary Club in Red Springs and Laurinburg. The music building at St. Andrews College is named Vardell Building in honor of his family. Vardell died in the hospital in Winston-Salem and was buried in Salem Cemetery. His portrait hangs in the Fine Arts Building at Salem College, and there are numerous photographs of him in the *Winston-Salem Journal-Sentinel* newspaper archives.

SEE: Raleigh *News and Observer*, 24 Apr. 1941, 31 Jan. 1955, 10 Feb. 1960, 20 Oct. 1962; Margaret Vardell Sandresky and Anna Withers Bair, personal recollections; *Who Was Who in America*, vol. 4 (1968); *Winston-Salem Journal and Sentinel* (archives, Winston-Salem).

ANNA WITHERS BAIR

Varnham (Vernham), John (*fl. 1663–81*), Council member, Assembly member, and leader in Culpeper's Rebellion, was one of the early landholders in North Carolina. On 25 Sept. 1663 he was granted a patent for 250 acres in the Chowan area by Sir William Berkeley, governor of Virginia and one of the recently created Lords Proprietors of Carolina. The grant was confirmed by the North Carolina colony, then called Albemarle, on 27 Nov. 1679, when officials of the colony granted Varnham the same land in the name of the Carolina Proprietors. At the time he received the patent from Berkeley, Varnham probably was officially a resident of Virginia, to which a settler bearing his name migrated before 3 Oct. 1656. It is likely, however, that he, as other early Albemarle settlers, was living on the land he patented before he received legal title to it.

Little is known of Varnham's life, as his name seldom appears in surviving records. The earliest known references to him are in accounts of the Albemarle uprising of December 1677, called Culpeper's Rebellion, in which Varnham is said to have commanded some of the armed forces of the "rebels." Varnham served in the Assembly held by the acting governor, Thomas Miller, in the fall preceding the uprising, which enacted measures responsible in part for the ensuing violence. Like a number of other members of that Assembly, however, Varnham took a leading part in overthrowing Miller. He also sat in the Assembly elected by the rebels after Miller's imprisonment.

In November 1679 Varnham was a Council member in the government headed by John Harvey, which recently had been established under authority of the Proprietors. Varnham held his seat as an "assistant," which indicates that he again was a member of the Assembly and had been elected to the Council by that body. He remained on the Council at least through March 1679 / 80.

Varnham's plantation was in Chowan Precinct. He was called captain, but it is not certain whether the title referred to rank in the militia or as a seaman. There are indications, however, that he was a seaman engaged in the coastal trade. He had contacts with New Englanders and served as attorney for a New England merchant in the settlement of an estate and other business in Albemarle. A connection with shipping also is implied in a reference to Varnham that occurs in a deposition relating to the handling of shipments of pork in 1680 and 1681. A Mrs. Alice Varnham mentioned in the deposition may have been his wife but is not so identified.

The fact that Varnham himself did not give evidence concerning the matters under investigation when the deposition was made indicates that he had either died, moved away from the colony, or become incapacitated by that time, which was the fall of 1682. No evidence of his being active in Albemarle after 1681 has been located.

SEE: J. R. B. Hathaway, ed., *North Carolina Historical and Genealogical Register*, 3 vols. (1900–1903); North Carolina State Archives (Raleigh): various papers, particularly in Council Minutes, Wills, and Inventories (1677–1701); Mattie Erma Edwards Parker, ed., *North Carolina Higher-Court Records, 1670–1696* and *1697–1701* (1968, 1971); William L. Saunders, ed., *Colonial Records of North Carolina*, vol. 1 (1886).

MATTIE ERMA E. PARKER

Vass, William Worrell, Sr. *(19 Feb. 1829–6 Dec. 1896)*, railroad executive, was born near Oxford in Granville County, the son of Thomas, Jr., a planter, and Lucy Hester Vass. The family of Thomas Vass, Sr., a Baptist minister and descendant of French Huguenots, had moved to North Carolina from Virginia in 1790.

Young Vass was educated in the common schools. While still in his teens, he clerked in the mercantile store of Major John S. Eaton at Henderson and became Eaton's full partner in 1843. Eaton, who retired from the business two years later, was a director of the Raleigh and Gaston Railroad, chartered in 1835. He secured Vass an appointment as treasurer of the railroad on 1 Jan. 1845. Because of the bankrupt condition of the line, the state bought it in 1848 and appointed Vass president. Vass proved to be an excellent administrator, and in 1851, when the line was again profitable, he returned to his duties as treasurer.

In October 1862 Vass was elected treasurer of the Chatham Railroad Company, later the Raleigh and Augusta Airline Railway Company. He maintained his appointment as treasurer of the Raleigh and Gaston, which consolidated with Seaboard Airline in 1893 and moved its headquarters to Norfolk, Va. On his resignation as treasurer owing to advanced age and ill health, he was appointed honorary secretary of the new consolidated railroad. By 1896 he had achieved the distinction of being perhaps the longest continuously serving railroad official in the United States.

Vass also served as a Confederate major, a director of the Raleigh Institute for the Deaf, Dumb, and Blind, and a trustee of Wake Forest College. He was an active member of the First Baptist Church of Raleigh for fortyeight years.

Vass's first wife, Amanda Freeman of Granville County, died without issue. Vass then married Lillias (Lillie) Margaret McDaniel, daughter of the Reverend James

McDaniel of Fayetteville, on 11 Oct. 1866. Vass and his second wife had three children: Eleanor, Lilla May, and William W., Jr., who became a prominent banker. Vass died in Raleigh and was buried in Oakwood Cemetery.

SEE: Moses N. Amis, *Historical Raleigh from Its Foundation in 1792, with Sketches of Wake County and Its Important Towns* (1913); Samuel A. Ashe, ed., *Biographical History of North Carolina*, vol. 6 (1907 [portrait]), and *Cyclopedia of Eminent and Representative Men of the Carolinas*, vol. 2 (1892); Grady L. E. Carroll, Sr., *They Lived in Raleigh* (1977); *Minutes of the Sixty-seventh Annual Meeting of the Baptist State Convention of North Carolina* (1897).

RONNIE W. FAULKNER

Vassall, John *(1625–July 1688)*, colonial entrepreneur and chief promoter of the Clarendon County settlement on the Lower Cape Fear in the 1660s, was born in Stepney, Middlesex County, England, the son of William and Anne King Vassall. His grandfather John Vassall had emigrated as a religious refugee from France to England, where he turned to merchandising with considerable success, developing his own fleet of vessels (two of his ships took part in the campaign against the Spanish Armada), and later to overseas colonization as a member of the Virginia Company. His uncle Samuel Vassall too became involved in overseas colonization as an incorporator of the Massachusetts Bay Company, in whose territory he secured huge patents of land. He also was actively, if unsuccessfully, interested in Sir Robert Heath's attempt to settle Carolana, challenging in 1663 Charles II's grant of the Carolana territory to the Lords Proprietors on the grounds that he held an assignment from Heath of the southern half of the old Carolana grant. Although his claim was disallowed, it showed that he had a strong continuing interest in the area. William Vassall (John's father) became an assistant in the Massachusetts Company and one of its early settlers, bringing his family (which now included John at age ten and five daughters) in the summer of 1635 to Roxbury. Within a year the Vassall family moved to Scituate in the Plymouth colony. Important by virtue of both wealth and ability, William Vassall became a leader in both colonies, especially in the movement to liberalize the suffrage. In 1646 he returned to England but two years later moved to Barbados, where he acquired sizable landholdings and died in 1655.

John Vassall remained in Scituate and joined the militia, ultimately achieving the rank of captain. Sometime in the 1650s he migrated first to Jamaica and then to Barbados, where he resided when Charles II granted the Carolina territory in 1663 to the eight Lords Proprietors. Perhaps influenced by his uncle Samuel Vassall, he and his cousin Henry Vassall (Samuel's son) became involved in an effort to colonize the area. They joined a group of Barbadians in financing an expedition led by William Hilton in the fall of 1663 to explore the territory around the Cape Fear River (a year earlier Hilton, from Massachusetts, had led an unsuccessful attempt by people from that colony to settle the Cape Fear but still felt the area had real possibilities for colonization). The Barbadians who remained behind organized the Corporation of Barbados Adventurers and chose Thomas Modyford, a prominent planter and former governor of the island, and Peter Colleton, son of John Colleton (one of the Lords Proprietors), to negotiate the conditions on which they might settle in Carolina. However, John and Henry Vassall were not willing to work through the corporation, choosing rather to follow an independent course in dealing with the Lords Proprietors.

Accordingly, about the same time that Modyford and

Colleton first communicated with the Proprietors, John Vassall wrote his own letter relative to a colony in Carolina. The Proprietors chose to deal with Modyford and Colleton. In response, the Vassalls, claiming to represent a majority of the corporation members, formed a separate body known as "the Adventurers and planters of Cape Feare." Henry Vassall was dispatched as agent for the group to London to obtain from the Proprietors the best possible terms of settlement. When Vassall met with the Lords, he was offered tentative terms that differed little if any from the "Declarations and Proposals" (a treatise issued earlier by the Proprietors to govern settlement in the Carolina territory). Although the terms were not altogether pleasing to the Adventurers back in Barbados, they were accepted, and Henry Vassall was instructed to complete a formal agreement with the Lords Proprietors.

However, John Vassall chose not to wait for the final agreement. With the promise of support from associates left behind on the island, he set out with a group of Barbadians in the spring of 1664, reaching the Cape Fear on 29 May. By November 1664 the settlement was incorporated in Clarendon County by the Proprietors, with John Vassall as deputy governor and surveyor-general. Using the inducements of the promise of land, freedom of religion, and the right to vote, the Vassals were able to attract settlers from New England, the West Indies, and Europe. Ultimately, Clarendon County would number about eight hundred inhabitants.

John Vassall's decision to migrate to the Cape Fear before Henry Vassall had reached a final decision with the Lords Proprietors proved to be a critical mistake. Henry Vassall was never able to conclude the agreement. A rival faction in Barbados led by John Yeamans proposed a settlement farther to the south at Port Royal under conditions more favorable to the Proprietors. The Lords largely turned their back on Vassall's settlement and supported a move to develop Craven County (later to become South Carolina) below Cape Romain. John Colleton alone of the Proprietors maintained an active interest in Vassall's efforts, and he unfortunately was removed by death in 1666. England's resumption of war with the Dutch in 1664 and the Great Plague and Great Fire in London in 1666 would have made it difficult for the Proprietors to provide much support for the Clarendon settlement; as it was, they provided none. Too, the Indians in the area became exceedingly hostile towards the settlement.

More and more people began to abandon the settlement until the whole effort was given up in 1667. Through it all, John Vassall acted with considerable courage and perspicacity. Even to the extent of using his personal fortune, he tried desperately to hold the colony together. In the fall of 1666, he sent at his own expense an emissary to the Proprietors to convey the terrible state of affairs in Clarendon with the hope of securing aid, only to have the emissary captured en route to England. Moreover, Henry Vassall died in 1667, ending the settlement's only immediate link with the Proprietors. As a last resort, John Vassall appealed to Massachusetts for aid, and in May 1667 the Massachusetts colony voted to send relief to the Cape Fear. If such aid was ever forthcoming, it was too little and too late. In the summer of 1667, Clarendon was abandoned, with its settlers going to Virginia or Massachusetts. Vassall, by now a financially ruined and dejected man, went to Virginia, where on 6 October he wrote to John Colleton a melancholy account of the last days of Clarendon. Unknown to him, Colleton was already dead. He seems to have remained in Virginia for some time trying to obtain redress of grievances against the Lords Proprietors.

By March 1672 Vassall had migrated to Jamaica, where he and his wife, Anne Lewis Vassall, settled in St. Elizabeth's Parish. For the remainder of his life, however, he maintained connections with the mainland colonies, engaged in the carrying trade among them, the West Indies, and Europe. In his will, proved in Jamaica on 6 July 1688, he provided for his son Samuel to be educated at Harvard College. Another son, Leonard, would live most of his life in Boston and die there. His descendants (notably his great-grandson, John Vassall) were living in the Boston-Cambridge area at the time of the American Revolution. They chose the English side, with many of them moving to England. Their vast estates were confiscated, and the family name soon lost any significance in the United States.

SEE: Thomas Bridgman, *Memorials of . . . King's Chapel Burial Ground* (1853); C. M. Calder, *John Vassall and His Descendants* (1921); Samuel Deane, *History of Scituate, Massachusetts* (1831); *Great Britain Public Record Office: Calendar of State Papers, Colonial Series: America and West Indies, 1663–1668* (1880), *1669–1674* (1889), *1675–1676* with addenda (1893), and *1677–1680* (1896); Lawrence Lee, *The Lower Cape Fear in Colonial Days* (1965); Library of Congress Transcripts of Public Record Office Papers and British Museum Additional MSS; *Massachusetts Historical Society Collections*, 2d ser., vol. 4 (1816), and 3d ser., vol. 8 (1843); *New England Historical and Genealogical Register*, January 1863; William L. Saunders, ed., *Colonial Records of North Carolina*, vol. 1 (1886); C. K. Shipton, *Biographical Sketches of Those Who Attended Harvard College in the Classes 1690–1700* (1933); N. B. Shurtleff, ed., *The Records of the Colony of Massachusetts Bay*, vol. 4 (1854); James Sprunt, *Chronicles of the Cape Fear River* (1916).

JAMES M. CLIFTON

Vaughan, Frank *(22 July 1828–3 June 1912)*, lawyer, novelist, and inventor, was born in Elizabeth City, the son of Thomas and Claudia Hamilton Elligood Vaughan. His mother was from Virginia, and the Reverend Maurice Vaughan of Maryland was his younger brother. The 1850 census recorded young Vaughan's given name as Francis.

Vaughan received his early education at the Pool School House at Elm Grove, the Pool family home some five miles southeast of Elizabeth City, and he became a teacher himself for about seven years. He worked briefly as a clerk in the Norfolk, Va., post office but returned to Elizabeth City to operate a mercantile establishment. In 1851 he was engaged by the Elizabeth City commissioners to draw up a plan of the town, and when it was finished the streets were named. In 1860, after studying law under state senator John Pool in Elizabeth City, he was licensed to practice and opened an office there. During the Civil War he held "a civil appointment" in the district in which he lived.

Resuming his law practice after the war, he also was active for a number of years in the movement to construct a railroad from Elizabeth City to Norfolk. On 8 Dec. 1880 the first number of a four-page periodical with a newspaper format, *The Railroad*, began publication with his support. He served both as president of the board of directors of the Elizabeth City and Norfolk Rail Road Company and, after its construction, as attorney.

In 1878 his novel, *Kate Weathers; or, Scattered by the Tempest*, was published by J. B. Lippincott and Company in Philadelphia. Set on the Outer Banks of North Carolina, it deals with the survivors of a wrecked ship and Kate Weathers, the wife of a banker. A Chapel Hill reviewer writing in a student publication praised it as superior to recent novels that he had read and commented particularly on the excellent characterization it presented. Another manuscript, "Tales of the Old South," was sent to a publisher in Louisville, Ky., in 1895, but it never appeared. Vaughan also assisted his son, Frank, Jr., in the preparation of two promotional pamphlets on behalf of northeastern North Carolina. *The Albemarle Section of North Carolina Traversed by the Norfolk Southern Railroad* was for distribution at the North Carolina State Exposition of 1884. For prospective settlers in the area they prepared a guidebook, *The Albemarle District of North Carolina*, published in 1895.

Over the years Vaughan was granted a dozen patents for inventions, many of which concerned marine and railroad equipment. Among them were a car-coupling device, a self-bailing boat, and submarine diving apparatus. In 1879 he secured a patent on a life preserver.

Probably because of the demands of his law practice Vaughan moved to Norfolk, where he died. He was buried in Elizabeth City, reportedly in the cemetery of Christ Episcopal Church of which he had been a member, but no record has been found there of his burial.

On 22 Nov. 1855 Vaughan married Annie Mae Scott, and they had seven children: Bertha Hamilton, Frank Elligood, William Kent, Percy Scott, Harold Cowper, Annie Almira, and Archie Musgrave. His son, Frank, after editing and publishing the *Elizabeth City Falcon*, a pro-redemption newspaper for ten years, moved to New York to work on the *Star* before he became city editor of the *New York Herald*. His daughter, Annie, who held degrees from the North Carolina College for Women, the University of California, and Columbia University, was recognized by the British government for her work with wounded soldiers during World War I.

SEE: John C. Emmerson, *The Emmersons and Portsmouth* (1966 [portrait]); William A. Griffin, *Ante-Bellum Elizabeth City: The History of a Canal Town* (1970); *Historical and Descriptive Review of the State of North Carolina*, vol. 2 (1885); *North Carolina University Magazine* 2 (November 1878); Bettie F. Pool, *Literature in the Albemarle* (1915); Raymond Sheely (Museum of the Albemarle, Elizabeth City), personal contact, 4 Feb. 1992.

B. CULPEPPER JENNETTE, JR.

Vázquez de Ayllón. *See* **Ayllón, Lucas Vázquez de.**

Velasco, Don Luis. *See* **Luis, Don.**

Venable, Abraham Watkins *(17 Oct. 1799–24 Feb. 1876)*, planter and congressman, was born at Springfield, his father's large plantation in Prince Edward County, Va. His parents were Samuel Woodson and Mary Scott Carrington Venable, both of Virginia. His paternal grandfather had immigrated to Virginia from England about 1765. Young Venable studied at home for several years under private tutors, then entered Hampden-Sydney, from which he was graduated at age seventeen. He next studied medicine for two years at what was to become the Medical College of Richmond, believing that this skill would be beneficial to a slaveholder. But he took a standard academic course at Princeton in 1818, read law, and was admitted to the bar in 1821. After engaging in planting and the practice of law in Prince Edward and Mecklenburg counties, he moved to North Carolina in 1829 and settled in Granville County in the now defunct town of Brownsville. By 1860 he owned forty-three slaves and real estate worth $69,000.

Venable was a Democratic presidential elector in 1832 and 1836. In 1846 he was elected to the first of three consecutive congressional terms. He was defeated for renomination in 1852 largely because of his opposition to the moderate Compromise of 1850. Although entering Congress as a moderate, he had become a strong champion of Southern rights by 1848. In denouncing Abolitionists that year, he said: "I hail dissolution with contentment, yes, even with satisfaction, if the bonds of the union are to be maintained only to expose us to the taunts of fanatics and hypocrits."

On 22 Feb. 1853, with suitable remarks, he delivered a block of North Carolina marble to the Washington Monument Society for the monument to the first president. Measuring four feet by two feet, it bore a sculptured bas relief and the name of the state.

During the winter of 1860–61 Venable campaigned for a secession convention, arguing that the North would not dare to oppose dissolution. After the ordinance of secession was adopted in May 1861, the Democrats to the state convention secured his election as a representative to the Confederate Provisional Congress. Here his strong states' rights convictions compelled him to oppose the Davis administration's moderate tax program, but otherwise he was its energetic supporter. In the fall of 1861 he announced for reelection but refused to campaign. The vigorous race conducted by his two rivals overshadowed his candidacy, and he received few votes, the district going for A. H. Arrington. At this juncture Venable retired from politics and soon from his law practice. He spent the last four years of his life at the home of his son in Oxford, where he died. He was buried in the Shiloh Presbyterian churchyard in Granville County.

Shortly after his death an article in the Richmond (Va.) *Dispatch* described Venable as "a true Virginia gentleman," "easy and independent," "exceedingly kind, social, and frank," and "genial and good humored." He was apparently notoriously voluble and, according to the Raleigh *Sentinel*, had once participated in a talking contest with the biggest talker in Kentucky. When morning came, the Kentuckian was dead and Venable was found still whispering in his ear.

In 1824 Venable married Isabella Alston Brown of a neighboring Virginia family. Her parents' wedding gift to the couple was a plantation. The Venables had five children: Thomas Brown, Samuel Frederick, Belle, Martha Elizabeth, and Grace.

SEE: *Biog. Dir. Am. Cong.* (1971); Lindley S. Butler, ed., *The Papers of David Settle Reid*, vol. 1 (1993); *Congressional Globe*, 1847–52; Raleigh *North Carolina Standard*, 1860–61; Raleigh *Sentinel*, 29 Feb. 1876; Ezra J. Warner and Wilfred B. Yearns, *Biographical Register of the Confederate Congress* (1975).

W. BUCK YEARNS

Venable, Francis Preston *(17 Nov. 1856–17 Mar. 1934)*, educator and chemist, was born in Prince Edward County, Va., near Farmville, the son of Charles Scott and Margaret Cantey McDowell Venable. His half brother, Dr. Charles S. Venable, was a physician of San Antonio, Tex. His Venable ancestors, who had resided in the Old Dominion continuously since 1685, included in the direct line members of the House of Burgesses and the General Assembly and men who had fought for American independence as officers in the armies of the American Revolution and the War of 1812. His grandfather was an officer of dragoons in the Revolutionary Legion of Light Horse Harry Lee. His great-grandfather, Nathaniel Venable, a mathematician of some reputation in the county of his residence, was the principal founder of Hampden-Sydney College, long the citadel of Virginia Presbyterianism. Most of the Venable men had been successful as farmers and planters and some as merchants and bankers. But Venable's father had rejected agriculture and business for a career in higher education.

Charles Scott Venable was graduated from Hampden-Sydney College at age fifteen and studied at the University of Virginia. At eighteen he returned to Hampden-Sydney as professor of mathematics and remained there until 1856. After attending lectures at the German universities of Bonn and Berlin he became professor of mathematics at the University of Georgia, where he taught for a single session before accepting the professorship of mathematics and astronomy in South Carolina College. When South Carolina withdrew from the Union in 1862, he joined the Congaree Rifles as a second lieutenant and participated in the bombardment of Fort Sumter. He later fought at the first Battle of Manassas as a private, took part in the defense of New Orleans as a lieutenant of artillery, and assisted in the fortification of Vicksburg as a captain of engineers. From 1862 to 1865 he served as an aide to General Robert E. Lee. In August 1865 he became professor of mathematics in the University of Virginia, where he remained to the end of his career. For a time he also served as chairman of the faculty, at that time the university's principal administrative officer.

Francis Preston Venable, like his father, early showed an inclination towards the teaching profession, but, unlike his father, he was interested in chemistry rather than mathematics. After his graduation from the University of Virginia in 1876, he taught for one year in the University High School, New Orleans, La., before returning to the University of Virginia for a year of graduate study. In 1880, while at Bonn, where he had been studying for a year, he was named professor of chemistry in The University of North Carolina and immediately proceeded to Chapel Hill to assume his new duties. In 1881, however, he went back to Germany, where he received that year the A.M. and Ph.D. degrees magna cum laude from the University of Göttingen. His dissertation, on B-heptane, contributed to knowledge of the hydrocarbons. Additional study at the University of Berlin in 1889 completed his formal education.

In 1900, on the resignation of President Edwin Anderson Alderman, who moved to the same post at Tulane University, Venable was elected president of The University of North Carolina. He soon proved to be both a capable administrator and an effective lobbyist who secured increased state financial support for the university. During his fourteen-year administration student enrollment increased steadily, and the university's financial position was greatly strengthened. The physical plant was enlarged and improved, faculty research was stressed, and athletics, in which Venable took a keen interest, were encouraged. The quality of the graduate school, organized in 1903 although graduate work had been offered earlier, and of the various professional schools was upgraded, and a number of departments achieved national recognition.

Following a physical breakdown caused by overwork, Venable took a leave of absence in 1913–14 and went to Europe in a vain attempt to regain his health. Still plagued by shattered nerves, he left the presidency in May 1914, to be succeeded by Harry Woodburn Chase, who had served as acting president in 1913–14. On his resignation, the trustees named Venable the chair of the Chemistry Department. In 1918 he became one of the university's first five Kenan professors. He retired in 1930 after fifty years of service to The University of North Carolina.

In 1883 Venable helped organize at The University of North Carolina the Elisha Mitchell Society for the advancement of science. The society soon began to publish a journal, and in it Venable reported much of his research in chemistry. He also furnished many articles to the *Journal of the American Chemical Society* and other scientific reviews. He was the author of a number of well-received books, including *Short History of Chemistry* (1894), *Study of the Atom* (1904), *Radioactivity* (1917), and *Zirconium and Its Compounds* (1921). According to one authority, Venable was the true discoverer of calcium carbide, although another chemist claimed a patent. Especially noteworthy was Venable's work on light atomic-weight elements, particularly zirconium, whose atomic weight he helped to determine.

A member of the American and German Chemical Societies and a Fellow of the British Chemical Society, Venable received numerous honors in recognition of his contributions to both education and chemical research. In 1905 he served as president of the American Chemical Society. The Universities of Pennsylvania, Alabama, and South Carolina and Jefferson Medical College honored him with the LL.D. degree, and Lafayette College and The University of North Carolina awarded him the honorary Sc.D.

On 3 Nov. 1884 Venable married Sally Charlton Manning, the daughter of John Manning, professor of law at The University of North Carolina, and the sister of Isaac H. Manning, later dean of the university's medical school. The Venables had five children: Louise Manning, Cantey McDowell, Charles Scott, John M., and Frances Preston. An active sportsman, Venable was a good tennis player and a fair golfer. He loved to work in his flower garden, to which he gave much time during his retirement. A devout Presbyterian, he served as an elder of his church. In politics, as befitted the son of an aide to General Lee, he was a Democrat. His physical monument on the Chapel Hill campus is Venable Hall.

SEE: Kemp P. Battle, *History of the University of North Carolina*, vol. 2 (1912); James Munsie Bell, "Dr. F. P. Venable's Contributions to Chemistry," *Journal of Chemical Education* 7 (June 1930); Philip Alexander Bruce, *History of the University of Virginia, 1819–1919*, vol. 4 (1921); Frank K. Cameron, "Francis Preston Venable," *Journal of the American Chemical Society* 59 (1937); E. Merton Coulter, *College Life in the Old South* (1928); "Francis Preston Venable, Ph.D.—A Brief Sketch," *North Carolina University Magazine*, n.s., 8 (October 1900); Daniel Walker Hollis, *University of South Carolina*, vol. 1 (1951); A. C. Howell, *The Kenan Professorships* (1956); William Rand Kenan, Jr., Papers and Charles Scott Venable Papers (Southern Historical Collection, University of North Carolina, Chapel Hill); *Who's Who in America, 1928–1929*.

W. CONARD GASS

Verrazano, Giovanni Da *(ca. 1485–1528)*, Florentine navigator, was born of noble parentage at his family villa in Tuscany, about 30 miles south of Florence. About 1506 he went to Dieppe, France, to pursue a maritime career. There is evidence that he sailed to Newfoundland in 1508 and later made trading voyages to the eastern Mediterranean.

In 1523 a group of Florentine bankers and merchants residing in Lyons, inspired by the riches accruing to Portugal from Asia, persuaded Francis I of France to lend royal patronage and a 100-ton royal ship, *La Dauphine*, to a western venture to explore north of the Spanish New World settlements in search of Cathay. The *La Dauphine* and three private vessels were outfitted by Jean Ango at Dieppe for an eight-month voyage, and Verrazano was chosen to command them.

That autumn, the fleet set out from Dieppe. Shortly afterwards, a storm destroyed two of the ships and forced Verrazano to put into a Breton port for repairs to *La Dauphine* and his remaining private ship. He then sailed south to Portuguese Maderia, taking Spanish prizes en route. There, he sent his second vessel back to France with the prizes and continued across the Atlantic in the *La Dauphine*.

About 1 Mar. 1524 he made landfall in the vicinity of Cape Fear. From there, according to him, he sailed south about 110 nautical miles to Florida, then returned to Cape Fear "in order not to meet with the Spaniards." In fact, he apparently turned back somewhere north of Charleston, as he also stated that he had been unable to find a suitable anchorage en route. From Cape Fear, he sailed north, making two or more landings between there and Cape Hatteras, visiting with the natives, whom he found friendly, and examining the flora and fauna of the land. Observing Pamlico Sound, he determined that this was not Asia but a new land, and the sound was the Pacific Ocean.

After spending about a month on the Carolina coast, he sailed north to New Jersey, New York, New England, Newfoundland, and back to France. On his return, he found the king preparing for war in Italy and his other backers unimpressed with the plants and mineral samples he brought. He thus was left without backers for a second venture.

Finally, in 1527 he persuaded Jean Ango and a high French nobleman to support him and he set forth again. This venture, beset with storms and mutiny, failed to reach North America, sailing instead to Brazil, and returned with a cargo of "Brazil wood," valued for making dye. In the spring of 1528 he sailed a third time for the New World. Taking a more southerly course, he made landfall in the Lesser Antilles. Mistaking the natives to be friendly as they had been in Carolina, he went ashore and was killed by the hostile Carib Indians.

During his North American voyage of 1524, Verrazano compiled a description of the lands and people he found and drew a map of the coastline. The account of the voyage was sent by him in a letter to Francis I, a copy of which was later obtained and translated into English by Richard Hakluyt. A copy of his map was given to King Henry VIII of England, apparently during the time the navigator was searching for a backer for his second voyage. This later came into the possession of John Lok, a London merchant, who like Hakluyt, was among the foremost proponents of English western expansion. Both of these documents were used in the planning and promoting of the English colonial movement that led to the colonies planted on Roanoke Island.

Verrazano in 1524 was probably the first European to sail the coast of North America. His map and account of his findings comprise the earliest description of the land and people of North Carolina and pioneered the way towards the eventual European settlement of North America.

SEE: Richard Hakluyt, *Divers Voyages Touching the Discoverie of America* (1582); S. E. Morison, *The European Discovery of America; The Northern Voyages* (1971); E. G. R. Taylor, ed., *The Original Writings and Correspondence of the Two Richard Hakluyts* (1935).

THOMAS M. GLASGOW, JR.

Vierling, Samuel Benjamin *(5 June 1765–15 Nov. 1817)*, apothecary, physician, and surgeon, was born in Rudelstaedt, Silesia. His parents, George Ernest and Maria Rosina Klein Vierling, were devout Lutherans who, having baptized their son in infancy, instilled in him the Christian precept of doing good unto one's fellow man. Heeding his father's advice, Samuel Benjamin decided that a medical career would enable him to realize his father's highest ambition for his son—administering to the needs of the physically distressed. While studying medicine at the University of Berlin, Benjamin associated with the Brethren of the Unitas Fratrum (Moravian church) and wrote to the Unity Elders Conference for permission to serve in one of the German congregations. Instead, he was called in 1789 to be the physician of the Moravians who, in 1766, had established the town of Salem, N.C., in the frontier of America.

Having bade farewell to his family, whom he would never again see on earth, he commended his life to the guidance of God, and on 27 Sept. 1789 he was joyfully received into the Moravian church by the congregation at Zeist, Holland. On 15 October, with other Moravians destined for America, he sailed from Amsterdam, safely landing in New York on 26 December. After spending a few days in the Moravian settlement at Bethlehem, Pa., he proceeded to Salem, where he arrived on 22 Feb. 1790 at age twenty-five. On the first day of his residence in the town, his knowledge of obstetrics enabled him to save the life of Magdelena Kraus.

As an apothecary, Vierling maintained an herb garden and dispensed his drugs with discretion. During an epidemic of scarlet fever, he abated the pestilence by prescribing less strong medicine and more fresh air. Smallpox, another disease that occasionally reached epidemic proportions, taxed his resources as a physician. In 1805, seven years after Edward Jenner had perfected his cowpox vaccine, Vierling successfully vaccinated more than two hundred persons throughout Salem and its environs.

The Salem Board Minutes and the Salem Diaries are interspersed with entries attesting to Vierling's renown as a surgeon in North Carolina and the adjoining states of Virginia and South Carolina. Supplications to Christ, the Great Physician, always preceded and accompanied his major operations. In his memoir, it is written of Vierling: "He did not depend upon his knowledge and skill alone, but trusted in the help and blessing of God, and often prayed to Him concerning the serious cases which frequently came into his hands."

Vierling also sang in the church choir and played the violin. He was a member of the Aufseher Collegium (the governing board) and the Music Committee in Salem, but he declined appointment (by the General Assembly) as a justice of the peace, an office that he believed would interfere with the demands of his medical practice.

In accordance with the "omniscient wisdom of the Lord," as divined through the Moravian custom of submitting the question of marriage determination to the Lot, Vierling married the Single Sister Anna Elisabeth Bagge on 19 Mar. 1790. They had one daughter, Maria Rosina. To Vierling's deep sorrow, his wife died on 14 Mar. 1792 during a scarlet fever epidemic. On 28 July Vierling, left with the responsibility of caring for a six-month-old daughter, proposed the name of Martha Elisabeth Miksch (the stepgranddaughter of Bishop Augustus Gottlieb Spangenberg and the daughter of the proprietor of the Miksch Tobacco shop) to the members of the Elders Conference as his second wife. The decision of the Lot was affirmative, and on 4 August Vierling married her. The couple had three sons—August Ernst, Friedrich Benjamin, and Theophilus—and five daughters—Henriette Friederika, Carolina Juliana, Johanna Eleonora, Theodora Amalia, and Eliza Wilhemina.

Five of Vierling's children by his second marriage were born in the imposing home on 463 South Church Street, built in 1802; it was large enough to accommodate not only his large family but also his medical practice. At the rear of the house was a stable, against which leaned a high pile of cordwood. One day his youngest daughter, who had been playing nearby, suddenly ran to the house to tell her mother that she had seen an angel on the woodpile. The mother hurriedly accompanied Eliza Wilhemina to discover what had excited her daughter. As Mrs. Vierling approached the backdoor of the house, she was astonished to see the tremendous pile of wood tumble down on the ground where Eliza had been playing. Who would doubt that the child had experienced the special protection of the Lord and had seen her Guardian Angel?

During the summer of 1817, while battling an epidemic of typhoid in Salem, Vierling was stricken with the fever. The remedies used for his relief had some effect, but during the ensuing months, the fever returned intermittently. Enfeebled by the disease, he was served Holy Communion in his home during the Moravian Festival of 13 August. He died three months later surrounded by his family and members of the congregation, who sang Moravian hymns.

SEE: Adelaide L. Fries, ed., *Records of the Moravians in North Carolina*, vols. 5–7 (1941–47); "Memoir of the Married Brother, Samuel Benjamin Vierling, Who Fell Asleep in Peace in Salem, November 15, 1817" (Moravian Archives, Winston-Salem); Dorothy R. Nifong, *Brethren With Stethoscopes* (1965); Edwin L. Stockton, Sr., "The Vierling House," in Mary Barrow Owen, ed., *Old Salem, North Carolina* (1941).

EDWIN L. STOCKTON, JR.

Vogler, John *(20 Nov. 1783–15 June 1881)*, gunsmith, silversmith, and watchmaker, was the son of George Michael and Anna Maria Kunzel Vogler of Friedland. At age eleven John was left an orphan and lived with his maternal grandfather for a few years after his father's death. There is no record that his father was anything but a farmer, yet John grew up with the desire and skill necessary to become a fine craftsman. It is unclear when he moved to Salem to begin an apprenticeship under his uncle, Christoph Vogler, who was a gunsmith. It must have been before 1803, however, because the town records show that in that year, after Vogler had been working for his uncle for "a few years," he made his second application to the Moravian authorities for admission to the Salem congregation, and this time it was approved. Thus at age nineteen he finally belonged to a community and was beginning to learn a craft.

It did not take long for Vogler to establish a reputation as a skilled craftsman, diligent worker, and responsible young man. In 1806 he was chosen to assist as a supervisor of the boys in Salem, and two years later he was elected to the Aufseher Collegium, one of the governing bodies of Salem. He refused a call in 1807 to move to Nazareth, Pa., to become the Vorsteher (warden) of the Single Brethren, saying that he was unfit for the job. By then he was already surpassing the talents of the master watch- and clockmaker in Salem, Ludwig Eberhardt, and it is likely that he could foresee a secure financial future in Salem and wanted to stay.

In 1809 he was granted permission to set up his own shop as a silversmith and watchmaker. There is little evidence that he continued to work as a gunsmith after leaving his uncle's shop, but it is possible that he made pieces of inlay for Christoph's rifles. During his most productive years John Vogler made many of his own tools, watches and clocks, spoons, ladles, and various trinkets out of silver and gold. He also supplied surveyors' tools and other brass implements to the Moravian congregation.

His ambitious and industrious nature was not only exhibited in his work but also in his many contributions to the community. He was reelected to the Aufseher Collegium many times in the decades following his first term in 1808. In different years he served as road master, sick nurse for the Single Brethren, fire master, and curator for the Single Sisters (1832–38). He sat on the Congregation Council and on the committee to investigate the Salem waterworks system. Vogler made several trips to Pennsylvania for both pleasure and business. In 1829 he visited the Indian missions in the South, and at home he was responsible for setting up Sunday schools in the neighboring communities where there previously had been no religious instruction for children.

In 1819 Vogler married Christina Spach in Salem. That year they moved into a new house that he had had built in the most modern style of the period. There they raised three children: Lisetta Maria, Louisa Lauretta, and Elias Alexander. Elias learned the silversmithing trade and was a partner with his father for a while but abandoned that to become a merchant. John Vogler died after a long and productive life. His house is now one of the exhibit buildings belonging to the Old Salem, Inc., restoration in Winston-Salem. Photographs and paintings of the Vogler family, memorabilia, and many objects made by the Vogler craftsmen are in the museum collection.

SEE: Adelaide L. Fries and others, eds., *Records of the Moravians in North Carolina*, vols. 6–11 (1943–69); John Vogler personal memoirs (Moravian Archives, Winston-Salem, N.C.).

ROSAMOND C. SMITH

Vollmer, Lula *(1898–2 May 1955)*, playwright, christened Louisa Smith, was born at Keyser (afterwards renamed Addor) in Moore County, the daughter of William Sherman and Virginia Vollmer. Her father was in the lumber business, and consequently the family made frequent moves as the locale of his work changed. She spent her early girlhood in Carthage and Cameron but went to boarding school at age eight. In 1918 she was graduated from the Normal and Collegiate Institute of Asheville and then went to New York for a time and became associated with the business office of the Theater Guild. She also worked in Atlanta.

Her first and most successful play was *Sun-Up*, which depicted the people of the southern mountain region. It was produced at the Provincetown Theater in New York, opening on 24 May 1923; subsequently, it played in Chicago, London, Amsterdam, Paris, and Budapest. She donated her royalties, amounting to over $40,000, to educational projects for the mountain people. In 1925 *Sun-Up* was published in book form. Between 1923 and 1946 other plays followed, among them *The Shame Woman*, *The Dunce Boy*, *Trigger*, and *Sentinels*. About 1930 she adapted *Troyka: A Play*, by Imre Fazekas, from Hungarian.

Hundreds of hopeful young actors performed in her plays, which were produced by amateurs across the United States. Grant Wood was scene designer for one of her early works. She also wrote a variety of radio serials including *Moonshine and Honeysuckle*, *Grits and Gravy*, *The Widow's Son*, and *The Hill Between*. In later years she wrote short stories for the *Saturday Evening Post, Collier's Magazine*, and others.

Except for Paul Green, Lula Vollmer had more plays produced in New York than any other North Carolina dramatist. An Episcopalian, she was a member of the Author's League of America and made her home at 1 MacDougal Alley, New York City. She was buried in Attalla, Ala., survived by two sisters and a niece.

SEE: Mrs. May Gardner (Carthage), personal contact; Stanley J. Kunitz, *Twentieth-Century Authors* (1922); *National Union Catalog,* vol. 641 (1979); *New York Times,* 21 Oct. 1923, 26 Dec. 1931, 3, 15 May (sec. II, p. 3) 1955; *North Carolina Authors: A Selective Handbook* (1952); Richard Walser Papers (Southern Historical Collection, University of North Carolina, Chapel Hill); *Who Was Who in America,* vol. 3 (1966).

KATHARINE S. MELVIN

Von Ruck, Karl (*10 July 1849–5 Nov. 1922*), physician and pioneer in the treatment of tuberculosis, the son of Baron Johann and Clara von Ruck, was born in Constantinople, Turkey, where his father was the German minister. Spending his youth in Württemberg, Germany, he was educated in Stuttgart where he received the B.S. degree in 1867. He entered the medical course at the University of Tübingen, but the Franco-Prussian war interrupted his studies. After the war he returned to the university, from which he received the M.D. degree with honors in 1877.

Von Ruck went to England for a time and then to the United States, where he enrolled in the medical department at the University of Michigan. Following his graduation in 1879 with a second M.D. degree, he spent almost a year working in hospitals in New York before establishing a private practice in Norwalk, Ohio, where he remained until 1883. News of the discovery by Professor Robert Koch in Germany of the germ that caused tuberculosis prompted von Ruck to return to Germany to work under Koch. He spent about eight months in Koch's Hygienic Laboratory and at Professor Rudolf Virchow's Pathological Institute. Von Ruck was present on 21 Mar. 1882 at a meeting of the Berlin Physiological Society when Koch announced his detection of the tuberculosis bacillus. Before returning to the United States he also visited private clinics that treated tuberculosis. Again in Ohio in 1884, he established a private hospital for the treatment of tuberculosis.

Because of the therapeutic climate in Asheville, N.C., he moved there in 1888 to establish the Winyaw Sanitarium for the treatment of diseases of the lungs and throat. Modeled and conducted along the same lines as those in Germany, the sanitarium soon was receiving patients from all over the United States.

After Koch discovered a serum for the treatment of tuberculosis, von Ruck was the first physician to obtain it for use in a private institution. Together with "the climatic, dietetic, hydropathic and other methods of treatment" at the Asheville clinic, the serum produced notable results. An 1892 account reported sixty-nine cases cured and a large number "permanently arrested and greatly improved." Von Ruck continued to operate the sanitarium until 1910, when he became consulting physician. In 1895 he founded the Von Ruck Research Laboratory for Tuberculosis in Asheville as a center for original investigation only, and in 1912 he found a vaccine for the prevention and cure of tuberculosis. During the summer of 1914 he went to London to present his observations on the treatment of tuberculosis to the medical profession of England and other countries. He was well received and

likely would have pursued his work there and on the Continent if World War I had not intervened.

Von Ruck contributed to a number of professional journals, and with his son, Dr. Silvio von Ruck, he was the author of *Studies in Prophylactic and Therapeutic Immunization against Tuberculosis* (1916).

On Christmas Day 1872 von Ruck married Delia Moore of Ottawa County, Ohio. They had two children—a daughter, Calla, who died in 1897, and a son, Silvio Henry, a physician who collaborated with his father and eventually took over much of his work before dying of pneumonia in 1918. Their only grandchild, Silvia, also died of pneumonia a few days later. Mrs. von Ruck died in December 1921, and Karl von Ruck, who had been in declining health from nephritis, was the last of his immediate family. His funeral was conducted at his home by the minister of the Congregational church, and he was buried in Riverside Cemetery. Both the laboratory, which had been endowed by von Ruck, and the sanitarium, under the direction of its staff, continued to operate for a number of years.

SEE: Samuel A. Ashe, ed., *Cyclopedia of Eminent and Representative Men of the Carolinas,* vol. 2 (1892); *Asheville Citizen,* 6 Nov. 1922; *A Critical Examination of Dr. [Arthur Marston] Stimson's Report on the Investigation of the Methods and Practices Employed by Drs. Karl and Silvio von Ruck, in Treating Tuberculosis and in Rendering Persons Immune from Tuberculosis* (1915, S. Doc. 641); Howard A. Kelly and Walter L. Burrage, *Dictionary of American Medical Biography* (1928); *Nat. Cyc. Am. Biog.,* vols. 18, 20 (1922, 1929 [portrait]); *Who Was Who in America,* vol. 1 (1981). For a bibliography of von Ruck's publications see *National Union Catalog: Pre–1956 Imprints,* vol. 642 (1979).

WILLIAM S. POWELL

Waddel, Moses (*29 July 1770–21 July 1840*), educator and Presbyterian minister, the son of William and Sarah Morrow Waddel, was born in a settlement located along the South Yadkin River in Rowan County, an area that became part of Iredell. The Waddels had emigrated from County Down, Ireland, landed in Charles Town, S.C., in early 1767, and from there moved immediately to the South Yadkin region where land was cheap and could be purchased on easy terms.

Moses Waddel appears to have been a frail child, yet this did not deter his parents from sending him, at age six, to a neighborhood school, where he made good progress in reading and writing. In 1778 the Reverend James Hall founded Clio's Nursery as a grammar school, and young Waddel enrolled; his teachers were James McEwen and Francis Cummins, both candidates for the ministry. The invasion of the backcountry by British soldiers caused a suspension of the school in 1780, but when it reopened two years later Waddel was again a pupil. He remained at Clio's Nursery until 1784; his studies included Latin, Greek, arithmetic, geometry, and ethics.

Though only fourteen at the time he left Clio's, Waddel was offered the position of teacher in a school located a short distance from his home. There he instructed seven pupils in Latin and "twenty or more in the ordinary English branches." In 1786 he made a trip to Greene County on the Georgia frontier where for a brief time he was engaged as a teacher, relinquishing the post when threats from the Creek Indians became imminent. For the next four years he taught in several other Georgia schools. By 1787 his parents had also moved to Greene County, being convinced that the land offered good opportunities for farming.

Religion played a minor part in Waddel's life until he was a young man of nineteen. At that time Presbyterian missionaries who had been sent from North Carolina awakened his interest and led him to unite with the church; a decision to enter the ministry soon followed. In September 1790 Waddel left for Prince Edward County, Va., where he applied for admission to Hampden-Sydney and entered the senior class the following January. He was graduated in September 1791 and the following May received from Hanover Presbytery his license to preach. At his own request Waddel was dismissed from the care of Hanover and received by South Carolina Presbytery, where he served in an interim capacity as minister to the people of James Island, John's Island, Wadmalaw Island, and Dorchester. In April 1794 he accepted the call to a charge in Georgia, identified only as Carmel Church, and there was ordained as a Presbyterian minister. The Reverend Francis Cummins, one of his first teachers, preached the ordination sermon.

But Waddel could not long resist the classroom, for soon he had organized a school outside the village of Appling in Columbia County. In 1801 he moved to Vienna, across the Savannah River in Abbeville District, S.C., where he opened a school and continued his preaching ministry. Three years later he moved the school to Willington, about six miles away, and there began an academy for boys that became one of the better-known institutions of the antebellum South. Its location was on a high ridge near the river, in a community that had been settled by Scots-Irish and Huguenots. The first building was a two-room log structure that was soon replaced by one with four classrooms and a chapel. Students obtained board and lodging in the homes of nearby residents and studied in small brick or log huts clustered around the main building. The curriculum was heavily weighted in favor of the classics, and the quality of instruction resulted in a remarkable number of graduates who, for their day, were well educated. Estimates of enrollment ranged from 180 to 250 students per year, with the total number of students coming under Waddel's influence at Willington being perhaps as many as 4,000.

Willington Academy is also remembered for its system of student government. Monitors, who were apparently not regarded as detectives, were appointed to supervise the various classes, and each Monday morning these monitors brought cases of rules infractions before a jury of five students. The student court was presided over by a teacher, with Waddel holding the position of final arbiter. The list of students who were enrolled at Willington is noteworthy. Among the names are William H. Crawford, a pupil in the Appling school and an assistant at Willington; John C. Calhoun, A. B. Longstreet, George McDuffie, and Patrick Noble, all governors of South Carolina; Henry W. Collier, governor of Alabama; George R. Gilmer and Thomas W. Cobb, governors of Georgia; and Hugh Swinton Legaré, James L. Pettigru, and Andrew Pickens Butler, U.S. senators. Good descriptions of the school and of Waddel appear in the second volume of David Ramsay's *History of South Carolina* (1809) and in A. B. Longstreet's *Master William Mitten* (1864). Few credit Waddel with great scholarship but instead find the secret of his success in complete mastery of the subject being taught, his impartiality in dealing with students, his insight into the character of youth, and, to a remarkable degree, his ability to stimulate the desire to learn.

In 1818 Waddel was elected president of the University of Georgia. The position was not one he sought, and he accepted it with reluctance. In May 1819 he and his family arrived in Athens, where he remained until retiring in 1829. His administration was marked by a greatly improved financial position for the university and a substantial increase in student enrollment.

On leaving Athens Waddel returned to Willington, where he owned a plantation and a home that had been recently built. Planting operations were left largely in the hands of an overseer, with much of Waddel's time being given to preaching. He enjoyed the association with other ministers and the opportunity it afforded him to visit the districts adjacent to Abbeville.

Waddel was twice married; in 1795 to Catherine Calhoun and in 1800 to Eliza Woodson Pleasants. Catherine Waddel, the only daughter of Patrick Calhoun and the sister of John C. Calhoun, lived for only a year after their marriage. The second Mrs. Waddel, whose name also appears as Elizabeth, was a Virginia native who had been a friend in earlier years. Eliza and Moses Waddel were the parents of six children who survived them—James Pleasants, Isaac Watts, William Woodson, Sarah Elizabeth, Mary Anna, and John Newton.

Moses Waddel continued to reside in Willington after the death of his wife in 1830. In September 1836, shortly after returning from a preaching mission, he suffered a severe paralytic stroke and in 1839 was moved to the home of his oldest son, James, who was then living in Athens. It was there that he died.

A. B. Longstreet described Waddel as being approximately five feet nine inches tall, "of stout muscular frame and a little inclined to corpulency," with a large head and a mass of dark hair. The surname was pronounced with the accent clearly on the first syllable, making it rhyme with model.

SEE: Robert P. Brooks, *The University of Georgia under Sixteen Administrations* (1956); *DAB*, vol. 10 (1936); Ralph M. Lyon, "Moses Waddel and the Willington Academy," *North Carolina Historical Review* 8 (1931); Colyer Meriwether, *History of Higher Education in South Carolina* (1888); William B. Sprague, *Annals of the American Pulpit*, vol. 4 (1858); John N. Waddel, *Memorials of Academic Life* (1891).

J. ISAAC COPELAND

Waddell, Alfred Moore (16 Sept. 1834–17 Mar. 1912), lawyer, newspaper editor, congressman, and author, was born in Hillsborough, the son of Hugh and Susan Moore Waddell, both of distinguished Lower Cape Fear lineage; he was the great-grandson of three of the state's greatest Revolutionary leaders, Hugh Waddell, Francis Nash, and Alfred Moore. He attended Bingham's School and Caldwell Institute in Hillsborough, was graduated from The University of North Carolina in 1853, studied law with such distinguished lawyers and jurists as John L. Bailey, William H. Battle, Frederick Nash, and Samuel H. Phillips, and was admitted to the bar in 1855. Moving to Wilmington, the home area of his illustrious forebears, he began a legal practice. He remained there for the rest of his life, except for the year 1881–82, when he edited the *Charlotte Journal-Observer*. In 1857 he married Julia Savage, by whom he had two children, Elizabeth Savage and Alfred M., Jr. Following her death he married her sister, Ellen Savage, in 1878. A third marriage came in 1896 to Gabrielle de Rosset, of a prominent Wilmington family.

Waddell's first public office was clerk of the court of equity of New Hanover County (1858–61). At the same time, he became increasingly involved in politics, especially on the national level. Of a staunchly Conservative and Unionist bent, he backed the presidential ticket of the American party in 1856 and that of the Constitutional Union party in 1860, attending the latter party's convention as an alternate delegate from North Carolina. On the local level, he opposed the growing secession sentiment, even going so far as to purchase and edit a Unionist newspaper, the *Wilmington Herald*, in 1860–61. But with the coming of the Civil War he entered the Confederate service, first as adjutant and later (1863–64) as lieutenant colonel in the Third Cavalry, later designated Forty-first North Carolina Regiment, from which he was forced to resign because of ill health.

After the war Waddell advocated a readjustment of the Southern political system along Conservative lines, with limited Negro suffrage (a position that came back to haunt him in his own political career a few years later). On the Conservative-Democratic ticket, he was elected to the Forty-second Congress in 1870 and to the three successive Congresses. Democratic overconfidence and consequent inactivity, and especially a wide distribution of his 1865 speech advocating limited Negro suffrage (now very much resented in his home constituency), caused his defeat in the 1878 campaign and ended his congressional career.

During his four terms in the House of Representatives, he served with distinction, ever quick to defend in eloquent terms the position of the South and to advocate the end of partisanship and sectionalism and the working together of both sections for the solidification of the American Union. He resented the Radical Republican policies towards the South, especially the Ku Klux Klan Act of 1871, which he regarded as both unconstitutional and unnecessary. However, he did vote for congressional investigation into purported Southern outrages and even served on the investigating committee in 1871, signing the minority report. During his last term in Congress, he was chairman of the House committee on post offices and post roads, where he worked for improvements in the postal service and the establishment of postal savings banks. When no longer an officeholder, he continued his strong affiliation with the Democratic party, serving as a delegate to the national conventions of 1880 and 1896, and as elector-at-large in 1888.

Retirement from public life gave Waddell an opportunity to engage in the other pursuits for which he had a considerable liking, oratory and historical authorship. His polished eloquence and commanding stage presence brought to him a continuous flood of requests throughout the state and elsewhere to deliver addresses of all kinds—commencement, patriotic, and historical. And he was ever sought after to assist in political campaigns—in the presidential contest of 1880 he campaigned in behalf of the Democratic ticket in Vermont, Maine, and New York. In the realm of historical authorship (inspired especially by his pride in his distinguished lineage and in the Lower Cape Fear as a region), he contributed three works of considerable merit: *A Colonial Officer and His Times, 1754–1773: A Biographical Sketch of General Hugh Waddell of North Carolina* (1890), *Some Memories of My Life* (1908), and *A History of New Hanover County and the Lower Cape Fear Region, 1723–1800* (1909).

The trying times of the late 1890s in North Carolina and especially in the Wilmington area brought Waddell back to the political fore. With the Republican-Populist-Negro abuses rampant (and a fellow Wilmingtonian, Daniel Lindsay Russell, as governor), he came to the aid of the Democrats with fervent speeches in the bitter "White Supremacy" campaign of 1898. Leader of the white citizens group in Wilmington, he and his followers in November 1898 ousted from power a corrupt and unpopular municipal government and forcibly shut down a Negro newspaper (whose editorials had been quite inflammatory), precipitating perhaps the bloodiest race riot in North Carolina history, during which ten Negroes were reported killed, ten others jailed on charges of having instigated the riot, and the remaining Negro political leaders forced to flee the city. Elected mayor, Waddell quickly restored sobriety and peace, demonstrating his capacity to act with courage in critical times. He continued as mayor until 1905, providing for the city an honest and wholesome government no longer racked with racial turbulence, with which position his long and fruitful public career ended. He died in Wilmington and was interred in Oakdale Cemetery.

SEE: *DAB*, vol. 19 (1928); *Biog. Dir. Am. Cong.* (1961); J. G. de Roulhac Hamilton, *Reconstruction in North Carolina* (1906) and *North Carolina since 1860* (1919); James Sprunt, *Chronicles of the Cape Fear River* (1916); A. M. Waddell, *Some Memories of My Life* (1908); *Wilmington Messenger*, 6 Jan. 1889; *Wilmington Morning Star*, 19 Mar. 1912.

JAMES M. CLIFTON

Waddell, Charles Edward *(1 May 1877–20 Apr. 1945)*, civil and electrical engineer, was born at Moorefields near Hillsborough, the son of Francis Nash and Anne Ivie Miller Waddell and a descendant of Colonel Hugh Waddell. With his parents and younger sister Maude he moved to Asheville, where he attended city schools and was graduated from Bingham Military School in 1894. Self-taught in electricity, he became superintendent of the Asheville fire alarm system at age fourteen. After training in engineering in the shops of the General Electric Company in Schenectady, N.Y., he became assistant superintendent of the electrical system of Bangor, Maine, during the year 1895–96.

One of his earliest achievements after opening an office in Asheville was the design and installation of a pioneer electrical heating system for George W. Vanderbilt's Biltmore House. From 1901 he was the consulting engineer for the Biltmore Estate. In the forefront of hydroelectric development in the South, he built power plants in 1903 and 1910, and later the steam plant of the Weaver Electric Company (afterwards the North Carolina Electric Company), of which he was also a director from 1908 to 1923.

This was a period of rapid development and industrial growth for western North Carolina, and Waddell worked in several branches of engineering involving reservoirs, roads, dams, street railways, street lighting, and heating and water systems. His bridge over the Swannanoa River at Biltmore was one of two that withstood the flood of 1916, the greatest flood of memory in the area. Bee Tree dam, built for the city of Asheville's water supply, was the highest semihydraulic fill dam in the East at the time. Among his projects for industry were the steam plant of the Champion Fiber Company at Canton and the filter plant for the American Enka Corporation at Enka. He also served as consultant on the water system for the city of Medellín in Colombia, South America.

For the state of North Carolina he was founder and chairman of the Board of Engineering Examiners (1921–25), engineering member of the Board of Health (1922–23), and a member of the Ships and Water Transportation Commission (1923–25). During World War I he was consulting engineer for the power section of the Council of Defense for the southern states, the North Carolina director of fuel conservation, and a consultant to the Quartermaster Department of the Army for construction of the Kenilworth and Oteen hospitals. In 1925 North Carolina State College of Agriculture and Engineering conferred on him the honorary degree of doctor of science for electrical engineering.

Waddell was a member of the American Society of Civil Engineers (president of the North Carolina section, 1923–24), American Society of Mechanical Engineers, and American Society of Electrical Engineers of which he was a Fellow. He was president (1919–23) of the Biltmore Hospital, a trustee of the Western North Carolina Diocese of the Episcopal church, vestryman for twenty years of All Souls Church in Biltmore, president (1923) of the Asheville Civitan Club, and an early member and president of the Pen and Plate Club of Asheville.

He married Eleanor Sheppard Belknap of Louisville, Ky., in 1904, and they were the parents of Eleanor Belknap (m. George M. Stephens) and Charles Edward, Jr.

During the final ten years of his life he was unable to walk and often in pain as the result of an operation for a brain tumor, but he continued to practice his profession from a wheelchair. It was during this period that he built the Sunburst dam for the Champion Fiber Company. He was buried in Riverside Cemetery, Asheville.

SEE: *Asheville Citizen*, 10 June 1925, 30 Oct. 1941, 21 Apr. 1945; *North Carolina Biography*, vol. 4 (1929); *Who Was Who in America*, vol. 2 (1950).

ELEANOR WADDELL STEPHENS

Waddell, Hugh (*ca. 1734–9 Apr. 1773*), colonial military and political official, merchant, and planter, was born in Lisburn, County Down, Ireland, the son of Hugh and Isabella Brown Waddell, both of Scots-Irish ancestry. His mother may have been the Isabella Waddell buried in Holywood Graveyard, County Down. Little is known about Waddell's early life, as his papers, lent to Dr. Hugh Williamson for his history of North Carolina, were lost. According to tradition, he accompanied his father to Boston when the elder Waddell fled Ireland after involvement in a duel. When the father and son returned to Ireland the family fortune had been dissipated, and the father died leaving his son in poverty. However, there is evidence that the senior Waddell was for a while a successful merchant in New York. Certainly young Hugh received a credible education and perhaps some military training.

Waddell's association with North Carolina began prior to 1754. Early in that year he was commissioned by Matthew Rowan, acting governor and president of the Council, as a lieutenant in one of the companies commanded by James Innes that was sent to Winchester, Va., to guard against incursions by the French and their Indian allies. These troops constructed on Wills Creek a fortification later known as Fort Cumberland. Captain Waddell was sent with a detachment to escort the captured French partisan leader, La Force, to Williamsburg in September 1754. It is not known whether Waddell remained in Williamsburg to greet Arthur Dobbs, who arrived the following month on his way to commence his duties as governor of North Carolina. Supposedly, the Dobbs, Rowan, and Waddell families were acquainted in Ireland, and this served to promote the interests of young Hugh. Soon after Dobbs qualified as governor, Waddell was appointed as one of two clerks of the Council, along with Richard Spaight, a nephew of the governor. Spaight and Waddell were corecipients of numerous grants issued by the Crown in Anson County.

British and colonial forces commanded by Edward Braddock were defeated at the Battle of the Wilderness in the summer of 1755. In response to a request by Dobbs and in fear of impending frontier hostilities, the North Carolina Assembly authorized the establishment of a company of rangers to protect the backcountry. Waddell was placed in command of the rangers. During the spring of 1756, Dobbs and Virginia governor Robert Dinwiddie entered into negotiations with the Cherokee and Catawba Indians to bind them more closely to the British cause and at the same time lessen the domination of South Carolina over the two tribes. Waddell served as the North Carolina commissioner at the Broad River meeting. During the discussions the Catawba leaders requested that a fort be built near their villages. By July 1756 construction of a fortification on the North Carolina frontier was in progress under Waddell's direction. This fort, named for Governor Dobbs, was located on a branch of Fourth Creek just north of the present city of Statesville. Later that year workmen under Waddell's supervision commenced a second fort located within the Catawba Nation in an area claimed by both Carolinas. Due to intrigue by Governor William Lyttleton of South Carolina, the Catawba chief asked that work on the fort by North Carolinians be discontinued in 1757. William L. Saunders and subsequent writers were in error in supposing that this "Catawba Fort" was located at present Old Fort. Instead, it was situated near what is now Fort Mill, S.C.

In the spring of 1758, Waddell, who had been advanced to the rank of major, was in charge of three companies of North Carolina provincials and a number of Tuscarora auxiliaries sent to Virginia to participate in the Forbes expedition. One of the North Carolina soldiers, Sergeant John Rogers, was instrumental in securing information that led to the abandonment of Fort Duquesne by the French the following November. The first warm days of 1759 witnessed a new wave of slaughter in the backcountry by disgruntled Cherokee braves. Waddell, now a colonel, moved swiftly to establish a force capable of delivering a retaliatory strike. In response to South Carolina's plea for aid, Dobbs ordered Waddell to march to its relief. This effort failed when the North Carolina troops mutinied rather than leave the province. Events on the frontier were made more critical following the atrocities committed by both Indians and whites at Fort Prince George in mid-February 1760. Ten days later, on 26 February, the Cherokee attacked Fort Dobbs. Waddell's strategy in throwing the Indians off guard was credited with saving the fort. Fort Loudon was besieged the next month, and once again South Carolina's governor asked for assistance, but to no avail. Dobbs and the Assembly were deadlocked over how to finance any new military venture. Thus, Waddell and the North Carolinians did not join with British and South Carolina troops in Archibald Montgomerie's unsuccessful attempt to subdue the Cherokee in the spring of 1760.

Ultimately British officials prevailed on North Carolina to join Virginia in establishing a second front to the north to coincide with an invasion of Cherokee lands through South Carolina by British and provincial troops commanded by Colonel James Grant. This was to occur early in 1761. Again political quarrels between Dobbs and the Assembly prevented a timely intervention by North Carolina troops. By midsummer Grant's forces had defeated the Cherokee, but it was not until late October that Waddell's troops, along with Tuscarora auxiliaries, left Fort Dobbs marching north through Piper's Gap and then west to join Virginia forces at the Great Island of the Holston. By the time the troops reached their destination, nearly one half had deserted. Their terms of enlistment over, many North Carolina soldiers went home. Fortunately the Cherokee sued for peace, and a treaty was concluded in Charles Town on 18 Dec. 1761.

In the fall of 1757 James Carter of Rowan County was removed from the Assembly on charges of misusing funds allocated for the purchase of arms. Waddell was seated as a delegate from Rowan and was subsequently commissioned a justice of the peace for both Rowan and Bladen counties. He represented the backcountry county in the Assembly from 1757 to 1760 and served as a delegate from Bladen County in 1762, 1766, 1768, and 1771. He was unsuccessfully recommended by both Governor Dobbs in 1762 and Governor William Tryon in 1771 for appointment to the Provincial Council. Tryon noted in his recommendation that Waddell had met with Lord Hillsborough when he journeyed to Ireland and England in 1768.

Although he took a prominent role in the armed opposition to the implementation of the Stamp Act in North Carolina in 1766, this did not reduce his standing within royal circles in the colony. No doubt his opposition was all the more increased by his growing mercantile interests. Waddell had trading associations with James Bailey, Robert Campbell, Faithful Graham, and Richard Spaight. However, by far his most extensive commercial connections were with his brother-in-law, John Burgwin, at Wilmington. In addition, Waddell maintained trading stations at Elizabethtown, Salisbury, Deep River, and Brown Marsh.

From mid-May to mid-June 1767, Waddell commanded Rowan and Mecklenburg militia detachments accompanying Governor Tryon to establish a boundary between North Carolina and the Cherokee. The troops marched to Dewitts Corner, a point located more than fifty miles south of the present border between the two Carolinas, in an effort to advance North Carolina's claim to this area in dispute between the two provinces. Later Waddell introduced legislation in the Assembly to pay for the cost of the expedition.

Waddell's final military venture occurred in the spring of 1771, when Tryon commissioned him a general, the highest military rank issued in North Carolina during the colonial period. Tryon's strategy called for Waddell to head west gathering militia troops from Bladen, Cumberland, Anson, Mecklenburg, and Rowan counties as he marched. While forming his army at Salisbury, he learned that his powder train advancing overland from Charles Town had been destroyed by a group of disguised Regulators who would later be known as the "black boys." This setback, along with considerable sympathy for the Regulator cause among his own troops, forced Waddell to abandon his encampment on Potts Creek and fall back to Salisbury when confronted by a large group of Regulators on 19 May. Thus, he was unable to effect a juncture of his troops with those under Tryon. Meanwhile, Tryon had met and defeated the Regulators at the Battle of Alamance on 16 May. Waddell then sent his troops into various backcountry areas to administer oaths of allegiance to the disaffected.

In 1762 Waddell married Mary Haynes, one of two daughters of Captain Roger and Margaret Marsden Haynes of Castle Haynes. Their other daughter earlier married John Burgwin. Margaret Marsden Haynes was the daughter and heiress of the controversial Reverend Richard Marsden. Both Castle Haynes and the Marsden estate, the Hermitage, were located on Prince George's Creek off the Northeast Cape Fear River just above Wilmington. Hugh and Mary Haynes Waddell were the parents of three sons: Haynes (b. 1785), Hugh (d. 1823), and John Burgwin (d. 1830). All three children were sent to England to be educated. Haynes died before reaching his majority aboard the brig *Hope* en route from England to Charles Town. The remaining two sons had large families, and twenty-one of their descendants were in Confederate service.

Although Hugh and Mary Waddell made their home at

Bellefont located in Bladen County on the Cape Fear River, it appears that on the death of Margaret Marsden Haynes in 1770, the mansion house at Castle Haynes was being renovated for the Waddell family. When General Waddell died at Fort Johnston "after a long and painful illness," he was buried at Castle Haynes. His widow died in 1776.

A communicant of the Church of England, Waddell was described as being approximately six feet in height with blue eyes and weighing nearly two hundred pounds. An engraving of him taken from a miniature appears in Alfred Moore Waddell, *A Colonial Officer and His Times, 1754–1773: A Biographical Sketch of Gen. Hugh Waddell*. There has been much speculation that had he lived, Waddell might have been "the Washington of North Carolina" during the Revolution. But those who engage in such speculation should take note of the fact that many of his friends and his trusted overseer, Faithful Graham, remained loyal to the Crown, and even his executor and brother-in-law, John Burgwin, was accused of Tory leanings.

SEE: James S. Brawley, *The Rowan Story, 1753–1953* (1953); Jerry C. Cashion, "North Carolina and the Cherokee: The Quest for Land on the Eve of the American Revolution, 1754–1776" (Ph.D. diss., University of North Carolina, 1979); John L. Cheney, Jr., ed., *North Carolina Government, 1585–1979* (1981); Draper MSS, 3FF (microfilm, 1980, reel 89, State Historical Society of Wisconsin); Homer M. Keever, *Iredell Piedmont County* (1976); William S. Powell and others, eds., *The Regulators in North Carolina* (1971); William L. Saunders, ed., *Colonial Records of North Carolina*, vols. 5–9 (1887–90); Alfred Moore Waddell, *A Colonial Officer and His Times, 1754–1773: A Biographical Sketch of Gen. Hugh Waddell* (1890).

JERRY C. CASHION

Waddell, Hugh (*21 Mar. 1799–2 Nov. 1878*), lawyer and legislator, was born at his father's plantation, Newfield, in Bladen County. He was the son of John W. and Sarah Nash Waddell and the grandson of General Hugh Waddell, colonial military officer and hero of the War of the Regulators, and of General Francis Nash, who was killed in the Battle of Germantown, Pa., in October 1777. Waddell was graduated in 1818 from The University of North Carolina, where he was a classmate of James K. Polk, who became the eleventh president of the United States.

Waddell planned to study medicine, but his interests changed and he read law instead. In 1823 he began to practice in Hillsborough and Orange County, where he quickly gained an excellent reputation in his profession. Elected to the House of Commons from Orange County, he served in the 1828–29 and 1835 sessions. From there he was sent to the state senate for the sessions of 1836–37, 1840–41, 1844–45, 1846–47, and 1848. In 1836 he was president of the senate. At that time there was no office of lieutenant governor, and the senate president acted in that capacity. In politics he was a Whig.

In 1842 in Hillsborough Waddell opened a school to prepare young men for the bar. He maintained his law practice in Hillsborough until 1867, when he went to live with his son Alfred in Wilmington. He died there, and his funeral was held at St. James's Episcopal Church.

Waddell married Susan Moore, the daughter of Alfred Moore, in 1824. They had four sons: Hugh, Cameron, Douglas, and Alfred Moore, who was also a well known lawyer and congressman.

A man of much charm and ability, Waddell was esteemed by his peers. He was described by one of his contemporaries as "an admirable specimen of refined manners, unrivalled address, and a nice sense of humor" and by another as "an excellent debator and speaker, and a jurist of much renown."

SEE: Ruth Blackwelder, *The Age of Orange: Political and Intellectual Leadership in North Carolina, 1752–1861* (1961); *DAB*, vols. 2, 10 (1936); Daniel L. Grant, *Alumni History of the University of North Carolina* (1924); Hugh T. Lefler and Paul W. Wager, eds., *Orange County, 1752–1952* (1953); Griffith J. McRee, ed., *Life and Correspondence of James Iredell*, vol. 2 (1857); Alfred M. Waddell, *Some Memories of My Life* (1908); John H. Wheeler, ed., *Reminiscences and Memoirs of North Carolina and Eminent North Carolinians* (1884); *Wilmington Daily Review*, 2 Nov. 1878.

MARY R. KEATING

Waddell, James Iredell *(13 July 1824–15 Mar. 1886)*, captain of the Confederate cruiser *Shenandoah*, was born in Pittsboro, Chatham County, the son of Francis Nash and Elizabeth Davis Moore Waddell. He was the grandson of Alfred Moore and the great-grandson of Hugh Waddell. Reared by his maternal grandmother, Waddell received his early education at the Hillsborough Academy. In 1841 he obtained an acting midshipman's commission in the navy. Shortly after reporting for duty to Norfolk, Va., Waddell challenged another midshipman to a duel and received a serious leg wound that left him with a limp for the rest of his life. In 1846 he served in the Mexican War aboard the *Somers* in the Gulf of Mexico. Distinguishing himself as a navigator, he was later transferred to Annapolis to take advanced navigation courses.

Between 1850 and 1857 Waddell served on the *Germantown* and *Release*, patrolling the waters around South America. In 1857 he was again transferred to Annapolis to teach navigation. After visiting Waddell in 1858, Samuel A. Ashe described him as "six feet one inch in height, with a powerful frame weighing more than two hundred pounds." In 1859 Waddell was assigned to duty in the Pacific, where he remained until the Civil War began.

At that time he resigned his commission and went to Richmond to join the Confederacy. On 27 Mar. 1862 he was commissioned a lieutenant in the Confederate navy and after one year of service in the South was ordered to Europe. On 19 Oct. 1864 to took command of the *Sea King*, a British merchant ship that had been purchased by the Confederacy and refitted as a maritime raider. Rechristened the *Shenandoah*, it set a course for the Pacific with orders to destroy the New England whaling fleet. The *Shenandoah* was enormously successful, capturing thirty-eight ships and destroying thirty-two, worth $1,772,223.

The cruise of the *Shenandoah*, which had been a glorious adventure for Waddell and his crew, ended on a note of tragic irony. On 23 June 1865 they learned from newspaper accounts aboard a captured ship of General Robert E. Lee's surrender at Appomattox the previous April. However, the same dispatches contained Jefferson Davis's Danville proclamation urging the South to fight on. This Waddell and his men proceeded to do. Only in August did they receive definite word that the war was over.

Official Union policy had always considered the Confederate cruisers as pirates. Without a government the *Shenandoah* was most vulnerable to charges of piracy, and Waddell regarded surrender to the United States as impossible. Deciding that their chances were better in Europe, he set a course by way of Cape Horn for Liverpool, 17,000 miles away. On 6 Nov. 1865 the *Shenandoah*, the last Confederate cruiser and the only one to sail around the world, reached Liverpool and surrendered to the British government.

Remaining in England until adverse public opinion towards him in the United States subsided, Waddell returned in 1875 and took a position as captain of the *San Francisco* for the Pacific Mail Company. In 1877, while commanding the *San Francisco*, he struck an uncharted reef, and the ship sank without losing a passenger. Returning to Annapolis, he took command of a small police force that controlled the oyster fleets in the Chesapeake Bay.

Waddell died of a brain disorder and was buried at St. Anne's Church (Episcopal), Annapolis. He was survived by his wife, the former Ann S. Iglehart of Annapolis, whom he had married in 1848. They had no children. Photographs of Waddell are on file at the North Carolina State Archives, Hillsborough Historical Museum, and North Carolina Collection at the University of North Carolina.

SEE: Samuel A. Ashe, "Captain James Iredell Waddell," *North Carolina Booklet* 13 (1912) and "The Shenandoah: A Sketch of the Eventful Life of the Confederate Cruiser," *Southern Historical Society Papers*, vol. 32 (1904); Jesse N. Bradley, "A Rebel Officer's Revenge . . .," *Smithsonian* 8 (November 1976); John Grimball, "Career of the Shenandoah," *Southern Historical Society Papers*, vol. 25 (1897); James D. Horan, ed., *C.S.S. Shenandoah: The Memoirs of Lieutenant Commander James I. Waddell* (1960); Cornelius E. Hunt, *The Shenandoah; or, The Last Confederate Cruiser* (1867); Charles Lining, "The Cruise of the Confederate Steamship 'Shenandoah,'" *Tennessee Historical Magazine* 8 (1924); *New York Times*, 24 Nov. 1865, 13 Feb. 1866; William C. Whittle, "The Cruise of the Shenandoah," *Southern Historical Society Papers*, vol. 35 (1907).

E. M. CHAMBERS

Wade, Thomas *(1720–Fall 1786)*, merchant, Revolutionary soldier, and legislator, was born possibly in Craven County. His father was probably the English immigrant John Wade. About 1743 Thomas Wade married Jane Boggan, a sister of Captain Patrick Boggan of Anson County. They had five children: Holden, Thomas, George (b. 1747), Mary, and Sarah. Throughout his life Wade was a communicant of the Anglican church.

In 1746 he received a land grant in Surry County, Va., but returned to North Carolina and settled in Granville County a year later. From 1761 to 1774 he owned land on Lynch's Creek and in Saint David's Parish (Chesterfield District), S.C., where he was the commissary general of purchases for the colony. Moving to Anson County in 1770, he became a tavern keeper at Anson County Courthouse and a large landowner in Mount Pleasant. For the next two years he served as a justice of the Anson County Inferior Court of Pleas and Quarter Sessions.

Wade was a staunch opponent of British imperial policies. While serving as chairman of the Anson County Meeting of Freeholders (1774), he was elected a member of the Anson Committee of Correspondence. The next year he signed a petition protesting the establishment of the North Carolina–South Carolina boundary line and was elected a delegate to the Provincial Congress held in Hillsborough. During 1775 Wade was a captain of the Anson committee to recruit men and to procure firearms for the rebel cause. As a member of the Provincial Congress (1775–76), he was appointed to reorganize the Anson County Inferior Court of Pleas and Quarter Sessions on which he again served from 1776 to 1778. In addition, he was chosen a commissioner for Anson County to supervise prisoners, especially former Loyalists, and to take care of "unhappy women and children."

The Provincial Congress of 1776 selected Wade as colonel of the Salisbury District of Minute Men. After pursuing Tories in the Pee Dee River area in 1778, he worked to obtain such needed supplies as salt, shoes, and cattle for the state Board of War. In 1780 Tories used his home as a rendezvous and took £50,000 worth of property and his crop. In the following year he participated in several encounters with the British. He won a battle at Raft Swamp in August 1781 against the Tory officers Neil and Ray, identified only as Loyalists from Bladen County. Later, while returning from fighting in the Neuse River area, Wade's troops were surprised by the Loyalist John Neil at Piney Bottom on Little Rockfish Creek. During the skirmish Wade's protégé, "a motherless boy," was killed although he had begged for mercy. Returning to Anson County, Wade raised a force of a hundred men and avenged the boy's death by executing many of the Loyalists and destroying their property. On 1 Sept. 1781 he lost a battle at Drowning Creek to Colonel David Fanning. Wade's final battle was at Lindley's Mill in present Alamance County, where he fought under General John Butler.

When the war ended, Thomas Wade was elected to represent Anson County as a senator in the General Assembly. While serving in New Bern, Hillsborough, and Halifax where the Assembly met in 1780, 1782, and 1783, he was chairman of the Committee on State Papers and on Petitions. In the 1783 session he sat on the committee that laid out the streets of Fayetteville. In addition to his senatorial duties, he was sheriff of Anson County in 1785. He was elected in 1786 to serve another term in the senate but died before taking his seat after becoming ill in Cheraw, S.C. He was buried in the family burial ground in Mount Pleasant. The next year, the General Assembly voted to change the name of New Town to Wadesborough in his honor.

SEE: Anson County Court, Minute Docket, Court of Pleas and Quarter Sessions, 1772–74 (microfilm, North Carolina State Archives, Raleigh); W. K. Boggan, "Colonel Thomas Wade: Distinguished Citizen, Patriot, and Soldier," in *The Colonial History of Anson County from Its Erection to the War of the Revolution* (mimeographed, 1923); Walter Clark, ed., *State Records of North Carolina*, vols. 11, 14–16, 19, 22 (1895–1907); David Fanning, *Colonel David Fanning's Narrative of His Exploits and Adventures as a Loyalist in North Carolina in the American Revolution* (1908); Brent Holcomb, comp., *Anson County, North Carolina, Wills and Estates, 1749–1795* (1950); May W. McBee, comp., *Anson County, North Carolina, Abstract of Early Records* (1950); Robert L. Meriweather, *The Expansion of South Carolina, 1729–1765* (1940); New Bern *North Carolina Gazette*, 2 Sept. 1774; North Carolina Daughters of the American Revolution, *Markers Placed by the North Carolina Daughters of the American Revolution, 1900–1940* (1940); William L. Saunders, ed., *Colonial Records of North Carolina*, vols. 4, 10 (1886, 1890).

CAROL E. DALTON

Wagstaff, Henry McGilbert (27 Jan. 1876–28 May 1945), historian and university professor, was born on a farm near Roxboro, the son of Clement McGilbert and Sarah Elizabeth Paylor Wagstaff. During his boyhood he developed a sound understanding of agricultural techniques and processes and a deep affection for field, forest, and stream, but in his late teens he became interested in the history of his state and favored an academic career, which his parents encouraged. In 1895 he entered The

University of North Carolina, where he was elected to Phi Beta Kappa and awarded a Ph.B. degree in 1899. For the next two years, while he taught at Rutherford College, his interest in history grew steadily. He entered the Johns Hopkins University for graduate work in history in 1901 and received the Ph.D. degree in 1906.

After teaching history and economics at Allegheny College, Meadville, Pa., for a year, Wagstaff was invited to join the faculty of The University of North Carolina as associate professor of history. He was delighted with this opportunity not only because it enabled him to teach at his alma mater, but also because it put him fairly close to the farmlands that he had roamed and plowed as a boy and to which he remained deeply attached. In the summer of 1907 he married and settled in Chapel Hill, where he spent the remaining thirty-eight years of his life as professor of history.

Since the history department was relatively new and the staff small, Wagstaff had to teach in several areas, including ancient, medieval, and Latin American history, until additional staff made it possible for him to devote all of his time to the history and government of Great Britain. Indeed, this diverse teaching experience helped him acquire a basic command of nearly all fields of history, an asset that was an inspiration to his students and a never-ending surprise to his colleagues. And even though he gained a remarkable mastery of English history as a whole, most of his writing and editing concerned the history of North Carolina. In addition to articles dealing with the history of the state, Wagstaff published *States Rights and Political Parties in North Carolina, 1776–1861* (1906) and *Federalism in North Carolina* (1910). Later he edited several collections of letters and documents: *The Harrington Letters* (1914), *The Harris Letters* (1916), *The Papers of John Steele*, 2 vols. (1924), *The James A. Graham Papers, 1861–1884* (1928), *Minutes of the North Carolina Manumission Society, 1816–1834* (1934), and the *Letters of Thomas Jackson Strayhorn* (1936). He also published a little volume of short stories dealing with the community of his childhood: *The Concord Community: A Retrospect* (1941), and he left unfinished an analytical account of The University of North Carolina from 1876 to 1940, later published under the title *Impressions of Men and Movements at the University of North Carolina* (1950).

As well as a sound scholar and gifted teacher, Wagstaff was a versatile, judicious, and public-spirited citizen with a wide variety of interests. He was an officer for many years in the Orange County Building and Loan Association, the owner and overseer of farmlands in Person County, and president (1928–29) of the North Carolina Literary and Historical Association. In the last year of his life he won first prize in a short story contest conducted by the Charlotte Writers Club. Kind, sturdy, and compassionate, his deep love of field and forest, and of all that lived therein, was lifelong. On 28 June 1907 he married Mary Jefferson Stephens, and they were the parents of Mary Frances, wife of Captain A. B. Coxe USN (Retired) of Chapel Hill, and Henry McGilbert, Jr., who was killed in action off Leyte on 29 Oct. 1944. Wagstaff was a Methodist and a Democrat. He died in Watts Hospital, Durham, and was buried in the Old Chapel Hill Cemetery.

SEE: *American Historical Review* 51 (October 1945); *Chapel Hill Weekly*, 5 Jan., 1 June 1945; Raleigh *News and Observer*, 29 May 1945; University of North Carolina History Department Records (University Archives, Chapel Hill); H. M. Wagstaff Papers (Southern Historical Collection, University of North Carolina, Chapel Hill).

CARL HAMILTON PEGG

Wait, Samuel (*19 Dec. 1789–28 July 1867*), Baptist minister, educator, and college president, was born in White Creek, Washington County, N.Y., the son of Joseph and Martha Wait. During his youth the family moved near Middletown, Vt. A convert of the Second Great Revival, Wait prepared for the ministry and in 1816 accepted a call as minister of the Baptist Church in Sharon, Mass. There he married Sally Merriam of Brandon, Vt.

Believing that he needed additional study, in 1819 he began theological studies with Dr. William Staughton, first in Philadelphia and then at Columbian College (now George Washington University) in Washington, D.C. Due to their limited funds, Mrs. Wait remained in New England until 1822, when Wait was employed as a tutor at Columbian. For reasons that are unclear, he received an M.A. degree from Waterville College, Maine, in 1825. While in Washington, the Waits briefly considered being missionaries to the Orient but were dissuaded by her relatives. Eventually, mismanagement of Columbian's finances by Luther Rice, the school's treasurer and a pioneer Baptist missionary, led indirectly to Wait's subsequent move to North Carolina, which he also considered to be a mission field.

In late 1826, to alleviate Columbian's monetary problems, its trustees sent President Staughton and Wait into the South to solicit funds. While in New Bern Wait preached several times for the Baptists, having been given a letter of introduction to the parish by Thomas Meredith, their former minister, who was also a former student of Staughton's. Later, when Rice reasserted his primacy in the college's affairs, Wait resigned his agency and returned to New Bern for a trial pastorate.

In the autumn of 1827 he moved his family to North Carolina, which he noted was largely bereft of religious enlightenment. For the last forty years of his life he worked to improve the religious and educational conditions in his adopted homeland. In 1830, as one of five college-trained Baptist ministers in the state, Wait was instrumental in founding the Baptist State Convention, an organization espousing the causes of missions and an educated ministry. For three years he was the convention's agent, traversing the state with his family in a covered wagon to solicit financial and organizational support.

In 1833 the Baptist State Convention authorized the establishment of a literary institute largely for the training of ministers. To help reduce tuition the convention endorsed a program of manual labor and purchased a farm in Wake County as the site for the school, called the Wake Forest Institute. Chosen principal, Wait had sole responsibility for the care of over seventy students from the time the school opened in early 1834 and until the following year. To demonstrate his regard for the manual labor plan, he worked in the fields with the students. Even so, the work plan was soon scuttled. In 1839, after the legislature had amended the charter, the school became Wake Forest College, of which Wait served as president until 1845.

Often during his tenure, the school's precarious financial condition caused Wait to spend much time traveling to raise funds, a task complicated by the nation's economic problems and by the general indifference of many Baptists. Following his resignation he immediately became chairman of the board of trustees, and in 1849 Wake Forest awarded him an honorary doctor of divinity degree.

When the Waits moved to North Carolina, their northern relatives frequently criticized them for living in the slave region. Wait maintained that ministers should say nothing about the issue, and Wake Forest owned a few slaves. After the creation of the Southern Baptist Convention in 1845, he declined an overture to accept appointment as secretary of a convention mission board. Instead, he remained in North Carolina as minister in several par-

ishes from 1845 to 1851. He later called this the happiest period of his life. In 1851 he returned to education as president of Oxford Female College, a post he held until his retirement in 1857. He then moved to Forestville, where he resided for the rest of his life.

Still possessing physical vigor and intellectual clarity, Wait in 1858 evidently considered accepting the presidency of Mississippi Female College in Hernando, Miss. During the Civil War he continued to be active in Baptist association matters as well as chairman of Wake Forest trustees until November 1865. Thereafter he still remained on the board. Such was his devotion to his beloved Wake Forest that even with the onset of mental debility, "he was devising ways and means by which he could promote the interests" of the school.

The Waits had two children: Ann Eliza, who married John Brewer, a Wake County merchant; and William Carey, who died in 1831 as an infant. Wait died in Forestville and was buried in Wake Forest. His portrait hangs in Reynolda Hall at Wake Forest University. A few months before Wait's death, a colleague assessed his impact in North Carolina: "You were always a working man. . . . Working men are rare. . . . If for the last 30 years we had had 50 such men as you, N.C. would have been a garden."

SEE: W. Ronald Wachs, "Conflict on College Hill: Luther Rice, Samuel Wait, and Columbian College's Financial Embarrassments," *Quarterly Review: A Survey of Southern Baptist Progress* 29 (1969), " 'Duty' Against Family: A Vermont Minister Adopts a Slave State," *Vermont History* 41 (1973), and "Samuel Wait: Evangelical Crusader" (M.A. thesis, Wake Forest University, Winston-Salem); Samuel Wait Papers (Baptist Historical Collection, Wake Forest University, Winston-Salem).

W. RONALD WACHS

Walden, Islay (*1843–January 1884*), black poet and Congregational minister, was born in Randolph County, the son of a slave named Ruth belonging to James Gardner. At Gardner's death in 1843 Ruth and her two children were sold to Dolphin Gardner. Islay was at that time a babe in arms while his sister, Sarah, was two. How many times he was sold after that is unknown. His father was William D. Walden, a free black who was highly respected in his community.

Islay Walden was blessed with abilities in mathematics and language, which expressed themselves before he was able to read. He was able to calculate difficult arithmetic problems with great speed in his head. His master delighted in exhibiting his prowess and in taking bets on Islay's accuracy with numbers. The youth's ability to form verses was also discovered by his master, who referred to him as a poet. In 1865, at the end of the Civil War, Walden was driving mules in a Randolph County gold mine.

Although threatened all of his life with blindness because of severe nearsightedness, he was determined to learn to read and to become a minister. In 1867 he walked from North Carolina to Washington, D.C., where he supported himself by manual labor and peddling political ballads of his own composition on the street. Meanwhile, he played the good samaritan to indigent black children, giving them what spiritual guidance he could and organizing some of them into a Sunday school.

In 1871, having memorized from an anatomy textbook selected chapters that he delivered—apparently verbatim—as a lecture entitled "Anatomy and Hygiene," he worked his way through Pennsylvania and New Jersey to New Brunswick. In New Brunswick he tarried and acquired friends and patrons. Indeed, in 1872 the Second

Reformed Church of New Brunswick gave him a scholarship of $150 a year to Howard University, and he returned to Washington.

Walden finished the normal school at Howard in 1876. Principally to help with his expenses he had published his *Miscellaneous Poems* in 1872, with a second edition in 1873. Returning to New Brunswick in 1876, he enrolled in the New Brunswick Theological Seminary. The next year he published his *Sacred Poems*, again as a means of helping to pay for his education. In New Brunswick, as he had done in Washington, he took a philanthropic interest in the local black community. In October 1877, for example, he started a "Student's Mission" for sixty boys and girls whose needs were extremely dire. He maintained this mission for two years.

In May 1879, after completing three years at the New Brunswick seminary, Walden was ordained to the ministry. In the fall of 1879, under the auspices of the American Missionary Association, he went to Lassiters Mills, in the county of his birth, as a teacher and a clergyman. In a forest clearing he began a Congregational church with twenty members. Within a year the membership tripled. His parishioners had no money, but they contributed their labor to construct a school and a church. In dedicating their house of worship in 1880, they named it the "Promised Land Church." Walden had, however, only four years of life left. In 1880 he was a boarder in his sister's home. His wife, Elinora Farmer, is first mentioned in a deed dated 1883. He died childless in 1884 and was buried in the churchyard at Strieby Congregational Church.

Walden's gift for poetry was slight. His verse was trite; his versification, often pathetically awkward and childish. But his gift for serving other human beings was great. It was in what he did rather than what he wrote that he truly paid his dues to art. The Randolph County Historical Society, Asheboro, has a copy of a photograph of Walden.

SEE: Archives of the Reformed Church in America (New Brunswick, N.J.); List of Sales of Personal Property of James Gardner, May Term 1844, Randolph County Will Book 8 (Randolph County Courthouse, Asheboro); Joan R. Sherman, *Invisible Poets* (1974); Islay Walden, Walden's *Miscellaneous Poems*, 2d ed. (1873), and Walden's *Sacred Poems, with a Sketch of His Life* (1877).

BLYDEN JACKSON

Walker, Carleton (5 Jan. 1777–12 Oct. 1840), British-born collector of the Port of Wilmington, paymaster of troops in the War of 1812, and Cape Fear planter and lavish speculator, was the youngest of three sons of James (d. 1785) and Jane Woodhouse Walker of Wooler in the Cheviot Hills near Alnwick Castle and Berwick-on-Tweed, County of Northumberland, in northern England. In 1791, at age fourteen, he immigrated with his widowed mother to Wilmington to join various other members of the Walker family already solidly established in the Cape Fear area, notably his picturesque, highly successful bachelor uncle, Major John (Jack) Walker (1741–1813), who had immigrated in 1761; three other uncles, Dr. Edward, George, and William Walker; and his own older brothers, Dr. James (d. 1807) and Thomas (d. 1797).

The Walkers had been landholders in the vicinity of Alnwick (one of the gates of the town of Alnwick is called the Walker Gate), and one of the Walkers served as high steward to the Duke of Northumberland whose ducal seat, Alnwick Castle, had been the fortress home of the Percy family for centuries. The Woodhouse clan apparently ranked somewhat higher than the Walkers in the

Northumbrian scale of values because they owned several choice estates, including Broadstruther, in the Cheviot Hills near Wooler.

Major Jack Walker, the shrewd, eccentric pioneer of the family in America, quickly established himself as a popular citizen of the Wilmington area. He early became a colorful figure in Cape Fear folklore, served as an aide on George Washington's staff, and gradually amassed a considerable fortune in rice plantations and other property. His elder brother James came to America in 1785 "to spy out the land," as James's granddaughter wrote many years later, but died on board ship on the return trip to England to join his family. Six years later, in 1791, James Walker's widow, Jane, and his youngest son, Carleton, went alone to Wilmington.

By 2 July 1801 twenty-four-year-old Carleton Walker was mentioned in the *Wilmington Gazette* as "Clerk" of the Port of Wilmington, and by 17 December as "Register" of the Port. His marriage notice, published in the *Gazette* of 31 Dec. 1801, states that "On Thursday evening last [i.e., on Christmas Eve, 24 Dec. 1801], Carleton Walker, Esq., Naval officer of this Port, was married to Miss Mariah Moseley." His daughter's [Margaret Isabella Walker Weber's] "Reminiscences," written in 1904 when she was eighty, vividly describe her father's departure on his wedding journey in a coach and four accompanied by liveried postillions: "All was merry as a marriage bell." The new bride, however, who was the daughter of Colonel Sampson Moseley and a member of the prominent Lillington family as well as a niece of Sir Walter Blake of Oran Castle, County Mayo, Ireland, died a year later, leaving an infant son, John Moseley Walker, who inherited Moseley Hall and its valuable 3,500-acre plantation at Rocky Point.

Margaret Isabella's "Reminiscences" note that she was once told that her father was "renowned for having married the three handsomest women of his day and for his facility in acquiring fortunes and losing them." Carleton Walker's second wife was Sabina T. Legaré of Charleston, S.C., whom he married in Charleston on 20 Mar. 1804. She also lived "but a short time," and on 11 June 1807, the twenty-nine-year-old widower took a third wife, eighteen-year-old Caroline Mary Mallett of Fayetteville, the daughter of the late Revolutionary figure, Peter Mallett (1744–1805), and his second wife, "pretty Sallie" Mumford. Caroline Mary, on a visit to Wilmington in 1806, had found young Walker "handsome, graceful, and of marked courtesy of manner" and regarded as the "catch of the town" with his own establishment, which included his mother, his infant son, and a very sizable staff of servant. Extravagance and impracticality marked all of Walker's undertakings, possibly in part because he regarded himself as the certain heir to his uncle Major Jack Walker's fortune and also as the chief "heir-at-law" to the choice Woodhouse estate, Broadstruther, in Northumberland.

Even this early Walker found himself in extreme financial difficulties. Wealthy Benjamin Smith, of Belvidere Plantation on the Lower Cape Fear, senator of the state, governor, and longtime trustee of the university, had become his surety for a debt of some $50,000 which involved the university trustees. Smith owned over 60,000 acres of North Carolina lands as well as some 204 slaves in 1810. The university in 1812 sued Walker and Smith jointly for the $50,000 debt, and a complicated legal battle was waged for the next six years. The former governor was arrested and jailed although fellow trustees finally came to his rescue. Smith's extreme anguish over "my cruel situation with Walker" and his bitterness towards Walker are reflected in letters preserved in the Ernest Haywood Collection. It was Smith's contention that Walker actually had sufficient money in hand to pay the debt, which Smith insisted was not of his making, and that Walker had gone into hiding until he should hear that Smith had paid it. The debt, as it appears, was finally paid almost wholly by Smith. In 1904 Carleton Walker's daughter in her old age wrote that this murky, bitterly contested affair had been caused by the "treachery" of the governor of the state and that "my father failed honestly and gave up everything he possessed."

Carleton Walker served in the War of 1812 on General Edmund P. Gaines's staff as paymaster of troops and attained the rank of major. On 6 Sept. 1813 Major Jack Walker died and unexpectedly left his large estate to another nephew, Major John Walker, Jr., the son of his brother Thomas, who had arrived from England in 1803. Carleton Walker, now under the most urgent pressure for funds, began the long, tedious process of attempting to resolve his claim to the Broadstruther estate in the Cheviot Hills. It took over twelve years, from 1815 to 1827–28, according to preserved records of the matter. The estate was sold in 1825 to the Governors of Greenwich Hospital in London for £3,150, of which £1,400 was remitted to Carleton Walker.

After the War of 1812 Walker seems to have devoted himself to the Smith affair and his Broadstruther claim, and to supervising the operation of his son's inheritance, Moseley Hall, and its extensive plantation. James Sprunt wrote in his *Chronicles of the Cape Fear River* that "this was a large and quite valuable place and was said to have been handsomely improved, but all that the writer remembers seeing were the remains of what were said to have been fine old avenues."

The Walker family now spent each summer at their Chatham County residence, Walker's Hill, "on the highest point in Chatham County," about seven miles from Pittsboro, near Rock Rest, home of their kinsman, Colonel Edward Jones. When the house at Walker's Hill burned, apparently in 1822 or 1823, the family looked to Hillsborough for a summer home.

Peter Mallett, Caroline Mary Walker's father, had in 1778 purchased Hillsborough property, and during the Revolution he and William Watters of the Cape Fear had bought Francis Nash's old mill property at the foot of Wake Street—three town lots and a narrow bordering strip called the Mill lands. The two Mallett mills were in 1823 broken and derelict, and townspeople had almost forgotten to whom "the old Mallett property" belonged. The Mallett heirs, Caroline Mary's five brothers, united on 29 Oct. 1823 to convey their interests in the lots to John Moseley Walker, Caroline Mary's stepson, now just barely of age, "for the separate and exclusive use of Caroline Mary Walker."

Margaret Isabella Weber's "Reminiscences" state that John Moseley Walker "lived to the age of twenty-one" (he died on 28 Oct. 1824) and that he was buried in Hillsborough "near the wall" of St. Matthew's Episcopal Church. He bequeathed his own inheritance, Moseley Hall and its plantation, to his half brothers and sisters. It would appear from all indications that Carleton Walker used part of the Broadstruther money to build the charmingly elegant small house, the Walker-Palmer house (still standing and restored) on the corner of Lot 19 on West Margaret Lane in Hillsborough. Walker had drawn on the Governors of Greenwich Hospital, London, even before the English deeds of sale were signed, and sizable "three drafts" sent to London by the Hillsborough merchants Cain & Moore (£600) and Thos. Clancy & Co. (£113) were rejected. (These two bills were later accepted and paid once the Broadstruther sale was completed.) The Walkers lived permanently in Hillsborough, both summer and winter after about 1826, for nearly twenty years.

The large Walker family now included eight surviving children: Sarah Jane, Eliza Henrietta, Mary Pearson, Peter Mallett, Caroline de Bernière (always called de Bernière), the twins Margaret Isabella and another John Moseley, and Catherine Burke. Three children had died in infancy. Although the family lived in reduced circumstances, the family lived well in Hillsborough as preserved account books show. Their servants still included the cooks "Aunt Dolly" and Anneke, the valet Glasgow, and a whole retinue of nurses and housemaids. The children attended Hillsborough's various excellent schools of the period. Carleton Walker himself died after a long bout with a kidney ailment. Although the "Reminiscences" state that four members of the family—John Moseley Walker, Mrs. Jane Woodhouse Walker (Carleton's mother), an infant Sophia Woodhouse Walker, and Carleton Walker—were all buried "near the wall" of St. Matthew's, no Walker graves are visible today in the vicinity of the church, and it seems possible that the ten-foot eastward expansion of the church in 1868–69 may have covered the four graves, perhaps left unmarked. Caroline Mary Mallett Walker sold her Margaret Lane home on 14 Feb. 1842 and left Hillsborough. She died on 20 Nov. 1862 and was buried in the old Mallet family graveyard in Fayetteville.

SEE: Kemp P. Battle, *History of the University of North Carolina*, 2 vols. (1907, 1912); Carrie L. Broughton, comp., *North Carolina Marriage and Death Notices, 1799–1825* (1966); Marian Camper Fuller, *Marriage and Death Notices in the Hillsborough Recorder, 1820–1877* (1946); Ernest Haywood Collection, Peter Mallett Papers, Margaret Isabella Walker Weber's "Reminiscences," and Caroline de Bernière Walker album (Southern Historical Collection, University of North Carolina, Chapel Hill); Donald Ray Lennon, "The Political Views and Public Activities of Benjamin Smith of Brunswick County, 1783–1816" (master's thesis, East Carolina College, Greenville, 1961); James Sprunt, *Chronicles of the Cape Fear River* (1914); Alfred M. Waddell, *A History of New Hanover County, and the Lower Cape Fear Region, 1723–1800* (1909); *Wilmington Gazette*, 1799–1816, and John Walker Papers (Southern Historical Collection, University of North Carolina, Chapel Hill).

MARY CLAIRE ENGSTROM

Walker, David (*28 Sept. 1785–28 June 1830*), black author of an incendiary antislavery pamphlet, was born in Wilmington to a free mother and a slave father who died before his birth. Despite his free status inherited from his mother, he grew up stifled by life in a slave society and developed a strong hatred of the institution. He left the South, stating that "If I remain in this bloody land, I will not live long. . . . I cannot remain where I must hear slaves' chains continually and where I must encounter the insults of their hypocritical enslavers." He traveled extensively around the country and by 1827 had settled in Boston, where he established a profitable secondhand clothing business. Active in helping the poor and needy, including runaway slaves, he earned a reputation within Boston's black community for his generosity and benevolence. In 1828 he married a woman known only as Emily, most likely a fugitive slave herself.

In September 1829 Walker first published his famous seventy-six-page pamphlet entitled *Walker's Appeal in Four Articles; Together with a Preamble, to the Coloured Citizens of the World, but in Particular and Very Expressly to Those of the United States of America*. In this emotional but carefully reasoned invective, he urged slaves to rise up against their masters and free themselves, regardless of the great risk involved. "Had you rather not be killed," he asked, "than to be a slave to a tyrant, who takes the life of your mother, wife, and dear little babies?" He warned white Americans to repent, for their day of judgment was at hand. They should not be deceived by the "outwardly servile character of the Negro," he wrote, for there was "a primitive force in the black slave that, once aroused, will make him a magnificent fighter." He condemned the colonization movement as a solution, claiming that America belonged more to blacks than to whites because "we have enriched it with our blood and tears." Two revised editions, each increasingly militant and inflammatory in tone, were published early in 1830.

The circulation of the *Appeal* in the South by the summer of 1830 caused great alarm, particularly in Georgia, Virginia, and North Carolina. It made its first appearance in Walker's home state in Wilmington, where copies were smuggled on ships from Boston or New York and were distributed by a slave thought to have been an agent of Walker's. Excitement among whites soon spread to Fayetteville, New Bern, Elizabeth City, and other towns in the state, particularly where news of the pamphlet was accompanied by rumors of slave insurrection plots scheduled to take place at Christmas. Many communities petitioned Governor John Owen for protection as their slaves became "almost uncontrollable." The governor sent a copy of the *Appeal* to the legislature when it met in November 1830 and urged that it consider measures to avert the dangerous consequences that were predicted. Meeting in secret session, the legislature enacted the most repressive measures ever passed in North Carolina to control slaves and free blacks. Harsh penalties were to be levied on anyone for teaching slaves to read or write and for circulating seditious publications. Manumission laws were made more prohibitive, and the movements of both slaves and free blacks were severely restricted. (The fact that Walker was a free black aroused particular suspicion of those of similar status in the state.) Finally, a quarantine law called for any black entering the state by ship to be confined, and any contact between resident blacks and incoming ships was prohibited.

The impact of Walker's *Appeal* in North Carolina and elsewhere in the South has been overshadowed by the even more alarming Nat Turner Rebellion just across the North Carolina border in Southhampton County, Va., in August 1831. The two events together led to a major turning point in antebellum race relations throughout the South. Because of the violent and extreme measures it advocated, the *Appeal* failed to win the support of most Abolitionists or free blacks. But in 1848 it found a new and wider audience when it was reprinted, along with a biographical sketch of Walker, by Henry Highland Garnet, a prominent black minister, newspaper editor, and Abolitionist in New York City.

Walker died in Boston three months after the publication of his pamphlet's third edition. The cause of his death remains a mystery, though it was widely believed that he was poisoned, possibly as a result of large rewards offered by Southern slaveholders for his death. His only child, Edward G. Walker, was born after his death and in 1866 became the first black elected to the Massachusetts state legislature.

SEE: Herbert Aptheker, *One Continual Cry: David Walker's Appeal to the Colored Citizens of the World, 1829–30* (1965); Benjamin Brawley, *Early Negro American Writers* (1935); DAB, vol 19 (1936); Clement Eaton, "A Dangerous Pamphlet in the Old South," *Journal of Southern History* 2 (August 1936); John Hope Franklin, *The Free Negro in North Carolina, 1790–1860* (1943); Derris Lea Raper, "The Effects of David Walker's Appeal and Nat Turner's Insurrection on North Carolina" (master's thesis, University of North Carolina, Chapel Hill, 1969).

JOHN C. INSCOE

Walker, Felix *(19 July 1753–1828)*, soldier, politician, and pioneer, was born in Hampshire County, Va. His grandfather, John Walker, emigrated from Derry, Ireland, in 1720 and settled in Delaware. His father, John Walker, Jr., was a soldier in the French and Indian War and moved to Rutherford County, N.C., in 1768. His mother was Elizabeth Watson. At age sixteen Felix was bound to a Charleston, S.C., merchant but went home early in 1775 and took part in the expedition of Judge Richard Henderson that established the Transylvania colony in Kentucky. After briefly returning to the North Carolina coast, he joined the settlers in the Watauga Valley in the Tennessee country and helped them reorganize their government as Washington County (now in Tennessee). He served for four years as the county clerk. After learning of the invasion of southern colonies by the British army, he went back to Mecklenburg County, N.C., and became a lieutenant in a regiment commanded by Colonel Isaac Huger, which marched eastward to aid in the defense of Charleston, S.C. He soon resigned his commission and crossed the mountains to help the frontiersmen repel Indian attacks and then accompany them to the Kings Mountain battleground.

He became clerk of Rutherford County, N.C., in October 1789; served in the North Carolina legislature in 1792, 1793, 1800–1802, and 1806; and represented Buncombe County in the U.S. Congress from 1817 to 1823. In the latter capacity he commented that he would make a speech for Buncombe and thus added the phrase "talking buncombe" to the English language. He wrote an autobiography that was published by his grandson. Felix Walker married Susan, a daughter of Major Charles Robertson. He died in Clinton, Miss.

SEE: George M. McCoy, "Mountain Memories: Felix Walker . . ." and John Parris, "Felix Walker," *Asheville Citizen-Times*, 25 June 1950 and 28 Aug. 1966; Clarence W. Griffin, *History of Old Tryon and Rutherford Counties* (1937) and *Revolutionary Services of Col. John Walker and Family and Memoir of Felix Walker* (1930); F. A. Sondley, *History of Buncombe County*, vol. 2 (1930).

STANLEY J. FOLMSBEE

Walker, Henderson *(ca. 1659–14 Apr. 1704)*, president of the Council and acting governor, justice of the General Court, Court of Chancery, and Admiralty Court, settled in the North Carolina colony about 1682. His early history is unknown, but it is evident that he had had educational advantages. Although he was in his early twenties, he became clerk of the county court, then the highest court of law in the colony, soon after his arrival. Appointed about March 1682/83, he served at least until 1689. He was clerk of the Council during part or all of that period.

In 1692 and 1693 Walker was secretary of the colony, a position that he apparently held until about January 1693/94. Presumably he sat on the Council while serving as secretary. He clearly held a seat by January 1693/94, when he was a Lord Proprietor's deputy, and did so until his death. As a Council member Walker was ex officio justice of several courts, including the General Court before 1698 and the Court of Chancery throughout his tenure. From March 1697/98 through March 1698/99 he was justice of the General Court by commission from the Council, which named him one of the justices of the quorum. In May 1698 he became the chief judge of the Court of Admiralty by appointment from the Council. He probably presided over the Admiralty Court for the remainder of his life.

At various times Walker held other offices, serving as member of the Assembly (1689), customs collector (1694), quit rent collector (ca. 1694), clerk of Chowan Precinct Court (1693–94), attorney general (1695), and escheator (1697). In 1699 he was a member of a commission appointed to settle the boundary with Virginia, but the boundary dispute was not resolved at that time.

On the death of Deputy Governor Thomas Harvey on 3 July 1699, the Council elected Walker to be its president and acting governor of the colony until appointment of Harvey's successor. Walker was serving as acting governor by 7 July and continued in that position until June or July 1703, when Robert Daniel assumed office as deputy governor.

Walker's administration was a relatively tranquil period for the North Carolina colony, but it was not free from problems. He came to office during a campaign by Crown officials in America and England who were seeking resumption of the Proprietary charters by the Crown and the consequent abolition of the Lords Proprietors' right to govern their American colonies. Particularly troublesome for Walker were Virginia officials who strenuously promoted charter resumption by strategies consisting in large part of allegations charging North Carolina officials with such offenses as harboring runaway slaves, pirates, and debtors and neglecting to punish Indians guilty of murder. Virginia officials also created incidents aggravating the long-standing boundary dispute. Such tactics provided excuses for sending arrogantly worded "protests" to Walker. The protests appear to have been drafted primarily for the eyes of London officials, to whom copies were sent as enclosures in lengthy complaints concerning the alleged difficulties of being neighbor to a Proprietary colony. Nonetheless, they required attention from Walker.

Crown officials in London also caused trouble for Walker by attempting to increase Crown control over Proprietary colonies without formal nullification of the Proprietors' charters. Those efforts occurred particularly in connection with implementation of navigation laws and establishment of vice-admiralty courts. Such actions often violated rights claimed by the Proprietors under their charters, and Walker was faced with the choice between disobeying his orders from the Proprietors or disobeying those of Crown officials. Walker sought to protect the Proprietors' interests and when possible evaded or temporized with respect to orders conflicting with those interests. Except for a few sharp replies denying charges by Virginia officials, he was diplomatic but unyielding in relations with officials of that colony. In 1701 the resumption movement was laid to rest for a time by Parliament's refusal to support it, and Walker's relations with Virginia and London improved.

Perhaps Walker's most significant accomplishment was initiation of the organization and establishment of the Church of England in North Carolina. Although many colonists held the Anglican faith, there was no organized Anglican worship in the colony in the seventeenth century—nor indeed in any faith except that of the Quakers. Under Walker's leadership the Assembly of 1701 passed a vestry act providing for Church of England parishes, vestries, church buildings, and clergy, and levying a poll tax to support them. Although the Proprietors later disallowed that act on a technicality, parishes were organized under it and foundations were laid for the subsequent establishment of the Anglican church in the colony.

Walker was not only an ardent Anglican, but also a loyal resident of the colony and an adroit politician. Consequently, he was able to secure passage of the vestry act of 1701 without engaging in the ruthless oppression of dissenters that characterized later efforts to establish the Anglican church. He died before such tactics were fully developed, so he was spared the pain of seeing the oppression, dissension, and violence that the colony later suffered in connection with the establishment movement he initiated.

Walker was Council president and acting governor in a period of relative prosperity for the colony, and he shared personally in that prosperity. He had extensive landholdings in Perquimans and Chowan precincts, was partner in an enterprise for buying and selling cattle, and was part owner of a sloop, the *Dubartus*, which traded with New England. He also had a large practice as a leading attorney in the colony, which the custom of the time permitted despite his position as judge on the higher courts.

Walker settled originally in Perquimans Precinct, but in the 1690s he was living in Chowan. In his last years his home plantation was about five miles from the present town of Edenton on a point in Albemarle Sound later called Moseley's Point and yet later, Skinner's Point. He was a member of the first vestry of Chowan Parish (now St. Paul's Parish) in Edenton. In that capacity he added his personal efforts and substance to his official influence on behalf of the Church of England.

Walker was married twice. His first wife was Deborah Green, whom he married on 7 Apr. 1686. Their daughter, Elizabeth, was born on 22 Feb. 1686/87. His second wife was Ann Lillington, the daughter of Alexander Lillington and his second wife, Elizabeth Cook. Walker married Ann on 20 Feb. 1693/94; there is no evidence that they had any children.

On his death at age forty-four, Walker was survived by his daughter Elizabeth and his wife Ann. He bequeathed a plantation, cattle and other stock, and household furnishings to Elizabeth; made bequests to his church, to the poor, and to several friends and relatives; and left the remainder of his estate to his wife. He was buried on his plantation, but his remains were later moved to St. Paul's churchyard, Edenton.

In 1705 Walker's widow married Edward Moseley, who had recently settled in the colony. She died on 18 Nov. 1732 and was buried beside Walker in the plantation cemetery. Her remains, like Walker's, were later moved to St. Paul's churchyard, Edenton.

SEE: Samuel A. Ashe, ed., *Biographical History of North Carolina*, vol. 5 (1906); J. Bryan Grimes, ed., *Abstract of North Carolina Wills* (1910); J. R. B. Hathaway, ed., *North Carolina Historical and Genealogical Register*, 3 vols. (1900–1903); North Carolina State Archives, Raleigh, various manuscripts, particularly Albemarle Book of Warrants and Surveys (1681–1706), Albemarle County Papers (1678–1714), Chowan County Miscellaneous Papers (1685–1738), Colonial Court Records (Boxes 139, 186, 187, 189, 192), Council Minutes, Wills, Inventories (1677–1701), Diary of David L. Swain (1832), Perquimans Births, Marriages, Deaths and Flesh Marks (1659–1739), Will of Henderson Walker (proved 4 July 1704); Mattie Erma Edwards Parker, ed., *North Carolina Higher-Court Records, 1670–1696* and *1697–1701* (1968, 1971); William L. Saunders, ed., *Colonial Records of North Carolina*, vol. 1 (1886).

MATTIE ERMA E. PARKER

Walker, Hugh (*ca. 1740–27 Nov. 1800*), Revolutionary soldier and printer of state currency, is an elusive subject, but he went to Wilmington apparently from Virginia before the American Revolution. Printer Adam Boyd acquired Andrew Steuart's press there when it closed in 1767, and Boyd continued it until 1775. Walker possibly succeeded Boyd, as he was identified as the printer in Wilmington of North Carolina's 1779 issue of bills of credit.

There are no surviving Wilmington newspapers between 1775 and 1788, when one Bowen and Caleb Howard began publishing the *Wilmington Centinel*. Hugh Walker, however, enlisted in the North Carolina militia in the Wilmington District and served in Virginia. He also was among the taxables listed in New Hanover County in April 1780. The name does not appear in the census of North Carolina for 1790, but he may have returned to Virginia, for the census for Middlesex County in that state lists one of this name in a household of ten whites and twenty-six blacks. Walker was married first to Mary Thurston and afterwards to Mrs. Catherine (Montague) Morgan.

SEE: Walter Clark, ed., *State Records of North Carolina*, vol. 15 (1898); *Roster of Soldiers from North Carolina in the American Revolution* (1932); Virginia census, 1790; Alexander McD. Walker, *New Hanover Court Minutes*, Part 2 (1959).

WILLIAM S. POWELL

Walker, John (*1728–25 Jan. 1796*), Indian fighter and Revolutionary officer, was born in Appoquinimink Hundred, New Castle County, Del., the son of John Walker of Derry, Ireland, who immigrated to Delaware in 1720. The elder Walker was the grandson of the Reverend Governor George Walker of Donaghmore County, Londonderry, Ireland, who successfully commanded the Siege of Derry in 1689 against the forces of King James II.

As a young man Walker settled on the south fork of the Potomac River in Hampshire County, Va., and in 1751 married Elizabeth Watson. He served as a volunteer under Colonel George Washington in the Virginia colonial troops suffering in the disastrous defeat of the army of General Edward Braddock in 1755 near Fort Duquesne and fought the rear action during the retreat of the colonial troops. Shortly afterwards he moved to the area that became Lincoln County, N.C., on Lee Creek, about ten miles east of the present town of Lincolnton. While residing there he enlisted in Colonel James Grant's regiment and served in a campaign against the Cherokee Indians in 1761. Two years later he settled on Crowders Creek near Kings Mountain and lived there until 1768, when he moved to Cane Creek in what is now Rutherford County. He was appointed by the legislature of 1774 as one of the commissioners to "select a site and build thereon the court house, prison and stocks" for the county of Tryon. In 1775 he and his son Felix accompanied Colonel Richard Henderson and Daniel Boone on an expedition that explored Kentucky and founded the settlement of Boonesboro.

At the beginning of the Revolution he was appointed chairman of the Tryon Committee of Safety and was author of the Tryon Association Resolution of August 1775, when forty-eight settlers of that county resolved "firmly to resist force by force in defense of our natural freedom and constitutional rights." In the same month he represented Tryon County in the Third Provincial Congress at Hillsborough. Shortly after the war broke out he was commissioned a captain in the First Regiment of North Carolina Troops. Promoted to major on 20 Apr. 1777, he

resigned his commission on 22 December due to age and poor health. Tryon County was abolished by an act of the legislature of 1778, and Rutherford and Lincoln took its place the next year. The act designated John Walker as one of the four commissioners to survey the dividing line between the two counties and assist in setting up a government in those counties.

In 1779 he was appointed justice of the peace in the new county of Rutherford, and the first session of the Court of Common Pleas and Quarter Sessions was held at his home near the mouth of Cane Creek. The legislature of 1784 named him one of the commissioners of the Morgan District for disposing of confiscated Tory property. It also designated him one of the commissioners in that district "for the purpose of erecting a court house, prison and stocks in the County of Burke, for the use of said district, and for levying a tax to complete the same." Other duties of the commissioners consisted of laying out and establishing a town in Burke County by the name of Morgansborough (now Morganton).

In 1787 Colonel Walker moved to the forks of the Green and Broad rivers, in Rutherford County, where he died. All of his six sons served in the Revolution, five being commissioned officers in North Carolina regiments of the Continental line. One son, Captain Felix Walker, was also a member of the state House of Commons six times and served in the U.S. House of Representatives from 1817 to 1823. The other sons were John, Jr., James Reuben, William, Thomas, and Joseph.

SEE: John P. Arthur, *Western North Carolina: A History, 1730–1913* (1914); Walter Clark, ed., *State Records of North Carolina*, vols. 13 (1896), 16–17 (1899); Lyman C. Draper, *Kings Mountain and Its Heroes* (1929); John Graham, *The History of the Siege of Derry* (1823); Clarence Griffin, *Revolutionary Service of Col. John Walker and Family* (1930); Francis B. Heitman, *Historical Register of Officers of the Continental Army during the War of the Revolution* (1914); London *Times*, 13, 24 Aug. 1924; David Schenck, *North Carolina, 1780–81* (1889); Robert W. Walker and R. Frederick Walker, "Genealogy of John Walker from Ireland in 1720 and Some of His Ancestors in England and Ireland and Some of his Descendants in America" (manuscript in possession of H. L. Riddle, Jr., Morganton, N.C.); John H. Wheeler, *Historical Sketches of North Carolina* (1851).

H. L. RIDDLE, JR.

Walker, John (Jack) (*10 Dec. 1741–September 1813*), Revolutionary officer and planter, was born in the parish of Reavley, near Alnwick Castle, Northumberland County, England. His parents were James and Anne Wodehouse Walker of a distinguished family; they moved directly to Brunswick, N.C., from England in 1761. Young Walker established himself as a planter and merchant and in 1762 was deputy collector of taxes for New Hanover County. In 1765, when a naval officer and the master of his vessel engaged in a duel over a woman and the officer was fatally wounded, Walker was foreman of the corner's jury.

Royal governor William Tryon made his home at Brunswick, and Walker and Tryon undoubtedly were well acquainted; in 1771 Walker delivered a message from Tryon to Attorney General Thomas McGwire about conditions on the frontier. Soon afterwards Walker was active in the militia against the Regulators in the backcountry and served as hospital steward with the rank of captain shortly before the Battle of Alamance. Just prior to the battle, however, he was made captain of artillery. On the eve of the battle, while on reconnaissance, he and Lieutenant John Ashe were captured, severely flogged, and threatened with use as a shield should their captors be attacked. An agreement was reached between the opposing sides to exchange prisoners, but after the Regulators had been released Walker and Ashe were still being held. The battle began before they were freed, and after the fighting ended the two were found in the garret of a house where the Regulators had left them.

With the coming of the American Revolution Walker participated in the organization and equipping of the New Hanover County militia and was present at the Battle of Moore's Creek Bridge on 27 Feb. 1776. He was elected captain in the First North Carolina Continental Regiment and was sent to Charles Town, S.C., on 11 June 1776; he was on Sullivan's Island when the British under Sir Peter Parker and Lord Charles Cornwallis attacked the fort and were repulsed. Returning to Wilmington, Walker and his troops were ordered to join General George Washington in June 1777. They were at the battles of Germantown and Brandywine and present at Valley Forge. Following action there, Walker was promoted to the rank of major.

In December 1777 he was on Washington's staff as aide-de-camp with the rank of lieutenant colonel but afterwards was promoted to colonel. Assigned to duty in the southeastern region of North Carolina, he was there when the British under Major James H. Craig occupied Wilmington.

When the war ended Walker returned home to begin rebuilding his fortune, which had suffered during the war, particularly when his property was occupied by the British. At the legislative session of 1790–91 the General Assembly awarded him, for his services, 5,000 acres of land on Duck River, then in far western North Carolina (now Tennessee).

Walker may never have married, as he bequeathed his large fortune for the most part to nephews and nieces in England and Scotland, at least one of whom moved to North Carolina to claim the estate. An early member of the Society of the Cincinnati, he died in Wilmington and was buried in the churchyard of St. James's Church, of which he was a member.

SEE: Leora H. McEachern and Isabel M. Williams, *Wilmington–New Hanover Safety Committee Minutes* (1974); William S. Powell, ed., *The Correspondence of William Tryon and Other Selected Papers*, 2 vols. (1880–81); James A. Walker, *Life of Col. John (Jack) Walker* (1902).

WILLIAM S. POWELL

Walker, Mamie Dowd *(11 May 1880–12 July 1960),* civic leader and judge, was named Mary Rebecca but became known to all as Mamie. She was born in the Lipscombe family home north of Durham and grew up in that city. She and her brother, William Lipscombe Dowd, were the only children of John Watson, a tobacconist, and Susan Lipscombe Dowd. Mamie was graduated from Durham High School and the Greensboro Female Seminary in Greensboro. On 26 Oct. 1904 she married Fielding Lewis Walker, Jr., who became an official of the Liggett and Myers Tobacco Company in Durham. They were the parents of Fielding Lewis III and of Mary Lipscombe, who married George C. Pyne, Jr.

Although untrained in the law, Mrs. Walker, whose husband had died several months previously, sought and received appointment as the first judge of the Juvenile Court for both Durham City and Durham County. She was also the first woman judge in North Carolina. During her many years of serving on the Durham Board of Edu-

cation and on the City Recreation Commission, of which she was the first chairman, she had demonstrated how effectually she could work with young people. She was sworn in as judge on 3 Dec. 1934 and, except for one term (1941–42) for which she was not reappointed, served until her retirement on 5 Dec. 1949.

Immediately on taking office Judge Walker sought counsel from the National Probation and Parole Association, knowing that it set the standards for juvenile and domestic relations courts. She continued to be guided by that organization throughout her fourteen years on the bench. The program she developed for the prevention and treatment of delinquency became a model for many similar programs over the nation. In February 1935 she organized two Co-ordinating Councils, one for whites and one for blacks, as auxiliaries to the juvenile court in its program to prevent delinquency and rehabilitate delinquents. According to her, the results of the combined efforts of the court and these councils were manifold.

Judge Walker was convinced that supervised play for children was both preventive and corrective of antisocial behavior. She was one of the leaders in developing playgrounds in Durham, and under her leadership several youth clubs were formed. Among the many local, state, and national organizations in which she was active was the National Recreation Association. For at least twenty-five years she sponsored the association's letter of appeals.

In great demand as a public speaker, Judge Walker had to decline many invitations to speak. However, during her years as judge she addressed various groups and organizations over 450 times. Her principal topics were prevention and treatment of delinquency, the work of the Durham Juvenile Court, and how various agencies could contribute to the success of the court. She attended numerous conferences over the country and visited a number of juvenile courts and detention homes. Likewise, her own court was visited occasionally by specialists in the field of juvenile justice.

Although inactive professionally during retirement, Judge Walker kept in touch with professional friends. She remained active in the St. Philips Episcopal Church (her parents had been Methodists), and it was from that church that she was buried in Maplewood Cemetery, Durham.

SEE: *Durham Morning Herald*, 13 July 1960; *North Carolina Biography*, vol. 4 (1941); Mrs. George C. Pyne, Jr. (Durham), personal contact.

MATTIE U. RUSSELL

Walker, Nathan Wilson *(7 Mar. 1875–13 Feb. 1936),* professor and educator, was born at Poplar Branch, Currituck County, the son of William Henry and Ellen Anthony Walker. He was graduated from The University of North Carolina in 1903 and received the Ed.M. degree from Harvard in 1921. In 1903 he became superintendent of the Asheboro public schools, serving until 1905, when he was appointed professor of secondary education at The University of North Carolina and state inspector of high schools. He was state high school supervisor for the State Department of Education from 1907 to 1920. Also in 1907 he revived the summer school program at the university and then served as its director for twenty-seven years.

In 1910 Walker founded and edited until his death the *North Carolina High School Bulletin* (later renamed the *High School Journal*), published by the department of education at the university. Walker was president of the North Carolina Teachers' Assembly (1918–19); he served two terms on the North Carolina Textbook Committee and was chairman of the state's high school textbook committee. In 1921 he became acting dean of the School of Education at The University of North Carolina.

He was active in the Southern Association of Colleges and Secondary Schools, which set educational standards in the South. He served as secretary (1912–16) and chairman (1924) of the association's Commission on Accredited Schools of Southern States and was elected president of the association in 1925. Walker became a member of the board of trustees of the North Carolina College for Negroes in Durham in 1925 and served as chairman of the board of governors of The University of North Carolina Press. He was a member of the Methodist church, the Democratic party, Phi Beta Kappa, and Phi Delta Kappa.

Walker married Eva Pritchard on 29 Dec. 1903, and their children were Mildred, Katherine, Thomas Henry, Nathan Wilson, Jr., and John Anthony. He died at his home in Chapel Hill and was buried in the Chapel Hill Cemetery.

SEE: *Durham Morning Herald*, 14–15 Feb. 1936; Daniel L. Grant, *Alumni History of the University of North Carolina* (1924); *High School Journal* 19 (1936); Raleigh *News and Observer*, 14–15 Feb. 1936; *Who Was Who in America, 1897–1942* (1942).

J. MARSHALL BULLOCK

Walker, Platt Dickinson (25 Oct. 1849–22 May 1923), lawyer and associate justice of the North Carolina Supreme Court, was born in Wilmington, the only son of Thomas O. D. and Mary Vance Dickinson Walker. His father, a graduate of The University of North Carolina in 1843, was a wealthy lawyer, businessman, and railroad president. His maternal grandfather was Platt K. Dickinson, New England–born capitalist, head of a profitable Wilmington lumber business, and founder and investor in and lifetime director of the Wilmington and Weldon Railroad.

Born to privilege, young Platt grew up in a home of culture and refinement under his mother's guidance. He received his early formal education at Mr. or Mrs. George W. Jewett's school in Wilmington and then was sent to the Horner School in Oxford, an academy run by James H. Horner that trained a sizable number of future leaders of the state. Like his father and teacher Horner, Platt then went to the state university at Chapel Hill, one of only fifteen applicants in 1865 for a greatly diminished freshman class. At the commencements in 1866 and 1867 he distinguished himself as a speaker representing his class. By the latter year, however, the shrunken university (which soon would close for a few years) was in desperate straits and short of both money and students. Platt Walker transferred to the University of Virginia and studied law under the dean of the law school, Professor John B. Minor, graduating in 1869 with the LL.B. degree.

In June 1870 young Walker, earnest and hardworking, passed the first examination given by the North Carolina Supreme Court and was licensed to practice before that body. In the same year he became the law partner in Rockingham of locally prominent Walter L. Steele, a former state legislator and leader in the secession convention. Steele, a classmate at Chapel Hill of Horner and one year behind Walker's father, was also a cotton manufacturer and banker. Competing for several years against other able attorneys far more experienced in life and law than he, Walker grew in stature as an able trial lawyer who carefully studied case law and marshaled his arguments adroitly before each day of court. To him, as a col-

league later stated, the majesty and dignity of the law demanded respect and obedience from all. With such beliefs Walker, too learned an attorney to be a popular advocate, had a natural conservatism and maintained that citizens had a duty to obey both just and unjust laws.

In 1876 Steele was elected to Congress, and Walker moved to Charlotte, where he again joined forces with a prominent Chapel Hill graduate. His new partner, seventeen years Walker's senior, was Civil War veteran and local politician Clement Dowd, who for several postwar years had been law partner with popular wartime governor and governor-elect in 1876 Zebulon Vance. When Dowd was also elected to Congress in 1880, Walker associated with Armistead Burwell, another former partner of Vance and an acknowledged leader of the Charlotte bar.

Walker and Burwell were partners for twenty years, interrupted only for two years in the early 1890s when Burwell served as an associate justice of the state supreme court. Up to that time, despite his string of politically connected partners, Walker had held public office on only one occasion, serving a term as Democratic legislator from late 1874 to early 1875 for then-Republican Richmond County. In 1884 he was defeated as the Democratic nominee for state attorney general. Turning their attention to their legal practice, Walker and Burwell developed an enviable reputation and appeared on one side or another in nearly every important lawsuit in the Mecklenburg region. The partners had many corporate clients and frequently worked on litigation in other parts of the state. Perhaps as a result of these endeavors, Walker was unanimously elected the first president of the North Carolina Bar Association in 1899.

In 1902 Walker won election as a Democratic associate justice of the state supreme court. He was reelected and served until he died in 1923. His over two decades on the court were surpassed at that time only by Chief Justices Thomas Ruffin, Richmond Pearson, and Walter Clark. Devoted to duty and legal study, Walker likely wrote over two thousand opinions for the court and placed extremely high value on precedent and legalism. He reportedly recognized that new conditions might require new laws but refused to alter his conservative belief that legislatures, not courts, should write laws. To Walker it was a greater evil for a court to correct a social or economic wrong by unconstitutional judicial legislation than to leave the issue uncorrected. In such conservatism he generally was aligned with most of his colleagues and many North Carolinians of the era. One notable exception was Walter Clark, who became chief justice when Walker joined the court. A Civil War veteran and 1864 graduate of The University of North Carolina, Clark vigorously fought the large railroads and tobacco companies while supporting numerous progressive social reforms and writing many dissenting opinions.

Conservative on a chiefly conservative court, Walker was active in legal societies. He divided the rest of his life between home and organizations, marrying Henrietta Settle Covington (d. 1907) in 1878 and Alma Locke Mordecai in 1910; apparently there were no children by either marriage. An Episcopalian, Walker served as a vestryman for many years. He also was a trustee of The University of North Carolina (1901–5) and president of the North Carolina Literary and Historical Association (1909–10). For years he maintained an interest in politics and business in Charlotte. He was buried in Wilmington.

SEE: Kemp P. Battle, *History of the University of North Carolina*, vol. 2 (1912); Aubrey Brooks, *Walter Clark, Fighting Judge* (1944); John L. Cheney, Jr., ed., *North Carolina Government, 1585–1979* (1981); Daniel L. Grant, *Alumni His-*

tory of the University of North Carolina (1924); *Greensboro Daily News*, 23 May 1923; North Carolina Bar Association, *Proceedings* (1923), *Report* (1900); *North Carolina Reports*, vol. 191 (1926); Raleigh *News and Observer*, 23–24 May 1923; *Who Was Who in America*, vol. 1 (1943).

RICHARD F. KNAPP

Walkup, Samuel Hoey *(22 Jan. 1818–26 Oct. 1876)*, Confederate officer, legislator, and lawyer, was born in Jackson Township, Mecklenburg County, which became a part of Union County when it was formed in 1842, the son of Robert and Elizabeth Johnston Hoey Walkup. His mother was a first cousin of General Andrew Pickens of South Carolina. The Walkup family probably was descended from Samuel Walkup, of Camden County, who was the only person of that surname in the 1790 census of North Carolina. Samuel's half sister, Sarah Walkup, was the mother of William Henry Belk, the founder of Belk stores.

Samuel H. Walkup was graduated from The University of North Carolina in 1841. An essay he wrote on 30 Oct. 1839 was entitled, "Is it likely that poetry will ever flourish in America?" Another, on 30 Apr. 1840, was on a topic widely discussed at the time: "Should literary distinctions be awarded in colleges as incentives to exertion?"

Walkup began to practice law in Monroe and in 1844 was awarded the customary M.A. degree granted by the university to graduates who were engaged in promising professions. As early as the summer of 1845, he was interested in trying to identify the birthplace of Andrew Jackson. In addition to talking with people on both sides of the North Carolina–South Carolina line, he wrote to and received letters from others relating what they knew or had heard on the subject. His findings and conclusions were published in the Wadesboro *North Carolina Argus* in September 1858 and later in other publications. James Parton's three-volume *Life of Andrew Jackson* (1860) accepted and reported his findings.

Politics interested Walkup, and he served as county solicitor from 1848 to 1858. He represented Union County in the General Assembly for the terms 1858–59 and ran for Congress as a Whig in 1859 but was defeated by Burton Craige. He again served in the legislature for the term 1860–61. During much of this time he also was brigadier general of the Eleventh Regiment, North Carolina Militia.

On 4 Oct. 1860 Walkup was married by the Reverend Jethro Rumple, Presbyterian minister of Salisbury, to Pamelia R. Price. The 1870 census lists their children as Lelia, nine; Alice, seven; Minnie, four; Willie, two; and Josephine, six months, whom relatives referred to as Daisy.

In 1862, at age forty-four, Walkup joined Company F, Forty-eighth Regiment, North Carolina Troops, for service in the Civil War. He was appointed captain on 4 Mar. 1862 and elected lieutenant colonel of the regiment in April. He was wounded in the hip at Fredericksburg in December 1862. Promoted to colonel in December 1863, he was again wounded at or near the Wilderness in May 1864, but was with his regiment at the surrender at Appomattox Court House, Va., on 9 Apr. 1865. It was said that he was one of the bravest officers in the Army of Northern Virginia. It is also recorded that "he was often laughed at on dress parade and brigade drill for his awkwardness, but when in battle all that knew him were satisfied that Walkup was there and that his regiment would do its duty."

As a Democrat he was elected to Congress for the 1865–67 term, but Southerners were denied seats at that time. He did, however, serve in the North Carolina Constitutional Convention of 1865–66 and was a member of the board of trustees of The University of North Carolina (1874–76). He died of chronic dysentery and was buried in the Monroe cemetery.

SEE: John L. Cheney, Jr., ed., *North Carolina Government, 1585–1979* (1981); Walter Clark, ed., *Histories of the Several Regiments and Battalions from North Carolina in the Great War*, vols. 2–3, 5 (1901 [portrait]); Daniel L. Grant, *Alumni History of the University of North Carolina* (1924); Weymouth T. Jordan, comp., *North Carolina Troops, 1861–1865: A Roster*, vol. 11 (1987); [John Nichols, comp.], *Directory of the General Assembly of the State of North Carolina for the Session Commencing Nov. 19, 1860* (1860); Ronald W. Walkup, Rutherfordton, N.C., 31 May 1994, to William S. Powell; Samuel Hoey Walkup Papers (Southern Historical Collection, University of North Carolina, Chapel Hill).

WILLIAM S. POWELL

Wall, Zeno, Sr. *(20 Aug. 1882–12 Sept. 1967)*, minister, World War I chaplain, and college president, was born in Mooresboro in eastern Rutherford County near the Cleveland County border. One of eleven children of Sidney F., a carpenter, and Elora Jane Robinson Wall, he attended Mars Hill College and the Southern Baptist Theological Seminary before his ordination to the ministry in 1908. In 1917 he was awarded the honorary doctor of divinity degree by Mississippi College, Clinton.

His first pastorate was at Marshall, N.C., in 1908–9. From 1911 to 1914 he was pastor of the Mount Olive, Mississippi, Baptist Church. For twelve months in 1914–15 he served as an enlistment secretary with the Southern Baptist Missionary Board. In 1915 he became pastor of the First Baptist Church in Columbus, Miss., where he remained until 1922. There he began a close association with Mississippi College. Between 1916 and 1921 he was secretary of the board of trustees of the college and treasurer of the Baptist board of ministerial education of Mississippi, except for the time he served as a chaplain with the 140th Field Artillery during World War I (1917–18).

In 1922 the Reverend Mr. Wall returned to North Carolina as pastor of the First Baptist Church in Goldsboro. In 1925 he moved to the First Baptist Church in Shelby in his native county. The church had a membership of 600, but when he left in 1948 there were 2,600 members, making it one of the five largest of its denomination in the state. During the years 1933–36 he was president of the North Carolina Baptist State Convention. He left Shelby to become superintendent of the Baptist Children's Home in Thomasville (1948–51). In 1952 he began an unusual ministry at the Elizabeth Baptist Church, near Shelby, where he was invited to preach for five Sundays. Instead, he remained for five years during which the congregation erected a new building.

Soon after going to Shelby in 1925, Wall became concerned about the status of Boiling Springs High School, which had been established in the county in 1905 as a private denominational school financed largely by the Kings Mountain, Sandy Run, and Gaston Baptist Associations. The development of a system of public high schools in the state caused it to lose support, and the trustees were concerned about how to maintain it. Under Wall's leadership the board recommended to the sponsoring associations that the high school be made a junior college beginning with the 1927–28 academic year. The first president remained for only a brief time, and then Wall assumed charge—without a salary. He helped the school to become established and to fill a need in the region. In time Boiling Springs Junior College evolved into Gardner-Webb College, an endowed four-year institution. After his initial service to the college, Wall retired but afterwards filled many engagements as interim pastor.

In 1919 a sermon that the young Wall preached before the faculty and student body at the Southern Baptist Seminary in Louisville, Ky., was published in pamphlet form; similarly, another one preached at the First Baptist Church in Goldsboro was brought out in 1922. A collection of his sermons, *Heartening Messages*, appeared in book form in 1944. He was the author of two other books: *Verities of the Gospel* (1947) and *A Day for God-Called Men* (1948).

On 4 May 1911 Zeno Wall married Ada Katherine Ramsey of Marshall. They had five children: Zeno, Jr., Mrs. Ollie Harris, Mrs. Walter Fanning, Woodrow Wilson, and Yates. He died at a nursing center in Charlotte and was buried in the Elizabeth Baptist Church cemetery in Cleveland County.

SEE: Cleveland County Historical Association, *The Heritage of Cleveland County* (1982); North Carolina Baptist State Convention *Minutes* (1967 [portrait]); John S. Raymond, *Among Southern Baptists* (1936); *Who's Who in the South and Southwest* (1950).

FRANCIS B. DEDMOND

Wallace, Lillian Frances Parker (*11 Apr. 1890–30 May 1971*), educator, historian, author, lecturer, antiquarian, musician, watercolorist, and linguist, was born in Pine City, Minn., the daughter of Saidie Althea Feetham and the Reverend George Selby Parker (13 Apr. 1857–1 Sept. 1926). The Feethams were Canadian, with English forebears; the Parkers originated in Ireland. Mrs. Parker was a teacher and her husband, a Methodist minister. Lillian Parker Wallace had one brother, Selby Carlyle Parker, an investment banker who lived most of his life in Buffalo, N.Y.

She was educated in the public schools of Minnesota and Colorado, where her father's church assignments took the family. After graduation from the Leadville, Colo., high school, she earned an A.B. degree in languages in 1910 from the University of Denver, where she was an assistant as an undergraduate and where she taught for several years. Relocating in North Carolina, she took summer courses at Wake Forest College and The University of North Carolina; in 1929 she received an M.S. degree in education from North Carolina State College at Raleigh. She received a Ph.D. degree in history from Duke University in 1944, when she was elected to Phi Beta Kappa.

After teaching Latin at the Bainbridge, Ga., high school from 1919 to 1921, Mrs. Wallace moved to Raleigh, where she became an instructor in history and education at Meredith College. Advancing to the rank of professor, she devoted full time after 1944 to the history department. She was acting head from 1946 to 1948 and then department chairman until her retirement in 1962, when she was named professor emerita. During the summers she taught at Wake Forest and North Carolina State.

In 1948 her department and the North Carolina Department of Archives and History introduced the first undergraduate course in the nation to offer museum and archival training. She and Director Christopher Crittenden jointly supervised the students, who became junior archivists. The program received special commendation from the American Association for State and Local History.

Dr. Wallace became a patron and life member of the Japan Society, in which she held a fellowship as a Scholar in 1958. In 1960–61 she won a Southern Fellowships Fund grant to complete a book published in 1966. Beginning in 1958 she was a consultant and lecturer for North Carolina's televised in-school classes on American and world history and a panel member on world affairs for other WUNC-TV programs. She was a frequent lecturer and panelist on international affairs before professional organizations, other colleges, and civic groups, including the American and Southern Historical Associations, Raleigh's Institute of Religion, the Sir Walter Cabinet, and other groups. She was a member of the North Carolina Literary and Historical Association (executive committee), Trinity College Historical Society, Southern and American Historical Associations, American Association of University Professors (president, Meredith College chapter, and executive committee member, North Carolina division), American Academy of Political and Social Science, Asian Society, Societies for French and Italian Historical Studies, Conference on British Historical Studies, American Institute of Archaeology (life member), Southern Baptist Historical Society, and American Association of University Women.

She was president of the Higher Education Association of North Carolina and of the Social Studies Council of North Carolina, chairman of the social studies section for the Baptist colleges of North Carolina, secretary of the Cooperative Research Committee of the North Carolina College Conference, secretary of the Social Studies Committee of the North Carolina Curriculum Study (1959–60), and permanent secretary of the Wake County Association of Phi Beta Kappa, of which chapter she was a founder and charter member in 1949. She was also a member of the National Triennial Council of united chapters and the National Committee on Associations of Phi Beta Kappa.

In 1964 an honorary doctorate awarded by North Carolina State College cited her significant contributions to the development of education at all levels throughout North Carolina and the region, recognized her as an accomplished linguist, and noted her extensive accomplishments as a professional pianist and organist. The 1946 Meredith College annual *Oak Leaves* was dedicated to "Dr. Lillian Parker Wallace, whose friendly smile and kindly heart is an encouragement to all, whose genuine interest and enthusiasm, an inspiration, and whose willing cooperation and versatile talents, an incentive to greater accomplishments."

Dr. Wallace combined a musical career with teaching, having become an able pianist and organist largely through self-instruction. In the 1920s she played organ accompaniment for traveling plays and silent movies in local theaters. She was a member of the Bessie Rae McMillan orchestra, a quintet that played nightly during the dinner hour at the Hotel Sir Walter in Raleigh; played piano with the WPTF radio orchestra and ensembles; and performed for events at the Executive Mansion. In the 1930s she was pianist and choir director at Pullen Memorial Baptist Church, Raleigh, and later was organist and choir director at Hillyer Memorial Christian Church, also in Raleigh. For over thirty years she was accompanist for the North Carolina State College Glee Club and quartet and accompanied the college orchestra's public concerts. A life member of Local 500 of the American Federation of Musicians, she was its president for some years as well as dean of the Central North Carolina Chapter of the American Guild of Organists. With Dr. Harry E. Cooper, she founded the Raleigh Chamber Music Guild in 1941, serving as director and later as vice-president. Also with Dr. Cooper in 1942 she helped organize the Raleigh Oratorio Society and was long its accompanist and assistant director. For nearly thirty years she was a member of the Saint Cecelia Choral Club, first as a singer and then as a pianist.

For many years she was director and vice-president of the Raleigh Civic Music Association and a member and patroness of Sigma Alpha Iota, the national music sorority. With other officers of the North Carolina Literary and Historical Association, she helped initiate Music Day of Culture Week on 3 Dec. 1957. In 1969 the North Carolina Federation of Music Clubs presented her an award of merit "for distinguished service to the cultural, musical, and artistic life of the State."

A talented watercolorist, Dr. Wallace annually exhibited her paintings as well as drawings, cartoons, and calligraphy in the Meredith College art gallery, beginning in 1947, and in other years in the Raleigh Woman's Club Sidewalk Art Show. Many of her watercolors depicted local scenes; others were executed during summer vacations at Lake Chatauqua, where she joined artists from the Lake Chatauqua Artists' Colony in afternoon painting groups. Her works are owned by a number of personal friends and collectors in the Raleigh area, as well as by Meredith College.

At Meredith, Dr. Wallace created the role of the White Rabbit in the faculty's quadrennial presentation of "Alice in Wonderland," playing that part in all twelve productions between 1924 and her death (even after her retirement). In sports, she was an expert marksman, an archer, a bowler, and an avid tennis player. Long after her health forced her off the courts about 1953, she retained her membership in the Raleigh Tennis Club and the National Tennis Foundation. She was also a skilled chess and scrabble player.

Dr. Wallace collaborated with Dr. Alice Barnwell Keith of the Meredith history faculty in writing *A Syllabus of the History of Civilization*, which they revised ten times between 1933 and 1962 for use by their students. She was the author of *The Papacy and European Diplomacy, 1869–1878* (1948), *Leo XIII and the Rise of Socialism* (1966), and "Bismarck and Decazes: The War Scare of 1875," *South Atlantic Quarterly* (Spring 1958). She was coeditor with William C. Askew of *Power, Public Opinion, and Diplomacy: Essays in Honor of Eben Malcolm Carroll, by His Former Students* (1959), to which she also contributed a chapter. The volume was one of the twenty-two winners of the eighth annual Southern Books Competition in 1959. Unpublished at the time of her death were two other manuscripts of history, "The Vatican and the Rise of Mussolini" and "The Vatican and European Diplomacy before World War I." She also was coauthor with a former student, Rachel Rawls, of an unpublished historical novel set in the fifteenth century.

In political preference she was a Democrat. A Baptist, she was a member during all her years in Raleigh of the Pullen Memorial Baptist Church, where in addition to her musical role she was an adult leader in the young people's organization.

Mrs. Wallace's marriage on 12 June 1911 to William Harvey Wallace ended in separation. A son, Wesley Herndon Wallace (b. 18 Apr. 1912), became a radio announcer, general manager of the Manila (Philippines) Broadcasting Company, and professor in the Department of Radio, Television and Motion Pictures Department of The University of North Carolina, where he was chairman from 1962 to 1977. A daughter, Marian Frances Wallace (b. 18 Sept. 1916), married Preston W. Smith and was for some years head of the immunology laboratory at Duke Hospital, Durham.

On 14 May 1971, sixteen days before Dr. Wallace's death, the Meredith College class of 1971 announced that it was establishing the Lillian Parker Wallace Fund to finance visiting lecturers and eventually a visiting professorship. By commencement it had given or obtained gifts totaling $7,000, with plans for enlarging the fund annually. The first Lillian Parker Wallace Lecture, presented in the college auditorium on 18 Sept. 1978, featured the Right Honourable Sir Harold Wilson, former prime minister of Great Britain.

Dr. Wallace's died after a short confinement at Rex Hospital in Raleigh. She was buried in Oakwood Cemetery.

SEE: "Brush Strokes of Lillian Parker Wallace" (phonograph recording of a partial interview with James W. Reid, March 1970, issued by Meredith Alumnae Association, 1971); Anne Bryan (president, Meredith class of 1971), introductory remarks at first Wallace Fund lecture, 18 Sept. 1978; *Dictionary of International Biography*, vol. 8 (1972); *Directory of American Scholars* (1957); Maxine Eleanor Taylor Fountain, ed., *Enthusiasts All* (1974); Mary Lynch Johnson, *A History of Meredith College* (1972); *Meredith College Alumnae Magazine* 16 (July 1962); William S. Powell, ed., *North Carolina Lives* (1962); Raleigh *News and Observer*, 22, 24 Oct. 1949, 28 May 1950, 31 May, 1 June 1971; *Raleigh Times*, 15 July 1950, 1 Apr. 1959, 29 May 1964, 9 May 1969, 31 May, 1 June 1971; *Sanford Herald*, 17 Oct. 1967; Lillian Parker Wallace Papers (Southern Historical Collection, University of North Carolina, Chapel Hill); Lillian Parker Wallace to James W. Reid, personal contact, March 1970; *Who's Who of American Women* (1958–59 and succeeding editions); *Who's Who in the South and Southwest* (1969–70).

ELIZABETH DAVIS REID MURRAY

Wallis (Wallace, Wallice), Robert (*d. 25 Mar. 1712*), Council member, Assembly member, and justice of the General Court and precinct court, settled in the North Carolina colony before 1668. Although a deposition made many years later places him among the early settlers of the colony, Wallis's name has not been found in surviving records before the 1680s, when it occurs occasionally in court records naming him as a juror, constable, or road surveyor. In January 1689/90 he was a justice of Pasquotank Precinct Court, but the full period of his tenure is unknown.

By 1 Jan. 1693/94 Wallis was a member of the Council, sitting as an "assistant," which indicates that he also was a member of the Assembly and had been appointed to the Council by that body. He remained on the Council at least through March 1694/95. As Council member he was ex officio justice of the General Court, but he attended as justice only in November 1694. In the early 1700s he advocated the establishment of the Anglican church and the placing of political disabilities on Quakers. His role in the establishment movement, however, probably was that of a private citizen, as he does not appear to have held public office after serving on the Council until 1711, when he was a member of the Assembly.

Wallis lived in Pasquotank Precinct, where he owned at least 400 acres of land. In addition to planting, he seems to have been engaged in a mercantile business. From time to time he also appeared as an attorney before the General Court. He was a member of the vestry of Pasquotank Parish in 1710 and probably was one of the original vestrymen.

Wallis's headrights included an Elizabeth Wallis, who may have been his wife. A Thomas Wallis also listed in his headrights may have been a son, but no later mention of him has been found. Wallis's only child known to have survived to adulthood was a son named William, who died shortly before his father's death. Robert Wallis left as his heir at law a grandson, William, son of the recently deceased William.

SEE: J. Bryan Grimes, ed., *Abstract of North Carolina Wills* (1910); J. R. B. Hathaway, ed., *North Carolina Historical and Genealogical Register*, vols. 1, 3 (1900, 1903); North Carolina State Archives, Raleigh: various papers, particularly in Albemarle Book of Warrants and Surveys (1681–1706) and Council Minutes, Wills, and Inventories (1677–1701); Mattie Erma E. Parker, ed., *North Carolina Higher-Court Records, 1670–1696* and *1697–1701* (1968, 1971); William S. Price, Jr., ed., *North Carolina Higher-Court Records, 1702–1708* and *North Carolina Higher-Court Minutes, 1709–1723* (1974, 1977); William L. Saunders, ed., *Colonial Records of North Carolina*, vol. 1 (1886).

MATTIE ERMA E. PARKER

Walls, William Jacob *(8 May 1885–23 Apr. 1975)*, Methodist clergyman, editor, and author, was born at Chimney Rock, the son of Edward and Mattie Edgerton Walls. He received his early education in the Asheville public schools and the Allen Industrial School in Asheville. Shortly before his fourteenth birthday he was ordained to the African Methodist Episcopal Zion ministry at the church's Hopkins Chapel in Asheville. From Livingstone College in Salisbury he received an A.B. degree in 1908, a B.D. degree in 1915, and a D.D. degree in 1918. In 1922 he studied philosophy and journalism at Columbia University and Bible history at Union Theological Seminary in New York. He earned an M.A. degree at the University of Chicago in 1941.

Walls served in the pastoral ministry at Cleveland in Rowan County (1905–7), Lincolnton (1908–10), and Salisbury (1910–13). While officiating in Louisville, Ky., between 1913 and 1920, he built Broadway Temple. Back in North Carolina between 1920 and 1924 he was at Charlotte as editor of the *Star of Zion*, the official organ of the African Methodist Episcopal church. In Indianapolis in 1924 he was elected bishop and served as senior bishop from 1951 to 1968.

He was fraternal messenger to the General Conference of the Methodist Episcopal Church, South, in Atlanta (1918); a delegate to the Ecumenical Methodist Conference in London, England (1921), a fraternal delegate to the General Conference of the Methodist Episcopal church in Kansas City (1928); a delegate to the Ecumenical Methodist Conference, in Atlanta, where he made the only address by a member of his race (1936); a delegate to the Twelfth World Sunday School Convention, at Oslo, Norway, where he delivered an address on "Christianity: The Unturned Key" (1936); and a member of the President and War Secretary's Clergymen's Commission to occupied countries in Europe (1947). He also was a delegate to the World Council of Churches in Amsterdam (1948), Evanston (1954), New Delhi (1961), and Uppsala (1968).

Walls was the author of *Wisdom for the Times, What Youth Wants, The Negro in Business and Religion, Joseph Charles Price: Education and Race Leader, The Romance of a College, The Dreams of Youth, Living Essentials of Methodism, Harriet Tubman,* and *The African Methodist Episcopal Church: Reality of the Black Church.*

During the period 1941–73 he was chairman of the trustees of Livingstone College and of the Harriet Tubman Foundation; vice-president of the National Association for the Advancement of Colored People; and a member of the World Sunday School Association, National Council of Churches of Christ in America, and American Bible Society (advisory council, 1941–70). He was also a member of the American Academy of Political Science, Phi Beta Sigma, the Masonic Order, the Odd Fellows, and the Elks.

On 6 Dec. 1956 he married Dorothy L. Jordan. In 1958 he founded Camp Dorothy Walls in Black Mountain. At the time of his death his home and office were in Yonkers, N.Y. Interment was in a family crypt in Lincoln Cemetery, Chicago. Portraits of him are in the Walls Center, Hood Theological Seminary Building, Salisbury; Heritage Building, Livingstone College; and administration building, Camp Dorothy Walls.

SEE: Emory S. Bucke, ed., *The History of American Methodism*, vol. 3 (1964); Bishop Herbert Bell Shaw (Wilmington), personal contact, 4 Jan. 1976; Mrs. Dorothy J. Walls (Yonkers, N.Y.), personal contact, 20 Jan. 1976; William J. Walls, *Joseph Charles Price* (1943, biographical data on dust jacket); *Who's Who in America, 1974–1975* (1974); *Who's Who in Colored America, 1838–1940* (1940).

GRADY L. E. CARROLL

Walser, Henry *(10 Sept. 1803–22 Sept. 1875)*, politician and college founder, was born in northern Davidson County near the Yadkin River, the youngest son and penultimate of nine children of Frederick and Margaret Earnest Walser, six of whom migrated to Tennessee and the Midwest. In 1825 Henry married Elizabeth Warner, and the couple had eight children: Margaret (Phillips), Priscilla (Owen), Daniel E., Cynthia (Smith), Gaither, Lucy Norfleet (Oakes), Henry Clay, and Frederick Taylor. He became a prosperous farmer with large holdings and in the 1830s aligned himself with the Union element of the Whig party, promoting such internal improvements as navigable streams, railroads, and mail routes.

Walser served in the North Carolina House of Commons for six terms: 1842, 1846, 1848, 1854, 1858, and 1862. His enthusiasm for education led in 1855 to the founding of Yadkin Institute (later Yadkin College) on land he donated. He was its principal builder, financial supporter, and president of the board of trustees until his death. As a Methodist Protestant institution, it was the immediate predecessor of High Point College. In 1860, with the oldline Whigs in disarray, he joined the short-lived Constitutional Union party and attended the Baltimore convention to nominate the Bell-Everett ticket. Though a strong Unionist, he actively supported the Confederate troops during the Civil War, and two of his sons, Gaither as a private and Henry Clay as a major, served in the army.

The race issue was never a divisive one in Davidson County, and after the war, his wealth depleted but his Union loyalties intact, he became a Republican. He was a local magistrate and, for six months before his death, first mayor of the town of Yadkin College. He was buried near the college building. A watercolor of Henry Walser was in the possession of his great-granddaughter, Mayree Oakes Greene.

SEE: *Journal of the House of Commons* (1842–63); Olin B. Michael, *Yadkin College, 1856–1924* (1939); *The State* magazine, 21 June 1941; Walser Family Papers (Southern Historical Collection, University of North Carolina, Chapel Hill).

RICHARD WALSER

Walser, Richard Gaither *(23 Oct. 1908–25 Nov. 1988)*, college professor, author, and cultural leader, was born in Lexington in a family of lawyers and teachers of Wachovia Moravian descent, the son of Zeb Vance and Frances Estelle Adderton Walser. His father, a Republican, had served in both the North Carolina Senate and House of Representatives, where he was speaker in 1895 during the Fusion period, and as attorney general (1897–1900). Richard was also a Republican and in his later years took considerable pride in pointing out that he was an original Republican, not a retread Democrat.

He first became interested in North Carolina literature and history under the influence of his father, an avid collector of North Caroliniana. His enthusiasm was furthered by his public school teachers who were themselves North Carolina partisans. At the insistence of his family he entered Davidson College as a freshman even though his heart was set on Chapel Hill. Transferring to The University of North Carolina the next year, he was graduated in 1929. He returned in the fall to begin graduate work, but the depression limited his stay to a single year. From then until 1942 he taught high school English, first at Linwood and Lexington in his native county and then in Durham and Greenville. Returning to the university for several sessions of summer school, he received a master's degree in 1933. His thesis dealt with anti-Catholicism in the Gothic novel. In 1938 he went to Greenville, where, as a critic teacher, he worked with East Carolina college students who were training to become teachers. While in Greenville he published his first book, *North Carolina Poetry* (1941), an anthology that he had begun eight years earlier.

During World War II he served in the U.S. Navy and afterwards in the Naval Reserve, retiring with the rank of lieutenant commander. Assigned to the southwestern Pacific, he participated in a number of the landings that led to Tokyo. While in that part of the world he built up a splendid collection of books on Australia that he later donated to the university library in Chapel Hill. Returning home near the end of the war, he requested a tour of duty in Panama; he also gave the university the books he had collected on that region.

Although the story is apocryphal, it was often said that at one point in his career he inquired about beginning doctoral work at Chapel Hill. He insisted that he would write a dissertation on North Carolina literature, but the faculty in very strong terms announced that that was not an acceptable subject. It may have been this rejection that prompted him to pursue his study of North Carolina poets, novelists, and dramatists and their work.

Walser published more than thirty books and pamphlets, clearly succeeding in the goal of his youth—to recall to mind the varied creative writings of our literary ancestors. He was a fair and objective critic, and where condemnation was in order he spoke clearly. His humorous anthology, *Nematodes in My Garden of Verse*, contains some excellent examples of poetry gone wrong. On the other hand, by scholarly research and writing and by publishing facsimiles of long-out-of-print books (which he largely financed himself), he helped to create an appreciation of North Carolina writers who lived between the eighteenth century and his own time. Walser came to be recognized as a national authority on Thomas Wolfe with books on him published by Harvard University Press as well as in the state.

His 1941 anthology of North Carolina poetry was followed by *North Carolina in the Short Story* in 1948. His *Short Stories from the Old North State* (1959), *North Carolina Miscellany* (1962), *North Carolina Parade* (1966), *Tar Heel Laughter* (1974), and *North Carolina Legends* (1980) served to broaden readers' understanding of the contributions of North Carolinians to a varied literary heritage. He also wrote biographical studies of Bernice Kelly Harris and Inglis Fletcher, writers of popular fiction, as well as books and pamphlets on Wolfe and other subjects. He contributed to study guides used by correspondence students through the university at Chapel Hill and North Carolina State College. Several of his works, published by the

North Carolina Division of Archives and History, were designed for use by children and young people in the schools of the state. Many of these were revised and reissued over a long period of time.

Through his participation in the North Carolina Library Association, North Carolina English Teachers Association, and State Literary and Historical Association, Walser was instrumental in the compilation of bibliographies, indexes, and assorted lists that advanced research and understanding of the state's culture. As a member of the later organization he played a prominent role in redefining the state's literary awards, consolidating the rules, and laying the groundwork for new awards.

A skilled teacher, Walser enlightened classes in Chapel Hill, where he taught briefly, and at North Carolina State University, where he spent most of his academic career beginning in 1946. As a guest lecturer at many other institutions, he entertained and informed hundreds of people. He was a popular speaker before civic and patriotic organizations. Active in the work of a local history group, the Folklore Society, the Society for the Preservation of Antiquities, and others, he further left his mark on North Carolina culture. His service on numerous hardworking committees led to growth and improvement in many facets of life in the state. A devotee of the opera and other forms of music, dance, and drama, he frequently went to New York and abroad to enjoy them, but he supported these in North Carolina as well.

He was an active member of the Watauga Club, composed of important leaders of the state who, as an organization, shunned publicity but whose ideas and advice, known to very few, were extremely important in charting the course of events in North Carolina for many decades. The three awards that most highly pleased him were a Guggenheim Fellowship in 1957, the North Carolina Award for Literature in 1976, and an honorary doctorate from North Carolina State University in 1988.

Never married, Walser died in Raleigh following several months of declining health and was buried in the National Cemetery, Raleigh.

SEE: William S. Powell, ed., *North Carolina Lives* (1962); Raleigh *News and Observer*, 18 Jan., 27 Mar. 1953, 1 May 1955, 24 Apr. 1961, 27 Nov. 1988; Richard Walser and E. T. Malone, Jr., eds., *Literary North Carolina* (1986).

WILLIAM S. POWELL

Walser, Zeb Vance (17 June 1863–17 Feb. 1940), lawyer and politician, was born near Yadkin College in Davidson County, the oldest son of Frances Edith Byerly and Gaither Walser. He attended Yadkin College, founded by his grandfather Henry Walser, and The University of North Carolina, then received an LL.B. from the University of Michigan in 1886. In politics, he inherited Whig and Unionist principles and became a Republican. He began practicing law in Lexington and for several years was deputy collector of internal revenue.

In 1888 Walser was elected to the state house of representatives and in 1890 to the state senate, where he was minority leader. Chosen speaker of the house by his Populist and Republican colleagues in 1895, he returned to Raleigh as attorney general in 1897, when the entire state Fusion ticket was elected. On 24 Nov. 1900, less than two months before the end of his term of office, he resigned on being appointed reporter to the state supreme court; by March 1905 he had compiled eleven volumes of the *North Carolina Reports*. In 1908 he was defeated for Congress by Robert N. Page. His admiration for Theodore Roosevelt prompted his joining the Progressive party in 1912, when

Roosevelt led his followers out of the national convention at which William Howard Taft was nominated. He then undertook the management of Roosevelt's campaign in North Carolina, a task he similarly performed for General Leonard Wood in the 1920 contest for the Republican nomination.

Throughout his life, Walser was a crusader for education, attested by his long service as trustee of The University of North Carolina and member of the Lexington School Board. He was a Presbyterian. For the Sunday supplements of the state newspapers, he wrote feature stories, but ill health prevented his completing a book on "Senators and Representatives from North Carolina in the Congress of the Confederate States, 1861–1865." He married Frances Estelle Adderton of Lexington, and they had five children: Pattie A. (Mrs. H. B. Turner), Zeb Vance, Jr., Donald Adderton, Frances Harcourt, and Richard Gaither. He was buried in the Lexington City Cemetery. A portrait by Paul Knepper hangs in the courtroom of the Davidson County Courthouse.

SEE: *North Carolina Biography*, vol. 4 (1919); Raleigh *News and Observer*, 24 Aug. 1899; Richard Walser, *Five Walsers* (1976); Walser Family Papers (Southern Historical Collection, University of North Carolina, Chapel Hill).

RICHARD WALSER

Walters, Sarah (Sadie) Wharton Green Jones

(1859–6 June 1943), society leader and the creator of Airlie garden, near Wilmington, was born at the residence of her maternal grandparents in Jamaica Plains outside of Boston, the daughter of Colonel Wharton and Esther Ellery Green. Her grandfather Thomas Jefferson Green was among the noted men of his day in North Carolina, and her mother was from a prominent New England family. Taken to North Carolina in infancy, Sarah was reared at her father's plantation, Esmeralda, on Shocco Creek in Warren County. Here were spent the difficult years of the Civil War. When the conflict was over, Wharton Green and his family moved to Tokay in Cumberland County. In St. John's Church, Fayetteville, Sarah Green married Pembroke Jones of Wilmington on 27 Nov. 1884. For some months thereafter, the young couple lived in Washington, D.C., where Mrs. Jones acted as hostess for her father who was then a congressman.

On settling in Wilmington, the Joneses bought the Edward Bishop Dudley Mansion on Front Street in 1885 for their residence. Shortly afterwards they also acquired a 150-acre tract on Wrightsville Sound, near Wilmington, and built a small cottage as a weekend retreat, naming the property Airlie after a Jones ancestral seat in Scotland. The cottage, gradually expanding to a large rambling house, became their principal home in Wilmington; they sold the Dudley house to James Sprunt in 1894.

Impressed with the native magnolias and wild azalea, or honeysuckle, growing in the Airlie woods, Sarah Jones decided to create a spring garden there. Over the years, the project expanded with pools, paths, and carriage ways laid out in an informal manner, embellished with statuary and other ornamentation. The garden was largely devoted to azaleas, camellias, wisteria, and other spring flowering plants. R. A. Topel, a former under-gardner of the German kaiser, was engaged to assist Mrs. Jones. Here he developed the topel tree, an unusual hybrid formed from grafting the mistletoe juniper on an other holly. In its prime, the Airlie garden was considered among the best of its kind.

The Joneses also bought several thousand acres adjoining Airlie that they maintained as a hunting preserve.

Here in 1908 they had a pavilion built in the Italian Renaissance style for entertainment purposes. Designed by their son-in-law, John Russell Pope, the building gradually fell into ruin after Mrs. Jones's death.

Sarah and Pembroke Jones were the parents of a son, Pembroke, who married but left no issue, and of a daughter, Sarah, who married John Russell Pope of New York. Pope, a noted neoclassic architect, designed many public buildings in Washington and was responsible for the wing added to the British Museum in London to house the Elgin Marbles. The Popes had a daughter, Jane, who married Anthony Akers.

Pembroke Jones died in 1919, and Sarah Green Jones married in 1922 Henry Walters, their lifelong friend. Walters was a noted railway magnate, yachtsman, and art collector whose main residence was in Baltimore; he was the son of William T. Walters, an organizer of the Atlantic Coast Line system that resulted in untold benefit to North Carolina. After their marriage, Mrs. Walters continued to winter at Airlie and summer at Newport. Walters was active in the affairs of Wilmington and a portrait of him, commemorating this association, hangs in the city hall there. At the time of his death in 1931, he was chairman of the board of the Atlantic Coast Line, which then had its main office in Wilmington. Having no children, Henry Walters bequeathed his fine art collection and a gallery to house it to the city of Baltimore.

Mrs. Walters survived her second husband by over a decade. In 1941 her own art collection, consisting mostly of eighteenth-century French furniture, statuary, and tapestries, was sold at Park-Bernet for over $600,000, which was considered a large sum for the times. Sarah Green Jones Walters died in her apartment at the Plaza Hotel in New York after a short illness and was buried beside her first husband in Oakdale Cemetery, Wilmington. A portrait of her as a young girl of fifteen was owned by her granddaughter, Mrs. Jane Pope Akers, of Palm Beach, Fla.

SEE: Herbert B. Battle and others, *The Battle Book* (1930); Elizabeth Drexel Lehr, *King Lehr and the Gilded Age* (1935); *New York Times*, 18 June 1943; Raleigh *News and Observer*, 1 Dec. 1931; Blackwell P. Robinson, ed., *North Carolina Guide* (1955); E. T. H. Shaffer, *Carolina Gardens* (1939); James Robert Warren, "History in Towns—Wilmington, N.C.," *Antiques* magazine (December 1980); U.S. Census, Warren County, N.C. (microfilm, North Carolina State Archives, Raleigh); Cicero P. Yow (Wilmington, N.C.) to Claiborne T. Smith, 9 July 1980.

CLAIBORNE T. SMITH, JR.

Wanchese *(fl. 1584–86)* (name from bird-gens), was an Algonquian Indian of the Roanoke tribe living on or near the present Roanoke Island. He was taken to England in September 1584 by Arthur Barlowe, who had been sent to the New World by Walter Raleigh to search out a site for a settlement. Wanchese was probably in the company of Granganimeo, elder of the tribe, when he was induced to go away with the English reconnaissance party in August 1584.

Wanchese was described as a "lusty" (physically strong) person, and he and his companion, Manteo, were said on 18 Oct. 1584, to look like "white Moors," originally dressed in mantles of rudely tanned skins, no other covering about their private parts. In England however, they were soon fitted out in English clothing of brown taffeta. He was at the time wholly unintelligible to the Europeans. Whether he learned much English or taught much Algonquian to his captors before he sailed back to North America with Sir Richard Grenville on 19 Apr. 1585, we cannot say. He appears to have been on the flagship, the *Tiger*, and thus saw a number of places in the Caribbean, mainly in the islands of San Juan de Puerto Rico, and Española before the *Tiger* ran aground on Wokokon (now Ocracoke Island) on 29 June.

At some time before Ralph Lane established his settlement on Roanoke Island in August 1585, Wanchese returned to his own people. This was a disappointment to the English settlers, but it appears natural that there was at least an even chance that an uprooted Indian would prefer to identify on his return with his own people rather than with the intruding Europeans.

During the period of growing hostility between the Roanoke tribe and Lane's men from March to June 1585, Wanchese was identified by Lane with the hostile group in the tribe, centering around the chief Pemisapan, which objected to the continuing presence of the English and to the burden of their food demands. After Lane's departure (Pemisapan having been killed), Wanchese, according to Manteo later, was a leading member of the group that harassed the small band of settlers left on Roanoke Island by Grenville in 1586 and eventually drove them off. We hear nothing further about him. Traditionally the villain who betrayed his white benefactors, he now can take on the image of a defender of the Amerindian peoples against the white invaders, though we know too little of his personality to pronounce on it.

SEE: David B. Quinn, ed., *The Roanoke Voyages*, 2 vols. 1955, which contains all of the extant sources.

DAVID B. QUINN

Wannamaker, William Hane *(28 Sept. 1873–2 Aug. 1958)*, educator and university administrator, was born in Bamberg, S.C., the son of Francis Marion and Eleanor Margaret Bellinger Wannamaker. His father, a scholarly planter and lawyer, saw that William was educated by private tutors and in the public schools of St. Matthews, S.C. In 1891 the young man entered Wofford College, in Spartanburg, S.C., where he lived in the home of President Henry N. Snyder, joined Chi Phi fraternity, and was graduated with Phi Beta Kappa honors in 1895. Wannamaker earned a portion of his college expenses by working during the summers as a railroad telegrapher. Among his instructors at Wofford were John C. Kilgo and William Preston Few; Kilgo was named president of Trinity College in Durham, N.C., in 1894, and Few joined the Trinity faculty as professor of English in 1896. After his graduation from college Wannamaker was a school principal in Mullins, S.C., for a year before becoming principal of the first public high school in Spartanburg, a post he held for four years.

In 1900 W. P. Few invited him to enroll at Trinity College as a graduate student and instructor in English and German. After receiving an A.M. degree from Trinity the next spring, Wannamaker entered the graduate school of Harvard University, where he studied German and earned a second master's degree in 1902. Although offered a faculty position at Trinity College, he first spent additional time studying at Harvard and at the universities of Berlin, Tübingen, Leipzig, and Bonn before accepting the post of professor of Germanic language and literature at Trinity in the fall of 1905.

Wannamaker soon became known as an effective and dedicated teacher, but, with some misgivings, he became increasingly involved in the administration of the college. When Few was named president of Trinity in 1910, Wannamaker joined the school's administrative committee. In the summer of 1917 he became dean of the college. This duty was delayed briefly by military training in 1918 at Plattsburgh, N.Y., where he earned the rank of second lieutenant and was named adjutant of the Trinity College detachment of the Student Army Training Corps. As dean, Wannamaker was responsible for such areas as curriculum and student life. A stern but fair disciplinarian, he took a personal interest in the welfare of each student. After assuming the deanship, he remained an active member of the German department for several years.

In 1926, two years following the metamorphosis of Trinity College into Duke University, Wannamaker was name vice-president in the Division of Education and dean of the university, responsible for its academic activities, including faculty recruitment and development. He also continued as dean of Trinity College, now the undergraduate men's unit, until 1942. Under the "triumvirate" of President W. P. Few, Vice-President Robert L. Flowers, and Wannamaker, Duke University became a respected leader of higher education in the South.

In addition to his administrative duties, Wannamaker was an editor of the *South Atlantic Quarterly* (1919–55) and for many years headed the university's faculty committee on athletics. In the latter role he was largely responsible for the growth and success of the school's intercollegiate sports program. He brought famed football coach Wallace Wade to Duke and supported the construction of new athletic facilities, but he was equally concerned about the proper relationship between academic and athletic affairs. He represented the university in the Southern Conference and for several terms was president of that rule-making athletic body.

Active as well in civic affairs, Wannamaker served on the Durham County (1916–18) and city (1923–47) boards of education; he was chairman of the city board for twenty-two years (1925–47). He was a trustee of Durham's Watts Hospital and an active Rotarian. During World War II he was a member of both the university and state Councils of Defense.

Wannamaker was small in stature and unassuming by nature, but his industriousness and diligence made him a most successful administrator. He was awarded honorary degrees by Wofford College (Litt.D., 1917) and Duke University (LL.D., 1953). On his retirement in 1948 he was named vice-chancellor of Duke University, an advisory post with lifetime tenure. A dormitory and a roadway at Duke are named in his honor, and a portrait of "Dean" Wannamaker, given by former students, hangs in the Duke University Library.

Wannamaker married Isabel Stringfellow (d. 1957) of Chester, S.C., on 30 June 1903. They had four children: Margaret Elizabeth, William Hane, Isabel, and Harriet Foote. Wannamaker, a Democrat and a Methodist, died in Pinebluff and was buried in Maplewood Cemetery, Durham.

SEE: *Duke Alumni Register* (May 1925); J. Skottowe Wannamaker, *The Wannamaker, Salley, Mackay, and Bellinger Families* (1937); William Hane Wannamaker Papers (Duke University Archives, Durham); *Who's Who in America* (1948–49).

MARK C. STAUTER

Ward, Hallet Sydney *(31 Aug. 1870–31 Mar. 1956)*, lawyer, state senator, solicitor, and congressman, was born near Gatesville, the son of Nathaniel Owens, a farmer and a soldier for the Confederacy, and Elizabeth Matthew Ward. Young Ward received a limited education so far as public schooling was concerned due to his rural surroundings. In the home setting, his maternal aunt instructed him using the McGuffy Readers Series. For a short time during his teenage years Colonel George V. Cowper taught him, and he received training from Captain Julien Picot at Como in Hertford County. He then studied law at The University of North Carolina, from which he was graduated in 1893. He was admitted to the bar in the same year and set up a practice in Winton, moving on to the town of Plymouth in 1895. Beginning in 1899 he served in the state senate, and in 1902–3 he was mayor of Plymouth. From 1904 to 1910 he was solicitor of the First Judicial District, an appointment made by Governor Charles B. Aycock. In this capacity as prosecutor for the state, he acquired the nickname "Hot Stuff," a play on his initials.

One of his cases, in particular, stands out as being controversial. In *State v. Harrison*, more popularly called the "Beasley Kidnapping Case," Ward was able to obtain a conviction of Joshua Harrison for abducting Kenneth Beasley, the only son of Samuel M. Beasley, a farmer and state senator. The accused was defended by two governors, Thomas J. Jarvis, his brother-in-law, and Charles B. Aycock, as well as Ike Meekins, later a federal judge. Despite the personalities involved and the circumstantial evidence, the jury brought in a guilty verdict, which was upheld on appeal. The boy, however, was never found.

Ward was elected to the Sixty-seventh and Sixty-eighth Congresses (1921–25) but declined the candidacy for a third term. Relocating in Washington, N.C., he formed a law partnership with Junius D. Grimes, the son of General Bryan Grimes. In 1931 he returned to the state senate with a specific mission: to fight the proposal for a minimum eight-month school term. When Ward was eighty-two, the lawyers of Beaufort County presented him with a gold medal for his service to the community. He wore that medal for the rest of his life.

Ward married Aileen Latham of Plymouth in 1898. Two daughters were born, but they both died in infancy. Mrs. Ward died in 1927 shortly after they moved to Washington, N.C. In 1929 he married Dora Bonner of that town. They had one son, Hallet S., Jr., who became chief judge of the Second Judicial District. An Episcopalian, Hallet Ward, Sr., taught the Men's Bible Class at St. Peter's Episcopal Church in Washington for thirty-four years. He was a member of the Democratic party and of the Patriots of North Carolina. Ward was buried in Oakdale Cemetery, Washington, N.C. His portrait was hung in the district courtroom of the Beaufort County Courthouse.

SEE: *Biog. Dir. Am. Cong.* (1971); Ursula F. Loy and Pauline M. Worthy, *Washington and the Pamlico* (1976); *Prominent People of North Carolina* (1906); Hallet S. Ward, Jr., to Julia J. Hicks, February 1979; Manly Wade Wellman, *Dead and Gone: Classic Crimes of North Carolina* (1954).

JULIA JONES HICKS

Warlick, Absalom (*May 1785–February 1873*), skilled ironworker, was born near Warlick Settlement in West Lincoln County, the son of Daniel II and Maria Margaretta Mosteller Warlick. Daniel Warlick I and Marie Barbara Schindler, the pioneers, were his grandparents. Absalom married Sally Crowder, who gave birth to three children. His sister married Michael Schenck, his partner in the Schenck-Warlick cotton mills.

In 1813 Michael Schenck built the first cotton mill in North Carolina. The seventy-two spindle mill was water-powered like most early mills. It was engaged in spinning, not weaving. Warlick made gears and shafting for the machinery, as he did in their mill built in 1816. Both mills were located near McDaniel's Springs, two miles east of Lincolnton. The second mill was built because the dam broke in 1816. Farther down the branch on Warlick's land, the second dam was constructed on a solid rock shoal that can be seen today. Warlick and Schenck agreed in 1816 to pay Michael Beam $1,300 for machinery for the second mill. The rest of the machinery came from Providence, R.I. According to Warlick family history, Absalom's three brothers—Daniel, David, and John—had shares in the cotton mill. Because their sister Barbara died in 1815, they were not tied to Schenck. Thus, they sold their shares and moved to Cleveland County. Schenck formed a new partnership in 1818 that constructed a larger mill at what became Laboratory, near Lincolnton.

Before 1820, Warlick moved to Lawndale. After his wife died in 1856, he lived with his daughter, Jane Jones. On his own death he left an estate worth $744. At that time he owned 122 acres. He was buried at Palm Tree United Methodist Church near Lawndale.

SEE: Curtis Bynum, *Marriage Bonds of Tryon and Lincoln Counties* (1929); Cleveland County Records of Accounts, 1868–77 (North Carolina State Archives, Raleigh); Richard W. Griffin, "The Schenck-Warlick Cotton Factory near Lincolnton, N.C." (a folder published by the American Cynamid Co., 1965); Lincolnton *Lincoln Times*, 28 Sept. 1959; William L. Saunders, ed., *Colonial Records of North Carolina*, vol. 8 (1890); David Schenck, *Historical Records of the Schenck and Bivens Families* (1884); William L. Sherrill, *Annals of Lincoln County, North Carolina* (1937); Alfred Caldwell Warlick, Sr., *Daniel Warlick of Lincoln County, North Carolina, and His Descendants* (n.d.).

MICHAEL EDGAR GOINS

Warlick, Wilson (*8 Mar. 1892–30 Jan. 1978*), judge and lawyer, was born in Catawba County, the son of Thomas McCorkle and Martha Elizabeth Wilson Warlick. He spent his entire life in Catawba County, where he owned 300 acres inherited from his great-great-grandfather, Mathew Wilson, a Scottish Presbyterian who obtained the land by a grant from King George II on 3 Oct. 1775. Warlick was graduated from Catawba College with a bachelor of science degree and received a bachelor of laws degree from The University of North Carolina in 1913, when he passed the bar. He practiced law in Newton for four years before enlisting as a private in World War I. He served in France with the Army's Corps of Intelligence Police, then returned to Newton to resume his career.

On 13 Jan. 1949 President Harry S Truman nominated Warlick to be a federal court judge in the Western North Carolina District. Succeeding Judge E. Yates Webb, who retired, Warlick was sworn in on 14 February in Charlotte.

A staunch believer in the probation system, Judge Warlick developed an installment plan by which federal prisoners who received suspended sentences could work out monthly payments on fines accompanying the time given. His plan paid off, with only a 6 percent return of offenders on later charges by 1963, a record for which he credited the close supervision of probation authorities.

Warlick was an elder in the Presbyterian church and a member of the Masons, Kiwanis Club, Elks Club, Moose Lodge, and Catawba Country Club. He also helped organize Newton Post 16 of the American Legion. On 24 Oct. 1925 he married Kittie Reed Hipp of Ellijay, Ga. They had two children: Mrs. William I. (Martha) Brame of North Wilkesboro and Thomas Wilson, an attorney in Newton.

Once asked what characteristics made a good judge, Warlick replied that patience, clear-minded and logical thinking, and "the ability to see both sides of the controversy" were the most important. He summed up his philosophy in this verse: "Whip light and drive slow, and pay your way before you go." He died in an automobile accident in Newton and was buried there.

SEE: *Asheville Citizen*, 14 Jan. 1949; *Charlotte Observer*, 31 Jan. 1978; *Durham Morning Herald*, 17 Mar. 1963; *Greensboro Daily News*, 7 Apr. 1948; *North Carolina Biography*, vol. 4 (1929); Raleigh *News and Observer*, 18 June 1948; *Who's Who in the South and Southwest* (1967–68, 1969–70).

KEVIN B. HANEY

Warner, Yardley (*2 Nov. 1815–4 Jan. 1885*), educator, lawyer, minister, and freedman's friend, was born at Warner homestead, Penn's Manor Farm, in Bucks County, Pa., the son of William and Letitia Field Warner, both of whom descended from generations of Quakers. He attended Westtown School in Pennsylvania, studied law under John Cadwallader in Philadelphia, and was admitted to the bar in 1838 at age twenty-three. Warner did not practice long, for in the same year he returned to Westtown as a teacher. He stayed until 1841, when he opened a private boarding school for Quaker girls at East Whiteland, Chester County, Pa. In 1842 he married Hannah Allen, who died on 25 Oct. 1872.

From 1858 to 1861 Yardley and Hannah Warner were joint superintendents of the Ohio Yearly Meeting Boarding School at Mount Pleasant, Ohio. After resigning this position they returned to Pennsylvania, but little is known of them until 1863, when they were again at Westtown.

Following the Emancipation Proclamation in 1863 Friends (Quakers) in New England, Pennsylvania, Ohio, and elsewhere saw the urgent need for assisting the freed slaves. The Friends Freedman's Association, formed in Philadelphia, raised money to establish schools for the former slaves but soon realized that there was a greater demand for well-trained black teachers. The association established normal schools in Virginia, Tennessee, North Carolina, and other Southern states. Warner spent several years traveling to these places, helping to open new schools, visiting those already in existence, distributing literature, and giving aid as required.

As a part of this work, he left Philadelphia in 1865 and went to Greensboro, where he bought 35.5 acres of land in the southeast quadrant of the city and sold it to free blacks in small parcels at a low cost. He also built a schoolhouse, organized the Warner Day School for black children, and taught black adults crafts and agriculture. Warner, who maintained his home in this black community, was severely criticized, even ostracized, by whites. The area became known as Warnersville, and, although the old homes were replaced by a redevelopment housing project, its residents still referred to it by this name in the late twentieth century. In 1972 grateful descendants of these early residents erected a monument to Warner's memory.

When this phase of his work in the South was completed, he spent several years as the superintendent of Pales Monthly Meeting School in Radnorshire, Wales. While there he married Anne Elizabeth Horne, matron of the Hospital for Children in London, and they became the parents of Stafford Allen, Joseph Yardley, and Charles Horne. The family returned to America in 1881 and lived in Jonesboro, Tenn., where Warner conducted the Freedman's Normal School, also known as the Warner Institute. In 1883 they went to Burlington, N.J., for a brief time before being received into the membership of Springfield Monthly Meeting of Friends, near High Point, N.C., in 1884. They resided at Bush Hill, now Archdale, where

Warner taught in the Little Davie, a private school for black children.

Warner died of typhoid fever at age seventy and was buried in the Springfield Monthly Meeting Cemetery. After his death Anne Warner and her three young sons returned to England.

SEE: *Greensboro Daily News*, 30 Aug. 1964, 1 Mar. 1976; *Greensboro Record*, 22 Feb. 1972; Stafford A. Warner, *Yardley Warner the Freedman's Friend . . .* (1957 [portrait]); Evelyn S. Whiting Paper (Quaker Collection, Guilford College Library, Greensboro).

TREVA W. MATHIS

Warren, Edward (*22 Jan. 1828–16 Sept. 1893*), physician and surgeon, the son of Dr. William C. and Harriet J. Alexander Warren, was born in Tyrrell County, but both of his parents were of prominent Virginia families. His father was a physician who practiced in Edenton. After attending the local school, Edward Warren, at fifteen, went to a boarding school in Fairfax, Va. He was graduated from the medical department of the University of Virginia in 1850 and received an M.D. degree from Jefferson Medical College in 1851. Warren practiced with his father until 1854, when he went to Paris for further study. While there he acted as correspondent for the *American Journal of Medical Sciences*. He had several noted teachers and made a special friend of Jean Martin Charcot, who years later helped him to begin a practice in Paris.

Warren returned to Edenton in the summer of 1855 and resumed his practice with his father. In 1856, for an essay on "The Influence of Pregnancy on the Development of Tuberculosis," he won the Fisk Fund prize, given by the Rhode Island Medical Society, which later published his essay. In 1857 he became editor of the *Medical Journal of North Carolina*, the first issue of which was published in August 1858; its last issue appeared in September 1861. Also in 1857 he married Elizabeth Cotten Johnston of Edenton. In 1860, partly because of the fact that his wife suffered from malaria, he accepted an offer to become professor of materia medica and therapeutics at the University of Maryland in Baltimore. With the outbreak of war in 1861 he returned to the South and held several important positions in the medical service of the Confederacy. Among these were chief surgeon of the navy of North Carolina, medical director of the Department of the Cape Fear, chief medical inspector of the Department of Northern Virginia, and surgeon general of North Carolina.

In 1865, after the war, Warren went back to Baltimore. As his former position at the University of Maryland was not available, he joined with some other physicians in reorganizing the old Washington University Medical School, whose charter was renewed in 1868. The school reopened, but in 1871 he and several other faculty members withdrew because of differences of opinion in regard to management. He then helped to develop the College of Physicians and Surgeons, which later absorbed the older Washington University school.

In 1875 Warren accepted service with the khedive and moved to Egypt, where he was appointed chief surgeon of the General Staff. He performed a successful operation, removal of a tumor and relief of an inguinal hernia, on Kassim Pasha, the minister of war, whom Egyptian surgeons had been unable to treat. Because of this he was given the honorary or courtesy title of "Bey" by the khedive and became so well known that he immediately had a large practice. However, he remained in Egypt less than two years, as he developed ophthalmia and went to Paris for treatment. His physician there advised against returning to Egypt. His excellent reputation, together with the help of Charcot and other friends, enabled him to shortly establish a practice in Paris, where he remained until his death. His wife, who was much younger than he, died in 1879 when she was six months pregnant. Warren was survived by two daughters. His two sons had died in infancy.

Edward Warren became a licentiate of the University of France and received many other honors. Among them, he was made a Knight of the Order of Isabella the Catholic by the Spanish government, was awarded the Cross of the Legion of Honor by France, and held the honorary LL.D. degree from the University of North Carolina (1884). He was one of the first to use a form of hypodermic medication, and he invented a splint for treatment of fracture of the clavicle.

In 1854, when Warren was twenty-six and just beginning his medical career, he contributed six poems to an anthology, *Wood-Note; or, Carolina Carols: A Collection of North Carolina Poetry*, compiled by Mary Bayard Clarke. *"The Rule of Life," An Address Delivered Before the Two Literary Societies of Wake Forest College, June 8, 1859* appeared in 1859 and his *Introductory Lecture Delivered in the University of Maryland . . . October 15, 1860* in 1860. In 1863, in the midst of the Civil War, his 401-page *An Epitome of Practical Surgery for Field and Hospital* was published in Richmond. After the war, when he had returned to Maryland, his *Introductory Lecture, Delivered Before the Faculty and Class of the Medical Department of Washington University . . . October 1, 1867* was also brought out. A volume of 613 pages, *A Doctor's Experiences in Three Continents: In a Series of Letters Addressed to John Norris, M.D., of Baltimore, Md.*, appeared in 1885.

SEE: *Confederate Veteran* 34 (May 1926); Archibald Henderson, "Famous North Carolina Physician Man of Rare Genius," Raleigh *News and Observer*, 5 Apr. 1941; Howard A. Kelly and W. L. Burrage, ed., *Dictionary of American Medical Biography* (1925); *North Carolina Medical Journal* 2 (August 1878); Hubert A. Royster, *The Adventurous Life of Edward Warren Bey* (1937); Edward Warren, *A Doctor's Experiences in Three Continents* (1885); John H. Wheeler, ed., *Reminiscences and Memoirs of North Carolina and Eminent North Carolinians* (1884).

DOROTHY LONG

Warren, Edward Jenner *(23 Dec. 1824–10 Dec. 1876)*, lawyer, jurist, and legislator, was born in Wardsboro, Vt., the third of twelve children of John Parker and Lucy Maynard Wheelock Warren, both of whom descended from a long line of prominent New England Puritans. Two of his great-grandfathers, Nathaniel Warren and Ebenezer Read, and his two grandfathers, Stephen Warren and Asa Wheelock, fought in the American Revolution. Read and Stephen Warren were minutemen who took part in the Battle of Lexington. E. J. Warren's father was a noted physician and botanist in Vermont.

Due to family financial problems, Warren—after graduation from Dartmouth in 1847—moved to North Carolina and became a teacher. While employed at the Washington Academy and the Greenville Male Academy, he studied law. After his admission to the bar in 1848, he established a law practice in Washington, N.C., and soon became one of the most prominent lawyers in eastern North Carolina. One case in particular brought him much unwanted notoriety. During the fall term of 1853 in the Beaufort County Superior Court, Warren had conducted the prosecution of his case masterfully, and the jury convicted the accused of murder. On hearing the verdict, the defendant pulled a

pistol and fired it point blank at Warren. However, the bullet was stopped by a large pocketbook in Warren's breast pocket, just above his heart. The convicted murderer then turned the gun on himself, committing suicide.

Besides his legal career, Warren pursued financial and community interests. In 1855 he helped found the Pamlico Bank in Washington. By the start of the Civil War, he had also become active in politics. From a Federalist-Whig background and himself an old-line Whig, he initially opposed secession. Yet at the same time he believed that Congress should protect Southern rights. When he was running for a seat in the state constitutional convention in February 1861 (which was not held because North Carolinians voted against its convening), he, as he explained it, "advocated the experiment of a peaceable and honorable adjustment of our difficulties upon the basis of constitutional guarantees acceptable to the South," such as the Crittenden Compromise. But by May 1861, as a candidate for the North Carolina Constitutional Convention that voted for secession, he had come to believe that compromise was no longer possible. He argued that the North had demonstrated that it was "united in support of the infamous policy of Lincoln. They intend our subjugation. . . . War exists." Therefore, he contended that "duty, self-respect, safety, [and] liberty" required North Carolina to "dissolve her connection with the Federal Government." Consistent with these beliefs, Warren, as a member of the 1861 convention in May, voted for secession.

During the war he aligned himself with the Conservative party. At the 1861 convention he had voted for former Governor William A. Graham as president of that body and for a resolution that would have required the convention to submit the ordinance of secession to the people for ratification. As a member of the state senate in 1862–64 he consistently voted with the Conservatives and supported Governor Zebulon Vance, one of his closest personal and political friends.

After the war Warren was seated in the 1865 state constitutional convention and voted for the resolution that declared the ordinance of secession, for which he had previously voted, null and void. In the same year, Governor William Holden appointed him one of seven circuit judges in the provisional government. In 1866 Governor Jonathan Worth named him a judge of the superior court, a position he held until July 1868, when a new state constitution was adopted under the provisions of congressional Reconstruction. Warren then formed a law partnership with David M. Carter and devoted his time to the legal profession while the Republicans controlled the state.

In 1870 Warren, now a Democrat, again won a seat in the state senate. During the campaign, he had claimed that he had no desire for the office but felt obligated to accept his party's nomination—which had been made without his knowledge. Explaining his political views, he said that he believed the South should have been treated with less severity and that congressional Republicans had been harsh with the South for political reasons. Yet he acquiesced to many of the Reconstruction measures. He stated that he would retain such Republican-initiated changes as the new suffrage provisions enfranchising blacks, the reestablishment of the common schools, and the homestead and personal property exemptions. But he opposed many innovations that the Republican-dominated state legislature had recently passed, including the change to a criminal code similar to that of New York and the abolition of the county court system. He also attacked the large state debt, as well as the supposed corruption and wastefulness in the state under Republican rule. However, he maintained that he did not favor "violent, revolutionary, or vindictive actions."

Elected president of the senate, Warren presided over Governor William Holden's impeachment trial during the 1871–72 session.

On 16 May 1849 he married Deborah Virginia Bonner, the daughter of Colonel Richard H. and Elizabeth Lee Bowen Bonner. Deborah's grandfather, the Reverend Thomas Bowen, was one of the early leaders and founders of Methodism in North Carolina. The Warrens had two children: Charles F., a successful lawyer and second president of the North Carolina Bar Association, and Lucy, who married William Rodman Myers.

Warren died at age fifty from a slow, crippling rheumatism that had inflicted him for fifteen years. For the last six years of his life he had to travel back and forth to his law office in a wheelchair. He was buried in the Episcopal churchyard in Washington, N.C. One biographer described him as a tall man, "with clear-cut features, rather fair complexion, light brown hair and piercing hazel eyes." A photograph is among his papers in the Southern Historical Collection at The University of North Carolina.

The North Carolina Bar Association eulogized Warren as a "very able lawyer, and a great judge." His law partner, David M. Carter, said that he was "a man of the strictest and sternest integrity." Chief Justice Walter Clark of the North Carolina Supreme Court believed that he was "one of the most forceful and able men that this state had produced."

SEE: David M. Carter Papers and Van Noppen Papers (Manuscript Department, Duke University Library, Durham); J. G. McCormick, "Personnel of the Convention of 1861," *James Sprunt Historical Monographs*, no. 1 (1900); North Carolina Bar Association, *Proceedings*, vol. 5 (1920); *North Carolina Biography*, vol. 4 (1919); Edward J. Warren Papers (Southern Historical Collection, University of North Carolina, Chapel Hill); L. C. Warren, *Beaufort County's Contribution* (1930); John H. Wheeler, ed., *Reminiscences and Memoirs of North Carolina and Eminent North Carolinians* (1884).

ROBERTA SUE ALEXANDER

Warren, Julius (Jule) Benjamin *(12 Oct. 1887–24 June 1960)*, newspaperman and editor, was born in Durham, the son of Julius B., a tobacconist who built the Globe warehouse, and Corinna Burch Warren, who taught school in Durham. The elder Warren died at age thirty-five when his son was two. Young Jule Warren attended the schools of Durham and was graduated from Trinity College in 1908. At Trinity he was sports editor of the student newspaper, the *Chronicle*, and on the staff of the literary magazine, *Archive*. In 1908 he became athletic coach, history and science teacher, and principal of the Gastonia high school. In 1910 he joined the staff of the *Durham Herald*, where he filled various posts: city editor, advertising manager, circulation manager, managing editor, and editor. From September 1918 to January 1919 he saw limited service with the army, working particularly with the draft boards in Statesville and Durham.

At the completion of his military service Warren moved to Raleigh as political writer and capital correspondent; his articles were syndicated to morning daily papers in Asheville, Charlotte, Durham, Wilmington, Winston-Salem, and elsewhere in the state. In 1922 he helped organize the North Carolina Educational Association and became its chief executive officer, a post he held for twenty years. During that time he served the educational profession well, gaining respect and support for its members. He was also editor of the journal *North Carolina Education*, which he established in 1924. During his tenure a perma-

nent headquarters building was erected on West Morgan Street in Raleigh. Also under his direction numerous publications were issued for teachers and other educators including the effective *Public Relations Handbook*. The February 1936 issue of *North Carolina Education* dealt with the 100-year history of public education in the state. He also spoke frequently to educational, civic, patriotic, religious, and other groups around the state. In 1937 Governor Clyde R. Hoey named Warren to a four-year term on the board of trustees of the North Carolina College for Negroes and to the State School Commission.

In 1941 Warren published a 328-page textbook, *North Carolina Yesterday and Today*, intended for use in the public schools. It was approved for adoption by the State School Commission (of which Warren was a member) in preference to one prepared by Professors Albert Ray Newsome and Hugh T. Lefler of The University of North Carolina faculty. Warren's book contained a commendatory foreword signed by Professor William K. Boyd, a highly regarded professor at Duke University. Almost immediately after copies became available for classroom use, the text fell under severe criticism. Initially several hundred factual errors were pointed out, and in the end more than a thousand were cited.

State education officials were criticized for not having reviewed the text themselves (or having it reviewed by a competent authority), and the role of the State School Commission in accepting a book prepared by one of its own members aroused suspicion of complicity. A considerable sum of public money had been expended in the book's preparation, and various remedies were proposed to make it acceptable. Those already printed were used as long as copies remained in stock, with pages of corrections to accompany them. At his own expense Warren corrected the text for a subsequent printing. At the next selection of textbooks the Newsome-Lefler 472-page book, *The Growth of North Carolina*, was approved, and in updated revisions it remained the choice for many years.

Warren ceased to serve as an officer of the North Carolina Educational Association and instead accepted a position with the North Carolina Citizens Association as editor of its magazine, *We The People*. The first issue under his leadership appeared in May 1943 and the last in June 1960. Continuing his earlier practice of issuing publications useful to the organization he served, he brought out *The People Govern North Carolina* in 1946 and the forty-page *North Carolina Atlas and Outline Maps* in 1947.

On 15 Sept. 1917 he married Hilda Gipe of Chicago, and they became the parents of a daughter, Elizabeth. He was a president of the Raleigh Rotary Club and an officer of the Knights of Pythias. An active member of the Presbyterian church, he served as a deacon and Sunday school superintendent.

SEE: *Asheville Citizen*, 25 June 1960; Clipping files, North Carolina Collection (University of North Carolina, Chapel Hill); David L. Corbitt, ed., *Addresses, Letters, and Papers of Clyde Roark Hoey* (1944); *North Carolina Biography*, vol. 3 (1941); *Trinity Alumni Register*, vols. 4 (January 1910), 8 (July 1922); Jule B. Warren, *North Carolina Yesterday and Today* (1941) (a copy with pencilled corrections by the author is in the North Carolina Collection, University of North Carolina, Chapel Hill); *We the People* 18 (July 1960 [portrait]).

WILLIAM S. POWELL

Warren, Lindsay Carter *(16 Dec. 1889–28 Dec. 1976)*, lawyer, legislator, congressman, and comptroller general of the United States, was born in Washington, Beaufort

County, the son of Charles Frederic and Elizabeth Mutter Blount Warren. He attended the Bingham School in Asheville and The University of North Carolina (1906–8), where he also studied law in 1911–12. Admitted to the bar in 1912, he served as Beaufort County attorney and chairman of the county Democratic executive committee from 1912 to 1925. In 1917 and 1919 he was a member of the state senate. Associated with O. Max Gardner politically, he succeeded Gardner as president pro tempore of the senate when Gardner became lieutenant governor. Gardner, Warren, and J. Melville Broughton were the mainstays of a group of Young Turks in the Democratic party that opposed the Simmons-Bailey faction.

In the 1920 special session of the legislature on woman suffrage, Warren opposed its champion, Gardner; outmaneuvering the proponents, he defeated the proposed amendment in the senate. He served in the house in 1923–25, including the special session in 1924 on state ports.

Warren was elected as a Democrat from the First District to the Sixty-ninth Congress in 1924 and to the seven succeeding Congresses. He remained extremely active in both state and Democratic party affairs. At home he was chairman of the Democratic conventions of 1930 and 1934 and temporary chairman and keynote speaker of the 1938 convention. In 1929 and 1931 he was seriously mentioned as a candidate for governor but refused to run. In 1931 he served on the North Carolina Constitutional Commission and joined Josiah Bailey and Robert R. Reynolds to lead the fight for the repeal of Prohibition.

Warren's career in Congress was greatly influenced by his close friend and political mentor, Speaker and later Vice-President John Nance Garner. Warren was chairman of the House Accounts Committee and served on the following committees: Roads, Special Conservation of Wildlife Resources, Merchant Marine and Fisheries, Select Government Reorganization, and Expenditures in the Executive Departments. His areas of legislative expertise included agriculture, rivers and harbors, the Coast Guard, conservation, and government reorganization. He sponsored and acted as floor leader for the passage of the Merchant Marine Act, Cape Hatteras National Seashore Act, Wright Brothers National Memorial, Executive Reorganization Act of 1939, and Congressional Reapportionment Act of 1940.

On Capitol Hill he was recognized as a skilled parliamentarian and a master of House rules. Although he had a reputation as an effective and influential New Dealer, he did not support President Franklin D. Roosevelt's proposal to pack the Supreme Court. He was twice elected Speaker pro tempore of the House and for a short period after Speaker William B. Bankhead's death, he acted as majority leader. Warren left the House on 1 Nov. 1940 to become comptroller general of the United States; it was as head of the General Accounting Office that he made his most indelible contribution to the nation.

The GAO was in disorder when Warren took over. Since its creation by the Budget and Accounting Act of 1921, the GAO had lacked progressive and innovative leadership. In August 1941, to try to bring some order to the GAO, he created a special planning and budget section. As war spending escalated, he separated cost-plus and other war contracts from the regular audits. On 18 Aug. 1942 he established a division to audit war contracts with field offices throughout the country. Warren argued often and long, but unsuccessfully, for a GAO audit of terminated war contracts, but the Contract Settlement Act of 1944 excluded a meaningful GAO audit from the settlement process.

Another initial concern was the GAO's limited, or total absence of, review of government corporations. From early 1943 to December 1945, when the Government Corporation Control Act was passed, he required GAO audits of the financial transactions of these corporations. To carry out the new commercial-type audits, he created a Corporation Audits Division staffed by professional public accountants. He also was instrumental in including in the 1946 Legislative Reorganization Act provisions that the GAO was authorized to determine whether public funds were administered economically and efficiently, and the Committee on Expenditures in the Executive Department was established to receive GAO reports. In 1952 this became the Committee on Government Operations.

By 1947 Warren's initiatives were taking new directions, as he, Secretary of the Treasury John W. Snyder, and Director of the Budget James E. Webb joined forces to improve accounting, budgeting, and financial reporting procedures. The agenda of these men, their staffs, and the Senate Committee on Expenditures became public knowledge, but the real work in this area was the result of the problem-solving approach of the North Carolina triumvirate: Warren, Webb, and Undersecretary of the Treasurer O. Max Gardner. These three Tar Heels laid the foundations for the Joint Accounting Improvement Program, and Warren formed an Accounting System Division in the GAO to supervise it. The program's significance lay in recognizing the executive branch's concern with management in accounting systems. The GAO redirected its approach from prescribing accounting systems to consulting with agencies in developing accounting methods.

During the same period Warren adopted a comprehensive audit program employing commercial-type audits. These were built on the GAO's experiences in auditing government corporations and its new responsibilities under the Federal Property and Administration Services Act of 1949 for prescribing property accounting systems and auditing them. The Joint Accounting Improvement Program and the Comprehensive Audit Program required the GAO to recruit experts to develop modern financial management practices. These basic changes were enacted into law by the Budget and Accounting Procedures Act of 1950, which placed the major responsibility for financial management practices on the departments and agencies. It allowed the GAO to use the comprehensive audit approach to look beyond simple legality and the propriety of expenditures.

Warren's tenure was characterized by basic redirections in the GAO's role: from antagonism towards executive departments and agencies to cooperation, from limited support of Congress to extensive and detailed programs of aid (audit reports and reviews to Congress increased fivefold), from cursory audits of millions of vouchers to a comprehensive audit, from a policy of concentrating auditing in Washington to audits at regional offices, and finally, a European office, and from GAO mandates on accounting systems to a cooperative program with the Bureau of the Budget and the Treasury Department—the Budget and Accounting Procedures Act of 1950. During the same period Warren withstood an attack by the first Hoover Commission, which had recommended severely limiting the GAO's independence of the executive.

During Warren's last years as comptroller general he reorganized the GAO so that it could better carry out the new directions in accounting procedures he instituted. He proudly pointed to the 1941–54 collections of the GAO, $915 million—more than twice the cost of running the GAO. He also reduced the GAO staff from a peak of 14,906 in 1946 to 5,890 in 1954 while, at the same time, upgrading the personnel.

For reasons of health Warren retired on 30 Apr. 1954 and returned to North Carolina, where he spent much time on the Outer Banks. On 24 Apr. 1958 he participated in the dedication of the Cape Hatteras National Seashore, celebrating his bill of 1937 that created the first national seashore park.

In 1959 he returned to the scene of his earliest legislative battles, the state senate. He successfully led fights against legislative reapportionment and court reform, and for toll-free bridges across Alligator River and Oregon Inlet.

Warren ended his public service in that same chamber. The *News and Observer* explained that although he chaired no committee, represented only a rural area, and was not any more brilliant than several of his peers, he was "the most powerful man in the 1961 Legislature." He dominated its last session—the last to meet in the old state capitol—by controlling a sizable bloc of votes on three key issues: state senatorial redistricting, court reform, and congressional redistricting. His plan for the redistricting of the state senate was accepted despite the objections from representatives of the more populous areas. Further, he amended the proposed Bell-Taylor amendment to the constitution by maintaining the control of the courts with the legislature. Warren believed that the legislature—not the executive or the judiciary—was the true instrument of the people's will. Last, he redrew the congressional boundaries so that eastern North Carolina, though losing population, did not lose a representative. His arguments to sacrifice a Republican and not a Democrat, and his balancing of the political powers in the state, led to the Jonas-Kitchen Bill.

On 10 May 1962 he attended the dedication of the Lindsay Warren Bridge connecting the mainland of the state to the Outer Banks. His health prevented his attending the dedication of the Lindsay Warren Visitor Center at the Fort Raleigh National Historic Site in 1966.

On 27 Jan. 1916 Lindsay married Emily Diana Harris. They had two sons, Lindsay C., Jr., and Charles Frederic, and a daughter, Emily Carter Warren (Jones). He was an Elk and a member of St. Peter's Episcopal Church in Washington, N.C. He was buried in Oakdale Cemetery, Washington.

SEE: *Biog. Dir. Am. Cong.* (1971); J. D. Brown, "The U.S. General Accounting Office's Changing Focus as the Federal Government's Auditor, 1921–1972" (Ph.D. diss., George Washington University, 1973); *Charlotte Observer*, 30 May 1959; *Life* magazine, 20 Mar. 1939; "Lindsay Carter Warren: Comptroller General of the United States, 1940–1954," *GAO Review* (Spring 1977); Manteo *Coastland Times*, 11 May 1962; Joseph L. Morrison, *Governor O. Max Gardner: A Power in North Carolina and New Deal Washington* (1971); David Porter, "Representative Lindsay Warren, the Water Bloc, and the Transportation Act of 1940," *North Carolina Historical Review* 50 (July 1973); Elmer L. Puryear, *Democratic Party Dissension in North Carolina, 1928–1936* (1962); Raleigh *News and Observer*, 12 Dec. 1959, 29 Apr., 25 June 1961; C. Wingate Reed, *Beaufort County: Two Centuries of Its History* (1972); Anna Rothe, ed., *Current Biography: Who's News and Why, 1949* (1949 [portrait]); *Time* magazine, 3 Apr. 1939; Mrs. Emily Harris Warren, personal contact, 25 Apr. 1979; Lindsay C. Warren Papers (Southern Historical Collection, University of North Carolina, Chapel Hill); *Washington [D.C.] Post*, 1 Jan. 1977; *Winston-Salem Sentinel*, 1 June 1961.

W. LEE JOHNSTON

Washburn, Benjamin Earl (*29 Dec. 1885–28 Dec. 1979*), physician and public health officer, was born in Rutherfordton, the son of John Rutherford and Camila Miller Washburn. He was graduated from The University of North Carolina in 1906 and received a master's degree in 1909; in his thesis, entitled "The Uncle Remus Stories," he made a careful study of the language ascribed by the author Joel Chandler Harris to blacks.

Awarded the M.D. degree from the University of Virginia in 1911, he began practicing medicine in the South Mountains of Rutherford County, but after fourteen months he became field director in North Carolina for the Rockefeller Sanitation Commission (1913–14) in campaigns against hookworm disease. He next became health officer of Nash County, one of the first counties in the United States to provide full-time health service. As a member of the staff of the Rockefeller Foundation, he organized the Bureau of County Health Work in the North Carolina State Board of Health in 1919–20. With time out in 1930, he attended the London School of Tropical Medicine and Hygiene, from which he received a certificate in tropical diseases.

Between 1920 and 1940 Washburn was director in foreign service with the Rockefeller Foundation in the West Indies, Central America, and Colombia, Venezuela, and British Guiana in South America. Here he was involved with plans to eradicate hookworm, malaria, tuberculosis, and yaws. Returning home during World War II, he became district health officer with the North Carolina State Board of Health and on the Rutherford County Selective Service Board. Afterwards for several years he held a seat on the District Selective Service Appeal Board.

Washburn was a member of the Governor's Commission on Hospitals and Medical Care (1944), director of the North Carolina Good Health Association (1946), and secretary of the board of trustees of the Rutherford Hospital. For a time he served as health editor of the *Progressive Farmer* magazine. Among other publications, he was the author of *Jamaica Health Stories and Plays*, *The Health Game*, *A County Doctor in the South Mountains*, *As I Recall*, and *Rutherford County and Its Hospital*.

In 1912 Washburn married Zillah Howe, and they had a daughter, Zellah Howe (Mrs. John Pike).

SEE: *Charlotte Observer*, 30 Dec. 1979; *Forest City Courier*, 12 June 1969; Daniel L. Grant, *Alumni History of the University of North Carolina* (1924); William S. Powell, ed., *North Carolina Lives* (1962); *Who's Who in the South and Southwest* (1950).

WILLIAM S. POWELL

Washington, William Henry (*7 Feb. 1813–12 Aug. 1860*), lawyer, congressman, and politician, was born in Wayne County near Goldsboro, the son of Nicholson Washington. He studied law and, after being admitted to the bar in 1835, began to practice in New Bern. A Whig, he was a member of the Twenty-seventh Congress from 1841 to 1843. Declining to seek renomination, he served instead in the North Carolina House of Commons in 1844–45 and 1846–47 and in the North Carolina Senate in 1848–49, 1850–51, and 1852. From 1842 to 1858 he owned the Stevenson House, now a part of the Tryon Palace complex in New Bern.

In 1834 Washington played a significant role in securing passage of legislation to establish the North Carolina Railroad. He also was active in the creation of the New Bern Literary Society, organized in 1843, which he once headed. In an address to the society on one occasion, he contrasted the nature of the English and French as demonstrated by the difference in their revolutions.

On 12 Aug. 1835 in Christ Episcopal Church, New Bern, he married Caroline H. Blount, the second daughter of Dr. Frederick Blount of New Bern. They had two children, Frederick Nicholson and Anna Maria. Washington died in New Bern and was buried in Cedar Grove Cemetery.

SEE: *Biog. Dir. Am. Cong.*, (1950); John L. Cheney, Jr., ed., *North Carolina Government, 1585–1979* (1981); Christ Episcopal Church Register, New Bern; *Raleigh Register and North Carolina Gazette*, 12 Aug. 1835; Alan D. Watson, *A History of New Bern and Craven County* (1987).

JOHN D. NEVILLE

Waters, Vincent Stanislaus (15 Aug. 1904–3 Dec. 1974), Roman Catholic prelate, was born in Roanoke, Va., the son of Michael Bernard, a railroad machinist, and Mary Francis Crowley Waters. He attended St. Andrews School (1911–20), Belmont Abbey College, Belmont (1920–25), St. Mary's Seminary, Baltimore (1926–28), and North American College, Rome, Italy (1928–32). On 8 Dec. 1931 he was ordained to the priesthood at North American College. Waters was assistant pastor of Holy Cross Church, Lynchburg, Va. (1936); chancellor of the Diocese of Richmond (1936–43); and director of Diocesan Missions Fathers and work with Trailer Mission (1943–45). Appointed bishop of Raleigh on 10 Mar. 1945, he was consecrated on 15 May and installed on 6 June. The Diocese of Raleigh covered 52,000 square miles.

The Most Reverend Vincent S. Waters, who traveled widely in North Carolina, founded the *North Carolina Catholic* (1947) and the North Carolina Catholic Laymen's Association, which later included the "Confraternity of Christian Doctrine." He made wide use of motor chapels. At his invitation two orders of Carmelites founded convents in eastern and western parts of the state. In 1953 he issued a pastoral letter ordering racial integration in Catholic churches in the diocese. He made a pilgrimage to the Holy Land in 1959 and participated in the sessions of Vatican Council II, the twenty-first general council of the Roman Catholic church.

The holder of an honorary doctor of divinity degree, the churchman was selected "Tar Heel of the Week" by the Raleigh *News and Observer* in 1964. In 1961 he had moved into Little Maryknoll, the new residence of the bishop of Raleigh at 600 Bilyeu Street (formerly the episcopal residence had been at Sacred Heart Cathedral on McDowell Street). He was six feet two inches tall, dignified, genial, scholarly, and a good public speaker. In early years he had been a member of the Appalachian Trail Club.

In 1972 the Diocese of Raleigh was divided: the forty-six western counties became the Diocese of Charlotte (under the supervision of Michael J. Begley), and the fifty-four easternmost counties remained in the Diocese of Raleigh.

Bishop Waters died five days before the Fiftieth Anniversary Celebration and Solemn Commencement of the 1975 Holy Year, held in December 1974. His funeral was at Sacred Heart Cathedral, Raleigh, with interment in the city's Memorial Park.

SEE: *American Catholic Who's Who, 1968–1969* (1968); Biographical sketch of Vincent S. Waters (provided by the Most Reverend Gerald Lewis, Chancellor, Diocese of Raleigh); Raleigh *News and Observer*, 23 Oct., 4–9 Dec. 1974, 9 Apr., 17, 20 May 1975, *Raleigh Times*, 8, 9 Dec. 1974, 18 Jan., 8 Apr., 17, 20 May 1975; Vincent S. Waters, personal contact, 15 July 1970.

GRADY L. E. CARROLL

Watkins, Franklin Chennault (30 Dec. 1894–4 Dec. 1972), artist, was born in New York City, the son of Benjamin Franklin and Shirley Chennault Watkins. His father, a Reidsville, N.C., native, was an inventor and made a career of developing and marketing patents. Having sold a patent to the British government for a new method of gold mining for a large sum, he maintained a bachelor existence in Europe for many years prior to marriage. His wife, a native of Louisville, Ky., was eighteen years younger than he. Her sister was the mother of the poet Ogden Nash, whose paternal ancestors were prominent in the history of North Carolina. Benjamin and Shirley Watkins were the parents of two sons and two daughters. The other son, Edmund, was a newspaperman in the Philadelphia area and an author of some note, contributing short stories to *Scribner's* magazine and the *Southern Review*. A novel, *The Palace of Dim Night*, was published in 1965.

As an infant Watkins was taken to London, where the family then resided. During childhood and adolescence he lived at various times in Rye, N.Y., Louisville, Ky., and Winston-Salem. Due to the uncertain nature of his father's income, Watkins was reared in an atmosphere of alternating affluence and financial difficulties. Entering Groton in 1908, he had to leave in 1910 because money was tight. He then matriculated at The University of North Carolina but left after four days, not finding the school congenial. Watkins then spent a year at the University of Virginia. Several terms at the University of Pennsylvania followed. In 1913, having decided on art as a career, he entered the Academy of Fine Arts in Philadelphia, an institution with for the remainder of his life. During World War I he did camouflage work for the U.S. Navy, and from 1918 to 1923 he was employed as an artist by the Philadelphia advertising firm of N. W. Ayer.

Franklin Watkins was little known in the art world until, at age thirty-seven, he suddenly received national recognition when his entry *Suicide in Costume* won first prize at the Carnegie International Exhibition in 1931. The oil painting, in an oval frame with a horizontal orientation, shows a male figure in a clown costume, lying on a table and holding a smoking gun. This picture, touching as it does on such basic human feelings, aroused so much controversy that the artist kept a low profile for several years afterwards. The painting now hangs in the Philadelphia Museum of Art.

On achieving success, Watkins enjoyed a wide patronage among the rich and prominent in Philadelphia. He became chiefly known as a portrait painter, though he painted still lifes, landscapes, and animals as well and executed the murals in the Rodin Museum on Philadelphia's parkway. Commissioned to paint President Franklin D. Roosevelt in 1941, he and his wife went on a short vacation to North Carolina's Outer Banks prior to beginning the work. While they were there, Pearl Harbor was attacked, and the president never had time to sit for the portrait. Among Watkins's many sitters were Dr. Jefferson B. Fordham, a North Carolina native and dean of the University of Pennsylvania Law School, and Dr. Eugene Strecker, the noted psychiatrist. An important commission was his portrait of the three Beinecke brothers, painted in 1969 for the Beinecke Rare Book room and manuscript library at Yale.

Watkins's portraits were at times controversial. He said that he painted what he saw in the sitter and did not strive for an exact likeness. His portrait of Joseph Clark, the Democratic reform mayor of Philadelphia, which showed the subject standing with arms folded and looking down, was not well received. It was only at Clark's insistence that the city accepted the picture. In his portraits Watkins has been said to have been influenced by Thomas Eakins, his great predecessor at the Academy of Fine Arts.

During his distinguished career Watkins, or Watty as he was known to his friends, received innumerable awards and honors both in Europe and America. His alma mater, the Academy of Fine Arts, gave him the three gold medals at its disposal. In 1934 he held his first one-man show at the Rehn Gallery in New York. The Philadelphia Museum of Art honored Watkins and his close friend Arthur B. Carles with an exhibition in 1946. A major show of his work took place at New York's Museum of Modern Art in 1950, and a retrospective was staged at the Philadelphia Museum in 1964. A member of many prestigious organizations and boards, including the American Academy in Rome, he was awarded a doctorate in fine arts by Franklin and Marshall College in 1954. His paintings now hang in thirty major museums. Watkins occasionally contributed articles to art periodicals, the most important of which, "An Artist Talks to His Students," was published in the *Magazine of Art* in December 1941.

Throughout his life he painted pictures of a religious nature. Critics have noted the influence of William Blake. The Vatican Museum in Rome, having built a wing for contemporary art, selected Watkins as one of six American artists to be represented and chose a large painting of the Crucifixion. The wing had been scheduled to open in October 1972, and Watkins and his wife went to Italy for the event. The opening was delayed and they decided to remain in Europe. However, he was stricken and died in Bologna.

Franklin Watkins was a tall, handsome, urbane man. A self-portrait, exhibited in the 1964 retrospective at the Philadelphia museum, is in a private collection. He was married first in 1927, to Fredolyn Gimble, daughter of Ellis Gimble, the department store magnate. The marriage ended in divorce in 1942. He then married Mrs. Ida Quigley Furst, a native of Lock Haven, Pa. There were no children by either marriage.

Watkins, though born in New York City, was proud of his southern heritage and claimed North Carolina as home. The family had lived on Fifth Street in Winston-Salem in 1910 and 1911. As a former resident of that city, he exhibited oil paintings at the Piedmont Festival of Music and Art in 1944 and 1946. A few years before his death, he and his wife visited the Watkins ancestral home in Reidsville. An early study in oil of a reclining nude is in the collection of the Ackland Museum at Chapel Hill.

SEE: Henry Clifford, introduction to *Catalogue, Philadelphia Museum of Art* (1964); Jaquelin Nash (Tarboro), personal contact; *Philadelphia Inquirer*, selected articles; Andrew Richie, introduction to catalogue, *Museum of Modern Art* (1950); Francis Speight, personal contact; F. W. Watkins, personal contact; Ben Wolfe, *Franklin C. Watkins: Portrait of a Painter* (1966); *Who's Who in America* (1976); *Who's Who in American Art* (1989).

CLAIBORNE T. SMITH, JR.

Watson, Alfred Augustin (*21 Aug. 1818–21 Apr. 1905*), Episcopal bishop, was born in Brooklyn, N.Y., to Jesse and Hannah Maria Watson. He was graduated from New York University with a B.A. degree in 1837 and studied law in the office of Chancellor James Kent. Admitted to the bar in 1841, he gave up the practice of law to tutor the children of Josiah Collins of Somerset Plantation in Washington County, N.C. His parents were Presbyterians, but Watson became interested in the Episcopal services of the plantation household. Confirmed in the Episcopal church,

he decided to study for its ministry and entered the General Theological Seminary in New York City. He was ordained deacon on 3 Nov. 1844 by Bishop Benjamin Onderdonk of New York and took charge of Grace Church, Plymouth, N.C., also serving St. Luke's, Washington County, and other missions, and helping to establish the Church of the Advent, Williamston. On 25 May 1845 he was ordained priest by Bishop Levi Silliman Ives, to whom he remained loyal until the bishop went over to the Church of Rome. After traveling in Europe for his health in 1855, Watson launched a campaign for a new church building in Plymouth.

After twice refusing calls to Christ Church, New Bern, he deferred to Bishop Thomas Atkinson's advice and accepted a third invitation in August 1858. To his new parish and its school he gave the same zeal and devotion that he had demonstrated at Plymouth. In July 1861 he became chaplain to the Second Regiment of Infantry, North Carolina State Troops, while continuing as rector of Christ Church. The next year, having resigned his commission and no longer being able to officiate in occupied New Bern, he was attached to the military hospital at Goldsboro.

In March 1863 Watson became assistant to Bishop Atkinson, who had taken over as rector of St. James's Church, Wilmington, on the death of the Reverend Dr. Robert B. Drane. Watson succeeded to the rectorship in December 1864. When, at the bishop's direction, he refused to offer prayers for the president of the United States, Federal forces occupied his church as a hospital and ordered him to leave Wilmington. Nevertheless, he remained on suffrance and continued to minister in private homes and at St. Paul's Church. In December 1865 he resumed services at St. James's, which his parishioners repaired without Federal compensation, and together they brought about a full recovery of the parish with increases in members, contributions, and property valuation.

In the matter of reunion with the Northern dioceses he differed with Bishop Atkinson, who participated in it. The University of North Carolina honored Alfred Watson, the New York native, in 1868 with a doctorate in divinity. During his rectorship, St. James's Parish supported St. Mark's Mission for the Negroes and St. James's House, later the Mission of the Good Shepherd. Watson played an important part in diocesan affairs, serving as a member and chairman of major committees and president of the diocesan convention, examining chaplain, delegate to the General Convention, and trustee of the General Seminary.

When, in 1883, the new Diocese of East Carolina was created after nearly twenty years of debate over division, Watson, who presided over the organizing convention, was unanimously chosen its first bishop. He was consecrated in his parish church of St. James on 17 Apr. 1884. The University of the South conferred on him the D.D. degree. Bishop Watson was preoccupied with continuing problems of men and money—finding and holding clergymen and securing adequate financial support from a relatively poor rural and agricultural area for diocesan missions. He commended the church's institutions of learning, particularly those in East Carolina: Trinity School at Chocowinity and St. Paul's School at Beaufort. In 1890 he traveled in Europe. Until overtaken by bodily infirmities he performed faithfully his duties as rural parish priest and later as chief pastor of the diocese, which he shepherded through its formative years and only relinquished at his death. He was buried in Wilmington's Oakdale Cemetery, leaving to his beloved diocese his library and part of his estate, which became the Bishop Watson Fund for the Support of the Episcopate.

Alfred Watson was married three times. His first wife soon died, as did their infant child. Watson then married Fannie Livingston of New York and after her death, Mrs. Mary Catherine Lord. He had a sister, Elizabeth Watson, and two half sisters, Mary Wendell and Mrs. Augusta Palfrey. Elizabeth and Mary lived in his home and shared with his wife in his estate.

SEE: *Appleton's Cyclopedia of American Biography*, vol. 6 (1899); Samuel A. Ashe, ed., *Cyclopedia of Eminent and Representative Men of the Carolinas*, vol. 2 (1892); Lawrence F. Brewster, "Alfred Augustin Watson: Episcopal Clergyman and the New South," *East Carolina College Publications in History* 3 (1966); Gertrude Carraway, *Crown of Life* (1940); *Journals of the Diocese of East Carolina* (1883–); *Journals of the Diocese of North Carolina* (1844–); *Mission Herald*, 1894–; Charles L. Van Noppen, "Biographical Sketch of Bishop Watson," in Additional Sketches for Ashe's *Biographical History of North Carolina* (Manuscript Department, Duke University Library, Durham); Wilmington *Morning Star*, 22 Apr. 1905.

LAWRENCE F. BREWSTER

Watson, Cyrus Barksdale (14 Jan. 1845–12 Nov. 1916), legislator, attorney, and politician, was born in that part of Stokes County, near Kernersville, that is now in Forsyth County. He was the son of John W. and Maria Folger Watson. His paternal grandfather was Drewry Watson, a native of Scotland who settled in Prince Edward County, Va., in 1740 and married a Barksdale of Halifax County, Va., for whom his grandson was named. Watson's formal education began when he entered the school at Kernersville at age fifteen, but he soon left to join the Confederate army.

In the spring of 1863 he enlisted as a private in Company K, Forty-fifth North Carolina Regiment, at Camp Mangum near Raleigh. This unit saw action in the Army of Northern Virginia, Ewell's Corps, Rhodes's Division. Watson, whose highest rank was second sergeant, was wounded three times; on the third occasion, at Spottsylvania in May 1864, his shoulder was shattered. Though not expected to live, he recuperated at home and returned to action before the end of the year. The wound reopened, however, and he went home. In March 1865 Watson again joined his regiment, this time near Richmond, unable to bear a gun. His unit was then ordered west to Appomattox. His shoulder wound continued to trouble him for the rest of his life.

After the war Watson was employed in farming and as a store clerk, first in Kernersville and later in High Point. In 1866 he began to study law in Lexington under James Madison Leach, who had served in both the U.S. and Confederate Congresses. Admitted to the bar in 1869, he entered the legal profession in Winston, then a village of between four and five hundred people. His lifelong practice there was interrupted only by his service in the General Assembly.

On 14 Nov. 1869 Watson married A. E. Henley, the daughter of W. F. Henley. They had five children: Mary, Alice, Fred, Netta, and Thomas.

In 1868 Watson was elected as a Democrat to the state senate and served two terms. A fluent debater, he was a practical and hardworking senator. In 1892 he was elected to the lower house of the General Assembly and served a single term. Among his committee assignments in the legislature were those on internal improvements, the judiciary, the code, and redistricting.

In 1896 Watson was nominated by his party for governor. The election came during the period of Republican-Populist fusion when three parties ran gubernatorial candidates. Republican Daniel L. Russell won a plurality, and Watson became the first Democrat to suffer defeat since Reconstruction. In 1898 the Democrats regained control of both houses in the General Assembly. The next year Watson was one of the attorneys in the impeachment trial of Republican Chief Justice David M. Furches and Associate Justice Robert M. Douglas. In 1903 he was an unsuccessful candidate for the Democratic nomination to the U.S. Senate and thereafter continued to practice law in Winston.

Watson was a member of the Methodist church, the Norfleet Camp of Confederate Veterans, and the Winston-Salem Bar Association. He died after a long illness and was buried in the Salem Cemetery, Winston-Salem.

SEE: Samuel A. Ashe, ed., *Biographical History of North Carolina*, vol. 4 (1906 [portrait]); Walter Clark, ed., *Histories of the Several Regiments and Battalions from North Carolina in the Great War*, vol. 3 (1901); Robert F. Durden, *Reconstruction Bonds and Twentieth-Century Politics* (1962); Daniel H. Hill, Jr., ed., *Confederate Military History*, vol. 4 (1899); Weymouth T. Jordan, comp., *North Carolina Troops, 1861–1865: A Roster*, vol. 11 (1987); *North Carolina Biography*, vol. 4 (1928); Raleigh *News and Observer*, 26–27 June 1896, 12, 19 Nov. 1916 [portrait]; Donald W. Stanley, comp., *Forsyth County, North Carolina, Cemetery Records*, vol. 4 (1976); John S. Thomlinson, *North Carolina Assembly Sketch Book* (1883).

THOMAS H. JOHNSON, JR.

Watson, Henry Bulls (16 Oct. 1812–25 Jan. 1869), professional military officer, was born in Johnston County, the son of Willis and Elizabeth (Betsy) Bulls Watson. Nothing is known of his early education, but on 5 Oct. 1836, more than a year after he sought acceptance, he was commissioned a second lieutenant in the Marine Corps. Like other new officers at that time, he was assigned to Marine Corps headquarters in Washington for military and administrative training. While stationed there, he met and on 18 Apr. 1837 married Mary Ann Higdon. Their son, Josiah Ogden Watson, was born on 14 Jan. 1838. In late October of that year the twenty-six-year-old lieutenant, with twenty-eight enlisted men in his charge, departed for New York. Early in December they became a part of the guard aboard the 74-gun ship of the line *Ohio* bound for the Mediterranean.

It was late summer of 1841 before Watson returned to the United States. Following a leave of absence to visit North Carolina, he was assigned to duty in Washington for the winter. At his own request he was stationed in Norfolk in the spring of 1842 and afterwards assigned to the Marine barracks at Gosport, Va., settling his wife and son in Portsmouth. In December 1844 orders came from fellow North Carolinian Brevet Brigadier General Commandant Archibald Henderson to "join one of the Sloops of War to sail from Norfolk on a cruise." Watson elected to sail on the *Jamestown*, headed for the coast of Africa. A more senior lieutenant than Watson took charge of the Marine Guard. Watson, however, on 9 Jan. 1845 was given command of the Marine Guard on the sloop-of-war *Portsmouth*. His orders directed him to pay "careful attention to the Military efficiency of the guard under your command, and to the health and comfort of the soldiers comprising it."

When the commission and the jurisdiction expired together on 26 Jan. 1845 it seemed that the United States and Mexico were on the verge of war. The United States had recently annexed Texas; Mexico considered this an act of aggression and was about to take steps to recover its lost territory. North Carolina–born President James K. Polk was unable to stem the tide sweeping the nation to war. In California a general from Mexico arrived to take charge of that region as governor, but Californians promptly drove him out. Fear that a foreign power, including Great Britain, might move in to occupy California led the United States to take steps to prevent such action. A squadron of U.S. ships kept watch over movement along the Pacific coast, and the *Portsmouth* joined them.

Lieutenant Henry Watson kept detailed journals of this cruise, which lasted more than two and a half years. He was in San Francisco Bay aboard the *Portsmouth* when its commodore claimed California for the United States. A small band of Marines and sailors under Watson occupied Yerba Buena (now San Francisco) and displayed the American flag. Soon afterwards he was placed in command of the force that occupied the town and held it from July to November 1846. Watson also participated in the overland march from San Diego to take Los Angeles in January 1847. His journal with its detailed account of these and other events has been described as "a valuable historical document in the American conquest of California," and his comments and critical accounts concerning the more senior leaders of this brief period in the history of California are particularly expressive.

The *Portsmouth* was next engaged in blockade duty along the western coast of Mexico, and Watson described long periods of boring duty with only an occasional excursion ashore. With tours frequently extended, the crew at times appeared to be almost at the point of mutiny. Finally on the morning of 3 Jan. 1848 the *Portsmouth* sailed, and Watson expressed his relief in these words: "I hope for a very long time, I dios, California." During these long months Watson's devotion to duty had not gone unnoticed. He was promoted to first lieutenant on 3 Mar. 1847 and was breveted captain on 29 November.

Having returned to home port in Virginia, Watson was assigned to the Marine barracks at Gosport until July 1852. He next served brief tours in the Mediterranean until 1853, first aboard the *Levant* and then the *Cumberland* (the ship that was rammed and sunk by the Confederate ironclad *Virginia* in March 1862). An extended furlough followed upon his return to the United States and then further shore duty. On 1 Jan. 1855 Henry B. Watson resigned his commission and made plans to return to rural Johnston County.

With the opening phase of the Civil War, he seems to have participated in the initial training of neighborhood youths. On 15 Apr. 1862, however, he was assigned to command a camp of instruction at Weldon. Addressed as colonel, he was given instructions for defending the Roanoke River from possible enemy attack. Some weeks later new orders sent him to Camp Mangum, located on the North Carolina Railroad four miles west of Raleigh, where new recruits were being trained. After these raw troops were equipped and introduced to military life, they were sent off to join the North Carolina regiments. His assignment completed, Watson returned home.

Not for long, however, could this experienced military man remain idle when there was need for his service. Without delaying to seek a commission, Watson enlisted in the Confederate navy on 8 Oct. 1863 but apparently because of ill health served a mere five months until 16 Mar. 1864. He then finally settled down on his 827-acre farm along the the Neuse River south of Smithfield which he had been given by an uncle, Dr. Josiah O. Watson, in 1852. But he had only a few months of family life, as Mary Ann Watson died on 17 Aug. 1864 shortly before her fiftieth birthday. Five years later he, too, died at age fifty-six and was buried in the family cemetery near the front door of

his home. With the death in 1912 of Mary Ann's sister, Fannie Higdon, who had made her home with the Watson family for many years, a plot was acquired in Riverside Cemetery, Smithfield, to which those buried in the family cemetery were moved. In addition to their first child, Josiah Ogden, who died in 1847 at age nine, Henry and Mary Ann Watson were the parents of Henry Lyndall (b. 1842), Mary Ferguson (1843) and Aline Elizabeth (1845) both of whom died in infancy, Mary Aline (1849), Elizabeth Bynum (1852), and Agnes Alwyn (1855). Henry L., a lieutenant in the Fifth North Carolina Regiment in the Civil War, was wounded at Gettysburg, captured at Winchester, and imprisoned at Fort Delaware until the end of the war.

SEE: Walter Clark, ed., *Histories of the Several Regiments and Battalions from North Carolina*, vol. 3 (1901); *Fortitude, Newsletter of the Marine Corps Historical Program* 15 (Summer 1985); Weymouth T. Jordan, comp., *North Carolina Troops, 1861–1865: A Roster*, vol. 4 (1973); Memorandum book of Mary Ann Watson (possession of descendants); *North Carolina Century Farms: 100 Years of Continuous Agriculture Heritage* (1989); *Official Records of the United States and Confederate Navies in the War of the Rebellion*, Ser. II, vol. 1 (1921); Raleigh *Daily Sentinel*, 1 Feb. 1869; Charles R. Smith, ed., *Journals of Marine Second Lieutenant Henry Bulls Watson, 1845–1848* (1990).

WILLIAM S. POWELL

Watson, John Fanning (15 June 1779–23 Dec. 1860), historian, financier, and correspondent of John Hill Wheeler, was born at Batsto, N.J., the son of William and Lucy Fanning Watson. His father, a Philadelphia shipowner and sea captain, was lost in a storm off Cape Hatteras. His mother was a member of the large Fanning connection of Connecticut and Long Island, to which Edmund Fanning and the Reverend William Fanning, active in eighteenth-century North Carolina, also belonged. John H. Wheeler, in his 1851 history of North Carolina, referred to Watson's published genealogical material in his sketch of Edmund Fanning.

John Watson's education was at sea and in the countinghouse. A onetime clerk in the War Department, he resigned in 1804 and was later appointed commissary of provisions for the army posts in Louisiana. Returning to Philadelphia after the death of his father in 1806, he first was a bookseller and then tried publishing. In 1814 he became cashier of the newly organized Bank of Germantown, a position he held until 1847, when he became secretary-treasurer of the Philadelphia, Germantown, and Norristown Railroad. He resigned in 1859. As a resident of Germantown he devoted much of his time to the study of the early history of New York and Philadelphia and published several books on each. He also was the author of many other books, pamphlets, and articles in journals.

Having a particular interest in the Revolutionary Battle of Germantown, Watson had a monument erected over the grave of General Francis Nash of North Carolina at Kulpsville, where Nash had been taken when mortally wounded during the battle. He also placed a monument over the mass grave in the Upper Burial Ground in Germantown to six soldiers who had been killed in the battle. He himself composed the inscriptions on both monuments.

Watson was married in 1812 to Phoebe Barron Crowell of New Jersey. From an 1817 genealogy of the Crowell family that he compiled, it appears that he was aware that two members of this family, John and Edward, had moved from New Jersey to Halifax County, N.C., in the mid-eighteenth century. The manuscript also cited the un-validated legend that the New Jersey family was founded by two brothers of Oliver Cromwell who fled to America at the time of the Restoration.

In the fall of 1851, John H. Wheeler went to Phila-delphia to arrange for the publication of his *History of North Carolina*. He had not previously met Watson and called on him in Germantown with a letter of introduc-tion. Not finding him at home, Wheeler wrote Watson a note dated 18 September asking for an interview, saying that he had called without success to thank him in person on behalf of the state of North Carolina for honoring its heroes who had died in the Battle of Germantown. He also sought copies of the epitaphs and excerpts from Wat-son's manuscript history of the Crowell family that were included in Wheeler's history.

It is interesting to speculate on whether Watson had any effect on Wheeler's 1860 trip to Nova Scotia to obtain a copy of the narrative of David Fanning in possession of descendants there. Fanning, the notorious North Carolina Tory partisan leader, had gone to Nova Scotia to live in exile at the end of the American Revolution.

Watson and his wife Phoebe were members of St. Luke's Episcopal Church and were buried in its church-yard. Their children were Barron E., John H., Myra, Selina (m. Charles Willing), and Lavinia (m. Harrison Whitman of Portland, Maine). In a footnote in his 1851 history, Wheeler stated that one son of John Watson was then liv-ing in Wilson, N.C.; however, he eventually returned to the Philadelphia area.

John F. Watson was regarded as one of the greatest local historians in the United States. In compiling the *Annals of Philadelphia* (1830) and the *Annals and Occurrences of New York City* (1846) he interviewed many elderly residents, mostly illiterate people with prodigious memories, and thus obtained information about the early period of both cities that would have soon been lost. Not the least of his endeavors was his role in the establishment of the Histor-ical Society of Pennsylvania in 1824. A portrait of Watson, painted by A. B. Lockey, is in the society's collections, do-nated by Watson in 1852.

SEE: *DAB*, vol. 19 (1937); *National Union Catalog*, vol. 651 (1979); Register of St. Luke's Episcopal Church, German-town, Philadelphia, Pa.; William Sowitzky, *Paintings and Miniatures in the Historical Society of Pennsylvania* (1942); John F. Watson Papers (Manuscript Department, Histor-ical Society of Pennsylvania); John H. Wheeler, *History of North Carolina* (1851).

CLAIBORNE T. SMITH, JR.

Watson, Josiah Ogden (14 Sept. 1784–12 June 1852), army surgeon, politician, and planter of immense wealth, was a son of John Watson of Pineville in Johnston County. About 1815 he married Penninah Tartt (1790–30 Jan. 1848), the daughter of Elnathan and Obedience Thomas Tartt of Edgecombe (now Wilson) County. Their only child, Elizabeth Obedience, died in Wilmington on 3 Dec. 1839 at age twenty.

As early as 1802 Watson studied under Dr. William Haywood of Tarboro before attending the Medical Col-lege at Philadelphia. In 1807 he sold two lots in Tarboro and moved to Charleston, S.C., where he "enjoyed the friendship of the family of Gov. Alston" as well as a "lu-crative practice." During the War of 1812 he became a sur-geon in the U.S. Army under General Andrew Jackson and "attracted the warm regards and friendship of that great man, which he retained in full force until his death."

Having returned to Johnston County after the war, Wat-

son served as its representative in the General Assembly of 17 Nov. 1828–10 Jan. 1829. He was a member of the Electoral College of 1836 and ran unsuccessfully for the U.S. Congress in 1841. For many years he was chairman of the Johnston County Court and of the Democratic state central committee; he was numbered among the distin-guished men under Governor John Motley Morehead "to superintend on behalf of the State works of public utility."

In addition to his medical practice, Watson engaged in numerous land transactions in Wake, Johnston, and Edge-combe counties and in the states of Alabama and Missis-sippi. He owned a wool factory in Raleigh, the Neuse River Mill, 40 shares of North Carolina Railroad Com-pany stock, and about 350 slaves. He died at his Sharon plantation near Raleigh leaving a lengthy will in which he divided his great wealth among friends and kinsmen af-ter providing money for "a steeple or tower to the new church edifice" and annually "a teacher for the Parish School of Christ Church."

SEE: Johnston County Wills (North Carolina State Ar-chives, Raleigh); *Raleigh Register*, 14 Dec. 1839, 2 Feb. 1848, 15 June 1852.

HUGH B. JOHNSTON

Watts, Alston Davidson (12 Mar. 1866–15 July 1927), Democratic political leader, legislator, public official, and newspaper publisher, was born in Shiloh Township, Ire-dell County, near Statesville, the son of Margaret Mor-rison and Thomas Alexander Watts. His father was a sher-iff of Iredell County (1874–88), and the Watts and Morrison families were early settlers of the region.

Watts attended Professor J. H. Hill's school in States-ville, briefly high school at Huntersville, Bingham School in Mebane, and Davidson College in the class of 1887. Al-though he read law privately, he never applied for a li-cense. Initially he held a number of clerkships in various county offices. Broadening his political horizon, he went in the early 1890s to Washington, D.C., as secretary to Representative John S. Henderson of Salisbury. In 1897 he and James A. Hartness, later secretary of state, purchased the *Mascot*, a weekly newspaper in Statesville. For a num-ber of years Watts devoted his attention to the paper, building a solid political base along with Hartness, Iredell's chief Democratic leader at that time.

He was elected to the state house of representatives in 1901 and 1903 and to the state senate in 1913. In the house he was the leader in the 1903 adoption of the Watts law, the harbinger of Prohibition. Not considered a moral is-sue but a popular political move, the idea did take on a moral appeal for the Democratic party. Watts rapidly be-came one of the top figures in the political network of U.S. Senator Furnifold Simmons. He was recognized for his organizational ability and early on became the target of anti-Simmons partisans. On 11 July 1913 he resigned his seat in the senate to become secretary to Simmons, as the partisan political wars were being waged in earnest be-tween the Simmons and anti-Simmons groups. From his job with Simmons he was able to keep a tight hand on po-litical patronage. Watts was described as the alter ego of the senior senator; his political knowledge was consid-ered astute and his actions daring. Later President Wood-row Wilson appointed him collector of internal revenue for western North Carolina with headquarters in States-ville. After leaving that position, he established a tax au-diting firm in Statesville in 1919.

Although Watts had been identified with the young politicians who returned the state to the Democratic party, his loyalties moved to the Simmons organization.

He practiced the art of practical politics, possessed a unique ability to remember names and election statistics, and mastered detail and political technique. These qualities were helpful in electing Cameron Morrison governor in 1920 over O. Max Gardner. When the General Assembly enacted legislation in 1921 creating the Department of Revenue, Morrison appointed Watts the first commissioner of revenue, effective 1 May. Watts served until personal scandal forced him to resign on 29 Jan. 1923. Early Sunday evening, 28 January, police made a surprise raid on his Fayetteville Street apartment, found a woman and others, and charged him with an indiscretion. Strongly defending his innocence, he refused to put the blame on others, handed his resignation to Governor Morrison, and returned to Statesville, where he was hospitalized. The incident was hailed by his opponents and condemned as a frame-up by his partisans. The *News and Observer* kept the episode alive. In defense of Watts, the *Greensboro Daily News* attacked his accusers and said that he was more honorable than they, noting his long service and record of honesty in financial affairs and his contributions to the Democratic party.

Watts did not lose the support of his political friends or the conservative leaders of his party, and he attended the 1924 Democratic National Convention. Although failing health restricted his activities, he continued his income tax business. When he died in the H. F. Long Sanatorium in Statesville at age sixty-one, the *Greensboro Daily News* published an obituary with a photograph on the front page, lauded his career, and noted that he "has for years been on his way to becoming a legendary figure." At his funeral were a majority of the state's top political figures, who recalled his career in the Democratic faith. Watts, who never married, was buried beside his parents in the New Sterling Associate Reformed Presbyterian Church cemetery in Shiloh Township, six miles west of Statesville.

SEE: Aubrey L. Brooks, *Walter Clark: Fighting Judge* (1944); Josephus Daniels, *Editor in Politics* (1941); Davidson College, *Alumni Catalogue of Davidson College, 1837–1894* (1924); *Greensboro Daily News*, 30–31 Jan. 1923, 16–17 July 1927; Homer Keever, *Iredell—Piedmont County* (1976); Hugh T. Lefler and Albert R. Newsome, *North Carolina: The History of a Southern State* (1954); Raleigh *News and Observer*, 29 Jan. 1923 and subsequent issues; Statesville *Landmark*, 1 Feb. 1923, 18 July 1927.

T. HARRY GATTON

Watts, George Washington *(18 Aug. 1851–7 Mar. 1921)*, industrialist and philanthropist, was born in Cumberland, Md., the son of Gerard S. and Annie Wolvington Watts. In 1858 the family moved from Cumberland to Baltimore, where George W. Watts attended the local public schools. He subsequently entered the University of Virginia, from which he was graduated in 1871 with a degree in civil engineering. For seven years thereafter he was associated with G. S. Watts and Company, his father's wholesale tobacco business in Baltimore.

The turning point in Watts's career occurred in 1878, when his father purchased for him one-fifth interest in the small but promising tobacco manufacturing firm in Durham owned and operated by Washington Duke and his sons James B. (Buck), Benjamin N., and Brodie L. This event marked the beginning of a harmonious and exceedingly profitable business alliance between Watts and the Dukes, particularly James B. and Benjamin N., that endured until Watts's death forty-three years later. Robert F. Durden, biographer of the Duke family, characterized

Watts as a "[q]uiet, sober, and hard-working" man who "possessed considerable business ability."

Formally organized as a partnership in 1878, the year that Watts joined the firm, W. Duke, Sons and Company was reorganized as a joint-stock company in 1885 with James B. Duke as president, Ben Duke as vice-president, and George Watts as secretary-treasurer. When the firm merged with four other cigarette companies in 1890 to form the American Tobacco Company, a business combination organized somewhat along the lines of a conventional trust, James B. Duke became president of the new company and Watts and Ben Duke were members of the board of directors. By 1911, when it was dissolved by the U.S. Supreme Court in a celebrated antitrust suit, the American Tobacco Company had acquired a virtual monopoly on the domestic manufacture of tobacco products, except cigars.

As they accumulated wealth over the years from their profitable tobacco business, George Watts and the Duke brothers sought other outlets for their capital. They invested particularly large sums, either jointly or independently of one another, in the rapidly developing North Carolina textile industry. By 1912 Watts, James B., and Ben Duke jointly controlled Erwin Mills, consisting of four plants, and four other mills located either in Durham or elsewhere in North Carolina. Meanwhile, as his business interests expanded, George Watts was elected to the governing boards of numerous corporations, among them the Seaboard Air Line, Southern Cotton Oil Company, Virginia-Carolina Chemical Company, and Republic Iron and Steel.

When Watts settled there with his wife and young child in 1878, Durham was a small, essentially rural-oriented town that offered little in the way of community services. By the time of his death in 1921, it had become an important commercial and manufacturing center of the New South, providing many of the public services it once lacked. George Watts and the Duke family, by investing in local tobacco and textile manufacturing and by giving liberally to local schools, hospitals, and churches, contributed significantly to this transformation.

Watts, unlike James B. and Ben Duke, was a permanent resident of Durham after 1878. A civic-minded individual, he devoted much of his time and money over the years to the betterment of his community. He served on the school board and as president of the YMCA and of the Commonwealth Club, the local booster organization.

In 1885 Watts, Eugene Morehead, and Julian S. Carr organized the Durham Electric Lighting Company, which for fifteen years had the exclusive privilege of supplying electricity to the city. Durham thus became one of the first communities in North Carolina to enjoy electric lighting. In 1904 Watts was instrumental in the founding of the Durham Loan and Trust Company and the Home Savings Bank, in both of which he, as well as James B. and Ben Duke, retained a financial interest. Perhaps his most notable contribution to the betterment of Durham was Watts Hospital, donated to the city in 1895 and at that time only one of six general hospitals in North Carolina. When it became apparent that the original Watts Hospital could no longer adequately serve the needs of the growing community, Watts in 1909 contributed large sums for the construction and maintenance of a new facility.

During his remarkably successful business career George Watts amassed a modest fortune, part of which, in the manner of Andrew Carnegie, James B. Duke, and other truly wealthy business tycoons of the era, he disposed of in his own lifetime. Among the beneficiaries of his philanthropic activities were the First Presbyterian

Church of Durham, the Durham YMCA, the Barium
Springs Orphanage, and numerous colleges, including
Davidson, Flora Macdonald, Agnes Scott, Lees-McRae In-
stitute, and especially Union Theological Seminary, in
Richmond, of which he was board president from 1904
until his death.

Although confirmed in the Lutheran church in his
youth, Watts, by all accounts a sincerely devout man,
joined the Presbyterian church after moving to Durham.
He served the First Presbyterian Church of Durham for
many years as elder and as superintendent of the Sunday
school class and contributed large amounts to the home
and foreign mission activities of the church. On 19 Oct.
1875 he married Laura Valinda Beall of Cumberland, Md.
Their only child, Annie Louise, was married in 1899 to
John Sprunt Hill, a resident of New York City who later
returned with his family to his native North Carolina and
settled in Durham. Mrs. Watts died on 26 Apr. 1915, and
two years later, on 25 Oct. 1917, George Watts married
Sarah V. Ecker of Syracuse, N.Y.

He died in Durham and was buried in Maplewood
Cemetery. His executors placed the value of his estate at
$11.4 million.

SEE: W. K. Boyd, *The Story of Durham: City of the New South*
(1925); Robert F. Durden, *The Dukes of Durham, 1865–1929*
(1975); *Durham Morning Herald*, 8–10 Mar. 1921; *North Carolina Biography*, vol. 4 (1919); Raleigh *News and Observer*, 8
Mar. 1921; Charles L. Van Noppen, comp., *In Memoriam:
George Washington Watts* (privately printed, 1922); George
Washington Watts Estate folder, Josiah William Bailey Papers (Manuscript Department, Duke University Library,
Durham).

NATHANIEL F. MAGRUDER

Way, Joseph Howell (*22 Nov. 1865–22 Sept. 1927*), physician, was born in Waco, Tex., the son of Charles Burr
and Martha Julia Howell Way. Ancestors on his father's
side had emigrated from England to Connecticut and
Massachusetts in 1630; his mother, a native of Haywood
County, N.C., was a descendant of a pioneer family in
western North Carolina. Charles B. Way, a native of Mississippi and a major on the staff of Confederate general
John B. Hood, moved to Texas after his plantation was destroyed during the Civil War. In the 1870s, however, the
family settled in Asheville where the elder Way farmed
and taught school. He became a judge of the county court
and was superintendent of schools.

Joseph Way was educated by his father and under
other private tutors. At age sixteen he was teaching
school in Buncombe County and studying medicine under Dr. W. L. Hilliard in Asheville. In 1884 he entered the
Medical College of Virginia, and in 1885, at age nineteen,
he was licensed to practice by the North Carolina State
Board of Medical Examiners. He made the highest grade
in a class of fifty-three. Nevertheless, he promptly enrolled in Vanderbilt University in Nashville, Tenn., and
was graduated with the degree of doctor of medicine in
1886. Before the end of the year he began a general practice in Waynesville that he continued, except when military service intervened, until shortly before his death.

Dr. Way specialized in the treatment of tuberculosis but
in general served as a country doctor. In anticipation of
war with Germany, he joined the Medical Corps of the
U.S. Army in 1916 and was commissioned a captain in
April 1917. Sent to Camp Greene in Greensboro, he was
a member of the First Officers' Training Camp. He was assigned to the first ward opened at the camp hospital and

remained in charge until the spring of 1918. Promoted to
major, he was transferred to the hospital at the Rockefeller
Institute in New York City for three months. His next assignment was at a military hospital in New Haven, Conn.,
but after a very brief stay he was returned to Camp
Greene. There he organized the Reconstruction Service
and served until the hospital was closed in March 1919.
He was transferred to the medical reserve and promoted to lieutenant colonel. In 1924 he was advanced to
colonel.

At Atlantic City in 1919 Way became a charter member
of the Medical Veterans of the World War and began a
lengthy period of deep interest in the welfare of veterans
of the war. For more than three years he was medical director of the U.S. Veterans' Bureau Training School in
Waynesville. In 1923 he organized the section of Medical
Veterans of the World War and the Medical Officers Reserve Corps at Asheville. Way also was a surgeon for the
Southern Railway and a member of the North Carolina
medical examining board from 1897 to 1902. Governors
Robert B. Glenn, William Kitchin, Thomas W. Bickett, and
Cameron Morrison appointed him a member of the State
Board of Health, of which he was president for three
terms. He also was a longtime trustee of Trinity College
and Duke University and a member of the International
Tuberculosis Congress. An active member of state and regional medical associations and secretary and president
of several, he was editor of the *Transactions of the North
Carolina State Medical Society* for four years and of the Tri-
State Association for six years. He contributed articles to
several medical journals as well as state news to the *Journal of the American Medical Association* for many years.

A Democrat, a Mason, and a member of the Methodist
Episcopal Church, South, he married Marietta Welch in
1888. They were the parents of Hilda (Mrs. Thomas L.
Gwynn), Joseph Howell, and Robert B., who died in
infancy.

SEE: *North Carolina Biography*, vol. 4 (1928); Walton S. Rankin, *Joseph Howell Way* (1927?); *Who Was Who in America*,
vol. 1 (1942).

WILLIAM S. POWELL

Waynick, Capus Miller (*23 Dec. 1889–7 Sept. 1986*),
newspaper editor, public official, and ambassador, was
born in Rockingham County, the son of Joshua James and
Anna Moore Waynick. A son and grandson of black-
smiths and farmers, he was a student at The University of
North Carolina (1907–9) but withdrew. From 1911 to 1913
he was a reporter for the *Greensboro Record*. After a brief
stint as a salesman of novelties, he returned to journalism
as a reporter with the *Charlotte Observer* (1913–14) and as
editor (1915–17). During World War I he served as an infantry private. Afterwards he became publisher of the
Greensboro Daily Record (1920–22) and also for many years
was editor of the *High Point Enterprise*.

Waynick represented Guilford County in the General
Assembly in 1931 and served in the state senate in 1933.
For the period 1933–34 he was state director of the National Reemployment Service, one of the federal agencies
designed to counteract unemployment, and in 1933–37,
during the administration of Governor J. C. B. Ehringhaus, he was chairman of the State Highway and Public
Works Commission. In this position he directed the repair
of unsafe bridges and road maintenance, both of which
had been unavoidably neglected during the depression.
Waynick was commended by the press for his fairness in
allocating highway funds. It was perhaps because of his

personal knowledge of the subject that he was the author of volume one of *North Carolina Roads and Their Builders*, published in 1952.

In 1937 Governor Clyde R. Hoey named him chairman of the State Planning Board, and in 1942 during the administration of Governor J. Melville Broughton he founded and was the first director of the state's Health Education Institute. As chairman of the state Democratic party, he was campaign manager for gubernatorial candidate W. Kerr Scott in 1948 but declined to accept the traditional political preferment usually given to those who performed that service for a successful candidate.

President Harry S Truman named Waynick ambassador extraordinary and plenipotentiary to Nicaragua, where he served from 21 May 1949 to 18 July 1951. Waynick was fluent in Spanish (as well as proficient in French) and had served as unofficial translator for recent governors J. Melville Broughton and R. Gregg Cherry. In the summer of 1951 President Truman named Waynick to be ambassador to Colombia, where he served from 28 July 1951 to 24 Oct. 1953. Because of his friendly nature, his inquisitiveness as an experienced journalist, and his language skills, he endeared himself to people in many walks of life and proved to be an effective diplomat. The president called Waynick home briefly on temporary leave in 1950 to organize the Point-Four Program to aid backward countries. In 1955 he headed Governor Luther Hodges's Small Industries Program, which resulted in the establishment of the North Carolina Business Corporation.

When the adjutant general of North Carolina resigned on 18 Aug. 1957 following discovery that three National Guard colonels had agreed to a pact to rotate the brigadier generalship in turn, Governor Hodges appointed Waynick to become adjutant general with the rank of major general. Though regarded as a civilian, Waynick had maintained his rank in the National Guard and in the U.S. Army Reserve. He served as adjutant general from 12 July 1957 to 30 Dec. 1960. Between 1961 and 1963 he worked in New York City, where he was executive vice-president of the Richardson Foundation, a private North Carolina endowment that supported public causes. It was also in the decade of the 1960s that President Lyndon B. Johnson named Waynick to the national Human Relations Commission. For the remainder of his life Capus Waynick answered the calls of the governors of the state as well as others for consultation on various subjects but especially on race relations. He was coauthor of the book, *North Carolina and the Negro*, published in 1964.

In 1915 Waynick married Elizabeth Hunt McBee, of Lincoln County, the great-niece of Mrs. Thomas "Stonewall" Jackson. They had no children. Their home was a restored antebellum house on a 24-acre farm near High Point where Waynick had his own small golf course. He was an avid sportsman and for many years regularly played tennis, golf, handball, and other games. He and his wife were excellent bridge players, and he once wrote a bridge column for a local paper. In 1971 he was the recipient of the North Carolina Award for public service. A Presbyterian, a Democrat, and a Freemason, he died in High Point at age ninety-seven after a long illness.

SEE: John L. Cheney, Jr., ed., *North Carolina Government, 1585–1974* (1975); *Eighth North Carolina Awards* (1971); Daniel L. Grant, *Alumni History of the University of North Carolina* (1924); *Greensboro News and Record*, 8 Sept. 1986; Raleigh *News and Observer*, 8 Sept. 1986; Jack Riley, "Tar Heel of the Week: Capus M. Waynick," Raleigh *News and Observer* (undated clipping [portrait], North Carolina Collection, University of North Carolina, Chapel Hill); Capus

Waynick Papers (Manuscript Collection, East Carolina University, Greenville); *Who Was Who in America*, vol. 8 (1985).

WILLIAM S. POWELL

Weatherell, Mary E. (Mollie) Jordan Gorman

(1830–post-1897), assistant editor of the *Spirit of the Age* (Raleigh), was born in Sussex County, Va., the daughter of Martha and James M. Jordan. Her father, referred to as "a man of education," moved to Raleigh in late 1859 to become principal editor of the *North Carolina Planter* (1858–61). On 4 Dec. 1855 at Athelingay, Isle of Wight County, Va., she married Alexander M. Gorman, of Raleigh, the editor and publisher of a temperance and family newspaper, the *Spirit of the Age*, from its inception in 1849 to February 1864. Gorman was also owner and publisher of the *North Carolina Planter*.

Substituting as editor of the *Spirit of the Age* in the absence of her husband, starting on 10 Dec. 1856, Mollie Gorman was immediately so popular that she was urged to take a permanent job with the paper. At once she became "editress" of the erratic Ladies Department, to which she had been a contributor before her marriage, and made various improvements. Obviously well educated, Mrs. Gorman wrote in a positive, often trenchant, style. Her persistent theme was the status of women, and she urged recognition of the homemaker's contribution to society, a strengthened and more practical education for women, a view of wives as equal partners in marriage, and a position of social dignity for unmarried women. Secondarily, but warmly, she championed the development of southern literature, deploring the attachment of southerners to northern magazines and books and asserting that the South was able to contend boldly for the prize of excellence. With particular pride, she identified southern women then in journalism and free-lance writing, and her stated purpose for the Ladies Department of the *Spirit of the Age* was to make it the paper's most intellectual and attractive feature.

In 1856 Alexander Gorman claimed for his paper—an assertion supported elsewhere—the largest circulation in the state, a popularity that apparently continued through 1859. However, the Gormans quickly felt the impact of the Civil War, which obscured the temperance cause and strained the family newspaper. By late 1861 the Ladies Department appeared irregularly, although Mrs. Gorman's pen appeared intermittently until 1863 as she took her husband's place during his absences on business. On 29 Feb. 1864 A. M. Gorman offered his paper for sale. He died less than a year later, leaving his widow destitute with four small children. In the bankruptcy of the Confederacy, she was unable to collect debts, had only meager provisions on hand, and was without liquid assets. A statement by her pastor praises her exemplary and economical habits, the strict frugality and great resourcefulness required of her to support her family.

On 12 Mar. 1869 Mary E. Gorman married Wm. P. Weatherell, a native of Massachusetts who had settled in Raleigh. With the four Gorman children—Maxwell J., George H., Florence P., and Alexander M.—they made their home for many years at Martin and McDowell Streets, Raleigh, the site of the old *Spirit of the Age* office.

SEE: Marriage Records of Isle of Wight County, Va., Estate Records of Wake County, N.C., and Marriage Registry of Wake County (1839–1967) (North Carolina State Archives, Raleigh); *Spirit of the Age* (Raleigh), 1850–64; Wesley H. Wallace, "North Carolina's Agricultural Journals,

1838–1861: A Crusading Press," *North Carolina Historical Review* 36 (1959); R. H. Whitaker, *Reminiscences, Incidents, and Anecdotes* (1905).

HELEN R. WATSON

Weatherford, Willis Duke *(1 Dec. 1875–21 Feb. 1970)*, educator, religious leader, writer, and social pioneer, was born near Weatherford, Tex., the son of Samuel Leonard and Margaret Jane Turner Weatherford. His family was part of the extensive migration from the hills of North Carolina and Tennessee that moved into the western territories just before and after the Civil War. Weatherford received a B.S. degree from Weatherford College (1895) and A.B. (1899), M.A. (1900), and Ph.D. (1907) degrees from Vanderbilt University.

In college Weatherford was active in the student YMCA movement, and on leaving Vanderbilt he accepted a position with that organization. From 1902 to 1919 he was international student secretary for the colleges of the South and Southwest. The position required almost constant travel, as he periodically visited the approximately two hundred colleges for which he was responsible. During the summer he organized meetings and training sessions for YMCA personnel, and in 1907, seeking a permanent location for these programs, he proposed and founded the Blue Ridge Assembly on a tract near Black Mountain, N.C. He raised approximately $500,000 to finance the project and eventually acquired some 1,500 acres. As president of the organization he was largely responsible for the operation of the assembly until 1944. He built a house on the grounds that he maintained as his summer residence and after 1946 as his permanent home.

In 1919 Weatherford left his post as student secretary to devote full time to the establishment of the Southern College of the YMCA, later known as the YMCA Graduate School. The college was located in Nashville, Tenn., in the midst of an academic community consisting of Vanderbilt University, George Peabody College, and Scarritt College. Its purpose was to provide specialized training for the position of YMCA secretary. This was Weatherford's most enterprising educational project, and for the next sixteen years he was completely committed to its success. The school operated throughout the year; summer programs and courses were conducted at the Blue Ridge Assembly grounds in North Carolina. Economic conditions forced Weatherford to close its doors in 1936, with the loss of a recently completed half-million-dollar plant. The college survived as a summer operation at Blue Ridge until the early 1940s.

From 1936 to 1946 Weatherford taught in the Department of Philosophy and Religion at Fisk University, a predominantly black school in Nashville, This was consistent with a concern he had developed early in his career. During his years of travel for the YMCA he became increasingly sensitive to the plight of blacks in the South, and in 1910 he published *Negro Life in the South* as a study book for college students in YMCA programs. The volume was widely distributed and had a liberalizing effect on thousands of southern students. He published a number of other works on racial issues, among them *The Negro from Africa to America* (1924) and *Race Relations*, with Charles S. Johnson, (1934). Weatherford organized college-level courses on Negro life and race relations during summer sessions at Blue Ridge and eventually supported interracial clubs on campuses in the community generally. In 1910 he was instrumental in the founding of the Commission on Interracial Cooperation and served on the board until it was reorganized as the Southern Regional Council.

At age seventy Weatherford left Fisk University to accept a position at Berea College and to embark on a new phase of his long career. A trustee of the college since 1916, he had been concerned with the conditions of life in the southern mountains. He believed that education was the best means of improving life for the people of Appalachia, and at Berea he served as fund-raiser, teacher, and recruiter of students. He spent most of his time traveling in the mountains, especially in North Carolina. In 1957 Weatherford and Berea College received a grant of $250,000 from the Ford Foundation to conduct a survey of the problems of Appalachia. The resulting study, coauthored with Earl D. C. Brewer, was published in 1962 as *Life and Religion in Southern Appalachia*. The appearance of this study was a prime factor in encouraging the federal government to establish a number of programs to improve living conditions in the region.

In 1903 Weatherford married Lulu Belle Trawick of Nashville, Tenn. The marriage was tragically short as she died during childbirth in 1907. In 1914 he married Julia McRory of Evans, Ala. (d. 1957). A son, Willis Duke, Jr., was born in 1916. Weatherford was an elder of the Methodist church, a member of Phi Beta Kappa and Pi Gamma Mu, and a life member of the Southern Regional Council. He was buried on the grounds of the Blue Ridge Assembly.

SEE: George P. Antone, "Willis Duke Weatherford: An Interpretation of His Work in Race Relations, 1906–1946" (Ph.D. diss., Vanderbilt University, 1969); Wilma Dykeman, *Prophet of Plenty: The First Ninety Years of Willis Duke Weatherford* (1966); "The Y.M.C.A. Graduate School, Nashville, 1919–1936," *Tennessee Historical Quarterly* 32, no. 1 (Spring 1973).

GEORGE P. ANTONE

Weatherspoon, Walter Herbert *(7 Feb. 1884–8 Aug. 1972)*, attorney, utility executive, and philanthropist, was born at Nelson to William Hardy and Cynthia Hopson Weatherspoon. The operator of a general merchandise store, his father despaired of sending his five sons and two daughters through college; thus the family's limited financial resources went primarily to the education of Jesse Burton Weatherspoon, who became a minister and professor of homiletics at Southern Baptist Theological Seminary in Louisville, Ky.

Contrary to common practice at that time, the father freed Herbert from the obligation of pooling his own earnings with the family's, and the young man joined brother Jesse as he left for Wake Forest College. To pay his own expenses Herbert Weatherspoon sold students clothing for Cross and Linehan of Raleigh, operated a club for sixty students, represented a steam laundry, and worked for T. E. Holding's local bank. He organized and sang bass in the school glee club and worked as business manager of *The Student* magazine. His total earnings exceeded expenses. He was graduated from Wake Forest in 1907 with a bachelor's degree and a law license, which he had received during his junior year by passing the bar exam (administered then by the chief justice of the North Carolina Supreme Court). Forty-six years after his graduation, Wake Forest University honored him with the degree of doctor of laws.

Weatherspoon practiced law in Laurinburg from 1907 to 1928 with Stephen McIntyre and R. C. Lawrence as partners and thus was associated as one client. Politically active, he campaigned for Prohibition and represented Scotland County in the state legislature for two regular terms and one special term. In the General Assembly he introduced a bill that led to the creation of Caswell Training School at Kinston. He also wrote and managed passage of the so-called Weatherspoon law, designed to enforce Prohibition, which had won by a 40,000 vote margin in a popular referendum. Josephus Daniels, the lifelong "dry" editor, hailed the law with an editorial captioned "Blind Tigers Must Go!"

In 1928 Weatherspoon moved to Raleigh as a partner with Josiah William Bailey (later a U.S. senator) in the law firm of Bailey and Weatherspoon. One client was the Carolina Power and Light Company, which soon elected him as full-time counsel to succeed the late James H. Pou, Sr. During an association spanning forty-two years, he rose progressively to vice-president and general counsel, director, and executive vice-president of CP&L. The utility honored him in 1958 by naming its facility at Lumberton the W. H. Weatherspoon Steam Electric Generating Plant.

An active churchman, he taught Bible, sang bass, and served as a deacon and board chairman of the First Baptist Church of Raleigh. For four decades he was a trustee (and sometimes board president) of Meredith College, for which he launched a five-million-dollar advancement program. Its first large gift was a physical education-recreation complex donated by Herbert Weatherspoon and the family of his brother, the late James R. Weatherspoon, who had been treasurer of Durham Life Insurance Company. His gentle wit once broke a critical stalemate as churchmen debated the issue of dancing on Baptist college campuses. Weatherspoon was quoted as remarking in the heat of debate: "If you deny dancing on campus, students will leave the campus to dance; and that's where the rub comes." Resulting laughter broke the tension and led to a peaceful solution.

Herbert Weatherspoon served several corporate and community causes. He was president of the North Carolina Citizens Association, Raleigh Chamber of Commerce, and Lions Club. He won many formal citations for his keen intellect, oratorical eloquence, and uncompromising standards of personal and professional conduct; his wise judgment was sought on critical issues for decades by Louis V. Sutton, longtime president and chief executive of Carolina Power and Light, who called him "the conscience of the company." His hobbies included golf, fishing, hunting, horseback riding, and flower gardening. He invariably wore a tiny boutonniere, usually a sweetheart rose from the gardens at his home in Hayes Barton, Raleigh. When he stopped riding on a doctor's advice, he donated his mount to the already outstanding stable of saddle horses at Meredith College.

With characteristic modesty, he attributed his successes to kin, friends, professors, and business associates. He said that he owed his life to a classmate, John Lee of Durham. On the way to school they had to walk a log across a swollen, swirling creek. Nine-year-old Herbert lost his footing, fell in, and was swept helplessly downstream. The older Lee plunged in, grabbed the large collar of his shirtwaist, and towed Herbert ashore.

His first wife was Maude Lee of Laurinburg, the daughter of Robert E. and Matilda Jane Sutton Lee. Two years after her death in 1960, he gave the First Baptist Church of Laurinburg an organ containing 1,683 speaking pipes and twenty chimes in memory of her contribution to the church's music and work with children. His second wife was the former Mrs. William Benjamin (Margaret Calvert) Duncan, of Raleigh, who survived him. Weatherspoon died at Atlantic Beach and was buried at Montlawn Memorial Park, Raleigh. He left no children.

SEE: CP&L, Board of Directors minutes, 12 Dec. 1962, 13 Mar. 1963, 15 Sept. 1971, 20 Sept. 1972; *Charlotte Observer*, 1 Nov. 1957; *North Carolina* magazine, September 1972; Raleigh *News and Observer*, 17 Nov. 1957; *The Twig*, Meredith College, 13 Dec. 1972; Wake Forest University, *Commencement Program*, 1 June 1953.

JACK RILEY

Weaver, Charles Clinton *(21 June 1875–19 Mar. 1946)*, Methodist clergyman, educator, and church administrator, was born in Ashe County of Scots-Irish ancestry, the son of James Harvey and Jennie Burkett Weaver. His mother was a member of a prominent pioneer family in Ashe County. When he was about three years old, his father left a career teaching school to enter the pastoral ministry of the Methodist Episcopal Church, South, at Jefferson. Charles Clinton grew up in parsonages where his father served in Virginia, in Tennessee, and in Franklin, Weaverville, and Greensboro, N.C. In 1895 he received an A.B. degree from Trinity College (now Duke University), where he was elected to the Phi Beta Kappa Society. He spent a year in graduate study at Vanderbilt University before earning a Ph.D. degree at Johns Hopkins University, awarded in 1900. Duke University honored him with the D.D. degree in 1936.

In 1900 Weaver became president of Rutherford College near Morganton. He was president of Davenport College, Lenoir, from 1903 to 1910 and of Emory and Henry College in southwestern Virginia from 1910 to 1920. While he was at Emory and Henry, more buildings were erected than during any previous administration, the student body was almost doubled, the curriculum was modernized and new courses were added, the faculty was strengthened, and intercollegiate athletics was restored. In 1918 the school merged with nearby Martha Washington College.

Weaver became a minister in the Methodist Episcopal Church, South, by joining the Western North Carolina Conference in 1901. Returning to North Carolina in 1920, he was the pastor of Central Church, Monroe (1920–24), Centenary Church, Winston-Salem (1924–33), and Central Church, Asheville (1933–35). He was presiding elder of the Greensboro District for a year, then moved to First Church, Charlotte (1936–40). For the next four years he was superintendent of the Winston-Salem District. In 1944 he became the administrator of the church-related Hugh Chatham Memorial Hospital in Elkin but had served less than a year and a half when he died.

In recognition of his ability and leadership he was elected to represent his annual conference in the General Conference, the quadrennial law-making body of his church, for every session from 1918 through 1944 except the one in 1939, when he was a member of the Uniting Conference. For many years he was an influential member of both his conference and denominational boards of missions.

During his pastorate in Winston-Salem he led in merging Centenary and West End Methodist Churches and in building the great Centenary Church that stands on Fifth Street. He also was a leader in bringing the Goodwill Industries to the city. He and his wife extended their ministry to the black community in fostering the establishment of Bethlehem House, a day-care facility for children. His work on behalf of the needy and racial minorities was an outgrowth of his deep religious convictions and high spiritual ideals. After he observed that young working women had no suitable place to get meals downtown, a cafeteria operated in the church for several years.

On 18 June 1902 he married Florence Stacy, the daughter of the Reverend and Mrs. L. E. Stacy; her father was a Methodist minister. For many years Mrs. Weaver was president of the conference women's organization. One of her brothers, Marvin Hendrix Stacy, was dean of The University of North Carolina for a quarter century; another brother, Walter Parker Stacy, was for many years chief justice of the North Carolina Supreme Court. The Weavers had five children: James Harvey, Lucius Stacy, Charles Clinton, Janie, and Philip Johnson. Dr. Weaver was buried at Emory, Va.

SEE: *Journal of the Western North Carolina Annual Conference of the Methodist Church* (1940–46); *Minutes of the Western North Carolina Annual Conference of the Methodist Episcopal Church, South* (1901–39); *Who's Who in America* (1947).

GARLAND R. STAFFORD

Weaver, David Stathem *(19 June 1896–12 Nov. 1966),* educator and agricultural leader, was born in Westwood, Hamilton County, Ohio, the son of Samuel Alvin and Clara Stathem Weaver. He was educated in the public schools of Cincinnati, Ohio, and, with time out for service in World War I, was graduated from Ohio State University in 1920. From 1920 to 1923 he was assistant professor of agricultural engineering at Mississippi A&M College.

In 1923 Weaver began teaching at the North Carolina State College of Agriculture and Engineering while working on a master's degree in agricultural engineering. After receiving his degree in 1925, he remained on the faculty, rising to the rank of professor by 1936. In 1936–37 he was principal engineer for the Federal Rural Electrification Administration in Washington, D.C. In this position he continued work that he had already begun in North Carolina and completed the first statewide electrification surveys. Weaver returned to North Carolina State College in 1937 as head of the Department of Agricultural Engineering. He maintained his association with the Rural Electrification Administration, serving as secretary and sometime chairman through 1963. During the period 1937–48 he was also a specialist in charge of agricultural extension work.

He became assistant director of the Agricultural Extension Service in 1948. Succeeding I. O. Schaub as director in 1950, he served in the post until 1961. For two years afterwards he was special assistant to the dean of the School of Agriculture and Life Sciences at North Carolina State University.

David S. Weaver was the author of a number of articles on agricultural engineering topics that appeared in professional journals. He also wrote Agricultural Experiment Station *Bulletins* concerned with soil and water conservation and with the use of electricity on farms. Throughout his career he was especially interested in improving the productivity of human labor on farms through rural electrification and through the more efficient use of farm machinery. Weaver became interested in the use of electricity on farms at a time when electricity was thought of primarily in terms of illumination. His work in this area, which led to his being called "the father of rural electrification in North Carolina," influenced both national and state programs in the development of rural electricity use. He served on numerous governmental committees dealing with another of his concerns: soil and water conservation.

As head of the Agricultural Extension Service, Weaver was responsible for one of the largest adult education agencies in the United States. While in this position he helped found the North Carolina Board of Farm Organizations and Agencies in an effort to ensure cooperation among federal and state agencies seeking to serve farm people. For his contribution he received the Distin-

guished Service Awards of the North Carolina Farm Bureau and the North Carolina State Grange. Weaver was chosen the *Progressive Farmer* "Man of the Year in Service to Agriculture" and elected a Fellow of the American Society of Agricultural Engineers. In addition to numerous other honors he was admitted to the North Carolina Agricultural Hall of Fame. In 1964 North Carolina State University awarded him an honorary doctor of humanities degree, and in 1968 a complex housing the Biological and Agricultural Engineering Laboratories of North Carolina State University was named for him.

Weaver married Gertrude Marie Brickman on 10 Oct. 1919, and they had three sons—David, Jr., Donald, and Samuel Alvin. He died in Philadelphia while on his way to New York to make a speech on agricultural developments and was buried in Montlawn Cemetery, Raleigh.

SEE: David S. Weaver Papers (University Archives, North Carolina State University, Raleigh); Mrs. David S. Weaver, personal contact, 22 July 1981.

H. THOMAS KEARNEY, JR.

Weaver, James Harvey *(29 Mar. 1903–11 July 1970),* athletic administrator, was born at Rutherford College, of which his father was president. One of five children of the Reverend Charles Clinton and Florence Stacy Weaver, his mother was the sister of Walter Stacy, chief justice of the North Carolina Supreme Court. The Reverend Mr. Weaver was later president for a brief period of Davenport College in Lenoir and for a longer time of Emory and Henry College in Emory, Va. James Weaver attended Emory and Henry Academy, where he played football, baseball, and basketball. Matriculating at Emory and Henry College, he played football for two years. In the fall of 1921, when his father returned to a North Carolina pastoral circuit, James Weaver transferred to Trinity College. The next spring he left school over a hazing incident and enrolled in Centenary College in Shreveport, La., where he played football from 1922 to 1924 and was captain his final year. He also played basketball and baseball at Centenary, was a member of the student council, and was vice-president of the student body.

After graduation Weaver sold cars in Shreveport for a short time before taking a position in the fall of 1925 as coach of the Centenary freshman football team. In 1926 and 1927 he coached high school baseball, football, and basketball and taught history and geometry in Nacogdoches, Tex.

Weaver returned to North Carolina in the spring of 1928 to teach and coach football and basketball at Oak Ridge Academy, where he remained through the spring of 1933. For several years he also umpired minor league baseball games in the area. In the autumn of 1933 he became head football coach at Wake Forest College. The small Baptist school was having a hard time competing with larger schools in the state, and Weaver was unable to affect an immediate change. His first team was winless and only scored thirteen points for the season. By the 1936 season, however, he produced a winning season, with five victories and four defeats. After that season he became athletic director at Wake Forest and relinquished football coaching duties to Douglas Clyde (Peahead) Walker.

Weaver remained athletic director until 1953, with an interruption during World War II. He joined the U.S. Navy in December 1942 and served until November 1945. During that period he was an athletic director at Georgia Pre-flight and the Ward Island Technical Training Center. He left the service as a lieutenant commander.

While Weaver was athletic director, Wake Forest's sports program enjoyed unprecedented success. It joined the large and somewhat unwieldy Southern Conference in 1936. The football team won with regularity under Walker and played in the school's first two bowl games in 1945 and 1948. In 1939 the basketball team became the first team from North Carolina to play in the National Collegiate Athletic Association tournament. In 1951 the Wake Forest baseball team was selected to represent the United States in the Pan American games. Weaver assisted with the golf program and helped recruit Arnold Palmer for the team.

Wake Forest was one of seven schools that left the Southern Conference in 1953 to form the Atlantic Coast Conference. In May 1954, by which time the league had added an eighth school, Weaver was selected to become its first commissioner. His explicit duties included rules enforcement, public relations, and managing the staff. Behind the scenes he was active in arbitrating disputes among the member institutions and promoting the league in the NCAA. During his tenure the conference had its share of recruiting violations, probations, fights, and scandals, most notably the basketball point shaving episodes at The University of North Carolina and North Carolina State in the early 1960s. However, Weaver's leadership helped the league survive these problems and become a leading college athletic conference in the 1950s and 1960s. The conference won national championships in basketball, baseball, and soccer and put together a lucrative basketball television package. It also gained a reputation for academic integrity and boasted stricter eligibility requirements than those mandated by the NCAA.

In addition to his duties as league commissioner Weaver was a member of the NCAA executive committee, where he was an active proponent of strengthened eligibility requirements, and of the National Collegiate Commissioners Association (president, 1970). He died suddenly of a heart attack while attending the commissioners' annual convention in Colorado Springs. Funeral services were held at the Christ United Methodist Church in Greensboro, and burial was at Westminster Gardens.

Weaver married Louise Wooten in June 1934. She died later that year. In 1938 he married Kate Dunn of Scotland Neck, and they had a daughter, Florence. A large, amiable man, Weaver was an enthusiastic hunter and fisherman.

Weaver was inducted into the North Carolina Sports Hall of Fame, the Helms Foundation Hall of Fame, and the Wake Forest University Hall of Fame. In 1971 the Atlantic Coast Conference instituted the Jim Weaver Postgraduate Scholarship, which is awarded to the conference athlete who best distinguishes himself or herself in academic and leadership qualities.

SEE: Bruce A. Corrie, *The Atlantic Coast Conference, 1953–1978* (1978); *Greensboro Daily News*, 29 May 1954; Charlie Harville, *Sports in North Carolina: A Photographic History* (1977); George W. Paschal, *History of Wake Forest College*, vol. 3 (1943); Raleigh *News and Observer*, 11 Oct. 1953; Weaver file (Sports Information Department, Wake Forest University, Winston-Salem).

JIM L. SUMMERS

Weaver, John Van Alstyne (*17 July 1893–14 June 1938*), writer, was born in Charlotte, the son of Annie Randolph Tate of Charlotte and John Van Alstyne Weaver, Sr., of New York State. Of Scottish, Irish, Huguenot, German, English, and Dutch ancestry, he and his brother Randolph were related to the Allison, Overman, and Graham families in North Carolina. Before his first birthday, he "was

removed to Chicago," as he put it, and there his family became prominent in the social and literary circles of the city. In 1914 he was graduated from Hamilton College, where he was editor of the literary magazine and published poems and essays, one of them on O. Henry. For a year he attended George Pierce Baker's playwriting class at Harvard. Returning to Chicago, he prepared advertising copy for the *Chicago Daily News* and was assistant to the book editor. In 1917–19 he served in the army, where he was promoted from sergeant to lieutenant.

Weaver had been, he revealed, a "tea-hound in my youth," and the Jazz Age of the Twenties suited his style and personality. His first book of "shirt-sleeve poetry," *In American* (1921), went through thirteen printings and made him a prominent figure. As one of the Carl Sandburg and Ring Lardner school, he wrote in the dialect and vernacular of working people, of plumbers, clerks, soldiers, milkmen, shop girls, and taxi drivers. "I never write about anybody who makes over $40 a week," he said, and in his use of the "American language," he was, H. L. Mencken believed, "the first poet, as far as I know, to attempt that operation." The popularity of *In American* led to five more books of poetry similar to it: *Finders* (1923), *More in American* (1926), *To Youth* (1928), *Turning Point* (1930), and the autobiographical *Trial Balance: A Sentimental Journey* (1932). From 1920 to 1924 he was literary editor of the *Brooklyn Eagle*, then resigned to devote full time to writing.

His marriage to the celebrated actress Peggy Wood on 14 Feb. 1924 was a happy and lasting one, and he was devoted to his son David and to his farm in Stamford, Conn. Frequently he returned to North Carolina to visit relatives. In 1926 he collaborated with the established playwright George Abbott on a comedy *Love 'Em and Leave 'Em*, which had a successful Broadway run. In 1926–28 he was drama critic for *College Humor*. Of his three novels—*Margey Wins the Game* (1922), *Her Knight Comes Riding* (1928), and *Joy-Girl* (1932)—the most widely read was the second, about a Brooklyn stenographer's search for a dream-hero. In 1928 he made his first trip to Hollywood and after 1931 spent long periods there writing dialogue for motion pictures. Original scripts for Clara Bow and an adaptation of *Tom Sawyer* were his principal accomplishments. Meanwhile he appeared on the lecture platform throughout the United States and contributed poems, short stories, and articles to magazines. After becoming ill in Hollywood with tuberculosis, he was sent to Colorado Springs, where he died several months later. Weaver was a Congregationalist. *In American: The Collection Poems* (1939) had a foreword by the approving H. L. Mencken.

SEE: *Charlotte Observer*, 20 Mar. 1927, 24 June 1928, 16 Oct. 1932, 16 June 1938; Archibald Henderson, *North Carolina: The Old North State and the New*, vol. 2 (1941); Library of Congress card catalogue; *New York Times*, 16 June 1938; *North Carolina Authors: A Selective Handbook* (1952); *Who Was Who in America* (1942). Weaver's scrapbooks, papers, and unpublished manuscripts are in the New York Public Library.

RICHARD WALSER

Weaver, Richard Malcolm, Jr. (*3 Mar. 1910–3 Apr. 1963*), intellectual historian, rhetorician, and political philosopher, was born at Asheville in Buncombe County, the son of Richard Malcolm (1870–1915) and Carolyn Embry Weaver, who was originally from Fayette County, Ky. He was the great-grandson of the Reverend Jacob Weaver (1786–1868), of Reems Creek, patriarch of the Weaver family in western North Carolina.

Young Weaver was educated in the public schools of Asheville and of Lexington, Ky., where his family resettled in the years following his father's untimely death. In 1832 Dick Weaver took his A.B. degree from the University of Kentucky, where he was a member of Phi Beta Kappa. He enrolled at Vanderbilt University in September 1933 and received an M.A. in English in 1934. He left Vanderbilt in 1936 without taking the terminal degree. Three years of teaching at Texas A&M University (1937–40) strengthened his determination to finish his professional education and round out the sequence of studies that he had begun in Nashville with instruction from John Crowe Ransom and Donald Davidson. In the fall of 1940 he entered the Ph.D. program in the Department of English at Louisiana State University, where under the direction of Cleanth Brooks he completed his dissertation, "The Confederate South, 1865–1910: A Study in the Survival of a Mind and a Culture," in 1943. In this work Weaver laid the groundwork for his entire career. In 1944 he joined the faculty of the University of Chicago, where he remained for the rest of his life.

Dr. Weaver was an extremely productive scholar. The flow of his publications began while he was still in Baton Rouge, but increased rapidly once he had relocated in the North. In his 1950 essay "Agrarianism in Exile," he described his situation at Robert Hutchins's university, Chicago (and that of a number of his mentors among the southern agrarians), as a "strategic withdrawal," an effort to gain an audience that he knew was not available to southern intellectuals so long as they spoke *from within the patria*. Having begun his research in a close consideration of southern intellectual history, he turned to examine the larger context of radical change within which the struggles of his own people had their most lasting significance. In 1932 Weaver had been a Socialist. By the time of his arrival in Chicago, he had become a principled advocate of traditionalist conservatism. With the 1948 publication of his first important book, *Ideas Have Consequences*, he emerged a major figure in the postwar revival of intellectual conservatism in America. His policy had been to divest the vision of life inherited from his North Carolina forebears of its fortuitous regional overtones in idiom and preoccupation.

Soon Weaver became an advisory editor of *Modern Age* and a regular contributor to William Buckley's new magazine, *National Review*. His work covered a wide range of subjects, but his next book reflected his growing competence in a new area of specialization. With *The Ethics of Rhetoric* (1953), Weaver became a leader in the restoration of the ancient discipline of rhetoric to its proper dignity as a basic component of a liberal education. His main argument in these studies was that corruption in the use of language has been a major source of the confusion concerning the hierarchy of human values so characteristic of our time. How a thing is said and what it means, he insisted, are inseparable. Some of his best work concerned the operation of concealed pleading in the diction of social scientists and politicians and in the structures of famous debates. Weaver wrote a rhetoric textbook. He also composed distinguished commentaries on the rhetorical design of famous texts from Plato and Milton. A posthumous collection of his rhetorical papers, *Language Is Sermonic* (1970), contains further confirmation of his authority in this field.

In the last decade of his life, Weaver did a good deal of public speaking and produced some powerful commentary on the pressing political questions of the day. He was especially concerned by egalitarian attacks on his native culture, "the regime of the South." Philosophically this preoccupation resulted in his most important work in

political theory, *Visions of Order* (1964), and in the collection *Life without Prejudice and Other Essays* (1965), a defense of the prescriptive approach to social questions and an attack on the utopianism of liberal schemes. But throughout the Chicago years Weaver had kept ready for the press the book that he had made out of his dissertation. This study, as *The Southern Tradition at Bay: A History of Postbellum Thought*, finally appeared in 1968. To this opus he had planned to add an American Plutarch, a set of brief intellectual biographies matching figures from North and South. But there was not time to complete this final return to the intellectual interests with which he had begun his scholarly career.

In these last years Professor Weaver got back to North Carolina and Weaverville at every opportunity, to reassuring places, friends, and the magic circle of the blood. Furthermore, at the end of his life he was planning to leave Chicago and accept an appointment to the faculty of Vanderbilt University, where the odyssey of his intellectual life had begun. In moving to succeed Donald Davidson at Vanderbilt, he had completed the pattern and was, by general agreement, one of the most southern thinkers and conservative voices of his time. His public life was the solitary life of the mind. Yet a passion for dialectics was not the source of his achievements. During a 1950 family reunion, Weaver spoke of the necessity of knowing who you are and where you are from. Concerning these home truths he was not confused. Richard M. Weaver, who never married, died in Chicago and was buried at Weaverville.

SEE: *Asheville Citizen*, 4 Apr. 1963; M. E. Bradford, "The Agrarianism of Richard Weaver: Beginnings and Completions," *Modern Age* 14 (1970); George Core, "One View of the Castle: Richard Weaver and the Incarnate World of the South," *Spectrum* 2 (1972); Eugene Davidson, "Richard Malcolm Weaver—Conservative," *Modern Age* 7 (Summer 1963); John East, "Richard M. Weaver: The Conservative Affirmation," *Modern Age* 19 (1975); James B. Graves, Jr., *Proposal for the Establishment of Richard M. Weaver College* (1977); Willmoore Kendall, "How to Read Richard Weaver: Philosopher of 'We the (Virtuous) People,'" *Intercollegiate Review* 2 (1965); Frank S. Meyer, "Richard M. Weaver: An Appreciation," *Modern Age* 14 (1970); Marion Montgomery, "Richard Weaver against the Establishment," *Georgia Review* 23 (1969); George S. Nash, *The Conservative Intellectual Movement in America since 1945* (1976); Pearl M. Weaver, *The Tribe of Jacob: The Descendants of the Reverend Jacob Weaver of Reem's Creek, North Carolina . . .* (1962); Richard M. Weaver Papers (Vanderbilt University Library, Nashville, Tenn.).

M. E. BRADFORD

Weaver, Rufus Washington (*3 June 1870–31 Jan. 1947*), clergyman, college president, and author, was born in Greensboro, the son of Preston De Kalb, a farmer and merchant, and Elizabeth Jane Forbis Weaver. He was graduated from Wake Forest College in 1893 with both a bachelor's and a master's degree and was ordained to the Baptist ministry in the same year. From the Southern Baptist Theological Seminary he received the Th.M. degree in 1898 and the Th.D. degree in 1899. At other times he undertook graduate study at the University of Cincinnati and the Johns Hopkins University. For the next eighteen years he was a pastor at churches in High Point, Middletown, Ohio, Baltimore, Md., Cincinnati, Ohio, and Nashville, Tenn. In Nashville he also taught religious education in the School of Religion at Vanderbilt University (1913–17). He was president of the Educational Board of the

Tennessee Baptist Convention (1912–17) and secretary of Christian Education (1917–18). Elected president of Mercer University in Macon, Ga., in 1918, he served until 1927. Under his guidance the university grew in both financial resources and numbers of students; it also added schools of theology, law, education, and journalism.

Following his resignation he became secretary of the education board of the Southern Baptist Convention for a year and resided in Birmingham, Ala. Moving to Washington, D.C., he occupied himself with writing and publishing. He was the author of a number of books and pamphlets (including sermons). Among the books were *Christian Conversationalist* (1904), *Religious Development of the Child* (1913), *Christian's Faith in the Nation's Capital* (1936), *Revolt Against God* (1944), and *Champions of Religious Liberty* (1946). During the period 1934–36 he was pastor of the First Baptist Church in Washington and a member of the faculty at American University, where he taught psychology. He was executive secretary of the local association of Baptist churches, which became the District of Columbia Baptist Convention, where he served until 1943. While there he helped to create the Baptist Joint Conference Committee on Public Relations to speak for the major branches of the Baptist church in the United States, both white and black.

For the remainder of his life he was a member of the Ministers Council of the Northern Baptist Convention. Throughout his active career Weaver served in various positions not directly related to the Baptist church. For three years he was president of the Association of Georgia Colleges, director of the Georgia Education Association, member of the education committee of the National Council of Boy Scouts of America, and member of the Georgia State Board of Education.

Weaver was awarded honorary degrees by Wake Forest College, Bethel College (in Kentucky), and Baylor University. In 1911 he married Charlotte Lewis Mason Payne, widow of John Daniel Payne. They had no children.

SEE: *Encyclopedia of Southern Baptists*, vol. 2 (1958); *Greensboro Daily News*, 1 Feb. 1947; Samuel S. Hill, ed., *Encyclopedia of Religion in the South* (1984); *Nat. Cyc. Am. Biog.*, vol. 35 (1949 [portrait]); *New York Times*, 1 Feb. 1947 (portrait); *Who Was Who in America*, vol. 2 (1950).

WILLIAM S. POWELL

Weaver, William Trotter *(18 July 1858–6 Nov. 1916)*, pioneer in furnishing electric power to western Carolina, was born in the Reems Creek valley near Weaverville, the youngest son of James Thomas and Hester Trotter Weaver. When he was four his father joined the Confederate army and, as lieutenant colonel of the Sixtieth North Carolina Regiment, was killed in December 1864 while leading his regiment at the Battle of Murfreesboro, Tenn. Hester Weaver and the children took refuge near Spartanburg, S.C., where William for a time "went to school to a Miss Julia Lee." At the end of the war the family returned home, and young Weaver walked two miles each day to attend the Methodist Academy near Weaverville, which became a college for men in 1870. After completing the sophomore year at the college when he was eighteen, Weaver became a clerk in a store at $12.50 per month. This enabled him to pay for his own education and that of his younger sisters.

Weaver's business career began when he was employed by the Saluda Manufacturing Company, a cotton mill, in Columbia, S.C., for which he became sales manager. Returning to western North Carolina in 1882, he entered into a partnership to sell shoes in a general furnish-

ings store on Pack Square in Asheville. In September 1885, during the administration of President Grover Cleveland, Weaver was appointed postmaster at age twenty-seven. With the expiration of Cleveland's term, Weaver's political appointment ended, but he was long remembered for his successful delivery of the mail "during the great snowstorm of 1888." Also during the 1880s he was elected captain of the Asheville Light Infantry, a unit of the state militia. As was then the custom, he thereafter was referred to as Captain Weaver.

Joining the staff of the National Bank of Asheville, he became its president in 1896 on the eve of a national financial crisis. Although the other banks in the city collapsed, all of the depositors of the National Bank of Asheville were paid promptly and in full before the doors were finally closed in October 1897. Weaver's business acumen was credited for the bank's excellent condition.

During the period 1890–96 he was the moving spirit behind the establishment of the first electric street railway in Asheville. This line connected the center of town with the village of Biltmore near which George Vanderbilt was then building his splendid château, completed in 1896. After some financial difficulties the street railway was acquired by the Asheville Electric Company, which Weaver had formed in October 1897. Indeed, it was the necessity for providing power for the various street railways then operating in the city that inspired him to undertake his most imaginative and daring enterprise—one that would have a lasting effect on the region.

The city of Asheville saw its first electric street railway in 1886 and limited public electric service in 1889. In 1890 E. G. Carrier, a hotelman and entrepreneur, built the first hydroelectric plant near Asheville, producing 40 kilowatts of direct current. In 1892 two generators were erected on Upper Hominy Creek to produce 250 kilowatts for the rapidly expanding railways and street lighting. These facilities were incorporated into Weaver's electric company in October 1897. By 1900 this company was serving 100 street lights and 5,000 incandescent bulbs. At this time Weaver recognized the possibilities for a much larger plant on the French Broad River below Great Craggy Mountain, five miles north of Asheville.

In 1903 he was able to secure financing in Boston and began constructing his own power plant. The Weaver plant opened in 1904, generating power from a granite dam that fed the waters of the French Broad River through a canal to the turbines downstream. By 1908 the W. T. Weaver Power Company supplied all of the Asheville Electric Power Company's needs for the four consolidated street railway lines in the city. In subsequent years the W. T. Weaver Power Company completed other plants along the French Broad River at Ivy and Elk Mountain. On 1 July 1916 the Elk Mountain plant came on stream producing 13,000 kilowatts for the system.

July 1916 proved to be a fateful month, however. On the tenth, six days of torrential rain began, resulting in the failure of the dam on Lake Toxaway upriver near Brevard. In this greatest flood disaster of the century, power plants along the river were inundated, and 185 feet of the dam at the Craggy plant were washed away. Weaver was at the scene almost constantly, laboring with the workmen under nearly impossible flood conditions in an effort to save the equipment and repair the damage. Exhaustion and exposure took their toll. He became seriously ill in August and died three months later at age fifty-eight. He was buried in Riverside Cemetery, Asheville.

Weaver had been a steward in the Central Methodist Church of Asheville and a leader in the building program that produced an imposing stone church. He was also a leader in the Masonic lodge. Although a strong Democrat, he never sought public office but was a frequent public speaker. His avocation was raising livestock, and with Haywood Parker, a local attorney, he imported the first herd of Angus cattle into that section of the state.

After Weaver's death the power company continued under the direction of T. S. Morrison until 1923, when it became part of the Electric Bond and Share Company. Later consolidated with the Asheville Power and Light Company, it was acquired by the newly formed Carolina Power and Light Company in 1926.

Weaver was married on 1 Feb. 1887 to Annie Laurie Johnston, the daughter of businessman William and Lucinda Gudger Johnston and the sister of Thomas D. Johnston, a congressman from Buncombe County in 1885–89. They had one daughter, Dorothea Johnston.

SEE: John P. Arthur, *Western North Carolina: A History* (1914); Samuel A. Ashe, ed., *Biographical History of North Carolina*, vol. 6 (1907); *Asheville Citizen*, 7 Nov. 1916, 28 Jan. 1940, 10 Apr. 1949, 17 July 1960; Jack Riley, *Carolina Power and Light Company, 1908–1958* (1958); F. A. Sondley, *A History of Buncombe County*, vol. 2 (1930); Pearl M. Weaver, *The Tribe of Jacob* (1952).

WILLIAM WEAVER RHOADES
VERNE RHOADES, JR.

Weaver, Zebulon *(12 May 1872–29 Oct. 1948)*, congressman and North Carolina legislator, was born on a farm near Weaverville in Buncombe County to William Elbert and Hanna E. Baird Weaver. His lineage included two prominent families of western North Carolina. His great-grandfather John Weaver may have been the first settler in Buncombe County. The town of Weaverville was named for Zebulon's grandfather, Metroville Weaver. His father had fought in the Civil War, developed large land interests, and played an active role in Democratic politics, including service in the General Assembly. Zebulon's mother was a granddaughter of Zebulon Baird, another pioneer resident of the area.

Weaver was first employed as a teacher in the Madison County schools after receiving a B.A. degree from Weaverville College in 1890. He studied law at The University of North Carolina (1894–95), was admitted to the bar, and returned to Asheville to practice general corporate and civil law. Entering politics, he served in the North Carolina House of Representatives in 1907 and 1909 and was a state senator from 1913 to 1915. In the 1907 session of the General Assembly he helped to draft North Carolina's first conservation laws, an action that reflected his lifelong interest in the environment. As a boy he had been intimately acquainted with the ornithologist John S. Carnes, who instilled the abiding appreciation for wildlife.

In 1916 Weaver ran as a Democrat for Congress in the traditionally Republican Tenth District. In a very tight race he was declared elected locally after he won 9 more votes than Congressman James J. Britt out of 36,000 votes cast. Britt continued to contest the election although Weaver was seated in Congress in March 1917. On 1 Mar. 1919, a few days before the end of the term, Britt was declared legally elected and was paid for two years of service for which Weaver had already been paid. Meanwhile, Weaver had been formally elected to a second term in 1918. He resumed his service and continued to be reelected each succeeding term until 1946, except for the great Republican triumph of 1928. During those years Buncombe County's district was changed to the Eleventh and in 1941 to the Twelfth District. Seeking renomination for a fifteenth term in 1946, Weaver was defeated by Monroe M. Redden of Hendersonville.

In Congress Weaver was a strong advocate of the policies of Woodrow Wilson and Franklin D. Roosevelt. On foreign policy matters, he was an internationalist. He was the only member of the North Carolina delegation to vote for the woman suffrage amendment. Weaver is most remembered for his support of the Great Smoky Mountains National Park and the Blue Ridge Parkway. Indeed, when he ran for renomination in 1946, he sought to remain in Congress only one more term so that he could see the parkway completed.

Weaver married Anna Capus Hyman, the daughter of Theodore Hyman, a prominent lumberman of Goldsboro and New Bern, on 11 Oct. 1899. The couple had five children: Mary Danvers (Mrs. Carter H. Hites of Washington, D.C.), Hannah Baird (Mrs. J. Frank Johnson of Peterboro, N.H.), Theodore Hyman (d. 1946), Zebulon, Jr., and Frances (Mrs. Walter Cuthrell of Asheville). Weaver's wife died in 1938.

After being defeated for Congress, Weaver practiced law with his son, Zebulon, Jr., in Asheville until declining health forced him to retire. He was buried in Riverside Cemetery, Asheville.

SEE: *Asheville Citizen*, October–December 1916, January–March 1917, 30 Oct. 1948, 4 Apr. 1972, 27 July 1976; *Biog. Dir. Am. Cong.* (1961); John L. Cheney, Jr., ed., *North Carolina Government, 1585–1979* (1981); Daniel L. Grant, *Alumni History of the University of North Carolina* (1924); *North Carolina Biography*, vols. 4 (1929), 3 (1941); *North Carolina Manual* (1945); Raleigh *News and Observer*, 30 Oct. 1948; *We the People of North Carolina*, November 1943; *Who Was Who in America*, vol. 2 (1950).

THOMAS S. MORGAN

Webb, Charles Aurelius *(4 Nov. 1866–11 Dec. 1949)*, newspaper publisher, attorney, legislator, and teacher, was born in Warrenton, the son of Alexander S. and Anabelle Moore Webb. His father, whose family was long prominent in Orange, Person, and Granville counties, fought in some of the bloodiest battles of the Civil War, lost all of his holdings as a result of that conflict, and suffered severe financial setbacks during Reconstruction. Because of these difficulties, the fifteen-year-old Charles was taken into the home of his uncles, W. R. (Old Sawney) and J. M. Webb, who operated the noted Webb School in Tennessee. There he received his preparatory education before entering The University of North Carolina in 1886. Although he worked his way through the university, he was graduated in 1889 with the second highest honors in his class and received the Willie P. Mangum medal for oratory.

In the fall of 1889 Webb moved to Asheville, where he had accepted a teaching position. He continued the study of law, begun while he was at the university, and was admitted to the bar in 1891. For more than a quarter of a century he had a large and successful law practice. Regarded as one of the most resourceful trial lawyers in the region, he figured in many of the more important cases in western North Carolina around the opening of the twentieth century.

Always interested in political and public affairs, Webb, a Democrat, represented Buncombe County in the state senate in 1903, 1905, and 1907, serving as president pro tem in the last two terms. He was considered one of the best leaders on the senate floor and a parliamentarian of rare ability. In 1907 he became chairman of the Committee on Insane Asylums and was instrumental in securing passage of an appropriation for permanent improvements for the state hospitals for the indigent insane. He was named by the governor as a member of a commission to spend the funds and served as its chairman.

Earlier he had introduced and secured passage of a bill limiting the time attorneys could use in addressing juries in certain cases. He also prepared the legislation that established a separate police court of Asheville and enlarged the jurisdiction of municipal courts. Named chairman of the state Democratic executive committee in 1912, he served for a year before resigning to accept appointment by President Woodrow Wilson as U.S. marshal for the Western District. He held this position throughout the Wilson administration.

While a U.S. marshal he realized a boyhood ambition by purchasing a newspaper, the *Asheville Gazette-News*, an afternoon paper, in February 1916, changing its name to the *Asheville Times*. Three years later he and George Stephens of Charlotte bought the *Asheville Citizen*. Before long Webb sold the *Times* and, virtually abandoning the practice of law, devoted his time almost exclusively to directing publication of the *Citizen*.

In 1930 he bought Stephens's interest in the *Citizen*, and later in the year he and Don S. Elias, then owner of the *Times*, merged the two newspapers. Webb served as president of the Asheville Citizen-Times Company until March 1949, when, at his own request, he was relieved of his duties as president. He continued as chairman of the board until his death.

Webb served as president of the North Carolina Press Association, as a director of the Southern Newspaper Publishers Association, and as chairman of the open shop committee of the American Newspaper Publishers Association. He participated in the meeting in 1899 that launched the organized effort to establish a national park in the Southern Appalachian Mountains and labored forty years before seeing the plan realized. He served as a director of the Southern Appalachian National Park Association, which laid the foundation for establishment of the Great Smoky Mountains National Park. In 1956 an overlook about six miles from Newfound Gap along the road leading to Clingman's Dome was named for him. He also devoted much of his time and the influence of the *Citizen* and the *Times* to securing the Blue Ridge Parkway for western North Carolina. Webb was concerned about the welfare of black citizens of the community, and the Asheville Colored Hospital was largely his creation.

On 10 July 1895 he married Bruce Banks of Washington, D.C. She died in 1913 leaving four children: Charles Bruce, Robert Stanford, Julia Banks, and Mandeville Alexander. In 1914 Webb married Mrs. Jessie Close Shaw, a native of Michigan who died on 15 Nov. 1960 at age ninety-eight. Webb was buried in Riverside Cemetery, Asheville. His portrait, a gift of employees of the newspaper, hangs in the Asheville Citizen-Times Building.

SEE: *Asheville Times*, 12 Dec. 1949; *North Carolina Biography*, vol. 4 (1928); North Carolina Press Association, *Pro ceedings* (1950); F. A. Sondley, *History of Buncombe County, North Carolina*, 2 vols. (1930); Stephen B. Weeks Scrapbook, vol. 2, p. 93 (North Carolina Collection, University of North Carolina, Chapel Hill); *Who Was Who in America*, vol. 2 (1950).

MARY COWLES

Webb, Edwin Yates (*23 May 1872–7 Feb. 1955*), congressman and federal judge, was born in Shelby, the son of the Reverend George M., a Baptist minister, and Priscilla Jane Blanton Webb. He received an undergraduate degree from Wake Forest College (1893), studied law at The University of North Carolina (1893–94), did postgraduate work at the University of Virginia, and was awarded the LL.D. degree by Davidson College (1918). In 1894 he was both admitted to the bar and elected to the state senate. He won a seat in Congress in 1900 and served eight terms; he was coauthor of the Webb-Kenyon Act and the bill establishing the Boy Scouts of America. He introduced the Webb Export Act, helped to write the Eighteenth Amendment, and played a significant role in shaping the Pure Food and Drug Laws. He also submitted the bill for appropriations to erect a monument at Kings Mountain commemorating the American victory there on 7 Oct. 1780.

Webb and his brother, state senator and superior court judge James L. Webb, and other men in their part of the state associated themselves in support of political activities. For many years in the 1920s and 1930s they gave North Carolina and the nation leaders so outstanding that their effectiveness came to be labeled "The Shelby Dynasty." The Webbs' concerns were broader than mere politics, as they promoted broad educational and religious interests throughout a state in which their constructive involvement was widely acclaimed. Their role was recognized in the establishment of Gardner-Webb College, a four-year Baptist institution at Boiling Springs, near Shelby. Webb was honored with a testimonial dinner at the college on his eightieth birthday, and a portrait of him hangs in its library. Other portraits of Webb are in the federal courtroom in Charlotte and in the Cleveland County Courthouse, in Shelby, where he presided for thirty-six years.

He was a leading layman of the First Baptist Church of Shelby, moderator of the Kings Mountain Baptist Association, and a member of the Kiwanis Club. Webb's first wife was Willie Simmons of Wake Forest, and they were the parents of Elizabeth, Edwin, Jr., and William. His second wife was Mrs. Alice Pender Taylor of Tarboro and Asheville. He was buried in Sunset Cemetery, Shelby.

SEE: *Asheville Citizen*, 8 Feb. 1955; *Charlotte Observer*, 31 Oct. 1937; John L. Cheney, Jr., ed., *North Carolina Government, 1585–1971* (1981); Daniel L. Grant, *Alumni History of the University of North Carolina* (1924); *Men of Achievement in the Carolinas* (1952 [portrait]); *North Carolina Biography*, vols. 3 (1919), 3 (1941), 4 (1929); *Who's Who in the South and Southwest* (1952).

H. HOLT MCPHERSON

Webb, James (*20 Feb. 1774–17 Feb. 1855*), pioneer physician of Hillsborough and Orange County, Presbyterian educational leader and philanthropist, merchant, and banker, was born at Tally Ho, Granville County, the second child and eldest son of ten children of William (1745–1809) and Frances (Fannie) Young Webb (d. 1810), and the grandson of gentleman planter James (1705–71) and Mary Edmondson Webb (1712–95) of South Farnham Parish, Essex County, Va. During 1795–96 he attended The University of North Carolina, where, on or about 18 Aug. 1796, he made the significant motion to change the English name of the Debating Society to its Greek equivalent, Dialectic Society. This was done officially a week later, on 25 August, and four days after that the companion Concord Society followed suit and changed its name to Philanthropic Society. Thus, the time-honored names of the university's Di and Phi Societies are the result of James Webb's 1796 motion. He enrolled in 1798 for a medical course at the University of Pennsylvania under Benjamin Rush and established himself as a physician and merchant in the town of Hillsborough in the closing years of the eighteenth century.

Like most early doctors, Webb necessarily supplemented his uncertain income from the medical profession in other ways, and his busy mercantile and medical careers ran concurrently until the end of his life. From 1799 to 1801 or a little later, he appears to have been a silent partner in the Hillsborough store of the successful Raleigh mercantile firm of Messrs. Southey and William Bond. He was also the major partner for several years with his brother Thomas in a mercantile establishment, James Webb & Co., near their father's home in Granville County.

In the late autumn of 1799 Dr. Webb was a principal figure in the establishment of the North Carolina State Medical Society, which met in Raleigh on 17 December for its historic organizational meeting. Webb was elected vice-president and appointed a member of the Board of Censors created by this early society (the eighth in the nation) to examine and accredit would-be doctors. This important forerunner of the modern system of medical examiners was the pioneer regulation of its kind. At the society's second meeting on 1 Dec. 1800, Webb read a paper on the causes and prevention of gout and rheumatism. Although the new State Medical Society ceased to exist after only five years, probably because of bad roads and the difficulties of transportation, it was Webb's ward and best-known medical student, Dr. Edmund Charles Fox Strudwick, who, forty-five years later in 1849, revived it from its dormant state and served as president. The seventy-five-year-old Webb was then made an honorary charter member and signally honored by the society.

Numbers of Webb's lengthy orders for medicines, small equipment, and so forth, sent to New York suppliers in the 1840s, have been preserved in the James Webb Papers in the Southern Historical Collection at The University of North Carolina, an immensely valuable compilation of records detailing many essential aspects of the growth of Hillsborough and Orange County. Webb kept no case histories or formal medical records as such. But fascinating notations concerning specific cases are to be found hurriedly jotted down in dim pencil on the backboards of his own mercantile ledgers, and a few accounts of special cases are recorded in the Cameron Papers in the Southern Historical Collection. Webb's ledgers sometimes note prices charged—"$30 for leg amputation," "Death and Burial, $1," "For cuting his eye—$2," "By Death—$12," "Ex Dent Julia [charged]"—and often record that he was never paid at all, or perhaps in cider, oats, eggs, chickens, and watermelons.

For many years he published an annual Bill of Mortality (vital statistics) in the Hillsborough *Recorder* that frequently included other useful data—the Bill of Mortality for 6 Jan. 1842 noted that there were then 150 students in the Hillsborough area alone. In 1822 Webb gave free smallpox vaccinations every Wednesday for two hours—a landmark clinic effort in Orange County medical history. Like many early doctors, he provided a vast amount of charity work to both blacks and whites and to area students that was ultimately paid for by mercantile undertakings of one kind or another.

Numerous students went to Hillsborough to read medicine with Webb at his small, two-story "medical shop" (office) and dispensary on East Queen Street. No complete list has ever been made of his medical students, but they included Edmund C. F. Strudwick, William Webb, Henry Young Webb, Walter A. Norwood, Thomas H. Turner, H. O. W. Hooker, J. E. Williamson, Thompson N. Johnston, George H. Mitchell, and probably Johnston D. Jones and L. D. Schoolfield.

Webb's first recorded real estate transaction in Hillsborough was the notable purchase for £300 on 17 Oct.

1800 of two properties on Margaret Lane, Lots 10 and 13, later sold to his friend Duncan Cameron, for whom he served as second in a famous duel fought between Cameron and the lawyer William Duffy on Sunday, 17 Apr. 1803, just over the Virginia line. The lots were the site of Cameron's law office (later Chief Justice Frederick Nash's) and his home (later Frederick Nash's and the Nash and Kollock School). For two and a half years (1 Jan. 1805–1 July 1807) Webb served as postmaster of Hillsborough.

On 26 Jan. 1807, in preparation for his coming marriage, Webb bought from James Phillips the five lots on the northern side of East Queen Street where he lived for the rest of his life—Lots 63, 64, and 65 where there stood an old inn that he evidently gradually converted into a rambling L-shaped yellow frame house, Lot 83 on the southern side of East Queen Street where he built his office and dispensary (with a saddler's shop just above it), and Lot 102, "the barn lot" adjoining Lot 83 on the south. (None of these structures now survives.) This five-acre estate, once a landmark in Hillsborough, was kept intact for decades.

On 12 Feb. 1807 Webb married Annie Alves Huske (13 Jan. 1785–23 June 1852), the orphaned daughter of the Englishman John Huske (d. 1792) and Elizabeth (Betsy) Hogg (d. 1788) and the granddaughter of the Scottish merchant James Hogg (d. 1805) and Elizabeth McDowell Alves (d. 1801). Ten children, nine of whom survived, were born to them: Henry Young, Frances Helen, Elizabeth, Ann (Annie), James, William (d. aged two), John Huske, Mary, William, and Thomas. Two of the sons, Henry Young and William, became physicians; James, Jr., was a well-known Hillsborough merchant.

In 1810 Webb was appointed Hillsborough agent (cashier) of the Branch Bank of the Cape Fear, a post that he held until 1846. The bank, staffed by five directors, in addition to the agent, rented a small structure belonging to the William Whitted estate on West King Street. Scores of stockholders' lists, records of quarterly dividends paid, loans and debts outstanding, and so forth still exist, as does at least one of the massive ledgers of the bank.

As early as 1804 Webb had begun his long, varied, and devoted service to the cause of education for both males and females at every level in Hillsborough. On 13 Dec. 1804, as "Trustee," he signed advertisements in the *Raleigh Register* for the Hillsborough Academy under Richard Henderson. He was clerk of the academy's board in 1815 and still a member of its nine-man board of trustees in 1839, when William James Bingham was principal. In addition, Webb served as guardian for countless boys attending the Hillsborough Academy, many of whom boarded in his home and for whom he sometimes became financially responsible.

Webb also single-handedly initiated and underwrote two famed Presbyterian schools in Hillsborough—Miss Mary W. (Polly) Burke's School and the Burwell Female School. In 1817 he erected a log schoolhouse (still standing as part of the Thomas Webb House) on his own Lot 63 in which his friend and neighbor, Mary Burke, should conduct a day school for the Webb children and those of his neighbors. This small, very modest elementary school continued with high success until 1834 and is usually cited as the forerunner of Hillsborough's excellent Presbyterian female schools. After the death of James Hogg, Webb had become Miss Burke's staunch supporter and closest adviser and remained so—even after she moved to Alabama in 1834—until his death.

In 1837 Webb suggested to Mrs. M. A. Burwell that she should teach his daughter Mary and two other Presbyterian girls, and the idea of the Burwell Female School took root. The new school, which not only replaced Miss Burke's school but also provided an extra four-year curriculum for older girls, operated successfully for twenty years (1837–57), with Webb always listed as its "Patron" (trustee). Burwell School records preserved in the James Webb Papers show that Webb financially underwrote the first renovation of the Burwell house (then the Presbyterian Manse) and steadily supported the undertaking without stint. Both Miss Mary W. Burke's School and the Burwell Female School were unquestionably Webb's personal creations. In 1825 he was also the president of the Orange County Sunday School Union, which petitioned unsuccessfully to gain state support for twenty-two Sunday schools to teach poor and indigent children to read and write.

At the opposite end of the scale, Webb was a "faithful, strong, and wise" trustee of The University of North Carolina for thirty-eight years (1812–50). In 1827 he served on the board of visitors and in 1830 on an emergency committee to help restore the university to a sound financial basis after the panic of 1825. For nearly half a century his involvements with education were continuous, widely varied, and extremely demanding, ranging from his own "Medical School" to the state university.

Webb's philanthropic support to local churches was no less than his aid to local schools. Although only his wife was formally listed in 1816 as one of the nine organizers of the new Hillsborough Presbyterian Church, Webb signed the first "true copy" of pew rental lists on 20 Sept. 1816 and consistently made large contributions to the Reverend John Knox Witherspoon's salary and to other church expenses over a period of years. In 1835 he took in his own name a ninety-nine-year lease on the extreme southeastern corner (30' × 40') of the Old Town Cemetery lot (98) and there erected a frame Sessions House with bell tower, used as a Presbyterian Sunday School room and eventually as a public library until 1934. He also served as a Presbyterian elder from 1835 until his death.

In 1822 Webb had provided the trustees of the Methodist congregation with both money and lumber to erect the first Methodist church in Hillsborough on the southwestern corner (44' × 44') of his own Lot 102, and on 1 Feb. 1823 he leased to them for ten shillings the plot "on which part the house now stands." An interesting paper, written in 1832 by Joseph B. Bacon, a leading Methodist trustee, mentions in considerable detail the indebtedness of the church to Webb, noting his many voluntary gifts and loans "and that he has waited patiently Ten years for the money that we still owe him." Bacon noted that Webb and his wife had frequently entertained the minister "comfortably" on Sundays and had "looked after" his horses.

Webb's extensive mercantile undertakings included a general store and lumberyard, later known as Webb, Long & Co., in which his son-in-law Dr. Osmond F. Long was a partner, and a sizable brickyard (Webb & Hancock) operating near the Eno River. He also entered into brief partnerships with various townsmen on occasion, such as with J. J. Freeland under the title Webb & Freeland. A sideline that almost amounted to a business with both Webb and Justice Thomas Ruffin was the hiring out on an annual basis of the slaves of widows and of ailing or absent owners. Webb also served as clerk and master in equity in scores of estate settlements and as the executor of innumerable Hillsborough and Orange County wills. The paperwork involved in his undertakings was enormous, and his swift, sloping handwriting appears on innumerable preserved lists, bills, receipts, inventories, and the like.

On 1 Nov. 1842 Dr. James Webb was declared bankrupt, and on 11 December his possessions were sold at public auction—the inevitable result of four decades of open-handed generosity to Hillsborough schools and churches, to academy students and medical students, to the sick and poor, and to his friends and relatives, and of a huge backlog of unpaid debts. His friends and neighbors repurchased for Webb and his family almost every item offered at the sale except "an old copper kettle & an old pair of steelyards"—a tribute to his half century of undeviating honesty and service to the town.

Mrs. Webb, long ailing, died in 1852, and Webb died three years later at age eighty-one. Both were buried in the Webb-Long plot in Hillsborough's Old Town Cemetery. No likeness or portrait of Webb in his later years is known to exist; a portrait of him as a young man, the provenance of which seems not to be certainly known, is reproduced in various publications. There also is said to exist a "composite" portrait of "James Webb" in which leading characteristics of the successive James Webbs have all been blended together in a single portrait.

SEE: Kemp P. Battle, *History of the University of North Carolina*, vol. 1 (1907); Marshall De Lancey Haywood, "The N.C. Medical Society of 1799–1804," *North Carolina Booklet* 16 (1916–17); *Old Town Cemetery (1757), Hillsborough, North Carolina* (1966); Orange County Deed Books (Orange County Courthouse, Hillsborough); William N. Tillinghast Papers (Manuscript Department, Duke University Library, Durham); James Webb Account Book, 1813–20 (Hillsborough Historical Society, Hillsborough); James Webb Papers, Bank of Cape Fear (Hillsborough Branch) Books, and Cameron Family Papers (Southern Historical Collection, University of North Carolina, Chapel Hill); James Webb Papers (North Carolina State Archives, Raleigh); Robert D. Webb, *The Webb Family* (1894); W. J. Webb and others, *Our Webb Kin of Dixie: A Family History* (1940).

MARY CLAIRE ENGSTROM

Webb, James Edwin (*7 Oct. 1906–27 Mar. 1992*), administrator of the National Aeronautics and Space Administration and other federal agencies, corporate executive, management expert, and attorney, was born in Tally Ho, near Stem in southwestern Granville County, the second child and first son of five children of John Frederick and Sarah Edwin Gorham Webb. His father was a teacher and then superintendent of the Granville County schools for twenty-six years (ca. 1907–34). Webb's first paternal American ancestor of record was James Webb (1705–71) of Essex County, Va. A Phi Beta Kappa graduate of The University of North Carolina, John Webb was a strong believer in education; four of his children (including James) also were graduated from Chapel Hill, and the fifth finished her studies at the state woman's college in Greensboro. Such a highly educated generation of siblings was uncommon in 1920s North Carolina.

Completing his secondary education at Oxford High School in 1923, James enrolled in the university at Chapel Hill. For financial reasons he interrupted his studies in 1924 to spend a year in the accounting department and as secretary to the president of R. G. Lassiter Construction Company in Raleigh. He returned to Chapel Hill in 1925 and was graduated in 1928 with a degree in education. For the next year he was secretary of the Bureau of Educational Research in The University of North Carolina's education department. In 1929 he became a legal clerk and stenographer for a small Oxford, N.C., law firm. After a year, he enlisted in the Marine Corps Reserve, learning to fly at the Pensacola Naval Air Station in Florida and becoming a second lieutenant and naval aviator in 1931. He spent a year on active duty at Quantico, Va., and then moved to Washington in 1932 as secretary to longtime Tar Heel congressman Edward W. Pou of Johnston County.

While working for Pou, the energetic Webb continued his flying activity as a Marine reserve officer and began studying law at night at George Washington University. From 1934 to 1936 he was an assistant in the Washington law office of former North Carolina governor O. Max Gardner. At the time Gardner was general counsel to the Aeronautical Chamber of Commerce of America, a trade group of airlines and aircraft manufacturers; this situation gave Webb substantial insight into the developing aviation industry.

After graduation from law school and admission to the District of Columbia bar in 1936, Webb moved to New York to become assistant to the president and personnel director of the Sperry Gyroscope Company. In five years he became vice-president. During much of the period Sperry worked under some 1,800 contracts to produce a great variety of complex scientific equipment for the military buildup of World War II. The company had over 30,000 employees, and Webb, while not a scientist per se, worked with engineers and researchers as well as accountants and general managers throughout the concern. At the same time he continued his interest in aviation, serving in 1938 with a group aiding the Department of Commerce to establish federal airways as well as in several professional aviation associations. The same year he married Patsy Aiken Douglas, of Washington, with whom he had two children and a union lasting until his death fifty-three years later. In 1943 Webb applied for active duty in the Marine Corps; by war's end he was commander of the First Marine Air Warning Group, which was developing night uses for radar in military aviation at Cherry Point, N.C.

After the war Webb briefly rejoined O. Max Gardner's law firm in Washington and in 1946 became executive assistant to Gardner when the latter was appointed undersecretary of the U.S. Treasury. In the same year President Harry S Truman, at Gardner's suggestion, named Webb, a Democrat as well as a highly competent administrator, director of the Bureau of the Budget. For three years he supervised preparation of the federal budget and was a principal adviser to the president on organization and management of the executive branch. He simplified federal statistical control systems, guided a study of federal research that helped spawn the National Science Foundation, assisted in updating accounting procedures, and coordinated executive cooperation with the Hoover Commission to improve governmental efficiency. Truman next made Webb undersecretary of state, where Webb reorganized the 20,000 members of the Department of State along recommendations of the Hoover Commission and maintained direct overall supervision of the global agency.

In late 1952, when the Democrats vacated the White House for the first time in twenty years, Webb moved to Oklahoma City to head the Republic Supply Company from 1953 to 1958. There he plunged into the petroleum industry, becoming a leader in trade organizations, director and assistant to the president of Kerr-McGee Oil Industries (the company of Senator Robert Kerr), and a key player in local civic and business groups. Among his many public service activities in the 1950s, he was at various times regional vice-president of the National Municipal League, director of the Oak Ridge Institute of Nuclear Studies, and a member of various advisory committees for George Washington and Harvard Universities, the Massachusetts Institute of Technology and Oklahoma State University. He also was a member of the executive committee of the U.S. Committee for the United Nations,

the National Advisory Cancer Council of the U.S. Public Health Service, and several national groups of citizen consultants advising the federal government on particular issues. Near the end of the decade Webb devoted about one-third of his time to business activities and two-thirds to public service work. He was president and part-time executive officer of Educational Services, a nonprofit corporation set up by the National Science and Ford Foundations to improve physics in high schools. About 1960 he returned to Washington to chair another Ford Foundation venture, the Municipal Manpower Commission, to devise ways to attract able young people to local government service.

In early 1961 the Democrats reentered the White House, and Robert Kerr of Oklahoma succeeded Lyndon Johnson as chairman of the Senate aerospace committee. Kerr recommended that Webb be named director of NASA, a growing federal agency founded in 1958. Reportedly reluctant, Webb accepted and used his management skills and political sophistication to accelerate the rise of NASA into a major federal agency that came to include some 35,000 government employees working with an additional 400,000 or so people in 20,000 contracting companies. NASA became a rare federal agency popular with both Congress and the public, and Webb used his myriad administrative skills and legendary mastery of detail to keep it on course. That course, announced by President John Kennedy in late May 1961 shortly after the Soviet Union triumphantly launched the first manned space flight (it had sent up the first unmanned satellite in 1957), was to put an American on the moon by 1970.

Webb and Secretary of Defense Robert McNamara secretly had advised Kennedy that men in space would capture the world's fancy and, despite likely marginal or nonexistent economic justification, greatly enhance American prestige. Many scientists felt that the nation had a good chance to reach the moon first, and the president, Congress, and Webb's NASA went to work. In July Congress doubled the agency's budget, and within a few years NASA spent $5 billion annually. When Webb established the Apollo (moon mission) command center in Houston, NASA began development of liquid fuel booster rockets, unmanned probes to the moon, and a lunar auto or rover. North American Aviation won the prime Apollo contract in late 1961.

In January 1967 three astronauts died in an Apollo space capsule on a launch pad during a rehearsal for the first launch. The resultant Senate investigation included much criticism of NASA and North American's receipt and handling of the contract. NASA's internal examination had ignored a key document of its own making, and the agency contracted with Boeing and Martin Marietta to get Apollo moving again. Congress reduced NASA's budget for 1967 and 1968. Warning that the Soviets might surpass America in space, Webb criticized the budget cuts and resigned in late 1968. Yet the major program he had begun went on successfully, and in July 1969 an American astronaut became the first man on the moon. Possibly more admired than loved at NASA, Webb had a reputation for able management, stubbornness, and a seeming delight in keeping his staff partly off balance—in his words, "planned disequilibrium." A celebrity of modesty, he rarely appeared at NASA's rocket launches and returned his government limousine to ride around Washington in a black Checker cab.

On leaving NASA, Webb returned to the payroll of Kerr-McGee Oil Industries for another decade and was a public spirited, active director of the National Geographic Society and regent of the Smithsonian Institution for many years. For the final decade of his life he suffered from Parkinson's disease; he died at age eighty-five of a heart attack at Georgetown University Hospital in Washington.

Webb was the author of such works as *Governmental Manpower for Tomorrow's Cities* (1962), *Space Age Management* (1968), and *Management Leadership and Relationship* (1972). A Presbyterian, he retired as a reserve lieutenant colonel in the Marine Corps. He received honorary degrees from thirty-two colleges and universities including Chapel Hill, Duke, Wake Forest, Syracuse, and Notre Dame. Among his many honors and awards were the Silver Buffalo from the Boy Scouts; the Presidential Medal of Freedom; state awards from North Carolina and Oklahoma; and major awards and/or medals from NASA, the Smithsonian, the National Geographic Society, and the U.S. Military Academy.

SEE: James M. Beggs, *James E. Webb: A Force for Excellence* (1983); *Durham Herald*, 30 Mar. 1992; Nelson Lichtenstein, ed., *Political Profiles: III, The Kennedy Years* (1946) and *IV, The Johnson Years* (1976); John M. Logsdon, *Decision to Go to the Moon* (1970); *Nat. Cyc. Am. Biog.*, vol. H (1952); *New York Times*, 29 Mar. 1992; *Oxford Public Ledger*, 30 Mar. 1992; Raleigh *News and Observer*, 29 Mar. 1992; Hugo Young and others, *Journey to Tranquillity* (1969).

RICHARD F. KNAPP

Webb, John Maurice *(29 Nov. 1847–5 Apr. 1916)*, educator, was born in Alamance County at a place called Stony Point, near Oaks, the son of Alexander Smith Webb (1804–30 June 1849), who died several months before the last Webb child was born, and Cornelia Adeline Stanford Webb (d. 1889). In the 1850 census John was listed as the tenth of eleven surviving children. His brothers were James Hazel (1829–1902), Sidney Smith (1836–1910), Richard Stanford (1837–1901, father of William Alexander Webb, 1867–1919), Alexander Smith (1840–1928), William Robert (Sawney, 1842–1926), and Samuel Henry (b. 1849); his sisters were Henrietta (1830–82), Susan Ann (Suny, 1831–1905), Mary Caroline (1833–1904), Amy Pomfret (1838–39), and Adrianna Adeline (Addie, 1845–97). William Robert founded the Webb School, a secondary school for boys, in Tennessee in the 1870s.

John Webb attended the Bingham School (in Oaks) from 1862 to 1865. In 1866 he entered The University of North Carolina and joined the Dialectic Society. During his two and one-half years as a student, he held the offices of recorder, secretary, librarian, vice-president, and archives keeper. In February 1868 he was elected one of two junior debaters. On 4 June 1868 he asked for and received a diploma from the Dialectic Society. Because the university closed after the Civil War (1871–75), he was not granted an honorary degree until 1875. In 1869 Webb returned to the Bingham School, then in Mebaneville, to teach for a year, and by 1870 he had secured a post at an academy in Rockingham. The census of that year listed him as having resided with a Covington family in Wolf Pit, Richmond County. He remained at the Rockingham school until he joined his brother in Culleoka, Tenn., in 1873. From 30 Jan. 1873 until his death, he served as principal and a teacher at the Webb School, which moved from Culleoka to Bell Buckle in 1886.

On 7 Dec. 1876 in Nashville, Tenn., he married Lily Shipp (1849–1929), the daughter of Professor and Mrs. Albert M. Shipp, formerly at The University of North Carolina, then at Vanderbilt University. Their children were Albert Micajah (1877–1965), Cornelia (b. 1879), Mary Gillespie (b. 1881), Sarah (b. 1884), and another son, Hazel Alexander (1886–88). Albert taught Romance languages

at Trinity College (afterwards Duke University) from 1903 until his retirement in 1947.

John Webb was known for his wide reading and comprehensive learning. He had a keen interest in Dante's works and started a Dante club to encourage his children, nieces, nephews, and others to read good literature. He and his brother William were known for having taught some of Vanderbilt's first and best students. The University of Nashville (later George Peabody College for Teachers) awarded Webb an honorary doctorate in 1895.

Webb was a charter member and president of the Philological Society of Tennessee. He was also a member of the executive committee of the Southern Association of Colleges and Schools, serving as president in 1899. His reputation of having some business ability earned him a term as president of the Bell Buckle Bank. He was a Methodist and an Independent Democrat. Webb died of a stroke in Bell Buckle and was buried in the Hazelwood Cemetery, named for his infant son.

SEE: Dialectic Society Papers (Archives, University of North Carolina, Chapel Hill); Washington Duke Papers (Manuscript Department, Duke University Library, Durham); *Durham Morning Herald*, 9 Sept. 1965; Graham *Alamance Gleaner*, 20 Apr. 1916; Daniel L. Grant, *Alumni History of the University of North Carolina* (1924); Laurence McMillin, *The Schoolmaker: Sawney Webb and the Bell Buckle Story* (1971 [portrait]); Edwin Mims, *John Maurice Webb, 1847–1916, An Address . . .* (1946); Raleigh *News and Observer*, 30 June 1929; Richard Dickins Webb, *The Webb Family* (1894); Albert M. Webb Papers and biographical file (University Archives, Duke University Library, Durham); W. J. Webb and others, *Our Webb Kin in Dixie: A Family History* (1940); *Who Was Who in America, 1897–1942* (1943).

EVA BURBANK MURPHY

Webb, Sarah M. Norfleet *(1788?–1850s?)*, the earliest known female newspaper editor in North Carolina and perhaps the first in the United States, was the daughter of Elisha (1759–1811) and Ann Evans Norfleet. Although the dates of her birth and death are unknown, she was listed as sixty-one years old in the 1850 census and her name did not appear in the census for 1860.

She married, first, James Wills, a highly respected citizen of Edenton, on 7 May 1815, when she became his third wife. Their marriage bond records her given name as Sally. Wills edited the *State Gazette of North-Carolina*, which until 1797 was published in Edenton by his brother, Henry. James Wills then was either editor or printer of the newspaper, which underwent several changes of name. After the death of her husband on 7 Aug. 1826, Sarah Wills became the editor of the *Edenton Gazette*. Regrettably only three issues of this newspaper—26 Jan., 13 Mar., and 8 May 1827—survive with her name in the masthead. While editor she advertised that she was able to handle "Handbills and other Job Printing." The issue for 31 July 1827 lists J. H. Barclift as publisher "for N. Bruer." Nathaniel Bruer was Henry Wills's stepson, so some family association with the paper may have continued.

A marriage bond was issued on 2 Dec. 1830 for the marriage of Sarah Wills to John Webb.

SEE: Carrie L. Broughton, *Marriage and Death Notices in the Raleigh Register and North Carolina State Gazetteer, 1826–1845* (1968); Chowan County census for 1820 and 1850, Chowan County Marriage Bonds (North Carolina State Archives, Raleigh); J. R. B. Hathaway, ed., *North Carolina Historical and Genealogical Register*, vols. 1–2 (1900–1901); Stuart Hall Hill, "Norfleets of Perquimans, Chowan,

Gates, Bertie, Edgecombe, and Halifax" (North Carolina Collection, University of North Carolina, Chapel Hill); Guion G. Johnson, *Ante-Bellum North Carolina* (1937); Elizabeth Vann Moore (Edenton) to B. W. C. Roberts, 1975–78; Thad Stem, Jr., *The Tar Heel Press* (1973); Will of James Wills (North Carolina State Archives, Raleigh).

B. W. C. ROBERTS

Webb, Thomas (*2 Nov. 1827–29 May 1894*), lawyer and railroad executive, was born in Hillsborough, the youngest son of Dr. James and Annie Alves Huske Webb. His father, Dr. James Webb, practiced medicine in Hillsborough for fifty years. Numerous students read medicine with Webb, who also initiated and underwrote two famed Presbyterian schools in Hillsborough, Miss Mary W. (Polly) Burke's School and the Burwell Female School. Thomas Webb's mother, Annie Alves Huske Webb, was a granddaughter of the Scotsman James Hogg, a University of Edinburgh graduate, merchant, and realtor who immigrated to North Carolina in 1774 setting out with a shipload of 280 persons. Hogg was on the committee to establish The University of North Carolina, served as president of the board of trustees, and was a large land donor to the university, where Thomas Webb was graduated in 1847.

On 16 Nov. 1854 Thomas married his second cousin, Robina Norwood (18 July 1835–24 Dec. 1919), the second daughter of John Wall and Anna Bella Giles Norwood. The Webbs lived at Norwood's Grove (later known as Poplar Hill and now known as Oconeechee Farm) with Robina's parents in the ancestral home built by James Hogg. For several years Webb was a clerk and master-in-equity before going into partnership with his father-in-law in the firm of Norwood and Webb, which did a large business in Orange and adjoining counties. In Hillsborough Presbyterian Church he was ordained an elder in 1855 and served as clerk of session in 1861.

About 1858, after two children were born, Thomas and Robina gathered material for a new home to be built on the knoll between the Hogg-Norwood house and the mineral spring. In the meantime, they moved to the Webb house on Queen Street, the one originally built by James Webb for his children's schoolroom. Due, however, to the Civil War, their new house was never constructed.

At a meeting of the Union party in Orange County for the purpose of nominating delegates to the proposed state convention, Thomas Webb served on the committee of nineteen representing the different sections of the county. After the Civil War began the president of the North Carolina Railroad, Charles S. Fisher, who had raised and equipped the North Carolina Sixth Regiment, was killed leading his unit on Rickett's Battery at Manassas during the first major encounter of the war on 21 July. The state nominated Webb president of the North Carolina Railroad, which he managed through the years of strife.

The Hillsborough Soldiers Aid Society, a group of ladies, gave food and aid to wounded soldiers traveling on the North Carolina Railroad. In 1861 the Orange County Court assumed responsibility for the support of the destitute families of its soldiers and managed this by dividing the county into districts, with an appointed commissioner for each district who assisted these needy families and reported all disbursements to Thomas Webb, who was treasurer of the soldiers' fund. In 1862 the wife of a Confederate soldier received $1.50 a month.

Federal forces failed to capture the North Carolina Railroad during the conflict, but the line suffered from both enemy attacks and the state's inability to provide adequate maintenance, including the replacement of worn-out rails and crossties.

In the 1870s, after managing to endure the havoc and ruin of the war, the Webb family suffered an even more dreadful time as Robina lay in bed with inflammatory rheumatism and Thomas was brought home paralyzed. For about eighteen years before his death, this handsome and learned man was an invalid. He was buried in the Old Town Cemetery in the family plot, where his wife also was interred in 1919. Of the Webbs' nine children, seven survived to adulthood: Margaret Taylor (22 Sept. 1855–1939), John Norwood (25 May 1858–1934), Anna Bella Giles (10 Sept. 1860–8 Feb. 1935), Alves (24 Dec. 1865–1924), James (23 Aug. 1868–23 May 1927), Thomas (5 Mar. 1871–1939), and Robin (24 May 1874–27 Mar. 1941). The two who died young were Benjamin Huske (6 July 1863–7 July 1866) and Eliza Plumer (29 Oct. 1876–26 Mar. 1877).

SEE: Ruth Blackwelder, *The Age of Orange* (1961); John F. Gilbert, *The Tree of Life: A History of the North Carolina Railroad* (1972); Archibald Henderson, *The Campus of the First State University* (1949); Hillsborough *News of Orange County*, 30 Oct. 1975; James Iredell and William H. Battle, comp., *Revised Statutes of the State of North Carolina*, vol. 2 (1837); Robina Webb Mickle, "Margaret Taylor Webb Mickle Biography" and "Manuscript of Webb Family History" (1951) (possession of Andrew Mickle, Winston-Salem, N.C.).

DONNA R. MICKLE
MENA F. WEBB

Webb, William Alexander (*30 July 1867–4 Nov. 1919*), educator and administrator, was born in that part of Orange County that later became Durham County, the son of Richard Stanford (23 Feb. 1837–10 Nov. 1901) and Jennie Morrow Clegg Webb (d. June 1910). His father was an itinerant pastor in the Methodist Episcopal church, so the family moved frequently. William Alexander was the oldest of at least five children. His brothers were Albert Shipp (b. 1873) and Richard; his sisters were Cornelia Catharine (b. Oct. 1869) and Jenny (b. July 1879). William was graduated from the Webb School in 1885 and from Vanderbilt University in 1891. At Vanderbilt he belonged to Phi Delta Theta fraternity and was elected to Phi Beta Kappa. Later he spent time at the University of Leipzig (1895–97) and the University of Berlin (1903–4). In June 1911 Wofford College awarded him the honorary Litt.D. degree.

Webb began his career in the early 1890s as a teacher at the Webb School, in Bell Buckle, Tenn., where his uncles John Maurice Webb and William Robert Webb had established their reputations as educators. After his first sojourn in Germany, he was principal of Central Academy in Fayette, Mo. (1897–99), and then taught English at Central (Methodist) College, also in Fayette, before serving as its president (1907–13). In 1913 he became president of Randolph-Macon Woman's College in Lynchburg, Va., a post he held until his death. A building on the campus bears his name. During several summer sessions (1911–14) he taught English in Colorado. He contributed to a number of professional and literary journals, including the *South Atlantic Quarterly*, the *Educational Review*, *School and Society*, and *Religious Education*.

On 31 Jan. 1899 in Bedford County, Tenn., he married Mary Lee Clary (d. 17 Oct. 1919) of Bell Buckle. Their children were Stanford, Carolyn, Dorothy, and Mary Clary. A member of the Religious Education Association, he served in 1916–17 as vice-president of the Association of American Colleges and president of the Association of Colleges and Secondary Schools of the Southern States.

He died in Nashville, Tenn., and was buried in Bell Buckle on 6 Nov. 1919.

SEE: Roberta C. Cornelius, *The History of Randolph-Macon Woman's College* (1951); Eugene Russell Hendrix Papers and Washington Duke Papers (Manuscript Department, Duke University Library, Durham); Thomas N. Ivey, ed., *Handbook of the Methodist Episcopal Church, South, in North Carolina and Almanac for 1902* (1901); Laurence McMillin, *The Schoolmaker: Sawney Webb and the Bell Buckle Story* (1971); *Nashville Tennessean and the Nashville American*, 19 Oct. 1919; Raleigh *News and Observer*, 5 Nov. 1919; *Spartanburg* (S.C.) *Journal*, 12 Nov. 1919; Western North Carolina Conference, Methodist Episcopal Church, South, *Journal* (1901); *Who Was Who in America*, vol. 1 (1942).

EVA BURBANK MURPHY

Webb, William Edwards (*ca. 1777–1829*), educator, legislator, and first professor of classics at The University of North Carolina, was probably born in the town of Halifax, the son of John and Rebecca Edwards Webb. His mother was the daughter of Colonel William Edwards, of Brunswick County, Va., whose brother Isaac was the private secretary of Governor William Tryon; Rebecca Edwards, the second wife of Colonel Allen Jones, was a sister of Colonel Edwards. John Webb, the father of William Webb, was the only child of Anne, the daughter of Daniel Pugh of Nansemond County, Va., who married first one Webb. Circumstantial evidence is strong that he was the Reverend William Webb, a graduate of Oxford University who immigrated to Virginia in 1746, served as minister to the Upper Parish in Nansemond County (1747–60), and was master of the grammar school at the College of William and Mary (1760–62). There is no record of Webb thereafter. His widow Anne then married James Gibson, a merchant in Suffolk who was a Tory in the Revolution.

The Reverend William Webb's career is significant in view of the later achievements of his grandson William. John Webb, the father of William E. Webb, as of Chowan County, bought a house and lot in Halifax in 1774 and settled there to practice law. He represented the borough in the Assembly in 1775. Active in the Revolution, he was a delegate to the first three provincial congresses from the town of Halifax. John Webb's promising career was suddenly cut short and he died soon afterwards. Benjamin Edwards, the brother of Rebecca whom he had married in 1776, was appointed guardian of their only child. Benjamin Edwards was later the father of Weldon Nathaniel Edwards, the noted North Carolina statesman.

There is little known about William E. Webb prior to his attending The University of North Carolina. In the early days of that institution students arrived so poorly prepared that a preparatory school was established. In 1798 young Webb, as a promising member of the senior class at the university, was called to assist in this phase of the university teaching. In the following year, although he had not been graduated, he was made professor of ancient languages, being the first to hold this chair. These were difficult days for the infant university. In the term preceding the commencement of 1799, there was a student uprising in which William Webb was waylaid and stoned. He signed a newspaper advertisement for the next session of the university in February 1799 "by order of the President, William Webb, secretary." Intending to continue his academic career in Chapel Hill, he bought Lots 1 and 2 in the village later in 1799.

There was a change of plan, however, and by 1802 Webb had returned to Halifax County. On 15 March of that year he advertised for sale his two lots in Chapel Hill which were described as commanding a good prospect of the public buildings. Becoming active in politics, he represented Halifax County in the House of Commons in 1809, 1810, 1811, and 1812. While serving in the legislature William Webb wrote and printed circular letters that he mailed to his constituents in which he detailed the activities currently taking place in the General Assembly and explained the positions he had taken in regard to them, a common practice in the late-twentieth-century America but possibly unique in early-nineteenth-century North Carolina.

From 1809 to 1818 Webb was a trustee of the university. After a lapse of twelve years, though a trustee, he returned to academic life and finished the work on his degree that had been interrupted when he joined the faculty. He was granted an A.B. degree in 1812 and an A.M. degree in 1815. William E. Webb then returned a second time to his native county. During 1817–19 he finally disposed of the Chapel Hill real estate that he had advertised for sale in 1802. In 1817 he sold Lot 2 and one-half of Lot 1 to William Pannill of Warrenton. Two years later Webb sold the remainder of Lot 1 to Lucy Hilliard.

On his final return to Halifax County, Webb devoted himself to teaching. In 1815 as "William E. Webb, A.M. former professor of Classical Languages at the University" he was listed as principal of the Union Academy, located in western Halifax County, roughly between the present towns of Littleton and Weldon. A former student from Scotland Neck wrote that from 1824 to 1827 he had attended the Hyde Park Academy, in the upper part of Halifax County, run by Mr. Webb whom he referred to as a famous classical scholar. It is not known whether this school succeeded the Union Academy. In an advertisement of the Hyde Park Academy in 1828 William Webb was not listed as a member of the faculty, but notation was made that boarding could be obtained at his residence nearby.

In 1804 William E. Webb married Sarah, the daughter of Lewis Williamson of Northampton County, and sister of Priscilla, the wife of his former guardian Benjamin Edwards. She died in 1807 without issue at Black Heath in Halifax County. Webb then married Ann, the daughter of George and Ann Lindsey Zollicoffer of Halifax County. On the death of his first wife William Webb had inherited a large plantation on Great Creek in Halifax County and here he resided. When he died intestate in 1829, the property was divided between his widow and their six children. One part of the division was referred to as the Hyde Park tract. William Webb and Ann Zollicoffer had three sons, Albert G., Richard, and William, and three daughters, Cornelia, Rebecca, and Ann S. Of the daughters, Rebecca married Charles C. P. Campbell and Ann married William Thweatt of Prince George County, Va. The son Richard is thought to have settled in Tennessee.

A French language textbook once owned by William E. Webb, printed in Philadelphia in 1804, has descended in the collection of the Alston family of Cherry Hill in Warren County. It bears his book plate, an oval with the inscription "—Libertas et Natale Solum—William E. Webb, Chapel Hill, North Carolina."

SEE: William C. Allen, *History of Halifax County* (1918); Kemp P. Battle, *History of the University of North Carolina*, vol. 1 (1907); John L. Cheney, ed., *North Carolina Government, 1585–1979* (1981); Charles L. Coon, ed., *North Carolina Schools and Academies, 1790–1840* (1915); Deeds of Gates, Halifax, and Orange Counties (North Carolina State Archives, Raleigh); Deeds, Wills, and Marriage Bonds, Brunswick County, Va. (Courthouse, Lawrenceville); Halifax, *North Carolina Journal*, 18 Feb. 1799, 15 Mar.

1802; Lois Neal, *Abstracts of Vital Records from Raleigh, North Carolina Newspapers*, vol. 1 (1979); Claiborne T. Smith, Jr., *Smith of Scotland Neck* (1976); Edgar Thorne (Inez, N.C.), personal contact; Frederick Weis, *Colonial Clergy: Virginia, North Carolina and South Carolina* (1976); Williamsburg, *Virginia Gazette*, 13 Oct. 1774; Zollicoffer Papers (North Carolina State Archives, Raleigh).

CLAIBORNE T. SMITH, JR.

Webb, William Robert (Sawney) *(11 Nov. 1842–19 Dec. 1926)*, educator and U.S. senator, was born near Mount Tirzah, Person County, of Scots-Irish ancestry, the son of Alexander Smith and Cornelia Adeline Stanford Webb. He was the grandson of Richard Stanford, a teacher and congressman. At an early age he moved with his parents to Orange County, where his family had acquired additional farmland. "Sawney" was a childhood nickname that stuck with him throughout his life and came to be spoken with affection. At age twelve he was enrolled at the noted school near Hillsborough conducted by William J. Bingham. He proved to be an assiduous and attentive student, and at seventeen he matriculated at The University of North Carolina, where he became a member of Delta Kappa Epsilon fraternity.

Although originally a Unionist, on 21 May 1861, when he was eighteen, Webb joined the Fifteenth Regiment of North Carolina Troops in Confederate service as first sergeant. Wounded in the right arm at Malvern Hill, Va., on 1 July 1862, he was unable to serve in that position, and as a consequence his rank was reduced to sergeant. While invalided at home recuperating from his injuries, he taught at the Classical School headed by Colonel J. H. Horner at Oxford and pursued his studies at the university. Returning to duty, he was appointed first lieutenant on 17 Mar. 1863. His disability persisted, however, and he resigned on 17 June. Reenlisting as a private on 5 Mar. 1864, he was captured at Amelia Court House, Va., on 5 Apr. 1865 and imprisoned at Hart's Island in New York Harbor.

After the war Webb related an account of one remarkable day that he spent while a prisoner. By diving around a parapet he escaped and went into New York City, where he spent the day sightseeing. Although he was wearing a Confederate uniform no one paid any attention to him. Although he had only a few cents in his pocket, he met a girl from Georgia who managed to get him a meal in a restaurant. At the end of the day he returned to the prison and went to the main entrance, but his account was not believed and he was denied admission. He was able to get back in only by following the same course he had taken in the morning—swimming around the barricade.

He resumed his interrupted studies at the university, which awarded him a B.A. degree in 1867 and an M.A. degree the following year. Webb then accepted a teaching position at the Horner School in Oxford. In 1870, disenchanted with conditions in North Carolina during Reconstruction, he moved west to the hamlet of Culleoka, Tenn., where he became principal of the Culleoka Institute—a moribund academy that he transformed into a thriving private boarding school. Three years later he married Emma Clary of Unionville, Tenn., the daughter of Benjamin Clary of Wilkesboro, N.C., by whom he had eight children.

Webb had a lifelong aversion to alcohol and objected strenuously without avail to Culleoka's open saloons. He determined to move his school to the dry community of Bell Buckle, Tenn., where local citizens had pledged a sixacre site and $12,000 for the new school. It opened there in 1886. Characteristically, Webb spent $8,000 of these funds for the acquisition of books for the school library. Within ten years, the Webb School had become the leading preparatory school of the South.

Slight of stature, redheaded, and physically fearless, Webb in personality and character was the quintessential southern puritan. At the same time, he was unorthodox in many of his moral, political, and social beliefs. Many of Webb's students feared him, a few hated him, but all respected him. His forte was character, his craft was wit and humor, his understanding of boys was intuitive and brilliant. Discipline at Webb School was generally fierce, often corporal, yet "old Sawney," as he came to be known, developed an honor system that was later adopted, with few modifications, by some of the most distinguished American universities.

Probably the heyday of Webb School was the period from 1904@ to 1930 when "Webb boys" received more Rhodes Scholarships than those graduated from any other American preparatory school. According to Horace Taft, founder of the Taft School in Connecticut, Webb "accomplished amazing results with such little equipment that he shames the rest of us."

For many years, Webb's younger brother, John Webb—an extraordinarily able teacher—shared the school's principalship. John Webb was no match for his aggressive and domineering brother, however, and was eventually forced to accept a subordinate position. In 1913 the state legislature of Tennessee elected Sawney Webb to the unexpired term of the late Senator Robert Taylor. His brief service in Washington (24 Jan.–3 Mar. 1913) was uneventful except that he did secure passage of a bill to prohibit desecration of the American flag and made an impressive speech favoring Prohibition. On his return to Tennessee he resumed the principalship of the Webb School, assisted by his son, William Robert Webb, Jr.

In 1922 he received honorary doctorates from The University of North Carolina and Erskine College. He lived to see his youngest son, Thompson Webb, found the successful Webb School at Claremont, Calif. For much of his life, Sawney Webb was the most successful and celebrated schoolmaster in the entire South. Active in the Methodist Episcopal Church, South, he was buried in Hazelwood Cemetery, Bell Buckle.

SEE: *Biog. Dir. Am. Cong.* (1971); *DAB*, vol. 10 (1936); *Durham Morning Herald*, 29 Sept. 1946; *Greensboro Daily News*, 10 Nov. 1924, 29 Sept. 1946; Nolan B. Harmon, ed., *Encyclopedia of World Methodism*, vol. 2 (1974); Weymouth T. Jordan, comp., *North Carolina Troops, 1861–1865: A Roster*, vol. 5 (1975); Laurence McMillin, *The Schoolmaker: Sawney Webb and the Bell Buckle Story* (1971); Louis H. Manarin, comp., *North Carolina Troops, 1861–1865: A Roster*, vol. 2 (1968); *Nat. Cyc. Am. Biog.*, vol. 37 (1951); John Ohleo, ed., *Biographical Dictionary of American Educators*, vol. 3 (1978); Raleigh *News and Observer*, 20 Dec. 1926 (portrait); John Andrew Rice, *I Came Out of the Eighteenth Century* (1942); *Who Was Who in America*, vol. 1 (1942); *Who Was Who in American Politics* (1974).

MATTHEW HODGSON

Wechter, Nell Carolyn Wise *(6 Aug. 1913–20 June 1989)*, teacher and writer, was born at Stumpy Point, Dare County, the daughter of Enoch Raymond, a fisherman, and Edith Casey Best Wise. She was graduated from East Carolina College in 1951 and received a master's degree from both her alma mater and the University of North Carolina at Greensboro. From 1933 until her retirement in 1964 she taught in the public schools of the state.

A free-lance feature writer for North Carolina newspapers between 1943 and 1968, she also was associate editor of the *Hyde County Herald* at Swan Quarter during the period 1948–50. In 1972 she taught creative writing and English at the College of the Albemarle in Elizabeth City. Her first novel, *The Romance of Juniper River*, appeared in 1937. She wrote for young people as well as adults, notably *Taffy of Torpedo Junction* (1957), *Betsy Dowdy's Ride* (1960), and *The Mighty Midgetts of Chicamcomico* (1974). Mrs. Wechter won numerous awards for her books, including those offered by the American Association of University Women and the Catholic Children's Book Club of America.

In 1943 she married Robert William Wechter, of Madison, Wis., a naval officer stationed on North Carolina's Outer Banks. They were the parents of a daughter, Marcia. Mrs. Wechter was a member of the Methodist church.

SEE: *Contemporary Authors*, vol. 57–60 (1976); *Greensboro News and Record*, 22 June 1989; William S. Powell, ed., *North Carolina Lives* (1962); Raleigh *News and Observer*, 21, 27 June 1989.

WILLIAM S. POWELL

Weddell, Alexander Watson (*20 May 1840–6 Dec. 1883*), clergyman, was born in Tarboro, the son of James and Margaret Ward Weddell. James Weddell and several of his brothers emigrated to North Carolina from Musselburgh, Scotland, near Edinburgh, and he became president of the Tarboro branch of the State Bank of North Carolina. Margaret Ward Weddell was a native of Edgecombe County. Their son, Alexander, was named for a family friend, Alexander Watson, who had accompanied the Weddell brothers to North Carolina; Watson was a merchant in Nashville before relocating in New York City. About 1854 James Weddell and his family moved to Petersburg, Va., where Alexander attended a private academy conducted by the historian Charles Campbell. After several years at Hampden-Sydney College, he studied law at the University of Virginia in 1860–61. Young Weddell left the university to join the Confederate army as a lieutenant. Wounded in June 1862, he was invalided out of the service and for the remainder of the war was private secretary to Judah P. Benjamin, Confederate secretary of state.

Returning to Petersburg, Weddell was both editor of a local newspaper and a lawyer. Deciding to enter the Episcopal ministry, he attended the Virginia Theological Seminary, and after his ordination in 1871 he was assigned to Emmanuel Church, Harrisonburg, Va. In 1875 he was called to historic St. John's Church, Richmond, a charge he continued to hold until his death. He was buried in front of the main entrance to the church. In 1942 his son, Alexander, presented a bronze plaque in memory of his father and his father's two brothers, John Archibald and Virginius Loraine Weddell, who had died in the Confederate army. This tablet, which contained the "Prayer before the study of law" written by Samuel Johnson in 1765, was placed at the entrance of the first-year law room in Clark Hall at the University of Virginia.

On 31 Jan. 1866, in North Carolina, Weddell married Penelope Margaret Wright, the daughter of Dr. David Minton Wright of Chowan County and Norfolk, Va. They had three sons, James, William, and Alexander, and three daughters, Margaret, Penelope, and Elizabeth. A son, Alexander Wilbourne Weddell, became U.S. ambassador to Spain and to Argentina; he bought Warwick Priory in England and reconstructed the house in Richmond in 1925. After he and his wife died, the residence—named Virginia House—and a large endowment were left to the Virginia Historical Society. Elizabeth Wright Weddell, the daughter of the Reverend Mr. Weddell, was the author of a history of St. Paul's Church, Richmond.

SEE: Philip A. Bruce, *History of Virginia: The Rebirth of the Old Dominion*, vol. 4 (biography, 1929); Edgecombe County Wills and Deeds (Edgecombe County Courthouse, Tarboro); *Genealogy of Members, 1896–1946: Sons of the American Revolution in Virginia* (1939); Richmond *Times-Dispatch*, 21 Oct. 1942.

CLAIBORNE T. SMITH, JR.

Weeks, Stephen Beauregard (*2 Feb. 1865–3 May 1918*), historian, bibliographer, collector of North Caroliniana, and government official, was born near Nixonton, Pasquotank County, to James Elliott and Mary Louisa Mullen Weeks. On the death of his parents, the child was reared by his father's sister and her husband, Robertson Jackson.

After attending the Horner School at Henderson, Weeks entered The University of North Carolina, where he was graduated with second highest honors in 1886. He remained there, earning a master's degree the next year and in 1888 receiving the first doctor of philosophy degree ever given by the Department of English. That fall he entered Johns Hopkins University, where he came under the influence of Herbert Baxter Adams, America's foremost exponent of the German or "scientific" school of historical investigation. In 1891, after receiving his second doctoral degree, Weeks joined the faculty of Trinity College in Randolph County. Within the year he organized the Department of History and Political Science, founded the Trinity College Historical Society, and established himself as the first "professional" historian in North Carolina. He moved with the college to Durham, but in 1893 he resigned and returned to Johns Hopkins on a one-year fellowship.

The following year Weeks joined the Bureau of Education of the Department of the Interior in Washington, D.C., as a specialist in educational history and associate editor of the bureau's annual report. For five years this position provided him with time for historical research and his consuming passion, the collection of books and articles relating to North Carolina. In 1895 he delivered the centennial address at The University of North Carolina, and in 1896 he was temporary chairman of the organizational meeting of the Southern History Association.

Just before the turn of the century, Weeks developed a severe lung ailment, and his request for assignment as principal teacher in the Indian School at Santa Fe, New Mexico Territory, was granted. Four years later he was promoted to the superintendency of the San Carlos Agency School in Arizona Territory, where he remained until 1907, by which time his health had been restored. Impressed by Weeks's sketches written for inclusion in Samuel A. Ashe's *Biographical History of North Carolina*, the publisher Charles L. Van Noppen persuaded Weeks to join his firm as an editor, assisting with the seventh volume of the biographical series and revising the first volume of Ashe's *History of North Carolina*. Then, in 1909, Weeks returned to the site of the old Trinity College in Randolph County as principal teacher in a public school. He rejoined the Bureau of Education in Washington as historian in 1911 and remained there until his death.

Weeks distinguished himself in four ways: he was the first professionally trained historian in North Carolina to earn his living from his speciality, he wrote prolifically—more than two hundred books and articles—on a variety of historical subjects, he was the state's first important bibliographer, and he amassed the finest collection of published North Caroliniana then in existence. His bibliography of North Caroliniana, published as Number 48 of Justin Winsor's *Bibliographical Contributions* (1895), listed 1,491 titles, 863 of which Weeks already possessed. By 1913 his collection had grown to 7,100 volumes. After his death the approximately 9,000 books and pamphlets in the Weeks Collection of North Caroliniana were purchased by The University of North Carolina to form the nucleus of its North Carolina Collection.

Though Weeks's monographs and articles were generally sound, not all of his early writings—for instance, his article on the Robeson County Indians—have stood the test of time. However, he himself recognized that "Historical truth is a progressive evolution, the product of successive generations of painstaking scholars. . . . It is only by continued research, by repeated investigation and reweighing of old beliefs in the light of fuller evidence that we can hope to arrive at ultimate truth." His single most useful publication was the monumental four-volume index to the combined *Colonial Records of North Carolina*, edited by William L. Saunders, and *State Records of North Carolina*, edited by Walter Clark, to which was added an exceedingly informative "Historical Review." Among his publications on non–North Carolina subjects were *History of Public School Education in Alabama* (1915) and *History of Public School Education in Arizona* (1918).

Weeks on 12 June 1888 married Mary Lee Martin, the daughter of the Reverend Joseph Bonaparte Martin, and they had two children, only one of whom—Robertson Jackson Weeks—lived to adulthood. On 28 June 1893, two years after her death, Weeks married Sallie Mangum Leach, a daughter of Martin W. Leach of Randolph County and a granddaughter of Senator Willie P. Mangum. By her he fathered four children, two of whom—Willie Person Mangum and Sallie Preston—lived to adulthood.

A man of medium build—about 5' 11" and 170 pounds—Weeks had wavy brown hair, blue eyes, and a somewhat ruddy complexion. He had a mustache and a Vandyke beard, and he often wore a high collar with a plain white bow tie. He was "an erect, rapid walker, a good though not scintillating public speaker, and a provocative conversationalist."

Although he recovered sufficiently from a mild stroke in 1917 to return to work, Weeks died the following year from a heart and kidney complication and was buried on the Willie Person Mangum farm cemetery in northern Durham County. The *News and Observer* editorialized: "His career ought to be given liberal mention in every history of the State. . . . It is likely that Dr. Weeks died a poor man. There is little reward of a financial kind in ransacking old libraries and musty correspondence files to establish the facts of history. But few men have wrought more capably and helpfully for the State than he did and the heritage of duty faithfully and efficiently rendered is more to be prized than great riches."

SEE: Samuel A. Ashe, ed., *Biographical History of North Carolina*, vol. 5 (1906); *DAB*, vol. 10 (1936); H. G. Jones, "Stephen Beauregard Weeks: North Carolina's First 'Professional' Historian," *North Carolina Historical Review* 42 (1965); William S. Powell, *Stephen Beauregard Weeks, 1865–1918: A Preliminary Bibliography* (1965); Raleigh *News and Observer*, 4 May 1918; *Who's Who in America* (1916–17). Many of Weeks's papers are in the Southern Historical Collection, University of North Carolina, Chapel Hill, his library and an oil portrait by Paul E. Monzol are in the university's North Carolina Collection.

H. G. JONES

Weil, Gertrude (*11 Dec. 1879–30 May 1971*), social reformer, humanitarian, and philanthropist, was born in Goldsboro, the older daughter of Henry and Mina Rosenthal Weil. Beginning in 1865 the Weil family and Weil department store became eastern North Carolina institutions. Herman Weil, Gertrude's uncle and a Confederate war veteran, chose Goldsboro as a promising site for a general store and there founded H. Weil & Bros. with the help of his brothers, Henry and Solomon. Gertrude attended Goldsboro public schools and Horace Mann High School in New York City. She was graduated from Smith College in 1901, the first Smith student from North Carolina.

Inculcated with the ideals of public service by her mother, Gertrude Weil was a founder and president of the North Carolina Suffrage League in 1920, founder and officer of the North Carolina Federation of Women's Clubs, pioneer president of the North Carolina League of Women Voters, and founder and officer of the Legislative Council of North Carolina Women. Recognizing the necessity for local public health assistance, she personally paid the salary of a public health nurse for Wayne County to demonstrate this need shortly after she helped create the County Health Department. Her coworkers dubbed her the "one-woman Welfare Department."

A Sunday school and adult Bible study group teacher for over fifty years, she was a charter member and three-time president of the North Carolina Association for Jewish Women. As district officer for both Sisterhood and Hadassah for the eastern states, she vigorously promoted interfaith activities. In the late 1950s she turned her efforts towards civil rights, building a park and swimming pool for Negroes, holding integrated meetings in her home, and founding the Bi-Racial Council in 1963. When the cast-iron black groom hitching posts adorning many Goldsboro lawns became a focus of racial tension, Gertrude Weil, with typical incisive wit, defused the situation by publicly painting her statue white.

The Weil family—Gertrude, her brothers Herman and Leslie, her sister Janet Weil Bluethenthal, and her cousin Lionel—established the Weil Lectures on American Citizenship at The University of North Carolina, gave the Weil and Rosenthal buildings at Woman's College in Greensboro, and endowed there the first scholarships for foreign students. In Goldsboro and Wayne County, the family donated Herman Park and made possible the Wayne County Memorial Community Building, the Public Library in the former Lionel Weil home, Boy Scout and Girl Scout camps, and the Wayne Memorial Hospital.

In 1951 Gertrude Weil was named Outstanding Woman of the Year by Chi Omega sorority. The citation for the honorary degree in doctor of humane letters bestowed by Woman's College in 1952 began, "Daughter of North Carolina and leader among North Carolina's daughters." Dr. Frank Porter Graham, president emeritus of The University of North Carolina, presided at the testimonial dinner for Miss Weil held at the B'nai B'rith Lodge of Greensboro in 1956. The biographical sketch accompanying the award of the Smith College Medal in 1964 stated: "It would be a great deal more difficult to find, in the State of North Carolina, a cultural, charitable, educational organization or drive with which the name of Miss Gertrude Weil is *not* connected, than to attempt to summarize her contributions to the civic welfare of this State." In 1965 she received the Howard Odum Award from the North Carolina Council on Human Relations.

Straight-backed, straightforward, but never straitlaced, diminutive Gertrude Weil continued her active and knowledgeable participation in such diverse additional interests as gardening, theater productions, and historical restoration until her death in Goldsboro at age ninety-one. Burial was in the Hebrew section of Willow Dale Cemetery, Goldsboro.

SEE: Emma R. Edwards, "In Love with Life" (typescript updating and amending article in *American Jewish Times* [October 1956], 1964, North Carolina Collection, University of North Carolina, Chapel Hill); Raleigh *News and Observer*, 3, 8 June 1952, 14 Mar. 1965 (portrait), 6 Mar. 1968, 31 May 1971; Moses Rountree, *Strangers in the Land* (1969 [portrait]); Harriette Hammer Walker, *Busy North Carolina Women* (1931); Gertrude Weil Papers (North Carolina State Archives, Raleigh); *Who's Who in the South* (1927).

ELLEN-FAIRBANKS DIGGS BODMAN

Weil, Henry (*9 Apr. 1846–9 Aug. 1914*), merchant, was born in Oberdorf, Würtemberg, Germany, the fourth child and second son of Jacob Weil (d. 1886), an antique dealer, and his Bavarian-born wife Yetta (d. 1889). Henry and his older sisters and brothers attended public schools first in Oberdorf and then in nearby Bopfingen, where they studied English and French. In April 1860 Henry emigrated to the United States.

Herman (1842–8 Dec. 1878), Henry's older brother, had left Germany in 1858, first joining his two older sisters in Baltimore and then moving to Goldsboro to work as a clerk in Oettinger's general store. On 28 June 1861 he enlisted in Captain J. B. Whitaker's company of the Goldsboro volunteers that later became Company D of the Fourth North Carolina Infantry Regiment, Confederate army. Returning to Goldsboro soon after Appomattox and just two months after Sherman's army had billeted briefly in Goldsboro, Herman was joined by Henry. The two brothers opened H. Weil & Bros. on 21 June 1865, inscribing in their first ledger the words "Mit Gott!" The original general store was a small frame building on a half-acre lot purchased for $1,050 and located in the center of town, opposite the juncture of two railroads. The following year a younger brother Solomon arrived to become part of the firm, which expanded rapidly into a major mercantile establishment in the state, reaching a million-dollar annual sales record by 1900. Herman died of cerebrospinal meningitis at age thirty-six but had lived to see his business well established and the original building replaced in 1870 by a two-story brick structure adorned with cast-iron fluted columns.

Henry Weil, besides his active participation in the varied interests of H. Weil & Bros., which included cotton, real estate, a brickyard, coal, and ice, was, together with his brother Solomon, incorporator of the major town business firms inaugurated between 1880 and 1900: the Goldsboro Oil Company, Pioneer Tobacco Company, Wayne Agricultural works, Goldsboro Savings Bank, and Goldsboro Storage and Warehouse Company. One of the founders of the Bank of Wayne, Henry remained a director until his death.

Renowned for his absentmindedness regarding domestic and personal details and his good-humored recognition of his lapses, Henry Weil was imaginative in venturing into new areas of investment. His Carolina Rice Mills experimented briefly with the production of Carolina Rice Flakes at the turn of the century. His dream of a Harnett Railroad, a narrow-gauge track between Dunn and Goldsboro, funded in 1879, remained a blueprint. In 1896 the bid of the Goldsboro syndicate to lease the Goldsboro-Morehead railroad line was turned down, but Henry received a compensatory appointment to the board of directors of the Atlantic and North Carolina Railroad.

A staunch advocate of public education, he served on the board of trustees of the Goldsboro Graded Schools from its establishment until his death—more than thirty years. In 1897 he was appointed to the board of trustees of The University of North Carolina. A lover of books with a fine personal collection in history, religion, and finance, he donated $1,000 in 1899 to The University of North Carolina Library for the purchase of volumes on political and social science.

Weil was among the founders of the Oheb Sholom Congregation in Goldsboro in 1883 and elected director. Although he supported wholeheartedly many Jewish causes, he did not approve of the Zionist movement. In 1910, writing from Palestine, he called it "criminal" to plan "the settling of poor Jews in Palestine on barren soil."

On 24 Mar. 1875, after a two-year engagement, Weil married sixteen-year-old Mina Rosenthal (2 Feb. 1859–18 Oct. 1940), the daughter of Emil Rosenthal, a merchant from nearby Wilson. The young couple moved into the new frame home next door to the house—identical in design and built at the same time—for his brother Solomon and his bride Sarah.

Henry and Mina Weil had four children: Leslie, Gertrude, Herman, and Janet. Weil became ill while returning to Goldsboro from his daughter Janet's graduation from Smith College. He died in the Johns Hopkins Hospital, Baltimore, and was buried in Willow Dale Cemetery, Goldsboro, in the plot purchased by the Oheb Sholom Congregation in 1875.

SEE: *Goldsboro Argus*, 1869–1914; *Greensboro Daily News*, 20 Oct. 1940; Bob Johnson and Charles S. Norwood, eds., *A History of Wayne County, North Carolina* (1979); *North Carolina Biography*, vols. 4 (1941), 6 (1919); Raleigh *News and Observer*, 11 Aug. 1914, 5 Feb. 1933; Moses Rountree, *Strangers in the Land* (1969 [portraits]).

ELLEN-FAIRBANKS DIGGS BODMAN

Weil, Herman (*1 Jan. 1882–21 Oct. 1961*), manufacturer and philanthropist, was born in Goldsboro, the son of Henry and Mina Rosenthal Weil. In 1901 he was graduated from The University of North Carolina, where he was a trustee from 1949 until his death. His business interests included a plywood box industry, a brick manufacturing plant, the Goldsboro Ice Company, a storage warehouse, and the Carolina Rice Company. He served on the board of the Goldsboro Hotel Company and was a director of the Borden Manufacturing Company. Weil was treasurer of the Tuscarora Boy Scout Council from its establishment until his death and in his will left funds for the council. He also bequeathed a sum for the Wayne Foundation, a charitable organization.

Weil married Elizabeth Bogle, and they had two daughters, Elizabeth and Mina Anne.

In the knowledge that the board of trustees of The University of North Carolina would prepare a tribute to him following his death, he wrote it himself and asked that it be read at the customary time:

"Herman Weil was born in Goldsboro in 1882 and lived there all of his life.

"After attending public schools he entered the University of North Carolina in 1897. As the standards were not too high he was graduated in 1901.

"He was connected with a number of local industries and his record was in no way outstanding.

"He developed a liking for the university by association. His father, Henry Weil, was a trustee from about 1890 until his death in 1914. He was succeeded by his son, Leslie Weil, who was succeeded by Lionel Weil, who was succeeded by Herman Weil.

"He leaves a widow, two daughters and three grand-daughters. The daughters graduated from UNC and the grand-daughters all under 5, have been instructed to attend the university if they can qualify.

"There is no need to send any resolution to his widow as she is thoroughly familiar with his long and short comings.

"If Herman Weil passes on while he is a trustee, please use this instead of the usual 5 per cent true eulogy."

SEE: *Chapel Hill Weekly*, 23 Oct. 1961; Daniel L. Grant, *Alumni History of the University of North Carolina* (1924); *Greensboro Daily News*, 22 Oct., 3 Nov. 1961, 27 Feb. 1962.

WILLIAM S. POWELL

Weil, Leslie *(29 June 1876–8 June 1943)*, public-spirited merchant, county and state official, and university bene-factor, was born in Goldsboro, Wayne County, the older son of Henry and Mina Rosenthal Weil. After attending the Goldsboro graded schools he entered The University of North Carolina, graduating with the Ph.B. degree in 1895. At Chapel Hill he was on the class football team, assistant editor of the *Carolina Magazine*, and a member of Phi Gamma Delta fraternity and the Philanthropic Assembly.

In 1896 Weil joined the family firm of H. Weil & Bros., becoming a partner in 1910. Following in the footsteps of his extended family, he assumed civic and community responsibilities: charter member and president of the Rotary Club (1923), member of the Elks and the Odd Fellows, president of the Goldsboro Chamber of Commerce (1917) and of the Goldsboro Citizens Building and Loan Association, director of the A. T. Griffin Manufacturing Company, director of the Farmers Cooperative Service and Exchange, and member of the executive committee of the Eastern Carolina Broadcasting Company.

Besides serving as president of the Oheb Sholom Congregation, Weil was a member of the National Hillel Commission and, in 1938, treasurer of the state organization to resettle Jewish refugees. After organizing the Tuscarora Council of Boy Scouts in 1923, he became a member of the interracial commission of the national Scout board. In 1936 he assumed the presidency of the National Association of Governing Boards of Land Grant Colleges.

Weil's loyalty to his alma mater continued throughout his life. He was a member of the board of trustees (1915–43), the Finance Committee (1920), and the Executive Committee (1923); assisted in founding The University of North Carolina Press, serving on its board; was both director and vice-president of the Alumni Association and chairman of the Alumni Fund; and, with other members of his family, established and endowed the annual Weil Lectures on American Citizenship. In 1926 the university annual, the *Yackety Yack*, was dedicated to him; in 1941 he was awarded an honorary LL.D. degree. Described by his fellow university trustees as having the "quality of quietness," Weil gave generously and inconspicuously of his business acumen, his enthusiasm, and his wealth, not only to the university but also to many individuals in need.

On 26 June 1900 he married Hilda Einstein (27 Dec. 1876–19 May 1969), the younger sister of his aunt Sarah (Mrs. Solomon) Weil. Their five children were Abram, Hilda (Mrs. Robert L. Wallerstein), Henry, Margaret (Mrs. Jay Pressley), and Marian (Mrs. Sidney Reitman). Weil died of a heart attack in Goldsboro and was buried in Willow Dale Cemetery.

SEE: Alumni Files (University of North Carolina, Chapel Hill); *Chapel Hill Weekly*, 11 June, 3 Sept. 1943; *Greensboro Daily News*, 9 June 1943; *North Carolina Biography*, vol. 6

(1919); Raleigh *News and Observer*, 9 June 1943, (1914–43); Moses Rountree, *Strangers in the Land* (1969 [portraits]); *University of North Carolina Alumni Review*, 1914–43.

ELLEN-FAIRBANKS DIGGS BODMAN

Weil, Lionel *(1 Sept. 1877–11 Feb. 1948)*, agronomist, conservationist, and merchant, was the son of Solomon and Sarah Einstein Weil of Goldsboro, Wayne County. After attending the Goldsboro public schools, he received a Ph.B. degree, magna cum laude in geology, in 1897 from The University of North Carolina, where he was a charter member of Phi Beta Kappa and a member of Alpha Theta Pi fraternity and the Philanthropic Society. On 30 Nov. 1910 he married Ruth Kaufmann Heyn (24 Aug. 1887–21 Dec. 1941), of Toledo, a graduate of the Vassar class of 1901. They had three children: Lionel Solomon, Helene Marie (Mrs. David B. Young), and Ruth (Mrs. William Harris). Weil's second marriage was to Jeanette Wolff Schallek in Baltimore on 22 Nov. 1944.

After graduation from college, he was eager to pursue graduate studies in chemistry at the Massachusetts Institute of Technology but was persuaded by his father to enter the family firm of H. Weil & Bros., in which he became a partner in 1910. From 1904 to 1923 he was an alderman in Goldsboro. As secretary of the City Charter Committee in 1917, he led Goldsboro to become the first municipality in the state to adopt the city manager form of government. A trustee of the Goldsboro city schools for twenty-three years, he also organized the first Community Chest, chaired the Zoning and Planning Committee, headed three drives to raise funds for the building of the Wayne County Memorial Community Building honoring World War I veterans, and helped establish the Orthopedic Clinic for Eastern North Carolina. A member of the Elks, Rotary, and Knights of Pythias, he made time to publish monographs on various aspects of city government.

Treasurer of the Oheb Sholom Congregation in 1917, Weil later became district president of B'nai B'rith, president of the North Carolina Jewish Relief Committee (1918, 1922), director of Samarcand Manor for delinquent girls, vice-president of the Hebrew Orphan Home in Atlanta, Ga., honorary vice-president of the United Palestine Appeal, North Carolina chairman of the National Jewish Welfare Board, and member of the state executive committee of the United War Work Campaign and European Relief.

Knowledgeable in agronomy and preaching diversification of crops, Weil took charge of the agricultural interests of H. Weil & Bros., personally supervising the extensive farms during the depression and experimenting successfully with fertilizers for specific soil deficiencies. He invented an effective device for transplanting longleaf pines and published a practical handbook on *Our Native Trees* as well as other tracts on farming. In 1932 he started the Weil Fertilizer Works and in 1941 patented a method for stabilizing plant hormones in fertilizers. He was the first president of the State Farm Debt Adjustment Committee; vice-president of the State Tobacco Advisory Commission; director of the North Carolina Forestry Association, National Fertilizer Association, and Rural Industry Committee; and president of the Plant Institute of North Carolina and Virginia. An ardent and foresighted conservationist, Weil donated to the state in 1945 the original 291 acres for the Cliffs of the Neuse State Park. With other members of the Weil family, he established and endowed the Weil Lectures on American Citizenship at The University of North Carolina in 1915. A charter member of the Friends of the Library of his alma mater, he was elected vice-president in 1946. In memory of his wife he created the Weil Collection of Classics in the Rare Book Room of Wilson Library. His university appointed him a trustee in 1943 and awarded him an honorary doctorate of humanities in 1947.

Lionel Weil died in the Johns Hopkins Hospital after an extended illness. His grave is in the Willow Dale Cemetery, Goldsboro.

SEE: Alumni Files (University of North Carolina, Chapel Hill); *Goldsboro News-Argus*, 15 Apr. 1923; *North Carolina Biography*, vol. 6 (1919); Raleigh *News and Observer*, 16 Nov. 1947, 12 Feb. 1948, 30 June 1949; Moses Rountree, *Strangers in the Land* (1969 [portraits]); *University of North Carolina Alumni Review*, 1910–48; Lionel Weil, *Fertilizer Suitable for Your Soil* (ca. 1937), *Goldsboro: Its Government from the Beginning to the Present Time* (1923), and *Our Native Trees* (1924).

ELLEN-FAIRBANKS DIGGS BODMAN

Weil, Solomon (*7 Jan. 1849–27 Sept. 1914*), merchant and religious leader, was born in Oberdorf, Württemberg, Germany, the youngest son of Jacob and Yetta Weil. Educated in public schools in Oberdorf and nearby Bopfingen, he emigrated to the United States in 1865 and joined his older brothers Herman and Henry as a partner in the firm of H. Weil & Bros. in Goldsboro in 1866. On 5 May 1875 he married Sarah Einstein (18 May 1859–11 Nov. 1928) of Boston and took his bride to a spacious new home in Goldsboro, a house identical in architecture to that of his brother Henry and built on the adjoining lot. Solomon and Sarah had three children: Edna (Mrs. Adolph Oettinger, 3 Feb. 1876–8 Feb. 1958), Lionel (1 Sept. 1877–11 Feb. 1948), and Helene (Mrs. Leon Strauss, 8 July 1884–31 May 1935).

In 1883 Solomon Weil helped organize the Oheb Sholom Congregation, of which he became treasurer; he then planned the building of the synagogue, completed in 1886. For many years he was a trustee and benefactor of the Hebrew Orphan Home in Atlanta, Ga., and served as president of the southeastern district of B'nai B'rith.

Elected alderman in May 1881, he was an energetic promoter of civic and community improvements, keeping a canny eye on the sound fiscal policies of the growing municipality of Goldsboro. He and his brother Henry marked the twenty-fifth anniversary of H. Weil & Bros. in 1890 by donating Herman Park to the city in memory of their older brother. Solomon celebrated his sixtieth birthday in 1909 by presenting $5,000 to the Goldsboro Hospital Association to start a successful fund drive for building the Goldsboro Hospital. A Democrat, Solomon was more interested in local than in state and national politics.

He shared his love of travel, art, and books with his wife Sarah, who had started a Woman's Club library in Goldsboro. After his death, the Weil family founded and endowed the Weil Lectures on American Citizenship at The University of North Carolina in memory of Henry and Solomon. His home was donated to the city for a public library in 1929 as a memorial to Solomon and Sarah.

Each year in late summer the Weils vacationed in New Hampshire to escape the hay fever season in the South. Solomon died in Fabyans, N.H., just six weeks after the death of his brother Henry. He was buried in Willow Dale Cemetery, Goldsboro.

SEE: Bob Johnson and Charles S. Norwood, eds., *A History of Wayne County, North Carolina* (1979); *North Carolina Biography*, vols. 4 (1941), 6 (1919); Raleigh *News and Observer*, 28 Sept. 1914; Moses Rountree, *Strangers in the Land* (1969).

ELLEN-FAIRBANKS DIGGS BODMAN

Welch, Robert Henry Winborne, Jr. (*1 Dec. 1899–7 Jan. 1985*), businessman and founder of the John Birch Society, was born in Chowan County, the son of Robert H. W. and Lina V. James Welch. The first of his paternal ancestors immigrated from Wales in 1720, and his forebears worked primarily as farmers and preachers.

Young Welch showed early signs of genius. He read at age three, was graduated from high school at the top of his class at age twelve, and, still wearing knee breeches, promptly matriculated at The University of North Carolina, where he was dubbed a "boy wonder." He was graduated at seventeen and enrolled at the U.S. Naval Academy for two years, followed by two years of study at Harvard Law School, where he took courses from Felix Frankfurter, but dropped out in disgust at academia.

Welch quit Harvard to found a candy business based in a loft in Cambridge, Mass. He prospered and in 1922 married Marian Lucille Probart of Akron, Ohio. In 1932 he joined the largest candy manufacturer in the country, E. J. Brach and Sons, from which he resigned in 1934 to work as a sales manager for the James O. Welch Company, his younger brother's candy business. Over the next twenty-two years, Welch's candy sales soared from $28,000 to more than $2 million annually. Robert Welch's expertise is reflected by the powerful positions he held: OPA Advisory Committee during World War II, vice-president and member of the board of directors of the National Association of Manufacturers, and board of directors for the United Prison Association and U.S. Chess Federation; he won the candy industry's Man of the Year award in 1947. In 1950 Welch ran for the Republican nomination for lieutenant governor of Massachusetts, placing second out of four candidates. In addition, he competed against chess masters without a handicap.

By the mid-fifties Welch was independently wealthy and obsessed with the political threat that he believed international communism posed to the country. He had already written three books. *May God Forgive Us* (1952), which analyzed President Harry S Truman's firing of General Douglas MacArthur, sold nearly 200,000 copies in its first year. In 1956 Welch left his job to become a full-time pamphleteer against communism. He published his own magazine, *One Man's Opinion* (later, *American Opinion*), and established his own publishing operations. In 1958 he delivered a marathon seventeen-hour speech to eleven followers that he later published as *The Blue Book*, which formed the basis for the John Birch Society.

The most commonly used word to describe Welch's conspiratorial views is "bizarre." Books, magazine articles, and roughly one thousand newspaper stories a day in 1963 reported on the John Birch Society and its founder. Welch set off a political storm by crusading against the Communist conspiracy. His bleak assessment of Communist penetration into the U.S. government made Joseph McCarthy's indictments appear tame. The original version of his *Blue Book* reached the unlikely conclusion that President Dwight D. Eisenhower "is a dedicated, conscious agent of the Communist conspiracy." This phrase generated so much controversy that Welch changed it in later editions, saying that Eisenhower "has been sympathetic to ultimate Communist aims." Welch thereby offered two possibilities: either "he is a mere stooge or . . . he is a Communist." Welch believed that Communists controlled 60 to 80 percent of the United States.

Welch founded the John Birch Society to defeat this threat. Thriving on secrecy, the society created a disciplined following of its absolute leader, Robert Welch. Members studied Welch's monthly *Bulletin* in their meetings, seeking to counter Moscow's advances by implementing his prescribed agenda. Birchers recorded what activities they had completed and sent their sealed reports to Welch's headquarters in Belmont, Mass., for review. A member completing less than 50 percent of Welch's directives could be dismissed. This self-styled counterrevolutionary vanguard prized vigilance and devotion. The *Bulletin* included demands for letter-writing campaigns to impeach Chief Justice Earl Warren, infiltration of organizations like the PTA and the Republican party, and censorship of suspect library books; members displayed an intense commitment to stamp out communism, which Welch saw permeating most of American society. Copying Communist organizational tactics, he had associates form small "cells" of roughly twelve members each.

As the press launched an exposé-style attack on the Birch Society, observers feared that the organization posed a threat to democracy—a value that Welch roundly assaulted. Tapping into North Carolina's political culture, the society's motto proclaimed: "A republic, not a democracy." In his *Blue Book*, he argued that democracy was merely a deceptive phase, a weapon of demagoguery. The authoritarian structure and potentially subversive ends to which the society's efforts could be directed fed media charges of extremism. Yet right-wing apologists such as WRAL radio editorialist Jesse Helms (later a U.S. senator) countered these indictments with regular defenses of the organization.

The John Birch Society's membership peaked in the mid-1960s, with many ultraconservative enthusiasts joining during Barry Goldwater's presidential campaign. Its roughly 100,000 members supported an $8 million budget, 270 paid employees, 400 bookstores, and a publishing house. Welch never drew a dime's salary for his crusading efforts.

He retired as chairman of the John Birch Society in March 1983 after suffering a stroke. The ever energetic Welch had published seven books, edited the *American Opinion* for twenty-seven years, and produced innumerable films, pamphlets, and radio programs. He died almost two years later in the Winchester Nursing Home in Winchester, Mass. Welch was survived by his wife, two sons, Hillard Walmer and Robert H. W. III, and six grandchildren.

SEE: *Boston Globe*, 8 Jan. 1985; J. Allen Broyles, *The John Birch Society* (1966); Benjamin R. Epstein and Arnold Forster, *The Radical Right* (1967); Daniel L. Grant, *Alumni History of the University of North Carolina* (1924); Jonathan Houghton, "The North Carolina Republican Party: From Reconstruction to the Radical Right" (Ph.D. diss., University of North Carolina, 1993); *New York Times*, 8 Jan. 1985 (portrait).

JONATHAN HOUGHTON

Weldon, Daniel (*ca. 1720–ca. 1763*), was born in Henrico County, Va., the son of Samuel Weldon and the grandson of the Samuel Weldon who settled in Virginia in 1675 as factor of a London merchant. His mother was Elizabeth Allen Cobbs Weldon, the widow of Robert Cobbs. By her first husband Mrs. Weldon was the mother of Sarah Cobbs, first wife of Robert Jones, attorney general of North Carolina. The will of Samuel Weldon in Henrico in 1748 mentioned among others his wife's grandchildren, Allen, Willie, and Martha Jones. Samuel Weldon, the youngest son of Samuel, later moved to North Carolina and was prominent in the Revolution. Priscilla Weldon, sister of Daniel and Samuel, married Lewis Williamson of Northampton County, N.C., and was the grandmother of Weldon Nathaniel Edwards.

About 1745 Daniel Weldon moved to Granville County, N.C., where he was clerk of court from 1748 to 1763. In October 1749 he and William Churton on behalf of North Carolina and Joshus Fry and Peter Jefferson on behalf of Virginia were the commissioners to run the line between the two colonies from Peter's Creek, where the Byrd survey had stopped, to the Holston River, a distance of ninety miles. In 1756 Weldon was appointed one of the commissioners to lay off a town on the land of James Leslie on the banks of the Roanoke River in Halifax County. This was the town of Halifax, of which Weldon was appointed a trustee and director by the General Assembly in 1759. On 11 Jan. 1753 Marmaduke Kimbrough sold him 1,273 acres of land on the south side of the Roanoke River on both sides of Chockoyotte Creek. This plantation, which became the residence of Weldon and his descendants, is the site of the present town of Weldon.

On 17 Jan. 1753 Weldon married Elizabeth Eaton, the daughter of Colonel William Eaton, a prominent settler in Granville County. Daniel and Elizabeth had only one child, a son William. No record of Weldon's estate has been found. His widow married William Park of Warren County and died in 1804. By her second husband she had Robert Park and Eliza, who married as her third husband and she his third wife, Governor James Turner of North Carolina. They had two daughters who married and left issue.

SEE: J. B. Boddie, "The Weldon Family," in *Southside Virginia Families* (1955); Walter Clark, ed., *State Records of North Carolina*, vols. 24–25 (1905–6); Deeds and Wills of Halifax and Granville Counties (North Carolina State Archives, Raleigh); William L. Saunders, ed., *Colonial Records of North Carolina*, vols. 4–5 (1886–87).

CLAIBORNE T. SMITH, JR.

Weldon, Samuel (*ca. 1730–82*), Revolutionary patriot, was born in Henrico County, Va., the youngest son of Samuel Weldon and the brother of Daniel, who settled in Granville County, N.C. In 1760 "Samuel Weldon, Gentleman, of Northampton County, [N.C.]" sold a lot in the town of Halifax that he had inherited from his brother-in-law, John Jones. At an undetermined date he married Penelope Short, the daughter of William Short, whose will was probated in Northampton County in 1764. Weldon, according to the records of Northampton, never owned property in that county, however. He appears to have settled in Halifax County in 1772, when he bought land on Chockoyotte Creek near the property of his nephew, William Weldon.

With the advent of the American Revolution Samuel Weldon was a member of the Safety Committee of Halifax County and of the Committee of Observation to prevent overcharging for salt. On 22 Apr. 1776 the Provincial Congress meeting in Halifax elected him a major in the Halifax regiment of militia, and he was a member of the Provincial Congress that met in the same town in the fall of that year. On 23 Nov. 1776 he was transferred with the same rank to a battalion of volunteers then being raised for the assistance of South Carolina in quelling an uprising of Tories. He was promoted to lieutenant colonel on 23 Dec. 1776 and elevated to colonel on 24 Apr. 1778. A few months later, however, he resigned his commission, probably because of poor health.

On 10 May 1778 it fell to Weldon to transmit to Governor Richard Caswell the proceedings of the Committee of the Willis Alston that had convened in Halifax on 5 April. For several years Weldon served as a justice of the Halifax

Court, and it probably was in that capacity that he carried out this assignment.

The will of Samuel Weldon, dated 16 May 1779, was probated in Halifax County in 1782. It mentioned his wife Penelope, sons Benjamin Allen and William, and daughters Martha and Penelope. David Short and brother-in-law William Short were appointed executors. According to the county deeds, Weldon had a posthumous son, Thomas Short Weldon. His widow married one Simmons. The children of Samuel Weldon moved away from Halifax County in the early nineteenth century.

SEE: W. C. Allen, *History of Halifax County* (1918); Samuel A. Ashe, ed., *Biographical History of North Carolina*, vol. 7 (1908); 1J. B. Boddie, "The Weldon Family," in *Southside Virginia Families* (1955); Walter Clark, ed., *State Records of North Carolina*, vols. 12–3, 15 (1895–98); William L. Saunders, ed., *Colonial Records of North Carolina*, vols. 9–10 (1890); Williamsburg *Virginia Gazette*, 12, 18 Jan., 31 Mar. 1775; Wills and Deeds of Halifax and Northampton Counties (North Carolina State Archives, Raleigh).

CLAIBORNE T. SMITH, JR.

Welfare (Wohlfahrt), (Christian) Daniel *(12 June 1796–30 Aug. 1841)*, Moravian painter, was born in Salem, the youngest son of Johann Jacob Wohlfahrt, who in 1769 had moved to North Carolina from Maine, and Anna Elizabeth Schneider of Pennsylvania. His two older brothers were Samuel Jacob and Johann Thomas. Eventually, for professional purposes, he was known as Daniel Welfare, the surname a simple translation from the German. Both parents died while he was a boy. He was educated in Salem and at age fourteen was an apprentice in the cabinetmaker's shop, where his artistic talents were first observed. After attending the boys' school (Anstalt) in Salem for two years, he taught there for a short time until poor health, which troubled him for the rest of his life, compelled him to travel south to a warmer climate.

In March 1824 Welfare went to Philadelphia and studied under the noted painter Thomas Sully. Sully, who became his close friend and patron, saw to it that he had an exhibition in 1825 at the Pennsylvania Academy. After returning to Salem, he began planning a gallery where he could earn a living from the sale of paintings by himself and others. Several years later his intention became a reality, although the installation of skylights ("windows in the roof") somewhat puzzled and alarmed the staid citizens of Salem.

On 9 Dec. 1829 he married Catherine Hege of Friedberg, and they became the parents of daughters Jane Edith and Theophila and a son, Thomas Sully, named for his father's benefactor. For over two years (1831–33) Welfare and his wife successfully operated the Salem Tavern, but poor health again forced him to seek a less arduous occupation. Despite his physical weakness, he persisted in carrying out what he considered to be his obligations, often traveling to Pennsylvania by horseback and reportedly, on one occasion, by foot. Late in 1835 he was chosen to represent the Salem congregation at the Synod of the Brethren's Unity at Herrnhut, Saxony. Although fearing that he might be unable to endure the strenuous eight-month journey, he set out in March 1836 for England, Germany, Switzerland, and France. In 1839 he moved just outside Salem to a new home, where he had a picture gallery and a garden. He died there, never having fully recovered from a serious illness in February 1840. Welfare, deeply religious, was of an affable, though rather solemn, demeanor.

The subjects for his art were varied. He painted reproductions of portraits of U.S. presidents and of famous religious canvases, "all in dark monotone." His still lifes and his portraits of Moravian worthies and their families are rather flat, almost primitive. More appealing are watercolors of Salem streets and scenes. Perhaps his best-known canvas is an oil copy he made of a self-portrait Sully dispatched from Philadelphia to Salem in 1839 in honor of his namesake, born in 1835. Work by Welfare can be found in the Pennsylvania Academy of Fine Arts, the North Carolina Museum of Art, Old Salem, Inc., and private collections.

SEE: James H. Craig, *The Arts and Crafts in North Carolina* (1965); Ola Maie Foushee, *Art in North Carolina* (1972); Adelaide L. Fries and others, eds., *Records of the Moravians in North Carolina*, vols. 7–9 (1947–64); "Memoir" of Welfare (Moravian Archives, Winston-Salem); Winston-Salem Public Library files.

RICHARD WALSER

Wellborn (Welborn), James *(29 Nov. 1767–4 Dec. 1854)*, army officer and legislator, was born in that part of Rowan County that first became Surry County and then Wilkes County in 1778. Here he made his home during a long life, holding public office and operating a large plantation on land that both he and his wife had inherited some two miles from the county seat town of Wilkesboro. In 1800 Wellborn owned 12,321 acres of land and seventy-five slaves. Willie P. Mangum, who visited Wellborn in the spring of 1820, praised the beauty of the Wilkes County area. He further commented: "I have seen in one stock at Col. Welbourns [sic] 340 Cattle, & 70 or 80 of them that are fattening are in better order than I ever saw any animal of that description. They are raised without expense by sending them into the inexhaustible range of the mountains in the warm season of the year."

There seems to be no account of Wellborn's parentage, early life, or education, but as an adult he served as a county justice, a member of the board of education, and a trustee of the Wilkesborough Grammar School. He was a trustee of The University of North Carolina from 1804 to 1814. In 1805 Governor James Turner named him one of three commissioners to settle a North Carolina–South Carolina boundary dispute. In 1809 Wellborn and General William R. Davie attended the formal close of the Salem Boarding School and "noted with pleasure the progress made by the pupils." Except during the period 1812–17, when he served in the army, and eight other years, when he was not elected, Wellborn represented the county as a senator in the General Assembly for twenty-seven years between 1795 and 1835. His final legislative service, in 1846–47, was in the House of Commons. As a legislator he worked unsuccessfully to have a road built across North Carolina from Beaufort to the mountains, a route followed many years later by the North Carolina Railroad. Earlier, Wellborn had been a delegate to the Convention of 1835, which revised the state constitution.

During the final months of 1799 the trustees of The University of North Carolina undertook to acquire some land in western North Carolina that was presumed to have escheated to the state and thence to the university as having belonged to Tories—in this case, the Moravians. Through the efforts of Wellborn and his brother-in-law, Montfort Stokes, the university conceded that the Moravians' claim to the land was valid (the Moravians had been more neutral than Tory), and title was restored to the Moravians. Hugh Montgomery, the father-in-law of both Wellborn and Stokes, had once held the land in trust for the Moravians and then bought it.

Wellborn had risen to the rank of brigadier general in

the North Carolina militia by 1812, when he resigned to accept a commission as colonel in the Tenth Regiment of the regular army to serve during the War of 1812. At an encampment on Cane Creek in Rowan County, he was responsible for training troops from western North Carolina, South Carolina, and Georgia. From here troops were dispatched as needed in the Canadian theater and against Indians in Georgia and Alabama following a massacre of 283 refugees at Fort Mims.

Recruiting in the Southern Department was one of Wellborn's duties, and he visited Columbia, S.C., Georgia, and the Mississippi Territory to organize recruiting offices. He reported securing 300 recruits in Georgia, 250 in South Carolina, and 500 in North Carolina. His officers spent $60,000 for bounties in North Carolina alone. At recruiting stations Wellborn reported that he employed fife and drum music to attract attention and appeal to patriotism and that "the judicious application of rum" was not overlooked. He was also involved in equipping the troops under his command and eventually accompanied his men briefly for duty in the vicinity of Washington and Baltimore. For the most part, however, he was engaged in recruiting, and his requests for more active duty were not acted upon. His fellow officers reported him difficult to work with and seldom mentioned him. No reference to any commendation for his services has been found, but he is known to have been a diligent, effective worker and quite patriotic.

In February 1813 Wellborn married Rebecca Montgomery, the daughter of Colonel Hugh Montgomery, of Salisbury, a native of England. Her twin sister, Rachel, married Governor Montfort Stokes. The two sisters inherited large tracts of land from their father and, with their husbands, donated land for the town of Wilkesborough. Wellborn and his wife were the parents of several children, but his eighteen-year-old son, James, Jr., died in November 1827.

In a journal kept by Elisha Mitchell in 1827–28 on a journey to the mountains when he called on James Wellborn, he wrote: "What Wellborn's real character is I cannot make out. He has been a member of the Baptist church and will not allow of no swearing about him. He left the church under the idea that he was unfit to remain in it. He seems to have a religious paroxysm." An obituary in an Asheville newspaper noted the he was "highly esteemed for his strict integrity, great liberality and sterling patriotism." Wellborn died at his residence in Wilkes County and was buried in a nearby family cemetery enclosed by a stone wall. In 1992 Wendell H. Edgerton, of Wilkesboro, the owner of a new factory nearby, pleading ignorance, had the cemetery bulldozed and the site leveled.

SEE: *American State Papers: Military Affairs*, vol. 1 (1832); J. Jay Anderson, *Wilkes County Sketches* (1976); *Asheville News*, 15 Feb. 1855; John W. Clauser, Jr., and Stephen R. Claggett, *Investigation of the Wellborn Cemetery, Wilkes County, North Carolina* (1992); Adelaide L. Fries, ed., *Records of the Moravians in North Carolina*, vol. 6–7 (1943–47); Johnson J. Hayes, *The Land of Wilkes* (1962); Francis B. Heitman, *Historical Register and Dictionary of the U.S. Army*, vol. 1 (1903); T. Felix Hickerson, *Happy Valley: History and Genealogy* (1940); Sarah M. Lemmon, *Frustrated Patriots: North Carolina and the War of 1812* (1973); William H. Powell, comp., *List of Officers of the Army of the United States from 1779 to 1900* (1900); Marvin L. Skaggs, *North Carolina Boundary Disputes Involving Her Southern Line* (1941); John H. Wheeler, ed., *Reminiscences and Memoirs of North Carolina and Eminent North Carolinians* (1884); *Winston-Salem Journal*, 1 June, 1 Sept. 1992.

WILLIAM S. POWELL

Weller, Sidney *(1791–1 Mar. 1854)*, physician, nurseryman, clergyman, and planter, was born in Crawford, Orange County (then the town of Montgomery in Ulster County), N.Y., the eldest of seven children of Hendrick (Henry) and Ann Kidd Weller. They were of a German Palatine family that had settled in the colony of New York in 1709. There seems to be no record of Sidney's early life, but he clearly was well educated and, inasmuch as other members of the Weller family were baptized in the Goodwill Presbyterian Church in Montgomery, he probably was as well. On 14 Aug. 1813, however, he was admitted to Graham's Associate Reformed Church in Montgomery and described as a teacher. At one time, when he resided in Crawford, he was identified as a minister. He witnessed a will in Montgomery, N.Y., on 1 May 1811. In the 1820s Weller moved to Halifax County, N.C., and in the community of Brinkleyville acquired a 400-acre farm on very poor-quality land for which he paid $1.50 an acre. He intended to demonstrate how the soil could be improved and the land made productive.

On 6 July 1820 Weller married twenty-year-old Laura Maria Meachan. She died childless on 17 June 1826. On 16 Sept. 1828 twenty-five-year-old Elizabeth McCarrel became his second wife, and they had nine children: Mirzah (or Mercer) Leander, John Henry, Mary Ann, Sarah Adelia, Jane Elizabeth, Irene, Joseph McCarrel, Howard William, and Laura Addie. Mirzah Leander was killed in the Battle of Shiloh, Miss., on 6 Apr. 1862; Joseph McCarrel enlisted in the Seventeenth Regiment of North Carolina Troops in May 1861 but was discharged the next year because of disability.

About the time Weller arrived in North Carolina agriculture was in a decline. Soil fertility was becoming exhausted, and hundreds of families were leaving the state to settle in newly opened regions in the South and Southwest, notably Alabama, Mississippi, and Louisiana. Weller set about to publicize his ideas for reform, and instead of becoming a planter he engaged in general farming, grew grapes, and operated a small nursery. He also planted and propagated mulberry trees in a plan to make the South a region of silk production. In a six-year period he reported having sold $10,000 worth of mulberry trees that he produced in his nursery. He advocated and demonstrated methods for improving the fertility of the soil through the use of livestock manure and other natural fertilizers, rotating crops, and cover crops to prevent erosion.

He wrote for agricultural journals in North Carolina and elsewhere and for DeBow's *Commercial Review* in New Orleans, spoke before agricultural societies, and advocated the growing of grapes for the production of wine. He pointed out the qualities of native grapes, particularly the scuppernong, which he may have been the first to describe. After experimenting with over a hundred varieties of grapes, he settled on twenty-six that he considered suitable for the South. By making grafts and propagating cuttings, he improved a wild grape that was given his name and that of his county—Weller's Halifax. His Medoc Vineyard in western Halifax and his commercial winery attracted attention even outside the state. In 1840 North Carolina was the leading wine-producing state in the nation. After his death his vineyard was acquired by the neighboring Garrett brothers, Charles and F. M. From Weller they had become familiar with the business and in time moved it to New York and California as pioneer producers of wine.

In addition to offering grape vines and mulberry trees, Weller's nursery stocked strawberries, vegetable seeds, a variety of fruit trees, and ornamentals. Armanino and okra were in particular demand at one time, and okra seed were recommended as a substitute for coffee. Packed in damp sawdust or moss, his plants could be shipped as far as New Orleans and St. Louis.

Weller was generous in sharing his knowledge, and he published practical articles on many related subjects. As a further means of encouraging improved agriculture, he played a leading role in creating the State Agricultural Society and in organizing the first North Carolina State Fair in 1853.

Little appears to be known of Weller's roles as clergyman and physician, but one of his publications in 1845 referred to him as "Reverend" and the Tarboro newspaper in 1847 called him "Dr. Weller." Nevertheless, he may have abandoned both professions when he moved to North Carolina. He was a frequent contributor to regional newspapers not only on agriculture, but also on theology and politics. As an active candidate for election to Congress in 1847 as a Whig, he attracted considerable attention but withdrew before the election.

SEE: C. O. Cathey, "Sidney Weller: Ante-Bellum Promoter of Agricultural Reform," *North Carolina Historical Review* 21 (January 1954); *History and Genealogy of William Bull and Sarah Wells Family of Orange County, N.Y.* (1974); *Raleigh Register*, 11 Mar. 1854; *Tarborough Southerner*, 22 May 1847; Ralph H. Weller (New York City) to William S. Powell, 20 Aug. 1980.

WILLIAM S. POWELL

Wellman, Manly Wade (*21 May 1903–5 Apr. 1983*), writer, was born in Angola, West Africa, the son of Frederick Creighton, a medical officer, and Lydia Jeanette Isely Wellman. In 1926 he was graduated from Wichita Municipal University in Kansas (now Wichita State University) and in 1927 received a bachelor of laws degree from Columbia University. From 1927 to 1934 he was a reporter for the Wichita *Beacon* and *Eagle* before embarking on a successful, lifelong career as a free-lance writer. In 1947 he moved to Pinebluff, N.C., but soon settled in Chapel Hill to take advantage of the resources of The University of North Carolina library.

Wellman wrote both fiction and nonfiction for periodicals of many types including mystery, sports, juvenile, scholarly, and general popular magazines. His numerous books were also varied: biography, history (particularly Civil War and local history), folklore, murder, science fiction, travel, and animals, among others. In 1955 he was the recipient of the Edgar Allan Poe Award for nonfiction by the Mystery Writers of America, and in 1978 he was given the North Carolina Award for literature.

He taught classes in creative writing in the Evening College of The University of North Carolina and was widely appreciated for the aid he extended to would-be writers. He read and commented on their efforts and patiently guided many of them to fruitful careers.

In 1930 he married Frances Obrist, and they had a son, Wade. Wellman was a Democrat, an Episcopalian, and an active member of folklore and historical organizations.

SEE: *Chapel Hill Newspaper*, 8 Apr. 1986; Raleigh *News and Observer*, 6 Apr. 1986 (portrait); Frances Wellman, personal contact, 4 Aug. 1994; *Who Was Who in the South and Southwest* (1961).

WILLIAM S. POWELL

Wells, Bertram Whittier (*5 Mar. 1884–30 Dec. 1978*), botanist, teacher, and author, was born in Troy, Ohio, the son of the Reverend Edward T., a Methodist minister, and Lucia Morehouse Wells. Identification of a rare wild-

flower as a high school youth sparked his interest in botany, which he pursued at Ohio State University, earning an A.B. degree in 1911 and an M.A. degree in 1916. He received a Ph.D. in ecology from the University of Chicago in 1917.

Now prepared to teach, Wells accepted a post at Knox College in Illinois. His stay there was short-lived as he moved first to Connecticut Agricultural College and then to the Kansas State Agricultural College. Late in 1918 he was named head of the Botany Department at the University of Arkansas. When the chairmanship in botany opened up at North Carolina State College in 1919, Wells was offered the position. He accepted and served until 1949. Under his leadership the department grew from three to thirty professors. Wells continued teaching ecology at State College until 1954.

During his thirty-five years of service in North Carolina, Wells made three significant discoveries. First, he postulated that salt activity causes brush along the ocean shore to slope away from the seaside. Until his observation winds were considered to be the causal factor of such distributions. Second, he suggested the most widely accepted origin for the Carolina Bays—that these strange depressions in eastern North Carolina were the result of scooping activity by showers of meteorites. And third, Wells indicated that "balds," grasslands in the midst of forested mountains, were sites of former Indian summer camps. Man's presence for the duration of the summer prevented tree growth.

Wells wrote many technical papers. His most famous work, *The Natural Gardens of North Carolina* (1932), described the flora of various habitats in the state. Although never one to be described as a joiner, he was a member and served as president of the Southern Appalachian Botanical Society and the North Carolina Academy of Science.

After his retirement in 1954, Wells lived the remainder of his life on his farm alongside the Neuse River in northern Wake County. He was married twice, first to Edna Mety, of Jewell City, Kans., in 1917; after her death in 1938, he married Maude Barnes of Raleigh in 1941. There were no children of either marriage. Wells died in Raleigh.

SEE: Raleigh *News and Observer*, 14 Jan. 1937, 6 Dec. 1959, 3 Jan., 30 Dec. 1979; James W. Troyer, *Nature's Champion: B. W. Wells, Tar Heel Ecologist* (1993).

JAMES MERCER THORP, JR.

Wells, Warner Lee (*24 Dec. 1913–27 May 1991*), surgeon and author, was born in Durham, the son of Warner Lee and Narvie Elisabeth Hobby Wells. He received his undergraduate degree (1934) and the M.D. degree (1938) from Duke University. Remaining at Duke for a general surgical residency, he was an instructor and associate in surgery from 1943 to 1949. Between June 1944 and November 1946, however, he was an army medical officer in neurosurgery, attaining the rank of lieutenant colonel.

He returned to Europe in 1949 as a consultant to the surgeon general; he also edited colored movies on nerve and spinal cord injuries suffered in combat and wrote a section on nerve surgery for the surgeon general's history of medicine in World War II. As a surgical consultant to the Atomic Bomb Casualty Commission in Hiroshima, Japan, from 1949 to 1952, he served with a team of professionals sent to the country in 1950 to learn whether there were any delayed effects of the atomic bombs dropped on Hiroshima and Nagasaki in 1945. In the final year of his tour he was also an honorary professor of surgery at the Hiroshima Medical School.

During the seventeen-day passage by ship from San Francisco to Japan, Wells made the acquaintance of Dr. Robert B. Hall, an authority on Japanese studies at the University of Michigan and for twenty-five years cultural attaché to Emperor Hirohito. He also met a Dr. Kusama, dean of the medical school and head of public health at Keio University in Japan. From these two men Warner Wells then and later acquired an unusual knowledge of Japan and its people and began to learn the Japanese language. He was able to serve informally as liaison between the medical profession of Japan and the commission.

The Casualty Commission sought information about Japanese culture before and after the bombs fell as well as their immediate and long-term effects. What the members saw produced a sense of guilt, Wells later remarked. "But we had to assume a philosophical pose and accept the bombing as something that was done that couldn't be undone and that the Japanese would have dropped it on us if they'd had it."

Wells was still in Tokyo when the Korean War began, and he took time from the bomb damage investigation to help train American general surgeons in his speciality, neurosurgery. Beginning on Thanksgiving Day in 1950, he assisted in and supervised thirty-one brain operations that lasted thirty-six hours without a break.

Wells encountered Dr. Michihiko Hachiya, who had been director of a hospital in Hiroshima and kept a diary from the day of the bombing, 6 Aug. 1945, until 30 September, when he almost died. Hachiya turned over his diary to Wells, and with the help of young Dr. Neal Tsukifuji, born in Los Angeles and educated in America and Japan, Wells began a rough translation.

In 1952 Wells joined the surgical faculty of the new four-year medical school at The University of North Carolina and began a refined translation of Hachiya's diary. Published by the University of North Carolina Press in 1955 as *Hiroshima Diary*, it was an immediate best-seller. Early versions of the work, including a full typescript of the diary, are in the North Carolina Collection at The University of North Carolina. The book was translated into more than nineteen languages and sold around the world. Drs. Wells and Hachiya set up an educational foundation through which royalties from the book were used to provide care for orphan victims of the atomic bombs.

Wells served on the editorial board of the *Journal of the History of Medicine and Allied Sciences* and contributed articles to such journals as *Surgery, Gynecology, and Obstetrics*, the *North Carolina Medical Journal*, the *Bulletin of the* [University of North Carolina] *School of Medicine, American Surgeon*, and the *Bulletin of the Atomic Scientists*. In 1957 he received the Oliver Max Gardner Award from The University of North Carolina. On 16 Dec. 1959 in Chapel Hill he delivered the Humanities Lecture, entitled "Our Technological Dilemma; or, An Appraisal of Man as a Species Bent on Self-Destruction."

In 1939 Wells married Rebecca Atzrodte of Clarksburg, W. Va., a graduate of the Duke School of Nursing. They had four daughters, Rebecca Agnew, Mary Hobby, Sara Allan, and Elisabeth Fumi (born in Japan), and a son, Warner Lee, III, born after they returned to North Carolina. Dr. Wells was in poor health for a number of years before his death in Chapel Hill.

SEE: *Oliver Max Gardner Award* (1957 [portrait]); William S. Powell, ed., *North Carolina Lives* (1962); Raleigh *News and Observer*, 14 Aug. 1955, 23 Mar. 1957, 24 May 1972, 29 May 1991.

WILLIAM S. POWELL

Welsh, John Rushing, III (*19 May 1916–4 Oct. 1974*), teacher, administrator, and scholar in the field of southern letters, was born in Monroe, the son of John R., Jr., and Hallie Hamilton Benton Welsh. He received an A.B. degree from the University of the South in 1939 and a master's degree from Syracuse University in 1941, the year he married Ruth Elizabeth Davis on 9 August. From 1941 to 1942 he was head of the Department of English of the Linsly Institute in Wheeling, W.Va., before serving as a captain in the U.S. Army, Pacific theater, where he was often under enemy fire.

In 1946 he became adjunct professor of English at the University of South Carolina, a post he held until 1947 and again from 1949 to 1951. In 1951 he received a Ph.D. from Vanderbilt University with a dissertation on "The Mind of William Gilmore Simms: His Social and Political Thought," a summary of which was published by the Vanderbilt Joint University Library (1952). At Vanderbilt, Welsh was much influenced by the Fugitive poets and developed a close friendship with Donald Davidson of that group. In 1951 he was appointed associate professor of English at South Carolina, where he became a full professor in 1960. In 1958 Welsh was co-recipient of the USC Russell Award for Distinguished Teaching, and in 1963 he won the Wingate College Alumni Achievement Award.

Divorced in September 1962, he married Sevena Molair of Barnwell, S.C., on 20 Dec. 1963. In 1973 he was named head of the University of South Carolina English Department, and in 1974 he became the first vice-president for instruction at the university. At the time of his death he was serving as director of the university's Educational Foundation, a post he had held since the foundation was established in 1958; as associate editor of the *South Atlantic Bulletin* since 1969; as a member of the editorial board for the Centennial Edition of the Writings of William Gilmore Simms, University of South Carolina Press; and as a member of the Presbyterian College Board of Visitors.

Welsh was a member of the Modern Language Association and the Society for the Study of Southern Literature, as well as Blue Key, Phi Beta Kappa, Pi Gamma Mu, and the South Caroliniana Society. At South Carolina he served as faculty secretary (1964–70), secretary to the faculty senate (1970–73), president of the Faculty Club, and president of the campus chapters of Phi Beta Kappa and the American Association of University Professors. Among his publications are "Egdon Heath Revisited—Glasgow's Barren Ground" in *Reality and Myth: Essays in American Literature* (1963), *John Esten Cooke's Autobiographical Memo* (1969), and numerous articles in scholarly journals such as the *Journal of American Studies* and the *Journal of Southern History*. A partial list of his publications may be found in the card catalogue of the university's South Caroliniana Library.

Welsh died suddenly in Columbia, S.C. He was survived by his wife; his two children from his first marriage, Nancy Benton and John R., IV; and an adopted son, William L. He was buried in Monroe City Cemetery, Monroe, N.C.

Welsh was perhaps best known for his easy familiarity and rapport with students. In an unsigned eulogy in the student newspaper, he was judged "an anachronistic and very human man," one of the last of the sort known as the "Southern gentleman," an appellation that, "according to the values of a romanticized age" which Welsh represented, "characterized the finest qualities attainable by man." In tribute to his long years of service to the University of South Carolina, the building housing the English Department was renamed the John R. Welsh Building.

SEE: *Directory of American Scholars, English, Speech and Drama,* vol. 2 (1974); Columbia, S.C., *The Gamecock,* 7 Oct. 1974, and *The State,* 5 Oct. 1974 (portrait); *Who's Who in America* (1974).

STEVE A. MATTHEWS

Wenger, Arthur Daniel *(15 Oct. 1916–25 Feb. 1977),* college president and clergyman, was born on a farm in Aberdeen, Idaho, the son of Frank L. and Anna Toevs Wenger, both members of the Mennonite church. His father came from a Swiss Mennonite family that had immigrated to Pennsylvania in 1717 and then to the Valley of Virginia, Missouri, Kansas, and, later, Idaho. His mother's ancestors were German Mennonites who had wandered through Russia to Turkestan, Canada, and Kansas before settling in Idaho. Wenger attended Bethel College in Newton, Kans., his father's alma mater, earning a A.B. degree in history in 1941. He attended the San Francisco Theological Seminary in San Anselmo, Calif., in 1941–42, was ordained to the ministry of the Mennonite church in 1942, and became the minister of First Mennonite Church in Shafter, Calif.

From 1944 to 1946 Wenger was a captain in the Army Chaplains Corps and served with combat infantry units in Western Europe during the final year of World War II. On his return in 1946, he was ordained to the ministry of the Christian Churches (Disciples of Christ) and attended Brite College of the Bible, Texas Christian University, earning a B.D. degree in 1948. He served the Christian Church of Hamilton, Tex. (1948–49), before becoming associate minister of First Christian Church in New Castle, Pa., in 1949.

Wenger entered the ministry of higher education in 1950, when he was appointed assistant to the president of Atlantic Christian College (now Barton College) in Wilson, N.C. He then moved to Texas Christian University as director of promotion (1952–56) and director of religious activities (1954–56).

In 1956 he was called to be the eighth president of Atlantic Christian College, a position he filled until his death in his twenty-first year in office. During the two decades of his administration he was influential in the development of the institution, in higher education in North Carolina, in civic affairs in Wilson, and in his church from the local to the national level.

Under his leadership the college, with very limited resources, developed a sound financial foundation by means of a Fifteen-Year Development Program and balanced budgets. Development of the campus facilities— four dormitories, a library, a gymnasium, a student center, and four classroom buildings—was a major achievement. Accreditation by the Southern Association of Colleges and Universities was obtained in 1956 and renewed thereafter. The programs of nursing, art, and teacher education also were accredited.

President Wenger guided the college into sound development during the educational expansion of the fifties and sixties and prepared it to meet the decline of the seventies without serious problems. He insisted that religion was not solely an academic field to be studied, but an influence to permeate the campus. A vigorous, optimistic personality, strong religious commitment, and spirit of service made a lasting impression on students and faculty alike.

His wisdom, public-speaking ability, and temperament facilitated Wenger's leadership in higher education in the state. He was a North Carolina delegate to the National Education Compact of the States (1956); president of the North Carolina Council of Church-Related Colleges (1959), North Carolina Association of Colleges and Universities (1965–66), and Association of Eastern North Carolina Colleges (1969–70); and a prominent member of the board of directors of the North Carolina State Educational Assistance Authority (1966–71). He was active in the formation of the North Carolina Association of Independent Colleges and Universities; while serving as president (1972–74), he pioneered the development of the Legislative Tuition Grants Program for students attending private colleges and universities. At his death he was the dean of college presidents in the state, and often his peers had called upon him for counsel.

In Wilson his interests included the Chamber of Commerce (board of directors), Arts Council (president, 1968–69), Salvation Army Advisory Board, Boy Scouts of America (Eastern North Carolina Council), and Wilson County United Fund. He also sat on the Wilson County Economic Development Council and was president of the Wilson Rotary Club.

As a member of the Christian Churches, Wenger served as elder in First Christian Church, Wilson, as well as on the board of the North Carolina Christian Churches, the Board of Higher Education of the Christian Churches (chairman, 1959), and the General Board of Christian Churches. He was active in the Commission on Brotherhood Restructure, which conducted a reorganization of the Christian Churches. For his achievements he received the LL.D. degree from Texas Christian University (1956) and the Litt.D. from William Woods College, Fulton, Mo. (1975). He was one of three recipients of the Texas Christian University Distinguished Alumnus Award and a member of Delta Sigma Phi fraternity and Alpha Psi Omega honorary drama fraternity.

On 29 May 1944 he married Doris Kellenbarger, of Kansas, a graduate of Bethel College. They had three children: Arthur Frank, Jon Michael, and Mark Randolph. Wenger was buried in Maplewood Cemetery, Wilson.

SEE: Milton L. Adams, personal contact, 31 Aug. 1978; *North Carolina Christian* 58, no. 2 (April 1977); W. Burkette Raper to Mrs. Doris Wenger, 11 Apr. 1977; Jacob Toevs, *A Short Sketch of My Life* (n.d.); Arthur D. Wenger, "Responsible Education," response to charge at his inauguration, 3 May 1957; Doris K. Wenger, personal contact, 30 Aug. 1978; Cameron West to Mrs. Doris Wenger, 26 May 1978; *Who's Who in America* (1976).

WALTER W. ANDERSON, JR.

West, Robert *(1677–27 Mar. 1743),* member of the colonial Assembly and the Council, active in Indian affairs, and a militia officer, was born in Chowan County, the son of Robert and Martha West. After his father died in 1689, his mother reared Robert and his three brothers, Thomas, John, and Richard. Robert became involved in land speculation in the early eighteenth century and on 8 May 1713 was appointed a land appraiser for Chowan County, his first public office. Two years later he served as church warden of St. Paul's Parish, Edenton, and was elected a member of the Provincial Assembly, a post he filled until 1728. In 1716 he was granted 500 acres of land near Sandy Point on the northern side of Albemarle Sound. He was a justice of the peace for Chowan County from 1716 to 1727. West became active in Indian affairs, serving first as a commissioner to settle the boundaries of Tuscarora lands in 1722 and then as a commissioner to Indians in 1725. He was appointed the Indian commissioner for the province on 22 Jan. 1731 and held the position for five years.

In 1717 West was commissioned a major in the militia and thereafter appears in public records as Major Robert West (as opposed to his son, Colonel Robert West, who made a name for himself in Bertie County beginning in the mid-1730s). Appointed to the Council in April 1724, West served until 1730. He was buried in the county of his birth.

SEE: Robert J. Cain, ed., *North Carolina Higher-Court Minutes, 1724–1730* (1981), *Records of the Executive Council, 1664–1734* (1984), *1735–1754* (1988); John L. Cheney, Jr., ed., *North Carolina Government, 1585–1979* (1981); William S. Price, ed., *North Carolina Higher-Court Minutes, 1709–1723* (1974); William L. Saunders, ed., *Colonial Records of North Carolina*, vol. 1 (1886).

NEIL C. PENNYWITT

Weston, James Augustus (*6 May 1838–13 Dec. 1905*), Confederate officer, clergyman, and author, was born in Hyde County, the son of Samuel and Dinah Bartee Watson Weston. He was a descendant of Colonel John Easton, a Revolutionary leader, and Colonel William Watson, a militia officer in the War of 1812. Weston attended the common schools of Hyde County, Jonesville Academy in Yadkin County, Trinity College in Durham, Trinity College in Connecticut, and the University of the City of New York.

He read law under John E. Young, Leesburg, Va., and John S. Hawks, Washington, N.C., but abandoned his studies to enlist in the Confederate army in the spring of 1861. Appointed first lieutenant on 19 Sept. 1861 in Company F, Thirty-third Regiment, he was captured at New Bern on 14 Mar. 1862 and confined at Fort Columbus in New York Harbor. Transferred to Johnson's Island, Ohio, in June 1862, he was promoted to captain (5 Aug. 1862) while still a prisoner. He was declared exchanged at Aiken's Landing, James River, Va., on 10 November and returned to duty on New Year's Day 1863.

Wounded in the leg at Jericho Mills, Va., on 23 May 1864, he was promoted to major in July while absent wounded. With the promotion he was transferred to the regimental Field and Staff command, to which he reported for duty early in 1865. Having fought at Antietam and Gettysburg, he was present at General Lee's surrender in 1865. The colonel of his regiment refused to surrender and instead simply mounted his horse and rode away, leaving Major Weston to conduct the formalities. The two men never saw each other again. Weston was the author of the regimental history published in Walter Clark's history of North Carolina troops.

During the war Weston made a vow to enter the ministry, and after studying at the Protestant Episcopal Theological Seminary in Alexandria, Va., he was ordained deacon in 1870 and priest in 1876. He served churches in Hertford, Raleigh, Hickory, and Lenoir, conducted services at numerous missions, was a prominent church leader in western North Carolina, and took an active interest in the Episcopal School at Valle Crucis. He published *Historic Doubts as to the Execution of Marshal Ney* (1895), a book that he started in 1882, and was an honorary member of the North Carolina Historical Society.

Weston never married. He suffered a fatal stroke while attending a church convocation in Shelby and was buried at Hickory.

SEE: Samuel A. Ashe, ed., *Biographical History of North Carolina*, vol. 7 (1908); Walter Clark, ed., *Histories of the Several Regiments and Battalions from North Carolina in the Great War*, vol. 3 (1901); Weymouth T. Jordan, comp.,

North Carolina Troops, 1861–1865: A Roster, vol. 9 (1983); James B. Sill, *Historical Sketches of Churches in the Diocese of Western North Carolina (Episcopal Church)* (1955); J. Weston and William L. Clinard, *A Brief History of the Church of the Ascension (Episcopal)* (1950); James A. Weston Papers (Southern Historical Collection, University of North Carolina, Chapel Hill).

FRANK P. CAUBLE

Wetmore, Thomas Cogdell (*22 Aug. 1869–3 Aug. 1906*), clergyman and educator, was born in Lincolnton, the son of the Reverend William Wetmore, rector of St. Luke's Episcopal Church, Lincolnton, and Mary Bingham Wetmore. There is no evidence that the son attended or was graduated from college. In March 1886, at age seventeen, he and his brother, L. C. Wetmore, started a small weekly newspaper, *The Trumpet*, which they published until September 1888. There are accounts that he later traveled to the foothills and mountains of western North Carolina on business or missionary work. In 1893 he married Susan Boone Allen, and they had two children.

Wetmore was ordained deacon in the Episcopal church by the Right Reverend Joseph B. Cheshire at St. Luke's Church in Lincolnton on 14 Feb. 1894 and priest by the same bishop in 1899. For a while he represented the Missionary District of Asheville as a general missionary and aroused much interest in the mission work of the mountain region. Apparently, however, he was much more drawn to the educational side of his ministry. At this time the few schools that existed in rural western North Carolina were open no more than three months a year. Wetmore wanted to establish a school that provided at least an eight-month term.

In 1894 he became rector of St. James's Church in Hendersonville, and his first report the following year showed a considerable increase in communicants. In his report for 1897 he noted that "a suitable and attractive church" in the community of Upward would soon be completed. For 1898 he said that "the many people here from the South during the summers take a great interest in the Church, which had not been the custom heretofore." Previously there had been much prejudice towards St. James's, "but it is gratifying to know that now there exists a kinder feeling toward it."

In 1897 Wetmore left his parish duties to found Christ School at Arden. Begun as "a work of love, faith, and high vision on eight hundred dollars," the school was established in 1900 by the Reverend and Mrs. Wetmore. Because it was intended for mountain boys whose education was being neglected, Thomas Wetmore became known as the founder of "The Rugby of the Mountains." Young and energetic, he made many friends who contributed financially to the school. His friends in the New York Stock Exchange on one occasion stopped the bidding for five minutes while the members gave a fairly large sum for the work of Christ School.

For six years Thomas and Susan Wetmore worked together, sharing the vision, the labors, and the hardships to make the dream a reality. But in 1906 he died following an operation for appendicitis, leaving his wife to carry on their work. With high courage she accepted the responsibility, and for many years the entire burden rested on her. The school prospered and grew with a large campus, new buildings, and an increasing enrollment. A portrait of Wetmore hangs in the library at Christ School, Arden.

SEE: Arden, *Christ School News*, March 1949; Asheville *Citizen*, 4 Aug. 1906; *Charlotte Daily Observer*, 4 Aug. 1906; *His-*

torical Sketches of the Diocese of Western North Carolina (1941); *Journal of the Thirteenth Annual Convention of the Missionary District of Asheville* (1907); Thomas C. Wetmore Diary, 14 Feb. 1894–1897 (Pack Memorial Library, Asheville).

ARTUS MONROE MOSER

Wharton, Robert Leslie *(Sept. 1871–2 Aug. 1960)*, foreign missionary and teacher, was born in McLeansville, the son of William P. and Jane N. Rankin Wharton, who were married in 1856. After graduation from Davidson College in 1892, he enrolled at Trinity College, Durham, in September 1893 for postgraduate courses. He may also have taught in the Durham school then as well as in the 1894–96 interval in his theological training. Wharton is recorded as attending Union Theological Seminary in Virginia during the periods 1893–94 and 1896–98. He was licensed and ordained by the Orange Presbytery on 25 May 1898 and served as an assistant pastor in Durham in 1898–99.

With the end of the Spanish-American War Wharton became a foreign missionary in Cuba. For two years beginning in 1899, he taught school in Cárdenas, about 100 miles east of Havana on Cuba's northern shore, and from 1901 to 1903 he was an evangelist in Caibarien. Returning to Cárdenas he was an evangelist during the years 1903–12; again at Caibarien, he served as pastor to the Presbyterian congregation from 1912 to 1918. In 1919, however, he began the work for which he was best known—superintendent of mission schools in Cárdenas, where, in 1900, he had founded a boys' school, La Progresiva, with fourteen students. Both a high school and a junior college, La Progresiva in time became coeducational, with an enrollment of two thousand students. Wharton also became editor of *El Heraldo Cristiano* and in 1922 was awarded an honorary doctor of divinity degree by Davidson College.

Wharton's school was recognized by the Cuban government as one of the strongest teaching centers in the country and soon had the largest number of students of any private school there. Its role in relief projects (a hurricane almost destroyed Cárdenas in 1931) and civic work was commended by the Red Cross and the Cuban government. To meet some urgent needs, Wharton created committees of a thousand people (called *Mil Hombres*) in each of forty towns who agreed to give a dollar every month to pave the nearly impassable streets of their town, provide pure water, control mosquitoes, or support some other community project. Wharton was given the highest honor Cuba could bestow on a private citizen—the Carlos Manuel de Céspedes medal. He was president of the school and superintendent of all Presbyterian educational work in Cuba for almost forty years. (There were thirteen schools in the system maintained by the Presbyterian church.) On his retirement from these positions in 1941, many national and local officials from across Cuba went to Cárdenas to honor him.

He next began to teach church history at the Interdenominational Seminary in Havana and to work among University of Havana students. For several years he also took a group of Cuban students to Presbyterian Junior College in Maxton, N.C., for summer school. In 1947 Wharton joined the Queens College faculty in Charlotte as professor of modern languages. In 1956 he moved to Arlington, Va., to live with a daughter, and it was there that he died. He was buried temporarily in Arlington until his body could be transferred to Cuba for burial in Cárdenas near that of his wife. Thousands of people lined the streets there as his body passed; stores, banks, and factories closed, and bells in churches of all denominations were rung in salute to him.

In 1902 Wharton married Anne Elizabeth Ramsey, of Durham, who died in 1953. They had three daughters, Elizabeth (Mrs. John P. McKnight), Anita (Mrs. Val John Guthery), and Josephine, and one son, Robert L., Jr.

SEE: *Charlotte News*, 22 Aug. 1947 (portrait); *Charlotte Observer*, 3 Aug. 1960; Mrs. Anita W. Guthery (Naples, Fla.) to William S. Powell, 18 Nov. 1994; *Historical Foundation News*, 10 Mar. 1974; *Presbyterian Outlook*, 20 Feb. 1961 (portrait); *Reader's Digest*, December 1944; Eugene C. Scott, comp., *Ministerial Directory of the Presbyterian Church, U.S., 1861–1941* (1942); *Trinity Alumni News*, vol. 2 (April 1916); *Washington Evening Star*, 3 Aug. 1960.

WILLIAM S. POWELL

Wheat, John Thomas *(15 Nov. 1801–2 Feb. 1888)*, Episcopal priest and university professor, was born in Washington, D.C., the son of Thomas and Mary Chatham Wheat. The founder of the line, Francis Wheate, emigrated from England in 1724, settled in Prince George County, Md., and married, though no record of his wife's name exists. Francis had at least two sons, John (b. ca. 1730) and Francis (b. ca. 1745). John Wheate married Mary Mullikan, and from this union came nine children, one of whom, Thomas, married Mary Chatham. The family estate, Cool Springs, was located in Maryland almost directly across the Potomac River from Alexandria, Va.

John Thomas Wheat (he dropped the final *e* from his name) was trained for the ministry at the Virginia Theological Seminary, in Alexandria, Va., and while there he conducted a school for about thirty advanced students. During this period he fell in love with Selina Blair Patten and married her on 10 Mar. 1825. She was the daughter of Thomas and Mary Roberdeau Patten and the granddaughter of General Daniel Roberdeau, a wealthy merchant of Philadelphia and a general in the Pennsylvania troops. The Wheats had eight children, five of whom reached maturity. Roberdeau Chatham, the oldest, was a soldier of fortune and was killed during the Civil War as was a younger brother, John Thomas. The last child, Leonidas Polk, named for the distinguished Episcopal bishop who became a Confederate major general, studied in Paris under Franz Liszt and became a concert pianist. One of Wheat's daughters, Selina Patten, married Dr. John Seay of Nashville, Tenn., and the other, Josephine May, married Francis E. Shober.

Wheat was admitted to the diaconate of the Episcopal church by Bishop William Channing Moore at Christ Church, Alexandria, in 1825 and the next year was ordained a priest in St. Paul's Church, Baltimore. During 1826 he served as rector at St. John's, Anne Arundel County, Md. From this time on Wheat made frequent changes of parishes. In 1829 he took charge of St. Matthew's Church, Wheeling, then in Virginia, and in January 1833 he moved his little family, which now numbered three children, to Marietta, Ohio, where he became rector of St. Luke's for three years. In 1836 Wheat went to New Orleans to recuperate from a severe illness. While there, he was engaged for three months by the vestry of Christ Church, which was temporarily without a rector. Shortly after he returned to his parish in Marietta, the Domestic Committee of the Episcopal church sent him back to New Orleans to establish a mission in the upper part of the city. The many friends he had made there supported the mission to such an extent that it soon grew into the self-supporting parish of St. Paul's. Two events, however, induced Wheat to leave New Orleans. A subscription of $40,000 to build a church was wiped out by the panic of 1837. And during this financial crisis he was called to

Christ Church, Nashville, Tenn., to which he moved his family in 1837.

In 1849 the chair of Rhetoric and Logic at The University of North Carolina was left vacant by the resignation of the Reverend William Mercer Green, and through the influence of Bishop James H. Otey of Tennessee Wheat was recommended for the position. At Otey's suggestion Wheat accepted it and moved to Chapel Hill. According to Kemp P. Battle, the university historian, Wheat proved to be an active and energetic professor, and his family added "much to the social attractions of the village." Mrs. Wheat took an interest in ill students, often nursing them and even offering the university a corner of her own yard for the site of an infirmary. The trustees accepted her generosity, and a two-room, one-story cottage was erected in 1858 on that lot—located where Spencer Hall now stands—and universally called "The Retreat."

In June 1859 Wheat resigned as professor and as rector of the Chapel of the Cross in Chapel Hill to accept a call to Christ Church, Little Rock, Ark. During the Civil War, while cut off from his parish by the fall of Vicksburg in 1863, he was a chaplain in the Confederate army, serving principally in North Carolina. After the war he returned to Little Rock where he remained until 1867, when he accepted a call to a recently organized church in Memphis, Tenn. This church was formed from members of other Episcopal churches in the city who did not wish to worship in the presence of carpetbaggers, occupying troops, and others who went south after the war. Determined to organize another parish, they called upon the Reverend John Thomas Wheat to become its rector. St. Lazarus was the name chosen for the new church because as Jefferson Davis, one of its founders, said, "We, like Lazarus, were licked by dogs." Mrs. Davis, wife of the former Confederate president, went out to the women of the congregation, and on a Sunday shortly after Wheat arrived the alms basins were "heaped high with brooches, rings, bracelets, chains, and gifts from loved ones" and laid on the altar. Enough precious metal was given to make a communion service consisting of a chalice, a paten, and a flagon. This beautiful service was later given to Saint Luke's Church, Salisbury, as a memorial to Wheat.

In 1873 Wheat resigned his charge at St. Lazarus's and went into partial retirement. He soon moved to Salisbury to live with his daughter, Mrs. Francis E. Shober. In the next year and afterwards he planted churches in Berkeley, Calif.; Lewisburg, W.Va.; and Greensboro and Concord, N.C. During his long ministry he had the honor of being a delegate to six General Conventions of the Episcopal church. He was awarded the D.D. degree by the University of Nashville and published a pamphlet entitled *Preparation for the Holy Communion* (1866).

He died in Salisbury at the home of his granddaughter, Mrs. A. H. Boyden, and was buried from St. Luke's Church in the English Cemetery near the church. His wife died on Christmas Eve 1896.

SEE: Kemp P. Battle, *History of the University of North Carolina*, vol. 1 (1907); Ellen Harrell Cantrell, *The Annals of Christ Church Parish, Little Rock, 1839–1899* (1900); Charles L. Dufour, *Gentle Tiger: The Gallant Life of Roberdeau Wheat* (1957); Archibald Henderson, *The Campus of the First State University* (1949); William S. Powell, *St. Luke's Episcopal Church, 1753–1953* (1953); Salisbury *Carolina Watchman*, 9 Feb. 1888.

JAMES S. BRAWLEY

Whedbee, Charles (7 Sept. 1875–26 June 1945), lawyer, legislator, and prime mover in the establishment of county libraries in North Carolina, was born in Hertford, the son of James Monroe and Fannie Skinner Whedbee. He was the nephew of Thomas Gregory Skinner, who served two terms in the U.S. House of Representatives, and of Harry Skinner, who served one term in the House, and the brother of Judge Harry Whedbee, of the superior court. He received his secondary education at Hertford Academy and afterward studied law independently. Prior to taking the bar examination, he attended one summer session of The University of North Carolina Law School. He began practicing law in Hertford around 1898 and was attorney for Perquimans County from 1920 to 1945. Under his leadership, the white high schools in 1926 were consolidated into the Perquimans County High School, the first such merger on a countywide basis in the state. For forty years he was affiliated with Major and Loomis, a lumber company, filling the office of secretary.

Much of his professional life was devoted to statewide activities. He was a trustee of The University of North Carolina from 1903 to 1945, and for almost all of that time he served on the executive committee. In 1929 and 1931 he held a seat in the state senate. As chairman of the finance subcommittee in 1931, he was instrumental in the passage—through the senate and the house of representatives—of the local government act that more than anything else stabilized the economy in urban areas and reportedly "controlled and saved millions in debt service for constructive social and civic enterprises." Also in 1931, in connection with a controversial school tax bill, Whedbee declared publicly: "I may be consigned to the pit of everlasting destruction, so far as politics goes, but I will never, as long as I keep my proper sense of right, hold out to my people a false hope that they have attained something they may desire when I know in my heart this is false and untrue and as baseless as the fabric of a dream." During the administration of J. C. B. Ehringhaus he was appointed to the State Highway and Public Works Commission, and he played an important part in the establishment of rural electrification in North Carolina. His most significant service in the mid–1930s was as legislative adviser to Governor Ehringhaus during the 1933 and 1935 sessions of the legislature.

Whedbee worked steadily for an appropriation for statewide library service; in 1940, at his own expense, he visited every county and consulted every legislator. He awakened such interest in public libraries and created so much demand for them that on 8 Mar. 1941 the North Carolina Assembly passed an act appropriating money for the purpose of "promoting, aiding and equalizing library service in North Carolina. . . . [The fund] shall be known as the Public Library Service Fund." The American Library Association later cited him for his unparalleled accomplishment, but illness prevented his attending its annual meeting and receiving an award.

In 1943 The University of North Carolina conferred on him an honorary LL.D. degree. Dr. Frank P. Graham summarized his achievements in the citation, which reads in part: "Charles Whedbee of Hertford, N.C., alumnus, lawyer, legislator . . . constantly and quietly in the center of movements for the building of better roads, better institutions and a better state. For over a quarter of a century a devoted trustee of the University . . . one of the builders of the present University and of the consolidated University of North Carolina. . . . With a solid background of legislative competence and distinctions in his own right it was in the critical sessions of 1933 and 1935 as the personal representative of the governor he drafted and helped pilot through both houses the administrative bills all but two of which became the law of the land. . . . In the last several sessions of the legislature he tirelessly and effectively worked for state appropriations for the countywide library service which now takes books to the people everywhere in North Carolina."

He was twice married: to Mabel Martin of Wilmington on 13 Jan. 1901, and to Evelyn Copeland of Hertford on 3 Jan. 1917. By his first marriage he was the father of one son, Silas M., and one daughter, Jocelyn (Mrs. Robert O. Applewhite). An Episcopalian, a Democrat, and a charter member of the Hertford Rotary Club, he died in a Norfolk, Va., hospital after an extended illness and was buried in Cedarwood Cemetery, Hertford.

SEE: Elizabeth City *Daily Advance*, 5 Feb. 1931, 4 June 1943, 27 June 1945; Raleigh *News and Observer*, 2 June 1943, 27 June 1945; University of North Carolina *Alumni Review*, vol. 31, no. 8 (1943); Mabel Martin Whedbee, "A History of the Development and Expansion of Bookmobile Service in North Carolina, 1923–1960" (master's thesis, University of North Carolina, 1962); Whedbee family, personal contact.

ESTHER EVANS

Wheeler, Alvin Sawyer *(2 Nov. 1866–12 May 1940)*, the first organic chemist in North Carolina, was born in Holyoke, Mass., the son of William Carleton and Sarah Elizabeth Couch Wheeler. When he was two, the family moved to Dubuque, Iowa, and Wheeler entered Beloit College from the Dubuque public schools. After receiving an A.B. degree in 1890, he moved to Tacoma, Wash., and worked in the family lumber business until 1893. As a substitute high school science teacher in Tacoma from 1893 to 1896, he discovered a great love for science—he built the first X-ray generator on the West Coast—and to pursue this new interest he enrolled at Harvard, where he was assistant in chemistry and received M.A. (1897) and Ph.D. (1900) degrees. He joined The University of North Carolina almost immediately as associate professor of chemistry.

In order to assume a more specialized career in organic chemical research, Wheeler spent a sabbatical year (1910–11) at the University of Berlin and the University of Zurich studying under the Nobelists Emil Fischer and Richard Willstätter, respectively. From this year there originated his internationally recognized series of studies on the organic chemistry of dyes. Several of his discoveries were patented, preeminently a dye named "Wheeler Brown" by the National Aniline Company, whose color was responsible for the tint of women's hosiery for many years beginning in the 1920s. He spent further study on dyes at the University of Manchester in 1928. His specialties were in the dyes formed from the chemical families of juglone, the principle of black walnut trees by which they prevent competition from other vegetation, and *para*-cymene; he drew attention to the fact that spruce turpentine, when distilled, was fairly pure *para*-cymene, and that if collected instead of discarded this type of turpentine could become the basis of a southern dyestuff industry. Demanding much of his students, he was nevertheless a memorable, animated lecturer, and it was once said of him that "as he describes or demonstrates some new dye he has just discovered, his face beaming with enthusiasm, . . . the magnitude of his smile usually is proportional to the tinctorial property of the dye."

Wheeler was promoted to professor in 1912 and at his retirement in 1935 was named Kenan Professor Emeritus. He published about sixty-six papers, mostly on the synthesis of dyes and of chemical compounds related to them, including the first chemical paper from North Carolina appearing in a European scientific journal. He was

president of the Elisha Mitchell Scientific Society, the North Carolina Section of the American Chemical Society, and Sigma Xi, the honorary society in scientific research. In Chapel Hill he was a charter organizer of the Carolina Playmakers and later treasurer, twice president of the Chapel Hill Country Club, the organizer and permanent president of the Faculty Club, and treasurer of the Presbyterian church for over twenty years.

A great traveler, he planned his vacations meticulously, crossing the United States by car many times and visiting Europe repeatedly. He often told friends that his greatest thrill had been standing at the crater of Mount Etna as it erupted.

On 24 Aug. 1899 he married Edith Myra James, of Cleveland, Ohio, the daughter of the prominent educator Henry M. James and a graduate of Wellesley College; she was well known as a music teacher in Chapel Hill for many years. They had three sons: James Robert, who died young; William Couch, born 23 Aug. 1903; and Henry James, born 26 Dec. 1904.

SEE: M. M. Bursey, *Carolina Chemists* (1982); *Greensboro Daily News*, 13 May 1940; *Industrial and Engineering Chemistry* 12 (1934); Raleigh *News and Observer*, 13 May 1940; *Who Was Who in America*, vol. 1 (1943).

MAURICE M. BURSEY

Wheeler, John Hervey *(1 Jan. 1908–6 Jul. 1978)*, black businessman and civil rights leader, was born in Kittrell on the campus of Kittrell College, an African Methodist Episcopal church school of which his father was president. His mother was Margaret Hervey Wheeler. The elder Wheeler (John Leonidas, 1869–1957), a graduate of Wilberforce University and the University of Chicago, gave up his academic career in 1908 for an executive position with the North Carolina Mutual Life Insurance Company in Durham. As the firm expanded throughout the South to become America's largest black business, he was transferred to Atlanta to direct the Georgia district. There John H. Wheeler spent his early years, attending the Atlanta public schools and graduating summa cum laude from Morehouse College in 1929.

In the same year he left Atlanta for Durham, where he went to work for the Mechanics and Farmers Bank, a sister institution to North Carolina Mutual. Under the tutelage of Richard L. McDougald, bank president and community leader, Wheeler adopted a model of black leadership. In 1952 he assumed the presidency of Mechanics and Farmers Bank. But for Wheeler, as for McDougald before him, the bank served as a base for action that ranged well beyond providing financial services. Much of this higher purpose was a given in Afro-American culture, the special burden of race relations. Even in the day-to-day granting of loans to black citizens, Mechanics and Farmers was more than a bank. Under Wheeler's direction it became an instrument for social change, making possible the purchase of decent homes, the acquisition of federal loans for housing projects, and the relaxation of racial barriers among white banks that learned from Wheeler that black borrowers were good risks.

Wheeler was never content, however, to work for change through economic uplift and indirect means. Happily for him, black Durham offered support and inspiration for direct politics. In 1935 he joined others to found the Durham Committee on Negro Affairs, a black political organization that became one of the South's most effective local movements in the struggle for reenfranchisement, civil rights, and economic justice. It was in the

DCNA that Wheeler served his apprenticeship and developed his mastery of New South politics. He presided over the committee from 1957 until his death, generally choosing to work behind the scenes as strategist and statesman. His choice of political style may have been limited, however, because he typically stood ahead of the times and was judged as too radical for the DCNA to put forward as a candidate for public office.

His reputation for "radicalism" stemmed from his efforts to build a local coalition of black and white workers, from his battle to integrate The University of North Carolina and the Durham public schools, from his unflinching endorsement of the sit-in movement, and, overall, from his lifelong demands for full equality. It would be correct, for example, to consider the completion of his law degree from North Carolina College in 1947 as instrumental to his quest for justice rather than as a supplement to his banking career. In a theoretical sense he played a key, functional role in the racial politics of the New South, especially in the difficult years before 1964. In these "forgotten years," figures like Wheeler made the "impossible" demands out of which "safer" black leaders could negotiate the "possible," and out of which younger black leaders could find a historical base to continue the process.

By the 1960s history began to fall into step with Wheeler, and public recognition quickly followed. In 1961 President John F. Kennedy appointed him to the President's Committee on Equal Employment Opportunity; in 1968 President Lyndon B. Johnson assigned him to the National Housing Corporation, a body created by the Housing and Urban Development Act of 1968. In the meantime the federal government had commissioned him to tour West Germany as part of a team evaluating the long-term effects of the Marshall Plan. In 1966 the State Department sent him to Egypt and Syria as a consultant and lecturer. His relationship with President Johnson earned him an invitation to participate in the drafting of the civil rights legislation of the 1960s. During the period 1963–68 he also served as president of the Southern Regional Council.

Such recognition in the nation and abroad made it difficult to deny him visibility at home. In 1964 he became North Carolina's first black delegate to the National Convention of the Democratic party; he continued his formal role in the state party and eventually served as its financial director. In 1970 Duke University awarded him an honorary doctor of humanities degree.

In his personal life Wheeler was an ardent tennis player and an accomplished violinist. His friends and colleagues remembered him as a renaissance man and a few months after his death established the John H. Wheeler Foundation, with the first Wheeler Scholarship awarded in 1979. He married Selena Warren, and they had two children, Warren Hervey and Julia. Wheeler was a life member of the NAACP and a member and trustee of St. Joseph's AME Church in Durham; he belonged to Omega Psi Phi fraternity and was a Mason and a Shriner. He was buried in Beechwood Cemetery, Durham.

SEE: Robert Louis Bowman, "Negro Politics in Four Southern Counties" (Ph.D. diss., University of North Carolina, 1964); Margaret Elaine Burgess, *Negro Leadership in a Southern City* (1960); *Durham Morning Herald*, 2 Aug. 1953; William R. Keech, *The Impact of Negro Voting* (1968); Everett Carll Ladd, *Negro Political Leadership in the South* (1966); Murray J. Marvin, correspondence (May 1979) and personal contact (1968, 1970, 1978, 1979), *Nat. Cyc. Am. Biog.*, vol. 61 (1982 [portrait]); Conrad O. Pearson, personal contact, 1968, 1979; Charles Clinton Spaulding Papers (North

Carolina Mutual Life Insurance Company, Durham); Viola G. Turner, personal contact, 1968, 1979; Walter B. Weare, *Black Business in the New South: A Social History of the North Carolina Mutual Life Insurance Company* (1973); John Hervey Wheeler, personal contact, 1972.

WALTER B. WEARE

Wheeler, John Hill (*2 Aug. 1806–7 Dec. 1882*), historian, lawyer, and diplomat, was born in Murfreesboro, the son of John, a prominent shipping merchant, and Elizabeth Jordan Wheeler. He studied at Hertford Academy under the Reverend Jonathan Otis Freeman and at age fifteen entered Columbian College (now George Washington University) in Washington, D.C., receiving his bachelor's degree in 1826. After reading law under Chief Justice John Louis Taylor, he was admitted to the bar in 1827, and the following year he received a master's degree from The University of North Carolina. At age twenty-one Wheeler was elected to the House of Commons from Hertford County, and he served for four years. At the end of his term President Andrew Jackson appointed him secretary of the board of commissioners established to adjudicate spoliation claims of Americans against France under the treaties of Berlin and Milan. He was an unsuccessful candidate for Congress in 1831.

In 1837 President Jackson appointed Wheeler superintendent of the Charlotte branch of the U.S. Mint. On his resignation in 1841, Mecklenburg Democrats nominated him to the House of Commons, but he declined because of his impending move to Lincoln County. The next year the legislature elected Wheeler treasurer of the state. In 1852 he again served in the House of Commons, that time from Lincoln County. A Mason, he was grand master of North Carolina in 1842 and 1843.

Long interested in history, Wheeler as state treasurer arranged for the printing of *Indexes to Documents Relative to North Carolina*, a list of papers prepared in London in 1827 for Archibald D. Murphey. After his defeat for reelection as treasurer in 1844, he devoted much time to an attempt to obtain copies of original sources relating to North Carolina history. He carried on frequent correspondence with George Bancroft, U.S. minister to England; Peter Force, Washington publisher and historian; and David L. Swain, former governor and then president of The University of North Carolina. To the three of them he dedicated his *Historical Sketches of North Carolina, from 1584 to 1851*, published in 1851. With all its defects (it has been characterized as having perpetuated more errors than any nineteenth-century history of the state), *Historical Sketches* was the first publication to utilize a substantial body of original source materials from both home and abroad. Whigs, piqued by the flowery sketches of their political rivals, referred to the two-volumes-in-one as "the Democratic Stud-Book."

James C. Dobbin of Fayetteville, secretary of the navy in President Franklin Pierce's cabinet, aided Wheeler in obtaining an appointment as assistant secretary to the president in 1854, and a few months later the historian was appointed U.S. minister to Nicaragua. Arriving there late in 1854, the inexperienced diplomat found himself caught between shifting factions in a civil war complicated by the involvement of American filibusters. Wheeler wrote that "the race of Central Americans have conclusively proved to all observant minds that they are incapable of self-government" and that Nicaragua was surely destined to "become part and parcel of the U.S." With that bias he allowed himself to be influenced by William Walker, a young Tennessean who, with a group of American mercenaries, sought to gain control over the country. Eventually Walker manipulated himself into the presidency of the republic, and Wheeler quickly recognized the new regime. Whether or not this action represented intentional disobedience to his instructions from Washington, Wheeler was recalled by Secretary of State William L. Marcy in 1856, and he resigned in March 1857. Strangely, the "List of U.S. Diplomatic Officers, 1789–1939" in the Federal Records Center, East Point, Ga., indicates that Wheeler was reappointed on 23 Dec. 1857, but, if so, he apparently declined to serve.

In July 1855, while traveling from Washington to New York for a return trip to Nicaragua, Wheeler became embroiled in a dramatic confrontation with Abolitionists. With him were a slave woman, Jane, and her two sons, Daniel and Isaiah. Boarding their steamer in Philadelphia, a group of Abolitionists informed Jane that from the moment the group crossed into Pennsylvania, the three blacks had shed their bondage. Over Wheeler's resistance, the woman and her sons were removed from the ship and put into a waiting carriage. Wheeler immediately applied to the federal district court for a writ of habeas corpus requiring Passmore Williamson, one of the leaders of the abducting group, to produce the trio. When he denied that the woman and boys were under his control or influence, Williamson was cited for contempt and imprisoned by Judge John K. Kane. The judge ruled that there was no Pennsylvania law that "affects to divest the rights of property of a citizen of North Carolina, acquired and asserted under the laws of that State, because he has found it needful or convenient to pass through the territory of Pennsylvania." Williamson's attorneys appealed the contempt citation to the state supreme court, which ruled that it had no authority to interfere with the federal court's actions. Two of the Abolitionists were fined and given a week's imprisonment for assault and battery on Wheeler, and Williamson was released after more than two months in prison. Wheeler failed in his efforts to reclaim the three blacks.

After a brief period at his home in Lincoln County following his resignation as minister to Nicaragua, Wheeler returned to Washington as superintendent of documents in the Department of the Interior, headed by Jacob Thompson, a native of Caswell County. In 1859 Wheeler accompanied Thompson and President James Buchanan on a state visit to North Carolina.

As civil war threatened, the historian unsuccessfully sought an appointment to the faculty of The University of North Carolina, where he hoped to resume research and historical writing. Though a Unionist at heart, he returned to North Carolina and in 1861 edited *The Narrative of Colonel David Fanning*. . . . One of his sons, Charles Sully, served in the U.S. Navy; another, Woodbury, was a Confederate soldier.

For nearly two decades John Hill Wheeler had aspired to go to England to obtain copies of additional records relating to colonial North Carolina, but his efforts had been thwarted, probably because of his partisanship. However, in September 1863, at his own expense, he boarded the state-owned *Ad-Vance*, slipped through the Federal blockade to Bermuda, and from there proceeded to Nova Scotia and thence to London where he spent several weeks early in 1864 copying manuscripts in the Public Record Office. In April he was back in Bermuda, and, with a Union victory becoming more apparent, late in the war he chose to return to Washington, where, except for occasional visits to North Carolina, he spent the remainder of his life in minor government jobs. In his later years, he was engaged in indexing the *Congressional Record*.

Wheeler delivered the commencement address at The University of North Carolina in June 1870 and was elected president of the university's Historical Society. Five years later in Raleigh he helped organize a new North Carolina Historical Society. Meanwhile, he had edited the *Legislative Manual and Political Register of the State of North Carolina for the Year 1874*. . . . Apparently in need of money, he contracted with Bangs and Company in New York in April 1882 to sell his library of 1,882 titles. He died the following December and was buried in Oak Hill Cemetery in Georgetown. Two years after his death his *Reminiscences and Memoirs of North Carolina and Eminent North Carolinians*—a potpourri of articles, county sketches, genealogies, and lists of officials—was published. The most valuable portion of his papers went to the Library of Congress; Stephen B. Weeks purchased another portion in 1899.

Wheeler married Mary Elizabeth Brown, the daughter of the Reverend O. B. Brown of Washington, D.C., on 19 Apr. 1830, and they had a daughter. Mary died in 1836, and on 8 Nov. 1838 Wheeler married Ellen Oldmixon Sully, the daughter of Thomas Sully, the Philadelphia artist. They had two sons, Charles Sully and Woodbury. Wheeler's birthplace in Murfreesboro has been preserved by the Murfreesboro Historical Association with assistance from the North Carolina Department of Archives and History.

SEE: Samuel A. Ashe, ed., *Biographical History of North Carolina*, vol. 7 (1908); *Case of Passmore Williamson* (1856); *DAB*, vol. 10 (1936); *Diario de John Hill Wheeler: Ministro de los Estados Unidos en Nicaragua, 1854–1857* (1974); Joseph S. Fowler, "Memoir of Colonel John Hill Wheeler . . . ," *At Home and Abroad* 6 (1883); Randall O. Hudson, "The Filibuster Minister: The Career of John Hill Wheeler as United States Minister to Nicaragua, 1854–1856," *North Carolina Historical Review* 49 (1972); H. G. Jones, *For History's Sake* (1966); William Still, *The Underground Rail Road* (1872); John Hill Wheeler Diary and Papers (Manuscripts Division, Library of Congress).

H. G. JONES

Wheeler, Junius Brutus (*21 Feb. 1830–15 July 1886*), army officer, textbook author, and professor, was the son of John and Sarah Clifton Wheeler. He was a native of Murfreesboro, where his father was for many years a prosperous merchant and shipowner. After enlisting as a private in the Twelfth Infantry Regiment in May 1847, Wheeler served gallantly in the Mexican War and "was appointed Lieut. by the President for bravery in the field" during the same year. Discharged from the service in 1848, he gained appointment to the military academy at West Point in July 1851 determined, as he told his family, to graduate "with distinction" or "leave his brains there." The former he accomplished in 1855 and was breveted second lieutenant of cavalry that July. An outstanding engineer, he was transferred to the Topographical Engineers in 1856 and promoted to first lieutenant in 1860.

The secession crisis of 1861 tore apart the Wheeler family, leaving Junius's half brother Samuel a major in the Confederate army and his half brother John Hill Wheeler a Disunionist. In a letter to his cousin John W. Moore in North Carolina in February 1861, Lieutenant Wheeler regretted the election of Abraham Lincoln as a minority president but held firm in the belief that the outcome was legitimate and concluded with the declaration: "I am a Union man." He served throughout the Civil War with the Corps of Engineers, where he was promoted to captain in 1863 and breveted major in April 1864 for gallant and meritorious service at the Battle of Jenkins's Ferry in Arkansas. He was breveted lieutenant colonel and colonel in March 1865 and promoted to major in 1866.

In September 1871 Wheeler was appointed professor of civil and military engineering at West Point. Over the next thirteen years he published a series of textbooks on military topics, including *An Elementary Course of Civil Engineering* (1874), *Elements of Field Fortifications* (1880), *A Course of Instruction in the Elements of the Art and Science of War* (1878), and *A Textbook of Military Engineering* (1884). He was retired with the pay of colonel in 1884 and died two years later.

In Washington, D.C., in September 1855 Wheeler married Emily Truxton Beale. They had eight children: Emily Beale, Sarah Clifton, Mary Eliza, Gertrude, Julia, Amy, John, and William Mackall.

SEE: William H. Powell, comp., *List of Officers of the Army of the United States from 1779 to 1900* (1900); Albert G. Wheeler, Jr., *History of the Wheeler Family in America* (1914); Wheeler family manuscripts (copy in possession of T. C. Parramore).

T. C. PARRAMORE

Wheeler, Raymond Milner (30 Sept. 1919–17 Feb. 1982), physician, champion of the rights of the poor and hungry, and crusader for social justice, was born in Farmville, where his father, George Raymond Wheeler, was superintendent of schools. His mother was Sallie Kate Collins Wheeler. Young Wheeler attended The University of North Carolina (1936–39) and in the fall of 1939 entered the university's two-year School of Medicine. He received a certificate after completing the course of study, then entered the Medical School of Washington University, St. Louis, and was awarded a medical degree in 1943. Dr. Wheeler served his internship in Barnes Hospital, also located in St. Louis.

From 1944 to 1946 he served in the Army Medical Corps with the rank of captain. Wheeler participated in some of the war's heaviest fighting, including the Battle of the Bulge, and was awarded the Silver Star and a Purple Heart. After being mustered out of service he was a resident in medicine at North Carolina Baptist Hospital in Winston-Salem until 1948, when he entered the practice of internal medicine in association with the Charlotte Medical Clinic. From 1966 to 1970 he was clinical associate professor of medicine in The University of North Carolina Medical School. Wheeler's standing in the medical profession was soundly based; he was a diplomate of the American Board of Internal Medicine (1951), a Fellow of the American College of Physicians, and recipient in 1969 of The University of North Carolina Medical School's Distinguished Service Award.

Many remember him as a shy, smallish man who loved good jokes yet was unable to tell them, and as "a graying physician . . . who still made house calls." Dr. William Porter, a medical partner, was impressed by Wheeler's acute power of observation both in the examining room and in the field; he regarded him as a doctor who not only "understood the science of medicine . . . [but] had the art to underpin it." There were those who regarded Wheeler as cold, even abrupt, or at least not overly warm. This seemingly impersonal quality was a part of his nature for he was not one to engage in small talk with patients, nor was he a sympathetic handholder. However, any impression of coolness or indifference belied Wheeler's concern for the sick and for mankind in general.

In addition to being a knowledgeable and able physician there was another Raymond Wheeler, a man who for three decades worked to better the lot of simply the neglected ones. He was, indeed, a doctor cast in a different mold. Social concerns led him to active membership in the Southern Regional Council, the North Carolina Council for Human Relations, the National Sharecroppers' Fund, the North Carolina Hunger Coalition, the Voter Education Project, and Southerners for Economic Justice. For four of these organizations he was at one time or another a member of the executive committee (or board of directors) and later president. In recognition of his distinguished service to the cause of civil liberty the North Carolina Civil Liberties Union honored him in 1979 with the Frank Porter Graham Award.

In 1967 Wheeler joined a team of six doctors who conducted a study of the health and living conditions of Negro children in two rural Mississippi counties. A report of their findings was published by the Southern Regional Council under the title *Hungry Children*. Members of the team were later called to testify before the U.S. Senate's Employment, Manpower, and Poverty Subcommittee. Wheeler's testimony was devastating as he described the cases of lack of health care, malnutrition, and near starvation they had seen. His was the testimony most frequently quoted by the national press, and it brought him both support and a flood of hate mail. Mississippi's senators, James Eastland and John Stennis, though not members of the subcommittee, were in attendance and responded angrily. Eastland called the testimony "totally untrue," and Stennis labeled it as "gross libel and slander." These two lawmakers referred to the doctors as "outside agitators" and "quickie experts on Mississippi health." The Mississippi newspapers and a few others in the Deep South, plus a radio station or two, followed suit.

Wheeler was also a member of a group of physicians who surveyed health and living conditions among migrant farm workers in Texas and Florida, and he sat on the Citizens Board of Inquiry into Hunger and Malnutrition in the United States. The Citizens Board published *Hunger, U.S.A., 1967–1968*, with Wheeler selected by CBS for preparation of the television documentary *Hunger in America, 1967–1968*.

Wheeler's marriage in 1942 to Mary Lou Browning ended in divorce in 1956. In 1958 he married Julie Buckner Carr, who survived him. By his first wife he had three children—Linda Lou, Margaret Browning, and David Stewart.

Wheeler died suddenly at age sixty-two as the result of a heart attack. Long before his death he had let it be known that he wanted no funeral or memorial service. During his lifetime he had "gently sustained old people and fought for little children. He [had] comforted the afflicted and sometimes afflicted the comfortable." He was a southerner saddened by the twin blights of malnutrition and injustice and set out to do something about them. The path that he walked might well have led to self-righteousness, but modesty and sincerity were his hallmarks, not self-importance. It can be said that his influence over a period of almost two decades made a vast difference in the physical well-being of the poor.

Wheeler was a member of the Unitarian Fellowship and for a term was president of the Charlotte congregation. His papers—containing about 1,740 items—in the University of North Carolina's Southern Historical Collection and the newspaper clipping file of the university's North Carolina Collection are the prime sources of information about his career.

SEE: *Charlotte Observer*, 19, 21 Feb. 1982; Frye Gaillard, *Race, Rock, and Religion: Profiles from a Southern Journalist* (1982 [portrait]); *Greensboro Daily News*, 23 Feb. 1982; *New York Times*, 20 Feb. 1982; *Raleigh News and Observer*, 29 July 1970 (portrait); U.S. Senate, Subcommittee on Employment, Manpower, and Poverty of the Committee on

Labor and Public Welfare, *Hunger and Malnutrition in America*, 90th Cong., 1st sess., 1967; Raymond Milner Wheeler Papers, 1936–82 (Southern Historical Collection, University of North Carolina, Chapel Hill).

J. ISAAC COPELAND

Whistler, Anna Mathilda McNeill *(27 Sept. 1804–31 Jan. 1881)* was the mother of the artist James Abbott McNeill Whistler and the subject of her son's painting popularly known as *Whistler's Mother*, though actually titled *Arrangement in Grey and Black*. This painting, which hangs in the Louvre and was reproduced on the 1934 Mother's Day U.S. postal stamp, as well as in countless art books and encyclopedias, has come to symbolize world motherhood. Certainly her likeness is better known throughout the world than that of any other North Carolina woman.

Anna's father, a physician educated at the University of Edinburgh, settled in North Carolina about 1785 and set up a medical practice in Wilmington. It was here that Anna Mathilda McNeill was born, the fifth of six children. In addition to the two-story brick home on the southwestern corner of Fourth and Orange streets, Dr. McNeill owned a plantation in Bladen County, where young Anna spent many happy summers. She did not receive the formal education her brothers did, but she was interested in music, history, French, cooking, and the social graces, and she became a devout Episcopalian.

As a young girl Anna met and became quite impressed by Cadet George Washington Whistler, a classmate of her brother William at West Point. Whistler had been born at Fort Wayne, in the Indian territory, where his father was commandant of the garrison. Before William and Whistler were graduated, Dr. McNeill left Wilmington to practice in New York. In 1819 the two young lieutenants received their commissions, and Whistler married one of Anna's closest friends, Mary Swift, the daughter of Colonel Joseph Swift, superintendent of West Point. In 1827 Mary died, leaving Whistler with three small children: George, Joseph, and Deborah. Mary had told Whistler on her deathbed that if he were to remarry it must be to Anna and no one else. They were married in New York on 3 Nov. 1831, and for the children "Aunt Annie" became "Mother."

In 1833 Whistler resigned his commission with brevet rank of major and the following spring was made chief engineer of the Locks and Canals Company in Lowell, Mass. The couple's first child was born that summer and in November was christened James Abbott Whistler (he later changed the Abbott to McNeill). Anna's husband was so successful in building locomotives that by 1835 his engines were on the new railroad between Lowell and Boston. No longer did America have to look to England for engines to power the rapidly expanding railway systems.

After their second son, William, was born, they moved to Stonington, Conn., where their third son, Kirk, was born, and Joseph, the son of Whistler by his first wife, died. The Whistlers were stern but devoted parents who strictly observed the Sabbath, allowing no toys and no books but the Bible. The year 1841 brought a new son, Charles Donald, and at this time emissaries from the czar were visiting the United States to study railroads. These Russians were so impressed by Whistler's engineering that they invited him to take over the construction of the railroad from St. Petersburg to Moscow. Whistler left the decision to Anna. She said yes. Their last son, John Routtatz, born in 1845, was named after the chief Russian em-

issary. A quotation in Anna's handwriting on the first page of her journal of their six years in Russia sums up her outlook on her children and life in general: "Gentleness is a mild atmosphere, it enters into a child's soul like sunshine into the rose bud—slowly but surely expanding into beauty and vigor."

The Whistlers became friends of the czar and nobility. Occupying an estate in the most fashionable section of St. Petersburg, they had a retinue of tutors, maids, and servants, a summer house in the country, and a yearly salary of $12,000. For his monumental work of supervising some 60,000 mechanics and laborers building 200 locomotives, 6,000 cars, tracks, depots, and bridges, Major Whistler was held in the highest esteem. The Order of St. Anne was conferred upon him by the emperor. Anna saw that young James was instructed in art at the Academy of Fine Arts. In 1848, when cholera struck St. Petersburg, Anna took the children to England where she arranged more art lessons for James. Whistler stayed behind to supervise the construction. When cool weather came, Anna returned to Russia, but Whistler contracted cholera that winter and died on 7 Apr. 1849. The emperor offered to educate her two living sons at the Imperial School, but she determined to return to America. With her yearly income reduced from $12,000 to $1,500 she began a frugal life raising her family in Pomfret, Conn., then in Scarsdale, N.Y. She was able to get William through medical school and obtain an appointment to West Point for James. James, however, dropped out and after several years of study in Paris moved to London, where he established himself as a painter of note.

With the formation of the Confederate States, William entered service as a surgeon at Richmond. Mrs. Whistler decided to leave America and make her home in England with James, so in August 1863, after a brief visit with William, she went directly to Wilmington and in a notable show of bravery ran through the enemy fleet on the blockade steamer *Ad-Vance*.

Mrs. Whistler was delighted to find the painter's studio a charming three-story house at 7 Lindsay Row, Chelsea—one of London's most picturesque sections. There she entertained his friends including Ford Madox Ford, Dante Gabriel Rossetti, George Meredith, Charles Augustus Howell, and others in true North Carolina style with homemade biscuits and preserves and tea. William joined them while on furlough. During his visit news came of Lee's surrender, so he remained to set up a medical practice in London. In these years Mrs. Whistler raised funds for stranded Americans, nursed friends' children, and was in close touch with her two other living sons and her stepdaughter Deborah, who had married Seymour Haden, family doctor to the archbishop of Canterbury. Anna and James moved to 2 Lindsay Row, where the famous portrait was finished in 1871 and was sold for 4,000 francs to the French government.

After a severe illness in 1876 Mrs. Whistler moved to Hastings. She died there and was buried at Hastings Borough Cemetery. There is a portrait of George Washington Whistler in the Public Library, Springfield, Mass., and an excellent full-size copy in oils of Mrs. Whistler's portrait at City Hall, Wilmington, N.C.

SEE: Horace Gregory, *The World of James McNeill Whistler* (1959); Elizabeth Mumford, *Whistler's Mother: The Life of Anna McNeill Whistler* (1939); Hans W. Singer, *James McNeill Whistler* (1905); *United Daughters of the Confederacy Magazine*, December 1972; Anna McNeill Whistler, unpublished letters and Russian journal (Manuscript Division, New York Public Library). See also material concerning Mrs. Whistler given by the Joseph Pennell Family (Division of Fine Arts, Library of Congress, Washington, D.C.), and clippings, correspondence, and papers, Louis T. Moore Collection, Wilmington, N.C., Public Library.

HEUSTIS P. WHITESIDE

Whitaker, John Clarke (7 Aug. 1891–23 Apr. 1978), businessman and community leader, was born in Salem, the son of William A. and Anna Bitting Whitaker. His father served as a major in the Confederate army and later operated a small tobacco company that gave John his start in the tobacco business. Young Whitaker attended Guilford College for two years, then transferred to The University of North Carolina from which he was graduated in 1912. The next year he joined the Reynolds Tobacco Company as a factory hand; he was a machine operator on the Camel production equipment when the first ones rolled off in 1913. Whitaker moved up rapidly from foreman to superintendent before he volunteered for service in the navy in World War I. Entering as a seaman, he advanced to ensign before his discharge.

After the war he returned to find Reynolds in need of a personnel department and was offered the position of organizing it. He stayed in personnel for twenty-nine years, making it and Reynolds's medical program among the best in American industry. In 1935 Whitaker was elected a director, and in 1937 he became vice-president of manufacturing and personnel, a post he held until 1948, when he became president of the company. He was elected chairman of the board in 1951 and chairman of the executive committee in 1955. In 1958 the company named its gigantic new manufacturing plant Whitaker Park in his honor. Whitaker retired on 1 Jan. 1960 but remained a consultant for many years. His portrait, commissioned after his retirement, hangs in the lobby of Whitaker Park.

Also engaged in numerous community activities, Whitaker served as alderman of Winston-Salem from 1921 to 1925. He helped raise money, supported bond issues, and made financial decisions for the construction of Forsyth Memorial Hospital, whose convalescent care unit was named Whitaker Care for him. He served as chairman of the Housing Authority, Community Chest, YMCA, Winston-Salem Teachers College Board of Trustees, North Carolina Engineering Foundation, United Community campaign, and Winston-Salem Hotel Company and as director of the executive committee of the Wachovia Bank and Trust Company and of the Security Life and Trust Company.

Whitaker married Elizabeth Norman of Mooresville, and they were the parents of John C., William, Louisa Johnson, and Elizabeth.

A vestryman of St. Paul's Episcopal Church, Whitaker belonged to the Rotary Club, the Masonic lodge, and the Democratic party. He died in Winston-Salem and was buried in Salem Cemetery.

SEE: Biographical files for John C. Whitaker (Wake Forest Library, Winston-Salem, and Alumni House, Chapel Hill); *Winston-Salem Journal*, 1 Oct. 1959, 3 Oct. 1961, 24–26 Apr. 1978; *Winston-Salem Sentinel*, 25 Apr. 1978.

LARA JANE NANCE

Whitaker, Spier (18 July 1798–2 Dec. 1869), lawyer and politician, the sixth of ten children, was born in Enfield to Matthew Cary and Elizabeth Coffield Whitaker. Called David Spier Coffield Whitaker, he dropped David and Coffield from his name. Spier was a name in his mother's

family. He was imbued with a deep sense of duty and honor as a result of his father's having been a Patriot soldier during the Revolutionary War and seriously wounded at the Battle of Guilford Court House.

Spier Whitaker is best remembered as a distinguished lawyer and southern gentleman. Early in life he decided to pursue the study and practice of law as a profession. While completing a law course at The University of North Carolina in 1817, he was active in the Philanthropic Society, where he gained experience in debating. The combination of oratorical ability and a solid grounding in law contributed to his success as an attorney.

In the 1830s he became active in politics. As a Democrat, he was elected in 1838 to the North Carolina House of Representatives by one vote. The apex of his political career, meager as it was, occurred in 1842, when the General Assembly selected him to be state attorney general. His bid in 1846 for a second four-year term was unsuccessful. His flourishing law practice, however, afforded him the opportunity by the late 1830s to become a prominent stockholder in the Wilmington and Raleigh Railroad.

On 30 Dec. 1819, at age twenty-one, he married Elizabeth F. Lewis. They had seven sons, Matthew (1820–97), Exum Lewis (1823–47), John Henry (1827–63), Charles (b. 1832), William (1836–62), David Coffield (1838–65), and Spier (1841–1901), and four daughters, Anne Harrison (b. 1825), Elizabeth West (1830–55), Mary (1834–55), and Lucy (b. 1844). By the end of the Civil War only five of their eleven children were still living.

Whitaker's forays into the realm of military service were neither as glorious as his ancestors' nor as tragic as his sons'. In 1831 he commanded an indeterminate number of men who set out towards Southampton County, Va., to help suppress Nat Turner's rebellion of slaves. When news of Turner's capture reached them by express rider, they returned home. Nevertheless, for his service Whitaker acquired the title of colonel of the militia and henceforth insisted on being referred to as Colonel Whitaker. At the outset of the Civil War he offered to lead men into battle but was denied an active role in the conflict. Governor Henry T. Clark thought that he was too old to fight and instead offered him a position as his aide. Whitaker assisted the governor in military affairs from July 1861 until September 1862.

In 1854 Whitaker had moved his family to Davenport, Iowa, to join his nephew, Judge James Grant, in a successful law practice. He retired in 1860. Feeling that it was his duty to help protect the state that had given his family so much, however, he returned to North Carolina for the duration of the Civil War. Afterwards he spent the rest of his life in Iowa.

SEE: William C. Allen, *History of Halifax County* (1918); Samuel A. Ashe, ed., *Biographical History of North Carolina*, vol. 7 (1917); Philanthropic Society Minutes (Archives, University of North Carolina, Chapel Hill); Raleigh *North Carolina Standard*, 30 May 1838, 16 Dec. 1846; *Raleigh Register*, 13, 27 Aug., 10 Sept. 1838, 9 Dec. 1842, 25 Nov. 1843, 2 Dec. 1845, 4, 8, 11, 15, 22 Dec. 1846, 11 Dec. 1847; Fannie DeBerniere Hooper Whitaker, *Spier Whitaker, 1798–1869* (1907); Max R. Williams, ed., *The Papers of William A. Graham*, vol. 3 (1960).

MARK MOKRIS

Whitaker, Spier (15 Mar. 1841–10 July 1901), Confederate and Spanish American War officer, attorney, state senator, and superior court judge, was born in Halifax

County, the seventh and youngest son of Attorney General Spier and Elizabeth Lewis Whitaker, the daughter of Exum Lewis, a militia colonel in the Revolutionary War and long a leading citizen of Edgecombe County. He was the grandson of Matthew Cary Whitaker, who represented Halifax County in both houses of the legislature in the early nineteenth century. Matthew, on 13 Mar. 1787, married Elizabeth Coffield, the daughter of Spier Coffield of Edgecombe County, and bought land in the wilderness near Enfield, Halifax County. In 1790 he began constructing a manor that would remain in the family for generations. The house was built by slaves out of lumber and bricks from the estate; the lime was made of oyster shells brought from Norfolk, Va., where Whitaker's produce was sent to market and from where his supplies were purchased. The house received its name, Shell Castle, from one of the building materials. The manor was still occupied by descendants of its builder at the end of the twentieth century.

In 1854 young Spier's father moved to Davenport, Iowa, to practice law, but his attachment to his native state prompted him to send his son back to North Carolina the next year to attend the school of Major Sam Hughes at Cedar Grove in Orange County. In the summer of 1857 Whitaker entered The University of North Carolina as a freshman. Shortly before graduation, when his state called for troops to fight for the Confederacy, Whitaker volunteered for service as a private in the company raised by Captain Richard J. Ashe and was in training camp at the time of North Carolina's secession on 20 May 1861. His company became a part of the regiment of Lieutenant General D. H. Hill, then a colonel, which so distinguished itself in the Battle of Bethel. In March 1862 Whitaker was captured by Federal forces at New Bern and imprisoned for four months. On his exchange, he was appointed second lieutenant and assigned to Company K, Thirty-third Regiment North Carolina State Troops, and participated in several battles including Sharpsburg and Chancellorsville. For some time, he was his company's adjutant. Whitaker surrendered at Appomattox and then went to his father's home in Iowa.

In 1866 he returned to his native state and, having studied law under his father, obtained a license to practice in the county courts. Settling in Raleigh, he occupied an office with Colonel Ed Graham Haywood. In the winter of 1866 he moved to Halifax and made his home in Enfield. In 1876 he was licensed to practice in the superior courts and shortly afterwards was made solicitor of the county courts. He soon commanded a good practice and became prominent in county politics. By 1881 he was elected to represent Halifax County in the state senate. To enlarge his practice, he returned to Raleigh in 1882 and formed a partnership with John Gatling, a lawyer of noted ability. Whitaker was diligent in the prosecution of his profession, though occasionally he took part in state politics. In 1888 he was made chairman of the state Democratic committee.

Whitaker attracted much public attention in July 1889 with his skilled investigation of the conduct of certain officers of the state hospital. That November Governor Daniel Fowle appointed him judge of the superior courts of the Fourth District. Subsequently elected by the people, he held the office until 10 July 1894, when he resigned and returned to the practice of law.

In the summer of 1898, on the declaration of war with Spain, Judge Whitaker was urged by some of his friends to seek the post of brigadier general of volunteers of the U.S. Army. President William McKinley did not make that appointment but on 20 June 1898 signed him a commission as major with the Sixth Regiment, U.S. Volunteers.

He departed at once for Knoxville, Tenn., where his regiment was in camp, and assisted in its drilling and more thorough organization. Whitaker went with the regiment to Puerto Rico, but the war ended before it was called for active service.

About the time Whitaker began practicing law he married Fanny De Berniere, the daughter of the late John De Berniere Hooper, professor of Greek at the University of North Carolina, and the great-great-granddaughter of George Hooper, brother of William, who signed the Declaration of Independence. The Whitakers had five children: four sons, De Berniere, Percy, Spier, and Vernon Edelen, and one daughter, Bessie Lewis. An Episcopalian, Judge Whitaker was a member of Christ Church, Raleigh.

Whitaker died at his home in Raleigh and, according to a long-cherished wish, was shrouded in a Confederate battle flag. The flag was a gift from the local camp of United Confederate Veterans. He was buried in Raleigh's Oakwood Cemetery.

SEE: Samuel A. Ashe, ed., *Biographical History of North Carolina*, vol. 7 (1917); John L. Cheney, Jr., ed., *North Carolina Government, 1587–1979* (1981); Oakwood Cemetery Records of Interments, 1866–1974; Raleigh *News and Observer*, 11 July 1901.

ELIZABETH E. NORRIS

Whitaker, Spier *(16 Dec. 1881–4 Jan. 1948)*, was born in Davenport, Iowa, the son of Charles and Sallie Grant Whitaker. His grandfather, Spier Whitaker (1798–1869), had emigrated to Iowa from Enfield, Halifax County, before the Civil War, but the family had retained close ties with North Carolina, where his uncle, Spier Whitaker (1841–1901), had a distinguished career as a lawyer, judge, and Democratic political leader.

Like his two namesakes, Whitaker was a distinguished lawyer. Chief Justice Charles Evans Hughes once commended him on having one of the most brilliant legal minds in America. He enrolled in The University of North Carolina in 1898 but after one year transferred to Harvard University, where he received an A.B. in 1903 and an LL.B. in 1905. As an undergraduate he took courses in philosophy from George Santayana, whom he deeply admired. Throughout his life he remained a member of The University of North Carolina Alumni Association.

In 1905 he moved to Birmingham, Ala., the home of his aunt, Mrs. Fanny De Berniere Hooper Whitaker, and formed the legal firm of Whitaker and Nesbitt. In 1917 he became vice-president and on 1 Dec. 1917 president of the Birmingham Bar Association. He resigned that position on 1 Apr. 1918, when he moved to Washington, D.C., to join the staff of the Bureau of Law, Office of the Custodian of Alien Property. The same year he was promoted to assistant general counsel to the Custodian of Alien Property, and in 1919 he became special assistant to the attorney general. Whitaker was involved in litigation that upheld the constitutionality of the Trading with the Enemy Act of 1917 and the authority of the Custodian of Alien Property to seize property.

In 1920 he moved to New York and formed the partnership of Rogers and Whitaker. Two years later he successfully represented Paul Reinemann, a German-born naturalized U.S. citizen. Reinemann had been in Germany at the outbreak of World War I and remained there throughout the conflict; prior to 1914 his wife and child had not emigrated, and he had confined his residence in the United States to business trips. But in 1917 his passport was revoked and his property seized. Reinemann's suit to recover his property and regain his citizenship therefore raised important issues concerning naturalization and expatriation. A transcript of the case—the only surviving documentation of Whitaker's legal career—which includes his exchanges with the bench and examination of witnesses is in the records of the Custodian of Alien Property, National Archives.

In 1908 he married Haidee Meade of Birmingham. They had two sons, Charles (1916) and Meade (1919). In 1928 he partially retired from legal practice in New York and returned to North Carolina, where he purchased and restored the family home in Enfield known as Shell Castle. As late as 1938 he still retained his law office at 52 Wall Street. During his later years he became interested in the improvement of farming methods on land he owned in Halifax County.

SEE: Alumni questionnaire, 1938 (Alumni Office, University of North Carolina, Chapel Hill); Birmingham Bar Association Records; *Chapel Hill Weekly*, 9 Jan. 1948; Daniel L. Grant, *Alumni History of the University of North Carolina* (1924); Records of the Custodian of Alien Property (National Archives, Washington, D.C.).

ROBERT M. CALHOON

Whitaker, William Asbury (*7 May 1883–28 Feb. 1960*), teacher, scientist, and business executive, the son of William Asbury and Anna Bitting Whitaker, was born in Salem, where he attended the public schools and the Salem Boys School. In 1904 he received a bachelor of philosophy degree from The University of North Carolina. During his senior year he did graduate work in chemistry at Columbia University, earning an M.A. degree. In the summer sessions of 1911 and 1912 he was a graduate student at the University of Chicago.

Whitaker began his teaching career in 1906 as an instructor in chemistry at the College of the City of New York. The head of his department, Dr. Charles Baskerville, had been his chemistry professor at The University of North Carolina. Whitaker remained at City of New York until 1912, when he accepted the position of associate professor of metallurgy at the University of Kansas. Four years later he was promoted to full professor. While at Kansas he served for four years as director of State Chemical Research and for two years as chairman of the Missouri-Kansas section of the American Chemical Society. He was the founder of the *Kansan Chemallurgist* and its advisory editor. Whitaker frequently contributed articles to scientific journals, including *Metallurgical and Chemical Engineering, Economic Geology, State Geological Survey of Kansas,* and *Engineering and Mining Journal.* One of the results of his original research was the invention of a process for the flotation of oxidized ores. During World War I he was appointed an associate member of the U.S. Naval Consulting Board.

At the end of the war Whitaker left Kansas to become a foreign representative of the Standard Commercial Tobacco Company of New York, an importing and exporting firm. In a few years he became vice-president of the company. He spent a good deal of his time in the Mediterranean area, particularly in Greece and Turkey. Continuing his research, now in the field of tobacco culture, Whitaker patented a process for the improvement of tobacco technology and in 1925 published an article, "The Culture of Turkish Tobacco as Exemplified in the Smyrna Type," in the magazine *Tobacco.* In the late 1920s he left the tobacco business and devoted most of his time to travel.

Whitaker was unable to enjoy his leisure for many years, for with the onset of the Great Depression "I was kicked back," as he expressed it, into the financial world. In 1931 he joined with Francis I. du Pont and others to form the brokerage house of Francis I. du Pont and Company at One Wall Street. On 1 Mar. 1932 the company announced that it had opened an uptown office "under the management of Mr. William A. Whitaker, resident partner."

Whitaker retired on 31 Dec. 1940 in order to pursue his growing enthusiasm for collecting in the fields of literature, history, art, and archaeology. As early as 1921 he had begun compiling autographs of notable people. This modest beginning expanded over the years to include rarities in the fields of English and American literature, historical documents of the colonial and Revolutionary periods, and objects of art, all of which were ultimately given to The University of North Carolina. Throughout his life Whitaker maintained an active interest in his alma mater, serving for a time as president of the New York alumni chapter.

In 1947 he made his first gift to the university library, the second folio edition of Shakespeare's works. On that occasion, he wrote the university librarian: "I had no sooner acquired this treasure when I realized that it should never be hoarded, and kept hidden in a vault where few eyes could see it, but rather it should rest where its presence might bring continuous joy to scholars and book-lovers. There was for me, then, only one choice as to its proper resting place, and that was a dear old southern campus." Over the next ten years Whitaker established several major collections for the university library: the works of Samuel Johnson, James Boswell, and their friends; first editions of Charles Dickens and other Dickensiana; illustrations of George Cruikshank; first editions of William Makepeace Thackeray; and costume plates in color. In 1955, as a memorial to his parents, he created the William A. Whitaker, Sr., and Anna B. Whitaker Loan Fund for needy students. In recognition of Whitaker's "business and professional achievements and of his generous benefactions for the advancement of scholarship" The University of North Carolina awarded him the LL.D. degree in 1956.

Whitaker, a bachelor, died at the New York Athletic Club, where he had made his home for the past twenty-five years. He was a member of the Episcopal church and the Sons of the American Revolution and a thirty-second degree Mason. He was buried in the Salem cemetery, Winston-Salem. A portrait of him by Albert Murray hangs in the Rare Book Collection at The University of North Carolina Library.

Two months after his death the university held a memorial service for Whitaker in Gerrard Hall. At this service, presided over by Chancellor William B. Aycock, it was announced that Whitaker had left the university a bequest of $1.75 million for the establishment of the William A. Whitaker Foundation. The bequest provided that the income should be divided into three equal parts for (1) the purchase of books and manuscripts for the library, particularly the Rare Book Collection; (2) scholarships and fellowships; and (3) the acquisition of paintings and sculptures. Through the years the Whitaker legacy has contributed greatly to the growth of the university's programs in these fields.

SEE: *Bookmark*, nos. 10–11 (1948), 16 (1951), 17 (1952), 25 (1956), 30 (1960); *Chapel Hill Weekly*, 2 May 1960; Daniel L. Grant, *Alumni History of the University of North Carolina* (1924) in *Memorium: William Asbury Whitaker (1960)*; *New York Times*, 29 Feb. 1960; University of North Carolina *Alumni Review*, nos. 13 (1925), 11 (1956), 18 (1960); William A. Whitaker Correspondence (General Alumni Association office) and William A. Whitaker Papers (Southern

Historical Collection), University of North Carolina, Chapel Hill; *Winston-Salem Journal*, 29 Feb., 2 Mar. 1960.

LAWRENCE F. LONDON

White, Arnold Howard (27 Sept. 1920–28 June 1976), newspaperman, was born in Burlington, the son of George Otis and Mamie Beckom White. After graduation from Burlington High School in 1937 he attended Catawba College, where he majored in English with a minor in sociology. There he headed the news bureau all four years, served as president of the freshman and sophomore classes, was editor of *The Pioneer* his senior year, and won a medal in journalism. He was graduated in 1941, and the same year, on 22 June, he married Mary Elizabeth Barger of Kannapolis. They had four children: Karen (1947), Connie (1948), Craig (1952), and Janet (1954).

Known as Howard, White became a carrier for the *Burlington Daily Times-News* at age twelve and worked his way upwards through jobs in the mail room, high school correspondent, and summer employment while in college. After receiving his degree he became a reporter and sports editor. Entering the navy in January 1943 as an ensign, he received indoctrination training at Princeton University, then served in the Pacific theater in New Guinea and the Philippines, earning three battle stars. He returned to the United States as editor of the Naval Harbor Defense magazine for the Chief of Naval Operations in Washington, D.C. He also wrote an operational manual before being released to inactive duty in 1945 as a senior lieutenant. At home in Burlington he became city editor of the newspaper in 1946, managing editor in 1955, and editor in 1963. In 1967 he was graduated from the Urban Policy Conference of the Brookings Institution at UNC-Charlotte.

Howard White was a member of the American Society of Newspaper Editors and of the News Media Administration of Justice Council of the Institute of Government. The Associated Press Club of North Carolina elected him president in January 1970. In July 1975 he was named president of the North Carolina Press Association, having previously served for four years as chairman of the association's legislative committee. In the latter position he was influential in securing passage by the General Assembly of "sunshine" laws clarifying the openness of public meetings.

In addition, he was a trustee of Catawba College and of the Burlington YMCA and a member of the Alamance County Human Relations Council, School Advisory Committee of Burlington, and local library board. Catawba College awarded him an honorary doctor of letters degree. A member of the First Reformed United Church of Christ, he served as elder and deacon. He collaborated with Walter Whitaker in writing the *Centennial History of Alamance County* (1949) and was the author of *Builders of Alamance* (1951), *Two Hours of History* (1957), a booklet on the Battle of Alamance, and *The Piedmont Crescent* (1967), a collection of editorial features.

Because of internal problems at the Burlington newspaper, White considered a college teaching position but instead became editor and general manager of the Kannapolis *Daily Independent* on 1 Mar. 1976. Three months later he died of a heart attack in Concord. He was buried in the cemetery at Shiloh United Church of Christ at Faith in Rowan County.

SEE: *Burlington Daily Times-News*, 15 Aug. 1973 (portrait); Catawba College alumni records; *Chapel Hill Newspaper*,

29–30 June 1976; *Charlotte Observer*, 1 July 1976; *Greensboro Daily News*, 1 Feb., 7 Mar. 1976; Raleigh *News and Observer*, 30 June, 1 July 1976; *Salisbury Evening Post*, 23 Jan. 1970, 1 Feb. 1976, 29–30 (portrait) June 1976.

WILLIAM S. POWELL

White, George Henry (18 Dec. 1852–28 Dec. 1918), lawyer, legislator, congressman, and racial spokesman, was born near Rosindale in Bladen County, the son of Wiley F. and Mary White. It is possible that he was born into slavery, although the evidence on this is contradictory. He did attend public schools in North Carolina and received training under D. P. Allen, president of the Whitten Normal School in Lumberton. In 1876 he was an assistant in charge of the exhibition mounted by the U.S. Coast Survey at the Centennial Exhibition in Philadelphia. After graduation from Howard University in 1877, he was principal of the Colored Grade School, the Presbyterian parochial school, and the State Normal School in New Bern. He studied law under Judge William J. Clarke and received a license to practice in North Carolina in 1879.

Entering politics in 1881, he served in the North Carolina House of Representatives for Craven County. Although an unsuccessful candidate for the state senate in 1882, he represented the Eighth District in Congress for the 1885 term and was a member of the Judiciary, Insane Asylum, and Insurance committees. In 1886 he won election to a four-year term as district solicitor of the Second Judicial District. During this period White gained the respect of many whites and blacks in his district. In addition, he became more active in religious and fraternal organizations. A founder and elder of the Ebenezer United Presbyterian Church in New Bern, he served as grand master of both King Solomon Lodge No. 1 of New Bern (1899–90) and the Colored Masons of North Carolina (1892–93).

In 1894 White moved to Tarboro in order to live within the boundaries of the Second Congressional District. This district, known as "The Black Second," included nine counties in the coastal plain area, from Warren and Northampton on the Virginia border to Lenoir in the south. All the counties had a sizable black population; four blacks served in the U.S. Congress from the district between 1872 and 1900.

White lost his party's nomination for the U.S. House in 1894 to his brother-in-law, Henry Plummer Cheatham, in a bitter fight that had to be settled finally by the National Republican Congressional Committee. White was nominated by the Republicans in 1896, and in an election held under a liberalized election law enacted by the fusion legislature, he beat the incumbent Democratic representative, Frederick A. Woodard, 19,332 to 15,378. In 1898 White won reelection, defeating W. E. Fountain in a campaign dominated by the race issue.

As the only black representative in Congress, White was an eloquent and vocal spokesman for his race. He is perhaps best known for his valedictory speech on 29 Jan. 1901 in which he spoke of the accomplishments of African Americans and of the hope for a better future. In his first term he was a member of the Agricultural Committee, and in the 56th Congress (1899–1901) he served on the District of Columbia Committee. Many of his speeches condemned the brutal treatment received by Negroes in the South, and White introduced the first antilynching bill in Congress. He supported local bills and appointed blacks to federal positions (especially postmasters) in his district.

A successful campaign to disenfranchise blacks plus increasing anti-Negro feeling prompted White not to seek reelection in 1900. When his term ended in 1901, he and his family moved to Washington, D.C., where he practiced law until 1905. He then went to Philadelphia. While continuing his law practice, he became involved in banking, founding the first black-managed bank in Philadelphia. He also established an all-black community in Cape May County, N.J., called Whitesboro.

White married Fannie B. Randolph in 1879, and they had one child, Della. In 1886 he married Cora Lina Cherry, the daughter of Henry C. Cherry, a black politician from Tarboro. They had two children, Mary A. and George H., Jr.

SEE: Eric D. Anderson, "Race and Politics in North Carolina, 1872–1901: The Black Second" (Ph.D. diss., University of Chicago, 1978); *Biog. Dir. Am. Cong.* (1961); Helen Edmonds, *The Negro and Fusion Politics in North Carolina, 1894–1901* (1951); George W. Reid, "A Biography of George H. White, 1852–1918" (Ph.D. diss., Howard University, 1974) and "The Post-Congressional Career of George H. White, 1901–1918," *Journal of Negro History* 61 (October 1976).

WILLIAM Z. SCHENCK

White, Henry, Jr. *(1642–3 Aug. 1712),* Quaker leader, colonial official, and poet, was born in Isle of Wight County, Va. His father, Henry White, Sr., a cooper, married, first, Elener (surname unknown) and, later, Rebecca Arnold, and it is unclear which was the mother of Henry White, Jr. The younger White also was married twice; by his first wife Mary were daughters Ann (1669), Elizabeth, and Elkanah (1679), and sons Robert (1674), and twins James and John (1676), of whom only Robert and John survived childhood. By his second wife, Damaris Morison, were daughters Mary, Damaris, Content, and Naomy, and sons Henry III, Arnold II, and Isaac.

White, like his father, bought land in North Carolina in 1663; he eventually moved to a plantation along the west side of Little River in Perquimans Precinct at least by 1679, but probably much earlier. In the 1690s he served as a justice on the North Carolina Higher Court as well as in the precinct county court.

Between 1672 and 1679 he was converted to Quakerism and was one of the earliest members of the Little River Preparative Meeting, one of five meetings that made up Pasquotank Monthly Meeting. White served as the monthly meeting's "registrer" (recording clerk), it meeting alternately at his and Caleb Bundy's home until 1707, when the first meetinghouse was built. This structure was erected partly under White's leadership on land next to his plantation. He was active among North Carolina Friends both as organizer and seemingly as lay minister, evidenced by a few extant writings.

White's lasting contribution was a 302-line poem in rhymed couplet and doggerel verse, written in 1698. This seventeenth-century poem is the earliest known literary work of its kind produced in North Carolina. It is an account of the fall of man in the garden of Eden, his restoration through Christ, and "some holsom exhortations for everyone to take notis of."

SEE: J. Bryan Grimes, ed., *Abstracts of North Carolina Wills* (1910); Guilford College Library (Greensboro), for MS Quaker records; J. R. B. Hathaway, ed., *North Carolina Historical and Genealogical Register*, vols. 1 (July 1900), 2 (April 1901), 3 (January 1903); William L. Saunders, ed., *Colonial Records of North Carolina*, vols. 1–4 (1886). Thomas E. Ter-

rell, Jr., "Some Holsom Exhortation's: Henry White's Seventeenth-Century Southern Religious Narrative in Verse," *Early American Literature*, vol. 18 (1983).

THOMAS E. TERRELL, JR.

White, Hugh Lawson *(30 Oct. 1773–10 Apr. 1840),* lawyer, banker, judge, legislator, claims commissioner, U.S. senator, and presidential candidate, was born to James and Mary Lawson White in that part of Rowan County that is now Iredell County. About 1785 James White moved his family to the Holston River and led in founding Knoxville, Tenn. His service to the state of Franklin—in the territorial legislature, Tennessee Constitutional Convention, and state legislature—and his friendship with the Blounts, John Sevier, and Andrew Jackson connected the family closely to the fortunes of the young state and its pioneer leaders.

Hugh studied with the Reverend Samuel Carrick, the Presbyterian minister in Knoxville, and read law with Archibald Roane, who was later governor. For a time he served as secretary to William Blount, the territorial governor, and as clerk of the Knox County Court. In 1793 he participated in a campaign against the Cherokee. He spent about eighteen months in Pennsylvania, studying mathematics in Philadelphia and reading law in Lancaster. In 1796 White returned to Knoxville and began to practice law just as Tennessee became a state.

In 1798 he married Elizabeth Moore Carrick, the daughter of his teacher. They had twelve children; two died in infancy, and the mother and eight of the children died of tuberculosis within six years (1826–31). Only two children were living when he succumbed to the disease in 1840. He had married Mrs. Ann E. Peyton of Washington, D.C., on 30 Nov. 1832.

In a period of flamboyant orators, White made his reputation as a careful, scholarly lawyer dealing with the complexities of land law on the expanding frontier. At age twenty-eight he was elected to Tennessee's highest court, the Superior Court of Law and Equity. He resigned in 1807 to enter the state senate, where he supported revision of the land law and creation of a supreme court. He served as a judge on the Tennessee Supreme Court from 1809 until 1815. To most Tennesseans, he continued to be "Judge White," no matter what office he held.

White had become president of a state bank in Knoxville in 1811 and operated it until 1827. He declined to accept any salary from the bank while holding public office—an unusual attitude at that time. After Congress chartered the second Bank of the United States in 1816, White returned to the state senate and worked to secure both an expansion of state banks and heavy taxation on branches of nonstate banks. He also supported legislation to prevent duelers from holding public office.

President James Monroe appointed White to a commission to determine the validity and amounts of claims against Spain that the United States had assumed in the treaty acquiring East Florida. This service revealed White's judicial talents to numerous national leaders. It also allowed him to judge national leaders, and he resented the intervention of Secretary of State John Quincy Adams to secure reversal of a commission policy.

Not only did White disagree with the positions of Adams, but he also agreed with those of Andrew Jackson and supported him on principle as well as from friendship. When Jackson was a candidate for the U.S. Senate in 1823, White supported him, and when Jackson resigned the seat in October 1825, the legislature chose White unanimously.

Senator White promptly joined the attack on the Adams administration. He opposed the Clay-Adams plan for U.S. participation in the Pan-American congress in Panama, federal funds for internal improvements in the states, and the protective tariff. White's experience led him to support additional federal judges for the West even though Adams could appoint the judges. Although perfectly consistent with his principles, White's senatorial service supported Jackson's presidential campaigns effectively.

When Jackson became president in 1829, Senator White endorsed every major measure despite his possible disappointment at Jackson's failure to name him secretary of war and despite his growing skepticism of the "Kitchen Cabinet." White was elected president pro tem of the Senate on 3 Dec. 1832, and Vice-President John C. Calhoun's resignation put White in a vital position during the Nullification crisis.

White chaired the committee on Indian affairs in the Senate from 1829 to 1840 and appeared to be the principal architect of the plans for moving the Indians west of the line of white settlement. When the bill to recharter the bank was before the Senate in 1832, White opposed it in a speech that made many of the points later incorporated in Jackson's veto, especially the issue of constitutionality. Jackson sought White's advice on removing the government's deposits but removed them against his advice. Nevertheless, White opposed the resolution that passed censuring Jackson for the action. White was a strict constructionist, but he supported the force bill to collect the tariff in South Carolina and the compromise tariff to ease the dispute.

The long and genuine friendship between Jackson and White broke over Jackson's determination to make Martin Van Buren his successor. When a movement to nominate White began in late 1833, the senator discouraged it. Continued urging, his skepticism of Van Buren, and reports of Jackson's threats to humiliate him led White to make the race. In December 1834 a majority of the Tennessee delegation in Congress asked if White would run if nominated. Tennessee was not officially represented when the Democratic convention nominated Martin Van Buren early in 1835, and many declined to consider the nomination legitimate. When the 1835 elections were held, supporters of White won the governor's seat and legislative majorities. Then the legislature reelected White and nominated him for the presidency.

Because White, Daniel Webster, William Henry Harrison, and Willie P. Mangum shared the opposition vote, White only carried Tennessee and Georgia for 26 electoral votes. In Tennessee White received 36,000 votes to Van Buren's 26,000.

When the election was over, he returned to the U.S. Senate and served until 1840. His most vigorous fight was a futile one to prevent the Senate from "expunging" the resolution censuring Jackson for removing the bank deposits. When the Democrats regained control of the state in 1839, they made plans to get rid of White. The legislature passed six resolutions "instructing" the Tennessee senators how to vote. When the Sub-Treasury bill came to a vote on 13 Jan. 1840, White resigned rather than follow the instructions and vote for it.

He returned home as something of a martyr and died soon afterwards. He was buried in the cemetery of the Knoxville Presbyterian Church, but his influence survived. His treatment by the Democratic party probably had something to do with its failure to carry Tennessee in a presidential campaign again until 1856—even when Tennessee's own James K. Polk was elected in 1844.

In an era of aggressive, colorful leaders, Judge White was a quiet, thoughtful public servant. Surely he had faults, but a man who stood by his principles so honestly and served so disinterestedly deserved more gratitude and remembrance than was the lot of Hugh Lawson White.

SEE: *DAB*, vol. 10 (1936); L. Paul Gresham, "The Public Career of Hugh Lawson White" (diss., Vanderbilt University, Nashville, Tenn., 1943), "The Public Career of Hugh Lawson White," *Tennessee Historical Quarterly* 3 (1944), "Hugh Lawson White as a Tennessee Politician and Banker, 1807–1827," *East Tennessee Historical Society Publications* 18 (1946), and "Hugh Lawson White: Frontiersman, Lawyer, and Judge," *East Tennessee Historical Society Publications* 19 (1947); Ernest Hooper, "The Presidential Election of 1836 in Tennessee" (thesis, University of North Carolina, 1949); Robert M. McBride and Dan M. Robinson, *Biographical Directory of the Tennessee General Assembly*, vol. 1 (1975); Powell Moore, "The Revolt against Jackson in Tennessee, 1835–1836," *Journal of Southern History* 2 (1936); Nancy N. Scott, ed., *A Memoir of Hugh Lawson White* (1856); Hugh Lawson White Papers (McClung Collection, Lawson McGhee Library [Knoxville Public Library], Knoxville, Tenn.).

ERNEST HOOPER

White, James (16 June 1749–10 Dec. 1809), physician, legislator, congressman, and western pioneer, was born in Philadelphia, the son of James and Ann Willcox White. His father was a native of Ireland, and Jesuits established their first mission in Pennsylvania at the home of his maternal grandfather about 1730. Nothing is known of young White's early education, but he later attended a Jesuit school at St. Omer, France. After returning home he studied medicine at the University of Pennsylvania and read law in Philadelphia. His brother Thomas, two years younger, was a merchant in Philadelphia who, by early January 1775, had moved to Cross Creek (later Fayetteville), N.C.

It is not known precisely when James White settled in North Carolina, but he represented Currituck County (where he lived on Bells Island) in the three Provincial Congresses that met between August 1775 and November 1776. In 1777 and between 1784 and 1789 he represented Chatham County in one and Currituck County in four sessions of the state legislature, and between November 1785 and May 1786 he was a member of the Continental Congress. He also was a justice of the peace in Currituck County prior to 1787. Some of White's correspondence was dated from Chatham County, and he was a trustee of an academy chartered there in January 1787. He also sometimes was in Wilmington, where he may have had relatives, and he owned property in Fayetteville that was described as still productive rural land at the time of his death.

Sometime after October 1786 White relocated in that part of far western North Carolina that became Tennessee. The move followed his appointment by Congress on 6 Oct. 1786 as superintendent of Indian affairs in the southern district composed of North Carolina, South Carolina, and Georgia, a post he filled only briefly as it interfered with his duties in the Continental Congress. Nevertheless, on 1 June 1787 he wrote Governor Richard Caswell that he had made a tour of the Creek Indian nation and was submitting a report to Congress that he showed to the governor first. In 1789 he was elected to the November session of the North Carolina General Assembly to represent the recently created Hawkins County beyond the mountains. White was involved in soothing the fears of residents of the state living along the Mississippi River, where settlers were being murdered by Indians believed to have been inspired by the Spanish. White's inquiries revealed that this was not the case—that isolated Indian hunting parties had encountered whites who had intruded into their territory and acted entirely on their own. White received assurances from Spanish officials that they would do their utmost to establish good relations.

Neither North Carolina nor the Continental Congress was doing anything to protect the western frontier. Many people in the Tennessee country were about ready to yield to the enticements of one Colonel Stark and withdraw from the United States in favor of seeking "refuge under a foreign government." White, however, was able to convince them to abandon this idea.

About the same time that White reported to Governor Samuel Johnston the results of his negotiations with the Spanish minister, he was named a North Carolina delegate to the Convention of 1789, which approved the U.S. Constitution. White voted with the majority. North Carolina shortly thereafter ceded its western lands to the new national government, but this was a step that White opposed in the legislature.

In November 1789, when the legislature drew up a list of names from which to select the state's first nominees for U.S. senators, James White's was third on the list and other names followed his. A few days later, for reasons not stated, White's name was withdrawn. The first two names—Samuel Johnston and Benjamin Hawkins—were then nominated and elected.

White represented Davidson County in the legislature of the Territory South of the Ohio in 1794 until he was elected to Congress. He served from 3 Sept. 1794 to 1 June 1796, when the territory was admitted to the Union as the state of Tennessee. In 1799 he moved to Louisiana, where he was judge of the Attakapas District in 1804 and afterwards of St. Martin's Parish.

A Roman Catholic, he died at Attakapas near New Orleans. He had married Mary Willcox, presumably his cousin, and they were the parents of one son, Edward Douglas White, born in Nashville, Tenn., in March 1795; the son served three terms in Congress and was governor of both Tennessee and Louisiana. This White's son, also Edward D. White, represented Louisiana in the Senate and was chief justice of the Supreme Court of the United States.

SEE: Thomas Perkins Abernethy, *From Frontier to Plantation in Tennessee* (1932); *Biog. Dir. Am. Cong.* (1989); John L. Cheney, Jr., ed., *North Carolina Government, 1585–1974* (1975); Walter Clark, ed., *State Records of North Carolina*, vols. 17–22 (1899–1907); Albert V. Goodpasture, "Dr. James White: Pioneer, Politician, Lawyer," *Tennessee Historical Magazine* 1 (December 1915); Robert M. McBride and Dan M. Robinson, *Biographical Directory of the Tennessee General Assembly*, vol. 1 (1975).

WILLIAM S. POWELL

White, John *(fl. 1577–93)*, colonizer and artist, who was closely associated between 1585 and 1590 with the area that became North Carolina, has not been firmly identified, but arms granted to him in 1587 are those of the White family of Truro, Cornwall, in England. One John White of this family was a member of the Haberdashers Company of London but died in 1585. He might possibly have been the uncle of our subject—a John White who was trained as an artist craftsman and became a member of the Painter-Stainers Company of London by 1580.

During the late 1560s John White was a parishioner of St. Martin Ludgate in London—a parish dominantly pop-

ulated by haberdashers. On 7 / 17 June 1566 he married Tomasyn Cooper. The next year, on 27 April / 7 May, their son Thomas was baptized. On 9 / 19 May 1568 John White's daughter Elinor, who was destined to become the mother of the first child of English parentage to be born in the New World, was baptized. Near the end of that year, on 26 Dec. 1568 / 5 Jan. 1568 / 69, the infant Thomas was buried, and White seems to have left the parish shortly afterwards—at least he does not appear in any of the parish records after that date. The next reference to a John White who might be he is in January 1578 / 79. On Twelfth Night, *A Maske of Amazons* was presented at Richmond Palace for Queen Elizabeth. One John White and one Boswell were paid by the Office of Revels under the category of painters for the parcel gilding of two armors used by two Knights of the Masque. A William Boswell, painter, had been a parishioner in St. Martin Ludgate at the same time as John White.

John White may have accompanied Martin Frobisher on his expedition to Baffin Island to look for gold in 1577. If so, he was probably present as observer and recorder (although no narrative of his is extant); he drew pictures there of one of Frobisher's ships and an Eskimo in a kayak, a vigorous impression of an encounter between English and Eskimos. He certainly painted front and rear views of the man, woman, and child brought back to England. It appears that these pictures (and perhaps others) were engraved (conceivably by White himself) in a small volume of illustrations published in 1578 of which no copy survives, but for which we are fortunate in having several original drawings and a number of derivatives.

White is first found mentioned by name in connection with the Roanoke voyages on 11 / 21 July 1585 in a ship's boat in convoy with Sir Richard Grenville and a small exploration party. Crossing Pamlico Sound to Pomeioc on the mainland, he drew the Indian village and a number of its inhabitants. Later, going on to Aquascogok and then to Secotan a little farther south, he did the same there.

In 1584 Walter Raleigh's reconnaissance party had identified Roanoke Island as a suitable place to establish a settlement. An expedition under Grenville left England on 9 / 19 Apr. 1585 to plant a military post and a base for a survey of the coast and the interior. In July it landed from the *Tiger* at what is now Roanoke Island, where, before the end of August, Ralph Lane supervised the construction of crude cottages and a fort. John White and Thomas Harriot, the mathematician and navigator in Raleigh's employ, were members of the expedition.

Harriot remained with the Lane colony for its eleven-month tenure, during which time he recorded the physical, natural, and human resources of the area. John White drew, and subsequently painted, many components of the same resources. We can imagine the two men compiling from their field notes and sketches large illustrated summaries in fulfillment of the task assigned to them.

White had begun to prepare himself by drawing picture-plans of temporary camps made in Puerto Rico on the way over and putting on paper a number of plants, animals, birds, and fish seen in the Caribbean and along the sea route to the Outer Banks. From the base at Roanoke Island the pair proceeded to compile illustrated information on their Indian neighbors, ultimately penetrating up Albemarle Sound and probably the Chowan and Roanoke rivers. To improve their coverage, they possibly paid further visits to the southern parts of Pamlico Sound, working their way along the shores of the Outer Banks. Harriot must have compiled map sketches as he went, with White helping him to assemble them into districts as a base for the first map of the area. At the same time he must have drawn the animals, crustaceans, fish, birds, and plants that came to their notice. It must have been at this time that Harriot made notes about clay, sand, minerals, and the possible uses of timber, as he later published a little book with such information.

In the Indian villages, both men carefully observed plants grown for food and tobacco for smoking. Harriot, and perhaps White as well, tried to learn the language and gain some impression of Indian concepts. After the initial investigation of the area, Sir Richard Grenville and his fleet departed for England, leaving behind a contingent of settlers who were charged with the responsibility of conducting further explorations under the direction of Governor Ralph Lane. Harriot certainly remained with the colony for its full tenure, and White may have—although there is no evidence to support his remaining or his leaving. All of his extant paintings could have been made during the preliminary explorations. Because these paintings do not include renderings of the fort and houses on Roanoke Island, there is reason to believe that some, or even most, of White's work has been lost. If he did remain with the colony for the full time, then he certainly would have made more drawings, perhaps even of the area near the Chesapeake Bay. A small group of colonists wintered near the southern shore, and White and Harriot would logically have been included.

Certainly by the summer of 1586, when the colonists returned to England with Sir Francis Drake, Harriot had compiled copious notes and collected numerous natural history specimens. The transfer of men and materials from the shore to Drake's ships during a violent storm was haphazard. Some of Harriot's samples were lost; some of White's sketches could have been lost, and that would account for the absence of pictures of the fort, cottages and many plants, Indians, and natural history specimens. Even so, once back in England Harriot proceeded to write *A briefe and true report of the new found land of Virginia*, which he planned to publish in support of the 1587 enterprise but held over, for some reason, until 1588. It was not until the latter year that a White-Harriot collaboration took shape when Theodor de Bry obtained materials from both of them to put together his *America*, Part I (1590), uniting Harriot's tract with engravings of a selection of White's Indian drawings. Published in four languages, it spread their names throughout Europe, although Harriot received most of the credit.

White put together a selection of his drawings as a gift to some important person (and this is what survives of his original work in the British Library). Many of his own copies were recopied in his household. By this process a number of his subjects were saved that otherwise would have been lost.

John White was one of the few men who returned from Roanoke Island with the belief that English people could settle alongside the Indians and live in North America a better life than most of the middling sort—craftsmen, tradesmen, mildly Puritan Protestants not too happy about bishops, small farmers, and the like—could at home. It was for this reason that he promoted a plan to bring out a new kind of settler, colonists who would go as families and would be self-sufficient in a short time even if, in the end, the land would, he believed, make them moderately rich. Raleigh sympathized with White and granted him a substantial area to the south of Chesapeake Bay where the city of Raleigh could be created. A society, called "The Governour and Assistants of the Cittie of Ralegh in Virginea," was constituted in 1587. A seal and arms were made for it; the governor (White himself) and the twelve assistants (even the Portuguese pilot, Simão Fernandes) were all granted coats of arms. It is likely that Raleigh paid for all of this. The enterprise did not go

smoothly but well enough to be viable. More were willing to join the colonists later.

Departure was rather late (8/18 May), with arrival at the Outer Banks not until 22 July/2 August. At Roanoke Island they were to leave Manteo as the new lord or high chief of the area under the English Crown and pick up the holding party left by Grenville when he arrived in late summer of 1586 and found the first colony gone. There was no one left alive on the island, however. But Fernandes was determined that there should be: he told White he would not take the colonists to Chesapeake Bay, their real objective, and they must stay on Roanoke Island. His reasons were obscure. Was it because he wanted to get even with White for their disagreements during the voyage, or was it, as he alleged, that he wished to hurry to the Azores to catch stragglers from the Spanish *flotá*, or even was it because he knew what had happened between 1570 and 1572 when the Spanish and the Powhatan Indians were in conflict and that it was not safe for them to go within reach of this tribe?

Despite all of this, White set his settlers to restoring the cottages and the fort (the embankment around it had been flattened). At a personal level he had problems; his daughter Elinor, wife of Ananias Dare, one of the assistants, was pregnant and on 18/28 August gave birth to the girl christened Virginia on 24 August/3 September, while Manteo formally accepted Christianity and was installed as lord of Roanoke. Clearly, White envisaged Roanoke as a place where his people might stay, even winter, before going on to their final home near Chesapeake Bay. But his associates were not happy; they did not have enough supplies to last very long, and they may have been anxious that their final site should be known in England. Only White, they assured him, could bring them aid and reinforcements quickly. He allowed himself to be persuaded. He said farewell, forever as it turned out, to his family and set sail for England on 28 August/7 September, reaching Southampton on 8/18 November after a wretched voyage.

It would seem that he had taken every reasonable precaution in anticipation of his return. The main body of colonists were to move when they were ready "fiftie miles within the maine"—that is, into the territory of the Chesapeake tribe. If, when he arrived and they were gone, signs were agreed as to whether they were well or in distress, and the name of their destination was to be incised on tree trunks. In England Raleigh met White twelve days after his arrival and assured him that aid would be sent with all speed. But in truth this was not easy to arrange. A single vessel could scarcely risk the direct route west from Madeira that Grenville had taken in 1586 or a run through the Caribbean alone now that war at sea was general. Finally, Raleigh made up his mind. White must wait and go over with a new expedition in 1588. This was not destined for Roanoke Island or the city of Raleigh but to find a site for a base, probably farther south, from which active war could be carried into the Spanish Indies. Grenville, once again, was to command, but though he was almost ready with his fleet in March 1588, he delayed long enough to be stopped by the queen and sent out to join the great naval force preparing to resist the long-heralded but now imminent Spanish Armada. Raleigh and Grenville did all they could for White: he was to face the ocean and the enemies there in two small pinnaces, the *Brave* and the *Roe*, with fifteen or sixteen new colonists and what stores he could cram in. Not far from the Azores, the *Brave* became involved in a fight with a stronger French privateer and was boarded and robbed.

Arriving back in England wounded and penniless, White found the *Roe* also a victim of pirates but otherwise unharmed. His miserable voyage left White helpless, while the great sea fight in the English Channel went on and while all sailings overseas were stopped until the queen could assess what shipping she needed for her counterblow the following year. It was apparently William Sanderson, Raleigh's business manager, if we may so call him, who eventually arranged some new backing for White. Also providing support was a syndicate of sympathizers including Sanderson and Richard Hakluyt, whose *Principall navigations* within a few months would make public the story of the Roanoke voyages. Why, somehow, relief could not be sent after the formation of this group on 7/17 Mar. 1589 we cannot tell, as a few privateers did get permission to operate in the Caribbean. But its influence was not enough to get White to sea that year.

It was only in 1590 that Sanderson could offer any hope of getting one of his ships, the *Moonlight*, to sea. She was to sail under the protection of three privateering vessels belonging to the merchant prince, John Watts, but they were ready before the *Moonlight*, and so White thrust himself on board the *Hopewell* and was grudgingly promised transport to Roanoke Island. He spent some time on board until finally the *Moonlight* joined them off Cuba, having made her way there safely (and was no doubt carrying stores for the colonists). Eventually the *Hopewell*, having sent home a valuable Spanish prize, agreed to go north with White. The vessels arrived off Hattorask (roughly what is now Oregon Inlet) on 15/25 August. But because of high seas and strong winds, the first attempt to get ashore was disastrous. Captain Spicer of Sanderson's *Moonlight* and nearly half his crew were drowned when their boat overturned. Eventually, one of the *Hopewell's* boats got White ashore. After an absence of three years, the governor finally returned to the settlement on Roanoke Island where he had left his colony.

The colonists were gone; so were both fort and cottages, and instead a stout barricade enclosure, suitable as a defended camp, remained. In it were some deserted guns and pieces of metal. The remains of White's personal belongings were found buried "in the ende of an olde trench, made two yeares past by Captaine Amadas"; they had been dug up by Indians. His armor was rusted, and his maps and pictures were damaged. More encouraging, however, were signs indicating that all was well, and the word *Croatoan* cut on one of the chief trees or posts of the palisade entrance showed that the resident party, which had waited as long as it could, had gone south to Croatoan where Manteo's village was. This was good news, but White pleaded in vain for transportation across the sound to where he expected to find them. The sea was too rough; the sailors were anxious to get away. White sailed home in the *Moonlight*, with her crew further depleted after an accident on board. Almost by a miracle she got back. White was at Plymouth on 24 Oct./3 Nov. 1590 after his last voyage, as no one would take him out again, even though the syndicate remained nominally in existence in London.

Further action rested with Raleigh alone, and he decided he wanted none taken. His patent would expire in 1591 if he had not planted a permanent colony in America. White, though he had not found the colony, had brought home news that it was alive. This assumption was to keep Raleigh's control over English voyages to North America alive until 1603. In due course White was packed off to Ireland, perhaps as a freeholder in the Munster plantation, another bigger English colony. If so, he was settled at Newtown in the Great Wood of Kilmore on the lands of a prominent landholder, Hugh Cuffe, some nine miles above Edmund Spencer at his little castle at Kilcolan. Here he lived, possibly with wife and family,

and from here he wrote to Hakluyt an account of his last voyage, with a covering letter dated 4/14 Feb. 1592/93. He could only say that all his plans for an American colony had come to an end. "And wanting my wishes, I leave off from prosecuting that whereunto I would to God my wealth were answerable to my will." He could only commend the relief "of my discomfortable company, the planters in Virginia" to God's help. This is his last word.

The colonists, it would appear, did live on. Raleigh promised to stop to see them in 1595 on his way back from Guyana but did not do so. Cautiously, using small trading vessels from about 1599 onward, he tried to get word of them: an expedition of 1602 reached the Outer Banks but too far to the south. Ironically, they probably were heard of when two Indians were brought to London who possibly could tell of them, but his patent had expired and he was a prisoner in the Tower in 1603. The belief persisted that the colonists had survived and may have strengthened the Virginia Company's determination to colonize Chesapeake Bay, where they might have been of help. But it appears that as Christopher Newport rounded Cape Henry in April 1607, Powhatan, busy building his power over the peoples around the bay, struck at the Chesapeake tribe and their English associates of nearly twenty years' standing and killed them all except a few who got away to the Chowan River, where the local Indians kept them out of sight of parties from Jamestown searching for them. Powhatan later admitted his complicity in their slaughter. The Lost Colony, however, passed into myth and legend and became the stuff of fiction, not history, though its shadow kept the name of White and of his daughter and granddaughter alive for Americans, especially North Carolinians.

As an artist, White's reputation has grown slowly but surely in the present century, though more particularly since publication of fine versions of his drawings in 1964. It appears that he had some artistic training, revealing some Mannerist influence, and he learned much from Jacques Le Moyne de Morgues, the artist-explorer of French Florida who settled in London and had his own collection of Indian scenes to make and remake. Paul Hulton, the leading authority on White's paintings, described his "carefully finished water-colour drawings" as "more spontaneously naturalistic than anything known by an English artist at this period." He considered White's "quality so marked as to be more revolutionary than anything known by an English artist at this period." White drew rough outlines in black lead and applied his watercolors directly to the paper, without a ground, strengthening them with body color and with touches of gold, silver, and white. His use of perspective was intermittent: often he used a half plan, half bird's-eye view for his landscapes, but most of his figure drawings of Indians were formed with a rare fidelity to life, and so they have an authority that no other early pictures of North American Indians had or were to have for a very long time. They are consequently priceless ethnographic documents, detailing artifacts and clothing with care and understanding, and showing the two village communities he drew as living entities.

His natural history specimens are also remarkably true to life, especially birds and fish, though he had nothing like Le Moyne's expertise and taste in drawing plants and flowers. Thomas Penny, an early zoologist, used versions of White's swallowtail butterfly, fireflies, and other insects, and John Gerard included the milkweed in his *Herbal* (1597). White also discussed with him the virtues of sarsaparilla roots (*Smilax pseudo-china*), and so his own drawings came to Hakluyt as well. White's presentation volume has survived; his own collections have not.

John White wrote well and at times with a simple eloquence. In his narratives of the 1587, 1588, and 1590 voyages he portrays himself as an enthusiast for colonization and a moderately effective organizer of his enthusiasm into action. He clearly could inspire people like himself with a vision of a fruitful life in a wholly new environment. But he had insufficient experience of business or, indeed, of the harshness and intrigues of life at sea. He failed to make a sufficiently strong impression on the London merchants with whom he dealt to rally them into adequate action on his behalf. At sea, too, he was pushed around by the more violent and self-centered seamen. As a governor he would no doubt have been paternal and constructive, while he had an instinctive affinity with the Indian that few Englishmen were to show. But he may not have been strong enough to stand up against adversity or opposition.

His return to England in 1587, whatever the pressures on him, was a fatal mistake—his primary duty was to stay with the colonists. His failures to return to relieve them were due to misfortune and bad luck, but he did not stand up to Raleigh once it became clear—as it must have done after his return in 1590—that Raleigh considered his interest would best be served by not relieving the colony, for the time being at least, because the discovery in or after 1591 that the colonists were all dead would rob him of his stake in North America that he was determined to hold. White, it might seem, always gave way under pressure. He was, however, more farsighted than most of his contemporary enthusiasts for American colonization in believing that a small, mixed community of men, women, and children stood a better chance of establishing itself in America alongside its own inhabitants than a larger, mainly male colony based on military strength and bound to conflict with Indian rights. He thus has a significant place in English colonial relations with the New World.

SEE: Theodor de Bry, *America*, Part I (1590); Richard Hakluyt, *Principall Navigations* (1589) and *Principal Navigations*, vol. 3 (1600); Thomas Harriot, *A brief and true report of the new found land of Virginia* (reprint, 1972); Paul Hulton, *The Watercolor Drawings of John White* (1965) and *The Work of Jacques Le Moyne de Morgues*, 2 vols. (1977); Paul Hulton and David B. Quinn, *The American Drawings of John White*, 2 vols. (1964), and "John White and the English Naturalists," *History Today* 13 (1963); Ivor Noël Hume, *The Virginia Adventure* (1994); David B. Quinn, *England and the Discovery of North America, 1480–1610* (1974) and *Ralegh and the British Empire* (corrected ed., 1973). Lebame Houston and Olivia Isil, Manteo, N.C., have contributed to this entry new information that they found on several research trips to England in the late 1980s.

DAVID B. QUINN

White, John (*31 Aug. 1814–17 Dec. 1894*), merchant and commissioner for North Carolina in England during the Civil War, was born in Kirkcaldy, Fifeshire, Scotland, one of ten children of Andrew Whyte and his second wife, Hannah Bolton. In December 1828 young John Whyte sailed from Kirkcaldy for New York en route to Warrenton, N.C., where his half brother, Thomas White, had previously settled. After a few years in school he was employed in a firm operated by his half brother and Peter Mitchel. In 1836 he became a partner, and when Thomas moved to Petersburg, Va., he took over the business, which he conducted until the outbreak of the Civil War. Like his brother before him, he changed the spelling of his surname.

On 28 Nov. 1838 White married Priscilla Bella Jones of rural Warren County, who came from an old, well-established family in the county. Between 1850 and 1852 they engaged the services of the architect Jacob Holt to build for them a large Italianate house in Warrenton where they lived for the remainder of their lives.

Early in the Civil War the demand for cotton abroad made it a valuable commodity for those who could ship it through the Federal blockade of Southern ports. To support its war effort the state of North Carolina sent John White to England to borrow money and secure credit on state warrants payable in cotton and rosin. White was appointed agent and commissioner for the state and sailed in November 1862. Traveling by way of Nassau and Liverpool, he reached London on 5 Jan. 1863. He succeeded in selling a large amount of cotton bonds for bales of cotton to be delivered to blockade-runners at North Carolina ports. The London firm of Alexander Collie and Company, through which he negotiated these transactions, also sold most of the supplies that he purchased.

White was accompanied to England by Captain Thomas Morrow Crossan, his neighbor from Warren County, formerly of the U.S. Navy and an officer in the small North Carolina navy. With the proceeds of a £100,000 loan from Collie and Company, White purchased North Carolina's first blockade-runner, the *Lord Clyde*, a side-wheel passenger steamer running between Glasgow and Dublin. It was converted into a blockade-runner with high-pressure boilers at the shipyards of John Key, who married White's sister, Sarah Whyte. The *Lord Clyde* was renamed the *Ad-Vance* presumably in honor of Governor Zebulon B. Vance, his wife Adelaide, and the ship's pioneering purpose. With a cargo from Liverpool, the *Ad-Vance* ran the blockade for the first time on 3 July 1863. Under the command of Crossan, the *Ad-Vance* proved to be the state's most famous blockade-runner.

White's successful completion of his assignment paved the way for the eventual provision of $12 million worth of goods—including blankets, shoes, socks, jackets, shirts, trousers, munitions, and medicines (especially quinine)—about half of which went to Confederate states other than North Carolina. Not surprisingly, throughout the war North Carolina's regiments were better clothed and equipped than those of any other state in the Confederacy.

In the fall of 1864 White made a second trip to England. He left Warrenton on 2 August with his wife and their children Mary, Sue, Kate, Andrew, and Hugh, expecting to sail for Liverpool. After a stopover in Raleigh, they arrived in Wilmington on 5 August. For over a month they remained on board the *Ad-Vance* and at the home of a friend in Wilmington while making repeated attempts to run the blockade. After nine failures, in which the *Ad-Vance* continually ran aground and faced hostile Union vessels offshore, White decided that the risks were too great and returned his family to Warrenton on 10 September. Soon afterwards, having made a total of eleven successful trips between Wilmington and Nassau, the *Ad-Vance* was captured a few miles from Wilmington. The seizure resulted from the ship's use of North Carolina soft coal; on a bright moonlit night, the dense cloud of black smoke produced by the coal betrayed her presence to a Union cruiser near the mouth of the Cape Fear River.

White sailed alone from Smithville (now Southport) on 26 October on board the *Virginia*, arriving at Bermuda two days later. He did not go ashore, however, because of yellow fever. Nevertheless, White contracted what was diagnosed as bilious and yellow fever and as a consequence did not reach London until the day before Christmas 1864. After the fall of Wilmington, there was no word from him until late May 1865, when an open letter—sent through a friend in New York, ostensibly to arrive by truce boat but forwarded instead to White's nephew in Petersburg and from there to Warrenton—reached the family. White was unable to return to North Carolina until that summer.

The war having ended, White undertook business in Petersburg but in the fall of 1867 decided to establish a cotton brokerage office in Liverpool. This time he took his family with him but after nine months abandoned the project. He returned to Warrenton where, as a devoted member and vestryman of Emmanuel Episcopal Church and the grandfather of thirty-six children, he remained until his death.

In April 1870 Robert E. Lee and his daughter Agnes were the guests of White and his family at their home in Warrenton. The Lees were there to visit the Warren County grave of Annie Carter Lee, the general's daughter, who had died of typhoid fever at Jones's Springs in October 1862.

John and Priscilla White had ten children: Hannah Bolton (17 Nov. 1839, m. Samuel Peter Arrington), William Jones (7 Oct. 1842, m. Sue Blount Cawthorn), John Thomas (15 Jan. 1845, m. Apphia M. Williams), Andrew Robert (13 Apr. 1847, never married), Mary Johnston (21 July 1849, m. Edmund Ruffin Beckwith), Sallie Jones (17 June 1853, died young), Hugh Jones (1 Aug. 1855, m. Florence C. Young), Catherine Augusta (14 Jan. 1857, m. Solomon Williams, Jr., older brother of Apphia M. Williams), Sue Eaton (19 Sept. 1858, m. John Pretlow), and Lizzie Chiffelle (22 Jan. 1861, died in infancy).

John White died suddenly of a stroke at his home after returning from gathering wood chips in the backyard. He was buried beside his wife in the family cemetery behind the house. In September 1897 the Warren County Camp of United Confederate Veterans was named the John White Camp in his honor. The North Carolina Museum of History has a portrait of White.

SEE: Mary Johnston Beckwith Diary (Southern Historical Collection, University of North Carolina, Chapel Hill); Walter Clark, ed., *Histories of the Several Regiments and Battalions from North Carolina in the Great War*, vol. 1 (1901); R. D. W. Connor, *North Carolina: Rebuilding an Ancient Commonwealth*, vol. 2 (1929); "Thomas Morrow Crossan," in *Dictionary of North Carolina Biography*, vol. 1 (1979); Archibald Henderson, *North Carolina: The Old North State and the New*, vol. 2 (1941); Lizzie Wilson Montgomery, *Sketches of Old Warrenton* (1924); Raleigh *News and Observer*, 14 July 1937; *Warrenton Gazette*, 21 Dec. 1894, 1 Oct. 1897; Manly Wade Wellman, *The County of Warren, North Carolina, 1586–1917* (1959); Peter M. Wilson, *Southern Exposure* (1927).

JAMES P. BECKWITH, JR.

White, John Brown (10 Mar. 1810–12 Feb. 1887), college president and clergyman, was born in Bow, N.H., the son of David and Betsey Carter White. His father was a colonel in the War of 1812. White attended Pembroke Academy and Brown University, where he studied under Dr. Francis Wayland and in 1832 was graduated with B.A. and M.A. degrees. For several years he taught at the New Hampton Institute in New Hampshire.

White studied law and was admitted to the bar in Greenville, Ill., in 1836. He was elected judge of probate in 1837 and appeared to be settled in the legal profession. In 1838 his future wife, the niece of the wife of President Samuel Wait of Wake Forest College, convinced him to accept Dr. Wait's invitation to join the faculty as professor of mathematics and natural philosophy. White also served

as secretary, and later as treasurer, of the board of trustees. In 1838, when Wait went into the field as an agent of the college, White was appointed president in his absence. Ten years later, after the resignation of William Hooper as president of Wake Forest, White was chosen as acting president and then president of the college; he served from December 1848 to December 1853. He was licensed to preach by the Wake Forest Baptist Church in January 1839 and ordained in 1849. The college historian said that White, being a New Englander and against slaveholding, became increasingly obnoxious in a slave state as the sectional bitterness increased. He was not a good teacher according to one student and an even worse preacher. The college history also indicates that White was not in total harmony with some members of the board of trustees. His letter of resignation surprised some of the trustees, but he was persuaded to continue until the end of 1853.

He next was president of a girls' seminary in Brownsville, Tenn. (1853–55), before becoming the first president of Almira College (now Greenville College) in Greenville, Ill., in 1855. Except for a short time in 1864–65 when he was chaplain of the 117th Illinois Volunteer Infantry Regiment, White occupied the presidency of Almira until 1878. Afterwards he briefly served as principal of two girls schools in Upper Alton and Champaign, Ill.

White's first wife was Mary Powers Merriam, the daughter of Isaac and Mary Powers Merriam, whom he married on 5 Apr. 1838. The couple had seven children: John Conant, Annie Elizabeth, Emily, Lucy Carter (Merriam), William Henry, Mary Brown, and Juliet Powers. His second wife was Elizabeth Richardson Wright, of Vermont. They were married on 5 Aug. 1857 but had no children. White died and was buried in Greenville, Ill.

SEE: William Cathcart, *Baptist Encyclopedia*, vol. 2 (1881); *Greenville (Ill.) Advocate*, 19, 23 Nov. 1931; Ralph Merriam, comp., *Col. Jonathan Merriam and Family* (1940 [portrait]); George W. Paschal, *History of Wake Forest*, vol. 1 (1935 [portrait]); Raleigh, *Biblical Recorder*, 14 Apr. 1838, 28 Apr. 1854, 17 May 1855, 23 Feb., 30 Mar. 1887; *Wake Forest Student*, no. 14 (March 1895); John Brown White Papers (Baptist Historical Collection, Wake Forest University, Winston-Salem).

JOHN R. WOODARD

White, Newman Ivey (3 Feb. 1892–6 Dec. 1948), teacher, folklorist, and literary biographer, was born in Statesville, the son of James Houston and Harriet Ivey White and the grandson of Methodist minister George Washington Ivey. After attending the Greensboro High School, he entered Trinity College in 1909 and was graduated in 1913 magna cum laude. He received an A.M. degree from Trinity (1914) and A.M. (1915) and Ph.D. (1918) degrees from Harvard University.

From 1915 to 1917 White was an English instructor at Alabama Polytechnic Institute, then taught for two more years at Washington University in St. Louis. In 1919 he returned to Durham, where he was a professor of English at Trinity College and then Duke University until 1948. For the last five years of his life he served as chairman of the Department of English. He held membership in many honorary and professional societies, including Phi Beta Kappa, the American Folklore Society, and the Modern Language Association of America.

From 1916 to 1928 White's chief scholarly interest was Afro-American poetry and folk songs. With Walter C. Jackson he edited *An Anthology of Verse by American Negroes* (1924), and he subsequently compiled a collection entitled *American Negro Folk-Songs* (1928). Years later, in 1943, he accepted the general editorship of *The Frank C. Brown Collection of North Carolina Folklore*. The first of its seven volumes was in press at the time of his death.

White's study of Percy Bysshe Shelley, his major scholarly commitment, began in a course taught by Irving Babbitt at Harvard and led first to White's doctoral dissertation, "Shelley's Dramatic Poems." He thereafter contributed many articles about Shelley to major scholarly journals and in the latter half of his career produced a series of authoritative books: *The Best of Shelley* (1932), *The Unextinguished Hearth: Shelley and His Contemporary Critics* (1938), a definitive two-volume biography bearing the title *Shelley* (1940), and a one-volume abridgement of this work called *Portrait of Shelley* (1945). At the time of his death White was engaged in research on the life of William Godwin.

In 1922 White married Marie Anne Updike, of St. Louis, who also taught English at Duke University for many years. Their only child, Marie, was born in 1926 but died in infancy. In his community White was known as a man of liberal convictions. He freely gave time and leadership to many civic causes. He was buried Statesville.

SEE: Frank C. Brown Papers (Manuscript Department, Duke University Library, Durham); James Cannon and Lewis Patton, "Newman Ivey White: Scholar and Humanitarian," *Library Notes*, no. 24 (1950 [portrait]); Robert W. Christ, "The Published Writings of Newman Ivey White," *Library Notes*, no. 24 (1950); Newman Ivey White Papers (Manuscript Department, Duke University Library).

DANIEL W. PATTERSON

White, Philo *(23 June 1796–15 Feb. 1883)*, newspaperman, diplomat, and town developer, was born in Whitesboro (Whitestown), Oneida County, N.Y., the son of a man by the same name and the grandson of the town's founder, Hugh White. After brief periods of schooling in his hometown and in Utica, N.Y., he became a printer for the *Columbian Gazette* in Utica and probably the *Manlius Times*. In 1820 he went to Salisbury, N.C., and with Lemuel Bingham established the *Western Carolinian* in the old printing shop of Jacob Krider. In 1823 Bingham withdrew from the paper, and with the financial and polemical support of Charles Fisher, White made the *Western Carolinian* a powerful voice in support of western rights until 1830, when his health failed and he left the paper to become a purchasing agent for the U.S. Navy on the Pacific Coast. In 1834 he returned to the state and established the *North Carolina Standard* in Raleigh. The paper was an active Democratic organ, and its editor was made the state printer. In 1836 White's health deteriorated again, and he sold the *Standard* to Thomas Loring. Securing another post with the navy, he was a purser with the fleets for seven years.

In 1844 he moved to what is now Racine, Wis., becoming one of the founding fathers of the city and erecting the United States Hotel, which was the grandest structure in the new city. He bought property in Racine and Milwaukee and for two years published the *Racine Advocate* with the financial support of Solomon Juneau, a wealthy real estate developer. As a member of the Territorial Council from 1847 to 1848, White introduced plank roads to the territory. In 1848, after Wisconsin was granted statehood, he was elected to the state senate. An Episcopalian, he was active in establishing the Diocese of Wisconsin. He was also one of the founders and a trustee of Racine College, an Episcopal institution, which granted him an honorary doctor of laws degree in 1856.

In 1849 White was appointed U.S. consul in Hamburg. In 1853 he became chargé d'affaires in the Republic of Ecuador, and from 1855 to 1858 he was the resident minister located in Quito. In 1859 he returned to Whitesboro, where he found that the other White heirs had sold the town hall and green during his absence. After a great deal of work and expense, he succeeded in regaining the title in order to return the property to the town in accordance with his grandfather's wishes.

On 9 May 1822, while editor of the *Western Carolinian* in Salisbury, he married Nancy B. Hampton (2 Sept. 1803–29 Nov. 1877), the daughter of William and Mary Hampton. The Whites had two children, Esther (b. 1830) who died in infancy and Mary (1824–44) who married John W. Ellis. After Nancy White died, Philo White married Lydia M. Marsh of Whitesboro in October 1880. He died at age eighty-six in his hometown.

SEE: James Brawley, "Salisbury Editor Remarkable Character," *Salisbury Post*, 18 Feb. 1973; W. W. Holden, *Address on the History of Journalism in North Carolina* (1881); State Historical Society of Wisconsin, *Dictionary of Wisconsin Biography* (1960); *Wisconsin Magazine of History* 8 (December 1924).

D. A. YANCHISIN

White, Stephen Van Culen *(1 Aug. 1831–18 Jan. 1913)*, banker and congressman, was born in Chatham County, the son of Hiram and Julia Brewer White. His father was descended from a Pennsylvania Quaker who relocated in North Carolina after the Revolutionary War. His mother was from a prominent North Carolina family descended from Oliver Cromwell. An antislavery advocate, Hiram White refused police duty during the 1831 Nat Turner scare and moved his family to Otterville, Ill. There, Stephen White attended the free school of Dr. Silas Hamilton, helped at his father's farm and gristmill, and was a trapper. In 1850, with financial aid from an older brother, he entered Knox College, in Galesburg, Ill., where he received an A.B. degree in 1854 and an honorary LL.D. in 1886.

After graduation, White moved to St. Louis, Mo., to work in a mercantile house as a bookkeeper. Eight months later he joined the law office of B. Gratz Brown and John A. Kasson. (Brown became governor of Missouri, a U.S. senator, and the vice-presidential candidate with Horace Greeley; Kasson was subsequently minister to Austria and Germany and a U.S. representative.) During this period White studied law and as a staunch Republican wrote articles for the *Missouri Democrat* (a Republican paper) during the Fremont campaign of 1856. He was admitted to the bar on 4 Nov. 1856 and in the same year moved to Des Moines, Iowa, to practice law. A successful lawyer, he was defense attorney in the first treason case in Iowa, heard in January 1861. In 1864 he was acting U.S. district attorney for Iowa.

In 1865 White and his wife of eight years, Eliza M. Chandler, moved to Brooklyn, N.Y., where he joined the Plymouth Congregational Church, serving as a trustee (1866–1902) and as treasurer (1869–1902). He became a close friend of the church's minister, Henry Ward Beecher, for whom he testified and reportedly paid legal expenses in the famous Beecher-Tilton-Woodhull seduction trial of 1875. After his admission to the New York bar, White was associated with the banking and brokerage firm of Marvin and White on Wall Street until it failed in 1867. He then established his own brokerage business. In 1869 he joined the New York Stock Exchange, where, as a stock manipulator, he made a name for himself with Delaware,

Lackawanna, and Western Railroad stock. As many investors, White suffered his second financial setback in 1872 because of the great fires of Boston. By 1882 he had formed another banking and brokerage firm, S. V. White and Company, and by March 1884 he was worth over one million dollars.

An amateur astronomer, White was the first president (1884) of the American Astronomical Society, which later became the Department of Astronomy of the Brooklyn Institute of Arts and Sciences. In 1886, after serving as park commissioner for Brooklyn, he was elected as a Republican representative from Brooklyn to the Fiftieth Congress (1887–89). He declined renomination in 1888.

In 1891, while trying to corner the corn market, White lost over a million dollars. The loss was not entirely his fault, but he took total blame. Although he was in debt to over 250 individuals, his honesty and credit-worthiness helped him maintain assets of $200,000 on his word alone; within a year he paid back all of his creditors. He was readmitted to the New York Stock Exchange on 15 Feb. 1892 but sold his seat in 1902, when he returned to his law practice. Although not always successful on Wall Street, he was known there both for his honesty and daring.

Short and stocky, White usually wore a frock coat and black tie which attracted considerable attention on Wall Street; people called him "Deacon," though he never attained that designation in its true sense. Both he and his wife were active in civic affairs. He died after years of poor health and was buried at Greenwood Cemetery, Brooklyn. White had one daughter, Mrs. F. W. Hopkins of Alpine, N.J.

SEE: *Biog. Dir. Am. Cong.* (1971); *Brooklyn Daily Eagle*, 17 Jan. 1913; Paxton Hibben, *Henry Ward Beecher: An American Portrait* (1927); *Nat. Cyc. Am. Biog.*, vol. 5 (1894 [portrait]); *New York Times*, 19 Jan. 1913 (2d ed., p. 12); *North Carolina Teacher* 10 (September 1892); *Selections from Portfolio of Stephen V. C. White* (1893); Daniel Van Pelt, *Leslie's History of Greater New York* (1898) [extract in North Carolina Collection, University of North Carolina, Chapel Hill); *Who Was Who in America, 1897–1942* (1972).

DEBORAH B. WILSON

White, Thomas Jackson, Jr. (6 Mar. 1903–5 Feb. 1991), legislator, attorney, lobbyist, and adviser to governors, was born on a farm near Concord, the son of Thomas Jackson and Mary Isabelle Culp White. The given names of father and son were for Confederate General Thomas J. (Stonewall) Jackson. His mother was a schoolteacher from Quaero, Tex. White attended Cabarrus County elementary schools for five years, then moved with his family to Kershaw County, S.C., where he continued in school for two years before returning to North Carolina in 1917. After a year in a Charlotte school he entered Bailey Military Institute in Greenwood, S.C. for the 1918–19 term. Returning once again to North Carolina, he was graduated from Concord High School in 1920 and entered North Carolina State College. He withdrew two years later, because of his father's ill health, to work on the farm and elsewhere. He also served in the 120th Infantry, North Carolina National Guard, between 1921 and 1924.

Beginning in the fall of 1924, White began to study law at The University of North Carolina; he was admitted to the bar in 1927. After practicing in Durham for three years, he moved to Kinston, where he was a founding member of the law firm of White and Allen and where he remained for the rest of his life. From 1938 to 1964 he served as county attorney; he was president of the Lenoir County Bar Association in 1952 and of the Sixth District

Bar Association in 1954. White also was a member of other state and national bar associations and was elected a Fellow of the American College of Trial Lawyers.

His long career as a public servant in the state began with the creation of the North Carolina Wildlife Resources Commission by the General Assembly in 1947, largely in response to White's advocacy; he was a member and first chairman of the wildlife commission. He served in the state house of representatives in 1953, 1955, and 1957 and in the senate during the sessions of 1961, 1963, 1965, and 1967. White was chairman of the Senate Finance Committee in the 1961 session and chairman of the Senate Appropriations Committee in the 1963, 1965, and 1967 sessions. He was a member (1961–72) and chairman (1963–72) of the Advisory Budget Commission. In 1969 he served as legislative counsel to Governor Robert Scott.

His first term in the General Assembly is perhaps the best remembered because of his involvement in the "Battle of the Whammy" during the 1953 regular session. When White introduced a bill to abridge the use of speed detection devices by the State Highway Patrol, critics attacked him because, they said, he had presented the measure after receiving a speeding ticket via radar detection. White claimed that he had planned to introduce the "anti-whammy" bill before he received the ticket. After this legislative skirmish, White acquired the nickname "Whammy" from the press, with which he had many disagreements throughout his career.

Also during his first term White was instrumental in establishing a driver training program in the Lenoir County high schools—making them the first schools in the country to offer driver training. After convincing the Lenoir County Board of Commissioners to fund such a program, he secured passage of a bill in the General Assembly allowing every county in the state to appropriate funds for driver training in high schools.

During his legislative career White served on numerous commissions, including the Commission on Reorganization of State Government (1957–59), State Legislative Building Commission (chairman, 1959–73), Sir Walter Raleigh Commission, Legislative Council (1963–65), Legislative Research Commission (1965–68), Richard Caswell Memorial Commission (1972–79), Governor's Commission on Education beyond the High School (1961–62), Governor's Committee on Reorganization of Higher Education (1971), and Museum of Art Building Commission (chairman, 1967–83). White is noted for his role in guiding the planning and construction of the State Legislative Building and the State Museum of Art Building.

His commitment to higher education led White to serve on The University of North Carolina Board of Trustees (1965–71) and its executive committee (1967–71) and on The University of North Carolina Board of Governors and its preparatory planning committee (1971–77). He was a recipient of the William R. Davie Award for distinguished service to the University of North Carolina at Chapel Hill (1986) and the Distinguished Service Award given by the University of North Carolina School of Medicine.

White's first wife was Amie Jordan Parham, whom he married on 28 June 1927; their children were Amie Isabelle, Sarah Ellen, and Thomas J. III. He married Virginia Edwards Turley on 28 Dec. 1937. White, an Episcopalian, died at age eighty-eight and was buried in Pinelawn Memorial Park, Kinston.

SEE: Isabelle White Davis, personal contact; *Greensboro News and Record*, 6 Dec. 1981; *Heritage of Lenoir County* (1981); Charles R. Holloman and Talmadge C. Johnson, *The Story of Kinston and Lenoir County* (1954); *Kinston Daily*

Free Press, 6 Feb. 1991; *North Carolina Manual* (1967); Raleigh *News and Observer*, 28 July 1957, 3 Mar. 1963, 3 Feb. 1967, 1 Dec. 1968, 30 Apr. 1970, 28 Jan. 1971, 6 Feb. 1991.

BENJAMIN A. JOLLY
PATRICK S. WOOTEN

White, William Edgar *(19 Jan. 1861–29 Mar. 1935)*, furniture manufacturer, was born in Mebane, the son of Stephen Alexander and Mary Jane Woods White. He received his education at the Bingham Military Academy, located near his home, before working as a telegraph operator for the Southern Railway until 1881. With his brother, David A., and a capital investment of $420, he then established the White Furniture Company, of which he was president until his death over half a century later. The company made furniture of the highest quality and earned an international reputation.

As a Republican White was active in local political affairs and a member of the school board; he was a director of the State Fair and helped organize the Mebane tobacco market. A member of the Presbyterian church, he was involved in its work. White never married. The White Furniture Company ceased operations in 1994.

SEE: *Greensboro Daily News*, 31 Mar. 1935 (portrait); Raleigh *News and Observer*, 30 Mar. 1936; *Who Was Who in America*, vol. 1 (1943).

WILLIAM S. POWELL

Whitehead, Richard Henry *(27 July 1865–16 Feb. 1916)*, physician, anatomist, and educator, was born in Salisbury, the son of Dr. Marcellus and Virginia Coleman Whitehead. The family had moved in 1845 from Virginia to North Carolina, where Richard's father and older brother John became eminent physicians. Young Whitehead attended high school in Salisbury, Horner Military School in Oxford, and Wake Forest College where he was graduated in 1886 with a bachelor of arts degree. Returning to Salisbury, he spent the summer of 1886 studying anatomy and physiology with his father, an experience that crystallized his desire to practice medicine.

In 1887 he enrolled in the University of Virginia, where he completed the two-year curriculum in one year and received a doctor of medicine degree with high honors. At Charlottesville he was profoundly influenced by Dr. William Beverly Towles, professor of anatomy, who appointed Whitehead as demonstrator of anatomy for the period 1887–89 in recognition of his outstanding scholarship and teaching skills. Whitehead spent the winter of 1889–90 studying medicine at hospitals in Philadelphia and New York City. In the summer of 1890 he returned to Salisbury to form a medical partnership with his brother, Dr. John Whitehead.

Scarcely had he settled into his practice when he was called to Chapel Hill to guide The University of North Carolina School of Medicine during its early years. The Medical School had closed in 1885, when Dr. Thomas W. Harris resigned his position as dean. In 1889 the university's board of trustees and faculty recommended reopening the school with Dr. Paul B. Barringer as dean. When Barringer subsequently moved to the University of Virginia, he strongly recommended to The University of North Carolina Board that Richard Whitehead be considered as his replacement. Thus in the summer of 1890 Whitehead was asked to become professor of anatomy and dean of the University of North Carolina School of Medicine. It was a difficult decision to give up his private practice for an uncertain future at the fledgling medical school, but he finally accepted the position and moved to Chapel Hill in September 1890.

Whitehead immediately set out to reorganize the curriculum of the Medical School, where he taught anatomy, physiology, and medicine while concurrently serving as university physician for the students and local population. During these early years, the Medical School had few students, beginning with ten in 1890 and increasing to twenty-five by 1895. Most of the graduates transferred to institutions outside the state to complete their clinical training, among the more popular choices being the University of Maryland, Jefferson, South Carolina, or Vanderbilt medical schools. Under Whitehead's skilled leadership, the school in Chapel Hill enlarged its curriculum from one to two years by the time of the 1896–97 academic session. In 1896 Dr. Charles Staples Mangum joined the faculty as professor of physiology and materia medica, and in 1898 the school was admitted to the Association of American Medical Colleges in recognition of its academic excellence. By 1901 Whitehead had successfully incorporated the Medical School into the general university and had recruited Dr. Isaac Hall Manning as professor of physiology and bacteriology. In 1902 clinical studies were offered for the first time at Raleigh under the direction of Dr. Hubert Ashley Royster.

Through all of these changes, Whitehead maintained his vision of how medicine should be taught, with the first two years devoted exclusively to the basic sciences, emphasizing a mastery of the foundations without the "distractions" of clinical practice. He believed strongly in the separation of the basic and clinical sciences, and his pioneering work at The University of North Carolina laid the foundations for the educational system and philosophy followed by his successors. With his growing reputation as a diagnostician, teacher, and administrator, Whitehead was called to the University of Virginia in 1905 to reorganize the curriculum and serve as dean of the Medical Department and professor of anatomy.

Whitehead also was recognized for his scholarly abilities and research in endocrinology, neuroanatomy, and embryology. His best-known work, *Anatomy of the Brain*, was published in 1900 in collaboration with Drs. Francis P. Venable, William de B. MacNider, and Charles S. Mangum. Whitehead was active in the American Medical Association, Association of American Anatomists, North Carolina Medical Society. He was a member of the Baptist church, the Democratic party, and Kappa Alpha social fraternity. On 4 June 1891 he married his cousin, Virgilia Whitehead, of Amherst, Va. In recognition of his leadership in medical education, Whitehead was awarded an honorary doctor of letters degree from The University of North Carolina in 1910.

SEE: Samuel A. Ashe, ed., *Biographical History of North Carolina*, vol. 5 (1906); W. R. Berryhill and others, *Medical Education at Chapel Hill: The First Hundred Years* (1979); *Transactions of the Medical Society of the State of North Carolina* (1917); University of North Carolina School of Medicine, *Bulletin*, no. 2 (1955).

MARCUS B. SIMPSON, JR.

Whitehead, Zollicofer Wiley *(1862–1 July 1923)*, businessman, editor, and journalist, was born in Kenansville, one of three children of Wiley W. and Cordelia Hussey Whitehead. After attending the county public schools, he completed his education at Grove Academy in Kenansville under the tutelage of Dr. James Sprunt.

In 1881 Whitehead joined the staff of the *Greensboro Pa-*

triot as an office boy; from that position he became associate editor and half owner, and in 1886 editor and sole owner. Under his direction, the *Patriot* grew from a weekly to a daily paper and became a strong supporter of the Democratic party. The masthead read, "Democratic Supremacy for the Good of All, And a Democratic Administration Administered by Democrats." Ill health caused Whitehead to sell the paper in late 1888. Recovering his health, he purchased the *Fayetteville Observer* in 1889 and published it until 1892. He sold the *Observer* in 1893 in order to accept a position in the Government Printing Office in Washington, D.C.; the job may have been a political reward for his newspaper's strong support of President Grover Cleveland. Moreover, Whitehead had been a member of the National Democratic Committee that had nominated Cleveland.

Returning to North Carolina in 1896, he settled in Wilmington, where he established and published two trade journals, the *Southern Lumber Journal* and the *Carolina Fruit and Truckers' Journal*. The *Southern Lumber Journal* eventually opened offices in Norfolk, Va., and Savannah, Ga. Both journals were sold and continued publication after his death. In 1904 Whitehead organized a convention in Savannah of southern yellow pine manufacturers and northern wholesalers that developed a new set of grading and inspection rules for merchantable southern lumber; these much-needed changes were the first enacted since 1883. Also active in Wilmington business circles, he served as chairman of the board of directors of the Wilmington, Brunswick, and Southern Railroad, as a director and then president of two steamship companies, as secretary-treasurer of a Wilmington lumber company, and as a board member of six local banks. Whitehead was a commissioner of the 1903 St. Louis World's Fair. In 1918–19 he was president of the North Carolina Press Association.

In 1885 he married Warren Smith in Winston-Salem. They were the parents of Anna, Wiley, and Thomas Ruffin. Whitehead, a Presbyterian, died from a stroke and was buried in Oakdale Cemetery, Wilmington. His obituary noted that he "was one of the best beloved of the citizens of the city."

SEE: *Ayers Directory of Newspapers, Magazines, and Trade Publications* (1880–1923); *Charlotte Daily Observer*, 24 Nov. 1911 (portrait); Eugene G. Harrell and John B. Neathery, comps., *The North Carolina Speaker* (1887); James G. Kenan, "Zollicofer Wiley Whitehead," in Charles L. Van Noppen Papers (Manuscript Department, Duke University Library, Durham); North Carolina Press Association, *Bulletin*, 22 Oct. 1923; Thad Stem, Jr., *The Tar Heel Press* (1973); *Wilmington Morning Star*, 2 July 1923.

J. MARSHALL BULLOCK

Whitener, Basil Lee *(14 May 1915–20 Mar. 1989),* legislator and congressman, was born in York County, S.C., the son of Levi, foreman in a Cannon textile mill, and Laura Barrett Whitener. His father died at the age of thirty-six when Basil was eight, and his mother and her three children moved to Ranlo community near Gastonia, N.C. Young Whitener finished high school in Lowell at age sixteen and then completed the two-year course at Rutherford College in 1933. He was graduated from the University of South Carolina in 1935 and received a law degree from Duke University in 1937. As a boy he helped to support the family by delivering newspapers to pay his college expenses he worked in a cotton mill in the summer and held student jobs during the term.

Admitted to the bar in 1937, he began to practice in Gastonia, and between 1938 and 1940 he also was an in-

structor of business law at Belmont Abbey College. He held a seat in the state house of representatives in 1941 and was renominated in 1942 but resigned to enter the U.S. Navy as an ensign. After serving as a gunnery officer, he was separated from the navy in November 1945 with the rank of lieutenant. Subsequently he became a major in the U.S. Air Force Reserve.

Governor R. Gregg Cherry, a fellow townsman from Gastonia, appointed Whitener superior court solicitor of the Fourteenth District on 26 Jan. 1946 to complete an unfulfilled term. He was elected to a full term the following November and reelected in 1950 and 1954. In 1946 he was named a member of the General Statutes Commission, and in 1947–49 he served on the Commission to Study Improvement of Administration of Justice in the state. In 1948 and 1960 he was a delegate to the Democratic National Convention. Elected to the Eighty-fifth and the five succeeding Congresses, he served from 3 Jan. 1957 to 3 Jan. 1969 but was an unsuccessful candidate in 1968 and 1970.

Whitener was a member of the Masonic order and other fraternal, civic, and professional groups. He was awarded honorary degrees by Belmont Abbey College and Pfeiffer College. A member of the Methodist church, he married Harriet Priscilla Morgan on 26 Sept. 1942, and they had three sons and a daughter: John Morgan, Laura Lee, Basil Lee, Jr., and Barrett Simpson.

SEE: *Biog. Dir. Am. Cong.* (1989); David L. Corbitt, ed., *Public Addresses and Papers of Robert Gregg Cherry, Governor of North Carolina, 1945–1949* (1951); *North Carolina Manual* (1967); William S. Powell, ed., *North Carolina Lives* (1962); Raleigh *News and Observer*, 30 Sept. 1951, 21 Mar. 1989; Cameron P. West, *A Democrat and Proud of It* (1959); *Who's Who in American Politics, 1977–1978* (1977).

WILLIAM S. POWELL

Whitener, Daniel Jay *(17 Aug. 1898–23 Mar. 1964),* historian and college administrator, was born near Newton, the son of Daniel Wilfong, a farmer and schoolteacher, and Alice Amanda Kincaid Whitener. After attending local schools, he served in the U.S. Army during World War I, then entered Catawba College, located at that time in Newton. He transferred to The University of North Carolina, from which he received a bachelor's degree in 1922 and a master's degree in 1923; his thesis was titled "The Rise of the Standing Committee System in Congress."

Whitener began his career in education as a high school principal in Catawba County in 1923. In 1928–29 he was acting head of social sciences at Lenoir-Rhyne College in Hickory. Determined to apply his talents to higher education, he returned to The University of North Carolina and earned a Ph.D. degree, awarded in 1932. That fall he accepted appointment as professor of history and government and chairman of the social studies department at Appalachian State Teachers College; he was the school's first faculty member to hold a doctorate. In the next twenty-three years Whitener probably influenced more history teachers than any other person in North Carolina, for nearly all future teachers majoring in social studies were exposed to his popular classes. From 1955 until his death he was dean of the college.

Although Whitener devoted most of his energies to his classes and other college and community activities, he was the author of important books and articles on history and education. His revised Ph.D. dissertation appeared in 1945 as *Prohibition in North Carolina, 1715–1945* in the James Sprunt Studies in History and Political Science. In 1949 the same series published his article, "Public Education in

North Carolina during Reconstruction, 1865–1876." He also wrote a centennial souvenir booklet called *History of Watauga County, North Carolina, 1849–1949, and History of Appalachian State Teachers College, 1899–1949* (1949); the booklet, *Local History: How to Find and Write It* (1955); and a grade school textbook, *North Carolina History* (1958). The *North Carolina Historical Review, South Atlantic Quarterly*, and other journals carried his articles on education, temperance, Prohibition, and the dispensary movement.

State and local history was Whitener's passion, for he believed that all good history depended on a solid local foundation. His political and professional affiliations attested to that interest: He served on the Watauga County Board of Education and was an officer of the Historical Society of North Carolina, North Carolina Literary and Historical Association, and Western North Carolina Historical Association. At the annual banquet of "Lit and I list" in 1958, he delivered his presidential address, "Education for the People," in the presence of former President Harry S Truman, who also was a speaker. A founder and first executive director of the Southern Appalachian Historical Association, Whitener was instrumental in the inauguration of the outdoor drama, *Horn in the West*, on whose board of directors he served. Under appointment by Governor Luther H. Hodges, he was a member of the executive board of the North Carolina Department of Archives and History from 1959 until his death. In that capacity he drafted and shepherded through the General Assembly a bill encouraging improved teaching of state and local history in the public schools. No ivory-tower historian, Whitener also busied himself in community and civic clubs and in the activities of the Boone Methodist Church.

On 23 Sept. 1925 he married Annie Laurie Choate of Sparta. They had one son, Carr Choate (Jack), a career officer in the U.S. Air Force. Whitener died of a heart attack and was buried in Mount Lawn Cemetery, Boone. In 1975 the building formerly housing Appalachian Elementary School was renovated and renamed D. J. Whitener Hall for offices and classrooms of the college's departments of history, political science, and sociology.

SEE: *Durham Sun*, 23 July 1975; *Heritage of Watauga County, North Carolina*, vol. 1 (1984); H. G. Jones, "Daniel Jay Whitener: Historian" (typescript, North Carolina Collection, University of North Carolina Library, 1975); William S. Powell, ed., *North Carolina Lives* (1962); *Who's Who in the South and Southwest* (1961); *Who Was Who with American Notables*, vol. 4 (1961–68).

H. G. JONES

Whitfield, James Vivian (*23 July 1894–19 Nov. 1968*), foreign service officer and legislator, was born in Seven Springs, the son of James A. and Vivian Powers Whitfield. He received his college preparatory education at Wallace High School in Wallace and at the Horner Military School in Oxford. After graduation from The University of North Carolina in 1915, he returned to Horner as commandant, a position he held until 1917, when he became a military instructor at the university and began graduate study. Majoring in economics, he received a master's degree in 1919.

With the end of World War I and his graduate education completed, Whitfield entered the U.S. Foreign Service in which he served until 1927. He filled tours of duty in Uruguay, Argentina, Cuba, and Mexico.

Leaving the foreign service, he stayed briefly in New York City before settling in Pender County, N.C., where he became a farmer. He served in the North Carolina

General Assembly between 1945 and 1953, first in the house of representatives and then in the senate. Whitfield's efforts for a clean environment and the protection and development of natural resources began in the legislature. In 1947 he was chairman of the House Committee on Conservation and Development and introduced a bill to authorize the issuance of bonds for the development of the ports of Wilmington and Morehead City. His first attempt failed, but in the senate he sponsored successful legislation that authorized the original $7.5 million bond issue for this purpose. He helped establish the Stream Sanitation Commission in 1951 and served as chairman from 1956 to 1967, when the commission was merged into the State Board of Water and Air Resources. Governor Dan K. Moore appointed him chairman of the new board, where he served until his death.

Whitfield was president of the Moore's Creek Battleground Association, and in the period 1943–50 he was a director of the North Carolina Farm Bureau. At various times he was president of the Forest Farmer's Association, vice-president and director of the North Carolina Forestry Association, a member of the State Council of Natural Resources, president of the Off Shore Highway Association, and chairman of the Commission on Interstate Cooperation. He also was a member of the Wallace Baptist Church and of several civic organizations.

He married Vivian Bartlett Stevens, and they had a son, John S. The elder Whitfield died in Burgaw and was buried in Rockfish Memorial Cemetery, Wallace. A portrait of him hangs in the lobby of Pender Memorial Hospital, at Burgaw, an institution he helped establish.

SEE: John L. Cheney, Jr., ed., *North Carolina Government, 1585–1979* (1981); Daniel L. Grant, *Alumni History of the University of North Carolina* (1924); Greenville *Daily Reflector*, 21 June 1970; North Carolina State House of Representatives, *Joint Resolution No. 256* (1969); Raleigh *News and Observer*, 12 Mar. 1956 (portrait), 20 Nov. 1968; *Wilmington Star News*, 20 Nov. 1968.

GARY F. TRAWICK

Whitfield, Nathan Bryan (*19 Sept. 1799–27 Dec. 1868*), legislator, planter, and entrepreneur, was born at Pleasant Plains, Lenoir County, the son of Bryan and Winifred Bryan Whitfield. He attended The University of North Carolina from 1813 to 1816 but left following a dispute with the faculty. Young Whitfield was elected to the House of Commons in 1821 and to the North Carolina Senate in 1822, 1823, 1825, and 1827. He served on the Council of State in 1828 and 1830 and was commissioned a major general in the state militia.

After several trips to Florida and Alabama, Whitfield in 1835 moved his family and slaves to Marengo County, Ala., where he acquired large tracts of land. Eight years later he purchased from George S. Gaines a farm that he named Marlmont near the town of Demopolis. There he located his household and began constructing a sizable residence.

By 1850 Whitfield owned 167 slaves plus real estate valued at $53,000. The new house took on even more substantial proportions as Whitfield, an accomplished amateur artist, architect, and engineer, designed more and more rooms. By about 1860, Gaineswood, as he called the mansion, was a showplace. During the preceding decade Whitfield had assisted in building an Episcopal church and a plank road and had increased his fortune to $142,000 in real estate and $300,000 in personal property (mostly slaves).

Whitfield married Elizabeth Watkins in February 1819,

and they had twelve children: Sarah Watkins, Winifred Bryan, Nathan Bryan, Jr., Nathan Bryan III, Mary Elizabeth, Bryan Watkins, Needham George, Edith Winifred, James Bryan, Sarah Elizabeth Watkins, Edith James, and Betsy Winifred. His first wife having died on 4 Nov. 1846, Whitfield on 26 July 1857 married Bettie of Baltimore, and she bore him one daughter, Natalie Ashe.

The completion of Gaineswood and the period of Whitfield's greatest wealth coincided with the outbreak of the Civil War. Both his fortune and health suffered during the conflict; he died three years after it ended and was buried in Riverside Cemetery, Demopolis. In the following decades Gaineswood was neglected as it passed through several ownerships. Recognizing the structure as architecturally the most important mansion in the state, the Alabama Historical Commission in 1971 undertook its restoration. It is now a National Historic Landmark and open to the public.

SEE: Walter S. Patton, "General Nathan Bryan Whitfield and Gaineswood," 1972 (typescript, files of the Alabama Historical Commission); Whitfield Family Papers (Alabama State Archives).

H. G. JONES

Whitford, John Dalton *(1825–13 Sept. 1910)*, legislator, railroad president, soldier, and historian, was born in New Bern, the son of Hardy (1793–1841) and Mary James Clark Whitford (1800–1884), who were married on 23 Dec. 1820 at New Bern. His maternal grandfather was Elijah Clark (8 Nov. 1774–19 June 1862), a mayor of New Bern, trustee of the New Bern Academy, and sheriff and trustee or treasurer of Craven County. At the grandfather's home on 11 May 1809 the First Baptist Church of New Bern was organized.

When only twenty-one, John D. Whitford was elected mayor or "intendant" of New Bern. Under his administration local ponds were drained, creeks filled, streets improved, and brick sewers constructed. The old sewers were among the first, if not the first, underground aqueducts of the kind built in North Carolina. At his instigation was erected the shellrock wall that still protects Cedar Grove cemetery. In his day such a wall was essential, for hogs, goats, and cattle were allowed to roam through the city streets.

Upon organization of the state-controlled Atlantic and North Carolina Railroad company in New Bern, with the first general meeting of stockholders held during 20–21 July 1854, he was elected its president; he continued in the post for the next decade with gratifying success except during the Civil War. Whitford was a director of the North Carolina Railroad Company, which operated trains between Goldsboro and Charlotte. Also a later member of a state commission for the improvement of Neuse River, he was a delegate in 1884 to the River and Harbor Convention at Savannah, Ga.; for a period thereafter he was superintendent of certain river improvements in the state authorized by the federal government.

An early member of the New Bern Light Infantry, formed during the mid-nineteenth century, Whitford on 4 July 1859 was publicly presented with a pitcher cast from silver dollars donated by its members "as a token of respect and esteem." From this company he and Jacob Brookfield became the first two volunteers for the Confederate army. He had been a member of the 1861 state convention that passed the ordinance of secession. Whitford was commissioned first a captain, then a major, and later a colonel.

Serving with General Lawrence O'B. Branch, he partici-

pated in the Battle of New Bern in March 1862 and in the fighting around Kinston and other parts of eastern North Carolina. For some time he had charge of the transportation of troops and munitions of war through the state. He was also state agent for the purchase of cavalry equipment and other war materials. His work was so effective that he received a complimentary letter from General Robert E. Lee. At the close of the war he was elected to represent Craven County in the 1865–66 state senate, getting more votes than any candidate for public office had ever received in the county up to that time.

In June 1866 Whitford was again chosen president of the Atlantic and North Carolina Railroad, and he was re-elected several times afterwards. At the 1867 stockholders' meeting he was officially thanked for his "able and efficient administration of the affairs of this company during the last year. More especially does this company owe to his untiring energy the funding of the remainder of the debt due to the state, and thereby rendering it possible for the stockholders to realize within a reasonable time some return for their investments."

Immediately after his war service he was instrumental in establishing at New Bern the firm of Whitford, Dill and Company, shipping and commission merchants and agents for Murry, Ferris and Company, owners of the first line of steamers operated successfully between New Bern and New York.

For more than sixty years he was a member of St. John's Lodge No. 3, AFAM, of New Bern. In the mid-nineteenth century he financed the decorating of its Blue Lodge room, including the notable trompe l'oeil paintings still colorful on its walls and ceiling in the late 1990s. Apparently unique in the state, they helped qualify the Masonic temple for the National Register of Historic Places. In 1869 he was named a director of the North Carolina Masonic Mutual Life Insurance Company, formed in 1867 by Masons at New Bern. The lodge instructed a committee in June 1886 to work with Whitford in presenting claims against the government for occupation and damage in the lodge room and temple during the Civil War. Later he was thanked for his "kind efforts" in this regard, which helped to obtain a cash award for the lodge.

A longtime leader in the First Baptist Church, he was the author of "The Home Story of a Walking Stick—Early History of the Baptist Church at New Bern, N.C." Available in manuscript, it is a virtual history of his native town.

After his death and burial in Cedar Grove Cemetery, New Bern, Judge Romulus A. Nunn of New Bern wrote of him:

> Probably no man has ever lived in New Bern who was more useful in developing certain features of our commercial life. He provided transportation by land and water. Undoubtedly the people of the east who now enjoy the fruits of his labor owe to him a debt of gratitude, which should never be forgotten.
>
> He lived to see the great celebration which was held in 1910 to commemorate the 200th anniversary of the founding of the town. As a courtesy to him, the parade was arranged to pass his house and he was visibly affected as he witnessed from his window the floats depicting the events in our history in which he had had so large a share and which he had written up in his admirable manuscript, "Historical Notes." A few months later . . . he died and closed a long life of honor and usefulness, in the 86th year of his age.

Also interred in Cedar Grove Cemetery were his parents; his wife, Jeanie Reid Whitford (1829–65); two sons, William (1851–86) and Clark (1860–1902); and two daughters, Mary James Clark (1853–72) and Orleana (15–23 July 1865). Surviving him were a son, Reid, and three daughters: Jeanie Reid Whitford Fife, Bessie Whitford Slover, and Johnes D. Whitford Bailey.

SEE: Gertrude S. Carraway, *Years of Light* (1944); John L. Cheney, Jr., ed., *North Carolina Government, 1585–1979* (1981); John D. Whitford, "The Home Story of a Walking Stick—Early History of the Baptist Church at New Bern, N.C." (manuscript in New Bern–Craven County Public Library, New Bern); John Dalton Whitford Papers (North Carolina State Archives, Raleigh).

GERTRUDE S. CARRAWAY

Whitford, John Nathaniel *(4 May 1835–26 June 1890)*, merchant, Confederate officer, and planter, was born near Vanceboro, the son of Nathan, a farmer who represented Craven County in the General Assembly in 1862–64, and Hannah Bright Whitford. After his early education at the South Lowell school in Orange County, Whitford was employed as a merchant until the outbreak of the Civil War, when he volunteered his services and was made captain of artillery by Governor Henry T. Clark.

Assigned command of Company I, Tenth North Carolina (First Artillery) Regiment, Whitford was attached to the forces of Brigadier General Lawrence O'B. Branch defending New Bern. When Union general Ambrose Burnside's powerful forces attacked Branch's defenses on 14 Mar. 1862, Whitford and his company constituted part of the garrison of formidable Fort Thompson on the Neuse River. During the battle the company engaged the Union gunboat fleet passing up the river to attack New Bern. Following the defeat and withdrawal of Branch's forces to Goldsboro, Whitford was placed in charge of a special battalion of troops consisting of his own and three other artillery companies. Later this battalion was disbanded when it was evident that Burnside's forces would not advance farther inland, and Whitford's company was sent to the defenses of Wilmington, garrisoning the Old Brunswick Battery.

After a time the service of Whitford's company was changed from artillery to infantry, and the men were stationed around Swift Creek, Craven County, as scouts watching the movement of Union forces. Here they had skirmishes with Union troops. In April 1863 the company was augmented by the addition of a number of other companies to form the First Battalion of Local Defense Troops. Whitford was given command of this organization and promoted to major on 14 May 1863. The battalion soon became known as the Whitford Battalion of Partisan Rangers, and Whitford led it in numerous partisan operations against Union forces. On 18 Jan. 1864 the battalion was augmented by still more companies and was commissioned the Sixty-seventh North Carolina Regiment, with Whitford elected as its colonel. The regiment contained nine companies of infantry and one of cavalry and, rather than being turned over to regular Confederate service, was retained by North Carolina as a state unit, subject to the orders of the governor and limited to service within the boundaries of the state.

On 1–3 Feb. 1864 Whitford's new regiment participated in the unsuccessful efforts of Major General George Pickett's Confederate forces to recapture New Bern. It was to have taken part in the assault on Fort Anderson on the northern bank of the Neuse, but the attack never materialized and the entire operation against New Bern was abandoned. Early in May Whitford led his regiment in yet another attempt to capture the city by Major General Robert F. Hoke. For a time Whitford's regiment led the advance, driving back Union outposts near Deep Gully, and then remained to protect the rear of Hoke's forces while they attempted to capture the city. Again the attack was called off, as most of Hoke's command was ordered immediately to Virginia, and Whitford's regiment continued to serve in eastern North Carolina on picket and relief duty for Confederate garrison troops at Plymouth, Washington, and Kinston.

Whitford also led numerous raids and forays against Union forces. He and part of his command were sent to Fort Branch, at Hamilton, on the Roanoke River and there repelled an effort by Union gunboats to steam up the river and destroy the Weldon Railroad bridge. In March 1865 his regiment joined other Confederate forces to halt the advance of Sherman's and Cox's Union armies through the state. It was present at the Battle of Southwest Creek, or Wise's Forks, again under General Hoke. At Goldsboro, Whitford was assigned command of a brigade consisting of his own and the Sixty-eighth North Carolina regiment. The brigade was present on the battlefield of Bentonville, 19–22 Mar. 1865, and following that Whitford was instructed to operate with it on detached service from the main Confederate army. Moving by way of Tarboro and Greenville, he was to attack and harass Sherman's lines of communication. This was a daring assignment, but Colonel Whitford was quite competent in partisan tactics and of course familiar with the area. Unfortunately, soon afterwards it was learned that General Joseph Johnston's Confederate army had surrendered to Sherman and the war was virtually over. Accordingly, Whitford disbanded his two regiments and returned home to New Bern.

After the war he became the successful owner of the Whitford Hardware Store in New Bern and of a substantial plantation in Jones County. He was twice married, first to Mary E. Williamson, a descendant of North Carolina's first governor, Richard Caswell, on 26 Nov. 1861, with whom he had six children. After her death he married Sidney A. Taylor of Beaufort on 3 Jan. 1884. He was buried in the Whitford family cemetery in Jones County.

SEE: Walter Clark, ed., *Histories of the Several Regiments and Battalions from North Carolina*, 5 vols. (1901); Weymouth T. Jordan, comp., *North Carolina Troops, 1861–1865: A Roster*, vols. 7–8 (1979–81); Louis H. Manarin, comp., *North Carolina Troops, 1861–1865: A Roster*, vols. 1, 3 (1966, 1971); J. S. Tomlinson, *Assembly Sketch Book, Session 1883* (1883); *War of the Rebellion: The Official Records of Union and Confederate Armies*, ser. I, vols. 9, 18, 27, 29, 33, 42, 46–47, 51 (1883–97); Mrs. Vera H. Whitford and Miss Marjorie Williams (Colonel Whitford's granddaughter), personal contact.

PAUL BRANCH, JR.

Whiting, Seymour Webster *(15 Aug. 1816–2 Jan. 1855)*, banker, railroad official, and poet, was a native of Stratford, Conn. When about eighteen years of age, he moved to Raleigh and obtained a license to practice law. Whiting, however, chose a business rather than a legal career. He became an officer in the State Bank and for several years, beginning about 1839, served as treasurer of the Raleigh and Gaston Railroad.

Whiting also achieved recognition as a poet, with his works appearing in several nineteenth-century literary collections, including Mary Bayard Clarke's *Wood-Notes* (1854), Calvin H. Wiley's *North Carolina Reader* (1859), and Eugene G. Harrell and John B. Neathery's *North Carolina Speaker* (1887). His best-known poem seems to have been "Alamance," a celebration of the Regulator battle as a glorious struggle for freedom.

On 19 May 1841 he married Hannah M. Stuart, of Raleigh, the daughter of John Stuart. They had eight children: George M., Mary Stuart, Elizabeth F., Margaret, Seymour, Hannah, Brainard, and Chester. Whiting died in Raleigh and was buried in Oakwood Cemetery.

SEE: Eugene Clyde Brooks, *North Carolina Poems* (1912); Raleigh and Gaston Railroad, Reports (North Carolina Collection, University of North Carolina, Chapel Hill); *Raleigh Register*, 21 May 1841, 17 Jan. 1855; Whiting's estate papers in Wake County Estates Records, 1770–1941 (North Carolina State Archives, Raleigh).

ROBERT G. ANTHONY, JR.

Whiting, William Henry Chase (*22 Mar. 1824–10 Mar. 1865*), Confederate general and defender of Wilmington, a descendant of prominent seventeenth-century English settlers in Massachusetts, was born in Biloxi, Miss., the son of Levi, an officer in the regular army, and Mary A. Whiting, both natives of Massachusetts. Intellectually gifted, he was graduated at the head of his class from the Boston Public School, Georgetown College (1840) where he completed the four-year course in two, and West Point where he was top man in the class of 1845. It is said that his academic record at the U.S. Military Academy was not surpassed until the graduation of Douglas MacArthur in 1903.

Like most of the best graduates of West Point, Whiting was assigned to the engineers and as a result missed active duty in the Mexican War. Most of his antebellum career was spent at work on river and harbor improvements and fortifications on the Gulf, California, and South Atlantic coasts. In the latter assignment he was lighthouse engineer for the two Carolinas. Among other projects between 1856 and 1858 he reopened communications between Albemarle Sound and the Atlantic Ocean. During a two-year tour on the lower Cape Fear River in North Carolina, he married, on 22 Apr. 1857, Katherine Davis Walker, the daughter of John and Eliza Morehead Walker of Wilmington and Smithville, who survived him, childless.

Promoted to captain in 1858, Whiting spent the last few years before the Civil War in Georgia and Florida. Apparently he was the senior U.S. officer present at Savannah when state authorities took over that city's military posts in January 1861. Despite his Northern antecedents and a mother, brother, and two sisters in New York, Whiting unhesitatingly sided with the South during the secession crisis, and he resigned his commission on 20 Feb. 1861. Soon afterwards he joined General G. P. T. Beauregard as a staff engineer at Charleston. Following a brief appointment as inspector general of North Carolina in April, he was commissioned chief of staff to General Joseph E. Johnston in Virginia. Johnston praised highly his services in the destruction of the Harpers Ferry arsenal and in the rapid transfer of his Army of the Shenandoah from western Virginia to Manassas, as a result of which he was promoted to brigadier general on the field of First Manassas on 21 July 1861. The next year Whiting commanded a division with conspicuous ability in the heavy fighting of the Peninsula, Seven Pines, Valley, and Seven Days' campaigns. His services as both staff officer and combat commander were commended by Beauregard, Johnston, and T. J. Jackson, the last an officer not lavish with his praise.

In November 1862 Whiting became commander of the military district of the Cape Fear with headquarters at Wilmington, and six months later he was promoted to major general. To him belongs much of the credit for the skillful innovations in construction and artillery placement that developed Fort Fisher into one of the strongest

defense works in the world. As the defender of Wilmington, Whiting seems to have enjoyed public esteem in North Carolina, although he was criticized by D. H. Hill for lack of cooperation with operations outside his immediate sphere. For his part, Whiting repeatedly requested transfer to a more active front, an application that was granted in May 1864 at the special request of General Beauregard.

Beauregard, who was defending Petersburg with a small force while the main armies were still north of the James River, planned an ambitious offensive against the Federals at Bermuda Hundred on the Peninsula. Traveling rapidly to Petersburg by rail, Whiting was assigned a small scratch division and an important role in a plan that required him to cover Petersburg while conducting part of a complicated offensive. In the ensuing action of Port Walthill Junction, he failed to get his force into action and carry out his mission. A rumor circulating at the time that he was debilitated by drink or drugs seems to have been unfounded, and it is more likely that his deficiency was the result of prolonged loss of sleep. He was not disciplined in any manner but was returned to duty at Wilmington by his own request.

Whiting's forces repulsed a major Federal advance on Fort Fisher at Christmas 1864, but when the attacking expedition returned the next month he was superseded, on orders from Richmond, by Braxton Bragg. Discovering that Bragg intended to evacuate Wilmington without using the reinforcements that had been sent there and thus to sacrifice Fort Fisher, Whiting entered the fort during one of the heaviest naval bombardments in history. Perhaps remembering the recent blot on his reputation, he apparently determined to share the fate of the outnumbered garrison and outgunned fort with which he had been so long connected. He declined to take over the command from Colonel William Lamb but serving as a volunteer took a notable part in the hand-to-hand fighting during the last assault on the fort. While leading a countercharge on 15 Jan. 1865, Whiting was shot twice in the leg. Taken prisoner with the survivors of the garrison, he was sent to Fort Columbus (now Fort Jay) on Governors Island, New York harbor, where he wrote an official report maintaining that Fort Fisher could have been held if Bragg had committed the reinforcements on hand, an opinion shared by other officers present and by North Carolina public opinion. Although his wounds were not thought to be fatal, Whiting declined from depression and the hardships of his midwinter transport and confinement; he died within eight weeks, shortly before his forty-first birthday. After well-attended services at Trinity Episcopal Church, New York City, he was buried in Greenwood Cemetery, Brooklyn. In 1900 his remains were reinterred in Oakdale Cemetery, Wilmington.

Whiting was described as soldierly in appearance and of below average height. A wartime likeness that has been widely published seems to portray a slender, intelligent, sensitive face. An adopted North Carolinian, he was one of not a few Northerners who gave the last full measure of devotion to the Southern Confederacy. Whiting undoubtedly possessed superior ability but lacked the opportunity and perhaps the stolidity of character required of the most successful military commanders.

SEE: Claude B. Benson, *An Address . . . Containing a Memoir of the Late Major-General William Henry Chase Whiting* (1970); Walter Clark, ed., *Histories of the Several Regiments and Battalions from North Carolina in the Great War,* vol. 2 (1901), *Confederate Veteran,* 2–3, 6–8, 10–11, 13–24, 26–33, 35–38, 49 (1893–1932), and index by Louis H. Manarin, ed.; George W. Cullum, comp., *Biographical Register of the Officers and Graduates of the U.S. Military Academy*, vol. 2 (1891); Douglas S. Freeman, *Lee's Lieutenants*, 3 vols. (1942); Rod Gragg, *Confederate Goliath: The Battle of Fort Fisher* (1991); information from local records furnished by Mrs. E. M. McEachern, Wilmington; "Journal of William Henry Chase Whiting, 1849," in Ralph P. Bieber, ed., *Exploring Southwestern Trails, 1846–1854* (1938 [portrait]), vol. 7, *The Southwest Historical Series*; *Nat. Cyc. Am. Biog.*, vol. 4 (1895 [portrait]); James Sprunt, *Chronicles of the Cape Fear River, 1660–1916* (1916).

CLYDE WILSON

Whitmell, Thomas (1713–88), legislator and Indian agent, the son of Thomas and Elizabeth Whitmell, was born in Virginia shortly before the family moved to North Carolina. His grandfather, Thomas Whitmell, the first of the family in Virginia, settled in Charles City County prior to 1690. According to extant Bible records for the family of Thomas and Elizabeth Whitmell, Thomas was the oldest child and only surviving son. Five daughters, however, reached maturity.

The public career of Thomas Whitmell began on 14 Oct. 1736, when, although he was only twenty-three, the North Carolina Assembly appointed him, Robert West, John Gray, and one Spiers general commissioners for Indian affairs. On 18 Sept. 1737 the Council of the colony allowed Whitmell and Gray £77 for running the dividing line between Crown lands and those of Lord Granville. Granville was the only Carolina Proprietor who refused to sell to the Crown, and the northern section of the colony had been laid out as his district. A justice of Bertie County in 1739, Whitmell was sheriff for many years. In 1749 he was a vestryman for Society Parish, and in 1750 he was mentioned in county records as a merchant. He also represented the county in the Assembly during the period 1754–60 and while so serving was delegated to deal with Indian affairs. Late in 1757 some Indians appeared in New Bern to visit Governor Arthur Dobbs, producing a scalp to demonstrate that they had been in action against the "Swanees." Whitmell was allowed £10 from the public treasury to be laid out in presents for the Indian allies.

Whitmell had a special relationship with the remnants of the Tuscarora tribe who were then living on a reservation in Bertie at a place still called Indian Woods. In 1752 Moravian Bishop A. G. Spangenberg visited North Carolina to look for land for his followers who planned to move to the colony from Bethlehem, Pa. On 12 September of that year he wrote that Whitmell had taken him to the Indian settlement, noting that Whitmell had been a trader among the Indians and spoke their language fluently. He commented further that Whitmell was one of the wealthiest men in Bertie County and enjoyed an excellent reputation among all classes.

At the beginning of 1755, when the Tuscarora in the county had one hundred fighting men, the colony called on them for help in the French and Indian War then in progress. In May 1757 Whitmell was awarded £40 for the relief of the wives and children of the warriors from the Tuscarora and Meherrin tribes who had gone to the assistance of Virginia. In 1771 Governor William Tryon issued him a warrant to raise militia for use against the insurgents in the War of the Regulation. This proved to be Whitmell's last public service of record.

Thomas Whitmell married Elizabeth West, the daughter of Robert and Martha Blount West. His will, written in Bertie County on 15 Dec. 1779, was filed first (but not probated) in Martin County. He lived many years after making his will, but it probably was filed in Martin County

because he left 250 acres there to a son who was out of the country at the time. The will, on file at the State Archives in Raleigh, mentions other children, grandchildren, and relatives. Three grandsons who had moved to Alabama were dead without heirs by 1827, thus ending the surname. Nevertheless, Whitmell as a given name has continued to be used among descendants into the late twentieth century.

SEE: John B. Boddie, *Southside Virginia Families*, vol. 1 (1955); John L. Cheney, Jr., ed., *North Carolina Government, 1585–1979* (1981); *North Carolina Genealogical Society Journal* 6 (1980); William L. Saunders, ed., *Colonial Records of North Carolina*, vols. 4–6, 8 (1886–90); Benjamin B. Weigiger III, ed., *Charles City County, Virginia, Court Orders, 1687–1695* (1980).

CLAIBORNE T. SMITH, JR.

Whitsett, William Thornton (5 Aug. 1866–22 Mar. 1934), educator and historian, was born in what is now Whitsett, near Gibsonville, in eastern Guilford County. Of Scots-Irish and German ancestry, he was the only son of Joseph Bason and Mary Foust Whitsett. Instructed by tutors and in public and private schools, Whitsett began a career in education by teaching in public schools at age sixteen. He later attended The University of North Carolina (1886–88) and North Carolina College in Mount Pleasant (A.M., 1901; Ph.D., 1903).

Influenced by the efforts of Brantley York and other pioneer educators who had attempted to establish a school for young boys on the same site, Whitsett in 1888 founded Whitsett Institute, succeeding the earlier Fairview Academy. The village of Whitsett grew around the institute in later years. A boarding academy for boys, the institute operated until 1918, when it was destroyed by fire. Averaging from 200 to 250 students per year in liberal arts, business, and teacher preparatory courses, it drew the student body predominantly from North Carolina and other southern states and many from Cuba. In fact, Whitsett Institute was the first school in North Carolina to accept Cubans and the first to enroll Cuban students at The University of North Carolina. Whitsett also conducted teacher institutes in several counties in the state.

He organized the North Carolina Association of Academies and was secretary and treasurer of the North Carolina Teachers Assembly, serving as its president in 1905–6. A trustee of The University of North Carolina from 1897 to 1919, he was also a member of the Guilford County Board of Education from 1897 to 1918 (chairman, 1906).

In his later years Whitsett, a member of several literary and historical societies, turned to historical research and occasional literary activity, publishing numerous brief works. A volume of his poetry, *Saber and Song*, was published by Whitsett Institute in 1917, and he wrote short reviews and essays on contemporary literary trends, often for regional newspapers. As an active Lutheran, he devoted much of his historical research to the early church history of North Carolina. As the official historian of Guilford County, he carried out extensive research into the early history of Guilford and Alamance counties, particularly into the genealogical histories of their older families. The results of his research were often given in addresses before family reunions, where Whitsett was a familiar figure in the late 1920s and early 1930s. Many of these addresses later appeared as *Whitsett's Historical Monographs*. Whitsett also addressed civic clubs and state and national Lutheran groups. He received an honorary doctor of letters from Lenoir-Rhyne College in 1933.

In 1906 Whitsett married Carrie Brewer of Salem. A graduate of Salem College, she became president of the Women's Lutheran Missionary Societies of North Carolina and of the State Federation of Home Demonstration Clubs (33,000 members in 1929). The couple had four children: Lucille Elizabeth, William Thornton, Carrie Brewer, and Joseph Gordon.

Whitsett died at his home after a brief illness and was buried in the graveyard of Friedens Evangelical Lutheran Church near Gibsonville.

SEE: Daniel L. Grant, *Alumni History of the University of North Carolina* (1924); *Greensboro Daily News*, 23 Mar. 1934; J. H. Joyner, "Men of Mark in North Carolina," in Charles L. Van Noppen Papers (Manuscripts Department, Duke University Library, Durham); Raleigh *News and Observer*, 23 Mar. 1934; William Thornton Whitsett Papers (portraits) (Southern Historical Collection, University of North Carolina Library, Chapel Hill); *Who's Who in America, 1934–1935* (1934).

GILBERT EDWIN SOUTHERN, JR.

Whitson, Edward Maxwell (20 Mar. 1895–30 July 1973), cartoonist and illustrator, was born in Asheville, the son of William Roberts and Ida May Keith Whitson. In 1915–16 he attended The University of North Carolina, where he drew cartoons for the student yearbook, *Yackety Yack*, and the humor magazine, *Tar Baby*. Afterwards he became a cartoonist and illustrator for various magazines and newspapers. Among the state papers that used his work were the *Asheville Citizen*, the *Asheville Review*, and the *Asheville Times*. Popular magazines of the time that published his cartoons included *Judge* and *Country Gentleman*, while many others presented his commercial work.

He died at his home in Holly Hill, Fla., survived by his wife.

SEE: Alumni Files (University of North Carolina, Chapel Hill [portraits]); Daniel L. Grant, *Alumni History of the University of North Carolina* (1924).

WILLIAM S. POWELL

Whittlesey, Sarah Johnson Cogswell (24 Aug. 1824–14 Feb. 1896), writer, was born in Williamston, the oldest child of Luman and Elizabeth G. Peale Whittlesey. Her younger brother was Oscar Columbus. She had two half brothers, Edgar Augustus and Joseph Adolphus, by her father's first marriage to Sarah Johnson Cogswell, who died in 1821 and for whom his next child was named. Luman Whittlesey was a native of Washington, Conn., a descendant of New England forebears going back to 1635, and an 1816 graduate of Yale. His second wife was a North Carolinian. He moved to Williamston to teach at the new Williamston Academy in 1818. In 1830 he had a farm and a store in Palmyra but moved back to the academy in 1841. After an unfortunate business venture with his son-in-law, he taught in Edenton in 1846 and finally settled in Alexandria, Va., in 1848.

During these peregrinations Whittlesey was sooner or later joined by his daughter Sarah. Educated at home until she was fourteen, she attended a school in Hamilton for two years and was graduated from La Vallee Female Seminary in Halifax County in 1841. On 19 June 1842 she married Henry A. Smith, of Lenox, Mass., recently arrived in Williamston to conduct an evening writing school. Apparently she agreed to this unfortunate union to please her beloved father and brother. Four years later she abandoned Smith because of his "jealous tyranny,"

assisted in her escape by her friend D. William Bagley, who arranged to bring her and her trunk down a ladder from her locked room on the second floor of the house, and who transported her to a Roanoke River vessel making an instant departure. In 1850 she and her husband were divorced, and she resumed her maiden name.

Though her first literary effort had appeared in the *Edenton Sentinel* in the summer of 1846, it was not until she was comfortably at home with her parents and brother in Alexandria that her exceptionally honed talents for genteel "false-feminine" sentimentality got into full stride. The *Spirit of the Age* (Raleigh), the *Williamston Mercury*, and even the *Southern Literary Messenger* carried her poems. The *Times* of Greensboro serialized her short novels "The Hidden Heart," "Reginald's Revenge; or, The Rod and Reproof," and "The Broken Vow," and the *Southern Field and Fireside* (Raleigh) announced "The Unwedded Wife; or, Wrong and Remorse." The title of *Heart-Drops from Memory's Urn* (1852) indicates the nature of the poems therein. Seven moral tales in which pure-minded heroines are pursuing or being pursued appear in *The Stranger's Stratagem; or, the Double Deceit, and Other Stories* (1859). Virginia is the scene of her novel *Herbert Hamilton; or, The Bas Bleu* (1868). Yet *Bertha the Beauty: A Story of the Southern Revolution* (1872) is Miss Whittlesey's "glory," for this lengthy autobiographical novel, with scenes in Williamston and Palmyra, has a detailed narrative of the struggles of the long-suffering heroine with her wicked husband. To the poems in *Spring Buds and Summer Blossoms* (1889) she added some verses by her brother Oscar Columbus titled *Idle Hours*.

SEE: James Wood Davidson, *Living Writers of the South* (1869); *Greensboro Times*, 2 June 1860; David and Elizabeth Tornquist, three articles on the Whittlesey family, in sec. 5, Tobacco ed., Williamston *Enterprise*, August 1959.

RICHARD WALSER

Wicker, Rassie Everton (6 Mar. 1892–17 Oct. 1972), land surveyor and local historian, was born near Cameron at Hall's Planer in Moore County, the son of James A. and Lucretia Millis Wicker. He attended the Cameron School and entered the Agricultural and Mechanical College in Raleigh in 1910. When elected surveyor of Moore County in 1912 he left college and, except for a few brief intervals, worked as a surveyor for the remainder of his life. In time he was licensed as a civil engineer.

In 1918 Wicker enlisted in the U.S. Army and served overseas with the Fifty-sixth Pioneer Infantry in the Meuse-Argonne offensive. Returning home to Pinehurst he worked with Pinehurst, Inc., where he headed all local civil and landscape engineering for many years with the exception of a period during World War II when he was draftsman and plant engineer at the General Machinery and Foundry Company in Sanford.

Although he was a man of many talents and interests, his main love was for Moore County and its history. It is said that he measured and mapped most of Moore and was an authority on it, describing the geography of the county as a surveyor and the traditions of its people as a historian. He was an organizing member of the North Carolina Society of County Historians and served as its president. Wicker rendered the same service to the Moore County Historical Society. He frequently took interested persons on long hikes to points of interest in the Sandhills, and with Paul Green and Phillips Russell of Chapel Hill he searched out sites of early Highland Scots homes, including the residence of Flora MacDonald and graves of her children.

His monumental work on land deeds, grants, will books, court records, and Revolutionary data was published by the county historical society in 1971. He also wrote *The Home of Flora MacDonald in North Carolina* and *Owners and Occupants of the House in the Horseshoe on Deep River*. In addition to his interest in local history, Wicker was an amateur astronomer, musician, botanist, mathematician, and master craftsman. He designed and made over fifty pieces of furniture, including three grandfather clocks.

On 13 June 1917 he married Mary Loving of Cameron, and they had a daughter and a son. A lifelong Presbyterian, he was buried at Old Bethesda Cemetery, Aberdeen.

SEE: H. Clifton Blue, "A Brief Glimpse of Rassie E. Wicker," in *Ancient Miscellaneous Records of Moore County* (1971); Beth Cadiau, "Curiosity of Rassie E. Wicker," an undated clipping from the Southern Pines *Pilot* in possession of Katharine Melvin; Tony McKenzie, "Tribute to the Late Rassie E. Wicker," Carthage, *Moore County News*, 9 Nov. 1972; Raleigh *News and Observer*, 18 Oct. 1972; Southern Pines *Pilot*, 18 Oct. 1972.

KATHARINE S. MELVIN

Widgery, Alban Gregory (*9 May 1887–22 Mar. 1968*), teacher and philosopher, was born in Bloxwich, Staffordshire, England, the son of John Thomas and Ellen Thomas Widgery. His father was a liberal Anglo-Catholic clergyman of very old Devonshire stock; his mother was the daughter of a Welsh farmer of South Wales. When he had qualified through preparatory schooling, he was admitted to St. Catharine's College, Cambridge. In his first year he was a Prizeman but was raised to Scholar at the beginning of his second year. Graduated with a bachelor of arts degree in 1908, he received a master of arts degree from the same institution four years later. He never completed the prescribed work for the doctor of philosophy degree for this reason: "I am convinced that when I took my degree of Bachelor of Arts I had a far wider and more thoroughgoing knowledge of classical works of philosophy than the best of Doctor of Philosophy students with whom I have been concerned in America, even at the time they took the degree."

Throughout his collegiate and research work, his special interest was the philosophy of religion. Widgery "trained himself to be more constructive than critical, explicitly conscious of the importance of a proper balance in one's consideration of the present and the future." With that thinking, he pointed his life towards "an academic career as a scholar and teacher." In Great Britain beginning in 1908 he taught at Bristol University, St. Andrews University, and Cambridge University; he also held appointments in India at Bombay and Amalner. In 1928–29 he taught at Bowdoin College, Brunswick, Maine, and was at Cornell University, Ithaca, N.Y., in 1929–30.

Duke University was ready to expand its Department of Philosophy in 1930 and selected Professor Widgery to become chairman. He stepped down as head of the department in 1946 but continued to teach until 1952. He spent the academic year 1953–54 at Amherst College in Massachusetts and then made his home on a mountain near Winchester, Va., where he died at age eighty-one.

Before going to Duke University Widgery contributed to both scholarly and popular periodicals, was the author of a number of books, and saw some of his addresses and lectures in print. After moving to North Carolina he continued to publish; most notable among his later works are *Living Religions and Modern Thought* (1936), *Christian Ethics in History and Modern Life* (1940), and *What Is Religion?*

(1953). He was not an expansive "joiner," but two groups commanded his interest: the North Carolina Philosophical Society, of which he was founder in 1935, and the American Theological Society, of which he was president in 1940. He expressed considerable satisfaction in the fact that he was an Englishman but said that he found both America and India "always stimulating." He was described as an incomparable teacher, fluent, provocative, and erudite. Those who knew him in the classroom called him "a gracious individual, stern in his demand for individual thinking [and] never allowing placidity in his students." His role in helping to make Duke University a center of intellectual thought and research in a strategic period of its establishment and growth was acknowledged.

Widgery married Marion Wilkins on 21 July 1915, and they were the parents of Rhoda, Claude, and Rolande. Claude died as a young man.

SEE: Lewis White Beck, "Alban Gregory Widgery, 1887–1968" (News Bureau Clipping File, Duke University Archives, Durham); W. J. Burke and Will D. Howe, *American Authors and Books, 1640–1940* (1943); Robert F. Durden, *The Launching of Duke University, 1924–1949* (1993); A. Lawrence, ed., *Who's Who among Living Authors of Older Nations*, vol. 1 (1931); *National Union Catalog, Pre-1956 Imprints* (1979); *Who's Who in the South and Southwest* (1950); Alban G. Widgery, "A Philosopher's Pilgrimage," 1961 (Duke University Archives, Durham).

C. SYLVESTER GREEN

Wiggins, Archibald Lee Manning (*9 Apr. 1891–7 July 1980*), business executive, was born in Durham, the son of Archie Lee and Margaret London Council Wiggins. In 1913 he was graduated from the University of North Carolina, where he was editor of the student annual, the *Yackety Yack*, and a member of the Order of the Golden Fleece, a student leadership organization. As a result of advice from two of his professors, he began working with a seed company in Hartsville, S.C., and rapidly advanced to more responsible positions with the firm as well as elsewhere in South Carolina and in the nation.

Over the years Wiggins occupied significant positions in both private and public life, in some of which he began in less important posts and moved to the top. He became chairman of the board of three railroad companies and was president of banks and bankers' associations, including the South Carolina Bankers Association and the American Bankers Association. He was publisher of two newspapers and a lecturer between 1941 and 1957 in the Graduate School of Banking at Rutgers University; undersecretary in the U.S. Treasury Department (1947–48) and special assistant to the secretary (1948–53); and a member of the regional advisory council of the Federal Reserve System. He served as a college trustee, treasurer of an endowment fund, a director of the American Cancer Society, and president of both the Crippled Children's Society of South Carolina and the state's Conference on Social Work. A member of the Southern Baptist church, he held a seat on its home mission board and was president of the Baptist Foundation of South Carolina.

Wiggins received honorary degrees from The University of North Carolina, Duke University, the University of South Carolina, and Campbell College. He married Pauline Lawton in 1915, and they had four children: Margaret Coke, Joseph Lawton, Lee Manning, and Pauline Elizabeth.

SEE: Columbia, S.C., *The State*, 31 Dec. 1946; Daniel L. Grant, *Alumni History of the University of North Carolina*

(1924); *Who Was Who in America* (1981); A. Lee M. Wiggins, *Autobiography of A. Lee M. Wiggins* (1969 [portrait]).

WILLIAM S. POWELL

Wiggins, Ella May (ca. Mar. 1900–14 Sept. 1929), textile worker, balladier, and union organizer, was born in the mountains of Cherokee County, near Bryson City, the daughter of James and Elizabeth Maples May. Her father, a lumberjack, was killed in a job-related accident when Ella May was a young girl, and she and her brother Wesley went to work in a nearby mill to help support the family. Trained as a spinner, she married a fellow mill employee, Johnny Wiggins, who, like her father, had worked in the timber region, and together they left the mountains to seek work in the burgeoning industrial region of Gaston County.

Ella May and Johnny Wiggins settled in Bessemer City, where they both took jobs in the American Mill. Ten years later, at age twenty-nine, Ella May had borne seven children and been deserted by her husband. She sought work on the night shift in order to stay with her children by day. Money and food were scarce, and two of the children, suffering from malnutrition, developed rickets and died of respiratory infections. Living near her brother's family with a man named Charley Shope, Wiggins became the central figure in a network of family and friends to whom she looked for support. Her ties to the poor white and black families who lived near her developed into relationships that contradicted the rigid racial mores of the early twentieth-century South. Ella May understood the plight of southern black workers, for their lives mirrored her own situation. She came to realize that her future was inextricably bound to the collective destiny of those who lived around her, both black and white.

These stirrings in Ella May Wiggins's mind became more focused as economic and racial issues in the southern Piedmont gained public attention in the late 1920s. The leading textile county in the South, Gaston, formed the geographic center of the New South's textile industry. In twenty years, between 1909 and 1929, the number of mills in the county more than doubled until there were over one hundred in a ten-mile radius. Built with new equipment, these factories were caught in an economic squeeze brought on by declining markets and increasing prices of raw materials, machinery, and labor. Faced with a tightening economy, manufacturers began to change their operations in the late 1920s, initiating a series of layoffs and increasing the workload of weavers and spinners. Workers named the new system the "stretch-out," which, according to one North Carolina textile worker, meant: "They'd put more work on you for the same pay until the people couldn't stand it no longer." Employers in many mills not only increased hours but also reduced wages. But the margin between subsistence and starvation was already too narrow for most southern mill hands to tolerate a wage cut. Workers like Ella May Wiggins, struggling to support five children on $9.00 a week, faced a decrease in wages with disbelief, anger, and action.

Wiggins and other Gaston County workers, having suffered the effects of a stretch-out introduced during 1927–28, began to organize the fight for higher wages and better conditions during the spring of 1929. The Loray Mill in Gastonia, the county's largest employer with over 2,000 workers, became the focus of efforts by the National Textile Workers' Union (NTWU) to establish a southern stronghold. On 25 March five union members lost their jobs at the Loray Mill, precipitating a strike on 30 March of 1,000 workers on 30 March. On 1 April close to 1,800 workers stayed out on strike, but the Manville-Jenckes Company, northern owners of the Loray Mill, refused to negotiate with the workers and ignored the NTWU demands for a minimum weekly wage of $20, a forty-hour week, equal pay for women, abolition of the stretch-out, and union recognition. On 4 April the state militia arrived to quell scuffles on the picket line; by 20 April many strikers had returned to work, the militia had withdrawn, and newly sworn local deputies enforced an ordinance against picketing. The union retained a loyal force of several hundred members who continued to picket in front of the five-story red brick mill and to win converts among those workers who had returned to work.

The strike at the Loray Mill engendered support from workers in nearby mills, and in early April 1929 Wiggins and fellow workers from the American Mill in Bessemer City staged a spontaneous walkout and joined the NTWU. The American Mill contingent helped sustain the Loray strikers, and Wiggins emerged from among the workers in Bessemer City as a strong leader. Described by one NTWU organizer as "a person of unusual intelligence," Ella May frequently led the singing among workers attending mass meetings at Loray. She seemed to understand each facet of the complex Gastonia situation and spoke to many groups of workers about the strike and the union, urging men and women alike to stand firm in their commitment. Most significantly, Wiggins sought cooperation between black and white workers. Independently, she organized a group of black workers, friends and neighbors who lived near her in Stumptown, a small community outside of Bessemer City, and brought them into the NTWU.

Events in the Gastonia strike escalated during the late spring and early summer. In mid-April a mob tore down the NTWU Gastonia headquarters building and raided the strikers' relief store. Ironically, the raid did not result in apprehension of members of the mob, but in the arrest of nine union men. Such an outrageous assault brought nationwide publicity for the strikers, the denunciation of the raid by southern liberals, and increased relief contributions from across the country. The spirit of the strikers was aroused, and large crowds attended union rallies and joined the picket line. In early May the Manville-Jenckes Company evicted over sixty families of strikers from company housing, and the union set up a tent colony, called New Town, for the homeless strikers. Several weeks later Ella May Wiggins discovered that the spring she used for drinking water had been poisoned. She went into Loray to report the incident and found that there had been prowlers around the tent colony. In response, the strikers increased their guard.

On the evening of 7 June 1929 deputies disrupted a union rally and broke up a picket line composed of women and children; later the same night a shooting incident in the tent colony injured one unionist and four policemen and fatally wounded the chief of the Gastonia police, D. A. Aderholt. Seventy-one union members and organizers were arrested and held incommunicado in the Gastonia city jail for one week. Most were released, but sixteen defendants were detained in the Gaston County jail for six additional weeks before being indicted for the shootings. Following two days in court in Gastonia, the defense obtained a change of venue to Charlotte, in neighboring Mecklenburg County. On 26 August the trial of the sixteen union members began. After days of testimony a mistrial was declared on 9 September, when one of the jurors reportedly went violently insane upon viewing an effigy of Chief Aderholt brought into the courtroom by the prosecution. That evening in Gastonia an angry mob of over one hundred men formed in response to the dismissal of the case, wrecked the union's headquarters in

Gastonia and Bessemer City, and terrorized, kidnapped, flogged, and threatened to kill several union members. The next day, 10 September, the mob re-formed, raided the Charlotte headquarters of the International Labor Defense (ILD), the group handling the case for the NTWU defendants, and attempted to remove one NTWU organizer from jail in order to lynch him. To protest such lawlessness the NTWU announced that a huge rally of all union people in Gaston County would be held in South Gastonia on 14 September.

As the events of the Gastonia strike unfolded, Wiggins recorded them in song. The strike, the union, and the men and women in jail all became the subjects of her ballads. After the murder of the police chief, Wiggins sang to the strikers: "Come all of you good people, And listen to what I tell; The story of Chief Aderholt, The Man you all knew well." Drawing from traditional mountain ballads, Wiggins put new words to old tunes while carefully observing the conventions of the unfamiliar songs. Her lyrics, "Toiling on life's pilgrim pathway—Wheresoever you may be, It will help you fellow workers—If you will join the ILD," became a popular strike song. Wiggins, or Ella May, as she was always called, sang before large groups of workers in fervent tones, with great seriousness. As folklorist Margaret Larkin wrote in 1929, Wiggins's songs were "better than a hundred speeches." This quiet young woman's untaught alto voice rang out simple, monotonous tunes that captivated those who listened. Her six-versed ballad entitled "The Mill Mother's Lament" documented her personal struggle to support her children:

> We leave our homes in the morning,
> We kiss our children good bye,
> While we slave for the bosses,
> Our children scream and cry.
>
> But understand, all workers,
> Our union they do fear,
> Let's stand together, workers,
> And have a union here.

This ballad, as each of Wiggins's songs, expressed her faith in the union, the only organized force she had encountered that promised her a better life.

Ella May was to sing her ballads and speak to the strikers at the NTWU protest rally on 14 Sept. 1929. Early that morning the Manville-Jenckes forces mobilized hundreds of men, including many newly sworn-in deputies and vigilantes, to disperse those attending the rally; they set up roadblocks in all directions. A short time before the rally was to begin, a group of twenty-two unarmed union members, strikers, and sympathizers, Ella May Wiggins among them, traveled in a truck from Bessemer City to the rally site south of Gastonia. Wiggins had insisted that none of the strikers carry weapons. The truck was halted at one of the roadblocks where armed men ordered the workers to return to Bessemer City "on pain of death." The strikers turned their truck around and headed away from the meeting, as ordered, only to be pursued by several carloads of armed men. After a short distance, one of the cars passed the truck and stopped in its path. The truck driver, unable to brake quickly enough, ran into the car, and workers riding in the back of the truck tumbled out. For a moment, while the others scrambled back into the truck, Ella May Wiggins stood in the bright sunlight, leaning against the side rail. Then, the mob opened fire and she fell into the truck bed gasping, "Oh, my God, they've shot me." Wiggins died in the arms of Charley Shope, who had stood near her in the truck. The other

strikers, two of whom were wounded, fled into a nearby field as the mob continued to fire their guns.

Immediately after Ella May Wiggins's death the Communist leadership of the NTWU announced that there would be a one-day strike to protest the murder; the ILD demanded the arrest of the men who had killed Wiggins. Union leaders were certain that Ella May had been deliberately shot for her interracial organizing and her role as balladeer and speaker. Claimed by the NTWU as a martyr for its cause, she was heralded in union and ILD campaigns nationwide. Among North Carolina liberals opposed to the Communist NTWU but appalled by the turn of events in Gastonia, Wiggins became a cause célèbre. Frank P. Graham, president of The University of North Carolina, wrote: "Her death is, in a sense, upon the heads of us all." He argued that he saw in Wiggins "not her mistaken Communism, but her genuine Americanism."

After her death, pressure from local strikers, North Carolina liberals, and national political organizations led Gaston County mill owners to reduce working hours to fifty-five per week, to improve conditions in the mills, and to extend welfare work in the textile villages. Although liberal groups throughout the state and national organizations such as the American Civil Liberties Union and the ILD severely criticized Gaston County authorities, no bills of indictment were returned for the killing of Ella May Wiggins until six weeks after the murder when Governor O. Max Gardner, himself a mill owner, reopened the investigation. At that time, five employees of the Loray Mill were indicted. Despite the existence of over fifty eyewitnesses, however, these men were acquitted in a trial held in Charlotte in March 1930.

In the decades after 1929 Ella May became both a major figure in historical accounts of the Gastonia strike and a legendary character in southern fiction by authors including Mary Heaton Vorse, Loretto Carroll Bailey, Myra Page, and Grace Lumpkin. A mill hand known as the "songstress of the mill workers," she remains North Carolina's most famous folk heroine.

Ella May Wiggins was buried in an unmarked grave in Bessemer City's public cemetery. Wreaths from the NTWU, the ILD, and the Workers' Defense League adorned her plain pine coffin. The calm dignity of the funeral, attended by hundreds of mill workers, marked the end of the NTWU's organizing efforts in Gastonia. Wiggins, pregnant at the time of her death, was survived by her five children: Myrtle, 11; Clyde, 8; Millie, 6; Albert, 3; and Charlotte, 13 months. The children assumed their mother's maiden name to help hide their identity in the face of threats made to them amid the publicity surrounding their mother's murder. They were put in an orphanage. On 14 Sept. 1979, fifty years after the day of the 1929 shooting, North Carolina women from the Gastonia area held a memorial service in Bessemer City and placed a permanent marker on the grave of Ella May Wiggins.

SEE: Loretto Carroll Bailey and James Osler Bailey, "Strike Song: A Play of Southern Mill People" (typescript, North Carolina Collection, University of North Carolina, Chapel Hill); Fred E. Beal, *Proletarian Journey: New England, Gastonia, and Moscow* (1937); *Charlotte Observer*, 15–18 Sept. 1929; Eugene Feldman, "Ella Mae [sic] Wiggins: North Carolina Mother Who Gave Her Life to Build a Union," *Southern Newsletter* 2 (March–April 1957), and "Ella May Wiggins and the Gastonia Strike of 1929," *Southern Newsletter* 4 (August–September 1959); Frank Porter Graham Papers (Southern Historical Collection, University of North Carolina, Chapel Hill); *Labor Defender* 4 (October 1929); Margaret Larkin, "The Story of Ella May," *New*

Masses 5 (November 1929), "Tragedy in North Carolina," *North American Review* 208 (1929), and "Ella May's Songs," *Nation* 129 (9 Oct. 1929); Grace Lumpkin, *To Make My Bread* (1932); Dan McCurry and Carolyn Ashbaugh, eds., "Gastonia, 1929: Strike at the Loray Mill," *Southern Exposure* 1 (Winter 1974); F. Ray Marshall, *Labor in the South* (1967); National Organization of Women, *Let's Stand Together: The Story of Ella Mae [sic] Wiggins"* (pamphlet, Metrolina chap., Charlotte), September 1979; Dorothy Myra Page, *Gathering Storm* (1932); Liston Pope, *Millhands and Preachers* (1942); Raleigh *News and Observer*, September 1929; George Brown Tindall, *The Emergence of the New South, 1913–1945* (1967); Tom Tippett, *When Southern Labor Stirs* (1931); Mary Heaton Vorse, *Strike!* (1930); Mrs. Merritt Wandell, Waverly, N.Y., personal contact; Vera Buch Weisbord, *A Radical Life* (1977); *Workers and Allies: Female Participation in the American Trade Union Movement*, Smithsonian Institution (1975)

MARY E. FREDERICKSON

Wilcox, Cadmus Marcellus (*29 May 1824–2 Dec. 1890*), Confederate soldier, was born in Wayne County, the second of four children of Reuben, a native of Connecticut, and Sarah Garland Wilcox, a noted North Carolina beauty. His parents moved to Tipton County, Tenn., where he grew up. After attending the University of Nashville, he entered the U.S. Military Academy and was graduated in 1846. During the Mexican War he served under both Zachary Taylor and Winfield Scott, distinguishing himself at Chapultepec, where he led the storming party. Appointed aide to General John A. Quitman he was brevetted first lieutenant for his gallantry. He served in Florida before becoming assistant instructor of infantry tactics at West Point from 1852 to 1857. His failing health caused him to secure a year's leave for travel in Europe. In 1859 he published *Rifles and Rifle Practice* and a year later translated a French work on Austrian evolutions of the line.

Commissioned captain on 20 Dec. 1860, Wilcox was in New Mexico when the Civil War began. When Tennessee seceded, he reluctantly resigned his commission on 8 June 1861, accepting the colonelcy of the Ninth Alabama Infantry. He fought with the regiment at First Manassas. Promoted to brigadier general on 21 Oct. 1861 and to major general in January 1864 to rank from 3 Aug. 1863, he served with the Army of Northern Virginia until Appomattox.

A steady but unspectacular commander, Wilcox established a record as a reliable officer. During the Seven Days' campaign his brigade sustained casualties amounting to 56 percent. His defense of the army's right at Salem Church during the Chancellorsville campaign was notable, and his unsupported attack on 2 July 1863 at Gettysburg which carried to the crest of Cemetery Ridge became one of the great "ifs" of the war. His stubborn defense of Fort Gregg at Petersburg on 2 Apr. 1865 enabled Lee's army to cover its withdrawal and move westward towards Appomattox.

A lifelong bachelor, Wilcox moved after the war to Washington, D.C., where he lived with the widow and two children of his older brother, a Texas congressman who died during the war. He declined offers for commissions in the Egyptian and Korean armies, refusing to leave his adopted family. In 1886 President Grover Cleveland appointed him chief of the railroad division of the General Land Office, a position he retained until his death. Wilcox wrote a *History of the Mexican War* which his niece, Mary Rachel Wilcox, edited and published posthumously (1892). At his funeral, four pallbearers were former general officers of the U.S. Army and four were former Confederate generals. Wilcox was buried in Oak Hill Cemetery, Washington, D.C.

SEE: *DAB*, vol. 20 (1936); Clement A. Evans, *Confederate Military History*, vol. 8 (1899); Douglas S. Freeman, *Lee's Lieutenants*, 3 vols. (1942–44); *Nat. Cyc. Am. Biog.*, vol. 11 (1901); Ezra Warner, *Generals in Gray* (1959).

JEFFRY D. WERT

Wilcox, John Alexander (*18 Apr. 1819–7 Feb. 1864*), lawyer and congressman, was born in Greene County, the son of Reuben and Sarah Garland Wilcox. The family moved to Tennessee where he attended school; afterwards he settled in Aberdeen, Miss., and became secretary of the Mississippi state senate until the War with Mexico. During the war he was commissioned a lieutenant, served as adjutant, and was promoted to lieutenant colonel. Reuben Davis, a congressman from Mississippi and fellow resident of Aberdeen, is credited with securing advancement for Wilcox. Wilcox enlivened his camp in times of discouragement, and his men had unbounded confidence in him.

As a successful lawyer, Wilcox employed wit, humor, and anecdote to advance his cases. He was described as handsome, jovial, and popular with everyone. Twice a candidate for Congress, he was elected in 1851 from Mississippi's Second Congressional District. At that time he was a Union Whig and the only man to win the favor of both Whigs and independents. Although he had little political experience, his perception was keen and clear. Nevertheless, his bid for a second term in 1853 was unsuccessful.

Following this defeat, Wilcox moved to San Antonio, Tex., and became a member of the Know-Nothing (American) party. He also joined the Knights of the Golden Circle, a secret, pre–Civil War, pro-Southern organization. At the Know-Nothing state convention in Austin on 21 Jan. 1856, he was chosen a presidential elector for the state at large in the election of 1856. Wilcox again changed his political affiliation in January 1858, when he attended the Texas Democratic State Convention and made a speech pledging allegiance to the Democratic party. He went to Austin in January 1861 as a delegate to the secession convention and was a member of the Committee on Address, which prepared the Ordinance of Secession.

Wilcox was elected to represent the Texas First District in the House of Representatives of the First Congress of the Confederate States and was reelected to the Second Congress. He took office on 18 Feb. 1862 for his first term but died suddenly of apoplexy ten days before the First Congress adjourned.

In Congress Wilcox was appointed to the Inauguration Committee, Committee on Territories and Public Lands, Committee on Military Affairs, and Committee on Enrolled Bills. His correspondence with constituents indicated his deep interest in Texas affairs, and he worked hard for his state. The Confederate Congress paid for Wilcox's funeral expenses when he was buried in Hollywood Cemetery, Richmond, Va. He was survived by his wife and two children.

SEE: Thomas B. Alexander and Richard E. Beringer, *The Anatomy of the Confederate Congress* (1972); *Biog. Dir. Am. Cong.* (1905); Richard N. Current, ed., *Encyclopedia of the Confederacy*, vol. 4 (1993); Reuben Davis, *Recollections of Mississippi and Mississippians* (1889); *Journals of the Congress of the United States of America*, vols. 2–3, 5–7 (1904–5); Dorothy Williams Potter, comp., *1820 Federal Census of*

Greene County, North Carolina (1973); Dunbar Rowland, *History of Mississippi: The Heart of the South* (1925); Walter Prescott Webb, *Handbook of Texas*, vol. 2 (1952); *Who Was Who in America, 1607–1896* (1963).

JUANITA ANN SHEPPARD

Wilder, Gaston Hillary *(1 Apr. 1814–5 Aug. 1873)*, lawyer, legislator, and railroad president, was the son of Hillary (1784–1849), a planter and legislator, and Esther Avera Wilder, both natives of Johnston County. While Gaston was still a boy, his father established a plantation, Wilder's Grove, in Wake County, four or five miles east of Raleigh. Here young Wilder spent his childhood and youth before attending the Bingham School at Hillsborough. He was graduated from The University of North Carolina in 1838, making a commencement address on "The Spirit of the American Government." He then began to read law in Raleigh under William Henry Haywood, was licensed to practice in 1841, and received the customary M.A. degree in 1843. Wilder was a member of a committee that supervised the opening of the new capitol in 1840.

While practicing law in Raleigh, he became interested in the political scene, ran for a seat in the legislature, and represented Wake County in the lower house from 1842 to 1847. In the latter year President James K. Polk appointed him paymaster, with the rank of major, of the North Carolina regiment in the War with Mexico. Wilder anticipated the development of a statewide system of railroads, and in 1852 he persuaded the legislature to appropriate funds to finance study and planning for railroad expansion in western North Carolina. From 1854 to 1857 he again served in the General Assembly, this time representing Wake County in the senate.

In 1858 Wilder became president of the Raleigh and Gaston Railroad. On 1 June 1859, during a visit of President James Buchanan to North Carolina to make the commencement address in Chapel Hill, he arranged for a locomotive, named the *William A. Graham*, painted white and its brass polished, to pull a "Special" consisting of seven cars to carry U.S. soldiers, artillerymen, a military band, and guests from Weldon to Durham Station. The president and Governor John W. Ellis had the use of Wilder's own president's car. From the station to Chapel Hill, however, everyone traveled by buggy, arriving, it was noted, "covered with dust."

The Civil War ended Wilder's career as a railroad president but made him an active participant in the conflict as the receiver of funds collected from the sale of property sequestered by the state from Union sympathizers. This duty lasted throughout the war, near the end of which Wilder, fearing capture and punishment by Federal authorities, fled with his son to Chester, S.C., in a mule-drawn wagon. In 1866 he returned, took the oath of allegiance to the United States, and was pardoned.

Both Confederate and Union troops had alternately occupied his plantation; livestock had been removed, crops used by the soldiers, and fence rails burned. But the buildings still stood, and he began rehabilitating them. Some of his slaves remained on the plantation for nine years. Work at Wilder's Grove and his law practice in Raleigh occupied him until early in 1873, when he suffered a fractured leg. His health failed rapidly, and he died in the late summer and was buried on the plantation. Newspaper obituaries were glowing in their characterization of him, employing such terms as "impressive speaker," "plain in his habits and manners," "hospitable," "one of the most popular citizens of Wake County," and "he lived and died an honest man."

In Johnston County on 1 May 1850 Wilder married Sarah Elizabeth Hinton (b. 5 July 1831). The administration of his estate lists as heirs S. E., H. M., F. H., Samuel, Katy A., William, Gaston H., Sarah E., and James Wilder.

SEE: Kemp P. Battle, *History of the University of North Carolina*, vol. 1 (1907); Daniel L. Grant, *Alumni History of the University of North Carolina* (1924); J. G. de Roulhac Hamilton, ed., *The Papers of William A. Graham*, vol. 3 (1960); Elizabeth Reid Murray, *Wake: Capital County of North Carolina*, vol. 1 (1983); *North Carolina Biography*, vol. 5 (1919); *Raleigh Daily News*, 8 June 1859, 6–7 Aug. 1873; Mrs. Jane Rogers (Chapel Hill, a descendant), personal contact; John H. Wheeler, *Historical Sketches of North Carolina* (1851); Wilder's will (North Carolina State Archives, Raleigh).

RALPH M. WATKINS

Wiley, Calvin Henderson *(3 Feb. 1819–11 Jan. 1887)*, writer and North Carolina's first superintendent of common schools, was born in the Alamance section of Guilford County, the son of David L. and Anne Woodburn Wiley. Of Scots-Irish origin, he was descended from the William Wiley who moved from Pennsylvania to North Carolina in 1754.

Wiley attended the Caldwell Institute in his native county and was graduated with high honors from The University of North Carolina in 1840. Admitted to the bar in 1841, he settled in Oxford, where he began editing the Oxford *Mercury*. He sometimes contributed to his own paper the "memoirs" of "Demi-John," a fictitious down-home–type character. In 1843 Wiley gave up the newspaper and soon relinquished his law practice, moving back to Guilford to help his family and to continue work on his novel *Alamance*.

His *Alamance; or, The Great and Final Experiment* (1847) was followed by *Roanoke; or, Where Is Utopia?* (1849), which was published in England as *Adventures of Old Dan Tucker and His Son Walter* (1851). Other books included *Utopia: A Picture of Early Life in the South* (1852), *Life in the South* (1852), and *Scriptural Views of National Trials* (1863). Wiley was a founder of the *Southern Weekly Post* in Raleigh and of the *North Carolina Presbyterian*.

In addition to awakening readers to their state and culture through his writing, he became interested in the politics of education. Elected to the General Assembly by his home county (1850–52), he was instrumental in passing the law establishing the office of state superintendent of the common schools in 1852. He served as superintendent from 1 Jan. 1853 until 26 Apr. 1865, when all state offices were declared vacant after the surrender of the Confederacy.

During his thirteen-year tenure as superintendent, Wiley worked tirelessly for the establishment of common schools and for the improvement of education throughout North Carolina. He traveled widely, at his own expense, giving speeches on education. He contributed newspaper articles, made annual reports, and created and maintained interest in public education. Wiley established and edited the *Common School Journal* (later, *North Carolina Education*) and in October 1856 at a meeting in Salisbury organized the state education association. In cooperation with Braxton Craven, he began teacher training institutes. He established standards and examining boards for teachers that required annual certification of teachers and organized county school units giving instruction to county superintendents and school committeemen. During his superintendency the state office began to prescribe and distribute uniform textbooks for use in the schools.

His book *The North-Carolina Reader* (1851) was published at his own expense and became a standard school text. On becoming superintendent, he disposed of his copyright, sold all of the copies and the plates at cost, and refused to accept any further remuneration for his work.

Wiley promoted universal education, advocating acceptance and support of the common schools. During the Civil War he urged Governor John W. Ellis not to divert school funds to the war effort; Ellis supported Wiley's position and the schools were kept open. The annual report for 1863 showed that 50,000 children were enrolled in the common schools. The percentage of illiteracy within North Carolina's voting population declined from 29.2 in 1850 to 23.1 by 1860, with the decrease being attributed to the schools' movement spearheaded by Wiley.

Using his communication skills as a writer and speaker, he devoted himself to finding ways to awaken a spirit of pride in the people. Wiley saw education as a means of overcoming the backwardness and poverty of his state. He began his mission through books and newspapers and later turned to elective and then appointive office to serve his fellow citizens. He built respect for the schools both within and outside the state. At the National Convention of Educators in Cincinnati in August 1858, he was on the program with Horace Mann. Wiley corresponded with his counterparts in other states, and among his papers are letters seeking his counsel from as far away as California.

Through his vision of a strong, vigorous system of common schools meeting standards set forth by the state, Wiley completely changed the concept of public education in North Carolina. By 1860 the state was considered to have the best public school system in the South. He is now known as the "Horace Mann of the South." Wiley's contribution was in creating an awareness of the state's cultural backwardness and in providing ways of overcoming it. He was a part of a new age in North Carolina. That the state was deprived of his services during the last twenty-odd years of his life was a loss not easily overcome. It was well into the twentieth century before Wiley's standards and guidelines from the state level began to influence public education again.

A religious person, Wiley in later years continued to serve his people, primarily through his work for the American Bible Society in Eastern and Middle Tennessee 1869–74 and afterwards in Salem, N.C. He had been licensed to preach by the Presbyterian church in 1855 and was ordained in 1866. In Salem he helped establish the local public school system.

On 25 Feb. 1862 Wiley married Mittie Towles of Raleigh, and they had seven children. He died at his home in Salem.

SEE: Samuel A. Ashe, ed., *Biographical History of North Carolina*, vol. 2 (1905); William K. Boyd, *History of North Carolina*, vol. 2 (1919); Howard Braverman, "Calvin Henderson Wiley: North Carolina Educator and Writer" (Ph.D. diss., Duke University, 1951); *DAB*, vol. 20 (1936); James Wood Davidson, *Living Writers of the South* (1869); *Who Was Who in America*, vol. 1607–1869 (1963).

BARBARA M. PARRAMORE

Wiley, Mary Callum *(14 July 1875–10 Mar. 1965)*, teacher, author, editor, and historian, was born in Salem, the daughter of Calvin Henderson and Mittie Towles Wiley. Her father was consecutively a lawyer, editor, member of the General Assembly, author of the *North Carolina Reader* and other educational publications, and North Carolina's first superintendent of public instruction. As the motivating force in the establishment of Winston's own graded school system, he became the first chairman of the Winston School Board and provided the school's first graduate—his daughter, Mary Callum Wiley.

Miss Wiley entered Woman's College (then the State Normal School) in Greensboro as a junior and was graduated in 1894. In those days, a graduate received a diploma but no degree. She returned to Woman's College in 1903 for a year to earn an A.B. degree. In 1946 she was awarded an honorary degree by her alma mater for her years of service as a "master teacher," author, editor, and historian.

Of the forty-nine years she spent in the classroom, forty-seven were in Winston-Salem, first at West End School, then at the Cherry Street High School, and, from 1923 to 1945 at Reynolds High School, where she was head of the Department of English. In the *Winston-Salem Journal* of 10 Mar. 1953, a staff reporter wrote: "Miss Mary, as she was affectionately called by her thousands of students, was an institution. But when her former pupils are asked to say why this is so, you quickly discover they are not talking in gray, granite-like institutional terms. Instead they seem to be describing a state of mind—a rather gay, somewhat strange and unpredictably wonderful state of mind."

Her teaching methods combined strict discipline (with a silent tongue and a speaking eye), enthusiasm, chuckles, smiles, and wit, portraying her irrepressible sense of humor. In clear evidence were her well-planned lessons. Her students enjoyed the variety of content and tempo to prevent any dullness, her "inspirational approach," her own dramatic impersonations of literary characters, and her pranks to enliven the class hour. She had strict requirements in regard to specific procedures, academic effort, "good study habits," and manners. For instance, students knew that on entering her class they were expected to say, "Good morning, Miss Mary." They could also expect her cheerful reply, "Good morning," and their name. Students knew to stand to recite, to enter through the back door and leave through the front door. "Class," she would sometimes say, "arise. We will now sing our state song." As one display of her strong loyalty to her beloved state, in an ardent—if not melodic—voice she would begin:

> "Carolina, Carolina, heaven's blessings attend her
> While we live we will cherish, protect and defend her."

Inspired by her enthusiasm, the class knew to chime in as heartily as she.

At other times she would instruct her students to condense a three-hundred-word paragraph into thirty words "with the exact core meaning of the author but in your own words." Many graduates of Reynolds High School, later in college or in the business world, praised "Miss Mary" for her insistence on a "perfect précis" and for instilling in them the understanding and appreciation of good literature. They were also grateful for the lessons in grammar and the drills that relentlessly weeded out the errors that she called "insults to our beautiful and effective English language."

She contributed many articles to *The State* magazine, and her essays on education were widely published in the state press. For many years following her retirement she wrote a daily column, "Mostly Local," for the Winston-Salem newspaper. An active member of the North Carolina Literary and Historical Association, she donated her writings and those of her father to the North Carolina Department of Archives and History; books and other family materials were given to The University of North Carolina Library in Chapel Hill.

After a long illness, Mary Wiley died at the age of ninety and was buried in Salem Cemetery.

SEE: William S. Powell, ed., *North Carolina Lives* (1952 [portrait]); *Some Pioneer Women Teachers of North Carolina* (1955); *Winston-Salem Journal-Sentinel*, 8 Mar. 1953, 10 Mar. 1965; *Winston-Salem Twin City Sentinel*, 29 May 1945, 10 Mar. 1965.

MARJORIE SIEWERS STEPHENSON

Wilkes, Jane Renwick Smedberg (22 Nov. 1827–19 Jan. 1913), Charlotte civic leader, was born in New York City, the daughter of Carl Gustave (1781–1845), a Swedish merchant, and Isabella Renwick (1797–1862) Smedberg. Her parents owned an estate in the Catskill Mountains. Shortly after Jane married former New Yorker John Wilkes (31 Mar. 1827–6 July 1908) on 20 Apr. 1854, the couple took up residence for about four years near St. Catharine's Mills in Mecklenburg County. By the mid-1870s they had moved to West Trade Street in Charlotte.

Although Mrs. Wilkes was brought up in the Presbyterian church, after her marriage the family belonged at one time to St. John's Episcopal Church in High Shoals (Gaston County) and later to St. Peter's Episcopal Church in Charlotte. She and her husband had nine children, several of whom died very young: Charles (d. 6 Aug. 1873), Jeanie Jeffrey (d. 5 Nov. 1868), Rosalie (September 1860–9 Oct. 1925, m. Lockwood Jones), Agnes (m. A. G. Rankin), John Frank (May 1864–4 Feb. 1953), Paul (d. 5 May 1894), Eliza Isabella (d. 19 Aug. 1868), James Renwick (July 1871–13 Jan. 1939), and Isabella Wilkes, whose tombstone in the family plot indicates the death date of 1 Sept. 1857.

Mrs. Wilkes's civic efforts centered around two institutions that she helped establish in Charlotte: St. Peter's Hospital and the Good Samaritan Hospital. She was on the board of managers of St. Peter's and nurtured the cause from suggestion to beginnings in the Church Aid Society and at last to a two-room building on East 7th Street in 1876. She served as president, secretary, and treasurer at various times during its growth. In the 1880s she also assisted in the establishment of the Good Samaritan Hospital for blacks.

Her other affiliations in Charlotte were with the Ladies Memorial Association, the Stonewall Jackson Chapter of the United Daughters of the Confederacy, the Woman's Auxiliary to the Board of Missions of the Episcopal Church, and the Episcopal Churchwomen. She helped place the United Daughters of the Confederacy tablet marking the Confederate Navy Yard on 3 June 1910. Mrs. Wilkes was the executive secretary of the Woman's Auxiliary in the Diocese of North Carolina for the terms 1882–95. In 1906 she was appointed "permanent president," having been a "President of former years." In the records of the diocesan Episcopal Churchwomen, she was listed as having been appointed honorary secretary of that organization in 1897 and president for the years 1904–9.

She died at her home on West Trade Street. The funeral, conducted by the Right Reverend Joseph Blount Cheshire, bishop of the Diocese of North Carolina, took place on 20 Jan. 1913 at St. Peter's. She was buried in Elmwood Cemetery, Charlotte.

SEE: Samuel A. Ashe, ed., *Biographical History of North Carolina*, vol. 5 (1906); Marion Frances Alston Bourne, "Seventy-five Years of Service," *Woman's Auxiliary to the National Council of the Protestant Episcopal Church: Seventy-fifth Annual Report and Handbook* (1957); *Charlotte Daily Observer*, 20–21 Jan. 1913; Charlotte *Evening Chronicle*, 6 July 1908, 20 Jan. 1913; *Charlotte News*, 20–21 Jan. 1913; *Charlotte Observer*, 21 Apr. 1904, 3 Apr. 1910, 15 Apr. 1978; Charlotte *Western Democrat*, 25 Aug., 10 Nov. 1868; Rev. Norvin C. Duncan, *Pictorial History of the Episcopal Church in North Carolina, 1701–1964* (1965); Protestant Episcopal Church, Diocese of North Carolina, *Journal of the Annual Convention of the Protestant Episcopal Church in the Diocese of North Carolina* (1887–1906), and Episcopal Churchwomen, *Annual Report and Handbook of Information* (1882–1912); James B. Sill, *Historical Sketches of Churches in the Diocese of Western North Carolina, Episcopal Church* (1955); Charles L. Van Noppen Papers (Manuscript Department, Duke University Library, Durham); Jane Renwick Wilkes, *History of St. Peter's Hospital, Charlotte, N.C., for Thirty Years* (1906).

EVA BURBANK MURPHY

Wilkes, John (Jack) (31 Mar. 1827–6 July 1908), sailor and businessman, was born in New York City of English descent. His great-grandfather was Israel Wilkes, the brother of the eighteenth-century English politician John Wilkes, for whom counties in both North Carolina and Georgia were named. Jack was the son of Charles and Jane Jeffrey Renwick Wilkes. Charles, a naval officer, rose to the rank of rear admiral on the retired list and commanded an Exploring Expedition (1838–42) to the Antarctic continent, the islands of the Pacific Ocean, and the northwestern coast of America. Mrs. Wilkes was the sister of James Renwick, a noted engineer and professor at Columbia University.

Immediately after his appointment as a midshipman on 9 Sept. 1841, young Wilkes was sent to sea. His initial voyage was on the U.S. ship *Delaware* to the South Atlantic and the Mediterranean. He then served on the U.S. steamer *Mississippi* in the Gulf Squadron during the Mexican War, including participation in the attacks on Brazos and Vera Cruz. His appointment to the U.S. Naval Academy at Annapolis came in 1846. He was graduated the next year, first in a class of 135. He next saw duty on the *Albany* as a master in the Gulf of Mexico, but in about 1848 his father had him transferred to work on the charts and calculations of the Exploring Expedition. Later as a lieutenant on the sloop of war *Marion*, he traveled to China, Manila, and other ports of the Far East. In June 1852 he returned to the United States, and on 3 Nov. 1854 he resigned his commission.

Wilkes settled in Charlotte in December 1853, probably during a leave of absence from the U.S. Navy. His purpose in moving to North Carolina was to supervise certain mining and milling property, including the Capps Gold Mine. In 1858 he turned his business interest to the Mecklenburg Flour Mills, which he purchased with William R. Myers. Wilkes became the proprietor, later called the manager, of a foundry the following year. This business had various titles including the Mecklenburg Foundry and Machine Shops, as well as the Mecklenburg Iron Works.

During the Civil War Wilkes took an active role in the Southern effort through his service in the local vigilance committee, in the Home Guards, and as a financial adviser to North Carolina state officials. From 1861 to 1865 the Confederate government took possession of the Mecklenburg Iron Works, which was used as an ordnance depot to supply the Confederate navy. Wilkes also became a railroad contractor in government service. He and his brother Edmund obtained a contract to build the section of the Piedmont Railroad from Greensboro to Danville. The brothers, who had formed a partnership, Edmund Wilkes and Brother, were involved in the construction in 1862 and 1863. Then they began building a railroad from Raleigh to Lockport but had to stop when General William Tecumseh Sherman occupied the area. In 1865 John Wilkes secured a pardon from the U.S. government.

In August 1865 he obtained a charter for the First National Bank of Charlotte and served as its president until 1869. This bank had the distinction of being the first national bank established south of Richmond. Wilkes also formed a business partnership with entrepreneur Miles Wriston and General John A. Young. They moved the Rock Island Woolen Mills to Charlotte, but eventually the enterprise failed. After this Wilkes devoted his energy to the Mecklenburg Iron Works, which became a successful business.

In April 1854 he married Jane Renwick Smedberg, of New York, who became a prominent Charlotte philanthropist. The couple had nine children, five of whom died young. Wilkes was a very active member of the Episcopal church both on the parish level and often as a delegate to the diocesan convention. He was a representative to the General Convention of the church on several occasions. Wilkes died in Charlotte and, after the funeral at St. Peter's Episcopal Church, was buried in Elmwood Cemetery.

SEE: Samuel A. Ashe, ed., *Biographical History of North Carolina*, vol. 5 (1905 [portrait]); C. K. Brown, "A History of the Piedmont Railroad Company," *North Carolina Historical Review* 3 (1926); Edward W. Callahan, ed., *List of Officers of the Navy of the United States . . .* (1901); Charlotte *Evening Chronicle*, 6 July 1908; Clement A. Evans, ed., *Confederate Military History* (1899 [portrait]); Daniel Henderson, *The Hidden Coasts* (1953); Jon L. Wakelyn, *Biographical Dictionary of the Confederacy* (1977); Wilkes Family Papers (Manuscript Department, Duke University Library, Durham).

SHARON E. KNAPP

Wilkins, Raymond Harrell (*28 Sept. 1917–2 Nov. 1943*), World War II Army Air Force officer, was born in Norfolk, Va., to William Samuel and Florida Alverta Harrell Wilkins of Columbia, Tyrrell County, N.C. He grew up in Columbia and attended school there in 1930–34 before entering The University of North Carolina in September 1934. He registered as a pharmacy major, intending to enter medical school. In 1936 he enlisted as a private in the U.S. Army Air Force and served at Langley Field, Va. Soon promoted to staff sergeant and assigned to clerical duty instead of flight training as he wanted, he managed to enter the Cadet Training Corps at Smith Air College, St. Louis. He afterwards was graduated at Kelly Field, Tex., where he was a Cadet Corps captain, received his pilot's wings on 31 Oct. 1941, and was commissioned second lieutenant. Remaining at Kelly Field as an instructor, he also received further training at Maxwell Field, Ala.

In 1941 he was assigned to duty in the Philippines, where he arrived four days before the Japanese attacked there. He saw his first combat service under General Douglas MacArthur, but when the United States withdrew, Wilkins flew with the aerial convoy of MacArthur and his forces en route to Australia. He participated in raids over Lae and other New Guinea bases where he destroyed three Japanese planes on the ground and knocked a Zero out of the air. He was awarded the Silver Star for distinguished service in a series of successful attacks on Japanese airdromes in which seventeen enemy bombers and other targets were destroyed.

Promoted to first lieutenant, Wilkins was a member of a light bombardment squadron that flew 180 missions against the Japanese in the Southwest Pacific, attacked seventy-five enemy vessels, and became the first outfit to introduce the parachute bomb in combat. He commanded a crew that flew 47 combat missions in Douglas Bostons.

Wilkins's daring and ability soon brought him promotion to captain, and in September 1943 he was made

squadron commander. For his flying exploits and extraordinary feats of daring and courage in the South Pacific, he was awarded the Air Medal, Distinguished Flying Cross with two Oak Leaf Clusters, and Silver Star. One year after his assignment to foreign duty he was promoted to the rank of major. The promotion came, however, just a few weeks before his death. He was killed while leading his squadron in an attack against a section of the Japanese fleet on 1 Nov. 1943 over Rabaul, New Britain. His last act was to dive his plane straight at a Japanese gunboat in an attempt to silence it and save the lives of his comrades. His thousand-pound bomb struck squarely amidships, causing the Japanese vessel to explode, and then, at low level, he attacked an enemy destroyer. After that he attacked a transport of some 9,000 tons, scoring a hit that engulfed the ship in flames. Turning next to strafe a heavy cruiser his plane was exposed to heavy fire, was hit, and crashed into the sea. He had destroyed two enemy vessels and made possible the safe withdrawal of the remaining planes of his squadron. After his death he was awarded the Purple Heart, and on 5 Apr. 1944 the War Department announced that he had been posthumously awarded the Congressional Medal of Honor.

Wilkins's successor as commander of the squadron said: "It was a privilege to serve under a man of his caliber. His ability as a combat pilot set the criterion that all of us strive to attain, but none ever equal, and his personal character was an example for every officer with whom he came in contact. His intelligence and high ideals, the high standards that he set for himself and his Squadron, and above all, his superb leadership make the task of attempting to take his place immeasurably difficult. He was truly the type of leader that could lead men anywhere under the most adverse conditions with the foreknowledge that they would follow him willingly and gladly. No other man that I have ever known came so close to achieving the standard set by ancient chivalry—that of being 'without fear and without reproach.'"

SEE: Alumni Files, especially Mrs. V. J. Vallier (Major Wilkins's mother) to J. Maryon Saunders, 21 Mar. 1944 (University of North Carolina, Chapel Hill); Gita Siegman, ed., *World of Winners* (1992); Norfolk, Va., *Ledger Dispatch*, 5 Jan. 1943; Raleigh *News and Observer*, 8 Apr. 1944.

WILLIAM S. POWELL

Wilkinson, Frank Smith (*25 Sept. 1833–13 Nov. 1919*), teacher and scholar, was born in Edgecombe County, probably in Lower Fishing Creek Township, the youngest of eleven children of Charles Wilkinson and the ninth child of his second wife Nancy. His father died at age forty when Frank was a year old. After graduation from The University of North Carolina in 1857 he began teaching in Raleigh and the following year was appointed principal of the Tarborough Male Academy. It was a private or quasi-public school established in 1813, when the General Assembly passed "an act for the erecting of an Academy in the Town of Tarborough"; two acres of land from the Town Common were given on which to build. The Tarborough academy, like a scattering of others throughout North Carolina, was private in the sense that policy was made and enforced by independent trustees but quasi-public because it did receive some aid from the local, state, and occasionally federal government.

In many ways Wilkinson was typical of the teachers during the years before public schools were established. A strict disciplinarian with a stout switch handy, he was the sole instructor much of the time, with pupils ranging from beginners to those preparing for college. As one writer remarked, his methods apparently were successful in view of the affection he instilled in his students, many of whom later became leaders in the state. His reputation as a teacher was such that The University of North Carolina would admit any student certified by him without requiring an entrance examination. The Right Reverend Joseph Blount Cheshire, bishop of the Diocese of North Carolina, who attended the academy from age eleven to sixteen (1861–66), was one of his pupils. Years later Cheshire wrote that Wilkinson "was devoted to the profession of teaching, laboring faithfully to interest his pupils and giving them the best of himself." According to the bishop, a large proportion of his students studied both Latin and Greek. His academic courses, consisting mainly of classical subjects, meant they were to be written down, memorized, and recited. Wilkinson was a man of "moral and gentlemanly deportment," stern in manner and exacting absolute obedience from his pupils.

On 24 Nov. 1885 the Tarborough Male Academy was destroyed by fire. It was never rebuilt, but Wilkinson opened a private school of his own for both males and females on the corner of St. Patrick and Wilson streets. He added a few business courses, two instructors for the girls, and an assistant to him for the boys. Wilkinson also served as county superintendent of public instruction, working diligently to improve the caliber of county schools and their teachers. During the 1890s, as superintendent in Edgecombe, his son, William Stronach Wilkinson, held the same position in the Nash County school system. When the Fusion party came into power in 1897–99, Frank Wilkinson was replaced, but his academy continued until well after 1910. He spent his last years at the home of his son William in Rocky Mount, where, approaching eighty years of age, he conducted special tutoring classes for older boys in a small one-room school on Main Street. Always the dedicated teacher, he continued his classes until a short time before his death, having devoted over sixty years to the education of the young. He was buried beside his wife and infant children in Calvary churchyard, Tarboro.

In the early 1860s Wilkinson married Annie Stronach (1837–1901), of Raleigh, the oldest child of William (1803–57) and Sarah Moody Savage (1814–66) Stronach. In 1833 Wilkinson's father-in-law had traveled to Raleigh from his native Scotland to be in charge of the stonework of the capitol then being built. The children of Frank and Annie who lived to maturity were Nancy W. Cheney, Sarah Ellen W. Roberson, William Stronach, Sue W. Jones, and George Alexander.

SEE: Harry Allen Jones, *Tarborough and Its Academies* (1975); Gaston Lichenstein, *Recollections of My Teacher Frank S. Wilkinson* (1953); Lawrence Foushee London, *Bishop Joseph Blount Cheshire: His Life and Work* (1941); "The Male Academy Burned," *Tarborough Southerner*, 26 Nov. 1885; "Tarboro Male Academy," *Tarborough Southerner*, 8 Aug. 1901; J. Kelly Turner and John L. Bridgers, Jr., *History of Edgecombe County, N.C.* (1920); Ruth S. Williams and Margarette G. Griffin, *Bible Records of Early Edgecombe* (1958).

DOROTHY BATTLE WILKINSON

Wilkinson, William (d. *September–November 1780*), Revolutionary leader in New Hanover County, was a member of the Safety Committee in 1775 and 1776, serving as deputy chairman in November 1775. He was a member of the committee to collect carriage guns and swivels in 1775 and of numerous local action groups during the war. Wilkinson also was paymaster for several in-

dependent companies of troops, a merchant, a constable of the peace, and a member of St. James's Anglican Church, of which he was a warden. In partnership with Cornelius Harnett he owned a rum distillery located on the Cape Fear River between Walnut and Red Cross streets as well as the schooner *Mary*.

In his will dated 22 September and proved in November 1780, he left property to his brother Robert of Duplin County. To his nephew William Wilkinson he left his house and lot in Wilmington near the church. Each of the other children of Robert received £5; William Maclaine, son of Archibald, £500; Elizabeth, the wife of Archibald Maclaine, £250; the Reverend James Tate, £5 yearly and the forgiveness of debts due Wilkinson; and William Henry Hill, the son of William Hill, £250. The will also provided £500 to build a Presbyterian church in Wilmington. To nephew John, the son of his brother Thomas, Wilkinson left his silver watch, buckles, buttons, and silver plate. He also freed a female slave and her daughter and supplied funds to establish them in Philadelphia on condition that they wash, mend, and make clothes for his nephew, John Wilkinson, during the time he was in school in Philadelphia. To Cornelius Harnett and Archibald Maclaine he left a cask, about thirty to forty gallons, of his oldest rum to be equally divided between them.

There is no evidence that Wilkinson ever married.

SEE: Walter Clark, ed., *State Records of North Carolina*, vols. 11 (1895), 13 (1896); Leora H. McEachern and Isabel M. Williams, comps., *Wilmington–New Hanover Safety Committee Minutes* (1974); William S. Powell, ed., *The Correspondence of William Tryon and Other Selected Papers*, 2 vols. (1980–81); William L. Saunders, ed., *Colonial Records of North Carolina*, vols. 7, 9–10 (1890); William Wilkinson will (North Carolina State Archives, Raleigh).

WILLIAM S. POWELL

Wilkison (or Wilkeson, Wilkinson), William (ca. *1645–1706*), Council member, justice, and speaker of the Assembly, moved from Maryland to the North Carolina colony, then called Albemarle, in the 1670s and soon became prominent politically. In November 1679 he was a member of the Albemarle Assembly and sat on the committee to oversee the public accounts. As a committee member and in other ways he aroused the hostility of Robert Holden, secretary and customs collector, who was using his offices to cheat and otherwise abuse the colonists. In the fall of 1860 Holden had Wilkison arrested on trumped-up charges and held prisoner for some months without trial. Two years later, however, Wilkison was among those who helped bring Holden to trial and rid the colony of his presence.

In 1684 Wilkison was a member of Governor Seth Sothel's Council, on which he appears to have sat also in 1687. He may have been on the Council through much of Sothel's administration, of which few records have survived. From March 1682/83 through October 1688 he was a justice of the county court, then the highest court of law in the colony. In 1688 or early the next year he was elected to the Assembly. By July 1689, however, he had resigned his Assembly seat and accepted reappointment to the Council.

Wilkison's resumption of Council membership came in the last days of Sothel's governorship, which apparently ended in late July or early August 1689. As a Council member Wilkison no doubt participated in the decisions and actions that resulted in Sothel's banishment, but records of those proceedings are not extant. He remained on the Council several years after Sothel's expulsion—at least through March 1694/95. He appears to have held no office from 1695 through 1698, but in July 1699 he was appointed to the General Court. He sat on the court through August 1701. Again elected to the Assembly in the early 1700s, he served as speaker in 1703. In addition to his major posts, Wilkison served from time to time in lesser capacities, including colonel of the militia, customs collector, and collector of quit rents.

In the 1690s, as in earlier periods, his public career was stormy, but few details of his controversies are known. It is evident that he was particularly hostile towards Daniel Akehurst, a leading Quaker who was secretary of the colony, and towards other Quakers who were prominent in the mid-1690s. There also is evidence that Wilkison used abusive language towards his fellow officials, and there are indications that he prepared and circulated written attacks on officials and governmental policies. In September 1694 the deputy governor, Thomas Harvey, in a letter to the Lords Proprietors, referred to Wilkison's "misdemeanors" and the fact that the Council had removed him from all his offices except that of Council member, from which, Harvey said, they would have removed him had they had legal power to do so. In March 1694/95 the Council ordered that Wilkison and his wife be arrested and brought before them to answer impeachment charges filed by the House of Burgesses. The charges are not specified, and the outcome is not indicated in the few surviving records pertaining to those proceedings. There is little doubt, however, that the result was Wilkison's removal from the Council, either by the Proprietors' action or through the impeachment procedure. Wilkison appears not to have served on the Council after March 1694/95.

In November 1695 the General Court partially disbarred Wilkison and another prominent colonist, Henderson Walker, prohibiting them from pleading as attorneys in that court, except for clients outside the colony, because of their "sundry affronts" to members of the court, all of whom at that time were Council members. Following the court's action, Wilkison burst into a Council meeting and engaged in "some violent discourse," directing his speech particularly to Daniel Akehurst and refusing to interrupt his harangue when Council members attempted to reply. In this episode, as in others, the basic subject at issue is unknown.

By the end of the decade Wilkison was again in good standing with the Council, as is evidenced by his appointment to the General Court, then composed of justices commissioned by the Council. However, the personnel and direction of the government had changed. The Quaker influence, so strong earlier in the decade, had now diminished, and a movement that eventually would result in the establishment of the Anglican church was under way. In 1701, when Anglican parishes were organized under the recently adopted Vestry Act, Wilkison served on the Chowan vestry and was chosen warden at its first meeting. These and earlier circumstances suggest that Wilkison's quarrels with his fellow officials may have been an early manifestation of those differences between Anglicans and dissenters that were to tear the colony apart in later years.

Wilkison lived in Chowan Precinct, where he had extensive landholdings. About 1680 he married Hester Sweatman, a widow, originally from Maryland, for whom he had served as attorney. Born Hester Jenkins, she was the daughter of Walter and Sarah Jenkins of Kent County, Md. Her father died in 1663, and her mother married George Harris of Kent County, who gave Hester a plantation and bequeathed her other property. The Wilkisons appear to have had no children.

In addition to his public concerns, Wilkison had many private interests. He frequently bought or sold land or bought headrights on which he patented land. As a planter he no doubt cultivated his home plantation and perhaps others that he owned. He also conducted a mercantile business involving the export of Albemarle products and the importation and distribution of goods from England and elsewhere. In the early 1700s he owned at least one ship, the *Reserve*, a vessel of fifteen tons. The *Reserve* was commanded by John Ingram, who appears to have been Hester's nephew. Also an attorney, Wilkison frequently represented residents of other colonies as well as Albemarle inhabitants in the General Court. He was executor of several large estates and was often appointed by the court to appraise an estate or audit an administrator's accounts.

After 1703 Wilkison took little or no part in governmental affairs. He may have been in failing health, but he attended a vestry meeting in January 1705/6. A month later he was on his deathbed. On 9 Feb. 1705/6 he had a will that he had made in 1704 brought out and read to him and confirmed it to be his last will and testament. On 9 May 1706 the will was proved in court. Depositions that Wilkison made at various times indicate that he was about sixty-one years old when he died.

Wilkison bequeathed his entire estate to his wife, whom he named executrix. Hester, or Esther as she was called in her later years, married Thomas Pollock after Wilkison's death. She died before 28 July 1713, when her will was proved.

SEE: Jane Baldwin Cotton, comp. and ed., *Maryland Calendar of Wills*, vol. 1 (1904–28); J. Bryan Grimes, ed., *Abstract of North Carolina Wills* (1910); J. R. B. Hathaway, ed., *North Carolina Historical and Genealogical Register*, vols. 1–2 (1900–1901); North Carolina State Archives (Raleigh), particularly Albemarle Book of Warrants and Surveys (1681–1706), Chowan County Miscellaneous Papers (1685–1738), Colonial Court Records (boxes 139, 148, 192), Council Minutes, Wills, Inventories (1677–1701), and Wills of Esther Pollock (1712) and William Wilkison (1704); Mattie Erma Edwards Parker, ed., *North Carolina Higher Court Records, 1670–1696* and *1697–1701* (1968, 1971); William S. Price, ed., *North Carolina Higher-Court Minutes, 1709–1723* (1977) and *North Carolina Higher-Court Records, 1702–1708* (1974); William L. Saunders, ed., *Colonial Records of North Carolina*, vol. 1 (1886–90); Gust Skordas, ed., *Early Settlers of Maryland . . .* (1968).

MATTIE ERMA E. PARKER

Willcox (or Wilcox), John *(21 June 1728–1793),* Chatham County iron manufacturer, was born in Concord, Chester County, Pa., the first son of Thomas and Elizabeth Cole Willcox. About 1759 he moved to Cross Creek where he operated a store and gristmill. Later he lived in Deep River, Orange County. An active supporter of the Regulator movement, he was one of those excluded from Governor William Tryon's pardon on 31 May 1771. Later that year Chatham County was created out of Orange, and Willcox was elected to represent the new county in the Provincial Assembly.

By 1771 Willcox had built an ironworks on Deep River where he discovered deposits of both iron ore and coal. Iron was in short supply during the Revolution, and Willcox operated one of the two ironworks in the province. His bloomery and forge supplied the area with good bar iron from which rough wrought iron utensils could be forged. In April 1776 the Fourth Provincial Congress sent a committee either to hire Willcox's ironworks or "purchase and repair" the Speedwell Works in Guilford County. Following the committee's recommendation, the Revolutionary government advanced Willcox the needed funds to complete a furnace under construction on Tick Creek about ten miles from his bloomery and forge and hired him slaves that had been confiscated as Loyalist property. Willcox and his brother-in-law and partner, William England, were to supply molten metal to founders employed by the state.

After various delays in getting the furnace into operation Willcox sold the ironworks to the state in February 1777 for £5,000. The state-appointed manager was no more successful than Willcox had been in keeping the furnace going. In April 1778 after months of haggling, the legislature restored Willcox's property and paid him £1,000 for damages he had sustained from public interference with his ironworks. When Willcox resumed management of the furnace, he turned out at least a few pots and possibly as much as five tons of pig iron. In June 1780 a freshet destroyed the furnace. When his accounts were settled in 1783, Willcox received £386.18s.6d. specie in payment "for sundries furnished for the use of the public."

In 1771 he married Rebecca Butler, of Philadelphia, by whom he had eight children. Willcox kept the Roman Catholic faith of his parents, and the records of St. Joseph's Church in Philadelphia indicate that at least three of their children were taken to Philadelphia for baptism. Willcox died in Richmond County.

SEE: Chatham Furnace Papers (Southern Historical Collection, University of North Carolina, Chapel Hill); Walter Clark, ed., *State Records of North Carolina*, vols. 11–12, 14–15, 17, 22 (1895–1907); Morris Family Papers (North Carolina Collection, University of North Carolina, Chapel Hill); William L. Saunders, ed., *Colonial Records of North Carolina*, vol. 10 (1890); John Willcox Papers (Manuscript Department, Duke University Library, Durham); Joseph Willcox, "Historical Sketches of Some of the Pioneer Catholics of Philadelphia and Vicinity," *Records of the American Catholic Historical Society* (December 1904), and *Ivy Mills, 1729–1866: Willcox and Allied Families* (1911).

GEORGE W. TROXLER

Williams, Alfred *(10 June 1805–9 Jan. 1896)*, businessman, was born in Franklin County to John (d. 1821) and Nancy A. Williams. He was the grandson of Jesse Williams and the great-grandson of Thomas Williams of Northampton County. At sixteen Alfred moved to Raleigh and worked as a clerk in the drugstore of Randolph Webb; at twenty-two he bought Webb's interest and became sole owner. In 1827 Dr. Fabius J. Haywood, a prominent Raleigh physician, was admitted to partnership and the firm became Williams and Haywood. For more than sixty years Williams and Haywood, with different names after Williams's withdrawal in 1851, continued as one of the state's leading drugstores. Williams was clerk of the Wake County Superior Court from September 1835 to September 1841 but thereafter did not seek reelection. In 1836 he purchased land in Alabama and for thirty years made annual inspection tours of that state's farming operations. In 1854 he began a new career by forming a copartnership in dry goods with Thaddeus McGee; the company of McGee and Williams remained operative for eight years and closed because of the Civil War.

In 1867, in the seventy-fifth year of Raleigh's history, Williams established a book-selling and publishing house at a site on the second block of Fayetteville Street. (Earlier booksellers in the city had been Joseph Gales, editor of the *Raleigh Register*, and Elijah Weems.) By 1883 the Alfred Williams Company published a magazine for teachers, *North Carolina Teacher*, as a private venture. For decades the company sold chalk, blackboards, office equipment, and textbooks. By 1911 the textbook business had become so brisk that the North Carolina School Book Depository was formed from the company and remained in Raleigh for many years. In 1878 Williams was one of the incorporators in the Articles of Incorporation of the Peace Institute of Raleigh. He retired in 1888.

In 1829 Williams married Eliza Caroline King (1810–29 Jan. 1832), the daughter of Mary Ann Cummings and Benjamin Seawell King, one of Raleigh's leading merchants and clerk of the superior court from 1814 to 1835. Her grandfather, John King, a native of England, was one of the pioneer Methodist clergymen in America. Alfred and Eliza had only one child, Lucy Ann (18 Dec. 1829–1920), who in 1850 married Dr. E. Burke Haywood, a prominent Raleigh physician. The Haywoods had nine children: E. Burke, Jr. (banker and planter), Alfred Williams (lawyer and manufacturer), Hubert (physician), Eliza Eagles (m. P. L. Bridgers of Wilmington), Ernest (lawyer), Edgar (bookseller and publisher), John (cotton dealer), and Eugene and Carolina Frances, both of whom died in infancy. In July 1850 Alfred Williams married Mrs. Sarah A. Jones Stone, the widow of David W. Stone; they had no children.

In 1895 Alfred Williams's grandson Edgar Haywood and his grandnephew Alfred William II, a namesake who moved from Hamilton, Ga., to Raleigh about 1886 at Alfred Williams's invitation, assumed leadership of his company. After Haywood's death in 1924, operations were directed by the founder's grandnephew and his two sons, Alfred Williams III (b. 1900) and B. Grimes Williams (b. 1902). Following their father's death in 1937 Alfred III and B. Grimes took over the company's management. Alfred III's sons, Alfred IV and Murray, became the fourth generation of leaders of the firm. In 1936 the company ceased book publication. In 1960, after ninety-three years on Fayetteville Street, the company moved to 705 Hillsborough Street, where it became a complete office outfitter (furniture, machines, and supplies). Alfred III retired in 1960 and B. Grimes in 1958.

The Alfred Williams home stood on lower Fayetteville Street from 1840 to 1924, when it was torn down. Williams was a Baptist and "probably a Democrat." A portrait of him as a young man (artist's name illegible) and a portrait of Alfred Williams II are on display at the firm's headquarters; a portrait of Williams's second wife, done by Garl Brown in 1850, and a portrait of Alfred Williams II as a young man are at the home of Alfred Williams III in Raleigh. Alfred Williams, Eliza Caroline King Williams, Dr. E. Burke Haywood, and Lucy Ann Haywood were buried in Oakwood Cemetery, Raleigh; the final resting place of Alfred Williams's second wife is unknown.

SEE: Ernest Haywood, *Sketch of Mr. Alfred Williams* (1933); Marshall De Lancey Haywood, *Builders of the Old North State* (1968); *North Carolina Education* 4 (October 1973); sketches of Alfred Williams and Ernest Haywood in Charles L. Van Noppen Papers (Manuscript Department, Duke University Library, Durham); Alfred Williams III, personal contact, July, October 1973; Alfred Williams IV, personal contact, July 1974.

GRADY L. E. CARROLL

Williams, Archibald Hunter Arrington *(22 Oct. 1842–5 Sept. 1895)*, businessman and congressman, was born in Franklin County near Louisburg. His father,

Henry G. Williams, had been a state senator representing Granville County. Archibald had four brothers, one of whom, H. G., was assistant superintendent of the U.S. House of Representatives Document Room. Another brother, Sam, edited the *Raleigh News*. Archibald Williams received his education at Emory and Henry College in Emory, Va. He enlisted as a private in the Army of Northern Virginia and by the end of the Civil War held the rank of captain and commanded the Fifty-sixth North Carolina Regiment.

After the war Williams entered retail trade in Oxford. He was instrumental in the completion of the Oxford and Henderson Railroad and served as its president. He sat in the North Carolina House of Representatives from 1883 to 1885. In 1890 he was elected to the U.S. House of Representatives as a Democrat from the Fifth Congressional District, a former Republican stronghold. Williams lost his bid for reelection in 1892 to Thomas Settle in a hotly disputed contest. He was a member of the Masonic lodge and the Order of Odd Fellows. For many years he served as one of the directors of the Oxford Orphan Asylum. He died in Chase City, Va., and was buried in Elmwood Cemetery, Oxford.

SEE: *Biog. Dir. Am. Cong.* (1961); *Oxford Public Ledger*, 6, 13 Sept. 1895; *Person County Courier*, 11 Sept. 1895; *Who Was Who in America, 1607–1896*.

ROBIN A. PUCKETT

Williams, Benjamin (1 Jan. 1751–20 July 1814), governor, congressman, and soldier, was the son of Colonel John and Ferebee Savage Pugh Williams of Craven County. A maternal ancestor, Thomas Savage, on 2 Jan. 1608 joined the colonists at Jamestown, Va. The grandson of William Williams, who had immigrated to North Carolina from Wales by 1735, Colonel Williams was a merchant, justice of the peace, and trustee of the 1764 New Bern School. His oldest daughter, Ferebee Pugh, born on 20 May 1746 at their home at Fort Barnwell in Craven County, married first Dr. John Leigh and second Dr. Isaac Guion, of New Bern, a Revolutionary surgeon, state councillor, and legislator. His other son, John Pugh Williams, was a militia colonel during the Revolution.

After attending rural schools and engaging in farming, Benjamin Williams represented Johnston County, which had been formed in 1746 from Craven, at the First Provincial Congress (25–27 Aug. 1774) in New Bern, the last Assembly in North Carolina under authority of the British Crown (4–8 Apr. 1775) in New Bern, and the Third Provincial Congress (20 Aug.-10 Sept. 1775) in Hillsborough.

By this third congress he was appointed (1 September) a lieutenant of the second regiment and (9 September) a member of the Committee of Safety for the New Bern district. On 19 July 1776 he was promoted to captain. Resigning his commission on 1 Jan. 1779, he represented Craven County that year in the House of Commons. Returning to military duty when the British invaded North Carolina, he received the rank of colonel on 12 July 1781 for gallantry as a volunteer officer at the Battle of Guilford Court House and was put in charge of a regiment of state troops.

From Johnston County Williams served in the state senate in 1780, 1781, April 1784, October 1784, and 1786; and in the state house in 1785 and 1789. From Craven County he was a state senator in 1788 and a delegate to the state constitutional convention. From Moore County he was a senator in 1807 and 1809. For one term (4 Mar. 1793–3 Mar. 1795) he was elected to the third U.S. Congress but was not a candidate for reelection. His application for membership in St. John's Lodge, AFAM, was approved

on 16 Apr. 1795, and he was raised on 19 December to Master Mason "at the Palace" in New Bern.

On 23 Nov. 1799 Williams became governor of the state as well as president of the board of trustees of The University of North Carolina. Since 1789 he had been one of the first trustees and had taken an active role in the 1792 selection of the university site. Twice he was reelected the state's chief executive, serving until 6 Dec. 1802. Shortly before his third term ended he pardoned Congressman John Stanly for fatally shooting former governor Richard Dobbs Spaight, Sr., in a political duel on 5 Sept. 1802 at New Bern. By then a Republican, Williams was defeated by Nathaniel Alexander for the 1805 gubernatorial nomination but again was elected governor for the term from 1 Dec. 1807 to 12 Dec. 1808.

Previously he had resided for a time at Raleigh but in 1798 had bought a home on Governor's Creek in Moore County, where he became a successful farmer and one of the largest cotton planters of the period. "In no pursuit have I yet found that enjoyment of contentment which agriculture affords," he wrote in 1804 to Major John R. Eaton of Granville County, "& nothing is wanting among our North Carolina Farmers for possessing wealth enough but a better sett of Merchants & change in System of farming, which by the bye is hard to effect, for we are but too unwilling to forsake old habits to adopt new ones; & as to the Merchants, I fear the grave will close on your great grand children before much amendment among this class of Men will take place. The Navigation of our State has I fear doomed us to the Dregs of Commercial Men."

Williams spent his last years at the Chalmers homestead, which he purchased with a large acreage and called "Retreat." The house had been built about 1772–73 in a wide bend of Deep River by Colonel Philip Alston. Now known as "the house in the horseshoe," the residence was acquired in 1954 by the Moore County Historical Society, which restored it to its appearance in 1781, when Alston's Whigs were defeated there by David Fanning's Tories. Bullet holes are still in the front wall. Since 1955 it has been open to visitors. A portrait of Williams painted by William C. Fields of Fayetteville from an original portrait owned by the state at Raleigh is one of its appropriate furnishings. The property is a state-owned and -operated historic site and is listed in the *National Register of Historic Places*.

Within an enclosure in its side yard are the large slab tombstones of Williams and his wife, Eliza(beth) Jones, moved there in 1970 from the family cemetery a mile and a half away on Governor's Creek. Also moved there were the unmarked vaults of their only son, Colonel Benjamin William Williams (28 July 1797–14 Feb. 1828), and his first wife, Mary Chalmers (1800–1821), who were married on 19 Oct. 1820 at Fayetteville, their tombstones having been vandalized in the original locations.

On 10 Aug. 1781 Benjamin Williams married Eliza Jones, the daughter of Marmaduke Robin Jones, attorney general under royal governors Arthur Dobbs and William Tryon, and his second wife, Mary Eaton Jones; she was the half sister of Willie Jones and General Allen Jones, Revolutionary patriots. Eliza died at New Bern on 24 Nov. 1817, "aged 54 years and 10 months . . . an affectionate wife, a tender mother, and one whose memory is now embalmed in the hearts of the poor of this extensive neighborhood."

The epitaph on the governor's tomb reads: "Providence blessed him with a large share of its bounties, and he acted as her faithful steward; for 'large was his bounty, and his soul sincere.'" His obituary published on 29 July 1814 by the *Raleigh Register* stated. "He died, as he had lived, much respected and highly esteemed by those who knew him; and, from his general demeanor and devout professions as well previously to us as during his last illness, has left to his relations and more intimate friends the cheering consolation that he died a believer, resigned and happy, in the hope of mercy, through the atonements and merits of the redeemer."

His son married, on 2 Jan. 1823, a second wife, Mary McBride, the daughter of Archibald McBride of nearby Carbonton. The only surviving grandchild, Dr. Benjamin Chalmers Williams (20 Dec. 1821–24 May 1873), born to the son's first wife, married on 20 Apr. 1858 Catherine McDougal. He was the last of the direct line. Hence, there are now no living descendants of Governor Williams.

SEE: W. J. Adams, *A Sketch of Governor Benjamin Williams* (1920); Samuel A. Ashe, ed., *Biographical History of North Carolina*, vol. 5 (1906); John L. Cheney, Jr., ed., *North Carolina Government, 1585–1979* (1981); Walter Clark, ed., *State Records of North Carolina*, vols. 17–23 (1899–1904); *Durham Herald-Sun*, 22 May 1938; Minutes, St. John's Lodge No. 3, AFAM, New Bern; Raleigh *News and Observer*, 10 Dec. 1950; Southern Pines, *The Pilot*, 12 Sept. 1963.

GERTRUDE S. CARRAWAY

Williams, Benjamin Brown (1815–15 Feb. 1894), physician, was the son of Robert, a planter and large slave owner of Pitt County, and Mary Williams. Benjamin's brother William (1785–1850) married Nancy May (1792–1858); their daughter Frances May Williams married James Lang Cobb, whose descendants were the noted Cobb family in North Carolina. After receiving an M.D. degree from the Eclectic Medical Institute of Ohio in 1847, Benjamin practiced in Meadville, Pa. He was the author of *A Treatise Upon the Electrical Philosophy and Cure of Cholera* (Richmond, Va., 1849), *A Treatise on Mental Alchemy, Electro-psychology, Biology, Magnetism and Mesmerism with the Cards of Classes, Editorials, &c* (Brooklyn, 1852), *Mental Alchemy: A Treatise on the Mind, Nervous System, Psychology, Magnetism, Mesmerism, and Disease* (New York, 1854), and *Primal Man, and the Science of Self-control, Psychology, and Mesmerism* (Meadville, 1887). In all four books the author's name appears as B. Brown Williams.

His 1852 work was dedicated to James Joiner, then an attorney in Washington, N.C., identified as "a boyhood friend of the author's," but who actually was six years younger than Williams. Prefatory notes indicate that Williams lectured on nature and the mind, and the chapters in this book were outlines of his lectures. Included were discussions of the relationship of mind to matter, man's spiritual system, and the natural and spiritual world. The reader was further informed that the author's "deductions . . . are the fruits of an humble plant of the old north state, and they are respectfully presented to the reader for his approval or disapproval."

Williams, survived by his wife who had been an invalid for several years, was buried in Greendale Cemetery, Meadville. His obituary reports that during his final days he was well cared for by "his housekeeper and family, who were with him until he went to sleep about two hours before he passed away." It is not clear whether *family* refers to that of the housekeeper or of Williams.

SEE: *Journal of the American Medical Association* 22 (3 Mar. 1894); Roger Kammerer, comp., *Tyson and May Genealogy of Pitt County* (1987); Meadville, Pa., *Crawford Journal*, 22 Feb. 1894; *National Union Catalog, Pre-1956 Imprints*, vol. 664 (1979); *Polk's Medical & Surgical Directory of the United States* (1886).

WILLIAM S. POWELL

Williams, Christopher (Kit) Harris (18 Dec. 1798–27 Nov. 1857), lawyer and Whig congressman from Tennessee, was born near Hillsborough, Orange County. He was the son of John, a veteran of the French and Indian War and of the Ninth North Carolina Continental Line in the American Revolution, and Elizabeth Duke Williams. Of Welsh origin, the family moved to Virginia in the late seventeenth century but settled in Piedmont North Carolina in the eighteenth century, afterwards living along Panther Creek in Surry (now Jackson) County. Christopher Williams studied law and was admitted to the bar about 1820.

By the early 1830s Williams was living in Lexington, Henderson County, Tenn. In 1831, described as "a Clay man," he was defeated for a seat in the General Assembly but soon participated in the successful campaign to elect Davy Crockett to the U.S. Senate. His work for William Henry Harrison for president in 1836, however, was ineffective. Williams, soon recognized as an outstanding speaker, contributed to the election of John Bell to the U.S. Senate. Williams himself was elected as a Whig to the Twenty-fifth, Twenty-sixth, and Twenty-seventh Congresses, serving from 4 Mar. 1837 until 3 Mar. 1843. He failed to win reelection in 1842. A delegate to several state and national conventions, he was elected to the Thirty-first and Thirty-second Congresses, during 4 Mar. 1849–3 Mar. 1853, but did not run for another term. Returning to Tennessee, he resumed the practice of law in Lexington, where he died and was buried in the Lexington Cemetery.

Williams and his wife, Jane Allison (b. ca. 1805), had two sons, Duke (1827–56) and Christopher (ca. 1830), four daughters, Nancy Allison (1832–40), Sarah C. (ca. 1837), Laura J. (ca. 1840), and one born between 1830 and 1835 whose name has not been found. They were the grandparents of John Sharp Williams (1854–1932), a U.S. representative and senator from Mississippi (1893–1909, 1911–23) who was the Democratic minority leader in the Fifty-eighth, Fifty-ninth, and Sixtieth Congresses.

SEE: *Biog. Dir. Am. Cong.* (1989); S. J. Folmsbee, *History of Tennessee* (1960); George C. Osborn, *John Sharp Williams: Statesman of the Deep South* (1943); information from records of Henderson County, Tenn., supplied by Mrs. Laura Waddle, Lexington, Tenn.; G. Tillman Stewart, *Henderson County* (1979); Herbert Weaver and others, eds., *Correspondence of James K. Polk*, vols. 1, 4–6 (1969, 1977–83).

VERNON O. STUMPF

Williams, Cratis Dearl (5 Apr. 1911–11 May 1985), folklorist, ballad collector and singer, linguist, professor, and college administrator, rose from humble beginnings in the Caines Creek community of Big Sandy Valley in eastern Kentucky's Lawrence County to become a specialist in the culture of the region and win the sobriquet "Mr. Appalachia." Runty in body and backwoodsy in appearance and speech, young Williams endured the condescension of his more affluent classmates at Louisa, a boarding school, to become the first person from his community to earn a high school diploma. He later credited this ridicule with his early interest in the history, folklore, ballads, songs, hymns, and tales of his region. He was only seventeen when the *Louisian*, a local newspaper, on 12 Dec. 1927 published his essay titled "Why a Mountain Boy Should Be Proud." He dedicated his career to that proposition.

The principal of the school, encouraging the student to "rise above his background," helped him get work at little Cumberland College, but after a year financial considerations forced Williams to return home and teach in a one-room school while, despite the depression, simultaneously taking classes at the University of Kentucky, from which he was graduated in 1933. As teacher and principal at Blaine High School during the next four years, he took graduate courses and received an M.A. degree from the university with a thesis on the ballads and songs of eastern Kentucky. For three more years he was the English teacher and principal at Louisa High School. Fired from that job because of his openness and candor—characteristics of his upbringing—Williams held menial jobs until he was appointed English critic teacher at the Demonstration High School at Appalachian State Teachers College in 1942. Four years later he joined the faculty of the college as teacher of English, speech, folklore, and dramatics. After a dozen years as a popular professor, he became director of the graduate school, which was named for him, and for a few months he served as acting chancellor of the college, by then renamed Appalachian State University.

His parents, Curtis [sic] and Mona Whitt Williams, lived on a farm owned by Cratis's grandfather, David Williams, one of the last legal distillers in Kentucky. This grandfather epitomized the true spirit of the mountaineer and was often a subject of Professor Williams's stories that regaled and informed those who attended his classes and lectures, heard him on radio and television, and read about him in the press. Proud that he was descended from Indian fighters, long hunters, veterans of the American Revolution, Tory escapees, refugees from the Whiskey Rebellion, and mountain feudists, he considered himself a "complete mountaineer" whose scholarly pursuits only reinforced his respect for the independent people often ridiculed by his elitist colleagues. Cratis Williams believed that all people, including his, should be judged within the context of their time, opportunity, good or bad fortune, and full character. Thus he fought the stereotype of mountaineers while celebrating many of their peculiarities. Although impeccable in his scholarly use of the English language, he found music in the expressions of the unschooled. "They had unique ways of saying things," he once said. "It glittered and sparkled with colorful language of all kinds. It was rich in metaphor. And yet, nowhere in the English-speaking world have 13 million people been made to feel so ashamed of their speech."

Throughout his career Williams spoke, wrote, and sang about the heritage of Appalachia. Long before the subject became fashionable in other universities, he collected materials and laid foundations for an Appalachian studies program at the Boone institution, and he was a consultant to other universities as they too began offering similar work. He helped found the Appalachian Consortium with its emphasis on publications relating to the region. He chose New York University for his doctoral work, and his Ph.D. dissertation, "The Southern Mountaineer in Fact and Fiction," was hailed as a pacesetter in the study of Appalachian literature. The 1,661-page tome was abridged and serialized in volume 3 of *Appalachian Journal*. A Founders Day citation from the university for outstanding scholarship reminded Williams of his long journey from a remote hollow in Kentucky to an academic life in New York City.

In accepting the Oliver Max Gardner Award in 1973 from the Board of Governors of The University of North Carolina for "contributions to the human race," Williams explained that a synthesis of folk culture of the mountains and humanistic traditions of Western civilization inspired him to devote most of his career to "the salvaging, perpetuation, and interpretation of the relatively neglected heritage of indigenous southern Appalachians whose struggle with grinding poverty, self-seeking outriders of economic exploitation, and political compromise had eroded their self-respect, made them ashamed of their

heritage, subverted their ethical values, and left them only half articulate about their own history and traditions." That he succeeded is attested to by other awards, including honorary doctoral degrees from Berea and Cumberland Colleges, Marshall University, Morehead State University, and the College of Idaho. He died one day before he was to receive still another honorary doctorate, this one from Appalachian, the university that he had served for four decades.

Williams valiantly fought the mispronunciation of the name of his native region that infiltrated through radio, television, and academicians after World War II. He pointed out that the word was derived from the Apalachee Indians, who would have been insulted to have a syllable in their name pronounced with a long "a." The new chairman of the Appalachian Regional Commission quickly discarded the errant pronunciation when Williams courageously told him that if he wanted to maintain credibility among mountaineers whom the commission was created to help, he must first "to learn how to pronounce Appalachia and Appalachian."

He married first Sylvia Graham, who died in 1942. On 31 July 1949 his marriage to Elizabeth Lingerfelt received widespread publicity as the first wedding in the new town of Levittown on New York's Long Island. They had two children, David Cratis and Sophie. Williams's ashes were returned for burial in the Williams family cemetery in his native Caines Creek community. At a memorial service his family and friends carried out his final request, "Remember me with joy and laughter," by sharing "Cratis stories" that have become a part of the culture to which he devoted his career.

SEE: *An Appalachian Symposium: Essays Written in Honor of Cratis D. Williams* (1977); *The Cratis Williams Symposium Proceedings: A Memorial and Examination of the State of Regional Studies in Appalachia* (1990); H. G. Jones, "Cratis D. Williams: A Personal Reminiscence" (typescript, North Carolina Collection, University of North Carolina, Chapel Hill); Loyal Jones, "A Complete Mountaineer," *Appalachian Journal* 13 (Spring 1986); Ron Larson, "The Appalachian Personality," *Appalachian Heritage* 11 (Spring 1983); Jim Lloyd and Anne G. Campbell, eds., *The Impact of Institutions in Appalachia* (1986); Raleigh *News and Observer*, 6 June 1976; Harold F. Warren, "... a Right Good People" (1974); *Who Was Who in America*, vol. 8 (1982–85).

H. G. JONES

Williams, David Marshall (Carbine) (13 Nov. 1900–8 Jan. 1975), firearms inventor, was born in Cumberland County, the first of seven children of James Claud and Laura Kornegay Williams (his father had four other children by a previous marriage). The youngster worked on the extensive family farm, dropped out of school after eight grades, worked in a blacksmith shop, served a short time in the navy (he was discharged for being underage), and then spent one semester at Blackstone Military Academy before being expelled. In 1918 he married Margaret Isobel Cook, who bore him one child, David Marshall, Jr.

Following his marriage, Williams worked for a short time for the Atlantic Coast Line Railroad, but, unbeknownst to his wife, he built and operated several illicit distilleries near Godwin. During a raid on one of the stills in 1921, Deputy Sheriff Al Pate was shot to death and Williams was charged with first-degree murder. The trial ended in a hung jury, but, rather than face a second trial and a possible death sentence, Williams pleaded guilty to a reduced charge of second-degree murder and was given a twenty- to thirty-year sentence. At Central Prison in Raleigh and at a camp near Robbinsville, he proved to be something less than a compliant prisoner, but when the chained man was transferred to Caledonia State Prison in Halifax County, the superintendent, H. T. Peoples, began to observe in him a certain genius.

Even as a child "Marsh" Williams had shown a talent for fashioning objects with his hands, and as an adolescent he took a special interest in guns. When he was only ten he had made a workable pistol from a hollow reed and pieces of juniper wood, and in prison—for self-defense—he shaped daggers from scrap iron. He also squirreled away paper and pencils and stayed up late at night drawing designs for firearms. Increasingly impressed by the talents of his ward, Peoples assigned Williams to the prison machine shop, where the prisoner repaired the weapons carried by the guards. His remarkable skill permitted him to keep ahead of his work, leaving a great deal of spare time to apply to his own hobby. With scrap metal, hand files, and hacksaws, he began building lathes and other tools, then parts for guns. Tractor and automobile axles became receivers, bolts, and movable chambers; drive shafts became gun barrels and operating handles; magnets became cocking cams and extractors; walnut fence posts became stocks. Peoples, marveling over Williams's ingenuity and precision, risked his own safety and job security by allowing the convict to build complete weapons, some of which were hidden in the walls of the shop. The prisoner was aided by his mother who, in response to his letters, obtained technical data on various models of guns for him and provided his contacts with patent attorneys.

While in prison Williams invented the short-stroke piston and the floating chamber principles that eventually revolutionized small arms manufacture. Inevitably news of these experiments reached the outside, and on 28 Apr. 1928 the *Charlotte News* reported: "An invention that may revolutionize the firearms world, involving radical departures in rapid fire mechanisms as applied to the automatic rifle, has apparently been perfected by Marshall Williams." Within a few days the Colt Patent Firearms Company wrote to George Ross Pou, superintendent of prisons, who forwarded the letter directly to Williams. Later the company sent representatives to interview the prisoner.

Meanwhile, the respected Williams family and their friends in Cumberland County started a campaign to obtain a commutation of Marsh Williams's sentence. They were joined by the sheriff to whom Williams had surrendered and the widow of the man he was accused of killing. Governor Angus W. McLean reduced the sentence, and in September 1929 David Marshall Williams left prison.

Back on the farm in Cumberland County, Williams concentrated on perfecting his inventions; after two years he went to Washington and showed them to the War Department. His first contract was to modify .30 caliber Browning watercooled machine guns to fire .22 caliber long rifle smokeless ammunition. He accomplished the task with his floating chamber principle, the only known way of obtaining great operating energy from small cartridges. Patenting firearms improvements by the dozens, Williams launched a career that was to bring him fame and fortune. For instance, his floating chamber was used in a semiautomatic pistol by Colt, in a rifle by Remington, and in a machine gun by the U.S. Army. But it was the use of his short-stroke piston in the M1 carbine, manufactured by Winchester and other companies, that brought him his greatest fame and his nickname, Carbine (which, he insisted, was pronounced to rhyme with "grapevine").

More than eight million of these guns were made, and General Douglas MacArthur called the light, rapid-fire carbine "one of the strongest contributing factors in our victory in the Pacific."

Williams worked at various times as a consultant for the army and for firearms manufacturers, particularly Winchester. He bought a large house in New Haven, Conn., and spent liberally on classical music, diamonds, and whatever captured his fancy. But his wealth lasted only a short time.

Marsh Williams became a legend when in 1952 James Stewart portrayed him in the MGM motion picture *Carbine Williams*. As technical director of the movie, Williams spent time in Hollywood, then returned to Fayetteville to be honored on "David Marshall Williams Day," 24 Apr. 1952. In the *Reader's Digest* he was hailed by his former prison superintendent, H. T. Peoples, as "The Most Unforgettable Character I Ever Met." Other favorable magazine articles facilitated his return to Godwin, where in his machine shop he continued to perfect other improvements on firearms. In all, he eventually held more than five dozen patents. His reputation was largely rehabilitated (he always denied having fired the shot that killed the deputy sheriff, though he had taken the blame because he was the head of the crew), and he became something of an idol of law enforcement officials: he held honorary membership in the National Sheriffs Association and was appointed honorary deputy U.S. marshal and a second deputy sheriff of Cumberland County.

The General Assembly of 1971 adopted a joint resolution paying tribute to Williams for the "exemplary citizenship" that he had practiced since his release from prison. At the urging of Governor Robert W. Scott, Williams gave his machine shop—building, tools, models, and all—to the State Department of Archives and History. The structure and its contents were moved to Raleigh and reinstalled in the department's Museum of History.

In his prime, Williams was 5 feet 9 inches tall, 180 pounds, with a ruddy complexion, reddish-brown hair, piercing blue eyes, and incredibly strong hands. He wore flaring sideburns down to the level of his mouth, and his dress was characterized by a wide-brimmed hat, a tooled leather belt with ornate buckle, and a revolver in a fancy holster. He was a man of unpredictable moods whose deep wounds of the past exhibited themselves in his suspicion of strangers. Yet, once his confidence was won, he could be a warm and generous being. Following his return to Godwin after the war, he and "Miss Maggie," who earned a teacher's certificate and taught school while he was away, lived quietly in a small, exceedingly modest country cottage without television or telephone. His name did not even appear on the mailbox beside the road. He continued to work regularly in his marvelously equipped machine shop until his health began to fail. Then, almost immediately following the ceremony opening the relocated shop in the Museum of History, he was hospitalized. He died at Dorothea Dix Hospital in Raleigh and was buried in the cemetery of the Old Bluff Presbyterian Church near Wade.

A portrait of Williams by Walter Keul is owned by the family.

SEE: Ross E. Beard, Jr., *Carbine: The Story of David Marshall Williams* (1977); Lucian Cary, "Big Trouble and a Big Idea," *True*, March 1951; John Kobler, "The Story of 'Carbine' Williams," *Collier's*, 3 Mar. 1951; H. T. Peoples, "The Most Unforgettable Character I Ever Met," *Reader's Digest*, March 1951.

H. G. JONES

Williams, Henry (*fl. 1778–1807*), active Loyalist during the Revolution, was a native North Carolinian who owned 369 acres on or near the Pee Dee River in Anson and Bladen counties. His father, Samuel Williams, raised a company of Loyalist militia in Anson County in January 1776. After the defeat at Moore's Creek Bridge Samuel left North Carolina with at least four sons: Samuel, Jr., Henry, Jacob, and William. They went to the frontier of Georgia, and Henry bought 200 acres. In the autumn of 1778 they moved to East Florida, where the father commanded a company of the East Florida Rangers.

After the British took Georgia, Henry accompanied the East Florida Rangers to the Georgia backcountry and also served as a major in the Georgia Loyalist militia. He was captured and released and finally driven from his Georgia land. He fled to the British post at Augusta and was taken prisoner when the Americans took the fort. His wife and seven children had joined him in Georgia. In the summer of 1782 he was exchanged to Savannah, and his family went to East Florida with him at the evacuation.

The postwar experiences of the greater Williams family illustrate Loyalist dispersion. The father, Samuel, lost his sight during the war and died prior to 1787. Samuel, Jr., who had joined the British forces in East Florida in 1777, ended the war with the Barrackmaster General's Department in New York. He participated in the Loyalist exodus from New York to New Brunswick. In 1792 he left his New Brunswick property for the newly opened lands of Upper Canada, where he was given 300 acres in 1794. In 1785 Jacob Williams entered a London workhouse and ended his days there, blind and insane. Meanwhile, in 1784 Henry and William Williams left East Florida for the Bahama Islands, where they lived several years as planters. Henry seems to have returned to Anson County, for in 1807 a Henry Williams owned land near the family's pre-Revolutionary home.

SEE: Anson County Deed Books N and O, Treasurer's and Comptroller's Papers, boxes 1 and 4 (North Carolina State Archives, Raleigh); Audit Office 12:36, 65, 109, 13:82, 138 (Public Record Office, London); Bahamas Register General, B/1, pp. 157, 159 (Archives, Commonwealth of the Bahamas, Nassau); Upper Canada Land Petitions, "W", bundle 1 (Public Archives of Canada, Ottawa); Wilkes County Court Minutes, August 1779 (Georgia Department of Archives and History, Atlanta).

                                     CAROLE WATTERSON TROXLER

Williams, Henry Horace (*16 Aug. 1858–26 Dec. 1940*), philosopher, was head of the Department of Philosophy at The University of North Carolina for all but the last five emeritus years of the fifty he taught there. Born in the isolation of Gates County, on the edge of the Dismal Swamp, he was the eldest of eight children of a country doctor, Elisha, and his second wife, Mary Taylor Williams. A life of teaching in an epochal period brought him into prominence. As teacher he inaugurated the department and became its first Kenan Professor. As philosopher he managed to convey the current and complex ideas of idealism, particularly Hegelian dialectic, with a mastery that prompted his most famous student, Thomas Wolfe, to call him the "Hegel of the Cottonpatch." As a person he had wide impact. He continued to be talked about in legislative halls as well as at dinner tables. In June 1968 he was the subject of the *Reader's Digest* series, "My Most Unforgettable Character," by Dr. C. B. Ross, Sr.

From farm boy on poor land devastated by the Civil War to Heidelberg, Germany, getting educated was difficult for him. After brief but crucial preparation and an in-

terval of clerking, he entered the state university in 1879. Admission was a feat hardly more difficult than the trip to reach Chapel Hill through winter floods by mule-drawn cart, train, and stagecoach. There he distinguished himself in ancient languages, moral philosophy, and mathematics and was active in the Philanthropic Society, one of the two debating societies that in those days governed the campus life and the honor system. As a senior he read German and Greek intensively and in 1883 was granted an M.A., the first advanced degree ever to be awarded for achievement rather than honor, as well as the B.A. degree. President of his senior class and winner of three medals, he became engaged to a lady considered by his college mate and biographer Robert Winston to be one of the most eligible in the village, although marriage did not then follow. In 1891 he was married by Bishop Phillips Brooks at the home of C. J. Havemeyer, the "sugar king," at Yonkers-on-the-Hudson to Bertha Colton of Middletown, Conn., the daughter of an Episcopal minister.

Williams studied further at the Yale Divinity School (B.D. 1888) and won a fellowship at Harvard. There were teaching posts and study in Germany. The most influential teachers were Timothy Dwight at Yale and Dean Edward Everett, William James, and Josiah Royce at Harvard, where Williams's independent mind was stimulated by Hegel's works and the literature of the religions of the world just coming from the East. Both permeated his teaching and writing, particularly logic, ethics, and history. His use of the dialectic, with force of drama that every successful teacher employs, is typified in his summary: ". . . the schools were like departments. Each stood for something definite and true. Spinoza had explored the absolute. He found no place for the individual. Kant had explored the individual. He found no place for the absolute. Science had explored nature. It found no place for the absolute or the individual. Then philosophy will be the synthesis of Spinoza, Kant and science. This is the system of Hegel."

Acceptance of the post at The University of North Carolina was his deliberate choice to help liberalize the institution intellectually and thus free the state and the South from the grip of orthodoxy. Williams proved equal to the task from the first, agreeing that he would teach Christian philosophy if the professor of mathematics would teach Christian math. Long before it became a civil rights issue he declared that all persons have equal rights to opportunities. His classes were well attended, and no leader on campus could afford to miss studying under him. Yet he said in his autobiography, *The Education of Horace Williams* (1936), that for twenty-five years he did not know whether his official life would last until commencement. Popular with students and active on the faculty, he championed the honor system. He ferreted out violations of training rules by football team members while chairman of the athletic committee, and at the suggestion of two students he helped form an honorary society, Golden Fleece—for senior men as it turned out, though not for Williams: exclusion of women was one of his rare failures. On appeal from an editor of the *Tar Heel* for advice when the university president ordered him to submit editorials for approval before publication, Williams demurred from giving advice but said that he himself would write his own editorials and invite the president to write any he wished if he would agree to sign them.

This ability to find and hold his students was based on genuine interest in them as well as in philosophy. He learned to master those educational techniques universally admired: thorough preparation of lectures, wide knowledge of subject, wit, involvement of students in discussion, strong and continuous personal contacts, and pretesting of ideas. Subjects were abstract but illustrations homely; problem-solving and formulation of realizable goals were encouraged. His own involvement in campus ethical and political issues was honest and courageous, which attracted hostility as well as admiration. The teaching of evolution was not banned as elsewhere; in his words, "There were no heresy trials."

His first book was *Evolution of Logic* (1925) and his major work was *Modern Logic* (1927). Style, form, and substance were Hegelian, which as a discipline had by then a strong adversary in pragmatism. Preferring a holistic approach, Williams countered this and other trends towards fragmentation. No less an activist, he concentrated on training leaders, rather than professionals, for free and rounded development of individuals and institutions in the South. His students formed a school of "Horatians" which did in fact dominate and direct social change in church, school, and courts to such an extent that it is credited with having "broken the fetters of a beautiful caste-ridden past" (*Horace Williams: Gadfly of Chapel Hill*, Robert W. Winston, 1942 [portraits], p. 299). Horatians organized the Horace Williams Philosophical Society in 1943 and formed local philosophical discussion groups. In Charlotte one survived, but most declined as did the St. Louis School and American Hegelianism generally, due as much to the dispersal of philosophers into other fields as to the competition of other theories. The Horace Williams Philosophical Society issued two publications, *Logic for Living: Dialogues from the Classroom of Horace Williams*, edited by Jane R. Hammer (1951 [portrait]), and *Origin of Belief*, by Williams (posthumous, 1978 [portrait]).

After the death of his wife in 1922, he adopted Miriam Young Bonner, a young teacher at a nearby college. Following a trip to England and a few months at home in Chapel Hill, Miss Bonner accepted teaching posts in various cities in the East and in California, where she married. Williams gave all of his property to The University of North Carolina in trust, the income to be used for fellowships in philosophy. He died at age eighty-two and was buried in the Old Chapel Hill Cemetery.

SEE: Kemp P. Battle, *History of the University of North Carolina*, vol. 2 (1912); Paul Green, *In Abraham's Bosom* (1929); Archibald Henderson, *Campus of the First State University* (1949); Philips Russell, *These Old Stone Walls* (1972); Horace Williams Papers (Southern Historical Collection, University of North Carolina, Chapel Hill).

JANE ROSS HAMMER

Williams, Isham Rowland (*19 June 1891–23 Apr. 1959*), attorney and World War I winner of the Distinguished Service Cross, was born in Spout Springs, Harnett County, the son of Marshall McDiarmid, a bank president, and Mary Lyde Hicks Williams of Faison. He attended the Horner Military School and in 1913 was graduated from The University of North Carolina, where he was editor of the student annual, *Yackety Yack*. Williams taught history at the Bingham School in Asheville during the years 1913–16 while also studying law and then did further work at the university before being admitted to the bar in 1917. He began to practice in Dunn, but with the entry of the United States into World War I he volunteered for service.

Commissioned second lieutenant in the infantry on 26 Oct. 1917, he went overseas with the Third Division and participated in numerous engagements. He was promoted to first lieutenant and then to captain. During the Marne offensive he was severely wounded on 23 July

1918. For his role in the battle he was awarded the Croix du Guerre by the French government and the Distinguished Service Cross and the Purple Heart by the United States. The citation read: "He led a patrol across the Marne river under intense machine gun fire, and when his boat sank, twice swam the river to correct the fire of his covering detachment and to bring his patrol to safety, after their mission had been accomplished." When he had recovered from his wounds he rejoined his unit, serving in Germany with the Army of Occupation until February 1919. Before returning to the United States he enrolled for a law course at Jesus College, Oxford University.

Back home in Dunn Williams resumed his law practice and successively became county attorney, city attorney, and solicitor of the Recorder's Court. He engaged in general civil and criminal practice but largely gave his attention to corporation work.

On 24 Jan. 1924 at Rocky Mount he married Lenoir Mercer; they had two children, Isham Rowland, Jr., and Lenoir (Mrs. Leslie Tucker). A Democrat and a member of the Presbyterian church, he was buried in the family cemetery at Faison.

SEE: Daniel L. Grant, *Alumni History of the University of North Carolina* (1924); *North Carolina Biography*, vol. 3 (1928), vol. 4 (1941); Raleigh *News and Observer*, 24 Apr. 1959; Charles L. Van Noppen Papers (Manuscript Department, Duke University Library, Durham).

WILLIAM S. POWELL

Williams, Jesse Lynch (*6 May 1807–9 Oct. 1886*), civil engineer, was born at Westfield, in Stokes County, the youngest child of Jesse and Sarah Terrell Williams, both of prominent families of the Society of Friends (Quakers) in the Guilford County area. He was the first cousin of three other men of note: on his father's side, of Levi Coffin, a leader in the Underground Railroad movement, and Elkanah Williams, a pioneer in the science of ophthalmology, and on his mother's side, of Charles Lynch, governor of Mississippi during 1835–37. The Williams family was also renowned for a major part of the Battle of Guilford Court House having been fought on the farm of Richard Williams, the grandfather of young Jesse.

In 1814 Williams and his family were among the people who left North Carolina during its "Rip Van Winkle" period, moving first to Cincinnati, then to Warren County, Ohio, and finally, by 1820, to a place near Richmond in Wayne County, Ind. He received an education in the small local schools where he lived as well as, for a time, at Lancastrian Seminary in Cincinnati.

Even though he had no formal training in civil engineering, it came to be his greatest interest, especially after the idea of a canal to connect the Great Lakes with the Ohio River was aired in the internal improvements boom of the 1820s. In about 1824 he signed on as a rodman with the first survey of the feasibility of such a project, and when the state of Ohio decided to undertake it in the form of the Miami and Erie Canal in 1828, Williams was hired as an engineer. While on this project he made a name for himself by developing such things as the feeding of the canal by a system of reservoirs instead of long feeder streams and designing an aqueduct for the canal across the Scotio River. Largely as a result of his work on the Miami canal, he was chosen by the Indiana legislature in 1832 to be chief engineer of the Wabash and Erie Canal, a position he held until 1876. In 1835 he was appointed chief surveyor of all canals in Indiana and in 1836, the state's chief engineer of canals. In 1837 he was also named to oversee all railroads and turnpikes.

With his career now encompassing railroads, Williams became the chief engineer of the Fort Wayne and Chicago Railroad, a corporation for which he was instrumental in many mergers until it became one of the largest railroads in the Midwest. He was its director from 1856 to 1873. In working with this railway through Indiana and Illinois he came to know and become a close friend of Abraham Lincoln, a friendship that brought him an appointment as government director of the Union Pacific Railway in 1864. He was annually reappointed to this post for five years by presidents Lincoln, Johnson, and Grant. In this job he directed the survey of the most easily traversable path over the Rocky Mountains that the rail was to take; it was said to be one of the greatest engineering feats in railroad building to that time. Further, his report to the secretary of the interior about the overcharges of contractors led to the famed Credit Mobilier investigation.

He resigned his position with the Union Pacific in order to accept the receivership of the Grand Rapids and Indiana Railway. Williams directed the completion of this floundering project acting as both receiver and engineer. Afterwards he took on a similar post with the Cincinnati, Richmond, and Fort Wayne Railroad.

Williams had left the Quaker church in 1830 to join the Presbyterians, and on his settling in the then small town of Fort Wayne in 1832 he joined the First Presbyterian Church. The next year he was named a ruling elder, a position he held for the remainder of his life. Active in the workings of the church, he frequently served as a commissioner at the meetings of the Presbytery, Synod, and General Assembly and was one of the original directors of the Presbyterian Theological Seminary of the Northwest, which later became the McCormick Theological Seminary.

On 15 Nov. 1831 he married Susan Creighton, the daughter of William Creighton, the first secretary of state of Ohio. They had three sons who lived to adulthood: Edward Peet, Henry Martyn, and Meade Creighton. Meade became an influential leader in the Presbyterian church and was the father of Jesse Lynch Williams (1871–1929), the author and playwright.

Williams died in Fort Wayne, where he was buried.

SEE: Mabel Williams Bean, *Williams-Enoch Genealogy with Allied Families* (1953); *DAB*, vol. 10 (1936); Hugh McCulloch, *Men and Measures of Half a Century* (1888); David W. Moffatt, *Jesse Lynch Williams* (1886); Alfred Nevin, ed., *Encyclopedia of the Presbyterian Church* (1884); C. B. Stuart, *Lives and Works of Civil and Military Engineers* (1871); *Who Was Who in America* (1967).

MARTIN REIDINGER

Williams, John (*14 Mar. 1731–10 Oct. 1799*), planter, judge, land speculator, and legislator, was born in Hanover County, Va., the son of John and Sarah Henderson Williams, both from long-established Virginia families. Around 1742 the Williamses, along with the Hendersons, Bullocks, and others of the Hanover County area, moved to North Carolina and acquired large tracts of land in eastern Granville (now Vance) County near the tiny village of Nutbush. During the next fifteen years the elder John Williams was instrumental in the growth of this town, donating large tracts of land for church and civic buildings. After his death, the town was renamed Williamsboro in appreciation of his services.

There is no record of young Williams's formal education, if any, but he did study law sufficiently to be granted a license. In 1763 he and his partner (and double first cousin) Richard Henderson were handling a considerable practice in the Oxford-Hillsborough area. On 12 Nov.

1759 Williams married the widow Agnes Keeling, formerly Agnes Bullock. They had only one child, a daughter Agatha.

Williams was appointed deputy attorney general for the Hillsborough district in 1768. After the Regulation disturbance in Hillsborough on 8 April of that year, he signed the order by which two of the ringleaders, Herman Husband and William Butler, were sent to jail. Perhaps as a result of this action Williams was among those attacked during the Regulator riot of 23 Sept. 1770 in Hillsborough. Beaten with sticks and clubs, he reportedly saved his life by hiding in a storehouse.

Early in his law practice Williams, along with his partner Richard Henderson and Thomas Hart, sheriff of Orange County, had made the acquaintance of the explorer Daniel Boone. As early as 1764 they hired Boone to investigate the western Carolina frontier for possible speculation and development. In 1774 Williams, Henderson, and Hart formed the Louisa Company (soon renamed the Transylvania Company) in order to explore, purchase, and settle lands in present-day Kentucky. In connection with the company, Williams spent the winter and spring of 1775–76 in the frontier settlement in Boonesborough.

Just prior to leaving for Boonesborough, he served as a delegate from Granville in the Provincial Congress that met in Hillsborough in August 1775. On his return from the frontier he was elected to the state House of Commons in 1777 and again in 1778, when he was speaker of the house. On 28 Apr. 1778 he was elected as a delegate to the Continental Congress. Apparently his only activity in the congress was to sign the Articles of Confederation. Williams returned to North Carolina, and on 1 Feb. 1779 he resigned, stating that he felt inadequate for the position.

Elected a judge of the superior court of North Carolina (the predecessor of the state supreme court) on 9 May 1779, he served until his death. During his twenty years on the bench he was involved in several precedent-setting decisions, the most important of which was *Bayard v. Singleton*. This decision, upholding the right of judicial review, was one of several used as precedent by the U.S. Supreme Court in *Marbury v. Madison*.

Throughout his career Williams sought to promote education in his community and the state. For many years he was the financial patron of Williamsboro Seminary, and he served as one of the original trustees of The University of North Carolina. His personal library of 234 volumes was the largest in eighteenth-century Granville.

In April 1799, while presiding over court in Hillsborough, Williams became ill. After a lengthy sickness he died on his estate, Montpelier, outside Williamsboro, one of the largest and most successful plantations in Granville County. Buried there, Williams was survived by his wife Agnes (d. 1803), his daughter Agatha, her husband Colonel Robert Burton, and their numerous children.

SEE: Samuel A. Ashe, ed., *Biographical History of North Carolina*, vol. 3 (1905); Kemp P. Battle, *An Address on the History of the Supreme Court* (1889); James R. Caldwell, "A History of Granville County, North Carolina: The Preliminary Phase, 1746–1800" (Ph.D. diss., University of North Carolina, 1950); Walter Clark, ed., *Colonial Records of North Carolina*, vols. 8, 10 (1890); W. S. Lester, *The Transylvania Company* (1935); William L. Saunders, ed., *State Records of North Carolina*, vols. 11–13 (1895–96), 15–22 (1898–1907), 15 (1906).

M. M. EDMONDS

Williams, John (*29 Jan. 1778–10 Aug. 1837*), lawyer, soldier, U.S. senator, diplomat, and legislator, was born at

Panther Creek in Surry County three miles from Shallow Ford on the Yadkin River. The third of twelve children of Welsh and French Huguenot parents, Joseph and Rebecca Lanier Williams, he received his early education in an old-field school in the county. Encouraged and financed by his father, who had been active in political and military affairs during the American Revolution, John studied law in Salisbury. His brothers Robert and Lewis also excelled in their studies and later became North Carolina congressmen.

In 1800 John Williams moved from North Carolina to Tennessee. Three years later he was admitted to the state bar and began practicing in Knoxville. During 1807–8 he served as the state's attorney general and became a charter trustee of East Tennessee College in Knoxville.

When the War of 1812 erupted, Williams joined the East Tennessee Mounted Volunteers and in February 1813 led over 150 men against the Seminole Indians in Florida. Commissioned a colonel in the Thirty-ninth U.S. Infantry, he joined Major General Andrew Jackson in January 1814 and two months later fought against the Creek Indians at the Battle of Horseshoe Bend.

Recognized for his organizing ability, Colonel Williams was given the responsibility for recruiting men and supplies for the Seventh U.S. Military District. When he refused to release arms and ammunition to a militia regiment because they were designated by the secretary of war for the use of regular soldiers, General Jackson demanded to know why Williams had withheld the equipment at the risk of his country's safety. Because of Jackson's belief that his authority had been overruled and of Williams's feeling that his loyalty had been questioned, the Tennesseans developed a mutual distrust that extended beyond Williams's honorable discharge from the army in June 1815.

Williams's military service probably aided his election in 1815 to the U.S. Senate to fill the vacancy of resigning George W. Campbell. In 1817 he won a six-year term, during which time he served on the Committee for Military Affairs, which reorganized the medical staff of the army and modified the organization of the U.S. Military Academy. Williams voted for legislation supporting the U.S. Bank, the protective tariff, and the Missouri Compromise.

In 1823 he was defeated for reelection to the Senate by General Jackson. The campaign was bitter, with Jackson accusing Williams of spreading a false rumor that Jackson had confiscated land from the Seminole Indians in 1818 for financial investment and charging that Williams's support of William H. Crawford for the presidency was an attempt to discredit Jackson's bid for that high office. Williams could not overcome these charges nor the popularity of Jackson, who won by a 35-to-25 vote.

After losing his bid for a seat in the state senate in 1825, Williams received an appointment by President John Quincy Adams as an ambassador to the Federation of Central America with headquarters in Guatemala. During the one-year term Williams made a study of existing facilities for a canal across Nicaragua and proposed several reforms to the existing civil code.

Despite serious opposition by Jackson supporters, he defeated incumbent James Anderson in 1827 in the state senate race. During the two-year term Williams served on a committee on internal improvements and introduced bills to relieve women debtors, to construct a turnpike to the Kentucky line, and to reform state banking laws. Even though he was unopposed for reelection in 1829, he decided not to run.

From 1829 to 1837 he practiced law in Knoxville and neighboring counties and promoted the projected Louisville, Cincinnati, and Charleston Railroad Company, serving as the first chairman of its board of directors. By 1835 he owned 531 acres of land, 17 slaves, and a carriage. Although retired from political office, he continued to express Whig sentiment by supporting the tariff and opposing Nullification and the growth of presidential power.

In 1805 Williams married Malinda White, the daughter of Knoxville founder General James White and the sister of presidential candidate Hugh Lawson White. They had twelve children but only six lived to maturity: Joseph Lanier, John II, Mary Lawson, Cynthia, Susan, and James. Joseph Lanier served in the U.S. House of Representatives from 1837 to 1843 and received an appointment by President Lincoln as a judge of the U.S. District Court of the Dakota Territory. John II won a seat in the Tennessee legislature in 1845, 1847, and 1857 and was instrumental in the calling of the 1861 Union conventions of Knoxville and Greeneville to denounce secession.

Regarded by friends as a man with a dignified but friendly manner who appealed to all classes of people, John Williams died at his home near Knoxville two days after he had written his will. Both a Mason and a Presbyterian, he was buried in the First Presbyterian Churchyard at Knoxville. His portrait, painted by Eleanor Wiley, hangs in the Tennessee state capitol in Nashville.

SEE: *Biog. Dir. Am. Cong.* (1971); Robert M. McBride and others, *Biographical Dictionary of the Tennessee General Assembly* (1975); Leota Driver Maiden, "Colonel John Williams," *East Tennessee Historical Publications* 30 (1958)

RICHARD A. SHRADER

Williams, John Taylor (*1 May 1859–8 June 1924*), educator, physician, and businessman, was born in the northern part of Cumberland County, the son of free black parents, Peter Williams, a successful lumberman, and Flora Ann McKay. Although his father was illiterate, his mother was not, and when the boy was six she began to teach him to read. In 1867 the family moved to Harnett County, where the father hired a white widow to teach his children in return for his working on her farm. Between 1868 and 1870 John mastered Webster's blue back speller and other books and became an avid reader. By age sixteen he had read widely among volumes of memoirs, history, and biographies.

His parents were active church members—his father was a Presbyterian and his mother a Methodist. John joined the African Methodist Episcopal Zion Church at age thirteen and set out on a course that led him to hold every church position open to a layman. He represented his denomination at quarterly, district, and annual conferences regularly for eighteen years and represented the Western North Carolina Conference in the General Conference of 1892, when it met in Pittsburg, Pa.

In 1876 he entered the State Normal School in Fayetteville (now Fayetteville State University) and in 1880 was graduated at the head of his class. Thereafter he taught school in Lillington, Monroe, Rutherfordton, Southport, and Charlotte. In Charlotte he was assistant principal but resigned in 1883 to study medicine at the Leonard Medical College in Raleigh. Following his graduation in 1886 with the M.D. degree, he was licensed by the State Board of Medical Examiners, one of the first of his race to qualify.

Settling in Charlotte, he soon had a large practice and became a surgeon in charge of the Union Hospital, visiting surgeon at the Samaritan Hospital, and a member of the Board of Health of Mecklenburg County. In 1888, as surgeon of the First Battalion, North Carolina State Guards he was appointed to the rank of captain by Governor Alfred M. Scales. In 1889 and 1891 he was elected to the board of aldermen of Charlotte. He also was a successful businessman as president of the Queen City Drug Company and with real estate and farming investments. He was a founding member of the Grace A. M. E. Zion Church on South Brevard Street, Charlotte, and a trustee of the A. M. E. Zion Publishing Company. President William McKinley in 1897 appointed him the U.S. consul to Sierra Leone, where Williams continued to serve until 1906 as one of the first black American diplomats.

In 1887 he married May E. Killian of Raleigh, but she died shortly afterwards. In 1890 Williams married Jennie E. Harris, of Concord, the niece of W. C. Coleman and a graduate of Scotia Seminary and Livingstone College. They were the parents of a daughter, Aurelia. He was buried in Ninth Street Pinewood Cemetery, Charlotte.

SEE: *Charlotte Observer*, 13 June 1980 (portrait); "Despatches from U.S. Consuls in Sierra Leone, 1858–1906" (microfilm, National Archives, Washington, D.C.); Thomas W. Hanchett, "Sorting Out the New South City: Charlotte and Its Neighborhoods" (Ph.D. diss., University of North Carolina, Chapel Hill, 1993); J. W. Hood, *One Hundred Years of the African Methodist Episcopal Zion Church* (1895 [portrait]); William J. Walls, *The African Methodist Episcopal Zion Church: Reality of the Black Church* (1974).

WILLIAM S. POWELL

Williams, Lewis (*1 Feb. 1786–20 Feb. 1842*), congressman, was a native of Surry County, the son of Joseph (1748–1827) and Rebecca (or Rebekah) Lanier Williams. His father, a native of Virginia who moved to Surry shortly before the Revolution, was a member of the Provincial Congress at Hillsborough in 1775 and at Halifax in 1776, then served as a colonel in the war for independence. His mother was the daughter of General Thomas Lanier of Granville County. The Williams family achieved great distinction. Lewis's oldest brother, Robert, was a congressman and governor of Mississippi. Another brother, John, served in the U.S. Senate from Tennessee, and Lewis's twin brother, Thomas Lanier, was a prominent politician and judge in eastern Tennessee. Congressmen Marmaduke Williams and Hugh Lawson White were both close relatives.

In 1808 Lewis was graduated from The University of North Carolina, where he became a tutor (1810–12) and was granted a master's degree (1812). In 1813 he was appointed a trustee of his alma mater, a post he held for the rest of his life. Surry County sent him to the General Assembly in 1813 and again in 1814. In 1813 he was an unsuccessful candidate for Congress, running against Edmund Jones and the incumbent, Meshack Franklin. Two years later Williams defeated Franklin and thereafter was returned to Congress every two years until his death. His service in Washington for fourteen terms (March 1815–February 1842) gained him the title "Father of the House."

During the Era of Good Feelings Williams, distrusting Monroe, Calhoun, and Jackson, supported William H. Crawford. His early efforts were devoted to a reduction of taxes and the size of the army. In February 1817 he offered a resolution to abolish all internal taxes. The following year he questioned the legality of Jackson's campaign against the Seminoles. Williams was generally opposed to Secretary of War Calhoun's program for internal improvements, but he supported the Missouri Compromise in 1820.

The Williams family feud with Jackson began with the Battle of Horseshoe Bend in 1813, when Colonel John Williams and General Jackson clashed. In 1823 Jackson forced John from the U.S. Senate. In the presidential campaign of 1824 Lewis was a leading supporter of William H. Crawford, and in February 1825, when the House of Representatives had to decide the election results, Lewis voted for Crawford. During the four years John Q. Adams was president, Williams was sympathetic to the administration, and by 1827 he had became a National Republican. Adams men in the state General Assembly tried in vain to reward Williams for his support by sending him to the U.S. Senate.

During the Jackson and Van Buren administrations Williams was in the opposition. Democrat Samuel King tried to capitalize on the fact that Williams opposed Jackson and Van Buren by running against him in 1829 and 1833, but Williams kept his seat. Williams was a bitter opponent of the Democratic presidents on the issue of the U.S. Bank, but he did support Jackson in the Nullification crises and on the Force Bill. In 1833 he was the Whig choice for Speaker of the House, but the Democratic candidate, Andrew Stevenson, was selected by the majority.

In the House of Representatives Williams served for several sessions as chairman of the Claims Committee. He was at different times a member of the Public Lands Committee, the Committee on Territories, the Committee on Indian Affairs, and the Committee on Rules. With the Whig victory in 1840 he emerged as one of the more important members of Congress. His death just over a year later came as a great shock to members of his party. Former president Adams on 23 Feb. 1842 recorded in his diary: "Lewis Williams was one of the best men in the House, or in the world." The "Father of the House" never married. After his death in Washington, D.C., his body was returned to Surry County for burial in Panther Creek Cemetery.

SEE: Charles F. Adams, ed., *Memoirs of John Quincy Adams*, vols. 5–7 (1970); *Biog. Dir. Am. Cong.* (1971); Daniel L. Grant, *Alumni History of the University of North Carolina* (1924); *Greensboro Patriot*, 1 Mar. 1842; J. G. de Roulhac Hamilton, ed., *The Papers of William Alexander Graham*, vol. 2 (1959); North Carolina Sons of the American Revolution, *Lineage Book* (1951); Herbert D. Pegg, *The Whig Party in North Carolina, 1834–1861* (1968); N. K. Risjord, *The Old Republicans* (1965).

DANIEL M. MCFARLAND

Williams, Marmaduke (*6 Apr. 1772–29 Oct. 1850*), congressman, legislator, and judge, was born in Caswell County, the son of Nathaniel, a member of the Provincial Congress, and Mary Ann Williamson Williams. Educated locally, he read law, was admitted to the bar, and established his practice in Caswell County. On Christmas Day 1798 he married Mrs. Agnes Payne Harris, a cousin of Dolley Payne Madison, wife of President James Madison. They had eight children.

Elected to the state senate, Williams represented Caswell County in the 1802 session. In the same year he was also named to the board of trustees of Caswell Academy. When his brother Robert was appointed governor of the Mississippi Territory by President Thomas Jefferson, Marmaduke succeeded him as a member of Congress. He then served three terms in Congress from October 1803 to March 1809.

Williams moved in 1810 to the Mississippi Territory and the following year to Huntsville, Madison County, Ala., where he remained until 1818, when he settled in Tuscaloosa. In 1819 he was a delegate to the state constitutional convention and with the adoption of the new constitution became a candidate for governor. He lost the election to former territorial governor William W. Bibb by a vote of 8,341 to 7,140.

In 1821 he won a seat in the Alabama House of Representatives. Reelected eleven times, he served until 1839. In the house he was known for his "character for usefulness and practical worth" and for his "inoffensive and business qualifications." During the period 1821–40 Williams was also secretary of the board of trustees of the University of Alabama.

In 1826 he was made one of the commissioners to adjust the unsettled accounts between Mississippi and Alabama dating from the time when both were claimed by Spain. In 1832 he was elected judge of Tuscaloosa County, a position he held until obliged to retire at the constitutionally mandated age of seventy.

In his later years Williams continued to practice law but restricted his services to that of counsellor and conveyancer. A member of the Methodist church, he died in Tuscaloosa and was buried in Greenwood Cemetery.

SEE: *Biog. Dir. Am. Cong.* (1961); William Garrett, *Reminiscences of Public Men in Alabama* (1872); L. L. Polk, *Handbook of North Carolina* (1869); Thomas Owen, *Annals of Alabama* (1900) and *History of Alabama and Dictionary of Alabama Biography* (1921); John H. Wheeler, *Historical Sketches of North Carolina* (1851) and ed., *Reminiscences and Memoirs of North Carolina and Eminent North Carolinians* (1884).

JAMES D. GILLESPIE

Williams, Mary Lyde Hicks (*27 Apr. 1866–17 Jan. 1959*), artist, was born in Faison, the daughter of Captain Lewis (Company E, Twentieth North Carolina Regiment, Confederate States of America) and Rachel McIver Hicks. She was a direct descendant of Captain Thomas Hicks, a member of the First, Second, and Third Provincial Congresses and of Henry Faison (1744–88), a soldier of the American Revolution.

Mary Lyde Hicks attended private schools in Faison and was graduated from St. Mary's Junior College in Raleigh. She then studied art and portrait painting in Washington, D.C., and New York. During her lifetime she painted more than five hundred portraits, many of them of political and military leaders. She also did a collection of Negro paintings that later were given to the North Carolina Museum of History.

Mrs. Williams helped organize the Faison-Hicks Chapter of the United Daughters of the Confederacy and from 1912 to 1914 was president of the North Carolina division. For several years she served on the board of the state hospital in Raleigh, and she filled several terms on the State Democratic executive committee.

On 13 Feb. 1889 she married Marshal McDiarmid Williams (1867–1939) of Cumberland County. They moved to Faison and lived in the antebellum home of her granduncle, Isham Faison, which she later inherited. The Williamses had four sons: Lieutenant Commander Lewis Hicks (1890–1931), U.S. Navy; Isham Roland (1891–1959), attorney; Major Marshal McDiarmid (1893–1935), U.S. Army; and Virginius Faison (1895–1977), attorney.

Mrs. Williams, a Presbyterian, was buried in the Faison Town Cemetery.

SEE: Gravestones, Faison Cemetery, Faison, N.C.; Raleigh *News and Observer*, 14 Dec. 1958; Mary Lyde Hicks Williams, *The Hicks Family* (1942).

CLAUDE H. MOORE

Williams, Robert (*25 Aug. 1758–12 Oct. 1840*), physician, legislator, and Revolutionary patriot, was born near Falkland in Pitt County, the son of Richard and Mary Williams. He was the grandson of one Robert Williams who reportedly came from Wales, settling first in Pennsylvania and finally in 1727 on the banks of Tar River at the mouth of Tyson's Creek; Robert, the pioneer, is said to have married four times and to have lived to the venerable age of 105.

The early life of Dr. Robert Williams is obscure. He allegedly obtained his medical education in Richmond and Philadelphia, but his name does not appear in the extant records of the medical school of the University of Pennsylvania. With the advent of the Revolution, he early became active in the Patriot cause. In 1832, at the age of seventy-four, Williams made an affidavit before the county court of Pitt concerning his wartime service in order to benefit from a pension that had that year been granted by Congress to veterans of the Revolution.

At age seventeen, young Williams served under Colonel Robert Salter, seemingly as an ordinary soldier, and was present at the Battle of Moore's Creek Bridge early in 1776. When the troops returned home to Pitt County, he was appointed quartermaster. For a short time Williams saw duty in the Continental line of the state as surgeon's mate under a Dr. Usher. It is possible that this experience stimulated his choice of lifework and that he received his medical training shortly afterwards, for in 1779 Williams was appointed surgeon to a regiment raised by the state under the command of Colonel John Herritage.

During his service of nine months he saw duty at various localities in North Carolina. When the South became the major theater of war, he enlisted in a regiment under Colonel James Gorham organized to aid General Horatio Gates. They joined the remnants of Gates's defeated army at Ramsey's Mill on Deep River, then under the command of General Jethro Sumner. Sumner appointed Williams a surgeon in his army. He sensed that the doctor had ability and offered to make him the chief surgeon, but Williams declined on the basis of his youth. After a skirmish with the enemy at Charlotte, Sumner's troops retreated to the eastern side of the Yadkin, where Williams kept a hospital for some months. When many years later Williams gave this account of his service, an old comrade in arms, one Willis Willson, who had served in the cavalry of Captain Benjamin Caswell in the 1779 campaign and who had also been a lifelong resident of Pitt, appeared in court and testified as to the veracity of the doctor's statement. This statement can be partially substantiated by state records. On 13 Oct. 1779 Colonel Herritage presented a certificate to the Council of State, meeting at Halifax, showing that Dr. Robert Williams, Jr., had been appointed surgeon to the state regiment on 15 Mar. 1779, and it was directed that he be paid from that date. On 6 April Williams wrote Governor Caswell from Camp Liberty Town asking for medicines for his men.

With the return of peace, Williams settled at Windsor in Bertie County where he practiced for a few years. He then returned to his native county and remained there for the rest of his life. In addition to his busy medical practice he was active in politics and represented Pitt in the House of Commons in 1786 and 1787. A member of the convention held at Hillsborough to consider the federal Constitution in 1788, he was again elected to the House of Commons in 1790 and 1791. Williams was elected senator from Pitt in 1793 and served intermittently in that capacity through 1814. As aide-de-camp to Major General Stephen W. Carney, he compiled *A Roster of the Names of the General Officers, and Their Command Respectively, in the North Carolina Militia* (1802). As his last public service, Williams was a member of the convention held at Raleigh on 4 June 1835 to consider changes in the state constitution.

He was buried in the family cemetery near Falkland. A copy of his will had been sent to Washington, D.C., to enable his heirs to obtain his pension prior to the destruction of the Pitt County wills by fire in 1857. From the will it appears that the doctor owned a plantation of several thousand acres and operated a turpentine distillery on the banks of the Tar River. In his will he devised to his youngest son, Dr. Richard Williams, his physic, shop furniture, medical books, surgical instruments, and clock.

Williams married first, on 4 Dec. 1781, Fanny Randolph, the daughter of Mathew Randolph of Virginia. She died on 4 Dec. 1790 leaving two daughters: Harriet (m. first James May and second John Joyner of Pitt County) and Fannie (m. John Hodges Drake of Nash). Williams's second wife was Nancy Haywood, the daughter of Colonel William Haywood of Edgecombe County, whom he married on 10 June 1792. She died on 11 Nov. 1800, leaving a son Robert F. J. H. (m. first Priscilla Foreman and second Caroline Drake), a physician like his father, and a daughter Marietta Eliza (m. Rev. John Singletary, an Episcopal priest). Dr. Robert Williams married for the third time, on 18 Mar. 1804, Elizabeth Hines Ellis, the daughter of John and Elizabeth Hines Ellis of Edgecombe County. By her he had four daughters and a son: Elizabeth (m. first William Foreman and second Edmund Freeman of Raleigh), Polly Ann (m. John Haughton of Pittsboro), Emily Adelaide (m. Dr. Noah Joyner of Pitt County), Adeline Edmunds (m. Rev. Nicholas Collin Hughes), and Dr. Richard of Greenville (m. Henrietta Green).

SEE: Henry T. King, *Sketches of Pitt County: A Brief History of the County, 1704–1910* (1911); Revolutionary Pension File S-7922 (National Archives, Washington, D.C.); John H. Wheeler, *Historical Sketches of North Carolina* (1851) and ed., *Reminiscences and Memoirs of North Carolina and Eminent North Carolinians* (1884); Dr. Robert Williams Family Bible, in the possession of a descendant.

CLAIBORNE T. SMITH, JR.

Williams, Robert *(ca. 1770–25 Jan. 1836)*, congressman and territorial governor of Mississippi, was born in Orange County (the present Rockingham County), the son of Nathaniel and Mary Ann Williamson Williams. His father (1741–1805), a native of Hanover County, Va., settled in the area that is now Rockingham County before 1770; he represented Guilford County in the Provincial Congress at Hillsborough in 1775 and was the first state attorney for the newly formed Rockingham County in 1786. Robert Williams was the brother of Congressman Marmaduke Williams (1803–9) and the first cousin of Congressman Lewis Williams (1815–42) and U.S. Senator John Williams of Tennessee (1815–23).

Robert Williams was reared in Rockingham County, where, after reading law, he was admitted to the bar. He purchased several tracts of land in the eastern section of the county, ultimately amassing nearly 5,000 acres. His home was a 2,000-acre plantation on the Dan River where in 1800 he had twenty-one slaves. In 1799 he secured a lot and house in the county seat, Wentworth, and resided there at least during court sessions. He married after 2 Oct. 1790 Elizabeth Winston (1772–1814), the daughter of Major Joseph and Elizabeth Lanier Winston of Stokes County.

A lifelong Jeffersonian Republican, Williams served in the state senate from 1792 to 1795 and in Congress from 1797 to 1803. On Capitol Hill he was an outspoken opponent of the Federalists. During the Quasi-War with France he was critical of administration policy and opposed all military expenditures. An early and strong supporter of President Thomas Jefferson, Williams was named to the land claims commission for the territory west of the Pearl River in Mississippi. While on the commission he was appointed the third territorial governor of Mississippi; he served from 10 May 1805 until his resignation on 3 Mar. 1809. During this period there was considerable political unrest in the territory, and twice the governor dissolved the legislature. Much of the opposition to Williams was fomented by the territorial secretary, Cato West, who had sought the gubernatorial appointment. A major issue during Williams's administration was the unresolved border with Spanish territory. This led to numerous intrigues and disturbances involving local citizens, the Creek Indians, General James Wilkinson, and Aaron Burr.

Several times as governor Williams traveled on business to North Carolina, where he still held property. Following his resignation he returned to North Carolina, and during the War of 1812 he was adjutant general of the state, the officer responsible for mobilizing the militia and overseeing the equipment and training of the state forces. From 1811 to 1813 he was grand master of Masons in North Carolina. At that time he retained a home in Washington, Miss., the old territorial capital, where his wife died on 25 July 1814. Williams later moved to Quachita, La. He died there and was buried on his plantation near Monroe, La.

SEE: *Biog. Dir. Am. Cong.* (1950); Lindley S. Butler, *Wright Tavern: A Courthouse Inn and Its Proprietors* (1973); Delbert H. Gilpatrick, *Jeffersonian Democracy in North Carolina* (1931); J. G. de Roulhac Hamilton, ed., *The Papers of Thomas Ruffin*, vol. 1 (1918); Sarah M. Lemmon, *Frustrated Patriots: North Carolina and the War of 1812* (1973); Rockingham County Court Minutes, Deeds, and Wills; Dunbar Rowland, *Encyclopedia of Mississippi History*, vol. 2 (1907); Second Census, Rockingham County, 1800; Irene Webster and Linda Veron, eds., *Early Families of the North Carolina Counties of Rockingham and Stokes with Revolutionary Service* (1977).

LINDLEY S. BUTLER

Williams, Samuel Clay *(24 Sept. 1884–25 Feb. 1949)*, lawyer and tobacco magnate, was born in Mooresville, the son of Thomas Jefferson and Willie Ada McCulloch Williams. He attended the local schools and then entered Davidson College. Elected to Phi Beta Kappa, he was graduated from Davidson in 1905 with a B.A. degree and from the University of Virginia in 1908 with an LL.B. degree. On 18 Oct. 1941 Davidson College conferred on him the LL.D. degree. Clay Williams was big physically (six feet two inches tall) and found enough time from his law studies to enjoy his position as guard on Virginia's varsity football team. He was admitted to the North Carolina bar in 1908 and practiced law in Greensboro as a member of the firm of Sapp and Williams (1908–14) and Brooks, Sapp, and Williams (1914–17).

In 1917, at Richard J. Reynolds's personal invitation, Williams moved to Winston-Salem to become assistant general counsel for the R. J. Reynolds Tobacco Company. He subsequently was general counsel (1921–25), vice-president and general counsel (1925–31), president (1931–34), and vice-chairman of the board (1934–35). He was chairman of the board from 1935 until his death fourteen years later. As head of one of the nation's largest tobacco companies, S. Clay Williams became the spokesman for the entire tobacco industry during the New Deal years. He engineered one of the New Deal's first successes: the tobacco marketing agreement of 1933. He was made chairman for industry on the National Labor Board (1933–34) and served on the U.S. Department of Commerce's Business Advisory Council (1933–49; chairman, 1934).

In September 1934, after much urging, President Franklin D. Roosevelt persuaded him to become chairman of the National Industry Recovery Board, and in this capacity S. Clay Williams served as head of the National Recovery Administration. The contrast between the former chief of NRA—the flamboyant, publicity- and power-seeking General Hugh S. Johnson—and the calm, dignified, reserved Williams was startling to Washington observers. The quiet efficiency with which Williams handled his duties, his impeccable conduct, his devotion to his church (Presbyterian), his belief in giving a full day's work, his thoughtful courtesy towards all with whom he came in contact, his lack of political ambition, his noblesse oblige attitude towards public service—these characteristics confused and confounded many of those whom Williams met on the national scene. And they misread him.

Although considered progressive and ahead of his time, especially regarding workers' benefits in the tobacco industry, he did not go as far as some labor leaders desired. The American Federation of Labor fought him as the symbol of big business interests and urged Roosevelt to fire him as head of NRA. The president refused. In March 1935, at the end of his six months' leave of absence from the Reynolds Tobacco Company, Williams asked President Roosevelt to accept his resignation so that he might return to his business and to his family. A Democrat in politics and a liberal in the best sense of that word, Williams remained a personal friend of the president. He served as trustee and member of the executive committee of the Infantile Paralysis Foundation from 1936 to 1946.

On 23 Nov. 1910 Williams married LuTelle Sherrill of Mooresville, and they had two children: Margaret Sherrill (Mrs. Thornton H. Brooks) and Samuel Clay, Jr., M.D. In the late 1920s Williams built a country home, Willsherr Lodge, in Davie County on a large farm bordering the Yadkin River, approximately twelve miles from Winston-Salem. He sold his house on Fifth Street but kept a suite of rooms in town at the Robert E. Lee Hotel, where the family lived during the gasoline shortage of World War II. Unless he was away on business, each Sunday morning found Mr. and Mrs. Williams in their accustomed pew at the First Presbyterian Church, where he also served on the church boards. *Fortune* magazine called him the "Squire of Willsherr"; Winston-Salem friends referred to him as one of their "gentlemen farmers." He raised thoroughbred Red Poll cattle on his model farm on the Yadkin, and his herd was reputed to be the largest and best of this breed in the nation.

On the day of his death Williams had been to his office at R. J. Reynolds as usual. Late that evening he suddenly became ill at his country home and died immediately, apparently of a heart attack. He was buried in Green Hill Cemetery, Greensboro.

Always active in community affairs, Williams served on boards of organizations like the Winston-Salem Chamber of Commerce, YMCA, and Community Chest. He made numerous generous financial gifts to institutions such as hospitals and colleges throughout the state. He was a trustee of Davidson College; trustee and member of the board and executive committee of the National Industrial Conference (chairman of the board, 1943–44); trustee of the U.S. Section, Inter-American Council of Commerce and Production; director and vice-president of the National Association of Manufacturers, 1936–39; and director of the U.S. Chamber of Commerce, 1937–39. Other memberships included the National Council of the Boy Scouts of America, Academy of Political Science, American and North Carolina State Bar Associations, Society of the Cincinnati, Newcomen Society of England, Omicron Delta Kappa, Delta Sigma Rho, Phi Delta Phi, and Beta Theta Phi. His directorships included the American Telephone and Telegraph Company, Security Life and Trust Company (now Integon), and Piedmont Aviation. His clubs were Winston-Salem Rotary, Twin City, Forsyth County, Sedgefield Country, and Congressional Country and Jefferson Island of Washington, D.C.

SEE: Anna W. Bair, personal recollections; "57,000,000 Worth of Whizz and Whoozle," *Fortune*, August 1938; Harold L. Ickes, *The Secret Diary of Harold L. Ickes* (ca. 1953); *New York Times*, 6 Mar. 1935; Arthur M. Schlesinger, Jr., *The Coming of the New Deal*, vol. 2, *The Age of Roosevelt* (1957); *Who's Who in America* 2 (1950); *Winston Salem Journal* and *Twin City Sentinel*, 24 Apr., 25 Aug. 1938, 26 Feb., 22 June 1949.

ANNA WITHERS BAIR

Williams, Thomas Hill (*14 Jan. 1773–7 Dec. 1850*), lawyer, planter, and U.S. senator from Mississippi, grew up just east of the Pee Dee River in the part of Anson County, N.C., that in 1779, when he was six, became Richmond County. Where and how he received his good academic education and sound legal training, except through close association with his civic-minded father, is unknown. Reticent almost to a fault, Tom had a perceptive intellect, a willingness to work, and seemingly independent resources. Only a year after he became of age the 1795 tax list of Richmond County showed that he owned 681 acres, perhaps a fortunate inheritance. Tagged later as a Jeffersonian Republican lacking partisan rancor, he may have been the Thomas H. Williams who in both 1796 and 1797 was elected clerk of the Tennessee House of Representatives. In any case, the flurry of U.S. preparations that accompanied the rise of the cold war with France in the John Adams administration must have accounted for Williams going to assist Caleb Swan, the New Englander who was paymaster general in the U.S. war office. One Thomas H. Williams, conceivably the same man, served honorably as a first lieutenant in the Twelfth U.S. Infantry for the brief period from 1 Apr. to 15 June 1800. The right Williams performed so well for the paymaster general that Swan warmly recommended him for future employment.

The Carolinian may have visited Mississippi territory in 1802 to file credentials towards getting a license to practice law there. In the autumn of 1803, endorsed by Meriwether Lewis, Williams was picked up at Louisville, Ky., by a river craft on which Thomas Rodney of Delaware was floating down to Natchez to begin a career as a territorial judge. Rodney and Williams arrived at Natchez the day before Wm. C. C. Claiborne, the territorial governor, took off for New Orleans to receive formal possession of Louisiana. On 16 Jan. 1804 Williams was in New Orleans acting as Claiborne's private secretary.

After Judge Rodney and Surveyor General Isaac Briggs praised Williams in letters to Secretary of the Treasury Albert Gallatin, Secretary of State James Madison sent down a commission on 3 Mar. 1805 naming Thomas H. Williams to the position of land register west of Pearl River. Pleased with the register's qualifications and popularity, the new territorial governor, Robert Williams, as well as Briggs wrote to President Thomas Jefferson in May 1805 quietly hoping that the register west of Pearl could be additionally appointed Mississippi's territorial secretary, an end effected by recess appointment on 1 July 1805.

None too happy about the doubling up of his engagements, register Williams did discharge the office of secretary of Mississippi territory on an acting basis through 2 June 1806.

Later that year, after Spanish forces intruded to the east side of the Sabine River, General James Wilkinson of the U.S. Army refused to attempt their dislodgement until reinforced by the Mississippi militia. Under Major Ferdinand L. Claiborne, Thomas H. Williams took to the field as captain, adjutant, and quartermaster to the Mississippi contingent. Displeased with Cowles Meade as territorial secretary, the Mississippi governor in the spring of 1807 let President Jefferson know that he wanted a man like "Mr. Williams, the late secretary." The hint resulted in another recess appointment of Williams, confirmed on 12 Nov. 1807. Meanwhile, after qualifying as secretary and with the governor's blessing, Williams left for Richmond, Va., expecting to attend the trial of Aaron Burr as a witness and then visit the president to report on conditions in Mississippi.

As far as known the territorial official made no venture into matrimony until quite late in life. In early 1809 he was contemplating getting extended leave to attend to some kind of private business in Kentucky, but the abrupt departure of Governor Robert Williams from Mississippi at the end of the Jefferson administration froze Secretary Williams in as acting governor of the territory from 4 Mar. to 30 June 1809. Territorial delegate George Poindexter pulled strings in Washington to keep the acting governor from the full governorship, which next went to David Holmes.

Wm. C. C. Claiborne, now governor of Orleans territory, was instrumental in getting Thomas H. Williams nominated on 3 Jan. 1810 (confirmed the next day) as U.S. collector of customs at New Orleans, but Williams continued to be paid as the Mississippi secretary until 25 May. In the new post he exerted valiant efforts to stamp out smuggling and to control erratic foreign shipping. He exchanged frequent correspondence with his superior, Secretary Gallatin, and in October 1812 conferred personally with him in seeking relief from a role that did not end until a new collector appeared on 9 Aug. 1813. Over the next three years he probably based most of his activities in Mississippi. In 1816 he served as secretary to a commission that concluded a treaty with the Choctaw Indians. Late that year, on behalf of John McKee, the U.S. agent to the Choctaws, he circulated through the nation compiling a list of worthy individual claims.

The Mississippi legislature that assembled on 6 Oct. 1817 chose Walter Leake of Red Bluff and Williams from Washington, the former territorial capital near Natchez, as the state's first U.S. senators. They took their seats in the national capital on 11 Dec. 1817, shortly after the Fifteenth Congress convened. Williams was reelected in 1823 for another full term and served through six Congresses (1817–29), most of the time as Mississippi's senior senator. He was appointed to the naval affairs committee in five of the six Congresses and to the public lands committee in three of them. The climax of his senatorial career came in the first session of the Sixteenth Congress when he was chosen both chairman of the standing committee on public lands and chairman of the select committee for the admission of Alabama. In the latter role he operated so promptly that Maine's petition for statehood was additionally thrown to his three-man select committee's care. It happened to be he, the former North Carolinian, who reported on 22 Dec. 1819 a bill declaring the consent of Congress to Maine's admission, but not actually effective until 15 Mar. 1820 because of jockeying for the Missouri Compromise.

Williams did not seek reelection, nor did he welcome any other type of public employment. An opportunity offered through George Graham, commissioner of the general land office, was declined on the ground that he did not financially need the job and "the confinement which would be required would not accord with my plan." He wrote this on 3 Sept. 1829 from Robertson County, Tenn., a healthful farming area from which he picked his wife and where he developed his permanent plantation home. A longtime friend of Andrew Jackson, he did become on 17 Sept. 1832 one of the commissioners who hoped to carry out the terms of the Rives convention with France. Even after settling in Tennessee he made visits to Mississippi, maintaining financial and property interests there.

Williams drew his will of 20 Nov. 1848 and codicil of 16 Mar. 1850 in his own hand but without witnesses. He left his books that were in Mississippi to his nephew Robert H. Wall, whom he had probably helped get established as a planter near Holly Springs. The house and lot he owned at Rodney, Miss., he willed to the widow and children of his deceased half brother Edward. There were legacies to other relations, but the bulk of his Tennessee property and assets, including chattels and cash, went to his wife, his sole executrix. He stipulated, however, that at her death the Williams farmstead near Tyrees Springs would go in fee simple to his grandnephew Tom Williams Turner of Simpson County, Ky. (fifth of the nine children of John and Betty Ann Blewett Turner). He further charged the executrix with obtaining a plain but durable vault in Nashville in which their ashes might rest together. In directing that the dates of his birth and death be inscribed, he categorically stated, "I was born on the 14th of January 1773."

He died in Nashville, obituaries said from dropsy. The Reverend Charles Tomes conducted the funeral services at Christ Episcopal Church, Nashville. Williams was buried with Masonic honors. His widow, Mary Cheatham Williams, born on 25 Sept. 1801, survived until 13 Apr. 1874, after which her remains too were consigned to the Williams vault at the old City Cemetery in Tennessee's capital.

SEE: George Edgar Blewett, *William Blewett Who Settled in North Carolina in 1746: A History and Genealogy of Him and His Descendants* (1954); Clarence Edwin Carter, *Territorial Papers of the United States*, vols. 4–6 (1936–38), 9 (1940), 15 (1951), 18 (1952); Goodspeed Publishing Co., *History of Tennessee from the Earliest Time to the Present: Together with an Historical and Biographical Sketch of the County of Knox and the City of Knoxville* (1887); Francis B. Heitman, *Historical Register and Dictionary of the United States Army*, vol. 1 (1903); W. Edwin Hemphill, *The Papers of John C. Calhoun*, vols. 2–9 (1963–76); *Nashville True Whig*, 10 Dec. 1850; Dunbar Rowland, *Official Letter Books of W. C. C. Claiborne, 1801–1816*, vol. 1 (1917), and *History of Mississippi, The Heart of the South*, 2 vols. (1925); John H. Wheeler, *Historical Sketches of North Carolina* (1851); Thomas H. Williams, will of 20 Nov. 1848, codicil of 16 Mar. 1850, proved at January 1851 term of court, Robertson County, Tenn., recorded at pp. 412–13 in a vol. of Estate and Guardian Settlements, 1848–51 (courthouse in Springfield, Tenn.); U.S. Congress proceedings: *Annals of the Congress of the United States*, 15th Cong.–1st sess. of 18th Cong., vols. 32–41 (1854–56), *Journal of the Senate of the United States of America*, 15th–20th Cong., 12 vols. (1817–30), and *Register of the Debates of Congress*, 18th Cong., 2d sess.–20th Cong., 5 vols. (1825–41).

H. B. FANT

Williams, William *(7 Oct. 1763–25 Aug. 1824)*, Quaker leader and author, was born in Chatham County. His father died when he was young, and he was educated by his mother. Apprenticed at age nineteen to a member of the Center Meeting of the Society of Friends, his feelings grew for the church under the kindly treatment of his master.

On 16 Mar. 1786 he married Rachel Kemp, and they settled in Tennessee where they joined the Lost Creek Quarterly Meeting. In 1799 or 1800 Williams became a minister. Setting off on a preaching tour in 1804, he visited Georgia, South Carolina, and North Carolina, and in 1807 he toured Ohio. The next year he moved to Blount County, Ohio, and helped to organize a new congregation. Finally in 1814 he settled in White Water Valley, in eastern Indiana, where he spent the remainder of his life as a minister. He traveled widely, however, visiting Friends and preaching in Virginia, Delaware, Pennsylvania, New Jersey, New York, and Rhode Island. His journal indicates that he frequently made his way back to North Carolina. Williams occasionally held services for other denominations. His final journey was to the Yearly Meeting in Philadelphia in 1823. He was ill when he returned home and was confined to his room and to bed for the remainder of his life.

It probably was shortly after his death that his followers published a four-page leaflet by him, entitled: *An Address: The following communication from our beloved friend, William Williams, dec., being presented to the Meeting for suffering of the Society of Friends of Indiana yearly meeting, was examined and approved by that body, and directed to be published.* There is a copy of this piece in the Haverford College library in Pennsylvania.

On his travels Williams kept a careful journal that was published in Cincinnati in 1828, four years after his death. Entitled *Journal of the Life, Travels, and Gospel Labours, of William Williams, Dec., A Minister of the Society of Friends Late of White-Water, Indiana,* it is regarded as a highly valuable source of information on the southern and midwestern states that he visited. A copy, now in the North Carolina Collection at the University of North Carolina in Chapel Hill, that belonged to Elijah Coffin of Milton, Ind., bears the neatly penned inscription: "Wm. Williams Journal was copied from his Manuscript which was amended & corrected by my father. It was so neatly done that the printer handed it over to the younger boys in the Office—one of these was David P. Holloway—afterwards a member of Congress." In 1839 a new printing, of which there also is a copy in the North Carolina Collection, was issued in Dublin by printers Webb and Chapman for William Robinson of Belfast.

SEE: R. E. Banta, comp., *Indiana Authors and Their Books, 1816–1916* (1949); Thomas D. Clark, ed., *Travels in the Old South,* vol. 2 (1956); William Williams, *Journal* (1828).

WILLIAM S. POWELL

Williams, William Sherley *(3 Jan. 1787–14 Mar. 1849),* trapper and guide better known as Bill or Old Bill Williams, was born on a farm on Horse Creek in Rutherford (now Polk) County, the fourth of nine children of Joseph and Sarah Musick Williams. His family was of Welsh origin on both sides. His mother was of a Virginia family that had migrated to Rutherford County; his father was born in North Carolina and served for seven years in the Continental army. They married in Rutherford County in 1777 and after the war received a grant of 274 acres on Horse Creek. They sold this in 1794 and moved westward to the vicinity of St. Louis, where they again took up farming.

At age seventeen, following some schooling, Williams became a traveling Baptist minister among the frontier settlements. After seven years he realized that this was not his calling and turned to trapping; at that time St. Louis was the hub of the U.S. fur trade. Settling among the Osage Indians, he hunted and trapped the year round. In 1825–26 he was a member of a surveying party that marked the greater part of the Santa Fe Trail. For the remainder of his life he was one of the ablest of the "mountain men," that hardy and colorful group that hunted and trapped in the West prior to 1850 and that often guided expeditions through wild and unexplored territory. Williams was on good terms with several Indian tribes and spoke their languages. His trapping and guide work took him to virtually every state west of Missouri; surveying and exploration groups sought out his services due to his expert knowledge of the climate and terrain.

In 1833–34 he was a member of the California expedition led by Joseph R. Walker; in 1841 and 1843 he was with parties exploring the Northwest and New Mexico. In 1848 he joined the fourth western expedition of John Charles Fremont as a guide. Mountain snowstorms slowed the party and led to eleven deaths; the group finally gave up and returned to Taos, N.Mex. Fremont blamed Williams for the disaster, rather unjustly in the view of most mountain historians. Several weeks afterwards Williams and another survivor, Dr. Benjamin Kern, returned to this trail in hopes of salvaging some lost medical equipment. They were attacked and killed by a band of Ute Indians.

Williams was probably the roughest, bravest, and most eccentric of all the mountain men, whose ranks included such vivid personalities as Kit Carson, Jed Smith, and Lucien Fontenelle. Albert Pike, for whom Pike's Peak is named, described him as "about six-feet-one, gaunt, red-headed, with a hard weatherbeaten face, marked deeply with small-pox. . . . a shrewd, cute original man, and far from illiterate. . . . the bravest and most fearless mountaineer of them all." His reckless sprees of fighting and drinking in the forts and trading posts of the time became legendary; still, his real love was the untracked solitude of the mountain West. Though reckless at times, he was a skilled trader at the fur posts and an accomplished negotiator with the Indians.

He is believed to have married, around 1813, an Osage woman by whom he had two daughters, and to have been buried by the Indians who killed him near the Del Norte River in lower Colorado. His name is perpetuated in Bill Williams Mountain, Bill Williams Fork of the Colorado River, and probably the town of Williams, all in Arizona, as well as the Williams River, in Middle Park, Colo., and the nearby Williams River Mountains.

SEE: *Asheville Citizen-Times,* 19 Apr., 6 May 1951, 17 Aug. 1961; *DAB,* vol. 10 (1964); Alpheus H. Favour, *Old Bill Williams: Mountain Man* (1936); William Terrell Lewis, *A Genealogy of the Lewis Family in America* (1893); Raleigh *News and Observer,* 27 Feb. 1955; C. P. Williams, *Lone Elk: The Life Story of Bill Williams, Trapper and Guide of the Far West,* 2 parts (1935–36).

JAMES MEEHAN

Williamson, Hugh *(5 Dec. 1735–22 May 1819),* educator, physician, legislator, merchant, scientist, scholar, and signer of the U.S. Constitution for North Carolina, was born near Octorara Creek in West Nottingham Township, Chester County, Pa., close to the Lancaster County boundary. His father, John W. Williamson, a clothier by trade, immigrated to America from Dublin, Ireland, in

1730, settling in Chester County. He married Mary Davison, the daughter of George Davison of County Derry, Ireland; immigrating to the colonies in 1718 at age three, she was captured for a short time by the notorious pirate, Blackbeard, during the crossing. She died in 1805. Her brother, or more likely her half brother, was Brigadier General William Lee Davidson, the North Carolina Revolutionary War leader, according to Williamson.

Hugh was the oldest of ten children—four girls and six boys—growing up under the influence of a typical Scots-Irish home, which taught thrift, industry, resourcefulness, self-reliance, and a deep Presbyterian devotion to the church. His father decided to provide him with a liberal education, and he was first taught by the Reverend Francis Alison at his academy in New London, Chester County. Alison, an "Old Light" or orthodox Presbyterian minister, was later described by Ezra Stiles as the "greatest classical scholar in America." He imparted to young Hugh a deep love for learning and stimulated his naturally inquiring mind. When Alison joined the faculty at the College of Philadelphia, his school was moved to Newark, Del., and taught by his pupil, the Reverend Alexander McDowell, with whom Williamson continued his studies. On completing this course, Williamson entered the College of Philadelphia (later the University of Pennsylvania) in 1753. Coming once again under the influence of his old mentor, Francis Alison, he taught Latin and English in schools associated with the college while he himself pursued the study of mathematics. On 17 May 1757 Williamson received a bachelor's degree in the first graduating class of the college.

Williamson's father died in 1757, just prior to Hugh's graduation, immediately after which he went home to Shippensburg, Cumberland County, to which the family had recently moved, in order to settle his father's estate. During the coming months Williamson continued his interest in theology by studying for the ministry at East Nottingham under the Reverend Samuel Finley, an emerging leader of the "New Lights" faction in the Great Awakening. In 1758 he moved on to Connecticut to pursue further theological training and while there was licensed to preach. On his return he was admitted to the Philadelphia Presbytery.

Doubting that he had the physical stamina required for a public speaking career and motivated by his own increasing personal disaffection with the growing theological debate between the orthodox Presbyterians and the New Lights, having been exposed to both through Alison and Finley, Williamson decided to leave the ministry and study medicine. Although licensed to preach, he was never ordained, nor did he ever accept the responsibility for a congregation. He first obtained a master's degree from the College of Philadelphia in 1760 and accepted an appointment to teach there while studying medicine.

In October 1763 Williamson resigned his teaching position in Philadelphia and sailed the following year for Scotland. He studied consecutively in Edinburgh, Scotland, London, England, and Utrecht, the Netherlands, where he received an M.D. degree. After some travel around Europe, he returned to Philadelphia by 1768 and began to practice medicine. Also in 1768 he was elected a member of the American Philosophical Society, perhaps as part of an attempt to infuse the organization with new blood. Being drawn more and more into the scholarly and scientific affairs, Williamson was appointed by the society to a committee for the observation of both Mercury's and Venus's transit across the sun. He wrote the society's report that was published in volume one of its *Transactions*. He joined other scientists and scholars in conducting experiments and is thought to have collaborated with Benjamin Franklin while in England. His "Observations on Climate" (1770) won him recognition among European scientists, and he read a paper on the electric eel before the Royal Society in London. The Holland Society of Science and the Society of Arts and Sciences in Utrecht made him a member, and the University of Leyden awarded him an honorary LL.D. degree.

Always working in support of his alma mater, the Newark Academy, he toured the West Indies in 1772–73 soliciting aid as a trustee of the school. Again, on 22 Dec. 1773, he sailed to Europe on a similar venture. Having spent some time before sailing in Boston becoming acquainted with many colonial leaders, he was present and observed the Boston Tea Party, leaving for England on the *Hayley*, one of John Hancock's ships, the first vessel to sail from Boston after the Tea Party. Bringing the first news of the event to England and being an eyewitness, Williamson was examined by the Privy Council, to which he remarked that if the British government continued to pursue its present course with regard to the colonies, civil war or revolution could be the only result. He also wrote an open letter to Lord Mansfield, England's lord chief justice, in defense of the colonies. The *Plea of the Colonies* was published on his return to Philadelphia. In March 1774 Williamson was one of twenty-nine Americans in London who signed a petition to the House of Lords protesting the Port Bill.

On learning of the signing of the Declaration of Independence, Williamson sailed for home on the brig *Salley* in December 1776 and was captured by a British man-of-war off the Delaware capes. After managing to escape in an open boat, he delivered important dispatches to the Continental Congress from its European envoys. Finding no suitable medical position available in the Continental army, he returned to his practice for a brief time. In the interim he was elected a ruling elder in the First Presbyterian Church of Philadelphia.

In 1777 he entered into a mercantile business venture with his brother John and sailed to Charles Town. Baltimore bound with a ship's cargo, Williamson stopped his journey at Edenton when impeded from continuing to his original destination by the southwards movement of the British under Lord Howe. Finding a situation to his liking, he decided to remain in Edenton and tried to help the war effort by engaging in shipbuilding operations at Winton and working with a tannery in the Edenton area. He continued in the mercantile business and also reentered private medical practice.

During this time he became acquainted with Governor Richard Caswell and offered his services to the state. After Williamson vaccinated North Carolina troops against small pox at New Bern, Caswell, then major general of the militia, appointed him surgeon general for the state. In August 1780 he served at the Battle of Camden, where he went behind enemy lines under a truce flag to care for American prisoners; he was even consulted by the British in the case of one of their general officers. In the fall he served under General Isaac Gregory in the Great Dismal Swamp, conducting experiments implementing dietary controls, instituting the use of proper clothing in keeping with local environmental conditions, and establishing specific sanitary procedures. Out of a force varying between 500 and 1,200 men during the winter, only two men died from disease and no one was granted sick leave. Williamson apparently advanced funds of his own to the state to buy medical supplies that would be needed in the event of a protracted campaign.

With his election to the North Carolina House of Commons from the Borough of Edenton in April 1782, Williamson embarked on both a political career and eleven years of service to his adopted state. He introduced eight bills, including one granting equity jurisdiction to the superior courts. His first three terms in the Continental Congress (1782–85) revealed him to be meticulous, energetic, and tenacious in discharging his duties. He made himself knowledgeable in areas of public finance, state and national debts, western lands, and Indian problems. Williamson remained in close contact with the state through correspondence with the leadership and through his business associates during the years he lived in Philadelphia and New York attending the congress. He was present at Annapolis in December 1783, when Washington resigned his commission as commander-in-chief of the Continental army and was represented in John Trumbull's painting of the event.

On his return to Edenton in 1785, he was immediately elected once again to the House of Commons from Chowan County and was responsible for the enactment of a law providing for the "Security of Literary Property," a precedent for the future copyright laws. He was instrumental in the founding of several academies and served on their boards of trustees.

One of five delegates to the Annapolis convention in 1786, Williamson was the only one actually to go, arriving on the day of adjournment. In March 1787 he was appointed to the Constitutional Convention at Philadelphia. Arriving on 14 June, he remained for the entire convention and signed the Constitution for the state of North Carolina. He served on five committees, offered twenty-three motions, and delivered over seventy speeches. Williamson's main role at the conference was in proposing and supporting certain compromises that ultimately made ratification a reality. He proposed an impeachment procedure for the chief executive, endorsed a six-year term for U.S. senators, recommended that a free and slave population census be taken in support of the Three-Fifths Compromise, and favored the extension of slavery until a future date in order to give all states conditions that they could accept in the Constitution. Never approving of slavery himself and never owning any slaves, he believed it better to have all the states within the Union, rather than excluding some by adopting provisions that everyone knew would not be accepted.

Williamson worked hard in North Carolina for ratification of the Constitution. He attended the Second Constitutional Convention at Fayetteville in 1789 as a delegate from Tyrrell County, making the initial motion on the floor to adopt the document that he had signed for the state. Meanwhile, he was reelected to the Continental Congress and was the last chosen delegate to serve, remaining in attendance until the old congress lapsed into disuse. He spent many long hours working to regulate the state's accounts from the Revolution with the central government; those records regarding the service of North Carolinians in the Revolution that have survived were saved largely through Williamson's efforts. Elected to the First and Second Congresses from North Carolina, he opposed the assumption of state debts, believing this unfair to states such as North Carolina that had already paid part of their own war debts. In the Second Congress he concentrated on obtaining tariff rates in the Revenue Bill that would be favorable to the state.

On 3 Jan. 1789 Hugh Williamson, a bachelor at age fifty-four, married Maria Apthorpe, the daughter of Charles Apthorpe, a wealthy New York City merchant and Tory colonial official. She died on 14 Oct. 1790, shortly after the birth of their second son. The Williamsons' first born, Charles Apthorpe, died on 18 Mar. 1811 while a law student at Columbia; the second son, John, died on 18 Nov. 1815.

After the death of his wife, Williamson retired from public life upon concluding his second term in Congress. Establishing a permanent residence in New York City, he devoted himself to study, writing, philanthropy, and private business enterprise. Among his numerous writings, principally scientific in nature, is a two-volume *History of North Carolina* (1812) that stands as the first post-Revolutionary history of the state. An original trustee of The University of North Carolina, he served as secretary to the board until 1801. As late as 1816 he corresponded with Nathaniel Macon, giving advice on artists and materials for the statue of George Washington that North Carolina was planning to commission.

A quiet, genial man of strong principal, Williamson died in New York City and was buried in the Apthorpe family tomb in Trinity Churchyard.

SEE: Samuel A. Ashe, ed., *Biographical History of North Carolina*, vol. 5 (1906); Kemp P. Battle, *History of the University of North Carolina*, 2 vols. (1907–12); *Biog. Dir. Am. Cong.* (1871); John L. Cheney, Jr., ed., *North Carolina Government, 1585–1974* (1981); Walter Clark, ed., *State Records of North Carolina*, 20 vols. (1895–1907); Josiah Collins Papers (North Carolina State Archives, Raleigh); Lawrence A. Cremin, *American Education: The Colonial Experience, 1607–1783* (1970); Governor's Letter Books, Alexander Martin (1791) and William Miller (1816) (North Carolina State Archives, Raleigh); W. B. Hannon, "Hugh Williamson: Historian, Minister, Doctor, and Congressman," *Journal of the American Irish Historical Society* 10 (1910–11); Don Higginbotham, ed., *The Papers of James Iredell*, vol. 2 (1976); David Hosack, *A Biographical Memoir of High Williamson, MD, LLD* (1820); *House of Lords Papers*, vol. 34 (1774); Helen Jenkins, "The Versatile Dr. Hugh Williamson, 1735–1789" (master's thesis, University of North Carolina, 1950); Alice Barnwell Keith, ed., *The John Gray Blount Papers*, 2 vols. (1952, 1959); William H. Masterson, ed., *The John Gray Blount Papers*, vol. 3 (1965); William James Morgan, ed., *Naval Documents of the American Revolution*, vol. 7 (1976); Office for the Bicentennial, U.S. House of Representatives, *History in the House*, vol. 3 (January 1987); Williamson Letters, 1778–1815 (microfilm, North Carolina State Archives, Raleigh).

JOHN L. HUMBER

Williamson, James Monroe *(1810–16 June 1877),* businessman and legislator, was born in Roxboro, the son of James and Susan Payne Williamson. His given name (James Monroe), his mother's maiden name (Payne), and the fact that the maiden name of North Carolina–born Mrs. James Madison was Dolley Payne suggests a relationship between these families of friendship if not blood. Williamson was graduated from The University of North Carolina in 1831, studied law, and opened a practice. He represented Person County in the House of Commons for three terms between 1834 and 1837 but in 1838 moved to Tennessee, where he began to practice law in Somerville, Fayette County, and represented the district composed of Fayette, Hardeman, and Shelby counties in the state senate from 1845 to 1849.

While in the legislature, he moved to Memphis in Shelby County and was clerk and master of the county court during the years 1847–54. Later he was president of the Memphis and Little Rock Railroad (1853–56) and cashier of the Bank of West Tennessee (1857–68). Simultaneously he was also president and director of the Memphis City Gas Light Company for twenty years.

Williamson, a Democrat and a Presbyterian, was married to Leonora J., whose surname has not been found.

Their children were Alice, Irene, Leonora (Mrs. William F. Shelley) and James Monroe, Jr. Williamson died in Memphis and was buried in Elmwood Cemetery there. Calvin Jones, a Raleigh physician and on whose land Wake Forest College was built, was Williamson's brother-in-law. Jones moved to Boliva in West Tennessee in 1832, and it may have been he who convinced Williamson in 1838 to move from North Carolina to Tennessee.

SEE: John L. Cheney, Jr., ed., *North Carolina Government, 1585–1974* (1975); Daniel L. Grant, *Alumni History of the University of North Carolina* (1924); Robert M. McBride and Dan M. Robinson, comp., *Biographical Directory of the Tennessee General Assembly*, vol. 1 (1975).

WILLIAM S. POWELL

Williamson, James Nathaniel (*6 Mar. 1842–21 Feb. 1921*), cotton manufacturer, was born at Poplar Grove, the family plantation in Caswell County, the youngest child of Thomas and Frances Pannill Banks Farish Williamson. Thomas Williamson was a wealthy planter and merchant who died when James was only six years old. In his will he left the management of his considerable property in his wife's capable hands. She was a descendant of prominent Virginia families; her maternal uncle, Linn Banks, was a member of the Virginia legislature for twenty-four years, eighteen of them as speaker of the house, and a member of Congress from 1838 until his death in 1842. This interest in public office did not descend to Banks's great-nephews James Nathaniel and his older brother, tobacco manufacturer Thomas Farish Williamson. In his will their father, Thomas Williamson, stressed the importance of a thorough education for all of his children, and his wife carried out his wishes. James attended the preparatory school of Dr. Alexander Wilson in Alamance County, where he was a good scholar, and from there entered Davidson College in 1860.

On 13 May 1861, two months after his nineteenth birthday, Williamson left college to enlist as a private in the Confederate forces in the first company raised in Caswell County, Colonel (later Major General) W. D. Pender's Third Regiment, North Carolina Volunteers. He was wounded at Chancellorsville, Gettysburg, and the Wilderness but always recovered in time to join his company in the next major battle. Promoted to captain of Company F, Thirty-eighth North Carolina Regiment, Williamson took part in the battle at Petersburg and was with his men at Appomattox when the war ended.

He returned to Caswell County to farm the plantation left him by his father and to assume his share of helping his mother run her plantation. Those were hard times indeed for a young man, family fortune gone, trying to restore formerly productive land that had perforce run down during the past four years. His father-in-law, pioneer cotton manufacturer Edwin M. Holt, strongly believed that his family should live and work together as a unit. In 1867 Williamson heeded Holt's wishes and moved to the Holt homeplace in Alamance County. He was made a partner in the firm of E. M. Holt's Sons, which ran the Alamance Cotton Mills, the first (1853) to weave dyed cotton yarn and colored plaid material in the South. Captain Jim, as he was now called, continued to oversee his plantation in Caswell County.

When the Carolina Cotton Mills were built on Haw River and put under the supervision of the Holt sons and Williamson, Captain Jim moved his family to Graham where he spent the remainder of his life. He later built and ran the Ossipee Cotton Mills in Alamance County under the firm name of James N. Williamson and Sons

and the Pilot Cotton Mills in Raleigh under the firm name of James N. and William H. Williamson.

A lifelong Democrat, Captain Jim supported the party but refused any nomination to political office. He was reared in the Presbyterian faith and active in the church wherever he lived. Known for his generosity and kindly manner, he was a favorite with young people.

On 26 Oct. 1865 Williamson married his first cousin, Mary Elizabeth Holt, the daughter of Edwin Michael and Emily Farish Holt, who was the younger sister of Frances Pannill Banks Farish Williamson. They had four children: William Holt (m. Sadie Tucker), Ada Virginia (m. O. H. Foster), James Nathaniel, Jr. (m. Mary Archer Saunders), and Mary Blanche (m. J. Harrison Spencer). Captain Jim Williamson died at his home and was buried in the town cemetery at Graham.

SEE: Samuel A. Ashe, ed., *Biographical History of North Carolina*, vol. 7 (1908); Greg Mast, *State Troops and Volunteers: A Photographic Record of North Carolina's Civil War Soldiers* (1995 [portrait of Williamson and his wife]); *North Carolina Biography*, vol. 4 (1919); Williamson Family Papers (possession of Anna W. Bair, Winston-Salem); Leonard Wilson, ed., *Makers of America*, vol. 3 (1917).

ANNA WITHERS BAIR

Williamson, James Nathaniel, Jr. (*28 Jan. 1872–17 May 1945*), cotton manufacturer, was born at the family home in Graham, the second son of James Nathaniel and Mary Elizabeth Holt Williamson. His paternal grandfather, Thomas Williamson, was a wealthy planter of Caswell County; his maternal grandfather was pioneer cotton manufacturer Edwin Michael Holt of Alamance County; and his grandmothers were sisters Frances Pannill Banks Farish Williamson and Emily Farish Holt, descendants of prominent Virginia families. James N., Jr., was educated at Pantops Academy near Charlottesville, Va., Bingham Military School at Mebane, and The University of North Carolina.

In 1894 he left the university and went to work at his father's Ossipee Cotton Mills in Alamance County. The elder Williamson had joined his father-in-law, E. M. Holt, in the cotton mill business in 1867 and later branched out for himself, building and running the Ossipee Mills and then the Pilot Cotton Mills in Raleigh with his older son, William Holt Williamson. With his grandfather, father, many Holt uncles and cousins, and his own older brother all engaged in the cotton mill business, young James N. naturally chose that field for his own vocation. He rapidly rose to the positions of secretary and treasurer and general manager of the Ossipee Mills. He added the offices of vice-president of Pilot Mills and president of the Hopedale Mills at Burlington. Williamson was not interested in holding political office but chose to serve the public by working as a member of North Carolina's Good Roads Commission. He also sat on the board of the American Trust Company of Charlotte (afterwards the North Carolina National Bank and later NationsBank).

On 9 Nov. 1898 Williamson married Mary Archer Saunders of Richmond, Va. Their children were James Saunders (m. first Ann Stuart Holcombe and after her death, Elizabeth S. Wilkinson), Mary Archer (m. first John Day Seely and after his death, Parker W. Morris), and Edwin Holt (m. Margaret Matilda Nelson). Williamson was reared in the Presbyterian faith, but after his marriage he joined his wife as a member of the Episcopal church, serving on the vestry of the church in Burlington. Around 1930 he and his family began to spend their winters at their home in De Land, Fla., and the rest of the year at their home in Biltmore. He died in Biltmore and was buried in the cemetery at Burlington.

SEE: *North Carolina Biography*, vols. 3 (1956), 4 (1919); *Who's Who in the South* (1927); *Who Was Who in America*, vol. 1 (1981); Leonard Wilson, ed., *Makers of America*, vol. 3 (1917 [portrait]).

ANNA WITHERS BAIR

Williamson, John Gustavus Adolphus *(2 Dec. 1793– 7 Aug. 1840)*, diplomat and legislator, was the son of James Williamson, a large landowner and slave master in Person County. His mother, whose first name is unknown, was the daughter of Dempsey Moore, the first settler of Roxboro. She died not long after John's birth. His father's second marriage was to Susan Paine, also of Person County. Nothing is known about John Williamson's early education, but in 1813 he enrolled in The University of North Carolina. He did not graduate, and although he studied for the bar, he never practiced law.

Williamson spent several years in the mercantile business in New York before returning to Person County, where he was elected to the General Assembly in 1823. He served three terms in the legislature (1823–25) and became known as an Andrew Jackson–John C. Calhoun man by his support of the Fisher Resolutions.

Governor Hutchins G. Burton and Bartlett Yancey recommended Williamson for a diplomatic post, and in March 1826 he was appointed U.S. counsel to La Guayra in the new nation of Gran Colombia. The North Carolina native returned to the United States in 1832, and on 8 May of that year he married Frances (Fanny) Travis of Philadelphia.

After running unsuccessfully for Congress in 1833, Williamson resumed his diplomatic career on 3 Mar. 1835, when he was appointed chargé d'affaires to Venezuela. He was the first U.S. diplomatic representative to that South American republic. There he became well acquainted with José Antonio Páez, who governed the country as president or as master of presidents from 1830 to 1846. One of Williamson's major accomplishments was the negotiation of a Treaty of Friendship, Amity, and Commerce between the United States and Venezuela in 1836.

Frances Williamson was unhappy in Venezuela, and she returned to Philadelphia in February 1840. After her departure Williamson's health deteriorated steadily; he died six months later and was buried in the English cemetery in Caracas. In his will he left two large paintings to the Dialectic Society in Chapel Hill. One of these was probably a portrait of Venezuelan president Páez painted by the English artist L. B. Adams. What happened to these paintings or whether the Dialectic Society ever received them is unknown. A manuscript copy of Williamson's diary is in the William T. Morrey Collection at Louisiana State University.

SEE: Jane Lucas DeGrummond, ed., *Caracas Diary, 1835– 1840* (1954) and *Envoy to Caracas* (1951); Walter Dupouy, *Sir Robert Ker Porter's Caracas Diary, 1825–1842* (1966); Nancy Jane Lucas, "Caracas Exile," *North Carolina Historical Review* 25 (October 1947).

CHARLES H. McARVER, JR.

Williamson, Robert Lynn *(14 Nov. 1860–6 May 1934)*, tobacco manufacturer and agriculturist, was born at Sunnyside, the family plantation in the Locust Hill section of Caswell County. He was the oldest son of Thomas Farish, a pioneer tobacco manufacturer and planter, and Lydia

Minerva Harris Williamson. His father's younger brother was James N. Williamson, Sr., a well-known early cotton manufacturer in Alamance County. Robert Lynn Williamson was named for his great-grandmother's brother, Linn (Lynn) Banks, a member of the Virginia legislature for twenty-four years (speaker of the house for eighteen of them) who was serving his third term in Congress at the time of his death. His maternal grandfather, William G. Harris, a Chatham County planter, was elected to the North Carolina Senate in 1860. Young Williamson found no interest in political office but chose to follow the family aptitude for manufacturing and agriculture. After private schooling in Caswell County, he worked in his father's plant, T. F. Williamson and Company, gaining practical experience in the manufacturing of plug and smoking tobacco.

In 1878 he moved to Winston, a town with many small tobacco factories, where he became superintendent of the T. L. Vaughn Tobacco Company. In Winston he met George T. Brown, the son of another early tobacco manufacturer; they became friends and, later, brothers-in-law. When Brown found himself with 100,000 pounds of tobacco that he could not sell because of the panic of 1893, the time seemed opportune to form a partnership with Robert L. Williamson in order to turn this leaf into saleable products. The two men complemented each other: Brown with experience in marketing and Williamson with expertise in manufacturing.

They rented from Harbour H. Reynolds a small building in Winston just over the line from Salem and on 1 Feb. 1894 began their operations as Brown and Williamson with thirty employees and a capital of $10,000. In their first year they took over T. F. Williamson and Company, Robert L.'s father's firm, which had been moved to Winston around 1880. To the older company's well-known products the young Brown and Williamson partners added their own Bugler, Bloodhound, Kite, and Shot chewing tobacco. The success of the partnership led to its incorporation in 1906 as the Brown and Williamson Tobacco Company, with Brown as president and Williamson as vice-president. The next year they began to manufacture snuff; one of their brands, Tube Rose, continued to be a best-seller for many years. After Brown's death in 1913, Colonel Francis H. Fries was elected president and Williamson continued as vice-president and general manager.

Through the years Brown and Williamson had bought several tobacco firms and added their brands—among them Sir Walter Raleigh smoking tobacco—to its original ones. Early in 1926 the purchase of R. P. Richardson Company of Reidsville brought Old North State tobacco and cigarettes. That summer Williamson suffered a heat stroke, which affected his eyesight, and he realized that he could not be as active in the firm as formerly. Fries's other business interests took so much of his time that he had become only a figurehead for Brown and Williamson, which until now had been a privately owned company with the few shares of stock in the hands of family members. In order to compete nationally in the cigarette market, additional personnel and new financing were needed, so a search was begun. On 23 Mar. 1927 the company was reorganized as Brown and Williamson Tobacco Corporation with Charles A. Kent as president and R. L. Williamson as first vice-president. Soon negotiations were concluded that made the firm a subsidiary of the British-American Tobacco Company.

Williamson had an abiding love of the land and a continuing interest in agriculture, as had his father and both grandfathers. He had owned several farms around Winston-Salem. His last one, on the southern border of town, received its name, Twilight Dairy Farm, from a group of his friends who pointed out that his busy days as a tobacco manufacturer left him only the early evening hours (twilight) in which to visit his farm. He believed in growing his own feed for his dairy herd and liked to try the latest improved varieties, particularly of lespedeza and alfalfa.

A big man physically, Williamson was over six feet tall and stout. He was extremely independent and very conservative in his opinions and business dealings, thrifty, but generous with his family and close friends. He had many of the latter. This was especially evident during the last five years of his life; as his health deteriorated they would come—young and old men alike—to sit and visit with him. "Mr. Rob" was well thought of by the workers in Brown and Williamson's factories; he knew them all, helped many of them through financial crises, and several named their sons for him. He owned one of the first automobiles in Winston and was among the early members of the Twin City and Forsyth Country clubs.

On 26 Nov. 1889 he married Minnie Thompson, whose younger sister Elsie married George T. Brown in 1893. Williamson and his wife had three children, all of whom died in infancy. After the birth of their third child and before their fourth wedding anniversary, Williamson's young wife died. He never remarried. He died at his home in Winston-Salem and was buried beside his wife and children in Salem Cemetery.

SEE: *The Brown & Williamson Story* (n.d.); Williamson Family Papers (possession of Anna W. Bair, Winston-Salem); *Winston-Salem Journal*, 24 Mar. 1927, 7 May 1934; Winston-Salem *Twin City Sentinel*, 26 Oct. 1970.

ANNA WITHERS BAIR

Williamson, Thomas Farish (*10 Feb. 1836–23 Mar. 1911*), early tobacco manufacturer, planter, and church leader, was born at the family plantation, Poplar Grove, in the Stoney Creek Township of Caswell County, the second son of Thomas and Frances Pannill Banks Farish Williamson. His father, a wealthy planter and merchant, died in 1848, leaving the care of their seven young children and of his lands and business interests to his capable wife, Frances. In his will he stated his full confidence in her fidelity, prudence, and sound judgment. Except for designated plantations left to each son, he gave her complete freedom in the management of his estate, and he authorized and directed her to provide for the education of their children "whether at school or at college or for a profession." Frances Farish Williamson was a descendant of prominent Virginia families. Her maternal uncle, Linn Banks, was a member of the Virginia legislature for twenty-four years and speaker of the house for eighteen of them; he was serving his third term in Congress at the time of his death. This interest in politics did not descend to Banks's great nephews Thomas Farish and his younger brother, textile manufacturer James Nathaniel Williamson; they never sought state or national offices but served from time to time in county or town political positions.

Thomas Farish Williamson's main interest was in agriculture, especially in growing and improving tobacco. Although he lived in town the latter half of his life, he always owned a farm close by. As soon as he was of age, he received the plantation willed him by his father and he called the place Sunnyside. It was here in the Locust Hill section of Caswell County in the early 1870s that he began the manufacture of plug and smoking tobacco. Two early chewing tobacco brands marketed by T. F. Williamson and Company were Red Juice and Red Crow. The firm's

Golden Grain granulated smoking tobacco, for its first sixty years a straight bright leaf blend, continued to be made by Brown and Williamson Tobacco Corporation for many years afterwards.

By 1878 T. F. Williamson and Company had a factory in Reidsville. Before 1880 Captain Tom, as he was called, moved the plant and his family to Winston, where his business prospered and expanded. In 1894 T. F. Williamson and Company was purchased by his oldest son, Robert Lynn Williamson, and George T. Brown as the foundation of their new firm, Brown and Williamson Tobacco Company.

By 1900 Captain Tom had moved to Leaksville (now Eden), where he owned and operated a general merchandise store. Maintaining his interest in agriculture, he bought a farm within sight of his home in town. Always concerned for the welfare of his community, he served on the town council where he was known for his sage advice and ability to conciliate opposing factions.

An active and devoted member of the Presbyterian church, Williamson served on its boards wherever he resided: first in his home church, Bethesda Presbyterian in Caswell County, then the First Presbyterian Church in Winston, and finally the Leaksville Presbyterian Church. In 1858 he married Lydia Minerva Harris of Pittsboro; they celebrated their fifty-first wedding anniversary before she died in 1909. They had eight children: Mary Alice (m. first Alexander T. Benton and second Judge Martin Byrd Wood), Robert Lynn (m. Minnie Thompson), Lulu Lee, who died in her teens, Charles Harris (m. Bettie Shepherd), Anna Banks (m. Walter R. Leak), Frances Cornelia (m. John C. Anderson), Thomas Farish, who died in childhood, and Carlton Adolphus, who died in his twenties, unmarried.

Thomas Farish Williamson died at the home of his daughter in Bristol, Tenn. He was buried beside his wife in the Leaksville (Eden) Cemetery.

SEE: Banks and Williamson Family Papers (possession of Anna W. Bair, Winston-Salem); Caswell County Wills (courthouse, Yanceyville); Price H. Gwynn, "Memorial of Capt. Thomas F. Williamson," *Leaksville Gazette*, March 1911; Winston-Salem *Twin City Sentinel*, 26 Oct. 1970; Winston, *Western Sentinel*, 7 Sept. 1882.

ANNA WITHERS BAIR

Willoughby (or Willoby, Willowby), John (*ca. 1622–ca. 1684*), Council member, public register, and leader in Culpeper's Rebellion, may have arrived in the North Carolina colony from Virginia, where at least one colonist bearing his name was living in the 1650s. On the other hand, he may have come from the Caribbean Islands, where the Willoughby family was prominent in his day and included members named John. Whatever his origin, a Captain John Willoughby was living in the North Carolina colony, then called Albemarle, by 1670 and was a member of the Council.

Willoughby was appointed to the Albemarle Council on 20 Jan. 1669/70, when he was made a Proprietor's deputy by Anthony, Lord Ashley, who later became the first Earl of Shaftesbury. At that time he also was named public register of the colony. The appointments were among a number of actions then being taken by the Lords Proprietors in order to bring the Albemarle government into conformity with the system provided in the recently adopted Fundamental Constitutions of Carolina. It is likely that the changes made were chiefly in organization, rather than personnel, and that some or all of the men named to the Council already were members. As the names of the previous Council members are not known, however, it is uncertain whether Willoughby was newly appointed or reappointed in January 1669/70.

He remained on the Council until the mid-1670s, when under a provision of the Fundamental Constitutions the terms of all members expired, including that of the president of the Council and acting governor, John Jenkins. For unknown reasons the Proprietors neither reappointed nor replaced the officials, so de jure government ceased to exist in Albemarle with the expiration of their terms. Despite the fact that their authority had not been renewed, Jenkins and the other Council members, including Willoughby, continued to govern for a time. But soon they were challenged by a faction headed by Thomas Eastchurch, who, as speaker of the Assembly, seized the powers of governor, imprisoned Jenkins, and issued a summons for Willoughby to appear before him and his "court." Willoughby, who as a Council member was an ex officio magistrate, apparently had continued to hold court despite Eastchurch's claim to power. Instead of submitting to the summons, Willoughby beat the man sent to serve it. Soon afterwards he fled to Virginia and remained there until about December 1677, when he returned to Albemarle and helped lead the uprising called Culpeper's Rebellion. He subsequently went to London, along with another leader of the uprising, as agent for the "rebels" in presenting their cause to the Proprietors.

By November 1679 the Proprietors had reestablished de jure government in Albemarle, and Willoughby was a member of the new Council. Again he sat as deputy to Lord Shaftesbury, and, as in his earlier period of service, he was public register for the colony. He remained in office at least until 1682 and probably until his death.

The date of Willoughby's death is unknown. He was alive in the fall of 1682, when he gave his age as "Sixty Yeares or upwards" in a deposition, but he was dead by 3 Apr. 1684, when suits involving his estate were tried in the county court. Little is known of Willoughby's private life. As he was called captain, it seems likely that he was a master seaman, but the title could have denoted rank in the militia instead. He appears to have lived in Perquimans Precinct. No records concerning his family have been located, but a John Willoughby and a William Willoughby who were living in the colony in the 1680s and afterwards may have been his sons.

SEE: J. R. B. Hathaway, ed., *North Carolina Historical and Genealogical Register*, vols. 1, 3 (1900, 1903); North Carolina State Archives (Raleigh): Albemarle Book of Warrants and Surveys (1681–1706), Albemarle County Papers (1678–1714), and Council Minutes, Wills, Inventories (1677–1701); Mattie Erma E. Parker, ed., *North Carolina Higher-Court Records, 1670–1696* (1968); William S. Powell, ed., *Yᵉ Countie of Albemarle in Carolina: A Collection of Documents, 1664–1675* (1958); Hugh F. Rankin, *Upheaval in Albemarle: The Story of Culpeper's Rebellion, 1675–1689* (1962); William L. Saunders, ed., *Colonial Records of North Carolina*, vol. 1 (1886).

MATTIE ERMA E. PARKER

Wills, George Stockton (3 Apr. 1866–27 Feb. 1956), educator, was born in Halifax County, the son of Richard Henry and Ann Louisa Norman Wills. At The University of North Carolina, where he was a member of the Philanthropic Society, he received a bachelor of philosophy degree magna cum laude in 1889 and was honored at his graduation with a special certificate in English. Afterwards Wills became an instructor of English at Oak Ridge Military Institute. Returning to Chapel Hill in 1894, he taught English until 1896, when he was awarded a master of philosophy degree in English; his thesis was entitled "William Cullen Bryant as a Poet." He received a master of arts degree from Harvard University in 1898.

From 1898 to 1900 Wills was professor of English at Western Maryland College in Westminster, and the next year he taught English at Battle Ground Academy in Franklin, Tenn. From 1901 to 1904 he was head of the Department of English at Western Maryland College.

In 1904 Wills became professor of English at Greensboro Woman's College. Three years later he left Greensboro for Baltimore Polytechnic Institute, where he was instructor of English (1907–12, 1914–22), acting head of the Departments of English and German (1911–12), and head of the Department of English (1914, 1920–22). From 1918 to 1920 he was a special instructor in English at the University of Maryland. He returned once again to Western Maryland College in 1922 to become head of the Department of English, a post he held until his retirement in 1944, when he was made professor emeritus. The college awarded him an honorary doctor of letters degree in 1935.

Wills was the author of numerous articles on southern history and literature. An early and important contribution to the Southern History Association's publication was a biographical sketch and complete, annotated bibliography of the works of the poet Sidney Lanier (1899). He also prepared biographies for Samuel A. Ashe and Charles L. Van Noppen's *Biographical History of North Carolina* and was a joint author of the *Freshman Handbook in English*. He wrote a *History of Western Maryland College, 1866–1886* (1949) and a *History of Western Maryland College, 1886–1951* (1952).

On 24 June 1903 Wills married Georgia M. Chidester. They had three children: Katharine Walker, Richard Norman, and Merillat Chidester Wills Frost. After a protracted hospital stay, Wills died of a stroke one month before his ninetieth birthday. His funeral was conducted at Ascension Episcopal Church in Westminster, Md., and he was buried in Druid Ridge Cemetery in Pikesville, Md.

SEE: Kemp P. Battle, *History of the University of North Carolina*, vol. 2 (1912); William Dougald MacMillan, *English at Chapel Hill, 1795–1969* (1970); Raleigh *News and Observer*, 29 Feb. 1956; *Who Was Who in America*, vol. 3 (1965).

BRENDA MARKS EAGLES

Wills, Henry (9 Apr. 1764–12 July 1827), was a printer and newspaper editor. The names of his parents and the place of his birth are unknown. His brother James was a newspaper editor and his sister-in-law, Sarah M. Norfleet Wills, was the first known female newspaper editor in North Carolina and perhaps the first in the United States.

In December 1787 or January 1788, several decades after the introduction of printing in North Carolina in 1751 by James Davis, Henry Wills, at age twenty-three, succeeded Andrew Blanchard as the partner of Abraham Hodge in the printing business. Hodge had gained printing experience during the Revolution operating a traveling press of Samuel Loudon of New York for George Washington. The printing office of Hodge and Wills was located on Pollock Street in New Bern opposite the area where tobacco was inspected. Judging from the numbering and date of the earliest extant issue of their weekly newspaper, the *State Gazette of North Carolina*, the firm apparently was established in 1785. The paper was eight pages or two folded sheets, and subscriptions cost twenty-five shillings per year.

In the summer of 1788 the printing business was moved to Edenton, where the newspaper was continued under the same title and with the same partners. According to Griffith J. McRee in *The Life and Correspondence of James Iredell*, the move to Edenton was a result of the persuasion of James Iredell. Maurice Murphy, who operated a printing business in Edenton, sold Hodge and Wills his printing office on 1 Nov. 1788 for £125. William Righton sold Hodge and Wills, for £125, the printing press, "tipes," and materials he had recently bought from Maurice Murphy.

In July 1792 Hodge and Wills began another newspaper, the *North Carolina Journal*, in Halifax. On 2 Mar. 1793, according to a newspaper notice, Hodge and Wills dissolved their partnership in newspaper publishing. Hodge became the sole proprietor of the Halifax newspaper and Henry Wills that of the *State Gazette of North Carolina* in Edenton. However, they continued their association as state printers. In the issue of 2 Nov. 1797 it was announced that Henry was retiring and that his brother James would become the publisher of an enlarged newspaper.

Between 1788 and 1797 Hodge and Wills were "Printers to the State," having been elected by the two houses of the legislature for the purpose of printing the laws and journals of the General Assembly, the Governor's proclamations, and any other bills that might be ordered. During that period, according to Douglas McMurtrie, considering both governmental and nongovernmental publications, they printed thirty-six titles in Edenton and ten in Halifax. William S. Powell, in his revision and supplement to the work of McMurtrie, added one imprint each to the Edenton and Halifax lists. McMurtrie also listed one imprint, not located, that was printed in Edenton by Henry Wills.

As early as 1788 Hodge and Wills were selling books and supplies at their printing office. By 1789 they offered such items as spelling books, ink, and sealing wax. In December 1794 Wills offered more than fifty books for sale at the printing office. By October 1797, shortly before he retired as a printer, he advertised "bed-ticks" and cloth goods for sale at his general store. By 1799 he was offering sugar, coffee, chocolate, spices, peach brandy, and rum. Later, in 1819, he dealt in family Bibles, stationery, blank books, and school books. From 1817 to 1819 Wills served as postmaster at Edenton, and in 1819 he was a deputy clerk of the court. He was listed as a member of the Bible Society of North Carolina in 1816.

Wills married twice. His first wife was Lydia Loudon (23 Oct. 1766–9 Apr. 1817), the daughter of Samuel Loudon, a New York printer with whom Abraham Hodge had worked before moving to New Bern. They had three sons: Samuel, Henry, and James. Samuel (according to the key to the lost St. Paul's Episcopal Churchyard map) died in 1802 and was buried next to his mother, although there is no gravestone. There were two daughters: Sarah Loudon (m. William Bennett Roberts) and Mary Louisa (m. Josiah Finch of Raleigh). The second marriage of Henry Wills took place on 9 Apr. 1820 to Mrs. Ann White, the widow of John D. White of Petersburg, Va.

Wills died at age sixty-three and was buried beside his first wife at St. Paul's Episcopal Church, Edenton.

SEE: Beth G. Crabtree, *Guide to Private Manuscript Collections in the North Carolina State Archives* (1964); Charles Christopher Crittenden, "North Carolina Newspapers before 1790," *James Sprunt Studies in History and Political Science*, vol. 20 (1928); Adelaide L. Fries, ed., *Records of the Moravians in North Carolina*, vol. 7 (1947); J. R. B. Hathaway, ed., *North Carolina Historical and Genealogical Register*, vols. 1–2 (1900–1901); George Blake Holmes, *History of Saint Paul's Episcopal Church in Edenton, North Carolina, Together with a Guide to the Churchyard Epitaphs* (1964);

Douglas C. McMurtrie, "A Bibliography of North Carolina Imprints, 1761–1800," *North Carolina Historical Review* 13 (1936), and *Eighteenth-Century North Carolina Imprints, 1761–1800* (1938); Griffith John McRee, *Life and Correspondence of James Iredell* (1857); Elizabeth V. Moore (Edenton), personal contact, 1975–76; George Washington Paschal, *A History of Printing in North Carolina* (1946); William S. Powell, "Eighteenth-Century North Carolina Imprints: A Revision and Supplement to McMurtrie," *North Carolina Historical Review* 35 (1958); Blackwell P. Robinson, *William R. Davie* (1957); Thad Stem, Jr., *The Tar Heel Press* (1973); Mary Lindsay Thornton, "Public Printing in North Carolina, 1749–1815," *North Carolina Historical Review* 21 (1944); Stephen B. Weeks, "Libraries and Literature in North Carolina in the Eighteenth Century," *American Historical Association Annual Report* (1895); John Hill Wheeler, "Printers and Newspapers in North Carolina," *North Carolina State Manual* (1874); Will of Henry Wills, Daybook and Ledger of Edenton Bookstore, 1800–1820, and Wills Family Bible (North Carolina State Archives, Raleigh).

B. W. C. ROBERTS

Wills, Sarah M. Norfleet. *See* **Webb, Sarah M. Norfleet Wills.**

Wills, William Henry (*4 Aug. 1809–22 June 1889*), Methodist Protestant minister, educator, and administrator, was born in Tarboro. In 1830 he became a member of historic Whitaker's Chapel, located between Enfield and Scotland Neck. His name was connected with the most significant events of the North Carolina Methodist Protestant Conference from 18 Apr. 1831, when he was licensed to preach, until he was stricken with paralysis in September 1884.

On 13 May 1835 Wills married Anna Maria Baker Whitaker (22 Feb. 1817–2 Feb. 1893), the daughter of Dr. Cary and Martha Susan Baker Whitaker of Enfield. They built a permanent home, Rocky Hill, near Brinkleyville in Halifax County, from which Wills traveled to preach over a wide area of North Carolina, and where his nine children were born and reared.

In 1853 Wills, then a member of the Union Methodist Protestant church, became one of the founders of and principal contributors to Bethesda Methodist Protestant Church, which was built near his home. As a result of his influence, the Annual Conference met at the Bethesda church in 1862.

In 1855 Wills and the Reverend Jesse Hayes Page, later his son-in-law, opened the Halifax Male Academy at Brinkleyville and, shortly afterwards, the Elba Female Seminary. Wills served as a trustee of the Lynchburg (Va.) Methodist Protestant College during the short period of its existence from 1855 to 1861. He received doctor of divinity degrees from Western Maryland College (1872) and Yadkin College.

Wills was secretary of the North Carolina Annual Conference for several years and president in 1848, 1849, and 1868. He served the following circuits or stations in the North Carolina Conference: Roanoke, Haw River, Granville, Halifax, Tar River, Greensboro, and LaGrange. A delegate to the General Conference of the Methodist Protestant Church eight times between 1846 and 1877, as well as a final time in 1880, he was appointed as conference evangelist in 1878. When the General Conference of 1866, of which he was president, met in the Georgetown section of Washington, D.C., the members went as a body to call on President Andrew Johnson in the White House. After Wills made a short address, President Johnson spoke. Reportedly Wills, clad in a suit of black homespun, later informed the president with pride: "Sir, the clothes that I have on are entirely of home production, my wife and daughters having dyed, and spun the wool, woven the cloth, cut out the garments and made them with their own hands."

At the General Conference held in Baltimore in May 1877, he was a member of the joint committee that recommended the adoption of the basis for union between the northern and southern branches of the denomination. On 16 May, when they were officially reunited, Wills and his neighbor, Dr. L. W. Batchelor of Brinkleyville, were among those who presented voluntary five-minute speeches. According to church historian Ancel H. Bassett: "Brother Wills proceeded to express the most liberal and kindly feelings and sentiments. . . . He admitted that in time past he had been opposed to the union, but now he felt happy to accept the situation, and pledged himself . . . to do, or say, or attempt nothing calculated to mar the peace of the united church. . . . He adopted the words of the Moabite convert: 'Entreat me not to leave thee.' " His "firm, conservative position on important questions won for him and his Conference the respect and good will of all. He was indeed an important factor in reaching amicable adjustment between the two divisions of the church."

Wills was said to have preached with "almost Pentecostal power," and, at a protracted meeting in Double Springs, Guilford County, a thousand hearers "seemed to have been swayed as by a strong wind." He was "a close student of the Bible, and made it the staple of his excellent sermons. He was also well versed in the economy of his church, clearly comprehended its principles, and was a parliamentarian of decided ability . . . so that as a presiding officer . . . he was preeminent, deciding points of order with readiness and dispatching business with speed."

SEE: Ancel H. Bassett, *A Concise History of the Methodist Protestant Church* (1887); J. Elwood Carroll, *History of the North Carolina Annual Conference of the Methodist Protestant Church* (1939); Lyman E. Davis, *Democratic Methodism in America* (1921); Edward J. Drinkhouse, *History of Methodist Reform*, vol. 2 (1899); Nolan B. Harmon, ed., *Encyclopedia of World Methodism* (1974); *Journal of the North Carolina Conference of the Methodist Protestant Church* and *Our Church Record*, scattered issues; J. L. Michaux and A. C. Harris, *Memorial of Reverend William H. Wills, D.D.* (1889).

RALPH HARDEE RIVES

Wilson, Alexander (1 Feb. 1799–22 July 1867), educator and Presbyterian clergyman, was born in Newforge, near Belfast, Ireland. He was the son of Alexander Wilson, Sr., a descendant of one of the Scottish families that had settled in Northern Ireland in the seventeenth century. The scant record of Wilson's early life suggests that his father had been moderately prosperous until he incurred financial losses as a result of standing security for friends. The son apparently received a good education and is reported in at least one account to have been awarded a diploma in medicine. Also, there are statements to the effect that his parents had been anxious for him to prepare for the ministry.

Wilson emigrated to the United States as a young man, arriving on 4 July 1818. He probably disembarked at Baltimore, as it is known that he was in the city from July until October of that year before going to Raleigh. Once located there he found ready employment as a teacher in the Raleigh Academy, headed by the Reverend Dr. William McPheeters. In 1821 Wilson moved to Granville

County to become principal of Williamsborough Academy, where he remained for fifteen or sixteen years as a teacher and minister. By 1837 he had moved to Greensboro and was principal of the Classics Department of Caldwell Institute; when the school was moved to Hillsborough in 1845, he continued his association until its closing in 1850.

When the decision was made to leave Hillsborough, Wilson purchased a tract of land in Alamance County known as Burnt Shop, located near the present community of Swepsonville and the town of Mebane. The name Burnt Shop was changed to Melville, and three structures were built on the property—a home for the family, a three-room school building, and a small dormitory. The school was opened in July 1851, and Wilson was its principal for the last sixteen years of his life.

While teaching at Williamsborough Academy Wilson began to conduct prayer meetings, and the people who attended urged him to become a minister. With this encouragement he made the request of Orange Presbytery that he be taken under its care and at the presbytery's meeting in Milton in 1826 was accepted as a candidate for the ministry. In 1830 he was licensed by Orange Presbytery when it convened at Hawfields Church in Alamance County. Wilson's first and only pastoral charge was the Spring Garden Church, located in Granville County, where he preached for four years. This record of his entrance into the ministry is unusual in view of the Presbyterians' insistence on theological training for their clergymen.

On his death at age sixty-eight, his funeral service was conducted at Hawfields Church with interment in the adjacent cemetery. He was survived by his wife, Mary Willis Wilson, who was also a native of Ireland and who had come to the United States to marry him. The couple was married in Baltimore on 9 July 1821.

The will of Alexander Wilson, signed on 11 June 1867, includes the names of five children—Alexander, Alice E. (Mrs. Edwin Heartt), Robert W., John B., and James W. From bits of information that can be pieced together, we know that Alexander and Robert Wilson were associated with their father in the operation of the school and can conclude that the school was continued after the elder Wilson's death. The manuscript copy of the 1860 census for Alamance County lists Alexander Wilson, Jr., as a teacher; he lived until 1880, as his will was probated on 5 July of that year.

A marker on North Carolina Highway 54, near Swepsonville, takes note of Alexander Wilson and his school, and only a few yards away stands a modern public school that bears his name.

SEE: Ruth Blackwelder, *The Age of Orange* (1961); Carrie L. Broughton, comp., "Marriage and Death Notices from *Raleigh Register* and *North Carolina State Gazette*, 1799–1825," in *Biennial Report of the State Librarian of North Carolina, July 1, 1942 to June 30, 1944* (n.d.); Carrie L. Broughton, comp., *Marriage and Death Notices in Raleigh Register and North Carolina State Gazette, 1846–1855*, [1948]; Charles L. Coon, ed., *North Carolina Schools and Academies, 1790–1849* (1915); Archibald Henderson, "Wilson School Famous throughout the South," *Greensboro Daily News*, 29 Apr. 1928 (portrait); A. G. Hughes, "In Memoriam," *North Carolina Presbyterian*, 31 July 1867; *Raleigh Register and North-Carolina Gazette*, 27 July 1821; Josephine Scott, "The Wilson School," *State Normal Magazine* (Greensboro) 8 (1904); Herbert Snipes Turner, *Church in the Old Fields* (1962); Will of Alexander Wilson, Alamance County, 11 June 1867 (North Carolina State Archives, Raleigh).

J. ISAAC COPELAND

Wilson, Alexander Erwin (11 Dec. 1803–13 Oct. 1841), missionary and physician, was born in Mecklenburg County, the son of the Reverend John Makemie and Mary Erwin Wilson. He attended Rocky River Academy in Cabarrus County and was graduated from The University of North Carolina in the class of 1822. After teaching in Morganton Academy, Burke County, he attended the Medical College (now University) of South Carolina in Charleston from 1826 to 1828, when he received an M.D. degree. Thereafter he practiced as a physician in Rocky River. From 1832 to 1834 he studied at Union Theological Seminary, then located in Hampden-Sydney, Va. In September 1834, thoroughly trained in both medicine and theology, he was ordained by the Concord Presbytery of the Synod of North Carolina.

In January 1834 the American Board of Commissioners for Foreign Missions accepted him as a missionary who would also be able to care for the health of colleagues. Together with five other Presbyterian missionaries, Wilson arrived in Cape Town, Cape Colony, in February 1835 to start a new mission in southern Africa. He worked first at Mosega, modern Zendelingspost, Transvaal (1836–37), then near modern Empangeni, Natal (1837–38). Armed conflicts between white settlers and blacks led to the destruction of these two mission stations as well as of other missions in southern Africa. Discouraged by the racial warfare, Wilson left southern Africa in June 1838 and returned to the United States.

Uncertain when circumstances in southern Africa might improve sufficiently for missionaries to be able to return to Natal and Zululand, Wilson volunteered for service in the western African mission of the American Board of Commissioners for Foreign Missions. In October 1839 he arrived at Cape Palmas in modern Maryland County, Liberia. Working as both physician and missionary, he helped to establish more firmly a mission that had been started there in 1834. After only two years in western Africa, Wilson died at Cape Palmas from dysentery. Colleagues wrote of his fervor, his meekness, and his holiness.

On 10 Nov. 1834, in Richmond, Va., he married Mary Jane Smithy (13 Nov. 1813–18 Sept. 1836). After her death he married, on 14 July 1839 in New York City, Mary Hardcastle (21 June 1815–31 Jan. 1849). By his first wife he had one child, Martha Smithey Wilson (15 Jan. 1836–1 Feb. 1906). Copies of paintings of Wilson and his first wife owned by her descendants are in the Africana Museum, Johannesburg, South Africa.

SEE: Archives of the American Board of Commissioners for Foreign Missions (Houghton Library, Harvard University, Cambridge); Archives of the American Board Mission, American Zulu Mission (Natal Archives Depot, Pietermaritzburg, South Africa); Boston, *Mission Herald*, 1833–49; William B. Ireland, *Historical Sketch of the Zulu Mission in South Africa, as . . . also of the Gaboon Mission in Western Africa* [1864]; Russell M. Kerr, *A History of Philadelphia Presbyterian Church* (1970); D. J. Kotze, ed., *Letters of the American Missionaries, 1835–1838* (1950); Eleanor R. Millard, *General Catalog of Trustees, Officers, Professors, and Students of the Union Theological Seminary in Virginia* (1975); Edwin W. Smith, *The Life and Times of Daniel Lindley (1801–1880)* (1949); Thomas H. Spence, *The Presbyterian Congregation on Rocky River* (1954); Vinton Books (transcripts, Congregational Library, Boston).

R. A. SHIELS

Wilson, Edwin Mood (26 July 1872–8 May 1968), teacher and school administrator, was born in Lenoir, the son of Jethro Reuben and Louisa Jane Round Wilson. He attended a public school in Lenoir from early August to December when he was six years old. This was followed by attendance at a subscription school from December to June. He continued this type of training for several years before transferring to Finlay High School, conducted by Captain E. W. Faucett with distinction and success.

In March 1886 he became a typesetter in the office of the *Lenoir Topic*, continuing his studies under the direction of his parents, both of whom were teachers. Two years later he entered Guilford College, where he was graduated in 1892. During this period he met his expenses by working in the college during the regular terms and summer vacations. At Guilford he participated in various student activities and was captain of the baseball team. In 1893 he transferred to The University of North Carolina, where he worked as secretary to President George Tayloe Winston and began graduate work. In Chapel Hill he became acquainted with problems and procedures of academic administration and earned a second A.B. degree.

While still at the university he was informed that he had been awarded a fellowship by Haverford College as a graduate designated by Guilford College. Beginning his work at Haverford in September 1893, he received an M.A. degree in English in June 1894. During the year he entered the contest for the John Sprunt Hill $100 cash prize in North Carolina history. His winning paper, entitled "The Congressional Career of Nathaniel Macon of North Carolina," was published later as Monograph No. 2 of the *James Sprunt Historical Monographs* of The University of North Carolina.

In the summer of 1894 Wilson and three college companions sold subscriptions for stereoptican views, produced by Underwood and Underwood, that featured the buildings and exhibits of the Columbian Exposition of 1892–93. In September, after a successful summer, Edwin became a teacher of English and Latin in Oakwood Seminary at Union Springs, N.Y. While there he accepted an appointment to teach history and Latin at the Haverford School in Haverford, Pa. That marked the beginning of forty-two years of teaching and administration at that preparatory school.

Appointed vice-principal in 1904, he gradually gave up classroom work for executive duties. On the retirement of the headmaster in June 1912, he was appointed to that position and occupied it until he was retired at age sixty-five as headmaster emeritus, on 1 Aug. 1937. During his administration the school made great progress in enrollment, physical plant, strength of faculty, and the quality and range of the curriculum. In 1916 the school became a nonprofit institution under the laws of Pennsylvania. As such, it was developed by trustees and officers into one of the very substantial preparatory schools of the Northeast. Wilson was the initiator of the change of direction and new program.

In 1939 he moved to Philadelphia and became an officer of the Presbyterian Social Union of Philadelphia and chairman for ten years of the Student Christian Association, an interdenominational organization of churches that maintained an educational center for students of the individual churches adjoining the campus of the University of Pennsylvania. He also served in the Westminster Foundation of the Presbyterian church in continuing its work at the university as a member of the interdenominational organization.

Wilson received honorary membership in the Headmasters Club of the Philadelphia area and of the National Headquarters Association, in both of which he had been an active member and officer. Honorary degrees were awarded by the University of Pennsylvania (A.M.), Dickinson College (Sc.D. in education, 1934), and Rutgers University (LL.D., 1935).

On 1 June 1904 he married Alice Green, of Wilmington, the niece of University of North Carolina president Edwin A. Alderman; she died in 1921. Their son, Edwin Mendenhall Wilson, died on 3 Feb. 1909.

In 1955 he moved to the Hillsborough home of another son, Hugh McLean Wilson, who survived him. Edwin was buried in the New Hope Presbyterian Church cemetery in Orange County. A Methodist in his early years, he became a Presbyterian and served as an elder in the Bryn Mawr Presbyterian Church while a resident of Haverford. He was a member of the Democratic party.

SEE: *Chapel Hill Weekly*, 12 May 1968; Daniel L. Grant, *Alumni History of the University of North Carolina* (1924); Louis Round Wilson Papers (Southern Historical Collection, University of North Carolina, Chapel Hill) and personal contact.

LOUIS ROUND WILSON

Wilson, Franklin Inge (Frank.) *(1822–16 June 1865),* teacher, newspaperman, and writer, was a native of North Carolina, but nothing convincing has been found about his origin except that one secondary account says he was born in Caswell County. His writing suggests a classical education and a knowledge of English literature. An attorney, he was in 1848–49 also principal of the Rutherfordton Male Academy as well as county solicitor.

In 1848 he also became coeditor of the *Mountain Banner*, a newspaper in Rutherfordton. In October 1850, in partnership with David S. Reid, he acquired the paper from Thomas A. Hayden but continued as coeditor until 1851, when Reid became governor and Wilson became the sole owner. In May 1851 he wrote to Governor Reid that he was editing the *Banner* and "doing a fair business," having increased its circulation from 300 to 540 copies; his purpose was "to induce the Whigs to read" his Democratic paper. Near the end of the year Wilson thanked the governor for assistance in getting him established with the newspaper.

Wilson was the author of an eight-chapter original novella, published first in his Rutherfordton paper, of which no copy appears to have survived, but which was reprinted in the *Carolina Watchman* in Salisbury on 11, 18, 25 Mar. and 1, 8 Apr. 1852. "Tom Fannon; The Celebrated Tory Partisan. A Revolutionary Romance," set around and in Salisbury, is based on an imaginary episode in the life of David Fanning, notorious Tory renegade in North Carolina in the 1780s. In 1861 a limited edition of David Fanning's own narrative of his activities was published, and it reveals that Wilson's account was remarkably accurate. Wilson obviously drew on what came to be regarded as "oral history," and some of the countryside was so flawlessly described that it could be easily recognized in the twentieth century. The novella is an engaging story of romantic love and rivalry with a touch of murder, suspense, and horsemanship. The characterization is good, and it is remarkably well written.

In Salisbury the issue of the *Carolina Watchman* for 24 Mar. 1853 advertised Wilson's *Mountain Banner* for sale. On 31 March he proposed publishing the *Republican Banner* to be issued in Salisbury as a Democratic organ.

Wilson sold the *Banner* to John C. Cannon, and after retiring to Marion in the mountains for a while he settled in Raleigh. At first he appears merely to have been in the employ of William Woods Holden, editor and publisher of the *North Carolina Standard*. From 1854 to 1859, however, Wilson was associate editor. Among his contributions were reports on the action of the lower house of the General Assembly while Holden covered the senate. The con-

venience of travel by train pleased Wilson in 1856, when he reported that he had gone from Raleigh to Salisbury in eleven and a half hours whereas previously the trip had required three and a half days over muddy roads. In the same year Wilson presided over the meeting of men when the Wake County Democratic Club was organized.

In 1859 he went to Charleston, Va. (now in West Virginia), to cover the execution of John Brown and John A. Copeland, a free black from Raleigh, who had been involved in the raid on Harpers Ferry. This apparently was the first time that a North Carolina newspaper had sent a representative out of the state to prepare a special report for a nonpolitical story. Returning home to Raleigh from a trip to Asheville, Wilson wrote in the *Standard* of 7 Sept. 1859 that the purpose of his trip had been "to soften the asperities of sectional feelings, and to convince the Eastern people that the people of the West are neither savages nor ignoramuses; but on the contrary, that they are intelligent, high-minded, hospitable, and civilized."

From a Raleigh address on 26 Nov. 1860 Wilson issued a prospectus for the *Ad Valorem Banner*, a weekly newspaper that he proposed to establish in early January 1861. To be published in quarto size, his paper would devote about half of its space to poetry, tales, essays, biographies, and other departments for which he would call upon "some of the best writers of the age." The remainder of the organ would deal with politics, news, and other features suitable for "a good Family paper." The "political principles of truth, justice and equality" would prevail, he promised.

The prospectus described Wilson as "a Democrat—one of the Old Guard—and under present circumstances a Union man." He had fought for equal suffrage, which brought the Democratic party to power in the state, and he intended to support "another great popular right— Equal Taxation." Nor was he blind to national concerns. "If Mr. Lincoln or any one else violates the Constitution," he proclaimed, "I shall advocate his removal from power and the infliction of a punishment commensurate with his crime; but I am not in favor of rashly overthrowing the fairest governmental fabric in the world, and of blotting out the last great hope of freedom, on account of the villainy of any man or set of men."

Perhaps as further assurance of his intention to produce a lively paper, he noted: "As occasion requires I shall use a set of editorial casters, well supplied with the vinegar of sarcasm, the mustard of irony, the pepper of ridicule, the horse-radish of invective, and other seasonings to suit times and circumstances."

It has not been possible to determine how deeply involved Wilson was in labor activities, but he presided at a meeting of the Wake County Workingmen's Association in October 1859. At the courthouse in Raleigh on 6 Feb. 1860 he attended another meeting of the association and delivered an address that was published as a 22-page pamphlet. These are presumed to be the first labor meetings in the state.

On the eve of the Civil War Wilson frequently wrote in his newspaper that he was a Union man, but at the same time he anticipated trouble if presidential candidate Abraham Lincoln persisted in ignoring what were regarded as Southern rights. During the course of the war his writings demonstrated no overt disloyalty to the Confederacy, yet something about him aroused suspicions—perhaps his association with W. W. Holden, who had begun to advocate an end to the war. He was at least *suspected* of smuggling copies of Holden's newspaper as "peace propaganda" across the state line into Virginia. This suspicion, however, ought to have been canceled by the publication in September 1864 of a 28-page pamphlet, *The Battle of Great*

Bethel, (Fought June 10, 1861), in which he commended North Carolina Troops in glowing terms for their critical role in winning this significant early encounter with the enemy.

In October 1864 Wilson published a 76-page paperback booklet, *Sketches of Nassau to which is added the Devil's Ball-Alley; An Indian Tradition.* Dedicated to Captain J. Julius Guthrie, Confederate States Navy, the first part of the book is an account of contemporary events in Nassau, in the Bahama Islands, frequently visited by North Carolina blockade-runners engaged in trade. Wilson sailed to Nassau (perhaps for his health, as he mentioned that he was a semi-invalid) aboard a blockade-runner. There he gathered information for this splendid journalistic report on the island, its people, religion, and government. Again he clearly demonstrated Southern ambition for independence.

The final portion of this publication is the author's version of an ancient Indian story. Set in the mountains where he lived briefly in 1854, it is a tale of rivalry between the Cherokee and the Catawba Indians with vivid descriptions of people and places. Told with sympathy and suspense, it may have originated in Wilson's contact with remnants of the Catawba nation in the vicinity of Rutherfordton and Salisbury where he had lived. This is a further example of his use of oral history.

The 1860 census for Wake County described Wilson as a 37-year-old printer and publisher; his wife, Jane, a native of Connecticut, was 34. She had taught in the Rutherfordton Female Academy when they lived in that town. Their children were Jefferson, 15, Ina, 12, David, 8, and Evai, 4. Living in his household were North Carolina–born J. N. Henson, 27, a printer, and Wilson Bliss, 27, a broom maker who was a native of Massachusetts. Wilson reported real estate valued at $2,500 and personal property at $1,000—respectable wealth for the time.

He died in Raleigh at age forty-three, the *North Carolina Standard* reported on 17 June 1865, "after a lingering illness." In the spring of 1859, when he delivered the commencement address at the Horner School in Oxford, he intimated that he had suffered at the hands of an unskilled doctor. No will has been found.

He was described by his contemporaries as "a ripe scholar and fine writer," and this judgment can be confirmed from his surviving writings. He made appropriate references to classical scholars and cited such writers as Shakespeare, Milton, and Byron, as well as Sir Walter Scott and other contemporary authors. He was commended as "an honest, direct, straightforward man. There was no guile or deceit in his character."

SEE: William T. Auman and David D. Scarboro, "The Heroes of America in Civil War North Carolina," *North Carolina Historical Review* 48 (October 1981); Lindley S. Butler, ed., *The Papers of David S. Reid,* vol. 1 (1993); Donald C. Butts, "The 'Irrepressible Conflict': Slave Taxation and North Carolina's Gubernatorial Election of 1860," *North Carolina Historical Review* 58 (January 1981); Charlotte *Western Democrat,* 20 June 1865; Clarence W. Griffin, *History of Old Tryon and Rutherford Counties* (1937); Guion G. Johnson, *Ante-Bellum North Carolina* (1937); Elizabeth Reid Murray, *Wake: Capital County of North Carolina,* vol. 1 (1983); Clarence C. Norton, *The Democratic Party in North Carolina, 1835–1861* (1930); Noble J. Tolbert, ed., *The Papers of John Willis Ellis,* vol. 2 (1964).

WILLIAM S. POWELL

Wilson, George Wood *(7 Apr. 1867–1 June 1930),* attorney and judicial officer, was born at Lenoir, the son of

Jethro Reuben and Louisa Jane Round Wilson. A strong, vigorous child, he spent his early years in his home and attended the local schools, including Finley High School and Davenport College. Following the example of his father, he taught in a county school. He frequently recalled with a chuckle an incident that occurred in a meeting of county teachers in which an eccentric teacher became annoyed with him because of his alertness and accuracy in answering a question that the teacher had badly missed. Smarting because of his discomfiture, the older instructor sharply remarked, "Young man, I have forgotten more than you know or ever will know."

After teaching he was employed by M. M. Courtney of Lenoir as a salesman in a general store for some time, and in 1883 he entered New Garden Boarding School for a year during which he had the measles. Not knowing that he should avoid using his eyes until he was well recovered, he continued his studies with the result that he injured his eyes and had to begin wearing glasses.

In 1884 he became a rodman on the Lenoir end of the Chester and Lenoir railroad, which was completed in 1885. When the first train entered the town, he, his father, and his three brothers were aboard. This job finished, he became a salesman in a general store in Morganton, operated by Claywell Brothers, where he remained until 1898.

At Morganton he became acquainted with a community that, unlike Presbyterian-Methodist–dominated Lenoir, was influenced largely by Episcopalians. However, although he became familiar with the phraseology and liturgy of the *Book of Common Prayer* and had friends among the younger set who danced, he acquired some of the different and more liberal attitudes of the community. More important for the future, he likewise became acquainted with the political life of the area and with the career of his great-uncle Joseph Wilson, a resident of Charlotte, who a generation earlier had become a distinguished district attorney for a large part of western North Carolina. In one of his most famous trials Joseph secured the conviction of a number of Burke County residents who had shortchanged the federal government in minting gold dollars in the branch U.S. Mint at Charlotte. Joseph Wilson and George's grandfather had studied law under Reuben Wood, of Asheboro, who had been a member of the North Carolina General Assembly.

In 1888 George returned to New Garden Boarding School and entered the junior class, joining his brother Edwin Mood, also a junior. Both men received an A.B. degree from Guilford College the first year after it was granted college status. In the next two years George read and studied extensively, took part in the activities of the debating society, and gained experience as a public speaker.

From 1892 to 1898 he was employed by the Holt, Gant, and Holt Manufacturing Company, at Altamahaw, N.C., which operated a large cotton mill and general store. In that position he assumed responsibility for visiting northern markets as buyer and director of the store. He also became acquainted with the methods of operating and financing a textile plant. In 1898 he entered the law school of Columbia University and studied diligently for two years. In August 1900 he passed the North Carolina bar examination in Raleigh and received a license to practice in the state. Returning to Columbia in September, he completed his course and was awarded an LL.B. degree in June 1901.

After considering various places in which to work, he selected Gastonia. In this decision he was assisted by Judge W. A. Hoke, a kinsman and descendant of Joseph Wilson. He was also influenced by the rapid industrial growth of Gastonia and the opportunities it offered for advancement. Thaddeus A. Adams, a Charlotte attorney who was designated as the memorialist of the Mecklenburg bar to prepare a sketch of George's life following his death, wrote that Wilson was by his inheritance a student and a thinker, which caused him to forsake the apparently certain profits or fortune of the industrial world and to devote himself to the legal profession.

Active in politics, and having a keen sense of civic pride, he served as mayor of Gastonia in 1903 and 1904. In 1910 he became solicitor of the old Twelfth Judicial District (later the Fourteenth District), serving continuously with distinction until he resigned in 1922 to return to private practice. In 1930 he moved his law office to Charlotte, where he remained until appointed in 1933 assistant chief counsel of the old Prohibition (later the Taxes and Penalties) unit of the U.S. Department of Justice, a post he held until his untimely death from a heart attack. The position frequently took him out of Washington to various district and circuit federal courts in which he was admitted to practice. He was also a member of the U.S. Supreme Court Bar.

On 2 Jan. 1907 Wilson married Osie Shuford, a teacher in Gastonia. He was survived by his wife and two children, George Wood, Jr., a graduate of The University of North Carolina, and Louisa, a graduate of Randolph Macon Womans College, both of whom received law degrees from George Washington Law School. He was also survived by his mother and his brothers E. W. Wilson of the Haverford School, Professor Robert N. Wilson of Duke University, and Dr. Louis R. Wilson of The University of North Carolina.

A member of the Methodist church, Wilson served as secretary of the Board of Stewards in Gastonia as well as in the Hawthorne Lane church in Charlotte and the Mount Vernon Place church in Washington, D.C. He was buried in Gastonia.

SEE: *North Carolina Biography*, vol. 6 (1919); *Proceedings of the Forty-first Annual Session of the North Carolina Bar Association* (1939); Louis Round Wilson, personal recollections.

LOUIS ROUND WILSON

Wilson, Henry Hall, Jr. *(6 Dec. 1921–22 July 1979),* businessman and presidential aide, was born in Monroe, the son of Henry Hall and Annie Vernon Sanders Wilson. He was graduated from Duke University in 1942, served in the army for three and a half years during World War II, and returned to Duke where he received a law degree in 1948.

Wilson established a practice in Monroe and remained there until 1961. He also represented Union County in the General Assembly for three terms (1953–57). While campaigning for gubernatorial candidate Terry Sanford he met John F. Kennedy, who, after winning the presidency in 1960, named Wilson an administrative assistant to serve as a congressional liaison. Under President Lyndon B. Johnson, Wilson remained in the same post until he resigned in 1967 to become president and chief executive officer of the Chicago Board of Trade. At the time he left Washington he was the senior White House staff member.

In 1968 President Johnson named Wilson to head a commission to promote trade with Eastern European countries. Resigning from the Chicago Board of Trade, he ran unsuccessfully in 1973–74 for the seat in the U.S. Senate formerly held by Sam J. Ervin. He then became a business consultant.

A member of the Baptist church, he was married in 1944 to Mary C. Walters, and they had two daughters and a son: Jean, Nancy, and Henry H. III. After nearly a year

of declining health, he died in a Charlotte hospital. He was buried in Monroe.

SEE: John L. Cheney, Jr., ed., *North Carolina Government, 1585–1974* (1975); *Greensboro Daily News,* 11 Nov. 1973, 23 July 1979 (portrait); *New York Times,* 23 July 1979; Raleigh *News and Observer,* 5 Mar. 1967, 26 Feb. 1972; *Who's Who in America* (1976); *Who's Who in American Politics* (1977).

WILLIAM S. POWELL

Wilson, Hugh *(16 Mar. 1794–8 Mar. 1868),* missionary, was born in the Bethany community of Iredell County, the son of the Reverend Lewis Feuilleteau and Margaret Hall Wilson. His father was a medical doctor. Hugh was graduated from the College of New Jersey, Princeton, in 1819 and received the customary M.A. degree in 1822. Between those two dates he attended the Princeton Theological Seminary and in 1822 was licensed by the New Brunswick Presbytery of the Presbyterian church.

Ordained by the Concord Presbytery in his home community in North Carolina on 14 Sept. 1822, he served as a missionary to the Choctaw Indians of Georgia during the years 1823–26 and to the Chickasaw Indians in Mississippi and Alabama during 1826–32. He was pastor of Portersville and Mount Carmel churches in Tennessee from 1832 to 1837. In the summer of 1837 he toured the Republic of Texas, where the next year he became a missionary. Moving to San Augustine in East Texas, he organized Bethel Presbyterian Church in June 1838; he then went to Washington County in south-central Texas and established a church at Mount Prospect in February 1839, remaining there until 1850.

Beginning in October 1838 Wilson taught for two years and served on the board of Independence Female Academy. When the Texas congress met in Washington-on-the-Brazos in 1844, he was chaplain of the lower house. Moving again, he organized in May 1852 a church at String Prairie in Burleson (now Lee) County, which he served for the rest of his life.

Called "the father of Texas Presbyterianism," Wilson was moderator of the Synod of Texas in 1857 and received an honorary doctor of divinity degree from Austin College (now the University of Texas), which he had helped found. In Princeton, N.J., on 12 June 1822, he married Ethalinda Hall. After her death in 1856, he married Mrs. Elizabeth Loughridge Reid in 1858. Wilson died in Burleson County and was buried near Tanglewood, survived by four daughters.

SEE: *General Catalogue of Princeton University* (1908); William S. Red, *A History of the Presbyterian Church in Texas* (1936); Eugene C. Scott, *Ministerial Directory of the Presbyterian Church, U.S., 1861–1941* (1942); Walter Prescott Webb, ed., *The Handbook of Texas,* vol. 2 (1952).

WILLIAM S. POWELL

Wilson, James Lewis *(ca. 1760–ca. 1802),* Episcopal clergyman. Little is known about Wilson, due in part to the partial destruction by fire of the records of Martin County where he seems to have spent most of his life. At the time of the Federal Census of 1790, he was residing in Martin with a wife and children. A few years later, as "of Williamston" he advertised in a Halifax newspaper. In 1789 Wilson made the then difficult journey to Philadelphia, where he was ordained to the Episcopal priesthood by Bishop William White on 21 July.

It is apparent that on his return to North Carolina there was not a great demand for his ministrations. In 1792 he

wrote his fellow clergyman, the Reverend Charles Pettigrew, that he had studied physic, as medicine was then
referred to, as early as 1780 and humorously commented
that he had quacked with some success without pay since
then. He further wrote that prominent persons in his
community were encouraging him to take up the practice
of medicine for profit, and that he was considering this, in
the sense that St. Paul was a tent maker, to sustain him
while he performed his clerical duties, which were not
economically rewarding. Wilson remained in Martin
County until 1795—in a list of the Episcopal clergy in
North Carolina drawn up by the Reverend Mr. Pettigrew
in that year, he is mentioned as serving in Martin and
Edgecombe counties.

Deciding to try a new area, he moved to Halifax
County sometime in 1795. On 25 June he was appointed
chaplain of the Royal White Hart Masonic Lodge in
Halifax town. By the fall Wilson had moved to Crowell's
Cross Roads in central Halifax County where, as he ad-
vertised in the *North Carolina Journal*, he had opened a
Latin school near Conoconary Church. In teaching school,
Wilson was fulfilling the dual role characteristic of the
Anglican clergy in colonial times. Conoconary Church,
where he had located, was the former parish church of
Edgecombe Parish, Halifax County, under the colonial establishment and the site of the residence of the Reverend
Thomas Burges, the old colonial parson who had died in
1779. Wilson undoubtedly held services in the old church,
which since the Revolution had been designated a free
church open to use by all. By 1798 he had moved again,
for in January of that year his school was located at New
Hope, described as a beautiful seat near Halifax, where
board, washing, and lodging with tuition could be had for
£20 Virginia money a year.

Before moving to the town of Halifax he may have had
some idea of returning to Williamston, because on 21
Sept. 1797 as of Halifax County he bought Lot 18 in that
town from Thomas Hunter. It is not known if Wilson ever
returned to Martin County. He does not appear in the
Federal Census of 1800 in either Martin or Halifax, but
this is not conclusive evidence. He was still in Halifax on
22 Jan. 1800, when he delivered the funeral oration at the
Royal White Hart Lodge in honor of George Washington,
who had died late in 1799. According to tradition he
preached a funeral sermon in Scotland Neck in lower
Halifax County in the summer of 1801. He is thought to
have died soon afterwards. There is no record of Wilson's
death or of his descendants.

James L. Wilson is best known for his work with the
Tarboro conventions. From 1790 to 1794 the few remaining Episcopal clergy and laity in North Carolina gathered
in Tarboro in four conventions in an attempt to establish
an Episcopal church organization in the state. Wilson was
the only clergyman who attended all of the conventions,
and he was president of one of them. The Reverend
Joseph B. Cheshire, the historian of the Tarboro conventions, said of Wilson's work at these meetings that he was
a most zealous and devoted minister and highly respected and trusted by all. In 1792 Wilson went to New
York City to attend the General Convention of the Episcopal Church as a delegate from North Carolina. However,
due to difficulties in travel, he arrived a few days after the
convention was over.

Two letters of Wilson have survived, both written to the
Reverend Charles Pettigrew on church matters. From
these letters, it is clear that Wilson was orthodox and took
his work seriously.

SEE: Joseph B. Cheshire, ed., *Sketches of Church History*
(1892); Halifax, *North Carolina Journal*, 29 Apr., 26 Oct.

1795, 8 Jan. 1798; Sarah M. Lemmon, *The Pettigrew Papers*,
vol. 1 (1971); Martin County Deeds (North Carolina State
Archives, Raleigh); Thomas C. Parramore, *Launching the
Craft: The First Half-Century of Freemasonry in North Car-
olina* (1979); Stuart H. Smith and Claiborne T. Smith, Jr.,
History of Trinity Parish (1955).

CLAIBORNE T. SMITH, JR.

Wilson, James William (*17 Dec. 1832–2 July 1910*), engineer, was born in Granville County, the son of the Reverend Alexander, a noted Presbyterian clergyman and educator, and Mary Willis Wilson. He grew up in Alamance
County, attended the Caldwell Institute in Greensboro,
and was graduated from The University of North Carolina in 1852. Choosing the profession of civil engineer, he
became a rodman on the survey of the Western North
Carolina Railroad and was soon promoted to assistant engineer. Wilson settled in Morganton in 1856 and in 1861
married Louise Erwin, of McDowell County, who bore
him ten children.

When the Civil War began, Wilson returned to Alamance County and raised Company F, Sixth North Carolina Troops. He became captain of the company and was
later promoted to major and assistant quartermaster on
the staff of General Stephen D. Ramseur. Wilson took part
in most of the campaigns of the Army of Northern Virginia from the Seven Days' Battle in 1862 to Cedar Creek
in 1864. In late 1864 Governor Zebulon B. Vance appointed him superintendent of the Western North Carolina Railroad. He was removed from the post during Reconstruction but continued to do work on the road under
contract.

After the war Wilson became active in the Democratic
party and with Alphonso C. Avery and Samuel McD. Tate
formed a triumvirate that dominated the politics of Burke
County and had a strong influence in the affairs of the
Western North Carolina Railroad. In 1876 he was elected
to the state house of representatives, where he championed the bill that reorganized the road, in which he
owned 1,400 shares of stock, making him one of the
largest private stockholders. In the spring of 1877 the new
board of directors elected Wilson president of the railroad, and in this post he achieved his major claim to fame.
Assuming the positions of chief engineer and general superintendent at a reduced salary, he worked to restore the
finances of the near-bankrupt company to a sound condition and pushed forward the work on the line, which had
virtually come to a halt during Reconstruction.

The building of the railroad through the mountains of
western North Carolina, in the face of forbidding terrain,
frequent landslides, and severe weather, as well as shortages of money, labor, and supplies, and sniping from political enemies, constituted an engineering feat that can only
be described as heroic. In 1880 the state sold the Western
North Carolina Railroad to a New York syndicate, which
soon lost control to the Richmond and Danville Railroad.
Wilson remained chief engineer until 1887, when he resigned to become chief engineer of the Knoxville, Cumberland Gap, and Louisville Railroad in Tennessee.

When North Carolina established a railroad commission in 1891, Wilson became its chairman. He was generally considered to be the member most sympathetic to the
railroads. In 1897 Governor Daniel L. Russell retaliated
against the commission's refusal to reduce railroad rates
by attempting to remove James W. Wilson and S. Otho
Wilson (no relation to him or his office). Russell charged
that James Wilson and Vice-President Alexander B. Andrews of the Southern Railroad owned the Round Knob
Hotel, which was worthless except as an eating house for

the Southern Railroad, and that they had persuaded S. Otho Wilson to lease the hotel in his mother's name with the understanding that the railroad would abandon its other eating houses and give its exclusive patronage to the hotel. Russell, a Republican, suspended the two Wilsons for conflict of interest, but the Democratic-controlled legislature, which met in 1899, reinstated them. S. Otho Wilson resigned immediately following his vindication, and James Wilson's term expired soon afterwards.

Wilson was a member of the Democratic state executive committee for several years. He served on the board of directors of the Western Insane Asylum at Morganton from 1882 to 1891, becoming president in 1888, and was a member of the board of trustees of The University of North Carolina from 1891 to 1899 and 1901 to 1905. He lived in Charlotte during the last four years of his life and was buried in Morganton.

SEE: Collier Cobb, "James Wilson," in Charles L. Van Noppen Papers (Manuscript Department, Duke University Library, Durham); *Charlotte Observer*, 3 July 1910, 15 Oct. 1939; Josephus Daniels, *Editor in Politics* (1941); Governors' Papers, 1877–81 (North Carolina State Archives, Raleigh); Daniel L. Grant, *Alumni History of the University of North Carolina* (1924); Weymouth T. Jordan, comp., *North Carolina Troops, 1861–1865: A Roster*, vol. 4 (1973); *Public Documents of the State of North Carolina, Session 1899*, Document 21 (1899); *Western North Carolina: Historical and Biographical* (1890).

ALAN B. BROMBERG

Wilson, John Makemie *(1769–30 July 1831)*, Presbyterian minister and schoolman, was the son of James and Margaret Makemie Wilson. Born in Mecklenburg County, about six miles east of Charlotte, he was a relative of Andrew Jackson, who, with his mother, spent several months (September 1780–February 1781) in the Wilson home as a refugee from the British army during its invasion of South Carolina. For his early education he was a student of Dr. Thomas Henderson of Charlotte, then attended Hampden-Sydney College from which he was graduated with high honors. Wilson studied theology under the Reverend James Hall of Iredell County. After his licensure by Orange Presbytery in the summer of 1793, he spent two months (December 1793–January 1794) on a missionary tour of eastern North Carolina, during which he "rode nearly a thousand miles." Orange Presbytery ordained him to the gospel ministry between May and 1 Oct. 1795, after which he served as pastor of the Quaker Meadows Church of Burke County until 1801.

In that year he accepted a call to the Rocky River and Philadelphia churches, situated in Cabarrus and Mecklenburg counties, respectively, where he served until the time of his death. During his early ministry at Rocky River, the church erected a new sanctuary that was completed in 1807. In addition to his ministerial duties, he established and operated Rocky River Academy (incorporated 1812) until about 1824. Twenty-five of his students entered the ministry, about fifteen of whom were from the Rocky River congregation.

While at Quaker Meadows, Wilson married Mary (Pretty Polly) Erwin of Burke County. They had five sons and four daughters. Two sons, John Makemie, Jr., and Alexander E., entered the Presbyterian ministry, the latter serving as missionary in Africa. In 1829 The University of North Carolina conferred on the Rocky River pastor the D.D. degree. He was the author of sermons on the deaths of the Reverend Samuel E. McCorkle and the Reverend

Lewis F. Wilson. John Makemie Wilson died suddenly at his home, which was located between his two churches, and was buried at Rocky River. No portrait of him has been located, nor have his papers been preserved.

SEE: William Henry Foote, *Sketches of North Carolina: Historical and Biographical* (1846); Minutes of the Synod of the Carolinas, vol. 1 (Presbyterian Historical Foundation, Montreat, N.C.); Richmond, *Watchman of the South*, 24 Nov. 1842; Thomas Hugh Spence, Jr., *The Presbyterian Congregation on Rocky River* (1954); William B. Sprague, Annuals of the American Pulpit, vol. 4 (1858).

THOMAS H. SPENCE, JR.

Wilson, Joseph *(28 Mar. 1780–27 Aug. 1829)*, lawyer, known in the legal annals of North Carolina as "The Great Solicitor," was born in Randolph County, the son of William, who was born near Edenton of Scottish ancestry, and Eunice Worth Wilson, who was born on Nantucket Island of English descent. She numbered among her lineal ancestors William Worth, the founder of the Worth family of North Carolina, who settled on Nantucket in 1662, and John Howland, a *Mayflower* pilgrim who landed at Plymouth Rock in 1620. William and Eunice Wilson were members of the Society of Friends.

After attending David Caldwell's school in Greensboro and Greeneville College in Greeneville, Tenn., Joseph studied law under Reuben Wood, an energetic, erudite lawyer and public servant who traveled on horseback carrying Bacon's *Maximims of the Law* and Blackstone's *Commentaries of the Laws of England* in his saddlebags to virtually all courts sitting in the vast area lying between his home in Randolph County and Jonesboro, Tenn. Licensed to practice law in 1804, Wilson settled in Stokes County, where the justices of the county designated him solicitor of the Stokes County Court of Pleas and Quarter Sessions. In this post he acquired valuable experience in prosecuting minor criminal offenses.

As a devoted Jeffersonian Democrat, he was elected to represent Stokes County in the North Carolina House of Commons, where he won substantial renown as a firm advocate of the rights of the United States in its controversies with Great Britain.

Although he was not a resident of the circuit, the North Carolina General Assembly in 1812 chose him solicitor of the Sixth Judicial Circuit over two formidable opponents, Robert H. Burton and Alexander McMillan. The results of the legislative poll was Wilson 94, Burton 41, and McMillan 37. His acceptance of the solicitorship necessitated his removal to the Sixth Circuit. As a consequence, he established his home at Charlotte in Mecklenburg County, where he resided for the remainder of his life. The Sixth Judicial Circuit, which was commonly known as the Mountain Circuit, included Mecklenburg, Cabarrus, Lincoln, Iredell, and all the other counties lying between them and Tennessee. When he accepted responsibility for prosecuting persons charged with crimes in the superior courts of his far-flung circuit, Wilson assumed a task of herculean proportions.

During the first quarter of the nineteenth century, a carnival of crime swept through the Mountain Circuit. Murder, robbery, and other violent offenses were widespread and aroused terror in all quarters. Even more nefarious because of its corrupting consequences was counterfeiting, which was rampant in parts of the circuit and, like all crimes motivated by greed, provoked other evil deeds. According to a tradition, which bears the earmarks of the apocryphal, Solicitor Wilson secured the conviction of a notorious counterfeiter in Burke County Superior Court, and the presiding judge ordered the culprit to pay a substantial fine. After he had done so and departed for parts unknown, it was discovered that he had paid the fine with counterfeit money.

By prosecuting wrongdoers without fear or favor, Wilson incurred the hatred of malignant evildoers, who frequently threatened his life and occasionally imperiled it. About August 1825, for example, Wilson, accompanied by his friend William Roane, his overseer, and a Negro, was traveling on horseback to a plantation he had purchased in Rutherford County. A contemporary account noted: "on their way thither, the party was fired at by some assassins in ambuscade, but fortunately their murderous intention was defeated. Mr. Roane was severely, though not dangerously wounded, a ball having passed through his body. The negro was shot through the thighs and legs, and Mr. Wilson's horse was shot. Mr. Wilson and his overseer received no personal injury."

Wilson disclosed his understanding of the perils that surrounded him by inserting these words in his will:

> I have written this, my last will and testament, in perfect health and sound mind, not with the expectation that I am about to die a natural death, but as a provision in the event of a sudden one which I have apprehended for several years, from someone of the banditry in my circuit, the extent of which is known to no one except myself; and I have lived, and now am, in daily expectation of a possibility, nay of a probability, of being destroyed by someone in this way. Should it be permitted by an inscrutable Providence, I ask of those who would, in that event, well knowing that I have fallen on account of a firm discharge of public duty, to extend a helping hand to my dear wife, and our helpless offspring, should they need it.

Although he hated evil, Wilson demonstrated his compassion for evildoers by writing to his wife while on his dangerous circuit: "How thankful we should be to Almighty God, to whose mercy we owe our better knowledge, our Christian education, our exemption from the temptations which have surrounded these unhappy men."

In restoring law and order in the Mountain Circuit, Joseph Wilson earned the gratitude of its law-respecting inhabitants, who bestowed on him their highest accolade by calling him "The Great Solicitor." His prowess as a prosecutor undoubtedly prompted Governor John Branch, acting with the advice and consent of the Council of State, to appoint him a superior court judge on 3 July 1819 to fill a vacancy caused by the resignation of James Iredell. But Wilson declined the appointment and remained a solicitor for the rest of his life, except for a brief period in 1825, when party spirit was running high in Mecklenburg County and he was induced to resign his office and make an unsuccessful canvass against Colonel Thomas G. Polk for a seat in the North Carolina House of Commons. After his defeat, he was reinstated in the solicitorship.

At the time of his death in Charlotte at age forty-nine, Wilson was regarded as a suitable successor to Senator John Branch, who had relinquished his seat in the U.S. Senate to accept President Andrew Jackson's commission as secretary of the navy.

Wilson married Mary Wood, the daughter of his legal preceptor, Reuben, and his wife, Charity Hayne Wood. After he moved to areas where Quaker meetinghouses did not exist, he affiliated with the Presbyterians. Mary Wilson was always a devout Episcopalian.

The Wilsons had four daughters: Catherine Elvira, Laura Theresa, Sarah Roxanna, and Mary J. Catherine married William Julius Alexander, of Charlotte, a distinguished lawyer and public servant; one of their daughters, Catherine Elvira Alexander, married Colonel John F. Hoke, of Lincolnton, an able lawyer, and became the mother of Chief Justice William Alexander Hoke of the North Carolina Supreme Court. Laura's first marriage was to Marshall Tate Polk, the youngest brother of President James Knox Polk; by Polk, who died at an early age while practicing law in Charlotte, she became the mother of Major Marshall Tate Polk, of Nashville, Tenn., state treasurer of Tennessee. By her second marriage, to Dr. William Caldwell Tate, of Morganton, a physician of note, she became the mother of Catherine Elvira Tate, the wife of William E. Powe. Sarah married Dr. Pinckney Colesworth Caldwell, of Charlotte, a distinguished physician, and became the mother of Catherine C. Caldwell, who married Benjamin Simons Guion, of Lincoln County. Benjamin S. Guion and Catherine C. Caldwell were the parents of Dr. Connie Guion, a noted woman physician of New York City. Mary, the Wilsons' youngest daughter, never married.

A portrait of Joseph Wilson was owned by his great-granddaughter, Mrs. Mary Hoke Slaughter, of Charlottesville, Va.

SEE: Samuel A. Ashe, ed., *Biographical History of North Carolina*, vol. 7 (1908); *Raleigh Register*, 26 Aug. 1825; *Raleigh Register and North Carolina Gazette*, 4, 17 Sept. 1829; Raleigh *Star*, 18 Dec. 1812; Salisbury *Western Carolinian*, 8 Sept. 1829.

SAM J. ERVIN, JR.

Wilson, Lewis Feuilleteau *(June 1752–11 Dec. 1804)*, physician and minister, was born on St. Christophers Island in the West Indies. The names of his parents are unknown, but his father was a wealthy English planter who, about 1758, moved his family from the West Indies to London so that they could receive a good education. On the voyage, young Wilson's older brother died. Lewis attended a grammar school in London and in 1769 went to New Jersey with an uncle and entered Nassau Hall (now Princeton University), where he was graduated with honors and an A.B. degree in September 1773.

Shortly after graduation he returned to England intending to enter the Anglican ministry. His father, who had become a wealthy merchant and a man of some influence in London, was able to procure for him "what they call, 'a good living' in the city, and urged him to take orders in the Episcopal church." Because he refused to do so, his father threatened to disinherit him, but young Wilson would not give in. Later, on his return to Princeton, he told friends that he had been unable to find "the least prospect of either influence or happiness" in the Church of England. About the time of his quarrel with his father, an aunt died and left him a legacy of approximately one thousand dollars, which he used to outfit himself, procure a small library, and pay for his passage to America. Here he entered into the study of theology under Dr. John Witherspoon, president of Princeton.

When the Revolutionary War forced the closing of the college, Wilson went to Philadelphia and studied medicine for two years. He then worked as a surgeon in both the Continental army and the incipient navy. In 1781 he received news of his father's death and of a legacy in his will of £500. He sailed for England, secured the money, and returned to Princeton to practice his profession. In

1786 the Reverend James Hall, D.D., a college friend, persuaded him to move to Piedmont North Carolina. This he did in August 1786 and shortly afterwards married Margaret (Peggy) Hall, the daughter of Captain Hugh Hall, a brother of his intimate friend, James Hall.

Wilson soon established a successful medical practice in the area, but his own conscience, troubled by his abandonment of theological studies, and the urging of friends and admirers led him to give up medicine and resume his pursuit of the ministry through study with James Hall. The Presbytery of Orange licensed him to preach in 1791, and on his acceptance of the calls of the Fourth Creek (now First Presbyterian, Statesville) and Concord (Iredell County) Presbyterian churches, the Presbytery ordained and installed him as pastor in June 1793.

In 1802–3 Wilson, Hall, and other ministers began participating in the revival that swept across the country. This led to a controversy with his church officers at Fourth Creek and threatened to split the congregation. To bring peace, Wilson resigned and devoted the last few years of his life to Concord alone. At age fifty-two he died at his home after a short illness and was buried beside his beloved friend James Hall in the Bethany Presbyterian Church cemetery, located on U.S. 21 north of Statesville.

Wilson and his wife had seven children, three sons and four daughters. Two of the sons followed their father into the ministry: the Reverend Hugh Wilson was the first settled Presbyterian minister in Texas, and the Reverend Lewis F. Wilson, Jr., served churches in Virginia and what is now West Virginia.

SEE: Louis A. Brown and others, *A History of Old Fourth Creek Congregation, 1764–1964* (1964); William Henry Foote, *Sketches of North Carolina: Historical and Biographical* (1846); "Minutes of the Synod of the Carolinas" and "Minutes of the Presbytery of Concord" (Davis Center for Historical Study, Princeton University); E. G. Scott, comp., *Ministerial Directory of the Presbyterian Church, U.S., 1861–1964* (1964); John M. Wilson, *The Blessedness of Such as Die in the Lord. A SERMON, Preached at Bethany, Iredell County, North Carolina, February 10, 1805, Occasioned By The Death of the Revd. Lewis F. Wilson, A.M. . . . To Which is Added by Way of Appendix, A Short Account of the Life of Mr. Wilson* (1805).

NEILL R. McGEACHY

Wilson, Louis Dicken (12 May 1789–12 Aug. 1847), merchant, military officer, and public servant, was born on the family plantation south of Tar River in Edgecombe County, the son of William and Elizabeth Dicken Wilson. After receiving a modest education at the local academy, he went to the town of Washington in 1807 and worked in a countinghouse while apparently reading law. A few years later he returned to Tarboro and qualified as a notary public on 28 May 1812 and as a justice on 24 Feb. 1817.

Wilson became an apprentice of Concord Lodge No. 58, AFAM, on 16 Mar. 1813 and a Master Mason on 20 July. He served as secretary (21 Dec. 1813–29 Dec. 1814) and junior warden (23 Dec. 1817–23 Nov. 1819). Elected senior grand warden of the Grand Lodge on 19 Dec. 1818 and junior grand warden on 19 Dec. 1825, he became the fourteenth grand master of Masons in North Carolina on 15 Dec. 1827. He was succeeded in the latter post by Richard Dobbs Spaight on 19 Dec. 1830. His last recorded Masonic office was grand lecturer (15 Dec. 1833–27 Dec. 1837).

In addition to representing Edgecombe County in the General Assembly (1814–19), Wilson collected the Tarboro taxes (1819–29) and served as a state senator (1820,

1824–32). On 30 Sept. 1827 he attended the Free Trade Convention at Philadelphia, and on 19 December he was elected brigadier general of the Fifth North Carolina Brigade, a rank that he appears to have held as late as 1846. He was one of the two delegates from Edgecombe County to the constitutional convention of 4 June-11 July 1835; later that year he was a delegate to the Democratic National Convention.

In 1829 Wilson first gave his support to the infant public school movement, even advocating the education of free blacks. On 4 Jan. 1831 he and Elder Joshua Lawrence were among the incorporators of the Hickory Grove Academy, and on 30 September he bought as his permanent home the handsome former residence of Congressman Thomas Blount, erected in 1810. In 1838 he was elected a member of the board of trustees of The University of North Carolina, and in 1844 the state senate placed him on the committee on education and the Literary Fund.

Returning to the senate in 1838, he represented Edgecombe County continuously until requesting a fateful leave of absence on 12 Dec. 1846 in order to support the patriotic honor of North Carolina by personally participating in the War with Mexico. He had served as speaker at the 1842–43 session. Wilson left Raleigh for the last time on 1 Jan. 1847 and returned to his native county, where on 5 January he was elected captain of Company A, First Edgecombe Volunteer Regiment, the first company to offer its services to Governor William A. Graham. The volunteers met the next day at Toisnot Depot (now the city of Wilson) "to partake of a barbecue dinner and arrange plans prior to their departure."

Captain Wilson's company arrived at Fort Johnston near Wilmington on 8 January for mustering into the U.S. Army and brief preparation before embarking from Smithville for Mexico in the schooner *E. S. Powell* on 22 February. Meanwhile he and several other officers had returned to Tarboro to attend a splendid dinner at Pender's Hotel on 9 January and the huge celebration on 18 January at which a beautiful silken banner provided by several patriotic ladies was received with an appropriate speech by Captain Wilson. It was not until 6 Mar. 1847 that the Edgecombe County companies A and E arrived at Brazos, from which they proceeded the next day to San Francisco on the Río Grande.

On 3 Mar. 1847 President James K. Polk offered Wilson the post of colonel of the Twelfth Regiment of U.S. Infantry, which Wilson accepted at Washington City on 9 April. It was expected that he and the 850 troops under his command would leave Vera Cruz and proceed towards Mexico City on 7 August as the guard with a train of supplies for General Winfield Scott's army, but Wilson was stricken six days earlier with the dreaded yellow fever and died. The military funeral and burial were held the next day, but his leaden casket was shipped subsequently to Edgecombe County and an appropriate oration was pronounced on 22 May 1850, on the occasion of the laying of the cornerstone of the monument erected to his memory. On 1 Nov. 1904 the casket from the neglected rural graveyard and the monument from the old Court House lawn were placed on the Tarboro Town Common.

Although Wilson never married and left no known descendants, he merits the remembrance and appreciation of posterity, not only because of his numerous public services but also because of his then-immense bequest of $40,000 to Edgecombe County for the future benefit of the public poor. About $12,000 was properly utilized, $10,000 lost by unsound investments, and $18,000 enjoyed by Reconstruction-period officials. It is more gratifying to remember that the town of Wilson was incorporated and named in his memory on 29 Jan. 1849, followed by Wilson

County on 13 Feb. 1855. An oil portrait is owned by Mrs. Becky White Johnston, Charlottesville, Va.

SEE: J. Howard Brown, *History of Concord Lodge No. 58* (1958); *Raleigh Register*, 2 Oct. 1847; J. K. Turner and J. L. Bridgers, Jr., *History of Edgecombe County* (1920).

HUGH BUCKNER JOHNSTON

Wilson, Louis Round *(27 Dec. 1876–10 Dec. 1979)*, librarian and educator, was born in Lenoir, the sixth and last child of Jethro Reuben and Louisa Jane Round Wilson. Both of his parents were teachers, and though they could not afford to keep their children in school on a regular basis, they were anxious for them to secure an excellent education. Louis attended local Lenoir schools and academies when the family finances did not require him to work. From 1891 to 1894 he was a typesetter and printer's devil in the office of the Lenoir *Topic*. In 1894 he attended Davenport College in Lenoir, and in 1895 he entered Haverford College, in Haverford, Pa., where he was employed as an assistant in the library. Wilson transferred to The University of North Carolina in the fall of 1898 and was graduated in May 1899.

Wilson's parents expected him to become a teacher, and in August 1899 he began teaching at Vine Hill Male Academy in Scotland Neck. After a year he moved to Catawba College, in Newton, where he taught Latin and English. In 1901 he accepted a position as librarian at The University of North Carolina and returned to Chapel Hill. There he also resumed his studies, receiving a master's degree in English in 1902. In 1905 he was awarded the Ph.D. degree in English and was elected to Phi Beta Kappa. From 1905 to 1907 he was an assistant in German at the university.

During his early years at Chapel Hill Wilson developed an interest in librarianship as a profession, and when in 1906 he had to decide whether to stay on at the university as librarian or seek employment elsewhere as a professor of English, he elected to stay in Chapel Hill. By the time he made this decision he was already well embarked on his career. In his first decade in the position he developed a library collection that would support graduate study and research. Recognizing the university's unique position in the state and region he repeatedly sought funds to obtain material that would reflect the history of North Carolina and the South. Later he obtained funds from university friends and alumni to develop a collection of rare books and incunabula in the library.

Also in the early years Wilson was absorbed in planning and supervising the building of the new Carnegie library, which opened in 1907. The building remained the main university library until 1929, when it was replaced by a larger structure that Wilson also planned. The new building was named for Wilson in 1956.

While building the library collection and supervising the construction of the new library, he began developing a trained staff of librarians. Wilson started teaching courses in librarianship in the summer school of the university in 1904. In 1907 he joined the faculty as an assistant professor of library science, and in 1920 he was appointed a Kenan Professor of Library Science.

Active in the library movement in the state and region, Wilson helped found the North Carolina Library Association in 1904 and drafted the legislation that created the North Carolina Library Commission in 1909, serving as chairman of the commission until 1916 and president of the library association in 1910, 1920, and 1930. He was an influential member of the Southeastern Library Association and served as president from 1924 to 1926. Wilson joined the American Library Association in 1904 and over

the years sat on many of its committees. While he was president in 1935–36, the national association made its first formal statement in support of federal aid to libraries, a position Wilson heartily endorsed.

A prolific writer, he contributed articles on every facet of his profession to library and education journals. One of his concerns, on which he expounded in local North Carolina newspapers in 1921, was in the phenomenon of reading. He viewed reading not only as an element in education but also as concomitant with the good life. Curious about ways to measure its use and test its effectiveness, he became interested in the research techniques of social scientists and in the use of those techniques to test the validity of some of his intuitive feelings about the value of books and reading. He was fortunate that The University of North Carolina was an early center for the development of the social sciences, for he was able to turn to his faculty colleagues for help in formulating devices to measure the extent and effectiveness of reading in the state and region. Wilson later expanded his interest in reading to include the entire United States and in 1934 published *The Geography of Reading*.

While pursing his career as university librarian and lending his time and talents to the burgeoning profession of librarianship, Wilson was also a creative and energetic member of the Chapel Hill faculty. An early advocate of the concept of university extension service to the state, he was appointed to the Committee on Extension in 1911 and served as chairman from 1912 to 1920. He envisioned the Alumni Association as another avenue to North Carolinians, and in 1912 he founded the *Alumni Review*, which he edited until 1924. From 1914 to 1932 he sat on the editorial board of *The University News Letter*, and in 1922 he was appointed director of the newly created University Press, a position he held until 1932. Wilson was a devoted friend and admirer of Edward Kidder Graham, president of the university from 1914 until 1918, and following Graham's death in 1918 he was made chairman of the Graham Memorial Building Committee. In the 1920s while planning and supervising the building of the new library and the Graham Memorial, he was also a member of the building committee of the University Methodist Church in Chapel Hill.

During these years Wilson was a respected member of the university faculty, as well as an admired citizen of the town of Chapel Hill. A witty man with a keen mind, he had many friends among his colleagues and the townspeople. He was an avid tennis player until he developed tuberculosis in 1916. Wilson went to Lake Saranac, N.Y., for treatment, and when he returned to Chapel Hill, he gave up tennis in favor of walking and gardening, hobbies that he continued will into his nineties.

Following the dedication of the new library in 1929, Wilson took a leave of absence from the university and made the first of three trips to Europe. Returning to Chapel Hill in the summer of 1930, he turned his attention to securing funds for a library school at the university. The Carnegie Corporation, whose president, Frederick P. Keppel, was an admirer of Wilson, awarded the university a grant of $100,000. The School of Library Science opened in 1931 with Wilson as its first dean.

Wilson's career had not gone unnoticed outside North Carolina. His sense of mission and service to the people of the state, his dedication to the concept of education for librarianship, his interest in formalizing the profession through professional associations and the development of a body of literature, and his curiosity about the use of social science techniques in librarianship made him the obvious candidate for the deanship of the Graduate Library School of the University of Chicago. He was offered and declined the position in 1926. In 1932, when offered the post again, he accepted it.

In his ten years at the Graduate Library School, Wilson rounded out and expanded every aspect of his varied interests in the profession. He assembled a faculty that developed a graduate curriculum designed to produce administrators for every type of library. At the same time, the faculty was engaging in research that sought solutions to some of the problems confronting librarians. Wilson taught courses in university library administration and library trends. The studies and papers produced at the Graduate Library School during Wilson's term as dean were published as part of the University of Chicago Studies in Library Science, of which he was general editor.

At Chicago Wilson continued to serve as a library consultant and surveyor, an activity he had begun in 1928 when he surveyed the library of the Union Theological Seminary in Richmond, Va. From 1928 until he retired as a consultant in 1955, Wilson surveyed many college and university libraries, as well as serving as a consultant to the Tennessee Valley Authority, Tennessee Valley Library Council, General Education Board, and American Library Association Board of Education for Librarianship.

He left the University of Chicago in 1942 and returned to Chapel Hill, where he rejoined the faculty of the School of Library Science. He taught courses in university library administration intermittently until 1959, when he retired from the faculty at age eighty-three. Also assuming many committee responsibilities, he was director of the university's Sesquicentennial Celebration in 1944–46 and edited the thirteen volumes that marked that event. He served on the board of the University Press and the Institute for Research in Social Science. In 1951 he was appointed special assistant for development to the chancellor of the university, and in 1959, following his retirement from the faculty, he became special assistant to the president of The University of North Carolina system. He retired from that post in 1969.

Wilson continued to write after he returned from Chicago. *The University Library*, written in collaboration with Maurice F. Tauber and published in 1945, was considered the authoritative work on the subject for many years. Wilson also produced a two-volume history of The University of North Carolina and wrote a series of articles about major events that reflected the influence of the university in the life of the state. These articles were compiled into a volume, *Louis Round Wilson's Historical Sketches*, which was published in October 1976, a few months before his one-hundredth birthday.

Throughout his life in Chapel Hill Wilson was a member of the University Methodist Church. He was a deeply religious man whose service to the church included many years on the Board of Stewards. An early and outspoken proponent of racial justice and equality, he wrote to newspapers frequently on the subject. He also maintained a lively correspondence with the North Carolina congressional delegation, encouraging its support of civil rights legislation. Wilson's political preference was for the Democratic party.

In 1909 he married Penelope Bryan Wright of Coharie. They had four children: Elizabeth, Louis, Jr. (d. 1913), Penelope, and Mary Louise (Mrs. Dean Stockett Edmonds, Jr.; d. 1978). He died a few days before his 103d birthday and was buried in the Old Chapel Hill Cemetery. A portrait of him hangs in the Wilson Library of The University of North Carolina.

SEE: Edward G. Holley, "The Centenary of a Giant of Librarianship: Louis Round Wilson," *The ALA Yearbook* (1976); *Louis Round Wilson Bibliography: A Chronological*

List of Works and Editorial Activities (1976); Maurice F. Tauber, *Louis Round Wilson: Librarian and Administrator* (1967); Louis Round Wilson Papers (Southern Historical Collection, University of North Carolina, Chapel Hill).

FRANCES A. WEAVER

Wilson, Peter Mitchel (*1 July 1848–24 June 1939*), lawyer, newspaperman, and clerk of the U.S. Senate, was born in Warrenton, the son of Thomas Epps, a physician, and Jane Marshall Mitchel Wilson. He attended Warrenton Male Academy and the Bingham School before entering The University of North Carolina in October 1865. With the decline of the university following the Civil War and the problems of Reconstruction, his parents withdrew him in October 1867 after his sophomore year and shortly before it closed. He was sent to the University of Edinborough, in part because his family did not want him to attend a Northern university, but also because they were of Scottish descent. He crossed the Atlantic in company with the family of John White, of Warrenton, who had been North Carolina's agent in England during the war purchasing needed supplies for the state. With many young men from the South being sent there, Southerners at Edinborough became a close-knit group and remained friends for the remainder of their lives.

Wilson was graduated with a master of arts degree in 1870 and returned to teach for a short while in Bellevue, Va., where his father was temporarily practicing medicine. Back in Warrenton he studied law with William Eaton, and after Wilson was admitted to the bar in June 1873 the two men practiced together. In 1877 Wilson, tiring of the routine of a lawyer's office, moved to Raleigh and became reading clerk of the state senate. During the years 1878–80 he was city editor of the Raleigh *Observer*, published by Peter M. Hale and William L. Saunders, both distinguished journalists. On 3 Dec. 1879 Wilson married in Christ Church, Raleigh, Ellen Williams Hale, the daughter of Peter Hale.

In some respects Wilson was a forerunner of Walter Hines Page in that he expressed concern for labor and the industrial development of North Carolina. Through his newspaper articles, for example, he described the comments and attitudes of people at a country store. His "What's the Matter with Farmin' in the South?" was widely circulated and frequently reprinted. In 1880 he became secretary of the State Board of Agriculture, a position he filled very competently for ten years. Wilson was in charge of both the U.S. and North Carolina exhibits at the World's Industrial and Cotton Centennial Exposition in New Orleans in 1884. In 1888, as secretary of the North Carolina Agricultural Society, he was the moving spirit behind the successful state fairs of that year and the next. He became state commissioner of immigration in 1889, when a great movement was under way to attract new labor and industry to the state. A large-scale advertising campaign, frequently in collaboration with railroad lines, was quite effective.

Near the end of the century Wilson moved from Raleigh to Winston, where he was secretary-treasurer of the West-End Hotel and Land Company and president of the Rowan Dunn Mountain Company. Exploration for minerals and the opening of new factories occupied him in those positions. He was executive commissioner for North Carolina's participation in the Chicago World's Fair of 1893. As an adult he found some consolation in recalling that mathematics professor Charles Phillips at Chapel Hill had told his mother that Wilson "knew less mathematics than any human being he ever saw." In retribution, Wilson noted, he served twenty years in the financial office of the

U.S. Senate. He actually was the assistant financial clerk between 1893 and 1915; in the latter year he became chief clerk, a position he held until his death at age ninety-one. Altogether he served for forty years in the Senate.

In 1927 The University of North Carolina Press published his autobiography, *Southern Exposure*. A delightful recounting of a happy childhood and youth, it is filled with the recollections of friends and acquaintances of a long life. His choice of words, his clear descriptions, the wide range of his knowledge, and the reach of his memory combine to make this book a Tar Heel treasure.

As a member of the Democratic party Wilson described himself as a laborer in the vineyard who "never kicked: never scratched 'reckon I never knew how.' " In 1923 he wrote that he was "Brought up in [the] Episcopal Church." He and Mrs. Wilson were the parents of a daughter, Mary Badger Wilson, the author of several novels and numerous short stories. He was buried in Oakwood Cemetery, Raleigh.

SEE: Alumni Files (University of North Carolina, Chapel Hill); *Chapel Hill Newspaper*, 27 Oct. 1985; *Charlotte Observer*, 19 Jan. 1941; Daniel L. Grant, *Alumni History of the University of North Carolina* (1924); *New York Times*, 25 June 1939; Raleigh *News and Observer*, 28 Nov. 1932, 23 June 1939; Randolph A. Shotwell and Natt Atkinson, eds., *Legislative Record*, vol. 1, no. 1 (1877); University of North Carolina *Alumni Review*, January 1933, July 1939; *Washington Post*, 25 June 1939; *Western North Carolina: Historical and Biographical* (1890); Peter M. Wilson, *Southern Exposure* (1927).

WILLIAM S. POWELL

Wilson, Ronald Bonar *(18 Nov. 1883–11 Sept. 1947)*, newspaperman and journal editor, was born in Greenville, the son of Lewis Henry and Jackie Anne Caroline Smith Wilson. After attending The University of North Carolina (1901–3) and North Carolina College of Agriculture and Engineering (1903–5), he lived for several years in Charlotte, where he was employed by the Elizabeth Manufacturing Company (1905–6) and Stone-Barringer, a book company (1906–7). He then became editor of *Textile Manufacturer* (1907–8) and *Real Estate Record* (1909). During this time he also was a sergeant in the First North Carolina Light Artillery.

Wilson was managing editor of the *Asheville Citizen* (1910–11), publisher of the *Brevard News* (1911–12) and the Statesville *Sentinel* (1912–13), and editor of the Rocky Mount *Daily Transcript* (1913). Later in 1913 he became editor and owner of the Waynesville *Courier*, where he remained until he joined the Raleigh *News and Observer* as state news editor in 1917. During the four years he resided in Waynesville Wilson was secretary of the Haywood County Democratic executive committee. For a time in 1918 he was city editor of the *Wilmington Dispatch*; later in the year he was an instructor at the North Carolina College of Agriculture and Engineering.

Wilson next became assistant to the secretary of the North Carolina State Board of Health, a post he held for fourteen years. He appears to have entered wholeheartedly into this work, becoming a member of the North Carolina Conference for Social Service, American Public Health Association, North Carolina Tuberculosis Association (of which he was a director) National Tuberculosis Association, and Southern Conference on Tuberculosis (vice president). Through his writings published in state papers, he made significant contributions to health care in the state.

On 11 Mar. 1909 Wilson married Anna Jackson Morrison. They had no children. He was a member of the Masons, the Pythians, and the Episcopal Church of the Good Shepherd, Raleigh. He was buried in Macpelah Church Cemetery in Lincoln County, his wife's home community.

SEE: Alumni Files (University of North Carolina, Chapel Hill); Daniel L. Grant, *Alumni History of the University of North Carolian* (1924); Raleigh *News and Observer*, 12–13 Sept. 1947.

WILLIAM S. POWELL

Wilson, Thomas D. (Big Tom) *(1 Dec. 1825–1 Feb. 1908)*, legendary hunter and mountain guide, was born at the family home on the Toe River in Yancey County, a region at that time of almost unbroken wilderness in the lofty Black Mountains. As a young man Wilson acquired an intimate knowledge of the region and was soon widely sought after as a guide for hunting and exploring trips. In 1852 he married Niagra Ray, the daughter of Amos Ray, and in 1853 the couple moved from the family homestead up to a cabin at the headwaters of the Cane River. Here he served as gamekeeper for the Murchison Preserve, a vast tract of virgin wilderness, and led innumerable forays through the high and remote areas of the Black Mountains and neighboring valleys.

Wilson first came to national attention as a result of his association with Dr. Elisha Mitchell (1793–1857), professor of geology at The University of North Carolina. Mitchell was convinced that the highest mountains in the eastern United States lay within the Black Mountain range, and in his attempt to establish this fact he became embroiled in a controversy that extended beyond the boundaries of the state. In an attempt to resolve the question, Mitchell and his son Charles planned a series of barometric measurements on the higher peaks of the range during the summer of 1857.

On Saturday, 27 June 1857, the Mitchells left William Patton's Black Mountain House on the southern rim of the Black Mountains, crossed the main ridge, and separated after planning for Dr. Mitchell to continue on to Tom Wilson's home. When Mitchell failed to arrive on schedule, Wilson was called upon to organize and lead a search party. The effort continued from Friday July 3 until Wednesday 8 July, when Wilson, who had located and followed the professor's route through the trackless wilderness, found Mitchell's body in the deep pool of a waterfall below the crest of the Black Mountains' eastern rim. The saga of Wilson's leadership, tracking ability, and knowledge of the mountains soon spread and established his fame far beyond the Appalachian valley where he lived.

After serving during the Civil War as chief musician for General Robert B. Vance's brigade, Big Tom Wilson returned to his home on the Cane River and resumed his life as a guide and hunter. In the following years, he was popular not only as a guide and leader for scientific explorations but also as a grand old man whose life and stories of the Mitchell search and early times soon became a central part of the folklore of the southern Appalachian Mountains. In 1885 Charles Dudley Warner (1829–1900) visited Wilson and incorporated the story into his widely read *On Horseback* (1888).

Wilson maintained remarkable physical vigor during his later years, and he was often known to walk on weekends the full 27 miles from his home into Asheville, where his striking physical appearance and familiar face often drew large crowds of friends and admirers. His stamina and reputation were such that on 10 June 1895, at age seventy, he was called upon to organize and lead the search party when the naturalist John S. Cairns (1862–95) disappeared and was accidentally killed near Balsam Gap in the Black Mountains.

Wilson lived out the remainder of his life at his family home in Yancey County, where a stream of visitors came to hear of his exploits as a guide, bear hunter, and leader. Years after his death the mountain peak previously known as "Black Brother," located just north of Mount Mitchell, was renamed "Mt. Tom" in honor of Wilson's contribution to the early exploration of the southern Appalachian Mountains.

SEE: *Asheville Citizen*, 5 Feb. 1908; *Asheville Citizen-Times*, 24 Oct. 1948; Asheville *Daily Citizen*, 20 Nov. 1889; *Asheville Gazette*, 10 June 1905; *Charlotte Observer*, 13 Nov. 1903; F. A. Sondley, *A History of Buncombe County, North Carolina*, vol. 2 (1930); Richard Sterling, *Sterling's Southern Fifth Reader* (1866).

MARCUS B. SIMPSON, JR.

Wilson, Thomas James, Jr. *(12 Jan. 1874–26 Oct. 1945)*, professor and university administrator, was born in Hillsborough, the son of Dr. Thomas James and Margaret Douglas Ross Wilson. In 1894 he was graduated from The University of North Carolina, which granted him an M.A. degree in 1896 and a Ph.D. in 1898. The next year he taught a ninth-grade class in the Charlotte public schools, reportedly the first man in the state with a Ph.D. degree to teach in a North Carolina graded school.

Returning to Chapel Hill in 1899 to teach Latin and Greek in the university, he was named associate professor in 1902. After additional graduate work at the University of Chicago in 1903 and 1906, he was appointed registrar in 1908 but continued to teach until 1915. Wilson became dean of admissions in 1930 and secretary of the faculty in 1934. Under his leadership the admissions officers of many colleges in North Carolina took steps leading to the designation of regularly accredited schools by the State Department of Public Instruction. High school units for college entrance were also standardized.

Wilson was editor of the University *Record* series and archivist in charge of maintaining historical records. He was noted among students for his supervision of several student organizations, notably Phi Beta Kappa, and for his remarkable memory for names.

He married Lorena Frank Pickard, and they had four sons: Thomas J. III, Peter P., Marvin P., and Walter W. Wilson was a member of the Episcopal church and was buried in the Chapel Hill cemetery.

SEE: *Chapel Hill Weekly*, 26 Oct. 1945; *Durham Morning Herald*, 27 Oct. 1945; Daniel L. Grant, *Alumni History of the University of North Carolina* (1924); Raleigh *News and Observer*, 20 Oct. 1945.

WILLIAM S. POWELL

Wilson, Thomas James, III *(25 Oct. 1902–27 June 1969)*, educator and publisher, was born in Chapel Hill, where his father was for many years professor of Latin and Greek, registrar, and dean of admissions at The University of North Carolina. Both his father and his mother, Lorena Franklin Pickard Wilson, were native North Carolinians. Educated in Chapel Hill's public schools and The University of North Carolina, he received an A.B. degree in 1921. Wilson continued his studies while employed as instructor in French, earning an A.M. degree in 1924. He then attended St. John's College, Oxford, as a Rhodes scholar, receiving a D.Phil. in 1927.

Returning to Chapel Hill, he was appointed assistant professor of French, a position he held until 1930. During this period he published a number of scholarly articles on seventeenth-century French literature and translated into English *The Correspondence of Romain Roland and Malwida von Meysenburg* (1934). In 1930 he turned to commercial publishing and was successively foreign language editor and vice-president of Henry Holt and Company and head of the college department and vice-president of Reynal and Hitchcock. When the United States entered World War II, he volunteered in the navy, where he rose in rank from lieutenant to commander, serving much of the time as hangar deck officer of the aircraft carrier *Enterprise*, which had a longer battle career than any other fleet carrier in the Pacific.

His war experience turned Wilson away from commercial publishing, and he decided to combine his two developed talents and go into the more scholarly field of nonprofit university press publishing. After slightly more than a year as director of The University of North Carolina Press, he was appointed director of the Harvard University Press in 1947. At that time university press publishing in the United States was in a formative stage. Although the Association of American University Presses had about thirty members, barely a handful could be considered fully professional organizations capable of handling major publishing projects. Indeed, the Harvard University Press, though founded in 1913, had fallen on hard times, so much so that President James B. Conant recommended its dissolution. He was overruled by the Harvard Overseers, whose decision to give the press stronger backing led to Wilson's appointment.

In the twenty years of Wilson's directorship, the Harvard University Press became one of the most distinguished publishing enterprises in the country. Its production of new titles increased from 67 in 1947 to 153 in 1967 and its sales volume from $500,000 annually to over $3 million, with a total backlist of over 2,500 titles. But the figures tell only a small part of the story. Wilson was always insistent that the press's publishing program serve the scholarly and educational aims of the university. While not neglecting the traditional disciplines, he developed strong lines in science and the history of science and in emerging academic fields, such as the many books emanating from the Harvard Russian Research Center and the East Asian Research Center.

With the help of a generous endowment provided under the will of Waldron P. Belknap, augmented by additional benefactions of his mother, the press was able to undertake a number of large publishing endeavors, such as the John Harvard Library of American Classics, the definitive edition of *The Poems of Emily Dickinson*, and the four-volume *Diary and Autobiography of John Adams*, initiating the monumental series of Adams Family Papers. Both of the last two works won the coveted Carey-Thomas Award, given annually by *Publishers' Weekly* for outstanding creative book publishing. Wilson's achievements at Harvard were summed up in the memorial minutes of the Harvard faculty after his death: "He made a greater contribution to scholarship at Harvard during his directorship than any single scholar."

Wilson's two decades at Harvard saw a period of unparalleled growth in university press publishing. The number of presses more than doubled, the number of new titles published tripled, and the dollar volume of sales increased fivefold. University presses became a highly skilled and highly respected part of the general publishing world. In this development Wilson was acknowledged by his fellow directors as their most forceful leader—through both his personal influence and his work for the Association of American University Presses, of which he was president in 1951–53.

Large in stature and of a commanding presence, he had an easygoing geniality that turned into forceful eloquence when important issues were at stake. At a time when increasing competence tempted university presses into a purely commercial approach to publishing, Wilson applied the full force of his energy and persuasive powers to the argument that however important sound business practices and promotional skills were to academic publishing, university presses must serve as tools of scholarship and stand on the solid rock of scholarly editorial decisions. His colleague Herbert S. Bailey, Jr., director of the Princeton University Press, spoke for the great majority of university press directors when he said of Wilson in 1973: "He was, I believe, the most respected member of our profession in the past quarter century."

Wilson's influence was felt well beyond university press circles, however. He was a director of the American Book Publishers' Council (now the Association of American Publishers) and a founding member and board chairman of Franklin Publications (now Franklin Book Programs), a nonprofit organization set up by American book publishers, with foundation and governmental support, for the diffusion of American books through indigenous publication in the developing countries in the Near and Far East. In 1962–64 and again in 1968–69 he served on the U.S. Government Advisory Commission on International Book Programs. For these agencies Wilson made a number of trips to the developing countries of Asia and had a significant impact on publishing in these areas. He was a trustee of the Massachusetts Historical Society and a member of the American Academy of Arts and Sciences. The University of North Carolina (1963) and Harvard (1965) awarded him honorary degrees.

In 1967, faced with mandatory retirement the next year and with the responsibility for a wife and two young children, Wilson decided to return to commercial publishing, and he became vice-president and senior editor of Atheneum Publishers. He was at the beginning of a vigorous new career when he suffered a fatal heart attack in his New York City home. He was married twice: first, to Dorothy Stearns, by whom he had a son, Thomas J. IV; and second, to Phoebe de Kay Rous Donald, by whom he had a son, Peyton Rous, and a daughter, Chase de Kay.

SEE: Mark Carroll, "Some Observations on the Harvard University Press" (MS, files of the *Dictionary of North Carolina Biography*); Lambert Davis, "The Director's Search for Identity," *Scholarly Publishing*, October 1973; *New York Times*, 18 June 1969; *Publishers' Weekly*, 1 Dec. 1946, 19 Apr. 1947, 14 Jan. 1956, 21 July 1958, 25 Jan., 21 Nov. 1960, 19 Feb. 1962, 11 Apr. 1963, 7 July 1969; *Who's Who in America* (1969).

LAMBERT DAVIS

Wimberly, Dred (1848–16 June 1937), member of the General Assembly, was born at Walnut Plantation near Tarboro, where he was raised and worked in the fields of James S. Battle prior to the Civil War. In 1865 Kemp Plummer Battle informed all his help that they were free to leave or stay and work for wages. Dred Wimberly elected to remain. Though his choice may have been for largely practical reasons, it was also indicative of the close relationship between Battle and Wimberly.

Placed in charge of supplies, Wimberly bought farm implements and dry goods for the plantation. During and after the Civil War, Battle lived in Raleigh and following Emancipation Wimberly was responsible for delivering poultry and other farm products from Flag Marsh and Walnut Creek farms to the Battle house in the city. The trip took two days by wagon with an overnight stop at Moccasin Creek.

It was probably soon after this that Wimberly moved to Rocky Mount, where he followed his trade as a carpenter. In 1879, or shortly before, he was approached by the Republican party and asked to run for a seat in the General Assembly. He did not think he was qualified. Reminiscing years later, he said, "I got into it when I wasn't looking . . . I hesitated at first and asked them to look around a lot more. They nominated me anyhow and I was elected."

Elected again in 1887, Wimberly won a seat the senate in 1889. To what extent the turbulence of Reconstruction influenced him is unknown. He does not appear as one given to charges and countercharges. And perhaps this was unnecessary because in 1887 black citizens outnumbered whites in Edgecombe County 2,523 to 1,304. Moreover, Wimberly had a "family" loyalty to the Battles, especially Kemp P. Battle, who was trying to obtain a substantial appropriation for The University of North Carolina, reopened only a half dozen years before.

Well after the turn of the century, when interviewed by the press, Wimberly firmly stated that *he* had cast the deciding vote for the appropriation. The vote had been called alphabetically, and just before it came to him the ayes and nays were tied, whereupon he cast an aye and thus earned the eternal gratitude of President Battle. This account has been disputed by later commentators, who point out that the appropriations of $5,000 and $15,000 were granted in 1881, when Wimberly was not in office. As there is no doubt of Wimberly's integrity, it is probable that, while in some education or finance committee meeting, he did cast a deciding vote to bring the matter to the floor, and this would not be on the record.

In any case, during the 1879 legislature he supported the improvement of roads and highways, and in 1887 he voted to establish the North Carolina College of Agriculture and Mechanical Arts. As he once stated, "I voted for Dr. Battle's appropriation because Dr. Battle had said voting for the University would help everybody. It might somehow help the colored folks too." Fifty years later, Josephus Daniels, in an editorial in the Raleigh *News and Observer* on the contribution of Wimberly and other black legislators, said: "they upheld education when no one else did. They laid the foundation for the common schools where the schools had few or no friends."

After retiring from the legislature, Wimberly remained active in Republican party affairs. In 1900 he attended the Republican National Convention in Philadelphia and voted to renominate William McKinley for president. He then went to Washington, D.C., and spent two years as a custodian in the House of Representatives, subsequently returning to Rocky Mount. Wimberly was twice married, the first time in 1869.

His first wife's name and that of their five children are unknown, and it is believed that most of these descendants moved to northern cities. His second wife was Ella Jenkins, whom he married on 11 Feb. 1891. Their children were Luther, Jim, Della, Lucy, Annie, John, and Allen. Wimberly spent the last years of his life at his house at 814 Raleigh Street, in Rocky Mount, in front of which a historical marker was erected in 1965. He was a member of the Primitive Baptist Church of Edgecombe County and held the position of deacon. He was buried in Unity Cemetery.

SEE: Herbert B. Battle, *The Battle Book* (1930) [portrait]; Edgecombe County Marriage Records (North Carolina State Archives, Raleigh); Raleigh *News and Observer*, 17 Feb. 1935, 17, 19 June 1937; *Rocky Mount Telegram*, 1 May

1965 (portrait); "Uncle Dred Wimberly—Slave Senator," *Carolina Magazine* (1935); Wimberly descendants, personal contact.

JOHN MACFIE

Wimble, James *(fl. 1696–1744)*, mariner, trader, distiller, landowner, and privateer, was a Carolina chart maker and the cofounder of Wilmington. Baptized on 31 Jan. 1696, he was born on the Sussex coast near Hastings, the sixth of ten children of James and Anne Wimble. Trained as a seaman, he built a small ship in which he sailed for the West Indies in 1718; with New Providence, the Bahamas, as a base, Captain Wimble was soon trading with the mainland. Evidently prospering, he acquired land in New Providence, in North Carolina, and in Boston. On 26 Mar. 1724 he married Rebecca Waters, the daughter of a substantial Boston citizen; James, the first of their several children, was born on 20 Dec. 1724. Wimble described himself variously in local deeds as a distiller, a mariner, and an innholder of Boston, but he continued a profitable trade with voyages to the West Indies and the Carolinas.

His activities in North Carolina prospered rapidly before disaster struck. In 1730 he became sole owner of a new brigantine, apparently built that year on the Cape Fear, which he named *Rebecca* after his wife. Of 128 tons burden, with a 54-foot keel and a 21-foot beam, she mounted ten guns with a crew of fourteen. Running into a violent storm on a 1731 voyage from Cape Fear to Boston, he was driven south and eventually reached New Providence in the Bahamas. There Governor Woodes Rogers illegally retained his papers and forced him to transport workers to the salt ponds. The ship was wrecked and lost in another storm. Wimble had to sell his slaves and even his Carolina lands before finding a passage from New Providence to Newport, R.I., which he reached on 10 Oct. 1732. He never recovered his losses, though he appealed repeatedly to the Board of Trade and Plantations in London for justice and redress.

With astonishing resilience, Wimble returned to North Carolina early in 1733, bought land on the Cape Fear River, sold lots, and became a cofounder with three others of a new settlement on the Cape Fear. Variously called New Carthage, New Liverpool, and Newton, it received in 1734 the support of the new governor, Gabriel Johnston, who named it Wilmington after his patron.

At the same time Wimble drew a crude but detailed and fairly accurate chart of the North Carolina coast, dated 16 Apr. 1733 (now in the Bodleian Library). Calling it "A Large and aisect [exact] Drafe. . . . By James Wimble wo as yausd [who has used] the Coast and trad this 12 yeare past," he sent the chart to William Mount, the publisher of the *English Pilot*. Mount may have been put off by the map's crudeness and its spelling, for not until 1738 did Mount and Page publish an improved version of Wimble's "North Carolina." This chart of the coast, the sounds, with soundings, inner passageways, and property owners, is dedicated to Thomas Pelham, the Duke of Newcastle and Secretary of State, the patron of Wimble and his relatives in Sussex, whom Wimble addressed as "The Duck of N. Castell." Wimble's work, with its hydrographic and topographic information, remained in spite of inaccuracies the best coastal chart of the region until the end of the century. On it "Wimble Shoals," north of Hatteras, is still a coastal landmark; "Wimblton Castel," which once rose on the high bluff near present Nun and Front Streets in Wilmington, stood against possible pirates and Spanish marauders.

How many vessels Wimble lost by storm and shipwreck is unknown, but the escalating War of Jenkins' Ear brought other misfortunes. In 1735 Captain Wimble wrote Newcastle that "Spanyords have takeing me 7 times." He attempted to retrieve his losses by turning to privateering. In April 1742 a chain shot from a Spanish ship that he was chasing in *The Rose* tore off his left arm, and he lost his ship. He lost another privateer, *The Revenge*, off Cuba two years later. Thereafter was silence; the life of a mariner and privateer was uncertain.

SEE: William P. Cumming, "The Turbulent Life of Captain James Wimble" and "Wimble's Maps and the Colonial Cartography of the North Carolina Coast," *North Carolina Historical Review* 46 (1969).

WILLIAM P. CUMMING

Winborne, John Wallace *(12 July 1884–9 July 1966)*, chief justice of the North Carolina Supreme Court, was born in Chowan County near Edenton, the eighth child and fifth son of Dr. Robert Henry and Annie Felicia Parker Winborne. He received his elementary education from his older sister, Martha Warren, who conducted a school for her younger brothers and sister and the children of tenants. From 1900 to 1902 he attended Horner Military School, Oxford, and in 1906 received an A.B. degree from The University of North Carolina. At Chapel Hill he earned monograms on the varsity track, baseball, and football teams, joined Delta Kappa Epsilon fraternity, and was a member of the Order of Gimghoul. He was, like his father, an active member of the Philanthropic Society and was tapped for membership in the Golden Fleece, the honorary order that selects only students who have been outstanding leaders.

Following graduation in 1906 he taught and coached at Bingham School in Asheville while studying law. Beginning in Marion in 1907, he practiced for thirty years. Winborne participated in many important cases of wide interest, served as special attorney for the state in connection with the condemnation of lands for the Great Smoky Mountains National Park, and was attorney for McDowell County and for the town of Marion from 1918 to 1937. He was a member of the North Carolina and American Bar associations and a Fellow of the American Bar Foundation.

When the state constitution was amended in 1936 to increase the number of supreme court members from five to seven, the General Assembly authorized the appointment of two additional associate justices. To fill these newly created positions Governor Clyde R. Hoey named Winborne and M. V. Barnhill, resident judge of the Second Judicial District. Because Justice Winborne was appointed directly from the bar and had no previous judicial experience, Hoey signed the commission designating Judge Barnhill first, thereby making Winborne the junior justice of the court. Elected for terms of eight years in November 1938, 1946, and 1954, Winborne was named chief justice by Governor Luther H. Hodges on the retirement of Chief Justice Barnhill on 21 Aug. 1956. In November of that year Winborne was elected to fill the term expiring on 31 Dec. 1958. In November 1958 he was elected to a full eight-year term, polling the largest number of votes of any candidate on the ticket.

Before joining the court, Winborne had been active in the civic, social, business, political, and religious life of his community and state. A member of the Marion Board of Aldermen from 1913 to 1921, he served during World War I as a member of the local Selective Service Board as well as chairman of the local committee of the American Red Cross and chairman of the Council of Defense in McDowell County. He was also chairman of the McDowell County Food Administration and a first lieutenant in the

Marion Company of the North Carolina Reserve Militia, the North Carolina National Guard having been called into service in the U.S. Army.

In politics Winborne was chairman of the Democratic executive committee of McDowell County (1910–12) and a member of the state Democratic executive committee (1916–37), of which he served as chairman from 1932 to 1937. He also sat on the local Government Commission from 1931 to 1933.

When the Kiwanis Club of Marion was organized in February 1923, Winborne became a charter member and its first president. He was one of the moving spirits in organizing and building the Marion General Hospital and was one of its incorporators as well as one of the original directors, a post he continued to fill until his appointment as an associate justice.

For many years he was a director of Clinchfield Manufacturing Company and served as chairman of its board of directors for several years prior to the time this large textile plant was merged with Burlington Industries, Inc. He was also one of the organizers of the Marion Manufacturing Company and a founder of the Marion Lake Club (afterwards the Country Club of Marion). A longtime director of the State Capital Life Insurance Company, he also was a director of and attorney for the First National Bank of Marion from 1929 until his appointment to the supreme court. He was an honorary member of the North Carolina Society of the Cincinnati, and in 1946 The University of North Carolina awarded him an honorary doctor of laws degree.

A member of St. John's Episcopal Church in Marion, Winborne served for many years as a vestryman and from time to time as senior warden. In addition, he was a longstanding teacher in the church school and for several years was superintendent. He was a licensed lay reader and frequently held services in his church in the absence of the rector.

Winborne also had a distinguished career in the Masonic fraternity. Long active locally, he was master of the Marion lodge during the period 1920–21 and was elected grand master of Masons in North Carolina in 1931. As typical of the man and his keen interest in the care and welfare of the children who were supported and educated at the Masonic Orphanage at Oxford, he served as a member of that institution's board of directors for thirty-two years (April 1930–April 1962).

On 30 Mar. 1910 he married Charlie May Blanton of Marion, and they had two children: Charlotte Blanton (Mrs. Charles M. Shaffer) of Chapel Hill and John Wallace Jr., of Atlanta, Ga. His wife died on 4 Nov. 1940, and on 14 June 1947 Winborne married Mrs. Lalage Oates Rorison. A portrait of the chief justice by Everett Raymond Kinstler hangs in the North Carolina Supreme Court, Raleigh. He was buried in Oaklawn Cemetery, Marion.

SEE: *Greensboro Daily News*, 14 Nov. 1932; *North Carolina Manual* (1961); *North Carolina Reports*, vol. 277 (1971); Raleigh *News and Observer*, 11 July 1966, 10 Feb. 1970; *Who Was Who in America*, vol. 7 (1981); Brodie B. Winborne, *The Winborne Family* (1905).

CHARLES M. SHAFFER

Winecoff, Thomas Edward (*29 Nov. 1867–29 May 1942*), minister and scientist, was born in Concord, the son of James and Margaret McKibben Winecoff. After he was graduated (1890) and obtained a master of arts degree (1893) from Davidson College, Winecoff studied law at The University of North Carolina in 1897–98. He left Davidson in 1890 to become an instructor of Latin at Cen-

tenary College in Louisiana. Although a Presbyterian by birth, he joined the Methodist church as a youth, and he left Centenary to become president of Cooper Normal College, a small Methodist college in Mississippi.

Winecoff was at Cooper for only a year, for in 1893 he turned to the Protestant Episcopal Church and was ordained to the ministry. From 1896 to 1898 he was in charge of the Chapel of the Cross in Chapel Hill, then spent some time at West Virginia University and the University of Washington while continuing work in the ministry. From Washington Winecoff went north to the Arctic Circle, where he became a U.S. marshal at Fort Yukon. He also collected arctic insects for the National Museum at Washington and the French national museum in Paris. A lover of outdoor life and biological science, he was able to enjoy both in the Arctic.

In 1918, near the end of World War I, Winecoff volunteered as a welfare worker in the French army. Ranking as an officer, he carried the official notice of armistice along the five miles of the French firing line on the morning of 11 Nov. 1918.

Winecoff returned to the United States to engage in home mission work in the Rocky Mountains, where he served an area more than four times the size of Delaware for over eight years. In 1927 he moved to Scranton, Pa., to become pastor of the Church of the Good Shepherd. He retired from the pastorate in 1929 and accepted a position as consulting biologist, in charge of research, for the Pennsylvania State Game Commission.

In 1892 he married Allie Estelle Black of Oxford, Miss. They had one daughter, Anna Thompson. Winecoff, a cousin of Thomas Dixon, author of *The Clansman*, died in Williamsport, Pa., and was buried in Concord, N.C.

SEE: Alumni Files (University of North Carolina, Chapel Hill); Clipping Files, including correspondence and family records (North Carolina Collection, University of North Carolina, Chapel Hill); Daniel L. Grant, *Alumni History of the University of North Carolina* (1924); *Scranton (Pa.) Times*, 2 Nov. 1927.

WARREN L. BINGHAM

Wingate, Washington Manly (*28 July 1828–27 Feb. 1879*), Baptist minister and college president, was born in Darlington, S.C., the son of William and Isabella Blackwell Wingate. After receiving an A.B. degree from Wake Forest College in 1849, Wingate continued his education at Furman Theological Institution from 1849 to 1851. He was ordained a Baptist minister on 3 Mar. 1852 by the Darlington, S.C., Baptist Church while pastor of Ebenezer Baptist Church and assistant pastor at Darlington.

In October 1852, at age twenty-four, he was elected agent of Wake Forest College to raise a $50,000 endowment, a task he completed in 1857. Wingate was elected both professor of moral and intellectual philosophy and rhetoric and president pro tempore of Wake Forest in June 1853. He served as acting president from 1854 to 1856 and as president from 1856 to 1879. Under his guidance the college grew steadily until the Civil War, when it was forced to close. Its buildings were used as a hospital, and its financial security was invested in Confederate States bonds.

During the war Wingate preached as an evangelist to the soldiers, was associate editor of the *Biblical Recorder*, and from 1862 to 1866 served as pastor of Baptist churches in Franklinton, Oxford, and Wake Forest. After the conflict Wake Forest College reopened, and Wingate began his second term as president in 1866. Faced with the problems of finance, he sent James S. Purefoy to secure endowments from Northern Baptists. The James W. Denmark loan fund was established, a new building was completed, and Wingate selected an excellent faculty. Though a strict disciplinarian, he was aware of the needs of the students; one biographer wrote, "He was so bright and cheerful and lovable." Wingate was an able preacher and speaker and presented the cause of Wake Forest College at many association and convention meetings.

He married Mary E. Webb of Bertie County in December 1850. They had seven children: Alice (Mrs. Needham Yancey Gulley), Lizzie (Mrs. W. J. Simmons), Walter Blackwell, William Jonathan, Belle (Mrs. Richard Battle), Sallie (Mrs. M. H. P. Clark), and Ruth (Mrs. Enoch Walter Sikes).

Wingate received an honorary D.D. degree from Columbian College (now George Washington University), Washington, D.C., in 1865 and from The University of North Carolina in 1871. He served as the first pastor of the Selma Baptist Church from 1872 to 1873. His only published work was a tract printed for soldiers entitled *I Have Brought My Little Brother Back* (1862?).

For fifteen years prior to his death, Wingate was aware of a heart condition. It finally proved fatal and he died of a heart attack. His funeral, conducted in the Wake Forest Baptist Church on 1 Mar. 1879 by William Bailey Royall, was attended by so many friends that a special train had to be chartered. He was buried at Wake Forest.

SEE: William Cathcart, *The Baptist Encyclopedia*, vol. 2 (1881); F. H. Ivey, *Memorial Address on the Life and Character of Rev. W. M. Wingate, D.D.* (1879); Luther Rice Mills, "My Recollections of Dr. W. M. Wingate," *North Carolina Baptist Historical Papers* 3 (July 1899, January 1900); George W. Paschal, *History of Wake Forest College*, 2 vols. (1935, 1943); Raleigh, *Biblical Recorder*, 5, 12, 19, 26 Mar., 2 Apr. 1879, 13 Mar. 1907; Raleigh *Observer*, 28 Feb., 1–2 Mar. 1879; *Wake Forest Student* 14 (May 1895 [portrait]); Washington Manly Wingate Papers (North Carolina Baptist Historical Collection, Wake Forest University, Winston-Salem [portraits]); Davis E. Woolley, ed., *Encyclopedia of Southern Baptists*, vol. 2 (1958).

JOHN R. WOODARD

Wingina. *See* **Pemisapan.**

Winslow, Caleb *(24 Jan. 1824–13 June 1895)*, physician, was the son of Nathan (1795–1873) and Margaret Fitz-Randolph Winslow (ca. 1781–1848), of Piney Woods Plantation near Belvidere, Perquimans County. After attending local schools, he entered Haverford School in Pennsylvania from which he was graduated in 1842. For a brief period he taught school and engaged in surveying. An accident in which he fractured his clavicle directed his attention to medicine, and he entered the University of Pennsylvania Medical School, from which he was graduated in 1849. For part of the time he had paid for his tuition by working as a pharmacist.

Settling in Hertford, Winslow soon enjoyed a large practice. During a smallpox epidemic he treated patients with considerable success and thereby enhanced his reputation. He also was known for his skill in gall bladder operations and amputations, and he anticipated the modern operation of trephining the skull for traumatic epilepsy. Because of his specialities patients were brought to him from a considerable distance.

Winslow became a member of the Medical Society of North Carolina at the session held in Edenton in 1857. He was a contributor to the pages of the *Medical Journal of*

North Carolina and was elected a member of the first Board of Medical Examiners of North Carolina, on which his special assignments dealt with surgery.

A Quaker, he was a pacifist and opposed slavery as well as secession on the eve of the Civil War. After Federal forces overran Hertford, however, he was accused by a soldier of having participated in the fight, was arrested, and taken to Roanoke Island, where he was held a prisoner for some weeks. At the end of the war, disheartened by the destruction around him, Winslow moved to Baltimore in 1866. There he found a number of surgeons with established practices, so he turned to general practice. He came to be appreciated as a family physician, and his services were in great demand. In one year he delivered an average of more than one baby a day. North Carolinians frequently went to Baltimore to consult with and be treated by him, and he sometimes returned to North Carolina to perform gallstone operations.

Winslow was offered the chair of materia medica in the Maryland College of Pharmacy, previously held by his brother, Dr. John Randolph Winslow, but teaching did not appeal to him and he declined the post. As a Quaker he served for many years as clerk of the Baltimore Monthly Meeting of Friends and frequently delivered papers before the Essay Meeting of the Society of Friends.

On 14 Jan. 1852, in Philadelphia, he married Jane Paxson Parry (1829–1910), the daughter of Oliver and Rachel Randolph Parry of Philadelphia and New Hope, Pa. Their children, all but the last born in Hertford, were Randolph (1852–1937), Olive Parry (1855–60), John Randolph (1856–60), Nathan (1857–58), Edward Randolph Parry (1859–62), Julianna Randolph (1861–1928), Margaret FitzRandolph (1 Apr.–8 May 1863), and John Randolph (1866–1937).

SEE: *Bulletin of the School of Medicine, University of Maryland*, 17 (January 1933); E. F. Cordell, *Medical Annals of Maryland* (1903); *North Carolina Medical Journal* 30 (August 1892).

ELIZA L. W. JONES

Winslow, John Ancrum *(19 Nov. 1811–29 Sept. 1873)*, naval officer, was born in Wilmington, the son of Edward and Sara Ancrum Berry McAllister Winslow. On his father's side he was descended from a prominent New England family and on his mother's he was connected with the Rhetts of South Carolina. At his father's insistence, John went to Massachusetts for schooling at age fourteen. But the boy's desire for a naval career led to his appointment as a midshipman, on 1 Feb. 1827, through the intercession of Daniel Webster.

His officer's career was fairly typical; it was marked by extensive sea and shore duty. In the Mexican War Winslow led a shore party with distinction in the capture of Tobasco in October 1846. But two months later he lost his first command in a gale. While a passenger on the USS *Raritan*, he became a friend and roommate of Raphael Semmes, who had suffered the same embarrassment. Illness, which sent Winslow home early in 1847, terminated his wartime services.

By his middle years in the 1850s he had come to regret his choice of profession. A confirmed Episcopalian, he turned increasingly pietistic, and, unlike many brother officers, he became an enthusiastic Abolitionist. At the beginning of the Civil War his attachments to North Carolina were virtually forgotten, and there was no question as to where his allegiance lay. When ashore he lived in Boston with his wife, the former Catherine Amelia Winslow, a cousin whom he had married in 1837. Two of their seven children (five sons, two daughters) were also navy men.

Winslow's Civil War career began at St. Louis, Mo., where he commanded the gunboat *Benton* under his friend, Flag Officer Andrew H. Foote. In December 1861 a freak accident, in which Winslow was struck in the arm by a piece of flying chain, deprived him of the chance to participate in the Fort Henry, Island No. 10, and Memphis operations. By the time he returned to duty in May 1862, Flag Officer Charles H. Davis had succeeded Foote. Winslow was dispatched to lead an expedition up the White River into Arkansas, but shallow water, river fever, and local guerrillas prevented his achieving anything substantial.

Although Winslow received his promotion to captain in July 1862, the choice three months later of Admiral David D. Porter, his junior on the naval officers' list, to replace Davis, as well as the Navy Department's discovery that Winslow had spoken disparagingly of President Abraham Lincoln and of General John Pope, a Republican favorite, raised the possibility that his usefulness might be over. His request for relief from unhealthy river duty got him placed on furlough—a seemingly dead end. Winslow wrote urgently to Secretary of the Navy Gideon Welles to make known his antislavery views; apparently the explanation was satisfactory, because in December 1862 he received command of the USS *Kearsarge*, a third-class screw steamer with seven guns and a crew of 163.

Despite continuing poor health, Winslow insisted on proceeding immediately to Fayal, Azores, where he was to join his new command. A three months' delay there, although exasperating, was probably a beneficial tonic. Winslow formally assumed charge on 6 Apr. 1863. The *Kearsarge*'s mission was the prevention of European-built and -manned Confederate raiding cruisers like the *Florida* and *Georgia* from putting to sea and the interception of the famous *Alabama* should it try to make port and refit. A shortage of Union cruisers allowed the first two vessels to get away, and Winslow's incessant patrolling soon led to an unpleasant incident with Great Britain. In November 1863 the *Kearsarge* recruited some Irish hands in Queenstown; Winslow immediately released the men when the British government protested, but he insisted on returning them to Ireland rather than risking their taking service with the Confederates. By early 1864 British pressure had compelled him to rely on Spain and the Low Countries instead of the British Isles for provisioning and refitting.

The *Kearsarge* was at Flushing when, on 12 June 1864, Winslow learned that the long-awaited *Alabama* had landed at Cherbourg; within two days he was outside the harbor. The refusal of French authority to permit Captain Semmes, Winslow's old shipmate, a long period in port for overhaul and Semmes's natural pugnacity led to send out a challenge. When the *Alabama* steamed out on the nineteenth, the *Kearsarge* dropped well beyond the three-mile limit to avoid any diplomatic complications. Seven miles offshore she put about; the two ships made seven opposite-course circuits with the range gradually dropping to seven hundred yards. Though their specifications were virtually identical, the *Kearsarge* was in much better condition than her adversary, which had been long at sea and had a foul bottom and deteriorated ammunition. Winslow had taken the added precaution of strengthening his ship's wooden sides by draped spare chains; moreover his gunnery, although slower, was considerably more accurate. Except for one lucky shot, which fortunately failed to explode, the *Kearsarge* escaped virtually unscathed and managed to sink the *Alabama*. The escape of Semmes and most of his officers aboard an English yacht later became a source of regret to the Union

captain because of Semmes's vindictive public pronouncements about his defeat. Unquestionably the vanquishing of the notorious raider *Alabama* strengthened the Federal government's diplomatic stance in Europe.

On returning home to Boston in November 1864 to decommission the *Kearsarge*, Winslow was voted the thanks of Congress and promoted to commodore with rank to date from his victory. He spent the remainder of the war at patriotic gatherings, on courts-martial, and in the supervision of ship construction in Boston. In December 1865 he assumed command of the Gulf Squadron for a brief period before it was merged with that of the North Atlantic. He hoisted his rear admiral's flag over the Pacific Squadron in 1870, but his ailments—he had already lost an eye due to long neglect of it at sea—forced him ashore to stay two years afterwards. He died at Boston Highlands.

A sea captain more in the dour tradition of puritan New England than of his native North Carolina, Winslow had made the most of a command that was less than his seniority called for. With it he won a dramatic naval duel in the romantic tradition of the War of 1812, one that stifled a late bid by the declining Confederacy for international prestige.

SEE: *Battles and Leaders of the Civil War*, vol. 4 (1888); *DAB*, vol. 10 (1936); John M. Ellicott, *The Life of John Ancrum Winslow, Rear Admiral* (1905); Jim Dan Hill, *Sea Dogs of the Sixties: Farragut and Seven Contemporaries* (1935); Clarence Edward Macartney, *Mr. Lincoln's Admirals* (1956).

RICHARD G. STONE, JR.

Winslow, John Randolph (*8 Nov. 1820–13 Feb. 1866*), physician, the first child of Nathan and Margaret FitzRandolph Winslow, was born on his father's plantation in Perquimans County. Because his family belonged to the Society of Friends, he very possibly was sent to the Friends' Boarding School at Providence, R.I. (later Moses Brown School). In 1838 he entered Haverford School in Pennsylvania (now Haverford College), from which he was graduated in 1840.

Winslow was a highly cultured man, and it is thought that on leaving Haverford he taught at Belvidere Academy. Soon, however, he began to study medicine at the University of Pennsylvania, from which he received an M.D. degree in 1846. Returning to his home, he established an office on his father's estate and remained some years in that locality. About 1851 he moved to Baltimore, where he continued to practice medicine until his death. He was also professor of materia medica in the Maryland College of Pharmacy (now the Department of Pharmacy of the University of Maryland). A nephew, Randolph Winslow, remembered being present at one of his lectures in 1865, although he was too young to understand the subject of his discourse. The late Professor Charles Gaspari, of Baltimore, told Randolph Winslow that he was a pupil of John R. Winslow at the time of his death.

Winslow invested extensively in western lands. Although he did not realize much from these transactions, the members of his family later profited when the land was sold. He died in Baltimore, reportedly from typhus fever that he had contracted from Negro patients. At his death he was unmarried and intestate, his father being his only heir. His nephew Randolph, who was living with him at the time, was the only member of his family present at his funeral.

In personal appearance, he resembled his brother Dr. Caleb Winslow so closely that they were often mistaken for each other, although John had darker coloring.

SEE: Winslow Family Papers, containing a biographical sketch by Randolph Winslow, M.D. (1852–1937) and other related papers (North Carolina State Archives, Raleigh).

ELIZA L. W. JONES

Winslow, Joseph (*ca. 1628–1679*), merchant, mariner, and landowner, was born in Marshfield, Mass., one of eight children of John of Plymouth Colony and Boston and Mary Chilton Winslow. John Winslow arrived in America on the ship *Fortune* in 1621, when he brought the furniture of the Pilgrims who had sailed in the *Mayflower* the previous year. Mary Chilton Winslow was among those who arrived on the *Mayflower*. Young Joseph was listed on the roster of the militia at Marshfield in 1643 and later accompanied his father to Maine, where John operated a trading post.

Among the eight Winslow children were Edward, a mariner, who was a leader in the foundation in 1664 of the Charlestown settlement on the Cape Fear River in North Carolina; John, a merchant and mariner, who contributed much to the growth of Maryland, North Carolina, and Virginia through seafaring and trade; and Mary, who married Elisha Hutchinson, the son of Anne Hutchinson, a quietist and an exile from the Massachusetts Colony. Uncle Edward Winslow was three times governor of the Massachusetts colony, served as minister to the court of Charles I, and was an associate of Oliver Cromwell.

Joseph Winslow was twice married. He last married Sarah Lawrence in 1673, and their children included Mary (b. 1674) and Joseph (b. 1677). By his first wife he was the father of Timothy, of Perquimans Precinct, N.C. His contribution to the population of the country has been called his greatest achievement. Although concentrated in eastern North Carolina, his descendants also spread out along the Atlantic seaboard and in significant numbers were part of the later Quaker exodus from North Carolina to the Midwest and among the Free-Soilers who contributed much to the westward expansion of the country.

Winslow was an opponent of the English Navigation Acts and a leader in Culpeper's Rebellion. In this connection he was the foreman of the jury that convened in 1677 at Nixonton on the Little River in Pasquotank Precinct and deposed Thomas Miller, variously known as governor and collector of customs. Governor Miller had acted without the consent of the Grand Assembly in enforcing the Navigation Acts.

As a master mariner, Joseph Winslow operated various vessels in the waters of North Carolina, Virginia, and Maryland. He was also an extensive landowner, with property in Massachusetts and Maryland as well as in North Carolina.

SEE: Louise Hall, "New Englanders at Sea: Cape Fear before the Royal Charter of 24 March 1662/3," *New England Historical and Genealogical Register* 124 (April 1970); Mattie Erma E. Parker, ed., *North Carolina Higher-Court Records, 1670–1696* (1968); Hugh F. Rankin, *Upheaval in Albemarle: The Story of Culpeper's Rebellion, 1675–1689* (1962); William L. Saunders, ed., *Colonial Records of North Carolina*, vol. 1 (1886).

JULIAN D. WINSLOW

Winslow, Milton (*21 May 1821–15 Nov. 1893*), Quaker minister and author, was born in Randolph County, the oldest child of Thomas and Anna (Nancy) Nixon Winslow, members of the Back Creek Quaker Monthly Meeting. His mother died after April 1827, and his father married Martha Bogue on 7 July 1830. In 1836 the family was granted a certificate of removal of membership to Mississinawa Monthly Meeting in Grant County, Ind., where Milton farmed and was ordained into the Society of Friends. In Indiana he married Mary Roberts on 23 Apr. 1846. Winslow indicated that he proposed to her in 1843 by sending her a poem that he composed proclaiming his love. They had ten children. As a Quaker minister Winslow traveled widely and even returned to North Carolina briefly in 1851.

Soon after the Civil War Winslow, his wife, and six other Quakers went to Mississippi as teachers of freedmen. They were well received by the former slaves but "very contemptuously" by white people. One night after the Winslows had retired, they were awakened by a soft knock at the door. On opening it Milton was greeted by one of his elderly black pupils who asked permission to stand guard during the night. They had seen signs, the man related, that the Winslows were to be harmed that night.

Over the years Winslow wrote numerous poems, most of them on folksy subjects and with local settings. In 1890 a 204-page edition was published in Fairmont, Ind., entitled *Winslow's Poems; or, Poems for Everybody*. A second edition, expanded to 287 pages with a pen-and-ink sketch of the author as a frontispiece, was issued by the same publisher in 1893.

His poems are devoid of literary merit but reflect the thoughts and sentiments of an ordinary citizen. One 72-line poem, however, is of interest to historians. "Mountain Meadow Massacre" is a dramatic and somewhat embellished recounting of an attack in September 1857 on a party of California-bound immigrants from Arkansas and Missouri by a mixed band of Mormons and Indians beyond Salt Lake City. Some 120 people were slaughtered, roughly one-fourth of all the California-bound immigrants who lost their lives in this manner. Winslow indicated that Mormon leaders refused to sell supplies to the tired and hungry people. Instead, after starting on their way, the immigrants were attacked, and all of them except seventeen young people were slaughtered; horses and wagons worth $300,000, jewelry, and clothes were taken. This is the only known attack on such immigrants by a collaborating band of whites and Indians, and Winslow's account in verse contains information not otherwise available. His sources are not noted, however, and it is difficult to separate fact from poetic license.

Winslow died in Grant County, Ind.. at age seventy-two.

SEE: Barbara N. Grigg and Myrle L. Walker, *Friends at Back Creek: Into the Third Century* (1993); Willard Heiss, comp., *Abstracts of Records of the Society of Friends in Indiana*, part 3 (1970); Elizabeth Doherty Herzfeld, *The Quaker and Southern Winslows* (1991); William W. Hinshaw, *Encyclopedia of American Quaker Genealogy*, vol. 1 (1937); Donald E. Thompson, comp., *Indiana Authors and Their Books* (1974); Milton Winslow, *Winslow's Poems* (1893).

WILLIAM S. POWELL

Winslow, Nathan (*4 Jan. 1795–29 Aug. 1873*), the eleventh child of Caleb (1749–1811) and his first wife, Ann Perry Winslow (1755–96) of Perquimans County, was born on his father's Piney Woods Plantation in Perquimans. Thirteen months later his mother died, and the duty of rearing him fell on his sister Rachel, twenty-five years older than he, who married Jonathan White. Little is known of his early life and his opportunities for getting an education; suffice it to say that he was a well-informed man and wrote a good hand.

By the will of his father, Nathan was made joint owner

of the home estate, and on the death of his stepmother, Peggy Scott Winslow, he came into possession of the whole property in 1833. It is probable that he added much by purchase to his land, for when the estate was sold in 1891, it turned out to comprise over 2,000 acres. This property is situated in the northern part of Perquimans County and to some extent in Chowan. In Nathan Winslow's day a large part of it was under cultivation and produced wheat, corn, oats, and other staple grains, fruits, sweet potatoes, and vegetables. The residence, which was destroyed by fire in 1921, was a two-story hip-roofed house with a wing extending back from the main building; the iron fireback in the large dining room fireplace bore the date 1768. The house was wainscoted throughout, the kitchen a detached building. In 1862, after the fall of Roanoke Island, Randolph Winslow (1852–1937), the grandson of Nathan, with his mother and his siblings took refuge there for several months.

On 29 Dec. 1819 Nathan Winslow married Margaret FitzRandolph (ca. 1781–3 July 1848), the daughter of Jacob and Elizabeth Pretlow FitzRandolph of Nansemond County, Va. The Winslows were the parents of John Randolph (1820–66), Rufus Kinsey (1822–43), Caleb (1824–95), and Margaret Ann Kinsey (1826–ca. 1830). Margaret FitzRandolph Winslow died at aged sixty-seven and was buried on Piney Woods Plantation. Remaining a widower for the rest of his life, Nathan Winslow lived alone on his plantation until the end of the Civil War, when, owing to the liberation of his slaves, he rented his place to J. Hardy Ward but continued to reside with the Wards in his own house.

Winslow was a birthright member of the Society of Friends but was disowned because he owned slaves; he continued, however, to attend meetings until his death. His father, Caleb, had manumitted his slaves, so Nathan did not acquire any by inheritance. The story is that he bought a Negro woman to keep her from being separated from her family. Having been "disowned" by the Society of Friends, he bought others and at the beginning of the Civil War owned a considerable number. He intended to free his slaves, and drafts of his will made in 1857 and 1858 provided that most of them be sent to Liberia; a few slaves were to be given the option of remaining in America. The Emancipation Proclamation precluded this intention.

Nathan Winslow was considered a rich man before the Civil War, but as a result of that conflict he became impoverished. He had a large estate but no one to cultivate it and no stock with which to till the soil. During the war a regiment of Union cavalry encamped on the place and used up his fences for fuel, killed his poultry, and stole his horses. Damage to the extent of $4,000 was done, and although the commanding officer gave him a receipt for the amount due, he was never able to collect it from the U.S. government.

As a farmer Winslow did not concern himself much about public affairs, but he did represent Pasquotank County in the state senate during the session of 1854–55. In those days he would drive to Hertford, about twelve miles from his plantation, in an old-fashioned gig drawn by one of his roan horses. After the war he spent several months each year with his son, Dr. Caleb Winslow, in Baltimore. About this time a small growth on one of his vocal chords affected his voice to such an extent that he could communicate only in a whisper. In the summer of 1873, after paying a visit to his Baltimore family, he took a sea voyage to Boston. On reaching Boston Harbor, he complained of pain in his chest. The ship's steward gave him some remedy and he retired. In the morning he was found dead in his bed. He was buried in the Friends' Harford Road Burying Ground in Baltimore.

SEE: John L. Cheney, Jr., *North Carolina Government, 1585–1974* (1975); Winslow Family Papers, containing a biographical sketch by Randolph Winslow, M.D. (1852–1937), the grandson of Nathan Winslow, and other related papers (North Carolina State Archives, Raleigh).

RANDOLPH WINSLOW

Winslow, Randolph (23 Oct. 1852–27 Feb. 1937), surgeon and educator, was born in Hertford, Perquimans County, to Dr. Caleb and Jane Paxson Parry Winslow. He attended Rugby Academy in Baltimore and in 1871 was graduated from Haverford College, from which he also received the customary master's degree in 1874. After obtaining an M.D. degree from the University of Maryland in 1873, he undertook additional study and training at the University of Pennsylvania and abroad in Berlin, Vienna, and Paris.

Winslow became a member of the teaching staff of the University of Maryland Medical School as assistant demonstrator of anatomy and rose through various positions to become chairman of surgery in 1902. He was one of the founders of the Woman's Medical College, Baltimore, where he also was professor of surgery (1882–93) and dean (1890–92). Additionally, in 1884 he held the chair of operative surgery and topographic anatomy at the Baltimore Polyclinic. He was on the surgical staff of a number of hospitals as well as a school for boys and an orphanage in Baltimore. A pioneer in performing several new operations in Maryland, he was among the first, if not actually the first, to introduce antiseptic surgery in Maryland.

Winslow was an active member of national, regional, and state medical societies, in which he held offices and contributed numerous important papers to their journals. He was a member of the North Carolina Society in Baltimore of which he once was an officer. In 1913 he was a founder of the American College of Surgeons and became a Fellow.

His role at the University of Maryland was an important one—it was largely through his efforts that the university hospital was built, and under his leadership the medical course was increased from two to three years and then to four. He was a regent of the university from 1891 to 1920 and on the board of trustees of the endowment funds of the university. He also served for twenty years on the executive council of the Association of American Medical Colleges.

In 1877 Winslow married Rebecca Fayssoux Leiper of Chester, Pa. Her great-grandfather, Dr. Peter Fayssoux of Charleston, S.C., had been surgeon general of South Carolina during the American Revolution. The Winslows had thirteen children: Nathan, John Leiper, FitzRandolph, Edwards Fayssoux, Mary Fayssoux, Jane Parry, Caleb, Eliza Leiper, George Leiper, Oliver Parry, Richard Randolph Parry, St. Clair Spruill, and Callender Fayssoux. A birthright Quaker, Dr. Winslow died in Baltimore and was buried in the Friends' Harford Road Burying Ground.

SEE: *Nat. Cyc. Am. Biog.*, vol. 28 (1940 [portrait]); University of Maryland, *Bulletin of the School of Medicine*, vol. 21 (April 1937 [portrait]); *Who Was Who in America*, vol. 4 (1968).

WILLIAM S. POWELL

Winslow, Warren (1 Jan. 1810–16 Aug. 1862), governor of North Carolina, congressman, and lawyer, was born and raised in Fayetteville, the son of John, magistrate of Fayetteville, and Caroline Martha Winslow. He had one brother, Edward Lee, and one sister, Lucy Ann Winslow Ochiltree. His grandfather was the Reverend Edward Winslow, a chaplain in the British army.

Winslow was educated at the Fayetteville Academy and at The University of North Carolina, where he received an A.B. degree in 1827. He entered business as a merchant in Fayetteville but was forced to abandon it following substantial losses during the panic of 1837. At this time, he began to study law and soon afterwards was admitted to the bar to practice in Fayetteville.

In 1853 Winslow gained his father's old spot as magistrate of police in Fayetteville. After serving for a year, he ran for a seat in the state senate. Not only was he victorious in this campaign, but he was also elected speaker of the senate. In the fall of 1854, when Governor David S. Reid resigned to take a U.S. Senate seat, Winslow, because of his office as speaker, succeeded him. After much debate over whether Winslow should resign as speaker to become acting governor, the senate decided by one vote to allow Winslow to hold both positions. Winslow, a Democrat, served as both governor of North Carolina and speaker of the Senate from 6 Dec. 1854 to 1 Jan. 1855. He was not a candidate in the 1854 gubernatorial election.

After leaving office in 1855 Winslow was sent to Spain by President Franklin Pierce as a representative during the Black Warrior Affair over the payment of a fine by an American vessel at Havana, Cuba. When he returned to North Carolina, Winslow won a seat in the U.S. Congress and then was reelected, serving from December 1857 to March 1861. In 1860, while a congressman, he was appointed chairman of the Military Board of North Carolina. In 1861 he negotiated the surrender of the Federal garrison in Fayetteville, thus securing over 37,000 stand of arms and munitions for the state. He also served as a member of the North Carolina Secession Convention from 20 May 1861 until his resignation late that year or early in 1862.

An Episcopalian, Winslow was buried in Cross Creek Cemetery, Fayetteville. He had married Mary Ivie Toomer (1811–43), a great-granddaughter of General James Moore; she was buried at Orton. Winslow left no will, but his estate was settled by his sister-in-law, Mary A. Winslow, and produced $14,682 from the trust estate he held for the children of his brother.

SEE: Kemp P. Battle, *History of the University of North Carolina*, vol. 1 (1907); Cumberland County Estate Records (North Carolina State Archives, Raleigh); *Fayetteville Observer*, 18 Aug. 1862; Daniel L. Grant, *Alumni History of the University of North Carolina* (1924); John A. Oates, *The Story of Fayetteville and the Upper Cape Fear* (1950); Robert Sobel and John Raimo, eds., *Biographical Directory of the Governors of the United States, 1789–1978* (1978).

CHRISTOPHER LEWIS WHITE

Winston, Ellen Black (*15 Aug. 1903–19 June 1984*), social worker, was born in Bryson City, the daughter of Stanley Warren and Marianna Fischer Black. She was graduated from Converse College, Spartanburg, S.C., in 1924 and received M.A. and Ph.D. degrees in sociology from the University of Chicago in 1928 and 1930, respectively. She was awarded five honorary doctoral degrees including those from The University of North Carolina and Duke University.

Mrs. Winston was a teacher of social science, the dean of girls, and the director of guidance in the Raleigh high schools from 1928 to 1934 and editor of technical publications on public relief in the Division of Research of the Works Progress Administration, Washington, D.C., from

1934 to 1939. She was chairman of the department of sociology and economics at Meredith College from 1940 to 1944, when she was appointed North Carolina commissioner of public welfare, a post she filled until 1963. During those years she served on numerous commissions and boards and in an advisory capacity to both state and national agencies.

In 1963 she began a four-year term as U.S. commissioner of welfare in the U.S. Department of Health, Education, and Welfare. She also was chairman of the Governor's Coordinating Commission on Aging (1956–63) and chairman or cochairman of the North Carolina White House Conference on Aging (1961, 1971, and 1981). In addition, Mrs. Winston served on the board of directors of such agencies as the International Council for Home Helps, Council on Social Work Education, North Carolina Conference for Social Service, Child Welfare League of America, and American Public Welfare Association, of which she was also president.

She was the American editor of *Nation and Family* (1941) and of a series of rural monographs for Works Projects administrators, a collaborator in the publication of *The Negro's Share* (1943), and coauthor of *Seven Lean Years* (1939), *The Plantation South* (1940), and *Foundations of American Population Policy* (1940). She wrote numerous professional articles.

Her husband was Sanford R. Winston, professor of sociology at North Carolina State College. They were married in 1928 but had no children. At her death memorial services were held at Meredith College with graveside services in Bryson City.

SEE: *Greensboro Daily News*, 30 Dec. 1962; Raleigh *News and Observer*, 1 Feb. 1940, 14–15 Mar. 1944, 15 Apr. 1951, 25 May 1982, 20 June 1984; *Who Was Who in America* (1976).

WILLIAM S. POWELL

Winston, Francis Donnell (*2 Oct. 1857–28 Jan. 1941*), lawyer, judge, state legislator, and lieutenant governor of North Carolina, was the third surviving son of prominent lawyer and planter Patrick Henry, Sr., and Martha Elizabeth Bird (or Byrd) Winston. Born in Windsor, Bertie County, Francis or "Frank" Winston obtained his early education at Windsor Academy, at Fetter's School in Henderson, and at Horner School in Oxford.

The closing of The University of North Carolina during the early 1870s for economic and political reasons made it necessary for him to travel out of state for his higher education. In 1873 he followed in the footsteps of his older brother, George Tayloe Winston, who two years earlier had entered Cornell University in New York. After studying journalism and literature at Cornell for a year, Francis enrolled at The University of North Carolina when it reopened in 1875. Reportedly, on arriving in Chapel Hill he beat his younger brother Robert in a foot race to campus, resulting in his being the first student to register at the university on its reopening. At Chapel Hill, Winston was president of his class, twice editor-in-chief of the reestablished *North Carolina University Magazine*, an active member of the Philanthropic Society, and a skilled player on the university's newly founded baseball team.

After graduating from The University of North Carolina in June 1879, Winston taught briefly at a school near Windsor and studied law with his father and later at the Dick and Dillard's Law School in Greensboro. One month after receiving his law license in January 1881, he was named clerk of the superior court for Bertie County, an appointment that stirred his interest in politics and provided him with important social and legal connections. In 1882 he opened his own law practice in Windsor, assuming responsibility for many of his ailing father's clients. He also began managing his father's extensive financial investments and real estate holdings.

In addition to administering his growing law practice, Winston steadily grew more involved in the political affairs of North Carolina. Though beginning as a Republican, he later became one of the state's leading Democrats and Bertie County's most influential politician. He was an unsuccessful Republican candidate for the office of state superintendent of public instruction in 1884, but two years later, again on the Republican ticket, he was elected to the state senate. In 1890, however, Winston joined the Democratic party and soon earned a reputation as an outspoken and fiery opponent of Republicans and of so-called Negro rule. He assisted in the planning of the white supremacy campaigns of 1898 and 1900, and he helped organize and promote statewide the establishment of "white supremacy clubs," or what he called "White government unions."

In 1898 Winston won a seat in the state house of representatives as a Democrat from Bertie County. In the 1899 session he introduced a discriminatory suffrage bill, one patterned after a Louisiana statute that—through educational and property qualifications—disfranchised poor and illiterate black voters. At the same time, the bill's inclusion of a grandfather clause protected the voting rights of most white voters with the same economic or educational deficiencies. Winston's bill passed and became the framework for the suffrage amendment that was placed on the ballot and approved by voters in the general election of 1900.

In 1901 Winston accepted appointment by Governor Charles B. Aycock as a judge of the Second Judicial District. He remained in this position until 1904, when he was elected lieutenant governor, serving during the administration of Governor Robert Brodnax Glenn (1905–9). In the 1904 campaign Winston had been bitterly attacked by his opponents, who reminded voters of his earlier membership in the Republican ranks and ridiculed past courtesies he had shown to fellow Republicans, most notably former black congressman George H. White. After his term as lieutenant governor, Winston continued to be very active in Democratic party affairs. For fifteen years he was a member of the Democratic Second Congressional District Committee and of the Democratic state executive committee, and in 1912 he was president of the North Carolina Democratic State Convention. At the request of President Woodrow Wilson in 1913, Winston served for two years as U.S. district attorney for the Eastern District of North Carolina. In 1916 he began serving as an "emergency judge" for the state's superior court, a duty he held for many years. Once again, in 1927, he was elected to represent Bertie County in the state legislature, but in 1929 he returned to the bench as a judge of the General Court of Bertie County.

Winston was grand master of Masons of North Carolina (1907–8), president of the State Bar Association (1911–12), a director of the Southern Conservatory of Music, a longtime member of the State Literary and Historical Association and the State Library Association, and a volunteer in many other civic organizations. He also served for over half a century as a trustee of The University of North Carolina, and he attended sixty-one consecutive commencements at his alma mater. In 1920 the university awarded him an honorary LL.D. degree.

On 30 May 1889, in St. Thomas's Episcopal Church, Windsor, Winston married Rosa Mary Kenney. She was the daughter of Stephen Bartlett Kenney, a U.S. Navy surgeon and a native of Maine. Although Judge Winston and his wife never had children of their own, they formally adopted one of Mrs. Winston's nephews, Stephen Etheridge Winston Kenney. Winston, "Bertie's Grand Old Man," died of heart failure at the age of eighty-three at Windsor Castle, the large family home built by his father. He died in the same room in which he was born, and he was buried in the cemetery of St. Thomas Episcopal Church, Windsor.

SEE: Samuel A. Ashe, ed., *Biographical History of North Carolina*, vol. 2 (1905); *Chapel Hill Weekly*, 31 Jan. 1941; Winfield S. Downs, ed., *Encyclopedia of American Biography*, n.s. (1942); Daniel L. Grant, *Alumni History of the University of North Carolina* (1924); *Greensboro Daily News*, 29 Jan. 1941; Archibald Henderson, *Francis Donnell Winston* (1942); Raleigh *News and Observer*, 4 Oct. 1936, 2 Oct. 1938, 30 Jan. 1941; Joseph S. Rowland, Jr., *Winstons of North Carolina and Their Descendants* (1982); Alan D. Watson, *Bertie County: A Brief History* (1982); Francis D. Winston, ed., *Sketch of the Class of 1879 of the University of North Carolina* (1889).

NEIL FULGHUM

Winston, George Tayloe (12 Oct. 1852–26 Aug. 1932), scholar, educator, and university president, a native of Bertie County, was the second son of Patrick Henry Winston, Sr., and Martha Elizabeth Bird (or Byrd). Like his older and younger brothers, he received much of his early education at Horner's School in Oxford. In 1866, at age fourteen, he entered The University of North Carolina, where he distinguished himself as not only the youngest but also the best student in his class. Winston remained in Chapel Hill until 1868, when classes were suspended due to declining enrollment and the university's increasing economic problems. The next year, by appointment of President Andrew Johnson, he was admitted to the U.S. Naval Academy in Annapolis, Md. Again he excelled in his studies, ranking first among seventy cadets in his class.

Despite his success in the classroom, Winston was unable to adjust to life aboard ship or to overcome bouts of acute seasickness during his training. These conditions forced him to resign his commission in 1870, after which he traveled to New York and entered Cornell University where he focused on foreign languages, literature, and mathematics. He received the university's highest award for Latin scholarship, and in his senior year, due to his exceptional abilities in mathematics, Winston was chosen to assume the teaching duties of a math professor who was away on leave. After graduation in 1874, he remained at Cornell for a year to pursue graduate work and teach mathematics.

With the reopening of The University of North Carolina in 1875, Winston accepted a teaching position on the Chapel Hill campus. Appointed assistant professor of literature at a salary of $1,500 a year, he administered the departments of Latin and German and was elected secretary of the faculty. A year later he was promoted to full professor, and on 5 June 1876 he married Caroline Sophia Taylor, of Hinsdale, N.H., whom he had met at Cornell. They had four children: Hollis Taylor, Patrick Henry, Lewis Taylor, and Isabella Byrd.

Although Winston studied law and had intentions of leaving the university to establish his own law practice, he continued to teach. In 1884 he traveled to Europe to study the culture of ancient Rome. During this time he wrote *The Greek, the Roman, and the Teuton*. On his return to Chapel Hill, he was appointed presiding professor in the university's enlarged Latin department. In addition to his teaching duties, he was elected president of the North Carolina Teachers Assembly in 1889.

In 1891 Winston was unanimously elected president of The University of North Carolina when Kemp Plummer Battle resigned. The seventh president of the university, Winston was at age thirty-nine among the youngest university presidents in the nation. He was also the first professional teacher to hold this post at Chapel Hill since the institution's first president, Joseph Caldwell. President Winston immediately began an expansion program, instituting changes that strengthened and modernized the school. During his five-year administration the university's income more than doubled, and the student population nearly trebled. Moreover, the university's summer school was also reopened for the first time in ten years.

Winston's accomplishments were impressive, especially at a time when the university was unpopular in some powerful political circles and among influential religious leaders, who insisted on a halt to public funding for higher education. These opponents of the state university, which included the presidents of Trinity College (now Duke University) and Wake Forest College, contended that it was not the public's responsibility or the state government's role to educate the masses beyond grade school, that only a few people could benefit by an education beyond elementary school, and denominational schools could better educate men for Christian leadership. Despite this serious and highly vocal opposition, Winston was ultimately successful in convincing the state legislature to continue its appropriations to public institutions of higher learning.

Winston was also a target of dissent by students, many of whom objected to his policies and management style. On the south side of Gerrard Hall, which served for many years as the campus's chapel, disgruntled students painted in bright red letters two feet high "Winston's Military Academy." This graffiti was a sarcastic reference to the iron hand with which Winston led the student body. In addition to strictly policing dormitory life, President Winston had forbidden any intercollegiate sports due to the ill will and brawling that had occurred during athletic contests with rival schools.

In 1896 Winston left Chapel Hill to become the first president of the University of Texas, which had offered to double his salary. But Winston stayed for only three years. Dissatisfied with the pace of administrative and educational reforms that he tried to install and uncomfortable with the general climate of Texas, he decided to return to his native state in 1899, this time to assume the presidency of the North Carolina College of Agriculture and Mechanic Arts in Raleigh (now North Carolina State University). Again, his skills as an administrator led to improvements in the young college's faculty and equipment and in the size of its student body and overall income.

Throughout his career Winston was a tireless campaigner for public education and a frequent lecturer, invited by many institutions and academic societies to express his views on a wide variety of educational and sociological issues. In some of his writings of the early 1900s, he also addressed race relations. Appearing in the July 1901 edition of *Annals*, published by the American Academy of Political and Social Science in Philadelphia, was Winston's "The Relation of the Whites to the Negroes." In this article he relies on sentimentality rather than detached scientific study to compare and assess the pre–Civil War and postwar conditions of southern blacks. Using personal childhood recollections, he recounts what he perceived as the happier, more secure time of slavery, when the races—both white and black—benefited from

the peculiar institution's rigid code of social conduct. With foreboding and unabashed condescension, Winston looks to a "dark and gloomy" future for African Americans if white civilization failed to support and nurture this recently liberated "child race."

Winston remained president of the North Carolina College of Agriculture and Mechanic Arts until 1908, when he retired at age fifty-six with a pension or endowment provided by the Carnegie Foundation. Although he spent time residing in New York and visiting England, he eventually returned to North Carolina to live out the rest of his life. His most significant publication during these years was his detailed biography of Daniel A. Tompkins, *A Builder of the New South* (1920). In poor health and an invalid in the last years of his life, Winston died of double pneumonia at age eighty in Watts Hospital, Durham. His cremated remains were buried in Asheville.

SEE: American Academy of Political and Social Science, *Annals*, July 1901; Kemp P. Battle, *History of the University of North Carolina*, vol. 2 (1912); Chapel Hill, *Daily Tar Heel*, 5 Apr. 1958; *Chapel Hill Weekly*, 23 June 1960; *Nat. Cyc. Am. Biog.*, vol. 13 (1906); William S. Powell, *The First State University* (1979); Raleigh *News and Observer*, 2 July 1896, 27 Aug. 1932; Joseph S. Rowland, Jr., *Winstons of North Carolina and Their Descendants* (1982).

NEIL FULGHUM

Winston, Hollis Taylor (25 Oct. 1877–5 June 1938), naval officer, was born in Chapel Hill, the son of George Tayloe and Caroline Taylor Winston. He attended The University of North Carolina between 1893 and 1895 and was graduated from the U.S. Naval Academy in 1900. Winston served on the USS *Columbia* in the West Indian campaign, on the USS *Charleston* during Secretary of State Elihu Root's diplomatic tour of South America in 1906, and as gunnery officer aboard the *Charleston*, which won the trophy in 1909. He was an instructor at Annapolis in 1910 and took part in the Nicaraguan and Mexican campaigns in 1913–14 aboard the USS *California*.

Winston was on engineering duty at the Brooklyn Navy Yard in 1917–19 and in charge of engineering inspection for the Philadelphia district in 1920–22. He retired from active service in 1922 as a lieutenant commander. An Episcopalian, he never married. Funeral services were held in the Fort Meyer Chapel, and he was buried in Arlington National Cemetery.

SEE: Daniel L. Grant, *Alumni History of the University of North Carolina* (1924); Raleigh *News and Observer*, 8 June 1938.

WILLIAM S. POWELL

Winston, James Horner (19 Sept. 1884–9 Apr. 1968), attorney, was born at Oxford, the son of Robert Watson, an eminent jurist, and Sophronia Horner Winston. After attending the Durham Grade School and Horner Military School in Oxford, he entered The University of North Carolina, where he was captain of the tennis team and a member of Zeta Psi social fraternity, Phi Beta Kappa, and the Order of Gimghoul. He was graduated with a B.A. degree in 1904. In the same year Winston achieved great distinction when he became the first Rhodes Scholar to be named from North Carolina. He studied at Oxford University from 1904 to 1907, when he was awarded the B.A. degree in jurisprudence from the law school.

Returning to the United States, Winston began to practice law at Norfolk, Va., in 1907. He moved to Chicago in

1911 to join the firm of Winston, Strawn, and Shaw. In 1947 he became associated with Miller, Gorham, Wescott, and Adams, where he remained until his retirement in 1953. Known as an authority on tax and antitrust law, he was a member of the American, Illinois, and Chicago bar associations. A prominent figure on the Chicago scene, Winston was a member of numerous organizations including the University Club of Chicago (of which he was president), Chicago Club, Law Club, Legal Club, Old Elm Country Club, and Indian Hill Golf Club. In addition, he served for many years on the selection committee for the Rhodes Trust. He was a Democrat and an Episcopalian.

On 26 Nov. 1908 Winston married Laura M. Flanagan of Chicago. They had four children: Robert W. III, Virginia (m. Herbert C. DeYoung), Albert F., and Laura Janet (m. Robert B. Wilcox). Following the death of his first wife in 1947, Winston married, on 19 Mar. 1949, Carita Reiss Bachmann of Sheboygan, Wis. There were no children of the second marriage. Winston died in Evanston, Ill.

SEE: Alumni Files (University of North Carolina, Chapel Hill); Daniel L. Grant, *Alumni History of the University of North Carolina* (1924); William S. Powell, ed., *North Carolina Lives* (1962).

JAMES ELLIOTT MOORE

Winston, John Reynolds (13 Apr. 1839–7 Mar. 1888), farmer, soldier, and politician, was born in Leaksville, the son of Edward and Susan Reynolds Winston. He received his early education in the local primary school and at the Leaksville Academy. In 1856 he entered Trinity College, where he was graduated with a master of arts degree in 1859.

Winston's plans for a career in law were cut short by the outbreak of the Civil War. He enlisted in the Confederate army in the spring of 1862 and was commissioned a captain in the Forty-fifth North Carolina Infantry. Wounded and captured at Gettysburg in July 1863, he was sent to Johnson's Island Prison in Lake Erie. There on the night of 31 Dec. 1863 he escaped across the frozen lake into Canada. With the help of a relative in New York, he obtained passage from Canada to Nassau and then ran the blockade into Wilmington, rejoining his regiment in time for the Wilderness campaign. When his commanding officer was killed at Spottsylvania in May 1864, Winston became colonel of the regiment and served with distinction until the war's end.

After being mustered out, he accepted a position as principal of the Memphis Academy in Memphis, Tenn., but he soon left and returned to North Carolina to take up farming. In 1867 he married Marian Long of Caswell County, and the couple had five children. Active in the Granger movement, he obtained the post of master of the New Hope chapter; however, Winston's interests in national finance and currency reform led him in other directions. Believing that the answer to the nation's fiscal woes lay in inflationary measures, he started a correspondence on that topic with farm and labor leaders across the country and participated in the formation both of the National Independent party in 1875 and its successor, the National Greenback Labor party, one year later. At the Greenback's national convention in 1880, he vigorously supported its presidential nominee, James B. Weaver.

Winston also agitated for the Greenback cause on the local level. In 1876 he published an open letter to the residents of his congressional district, the Fifth, urging them to support financial reform, and in 1878 and 1880 he was an unsuccessful Greenback candidate for the district's congressional seat. In 1880 Winston again at-

tempted to organize the party on the state level but failed miserably, attracting only five people to the state convention. He also served as political editor of a short-lived Greenback newspaper, the Greensboro *Beacon*. Still proselytizing for soft money, Winston ran for Congress in 1882 as a Republican and again in 1884 as a Liberal but was defeated both times. He died four years later at his home near Hycotee post office in Caswell County.

SEE: Walter Clark, ed., *Histories of the Several Regiments and Battalions from North Carolina in the Great War*, vols. 3–5 (1901); Graham, *Alamance Gleaner*, 15 Mar. 1888; *Greensboro Patriot*, 16 Mar. 1888; Weymouth T. Jordan, comp., *North Carolina Troops, 1861–1865: A Roster*, vol. 11 (1987); Irwin Unger, *The Greenback Era* (1964); Charles L. Van Noppen Papers (Manuscript Department, Duke University Library, Durham).

DONALD C. BUTTS

Winston, Joseph (17 June 1746–21 Apr. 1815), Revolutionary patriot, militia officer, legislator, and congressman, was born in Louisa County, Va. His ancestry can be traced to one of three Winston brothers who emigrated from Yorkshire, England, in the seventeenth century. Influential Virginia members of his family included his father Samuel, his aunt (or cousin) Sarah Winston Henry (Patrick Henry's mother), and his uncle Anthony (mentor and benefactor of the giant Revolutionary soldier, Peter Francisco). As a youth Winston fought with the Virginia militia and was wounded during a skirmish with border Indians in 1763. He moved to North Carolina in the late 1760s and by the early 1770s had settled on the Town Fork of the Dan River in Surry (now Stokes) County.

In 1775 Winston was elected a delegate to the Hillsborough Provincial Congress, where he signed the Continental Association, and he and the county's other delegates were constituted as the Surry County Committee of Safety. In April 1776 he represented Surry at the Halifax Provincial Congress and voted to instruct the state's delegation to the Continental Congress to vote for independence. In 1778 he was made entry taker (register of deeds) for Surry County. This position brought him into close contact with the Moravians (*Unitas Fratrum*) of Salem, and he assisted them in acquiring deeds to the Wachovia settlement. Although occasionally at odds with the Moravians, especially in his role as a Patriot militia leader, Winston was on friendly terms with them for the remainder of his life. This gave him a substantial base for a lengthy political career.

Shortly after the 1775 Hillsborough Congress Winston was named second major, then first major of the Surry County militia. In February 1776 he led a group of Surry volunteers to fight Tories at the Battle of Moore's Creek Bridge. Later that year he and his men joined a multistate effort against the Overhill towns of the Cherokee. Winston and his force served under Colonel Martin Armstrong and General Griffith Rutherford in subduing the Indians, and Winston participated in the negotiations that led to the signing of the Treaty of Long Island on the Holston on 20 July 1777.

During the remainder of the Revolution he had several opportunities to protect the peace-loving Moravians from marauding militia groups from both sides and to lead Patriot groups against Tory forces in the Surry County region. In September 1780 Major Winston and sixty Surry County militiamen joined Colonel Benjamin Cleveland and his Wilkes County troops. They met with the over mountain men and joined in the defeat of Major Patrick Ferguson and his forces at Kings Mountain on 7 Oct. 1780.

On 15 Mar. 1781 Winston and his militia served under General Andrew Pickens in the Battle of Guilford Court House. Some accounts report that Winston and his men were among the last Americans to leave the battle, and that Richard Talliferro, serving with Winston, was the last American to be killed. Years later Winston apparently was given the rank of lieutenant colonel in the Stokes County militia. In 1812 the North Carolina legislature presented him an "elegant sword" for his military services.

Winston represented Surry County in the House of Commons in 1777, 1779, 1782, and 1783. In 1788 he was a delegate to the Hillsborough convention to consider the ratification of the proposed U.S. Constitution. He voted with the majority neither to ratify nor to reject the Constitution apparently in hopes of forcing either a new convention or the addition of a bill of rights to the proposed document. Winston was also a delegate to the 1789 Fayetteville convention and voted with the majority to ratify the Constitution.

In 1787–89 he represented Surry County in the North Carolina Senate. He led the movement to divide Surry County and was senator from newly created Stokes County in 1790, 1791, 1802, 1807, and 1812. In addition, he represented the district consisting of Surry, Stokes, Iredell, Wilkes, and Ashe counties in the Third Congress of the United States (1793–1795) and in the Eighth and Ninth congresses (1803–7).

A hardworking state senator, Winston represented the interests of his Piedmont region in a generally Jeffersonian manner. On several occasions he called public meetings to determine the wishes of his constituents on local, state, and national issues. He favored education, limited government, and supremacy of the legislature and opposed the dominance of eastern over western counties. In the national Congress Winston attended and voted regularly, but he served on no important committees and never addressed the body on any issue. He backed the Jeffersonian position on almost every matter on which a vote was recorded. Thus he was an undistinguished but reliable representative. He served twice as a presidential elector, voting for Jefferson in 1800 and Madison in 1812.

In 1784 he became a trustee of the Salisbury Academy, and in 1807 he was tapped by the legislature to serve a six-year term as trustee of The University of North Carolina. In 1809 he was a trustee for the Germanton Academy, located only a few miles from his home.

As early as 1782 Winston owned 980 acres of land and fifteen slaves. In 1790 he had 1,362 acres and eighteen slaves; on his death he left a will in which he indicated ownership of 900 acres in Stokes County and 8,000 acres of western lands. He was married twice, first to Jane Dalton in 1769 and later to Minerva Elizabeth Lanier. His children numbered at least twelve, mostly boys. Triplet sons, Samuel L., Lewis L., and William H., moved to Mississippi and Alabama where one became a major general in the War of 1812, another a state supreme court judge, and the third lieutenant governor. Another son, Joseph, remained in North Carolina and also became a major general in the War of 1812.

Winston was buried in the family cemetery near Germanton. In 1849, when Stokes County was divided, the county seat of Forsyth, the new county, was named for him. In 1894 a statue of Winston was erected on the Guilford Court House Battlefield, and in 1906 his remains were moved to the battlefield, now a part of the Guilford Court House National Military Park.

SEE: *Biog. Dir. Am. Cong.* (1950); Walter Clark, ed., *State Records of North Carolina*, vols. 11–17 (1895–99), 19–24 (1901–5); *DAB*, vol. 20 (1936); Lyman Draper, *King's Mountain and Its Heroes* (1914); Adelaide L. Fries, ed., *Records of the Moravians in North Carolina*, vols. 1–7 (1922–47); Delbert H. Gilpatrick, *Jefferson Democracy in North Carolina, 1789–1816* (1931); J. Edwin Hendricks, "Joseph Winston: North Carolina Jeffersonian," *North Carolina Historical Review* 45 (1968); William L. Saunders, ed., *Colonial Records of North Carolina*, vol. 10 (1890); George T. Winston, *The Life and Times of Major Joseph Winston* (1895).

J. EDWIN HENDRICKS

Winston, Laura Annie Ballinger (9 July 1850–9 June 1922), temperance leader and educator of the deaf, was born at Swinton Lodge in Guilford County, the daughter of Yancey and Naomi Coffin Ballinger. Her father was of a line of French Huguenots who settled in South Carolina seeking religious freedom. Her mother was of the noted Coffin family line of Devonshire, England, which immigrated to Massachusetts in 1642. The Coffins were Friends (Quakers) and subsequently settled on the island of Nantucket, from which future lines moved to Guilford County, N.C.

She studied under her parents before entering the New Garden Boarding School (later Guilford College), where she was a student for seven years (1862–69). In 1869 she went to Raleigh to teach in the state school for the deaf. Demonstrating an unusual facility for working with the deaf, she was regarded as a dedicated and successful teacher. In 1872 she married Alonzo Hinton Winston of Raleigh. They had one daughter, Lonnie, born in 1873. Alonzo died five days after their daughter's birth, and his widow never remarried.

For about five years after her husband's death, Mrs. Winston served in a missionary field in Mexico. There, at the Hussey Institute in Matamoras, she was associated with her sister, Julia L. Ballinger, a longtime principal and teacher of that missionary school for Mexican girls. The school was a project of the Friends' Board of Missions of Philadelphia. About 1890 Mrs. Winston and her daughter returned to North Carolina, and within a few months the daughter died. It was then that Mrs. Winston said: "I'll try to live for somebody else's daughter."

When the State School for the Deaf was built in Morganton in 1894, she was invited to resume teaching deaf children and accepted what became a brilliant and enduring lifework. Her instruction of subject matter was considered spectacular, but her emphasis on religion and character-building was recorded as phenomenal. Initially Mrs. Winston was a supervising teacher in the sign department. Within three years, in 1897, the school's board of directors named her lady principal with full responsibility for the institution's educational program as well as social relationships. Among the latter she edited the school paper, the *Deaf Carolinian*. Reviewers praised her journalism, and the paper's circulation increased beyond any previous record. She also wrote instructive articles on various subjects, especially religion, temperance, and travel, and received wide recognition for her series on "My Trip to Palestine and the Holy Land." One of her professional papers, "How to Encourage the Use of English outside the Schoolroom," written for the Teachers' Association in 1904, brought a request for copies to be distributed in schools abroad.

In 1904 Mrs. Winston went to Jerusalem as a delegate from North Carolina to the World's Sunday School Convention, of which she was elected first vice-president, presiding over several sessions of a gathering that drew representatives from twenty-six nations.

As early as 1883 she participated in the first state convention of the Woman's Christian Temperance Union, serving as recording secretary. Active in the organization for over thirty-eight years, she was an effective promoter of temperance legislation that resulted in special instruction on the subject in the public schools. From time to time she was state president, state organizer, and a delegate to state and national conventions and to the World's Convention of the temperance union held in Edinburgh in 1900. Among her activities were lectures on temperance before various groups in North Carolina and adjacent states, cottage meetings and Bible readings, and special conferences with parents.

Mrs. Winston never allowed her work for temperance to supplant the principal mission of her life: teaching the deaf. She resisted many offers to go into the field—among them, invitations to teach in schools in China and Europe. She continued to travel widely and shared that enrichment with her pupils first and then with many groups around the state, especially churches and schools. From her early youth she was a devout Friend (Quaker) and ministered in many places and in many ways.

In early 1912, after a seventeen-year association with the school at Morganton, Mrs. Winston retired from teaching, but she continued her temperance work and other projects that had drawn her interest. She died at her home in Greensboro following a brief illness and was interred in a Greensboro cemetery.

SEE: Samuel A. Ashe, ed., *Biographical History of North Carolina*, vol. 8 (1917); Otis A. Betts, *North Carolina School for the Deaf: Education of the Deaf in North Carolina* (1945); *Deaf North Carolinian*, 24 Dec. 1910.

C. SYLVESTER GREEN

Winston, Patrick Henry *(9 May 1820–14 June 1886)*, lawyer and public official, was born in Franklin County, the son of George W. and Anne (Nancy) Fuller Winston. George Winston was a descendant of John Winston, uncle of Sarah Winston Henry, mother of the noted Patrick Henry. As a youth Patrick Henry Winston worked in the fields of his father's farm and studied under his mother's guidance. At age eighteen he entered Wake Forest College, where he completed three years of academic work in a single year. For the next three years he taught in Oak Grove Academy near Windsor, Bertie County, while continuing his own personal study. He then enrolled at Columbian University in Washington, D.C., from which he received an A.B. degree with highest honors. For a brief time Winston read law under Judge Robert B. Gilliam at Oxford before studying law at The University of North Carolina in 1844–45.

On New Year's Day 1846 he married Martha Elizabeth Bird of Bertie County, where the couple made their home. While establishing a law practice, Winston also taught school, but he soon gave that up as he came to be regarded as one of the foremost lawyers of northeastern North Carolina. In addition, he owned a number of plantations and operated fisheries on the Roanoke River.

In 1850 and 1854 he represented his county in the House of Commons. The General Assembly in 1861 named him one of the judges of the Court of Claims, and later Governor Zebulon B. Vance appointed him financial agent for North Carolina in fiscal relations with the Confederate government. In 1862, after Union forces occupied portions of eastern North Carolina, Winston acquired the 721-acre Springfield plantation on the Tar River in Franklin County and moved his family there for the duration of the Civil War. In 1864 he was president of the Council of State, and in 1865 he was the Franklin County delegate to the Constitutional Convention.

In the fall of 1865 the Winston family returned to their home, Windsor Castle, in the town of Windsor. The last three of the Winstons' ten children had been born while they lived at Springfield plantation in Franklin County. Patrick Winston resumed his legal practice and retired from politics. In 1868 he declined a nomination for the U.S. Congress, and in 1878 he did not pursue an opportunity to have his name submitted at the Democratic state convention for a seat on the North Carolina Supreme Court. He was in ill health for a number of years before his death in Windsor. He was buried in the churchyard of St. Thomas Episcopal Church, Windsor.

His five children who lived to adulthood were Patrick Henry, Jr., George Tayloe, Francis Donnell, Robert Watson, and Alice Capehart. Four others died in infancy and one at age three. The Winstons were noted for their learning and culture as well as for their sense of humor. Even near the end of the twentieth century funny stories by and about "Old Man Pat" Winston, as he was lovingly called, were still being related.

SEE: Samuel A. Ashe, ed., *Biographical History of North Carolina*, vol. 2 (1905 [portrait]); John L. Cheney, Jr., ed., *North Carolina Government, 1585–1979* (1981); Walter Clark, ed., *Histories of the Several Regiments and Battalions from North Carolina in the Great War*, vol. 1 (1901); Daniel L. Grant, *Alumni History of the University of North Carolina* (1924); Patricia Winston Norman (Flintridge, Calif.), personal contact, October 1981.

WILLIAM S. POWELL

Winston, Patrick Henry, Jr. *(22 Aug. 1847–3 Apr. 1904)*, lawyer and journalist, was born in Windsor, Bertie County, the son of Patrick Henry, Sr., and Martha Elizabeth Bird Winston. He attended the Horner School in Oxford, and during the Civil War, in December 1864 at age seventeen, he was an aide-de-camp to Governor Zebulon B. Vance. In March 1865 he entered the Confederate army and was en route to join the Fourth North Carolina Cavalry when word arrived of the surrender of General Robert E. Lee. There is a family story that Winston spent so much time saying goodbye to his many kinfolk that the war ended before he arrived.

Back home from his unsuccessful journey to find his unit, he entered The University of North Carolina and in 1867 was graduated as valedictorian of his class of eleven. He read law under his father and was licensed to practice on 8 June 1868. Like many other Southerners after the war, Winston moved to Baltimore, where he was also licensed and practiced law for two years. There he was introduced to Virginia Beeson Miller of Pittsburgh and proposed marriage to her at their first meeting. She was the daughter of Maria Morrow and Alexander Hamilton Miller, a prominent lawyer of Pittsburgh. They were married on 5 Jan. 1870 and lived in the Millers' home. Winston received a license in Pennsylvania and joined his father-in-law's law firm. The Winstons' son, Patrick Henry Winston III, was born on 10 Feb. 1871 but died on 3 July.

Winston was a delegate from Pennsylvania to the 1872 Democratic National Convention, in Baltimore, which nominated Horace Greeley. In December 1873 he moved his family, now consisting of a young son and a daughter, to North Carolina, where he began practicing in Windsor. In 1874 he became co-owner and editor of the local newspaper, the *Albemarle Times*, and in the fall of that year he was elected reading clerk of the state senate. In 1875 he became a trustee of The University of North Carolina, and in 1876 he was a North Carolina delegate to the Democratic National Convention in St. Louis, which nominated

Samuel Tilden. Governor Vance appointed him a director of the Albemarle and Chesapeake Canal in 1877.

Never one to put down deep roots, lawyer Patrick Winston had left Windsor by 1882 and moved to the Forsyth County seat of Winston. Soon afterwards he made another surprising move. In September 1883, in a published "open letter," he announced his switch of allegiance from the Democratic to the Republican party. This apparently precipitated his fall into disfavor among his Tar Heel peers. His new party, however, chose him as a delegate to the 1884 Republican National Convention in Chicago, where, in a brilliant speech, he seconded the nomination of Chester A. Arthur for a second term. In the same year President Arthur appointed him minister to Zurich, but his wife refused to move to Switzerland. Winston then was appointed registrar of the U.S. Land Office in Lewiston (now Idaho) and thereby became a southern émigré.

Apparently Winston went to Lewiston alone, but he returned to North Carolina in a couple of years to collect his family. He resigned his position as registrar in 1886, and by the end of 1887, or early the next year, the family settled permanently in what was then Spokane Falls, Washington Territory. On 4 Apr. 1888 Winston became the editor and one of four co-owners of the *Spokane Review*. By the end of November 1888 he had resigned as editor and soon resumed the practice of law.

In 1889, immediately following the admission of Washington into the Union, President Benjamin Harrison appointed Winston U.S. district attorney, a post he held until removed by President Grover Cleveland. He then became involved in Washington State political activity during the campaigns of 1892 and 1896. Joining the Silver Republicans in 1896, he was elected state attorney general on the Fusion ticket by a large majority.

Exertion during the state senatorial campaign of 1897 undermined Winston's health, and after a year's illness he spent nine months with his brother, George Tayloe Winston, in Austin, Tex. He then went back to North Carolina and subsequently entered a sanitarium in Maryland. In 1900 he returned to his law practice in Spokane. On 22 Aug. 1903 he published the first issue of a new newspaper, *Winston's Weekly*, which he continued until his death. Recounting his experiences, philosophy of life, and nostalgic recollections of his childhood in North Carolina, it proved to be a popular journal with a circulation far beyond the northwestern region. Following his death of apparent heart failure in a Spokane hotel he was buried in the city's Greenwood Cemetery. Winston was an Episcopalian.

In addition to the infant son who died in 1871, his other children were Alexander Miller, Virginia, Maria Ellis, Joseph Byrd, Crossan Cooke, George Hampton, Sally Shiras, Martha Elizabeth, and Francis Robert.

SEE: Samuel A. Ashe, ed., *Biographical History of North Carolina*, vol. 2 (1905 [portrait]); Daniel L. Grant, *Alumni History of the University of North Carolina* (1924); Patricia Winston Norman (Flintridge, Calif.), personal contact, October 1981; Spokane, Wash., *Winston's Weekly*, 22 Aug. 1903–9 Apr. 1904.

WILLIAM S. POWELL

Winston, Robert Watson (12 Sept. 1860–14 Oct. 1944), lawyer, judge, and author, was born in Windsor, the son of Patrick Henry and Martha Elizabeth Bird Winston. After attending the Horner School in Oxford, he entered The University of North Carolina where he was on the baseball team; he was graduated in 1879 and received an LL.B. degree in 1881. Admitted to the bar in 1881, he opened an office in Oxford, where he was treasurer first and then city attorney. In 1895 he moved to Durham and formed a partnership with other lawyers, ultimately with Victor S. Bryant during the period 1903–9. Moving to Raleigh in 1909, he was an associate of Charles B. Aycock until 1912 and thereafter with J. Crawford Biggs.

Politics attracted Winston, and for many years after 1895 he was a member of the state Democratic committee. He served in the North Carolina Senate during the years 1885–87 and as a superior court circuit judge from 1889 to 1895. As an attorney he represented a number of important business and financial firms, including the Metropolitan Life Insurance Company and the state of North Carolina in railroad cases. He successfully defended Raleigh newspaper editor Josephus Daniels in a contempt of court charge brought by a federal judge.

Judge Winston, as he was widely known, retired from his law practice in 1924 and for a brief time lived at the Cosmos Club in Washington, D.C. At age sixty-three he reentered The University of North Carolina as a freshman, taking the complete four-year course, he said, to reorient himself. He devoted the remainder of his life to study and writing, living most of the time at the Carolina Inn on the campus. In 1928 he published *Andrew Johnson: Plebian and Patriot*, a 549-page biography of the Raleigh native who succeeded Abraham Lincoln as president in 1865. In 1930 his biography of Confederate president Jefferson Davis, *High Stake and Hair Trigger*, appeared. *Robert E. Lee—A Biography* and *Gadfly of Chapel Hill: A Biography of Horace Williams, Socrates of Chapel Hill*, were brought out in 1934 and 1942, respectively. His autobiography, *It's A Far Cry*, in 1937 was a look at southern traditions that survived beyond their time. Also published were many of Winston's lectures and public addresses dealing with the law, the lives of prominent citizens, and the history of the state.

On 13 Dec. 1882 Robert Winston and Sophronia Horner were married in Oxford. She was the daughter of James Hunter Horner, whose school Winston had attended in his youth. Their children were James Horner, Annabel Conyers (m. Watts Carr), Gertrude (m. Frank Blount Webb), and Robert Watson. Winston received honorary degrees from Wake Forest College, The University of North Carolina, and Duke University. He also became an honorary member of Phi Beta Kappa. He was an Episcopalian and a Democrat.

SEE: Samuel A. Ashe, ed., *Biographical History of North Carolina*, vol. 2 (1905 [portrait]); John L. Cheney, Jr., ed., *North Carolina Government, 1585–1979* (1981); Daniel L. Grant, *Alumni History of the University of North Carolina* (1924); *Nat. Cyc. Am. Biog.*, vol. 45 (1962); *New York Times*, 15 Oct. 1945; Patricia Winston Norman (Flintridge, Calif.), personal contact, October 1981; Robert Watson Winston Papers (Southern Historical Collection, University of North Carolina, Chapel Hill)

WILLIAM S. POWELL

Winters, Sellie Robert (21 Sept. 1888–26 July 1953), writer, was born near Hester in Granville County, the son of William and Mollie Harris Winters. He was a student at The University of North Carolina during the years 1909–11. One of his first contributions to the press was a feature story on the university published in the *Norfolk Landmark* on 26 Nov. 1911 and reprinted in the *University Report*, No. 100, in April 1912. Initially he was the Durham and Washington, D.C., correspondent for the Raleigh *News*, and later he was a Washington correspondent for the *Asheville Citizen*, Raleigh *News and Observer*, *Wilmington Star*, and Winston-Salem *Journal*. Winters then became a free-lance journalist and sold his work to a large number of journals, including *American City, American Magazine, Breeder's Gazette, Commerce and Finance, Country Gentleman, Country Life, Field and Stream, Hygeia, Journal of Geography, Ladies Home Journal, Leslie's Weekly, Popular Mechanics, Review of Reviews, Science Digest,* and *Scientific America.* He also contributed regular features to the *Christian Science Monitor* and the *New York Times.*

In response to a questionnaire from The University of North Carolina Alumni Association, Winters once wrote: "If there is any one contribution that I have made it is this: Take the drab scientific fact and put that into popular expression and at the same time retain its authenticity. Around this idea I have developed what I believe to be an unusual journalistic career—writing about facts solely— ever subscribing to the dictum that facts are stranger (and more interesting) than fiction. That 50 or more journals should buy my copy is some evidence that I have succeeded in a small measure in putting the idea across." Apparently he made his last contribution to the press in 1949.

A member of the Methodist church, Winters married Lelia Frances Wyatt of Petersburg, Va., on 25 Dec. 1914. They had two sons, Early Wyatt and Herbert Gates. Winters died of a heart attack at his summer home on Reems Creek near Weaverville in Buncombe County.

SEE: Alumni Files (University of North Carolina, Chapel Hill); *Alumni Review . . . The University of North Carolina* 41 (July 1953); Daniel L. Grant, *Alumni History of the University of North Carolina* (1924); *Reader's Guide to Periodical Literature* (various dates).

WILLIAM S. POWELL

Withers, William Alphonso *(31 May 1864–20 June 1924),* agricultural chemist and founder of chemistry at North Carolina State University, was born in Riverview, near Davidson, and reared on a farm there, the son of William Banks and Sarah L. Rutledge Withers. He was graduated from Davidson College with a B.A. degree in 1883 and an M.A. in 1885. From 1888 to 1890 he was a Sage Fellow at Cornell University. Withers worked at the North Carolina State Agriculture Experiment Station as assistant chemist (1884–88), chemist (1897–1921), and acting director (1897–99).

In 1889 he was named the first professor of chemistry at the College of Agriculture and Mechanic Arts. There he spent his entire academic career, with a period as vice-president (1916–23) and one as director of the summer session (1917–23). In addition, he taught chemistry and physics at Peace Institute (1890–93), served as state statistical agent for the U.S. Department of Agriculture (1885–1902 and 1905–15), and sat on the executive committee of the National Food and Drug Congress (1898). From 1889 to 1903 he was chairman of the committee on Pure Food Legislation of the Association of American Agricultural Colleges and Experiment Stations.

Withers is best remembered as the author of the North Carolina Pure Food Law (1899) and the codiscoverer, with C. F. E. Carruth, of gossypol, the toxic principle of cottonseed (1915). He served as president of the American Association of Official Analytical Chemists (1909–10) and of the North Carolina Academy of Science (1917–18). Davidson College awarded him an Sc.D. degree in 1917, and, in recognition of his immense contribution to the college and to agriculture and health in the state, North Carolina State College named its new chemistry building in his memory in 1938.

Not merely an academic researcher, Withers had intense civic interests. During World War I he was a member of the North Carolina Council of Defense and of the Wake County Food Administrative Board and served on the executive committee of the Raleigh Red Cross. He was an elder of the First Presbyterian Church and president of the Young Women's Christian Association; from 1919 to 1924 he sat on the executive committee of the Wake County Board of Education. At his death he was president of the Raleigh Chamber of Commerce.

On 11 June 1896 he married Elizabeth (Bessie) Witherspoon Daniel (1874–20 Aug. 1905), the daughter of Dr. and Mrs. Eugene Daniel, then of Lewiston, W.Va.; her father had been minister of the First Presbyterian Church in Raleigh. They had two children, Susannah (1897–1903) and William Banks. Mrs. Withers contracted tuberculosis and spent the last years of her life in Saranac, N.Y., Lewiston, W.Va. and Brevard, N.C., where she died. On 29 July 1909 Withers married Jane (Jennie) Hinton Pescud (1874?–1962?); their children were Mary Laurens (Mrs. John T. Richardson) and William Alphonso, Jr., both of Raleigh, and John Pescud, of Elizabeth, N.J.

SEE: *Raleigh Morning Post,* 22 Aug. 1905; Raleigh *News and Observer,* 21 June 1924; *Who Was Who in America,* vol. 1 (1981); William Alphonso Withers Papers (personal papers 178, University Archives, North Carolina State University, and private papers 1477, North Carolina State Archives).

MAURICE M. BURSEY

Witherspoon, John Knox *(1791–25 Sept. 1853),* Presbyterian pastor and educator, was the only child of attorney David, of New Bern (d. 1801), and Mary Whiting Jones Nash Witherspoon (d. 5 Feb. 1800), the widow of Governor Abner Nash. He was the grandson of the Scottish-born Reverend Dr. John Witherspoon (1723–94), the only clergyman to sign the Declaration of Independence and president of Nassau Hall, N.J. (College of New Jersey, later Princeton University) and his first wife Elizabeth Montgomery (d. 1789) of Craighouse, Ayrshire. Young Witherspoon was born at Pembroke Plantation, across the Trent River from Tryon Palace, where his half brother Frederick Nash (later chief justice of North Carolina) had been born a decade before in 1781. Although it has been frequently claimed that he was in direct line of descent from the Scots Calvinist John Knox, modern genealogical research indicates that this was not the case.

Orphaned at about age nine, the boy had generally unsatisfactory experiences at two preparatory schools—in Baskenridge, N.J., and at New Bern. He was eventually placed under the guardianship of his half brother Frederick, "of a settled disposition," and sent to the Reverend Abner W. Clopton's preparatory school in Chapel Hill, where in 1808 he was enrolled in The University of North Carolina. In September 1809 he was briefly suspended because of a bell-ringing prank in which he was apparently not directly involved. In 1810 he was graduated with an A.B. degree, second in a class of three. Witherspoon read law in Frederick Nash's Hillsborough law office for a time and was "duly admitted to the Bar," but influenced heavily by members of the Kollock family and by Dr. Robert Hett Chapman, president of The University of North Carolina, he decided to pursue a career in religion instead.

On 1 July 1813 he married Susan Davis Kollock (21 Dec. 1792–31 Mar. 1854) of Elizabethtown, N.J., the daughter of Captain Shepard and Susan Arnett Kollock and the sister of Mrs. Frederick Nash. From 1814 to 1816 he pursued his theological studies at Elizabethtown and Princeton. By the early summer of 1816, at age twenty-five, he returned to Hillsborough to assume a double charge, the pastorate of the newly built Presbyterian church and the principalship of the closely allied Hillsborough Academy.

Despite his youth the Reverend Mr. Witherspoon's family and church connections automatically secured for him immediate and almost unlimited prestige in North Carolina and throughout the country. He was in constant demand to fill pulpits and to organize new churches such as the Presbyterian Church of New Bern in 1817. Early biographical sketches note that he was granted an M.A. in 1815 or 1816 by the College of New Jersey as well as by The University of North Carolina. Appointed to the University of North Carolina Board of Trustees in 1817, he served until 1834.

Witherspoon inherited a sizable estate from his parents, and in 1817 his half sister Ann's estate also came to him. On 26 July 1817 he bought a house in Hillsborough and carried out very considerable repairs there. Somewhat later he purchased two adjoining tracts one and a half miles south of the town, on one of which he erected a comfortable Piedmont farmhouse and a whole cluster of outbuildings including a schoolroom. This new establishment served as both a country home and his own private boarding school for boys.

Sometime after 1819 Witherspoon apparently terminated his connection with the Hillsborough Academy, perhaps because of differences with trustees or assistant teachers as to educational philosophy. At any rate, after a single session of the new school, which had opened in early July 1826, a disastrous fire on 1 Jan. 1827 completely destroyed the Witherspoons' rural home and its contents, including all but one volume of the invaluable old records of Orange Presbytery, which Witherspoon, as stated clerk, had temporarily in his keeping. Although the house was promptly rebuilt, the money losses involved an estimated $3,000, the first of a long series of financial reverses for the Witherspoon family, which by July 1827 included seven children: Frederick Nash (1 Apr. 1814), Susan Kollock (1 July 1815), John Knox (Sept. 1816), Henry Kollock (20 Feb. 1820), David Brainerd (10 Feb. 1822), George Burgwyn (18 Mar. 1826), and Mary Nash (9 July 1827).

In an affectionate, though reticent sketch, written after John's death, Frederick described his half brother as socially affable and graceful, with a melodious, sweet voice (mentioned elsewhere as "silvery") that could fill every corner of the little Presbyterian church, and with a marked gift for extempore speaking. Although Witherspoon was an enormously successful teacher with an excellent memory and a talent for calling up precisely the right illustration to illuminate a point, he was not a bookman or an intellectual in the usual sense. During his lifetime he wrote a number of religious articles, most of them controversial in character, including a rare little pamphlet, published by Hillsborough printer Dennis Heartt in 1825, reviewing a sermon preached before the Bible Society of North Carolina by Bishop John S. Ravenscroft, and two exegetical papers, "On the Right Interpretation of the Word of God," which appeared under the pseudonym "Knox" in the Charleston *Observer* of 30 Jan. 1836 and 6 Feb. 1836, as well as various essays in the Philadelphia *Presbyterian*.

In the late 1820s the slavery question was beginning to agitate the area, and Witherspoon took a position far ahead of his time in advocating religious education, Sunday schools, and preaching for slaves, a stand that ultimately resulted in strained relations between the pastor and his congregation. On 23 Aug. 1833 he severed his seventeen-year connection with the Hillsborough Presbyterian Church and somewhat reluctantly moved to Camden, S.C., to begin a brief, uneasy pastorate in the handsome Bethesda Presbyterian Church, designed by Robert Mills, on DeKalb Street.

In 1836 he found it necessary to place a second mortgage of $1,000 on his Hillsborough plantation and apparently, soon after, to mortgage his slaves. Part of the plantation mortgage may have been used to enable him to travel to Pittsburgh, Pa., for the annual convocation of the Presbyterian church, which he had always faithfully attended, thus keeping his own church abreast of the national currents of Presbyterian thought. At that time he received the highest honor of his life, and the highest within the gift of his church, when he was elected moderator of the General Assembly of the Presbyterian Church in America as his grandfather the Signer had been. (He had earlier served as moderator of Orange Presbytery in 1822, 1827, and 1831 although only one term was usual.)

Several honorary degrees now came to him, but there is confusion as to early records. Battle's *History of the University of North Carolina* states (1:186) that The University of North Carolina conferred a D.D. on Witherspoon and that Princeton awarded him an LL.D. The D.D., however, is not included in the University of North Carolina's official listing of honorary degrees. An early biographer, W. A. Withers, stated that the College of New Jersey granted Witherspoon a D.D. in 1836 as had Lafayette College at Easton, Pa., and that an LL.D. had been granted to him, although the grantor institution was not named. Despite the contradictions involved, it seems certain that Witherspoon received both degrees. But he was not elected president of Miami College, Oxford, Ohio, as Battle's *History* states (1:836), nor was he elected to any post at Hampden-Sydney College, Farmville, Va., as is sometimes said, although he did fill the pulpit of a Presbyterian church in the vicinity of the college.

Colds and rheumatism had steadily troubled Witherspoon in Camden, and he made an ominous discovery the next spring at the General Assembly meeting in the wet, chill May of 1837 in Philadelphia. Some large, painful internal "boil" or "affection of the heart," as he described it in a letter of 23 May to his daughter Susan, made it "exceedingly painful" for him to move about or turn his body. On his return to Camden, he decided after thought and consultation to accept a call to the Presbyterian Church in Columbia, S.C., and began his pastorate there in the summer of 1837.

However, persistent heavy chest colds and rheumatism incapacitated both Witherspoons in Columbia for months at a time throughout two unusually severe winters, necessitating the constant and expensive employment of substitute pastors. Finally, on 29 Aug. 1839, Witherspoon formally resigned his charge and went back to his mortgaged Hillsborough farm, Tusculum, named at about that time for his grandfather's New Jersey farm, also about one and a half miles from its village (Princeton). He had returned to his native state "to die," as he told his brother, but in fact he lived another fourteen incredibly difficult years.

An early ambitious plan of the Witherspoons on their return to Tusculum had been to establish a silk farm in order to earn a livelihood and pay their debts. They strained their slender resources to buy eggs and worms, plant "closely" some 5 acres of mulberry trees, and build a hundred-foot-long, one-and-a-half story cocoonery. But the project did not succeed. Neither did the idea of building up a purebred stock farm. They even thought vaguely of driving vast flocks of 500 to 1,000 turkeys overland to autumn markets in Charleston, and Witherspoon decided to attempt opening a boarding school for boys once again—but no boys came.

A crushing blow was the public sale of Tusculum at the

courthouse door on 29 Aug. 1845 to Dr. Edmund Strudwick, who had long and patiently held the mortgages. Witherspoon seems then to have departed on a curious *Wanderjahre* or trek through South Carolina and Alabama, preaching and teaching wherever he could, while his wife, still at Tusculum by special provision of Dr. Strudwick, tried to cope with the increasingly alarming nervous illness of their youngest daughter, Mary Nash, whom she managed to take to Philadelphia for prolonged treatment on three occasions.

In 1851 and 1852 Witherspoon, back at Tusculum, seems to have been well enough at intervals to conduct a baptismal service and even to preach now and then as supply pastor. His ailment, which he later called "dropsy," may have been cancer of the respiratory tract. He died at the Tusculum farmhouse, entirely penniless, on the thirty-seventh anniversary of the memorable organization service in the Hillsborough Presbyterian Church. His funeral services were held there, and he was interred a few yards to the northwest in the Nash-Strudwick plot of the Old Town Cemetery. The Presbyterian congregation and townspeople purchased the obelisk marking his grave.

A crayon portrait of Witherspoon as a young man was owned by the family of the late Reverend Dr. James Whitted Witherspoon, Lexington, N.C. It was reproduced in the Hillsborough Presbyterian church's anniversary publication, *One Hundred and Fifty Years of Service, 1816–1966* (1966). Mrs. Susan D. Witherspoon died a few months after her husband, on 31 Mar. 1854 in Camden, S.C.

SEE: Samuel A. Ashe, ed., *Biographical History of North Carolina*, vol. 5 (1905); Kemp P. Battle, *History of the University of North Carolina*, vol. 1 (1907); Charleston *Observer*, 30 Jan., 6 Feb. 1836; Francis Nash Collection (North Carolina State Archives, Raleigh); Frank Nash Papers and Witherspoon-McDowell Papers (Southern Historical Collection, University of North Carolina, Chapel Hill); Frederick Nash, "Rev. John Witherspoon, D.D., LL.D.," *University Magazine* 7 (April 1888); *One Hundred Fifty Years of Service, 1816–1966*, anniversary booklet of the Hillsborough Presbyterian Church (1966); Jesse Laing Sibbet, "Genealogy of the Witherspoon Family" (Presbyterian Historical Society, Philadelphia); Wills and deeds (North Carolina State Archives, Raleigh, and Orange County Courthouse, Hillsborough).

MARY CLAIRE ENGSTROM

Wittkowsky, Samuel (*29 May 1835–14 Feb. 1911*), merchant and building and loan executive, was born in Schwersenk, near Posen, east Prussia (now Poznan, Poland), the youngest child of Jacob and Mendel Wittkowsky. Misfortune had befallen his formerly comfortable parents, and he spent his youth in poverty, receiving only the free school education available in the neighborhood. In 1853, with the aid of a distant relative, he immigrated to New York and obtained modest employment. As soon as he had saved enough money for the voyage, he settled in Charleston, S.C., and found satisfactory work.

In 1855 he moved to Charlotte, N.C., and became a clerk in a store named Rintels. Towards the end of the next year Wittkowsky invested his savings in a partnership with Rintels, and they opened a store at Ellendale in Alexander County with a branch in Caldwell County that Wittkowsky managed. Soon after the Ellendale store was moved to Boone, Wittkowsky sold his interests and moved to Winnsboro, S.C., from which he returned to North Carolina, he became a partner in Koopman, Phelps, and Company in Concord. Withdrawing in 1861, he again joined Rintels and they opened a store in Statesville. At

the beginning of the Civil War Rintels went to the North, and Wittkowsky began a business to manufacture hats, an undertaking that proved to be very profitable. With Rintels's return, the business came to be known as Wittkowsky and Rintels, and the partners opened a wholesale store and a retail store in Charlotte. Their business was good, new stores were opened, and after Rintels's death in 1876 a new partnership was formed with H. Baruch.

At the end of the Civil War Wittkowsky was living in Statesville, where Governor Zebulon B. Vance and his family were located temporarily in a rented house. On 3 May 1865 Vance was arrested by Federal cavalrymen. They had only pack horses to take the governor away, so Wittkowsky volunteered to drive Vance in his carriage to the depot in Salisbury, where he was placed on a train for Washington and imprisonment. At Vance's death in 1894 Wittkowsky delivered a memorial address in his honor.

A very generous man, Wittkowsky aided various public causes and engaged in private charities. He served as an alderman of Charlotte during the years 1878–79 and was an active member of the Chamber of Commerce. In 1883 he organized the Mechanics Perpetual Association with assets of one million dollars. This building and loan association enabled a large number of people in Charlotte to buy homes.

In 1871 Wittkowsky married Carrie Bauman of New York City, and they had three children: Dr. Albert Wittson, Gerard Wittson, and Mrs. J. B. Harty. An active Mason, he held high office in that fraternal organization in Statesville and Charlotte as well as at the state level. His funeral was conducted by an Episcopal priest, and he was buried in Elmwood Cemetery, Charlotte.

SEE: *Charlotte Observer*, 17 Apr. 1894, 15 Feb. 1911; Jerome Dowd, *Sketches of Prominent Living North Carolinians* (1888); Van Noppen Papers (Manuscript Department, Duke University Library, Durham); *The State* magazine, 7 June 1941.

WILLIAM S. POWELL

Wolfe, Julia Elizabeth Westall (*16 Feb. 1860–7 Dec. 1945*), mother of Thomas Wolfe, was born on a farm near the Swannanoa River nine miles east of Asheville. She was the fourth of eleven children (Henry Addison, Sam, Sally, Julia Elizabeth, James M., William Harrison, Lee, Mary, Crockett, Elmer, and Greely) born to Martha Anne Penland and Thomas Casey Westall, a farmer and builder. On both sides she was descended from pioneer families of western North Carolina. Educated at Judson College in Hendersonville, she taught school for a time but gave it up to marry William Oliver Wolfe on 14 Jan. 1885.

The couple resided in Asheville, where their eight children were born: Leslie, 1885–86; Effie Nelson (Gambrell), 1887–1950; Frank C., 1888–1956; Mabel (Wheaton), 1890–1958; twins Grover Cleveland, 1892–1904, and Benjamin Cleveland, 1892–1918; Frederick William, 1894–1980; and Thomas Clayton, 1900–1938. In 1906 Mrs. Wolfe bought for $6,500 a boardinghouse at 48 Spruce Street, which she operated until her death. Called the Old Kentucky Home by the former owner, it was the Dixieland of *Look Homeward, Angel* and *Of Time and the River*. Purchased by the state of North Carolina in 1975 as a historic site, it was then opened to the public as the Thomas Wolfe Memorial.

In his novels Wolfe provided a largely autobiographical account of the family's life from the turn of the century on. Julia Wolfe became the fictional Eliza Gant, a small, compact, and persevering woman, determined to keep her family together and manage her boardinghouse in spite of marital discord and tragedies such as the deaths of Grover and Ben. An able talker with a remarkable memory, she provided her son with much raw material for his novels and short stories. Her talents in business, not only in running the boardinghouse but also in real estate purchases and sales, led to the family's relative affluence; thus Thomas was able to attend a private preparatory school and The University of North Carolina.

After her husband's death Mrs. Wolfe continued her business interests and was able to provide financial aid for her son, then teaching at New York University and traveling in Europe. When she lost much of her capital in the Florida real estate crash of the 1920s, which was followed by the 1930s depression in Asheville, she had to depend mainly on the Old Kentucky Home for income. As her son's books became famous, she in turn became noted as the real-life matriarch of the fictional Gants. From the early 1930s onward, her boardinghouse drew literary pilgrims to Asheville.

A close bond existed between Mrs. Wolfe and her son Thomas from childhood until his death, and some commentators have traced similar traits of character, such as a prodigious memory, ambition, verbal power, and determination. Their correspondence, which spanned thirty years, illumines one of the most moving mother-son relationships in American literary history. Always a champion of her son's writing, Mrs. Wolfe became ever more so after his death. Often she traveled to various parts of the country giving informal talks on his early life and influences. Spry, agile, and talkative to the last, she died in New York City while on one of these trips. She was buried in the family plot at Asheville's Riverside Cemetery. Mrs. Wolfe was a Presbyterian and a Democrat.

SEE: *Asheville Citizen*, 8 Dec. 1945; *Charlotte News*, 30 July 1945; C. Hugh Holman and Sue Fields Ross, eds., *The Letters of Thomas Wolfe to His Mother* (1968); Hayden Norwood, *The Marble Man's Wife* (1947); Mabel Wolfe Wheaton with LeGette Blythe, *Thomas Wolfe and His Family* (1961); Thomas Wolfe, "The Web of Earth," in *From Death to Morning* (1935).

JAMES MEEHAN

Wolfe, Thomas Clayton (3 Oct. 1900–15 Sept. 1938), novelist and short story writer, was born in Asheville, the eighth child of William Oliver, a stonecutter from Pennsylvania, and Julia Elizabeth Westall Wolfe, a native North Carolinian. In 1904 he went with his mother and some of the other children to St. Louis, where his mother kept a boardinghouse during the World's Fair and where his brother Grover died, an event that he was to use with distinction in his fiction. In 1905 he began attending public school in Asheville and in 1912 moved to a private school operated by Mr. and Mrs. J. M. Roberts. Margaret Roberts was a major influence on his life and work.

In 1916 Wolfe entered The University of North Carolina as a freshman. In the summer of 1918 he was a civilian war worker in Norfolk; that fall he enrolled in Professor Frederick H. Koch's playwriting course at The University of North Carolina. On 14 and 15 Mar. 1919 his one-act play, *The Return of Buck Gavin*, was performed with Wolfe in the title role on the first bill of the Carolina Playmakers. Wolfe edited *The Tar Heel*, The University of North Carolina student newspaper, and won the Worth Prize for Philosophy for an essay, "The Crisis in Industry." Another of his plays, *The Third Night*, was performed by the Playmakers in December 1919.

In June 1920 he was graduated from the university with a B.A. degree and in September entered the Graduate School for Arts and Sciences at Harvard University to earn an M.A. degree in English and to study playwriting under George Pierce Baker. Two versions of his play *The Mountains* were performed by the 47 Workshop at Harvard in 1921. In 1922 he completed the requirements for the M.A. degree, and in June of that year his father died in Asheville, another event of great importance in his fiction. Wolfe continued to study with Baker in the 47 Workshop, which in May 1923 produced his ten-scene play *Welcome to Our City*. In November 1923 he went to New York City, where he solicited funds for The University of North Carolina. In February 1924 he began teaching English as an instructor at the Washington Square College of New York University, a task that he continued to perform intermittently until January 1930. According to student reports, he was a conscientious and successful teacher.

In October 1924 he sailed for England on the first of what proved to be seven European trips. He traveled in France, Italy, and Switzerland, and on his return voyage in 1925, he met Mrs. Aline Bernstein, who was eighteen years his senior, a scene designer for the Theater Guild and the wife of a successful stockbroker. In October 1925 she became his mistress. Their affair was stormy, but Aline Bernstein was one of the powerful influences on his life. In the summer of 1926 he returned to Europe and there began work on the first version of his novel *Look Homeward, Angel*. In the summer of 1927 he made his third European journey, traveling in France, Austria, and Germany.

On 31 Mar. 1928 he completed the manuscript for the novel *Look Homeward, Angel*. That summer he made his fourth European trip, was injured in a fight at the Oktoberfest in Munich, and received news of Scribner's interest in *Look Homeward, Angel*, which was accepted for publication in January, beginning his long, close, and sometimes painful association with the editor Maxwell Perkins. The amount of editing done on the manuscript by Perkins has been greatly exaggerated. The novel, when published on 8 Oct. 1929, was of all Wolfe's long works the one closest to his original plan. It sold only moderately well, but it was a great critical success, and Wolfe was hailed as the most promising young American novelist.

In 1930 he received a Guggenheim Fellowship and made his fifth European tour. On his return in the late spring of 1931, he began living in Brooklyn. The following year his tempestuous affair with Mrs. Bernstein ended. Perkins, after first putting it into production, withdrew his second novel, *K-19*, which remained unpublished. His short novel, *A Portrait of Bascom Hawke*, appeared in *Scribner's Magazine*, and it was co-winner of the $5,000 Scribner's Short Novel Prize. In July he published a second short novel, *Web of Earth*, one of his best works.

During the period between 1932 and 1935 Wolfe prepared three books for publication, *K-19*, *No Door*, a short novel, and a collection of three short novels. Perkins, however, insisted that Wolfe must come forward with a long work continuing his saga of Eugene Gant, the protagonist of *Look Homeward, Angel*. Wolfe was having difficulty with the large book although he was publishing excellent short stories and short novels. In 1933 Perkins began to work with him daily on the "big book" and finally, in July 1934, over Wolfe's protests, sent the manuscript of *Of Time and the River* to the publishers. On its publication Wolfe was bitter about the shape of the book, declaring that had he been allowed to, he would have made it much better. The critics, although generally approving, did find the work to be sprawling and ill organized.

In 1935 he participated in the Writer's Conference at Boulder, Colo., and his speech made there was published as a serial in the *Saturday Review of Literature* and as a book, *The Story of a Novel*. This work recounts his struggle to produce *Of Time and the River*. In November 1935 *From Death to Morning*, a collection of short novels and short stories, was published.

In 1935 and 1936 Wolfe made his sixth and seventh European trips, spending much time in Germany, where translations of his works had made him a very popular figure. In 1936, leaving Berlin on a train, an incident with a Jew trying to escape Germany forced him to recognize the cruel nature of the Nazi state, and on returning home he wrote one of his most powerful short novels, "*I Have a Thing To Tell You*," a strong indictment of Germany, which was serialized in the *New Republic*. Like many of his short novels, it was later incorporated in expanded form in one of his novels, in this case *You Can't Go Home Again*.

In 1936 his quarrel with his publisher, Charles Scribner's Sons, began; it grew out of his sense that Perkins was preventing him from writing what he truly wished to write, and it was exacerbated by what he felt was Scribner's unwillingness to defend him in a libel suit and by his unhappiness about the reputation that *Of Time and the River* and *The Story of a Novel* gave him of being a prodigious but formless writer whose works were shaped by his editor. This struggle with Scribner's continued throughout 1937, until in December he signed a contract with Edward C. Aswell, of Harper and Brothers, for the publication of his later work. However turbulent this period was emotionally, it was one of the most fruitful for Wolfe in terms of short publications in such journals as the *New Republic*, the *New Yorker*, *Scribner's*, *American Mercury*, *Harpers Bazaar*, the *Yale Review*, and the *Saturday Evening Post*.

In 1938 he left New York for a western tour, depositing the large body of manuscript materials that he had with his new editor, Edward C. Aswell. On the way west, he stopped by Purdue University and gave a lecture, "Writing and Living" (published in 1964). In July 1938 he became ill in Seattle, and on 6 September he was sent to the Johns Hopkins University Hospital, where he died of tuberculosis of the brain, eighteen days before his thirty-eighth birthday.

After Wolfe's death, Edward Aswell assembled from the manuscripts the novels *The Web and the Rock* and *You Can't Go Home Again*, which were published in 1939 and 1940. A collection of short stories and sketches and fragments of a novel were published as *The Hills Beyond* in 1941. In assembling these works, Aswell worked from Wolfe's outline and organized the material in the huge but incomplete collection of manuscripts that Wolfe had left. *The Web and the Rock*, which deals with a new protagonist George Webber, is pretty much the novel that Wolfe would have produced, although the latter two-thirds would certainly have been greatly revised. *You Can't Go Home Again*, also about Webber, is largely a collection of materials, with narrative links written by Aswell to bridge the gaps. Thus only in his short stories, short novels, and *Look Homeward, Angel* does Wolfe's work survive in a form in which he himself was the principal agent of organization. *Of Time and the River* carries too much of Maxwell Perkins's intention rather than Wolfe's, even to being in the third person when Wolfe had written most of it in the first person. The last two novels had to be given their present shape by Aswell with only Wolfe's outline to assist him.

In 1991 The University of North Carolina Press and Paul Gitlin, administrator of the estate of Thomas Wolfe, brought out *The Good Child's River*, an unfinished novel "based loosely on the early life of" Aline Bernstein, edited and with an introduction by Suzanne Stutman. According to the jacket, "Some sections of this work were heavily edited and published after Wolfe's death. Here for the first time is *The Good Child's River*, as Wolfe wrote it, along with some fragments, contained in two appendixes, that Wolfe may have intended to include in the finished work."

Thomas Wolfe was a writer of enormous energy and imaginative force, marked by a richly rhetorical style and powerful command of language. The subject of the bulk of his writing was his own experience as an American. He was in the tradition of Walt Whitman, attempting through the record of himself to explain and to define what it meant to be an American. His work is marred by excesses and exuberance, and of his novels, only *Look Homeward, Angel* has the firm shape that he himself gave it. Out of these facts has grown the legend that Wolfe was an uncontrolled and excessive writer, blessed with the gift of language but unable to control the structure of his works. But his thirty-two short stories and his seven short novels indicate quite clearly that this was not true. In the short length of the story and the intermediate length of the short novel, he was able to write tightly organized, powerful, and convincing stories, and it was only when he began to assemble these works into large structures, such as those that Perkins imposed on him in the early 1930s, that his lack of artistic control became apparent.

Wolfe's subject was always himself and his experiences, transmuted by the imagination and elevated by the power of his rhetoric. His effort to put a person, himself, fully "on record" through the guise of fiction was a major and masterful accomplishment in the American novel, and at the time of his death he was ranked among the top three or four twentieth-century American novelists. His critical stock has fallen severely since his death in 1938, yet his command of language, the strength of his characterizations, and the power with which he could describe the experiences and feelings of youth were all such that his place as a permanent figure in American writing seems assured.

SEE: C. Hugh Holman, *The Loneliness at the Core: Studies in Thomas Wolfe* (1975); C. Hugh Holman and Sue Fields Ross, eds., *The Letters of Thomas Wolfe to His Mother* (1968); Elmer D. Johnson, *Thomas Wolfe: A Checklist* (1970); Richard S. Kennedy, *The Window of Memory: The Literary Career of Thomas Wolfe* (1962); Leslie A. Field, ed., *Thomas Wolfe: Three Decades of Criticism* (1968); Elizabeth Nowell, *Thomas Wolfe: A Biography* (1960); T. C. Pollock and Oscar Cargill, *Thomas Wolfe at Washington Square* (1954); Louis D. Rubin, Jr., *Thomas Wolfe: The Weather of His Youth* (1955); Andrew Turnbull, *Thomas Wolfe* (1967); Richard Walser, *Thomas Wolfe: Carolina Student* (1977).

C. HUGH HOLMAN

Wolfe, William Oliver *(10 Apr. 1851–20 June 1922)*, stonecutter and father of Thomas Wolfe, was born at Latimore near York Springs in Adams County, Pa., the seventh child and third son of Eleanor Jane Heikes and Jacob Wolf [sic], both of German stock. His siblings were Augusta Louisa (Martin), George Alexander, Sarah Ellen (Lentz), Huldah Emeline, Susan Rebecca, Wesley Emerson, Elmer Emerson, and Gilbert John. When only a boy, he was hired out to the more well-to-do farmers in the neighborhood. At the time of the Battle of Gettysburg, he observed the march of J. E. B. Stuart's invading Confederate cavalrymen and, according to family story, had a face-to-face encounter with General Fitzhugh Lee.

After the war Wolfe and his older brother Wesley went to Baltimore to learn stonecutting, a trade in which all five brothers were engaged at one time or another. Following brief stints in York, Pa., and Columbia, S.C., he went to Raleigh in 1870 to work on the state penitentiary, then set up his own monument works in the town. His marriage to Hattie J. Watson ended in divorce, and he then wed Cynthia C. Hill, with whom he moved to Asheville in 1880.

After Cynthia's death in 1884 of tuberculosis, he married Julia Elizabeth Westall. Wesley had meanwhile gone to Asheville and was engaged in various construction projects. For several years William Oliver was associated with James M. Westall, his brother-in-law, in the sale of sand, cement, plaster, lumber, and other building materials. In 1887 he and his wife purchased a lot at Market Street and Pack Square and on it erected a two-story building, a portion of which served as his stonecutting shop. He built a home (no longer standing) at 92 Woodfin Street, where Thomas Wolfe, the youngest of his eight children, all by his third wife, was born.

At the turn of the century he sold iron fencing and dealt in fruits and vegetables. His many ventures prospered. In both Raleigh and Asheville he was constantly involved in litigations, criminal as well as civil, most of the latter having to do with property disputes. In February 1906 he traveled to California with the notion of moving his business and family there, but when nothing came of it, his wife began operating a boardinghouse on Spruce Street. Wolfe and his daughter Mabel, and infrequently the older children, stayed on at Woodfin.

In November 1914 at Johns Hopkins Hospital he was operated on for cancer of the prostate, but in spite of many subsequent treatments there, his health slowly declined. From 1917 until his death he lived at Spruce Street. He was buried at Riverside Cemetery, Asheville.

Wolfe was a Presbyterian and a Republican. Though unlettered, he was a man of sharp business acumen, exuberant moods, sometimes violent actions, but always high spirits. His son's fictional portrait of him as W. O. Gant in *Look Homeward, Angel* and *Of Time and the River* is one of the glories of American fiction.

SEE: Buncombe County Civil Action Papers (North Carolina State Archives, Raleigh); Richard Walser, *Thomas Wolfe's Pennsylvania* (1978) and *The Wolfe Family in Raleigh* (1976).

RICHARD WALSER

Wolstenholme, Hugh *(1780 or 1785–1886?)*, Anglican priest, teacher, and hermit, was the son of Geoffrey Wolstenholme, of Horsley-Gate, Derbyshire, England, of an ancient family from the north of England. The clan claimed descent from Sir Geoffrey Wolstenholme of The Peak, Derbyshire, and from William Peverell to whom the Duke of Normandy had granted an estate in Derbyshire. Sir John Wolstenholme (1562–1639), also from Derbyshire, was a member of the Virginia Company Council in 1609 and had other American connections as well. Hugh studied at Sheffield Grammar School and entered Trinity College, Cambridge University, on 25 Oct. 1797 at age seventeen, according to university records. Graduated with a B.A. degree in 1802, he was ordained in the Church of England and became vicar of a parish in Lancashire and of Hope Parish in Derbyshire. Wolstenholme told members of his family that he had helped Sir Walter Scott collect information for his novel *Peveril of the Peak*. Scott's physical description of a character in the book, Geoffrey Crayon, closely fits that of Wolstenholme.

Wolstenholme became active in the cause of laborers and yeomen and joined them in expressing opposition to taxes considered to have been unjustly imposed. A man named Hunt organized the laborers, but troops were ordered to end their uprising. Wolstenholme was among those arrested and imprisoned, and he soon was dis-

missed from his church appointment. After his release, he entered into a partnership with James Montgomery, the poet and newspaper editor in Sheffield for whom Joseph Gales had also worked before migrating to North Carolina in 1799. Montgomery's former newspaper, the *Sheffield Register*, became the *Sheffield Iris*, a radical reform paper. In 1818, following a warning from authorities, Hugh Wolstenholme left for the United States, having inherited "a goodly estate" from his father of which he gave a portion to his sister, Mary Wolstenholme Reavis.

It was perhaps from family recollections of Sir John Wolstenholme that Hugh acquired an interest in the Lost Colony of Roanoke. He said that he chose to move to North Carolina in hope of finding some trace of relatives who had been among the Lost Colonists. His ship wrecked near Norfolk at what is now Virginia Beach, and he went to Norfolk to await the receipt of the proceeds from the sale of his father's property. The name of the North Carolina state capital, Raleigh, prompted him to settle there. His sentiments for reform remained with him in his new home, where he was described as "a man of strong convictions, aggressive spirit and fearless utterances." He spoke out against slavery and criticized the state's failure to support education for white youth.

In Raleigh Wolstenholme spent several hours each day reading to the apprentices in James J. Selby's tailor shop while they worked, and soon other people came just to listen to him. He read from the *Sheffield Iris* and the *London Quarterly Review*. One of the apprentices was Andrew Johnson, then illiterate but destined to become president of the United States. Wolstenholme's reading inspired some of his listeners, Johnson among them, to accept his invitation to gather at his home on certain evenings each week to learn to read.

In England Wolstenholme had been a member of the Anglican church, but in North Carolina he found the Moravian denomination more to his liking; after all, that had been the church of his friend, James Montgomery, in Sheffield. The academy operated by the Moravians in Salem won his approval, and on one occasion he mentioned that his favorite books were the Bible, the *Book of Common Prayer*, and Shakespeare. The Right Reverend John Starke Ravenscroft, bishop of North Carolina, once said in a letter of introduction that Wolstenholme was "reputed to be one of the most learned men in North Carolina." When Bishop Philander Chase was making plans to visit England in search of support for the establishment of the institution that in 1824 became Kenyon College, Wolstenholme provided him with letters of introduction to his old friend James Montgomery, to John Kenyon, vicar of Manchester, and to other prominent men.

When he grew tired of associating with so many people with whom he had little in common, Wolstenholme withdrew to far western North Carolina and built himself a small log cabin against the side of a precipice at the southern end of the Bald Mountain range. His abode was described by a great-nephew, who visited him, as "an embowered nook or nitche" covered by vines and furnished with homemade but comfortable furniture, a bearskin rug, and a few of his favorite books. He slept on a narrow, low featherbed under which he placed the casket he had made in anticipation of his last day. In the casket was the surplice in which he would be buried—the last of five generations of clergymen. His native county in England had been the site for centuries of hermits who lived in caves where they studied and prayed, sometimes taught, and often assisted travelers. Wolstenholme modeled his life on them. His wife and two children, a son and a daughter, had been dead for a number of years, but his sister's children and grandchildren lived not too far away.

When Wolstenholme was sixty-five, a visitor described him as over six feet tall, with steel gray eyes and shaggy eyebrows. He wore a Moravian or Quaker style hat, close-fitting corduroy jacket, knee breeches of "Kentucky jeans," buckskin leggings, high-top, rawhide shoes, and a beaver skin cloak.

Tradition relates that the hermit often had visitors and that he received them cordially. Governor Zebulon B. Vance is said to have called on him to discuss affairs of state and to seek his advice, and both local and state officials communicated with him.

Finally, disturbed about the Civil War and his money nearly exhausted, Wolstenholme abandoned his cabin and moved into Asheville. A long time afterwards, when he was over a hundred, he died in the public poorhouse; his funeral was conducted by the Reverend Jarvis Buxton of Trinity Episcopal Church, and he was buried in Asheville. Many years later a great-nephew visited the site of his hermitage and found the structure in ruins. There he discovered an issue of the *Sheffield Iris* from 1832, a copy of the will of the hermit's sister, and an old gold coin supporting the belief that Wolstenholme had secreted coins under trees and rocks around his retreat.

SEE: *DNB*, vol. 21 (1958); Christina Hardyment, "In Search of Cave Hermitages," *Illustrated London News* 271 (Christmas no. 1983); John Hewitt Memoir (Southern Historical Collection, University of North Carolina, Chapel Hill); *Nashville Tennessean Magazine*, 9 May 1965; J. A. Venn, comp., *Alumni Cantabrigienses*, part 2, vol. 6 (1954).

WILLIAM S. POWELL

Womack, Nathan Anthony (*14 May 1901–2 Feb. 1975*), surgeon and medical educator, was born in Reidsville, the son of James Henry and Susan Margaret Norman Womack. After receiving a bachelor of science degree from The University of North Carolina (1922) and an M.D. degree from Washington University, St. Louis, Mo. (1924), he served his internship and residency at Barnes Hospital, St. Louis, from 1924 to 1927. A traveling fellow in Europe in 1929–30, he returned to the Washington University School of Medicine and was named professor of surgery in 1947. From 1948 to 1951 he headed the Department of Surgery at the University of Iowa, then became professor of surgery and head of the department in The University of North Carolina's newly expanded School of Medicine, where he remained for sixteen years.

As a visiting professor for short courses, Womack taught at Yale University, Vanderbilt University, the universities of Michigan, Wisconsin, Arizona, Kentucky, and elsewhere. He was a member and an officer of a great many medical societies and contributed more than 120 articles to their journals. In addition, he served on the editorial boards of the *Annals of Surgery* and *American Surgeon* and on the editorial board of The University of North Carolina Press. Citations, distinguished service awards, and honorary memberships came to him from a variety of sources. At The University of North Carolina the Nathan A. Womack Surgical Society was organized by his former students.

On 23 Jan. 1937 Womack married Margaret Elizabeth Richardson of Reidsville, and they had a son and a daughter: James Anthony and Sarah Richardson (Mrs. Thomas A. Hruska). An Episcopalian, he was buried in Reidsville.

SEE: *Chapel Hill Newspaper, Durham Morning Herald*, and other newspapers of the state, 3 Feb. 1975; curriculum vitae (School of Medicine, University of North Carolina,

Chapel Hill); William S. Powell, ed., *North Carolina Lives* (1962); *University Gazette*, 21 Feb. 1975; *Who Was Who in America*, vol. 6 (1976).

C. SYLVESTER GREEN

Wood, Edward (*8 Dec. 1820–28 Nov. 1872*), businessman, was the son of Edward (d. ca. 1829) and Elizabeth (1793–1876) Wood. A resident of Gatesville, he opened a sawmill there in 1843 and made barrel headings and staves in addition to shingles. A year later he set up his Montpelier fishery, where his workers caught fish from the Albemarle Sound during the spring fishing season and salted them down or packed them in ice for sale at markets. In 1845 he had accumulated enough savings from his businesses to buy several town lots in Gatesville as well as slaves and approximately 800 acres of land belonging to his father-in-law's estate, which was in financial trouble. In 1850 he acquired partial ownership in a steam mill at Hertford.

During these years Wood moved his family to Greenfield Plantation, in Chowan County, which he had purchased from the Creecy family; it was located fourteen miles east of Edenton along the northern shore of the Albemarle Sound. At Greenfield he cultivated 800 of his 1,934 acres of land and grew wheat, corn, and oats. He also raised cattle, hogs, and sheep and set up another fishery. As Wood prospered, he channeled some of his profits into purchasing slaves to work in his fields and at his fisheries; by 1860 he owned forty-six. In 1856 he bought town lots in Edenton and became a co-partner in the mercantile firm of J. M. Cox and Company of Hertford. He also became president of the Albemarle Steam Navigation Company, which owned steamboats and schooners that carried freight and passengers.

During the Civil War Wood continued to operate his fisheries. With the occupation of North Carolina by Federal forces, however, his business routines were interrupted. The military government feared that fishermen would cross Federal lines in the Albemarle Sound to trade with enemies of the United States and so forbade fishing. In February 1863 Wood complained to authorities about the regulation, arguing that the residents of Edenton needed food, and received permission to fish. But almost as soon as he began spring fishing on a limited scale, he was arrested for having "become obnoxious . . . by the free expression of his sentiments"—evidence suggests that a Federal gunboat interfered with his fishermen—and held as a hostage pending the release of a prisoner taken by the Confederate forces. Fortunately, by the end of March Wood was released from his parole and obligations involved in the exchange of prisoners. Yet the brief episode showed Edenton citizens' loyalty to Wood, in particular that of James Cathcart Johnston, who participated in negotiations to free him. Shortly afterwards Johnston named Wood one of his heirs and a coexecutor of his estate.

In 1865 Wood inherited Johnston's Hayes Plantation, located east of Edenton across Queen Anne's Creek and Edenton Bay. Moving his family from Greenfield into the handsome house at Hayes, he began farming the approximately 1,400 acres of land. This property, in addition to his other land and fisheries that had survived the war unscathed, gave Wood economic security at a time when the state was struggling to recover its prewar strength, and he became instrumental in helping rebuild Edenton's economy. Countless persons asked him for loans and jobs on his steamboats or at his farms and fisheries. Managing about 5,000 acres at Hayes, Belvedere, Mulberry Hill, Atholl, Greenfield, Somerset, Ashland, Winslow, and Spruill farms, he hired laborers to work the fields in addition to renting land to sharecroppers. The major crops—cotton, corn, small fruits, and vegetables—were grown for sale at markets. His fishermen continued to harvest large quantities of shad, perch, rock, and herring from the Albemarle Sound. The fish were packed for market at five fisheries along the sound—Skinner Point, Greenfield, Montpelier, Frying Pan, and Drummond Point.

As Wood's wealth steadily grew, he invested some of it in stock of the Albemarle and Chesapeake Canal Company and the Seaboard and Roanoke Railroad Company. Both firms were ones in which Wood had a vital interest because he used their services to ship his fish and crops to market.

Wood married Caroline Moore Gilliam (1824–86), the daughter of Henry Gilliam (1784–1842), a Gates County judge, and his first wife, Mary. The Woods had ten children: Mary Francis (born and died in 1845), Sarah Elizabeth (1846–76), Mary Moore (1848–93), Edward (1851–98), John Gilliam (1853–1920), James (1856–76), Francis (1858–1926), Annie Augusta (b. 1861), Julian Gilliam (b. 1863), and Henry Gilliam (b. 1868). In 1869 their daughter Sarah married Octavius Coke, a North Carolina secretary of state. An Episcopalian, Wood was buried at Saint Paul's Episcopal Church, Edenton.

SEE: Hayes Collection (Southern Historical Collection, University of North Carolina, Chapel Hill).

MARTHA M. SMITH

Wood, Edward Jenner (*12 June 1878–16 Sept. 1928*), physician, was born in Wilmington, the son of Thomas Fanning (1841–92), also a physician, and Mary Kennedy Sprunt Wood (1848–1932), the daughter of cotton exporter Alexander and Jane Dalziel Sprunt Wood. The elder Wood was regarded as the father of the North Carolina State Board of Health because of his role in organizing and managing it; he also cofounded the *North Carolina Medical Journal*. Edward J. Wood was graduated from The University of North Carolina with a B.S. degree in 1899 and received an M.D. degree from the University of Pennsylvania in 1902. Returning to Wilmington, he passed the North Carolina State Medical Board examinations in 1903 and opened a practice in the town of his birth. In 1906 he went to Munich, Germany, for further medical study, and in 1910 he was elected president of the North Carolina Medical Society.

In 1918, during World War I, Wood was commissioned a lieutenant commander in the U.S. Naval Reserve. At the end of the war he served as an assistant in clinical medicine at Guy's Hospital in London and in 1920 received a diploma in tropical medicine from the Royal College of Physicians and Surgeons in London.

Wood's reputation was based on his expertise in tropical medicine, particularly pellagra and (tropical) sprue. Both diseases involved nutritional deficiencies endemic in the rural South in the 1920s. Wood was the author of many articles in his area of specialization, including "A Treatise on Pellagra" and the chapters on pellagra in *The Oxford System of Medicine* and sprue in *Nelson's Loose Leaf Medicine*. He delivered lectures before meetings of his colleagues as well as to the general public on how to identify these diseases and how to eradicate them through improved diet, sanitary practices in food handling and preparation, and changes in agricultural practices.

On 18 Apr. 1906 he married Louise Bellamy, and they had three children: Edward Jenner, Jr., John Dalziel, and Louise Bellamy, who married Donald Brock Koonce. Koonce was elected president of the North Carolina Medical Society in 1957.

Wood died at his home. Funeral services were conducted at the First Presbyterian Church, Wilmington, with burial in Oakdale Cemetery.

SEE: Daniel L. Grant, *Alumni History of the University of North Carolina* (1924); New Hanover County Medical Auxiliary, *The Lonely Road: A History of the Physicks and Physicians of the Lower Cape Fear, 1735–1976* (1978); *Wilmington Star-News*, 17 Sept. 1928, 13 July 1932.

DIANE COBB CASHMAN

Wood, Ernest Harvey, Jr. (*12 Dec. 1914–11 Feb. 1975*), radiologist and medical educator, was born in New Bern, the son of Ernest Harvey, Sr., and Lilliam Fordham Wood, a native of Kinston. His father was a native of New Bern and a lifetime practicing pharmacist who served as mayor of the town in the late 1940s. Young Wood was educated in the New Bern public schools and Duke University, from which he was graduated magna cum laude in 1935. At Duke he was a member of Phi Beta Kappa and of the university orchestra, having gained considerable note as a child virtuoso violinist. In 1935 he enrolled in the school of medicine at Harvard University, from which he was graduated in 1939. After interning at the Philadelphia General Hospital, Wood spent two years in New York as a resident in radiology at the Presbyterian Hospital and an instructor in radiology at the College of Physicians and Surgeons, Columbia University.

His residency at Columbia was interrupted in 1943, when he was inducted into the army. Serving in the medical corps, he had attained the rank of major by the time of his discharge three years later. Returning to Columbia, he was advanced to professor of radiology in the College of Physicians and Surgeons. In 1952 Wood was invited to serve as professor of radiology and director of radiological services in the newly expanded four-year school of medicine at The University of North Carolina. For thirteen years he devoted himself to the establishment of the department and its expanding services in the new school and its adjunct hospital. In 1965, however, he returned to his old post in New York City and remained there until his death.

Wood was active in a number of professional organizations and a member of the consulting staff of several hospitals and institutes. He served on the editorial boards of *Neurology* and *Radiology*. In 1958 he was president of the North Carolina Radiological Society and in 1966–67 of the American Society of Neuroradiology. He also was a member of the Society of Nuclear Medicine and of the World Federation of Neurologists. He distinguished himself as a world authority in academic neuroradiology with research in roentgenological methods of diagnosis and investigation of neurological diseases, especially cerebrovascular disease.

A prolific writer, Wood was the author of many articles and reviews on neuroradiological topics as well as of *An Atlas of Myelography* (1958), the first book published on the subject. In 1964 he was coauthor of a textbook, *Diagnostic Neuroradiology*. He contributed more than fifty articles to professional journals or as chapters in books on his special field. He was a pioneer in the development of thermography in the diagnosis of cerebrovascular diseases. The August 1975 issue of *Radiology* wrote: "His quiet charm, devotion to the highest ideals of professional integrity and his scientific curiosity have been sources of inspiration to many."

On 23 Aug. 1941 Wood married Ruth Eleanor Radcliffe of Melrose, Mass. They had three children: Ernest Harvey III, William Edward, and Janet Ruth (Mrs. William

Brown). At age sixty Wood died suddenly of a heart attack in his office in the Neurological Institute. After a memorial service at the United Methodist Church in Ridgewood, N.J., he was buried in the Chapel Hill cemetery.

SEE: *American Men and Women of Science* (1969); *Chapel Hill Newspaper*, 12 Feb. 1975; Duke University, *Alumni Register*, April 1975; *Radiology*, August 1975.

C. SYLVESTER GREEN

Wood, John Elliott (23 Feb. 1891–1 Oct. 1963), army officer, was born in Hertford, the son of John Q. A. and Julia Elliott Wood. He was graduated from The University of North Carolina in 1911 and received an M.A. degree in 1912 with a thesis entitled "Design of an Engineering and Physics Building for the University of North Carolina." In 1914 he obtained a B.S. degree from the Massachusetts Institute of Technology. Wood was a special student in the University School of Architecture in Venice, Italy, before World War I.

In 1917 he joined the army and was commissioned second lieutenant, serving in the Twenty-sixth Infantry Division in France in 1917 and 1918. At the end of that time he was commissioned in the Corps of Engineers, Regular Army, and was with the Army of Occupation in Germany in 1919–20. President Woodrow Wilson in November 1920 appointed him to the District of Columbia Commission, where until 1924 he was in charge of waterworks, sewers, street lighting, and the design and construction of municipal structures in the city. Included were school buildings, fire and police stations, hospitals, and other structures.

Between 1927 and 1930 Wood was with the First Cavalry Division on the Mexican border, and in 1931–34 he was federal instructor-inspector with the New England National Guard. He next was in the Philippines as assistant department engineer working on the fortifications of Corregidor, Manila, and Subic Bay in 1934–36. Returning to Washington, he was in charge of the map collection in the War Department from 1937 to 1940. In August 1940 he was assigned to Fort Bragg to organize the Forty-first Engineer Regiment, which he commanded successively as major, lieutenant colonel, and colonel, participating with the regiment in the Carolina maneuvers of 1941. Leading engineer units, he took part in amphibious training at Onslow Beach in 1941 and Cape Henry in 1942. He commanded a task force landing on the coast of Liberia in June 1942, composing the first U.S. troops in Africa.

Wood was assistant division commander of the Ninety-second Infantry Division throughout its training; that division's first combat team went to Italy in the summer of 1944. He served in Italy on the Fifth Army front from the August offensive of 1944, crossing the Arno, until the end of hostilities; his command was first attached to the First Armored Division and then to the Ninety-second Division. It advanced from Pisa to the French border, capturing Genoa and other cities in the offensive of April 1945. Now a brigadier general, Wood commanded the division in the occupation from August until it was demobilized in November.

He served as theater engineer in the Mediterranean theater of operations in 1946–47 and as assistant chief of staff, G-4, Army Field Forces, in 1948–49. On 31 July 1949 he retired after thirty-two years of active duty. For his contributions he was awarded the Silver Star Medal, Legion of Merit, Bronze Star, Army Citation Ribbon, and Order of the Crown of Italy and Military Cross—the latter bestowed in person by the former king Umberto in 1945. He also was made an honorary citizen of Viareggio, Italy.

Following his retirement General Wood settled on his farm on Currituck Sound to raise stock and engage in research and writing local history. He was a member of the Pasquotank Historical Society, which he served as president; he also was editor of the first two volumes of the society's *Year Book*. A Democrat and a member of the Episcopal church, Wood never married. He was buried in Cedarwood Cemetery, Hertford.

SEE: Daniel L. Grant, *Alumni History of the University of North Carolina* (1924); Pasquotank Historical Society, *Year Book*, vol. 3 (1975 [portrait]); William S. Powell, ed., *North Carolina Lives* (1962); Raleigh *News and Observer*, 2 Oct. 1963.

WILLIAM S. POWELL

Wood, Marquis Lafayette (23 Oct. 1829–25 Nov. 1893), Methodist clergyman, missionary, and college president, was born near Concord Camp Ground in Randolph County, the tenth of fourteen children of Jones Kendrick and Ruth Loftin Wood. After working on his father's farm until age twenty-one, he entered Union Institute Academy; in 1855 he was graduated from Normal College after the academy officially changed its name. Having grown up in the same section as President Braxton Craven and owing his opportunity for education to the financial assistance of the church, Wood had a special affinity for and lasting devotion to the Methodist institution later named Trinity College and Duke University. He was present at the organizational meeting of the college alumni association in 1858 and thereafter rarely missed a commencement celebration.

Wood was converted during a camp meeting in 1842, received into full fellowship at Salem Church in 1844, and licensed as an exhorter in 1852 and to preach in 1853. After joining the North Carolina Conference of the Methodist Episcopal Church, South, in 1855, he was ordained a deacon in 1857 and an elder in 1859. His lifelong emphasis of church-centered education and the relevancy of scripture was evident in his first appointments on the Wilkes (1856), Franklinsville (1857), and Surry circuits (1858–59). Carefully kept diaries and numerous sermons depict Wood as a disciplined, studious, ardent Methodist ever mindful of the duties and responsibilities of the itinerant preacher and presiding elder. He preached to slaves, distributed literature of the Methodist publishing concerns, founded Sabbath schools in every congregation where ten or more children were present, and established a reputation as a learned yet clearly understood and quotable preacher.

At a "China Missionary Meeting" during commencement week at Trinity in 1859, Bishop G. F. Pierce called for a volunteer from the North Carolina Conference to be its first missionary to China, and shortly afterwards Wood answered his appeal. Rapidly setting his affairs in order, he married Ellen E. Morphis (b. 1835), a member of the faculty of Greensboro Female College, on 19 Sept. 1859, traveled to Columbia, Tenn., to be ordained as elder on 16 October, and with his bride sailed for China from New York City on 17 December. Such momentous events could not be postponed for ordination at his own annual conference.

The seven-month voyage on the small sailing vessel, *Seaman's Bride*, was often grim despite the study of anatomy, geography, and church history and the companionship of another Methodist missionary couple from Georgia, Young J. Allen and his wife. Often going weeks without sighting land or even other vessels and after experiencing all manner of physical discomforts, it is little wonder that Wood sometimes recorded in his diary, "I feel dull physically, mentally, and spiritually today."

The relief and excitement of arrival in Shanghai on 13 July 1860 soon gave way to uncertainties of another sort. Assignment of the young couples to Soochow and then Hang-chow was canceled because of the unsettled conditions due to the Tai-ping Rebellion, and then Civil War at home cut off all communication and support from their church. Weekly interdenominational services and social occasions and trips into the surrounding area when conditions permitted counterbalanced the dire circumstances, but eventually the Methodists had to double up in their residences to create rental property as well as seek secular employment for income. Wood, who assiduously studied Chinese and preached his first native-language sermon in December 1861, contributed to the support of the mission as a translator for cotton brokers and as editor of the newspaper *North China Herald*. He also served on the committee that compiled the *Union Hymn Book* for use in the native churches of the various missions.

Only a strong faith sustained Wood. At the close of 1864, "the saddest year of all my life," he wrote of the death of his wife in March after a severe illness; the forced separation of his children, Edwin then age three and a half and Charles age fourteen months, who were placed in the care of a missionary family in another city; the news of the death of his favorite and youngest brother, Virgil; the Civil War at home; and the growing financial crisis at the mission. Yet at the same time he recalled his covenant made in Salem Church over a decade earlier where he consecrated himself to God, "becoming willing to trust Him anywhere in the world—even in China." To Wood, God's acceptance of his life and sanctification of his soul made him "perfectly happy in his Savior's love" as he faced another uncertain year.

On 1 Feb. 1866 Wood and Allen received their first communication from the Home Mission Board, which stated that they would be supported financially. Nevertheless, personal affairs dictated Wood's return to the United States. On 5 December he and his children sailed on the *Antelope* bound for home via the Cape of Good Hope. On 20 Mar. 1867 they arrived in New York City, and by 12 April he visited his aged parents and renewed acquaintances in Randolph County. Rejoining his home conference Wood received appointments to the Mount Airey Station (1867–70), Iredell Circuit (1875–76), Rockingham Station (1888–91), and St. John Station (1893). He also served as presiding elder for the Salisbury (1871–74), Greensboro (1877–79), Charlotte (1880–83), Shelby (1885–87), and Rockingham (1892) districts.

In November 1882 Trinity College faced a crisis on the death of Braxton Craven, its leader for over four decades, and in June 1883 the board of trustees asked Wood, a member of that body for ten years and perhaps Craven's closest friend in the conference, to be president. He accepted in an emotional speech, but soon, after a careful analysis of the condition of the college, he was cautioning that "all great enterprises require time and patience and labor and suffering and money." Despite diligent work and innovative attention to college-church relations, including holding district rallies where the first money ever was raised for endowment, Wood's greatest burden and disappointment was that the Methodists simply did not adequately support the college. When the annual conference meeting in December 1884 accepted the proposal of three wealthy laymen, John W. Alspaugh, James A. Gray, and Julian S. Carr, to serve as a Committee of Management to oversee the affairs of the college, Wood tendered his resignation.

Despite an "impossible task" and unpleasant intrigue for his position by a faculty member, Wood professed "abiding interest" in Trinity. Remaining on the board of trustees, he submitted the controversial and momentous resolution in 1889 calling for the removal of the college to Raleigh, a resolution that culminated in the relocation of the institution in Durham and the identity of the school with the philanthropy of the Duke family.

On 2 Mar. 1869 Wood married Carrie V. Pickett (1843–73) in Wilmington. They had three children: Francis Loftin, Thomas Pickett, and Margaret Graves. Widowed for the second time with young children, he married again on 29 Nov. 1875 in Statesville; his third wife was Mrs. Amanda Alford Robbins (1833–90), widow of Captain Julius Alexander Robbins, Confederate States of America.

Interested in church history, Wood carefully prepared a conference lecture on "Methodism: Its Rise, and Introduction into America; and into the Yadkin Valley, North Carolina." An active preacher he died in the parsonage at Gibson Station and was buried at Eastside Cemetery, Rockingham. In 1884 The University of North Carolina and Rutherford College awarded him D.D. degrees. He was a Royal Arch Mason.

SEE: Samuel A. Ashe, ed., *Cyclopedia of Eminent and Representative Men of the Carolinas*, vol. 2 (1892); Nora C. Chaffin, *Trinity College, 1839–1892* (1950); Duke University, *Alumni Register*, August 1932; *Journal, North Carolina Annual Conference, Methodist Episcopal Church, South, 1893* (1894); Marquis Wood Lawrence, "The Life of Marquis Lafayette Wood as Shown By His Diary" (B.D. thesis, Duke University, 1930); Marquis Lafayette Wood Papers (Duke University Archives [portrait]).

WILLIAM E. KING

Wood, Otto *(9 May 1895–31 Dec. 1930)*, criminal and escape artist, was born in Wilkes County of a law-abiding Baptist family. His father died when he was four years old; his mother's given name was Ellen. In his autobiography, published in 1926, he wrote that he was born in 1894 and had four brothers; other accounts state that he was born in 1895 and had two brothers and three sisters. Wood probably studied a total of three years in his life, although he claimed to have attended school for fewer than six months. His life of crime began at age seven when he ran away from home to live with an uncle in Vulcan, W.Va. There Wood witnessed battles between the Hatfields and McCoys and befriended several Hatfields.

At thirteen Wood began to work for the railroad, the only steady employment he ever had. Also during that year, he stole a bicycle in Wilkesboro for which he was jailed for five months and released with a reprimand. At fourteen he was convicted of breaking into a hardware store; sentenced to serve six months on the chain gang, he was, instead, sent home because of his youth.

During the six years he worked on the railroad, Wood lost his left hand in an accident. He used the $7,000 received in compensation to marry his fiancée, but a former girl friend charged him with seduction. At nineteen he began to serve his first prison sentence in the Virginia Penitentiary. Soon afterwards he made the first of ten prison escapes. He was recaptured in Portsmouth, Ohio, in 1916. After three months behind Virginia bars, Wood escaped again. He moved to Welch, W.Va., where he began to make and haul moonshine whiskey. His wife divorced him and he remarried. On a honeymoon trip to Kentucky Wood was convicted of car theft in Tennessee and sentenced to three years. His second wife divorced him and he never remarried. Nevertheless, he was the father of several children, both legitimate and illegitimate.

After six months in the Tennessee prison Wood made

his third escape. In two weeks he was arrested in his native Wilkes County. A year later he escaped from the Tennessee Penitentiary a second time, leaving in a dry goods box being hauled from the prison yard. Chased by bloodhounds through the night, Wood knocked out a 250-pound guard and grabbed onto the caboose of a freight train. After disguising himself as a brakeman, he joined the chase for himself.

When Wood reached Welch, W.Va., he was arrested and given a five-year sentence for car theft. But five months later, on 3 Jan. 1919, he escaped. There were reward offers for his capture in Virginia, West Virginia, and Tennessee. The West Virginia governor pardoned Wood, and he was sent to Tennessee where he made his third escape from the prison.

On 15 Oct. 1923 Wood committed murder for the first time when he killed A. W. Kaplan, a Greensboro pawnbroker who refused to return a watch that Wood had pawned. For that deed Wood was sentenced to thirty years in the North Carolina state penitentiary. In May 1924, however, he escaped. Following two days of freedom he was caught in Virginia and returned. This time he remained in the prison for eighteen months before hiding in a concrete culvert being shipped out of the prison in a box car. Two weeks later, on 8 Dec. 1925, he was caught in Wilkes County.

The escape artist spent the next year in the state prison writing his memoirs, but despite his repentant words walked out on 22 Nov. 1926 through an unlocked door. This time he was gone for seven months until wounded in a burglary attempt in Indiana and returned to North Carolina. Placed in solitary confinement on death row, he remained for two years and two months. His health declined, and Governor O. Max Gardner ordered that Wood be treated as other prisoners. Wood then vowed not to run away while Gardner was governor, but he broke that promise on 12 July 1930, when he made his fourth escape from the North Carolina prison—and the tenth in a long list of such activity.

Wood died on the streets of Salisbury when the chief of police, R. L. Rankin, shot him in an exchange of gun fire. Wood's mother claimed his body, and he was buried in Coaldale, W.Va.

SEE: *Charlotte Observer*, 11 July 1930; *Life History of Otto Wood* (an autobiography) (1926 [portrait]), (1931 [portrait]; Raleigh *News and Observer*, 11 July 1930, 18 Jan. 1931, 10 Jan. 1954; *Washington (N.C.) Daily News*, 15 Feb. 1979.

CATHERINE L. ROBINSON

Wood, Reuben (1750–July 1812), trial lawyer, member of the state constitutional convention, legislator, and councillor of state, the son of John Wood, a native of Massachusetts, and Sibbel Wilborne Wood, resided in Randolph County. Reuben Wood was well qualified for the law, which he chose as his vocation. Unlike most of his contemporaries at the early North Carolina bar, he devoted his chief efforts to the law rather than to politics. As a consequence, he became noted as a wise counselor and skillful advocate.

With horse and saddlebags, Wood attended virtually all of the courts that sat in the vast territory between his home in Randolph County and North Carolina's westernmost court town, Jonesboro, which now lies within the boundaries of Tennessee. He was among the lawyers considered by the North Carolina General Assembly in 1788 for appointment as attorney for the Washington District, embracing practically all of the territory that subsequently became the state of Tennessee.

Wood served as solicitor or prosecuting attorney in the Burke County Court of Pleas and Quarter Sessions in 1788 and 1789 and in the Buncombe County Court of Pleas and Quarter Sessions from the organization of Buncombe County in April 1792 until April 1795, when he resigned his office.

Like his older brother Zebedee, Reuben merited and received the undying confidence of his contemporaries. Both men were chosen delegates from Randolph County to the constitutional convention that met at Fayetteville in November 1789 and with their approving votes ratified the U.S. Constitution on behalf of North Carolina. Moreover, they were both elected in 1791 to represent Randolph County in the North Carolina House of Commons. Subsequently Reuben was designated a councillor of state by the General Assembly for seven terms between 1800 and 1806. The councillor's role was to advise the governor on affairs of state.

Wood married Charity Hayne of South Carolina, and they had four sons and four daughters: John L., Joseph, Alfred, Edwin, Sally (m. Augustine Willis of Randolph County in 1802), Laura (m. Joseph Wilson, "the Great Solicitor" of Charlotte and a brother of Jethro Starbuck Wilson), and Evalina (m. Augustine Willis in 1822 after the death of her sister, Sally, his first wife).

Reuben Wood died intestate in Randolph County, and the November 1812 term of the Randolph County Court of Pleas and Quarter Sessions settled his estate. At that term his son Joseph returned to the court "An Inventory and Acount of the Sales of the Estate of Reuben Wood, dec'd, both in One," which shows that Reuben possessed an unusually large and diversified library for his day and supports Maud Potter's assertion that he "was a lawyer of distinction and a man of education and culture."

SEE: John L. Cheney, Jr., ed., *North Carolina Government, 1584–1974* (1975); Walter Clark, ed., *State Records of North Carolina*, vol. 20 (1902); Minutes of Buncombe and Burke County Courts of Pleas and Quarter Sessions (North Carolina State Archives, Raleigh); Maud Potter, *The Willises of Virginia* (1964); *Raleigh Register*, 21 Aug. 1812.

SAM J. ERVIN, JR.

Wood, Thomas Fanning (23 Feb. 1841–22 Aug. 1892), physician, first secretary of the North Carolina Board of Health, and cofounder of the *North Carolina Medical Journal*, was born in Wilmington. His parents, Robert B. and Mary A. Wood, were of "Quaker extraction" and had migrated to North Carolina from Nantucket, Mass.

After completing his secondary education in the Wilmington public schools Wood worked in a local drugstore and studied medicine under several physicians. With the outbreak of the Civil War, he volunteered for military duty. In 1862 Wood was assigned to Richmond, Va., where he served as a hospital steward and, at the direction of the Confederate secretary of war, attended lectures at the Medical College of Virginia. After he passed a medical examination, the Army Medical Board appointed him an assistant surgeon with the rank of captain.

From February 1863 until the end of the conflict, Dr. Wood served with the Third North Carolina Regiment, Jackson's Corps, participating in several important battles, including Chancellorsville and Gettysburg. When the war ended he returned to Wilmington and soon established a successful medical practice. For at least a year he was in charge of Mount Tirzah Hospital, a facility just outside the city that was used during the 1865–66 smallpox epidemic to care for indigent black victims of the disease. As a result of his experiences during the smallpox epidemic, Wood developed a scholarly interest in the work of Dr. Edward Jenner, the English physician who introduced vaccination. Wood himself subsequently became a leading advocate in North Carolina of inoculation.

In the opinion of one medical historian, Wood was "probably the greatest contributor to the development of North Carolina medicine in the last half of the nineteenth century." This assessment is based largely on his activities in behalf of the North Carolina Board of Health. Established in 1877 by act of the General Assembly, the original board enjoyed only limited powers and was allocated a mere $100 in state funds. By acts of 1879 and 1885 the board's duties and powers were enlarged and its annual appropriations increased to $2,000. In 1877 the state medical society elected Wood secretary-treasurer of the Board of Health, a position he retained until his death fifteen years later. During these formative years of a state-sponsored public health program in North Carolina, he supervised virtually single-handedly the activities of the Board of Health. Although often discouraged and frustrated by the lack of adequate state support for public health services, Wood, operating out of his Wilmington office and on at least one occasion using personal funds to meet board expenses, worked diligently to fulfill the duties of secretary-treasurer.

Much of the early work of the North Carolina Board of Health was educational. During its first year of operation, the board began to issue pamphlets on good health and sanitation practices for public distribution. In 1886 Wood started to compile and edit the Board of Health's *Bulletin*, a monthly newsletter containing reports on health conditions in the state and articles on preventive medicine. Because his contributions in the early development of the board were so significant, he is often regarded as the "father of the North Carolina Board of Health."

In 1878 Wood and Dr. Moses John De Rosset III, also a prominent Wilmington physician, founded the *North Carolina Medical Journal*, of which Wood was the principal editor until his death. In his editorials he advocated increased state funding of public health work, the adoption of uniform procedures for performing autopsies, and the systematic recording of vital statistics by local authorities. Although skeptical in 1882 of "would-be sanitarians" who "greatly exaggerate the dangers of adulteration," he later endorsed the publication by state agencies of chemical analyses of adulterated foods and drugs.

Active in state and national professional organizations, Wood served as secretary (1867–71) and president (1881–82) of the North Carolina Medical Society. From 1867 to 1872 he was secretary of the State Board of Medical examiners and in 1878 was elected a member of the board as examiner in chemistry. In 1880 and again in 1890 he was elected to the committee to revise the *United States Pharmacopeia*. At the time of his death he was first vice-president of the American Public Health Association.

Although best known in his day as a medical journalist and public health administrator, Wood enjoyed at least a modest reputation as a medical researcher. His autopsy report on a heart disease victim and his description of a brain tumor and of a large tumor of the upper jaw—all published in either the *Transactions of the North Carolina Medical Society* or the *North Carolina Medical Journal*—were significant contributions to the development of medical pathology in North Carolina.

Though extraordinarily active in his professional life, Wood found time to study botany and, indeed, came to be recognized as one of the state's leading botanists. He presented several papers on botanical topics before the Wilmington Historical and Scientific Society and with Gerald McCarthy collaborated on "Wilmington Flora,"

published in 1887 in the *Transactions of the Elisha Mitchell Scientific Society*.

Wood was awarded an honorary M.D. degree by the University of Maryland (1868) and an honorary LL.D. degree by The University of North Carolina (1890). He married Mary Kennedy Sprunt of Wilmington and had five children: Edward Jenner, Thomas Fanning, J. Hunter, Jane, and Margaret. A member of the Episcopal church, Wood died in Wilmington and was buried in Oakdale Cemetery.

The North Carolina Museum of History has an oil portrait of Dr. Wood commissioned by the state medical society and presented to the state library in 1894.

SEE: George M. Cooper, "The Woods—Father and Son" and [Thomas Fanning Wood], "Autobiographical Sketch of Thomas Fanning Wood," *Southern Medicine and Surgery* 90 (1928); "Dr. Thomas Fanning Wood," *North Carolina Medical Journal* 30 (1892); Dorothy Long, ed., *Medicine in North Carolina: Essays in the History of Medical Science and Medical Service, 1524–1960*, 2 vols. (1972); *Wilmington Messenger*, 23 Aug. 1892; *Wilmington Morning Star*, 23–24 Aug. 1892; Edward J. Wood, "Thomas Fanning Wood," *Dictionary of American Medical Biography* (1928); Jane Zimmerman, "The Formative Years of the North Carolina Board of Health, 1877–1893," *North Carolina Historical Review* 21 (1944).

NATHANIEL F. MAGRUDER

Woodall, Charles Lawrence, Jr. *(26 July 1894–6 May 1963)*, professional baseball player and coach, was born in Staunton, Va., the son of Charles Lawrence, Sr., and Fannie Woodall. He grew up in Raleigh, where his father was a prominent businessman. Woodall was graduated from Wake Forest College with a B.A. degree in 1912 and then entered The University of North Carolina, where he was catcher on the baseball team and from which he received a master's degree in physics in 1915 with a thesis entitled "Development of Physical Science." After overcoming the objections of his father, he began a professional baseball career in 1915, playing catcher for the Asheville team of the North Carolina State League. He spent the next four seasons playing for the Fort Worth club in the Texas League.

Woodall's contract was acquired in 1920 by the American League's Detroit Tigers, which sent him to Toledo of the American Association for more seasoning. He finished that year in Detroit, playing in eighteen games. Woodall caught for the Tigers for the remainder of the decade. He was regarded as an intelligent player and an excellent defensive catcher, leading the American League in fielding percentage at that position in 1927 and 1928. He hit for a high average but had little power. His best season was 1927, when he batted .280 and drove in thirty-nine runs. In 1929 he finished his major league career with a lifetime total of 548 games, 353 hits, a .268 batting average, but only one home run. One writer characterized him as "always a gentleman . . . one of the finest characters professional sport has ever known."

After leaving the majors, Woodall kept his career alive in the Pacific Coast League, the most prestigious minor league during the 1930s. He managed the Portland Beavers in 1929 and 1930, caught for Sacramento in 1932 and 1933, and completed his playing career with the San Francisco Seals from 1934 through 1939. He was a coach for Sacramento in 1940 and 1941.

Joining the Boston Red Sox as a coach in 1942, Woodall was a member of Boston's 1946 American League champions. In 1948 he became director of publicity for Boston, a position he held until 1962. From 1954 to 1962 he also was a Boston scout and supervised the team's New England tryout camps. At his death he was survived by his wife, Dorothy E. Buckley Woodall; a daughter, Patricia (Mrs. Cornelius Ryan); a son, Paul B.; and ten grandchildren. His funeral was held in Rockville, Md.

SEE: *Boston Globe*, 7 July 1963; Daniel L. Grant, *Alumni History of the University of North Carolina* (1924); Raleigh *News and Observer*, 8 Mar. 1929 and scattered issues; *Sporting News*, 18 May 1963; Woodall file, Alumni Office (University of North Carolina, Chapel Hill).

JIM L. SUMNER

Woodard, Frederick Augustus (*12 Feb. 1854–8 May 1915*), congressman, state legislator, and lawyer, was a native of Wilson County, the son of Dr. Stephen and Mary Hadley Woodard. He was educated at the Reverend Joseph H. Foy's private school and studied law with Chief Justice Richmond M. Pearson, who immersed his students in Blackstone, Coke, and the principles of the common law. "Judge Pearson regarded Mr. Woodard as one of his best students and one of the most thoroughly prepared members of his class," according to Woodard's friend, the eminent jurist Henry G. Connor. Woodard received his law license in 1873 and began a private practice in the town of Wilson, which he made his home for the rest of his life.

A strong Democrat living in a strongly Democratic community, he soon became involved in partisan politics, serving as a leader in both the county and Second Congressional District Democratic organizations. He first ran for elective office in 1884, vainly seeking to unseat Republican congressman James E. O'Hara. In 1892 he again sought a seat in Congress, and in a three-way race that included a Populist candidate as well as incumbent Republican Henry P. Cheatham, Woodard won with a small plurality.

In 1894 Woodard was reelected, again a minority winner in a three-party campaign. His victory was one of the few successes for North Carolina Democrats as a Republican-Populist "fusion" seized control of the General Assembly and carried six of the state's nine congressional districts. One of Woodard's opponents, Henry Cheatham, contested the election in the House of Representatives, charging the Democrats with wholesale fraud. After sifting through voluminous testimony, the Republican-controlled House Committee on Elections concluded that the evidence did not support Cheatham's claim.

In his fourth race for Congress in 1896, Woodard lost to Republican George H. White. Thanks to a new election law that banned many of the unfair practices used by Democratic registrars to limit Negro voting, the Second Congressional District returned to its usual Republican allegiance. Woodard was a contender for the Democratic congressional nomination in 1900, but after a lengthy session, the convention selected Claude Kitchin, a young lawyer from Halifax County. After this defeat, Woodard returned to his law practice, limiting his public service to such nonpartisan positions as trustee of The University of North Carolina and board member of the Wilson graded schools.

Because of his extensive interest and experience in railroad matters, he was elected in 1910, without opposition, to represent Wilson County in a special General Assembly session devoted to the issue of railway freight rates. He died two years later and was buried in Maplewood Cemetery, Wilson.

Woodard was married twice, first to Fannie E. Rountree

and then, after her death, to Mrs. R. E. Holleman. He had one son, Graham. Woodard was an active member of the Methodist Episcopal church.

SEE: Eric Anderson, "Race and Politics in North Carolina, 1872–1901: The 'Black Second' Congressional District" (Ph.D. diss., University of Chicago, 1978); *Biog. Dir. Am. Cong.* (1971); Henry G. Connor, "Frederick A. Woodard," in Charles L. Van Noppen Papers (Manuscript Department, Duke University Library, Durham).

ERIC ANDERSON

Woodfin, John W. (*9 Apr. 1818–20 Oct. 1863*), lawyer and soldier, was born in the Mills River section of Buncombe County that became Henderson County in 1838, the son of John and Mary Grady Woodfin. Of his eleven brothers and sisters John was closest to his elder brother Nicholas W., who rose to prominence in his own right as a state senator and lawyer.

Woodfin was admitted to the North Carolina bar in 1845 and opened a law office in Asheville. Two of the more notable students who studied under him were Augustus Summerfield Merrimon and Zebulon Baird Vance. Merrimon reported Woodfin to be on the whole very genial but a master of sarcasm and invective.

With the coming of the Civil War Woodfin left his practice and helped organize the Buncombe Rangers, in Asheville, of which he was elected captain on 16 May 1861. On 1 August his unit was sent to Camp Beauregard in Warren County for cavalry drill and instruction. Here it was officially designated Company G, First Regiment, North Carolina Cavalry, with Woodfin as captain.

On 23 Sept. 1861 he was promoted to major and transferred to the field and staff of the Second Regiment of the cavalry. He spent much of the next year with the regiment harassing Major General Ambrose Everett Burnside's raiding parties in eastern North Carolina and picketing the roads around New Bern. On 6 Sept. 1862 Woodfin resigned from the regiment for reasons of poor health and returned to Asheville. There he organized and became major of a battalion composed primarily of conscripts and men who had formerly been exempted from service. This battalion was the basis of what would later become the Fourteenth Battalion, North Carolina Cavalry. Although never transferred to Confederate States service, Woodfin's battalion was mustered into state service and was in position to oppose a Federal force moving on Warm Springs in October 1863. At Warm Springs Woodfin was killed during a skirmish while leading a detachment from his battalion against the advancing Federals.

Surviving him was his widow, Mira McDowell Wood, formerly of Quaker Meadows, Burke County. She was the daughter of Captain Charles McDowell and the sister of Eliza Grace McDowell, who married John's brother Nicholas. John W. Woodfin was buried in Riverside Cemetery, Asheville. In a letter written just before a battle and probated as a will, he left his property to his wife asking her to be generous to "our little niece Mira."

SEE: Elizabeth Roberts Cannon, *My Beloved Zebulon* (1971); Frontis W. Johnston, *The Papers of Zebulon Baird Vance* (1963); Louis H. Manarin, ed., *North Carolina Troops, 1861–1865: A Roster: Volume 2, Cavalry* (1968); Wills, Buncombe County, Asheville.

ALAN C. DOWNS

Woodfin, Nicholas Washington (*29 Jan. 1810–23 May 1876*), lawyer, legislator, and planter, was deeply interested in internal improvements, public education, scientific agriculture, and industrial development. Born in the Mills River section of that part of Buncombe County that later lay in Henderson County, he was the fourth of twelve children of John, a prosperous farmer, and Mary Grady Woodfin. Nicholas not only became a distinguished member of the Asheville bar and a state senator for five terms, but he also acquired extensive acreage in the French Broad River valley and the largest number of slaves—122—owned by anyone in Buncombe County in 1860. That year he valued his real estate and personal property at $165,000. In 1870, however, the total value of his property was given as only $36,000.

Although the formal education of the Woodfin children was limited to the local school, three of them became professional men. Nicholas's younger brother, John W., also entered the law but was killed during the Civil War; another younger brother, Henry Grady, became a physician. Nicholas continued his education under attorneys Michael Frances and David Lowry Swain and at age twenty-one was admitted to the North Carolina bar. Preferring to remain an advocate, he refused the offer of a judgeship when he was thirty-two.

In 1840 Woodfin married Eliza Grace McDowell, the daughter of Colonel Charles McDowell of Quaker Meadows in Burke County. They had three daughters: Anna, Lillie, and Mira. The Woodfin home on the street that was named for him became part of the YMCA building in Asheville. Attesting also to his prominence is a community near Asheville that bears his name and the presence of his portrait in the Buncombe County Courthouse.

Woodfin's service as state senator from the Buncombe and Henderson District began in 1844 and ended with the 1852 term. He served on the Committee on the Judiciary and was its chairman during his last three terms. Recognizing that turnpikes and railroads were the key to the development of his region, he strongly supported their construction. During Reconstruction he was one of the commissioners appointed to investigate fraud and corruption connected with the Western Division of the Western North Carolina Railroad Company. It was he who was sent to London to make a settlement with Milton S. Littlefield, the president of the company who had fled the country.

Woodfin's activities in support of public education received the highest praise from the first superintendent of common schools, Calvin H. Wiley. Further, he instructed without compensation a number of young men training to become lawyers.

Because the mountains were particularly suited to tobacco production and dairying, Woodfin advocated those means, as well as diversified industries, to increase the prosperity of the region. After the Civil War he started and for a time operated a cheese factory. He was a member of the Buncombe County Agricultural Society and once spoke to the American Agricultural Society at Ithaca, N.Y.

A Whig with strong Unionist sympathies, Woodfin opposed secession until President Abraham Lincoln called for troops to coerce the seceded states. He represented Buncombe County in the secession convention, and after the war began he served without remuneration, so it developed, as the agent of the state to superintend the North Carolina Salt Works that were located at salt mines in southwestern Virginia. At the end of the war he returned to his previously extensive law practice.

During his middle years Woodfin was confirmed in the Episcopal church and served as a vestryman. A handsome man with a pleasant personality, he has been described as a "conspicuous example of eminent citizenship."

SEE: John Preston Arthur, *Western North Carolina: A History* (1914); Samuel A. Ashe, ed., *Biographical History of North Carolina*, vol. 2 (1905); *Asheville Citizen*, 22 Sept. 1960; Jonathan Daniels, *Prince of Carpetbaggers* (1958); *Journals of the Senate and House of Commons of the General Assembly of the State of North Carolina* (1944–52); John Gilchrist McCormick, "Personnel of the Convention of 1861," *James Sprunt Historical Monographs*, no. 1 (1900); U.S. Census, Buncombe County, 1860, 1870.

MATTIE U. RUSSELL

Woods, Freeman (*ca. 1766–20 Nov. 1834*), silversmith, was a native of New Jersey and worked in New York before moving to New Bern around 1794. For the three years prior to his departure he was listed in the New York directories, but by 27 Dec. 1794 he had established himself in New Bern as a goldsmith and silversmith. In his advertisements Woods professed to be able to execute almost any item in the newest fashion and on short notice. Flatware and holloware that bear his identifying mark support his claim, as they demonstrate his obvious familiarity with current styles in London and in the more affluent American cities.

A highly successful craftsman, Woods made silver unexcelled by pieces found in any other state. His work is especially notable for its simplicity, graceful lines, perfect proportion, and artful embellishment. As a skilled engraver, he employed bright-cut extensively on a number of pieces found. One of his apprentices was David Murdock.

Although Woods was a man of some prominence and well respected, there is little indication that he was active in politics or civic matters. However, when Andrew Jackson and John Quincy Adams were presidential candidates in 1827, Freeman Woods was a member of a committee of correspondence selected by supporters of Andrew Jackson.

Woods died and was buried in New Bern. Both the *Raleigh Register* and the *Raleigh Minerva* published on 1 Nov. 1811 carried notices of the death of "Mrs. Hannah Woods," wife of Mr. Freeman Woods" on 17 October, but nothing else could be learned of Mrs. Woods or of any surviving children.

SEE: Ernest M. Currier, *Marks of Early American Silversmiths . . . Lists of New York Silversmiths, 1815–1841* (1938); George B. Cutten and Mary Reynolds Peacock, *Silversmiths of North Carolina, 1696–1850* (1973); Lois Smathers Neal, comp., *Abstracts of Vital Records from Raleigh, North Carolina, Newspapers, 1799–1819*, vol. 1 (1979); New Bern *North Carolina Gazette*, 21 Feb. 1795; New Bern *Carolina Sentinel*, 18 July 1795, 18 July 1818, 7 Sept. 1822, 2 Oct. 1824, 14 Oct. 1826, 25 Aug., 24 Sept. 1827.

MARY R. B. PEACOCK

Woodward, Sara Griffith Stanley (*1836–1918*), antislavery activist and teacher and one of the earliest African Americans to attend college, was born in New Bern, the daughter of John Stuart and Frances Griffith Stanley. In 1830 her father, a prosperous merchant, owned eighteen slaves, most of whom probably were relatives he purchased so they could remain in North Carolina; he also operated a private school for free blacks. Her grandfather, John C. Stanly, a barber, was the free mulatto son of John Wright Stanly and a mulatto woman who was one of the founding members of the New Bern Presbyterian Church.

Educated by her mother, who taught in the school for blacks in New Bern, Sara G. Stanley was sent to Oberlin College in Ohio at age sixteen. Four years later, in 1856, the Stanleys moved to Cleveland, Ohio. Members of her family, particularly the women, were very fair with blue eyes and were often assumed to be white—Sara once described herself as "a colored woman, having a slight admixture of negro blood in my veins"—yet they always operated in the "colored social circle" and took pride in their African American ancestry.

The Stanleys may have lived briefly in the town of Delaware, Ohio, near the center of the state before moving north to Cleveland. The name Sara G. Staley [sic] appears in a printed antislavery petition drawn up in Delaware and read before a convention of black men in Columbus in 1856. It offered the support of black women to black men in a move for political liberty; citing the "conglomeration of hatred and prejudice against our race," it urged that religion and science cease attempts to justify racial inferiority. "One truth, the only essential truth, in incontrovertible," the petition recorded. "The Omnipotent, Omniscient God's glorious autograph—the seal of angels—is written on our brows, that immortal characteristic of Divinity—the rational, mysterious and inexplicable soul, animates our frames."

In an article in the Weekly Afro-American of 19 Apr. 1862 she praised the poet John Greenleaf Whittier for supporting the antislavery sentiment. Although his stance reduced his popularity at the time, she stated, because he possessed a "broader catholicity, a truer humanity, because founded upon an imperishable principle—'the fatherhood of God and the brotherhood of man,'" his poems would be more appreciated in the future. It was perhaps in recognition of this essay that she was one of several black women chosen for honorary membership in the National Young Men's Literary Association, a black organization.

Sara Stanley may have taught in the Cleveland public schools on the eve of the Civil War. Her application in 1864, when she volunteered as a teacher with the American Missionary Association, noted that she had taught in the Ohio public schools for several years. In her new position she was sent to Norfolk, Va., to teach blacks recently freed by Union troops. She reported less difficulty with her pupils than with white administrators and teachers who stressed "the inferiority of 'negroes'" and who opposed the social unity of the races even in the North. She maintained, however, that "Christian unity and sociality among those working as missionary-teachers in the South were essential as dissension would undercut the common goal of helping the freedmen." She particularly objected when a white matron in a teachers' dormitory wanted "all colored teachers removed," and she was articulate and outspoken in stressing the goal of racial tolerance among the staff. One Walker, a white male teacher in the Norfolk school, endorsed her views, and they became kindred souls, exchanging letters. A fellow teacher reported this friendship as a romantic involvement, and the American Missionary Association recalled Miss Stanley. Walker, it was revealed, was married and living with his newly pregnant wife.

After thanking the corresponding secretary of the association for his "kindness and compassion in dealing with her 'sin,'" Sara Stanley received a teaching assignment in St. Louis, Mo. In March 1865, in a final letter, she wrote: "I must tell you before ending that I have acknowledged all my wrong-doing before God and am fully and freely pardoned." In spite of poor conditions in this school, she tried to make the surroundings attractive and to improvise in the absence of equipment and supplies. Most of her pupils were free blacks, many of them mulattoes, and here there were no complaints of racism. But in the fall of 1865, when a new, all-white city school board was elected,

she applied for reassignment. Although she had requested a school on the Atlantic coast, she was sent to Louisville, Ky. Successful at the new school, where enrollment doubled to 190, she soon was promoted to principal.

Articles written by Sara Stanley appeared frequently in the American Missionary between 1865 and 1867, and the Annual Report of the American Missionary Association for 1866 included an account of some of her classroom experiences. By 1868 she was teaching in a freedman's school in Mobile, Ala., where she met Charles A. Woodward, a white man. He was twenty-eight, four years younger than she, a native of New York State, and a mason by training. A resident of Detroit on the eve of the Civil War, he had enlisted as a private and served as a regimental musician with the Michigan Infantry. At the end of the war he moved to Mobile and became head cashier of the Freedman's Bank.

Woodward discovered that he and Sara Stanley had many interests in common despite the fact that he was a blue-eyed, blond, white male and she an acknowledged black woman. They decided to marry, but the American Missionary Association disapproved, largely because it did not want to inflame local resistance when the association was on the verge of buying a large building in Mobile as a training school for teachers. Moreover, Ku Klux Klan activities were getting under way, and the marriage of a white man and a black woman would threaten the peace of the city.

The association attempted to dissuade Sara from marrying at all and certainly from marrying in the Mission House in Mobile. School officials suggested that the couple return to Cleveland, but she was insistent and after some delay they were married in the home of a friend. An infant girl born to them not long after their marriage died within six months; there were no other children. The 1870 census of Mobile recorded her as a teacher in the local Emerson Institute, the new training school. Woodward, perhaps with the assistance of his better-educated wife, was the author of a history of the Freedman's Bank.

For a time Sara Woodward was employed as an assistant cashier in the bank, but in 1874 her husband was accused (but not convicted) of embezzlement. They then moved to New Jersey, where he died in 1885. Afterwards she worked as an engraver in Philadelphia and received a widow's military pension but in 1894 taught briefly at Lucy Lainey's school for black women in Georgia. Her whereabouts are unknown until 1918, when she died, but she may have returned to Cleveland before then.

SEE: John Hope Franklin, The Free Negro in North Carolina (1943); Ellen N. Lawson and Marlane Merrill, "Sara Stanley: Documents of a 19th Century Pioneer in Race Relations" (research paper, Women's History Project, Mudd Library, Oberlin College, Ohio); Stephen F. Miller, Recollections of Newbern Fifty Years Ago . . . (1874); The Stanly (Stanley) Family and the Historic John Wright Stanly House (1969).

WILLIAM S. POWELL

Woodward, Thomas (1604–76), surveyor general of the Albemarle, was born in England. Assay master of the Mint under Charles I, he was dismissed from this position on 23 Oct. 1649 by John Bradshaw, president of the Council of State, because of his loyalty to the Crown. Woodward went to Virginia, publicly declaring never to see England again until the return of Charles II to the throne. In November 1661, after the Restoration, John Woodward, a son of Thomas who seems to have remained in England, petitioned the king; reciting the loyalty of his father, he requested that the house and office of assay master be put in his possession until his father's return or, if his father was dead, to have a grant of it himself. This request was granted, for when John Woodward died in 1665, King Charles II advised the warden of the Mint that the office of assay master was vacant by reason of the death of John Woodward and in the absence of Thomas Woodward, who, if alive, was at some plantation in Virginia. John Brattle was to exercise the office during Woodward's absence. Thomas Woodward, however, never returned to England.

Assuming a prominent role in Virginia, he served as clerk of court of Isle of Wight County from 1656 to 1662. On 25 Sept. 1663 Sir William Berkeley, governor of Virginia and himself one of the recently appointed Proprietors of Carolina, issued twenty-nine grants in the Albemarle region. These were the first grants of land made in what is now North Carolina. Thomas Woodward was the surveyor appointed to lay off these grants, and of the twenty-nine, three were made to Woodward and members of his family. These tracts, representing over 5,000 acres, lay on the Pasquotank River and on the western side of the Chowan.

Thomas Woodward seems to have remained in the Albemarle section for several years. On 2 June 1665 he sent an interesting report to John Colleton, one of the Lords Proprietors, concerning the new colony and acknowledged his official appointment as surveyor. The report revealed him to be a man of education, as he referred to Bacon's essay on plantations and quoted a proverb in Spanish. While in Carolina, he served as secretary for the colony and was a member of the governor's Council. He and Governor William Drummond were commissioners to treat with Maryland and Virginia for a cessation of tobacco planting for the year 1667. This conference, called in response to a sharp drop in the price of tobacco, was held at Jamestown on 12 July 1666.

Woodward returned to Isle of Wight, Va., where he died. In his will, dated 5 Oct. 1677 and probated the same year, he mentioned his wife, his son Thomas, and his daughters Katherine, Elizabeth, Mary, Rachel, and Philarite. Provision was made for the children, if any, of his deceased son John in England. The inventory of his estate listed a parcel of books. The surname of his wife Katherine is unknown; her will was probated in Isle of Wight in 1684.

SEE: John B. Boddie, *Seventeenth-Century Isle of Wight County, Va.* (1938); Isle of Wight County, Va., Wills, Isle of Wight; John Kennedy, *Colonial Transcripts, 1573–1772* (1905); Nell Marion Nugent, *Cavaliers and Pioneers: Abstracts of Virginia Land Patents and Grants*, vol. 1 (1934); William S. Powell, ed., *Yᵉ Countie of Albemarle in Carolina: A Collection of Documents, 1664–1675* (1958).

CLAIBORNE T. SMITH, JR.

Woody, John Warren *(17 Mar. 1841–6 Aug. 1920)*, educator, college president, and religious leader, was born at Saxapahaw, Alamance County, of English Quaker ancestry, the son of Nathaniel, a farmer, surveyor, and owner of land on Haw River originally granted to his great-grandfather, and Sarah Hornady Woody. He attended Spring Friends Monthly Meeting School and New Garden Boarding School. As a conscientious objector, he left North Carolina when the Civil War began and walked to the home of an uncle in Thorntown, Ind. He was graduated from Westfield Academy in Indiana and from the Old Lebanon National Normal University, in Ohio, where he received both bachelor's and master's degrees. Woody later stud-

ied at the University of Tennessee and earned an LL.B. degree law at the University of Michigan, Ann Arbor.

He began teaching at a time when Quaker colleges were developing across the United States. He assisted in the organization and growth of six educational institutions. In 1868 he became the first president of Whittier College in Salem, Iowa, and in 1871 he helped establish William Penn College in Oskaloosa, Iowa, serving as its first president. Returning to North Carolina in 1880 to teach at New Garden Boarding School, he was a member of the first faculty of Guilford College. After fourteen years as professor of history and instructor in surveying, natural science, philosophy, and Bible at Guilford, he went to teach in the new college at Whittier, Calif. Four years later he accepted an invitation to assist in the establishment of Friends University at Wichita, Kans. In 1899 he helped set up Slater Industrial and State Normal School for blacks in Winston, N.C. (now Winston-Salem State University).

Woody, who retired in 1908, taught with great patience and dignity, always encouraging students and showing a particular interest in plodders. He often took into his own home an unfortunate or handicapped student, giving him special attention and help. His surveying class at Guilford College, among other projects, in 1884 ran a line through the woods from Founders Hall to the Guilford depot—the location of present College Road. He was the author of *A Handbook of Pedagogics* (1884), *History by the Topical Method* (1889), and *The Elements of Pedagogics* (1891). His teaching of history and the Bible was enriched by travel to the Holy Land and to Greece and Rome in 1892.

A promoter of industry in North Carolina at the turn of the twentieth century, Woody founded a cotton mill at High Falls and served as president of the High Falls Manufacturing Company for twenty-five years. He constantly kept in view the development of the economic, social, moral and spiritual well-being of the employees and of the community as a whole.

Another great concern of his was to assist a number of families, both black and white, to acquire land and build homes of their own, making for a more stable community. His plan was to train them to develop and finance their own resources. As an instructor in summer institutes for teachers of both races, he tried to impress on them the importance of working for community betterment. Endowed with a well-balanced personality, he was a man of deep convictions and firm purposes but with enough wit and humor to relieve tense situations.

In 1868 Woody married Mary Chawner, then of Thorntown, Ind., a teacher with him and a Friends minister. They had three children: Hermon, John Waldo, and Alice. Oil portraits of John and Mary C. Woody hang in the foyer of Spencer Chapel at William Penn College, Oskaloosa, Iowa. Woody died at his home at Guilford College and was buried in the New Garden Friends Cemetery.

SEE: Charles W. Cooper, *Whittier: Independent College in California* (1967); *Friends University Bulletin* (1899); Dorothy Lloyd Gilbert, *Guilford: A Quaker College* (1937); Guilford College, *Friends Messenger*, September 1920; Arthur S. Watson, *William Penn College: A Product and a Producer* (1971); Stephen B. Weeks, *Southern Quakers and Slavery* (1896); *Wichita Daily Eagle*, 22 Sept. 1898; Woody family records (possession of Mary Edith Woody Hinshaw).

MARY EDITH WOODY HINSHAW

Woody, Mary Chawner *(22 Dec. 1846–25 Dec. 1928)*, Friends minister, teacher, and spiritual leader, was born in

Bartholomew County, Ind., of Quaker English and colonial ancestry, the daughter of Chalkley Albertson and Sarah Cox Chawner. Her father was the son of John Squires Chawner, an attorney at the King's Bench, London, who migrated to North Carolina and married the daughter of a Friends minister in Perquimans County. Her mother was of a Wayne County Quaker family. Among her ancestors were Francis Toms, a member of the colonial Council of Carolina, in whose home the North Carolina Yearly Meeting of Friends was organized in 1698, and Richard Cox, in whose home Contentnea Quarterly Meeting of Friends was organized in Wayne County.

Mary Chawner was educated in Sand Creek and Sugar Plain Friends Monthly Meeting Schools and at Bloomingdale Academy (Friends) and Earlham College, all in Indiana. In 1868 in Thorntown, Ind., where both were teaching, she married John Warren Woody, of North Carolina, who during the Civil War had walked to the Indiana farm of his uncle, who lived next to the Chawners. Mary C. Woody read law with her husband at the University of Michigan Law School at Ann Arbor; she also studied public speaking there.

A teacher by disposition, she assisted her husband in the establishment of Whittier College in Salem, Iowa, and, later, of William Penn College at Oskaloosa, Iowa. Her oil portrait hangs with his in the foyer of Spencer Chapel at Penn College. She also taught at Guilford College and for a shorter time at Whittier College in California and Friends University, Wichita, Kans. Her favorite subjects were English composition, rhetoric, literature, and the Bible. She gave lessons in elocution at Guilford College and, during her retirement, at home.

Mrs. Woody was recorded a minister in the Society of Friends in 1884 and became a strong leader in the North Carolina Yearly Meeting of Friends. As secretary of the evangelism and outreach committee she helped organize a number of Friends meetings across the state. She traveled in North Carolina for two years as acting superintendent of the Yearly Meeting at the time Friends meetings were beginning to accept the pastoral system. For a period she served as resident pastor of New Garden Meeting, which was attended by Guilford College students and faculty.

Taking the lead in 1884 in forming the state Woman's Christian Temperance Union, Mrs. Woody was elected first president at the organizational meeting held at Benbow Hall on South Elm Street, Greensboro. She served as president for ten years, traveling, preaching, and lecturing; at different times she spoke to the state legislature urging the passage of temperance laws. Mary Woody was vice-president of the national temperance union when Frances Willard was president.

In 1892 she traveled to England with "a minute to visit Friends Meetings and missions in London Yearly Meeting." Her companion, Lorena Reynolds, wrote: "from the time we left Greensboro until our return she was sowing seeds of truth which, I doubt not, yielded a rich harvest." Mrs. Woody was a delegate to the three national organizational conferences of American Friends and instrumental in helping to establish the Five Years Meeting of Friends in America (now Friends United Meeting), where she held important positions for several years.

Among her concerns for people, she demonstrated a lively interest in equal rights for women. She was one of a committee of three women Friends in 1895 who planned and raised money for a gymnasium for women at Guilford College. (Guilford was probably the first college in America to have a physical education department for women, eight years before it hired a coach for men.) Wishing to see a woman's college in Greensboro, she

worked with other Quaker women for the establishment of the State Normal and Industrial College (now the University of North Carolina at Greensboro). While her husband was associated with the Slater Industrial and State Normal School for blacks in Winston, she sought money from Quakers in Philadelphia with which to begin a school of nursing at Slater School. She promoted passage of the Nineteenth Amendment and continued to encourage women to vote.

Small in stature, Mary Woody was quick in movement, in perception, and in speech. She was a clear thinker, a good organizer, and a convincing speaker. The Woodys had three children: Hermon, John Waldo, and Alice. Mary Woody died at the home of her son Waldo in High Point and was buried in the New Garden Cemetery at Guilford College.

SEE: Dorothy Lloyd Gilbert, *Guilford: A Quaker College* (1937); Guilford College, *Friends Messenger*, 19 Feb. 1929; S. B. and M. E. Hinshaw, eds., *Carolina Quakers* (1972); Minutes of the North Carolina Yearly Meeting, 1882–1928 (Quaker Collection, Guilford College); Arthur S. Watson, *William Penn College: A Product and a Producer* (1971).

MARY EDITH WOODY HINSHAW

Woody, Robert Hilliard (*11 Mar. 1903–30 Dec. 1985*), historian and teacher, was born in the Little Cataloochee Creek community of Haywood County, the son of Stephen and Margaret Leona Hannah Woody. His father, a diabetic, died when he was two years old. When he was five, his mother left him for a few years in Little Cataloochee with his uncle, Valentine Woody, and his wife Laura. With a fourth-grade education she entered Berea College to study nursing; certified as a registered nurse in 1914, she became in 1922 the first female anesthetist in Kentucky.

Woody attended grammar schools in Berea and Louisville and was graduated from high school in London, Ky., in 1923. That fall he entered Emory University, where during his junior year Professor Francis Butler Simkins invited him to collaborate in a study of South Carolina during Reconstruction. After receiving a B.Ph. degree from Emory in 1927, he entered Duke University where he obtained the degrees of M.A. in 1928 and Ph.D. in 1930, his dissertation being part of his collaborative effort with Simkins. Their work, published in 1932 as *South Carolina during Reconstruction*, had been awarded the John H. Dunning Prize in American History by the American Historical Association the year before. The book was hailed by historians as a major revisionist study, but Woody always maintained that he and Simkins had only tried to "tell the full story."

From 1929 until his retirement in June 1970, as a full professor, Woody taught history at Duke University. For the first seven years his subject was modern European history, but in 1932 he began to teach U.S. history as well. In 1938 he took over the graduate course of the late William Kenneth Boyd entitled "Union, Confederacy, and Reconstruction." At various times he also taught graduate courses on American colonial history and the Revolution, the United States from 1850 to 1900, historiography of the South, the Old South, and a seminar in southern history.

Woody directed thirty-two doctoral dissertations and at least fifty-eight masters theses. He served on numerous graduate examining committees in the fields of U.S. history and American literature. He was coauthor of two books, edited another, published more than two dozen articles and over 220 book reviews, and presented papers at professional meetings. His edition of *William Preston Few:*

Papers and Addresses, for which he wrote an extensive biographical memoir, appeared in 1951. *Christopher Gadsden and the American Revolution* by E. Stanly Godbold, Jr., and Woody was published in 1982.

In 1937 he went on a part-time teaching schedule for eleven years in order to direct the George Washington Flowers Memorial Collection of Southern Americana in the Duke University Library. He served on the board of editors of the *Journal of Southern History,* on the executive council of the Southern Historical Association, as president (1954–55) of the Historical Society of North Carolina, and on several North Carolina state committees and commissions. He was a member of Phi Beta Kappa and of all the major historical organizations.

As a teacher Woody's style was to talk rather than lecture. Without pretense and always courteous and respectful of individuality in people, he never tried to make the writing styles of his students conform to his own skillful craftsmanship. Their writing, though, had to be clear and concise as well as grammatical.

Woody never ceased to appreciate his mountain heritage. Many summers of his youth had been spent helping his "Uncle Tine" on his farm, and he portrayed him and other self-sufficient mountaineers in his "Cataloochee Homecoming," published in the *South Atlantic Quarterly* in 1950. This bittersweet essay is about former residents of the communities of Big and Little Cataloochee creeks being forced off their lands during the creation of the Great Smoky Mountains National Park.

On 3 June 1929 Woody married Louise Wills (18 Aug. 1906–19 Mar. 1984), a musician and the daughter of a Methodist minister. They adopted two children, Dorothy Jean and Stephen Boyd. Due to failing health they moved in 1983 from Durham to San Diego, Cal., to live with their daughter. Woody died there, and his body was cremated.

SEE: Biographical file with photographs and personal papers of Robert H. Woody (Duke University Archives, Durham); Duke University theses and dissertations; "Robert Hilliard Woody: An Appreciation," in E. Stanly Godbold, Jr., A. V. Huff, Jr., and Mattie U. Russell, "Essays in Southern History in Honor of Robert H. Woody," *South Atlantic Quarterly* 73, no. 1 (Winter 1974): 3–9; Robert H. Woody, personal contact.

MATTIE U. RUSSELL

Wootten, Mary Bayard Morgan *(17 Dec. 1875–6 Apr. 1959),* photographer and artist, was born in New Bern, the daughter of Mary Devereux Clarke and Rufus Morgan. Her maternal grandmother was Mary Bayard Devereux Clarke, author and editor; her maternal grandfather was William J. Clarke, commander of the Twenty-fourth Regiment, North Carolin Troops, in the Confederate army. She attended New Bern Collegiate Institute and in 1892 enrolled for a year's instruction at the State Normal and Industrial College (now the University of North Carolina at Greensboro).

When she was seventeen financial necessity prompted her to accept a position as an art instructor in the Arkansas School for the Deaf. This opportunity came through the influence of her uncles, Francis D., head of a school for the deaf in Flint, Mich., and Thomas P. D. Clarke, a teacher of the deaf in Vancouver, Wash. It probably also was they who persuaded her to move the following year to the Georgia School for the Deaf, where she taught for four years. While there she met and in 1897 married Charles Wootten; they had two sons, Charles Thomas and Rufus Morgan. The couple separated in 1901, when she returned to New Bern to support her sons and to help her mother care for her aged stepfather, a half brother, and a half sister.

Painting flowers on calendars, greeting cards, fans, and china provided a meager livelihood for two years. In about 1902 she designed the first Pepsi-Cola trademark at the request of the pharmacist, Caleb D. Bradham, a neighbor who invented the drink. With a borrowed camera she supplemented one of her calendar paintings with a photograph. Orders for photographs followed and she soon bought her own camera. Basic instruction and encouragement from a local portrait photographer led her to open a studio on a lot by her mother's home in New Bern.

Business for a free-lance photographer was limited in the summer, and Mrs. Wootten sought supplementary work in nearby Camp Glenn, where the North Carolina Guard trained during the summer. The morale-boosting effect of her photographic services and the publicity they provided for the Guard prompted the commanding general to offer her official membership in the Guard with a uniform and the title, chief of publicity. This association continued until after World War I, when the U.S. commanding general at Fort Bragg asked her to set up a studio on the base.

In 1914 Bayard Wootten made perhaps the first aerial photographs by a woman. In a Wright Brother's plane, with a camera aimed straight down between her feet, which rested on the metal struts, she took views of New Bern and the Neuse River. In 1917 Albert Rogers, a New York advertising executive and manager of the Grand Central Palace, the city's exposition building, was so impressed with Mrs. Wootten's work that he used her photographs for sales promotion, and he appointed her official photographer for the Palace. This led to a brief period of operating her own studio in New York.

Mrs. Wootten bought her first car, a Ford touring model, in 1918 and began a statewide portrait photographic service. Through a chain of agents in various towns who made appointments for sittings according to a preplanned schedule, she had clients from the mountains to the coast. Her innovative idea of posing her subjects in their home or other familiar environment instead of before a velvet curtain in a studio attracted favorable notice and imitation. Later, before there were good roads in many parts of the state, she extended her work to taking scenic pictures all over North Carolina for book illustrations and murals.

Through her affiliation with the National Guard and her growing reputation over the state, Mrs. Wootten came to the attention of a wide range of people. Among them, in 1919, was Professor Frederick Koch, director of the Carolina Playmakers, who invited her to become the Playmakers photographer. This Chapel Hill association was expanded in 1921 to include the *Yackety Yack,* the university's yearbook, and these contracts continued until 1947. In 1928 she opened a studio in Chapel Hill, where her half brother, George Moulton, later joined her in business.

After 1928 she spent most of her time in Chapel Hill, where, in addition to doing portrait work at her studio and traveling across the state, she collaborated with a number of authors in providing illustrations for their books. Among these were *Backwoods America* by Charles Morrow Wilson; *Cabin in the Laurel* by Muriel Sheppard; *Charleston, Azaleas, and Old Bricks* by Samuel Gaillard Stoney; *Old Homes and Gardens of North Carolina,* published for the Garden Clubs of North Carolina with text by Archibald Henderson; *New Castle, Delaware, 1651–1939,* by Anthony Higgins; and *From My Highest Hill* by Olive Tilford Dargan.

Wide recognition also came to Mrs. Wootten through the exhibition of her work. In addition to numerous shows in North Carolina, her photographs were displayed in Charleston, Richmond, Boston, Chicago, and New York.

After taking approximately 600,000 pictures, she retired from working behind the camera in 1948 after suffering an eye hemorrhage. Nevertheless, she continued to direct the operations of her Chapel Hill studio until 1954, when she returned to New Bern. She died there five years later and was buried in Cedar Grove Cemetery. There is a large collection of Mary Bayard Wootten's photographs and negatives in the North Carolina Collection at the University of North Carolina, Chapel Hill.

SEE: *Durham Morning Herald*, 31 Oct. 1954; John B. Green, *A New Bern Album* (1985); T. C. Moore, personal contact, April 1974; New Bern *Sun-Journal*, 2 July 1976; Raleigh *News and Observer*, 5 Dec. 1937; Mary Bayard Wootten, personal contact, 1945–51; Charles and Rufus Wootten to Helen Dugan Allen, 1974.

HELEN DUGAN ALLEN

Word, Thomas Jefferson (*ca. 1809–ca. 1856*), lawyer and congressman from Mississippi, was born in Surry County, the son of Thomas Adams and Justiana Dickerson Word. His grandfather, Charles Word, died at Kings Mountain on 7 Oct. 1780. In 1827 the younger Word held 350 acres in one tract and 72 in another. Elected to represent Surry County in the House of Commons in the session of 1832–33, he served on the committee on internal improvements.

Soon afterwards Word moved to Pontotoc, in northeastern Mississippi, where he was admitted to the bar on 7 Nov. 1836. A contemporary who knew him at this time later described him as "a remarkably fine looking man" and mentioned his polished, agreeable manner. "Added to this," it was said, "he had a fine, humorous way of telling anecdotes, and could play well the violin." He contested a congressional election which was set aside, and Word was subsequently elected as a Whig. He served from 30 May 1838 to 3 Mar. 1839.

Word was married about 1839 and during the 1840s moved to the fast-growing Holly Springs, Miss., seat of Marshall County on the Tennessee state line. A convention of Mississippians at Jackson in October 1849 chose him from the state's First Congressional District to go to the Nashville Convention scheduled in June 1850 to consider the South's constitutional future. Though apparently not a slaveowner himself, Word supported those who believed that the national government had no jurisdiction over slavery. The next year he was again elected to represent his county at a states' rights convention in Pontotoc on 2 June.

Word's law practice made him a familiar figure in circuit, probate, and chancery courts in northern Mississippi, and some of his cases went to the High Court of Errors and Appeals, as the supreme court in Jackson was called. He spoke at various temperance, patriotic, and memorial gatherings but had faded from public notice by the mid-1850s. Neither the date of his death nor the place of his burial seem to be known.

The 1850 census records his wife as Mary E. Word, a native of Ireland, and their children as Justiana, 9; John J., 7; Jefferson, 4; and Sarah, 1.

SEE: *Biog. Dir. Am. Cong.* (1971); John L. Cheney, Jr., ed., *North Carolina Government, 1585–1979* (1981); A. M. Clayton, *Centennial Address on the History of Marshall County* (1880); Reuben Davis, *Recollections of Mississippi and Mississippians* (1890; rev. ed., 1972); Dallas C. Dickey,

"The Disputed Election of 1837–1838," *Journal of Mississippi History* 1 (1939); Richey Henderson, *Pontotoc County Men of Note* (1940); Jesse G. Hollingsworth, *History of Surry County* (1935); Holly Springs, Miss., *Empire Democrat*, 17 Mar. 1855, and *The Palladium*, 25 Apr. 1851–1 July 1852; James D. Lynch, *The Bench and Bar of Mississippi* (1881); E. T. Winston, *Story of Pontotoc* (1931); Thomas Jefferson Word folder (Mississippi State Archives, Jackson).

H. B. FANT

Work, Monroe Nathan (*15 Aug. 1866–2 May 1945*), bibliographer and historian, was born in Iredell County, the son of Alexander and Eliza Hobbs Work, both slaves until the end of the Civil War. He was the youngest of eleven children, six girls and five boys. In 1866 Alexander Work moved to a farm near Cairo, Ill., where his family joined him in 1867.

In 1876 the Works moved to Sumner County, Kans., where Monroe completed his elementary education. As the youngest son, he worked on the family farm until the death of his mother in 1889, when at age twenty-three he entered high school in Arkansas City. An excellent student, he was graduated at the head of his class in 1892. After trying his hand at both teaching and preaching, he entered the Chicago Theological Seminary in 1895 and was graduated in 1898. Deciding that he was not intended to be a minister, he entered the University of Chicago, paying his way by working as a janitor. He took most of his courses in the social studies and received Ph.B. and M.A. degrees in 1902 and 1903, respectively.

In the fall of 1903 he became instructor of history and pedagogy at Georgia State Industrial College, in Savannah, where he remained until 1908. On 27 Dec. 1904 he married Florence Evelyn Henderson of Savannah.

While at the University of Chicago Work began research and writing in the field of Negro history and sociology with an article on "The Negro and Crime in Chicago," published in the *American Journal of Sociology* in September 1900. Continuing this interest at Savannah, he attracted the attention of Booker T. Washington, who invited him to join the faculty of Tuskegee Institute in Alabama.

In September 1908 Work became director of the Department of Records and Research at Tuskegee, a position he held until his retirement thirty years later. Charged with collecting, recording, and preserving the history of the Negro in America, he began in 1912 to publish *The Negro Yearbook*, a compilation of information and statistics on the Negro in America: economic, social, and historical. Of particular interest was his continued record of lynchings in the United States. Work wrote widely for periodicals and newspapers, especially the *Southern Workman*, published at Tuskegee, and the *Journal of Negro History*. He was also instrumental in 1915, along with Washington, in starting the annual Negro Health Week, an event later sponsored by the U.S. Public Health Service.

In 1928 Work published his major contribution to scholarly research, *Bibliography of the Negro in Africa and America*, which contained over 17,000 entries, including many rare items found in a tour of European libraries. A review of this work called it "the whole history of the Negro race in outline." The next year he received the William E. Harmon Award for the *Negro Year Book* and *Bibliography*. Among other honors, he was awarded the University of Chicago Alumni Citation (1942) and the D.Litt. degree from Howard University (1943). In 1942 Mrs. Betsy Graves Reyneau painted his portrait for the American Negro Citizens series.

At various times he was a member of the American Association for the Advancement of Science, American

Academy of Political and Social Science, American Economic Association, American Sociological Society, International Institute of American Language and Culture, Southern Economic Association, Southern Sociological Society, NAACP, and other organizations.

Work died at his home in Tuskegee and was buried in the cemetery on the campus. His wife died on 27 June 1955. They had no children.

SEE: Gussie P. Guzman, "Monroe Nathan Work and His Contributions," *Journal of Negro History* 34 (1949); Linda O. McMurry, *Recorder of the Black Experience* (1985); *New York Age*, 12 May 1945; *New York Times Book Review*, 25 Nov. 1928; James Preston, "Monroe Work: A Black Scholar at Tuskegee Institute, 1908–1945" (MSS, Tuskegee Institute Archives); E. E. Thorpe, *Black Historians* (1971); Monroe Nathan Work autobiographical sketch (Work Papers, Tuskegee Institute Archives).

E. D. JOHNSON

Worley, John (*d. between 8 Feb. and 3 Mar. 1741*), justice of the General Court and a member of the Council, flourished in what is now Tyrrell County from 1715 until the mid-1730s. He first appears in colonial records as a vestryman for the South West Parish in the Chowan Precinct of the colony in 1715; thereafter his name shows up with great regularity.

Worley was appointed a justice of the General Court in August 1716 and remained a member until November 1732. It seems, however, that he was not an impeccable, law-abiding model for the community; twice he was tried for assault (in 1716 and 1727), though acquitted both times. Colonial records also note in 1716 that he was accused of keeping one Mary Haskins (the wife of John Haskins) in his household, along with several illegitimate children. Worley admitted that Mary Haskins was indeed a member of his household, but only as a "hierling," and he made no mention of the children. Apparently he was a man of action as well as a judge.

The Worley name was quite prominent in the Chowan area; concurrent with his General Court membership, John Worley was a justice of the peace from 1716 to 1727, was appointed road overseer for the "lower district" of Chowan precinct in 1716 (a very important post at the time), and served as a colonel in the local militia. Despite his questionable decorum, he must have been held in some esteem as a learned man, for in 1716 John Swain signed an agreement with the judge placing his orphaned sister Elizabeth in Worley's service for an undetermined period in return for Worley's teaching her to read.

Little appears of his later activities, although he was a member of the Provincial Council from August 1726 to December 1730. His family is also seldom mentioned, but apparently one of his sons followed in his legal footsteps, as John Worley, Jr., is listed as a justice of the peace for Tyrrell County in March 1735.

During his lifetime Worley acquired a rather sizable estate. According to the 1735 quitrents, he paid taxes on 1,050 acres in Tyrrell County; his son, John, Jr., is listed for 840 acres, and his son Joshua held 390 acres. Worley drew up his will on 8 Feb. 1741, and it was recorded on 3 Mar. 1741. Survived by sons John, Jr., and Joshua, two daughters, Elizabeth Lurry and Penelope Wright, and a grandson, John Norcom, he was buried somewhere in present-day Tyrrell County.

SEE: Robert J. Cain, ed., *Records of the Executive Council, 1664–1734* (1984); J. R. B. Hathaway, ed., *North Carolina Historical and Genealogical Register*, vol. 1 (1900); William S.

Price, Jr., ed., *North Carolina Higher-Court Minutes, 1709–1723* (1977) and *1724–1730* (1981); William L. Saunders, ed., *Colonial Records of North Carolina*, vols. 1–2 (1886).

NEIL C. PENNYWITT

Worth, Daniel (*3 May 1795–12 Dec. 1862*), missionary and Abolitionist, the son of Job and Rhoda Macy Worth, was born in the Old Center Quaker community of Guilford County. Although a member of the Methodist church, he probably received his formal education from the Friends who constructed the first schoolhouse in southwestern Guilford County where Levi Coffin taught for several years during the period Worth would have been of school age. Coffin later became the chief engineer of the Underground Railroad.

Because of the Quaker discontent with slavery in North Carolina, many Friends moved to Indiana after that territory became a state in 1816. Worth, with his mother and father, joined this emigration and settled in Randolph County, Ind., in 1823. He served four terms in the lower house of the legislature (1825, 1825–26, 1827–28, and 1828–29) and three in the state senate (1829–30, 1830–31, 1831–32). He also was a justice of the peace in his county in 1835.

In 1840 Worth became the first president of the first State Anti-Slavery Society of Indiana. In 1842 he joined the Wesleyan Methodist church, and in September 1843 he was licensed to preach in that denomination. He became president of its General Conference in 1848 at the annual meeting in New York.

Politically Worth was anti-Jacksonian, supported the Liberty party in 1844 and the Free-Soil party in 1848, and then became a Republican. In 1844 and 1848 he lost his bid to serve as a presidential elector, and in 1845 he lost a race for Congress as well as for the state senate.

From Indiana he moved to Ohio in 1850 and on to Kentucky in 1853 to continue his antislavery work. Two years later he was back in Ohio as the pastor of a church with sixty to seventy former slaves who had escaped through the Underground Railroad. In 1856 he once again returned to Indiana as president of his church in that state.

After some doctrinal disagreements with several of the younger members of the Indiana Conference, Worth decided to return to North Carolina in the fall of 1857 as a missionary. It is unclear whether he was working for the Wesleyan Methodist church or the American Missionary Association. The latter group provided him with fifty copies of Hinton Rowan Helper's antislavery book, *The Impending Crisis of the South: How to Meet It*, as well as antislavery tracts to be distributed in North Carolina. Helper was also a native of North Carolina, and historians have described his book as "probably the most caustic, scathing, and vituperative criticism of slavery and slaveholders ever written."

Worth preached his first sermon in New Salem, Randolph County, N.C., on 8 Nov. 1857, to a "large and attentive congregation." For the next two years he continued to preach and distribute antislavery literature in an area of the state with a small slave population.

Finally, after many of the state's newspapers campaigned against him for being an Abolitionist, Worth was arrested on 22 Dec. 1859 by the sheriff of Guilford County for circulating incendiary material against slavery. Under the statute, this offense was punishable by one year in prison, and, at the discretion of the court, a whipping might be added. Worth was first tried and subsequently convicted on 30 Mar. 1860 in Asheboro and sentenced to twelve months in jail, but the court omitted the whipping. He appealed his conviction.

His second trial was held in Greensboro on 27 April. It took the jury only fifteen minutes to return a verdict of guilty. Again he was sentenced to prison for a year. However, he was permitted to appeal to the North Carolina Supreme Court and was released on a $3,000 bond. Worth forfeited the bond and escaped in a closed carriage to Virginia, where he boarded a train for New York. Arriving on 5 May, he announced that he had been permitted to escape from the "den of slavery." The next day, Sunday, 6 May, he began a series of speaking engagements to raise money to pay his bond in North Carolina. His first stop was Henry Ward Beecher's church, where Beecher declared that he was unworthy so much as to unfasten Worth's shoes. Soon afterwards the North Carolina Supreme Court upheld the Guilford County Superior Court's verdict in Worth's case, and by 6 August Worth had raised all the money to pay his bondsmen for their loss; the sum included a $50 donation from Hinton Rowan Helper.

Worth returned to Indiana and later was elected president of the Indiana Conference of the Wesleyan Methodist church, a post he retained for the few remaining months of his life.

Before leaving North Carolina as a young man, Worth was married in 1818 to Elizabeth Swain, by whom he was the father of eight children. She died in 1858, and the following year he married Huldah Cude. Worth died in Fountain City, Wayne County, Ind.

SEE: *A Biographical Directory of the Indiana General Assembly* (1980); Noble J. Tolbert, "Daniel Worth: Tar Heel Abolitionist," *North Carolina Historical Review* 39 (July 1962).

NOBLE J. TOLBERT

Worth, David Gaston *(18 Dec. 1831–21 Nov. 1897)*, merchant and state salt commissioner during the Civil War, was born in Asheboro, the only son of eight children of Jonathan and Martitia Daniel Worth. His father was state treasurer during the Civil War and governor during Reconstruction. Young Worth acquired his early education at his home in Asheboro. He entered The University of North Carolina at age seventeen and was graduated as one of the first honor men in the class of 1853. At Chapel Hill Worth was a member of Delta Kappa Epsilon fraternity, an association he continued for the rest of his life, contributing to the building and furnishing of the fraternity hall. He was a large contributor towards the construction of the alumni hall and in 1891 donated $500 to help in remodeling the university chapel.

Following graduation he entered the turpentine business in Harnett County, and in 1861 he moved to Wilmington to associate with his uncle, N. Green Daniel, his mother's younger brother, in the merchandise and commission business. The store of Worth and Daniel was located on Water Street between Princess and Chestnut. After Daniel's death in 1870, Worth became a partner with his uncle, Barzillai Gardner Worth, in the firm of Worth and Worth, a wholesale grocery business. Their store was destroyed by fire in February 1885, and a new store was designed and built by James F. Post at Nutt and Mulberry streets. Mulberry afterwards became Grace Street.

Active in civic affairs, Worth served as president of the Produce Exchange and of the Chamber of Commerce; for several years he was a member of the board of aldermen. He also belonged to the Wilmington Steam Fire Engine Company No. 1 and Wilmington Lodge No. 319 of the Ancient Free and Accepted Masons. He was associated with the YMCA and sat on the board of directors of the First National Bank.

In July 1863 Governor Zebulon B. Vance appointed him salt commissioner of North Carolina in place of his uncle, John Milton Worth, who had resigned. The State Salt Works, located at Myrtle Grove Sound, was about seven miles from Wilmington. He held this position until the end of the war. Also during the war he was the overseer of his sister Roxana's plantation in Harnett County, as her husband, John McNeill, had died in 1857.

In 1839 his father was one of five commissioners appointed to raise funds to establish a school for girls in Asheboro. One of the first teachers in this academy was Julia Anna Stickney. Born on 23 Oct. 1830 in Rockwell, N.Y., Julia was the daughter of William and Caroline A. Stevens Stickney. She attended an academy in Sandy Hills, N.Y., a seminary in Poultney, Vt., and Troy Female Seminary (later the Emma Willard School) in Troy, N.Y. David Gaston Worth and Julia Anna Stickney were married on 7 July 1853. They had eight children, of whom only three survived childhood: Charles William (1861–1930), who became associated with his father in business; Dr. George Clarkson (1867–1936), a medical missionary in China; and James Spenser (1869–1900). At one time the Worths lived at 410 South Second Street in Wilmington. Julia's brother, Henry Stickney, entered Wilmington in February 1865 with the 169th New York Volunteers, one of the first units of the Federal troops to enter the city. Another brother, Charles, was killed at South Mountain, Md., during the war.

The Worths were members of the First Presbyterian Church, and he was elected a deacon in 1864 and became a ruling elder in 1891. His funeral was held in the church, and both he and his wife, who died in 1911, were buried in Oakdale Cemetery, Wilmington. A memorial service was held for Worth at The University of North Carolina. He was characterized by an associate as "quiet, modest, conscientious."

SEE: Malcolm Fowler, *They Passed This Way* (1955); *North Carolina Biography*, vol. 5 (1919); Isabel M. Williams and Leora H. McEachern, *Salt: That Necessary Article* (1973); Wilmington *Evening Dispatch*, 22 Nov. 1897; *Wilmington Messenger*, 23 Nov. 1897; Julia A. Worth to David Gaston Worth, 27 Feb. 1865 (copy in possession of Leora Hiatt McEachern); Richard L. Zuber, *Jonathan Worth: A Biography of a Southern Unionist* (1965).

LEORA HIATT McEACHERN

Worth, John Milton *(28 June 1811–5 Apr. 1900)*, physician, businessman, and politician, was born near Center (Friends) Meetinghouse, Guilford County, the son of David and Abigail Gardner Worth. He was a descendant of John Carver, the first governor of Plymouth Colony, and of Tristam Coffin, who as a member of a small colony bought land from the Indians and became one of the first settlers of Nantucket Island off the coast of Massachusetts. Daniel Worth, the founder of the family in North Carolina, was born in Nantucket, Mass., and moved to North Carolina in 1739; settling at Center Meetinghouse, he became a substantial farmer. Daniel's son David, the father of John Milton Worth, studied medicine in Philadelphia and practiced in Guilford County. Like John Milton himself, four of his brothers—Jonathan, Thomas Clarkson, Joseph Addison, and Barzillai Gardner—became prominent businessmen in the state, and Jonathan also served as state treasurer (1862–65) and governor (1865–68). A first cousin was the Reverend Daniel Worth, the Methodist minister and Abolitionist who was jailed in Guilford County in the winter of 1859–60 and was twice convicted of circulating incendiary literature.

John Milton Worth received his early education in schools in the Guilford County area and studied medicine in Transylvania University (now College), in Lexington, Ky. After practicing briefly in Guilford he largely abandoned medicine for goldmining, farming, and merchandising in Montgomery County. While representing Montgomery and Moore counties in the state senate in 1842, 1844, and 1848, he strongly supported internal improvements and the common schools. Worth later moved to Randolph County, where his brother Jonathan already lived. Like Jonathan, he was a Whig. Until the outbreak of the Civil War he was strongly pro-Union but thereafter supported the Confederate cause.

During the early years of the war Worth served as salt commissioner for the state. He was also colonel of the Sixty-third Militia Regiment but resigned his commission on 20 Dec. 1861 in order to give his full attention to his duties as salt commissioner. In 1864, however, he became colonel of the Seventy-sixth North Carolina Regiment, then known as the Sixth, or Senior, Reserve. His principal task seems to have been that of apprehending army deserters and draft evaders.

In 1870 Worth was elected to represent Randolph and Moore counties in the state senate, where he voted to impeach Governor W. W. Holden. He was reelected in 1872. From 1876 to 1885 he served as state treasurer, leading in the settlement of the state's debts and in the revision of its tax laws. Meanwhile he continued to manage his private business interests, to which he gave his full energies after retiring from the state treasurership. He was president of the Bank of Randolph and of the Southern Stock Mutual Fire Insurance Company and served as head of the Worth Manufacturing Company, which had large cotton mills at Worthville and Central Falls in Randolph County. Like many of his family for several generations before him, Worth was a member of the Society of Friends.

In 1832 he married Sarah Dicks. Their son, Captain Shubal Gardner of the Nineteenth North Carolina Cavalry, was killed in battle near Richmond on 31 May 1864. Their grandson, Henry M., became a lumberman and cotton manufacturer. John Milton Worth died in Asheboro and was buried in the Asheboro city cemetery.

SEE: Samuel A. Ashe, ed., *Biographical History of North Carolina*, vol. 3 (1905 [portrait]); J. G. de Roulhac Hamilton, ed., *The Papers of William Alexander Graham*, vol. 2 (1959); *North Carolina Biography*, vol. 6 (1919); *Public Laws of the State of North Carolina, 1871–1872* (1872); *Raleigh Register*, 1842–63; Wilfred Buck Yearns, ed., *The Papers of Thomas Jordan Jarvis*, vol. 1 (1969); Richard L. Zuber, *Jonathan Worth: A Biography of a Southern Unionist* (1963).

W. CONARD GASS

Worth, Jonathan *(18 Nov. 1802–5 Sept. 1869)*, Civil War treasurer, Reconstruction governor, legislator, lawyer, planter, and businessman, was descended from a line of Quaker ancestors extending back to colonial Nantucket. The third child and second son of David and Eunice Gardner Worth, he was born at Center, on the northern edge of Randolph County. After attending neighborhood schools and the Greensboro Academy, he moved to Hillsborough in 1823 to study law under the eminent judge Archibald DeBow Murphey. Murphey became Worth's friend and mentor and exercised perhaps the greatest influence on him. The bond between the two men was strengthened when Worth married Murphey's niece, Martitia Daniel, in 1824. On completion of his studies with Murphey, Worth and his bride settled in Asheboro,

where he opened a law practice and lived until he moved to Raleigh in 1860.

Worth's political activity began as early as 1830 and continued throughout his life, but in the years prior to 1860 it was intermittent. He served in the House of Commons in 1830 and 1831 at the height of the Nullification crisis, at which time he set the tone of his political career by introducing resolutions denouncing the states' rights doctrine. In the 1830s, while not in public office, he developed a keen admiration for Henry Clay and the emerging program of the Whig party.

While serving in the state senate in 1840, Worth wrote the law that established the basic structure of the state's antebellum public school system. He then served as superintendent of schools in Randolph County for twenty years under the system he had written into the 1841 law. During the early 1840s he twice ran for Congress but was defeated on both occasions. In 1858 he returned again to the state senate, spending most of his time in an unseemly squabble over the operation of the North Carolina Railroad.

Worth's nonpolitical activities in the years between 1825 and 1860 were extensive and varied. His primary work was practicing law, but he was deeply involved in business, including the development of textile mills and the operation of several general stores. Also heavily involved in the movement for internal improvements, he served from 1856 to 1860 as general superintendent of the Fayetteville and Western Plank Road Company. Before the Civil War Worth owned and operated several farms. He found it necessary to use slaves but felt increasingly uneasy about the institution of slavery.

As a state senator during the secession crisis, Worth opposed the call of a convention to consider withdrawal from the Union and was one of only three men in the legislature who rejected the convention bill in its final form. After making a painful decision to support his state, Worth accepted the position of public treasurer in the administration of Governor Zebulon B. Vance. He administered the wartime financial legislation in an able, but conservative manner, frequently disagreeing with Confederate treasury officials over financial relations between the two governments. Detesting the war from beginning to end, he became deeply involved in a peace movement led by William W. Holden in 1863 and, especially, 1864. His final months as treasurer were spent in an effort to recover lost, displaced, and stolen property belonging to the state.

Under President Andrew Johnson's plan of Reconstruction, Worth was elected governor in the fall of 1865 and reelected in a regular ballot in 1866. Almost all of the work of his office was concerned with problems created by the war or with reestablishing North Carolina's former position in the Union. Civil government was restored rapidly, but Worth consistently opposed the presence of Federal troops in the state, particularly those connected with the Freedmen's Bureau. He deeply resented the role of the bureau's courts and argued at length with bureau officials over the administration of justice. He was almost equally concerned about continuing conflicts between former Secessionists and Unionists.

From 1866 until his removal in 1868 Worth fought against the programs of Reconstruction emerging from Washington, D.C. He loathed the Fourteenth Amendment and the Reconstruction Acts, passed early in 1867, which provided for military rule, a new state constitution, Negro suffrage, and elections to replace the existing government. In June 1868, after these arrangements were carried out, Worth was removed from office.

With his withdrawal from public life, Worth's health

declined rapidly. Following a futile sojourn at a spa in the Virginia mountains in the summer of 1869, he died and was buried in Oakwood Cemetery, Raleigh.

Worth and his wife Martitia had eight children: Rosana Cornelia (m. John McNeill of Cumberland County), Lucy Jane (m. Joseph John Jackson of Chatham County), David Gaston (m. Julia Stickney of Sandy Hills, N.Y.), Eunice Louisa (died unmarried), Elvira Evelyna (m. first, in 1856, Samuel Spencer Jackson [d. 1875], second Samuel Walker [d. after three months], and third, in 1883, E. N. Moffit), Sarah Corinne (m. first Dr. William Roberts of Edenton and second Dr. Hamilton C. Jackson of Chatham County), Adelaide Ann (m. William Henry Bagley of Perquimans County), and Mary Martitia (died unmarried).

SEE: Samuel A. Ashe, ed., *Biographical History of North Carolina*, vol. 3 (1906 [portrait]); J. G. de Roulhac Hamilton, ed., *Correspondence of Jonathan Worth*, 2 vols. (1909); Jonathan Worth Papers (Southern Historical Collection, University of North Carolina Library, Chapel Hill, and North Carolina State Archives, Raleigh); Richard L. Zuber, *Jonathan Worth: A Biography of a Southern Unionist* (1965).

RICHARD L. ZUBER

Worth, Kathryn (*23 Aug. 1898–20 Jan. 1969*), writer, was born at the family summer cottage at Wrightsville Beach, the youngest of three children of James Spencer (1869–1900) and Josephine McBryde Worth. Her brother was David Gaston Worth II, her sister Frances McBryde Worth. The Worths were English Quakers who went to North Carolina in 1771 from Nantucket, Mass. The McBrydes moved into the Laurinburg area about 1788 from Argylshire, Scotland. Kathryn Worth's maternal grandfather was Duncan D. McBryde, a prominent Presbyterian preacher; her great-grandfather on her father's side was Governor Jonathan Worth. In 1905 the James Worths moved from Wilmington to Davidson, and during 1910–12 they were in Europe, where the three children attended private schools in Geneva and Neuchâtel.

Kathryn Worth was graduated from Converse College in 1920 and, after a period of teaching and writing, did graduate work at Radcliffe College in 1922; she received a bachelor of letters from the Pulitzer School of Journalism, Columbia University, in 1923. Soon she began publishing in national periodicals. On 27 July 1927 she married Walter Clyde Curry, professor of English at Vanderbilt University, and made her home in Nashville, Tenn. After the birth of her only child, Josephine (Mrs. Harold McNatt), her writing activity increased, with hundreds of poems appearing in a wide variety of publications. *Sign of Capricornus* (1937) is a book of poetry in which, she said, she "attempted to interpret metaphysically and intellectually the half world of very young childhood, as I have observed it in my daughter," who, at age eight, "memorized the poems as they were written; and though she does not wholly understand their meaning, she is very proud of them."

When Josephine asked her mother for a book she could "understand" as well as "memorize," Kathryn Worth wrote *The Middle Button* (1941), a juvenile novel using as its setting the Cumberland County home (Linden) of her mother's people and narrating the story of a Scottish girl in 1883 who wants to become a doctor. *They Loved to Laugh* (1942) recalls the Guilford County boyhood of Governor Worth in 1831–33, its central character a shy girl among five boys in a household of thrifty, fun-loving Quakers. After *Poems for Josephine* (1943), a collection of verses for children, came *New Worlds for Josie* (1944), a juvenile novel

of two American sisters in a Geneva boarding school. *Sea Change* (1948), a love story for teenagers, comes to grips with religious prejudice on the Carolina seacoast in 1893; in it a southern girl decides to accept the attentions of an attractive Irish Catholic boy who had come to an unfriendly region to help in the building of a bridge.

Kathryn Worth was a Democrat and a Presbyterian. She was buried in the churchyard of Dials Church, near Fountain Inn, S.C.

SEE: *North Carolina Authors* (1952); William S. Powell, ed., *North Carolina Lives* (1962); Richard Walser, *Young Readers' Picturebook of Tar Heel Authors* (1966); *Who's Who in the South and Southwest* (1950); Frances McBryde Worth (Greensboro) to Richard Walser, 20 Apr. 1974 (Richard Walser Papers, Southern Historical Collection, University of North Carolina, Chapel Hill).

RICHARD WALSER

Worth, William Henry (*13 July 1839–6 Feb. 1931*), Farmers Alliance leader, was born on a farm in the Polecat Creek community in Guilford County. His parents, Hiram Coffin and Phebe (or Phoebe) Henley Worth, were devout Quakers of moderate affluence. When the boy was three years old, the family moved to Greensboro, twelve miles from their rural home.

After attending the local free school, Worth completed his studies at New Garden Boarding School (now Guilford College) from 1854 to 1856. He then worked as a carpenter to pay for his education. In 1860 he moved to Company Shops (now Burlington), where he was employed as a clerk in the mercantile establishment of the John M. Worth and Company, a firm owned by relatives and managed by his brother Daniel. He left this position when the Civil War began, declined military service because of his Quaker convictions, and worked for the North Carolina Railroad Company at Company Shops until the conflict ended.

After serving as assessor of internal revenue for the Third North Carolina District from 1866 to 1870, Worth moved eastward to Lenoir County where he farmed successfully for nearly twenty years. A pioneer member of the North Carolina Farmers Alliance on its organization in 1887, he served first as business sub-agent, then in 1889 as business agent for Lenoir County, and finally as state business agent until 1894, when he resigned to run for political office. As a Populist (he later became a Republican), he was nominated for state treasurer on the Fusion ticket and won the office. Reelected in 1896, he served until 1900, when he was defeated by Benjamin R. Lacy. At the end of his last term, it was discovered that one of his subordinates was $12,000 short in his accounts. When Worth learned of the matter, though not legally required to do so, he made good the loss with his own funds at great personal sacrifice. He then retired to the old family home in Guilford County where he lived for the rest of his life.

Worth was a faithful member of the Pomona Friends Meeting for many years and in 1899 was elected a trustee of Guilford College, a position in which he served until nearly the end of his life. He spent much of his time in horticulture, and his garden, orchard, and vineyard became local showplaces. In 1927 a grateful state paid a tribute to his honesty by returning the $12,000 he had advanced two decades earlier to cover his clerk's shortage. Though Worth had sought no inducement, he accepted the gift with gratitude.

On 25 Apr. 1877 Worth married Samie M. Henley, and they became the parents of Hiram C. and Eunice L. (Mrs.

Charles D. Roberts), both of Greensboro, Ruth M. (Mrs. Charles W. Petty) of Clinton, and Annie Henley (Mrs. Smith) of Westfield, Ind. He died at his Greensboro home and was buried in New Garden Cemetery at Guilford College.

SEE: Samuel A. Ashe, ed., *Biographical History of North Carolina*, vol. 3 (1906); John L. Cheney, Jr., ed., *North Carolina Government, 1585–1974* (1975); R. D. W. Connor, *North Carolina: Rebuilding an Ancient Commonwealth*, vol. 2 (1929); *Greensboro Daily News*, 25 Apr. 1926, 22 May 1927, 7 Feb. 1931; William Wade Hinshaw, *Encyclopedia of American Quaker Genealogy* (1969).

DURWARD T. STOKES

Worthington, Samuel Wheeler (*28 Nov. 1875–14 Jan. 1956*), businessman and bibliophile, was born in Bertie County, the son of Colonel Dennison and Julia Wheeler Worthington, a niece of the historian John H. Wheeler. He attended The University of North Carolina (1893–95), and during his lifetime he was involved in various occupations and pastimes. His primary means of earning a livelihood, however, seems to have been in the mercantile field. The Wilson city directory for 1912–13 lists him as a general salesman. Then in 1924, as owner of the Dixie Land Company, he was regarded as a pioneer promoter of Dare County coastal property. In 1947–48 the Wilson directory identified him as a manufacturer's agent.

A knowledgeable book collector, Worthington frequently advertised for titles that he wanted to acquire. He once reported that Bruce Cotten, a noted collector of North Caroliniana, had inspired his interest in "the colorful history and hallowed traditions" of the state. In 1939 he prepared the manuscript for a book that he proposed to publish in a limited edition. The manuscript, now in the North Carolina Collection at the University of North Carolina at Chapel Hill, is entitled "Historic Glimpses of North Carolina: A Pictorial Review of the History, Memorials, Shrines, Public Buildings, Mansions, and Personages of North Carolina during the Colonial and Ante-Bellum Periods." Some of the photographic illustrations, he noted, had been made by himself; others were acquired from libraries and archives. Some of the text appears to have been researched, and some was based on his own knowledge.

Worthington published an undated illustrated pamphlet entitled *Ancient and Rare North Caroliniana: A Brief Resume of Some of the Early and Rare Publications on North Carolina from 1424 to 1929*. It contains no indication of its purpose—whether he was seeking to buy or to sell the publications it describes. The pamphlet was attractively designed and printed and undoubtedly has become a rarity itself.

On 7 Dec. 1899 Worthington married Lucy Roscoe Outlaw, and they had a son, Samuel Wheeler, Jr. His funeral was conducted at St. Timothy's Episcopal Church, Wilson, and he was buried in Maplewood Cemetery.

SEE: Daniel L. Grant, *Alumni History of the University of North Carolina* (1924); Raleigh *News and Observer*, 16 Jan. 1956.

WILLIAM S. POWELL

Wrenn, Manleff Jarrell (*25 Aug. 1858–18 Feb. 1934*), pioneer furniture manufacturer in High Point, was born near Liberty in Randolph County, the son of Merritt C. and Nancy Elizabeth Jarrell Wrenn. His father, a farmer, was a Confederate soldier in the medical department who died in Raleigh near the end of the war. His mother, who was educated in the New Garden Boarding School, suffered many hardships rearing her two sons; her daughter died in childhood. When her sons were still young, she sold the farm and moved to the small town of High Point, where they attended school and Manleff worked in his uncle's hotel and clerked in a grocery store.

At age twenty-two Wrenn invested his meager savings in the grocery business that he continued to operate until 1888. His brother, Thomas F., joined J. H. Tate and E. A. Snow in organizing the High Point Furniture Company. Soon Manleff acquired Snow's interest, and by 1898 he had obtained the shares of the other partners as well. This was the first furniture factory in the town, and as the sole owner of a flourishing enterprise, Wrenn began to expand his business interests. He became a director of the Atlantic Bank and Trust Company, half owner of the Wrenn-Columbia Furniture Company, and a stockholder in the Southern Furniture Exposition Building. He also was president of the North State Telephone Company from 1921 until his death. He was buried in Oakwood Cemetery, High Point.

Wrenn, a Democrat, was an alderman of High Point for seven years and mayor for four, as well as a steward in the Methodist Episcopal Church, South. In 1928 he was a delegate to the Democratic National Convention in Houston, Tex. On 11 June 1918 he married Louise Clinard, a graduate of the North Carolina State Normal School. On his death she became head of the High Point Furniture Company, and in 1937 she donated the M. J. Wrenn Memorial Library to High Point College.

SEE: *Greensboro Daily News*, 20 Feb. 1934; *North Carolina Biography*, vols. 5 (1919), 3 (1928), 5 (1941); Ray J. Shipman, *High Point: A Pictorial History* (1983 [portrait]); *Who's Who in the South* (1927).

WILLIAM S. POWELL

Wrenn, Thomas F. (*10 Sept. 1860–31 May 1940*), manufacturer and financier, was born near Liberty in Randolph County, the son of Merritt C. and Nancy Elizabeth Jarrell Wrenn. His father, a Confederate soldier, died near the end of the Civil War, and his mother reared their two sons, Thomas F. and Manleff J.; their daughter died in childhood. While her sons were still young, Nancy Wrenn moved to the small settlement of High Point where they attended school.

In 1888 Wrenn joined J. H. Tate and E. A. Snow in organizing the High Point Furniture Company, the first furniture plant in the town. Snow soon sold his interest in the business to Wrenn's brother, Manleff, as did Tate. In 1898, when he moved to Marion, Thomas also sold his share to Manleff. For many years Thomas Wrenn owned the Catawba Furniture Company in Marion and later also bought the Wrenn Hosiery Company in Thomasville.

On 10 Aug. 1898 Wrenn married Sadie Elizabeth Weedon, who died on 18 May 1909. In 1912 he married Mrs. Pearl Pitts Perry; she died on 24 Jan. 1930. Wrenn was in New York City for an operation on 22 May 1940 and died there after a short illness. He was buried in Marion.

SEE: Holt McPherson, *High Pointers of High Point* (1975 [portrait]); *Marion Progress*, 6 June 1940; Raleigh *News and Observer*, 1 June 1940.

WILLIAM S. POWELL

Wright, Charles Calvin (*14 Aug. 1862–14 July 1933*), educator, school administrator, and religious and civic leader, was born on a small farm at Hunting Creek in Wilkes County and lived there all of his life. His great-grandfather, Thomas Wright, emigrated from England in the early eighteenth century and settled in Surry County, which he later represented in both the lower house and senate of North Carolina. Wright was also a lineal descendant of Benjamin Cleveland, a Revolutionary war general who distinguished himself in the Battle of Kings Mountain. His grandfather, William W. Wright, moved to Hunting Creek in Wilkes County and served as a tax collector and justice of the peace until resettling in Alabama, where Wright's father, James W., was born on 28 Feb. 1826. In 1836 the family returned to North Carolina, and James Wright became a rural schoolteacher in Wilkes County. He later married Frances (Fannie) A. Transou, a descendant on her father's side of French Huguenots who had moved to Germany to escape religious persecution and there joined a group of Moravians who migrated to Pennsylvania. About 1760 the Transous moved to Bethania, N.C., and settled in the area around Salem.

In 1862 Wright's father joined Company C of the Twenty-sixth North Carolina Regiment of the Confederate army. He was wounded in Pickett's Charge on the third day of the Battle of Gettysburg; later he was captured and imprisoned at Point Lookout, Md., where he died in January 1865. At the time of his father's death, Wright, an only child, was unhealthy and less than three years old. His mother, who lived until 18 May 1907, cared for him and taught him to read. His only formal education came from the county's private schools, but he read voraciously in his youth and gradually acquired a considerable personal library. In later life he asserted that work on the family farm, which was "good for both body and mind," and the reading of "the lives of those who through adverse circumstances had won for themselves a name" had inspired him and shaped his character.

At seventeen Wright began his long teaching career in the public schools of Wilkes County. Before age twenty-one he was appointed postmaster of Hunting Creek but resigned because of his youth. At twenty-one he was elected justice of the peace, an office he held for ten years. After sixteen years as a teacher he was elected county school superintendent. He also served as president of the Wilkes County Teachers Association and of the West Central District Association of County Superintendents, and he was a member of the County Board of Education, State Board of School Examiners, State Text Book Commission, Library Commission, and executive committee of the State Teachers Association.

It was in his role as a county school administrator, however, that Wright made his greatest contribution to his community and to the emerging professional status of public school educators. In 1900 the Wilkes school system consisted of a few log and unpainted frame buildings, as well as an insufficient number of inadequately trained and paid teachers; it had no libraries. During his thirty-four-year tenure the county made great strides in public education due to Wright's tireless efforts to obtain better facilities, improved teaching methods, more qualified teachers, and adequate textbooks and libraries. He served as Wilkes County school superintendent until one month before his death.

Wright, who supplemented his income as a teacher through farming, was active in several farmers' organizations. During the late 1880s and early 1890s he was one of the relatively small number of lecturers and organizers who rapidly built the Farmers Alliance into a powerful force in North Carolina politics and economics. He was the first corresponding secretary of the Hunting Creek Farmers Sub-alliance, then president of the Sub-alliance,

president of the Wilkes County Farmers Alliance, and steward of the North Carolina Farmers State Alliance. In 1891 he traveled throughout western North Carolina as assistant district lecturer for the Alliance, recruiting members and promoting its program.

In 1890 he ran for the state senate on the Democratic ticket with Alliance support but lost in his heavily Republican county. Unlike many Alliancemen he did not join the People's party, and in 1896 he again ran as a Democrat for the senate and was unsuccessful. After the demise of the Alliance Wright joined the Farmers Union and held local and national offices in that organization. In 1915, as chairman of the union's National Education Committee, he helped organize a campaign to encourage greater consumption of cotton products. During this period he also was a member of the State Board of Agriculture.

At the Edgewood Baptist Church Wright was a deacon for over twenty years and superintendent of the Sunday school until his son took over the post in 1933. In 1913 he helped found the Mountain View Institute, a private school later supported by the Baptists. Beginning in 1905 and continuing for over twenty years, he served as moderator of the Brushy Mountain Baptist Association, and after 1917 he sat on the board of trustees of the Baptist orphanage at Thomasville.

On 23 Sept. 1891 Wright married Jennie Katharine Land, the daughter of Colonel J. C. Land. She also taught in the Wilkes County public schools and assisted in the work of the county superintendent's office. The Wrights had five children. The oldest, Mary Dorris, died on 10 Apr. 1913 just after completing high school. The remaining four children were James C., David R., Robert C., and Charles Calvin, Jr. Wright was buried in the Edgewood Baptist Church cemetery in Wilkes County.

SEE: J. Jay Anderson, *Wilkes County Sketches* (1976); Johnson J. Hayes, *The Land of Wilkes* (1962); *North Carolina Biography*, vol. 4 (1929); Raleigh *Progressive Farmer*, 4 Feb., 5 Aug. 1890, 12 May, 7 July, 3 Nov. 1891, 5 Jan., 31 May 1892; Charles Calvin Wright to Reuben Dean Bowen, 29 Jan. 1915 (Bowen Collection, Manuscript Department, Duke University Library, Durham); C. C. Wright questionnaire (Charles L. Van Noppen Papers, Manuscript Department, Duke University Library, Durham).

LOIS S. SELF

Wright, Claiborne *(1810–6 Mar. 1836)*, Alamo defender, was born in North Carolina, perhaps the son of Henrietta Claiborne (1754–1810) and William Wright (1752–1827), natives, respectively, of King William County and Fauquier County, Va., who moved to Surry County, N.C., in 1774. Young Claiborne Wright traveled to Texas, possibly to visit a family of the same name who lived at Pecan Point in Red River County. Eventually he settled in Gonzales, Tex., and enlisted as a private in the Texas army. On 29 Feb. 1836 he accompanied a group of thirty-one other Gonzales residents to San Antonio de Bexar to aid in the defense of the Alamo. The force arrived at San Antonio on 1 March and entered the Alamo under the cover of darkness that night. Wright died five days later when the besieged Alamo fell to the armies of General Antonio López de Santa Anna.

On 25 June 1851 the state of Texas awarded Wright's heirs a bounty of 1,920 acres of public land "for his having fallen with Travis in the Alamo." In 1860 the acreage of the land grant was doubled.

SEE: Robert F. Cole (Miami, Fla.) to Nathaniel C. Hale (Philadelphia), 10 Jan. 1956 (possession of Dr. Claiborne T.

Smith, Ardmore, Pa.); State of Texas, *General Land Office Files* (1851, 1860); Lon Tinkle, *The Alamo* (1958); Amelia W. Williams, "A Critical Study of the Seige of the Alamo and the Personnel of Its Defenders," *Southwestern Historical Quarterly* 37 (1933–34).

R. H. DETRICK

Wright, David Minton *(21 Apr. 1809–23 Oct. 1863),* physician, remembered because of the regrettable circumstances surrounding his death, was born in Nansemond County, Va., the son of David Minton (1775–1813) and Mary Armistead Wright (1777–1817). He received his earliest education locally and then, at a suitable age, was sent to the military school of Captain Patrick in Middletown, Conn. After completing its program, he moved to Edenton, N.C., to study medicine under Dr. William Warren, the father of the noted physician Dr. Edward Warren. Subsequently he entered the medical department of the University of Pennsylvania, where he received a doctor of medicine degree about 1833. Following further training at the hospital in Philadelphia, he settled in Edenton and joined the practice of William Warren, an association that lasted for eighteen years. During his second year in Edenton Wright married Penelope Margaret Creecy (1816–89).

In 1854 he moved to Norfolk, Va., for the better advantages that city offered his growing family. Wright soon established a large and lucrative practice. When an epidemic of yellow fever struck the city the next year, he remained steadfast at his post. All of his family and servants remained in the city with him as he worked tirelessly to aid the sick. Wright himself fell victim of the scourge but fortunately recovered "through the kind nursing of his loving companions, his indomitable will and the skill of his physicians, in the providence of God."

By the eve of the Civil War Wright's reputation as a skilled physician, a gentleman, and a useful citizen was well established. As war appeared inevitable, he, like thousands of other Southerners, was a staunch Union man. It was said that "as long as he could do so consistently with loyalty to his State and people, he used his influence to prevent war and to bring about a peaceful settlement of the dispute between the sections." With the final break, however, he became a firm supporter of the Confederacy, and two of his sons joined the army.

When Federal troops entered Norfolk on 10 May 1862, the noncombatant citizens were permitted to carry on undisturbed and peacefully. As a physician Wright was accorded the same privileges. This changed for him on 11 July 1863. There are numerous accounts of the precise events of that afternoon on the sidewalk of Main Street. Reports by Wright, his friends, and other witnesses do not conform to the findings of army investigators. Although civil government in Norfolk was presumed to operate, the city actually was under military authority, and it was the military, not the civil government, that interpreted the events of the day and that determined the fate of Dr. Wright.

According to the newspapers, Wright was walking on the sidewalk near his home when he met a column of Negro troops occupying the entire walk, "jostling men, women and children into the gutter."

"Dr. Wright stepped aside," it was reported, "and as he did so, in the heat of his indignation he uttered some sharp exclamation of contempt and disgust. A white lieutenant, A. L. Sanborn, heard this and advanced on Dr. Wright with sword drawn and threatening." The doctor was unarmed, but a friend who saw his danger handed him a pistol.

With the weapon held behind his back but facing Sanborn, Wright stood still as he called out "Stand off!" to the advancing lieutenant.

Eyewitnesses stated that Sanborn continued to advance and the doctor fired a single shot, striking the lieutenant in the hand. Sanborn called on his troops to assist in making an arrest, and "there was a short, hot altercation," a newspaper reported. "The feeling against negroes in United States uniform was then intensely bitter, especially among the older men who had been brought up to honor the army and the flag it represented."

Several shots were fired, but by whom was never known. Sanborn was hit again and "clinched" with Wright, who was said to have put the pistol to Sanborn's breast for a moment but did not fire. Negro troops rushed in with fixed bayonets but were turned aside, whereupon Sanborn relaxed his hold and fell dead into the adjacent store.

Wright was immediately arrested and tried by a military commission. During the course of the trial various points were made—that the military had no authority when a civilian was involved and there was a civil government in Norfolk, the fatal shot may well have been fired by someone else (even one of the troops), or insanity might have been pled. Various routes were followed with appeals to both civil and military authorities, even to the president of the United States, but, as Wright observed early in the proceedings, it had been determined that he was guilty before the first evidence was considered.

And indeed he was found guilty and hanged. He thereby came to be considered a martyr to the Southern cause and a hero. When Federal forces occupied Petersburg, where his wife had taken refuge, she moved to Chapel Hill, N.C., but in time returned to Virginia.

Dr. Wright's children were Elizabeth Minton, David Minton, Penelope Margaret, Minton Augustus, Elizabeth Minton, Mary Creecy Armistead, Joshua Creecy Armistead, Sarah Jordan Armistead, William Armistead, and Viola Jessica. Minton A. was killed at Gettysburg, but word of this was kept from Wright. Descendants of the family still lived in the region in the late twentieth century, keeping alive the memory of David Minton Wright.

While he was in prison awaiting final word as to his fate, the long-anticipated wedding of one of Wright's daughters was held in the prison so that he could give the bride away. Also while confined, he was baptized and received communion. He was visited often and for long periods of time by several clergymen of various denominations in Norfolk. Wright constructed his own coffin, of cypress wood, presumably while in prison. Inside the top were hung daguerreotypes of his wife and children. Initially Federal officials were reluctant to release his body to the family but eventually relented. Attending his funeral in Christ Church, Norfolk, was an overflow crowd, while hundreds of mourners lined the route to the cemetery. At the time of his execution and funeral the day was dark, rainy, and dismal.

SEE: Beth G. Crabtree and James W. Patton, eds., *"Journal of a Secesh Lady": The Diary of Catherine Ann Devereux Edmondston, 1860–1866* (1979); *"Expunged from the Record": David Minton Wright, M.D., 1809–1863* (a reprint from *Richmond News*, Richmond, Va., 10 May 1901); Ervin Leon Jordan, Jr., "A Painful Case: The Wright-Sanborn Incident in Norfolk, Virginia, July–October, 1863" (master's thesis, Old Dominion University, 1979); Norfolk *Landmark*, 31 Dec. 1892.

WILLIAM S. POWELL

Wright, Gideon (*ca. 1726–82*), Loyalist, one of the prominent men in early North Carolina who stood for law and order, was the son of John and Ruth Ludlam Wright. Gideon and his brother, Hezekiah, served in the French and Indian War in the colony of New York before moving to North Carolina. It was customary in each county to hold the court in the center of the county, and a man who had a house near the center and enough friends or a bit of influence could usually determine where the courthouse would be located. In 1771 Wright got the jump on his neighbors, the Armstrongs, and determined the location of the county seat of newly established Surry County. The legislative act authorized Gideon Wright to build the courthouse. The land on which it was located belonged to him and had been included in a grant from the Earl Granville in 1762.

Wright was a justice of the peace, and it was on his land that a muster ground had been reserved. The pendulum of power did not stop with this important local decision, however, but continued to swing. When it did, the Wright site, after four years as the courthouse, was abandoned. The Armstrong family was then in the ascendancy, and the recently built courthouse was abandoned and a new one authorized two miles north where a new town to be named Richmond was being formed.

During the Regulator uprising, Gideon Wright sided with Governor William Tryon and rose to the rank of colonel. When the American Revolution began, he remained loyal to the Crown. In January 1776 Governor Josiah Martin authorized him to erect the king's standard, to enlist and arm the loyal subjects of Surry County, and "to oppose all rebels and traitors." During the war Wright led the Tories at the Battle of Shallow Ford on 14 Oct. 1780. Land owned by both Gideon and his brother, Giery Wright, was confiscated after the war. Both men must have operated very cautiously, however, as they seem not otherwise to have been punished. Gideon was able to purchase 200 more acres of land at the very time land of Tories was being confiscated.

Wright died near the end of 1782. In 1790 his widow, Elizabeth Durling Wright, listed 69 acres for taxation, and in 1791 she and her son, Hezekiah, deeded the land to Leonard Scott. The other Wright children were Sarah, Elizabeth, Susannah, and Catherine. By inheritance the land passed to John W. Scott and then to his children, Wiley and Cora (m. Hoke Petree). The site of the early Wright courthouse was on land owned by the Petree family in the late twentieth century. The only evidence remaining of the early county power struggle was a depression in the ground where the courthouse cellar had been, together with a pile of stones that had once been the chimney of the Wright home. Nearby is the family burial ground.

Descendants of the Wright family continued to live in the community and took more than a passing interest in the fate of the newer courthouse. In August 1830 a cyclone destroyed the town, and the site was abandoned.

SEE: Walter Clark, ed., *State Records of North Carolina*, vols. 14 (1896), 22 (1907); Adelaide L. Fries, ed., *Records of the Moravians in North Carolina*, vols. 1–4 (1922–30); Hester Bartlett Jackson, ed., *The Heritage of Surry County, N.C.*, vol. 1 (1983); William S. Powell, ed., *The Correspondence of William Tryon and Other Selected Papers*, vol. 2 (1981); Alonzo Oakland, *Biographical Sketches of Loyalists in the American Revolution*, vol. 2 (1864); William L. Saunders, ed., *Colonial Records of North Carolina*, vols. 9, 10 (1890).

FRANK SALTER

Wright, Marion Allen (*18 Jan. 1894–14 Feb. 1983*), attorney, citizen of the two Carolinas, and firm supporter of civil rights, was born in Johnston, Edgefield County, S.C., the youngest of ten children of Confederate veteran Preston and Octavia Watson Wright. Both parents died before his sixth birthday, and he was reared by an older sister, Mabel, and her husband, William D. Holland, who lived in nearby Trenton. U.S. Senator Benjamin Ryan Tillman was a neighbor of the Hollands, and as a teenager Wright stayed in the Tillman home as protector for Mrs. Tillman and the daughters during the senator's frequent trips from home. The Tillman library was well stocked with the classics, and young Marion was encouraged to make use of its holdings. The Hollands were unenthusiastic about their ward's association with Senator Tillman because of his use of profanity and the fact that while governor he had instituted the dispensary system for state control of liquor sales; his racial views disturbed them not at all.

At sixteen Wright enrolled in the University of South Carolina, and at that tender age there was little to indicate that his future would be so dedicated to justice, tolerance, and the protection of human rights. True, as a boy he had witnessed racial incidents that had left an impression, but it was at the university and in the city of Columbia that his social conscience was fully awakened. By his own admission Wright was an indifferent student, but classes with President Samuel Chiles Mitchell and Professor Josiah Morse exerted a tremendous influence in shaping his outlook on society. President Mitchell in his political science class focused the attention of his students on the need for better public schools, the establishment of public library facilities, and the provision for public health agencies. Morse, a Jew who taught one of the first courses offered in the South dealing with race relations, openly criticized discrimination and prejudice of any kind. Wright became a friend and admirer of both men.

Also important was Wright's experience while working as a part-time reporter for the Columbia *Record* at a time when the Ku Klux Klan was particularly active in espousing anti-Jewish and anti-Catholic sentiments. Through friendship with his supervisor at the *Record*, William Carmack, a Catholic, Wright came to realize the prejudice faced by members of that religious body. But of more significance in the development of his social conscience were assignments by the *Record* to witness and report on the first sixteen electrocutions at the state penitentiary, a practice begun in 1912; thirteen blacks and three whites were the victims. The experience was revolting and explains why in later years Wright spent untold hours supporting efforts to abolish capital punishment.

Wright left the university in 1914 without receiving a degree. Moving to Winston-Salem, he worked with his brother in the real estate and insurance business, according to a statement he made in a 1978 interview. Arnold Shankman reported that the time was spent teaching school. The answer probably is that Wright did both. While living in Winston-Salem he married Lelia Hauser, and in 1916 the couple moved to Columbia, S.C.; Wright entered the university's law school, and his wife was employed by August Kohn, a prominent Jewish resident for whom both developed affection and respect.

After obtaining a law degree in 1919, Wright moved to Conway, S.C. There, and later in nearby Myrtle Beach, he established offices for what developed into a highly successful practice of corporate and business law. Conway's black population was small, but Wright soon took note of the unpaved streets in the black section of town, the lack of sanitary facilities available to Negroes, and the limits placed on their use of the Conway hospital. These facts moved him steadily forward in his commitment to equal treatment for all citizens. Wright was a gifted speaker, and as opportunities arose he began to call for justice to Negroes and the establishment of public libraries, and to express disapproval of the death penalty.

In 1919, shortly before or after settling in Conway, he was invited to deliver the commencement address to the high school seniors. Speaking on civil rights, he stated that black Americans should be allowed to vote in the Democratic primary and to serve on juries. These remarks received a cool reception, and following the exercises the chairman of the school board challenged Wright's views. To the credit of both, the gentleman later became a friend and valued client of Wright. In 1927 Wright accepted the invitation extended by citizens of Marion to be the speaker for the Memorial Day observance on 10 May. After paying due tribute to the Confederate dead, he declared that the time had come "when the political rights of the Negro must have ample protection"; no people could reach their full potential when deprived of political rights, he observed.

Neither these addresses nor other forthright expressions of his views appear to have affected Wright's popularity or to have diminished the esteem with which he was held. He was elected president of the University of South Carolina Alumni Association (1935–37) and served a term as president of the university's Law School Alumni Association. Such evidences of confidence and tolerance can best be explained by Wright's obvious ability, the wit and charm that characterized his handling of controversial issues, and his magnificent power of personal persuasion.

His championship of equal rights for all citizens, justice that is color blind, and abolition of the death penalty are common knowledge, but less known is the support he gave to public libraries. To him librarians were an indispensable agency in the education of the citizenry, and in the 1930s he joined wholeheartedly with a loosely organized group of South Carolinians known as the Citizens Library Association to promote library service. He was elected president of that organization and later became chairman of the South Carolina Library Board. South Carolinians are indebted to Marion Wright, as much as to any other person, for the evolution of small, locally operated, inadequate libraries into an effective statewide system. His interest in libraries and his belief in the importance of education led him to serve for a term as chairman of the South Carolina Commission on Adult Education. Furthermore, such interest did not end with retirement; after moving to North Carolina Wright opened his personal library, with its books and wide list of newspaper and magazine subscriptions, to the school children of Linville Falls.

In 1919, during the dark days of racial conflict and Ku Kluxism that followed World War I, the Commission on Interracial Cooperation was born. A number of southern liberals gave it their support, and in 1944 members from this group organized the Southern Regional Council with the primary objective of promoting racial justice. Many of these men and women believed in all honesty that the race problem could be solved through separate but truly equal facilities for schools, hospitals, rest rooms, and parks. Wright disagreed. He regarded it a waste of time and talent to teach the ABCs and multiplication tables separately to white and black children. To his well-meaning friends he posed the question of morality in expecting some citizens to await future delivery of their natural rights. In November 1945 Wright became a member of the board of the Southern Regional Council and was reelected continuously for some thirty years; from 1952 until late 1958 he was president of the council. After serving on the council's board and executive committee, he was honored with the title Life Fellow.

Wright's concern for educational opportunities for Negroes undoubtedly prompted his interest in Penn School, located on St. Helena Island off the South Carolina coast. He was a member of its board of trustees in 1947 and 1948 and chairman of the board from 1965 to 1971. For over three-quarters of a century Penn Normal, Industrial, and Agricultural School had operated as the educational agency for blacks living on the island, but in May 1948, following a study and recommendations by Dr. Ira DeA. Reid, the trustees decided to relinquish responsibility for the academic program to the state and to abandon the farm program. At the same time the name was changed to Penn Community Services, and future emphasis was to be on support of the island's economic development, with continued assistance for the improvement of public health facilities.

In 1947 Wright retired from the practice of law and moved to Linville Falls, N.C. By this move North Carolina gained a citizen who for the next three decades would be active in behalf of civil rights, efforts to abolish the death penalty, the support of public libraries, and the cause of equal educational opportunities for all. He became a member of the national board of the American Civil Liberties Union and of North Carolina's first State Advisory Committee to the U.S. Civil Rights Commission, and he continued his membership in the NAACP. In 1969 the North Carolina Civil Liberties Union presented him with the Frank Porter Graham Award. Yet no cause was closer to Wright's heart than abolition of the death penalty; becoming founder and first president of North Carolinians against the Death Penalty, he worked diligently for the remainder of his life to secure passage of the necessary legislation.

Lelia Wright died in October 1956, and Marion Wright remained a widower until 1970, when he married Alice Norwood Spearman, a widow with whom he had been associated as a fellow member of the South Carolina Advisory Committee for the Civil Rights Commission. Alice Wright shared her husband's devotion to civil rights and in 1973 was herself the recipient of the Frank Porter Graham Award. Wright died a few weeks after his eighty-ninth birthday, and his body was willed to the Duke University Medical School.

Though a man of deep religious feelings, Wright was not a member of any church. Detailed information about his private life, as well as the dates related to his public career, are in many instances difficult to establish. Information such as an entry in *Who's Who in America* would have contained must have seemed unimportant to him; until the end his chief concern was the establishment of fair treatment under law for all mankind and the removal of any statute that denied basic civil rights to any citizen.

Wright gave the bulk of his papers to the Southern Historical Collection of The University of North Carolina library; they consist largely of correspondence with the various agencies with which he was associated either by interest or membership, plus copies of his numerous speeches. Additional folders contain correspondence with his brother, Preston, his sisters, Helen and Kathleen, and his nephews. The Dacus Library of Winthrop College and the South Caroliniana Library of the University of South Carolina each hold smaller groups of Marion A. Wright Papers. Within the three collections there is some duplication.

SEE: *Asheville Citizen*, 15 Feb. 1983; *Chapel Hill Newspaper*, 25 Apr. 1983; Elizabeth Jackoway, *Yankee Missionaries in the South* (1980); Harriet Quinn, "Interview with Marion

Wright on N.C. and the Death Penalty," 7 June 1978 (mimeographed), and "General Correspondence" (Marion A. Wright Papers, Southern Historical Collection, University of North Carolina, Chapel Hill); *Southern Regional Council: Its Origin and Purpose* (1944); Marion A. Wright and Arnold Shankman, *Human Rights Odyssey* (1978).

J. ISAAC COPELAND

Wright, Orville *(19 Aug. 1871–30 Jan. 1948)*, aviation pioneer, the fourth of five surviving children, was born at Dayton, Ohio, the son of Milton and Susan Catherine Koerner Wright. He shared his brother Wilbur's interest in aviation and their careers were inseparable.

In 1914 Orville bought the stock of all but one of the other stockholders in the Wright Company as a step towards getting entirely out of business. He sold the company in 1915 to a group of eastern capitalists. In 1929 the Wright Aeronautical Corporation merged with Curtiss Airplane and Motor Company to form Curtiss-Wright.

In 1916 Orville built an office workshop in Dayton that remained his headquarters for the rest of his life. During World War I he served as a consultant to the Army Signal Corps and as director of engineering for the Dayton Wright Company, which built Liberty motors and the American version of the De Haviland airplane. He continued to carry on experiments and in 1924 patented the "split wing-flap" for use in slowing down an airplane for landing. He was present at the dedication of the sixty-foot granite monument on top of Kill Devil Hill in November 1932. The site is now a national park.

The airplane flown at Kitty Hawk in 1903 had a long and circuitous route to its place in the Smithsonian Institution. In an apparent attempt to emphasize the contribution to aviation of Samuel P. Langley, former director of the Smithsonian, the institution proposed in 1910 to place a model of the 1908 Wright machine flown at Fort Myer alongside a full-size model of the Langley machine of 1903, which had never flown. Dr. Charles D. Walcott, secretary of the Smithsonian, did not even ask the Wrights for their 1903 airplane. Relations were embittered by the Smithsonian's loan of the Langley airplane in 1914 to Glenn H. Curtiss, who made numerous changes in the structure and engine that enabled him to fly it for a five-second duration in the hope of strengthening his appeal of the patent infringement suit brought by the Wright Company. The Smithsonian Institution's annual reports of 1915–18 recorded the flights without noting the fundamental changes made by Curtiss. After an interview with Walcott in 1916, Orville concluded that the Smithsonian still did not want the 1903 Wright airplane exhibited beside the Langley machine.

In 1928 Orville acceded to the request of the Science Museum at South Kensington, London, to exhibit the airplane. The controversy with the Smithsonian was not settled until 1942, when Walcott's successor published a retraction of the earlier statements and a full apology. Orville then offered the original plane to the Smithsonian. Because of war conditions it was not returned to the United States until 1948. The airplane was formally installed at the Smithsonian on 17 Dec. 1948, eleven months after Orville's death at Dayton. Like his brother he never married.

For bibliographical references see the sketch of Wilbur Wright, below.

GEORGE W. TROXLER

Wright, Richard Harvey *(13 July 1851–4 Mar. 1929)*, industrialist, was born in Franklin County, the son of

Thomas Davenport and Elizabeth Glover Harris Wright. His grandfather, Griffin Wright, was a native of England. As a youth Wright attended Louisburg Male Academy and Horner Preparatory School near Oxford. His father died when he was six and his mother when he was fourteen. He then went to Oxford and apprenticed himself to a merchant for three years (1869–71). The inspiration to learn that he acquired from his teacher, T. J. Horner, never left him, and while serving the apprenticeship Wright studied diligently and read, particularly poetry and biographies of important men. At the end of three years Wright and his employer formed a partnership that lasted until 1874, when their business was destroyed by fire.

Taking another partner, Wright rented a building in Durham in 1877 and began to manufacture smoking tobacco. The next year he bought his partner's interest, erected his own building adjacent to Washington Duke's factory, and began to go on long sales trips around the country. He was an excellent salesman and acting alone impressed Duke to the extent that in 1880 Duke invited him to become a partner. For four years Wright traveled around the world—Africa, India, China, Japan, the Philippines, Australia, and elsewhere—making friends, becoming a true cosmopolite, and expanding the company's business.

Returning home after four years, he married Mamie Exum of Wayne County in June 1884; they became the parents of a daughter, Mamie Exum Wright. About this time he sold his interest in Duke's tobacco company and moved to Lynchburg, Va., where he bought an interest in another tobacco factory that he operated for four years. In December 1888 Wright became the agent for the Bonsack Cigarette Machine and soon had it installed in factories in China, Japan, the Philippines, India, and Africa. As president of Wright's Automatic Tobacco Packing Machine Company, he saw his machine used by most U.S. tobacco manufacturers. He also was director of two coal and coke companies in West Virginia, acquired an interest in the United Machine Company in London, was president of the Durham Traction Company, which installed streetcars, and was a large real estate owner in Durham. In addition, he had an interest in a press that manufactured soap, and he played a role in developing public utilities.

Wright was a member of the Masonic order and of the Methodist Episcopal church; with the exception of one election, he voted a straight Democratic ticket. He was extremely generous with his wealth, aiding numerous causes, particularly homeless children and education for women, but always privately and without fanfare.

Two of Wright's sisters and two nephews made their home with him. He was interred in the Wright mausoleum in Maplewood Cemetery, Durham.

SEE: Samuel A. Ashe, ed., *Biographical History of North Carolina*, vol. 5 (1906 [portrait]); *Greensboro Daily News*, 4 Mar. 1929 (portrait); *Nat. Cyc. Am. Biog.*, vol. 22 (1932); *Who's Who in the South* (1927).

WILLIAM S. POWELL

Wright, Robert Herring *(21 May 1870–25 Apr. 1934)*, teacher and educational administrator, was the first president of East Carolina Teachers Training School (later East Carolina University). He was a descendant of John (d. 4 Oct. 1814), a veteran of the American Revolution, and Penelope Clark Wright, and the son of John Cromartie and Dottie Vaidon Horring Wright of Coharie, located between the Big and Little Coharie rivers in Sampson County (now Parkersburg).

Wright belonged to the period of educational awakening in North Carolina that was ushered in by Governor Charles B. Aycock. In the quarter of a century from 1909—when Wright was named president of East Carolina Teachers Training School—until his death, he was involved in every major educational movement in the state.

In 1888, having completed the courses offered in the local neighborhood school, Wright took an examination for a teacher's certificate and began teaching at Hungry Neck in Bladen County. After two years he entered Oak Ridge Institute in preparation for college. He left Oak Ridge in 1892 and taught for the next two years in Marlborough County, S.C., before entering The University of North Carolina as a sophomore in the autumn of 1894. At Chapel Hill he served as president of two societies, became captain of the football and track teams, and was marshal at the commencement of 1896. After receiving a bachelor of arts degree in 1897, Wright taught for a year in Stanhope, Nash County, and from 1898 to 1901 he taught mathematics and coached football at Oak Ridge Institute.

He entered the Johns Hopkins University in Baltimore in 1901 and in June 1902 began teaching history in Baltimore City College. In 1903 he left Johns Hopkins to devote full-time to his duties at City College, where in the next year he became chairman of the Department of History, Civics, and Economics. In 1906 he was appointed principal of Eastern High School, one of two high schools for girls in Baltimore. Wright served as the first president of the Maryland History Teachers Association and was an active member of the North Carolina Society of Baltimore.

In 1909 he accepted the presidency of the newly established school for training teachers in Greenville. Wright was convinced that the most vital factor in improving the public schools of North Carolina was better teacher training, and he stressed the need for instructing future teachers in the most efficient way to integrate theory and principle in their classroom procedures. The new school was originally set up to offer a two-year professional course, but in 1920, through Wright's guidance, it was authorized to provide four years of professional work and was rechartered as a teachers' college. Under his leadership, the school grew from an institution of about 175 students to a college of 1,000. The number of graduates during the twenty-five years of his administration, including those with the A.B. degree and those holding diplomas, was 4,431; a total of 22,327 students had attended the school. The faculty had grown from 13 to 90, and the nine subjects taught in the first year had grown into twelve departments.

As a result of his special concern with the apprenticeship of student teachers and the importance of supervising teachers and critic teachers, a grammar school in the Greenville school system was located on the Training School campus in 1914. East Carolina Teachers College was received into full membership in the American Association of Teachers Colleges in 1926, and in the following year it was ranked as a Class A college by the Southern Association of Colleges and Secondary Schools. In 1929 the college was granted the right to offer graduate courses and to confer the master of arts degree.

Wright served as director of the college's summer school program for five years, and he guided the evolution in concept of summer school, which had developed from the earlier teachers' institutes. East Carolina Teachers College became one of the first colleges in North Carolina to offer only regular-term classes in summer school.

Wright collaborated in the preparation of a bulletin, *Training Courses for Rural Teachers*, issued by the U.S. Bureau of Education in 1913. He was the chairman of an educational commission appointed in 1917 to study the public schools of the state and make recommendations for their improvement. In 1920 he presented a series of ten lectures at Peabody College for Teachers. He fought vigorously in 1928 to persuade the General Assembly to pass a measure providing an eight-month public school term.

Among his professional honors were the doctor of education degree conferred by Wake Forest College in 1928 and the presidency of the American Association of Teachers Colleges. In Greenville he was an active member of the Jarvis Memorial Methodist Church and the Masonic order; he was a charter member of the Greenville Rotary Club and the Greenville Country Club. He also served as a director of the Home Building and Loan Association and as president of the East Carolina Shippers Bureau.

On 31 Dec. 1901 Wright married Charlotte Pearl Murphy (13 Feb. 1876–7 Mar. 1965) of Tomahawk. They had four children: Pearl (Mrs. Donald) Cadman of Chappaqua, N.Y.; Dr. Robert H., Jr., of Phoebus, Va.; Mary (Mrs. Durwood) Parker, and William.

At the time of his death, the Robert H. Wright Memorial Loan Fund was established at East Carolina Teachers College by colleagues, students, alumni, and friends. Wright Building on the campus of East Carolina University was named for him. He was buried in Greenwood Cemetery, Greenville.

SEE: Daniel L. Grant, *Alumni History of the University of North Carolina* (1924); C. H. Hamlin, *Ninety Bits of North Carolina Biography* (1946); Mamie E. Jenkins and others, *Robert Herring Wright—Educator, Executive, and Leader in Teacher Training* (1938); Raleigh *News and Observer*, 26 Apr. 1934; Robert H. Wright to Louis R. Wilson, 14 Jan. 1913 (Clipping files, North Carolina Collection, University of North Carolina, Chapel Hill).

RALPH HARDEE RIVES

Wright, Wilbur (*16 Apr. 1867–30 May 1912*), aviation pioneer, the third of five surviving children of Milton and Susan Catherine Koerner Wright, was born at Millville, near New Castle, Ind. His father was a bishop of the United Brethren in Christ Church and editor of the *Religious Telescope*. Scientific concerns of Wilbur and his younger brother Orville were encouraged by their parents, and their first interest in flying was stimulated by their father's gift of a helicopter type toy designed by the French aviation pioneer Alphonse Penaud. While in high school the brothers started a job printing office and later published a weekly paper, the *West Side News*.

In the spring of 1893 the Wrights opened a bicycle shop where, in addition to offering the usual bicycle repairs, they manufactured their own bicycles, the Wright Flyer and the Van Cleve. The seasonal nature of the bicycle business allowed time for study, and in 1896 news of the death of the German aeronaut, Gustav Lilienthal, aroused their interest in gliding. They soon obtained the most recent aeronautical data and began experimenting with kites. Their study was encouraged by correspondence with the noted engineer and aviator Octave Chanute beginning in 1900. He frequently informed them about the research of other experimenters and continued to show interest in their work.

Using Lilienthal's air pressure tables the Wrights calculated that a machine with a wing area of a little over 150 square feet would support a man when flown in a wind of 16 miles per hour. In July 1899 the brothers built a model biplane glider with a wing span of 5 feet that Wilbur flew as a kite. The flight demonstrated a major contribution of the Wrights to aeronautics—the system of lateral control by which the wings are warped or presented at different angles to turn the aircraft (the aileron principle).

Information received upon inquiry from the U.S. Weather Bureau led the Wrights to select Kitty Hawk as a location where the wind velocity and sand hills, free of trees or shrubs, would allow them to fly a man-carrying glider. Correspondence with Joseph J. Dosher of the Kitty Hawk weather station and William J. Tate, the former postmaster, confirmed their decision, and on 12 Sept. 1900 Wilbur disembarked from the decrepit flatbottomed schooner that had brought him to Kitty Hawk from Elizabeth City, the nearest railroad point to his destination. Orville arrived at the camp on 28 September. In the tests of their machine flown as a kite, and then with a man on board, the Wrights were pleased with the system of lateral control but disappointed with the machine's lifting ability.

In July 1901 the brothers returned to Kitty Hawk, where with a large machine they made several hundred flights ranging from 50 to 400 feet in length. These flights confirmed their suspicion, based on experiments during 1900–1901, that Lilienthal's tables and the current theories regarding air pressure were incorrect. The brothers also realized that the center of pressure on the wings moved backwards as the angle of incidence was decreased—in direct opposition to accepted theory.

The machine that the Wrights began assembling at Kitty Hawk in August 1902 incorporated changes based on their own air pressure tables and wind tunnel experiments. The glides made in September and October confirmed the Wrights' theories regarding air pressure and demonstrated the efficiency of their control system. The basic Wright patent filed in March 1903 incorporated the plans of the 1902 glider. The patent was granted on 22 May 1906.

On their return from Kitty Hawk in 1902, the Wrights began building a larger machine powered by a 12-horsepower motor of their own construction that drove two propellers of their own design. The Wrights returned to Kitty Hawk on 25 Sept. 1903, but due to a succession of bad storms the first successful flight was not made until 17 December. The machine was launched from a truck on a monorail track on level ground entirely through the power of the motor and the thrust of the propellers. Orville made man's first machine-powered flight, which lasted about 12 seconds and covered a distance of 100 feet. The fourth and last flight of the day made by Wilbur covered 852 feet in 59 seconds.

During the next two years the Wrights built two heavier and stronger airplanes, improving their design and increasing the reliability and range of flight. Both were tested at Dayton, where on 5 Oct. 1905 they made a circular flight of 24 miles.

On 8 Feb. 1908 they received a contract from the U.S. Army Signal Corps to build a machine capable of flying 40 miles per hour for 10 miles carrying a pilot and a passenger. Three weeks later they contracted with a French syndicate to manufacture the airplane in France. They redesigned their machine to permit the pilot and passenger to sit upright and in May 1908 returned to Kitty Hawk to practice for demonstrations at Fort Myer, Va., and in France. Immediately after the Kitty Hawk trials Wilbur went to France, where his demonstrations at the race course at Humandrieres near Le Mans created a sensation. After his return he made spectacular demonstration flights as part of the Hudson Fulton Celebration: on 29 September from Governors Island around the Statue of Liberty and on 1 October from Governors Island 21 miles up the Hudson to Grant's Tomb and back.

After the successful trials at Kitty Hawk in 1908, Orville demonstrated the contract machine at Fort Myer. However, an accident on 17 September in which his passenger,

army lieutenant Thomas E. Selfridge, lost his life delayed completion of the tests until July 1909. Orville then went to Germany and formed a German Wright Company.

In 1909 the American Wright Company was incorporated with Wilbur as president. The Wrights were to receive stock and cash and a 10 percent royalty on all airplanes sold. The company was profitable from the start, with the largest source of income from expedition flights.

Wilbur Wright, who never married, died at age forty-five.

SEE: Barbara Craig, *The Wright Brothers and Their Development of the Airplane* (1967); *DAB*, vol. 20 (1936); Fred C. Kelly, ed., *Miracle at Kitty Hawk* (1951) and *The Wright Brothers* (1943); Marvin W. McFarland, ed., *The Papers of Wilbur and Orville Wright*, 2 vols. (1953); Lloyd Morris and Kendall Smith, *Ceiling Unlimited* (1953); Orville Wright, *How We Invented the Airplane* (1953).

GEORGE W. TROXLER

Wyatt, Henry Lawson (*12 Feb. 1842–10 June 1861*), the first Confederate soldier from North Carolina to be killed in battle during the American Civil War, was born in Richmond, Va., the son of Isham Belcher and Lucinda N. L. Wyatt. In 1856 he and his family moved to Pitt County, N.C., and eventually settled in Tarboro, Edgecombe County, where young Wyatt was apprenticed to the carpenter's trade.

On 18 Apr. 1861 he enlisted as a private soldier with the Edgecombe Guards, which had been organized earlier on the same day. Originally composed of eighty-eight privates and nine noncommissioned and four commissioned officers, the company was commanded by Colonel Daniel Harvey Hill of Mecklenburg County and became A Company of the First Regiment of North Carolina Volunteers. After North Carolina had enlisted ten regiments, the First Regiment, which had been the earliest of all North Carolina troops to organize and take the field, became known as the Bethel Regiment.

In May the First North Carolina Volunteers were ordered to Yorktown, Va. They broke camp at Richmond on 24 May and reached Yorktown that evening. Under the orders of the commanding officer, John B. Magruder, the First North Carolina marched to Big Bethel Church, thirty miles from Yorktown, and eight or nine miles from Hampton and Newport News. On 10 June, at three o'clock on a Monday morning, the First Regiment was awakened for a general advance on the enemy. The Federals, under the command of Brigadier General E. W. Prince, had approached on the road leading from Fortress Monroe and Newport News.

A number of Massachusetts troops, led by Major Theodore Winthrop, soon occupied a house on the battlefield. At the suggestion of Colonel Hill, Captain John L. Bridges asked for volunteers to burn the house. Corporal George Williams and Privates Henry L. Wyatt, Thomas Fallon, John H. Thorpe, and Robert H. Bradley of Company A offered their services. Issued matches and a hatchet, the soldiers were to charge across an open field, two hundred yards wide, in the face of the enemy's lines. Wyatt was the next to the last man to leave the breastworks. A volley was fired not from the house but from a Federal company off to the left along a road. Thirty yards from the breastworks, Wyatt fell on his back with a musket ball in his brain. Three of the other men were wounded; they lay on the ground until a howitzer shell was fired on the house and the enemy was routed. After a battle of approximately two and one-half hours, the enemy retreated.

That night Wyatt was carried to Yorktown where he

died, never having regained consciousness. Eighteen Federals had been killed, yet he was the only Southern soldier to lose his life during the day's fighting. On Tuesday he was taken to Richmond and buried. A board of pine inscribed with Wyatt's name, regiment, and time and place of death was put on his grave.

A marker has since been placed where Wyatt fell bearing the inscription: "On this spot, June 10th, 1861, fell Henry Lawson Wyatt, private, Co. A, First Regiment of N.C. Volunteers. This stone, placed here by the courtesy of Virginia, is erected by authority of the State of North Carolina." A camp was named for him during the war, his portrait was hung in the state library, and the Virginia and North Carolina Monument Association erected a statue, unveiled on 10 June 1905, at Bethel. On 10 June 1912 a statue of Wyatt was dedicated in Raleigh.

SEE: James C. Birdsong, *Brief Sketches of the N.C. State Troops in the War between the States*, app. B (1894); E. J. Hale, address in Raleigh, 10 June 1912, in Raleigh *News and Observer*, 7 July 1912; "Henry Lawson Wyatt: The First Confederate Soldier Killed in Battle," reprinted from *National Magazine*, November 1892; Louis H. Manarin, comp., *North Carolina Troops, 1861–1865: A Roster*, vol. 3 (1971); Greg Mast, *State Troops and Volunteers: A Photographic Record of North Carolina's Civil War Soldiers* (1995 [portrait]).

DANIEL BURT VEAZEY

Wyche, Benjamin (12 Sept. 1869–6 May 1936), first full-time trained librarian at The University of North Carolina, was born in Williamsboro, the son of Benjamin and Sarah Hunter Wyche. He received his early education at Roxboro Academy and Mount Tirzah Academy. From 1889 to 1894 he attended The University of North Carolina, where he earned a B.Litt. degree, and then entered Amherst College for library training.

Wyche was librarian at The University of North Carolina (1894–97), the University of Texas (1897–1903), and Carnegie Library, San Antonio, Tex. (1903–11). He was secretary and then president of the Texas Library Association. Poor health led him to give up his profession, and in 1912 he became a special agent for the New York Life Insurance Company, in Charlotte, where he was an outstanding salesman.

His first wife was Knowlton Woodward, whom he married on 14 Oct. 1897. She died in 1910, and he married Ethel Cheshire Deaver on 14 Sept. 1914. Wyche had a son Benjamin and a daughter Barbara. A member of the Methodist church, he was buried in Riverside Cemetery, Asheville.

SEE: *Charlotte Observer*, 7 May 1936; Daniel L. Grant, *Alumni History of the University of North Carolina* (1924).

WILLIAM S. POWELL

Wyche, Ira Thomas (16 Oct. 1887–8 July 1981), army officer, was born at Ocracoke, where his father was pastor of the Methodist church. The son of Lawrence Olin and Lorena Howard Wyche, he attended the Quakenbush School at Laurinburg, was graduated from the U.S. Military Academy on 13 June 1911, and was commissioned second lieutenant in the Thirtieth Infantry. He then served at several posts in California, Alaska, Texas, and elsewhere. During World War I Wyche was transferred to the Field Artillery and promoted to captain. In France he had temporary ranks as major and lieutenant colonel. After the war he was a regimental commander at Camp

Jackson, S.C., and in 1919 he was assigned to duty in Washington, D.C. He was graduated from the Mounted Service School (1916), Field Artillery School (1924), Command and General Staff School (1925), and Army War College (1934).

When World War II began, Wyche was a brigadier general but in 1942 he was promoted to major general; he commanded the Seventy-ninth Division throughout its battle operation in the European theater. In 1945 he was named commanding general of the Eighth Corps in Germany. After the war he led the Third Corps at Camp Polk, La., and the First Service Command at Boston and in January 1947 was appointed inspector general of the army. After his retirement in 1948, he moved to Southern Pines, N.C. He died in Moore General Hospital following a stroke and was buried in the Fort Bragg Post Cemetery.

In 1917 he married Mary Louise Dunn, and they had a daughter, Elizabeth.

SEE: Raleigh *News and Observer*, 19 July 1941 (portrait), 10 Feb. 1949, 6 May 1951 (portrait), 10–11 July 1981; Wirt Robinson, ed., *Biographical Register of the Officers and Graduates of the U.S. Military Academy*, vol. 6-B (1920); Southern Pines *The Pilot*, 29 Nov. 1972 (portrait); *Who Was Who In America*, vol. 8 (1985); Ira Thomas Wyche Papers (Manuscript Collection, East Carolina University, Greenville, N.C.).

WILLIAM S. POWELL

Wyche, Mary Lewis (26 Feb. 1858–22 Aug. 1936), nurse, was born near Williamsboro in present Vance County, the daughter of Benjamin and Sarah Hunter Wyche. In 1889 she was graduated from Henderson College, where she had taught in the primary department while a student herself. Shortly afterwards she moved to Chapel Hill to keep house for her brothers, who were enrolled at The University of North Carolina; she also kept boarders and taught school. When she was no longer needed to assist her brothers, she gave thought to her own future and turned to medicine. Choosing nurses' training rather than medical school, she was graduated from the Philadelphia General Hospital in 1894 at age thirty-six.

Moving to Raleigh, Miss Wyche was active in the organization of Rex Hospital Training School for Nurses; of her first class of five student nurses, four were graduated. Three years later, in 1898, she resigned her post to enter private nursing in Raleigh. The next year she became nurse at the infirmary of the State Normal and Industrial College in Greensboro, and in 1901 she returned to Raleigh as a private nurse for a year.

In order to advance women in the nursing profession, Miss Wyche organized the Raleigh Nurses Association in 1902; in time it evolved into the North Carolina State Nurses Association. Also recognizing her own need for further training, she spent a year studying dietetics and massage in Philadelphia.

Through Miss Wyche's efforts the North Carolina General Assembly passed a law, signed by Governor Charles B. Aycock in March 1903, to raise nursing standards and to require the registration of nurses. In the same year she became superintendent of nurses at Watts Hospital in Durham, a position she held for ten years. During that time she was secretary-treasurer of the first Board of Examiners for Trained Nurses and served on the board for six years.

Still another successful project with which she was associated was the establishment of a home in Black Mountain for tubercular nurses. Miss Wyche together with Birdie Dunn, of Raleigh, who introduced the idea, coordinated the efforts of the State Nurses Association that led to its opening in 1913. No longer needed, the home was sold at the beginning of World War I and the money invested in Liberty Bonds. For several years afterwards Miss Wyche served as superintendent of nurses at Sarah Elizabeth Hospital in Henderson and then once again engaged in private nursing, first in Greensboro and then in Raleigh. During this time she led the movement to establish a prenursing course at the North Carolina College for Women in Greensboro, and she took the lead in seeking a school of nursing at Duke University in Durham.

In 1925, at age sixty-seven, she retired from nursing and returned to her family home, Wychewood, near Henderson, where she wrote *The History of Nursing in North Carolina*. She was an active member of the Methodist church.

SEE: *Greensboro Daily News*, 23–24 Aug. 1936; C. H. Hamlin, *Ninety Bits of North Carolina Biography* (1946); Raleigh *News and Observer*, 23 Aug. 1936, 14 Nov. 1948; Lou Rogers, *Tar Heel Women* (1949 [portrait]) and "Mary Lewis Wyche: Pioneer Nurse," *We The People of North Carolina* 3 (June 1945 [portrait]); Mary Lewis Wyche, *The History of Nursing in North Carolina* (1938).

WILLIAM S. POWELL

Wyche, Richard Thomas (*25 July 1867–5 May 1930*), lecturer and storyteller, was born in Henderson, the son of Benjamin and Sarah Elizabeth Hunter Wyche. He attended The University of North Carolina (1889–92), the University of Chicago (1901), and Columbia University (1911). Wyche was a bookkeeper and cashier in Raleigh for a few years and served as general secretary of the YMCA in Concord in 1892. He taught in the North Carolina schools in 1893 and 1897–98 and engaged in ministerial work in 1894–96 while also teaching. Experience at the YMCA as well as in the classroom led him to entertain as well as educate children and young people through stories. He soon perfected his skills and began to acquire a following.

Beginning in 1899 Wyche was acknowledged as a lecturer and storyteller. He made early appearances at the University of Chicago and on the circuit for the Chautauqua Institution. Soon he was also lecturing at the summer schools of colleges and universities on the art of storytelling. He spoke before women's clubs, social and civic organizations, library and educational conventions, and training schools. In 1903 he organized and was the first president of the National Story Tellers League; after 1917 he served as its honorary president. Storyteller leagues were organized in other states and abroad, and storytelling began to be taught in schools and colleges. In 1910 Wyche was the author of a book on his new profession, *Some Great Stories and How to Tell Them*, and in 1913 he cofounded and became editor of *Story Tellers' Magazine*.

Wyche was a member of the North Carolina Folklore Society, Philological Club in Chapel Hill, Knickerbocker Story Tellers League of New York City, and other organizations. He joined the Methodist Episcopal Church, South, as a young man but later became a Congregationalist. On 26 Feb. 1916 he married Maude Anna Ambrister of Norman, Okla., and they had two children: Richard Thomas, Jr., and Mary Elizabeth. He died in Washington, D.C., where he had made his home for a number of years, and was buried in Forest Lawn Cemetery, Greensboro.

SEE: Alumni Files (University of North Carolina, Chapel Hill [portrait]); Daniel L. Grant, *Alumni History of the University of North Carolina* (1924); *Greensboro Daily News*, 6

May 1930; *Nat. Cyc. Am. Biog.*, vol. 24 (1935 [portrait]); *Who Was Who in America*, vol. 1 (1943); *World's Work* 25 (March 1913).

WILLIAM S. POWELL

Wynn, Earl Raymond (*25 Nov. 1911–17 Sept. 1986*), educator and actor, was born in Coal Valley, Ill., the son of Zadoc Hardin and Mary Jane Ziegler Wynn. He was graduated from Augustana College, Rock Island, Ill., in 1932 and received an M.A. degree from Northwestern University in 1934. Wynn taught English and speech at Tarkio College in Missouri and speech at Northwestern. In 1938 he joined the faculty of The University of North Carolina, first in the dramatic arts and then in charge of radio. From 1947 until his retirement he was professor of radio, television, and motion pictures.

In the early 1940s, from Chapel Hill, Wynn produced and directed the program *Men of Action* for the Mutual Broadcasting System coast-to-coast network. During World War II, as an officer in the Naval Reserve, he was writer-producer for training films. At the university he introduced the idea of a communications center as well as organized and helped to develop it. He also was executive director of the North Carolina Communications Study Commission and executive secretary of the North Carolina Educational Radio-Television Commission.

Wynn was an actor in several summer outdoor dramatic productions: *The Lost Colony, Unto These Hills*, and *The Legend of Daniel Boone*, among others. He directed and performed in a number of Carolina Playmaker productions and contributed articles to journals on speech, television, radio, and acting. He retired in 1977 but occasionally taught classes until 1982.

In 1939 he married Irene Grace Schwartzinger; they were divorced, and in 1951 he married Rhoda Mabel Hunter. He was the father of two children, Stacy Hunter and Sherry.

SEE: Chapel Hill, *Daily Tar Heel*, 18 Sept. 1986; Raleigh *News and Observer*, 18 Sept. 1986; *Who's Who in the South and Southwest*, vol. 12 (1971).

WILLIAM S. POWELL

Wynne, William (Will) Andrew (*27 Mar. 1869–7 Aug. 1951*), bicyclist, professional baseball player, and radio pioneer, was born near the community of Neuse in Wake County, the son of William W. and Elizabeth Culbreth Wynne. In 1922 he opened a retail radio shop in Raleigh that he operated until his death. A man of many talents, he was fascinated as a youth by many of the inventions of the day—the telephone, the automobile, and the radio.

His first love, however, was sports. As a bicyclist he was a hero to the young boys of Raleigh. Will Wynne found out that he could do tricks with a bicycle that others could not and so became a contortionist and trick bicycle rider. In 1888 he won the National Trick Riding championship by defeating Harry Ward at Norfolk, Va. Wynne used a borrowed bicycle, whereas Ward rode a specially built nickle-plated one. In 1891 Wynne set a record for the longest bicycle trip—twelve days—when he pedalled from Raleigh to Portland, Maine, then a distance of 1,100 miles over dirt roads. He also staged exhibitions of his skill across the South and the East.

At the Southern Exposition in Atlanta, Ga., on 19 Nov. 1895, he rode a bicycle down the 300-foot incline of the shoot-the-chute and into a lake at the bottom of the track. He raced for time a shoot-the-chute boat with eight people in it. There was a clearance of only sixteen inches between the rails of the track on which he rode, and race officials clocked his speed at 75 miles per hour by the time he was midway down the incline. Wynne won the race but was knocked unconscious for three minutes. He went so fast down the last half of the course, he said, that he could not see or breathe.

Once when he was in Washington, D.C., Wynne was inspired to ride his bicycle down the steps of the Capitol. Having done so successfully, he wanted to do the same at the Washington Monument. For that purpose he and some of his baseball-playing teammates smuggled a disassembled bicycle to the top landing of the monument, but just before they finished putting it together they were discovered by guards.

Wynne also enjoyed a baseball career. He pitched for professional clubs in Columbia and Charleston, S.C., Atlanta, Brockton, Mass., Wilkes-Barre, Pa., and, finally, the National League. His sports career got under way with the Raleigh Amateurs, and he once pitched seven games in six days—with an open gunshot wound in his right arm. In the 1890s there were no eligibility rules in collegiate athletics, and as a unique contribution he pitched for the Wake Forest team one afternoon and for Trinity College the next.

On the first afternoon he pitched for Wake Forest against Trinity at Durham and won 17–7. The next day Trinity was scheduled to play the University of Vermont, whose talented pitcher, "Doc" Pond, had recently been signed by the Baltimore Orioles. On the spot, Trinity hired Wynne. As a result, Trinity won 1–0, with Wynne scoring the winning run as well as pitching.

Wynne became the pitcher for the Washington club of the National League, the only major league in the country. He lost his first game as a major league pitcher, but it was not his fault. Wynne's team played Philadelphia, fourth-ranked in the twelve-team league, and lost 11–5. But only three of the runs were earned off Wynne, as he held Ed Dilahanty, the Babe Ruth of his day, hitless.

Not one to hoard his talents, he early added to his multiple careers that of telegraph operator, becoming superintendent of that service for the Norfolk Southern Railroad. The telephone also attracted him, and from his careful examination and study of pioneer instruments, he developed the only direct and instantaneous telephone system. After forming the Raleigh Telephone Company, he installed the first telephones in the city. In 1897 he built the first long-distance telephone lines in the state—from Raleigh to Goldsboro and from Selma to Dunn. When the Raleigh-to-Goldsboro line was connected, the first person to use it was Josephus Daniels, editor of the *News and Observer*. In time Wynne sold his telephone lines to Southern Bell.

When Henry Ford built his first car in 1903, Wynne promptly saw in it more than personal transportation. He built what is considered to have been the first truck. At a reported cost of $908.52, excluding labor, he constructed the truck using railroad wheels and employed it to haul coal and telephone equipment and as his own private car.

When radio sets began to appear in Raleigh in the 1920s, Will Wynne lost no time in taking some of them apart and putting them together again. He came to understand the mechanism and to recognize its potential. He opened the first shop in the area devoted exclusively to radio in 1922 and operated it until his death. Two years later he established the city's first radio station, WRCO [*Wynne Radio Company*], which he sold to the Durham Life Insurance Company in 1929 after which it became WPTF ["*We Protect the Family*"].

Will Wynne married Mary Avera, and they had three daughters and a son—Elizabeth, who died young, Grace,

Louise, and William Avera. He was buried in Oakwood Cemetery, Raleigh.

SEE: Raleigh *News and Observer*, 8 Aug. 1951 (portrait); Raleigh *Spectator*, 25 July 1985; John R. Woodard (Wake Forest University), personal contact, December 1994.

WILLIAM S. POWELL

Wynns, Benjamin (1710s–1788), state assemblyman, militia colonel, and planter, was born in Chowan Precinct, the son of Captain George and Rose Bush Wynns. George Wynns was a large landowner on the Chowan River and Wiccacon Creek area of present Hertford County, as well as a justice of the peace, an assemblyman, and a captain in the county militia. The Wynnses descended from the inhabitants of the ancient royal residence of Gwydir Castle of northern Wales who lived in and around Canterbury, England, for three or more centuries before migrating to Virginia. Members of the family figured prominently in political and social circles in London as well as colonial Virginia as early as 1609.

Benjamin Wynns was mentioned in public life as early as 1740, when he was listed as a freeholder and juryman in Bertie County. A long and distinguished career as a public servant began in 1744 with his appointment as deputy clerk of court and justice of the peace in Bertie. From 1744 to 1746 he was deputy surveyor under the surveyor general of the Crown. His depositions taken on behalf of the Crown were used in an attempt to prove charges of corruption against Governor Gabriel Johnston for violating land grant laws. In 1748 Wynns was the clerk of court in nearby Edgecombe County, but he returned to Bertie in that capacity from 1756 to 1759.

Benjamin Wynns represented Bertie County in the colonial Assembly from 1754 to 1760. In 1759 he sponsored a bill in the Assembly that founded Hertford County from surrounding Bertie, Chowan, and Northampton counties. From 1762 to 1768 he represented this new county in the Assembly. He also served as the first clerk of court for Hertford County from 1760 to 1764. Since 1754 Wynns had tried to have a town incorporated on his plantation at Barfield Landing along the Chowan River. He competed for this honor with his neighbor, Alexander Cotton. Cotton's death in 1766 opened the way for Wynns, and in 1768 the Assembly passed a bill incorporating the town on 150 acres donated by Wynns and named Winton in his honor. This was the only incorporated town in the county for twenty years and was a public landing and area trade center. Wynns again represented Hertford County in the Assembly during the 1771–72 and 1773–74 terms.

At the general muster of the Hertford County regiment of militia on 28 May 1772, Benjamin Wynns was listed as the regiment's colonel. This appointment by the Crown was reaffirmed by the Provincial Congress at Hillsborough on 9 Sept. 1775. In late 1775 and early 1776 he led these troops as a part of the colonial force attempting to expel Lord Dunmore from Norfolk. They participated in the Battle of Great Bridge and the subsequent siege of Norfolk. When Wynns led his troops home to Hertford County in early 1776, he "was met with great rejoicing among the people and was rewarded with the unbounded praises of the Americans along his route."

After 1776 Wynns seems to have retired from public life to have more time for his growing interests along the Chowan River. He had been trained as a carpenter during his youth and had inherited land from his father along the Chowan River. In 1745 he acquired a gristmill near his holdings at Barfields. The Hertford County tax list of 1779 showed him owning over 2,500 acres and 23 slaves. His land's location along the river gave him access to foreign markets for his plantation wares and enabled him to engage in shipbuilding as well. The brig *Fair American* was built on his Barfields plantation in 1780 by two of Wynns's sons and their Edenton partners but was captured by the British on its maiden voyage. Relatives in England and the West Indies aided Wynns and his sons in carrying on a busy trade from his Chowan River plantation.

Benjamin Wynns married twice. His first wife was Catherine Baker, the daughter of Henry III and Catherine Booth Baker, sister of General Lawrence Baker. They had three children—George, William, and Benjamin, Jr.—all of whom represented Hertford County in the Assembly and served in the Revolutionary War. Benjamin Wynns's second wife was Margaret Pugh, the daughter of Colonel Francis and Ferebee Savage Pugh and the stepdaughter of Thomas Barker of Edenton. They also had three children: Mary, Margaret, and Thomas, who became a U.S. congressman and a general in the state militia. Benjamin Wynns died in Murfreesboro, where he was buried along with his son Thomas.

SEE: John L. Cheney, ed., *North Carolina Government, 1585–1971* (1972); Walter Clark, ed., *State Records of North Carolina*, vols. 22–23 (1907, 1904); John Wheeler Moore, *Historical Sketches of Hertford County, North Carolina* (1880); William L. Saunders, ed., *Colonial Records of North Carolina*, vols. 4–7 (1886–90), 9–10 (1890); John Hill Wheeler, *Historical Sketches of North Carolina* (1851); Benjamin B. Winborne, *The Colonial and State History of Hertford County, North Carolina* (1906).

THOMAS R. J. NEWBERN

Wynns, Thomas *(1760–4 June 1825)*, congressman, state legislator, and major general of state troops, was born at Barfields, the Chowan River plantation of the Wynns family, in Hertford County. His father, Benjamin, was a state legislator and a militia colonel during the Revolutionary War; he also introduced bills in the General Assembly creating Hertford County from sections of Bertie, Chowan, and Northampton counties, as well as founding the county seat of Winton, named in his honor and located on land that he donated. Thomas's mother was Margaret Pugh Wynns, the stepdaughter of Thomas and Penelope Barker of Edenton.

Wynns received his education at a local academy and at age twenty was allowed to tour Europe, a fashionable practice for planters' sons of the period. He sailed in the late spring of 1780 on the brig *Fair American*, which was built at Barfields and owned by his uncles, George and William Wynns, and by several Edenton businessmen. But only two weeks after leaving Ocracoke the brig was seized by the British frigate *Vestal*. The *Vestal* reached Spithead, near Portsmouth, England, on 14 November, with Wynns and several members of the *Fair American*'s crew securely locked up. Wynns was released soon after he was questioned by British magistrates and spent six weeks in the London area contacting friends and relatives of his acquaintances in North Carolina. In January 1781 he booked passage first to France, then to Boston, and arrived in North Carolina by the spring of 1781.

Wynns entered politics in 1786 with his election to the state senate from Hertford County. In 1787 he represented his county in the House of Commons but returned the next year to the senate, where he served continuously until 1800. In July 1788 Wynns and his uncle George were delegates to the convention at Hillsborough to discuss the new federal Constitution. The following year he attended the convention at Fayetteville that adopted the document.

Returning to the senate, Wynns pushed for the founding of the state university at Chapel Hill and was named one of the first trustees of the school. During this period he also served as Indian commissioner for the Southern District. In 1800 he was a presidential elector and voted for the Jefferson-Burr ticket.

In 1802 Wynns was elected to the U.S. House of Representatives to fill the vacancy created by the death of Charles Johnson of Edenton. He was reelected to serve in the Eighth and Ninth congresses, ending 4 Mar. 1807. He again served as a presidential elector in 1808, casting his vote for James Madison.

Wynns withdrew from the national political scene in 1808 and returned to Hertford County to oversee the running of his plantation on the old Barfields land. He was, however, persuaded to serve once again in the state senate from 1808 to 1817, after which he retired to Barfields. In this period he received the commission as major general in the First Division of state troops, a post that he held until 1813.

Wynns married Susanna Maney, the daughter of James Maney II of Maney's Landing, Hertford County. They had no children. Susanna died on 5 Jan. 1822, a few years before her husband. Both were buried on the old Maney plantation at Maney's Landing.

SEE: John L. Cheney, ed., *North Carolina Government, 1585–1979* (1981); *Hertford County: The First Two Hundred Years, 1589–1789* (1976); Betsy Overton, "Legacy of Barfield" (graduate research paper, Wake Forest University, possession of Thomas R. J. Newbern); Thomas C. Parramore, "The Great Escape from Forten Gaol," *North Carolina Historical Review* 45 (October 1968); Benjamin B. Winborne, *The Colonial and State History of Hertford County, North Carolina* (1906).

THOMAS R. J. NEWBERN

Yancey, Bartlett *(19 Feb. 1785–30 Aug. 1828)*, lawyer, congressman, and longtime state senator, was born at the Yancey family homestead in Caswell County, now within the limits of the county seat, later (1833) named Yanceyville in Bartlett Yancey's honor. He was the tenth child of Nancy Graves and Bartlett Yancey, Sr. Of Welsh extraction, his father was a semi-invalid who was unable to do any physical labor such as farming and eked out a living for his large family by teaching in country schools.

As a lad Yancey attended the neighborhood school near his home. At age fifteen he taught in the school for one term, performing his duties so well that he was invited the next year to teach in the academy located at the county seat. For two years he taught there and studied Latin and mathematics under the principal, the Reverend Hugh Shaw. When Shaw resigned in 1803, Yancey succeeded him as principal at an annual salary of $200, most of which he saved in order to finance his college education.

In 1805 Yancey enrolled at The University of North Carolina over the strenuous objections of his mother, who was convinced that no young man who attended the university was "ever of any account afterwards." After two years he left the university for the home of Archibald D. Murphey, under whom he studied law. On receiving his license, Yancey borrowed enough money from his brother James to open a law office in his native Caswell County in 1809.

Yancey possessed a rare personal magnetism, and that combined with his great legal skill, common sense, and powers of persuasion within a short time made him one of the most successful lawyers in the state. Soon he was able to pay off his debts and build a fine home, where he dispensed a generous hospitality. In 1813 he decisively defeated his former teacher, Archibald D. Murphey, in a race for Congress, receiving all but three of the votes cast in Caswell County. Elected as a Republican and a War Hawk, Yancey took his seat on 3 June 1813 and shortly became one of the House's leading members. Appointed during the second session to the Committee on Claims, he became chairman of the committee in the third session when Stephen Archer left that position to become chairman of the Committee on Ways and Means.

In the House Yancey was intimately associated with John Quincy Adams, John C. Calhoun, and Henry Clay. According to tradition, Speaker Henry Clay frequently called upon Yancey to preside over the House in his stead, a responsibility that Yancey discharged with great efficiency. Another of his intimates in Congress was Nathaniel Macon, already a friend of long standing. Yancey often differed with Macon on specific issues, however, and they frequently voted on opposite sides.

At the end of his second term Yancey refused to be a candidate for Congress again, as he wished to give more time to his law practice in order to support his growing family. Economic considerations also dictated his refusal in 1818 of an appointment to the superior court bench by Governor John Branch. In 1826 he similarly declined President John Quincy Adams's offer to name him U.S. minister to Peru. Yet the demands of Yancey's law practice did not prevent him from serving as Caswell County's representative in the North Carolina Senate from 1817 to 1827. During his first term he was unanimously elected speaker of the senate, and he held the position by successive unanimous elections until the end of his legislative service.

Yancey played a prominent role in almost all the important political developments of his time. He was extremely influential in obtaining the legislation that created the North Carolina Supreme Court, and he deserves much of the credit for reorganizing the office of the state treasurer and for reforming the method of selecting trustees for The University of North Carolina. Against the advice of his friend Nathaniel Macon, he earnestly advocated federal aid to finance internal improvements. Yancey shares with his mentor, Archibald D. Murphey, much of the honor for taking the first steps towards the establishment of public schools in North Carolina. In 1825 the legislature enacted a bill, drawn by Yancey and introduced into the senate by Charles A. Hill, that created a Literary Fund, from special sources, which was to be used to establish common schools when the fund had become sufficiently large.

Yancey was an early proponent of constitutional revision to grant the western portion of the state representation in the General Assembly commensurate with its population. Although this reform was not finally achieved until 1835, seven years after Yancey's death, his support of their cause was not ignored by grateful westerners, who in 1833 named a new county in his honor. In addition, Yancey was a trustee of The University of North Carolina for eleven years (1817–28). He had long wished to serve in the U.S. Senate, and had his own death not intervened, he would probably have been chosen to replace John Branch in the Senate when Branch became Andrew Jackson's secretary of the navy in 1829.

On 8 Dec. 1808 Yancey married Nancy Graves (1786–1855), a first cousin. They had two sons and five daughters: Rufus Augustus, Algernon Sidney, Frances (Mrs. Henry McAden), Mary (Mrs. Giles Mebane), Ann (m. a Womack), Carolina (Mrs. Temud Mebane), and Virginia (Mrs. George W. Swepson). On Sunday morning, 23 Aug. 1828, Yancey became seriously ill at Greensboro, where the preceding day he had completed a strenuous week in Guilford Superior Court. Against the urging of his friends, he immediately left for home, a distance of fifty-

two miles, and arrived at ten o'clock that night. His condition steadily worsened, and he died the following Saturday, only a few days after his election to an eleventh consecutive term in the state senate. Yancey's powerful mind remained clear to the end. As death drew near, he called his wife to his bedside and gave her instructions concerning the future management of his estate and the training of their children. Yancey's portrait was painted about 1810 by an unidentified primitive artist.

SEE: Samuel A. Ashe, ed., *History of North Carolina*, vol. 2 (1925, 1971); J. G. de Roulhac Hamilton, *The Political and Professional Career of Bartlett Yancey*, James Sprunt Historical Publications, vol. 10, no. 2 (1911); W. H. Hoyt, ed., *The Papers of Archibald D. Murphey*, 2 vols. (1914); Guion G. Johnson, *Ante-Bellum North Carolina* (1937); Alva B. Konkle, *John Motley Morehead and the Development of North Carolina, 1796–1866* (1922, 1971); Laura MacMillan, comp., *The North Carolina Portrait Index, 1700–1860* (1963 [portrait]); M. C. S. Noble, *A History of the Public Schools of North Carolina* (1930); William S. Powell, *When the Past Refused to Die: A History of Caswell County, 1777–1977* (1977 [portrait]); Bartlett Yancey Papers (Southern Historical Collection, University of North Carolina, Chapel Hill).

W. CONARD GASS

Yancey, James (*ca. 1768–27 Nov. 1829*), legislator, merchant, planter, public official, and educator, was born in Gloucester District, Orange (now Caswell) County, of English and Welsh ancestry, the son of Bartlett, Sr., and Ann Graves Yancey. He was the elder brother of Bartlett, Jr., and the first cousin of Calvin Graves, the Reverend John Kerr, and Senator James Kerr.

Yancey represented Caswell County in the General Assembly in 1798, 1801–3, 1807–8, 1811, and 1822. In 1802 he introduced a bill to establish Caswell Academy, the first chartered school in the county, of which he served as trustee. He was a justice of the County Court of Pleas and Quarter Sessions from 1802 to 1829 and attended most quarterly meetings. In 1822 he was elected the first permanent chairman of the county court, serving until his death. His leadership, important to the establishment of sound government in Caswell County, resulted in agreeable negotiations for a site for an enlarged courthouse, public square, and other public buildings. In 1793 Yancey's store was one of the landmarks of the county.

He was married twice, first to Lucy Kerr on 14 Jan. 1794, and second to Zilpah Johnston, the daughter of Dr. Lancelot Johnston, on 24 June 1811. His children were James Monroe, Mary Elizabeth, Albert Gallatin, William, and Mildred Yancey. James Yancey was buried on his plantation five miles south of Yanceyville, the county seat, near the tripartite house he built before 1800.

SEE: Mary Wilson Brown, "If Courthouses Could Only Talk," *Popular Government*, March 1935; John L. Cheney, Jr., ed., *North Carolina Government, 1585–1979* (1981); *Durham Morning Herald*, 28 Mar. 1948; Minutes, Caswell County Court of Pleas and Quarter Sessions (North Carolina State Archives, Raleigh); William S. Powell, *When the Past Refused to Die: A History of Caswell County, 1777–1977* (1977); *Public and Private Laws of North Carolina* (1802, 1833); *Raleigh Register*, 5 Dec. 1829; Yanceyville, *Caswell Messenger*, 23 June 1976.

KATHERINE K. KENDALL

Yarbrough, Mrs. J. A. (*28 Aug. 1879–5 Nov. 1961*), clubwoman and newspaper writer, was born Josephine Mc-

Donald in Ashland, Miss., the only child of James McLeod and Emma Josephine McDonald. After her marriage on 11 Dec. 1901, she was always referred to as Mrs. J. A. Yarbrough. She attended Flora MacDonald College in Red Springs, N.C., then moved to Radford, Va., where she met her future husband, Joel Alexander Yarbrough, a bank employee and recent graduate of Virginia Polytechnic Institute. Resettling in Charlotte, Yarbrough founded a coal and ice company and developed a chain of dairy stores. They became the parents of two sons, Joel A., Jr., and John McDonald.

Mrs. Yarbrough's talents were diverse, and her interest in public affairs was genuine and deep. She wrote a great many feature stories that were published in the *Charlotte Observer* and was especially well known for an extensive series on "Interesting Carolinians." Though most of her writings were of historical interest, based on serious research, others were on topics of current concern in the city and region. She held office in, conducted programs for, and otherwise was active in the Charlotte Woman's Club, Daughters of the American Revolution, Daughters of American Colonists, United Daughters of the Confederacy, Society for the Preservation of Antiquities, YWCA, a book club, and a needlework guild. She served on the board of directors of the Florence Crittenton Home, was active in the work of the Myers Park Baptist Church, and played an important role in the moving and restoration of the U.S. Mint in Charlotte (now the Mint Museum of Art).

She was described as a precise and well-organized person whose demeanor was always proper. After an illness of several years she died in Asheville and was buried in Elmwood Cemetery, Charlotte.

SEE: *Charlotte Observer*, 5 Nov. 1961; *Cranford Profiles: The First Hundred Years of a Charlotte Book Club* (1992); Pat Ryckman (Carolina Room, Public Library of Charlotte and Mecklenburg County), personal contact, 15 Dec. 1993, 10 Jan. 1994.

WILLIAM S. POWELL

Yates, Matthew Tyson (8 Jan. 1819–17 Mar. 1888), Baptist missionary to China, was born in Wake County, the second of ten children of William and Delilah Booth Yates. He grew up in the Mount Pisgah community and attended the Mount Pisgah Baptist Church, where he was baptized on 23 Oct. 1835. Yates attended the Hilliard School near his home. After studying for a year under G. W. Thompson at Forest Hill Academy, he began teaching school at the Mount Pisgah Baptist Church as well as helping on his father's plantation. Yates returned to Forest Hill Academy, and on the advice of his teacher visited Dr. Samuel Wait, president of Wake Forest College. Wait talked Yates into attending the next session even though he was twenty-one years old, and the young man entered Wake Forest College in August 1840. In October 1841 the North Carolina Baptist State Convention elected him one of their beneficiaries and paid his tuition to Wake Forest, from which he was graduated with an A.B. degree in 1846. In 1869 the college awarded him an honorary D.D. degree.

Yates had decided that he wanted to become a missionary. He had some debts to settle first and in this effort was assisted by Professor John Brown White, who took up a collection from the faculty and remaining students. On 3 Aug. 1846 he was accepted by the Southern Baptist Convention as missionary to China as candidate for service in China, and on 18 October he was ordained at the meeting of the Baptist State Convention.

Arriving in Shanghai on 13 Sept. 1847, Yates and his wife served under difficult conditions due to the Taiping Rebellion, isolation from America during the Civil War, occasional cholera scourges, and Yates's bad health. They began Sunday schools, churches, outstations, and chapels throughout the Shanghai area. Yates was constantly traveling, preaching, and baptizing converts. During the Civil War, when funds were cut off from the United States, he served as interpreter of the Shanghai Municipal Council and superintendent of Chinese taxes. For a short time he studied in Paris, France. In 1868 he was interpreter for the U.S. consul general.

Yates wrote a number of tracts. His letters and reminiscences appeared in the *Biblical Recorder* and other publications. He edited an enlarged edition of the Chinese Hymn Book and at his death had just finished translating the New Testament into the Shanghai dialect. Several of his lectures were published in pamphlet form.

On 27 Sept. 1846 at the Mount Pisgah Baptist Church Yates married Eliza Emmeline Moring, the daughter of John, Jr., and Anne Vorlander Moring of Chatham County. They had one daughter, Annie-James, who married John F. Seaman, a Shanghai merchant.

Yates was in Chinkiang on a preaching mission when he suffered a second paralytic stroke. D. W. Herring, a co-worker, took him home to Shanghai, where he died. He and his wife were buried in the Eight Fairies Bridge Cemetery in Shanghai. Yates Academy, a boys' school in Soochow, China, and the Yates Baptist Association in North Carolina were named in his honor.

SEE: Ferrebee Catharine Bryan, *At the Gates: Life Story of Matthew Tyson and Eliza Moring Yates of China* (ca. 1949); William Cathcart, *The Baptist Encyclopedia*, vol. 2 (1881); Raleigh, *Biblical Recorder*, 21, 28 Mar., 4, 11, 25 Apr., 2 May 1888; William R. L. Smith, *A Great Trio: Fuller, Jeter, Yates* (1896); W. S. Stewart, *Early Baptist Missionaries and Pioneers* (ca. 1925); Charles E. Taylor, "Estimate of the Character of M. T. Yates," *Wake Forest Student* 32 (March 1913), *General Catalogue of Wake Forest College, North Carolina, 1834–5–1891–2* (1892), and *The Story of Yates the Missionary, as Told in His Letters and Reminiscences* (1898); Davis E. Woolley, ed., *The Encyclopedia of Southern Baptists*, vol. 2 (1958); *Yates Baptist Association Minutes, 1953*; Matthew Tyson Yates Papers (Baptist Historical Collection, Wake Forest University, Winston-Salem [portraits]).

JOHN R. WOODARD

Yates, William James (28 Aug. 1827–25 Oct. 1888), newspaper editor, was a native of Fayetteville, the fourth of six children of James (1788–1850) and Elizabeth Roach Yates (ca. 1793–29 May 1879). One of Yates's younger brothers was the Reverend Edwin A. Yates (1829–1909).

At age thirteen Yates began work as an apprentice in the printing office of the Fayetteville *North Carolinian*, a Democratic newspaper then published by Hardy L. Holmes, a prominent lawyer. In October 1853 he purchased an interest in the *North Carolinian* from Robert K. Bryan, and the two men published the paper as joint proprietors until September 1854, when Yates acquired Bryan's interest and became sole proprietor of the journal. In December 1855, citing "impaired health and a large and arduous business," Yates named Josiah Johnson of Sampson County as joint editor and proprietor. In June 1856, again giving poor health as his reason, Yates sold his interest in the *North Carolinian* to Johnson and moved to Charlotte. The following September he bought the Charlotte *Western Democrat* from John J. Palmer and became its editor. With the exception of a brief period of retirement in the early 1880s, Yates remained connected with this paper for the rest of his life.

The *Western Democrat* was founded in Charlotte in January 1853 by Robert P. Waring and Rufus M. Herron. Under Yates's ownership it became an effective organ of the Democratic party in the western part of the state. A staunch, lifelong Democrat, Yates made no attempt to conceal his devotion to the party. The *Western Democrat* appeared without interruption throughout the Civil War; it was the only antebellum North Carolina newspaper that could make that claim.

After the war the paper continued to flourish despite increased competition from other Charlotte newspapers. Yates, who associated himself with the Bourbon or conservative element of the Democratic party, was vitally interested in North Carolina's economic welfare and in the growth and development of Charlotte. In December 1870 he changed the name of his paper from the *Western Democrat* to the *Charlotte Democrat*. On 1 Oct. 1881 he sold it to James M. Strong, then owner of the Charlotte *Southern Home*; the two papers were then merged into a new publication called the *Charlotte Home and Democrat* (later the *Charlotte Home-Democrat*). Yates retired, but finding himself "unable to stay away" from the printing office, he returned in February 1884 as editor and resumed an active role in the management of the paper until his death. In July 1887—slightly more than a year before he died—the name of the paper was changed back to the *Charlotte Democrat*. In 1896 James Strong disposed of the *Democrat*, and it was discontinued the next year.

Although implored by friends and associates to do so, William J. Yates never sought elective office. He was, however, appointed to several state boards and councils by various governors. During the first term of Governor John W. Ellis in 1859–60, Yates was a member of the Council of State. He served on the State Library Board during one term of the Civil War–era administration of Governor Zebulon B. Vance. From 1879 until his death Yates was a trustee of The University of North Carolina, in which he took a lively interest. From 1883 he distinguished himself as a member of the board of the Western North Carolina Insane Asylum at Morganton and at the time of his death was serving as first chairman. Yates was also a member of the state Democratic executive committee in 1884 and a director of two railroad companies. He was a close personal friend and adviser of Governor Vance and a number of other state political leaders.

On 13 Aug. 1850 Yates married Mary Louise Laurence, the oldest daughter of John Laurence of Fayetteville; before her death on 21 Jan. 1857 at age twenty-three, the couple had two sons, both of whom died as young children. On 24 Nov. 1857 Yates married Sallie Springs (14 Feb. 1838–18 Mar. 1899), the third child of Alexander and Eliza Marsh Springs of Mecklenburg County. They had three sons and six daughters: William J., Jr. (b. 1870), David Schenck, Clara (Mrs. James H. Ross), Sallie (Mrs. I. W. Faison), Laura (Mrs. Walter W. Watt, d. 13 Jan. 1889), Addie P. (d. 20 July 1889), Mamie (Mrs. E. L. Keesler), and Bettie (Mrs. H. N. Pharr, d. 3 Feb. 1899). A stepdaughter, Lizzie (Mrs. Thomas Simons Clarkson, 1856–1906), also lived with the family for many years.

Long a member of the Tryon Street Methodist Church, Yates was buried in Elmwood Cemetery, Charlotte.

SEE: John Brevard Alexander, *The History of Mecklenburg County from 1740 to 1900* (1902); *Charlotte Daily Observer*, 19 Mar. 1899, 1 June 1915; *Charlotte Democrat*, 26 Oct., 2 Nov. 1888; Charlotte *Western Democrat*, 7 Oct. 1856; Zebulon F. Curtis, "William J. Yates," *Trinity Archive* 10 (March 1897); Jerome Dowd, *Sketches of Prominent Living North Carolinians* (1888); Fayetteville *North Carolinian*, 28 Sept. 1850, 1 Oct. 1853, 23 Sept. 1854, 15 Dec. 1855, 28 June, 5 July, 30 Aug. 1856, 24 Jan., 3 Dec. 1857; *Fayetteville Observer*, 20 Aug. 1850.

ROBERT M. TOPKINS

Yeamans, Sir John *(February 1611–August 1674)*, Proprietary governor of Carolina and landgrave, was born in Bristol, England, where he was baptized at St. Mary Redcliffe on 28 Feb. 1611, the son of John, a Bristol brewer, and Blanche Germain Yeamans. He married a Miss Limp, who probably was the mother of his five sons, William, Robert, George, Edward, and one whose name is unknown, and three daughters, Frances, Willoughby, and Anne. He migrated to Barbados by 1638 and formed a partnership for land acquisition with Benjamin Berringer by 1641. In 1643 Yeamans and Berringer were living on the same plantation in St. Peter Parish, but after 1648 the partnership was dissolved.

Yeamans accumulated wealth as a successful planter and gained political prominence in the colony's assembly, on the council, and as a judge in the courts of common pleas. He acquired the confidence of John Colleton, a former royalist officer turned planter and politician. With the restoration of Charles II, Colleton successfully developed the concept, which appears to have been his idea initially, for the establishment of the Proprietary colony of Carolina. As the principal spokesman for the eight Lords Proprietors of Carolina, Colleton took the lead in trying to attract settlers to that colony.

Prior to his intense involvement in the settlement of Carolina, Yeamans married, on 11 Apr. 1661 Margaret Foster, the daughter of the Reverend John Foster and the widow of Yeamans's former business partner, Lieutenant Colonel Benjamin Berringer. The Berringers were the parents of Mary, Simon, John, and Margaret, who was born after the death of her father. Evidence has been uncovered that the last years of the Berringer marriage were unhappy, that Margaret had transferred her affection to John Yeamans, and that the Berringers were virtually separated. Berringer died in January 1661 after a prolonged and undetermined illness. Suspicion was raised at the time, admittedly by Yeamans's political enemies, that Yeamans and Margaret Berringer had conspired to murder her husband. Yeamans was cleared of these accusations by the council of Barbados, and the Berringer estate passed to Margaret Yeamans and her children. For a time the Yeamanses lived on Nicholas Plantation (now St. Nicholas Abbey), built by Benjamin Berringer after 1656 and considered one of the three great Jacobean houses surviving in the Western Hemisphere.

The attention of the first prospective Carolina settlers focused on the Lower Cape Fear region, which the Proprietors named the County of Clarendon. Here a colony sponsored by the Corporation of Barbadian Adventurers from Barbados and elsewhere established itself in 1664. The Lords Proprietors, however, soon shifted their interest to a more southerly site near Port Royal. Taking advantage of this interest, another group of Barbadians, led by Yeamans, Sir Thomas Modyford, and Peter Colleton, negotiated through Yeamans's son Major William Yeamans a Proprietary endorsement for a colony at Port Royal. As a mark of their favor and to add to Yeamans's prestige, the Proprietors prevailed on King Charles to confer upon him the honor of knight baronet on 12 Jan. 1665. On the preceding day the Proprietors had appointed him "Governor of our County of Clarendon neare Cape Faire and of all that tract of ground which lyeth southerly as farr as the river St. Mathias."

In October 1665 Yeamans sailed from Barbados for the Cape Fear with three ships planning to explore southward from there to Port Royal, where he hoped to found a colony. As Yeamans's fleet attempted to enter the Cape Fear River, his largest vessel ran aground and sank. Though most of the passengers were saved, his supplies were lost, including the cannon with which he intended to fortify the Port Royal settlement. Shortly after this Yeamans sent another of his vessels to Virginia to obtain food, clothing, and other supplies for the Clarendon settlers, only to have it wreck on the return voyage.

Yeamans remained on the Cape Fear from early November until shortly after Christmas. Here the governor made plans for Robert Sandford, secretary of the colony, to undertake an exploratory voyage to the south, which was later successfully carried out. Having presided over a meeting of the General Assembly of Clarendon, the governor boarded his one remaining vessel and sailed for Barbados never again to return. For another year and a half the Clarendon settlement hung on, but by the close of the summer of 1667 the last of its settlers departed, and Clarendon County ceased to exist. Its governor meanwhile was embroiled in the uncertain and often tempestuous politics of Barbados and seems to have made no effort to save his colony.

Under the vigorous leadership of Lord Ashley, soon to be created Earl of Shaftesbury, the Proprietors in 1669 renewed their efforts to settle Carolina and dispatched a fleet of three ships with colonists aboard bound for the Port Royal area. With the fleet went a blank commission as governor and commander-in-chief addressed to Sir John Yeamans, at Barbados, who was instructed to fill in the document with his own name or that of another of his choice. Yeamans took command of the expedition, hired the sloop *Three Brothers* to replace a vessel that had sunk off Barbados, and sailed for Carolina. A great storm scattered the fleet, and the two surviving ships sought safety in Bermuda. Here Yeamans decided, for reasons that are unclear, to withdraw from the expedition and to return to Barbados. He then appointed William Sayle, a septuagenarian and a former governor of Bermuda who had had some earlier connection with Carolina, to take his place as governor.

The expedition then proceeded to Carolina where it established a colony not at Port Royal, but at Albemarle Point on the Ashley River. This colony became the nucleus of South Carolina. Yeamans finally reached the colony in the summer of 1671 with his wife, some of his children, and about fifty immigrants from Barbados in his party. The Proprietors on 5 Apr. 1671 had bestowed upon him the title of landgrave. This was the highest rank in the colony's nobility created by the Proprietors under their new framework of government known as the Fundamental Constitutions. Yeamans expected to be immediately acclaimed as governor of the colony, for under the provisions of the Fundamental Constitutions when a Proprietor was not present in Carolina, the highest ranking member of the native nobility would become governor. Joseph West, who had been named governor following the death of William Sayle, refused to give up his office until he received orders from the Proprietors.

Meanwhile, Yeamans established a plantation on Wappoo Creek and reportedly introduced slavery to the colony. Despite repeated efforts to gain the governorship, he was stymied until the Proprietors, acting in accordance with the provisions of the Fundamental Constitutions, ordered that the landgrave be given preference to a commoner and sent him a commission.

On 26 Mar. 1672 the Council proclaimed Sir John governor. In an effort to provide needed food supplies for the colony in 1672 and 1673, Yeamans made liberal use of the Proprietors' credit without their approval. It was also charged in the colony that he had attempted to make huge profits from the food shortages and that his actions had helped bring on these shortages. Displeased at last with Sir John after years of the closest association, the Proprietors on 25 Apr. 1674 revoked his commission as governor and proceeded to appoint Joseph West as his successor. Before this news reached the colony, however, Governor Yeamans died, and on 13 Aug. 1674 Joseph West was named to succeed him.

Lady Margaret remained in South Carolina for several years securing additional land grants that she left to her daughter Margaret, who later became the wife of Colonel James Moore, the founder of a second and permanent settlement on the Cape Fear. Lady Margaret eventually married Captain William Walley and returned to Barbados, where she died.

Sir John Yeamans continues to be an enigmatic figure. He clearly deserves credit as a founder of the two Charles Townes—first on the Cape Fear and then in southern Carolina—but his terms as governor of each of the colonies were more controversial. Circumstances conspired to overwhelm the fledgling Cape Fear colony, but Yeamans initially tried to save the settlement. His interest, however, lay farther south. His tenure in the southern colony was marred by dissension, although again he attempted, even beyond Proprietary limits, to meet the colony's most pressing problems. The accusation that he alienated his friend's wife and then murdered him cannot be absolutely proven, but the circumstantial possibility seriously compromises his character. Seen in the best light, Yeamans may be viewed as an energetic and restless adventurer who was actively involved in the West Indian colonization of the mainland, playing a significant role in the founding of the Carolinas.

SEE: Agnes L. Baldwin, *First Settlers of South Carolina, 1670–1680* (1969); Langdon Cheves, ed., "The Shaftesbury Papers," in *Collections of the South Carolina Historical Society*, vol. 5 (1897); Wesley Frank Craven, *The Southern Colonies in the Seventeenth Century, 1607–1689* (1949); *DAB*, vol. 10 (1929); *DNB*, vol. 21 (1921–22); Richard S. Dunn, "The English Sugar Islands and the Founding of South Carolina," *South Carolina Historical Magazine* 72 (1971), and *Sugar and Slaves: The Rise of the Planter Class in the English West Indies, 1624–1713* (1972); Vincent T. Harlow, *A History of Barbados, 1625–1685* (1926); Lawrence Lee, *The Lower Cape Fear in Colonial Days* (1965); Prerogative Court of Canterbury, August–October 1663 (transcript, Barbados Museum and Historical Society); M. Alston Read, "Notes on Some Colonial Governors of South Carolina and Their Families," *South Carolina Historical and Genealogical Magazine* 11 (1910); *Records in the British Public Records Office Relating to South Carolina*, vol. 1 (1928); W. Noel Sainsbury, *Calendar of State Papers: Colonial Series: America and West Indies, 1661–1668* (1880); Alexander S. Salley, ed., *Narratives of Early Carolina* (1911); William L. Saunders, ed., *Colonial Records of North Carolina*, vol. 1 (1886); E. M. Shilstone, "Nicholas Plantation and Some of Its Associations," in Peter F. Campbell, ed., *Chapters in Barbados History: First Series* (1986); M. Eugene Sirmans, *Colonial South Carolina: A Political History, 1663–1673* (1966); Henry A. M. Smith, "Sir John Yeamans: An Historical Error," *South Carolina Historical and Genealogical Magazine* 19 (1918); John P. Thomas, Jr., "The Barbadians in Early South Carolina," *South Carolina Historical and Genealogical Magazine* 31 (1930); Will of Sir John Yeamans, 20 May 1671 (Barbados Archives, Bridgetown).

LINDLEY S. BUTLER
HERBERT R. PASCHAL

Yeardley, Francis (1624–55), explorer and Virginia official, was born in Virginia, the son of Governor Sir George and Temperance Flowerdew Yeardley. She was the cousin of John Pory, Virginia secretary and speaker of the 1619 Assembly. In 1643 young Captain Yeardley was appointed commander of troops in Accomack, and early the next year he received a grant of 3,000 acres for transporting fifty-eight people to the colony.

In 1647 he married Sarah Offley, who had been married first to Adam Thorogood, by whom she had a son, Adam, and second to John Gookin. There apparently were no children by her other two husbands. Yeardley was a member of the Maryland Council in 1652 but soon returned to Virginia and was a burgess of Lower Norfolk County in 1653. He was also a church commissioner for the county in 1651, 1652, and 1654 and a colonel of militia in 1653. He appears to have been a leader of the Cromwellian party in the colony.

Yeardley was interested in the land south of the settled portion of Virginia, and in a letter of 8 May 1654 to John Ferrars he reported that he had recently (apparently in September 1653) sponsored "an ample discovery of South Virginia or Carolana" which he described in glowing terms. He especially mentioned the fertile soil, mulberries, grapevines, timber, the longer growing season, and other natural features. He stated that he had invested £300 of his own money in the expedition and that he intended to go there himself in the summer of 1654. It appears that Nathaniel Batts, afterwards a pioneer settler of North Carolina, was among the explorers.

Information gathered at this time appeared on the map made in London in 1657 by Nicholas Comberford. The Roanoke Indians gave Yeardley a great deal of land, and he had a house built for the "Emperour of Roanoke." At the request of this Indian leader Yeardley received his only son in his home at Lynnhaven, Va., to be educated; he also was baptized there. Robert Bodnam, a carpenter, was sent by Yeardley in 1655 to build a house for Nathaniel Batts on what is now Salmon Creek, in Bertie County, where Batts established a trading post. The inventory of Yeardley's estate noted an impressive number of books "small & great."

SEE: Alexander Brown, *Genesis of the United States*, vol. 2 (1890); *Lower Norfolk County Virginia Antiquary*, vol. 2, part 3 (1898); Alexander S. Salley, Jr., ed., *Narratives of Early Carolina* (1911); *Virginia Magazine of History and Biography* 1 (1893), 4 (1897), 5 (1898), 6 (1899), 25 (1917), 28 (1920); *William and Mary Quarterly* 1 (1894); J. H. R. Yardley, *Before the Mayflower* (1931).

WILLIAM S. POWELL

Yeates, Jesse Johnson (29 May 1829–5 Sept. 1892), attorney and congressman, was the son of James Boon and Lucy J. Yeates of Hertford County. He attended schools in his native county and is said to have had "a hard struggle to secure his education and prepare himself for his profession." One of his teachers was Richard J. Gatling, subsequently inventor of the Gatling gun. After graduation from Emory and Henry College, Yeates taught school for two years as headmaster of an academy in the village of Harrellsville.

His first wife, Maria E. Piper of Cedarville, died in 1854 as he was beginning to study law with William N. H. Smith, of Murfreesboro, later chief justice of the state supreme court. In 1855 he was admitted to the bar and in the same year married Virginia Scott, the daughter of James A. Scott of Murfreesboro. He practiced in Murfreesboro for the next six years and served as prosecuting attorney for

Hertford County from 1855 to 1860, when he won election to the state House of Commons. During his term he also served as solicitor for the First Judicial District.

At the outbreak of the Civil War, Yeates resigned his seat in the legislature to raise a company that became part of the Thirty-first North Carolina Regiment. He was captured, along with most of his troops, at the Battle of Roanoke Island but was exchanged and spent the last part of the war as a purchasing agent for the Confederate army.

After the conflict Yeates served a term on Governor Jonathan Worth's Council but declined an appointment by Governor William W. Holden as a judge in the First Judicial District. In 1871 he was a delegate to both the state Democratic convention and the state constitutional convention. Elected as a Democrat to the U.S. House of Representatives in 1875, he held a seat in the Forty-fourth, Forty-fifth, and Forty-sixth congresses. His legislative efforts were directed towards securing appropriations for improvements in life-saving and lighthouse service and fostering the U.S. Fish Commission.

On leaving Congress in 1881, Yeates practiced law in Washington, D.C., until his death there eleven years later. He was the father of one daughter by his first marriage and four sons by his second. He was buried in Glenwood Cemetery, Washington, D.C.

SEE: *Biog. Dir. Am. Cong.* (1971); Weymouth T. Jordan, comp., *North Carolina Troops, 1861–1865: A Roster*, vol. 8 (1981); *Nat. Cyc. Am. Biog.*, vol. 13 (1906); John H. Wheeler, ed., *Reminiscences and Memoirs of North Carolina and Eminent North Carolinians* (1884).

T. C. PARRAMORE

Yeates, William Smith (15 Dec. 1856–19 Feb. 1908), first state geologist of Georgia, was born at Murfreesboro, the son of Jesse Jackson, a prominent attorney and U.S. congressman, and Virginia Scott Yeates. He attended the primary and high schools of Murfreesboro; Randolph-Macon College at Ashland, Va., for a year and a half; and Emory and Henry College, at Emory, Va., for three and a half years, where he received a B.A. degree in June 1878. Three years later Emory and Henry awarded him a master of arts degree in consideration of further literary and scientific studies.

In the spring of 1879 Yeates was appointed a messenger for the U.S. Fish Commission and was involved in the distribution of young fish from the hatchery at Avoca. He was then the principal of two high schools before becoming a clerk with the Fish Commission in 1880.

Long interested in geology, Yeates in 1881 was named assistant to the curator of the Department of Minerals and Economic Geology at the National Museum in Washington, D.C. He advanced rapidly in the system and soon became assistant curator of the mineral collection as well as professor of mineralogy and professor of geology at the Corcoran Scientific School of Columbian University. He also was responsible for organizing important mineral displays at the Cincinnati and New Orleans expositions in 1884 and the Chicago World's Fair of 1893.

In 1893 Yeates was appointed the first state geologist of Georgia and moved to Atlanta. During his tenure, he published nine works on Georgia's geological resources, including: *A Report on . . . Marbles . . .*, *A Report on . . . Corundum Deposits . . .*, *A Report on . . . Water Deposits . . .*, *A Report on . . . Gold Deposits . . .*, *A Report on . . . Phosphates and Marls . . .*, *A Report on the Artesian Well Systems . . .*, *A Report on . . . Clays . . .*, *A Report on the Roads and Road-Building Materials . . .*, and *A Report on . . . Granites and Gneisses . . . .* He also collected and organized an extensive display of Georgia's minerals, ores, and building stones and woods. During his career Yeates was a Fellow of the Geological Society of America and a member of the Philosophical Society of Washington, D.C., Geological Society of Washington, D.C., American Chemical Society, American Institute of Mining Engineers, American Association for the Advancement of Science, and International Congress of Geologists (1891).

On 16 Jan. 1884 he married Julia Wheeler Moore, daughter of the historian John Wheeler Moore. They had three children: Julia Moore (died young), William Smith, Jr., and Charles Moore. Still serving as state geologist Yeates, died in Atlanta and was buried at Glenwood Cemetery, Washington, D.C.

SEE: Henry Poellnitz Johnston, *William R. King and His Kin* (1975); *The Official Sketchbook, 1898–1899* (1899); *Who Was Who in America*, vol. 1 (1943).

JAMES ELLIOTT MOORE

Yellowley, Edward Clement (*22 Oct. 1821–23 Sept. 1885*), lawyer and politician, was born in Martin County, where his father, Edward Yellowley, settled after emigrating from England shortly following the end of the American Revolution. When E. C. Yellowley was a boy, the family moved to Greenville, where he received his early education at the Greenville Academy under J. M. Lovejoy, a noted southern teacher. After obtaining a bachelor of arts degree from The University of North Carolina in 1844, Yellowley became a lawyer and established a practice in Greenville. He also had some farming interests, owned a few slaves, and took an active interest in politics as a Whig. In the 1850s he was elected clerk of the superior court and then solicitor for the county court.

In 1847 Yellowley's strong political beliefs got him into grave personal difficulties with H. F. Harris, a member of the House of Commons from Pitt County. Harris, objecting to some of Yellowley's political statements against him, demanded satisfaction in a duel. The duel was delayed for a while because of interference by local authorities, but on 1 Oct. 1847 it took place near Portsmouth, Va. At the first firing Yellowley shot his pistol into the air. His opponent shot his through Yellowley's hat. Yellowley hoped that that would satisfy Harris, but the legislator demanded a second firing. This time Yellowley took deliberate aim and shot Harris through the heart, instantly killing him. Yellowley never spoke of this affair and always regretted it.

In 1860 he supported John Bell for president and opposed secession. After Abraham Lincoln's election, however, he switched sides and became an ardent supporter of the Confederacy. In 1861 he raised a company; commissioned a captain, he was assigned to Company G of the Eighth Regiment. In February 1862 he was captured at Roanoke Island but was paroled three weeks later and rejoined his regiment. In July 1863 he was promoted to major and in October to lieutenant colonel in the Sixty-eighth Regiment of North Carolina State Troops.

Although greatly respected by his men, Yellowley experienced a very embarrassing incident late in the war. His troops, wearing long cape overcoats, were marching just before dawn near Hamilton, N.C., at Butler's Bridge. Unbeknownst to Yellowley and his men, they were advancing side by side with the enemy, with Yellowley riding next to the Union colonel. Reportedly, Yellowley thought that the other man was another Confederate colonel's body servant. He did not discover his error until the Federal officer issued a command to Yellowley, thinking that he was his courier. When Yellowley did not obey

the command, both colonels realized the situation, the troops separated, and a face-to-face skirmish ensued. Soon both sides retreated.

Throughout the Civil War Yellowley retained his interest in politics. In 1862 he was an unsuccessful candidate for the Confederate Congress as a strong supporter of the war. In 1864 friends urged him to run for the state legislature. As one of them noted, Yellowley was sought because he would "properly represent the interests of the Southern cause" while still devoting himself "to the welfare and honor of North Carolina." According to the friend, Yellowley was "conservative in principle, *but not too conservative*"; he would not support peace meetings or "convention schemes."

After the war Yellowley served one term (1865) in the House of Commons. Though he remained an active Democrat, he held no further political office. Instead, he built a large, lucrative law practice, accumulating a substantial fortune. Late in life his health failed, so he moved to Asheville to recuperate and died there. He was buried in Cherry Hill Cemetery, Greenville. Yellowley never married.

SEE: Samuel A. Ashe, ed., *Cyclopedia of Eminent and Representative Men of the Carolinas*, vol. 2 (1892); Walter Clark, ed., *Histories of the Several Regiments and Battalions from North Carolina in the Great War*, vols. 1, 3 (1901); Wymouth T. Jordan, comp., *North Carolina Troops, 1861–1865: A Roster*, vol. 4 (1973); H. T. King, *Sketches of Pitt County* (1911); E. C. Yellowley Letters and Paper (Manuscript Department, Duke University Library, Durham); Yellowley Papers (Southern Historical Collection, University of North Carolina, Chapel Hill).

ROBERTA SUE ALEXANDER

Yelverton, Emory Harrison (*16 July 1890–8 May 1955*), diplomat, was born at his father's town house in Goldsboro, Wayne County, the son of William Thomas and Sarah Jane Sauls Yelverton, both natives of Wayne County. His father, a former clerk of the Wayne County Superior Court, was a partner in the hardware firm of Yelverton and Smith, later W. T. Yelverton and Sons. Through his father he was descended from Captain James Blount (fl. 1670), of Mulberry Hill, Chowan County, an influential Carolina planter, member of the Council, and founder of one of the colony's most powerful and prominent families, whose granddaughter, Elizabeth Blount, married John Yelverton sometime before 1706. The Yelvertons moved into what is now Wayne County in the mid-eighteenth century, and a later John Yelverton was commissioned an officer in the Dobbs County Militia in 1761. The family had produced justices of the peace, court officials, and members of the General Assembly.

Harrison Yelverton attended the public schools of Goldsboro and was graduated from the Goldsboro High School in 1908, when, like his four older brothers, he entered The University of North Carolina. There he was a member of the Beta Chapter of Phi Delta Theta social fraternity and was president his senior year. He continued to support this fraternity throughout his life and left it a generous bequest at his death. During the summer of 1910 he and four friends sailed on a freighter from Philadelphia to Manchester, England, where they toured the British Isles, returning for the opening of the university in the fall. He was graduated in 1912 and joined the family firm with his father and older brothers in Goldsboro.

Not satisfied in his father's business, Yelverton spent a year at the Harvard University Business School and decided on a career in the foreign service. After taking the foreign service examination on 19 Jan. 1914 and passing it, he was appointed American consular assistant on 14 Apr. 1914 and detailed to the Department of State in Washington, D.C. His father was a prominent member of and heavy contributor to the Democratic party in North Carolina and a close friend of Walter Hines Page, whom President Woodrow Wilson had appointed ambassador to the Court of St. James. On 1 Feb. 1915 Yelverton was detailed to the Consulate General at London. Showing promise as a young diplomat, he was then assigned to duty as vice-consul at Swansea, Wales, on 18 Nov. 1916, but on 3 Jan. 1917 he was transferred back and named vice-consul to London, serving in that post for the remainder of World War I. He was deeply saddened by the death of his only sister, Glendora, on 2 Sept. 1917 in Goldsboro and for a time was eager to return to the family. On 25 Aug. 1919 he resigned his post and left for the United States aboard the liner *Mauretania*.

In London he quickly had become well known in diplomatic and social circles, making many friends among people of the arts and letters and in the glittering social circles surrounding the British court even in wartime. He also studied the antique market and became an authority on seventeenth- and eighteenth-century furniture. Yelverton was named to the board of directors of the American University Union in London and was appointed by Lord Fortescue to membership on the committee for the celebration of the Sir Walter Raleigh Tercentenary in 1916.

After arriving in the United States he was detailed to the Department of State and appointed by the secretary of state to duty on the Conference for the Limitation of Armament, which convened in Washington from 15 Nov. to 31 Dec. 1921. During the conference he acted as private secretary to Oscar W. Underwood, of Alabama, one of the most powerful members of the U.S. Senate.

Returning to Goldsboro, he made his home with his aging father and brother Edgar, his mother having died in 1922. He was a member of the firm of W. T. Yelverton and Sons and sometimes listed his occupation as "merchant." He represented Wayne County in the General Assembly in 1925 and 1927.

In 1929 the legal suit and court trial over the will of his father, who had died the previous year, drew an extraordinary amount of sensational news coverage statewide and deeply divided his family. The settlement of the suit in favor of the brothers Harrison, Edgar (who died during the trial), and their widowed sister-in-law, Mrs. Leslie Yelverton, gave Harrison the financial independence that seemed essential to his happiness.

Long interested in architecture, he speculated in real estate development, and a number of Colonial Revival–style cottages with antique woodwork, built in southeastern Goldsboro, date from this period. He traveled extensively and returned to Britain and the Continent a number of times. Yelverton joined the Wayne Lodge of Ancient, Free, and Accepted Masons and was an active member of the North Carolina Art Society and of St. Stephen's Episcopal Church in Goldsboro. At his death he left St. Stephen's parish a large bequest that paid for a substantial capital improvement to the parish hall. The handsome iron fence that surrounds the churchyard came from the elegant town house designed, according to the family, by the New Jersey architect G. S. H. Appleget, that his father had built on John Street in Goldsboro. This large two-story home, constructed in a cruciform plan, was ornamented with marble mantles and elaborate parquet floors. Featuring a spiral stairway in the circular, center hall, it was one of the most sophisticated and elegant Italianate-style houses in the state and represented

the architectural and cultural renaissance that merchant-princes helped bring about in North Carolina during the postbellum period. The house was razed about 1957.

Yelverton never married. He was buried on the family lot in Willowdale Cemetery, Goldsboro.

SEE: John L. Cheney, Jr., ed., *North Carolina Government, 1585–1979* (1981); Stuart Hall Hill Papers, vol. 2 (North Carolina Collection, University of North Carolina, Chapel Hill); Talmage C. Johnson and Charles R. Holloman, *The Story of Kinston and Lenoir County* (1954); *Register of the Department of State*, 23 Dec. 1918; Pearl Ella Thompson and Mrs. Henry Bridgers Kennedy (Goldsboro), personal contact, 30 June 1960; E. Harrison Yelverton Papers (possession of Mrs. Plato Evans, Greenville, N.C.); Frank C. Yelverton (Fremont, N.C), personal contact, 6 July 1960.

JOHN BAXTON FLOWERS III

Yergan, Max *(15 Aug. 1892–11 Apr. 1975)*, world religious leader, educator, reformer, and consultant on African affairs, was born in Raleigh, the son of Lizzie Yergan and the grandson of Fred Yergan, a slave and apprentice carpenter. He attended St. Ambrose parish school and Shaw University, where he played football and was a member of the debating team until 1914. After graduate work at Springfield College, Yergan became affiliated with the YWCA in 1915. Beginning as an officer in the student Christian movement in the southern states, he remained with the YMCA for twenty-five years.

At the start of World War I, he was sent to organize YMCA units among the African regiments that the British army was activating in Kenya. Later he returned to the United States, joined the army, and was commissioned chaplain and sent to Europe, where he served in France.

After the war he was appointed senior secretary of the International Committee of the YMCA and stationed in South Africa. Working among young college men, he spent eighteen years teaching his students to put their faith to practical use and influencing them to become leaders and teachers. He also traveled and worked in India. In recognition of his labors he was presented the Harmon Award in 1926 and the Spingarn Medal in 1933.

With his appointment to teach Negro history at City College, New York, in 1936, Yergan became the first black studies teacher on a major campus in the United States. In 1938, in order to assure the perpetuation of his work in Africa, he organized the Council on African Affairs, whose directors included Dr. Ralph J. Bunche, Jawaharlal Nehru, and Paul Robeson. He was co-publisher with Adam Clayton Powell of *The People's Voice* during the 1930s and 1940s and was president of the National Negro Congress. Two years after the United States entered World War II, the congress—though supporting the war—demanded the right of colonial people to self-determination and the removal of every barrier to full Negro participation in the conflict. While still head of the Negro Congress in 1946, he led a delegation of the congress to petition the United Nations to eliminate political, economic, and social discrimination in the United States. He said he left the congress in 1946 because the Communists sought to frustrate the decisions of the board.

He also had to battle the Communists in the Council on African Affairs. In 1948 Communist infiltration had split the council into Communist and anti-Communist factions, causing a major crisis that threatened the purposes for which it was founded. His chief opponent was council chairman, Paul Robeson. In 1962 he was chairman of the American Committee for Aid to Katanga Freedom Fighters, which opposed U.S. support for the United Nations military action against secessionist Katanga Province in the Congo.

Yergan married Susie Wiseman of Salisbury. They had two sons, Dr. Charles, a specialist in internal medicine, and Fred, an engineer, and one daughter, Mrs. Mary Yergan Hughes, whose husband, Dr. Durward L. Hughes, also was a physician.

He was living on Pinebridge Road in Ossining, N.Y., when he died in Northern Westchester Hospital, Mount Kisco, N.Y. A eulogy was delivered by Andrew R. Tyler, and a testimonial—signed by Dr. J. Archie Hargraves, president of Shaw University, in behalf of the trustees, administration, faculty, staff, students, and alumni—was read at the funeral. His huge rare book collection was given to Shaw University and his papers to Howard University. He was buried in New York City.

SEE: Thomas Kee, personal contact, 22 Aug. 1978; *New York Times*, 13 Apr. 1975; Raleigh *News and Observer*, 13 Apr. 1975; Shaw University, *Alumni News*, April 1975.

JAMES H. BOYKIN

Yonaguska (or Drowning Bear) *(1760?–April 1839)* was head chief of the Cherokee middle towns in the crucial years from 1800 until his death. The exact date and place of his birth are unknown, but Charles Lanman, who visited the eastern Cherokee a decade after the old chief's death, reported that Yonaguska was "born in this mountain land . . . and died in the year 1838, in the seventy-fifth year of his age." Probably one of the last practitioners of polygamy among the Cherokee, Yonaguska was survived by two wives and many children.

As head chief he consistently urged peace with the United States and played a prominent role in the meeting between Cherokee chiefs and Tecumseh in 1811. This conference resulted in the Cherokee's refusal to join the Shawnee leader in his alliance with the British for an offensive against the United States.

In accordance with a provision of the treaty that delegates of the Cherokee Nation signed with the federal government in 1819, Yonaguska and the heads of at least fifty other families who lived along the Oconaluftee, Tuckasegee, and Little Tennessee rivers between the Balsam and Cowee mountains withdrew from the nation, received a reservation of 640 acres each, and became citizens of the state of North Carolina and the United States. Yonaguska's reservation was located on Governors Island at the confluence of the Oconaluftee and Tuckasegee rivers, and his followers obtained reservations along the Oconaluftee River and near Quallatown. In 1820 the chief sold his reservation for $1,300 and moved to Quallatown.

The extension of state laws over the Cherokee Nation in the late 1820s freed traders from the restrictions previously imposed on the sale of liquor and allowed unscrupulous speculators, whose appetite for land had been whetted by the discovery of gold in northern Georgia, to employ alcohol in frequently successful attempts to negotiate illegal sales of Cherokee property. Yonaguska realized that intemperance would destroy both himself and his tribesmen. According to William Holland Thomas, the white trader whom Yonaguska's clan adopted, the chief assembled the Oconaluftee Cherokee in 1830 and informed them that "he had been considering and devising ways to promote their happiness in the future." Citing the Oconaluftee Cherokee's "present state of improvement" as evidence of the injurious effects of intemperance," Yonaguska encouraged his people to refrain from the immod-

erate consumption of alcohol and then instructed his clerk to write down a pledge by which the Qualla Indians agreed to "abandon the use of spiritous liquors." The chief signed first, and all the residents of the town reportedly followed. In 1838 Thomas credited Yonaguska with the Oconaluftee Cherokee's "present state of improvement" because of his devotion to the cause of temperance.

When the Cherokee Council convened at New Echota in 1835 at the behest of the U.S. agent, the Reverend John F. Schermerhorn, to sign a treaty by which the Cherokee ceded all lands in the eastern United States and agreed to remove west of the Mississippi River, Yonaguska did not attend. He vehemently opposed removal, but after a minority of Cherokee led by John Ridge, Major Ridge, and Elias Boudinot accepted the government's proposal, Yonaguska dispatched Thomas to Washington. D.C., to ensure that the Oconaluftee Cherokee received their share of the benefits of the treaty. Thomas hesitated to take up the matter with the government for fear of delaying ratification by the Senate and thereby depriving the Cherokee who were desperately in need of financial aid of immediate assistance, but he did sign an agreement with the Ridge party in which the senators recognized the claim of the Oconaluftee Cherokee.

In 1837 Yonaguska and fifty-nine other Oconaluftee Cherokee submitted a memorial in which they stated to the commissioners who had been appointed to carry out the treaty of New Echota that they were opposed to removal. The commissioners acknowledged the provision in the 1819 treaty by which the Oconaluftee Cherokee had withdrawn from the Cherokee Nation and become citizens of North Carolina, granted them their memorial, and exempted them from forced removal. According to Thomas, the primary motivation for Yonaguska's resistance to removal stemmed from the chief's belief that North Carolina, the state that had recognized the Cherokee's land titles, was "better and more friendly disposed to the Red Man than any other. That should they remove west, they would there too be, in a short time, surrounded by the settlements of the whites, and probably be included in a State disposed to oppress them." Yonaguska demonstrated his loyalty to North Carolina and the federal government by ordering his warriors to assist U.S. troops in capturing those Cherokee who had hidden in the mountains. For rendering this aid he received a commendation from Colonel William L. Foster, commanding officer of the Fourth U.S. Infantry.

Yonaguska's leadership ability, his steadfast dedication to temperance, and his willingness to cooperate with the U.S. government enabled the Oconaluftee Cherokee to secure the enforcement of the treaty of 1819 and the recognition of their rights as North Carolina citizens. Thus the followers of Yonaguska managed to avoid removal.

SEE: John Finger, *The Eastern Band of the Cherokee, 1819–1900* (1984); Duane H. King, "The Origin of the Eastern Band of Cherokees as a Social and Political Entity," in King, ed., *The Cherokees in Historical Perspective* (1975); Charles Lanman, *Adventures in the Wilds of the United States and British American Provinces* (1856); James Mooney, *Myths of the Cherokee* (1900); Mattie Russell, "William Holland Thomas: White Chief of the North Carolina Cherokee" (Ph.D. diss., Duke University, 1956).

THEDA PERDUE

York, Brantley *(3 Jan. 1805–6 Oct. 1891)*, Methodist clergyman, educator, lecturer, and author, was born near Bush Creek in Randolph County, the seventh of nine children of Eli and Susanah Harden York. His grandfather, Henry York, immigrated to the United States from Yorkshire, England. Because of Eli's uncertain employment as a distiller and miner, the family fortunes fluctuated considerably, often depending on income from the children working as hired hands. Young Brantley thus attended school only thirteen months in a ten-year period; nevertheless, the excitement of learning and the challenge of obtaining an education captivated him. Obviously largely self-taught, by age nineteen York was reading a thousand pages a week through the auspices of the formally organized Library Society of Ebenezer Church, the place of his conversion at a camp meeting in 1823. Influenced strongly by the organizational structure of Methodist class, band, and camp meetings, York closely associated education and religion throughout his life. He began teaching at Bethlehem Church in Guilford County in 1831 and was licensed to preach in 1833.

In 1838, after ordination as a deacon and an unpleasant administrative mix-up that prevented his joining the newly organized North Carolina Conference of the Methodist Episcopal church, York consented to teach a subscription school in northwestern Randolph County. The school, in an infrequently used building, was called Brown's Schoolhouse after the owner of the land where it was located. Immediate success necessitated replacement of the rough log building with a hewn log building in the summer of 1838 and again with a two-room wooden frame structure in the summer of 1839.

York drew up plans for support of a permanent academy by an Education Association, and when they were implemented, he selected the name Union Institute not for patriotic reasons but because the school united nearby predominately Methodist and Quaker communities. Incorporated by the legislature in January 1841 as Union Institute Academy, the school later became Normal College, Trinity College, and after its move to Durham in 1892, Duke University in 1924. Though gratified with the success of the venture, York considered his years at Union Institute "truly onerous." It was a large school of over fifty male and female students requiring considerable time in raising money, and late at night while preparing for recitations in subjects he had not adequately studied, York noticed his vision failing in one eye.

The experience at Union Institute set the pattern for his lifework despite complete blindness that occurred in 1853 at age forty-eight. He organized Clemmonsville High School in Davidson County (1842), Olin High School in Iredell County (1851), York Collegiate Institute in Alexander County (1856), Ruffin-Badger Institute in Chatham County (1869), and New Salem and Randleman High School in Randolph County (1881). From 1873 to 1877 he was professor of belles lettres (higher English, logic, rhetoric, and elocution) at Rutherford College.

York published a successful series of original grammars beginning with *York's English Grammar* (1854), which had one additional revision in New York in 1859. His *Common School Grammar* (1860) and *High School Grammar* (1862) were published in Raleigh in at least four editions each. Appearing in 1873 was his *The Man of Business and Railroad Calculator*, a book of "applied arithmetic and legal forms."

Although York never joined the annual conference or itinerant ministry, he continued to preach, especially enjoying camp meetings. He preached in local churches in towns where he was delivering a series of lectures. Traveling with a member of his family and even alone, he would present from four to twenty lectures in a community mostly on English grammar but also on education or Prohibition. Income from the sale of his books, lecture fees, and donations provided the major means of support for his large family. Traveling throughout North Carolina and into South Carolina, Virginia, and Arkansas, he estimated late in life that he had preached or lectured over 8,000 times and taught more than 15,000 pupils.

York was president of the Randolph County Temperance Society in 1853, and he spoke widely in the statewide Prohibition campaign of 1881. He served as the first president of the North Carolina Local Ministers' Conference, and Rutherford College awarded him a D.D. degree.

He married Fannie Sherwood (1809–34) of Guilford County on 31 Jan. 1828. Then widowed with a young daughter, Rachel, he married Mary Wells Linebery (1818–1910) of Randolph County on 13 Nov. 1836. Their eleven children were Fannie Sherwood, Richard Watson, Jane, Wesley Clegg, Lucreta, Amos, Nelson Durant, Senora, William Brantley, Bascom Alfred, and Davidson Victor. York died in Forest City and was buried at Rocky Springs Methodist Church in the former York Collegiate Institute community in Alexander County. Grateful students purchased a suitable marker for his grave to honor "the unique nineteenth century educational circuit rider."

SEE: *Autobiography of Brantley York* (1910; revised, edited, and indexed by Charles Mathis, 1977); Nora C. Chaffin, *Trinity College 1839–1892* (1950); "In Memoriam," *North Carolina Teacher* 9 (December 1891); *Raleigh Christian Advocate*, 23, 30 Aug. 1893; Brantley York Papers (Duke University Archives, Durham [portrait]).

WILLIAM E. KING

York, Tyre (4 May 1836–28 Jan. 1916), physician and politician, was born in Rockford, Surry County, the son of Michael York, a Surry County farmer. After attending the common schools in his home county, young York entered the Charleston Medical College in Charleston, S.C. He completed his medical training in 1857 and the next year married Eliza Crumpler, also of Surry County. They had three daughters: Emma, Euaia, and Alice.

In 1859 he moved to Trap Hill in Wilkes County to pursue a career in medicine. Despite his later political duties, he always remained an active country doctor, serving the people of Wilkes, Surry, Ashe, and Alleghany counties. He also did some farming although he did not own slaves.

During the Civil War he was a peace man, sympathizing with the many western North Carolinians who evaded Confederate service. In fact, he often gave medical treatment to those hiding out in the mountains or caves and would supply certificates of ill health to others who were seeking to avoid army service. He himself served as a surgeon in the home guard to avoid active duty.

Before the war York was a Whig but was not politically active. Afterwards, however, he entered public life as a Democrat, serving as clerk of the Wilkes County Court in 1865, a member of the House of Commons in 1865, 1866, 1870, and 1879, and a state senator for the 1876 and 1881 terms. York was a successful Democratic politician in a predominantly Republican county because he fought for the interests of the common man. He favored such reforms as reduction of taxes and the salaries of elected officials; he worked for the people in every way. He also showed a willingness to treat blacks fairly. In 1881, as chairman of the Joint Committee on the Insane Asylum, he sought the appropriation of sufficient funds to complete the asylum at Goldsboro for the state's black residents. He also led the fight to get the state to donate a portion of its land to Shaw University in Raleigh for the construction of a building to house a new Department of Medicine.

In 1882 York changed his political affiliation, joining the liberal Republican–Anti-Prohibition Coalition in North Carolina. He said that he switched parties because the Democrats failed to keep their promise to the people to abolish the internal revenue laws and because they advocated Prohibition. Adamant in his opposition to Prohibition, York was the first person in the 1881 state legislature to speak against the issue when it was first introduced in the senate. He felt that the Prohibition bill was a "dangerous piece of class legislation" that violated people's rights, liberties, and privileges. Therefore, he accepted the nomination for Congress in the Seventh District on the liberal Republican–Anti-Prohibition Coalition ticket. Winning that campaign, he served in the Forty-eighth Congress (1883–85) but did not seek reelection in 1884. Instead, he was North Carolina's unsuccessful Republican candidate for governor that year.

In 1887, as leader of the Republican party in North Carolina's lower house, he displayed a keen interest in the common man, advocating all bills proposed for the benefit of the working classes and causing the formation of a Committee on Labor, of which he became chairman.

York retired from politics in the late 1880s except for serving as a presidential elector in 1896, returning to his medical practice and agricultural pursuits. He died at Trap Hill and was buried in the community cemetery.

SEE: *Alamance Gleaner*, 21 Aug. 1884; *Biog. Dir. Am. Cong.* (1950); John L. Cheney, Jr., ed., *North Carolina Government, 1585–1979* (1981); *Dr. Tyre York: Coalition Candidate for Congress* [1882] (broadside, North Carolina Collection, University of North Carolina, Chapel Hill); *Legislative Biographical Sketch Book* (1887); J. S. Tomlinson, *Tar Heel Sketch-Book* (1879).

ROBERTA SUE ALEXANDER

Young, Allen Lawrence (*5 Sept. 1875–17 Feb. 1957*), community leader, educator, and founder of the Wake Forest Normal and Industrial School for Negroes (1905–57), was born in northern Wake County, the eldest of ten children of Henry and Ailey Fowler Young. Seven of his own children were teachers, five of them employed at one time or another in their father's school before moving on to other careers. Arthur Allen (1897–1955) was a teacher, musician, and composer. Maude Elizabeth (b. 1901) was a librarian in Raleigh's Richard B. Harrison Public Library 1941 to 1968. Ailey Mae (b. 1903), after retiring from public school teaching, became in 1971 the first Negro to be elected to the Wake Forest City Council and received that town's 1976 Citizenship Award during her second term. James Terrence (1906–45) taught biology and music at his father's school until his early death. George Henry (b. 1913) was elected in 1977 to the Lumberton school board on retiring after forty-two years as teacher and principal of Lumberton Junior High School. Robert Trice (b. 1915) taught in the Raleigh public school system and was its last attendance counselor before merger with the Wake County system. Kathryn Lucille (b. 1917), who married the Raleigh realtor James A. Shepard, was professor of childhood education at Shaw University in Raleigh. Lewis Albert (1898–1917) died while a college student. Benjamin Lloyd (b. 1919) and Thomas Leon (b. 1920) went into government service after college.

Although all of his children who survived childhood attended institutions of higher education, Allen Young himself had little formal training. As a child attending Wake County public schools, he also had to help support his farming family. He found employment with the families of Wake Forest townspeople, including those of faculty members at Wake Forest College, several of whom gave him private instruction, including Professors W. R. Cullom, Gorell, J. H. Gulley, J. L. Lake, G. W. Paschal, W. L. Poteat, and B. F. Sledd. This preparation enabled him to enter Henderson Institute, then Kittrell College in Vance County, and eventually Shaw University. After obtaining his teaching certificate he taught in a county public school in the northern Wake County community of Wyatt. To augment his income, he and Mrs. Young established a dry cleaning business in their home in Wake Forest, catering especially to the faculty and students of the college.

In 1905 Young and Nathaniel Mitchell of Wake Forest were among the five charter members and elders of the Spring Street Presbyterian Church, founded that year in Wake Forest. In the same year the two men, together with other Negro leaders in the community, met in Young's home and organized the Presbyterian Mission School for Colored Boys and Girls. Classes opened on 6 Nov. 1905 in a corner of a bed springs factory on nearby White Street. Young was named principal and the school's only teacher for the first year. Thirty pupils enrolled in classes designed "to prepare colored boys and girls for practical duties of life," according to the first catalogue, and to equip those planning to enter college with basic English, Latin, and other courses. Boarding facilities were provided in neighborhood homes, including that of the principal. Young's first wife was instructor in general housekeeping until her death in 1910. The second Mrs. Young taught piano and primary grades. Financial assistance came from the growing membership of the church, into whose meetinghouse the school moved; from sympathetic white friends in and around Wake Forest; from philanthropists in other states; and from the Freedman's Board of the Presbyterian church, which commissioned him a missionary teacher "to the Freedmen at and about Wake Forest."

A catalogue for the second scholastic year beginning 8 Oct. 1906 listed tuition charges of 25 to 50 cents per month for courses in the literary department, and of $1.00 to $1.50 in the musical department. Room and board was $5 per month; the students furnished their own bedclothes, books, and lamp oil and were "required to do at least two hours' work each day." Boys received practical farming instruction and experience and eventually manual training. Girls learned housekeeping, sewing, and cooking and assisted in providing the meals for the boarding students. Students also raised and canned vegetables to be sold in a nearby store established by Young about 1914. For a bakery added later, they baked rolls and bread for sale. Night classes were conducted for adults in many of the school's departments.

The school's church-appointed board of trustees secured funds to erect permanent buildings for classrooms and dormitories for the growing student body. The school reached its zenith in the 1920s and 1930s, when more than three hundred students were instructed by about a dozen faculty members. The high school department was the first for Negroes in Wake Forest and one of the first in Wake County. Its private vehicle was the first school bus operated in Wake County for black students. Young's sons Arthur and James organized a music department and directed a choral group, a band, and a touring musical drama troupe, all of which performed in numerous localities in North Carolina and in states as far away as Connecticut. Close ties were maintained with Wake Forest College, whose faculty and student body often conducted chapel services and assisted in athletic programs at Young's school.

Enrollment began to drop after the state began improving public education for blacks. The high school was discontinued first, after a free public high school opened nearby. The earlier grades were gradually phased out, and in the school's final year (1956–57) only the kindergarten department was operating. In 1978 only one of the school's five buildings survived, relocating a few yards west of its original site. Young's daughters living nearby preserved a single sewing table and classroom chair.

Always a community leader, Young took an active role in annual Emancipation Day observances in the area. The facilities of his school were frequently used for meetings such as sessions of the Rural Progressive Uplift organization, for which the school's music department performed, and Principal Young spoke or chaired discussion groups. He was as early as the 1930s engaged in successful efforts to correct local abuses in voter registration requirements for Negroes and continued to spearhead drives for increased Negro registration and voting. In 1920 he was a delegate-at-large to the Republican National Convention in Chicago, which nominated successful presidential candidate Warren G. Harding. He later changed his party affiliation to Democrat. He led local efforts for community betterment, including especially street improvements in the black communities of Wake Forest, as well as increased recreational opportunities. He was himself an avid tennis player. He was also an Odd Fellow. A lifelong member and elder in the Spring Street Presbyterian Church, he served as clerk of its sessions and was commissioned elder to the General Assembly of the Presbyterian Church of the United States.

Young's first wife was the former Louzania Jones of Franklin County. Of their five sons and three daughters, a son and a daughter died in infancy and another son died as a young man. After her death on 10 Dec. 1910, Young married Geneva Trice, of Chapel Hill, a Shaw University alumna who assisted in the family school. They had four sons and a daughter. Predeceasing her husband, she died on 6 Nov. 1934.

The final year of his school was Young's last year of life. After gradually failing health, he died at home at age eighty-one. Funeral services were conducted from the Spring Street Presbyterian Church, with burial in the community cemetery at Taylor and Walnut streets, Wake Forest. Portraits of Young and of the buildings and student activities of his school are in the photographic collection of the North Carolina State Archives, Raleigh.

SEE: Raleigh *Carolinian*, 15 May 1971; Raleigh *News and Observer*, 18–20 Feb. 1957; *Raleigh Times*, 25 Oct. 1971; Wake Forest Normal and Industrial School, *Annual Catalogue* (1906), *Annual Bulletin* (1920–21), *Annual Report* (1930–31); *Wake Forest Student*, November 1941; Wake Forest *Wake Weekly*, 29 Apr., 6 May 1971; Yulan Washburn, "Allen Young's School," *Wake Forest Student*, 28 Mar. 1956; Ailey M. and Maude E. Young (Wake Forest), personal contact, 7, 26 July 1971, 19, 28 Oct. 1978; Maude E. Young, "Birth and Death of an Institution" (typescript, 1971) and other materials in vertical file (Richard B. Harrison Library, Raleigh); Young Family Bible (possession of Ailey M. and Maude E. Young, Wake Forest).

ELIZABETH REID MURRAY

Young, David Alexander (*19 May 1907–5 May 1994*), psychiatrist and hospital administrator, was born in Raleigh, the son of James Richard and Virginia Nicholls Young. His father, of Vance County, was North Carolina's first insurance commissioner. David A. Young was graduated from The University of North Carolina in 1928 and then attended the institution's two-year School of Medicine. In 1931 he received an M.D. degree from Harvard

University. He was trained in internal medicine and neurology at Massachusetts General Hospital in Boston, Bellevue Hospital in New York City, Worcester State Hospital, and McLean Hospital in Belmont, Mass.

Young completed his residency in psychiatry at Duke Hospital and Massachusetts General Hospital before entering private practice in neurology and psychiatry in Salt Lake City (1940–45), where he was also assistant clinical professor of psychiatry and neurology at the University of Utah for the four years he was in that state. In 1945 he became general superintendent of mental hygiene for the state of North Carolina. From 1955 to 1968 Young was also a clinical professor of psychiatry at The University of North Carolina Medical School. However, he was primarily in charge of five hospitals across the state—at Raleigh, Butner, Morganton, Goldsboro, and Kinston. When he arrived, North Carolina had only recently acquired from the U.S. Army the huge complex at Camp Butner for conversion into facilities for the treatment and care of the mentally ill. In addition, new construction was under way at Goldsboro.

In June 1955 Young resigned to enter the private practice of psychiatry and psychoanalysis in Raleigh. During his term as director the large facility at Butner had been put into use, as had the new quarters in Goldsboro. The patients treated in the various hospitals grew from 8,300 to more than 11,000.

Young participated in the establishment of The University of North Carolina–Duke Psychoanalytic Training Institute and served as a training analyst from 1960 to 1987. In 1984 he received the Faculty and Alumni Distinguished Service Award of the UNC Medical School and the George Ham Award from the UNC Department of Psychiatry in 1989. In the latter year a stone building on the Dorothea Dix State Hospital campus in Raleigh where he had lived was named the Young House.

Young married Alma Stanley, and they had four children: Francis Nicholls, Sidney Stanley, James Richard, and Carolina Alma. A memorial service for him was held at Christ Episcopal Church, Raleigh.

SEE: Alumni Files (University of North Carolina, Chapel Hill); *Biographical Directory of the Fellows and Members of the American Psychiatric Association* (1977); Raleigh *News and Observer*, 8–9, 24 June 1945, 8 June 1955, 7, 9 May 1994.

WILLIAM S. POWELL

Young, James Hunter (*26 Oct. 1858–11 Apr. 1921*), politician, editor, businessman, and racial spokesman, was born near Henderson. His mother was a slave belonging to Captain D. E. Young, and his father was "a prominent white man in Vance County" who assumed responsibility for his education and was instrumental in securing his first political appointment. Young attended common school in Henderson and in 1874 entered Shaw University in Raleigh, an institution to which he remained devoted throughout his life. In January 1877 he left Shaw to take a job in the office of Colonel J. J. Young, the collector of internal revenue for the Fourth District of North Carolina, a decision that marked the beginning of his career in Republican politics.

Young's industry and efficiency attracted the attention of state Republican leaders and resulted in his rapid advancement within both party circles and the Internal Revenue Service. By 1882 he had become chief clerk and cashier in the Fourth District revenue office. First chosen a delegate to the Republican state convention in 1880, Young was prominent in North Carolina party councils for more than three decades. He was an alternate delegate and delegate-at-large to the Republican National Convention in 1884 and 1892, respectively.

When Grover Cleveland entered the White House in 1885, Young was replaced in the revenue service by a white Democrat. Even though Democrats controlled federal patronage, the young black politician had influential Republican friends in local government. Through them he was appointed, in December 1886, chief clerk in the office of the Register of Deeds in Wake County, a position that he held for more than two years. By the time the Republicans returned to power in Washington in 1889, Young had emerged as one of the most influential black Republicans in North Carolina. During the next decade he "was easily the outstanding Negro in state influence."

In 1889, largely through the influence of his friend and political associate, Henry Plummer Cheatham, North Carolina's black congressman, Young was appointed a special inspector of customs. A year later President Benjamin Harrison selected him to be collector of the port of Wilmington, one of the most prestigious and lucrative patronage positions in the state. The appointment triggered a prolonged and acrimonious controversy, and despite the efforts of Cheatham and other North Carolina Republicans, the state's Democratic leadership was able to prevent his confirmation by the Senate. With the beginning of Cleveland's second administration in 1893, Young was relieved of his post as a special customs inspector and once again "returned to private life."

Early in the 1890s party politics in North Carolina underwent dramatic changes in large part because of the emergence of the Populists. An ambitious and skillful politician, Young took maximum advantage of these developments to advance his own political career as well as the welfare of black citizens in general. In June 1893 he purchased the *Gazette*, a weekly newspaper published in Raleigh. During the five years in which he edited the *Gazette* it was not only recognized as the principal mouthpiece of black Republicanism in the state, but its columns also reflected Young's personal interest in various programs of racial uplift, especially those concerning education, moral development, and economic self-help. An articulate, forceful individual whose talents won for him the respect of whites as well as blacks, Young entered upon the most significant phase of his political career in 1893–94, when negotiations between Republicans and Populists sought to effect an arrangement known in North Carolina as Fusion. A staunch advocate of Republican-Populist cooperation, he labored with considerable success in winning the support of those black Republicans who were wary of such an alliance. Indeed, he was one of the principal architects of the Fusionist strategy by which Populists and Republicans wrested control of state politics from the Democrats in the 1890s.

In 1894 Young was elected to the state legislature from Wake County on a Fusion ticket, and two years later he was reelected. Notwithstanding the carping criticism leveled at him by Josephus Daniels's *News and Observer*, his performance as a legislator provided abundant evidence of his ability, energy, and political astuteness. A member of the half-dozen important committees in the state House of Representatives, Young displayed particular concern for measures relating to education, penal reform, and charitable institutions, such as the school for the deaf, dumb, and blind. Nothing, however, provoked more hostility from Democratic quarters than his success in obtaining revisions in the Raleigh city charter that allowed blacks greater opportunities for participation in municipal affairs.

In the election of 1896 Young played a key role in the campaign of Daniel L. Russell, a Republican, who ran for governor on the Fusion ticket. During the four years following the triumph of the Fusionists in 1896, Young reached the apex of his political power and prestige. He enjoyed the confidence of both the governor and Republican senator Jeter C. Pritchard. Governor Russell appointed him chief fertilizer inspector in the state and a member of the board of directors of the deaf, dumb, and blind institutions whose interests he had consistently championed earlier as a legislator.

The Democratic press, already outraged by the selection of a Negro to serve as a director of the state's principal charitable institution, unleashed a barrage of racist rhetoric against Young when, on the outbreak of the Spanish-American War, Governor Russell appointed him colonel of a regiment of black volunteers designated as the Third North Carolina Infantry. Although the regiment never saw combat and remained in the United States, its existence was a source of considerable pride among black North Carolinians. Some of the white Democrats who had been most severe in their denunciation of Colonel Young in 1898 later admitted that he and his men "made much better soldiers than anybody expected."

By the time the black regiment was mustered out early in 1899, the Democrats had mounted an effective offensive against the Fusionists. Throughout their "white supremacy" campaign in the fall of 1898, they had equated Fusion rule with "negro rule"—a theme that proved useful not only in turning the Republicans and Populists out of office but also in disfranchising black voters. The Democratic legislature of 1899, intent on obliterating all reminders of "negro rule," passed a resolution directing that the name of James H. Young be removed from the cornerstone of the new school for the deaf, dumb, and blind, an institution that he had championed both as a legislator and as a member of its board of directors. This gesture aptly symbolized the political fate of blacks in North Carolina.

Although the return of the Democrats to power meant that Young was no longer a significant force in North Carolina politics, the Republican administrations in Washington did not ignore his services to the party. In 1899 President William McKinley appointed him deputy revenue collector for the Raleigh district, a position to which he was reappointed by both Theodore Roosevelt and William Howard Taft. In 1913, early in the Democratic administration of Woodrow Wilson, Young's career in the federal service, which altogether totaled more than a quarter of a century, came to an end. Observers interpreted his removal as deputy revenue collector as an event of major significance, because by 1913 he was the sole black man occupying a federal position of any consequence in North Carolina.

After his dismissal Young retired from politics and devoted himself to a variety of business, religious, civic, and fraternal enterprises with which he had been identified for many years. From a suite of offices in the Masonic Temple in Raleigh he conducted a profitable business in insurance and real estate. In addition, he was president of the Raleigh Undertaking Company and a director of the Mallette Drug Company. An example of sobriety and "clean living," he continued to maintain an interest in the affairs of the Baptist denomination, which he had served in various capacities including those of Sunday school superintendent in Raleigh's First Baptist Church (black) and president of the Baptist State Sunday School Convention. Widely known in fraternal circles, he held important posts in the Odd Fellows, Masons, Knights of Pythias, and the Household of Ruth.

Throughout the decade following his retirement from politics, Young functioned as an elder statesman among black North Carolinians. A social pacifist who abhorred violence, he sought to maintain harmony between the races. During World War I his services as a public speaker were much in demand at patriotic rallies, and Selective Service officials often called upon him for advice in regard to the drafting of black men. In the racially turbulent era immediately after the war his principal message was a call for "moderation" on the part of both whites and blacks—a position that caused some Negroes to charge that he was "recreant to the race."

Young was married three times. In 1881 he married Bettie Ellison, the daughter of Stewart Ellison, a prominent black politician and businessman in Raleigh. His second wife was a widow, Mrs. Mary Christmas, and his third was Lula Evans of Raleigh whom he married in July 1913. He was the father of two daughters, Maude and Martha. At his funeral on 13 Apr. 1921, "the high and low, irrespective of race, gathered in tremendous throng" in the First Baptist Church to pay tribute to a man who was credited with being in large measure responsible for "the friendly relations obtaining between the races in North Carolina."

SEE: *Biographical Sketches of the Members of the General Assembly of North Carolina, 1895* (1895); Helen G. Edmonds, *The Negro and Fusion Politics in North Carolina, 1894–1901* (1951); Willard B. Gatewood, Jr., "North Carolina's Negro Regiment in the Spanish-American War," *North Carolina Historical Review* 48 (October 1971); *National Cyclopaedia of the Colored Race* (1919); Raleigh *Gazette*, 1897–1898; Raleigh *News and Observer*, 12, 14 Apr. 1921; Washington, D.C., *Colored American*, 21 Jan. 1899.

WILLARD B. GATEWOOD

Young, John Smith (4 Nov. 1834–11 Oct. 1916), Louisiana lawyer, Confederate officer, jurist, legislator, congressman, and sheriff, had ancestral connections with Granville County but was born on his father's twenty-slave plantation in Wake County. He was the fourth son of Granville natives, planter-physician John Y. (16 Apr. 1793–27 Aug. 1868) and Eliza Henry Jones Young (27 July 1807–12 June 1882). When he was about two years old, his father acquired a 640-acre section of former Chickasaw land in Marshall County, Miss., but when the state line was resurveyed in 1837, the plantation to which the doctor moved his North Carolina household fell into Fayette County, Tenn. Ultimately, in 1848, the family settled at Calhoun, a cultured community in southwestern Arkansas.

At age eighteen Young entered the sophomore class of Methodist-oriented Centenary College of Louisiana, where he was graduated in 1855. After reading law under Judge W. B. Egan, he joined the Masonic lodge and was admitted to the bar in 1857. He also acquired land and slaves. In the spring of 1861 he became a third lieutenant in a company of Louisiana infantry. During the Civil War he was promoted through the grades to lieutenant colonel. He saw active service along the Mississippi River in Louisiana and in Virginia in the vicinity of Yorktown and Williamsburg, as well as elsewhere along the James River. After the war he returned to Louisiana and resumed his law practice.

In 1867 he married nineteen-year-old Fannie R. Hodges, and in November 1870, at age thirty-six, he was elected judge of Claiborne Parish Court. Reconstruction politics resulted in his removal from the court. He was then chosen as a candidate for lieutenant governor but was defeated. Instead, he was appointed parish attorney and served in that post until he was elected to the Louisiana legislature in 1874. There, through skillful political

maneuvering by his friends, Young was selected to fill a seat in Congress, where he served from 19 Dec. 1878 to 3 Mar. 1879. For a time during this period he and his family lived in Monroe, but in the 1880s they moved to Shreveport. As a lawyer there he was selected by the state legislature to compile and revise the state penal code as well as the code of criminal practice. His work appeared as part of the 759-page volume, *The Revised Statutes of the State of Louisiana*, published in 1886.

As chairman of a board that supervised a primary of the white voters of Louisiana in 1892, he cast a tie-breaking ballot that in effect doomed the "malodorous Louisiana lottery." In the same year he was appointed sheriff and ex officio tax collector of Caddo Parish, and in 1896 he was reelected to a four-year term.

Following the death of his wife in 1891, Young was married in 1896 to Mrs. Mattie Hamilton Morrison. A member of the Presbyterian church, he served a four-year term as elder of the church in Shreveport. Survived by sons Edward H., John L., and Joseph B., Young was buried in Oakland Cemetery, Monroe.

SEE: *Biog. Dir. Am. Cong.* (1928); Hope S. Chamberlain, *History of Wake County* (1922); D. W. Harris and B. M. Hulse, *The History of Claiborne Parish, Louisiana* (1886); Maude Hearn-O'Pry, *Chronicles of Shreveport* (1928); John S. Kendall, *History of New Orleans*, vol. 2 (1922); Mattie Hicks Kilgore, *History of Columbia County [Ark.]* (1947); Ella Lonn, *History of Reconstruction in Louisiana after 1868* (1967); Monroe *News-Star*, 12 Oct. 1916; New Orleans *Louisianian*, 18 Dec. 1870–28 Dec. 1878; *Shreveport Journal*, 11–12 Oct. 1916; Henry Clay Warmoth, *War, Parties, and Reconstruction: Stormy Louisiana* (1930).

H. B. FANT

Young, Richard Knox (18 Sept. 1913–31 Dec. 1974), clergyman and pioneer in pastoral care for the ill, was born on a farm in Person County, the son of Ernest Moore and Ethel Pugh Young. He became ill as an infant, and the family physician said that he would not live. His mother prayed for him, asking that he be spared and offering his life to the glory of God. As a youth Young felt a call to the Christian ministry but ignored it. The sense of being called persisted, yet he switched from job to job.

Finally, in 1941, at age twenty-eight, he entered Wake Forest College, graduating in 1943. From the Southern Baptist Theological Seminary in Louisville, Ky., he received a bachelor of divinity degree in 1946; he was ordained a Baptist minister in 1947 and earned a doctor of theology degree in 1952. To further prepare himself for the goal he had in mind, in the summer of 1945 he spent twelve weeks in a mental hospital in Elgin, Ill. He ate and slept on a ward with the patients and learned more about humanity in those few months, he said, than a lifetime at seminary would have taught.

Following his graduation from seminary, Young was invited to become chaplain at the Baptist Hospital in Winston-Salem, operated in conjunction with the Bowman Gray School of Medicine of Wake Forest College. From 1946 to 1970 he was director of the school of pastoral care at the hospital. The first session of a new program began in 1947, and within a few years more than 1,700 students representing thirty-six denominations and twenty-five foreign countries had been trained in the care of the sick. As of 1994, more than 3,000 persons, representing thirty-nine denominations from as many countries, had studied chaplaincy and pastoral work in the program begun by Richard Young. He served as the first professor of pastoral care at the Southeastern Baptist

Theological Seminary in Wake Forest, N.C., and as professor of pastoral care at Wake Forest College (later Wake Forest University) in Winston-Salem.

Physicians and nurses came to appreciate Chaplain Young's success with the ill, and he became the first clergyman invited to address the American Medical Association. In time he was called upon to lecture to ministers, students, physicians, nurses, and others, not only in the United States but in several foreign countries as well. His work became well known after an article in *Reader's Digest* was published in 1959. As a result of this article, the U.S. Air Force established a contract with Wake Forest College's Department of Pastoral Care to train chaplains.

Young was a member of the American Medical Association, in which he served on the medicine and religion committee, and of the National Conference on Clinical Pastoral Education, in which he sat on the executive committee. He was president of the Chaplain's Division of the American Protestant Hospital Association and of the Southern Baptist Hospital Chaplain's Association.

In 1962 chronic depression overcame Young, and two months of psychiatric observation and treatment followed. His friends and the community at large responded to his illness in the manner that he had been teaching. In May 1970 he retired from the medical school but continued to write as well as to teach at North Carolina Memorial Hospital at The University of North Carolina. After a year he moved to his birthplace, Roxboro, where he engaged in pastoral counseling and was an interim pastor.

He was the author of *The Pastor's Hospital Ministry* (1954) and *Spiritual Therapy: How the Physician, Psychiatrist, and Minister Collaborate in Healing* (1960), for which Albert L. Meiburg assisted in collecting information. Married to Mary Frances Vickers of Atlanta on 13 Nov. 1935, they had a daughter and two sons: Vickie, Richard, Jr., and David. Young died in Roxboro at age sixty-one and was buried in the cemetery at Providence Baptist Church north of the city.

SEE: *Contemporary Authors*, vol. 13–16 (1975); *Greensboro Daily News*, 1 Jan. 1975; Manson Meads, *The Miracle on Hawthorne Hill* (1988); Mrs. Otha Murray, untitled paper read in 1975 to a local historical society in Roxboro (copy in possession of William S. Powell); "Spiritual Therapy: Modern Medicine's Newest Ally," *Reader's Digest*, September 1959; *Winston-Salem Journal*, 8 Dec. 1962.

WILLIAM S. POWELL

Yount, George Calvert (4 May 1794–5 Oct. 1865), trapper and pioneer settler of California, was born near Dowden Creek in Burke County. His grandfather, John Jundt, a native of Alsace, moved to Lancaster County, Pa., in the mid-1700s when he was a child, changed his name to Yount, and settled in North Carolina. George C. was the son of Jacob, who served with General Nathanael Greene in the American Revolution, and Marillis Killian Yount; in 1804 the family moved to Cape Girardeau, Mo.

In 1818 Yount married Eliza Cambridge Wilds and became a cattleman in Howard County, Mo. In 1825 after a neighbor embezzled his savings, he set out on an expedition to Santa Fe. In 1827, after arriving in the West, Yount led a party that hoped to trap along certain rivers in Arizona, but the expedition failed when part of the group turned back after reaching the mouth of the Gila River. During 1828–29 he trapped in the northern part of the country, and a mountain at the mouth of the Yellowstone River was named Yount's Peak to commemorate his activities in the area.

After meeting Jedidiah Smith while accompanying

William Wolfskill, Yount became interested in the exploration of California. In 1831 he traveled along the Old Spanish Trail to Los Angeles and three years later moved north to Sonoma and San Rafael. At this time he converted to Roman Catholicism and adopted Spanish forenames: Jorge Concepción. He also became a Mexican citizen. Receiving a grant of land for a ranch in 1836, Yount settled in the Napa Valley and guarded the northern frontier of California against Indian attack. After an American emigrant party arrived in the area in 1841, he sent for his family. His two daughters joined him in California, but during his long absence his wife, thinking he may have been dead, sued for divorce in 1829 and married someone else.

In the 1850s Yount began to produce wine on his ranch in the Napa Valley, and in 1855 he married Mrs. Eliza Gashwiler. A Mason, he died at his home on the outskirts of the town of Yountsville, named for him. He was buried in the Yountsville cemetery, where his grave is marked by a monument with primitive carving.

SEE: Dick Byrd, "N.C. Connection in Napa Valley," *The State* magazine, November 1985 (portrait); Charles L. Camp, ed., *George C. Yount and His Chronicles of the West, Comprising Extracts from his "Memoirs" and from the Orange Clark "Narrative"* (1966); *DAB*, vol. 10 (1936); James D. Hart, *A Companion to California* (1978); Edith Warren Huggins, *The Yount (Jundt) Family in Europe and America* (n.d.); George F. Wilson and Maryhelen Wilson, *Early Missouri Ancestors*, vol. 1 (1987).

ROBIN A. PUCKETT

Zachary, Jonathan Thompson Walton (7 May 1896–24 Jan. 1969), professional baseball player, was born in Graham, one of eight children of Alfred, a farmer, and Mary Guthrie Zachary. He was educated at Springs School and Guilford College, where he was a standout baseball, football, and basketball player. Under his leadership Guilford's 1917 baseball team won 12 of 13 games and claimed the unofficial state championship.

Zachary was the rare player who never competed in the minor leagues. He made his major league debut in 1918 with the Philadelphia Athletics. He pitched two games under the name Zach Walton, winning one with one no-decision. The same year he volunteered for relief work in France through the American Friends Service Committee. He served with the American Red Cross in France through the end of the war and into 1919.

After returning from France, Zachary signed with the Washington Senators. From this point until 1936 he pitched in the major leagues. He played for seven major league teams in nineteen years, winning ten or more games in eleven of these seasons. It was Zachary's misfortune to spend much of the time playing for second-division teams. When given the chance to pitch for better teams, he frequently compiled impressive records. For the Washington Senators he won eighteen games in 1921 and fifteen games in 1922 and 1924. In the latter year his earned run average was second in the American League only to future Hall-of-Famer and Senators teammate Walter Johnson. This combination carried Washington into the World Series against the New York Giants in 1924. Zachary was the star of the Series, leading Washington to victory by winning game two 4–3 and game six 2–1. He slumped to 12–15 in 1925 and made only a brief relief appearance in the World Series of that year. In 1927, while pitching for the Senators, Zachary gave up Babe Ruth's famous sixtieth home run. This brought Zachary some notoriety for the rest of his life and tended to obscure his other accomplishments.

Ironically, Zachary was traded to the New York Yankees in 1928. He played in his last World Series that year and won one Series game for the victorious Yankees. The next year he won twelve games without a loss for the second-place Yankees. In the 1980s this remained the major league record for most wins without a loss in a single season. He was traded in 1930 to the Boston Braves and finished his career in the National League, mostly with losing teams. He retired after the 1936 season, at age forty.

Zachary finished his career with 185 wins, 191 losses, and an earned run average of 3.72. He pitched 3,134 innings in 533 games. A good hitting pitcher, he batted .226 with six career home runs. He also finished his career with three World Series victories, without a loss.

After his retirement from baseball Zachary returned to Alamance County, where he grew tobacco and invested in real estate. He married Etta McBane of Asheville on 16 Jan. 1931. They had two children: Tom, Jr., and Sally. Zachary died at Alamance County Hospital and was buried in Alamance Memorial Park, Burlington. He was inducted into the North Carolina Sports Hall of Fame.

SEE: Herb Appenzoller, *Pride in the Past: Guilford College Athletics, 1837–1987* (1987); Gene Karst and Martin J. Jones, Jr., *Who's Who in Professional Baseball* (1973); Shirley Povich, *The Washington Senators* (1954); Joseph L. Reichler, *The Baseball Encyclopedia* (1985); St. Louis, *Sporting News* (Zachary file); Zachary file, National Baseball Library, Cooperstown, N.Y.

JIM L. SUMNER

Zimmerman, Erich Walter *(31 July 1888–16 Feb. 1961)*, economist and educator, was born in Mainz, Germany, the son of Wilhelm and Eugenie Grünberg Zimmerman. Educated in the Mainz Volkschule and a graduate of the "humanistic" Gymnasium at Düsseldorf, he pursued graduate studies in the universities of Berlin, Munich, and Bonn, from which he earned a Ph.D. degree in 1911. His doctoral dissertation on British coal exports resulted from extensive travels that had led him to Scotland, Wales, and England, where he learned English for a time in the universities of Edinburgh and Birmingham.

Immediately on completing his graduate studies, he went to the United States, originally as a visiting scholar to gather materials for a study of the Great Lakes in the transportation pattern of North America. To finance his studies, he taught first in a mountain school in Kentucky and from 1912 to 1915 in the Riverdale Country School in New York City. He began his teaching career as an instructor in economics and sociology at New York University (1914–18). In the fall of 1918 he was appointed professor of economics at James Millikin University, Decatur, Ill., where he remained until he joined the faculty of The University of North Carolina as associate professor of economics in 1921. He became a naturalized U.S. citizen in 1925.

Already an active scholar, Zimmerman had published two books, *Foreign Trade and Shipping* (1917) and *Ocean Shipping* (1921), which attracted favorable comment in the United States and abroad. His most important contribution, however, grew out of a course entitled "Resources and Industries," which developed into a book, *World Resources and Industries* (1933; 2d ed., revised and enlarged, 1951). In the biographical notes he furnished for *The Kenan Professorships*, he described his approach to the work as "functional or operational . . . [transferring] the concept of resources from its static natural science prototype of inventory fixtures to a dynamic product of interacting processes and forces . . . [stressing] availability for human use as against mere physical existence."

World Resources won for Zimmerman in 1934 the Mayflower Cup for the best nonfiction book by a North Carolina author as well as a Kenan professorship. It also brought him into prominence as a consultant on resources, and his services were much in demand. At various times he served in that capacity at the U.S. Bureau of Mines, Brookings Institute Puerto Rico Survey, Interdepartmental Committee on Puerto Rico, and U.S. Department of State. His comprehensive studies on resources, set forth in the government publications on the Puerto Rican economy, were influential in bringing order out of the chaos that was the aftermath of the Great Depression in the Commonwealth.

In 1942 Zimmerman left The University of North Carolina to accept a Distinguished Graduate Professorship of Resources at the University of Texas; in 1948 he was also made Distinguished Graduate Professor of Economics. Before his retirement in 1958 he had continued his studies in resources as a contributor to the *Encyclopedia of the Social Sciences* (1937), *Resources of Texas* (1944), *Texas Academy of Science* (1944), *University of Texas Institute of Latin-American Studies* (1946), *Management Foundation* (1950), and articles in various journals.

In 1949 Washington and Lee University honored him with an LL.D. degree. His citation well summed up Zimmerman's career as teacher and scholar: "Grateful students without number call you Master, and officials of State acknowledge your manifold patriotic contributions; but all men who struggle with the human problem know the importance of your accurate and sympathetic analysis of the potential of earth's varied people."

Zimmerman married Margaret Hoff on 23 June 1917. His three children were Erika Sophia, Charles Hoff, and Margaret Eugenia. He died and was buried in Austin, Tex.

SEE: Chapel Hill, *Daily Tar Heel*, 6 Dec. 1941; A. C. Howell, *The Kenan Professorships* (1958); *Who Was Who among North American Authors*, vol. 2 (1976); *Who Was Who in America*, vol. 4 (1968).

A. C. HOWELL

Afterword

The first volume of the *Dictionary of North Carolina Biography* was published in 1979. Now, with the appearance of this final volume seventeen years later, I take pleasure in pointing out that all six volumes are the result of willing work by numerous individuals who have thereby demonstrated their sincere interest in North Carolina. This is an outstanding example of what can still be accomplished by following practices from the days before government grants and endowments became the source of inspiration for such undertakings.

The idea for this work was my own as I sought a worthwhile project to follow the *North Carolina Gazetteer*, which appeared in 1968. Drawing on many years of involvement with North Carolina history, I compiled the initial list of potential entries for a biographical dictionary and then called upon friends and acquaintances to add or delete names. This process continued throughout the course of the project.

I also established the rules to be followed in preparing the entries. No living people would be included. Each person profiled in the *DNCB* would have some significant association or connection with North Carolina. Birth in the colony or state would be considered as qualifying a person for inclusion, as would living in or serving the area, but the subject's role need not have been played out solely in North Carolina. Nor need the subjects necessarily have been *good*, hence noted pirates, criminals, and scoundrels in various categories would also be eligible. So would a noted hermit and the heaviest man known to have lived in the state. "Firsts" in many fields would be included. Adding to the usefulness of the work, people of widely assorted occupations, professions, and accomplishments were considered to ensure that pioneers and leaders of all sorts would not be overlooked. Persons who had been recognized or honored by the state or nation were considered for inclusion. Contributions in such areas as art, music, engineering, invention, discovery, religion, politics, medicine, teaching, architecture, transportation, and many more were reviewed. Membership in a few categories routinely warranted inclusion: governors, senators, and high federal officials, for example. Service in the General Assembly, however, unless accompanied by some accomplishment of further significance, was not deemed sufficient. I even included a few people simply because they had interesting names. One "person" who was included never actually existed; a fictitious biography of him, published more than a century ago, has been accepted as authentic by prominent but unsuspecting scholars. One of our writers discovered the hoax, and the record at last has been set right. With one exception, each entry is signed by its author. The one exception was written by a person who knew the subject well but declined to be identified, so I provided a pseudonym. I leave these two biographies to be discovered by some alert reader.

Among those who wrote biographies are published authors of local, national, and international note. Many are professors and teachers of various ranks, clergymen, physicians, journalists, novelists, housewives, and students.

When I was teaching North Carolina history at the University of North Carolina in Chapel Hill, I invited my students to volunteer to write biographical sketches, with the understanding that I would not necessarily publish their contributions, nor would their efforts affect their grades. Many gladly responded and now join me in looking with pride on their contributions. A professor at the University of North Carolina at Greensboro assigned subjects to students in his beginning seminars, and this resulted in many carefully researched and written biographies. Other friends in similar positions did the same, while many more excellent contributions came from teachers in community colleges and high schools who welcomed the opportunity to participate in such a scholarly project. Some of the best work was done by people who had never (or seldom) before undertaken this kind of writing. Since no one was paid for his or her work, it was all done at personal expense, and several contributors undertook research trips—even going abroad—in search of information. One prepared a sketch of a colonial governor that corrected errors first recorded years ago.

The sketches are not uniform in length, and length does not necessarily indicate the importance of the subject. Although I made an effort to keep the biographies brief and to the point, some were so interesting and well written, or so ably profiled persons heretofore relatively unknown, that I made little or no effort to limit them. In the case of some people of national importance, we attempted to stress the connection with North Carolina. On the other hand, we have discovered that some people with a North Carolina background possess a national significance yet to be recognized; we hope that their appearance in the *DNCB* will bring them to national attention.

As already indicated, the people who worked on the *DNCB* did so out of devotion to the state, and for their care and skill, so evident in the biographies, I am grateful. Several other states, using grants and public funds, have attempted to produce similar works, but they have either published less complete volumes or have become bogged down trying to work out their plans.

As mentioned in the acknowledgments to the first volume, the Research Council of the University of North Carolina provided resources (from alumni gifts) that were used for some of the initial mimeographing and postage and for the services of a student assistant who compiled lists of certain names. Three individuals, previously acknowledged in the appropriate volume, also provided funds for supplies. The North Carolina American Revolution Bicentennial Commission made a grant to the University of North Carolina Press to assist with the production costs of the first volume. After that volume appeared, the North Carolina Society of the Cincinnati volunteered to assist the Press with some of the production costs for Volumes 2 through 6.

Following each biography is a brief listing of works on which the sketch was based or sources for further information. In some cases this list may include all known sources, but in others it is selective. During the preparation of these bibliographies, one type of source posed a special problem. Between 1919 and 1956, four histories of North Carolina, written by outstanding state historians, were published. Each consisted of two or more volumes of history followed by several volumes of biographies—generally the biographies of those persons who subscribed in advance for the history. Sometimes referred to as "vanity publications," these biographical volumes were prepared by a staff of writers employed by the publisher. Though drawn primarily from completed questionnaires or notes supplied by the subject, the biographies nevertheless are useful and generally reliable. Bibliographically, these supplemental volumes could not be credited to the authors of the histories, so, even though they were published over a period of thirty-seven years, I have arbitrarily called all ten of them *North Carolina Biography*.

The state histories, with their accompanying biographical volumes, are:

R. D. W. Connor, William K. Boyd, and J. G. de Roulhac Hamilton. *History of North Carolina*. Chicago: Lewis Publishing Co., 1919. Vols. 1–3, history; vols. 4–6, biography.

R. D. W. Connor. *North Carolina: Rebuilding an Ancient Commonwealth*. Chicago: American Historical Society, 1929. Vols. 1–2, history; vols. 3–4, biography.

Archibald Henderson. *North Carolina: The Old North State and the New*. Chicago: Lewis Publishing Co., 1941. Vols. 1–2, history; vols. 3–5, biography.

Hugh T. Lefler. *History of North Carolina*. New York: Lewis Historical Publishing Co., 1956. Vols. 1–2, history; vols. 3–4, biography.

Readers can identify the particular volume cited by noting the year of publication and the volume number. Reference to the index will be helpful in each instance. In the case of Connor (1929), however, there were more available biographies than could be accommodated in two volumes but not enough for three. Therefore, the two volumes were printed twice with slightly different contents. This could be confusing, but the indexes should help locate the desired subject.

Research conducted during the preparation of the *Dictionary of North Carolina Biography* suggests that the *Biographical History of North Carolina* (8 vols.), edited by Samuel A. Ashe and others, also displays certain characteristics of a vanity publication, in that living subjects were included, as were people of little or no statewide significance, whereas some likely subjects may have been omitted for personal reasons. Evidence also suggests that it was possible to pay to be included.

North Carolina Lives, published in 1962 with only limited oversight by me, is yet another work with some features of a vanity publication. Those included therein did not pay, however, and were not obliged to buy a copy of the book. Most of the biographies were prepared by a staff of writers employed by the publisher but were written from questionnaires supplied by the subjects. I did write biographies of a number of people who did not return questionnaires but whom I thought should be included in a work of this kind. In the years since its publication, this work has proved a useful source of information about people not included in the more standard works of this nature.

Another discovery was that the standard *Biographical Directory of the American Congress*, more recently called *Biographical Dictionary of the United States Congress*, should be used with caution, as innumerable errors have been found in it. We have attempted to correct errors in the *DNCB* that were based on this source.

None of the above is intended to suggest that the *Dictionary of North Carolina Biography* is without error. Some errors there surely are, and they will be corrected in subsequent printings, as has already happened with certain inaccuracies in the first two volumes. It is worth noting here that what was believed to have been an error in Volume 2 was "corrected" in the second printing. It now develops, however, that the "error" was not an error after all! The first printing gave Judge William Gaston a middle name, heretofore unknown. The name was removed in the next printing, but we afterwards discovered that when Gaston enrolled in Georgetown College, he did so as William *Joseph* Gaston.

Errors brought to the attention of the University of North Carolina Press will be investigated for correction in subsequent printings. Interested readers may also send the Press names to be considered for a possible supplemental volume.

Finally, any contributors of biographical sketches who discover that their published work is not quite the same as when they submitted it may join me in expressing appreciation to our skilled copyeditor, Stevie Champion. Not only has she served us in that capacity, she has also read our words with a remarkable memory for names and facts. It is in large measure due to her that names of people and places, as well as many facts, are consistent throughout these six volumes. If something in a later volume did not agree with a related earlier entry, she sent me off in search of a resolution. It has been my pleasure and a real delight to work with her.

Chapel Hill   WILLIAM S. POWELL
November 1995